The Handbook of English Linguistics

Blackwell Handbooks in Linguistics

This outstanding multi-volume series covers all the major subdisciplines within linguistics today and, when complete, will offer a comprehensive survey of linguistics as a whole.

Already published:

The Handbook of Child Language
Edited by Paul Fletcher and
Brian MacWhinney

The Handbook of Phonological Theory
Edited by John A. Goldsmith

*The Handbook of Contemporary
Semantic Theory*
Edited by Shalom Lappin

The Handbook of Sociolinguistics
Edited by Florian Coulmas

The Handbook of Phonetic Sciences
Edited by William J. Hardcastle
and John Laver

The Handbook of Morphology
Edited by Andrew Spencer and
Arnold Zwicky

The Handbook of Japanese Linguistics
Edited by Natsuko Tsujimura

The Handbook of Linguistics
Edited by Mark Aronoff and Janie
Rees-Miller

*The Handbook of Contemporary
Syntactic Theory*
Edited by Mark Baltin and
Chris Collins

The Handbook of Discourse Analysis
Edited by Deborah Schiffrin, Deborah
Tannen, and Heidi E. Hamilton

*The Handbook of Language Variation
and Change*
Edited by J. K. Chambers, Peter Trudgill,
and Natalie Schilling-Estes

The Handbook of Historical Linguistics
Edited by Brian D. Joseph and
Richard D. Janda

The Handbook of Language and Gender
Edited by Janet Holmes and
Miriam Meyerhoff

*The Handbook of Second Language
Acquisition*
Edited by Catherine J. Doughty and
Michael H. Long

The Handbook of Bilingualism
Edited by Tej K. Bhatia and
William C. Ritchie

The Handbook of Pragmatics
Edited by Laurence R. Horn and
Gregory Ward

The Handbook of Applied Linguistics
Edited by Alan Davies and
Catherine Elder

The Handbook of Speech Perception
Edited by David B. Pisoni and
Robert E. Remez

The Blackwell Companion to Syntax,
Volumes I–V
Edited by Martin Everaert and
Henk van Riemsdijk

The Handbook of the History of English
Edited by Ans van Kemenade and
Bettelou Los

The Handbook of English Linguistics
Edited by Bas Aarts and April McMahon

The Handbook of World Englishes
Edited by Braj B. Kachru; Yamuna
Kachru, Cecil L. Nelson

The Handbook of English Linguistics

Edited by

*Bas Aarts and
April McMahon*

WILEY-BLACKWELL

A John Wiley & Sons, Ltd., Publication

© 2006 by Blackwell Publishing Ltd

BLACKWELL PUBLISHING
350 Main Street, Malden, MA 02148-5020, USA
9600 Garsington Road, Oxford OX4 2DQ, UK
550 Swanston Street, Carlton, Victoria 3053, Australia

The right of Bas Aarts and April McMahon to be identified as the Authors of the Editorial Material in this Work has been asserted in accordance with the UK Copyright, Designs, and Patents Act 1988.

First published 2006 by Blackwell Publishing Ltd

1   2008

Library of Congress Cataloging-in-Publication Data

The handbook of English linguistics / edited by Bas Aarts and April McMahon.
    p. cm. — (Blackwell handbooks in linguistics)
    Includes bibliographical references and indexes.
    ISBN: 978–1–4051–1382–3 (hardback : alk. paper)
    ISBN: 978–1–4051–8787–9 (pbk : alk. paper)   1. English language—Handbooks, manuals, etc.   2. Linguistics—Handbooks, manuals, etc.   3. English language—Grammar—Handbooks, manuals, etc.   I. Aarts, Bas, 1961–   II. McMahon, April M. S.   III. Series.

    PE1106.A27 2006
    420—dc22

                                                                                        2006006915

A catalogue record for this title is available from the British Library.

Set in 10/12pt Palatino
by Graphicraft Limited, Hong Kong
Printed and bound in Singapore
by COS Printers Pte Ltd

The publisher's policy is to use permanent paper from mills that operate a sustainable forestry policy, and which has been manufactured from pulp processed using acid-free and elementary chlorine-free practices. Furthermore, the publisher ensures that the text paper and cover board used have met acceptable environmental accreditation standards.

For further information on
Blackwell Publishing, visit our website:
www.blackwellpublishing.com

To my parents
Flor Aarts and Sjé Aarts-Postmes

Contents

Notes on Contributors

Bas Aarts is Professor of English Linguistics and Director of the Survey of English Usage at University College London. His publications include *Small clauses in English: the nonverbal types* (Mouton de Gruyter, 1992), *The verb in contemporary English* (Cambridge University Press, 1995; edited with Charles F. Meyer), *English syntax and argumentation* (Palgrave Macmillan, 1997/2001), *Investigating natural language: working with the British component of the international corpus of English* (John Benjamins, 2002; with Gerald Nelson and Sean Wallis) and *Fuzzy grammar: a reader* (Oxford University Press, 2004; with David Denison, Evelien Keizer, and Gergana Popova), as well as many articles in books and journals. With David Denison and Richard Hogg he is one of the founding editors of the journal *English Language and Linguistics*.

D. J. Allerton is Emeritus Professor of English Linguistics at the University of Basle (Switzerland), where he was professor from 1980 till 2003. He had previously been (senior) lecturer in general linguistics at the University of Manchester. He has published widely on valency grammar (*Valency and the English verb*, Academic Press, 1982; *Stretched verb constructions in English*, Routledge, 2002), but also on semantics, pragmatics, text linguistics, and phonetics. Another of his current interests is graphemics.

Laurie Bauer did his Ph.D. at the University of Edinburgh, and has since taught in Denmark and in New Zealand. He was appointed to a position at Victoria University of Wellington in 1979, and promoted to a personal chair in Linguistics there in 2000. He has published widely on New Zealand English and on morphological matters. He is on the editorial boards of three journals and three book series, spanning these two interests, and the subject editor for morphology for the Elsevier *Encyclopedia of language and linguistics*. His recent books are *Morphological productivity* (Cambridge University Press, 2001), *An introduction to international varieties of English* (Edinburgh University Press, 2002),

Introducing linguistic morphology (Edinburgh University Press, 2nd edn., 2003), and *A glossary of morphology* (Edinburgh University Press, 2004).

Ricardo Bermúdez-Otero is Lecturer in Linguistics and English Language in the School of Languages, Linguistics and Cultures at the University of Manchester. He previously held a postdoctoral fellowship of the British Academy at the University of Manchester, followed by a lectureship in Linguistics at the University of Newcastle upon Tyne. His research focuses on Optimality Theory, with particular attention to its diachronic applications and to problems in the morphology–phonology and phonology–phonetics interfaces. He has contributed articles and book chapters for *English language and linguistics*, *Lingua*, *Optimality Theory and language change* (Kluwer, 2003), the *Encyclopedia of language and linguistics* (Elsevier, 2006), and *The Cambridge handbook of phonology* (Cambridge University Press, 2006).

Douglas Biber is Regents' Professor of English (Applied Linguistics) at Northern Arizona University. His research efforts have focused on corpus linguistics, English grammar, and register variation (in English and cross-linguistics; synchronic and diachronic). His publications include books published with Cambridge University Press (1988, 1995, 1998), and the co-authored *Longman grammar of spoken and written English* (1999) and *Longman student grammar of spoken and written English* (2002).

Robert I. Binnick is a Professor in the Department of Linguistics of the University of Toronto, Canada, and author of *Time and the verb: a guide to tense & aspect* (Oxford University Press, 1991).

Betty J. Birner (Ph.D., Northwestern, 1992) is an Associate Professor in the Department of English at Northern Illinois University, where she has taught since 2000. Her primary research area is discourse/pragmatics, with specific interests in information structure, noncanonical syntactic constructions, and inferential relations in discourse. She is co-author, with Gregory Ward, of *Information status and noncanonical word order in English* (John Benjamins, 1998).

James P. Blevins took his Ph.D. at the University of Massachusetts at Amherst in 1990, then worked at the University of Western Australia before taking up the post of Assistant Director of the Research Centre in English and Applied Linguistics at the University of Cambridge in 1997. He has held visiting positions at the Universities of Texas, Stanford, Alberta, and Berkeley. His main research interests are in morphology (especially paradigmatic relations, syncretism, and productivity) and syntax (including impersonals, coordination, and discontinuous dependencies), and he has worked on Germanic, Balto-Finnic, Balto-Slavic, Kartvelian, and Celtic languages. His recent publications include articles in *Language*, *Journal of Linguistics*, *Transactions of the Philological*

Society. He is the Syntax editor of the second edition of the *Encyclopedia of language and linguistics.*

Kersti Börjars studied English Language and Literature at the University of Leiden and went on to complete a Ph.D. in Linguistics at the University of Manchester. After her Ph.D., she worked as a research assistant on EUROTYP, a European typological project. She is now Professor of Linguistics at the University of Manchester. She is the author of a research monograph, *The feature distribution in Swedish noun phrases* (Blackwell, 1998), and a text book *Introduction to English grammar* (Arnold, 2001; with Kate Burridge).

Deborah Cameron is Professor of Language and Communication in the English Faculty of Oxford University. She is the author of *Feminism and linguistic theory* (1992), *Verbal hygiene* (1995), and *Language and sexuality* (2003; with Don Kulick), and has edited *The feminist critique of language: a reader* (1998).

Devin Casenhiser is currently a postdoctorate researcher at Princeton University. His research focus is on soft constraints in the acquisition of form–meaning correspondences.

Julie Coleman is a Reader in the English Department at the University of Leicester, and has previously taught at the University of Lund, Sweden. Her research interests are historical dictionary studies and the development of the lexis. She is the chair and founder of the International Society of Historical Lexicography and Lexicology. Her main publications are *A history of cant and slang dictionaries. Volume I: 1567–1784* and *Volume II: 1785–1858* (Oxford University Press, 2004).

Peter Collins obtained his doctorate from the University of Sydney. He is an Associate Professor in Linguistics and Head of the Linguistics Department at the University of New South Wales in Australia, and has served as editor of the *Australian Journal of Linguistics.* His main areas of interest are grammatical theory and description, corpus linguistics, and Australian English. Throughout the 1990s he was involved in a project supervised by Rodney Huddleston which produced the *Cambridge grammar of the English language* (Cambridge University Press, 2002).

Ilse Depraetere is Professor of English at the University of Lille III. She has also worked at the Katholieke Universiteit Brussel and the Katholieke Universiteit Leuven. Most of her publications relate to tense and aspect in English; she also has a number of publications on collective nouns. Her broad research interests are semantics, pragmatics, corpus linguistics, and varieties of English.

Paul Foulkes is Reader in Linguistics at the University of York. He holds MA, M.Phil., and Ph.D. degrees from the University of Cambridge, and has previously held posts at the Universities of Cambridge, Newcastle, and Leeds. With Gerry Docherty he co-edited *Urban voices* (Arnold, 1999), a collection of sociophonetic studies of English in the British Isles. His other publications include articles in *Language, Journal of Sociolinguistics, Phonology, Journal of Linguistics, Language and Speech,* and the Laboratory Phonology book series. He is a co-editor of the *International Journal of Speech, Language and the Law.* His research interests include sociolinguistics, phonetics, phonology, first-language acquisition, and forensic phonetics.

Costas Gabrielatos is a Research Associate and Ph.D. student at Lancaster University, doing corpus research on English *if*-conditionals. He is also collaborating with Tony McEnery on the compilation of a corpus of MA dissertations. His main interests are the expression of time and modality in English, pedagogical grammar, and the use of corpora in language teaching.

Adele E. Goldberg is a Professor in the Program in Linguistics, and in the Humanities Council at Princeton University. She is author of *Constructions* (University of Chicago Press, 1995) and *Constructions in context* (Oxford University Press, to appear).

Liliane Haegeman is the author of a number of research books and papers in generative syntax and of textbooks and handbooks on syntax. She was Professor of English Linguistics and General Linguistics at the University of Geneva from 1984 until 1999. Since 1999 she has been Professor of English Linguistics at the University of Lille III.

Michael Hammond received his Ph.D. in Linguistics from UCLA in 1984. He is currently full Professor and Head of the Department of Linguistics at the University of Arizona. His research has focused on phonology and morphology with particular attention on English prosody. He has approached these issues using traditional linguistic language elicitation techniques, but also experimentally, computationally, psycholinguistically, and using poetry and language games as data. He is the author of numerous books and articles on English phonology, most notably *The phonology of English* (Oxford University Press, 1999).

Rodney Huddleston held lectureships in Britain before moving to the University of Queensland, where he has spent most of his academic career and was promoted to a personal chair in 1990. He has written numerous articles and books on English grammar, including *Introduction to the grammar of English* (Cambridge University Press, 1984) and, with Geoffrey K. Pullum and an international team of specialist collaborators, *The Cambridge grammar of the English language* (Cambridge University Press, 2002), winner of the Leonard Bloomfield Book Award. He is a Fellow of the Australian Academy of the Humanities; in 2005 he was elected an Honorary Life Member of the Linguistic

Society of America and a Corresponding Fellow of the British Academy, and awarded an Honorary D.Lit. by University College London.

Kate Kearns is Senior Lecturer in Linguistics at Canterbury University, and has published on syntax, semantics, and pragmatics. Her particular research interests lie in the syntax and semantics of verbal predicates (especially aktionsarten), argument structure, event semantics, and lexical semantics.

Bernd Kortmann is Full Professor of English Language and Linguistics at the University of Freiburg, Germany. He received his academic education at the Universities of Trier, Lancaster, and Oxford (Jesus College), and held positions as Assistant Professor at the University of Hanover and the Free University of Berlin. His publications include three monographs, several edited volumes, and some fifty articles in journals, collective volumes, and encyclopaedias. He is also editor of the Mouton de Gruyter series Topics in English Linguistics. His main research interest over the last years has been the grammar of non-standard varieties of English, especially from a typological perspective. As a result of his research efforts, three edited volumes on syntactic variation in English and Germanic dialects have been published in 2004 and 2005, among them a two-volume *Handbook of varieties of English* (Mouton de Gruyter, 2004; edited with Edgar W. Schneider, in collaboration with Kate Burridge, Raj Mesthrie, and Clive Upton).

Geoffrey Leech is Emeritus Professor of English Linguistics at Lancaster University, England, having taught in the same university since 1969. His publications include (with Randolph Quirk, Sidney Greenbaum, and Jan Svartvik) *A comprehensive grammar of the English language* (Longman, 1985), *A communicative grammar of English* (Longman, 1975; with Jan Svartvik, 3rd edn. 2002), *Meaning and the English verb* (Longman, 1971; 3rd edn. 2004), and *The computational analysis of English* (Longman, 1987; with Garside and Sampson). Since the 1970s, much of his research has been in corpus linguistics, and he has played a major role in the compilation, annotation, and use of the LOB Corpus and the British National Corpus.

Andrew Linn has published extensively on the history of English and Scandinavian linguistics. He is Professor of the History of Linguistics and Head of the Department of English Language and Linguistics at the University of Sheffield. His recent books are *Johan Storm: dhi grétest pràktikal lingwist in dhi werld* (Blackwell, 2004) and *Standardization: studies from the Germanic languages* (John Benjamins, 2002; with Nicola McLelland). He is the history of linguistics section editor for the second edition of the *Encyclopedia of language and linguistics* (Elsevier, 2005) and, from 2006, editor of *Transactions of the Philological Society*.

Christian Mair was Assistant and, subsequently, Associate Professor in the English Department of the University of Innsbruck, Austria, before being appointed to a chair in English Linguistics at the University of Freiburg in Germany in 1990. He has been involved in the compilation of several corpora (among them F-LOB and Frown and – currently in progress – a corpus of Caribbean English as part of the International Corpus of English and an extension to the ARCHER corpus). His research since the 1980s has focused on the corpus-based description of modern English grammar and regional variation and ongoing change in standard Englishes worldwide and resulted in the publication of one monograph (*Infinitival clauses in English: a study of syntax in discourse*, Cambridge University Press, 1990) and more than forty contributions to scholarly journals and edited works.

Tony McEnery is Professor of English Language and Linguistics, Lancaster University. He has published widely in the area of corpus linguistics, though within that field his major interests are currently the contrastive study of aspect, epistemic modality, and corpus-aided discourse analysis.

Michael K. C. MacMahon is Professor of Phonetics at the University of Glasgow. His research interests cover the pronunciation of English from the eighteenth century to the present, and the study of phonetics in the British Isles since the eighteenth century. A further teaching interest is Germanic Philology.

April McMahon is Forbes Professor of English Language at the University of Edinburgh. She previously worked in the Department of Linguistics at the University of Cambridge and held a chair in English Language and Linguistics at the University of Sheffield. Her research interests involve the interaction between phonological theory and historical evidence, as well as issues of language comparison and classification. Her books include *Understanding language change* (Cambridge University Press, 1994), *Lexical phonology and the history of English* (Cambridge University Press, 2000), *Change, chance, and optimality* (Oxford University Press, 2000), and *Language classification by numbers* (Oxford University Press, 2005; with Robert McMahon).

Charles F. Meyer is Professor of Applied Linguistics at the University of Massachusetts, Boston. He was co-editor (with Anne Curzan) of the *Journal of English Linguistics* and is author of *English corpus linguistics: an introduction* (Cambridge University Press, 2002), among other works.

Laura A. Michaelis is Associate Professor of Linguistics and a Faculty Fellow in the Institute of Cognitive Science at the University of Colorado at Boulder. She received her Ph.D. in Linguistics from the University of California at Berkeley. She is the author of two books, *Aspectual grammar and past-time reference* (Routledge, 1998) and *Beyond alternations: a constructional account of applicative formation in German*, with Josef Ruppenhofer (CSLI Publications, 2001). She is also the co-editor, with Elaine J. Francis, of a collected volume of papers, *Mismatch: form-function incongruity and the architecture of grammar* (CSLI Publications, 2004). She has published numerous papers on lexical semantics, the discourse–syntax interface, corpus syntax, and construction-based syntax. Her work has appeared in the journals *Language, Journal of Linguistics, Journal of Semantics*, and *Linguistics and Philosophy*.

Jim Miller until recently held a personal chair of Spoken Language and Linguistics at the University of Edinburgh. He is now Professor of Cognitive Linguistics at the University of Auckland, New Zealand. His research interests are spoken and written language, standard and non-standard language, grammaticalization, and the semantics of grammatical categories, and Slav languages.

Donka Minkova is Professor of English Language at the University of California, Los Angeles. She has published widely in the areas of English historical linguistics, with emphasis on phonology and meter. She is Vice-President of the Society for Germanic Linguistics. She has been Fellow of the Institute for Advanced Studies in the Humanities in Edinburgh, UC President's Research Fellow in the Humanities, and recipient of a Guggenheim Fellowship. She is the author of *The history of final vowels in English* (Mouton de Gruyter, 1991), *English words: history and structure* (Cambridge University Press, 2001; with Robert Stockwell), *Alliteration and sound change in early English verse* (Cambridge University Press, 2003), and co-editor of *Studies in the history of the English language: a millennial perspective* (Mouton de Gruyter, 2002; with Robert Stockwell), and *Chaucer and the challenges of medievalism* (Peter Lang Verlag, 2003; with Theresa Tinkle).

Gerald Nelson lectures in the Department of English Language and Literature at University College London and is coordinator of the International Corpus of English (ICE) project. His publications include the *Internet grammar of English* (www.ucl.ac.uk/internet-grammar), *English: an essential grammar* (Routledge, 2001) and *Exploring natural language: working with the British component of the International Corpus of English* (John Benjamins, 2002; with Sean Wallis and Bas Aarts).

Francis Nolan is Professor of Phonetics in the Linguistics Department at the University of Cambridge. His research interests range over phonetic theory, connected speech processes, speaker characteristics, forensic phonetics, and intonation. In this last area he has been involved in a major research project "English intonation in the British Isles" which made recordings, in a number of different speaking styles, of speakers in urban centers in the UK and Ireland and analyzed aspects of their intonation. He has also supervised Ph.D. dissertations on intonation in English, Estonian, and Catalan.

Pam Peters holds a personal chair in Linguistics at Macquarie University, NSW, Australia, where she is Director of the University's Dictionary Research

Centre, and a member of the Editorial Committee of the *Macquarie Dictionary*. She has led the compilation of several Australian computer corpora (ACE, ICE-AUS, EDOC, OZTALK) and is currently researching and writing a descriptive grammar of Australian English. Her major publications on usage include the *Cambridge Australian English style guide* (Cambridge University Press, 1995) and the *Cambridge guide to English usage* (Cambridge University Press, 2004).

Ingo Plag received his doctorate in 1993 at the University of Marburg, Germany, with his dissertation *Sentential complementation in Sranan* (Niemeyer, 1993). He is the author of numerous articles on the phonology, morphology, and syntax of English and other languages in journals such as *English Language and Linguistics, Journal of Pidgin and Creole Languages, Lingua*, and *Yearbook of Morphology*. He has published six books, including the more recent monographs *Morphological productivity: structural constraints in English derivation* (Mouton de Gruyter, 1999) and *Word-formation in English* (Cambridge University Press, 2003), and the edited volume *The phonology and morphology of creole languages* (Niemeyer, 2003). He was editor-in-chief of *Zeitschrift für Sprachwissenschaft* (1998–2003), and is a member of the editorial board of *Journal of Pidgin and Creole Languages* (1997–), consulting editor of *Yearbook of Morphology* (2004–), and member of the editorial board of the book series *Linguistische Arbeiten* (Niemeyer, 2000–). He is Professor and Chair of English Linguistics at the University of Siegen, Germany (2000–).

Geoffrey K. Pullum is Professor of Linguistics and Distinguished Professor of Humanities at the University of California, Santa Cruz, where he has worked since 1981. Between 1974 and 1980 he taught linguistics at University College London. He has published on a wide range of topics in linguistics, and is co-author with Rodney Huddleston of *The Cambridge grammar of the English language* (Cambridge University Press, 2002), winner of the Leonard Bloomfield Book Award from the Linguistic Society of America in 2004, and more recently a textbook on contemporary Standard English, *A student's introduction to English grammar* (Cambridge University Press, 2005).

Paulo Quaglio is Assistant Professor of TESOL and Applied Linguistics at the State University of New York at Cortland. His research interests include corpus linguistics, English grammar, lexico-grammatical variation in spoken versus written discourse, television dialogue, and second-language acquisition.

Susan Reed is currently working on a research project on the grammar of the verb phrase at the Katholieke Universiteit Leuven. She has also worked at the University of Brighton. Her publications are on tense, aspect, and conditionals.

Peter Stockwell is Professor of Literary Linguistics and head of modern English language at the University of Nottingham, where he teaches stylistics and sociolinguistics. His recent publications include *The poetics of science fiction* (Longman, 2000), *Contextualized stylistics* (Rodopi, 2000), *Cognitive poetics*

(Routledge, 2002), *Sociolinguistics* (Routledge, 2002), and *Language in theory* (Routledge, 2005). He edits the Routledge English Language Introductions series.

Robert Stockwell is Professor Emeritus in the UCLA Department of Linguistics of which he was one of the founders. His research has always focused on aspects of the history of the English language on which he has published over eighty articles. He was a Fellow of the American Council of Learned Societies and has been honored with a Festshrift entitled *On language: rhetorica, phonologica, syntactica* (Routledge, 1988). His publications include also: *Major syntactic structures of English* (Holt, Rinehart, and Winston, 1973; with Paul Schachter and Barbara Partee), *Foundations of syntactic theory* (Prentice-Hall, 1977), *English words: history and structure* (Cambridge University Press, 2001; with Donka Minkova), and *Studies in the history of the English language: a millennial perspective* (Mouton de Gruyter, 2002; co-edited with Donka Minkova).

Gregory Ward (Ph.D., Penn, 1985) is Professor of Linguistics at Northwestern University, where he has taught since 1986. His primary research area is discourse/pragmatics, with specific interests in pragmatic theory, information structure, intonational meaning, and reference/anaphora. In 2004–5, he was a fellow at the Center for Advanced Study in the Behavioral Sciences (Stanford) and currently serves as Secretary-Treasurer of the Linguistic Society of America.

1 Introduction

BAS AARTS AND APRIL MCMAHON

When you picked up this book you may have been struck by the phrase *English Linguistics* (EL) on the cover. What is English Linguistics? Is it like other areas of linguistics, on a par with psycholinguistics, computational linguistics, cognitive linguistics, forensic linguistics, or other topics in the Blackwell Handbooks in Linguistics series? Or is it perhaps linguistics as practiced in England by the English? In both cases the answer is 'no.' We define English Linguistics as a discipline that concerns itself with the study of all aspects of Present-Day English (PDE) from a variety of different angles, both descriptive and theoretical, but with a methodological outlook firmly based on the working practices developed in modern contemporary linguistics. EL arguably includes diachronic studies, though we have chosen not to include papers from this domain in this *Handbook*, mainly because there is a separate *Handbook of the history of English* (edited by Ans van Kemenade and Bettelou Los).

The phrase *English Linguistics* is not a recent one, and can be traced back at least to a number of publications that have it in their titles, e.g. Harold Byron Allen (1966) (ed.) *Linguistics and English linguistics: a bibliography* (New York: Appleton-Century-Crofts), R. C. Alston (1974) (ed.) *English linguistics: 1500–1800* (London: The Scolar Press), and John P. Broderick (1975) *Modern English linguistics: a structural and transformational grammar* (New York: Thomas Y. Crowell Co.). However, as these titles show, the phrase is either used in a very wide sense, as in Allen's and Alston's books, or quite narrowly, as in Broderick's.

In its present-day sense it is probably the case that the label *English Linguistics* is used more in Europe than in other parts of the world. In North America there are programs and courses in EL, but, as Bob Stockwell points out to us "I do not believe there exists in North America a field 'English Linguistics' that can be administratively defined. By 'administratively defined' I mean something like a faculty, a department, an interdepartmental program that is separately budgeted, or an independent research center. The field exists as a concept, as a set of shared research interests."

Things are quite different on the other side of the Atlantic. In the UK, while there are no Departments of English Linguistics, there is a university Department of English Language in Glasgow, and there are a number of departments which have both 'Linguistics' and 'English Language' in their titles (e.g. Bangor, Edinburgh, Lancaster, Manchester, Sheffield, Sussex). In addition, there are several research units dedicated to research in EL, as well as a number of academics whose title is Professor of English Linguistics. Of course, there are also many Departments of English Language and Literature, but in these units English literary studies are usually the main focus of interest.

On the continent of Europe the English language is mostly studied in departments of English which have two or three sub-departments, including language, literature and medieval studies. These departments often have names that includes the label 'philology,' e.g. *Seminar/Institut/Fachrichtung für Englische Philologie* or *Departamento de Filología Inglesa*, though this seems to be changing, and we also find *Seminar für Englische/Anglistische Sprachwissenschaft* and *Vakgroep Engelse Taalkunde*. Linguists in these departments, apart from doing research, also often teach English-language skills, such as writing, pronunciation, etc.

In the wider academic community there are a number of journals specifically devoted to the English language: the *Journal of English Linguistics* (Sage, since 1972), *English Linguistics* (Kaitakusha, since 1983) and *English Language and Linguistics* (Cambridge University Press, since 1997). In addition there are also now several specialist conferences in EL. For those interested in the history of English there's the bi-annual International Conference on English Historical Linguistics (ICEHL), while the more recent International Conference on the Linguistics of Contemporary English caters for those interested in PDE. Computer-oriented studies are the focus of the annual ICAME (International Computer Archive of Modern and Medieval English) conference.

The demonstrable fact that there is a field of English Linguistics with its own identity in terms of research interests does not, however, mean that this field is inward looking, or that its findings are irrelevant to colleagues working on other languages. Many general linguistic innovations can be traced to research on English: think of Chomsky and Halle's *Sound Pattern of English*; or the big reference grammars of English; or Labov's pioneering sociolinguistic investigations of the Lower East Side in New York. Influence from these works has spread to inspire descriptions and theoretical analyses of other languages: at least in some cases, it seems that English Linguistics sneezes, and general linguistics catches cold. Likewise, EL is sensitive to developments in other fields both within and beyond linguistics; the mention of the ICAME conferences above recalls the considerable influence which the construction and use of corpora has had in both historical and synchronic studies of English. At the same time, however, EL has been characterized by a sensitive awareness of variation; a focus on fine-grained description; and approaches which are informed by history, both as change in the language and change in the discipline, even when they are not explicitly or overtly historical or historicizing themselves.

The confluence of many traditions and approaches in EL means both a diverse range of possible audiences (a point to which we return below), and many possible ways of constructing and dividing coverage of the field. There is certainly no single, agreed syllabus, as it were, which determines the particular chapters and areas to be included in a book such as this one; and many traditionally recognized disciplinary divisions are rather fluid, so that while we have a section on syntax and another on lexis and morphology, there might equally have been a case for a composite section on morphosyntax. Some readers might take issue with the treatment of English phonetics, surely a particularly broad subject area, within a single chapter, while prosodic phonology and intonation are allowed to take up two. Phonological variation might equally have been in this phonetics and phonology section, whereas we have in fact located it in a separate grouping of chapters on variation, discourse, and stylistics. Similarly, we might have opted for a chapter on English syntax, say, from each of a number of theoretical perspectives, such as minimalism, LFG, cognitive and construction grammar. There are, it is true, certain theoretical Zeitgeist effects (like the presence of a good deal of Optimality Theory in the phonology chapters); but authors in general balance their theoretical predilections with accounts of the particular phenomena which are specific to English, but of more general theoretical relevance, in each domain.

Our decision in formulating the contents for this *Handbook* was to confront the various tensions within EL head-on, by commissioning chapters that deal with them: hence, our first part is on methodology, and includes chapters on description and theory; on data collection; on the use of corpora; and on the development and historical context of grammar writing. Although diachronic research is covered in our sister *Handbook of the History of English*, we have sought to maintain and encourage the historical awareness which we see as characteristic of EL, so that readers will find chapters on syntactic change in progress, and syntactic and phonological variation, along with an engagement with historical facts and legacies in the chapters on phonology and morphology, productivity, and English words, for example. After all, the history of the language has shaped its present, and is partly responsible for the fine line linguists attempt to tread between what is regular, patterned, and amenable to theoretical analysis on the one side, and the exceptions, language-specific oddities, and relic forms on the other.

Our selection of chapters is, unavoidably, driven partly by considerations of space, as well as by whether research in a specific area has been particularly colored by the fact that its data are from English. The prominence of dictionary writing in the history of English has led to the inclusion of a chapter on lexicography; likewise, the coverage of syntax is driven by the constructions and grammatical/semantic areas which may be encountered in English and not necessarily elsewhere, though they may also raise points of more general theoretical and typological interest. We have opted to cover English usage, differences between spoken and written English, and the interface between language and literature, since these are areas characterized by productive ongoing research and findings of general interest and relevance. But the same could be said of first or second language acquisition, where many pioneering studies have involved English; or of English in education; or of the development of new Englishes. Arguably, the one possible dichotomy we have not addressed explicitly through the structure of the *Handbook* is the equally amorphous one between theoretical and applied linguistics; again, considerations of space mean there must be some compromises, and we have only been able to dip a toe in the waters of variation and ongoing change with the chapters in our final section.

We hope this *Handbook* will be of use to colleagues and students in English Linguistics, who may be working on a specific area of syntax, say, but wish to update their knowledge of other aspects of the language and of current approaches to it. Each chapter is a self-contained summary of key data and issues in a particular area of the field, and should be accessible to advanced undergraduate or graduate students who are seeking an initial overview; a suggestion of where some of the unanswered questions are; and a list of readings to turn to as the next step. The chapters are relatively short, so that decisions have had to be made on what each author can include, but these decisions are flagged clearly in each case. This joint focus on data, description, and theoretical analysis means that chapters will also be useful for readers who work on other languages or are primarily concerned with particular theoretical models, and who wish to acquaint themselves with English data and with accounts inspired by such data. The introductory, methodological chapters, and the balance and interplay throughout between the more theoretical chapters focusing on a single area of the grammar, and the more global, later chapters dealing with issues of usage and variation, also make this *Handbook* relevant and potentially provocative reading for colleagues who already see themselves as working in English Linguistics, but who wish to contextualize their understanding of their field of research. Finally, although we have not sought contributions on particular varieties of English, the wide geographical spread of our authors ensures that attention is paid to the richness and diversity of English data. This perhaps highlights a further tension between the variation which we acknowledge and can increasingly exploit through corpus studies, for example, and the rather monolithic datasets sometimes used in particular theoretical approaches.

Tensions and oppositions have been mentioned at various points through this introduction – between broad description of a range of phenomena and deep, detailed theoretical analysis of a small number of facts; multiple, variable datasets and *the* English pattern; usage and documentation; history and the here and now. However, we certainly do not want to present English Linguistics as a field riven with division, disagreement, and factions; on the contrary, the field often seems a particularly harmonious and welcoming one. But tension can be a force for the good; physical tension holds up bridges, after all. The crucial thing is to be aware of the potential tensions and areas of disagreement, and to debate them openly; and this has been a characteristic of the best work in English Linguistics. It is to such lively, scholarly, and collegial debates that we hope this *Handbook* will continue to contribute.

We would like to thank all those who have helped with the production of this *Handbook*. In particular, we owe our authors a special, if obvious, debt of gratitude for their enthusiastic participation in the project; their (mainly) timely delivery of their chapters; and their good-humoured and swift attention to the comments of reviewers. We also thank these reviewers, some, though not all, authors themselves, for their involvement and for their detailed, careful, and sensible reports. Leaving author-reviewers aside, we wish to thank in particular Paul Buitelaar, Noël Burton-Roberts, Jenny Cheshire, Bernard Comrie, Bill Croft, Teresa Fanego, Susan Hunston, Koenraad Kuiper, Knud Lambrecht, Lynne Murphy, Frank Palmer, Carson T. Schütze, Peter Trudgill, and Richard Xiao. We are also grateful to our editors at Blackwell for commissioning the volume and seeing it cheerfully through the process thus far, and to our copy editor. Finally, we thank all those colleagues and students with whom we have debated the existence, health, definition, and future of English Linguistics; we have appreciated the many reminders of how friendly and vibrant a field this is, and why we enjoy working as part of it.

Bas Aarts, London
April McMahon, Edinburgh
November 2005

Part I   Methodology

2   Description and Theory

KERSTI BÖRJARS

1   Introduction

As reflected in many chapters in this book, English is probably the most well-studied language in the history of linguistics, so that there is a vast pool of examples of both excellent description and insightful theoretical analysis to be found in the literature. Still, concepts like 'description' and 'theory' are anything but clear. The issue of what the defining characteristics of a 'theory' are has received a lot of attention in philosophy and the history of science. However, in terms of distinguishing a theory from a description, that literature is not terribly helpful. Even though 'theory' may appear to be the more complex of the two notions, there are issues also with what constitutes a description of a language.

2   The Description of English

A description of any language should contain an inventory of the building blocks; sounds and morphemes, roughly. It should also contain the rules for how those elements can be combined; phonotactic constraints, information about which differences between sounds are distinctive, how morphemes can be combined to form words, and how words can be combined to form phrases. In spite of the attention that the language has received, no complete description of English in this sense has yet been provided. To take but one example, even though there are many insightful descriptions of the English passive, the exact rules that allow for sentences such as *This road has been walked on* have not been provided. The view of a grammatical description just described coincides with the original conception of a 'generative' grammar. A generative grammar in that sense takes the building blocks of a language and 'generates' all and only the grammatical sentences of that language. Needless to say, no complete such grammar has been defined, not for English and not for any other language.

Associated with the question of what constitutes a description of English is the question of what such a description describes. Traditionally, the object of description has been a variety of English referred to as the 'standard.' Many grammars of course aim not only to *describe* this variety, but also to *prescribe* it; to describe a variety which native speakers of English should aim to follow. Even though modern grammars of English such as Quirk et al. (1985) and Huddleston and Pullum (2002) avoid prescriptivism, descriptions which aim also to prescribe are still prevalent, as witness the popularity of books such as Trask (2002). Descriptions of varieties of English other than the standard do, however, also have a long tradition. There are many good grammars of geographical dialects within Britain (for examples and references, see for instance Hughes and Trudgill 1980, Milroy and Milroy 1993), the US (e.g. Wolfram and Schilling-Estes 1998) and to some extent Australia and New Zealand (e.g. Burridge and Mulder 1998). See also Kortmann (this volume). Increasingly, varieties of English which have arisen in countries where English has not traditionally been the first language are also considered varieties in their own right and are described as such and not as examples of "English not used properly." This has led to an area of study known as World Englishes (e.g. Trudgill and Hannah 2002).

A description of a language, regardless of how one selects the particular variety, has to be based on data and a further issue involved in description is how to select these data. Although most descriptions rely on a mixture of types of data collection, a number of types can be distinguished. These are described in more detail in Meyer and Nelson (ch. 5, this volume), but given the direct way in which they impact on the relation between data and theory, we will discuss them briefly here. Each approach has advantages and disadvantages, and all of them involve some degree of idealization.

An approach that has not been uncommon in descriptions and in theoretical work is introspection; the author of the description considers whether he or she would accept a particular pronunciation, a particular phrase or sentence and uses these judgments as a basis for the description. An advantage of this approach might be that a linguistically trained person can provide more subtle judgments, whereas non-trained native speakers might find it difficult to make the distinction between 'is grammatical' and 'makes sense,' a distinction which is crucial both for description and theory.[1] The disadvantages of this approach are, however, also obvious; even trained linguists might not have a good awareness of what they actually say. There are examples of linguistic articles in which a construction is attested which is claimed in the description or in the analysis not to exist.

The introspective approach is particularly dangerous in theoretical work within a particular framework, where the desire to provide a neat analysis within the favored theory may cloud the linguist's native speaker intuitions. A more reliable way of collecting the data is to elicit grammaticality judgments from a group of native speakers or to get their judgments in a more subtle way through picture description tasks or similar processes. In an approach like this, a consensus view can emerge and peculiarities of individual speakers are ruled out. However, data collected in this way may deviate from naturally occurring data. The notion of a simple grammaticality judgment is not a straight-forward one to most native speakers. If the speaker is aware of some high-status standard which differs from their own variety, this may also interfere with their judgments, and in cases where there is no obvious standard, it may actually be difficult to get a definite judgment from native speakers.

The use of corpora avoids many of the drawbacks identified with using native speaker judgments in that it allows wide-ranging studies of naturally occurring language. Especially with the existence of large-scale electronically available corpora, this has become an important tool for the study of all varieties of English (see McEnery and Gabrielatos, ch. 3, this volume). Biber et al. (1999) is an example of a corpus-based grammar of English. There are of course drawbacks, especially in that the absence of a particular construction in a corpus cannot be taken as evidence that this construction is absent from the language. This is a familiar problem for those working on varieties for which there are no longer any native speakers, for whom corpus study is the only option. Similarly, constructions which would be described as ungrammatical by the vast majority of the language community may occur in corpora, say as speech errors, or in historical texts in the form of scribal errors.

Most descriptions of English are based on the written language, though modern grammars do refer to alternative constructions which occur in the spoken language but which are infrequent in written form. Biber et al. (1999) is an exception in that it is partially based on spoken corpora. Miller and Weinert (1998) go one step further and describe spoken language as a separate variety with a partially different grammar from the spoken language (see also Miller, this volume).

3   Theory

Trying to establish a general definition of what is and what is not a theory would not be a fruitful exercise in this kind of publication, but for the reader who is interested in such issues, Chalmers (1982) provides an eminently read-able introduction and further references. Similar general issues are discussed specifically from the perspective of linguistics in the articles in Katz (1985). The relevant questions for our purposes are rather 'When does a linguistic description turn into something more abstract, which we can call a linguistic theory?' and 'What is the relationship between description and theory in linguistics?'

With respect to the first of these questions, it is worth pointing out that every description that is not just a list of actually occurring sounds or phrases involves some degree of abstraction, so that for instance as soon as we refer to a unit such as a 'phoneme' or a 'verb phrase,' we are abstracting away from the pure data. A theory should of course predict (or generate in the sense used above) the correct set of data that it aims to deal with. However, it is often assumed that a good theory should do more than this. Chomsky (1964) defined three properties which a theory should have: they are known as 'levels of adequacy' and have played a central role not only within the Chomskyan approach to linguistics. The notion of generating the correct set of data which we have already discussed is referred to as the 'observational adequacy' criterion. In addition, a theory must be 'descriptively accurate' in that it must abstract away from the actual phrases and describe the principles which allow a theory to make predictions about the grammaticality of strings. Finally, a theory must possess 'explanatory adequacy': it must provide an explanation for how human beings can acquire the principles captured under descriptive adequacy. All linguists can be expected to agree on the necessity of observational adequacy. Even though there is some disagreement as to what the exact principles are which are captured under descriptive adequacy, the idea of a theory being required to have such principles is relatively uncontroversial. The idea that a linguistic theory should also explain processing and more generally the cognitive underpinning of language is also fairly widely accepted. However, exactly when a theory can be said to have explanatory adequacy in this sense is a very controversial issue.

Within the Chomskyan tradition, there is great emphasis on the aim of linguistic theory being the potential for explaining the knowledge of a language that is in a native speaker's head and how it came to be there:

> To put the matter in somewhat different but essentially equivalent terms, we may suppose that there is a fixed, genetically determined initial state of the mind, common to the species with at most minor variation apart from pathology. The mind passes through a sequence of states under the boundary conditions set by experience, achieving finally a "steady state" at a relatively fixed age, a state that then changes only in marginal ways . . . So viewed, linguistics is the abstract study of certain mechanisms, their growth and maturation.   (Chomsky 1980: 187–8)

This general view of the ultimate goal of linguistic theory is shared by many theoretical approaches which differ from the Chomskyan tradition in other ways, as we shall see in the next section. In an introduction to Head-driven Phrase Structure Grammar (HPSG), we find the following statement on the aim of linguistic theory:

> Indeed, we take it to be the central goal of linguistic theory to characterize what it is that every linguistically mature human being knows by virtue of being a linguistic creature, namely, universal grammar.   (Pollard and Sag 1994: 14)

However, such assumptions are by no means a necessary part of a theory. Generalized Phrase Structure Grammar, which to some extent can be said to be a pre-cursor to HPSG, very explicitly did not contain any such assumptions:

In view of the fact that the packaging and public relations of much recent linguistic theory involves constant reference to questions of psychology, particularly in association with language acquisition, it is appropriate for us to make a few remarks about the connections between the claims we make and issues in the psychology of language. We make no claims, naturally enough, that our grammar is *eo ipso* a psychological theory. Our grammar of English is not a theory of how speakers think up things to say and put them into words. Our general linguistic theory is not a theory of how a child abstracts from the surrounding hubbub of linguistic and nonlinguistic noises enough evidence to gain a mental grasp of the structure of natural language. Nor is it a biological theory of the structure of an as-yet-unidentified mental organ. It is irresponsible to claim otherwise for theories of this general sort.   (Gazdar et al. 1985: 5)

This approach would then not have the property of explanatory adequacy and hence would not be an acceptable theory according to the Chomskyan tradition.

In this context it is, however, important to keep in mind that our empirical knowledge and understanding of how the human mind deals with language is incomplete. Many accounts that claim explanatory adequacy only do so based on the assumptions made about the language faculty within their particular theoretical framework. To someone who does not share those particular assumptions, the theory would not be considered explanatory. Explanatory adequacy is a contentious issue.

To place linguistics in a broader context, we can say that those systems which we refer to as linguistic theories are essentially models of systems, on a par with a model of a chemical compound or a traffic situation. Models in this sense provide an abstract description of a system, in our case a language or a subset of a language. They are, however, not assumed just to describe, but also to enhance the understanding of that which it models. This way of looking at linguistic theory leads us to consider the relation between the model and that which it models, which comes down to the issue of the relation between the data described and the theory.

In this section so far, I have used 'theory' to describe whole frameworks, such as HPSG or Chomskyan theory. In a sense this boils down to including both the actual theory and the machinery used to express the theory under the term. Even though this is the way the term tends to be used, it is not entirely accurate to include under 'theory' the metalanguage which is used to express the theory. The distinction is sometimes articulated in linguistic writing, for instance by Bresnan (2001: 43) with respect to Lexical-Functional Grammar (LFG):

Note, however, that the formal model of LFG is *not* a syntactic theory in the linguistic sense. Rather, it is an architecture for syntactic theory. Within this architecture, there is a wide range of possible syntactic theories and sub-theories, some of which closely resemble syntactic theories within alternative architectures, and others of which differ radically from familiar approaches.   Bresnan (2001: 32)

For the sake of simplicity, I will continue to use 'theory' in the more common, less precise meaning.

Current syntactic theories share some of their metalanguage, but they also vary substantially with respect to some of their fundamental assumptions. There are different ways of modeling the same data set. At a more abstract level, different theories would all like to claim properties such as ontological parsimony, i.e. a principle known as Ockham's razor should apply: as little theoretical apparatus as possible should be used to explain a phenomenon within the theory. This is often captured in terms of a principle of economy in theories, but as we shall see, the effect which this principle is assumed to have varies drastically. Theories will also claim to have decidability – formal procedures exist for determining the answer to questions provided by the theory, like whether or not a particular sentence will be generated by the grammar – and predictability – the theory makes predictions about what does or does not occur.

4   Description and Theory

Unfortunately, in some linguistic circles, there is a history of mutual disrespect between those linguists who would refer to themselves as descriptive and those who would call themselves theoretical linguists. This is particularly unfortunate since there is a strong interdependence between description and theory formation, as we have seen. Clearly, without description there could be no valid theory. Using the terminology introduced above, to model something, we need to know what we are modeling. To my mind, it is also the case that linguistic theory has allowed us to ask some interesting questions about the described data that we could not otherwise have asked. Indeed, the insight added in this way is the prime justification for theory construction.

Let's consider in a little more detail the link between a set of data and a theory. This involves a stage which we can refer to as pre-theory (cf. Lyons 1977: 25–31). Pre-theory involves something more abstract and general than just data, but it is not yet something sufficiently systematic for it to be referred to as a theory under anybody's definition of the term. Pre-theory can be described in terms of a trichotomy between 'problems,' 'issues' and 'constructs.' Problems are sets of data grouped together under the assumption that an analysis of one member of the set should also naturally extend to the whole set. Examples of core problem sets are English auxiliaries or *wh*-questions. This is then in a sense the first step on the path from a description to a theory. By 'issues' is meant aspects of linguistic structure abstracted from the data sets, which are generally recognized as being central to any theoretical approach to the data, even though the way in which they end up being dealt with in the syntactic theory may vary. Examples of such issues are the phoneme, syntactic constituency, and the classification of categories. Constructs are theoretical concepts set up in order to analyze and characterize the problems and to capture the issues. Some constructs are common to most theoretical approaches, for instance phonological or syntactic features. Some would be present in most frameworks but with different instantiations, like phrase structure rules, whereas others still are posited in some theories but not in others, for example movement rules. A set of interrelated theoretical constructs forms the building bricks for a theory.

Given that there is no complete description even of a well-studied language like English, theories will be based on partial data sets. Questions then arise as to the breadth of data one needs to take account of in order to formulate a sound theory of language. The answers to such questions vary widely between theoretical approaches. The particular view taken of universal grammar within the Chomskyan tradition says that the basic underlying structure of all languages is identical. In its pure form this means that the underlying structure of all clauses is the same. The more superficial variation between languages is due to 'parametric variation,' something we shall return to below. If all languages are the same underlyingly, then an in-depth study of one language should suffice to formulate a theory of universal grammar. This is indeed the position taken within transformational grammar:

> I am interested, then, in pursuing some aspects of the study of mind, in particular, such aspects as lend themselves to inquiry through the construction of abstract explanatory theories that may involve substantial idealization and will be justified, if at all, by success in providing insight and explanation. From this point of view, *substantial coverage of data is not a particularly significant result*; it can be attained in many ways, and the result is not very informative as to the correctness of the principles involved.   (Chomsky 1980: 11, my emphasis)

To many descriptive linguists and typologists, a statement like this would be anathema. However, it should be added here that much good descriptive work on a variety of languages has been carried out within the Chomskyan tradition; it is just that this is in itself not an aim and not a requirement for theory formation.

All other theoretical frameworks would disagree strongly with the suggestion that broad and thorough descriptive work had only a minor role to play in the development of syntactic theory. Quotes by proponents of Generalized Phrase Structure Grammar and Role and Reference Grammar, respectively, illustrate the point:

> A necessary precondition to 'explaining' some aspect of the organization of natural languages is a description of the relevant phenomena which is thorough enough and precise enough to make it plausible to suppose that the language under analysis really is organized in the postulated way.   (Gazdar et al. 1985: 2)

> Describing linguistic phenomena is one of the central goals of linguistics . . . Developing serious explanatory theories of language is impossible in the absence of descriptions of the object of explanation. Understanding the cognitive basis of

language is impossible in the absence of an adequate cross-linguistic characterization of linguistic behavior.   (Van Valin and La Polla 1997: 3)

Given what has been said so far about description, pre-theory and theory, the best distinguishing criterion for deciding whether something is a description, or possibly a pre-theoretical description, or indeed a theory seems to rest in its explanatory power. In the Chomskyan tradition, there is a strict dichotomy between, on the one hand, the abstract internal language ability, referred to as I-language (I for internal or individual; a similar, though not identical, concept in earlier versions of the theory was 'competence') and, on the other, the physical and perceptible language, referred to as E-language (E for external; in previous versions of the theory, 'performance' stood for a related concept). The latter also involves the communicative and social aspects of language. In this tradition, the explanations captured within the theory (and this is almost exclusively syntactic theory) refer to I-language. The aim is never to capture pragmatic or social aspects of the language. This means that it is difficult to judge the extent to which a particular theoretical analysis within this framework succeeds in the aim of explanatory adequacy, unless one shares the assumptions about the nature of I-language. Indeed, to linguists not working within this tradition, the use of the term 'explain' in some analyses proposed in the literature appears to rather stretch the meaning of the word. For instance, the assumption of some feature may be said to explain a particular linguistic patterning in one theory, whereas to others the feature seems contentless, unmotivated by data and introduced with the sole purpose of creating the desired solution. However, potential misuse of the word *explain* is of course not exclusive to Chomskyan linguistics and is certainly not a common property of Chomskyan analyses.

In most other theoretical frameworks within which explanatory power is also taken to be a litmus test for the status as a theory, the explanandum – that which is to be explained – is interpreted to be broader than the internal grammar, or abstract syntactic principles. In such theories, explanations refer also to more general cognitive capacities and to how the syntactic principles interact with areas like pragmatics.

5   Some Current Theories

Even though theories may disagree on the role of typological data, one property that all theories have in common is that work has been done on English within that theory. At the same time, linguistic theories will also want to have something to say about linguistic variation and it is in this area that the differences between theories are most apparent. What I will have to say here will be based on analyses of English, but in order to illustrate differences in philosophy between the theories, in particular in their approach to typological variation, it will sometimes be necessary to refer to other languages.

Especially within the general research area of syntactic theory, there are too many well-established and interesting theories to mention or describe here. Some have a limited following. The reason for this is rarely to be found in scientific merit, but rather in socio-geographic factors. Some approaches which I regret not to be able to include here, but for which I refer the reader to the literature are Head-driven Phrase Structure Grammar (Pollard and Sag 1994), Role and Reference Grammar (Van Valin and La Polla 1997), dependency grammars such as Word Grammar (Hudson 1984, 1990) and Categorial Grammar (for an introduction, see Wood 1993), but there are others. Here I will instead concentrate on the Minimalist Program (MP), Lexical-Functional Grammar (LFG) and Optimality Theory (OT). The latter is included here because it involves the most radical paradigm shift in linguistic theory in recent times. MP and LFG have been chosen not only because they encapsulate different approaches to syntactic theory, but also because they illustrate how two approaches with very different looking architectures can actually share some properties.

With any syntactic theory, researchers working within the same paradigm may interpret the details of a theory differently, and analyses may vary with respect to how the detailed technicalities are worked out. In the descriptions that follow, the focus is on those aspects of the theory on which there is broad consensus. The emphasis will also be on those aspects which illustrate the similarities and differences most clearly. By necessity, the account given here will be schematic and will avoid some of the technical details.[2] I refer the reader to Chomsky (1993, 1995) for the original statement of the Minimalist Program. There are a number of textbooks, such as Adger (2003) which gives a clear and faithful view of both the philosophy underlying the theory and the technicalities of MP. For LFG, Bresnan (2001) and Dalrymple (2001) provide statements of the theory, whereas Falk (2001) is in textbook format and also has the virtue of providing explicit comparison with Chomskyan approaches. General introductions to OT are Kager (1999), McCarthy (2001) and Prince and Smolensky (2004).

5.1 The Minimalist Program

The modern roots of syntactic theory can be traced back to Chomsky's earliest work (Chomsky 1957) and even those linguists who are critical of recent versions of this theory will acknowledge the influence of this early work. The theory has gone through developments and renaming: (Extended) Standard Theory, Government and Binding (GB) and, in the early 1990s, a radical shift to the Minimalist Program (MP). The term Principles and Parameters (P&P) is used in parallel with the latter two of these, but whereas GB and MP can be said to refer to the technicalities of the analysis, P&P describes the underlying assumption that all languages have a common universal core and that the variation which is evident from even a small typological study is the result of parameters being set differently. The common core of a language is innate and the parametric variation is acquired as a child acquires the language. In GB work, the parameters were represented as a finite set of binary choices, for instance 'a head precedes its complement' or 'a head follows its complement.' The underlying idea is that a child would need relatively little evidence to set a parameter, but once the parameter is set, the child will be able to correctly predict and produce a number of other constructions which depend on the same parameter. The P&P approach is then part of an explanation for the speed of language acquisition. As we shall see presently, the view of language variation and parameters is captured slightly differently in the most recent version of Chomskyan theory, MP.

Different terms are used to capture all the stages of development within this line of syntactic research and all of them have drawbacks in spite of their common usage. Here I have used 'Chomskyan,' which seems reasonable, given that work by Noam Chomsky started the tradition and every major change has been signaled by some publication of Chomsky's (e.g. 1965, 1982, 1986, 1993). However, the development and change of direction of the tradition does of course not depend solely on one person and it may therefore appear inappropriate to use this term. 'Generative theory' is also frequently used to mean Chomskyan syntactic theory. However, this term is wrong for two reasons. Firstly, in the narrow sense of viewing a grammatical theory as a machinery which generates all and only the grammatical sentences of a language it is an inappropriate representation of what modern Chomskyan theory is aiming to achieve. Secondly, if we take a broader interpretation of the term, to mean an explicit precise approach to grammar, then all the theories mentioned here and a few more too would be rightly described as 'generative' and hence it is not a useful term for singling out the Chomskyan tradition. Another term used is 'transformational theory.' This term arose early on, when one under-lying abstract representation of a sentence, d(eep)-structure, was assumed to 'transform' into a more concrete representation, s(urface)-structure, by means of a number of transformations. Even though d-structure, s-structure and trans-formations are not quite accurate terms for the mechanisms within Minimalism, these terms are still used to capture all the stages of the development from the Standard Theory to the Minimalist Program.

The Minimalist Program is built around two types of representation of a syntactic object, or rather, two interface levels. These are Logical Form (LF), which relates to meaning aspects of a linguistic object and Phonetic Form (PF), which relates to its pronunciation. Formally, LF and PF are interface levels because they are the representations of language with which our conceptual and auditory-perceptual abilities interact. A grammatical sentence can then be seen as an appropriate pair of LF and PF representations, a meaning compon-ent and a corresponding sound component. The objects which are eventually represented at LF and PF are built up from a list of elements taken from the lexicon. Such a list is referred to as the numeration. The lexical elements which are part of the numeration have the shape of feature bundles and as part of the derivation of, say, a clause, these elements merge in pairs to give a new unit, which can in turn be merged with another unit. Under this approach then, the operation Merge is central and since Merge is defined only to combine two elements at a time, only binary branching trees can be created by it.

In order to ensure that only grammatical phrases are built up in this way, there need to be restrictions on which elements Merge can combine. This is captured in MP as constraints on the feature content of the elements which are to be merged. All features need to be 'checked'; a theory of feature checking is central to the MP. Checking is a technical term, the essence of which is to ensure that elements do not occur in an inappropriate environment. For example, an element with a nominative case feature may only occur in a slot in the sentence where a nominative case is permitted, or, in this terminology, a nominative element can only Merge with an element which allows its nominative feature to be checked. There are detailed structural constraints on checking, but they are not directly relevant here.

There are two different ways of classifying features: with respect to their semantic content and with respect to their structural behavior. The semantic distinction gives two types; 'uninterpretable features,' which are not relevant to the semantics of the unit, but are purely formal, and 'interpretable features,' which have semantic content. Both types of features need to be checked against a matching feature in an appropriate place in the tree. The difference lies in the fact that uninterpretable features are erased as they are checked. If such a feature is not checked and erased before LF, it would result in an illicit LF representation, since meaningless features would have to be assigned an interpretation. Another way of putting this is that uninterpretable features which remain at LF cause a derivation to 'crash' at LF. Interpretable features too need to be checked, but they are not deleted on checking. These features have meaning, which will need to be included in the interpretation at LF. If all features are checked, the derivation is said to 'converge' at LF and we get a grammatical unit. Examples of uninterpretable features are Case features and those features which capture selectional restrictions of the kind traditionally known as subcategorization.[3] For instance, *the* would contain some feature which requires it to combine with a nominal. If *the* is successfully combined with a nominal, then that feature is checked and erased, and the resulting unit can merge with another element, say a verb. Without merging with a noun, *the* would retain an unchecked uninterpretable feature and could then not combine with anything else. Examples of interpretable features are the so called Φ-features (person, number and gender) and tense features.

Features can also be divided into 'strong' and 'weak' features. This distinction relates to constraints on the structural position of the elements whose features are to be checked. A strong feature can only be checked 'locally,' i.e. if the feature against which it is to be checked is near it in the tree. It is not necessary here to go into what types of structural relations there are or what 'near' means. The crucial point is that a strong feature can make an element move to a position in the tree from where its features can be checked. Weak features do not have this effect. Strictly speaking, weak features can cause movement, but so as to effect only LF and not PF, i.e. for the purposes of pronunciation, the element occurs in its original position, but for the interpretation it has moved to a new position. Whether a feature is strong or weak is not related to its semantics. It has been suggested in the literature that feature strength is connected to there being overt morphology marking the feature, but this connection is certainly not absolute. The difference between strong and weak features can be illustrated by *wh*-questions. In English neutral *wh*-questions, the *wh*-constituent occurs at the front of the clause and not in its canonical position. It is assumed that this involves a strong feature, say [+*wh*], which can only be checked if the *wh*-constituent moves to the front. In Chinese for instance, the *wh*-phrase is not fronted and hence the Chinese [+*wh*] feature is assumed to be weak.

Let's now turn to the way in which phrases are constructed. In the initial stages of this process, the derivation, lexical elements undergo Merge to form a lexical core for the sentence. Features like the selectional ones can be checked in this core. Functional features such as tense, on the other hand, can be represented on a lexical element in the core, e.g. *like-liked*, but since there is no identical feature to check against, they cannot be checked within the lexical core. Instead, it is assumed that for each such relevant interpretable functional feature there is a functional category which houses the relevant checking feature. This functional category can Merge with the lexical core and in doing so check the features within it. This checking can, however, only take place if particular structural relations exist between the checker and the feature to be checked. As we shall see, this reliance on structure to capture features is a major distinguishing feature between MP and other feature-based theories such as LFG.

Let's consider an example. For a sentence like (1a), the required lexical elements Merge successively to form the tree in (1b). The labeling of the nodes in this tree indicate that the V is the head and that the phrase is built up around this head to form a VP. In this approach to phrase structure, all phrases are endocentric, which means that one of the daughters is the head of the phrase, for instance in that it is of the same category type as the mother.[4]

(1)   a.   The dog ate the rats.

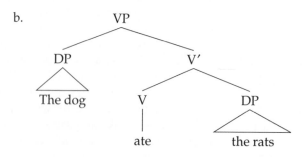

The words in (1b) would all have uninterpretable features indicating selectional restrictions. These restrictions are satisfied and it follows from the assumptions made within MP that the features are deleted. However, *ate* would also have an interpretable feature, *past*, which has not been checked. In order for this checking to take place, a functional category, T, containing the appropriate feature must be added, to give the tree in (2). This category heads a phrase TP. The structural relation between *past* under T and *past* under V is such that checking can take place.

(2)

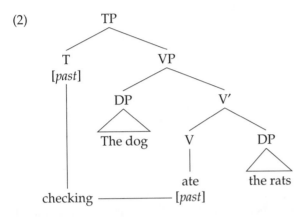

In this example, the presence of the category T is motivated by the presence of a feature without linguistic form – though the same feature does have lexical content on the verb under V. There are, however, also words which have the category T so that they can be lexically inserted under T, for instance modal verbs. For other interpretable functional features, like *perfect*, *progressive* or *negation*, new projections are added which can house the features against which elements need to be checked. Thus a hierarchy of functional projections is established. This hierarchy is assumed to be universal so that in principle all clauses have the same structure.

The position of the subject in (2) is licenced by the semantic role assigned to it by the verb. However, this noun will also have a Case feature, which will need to be checked. The Case feature is *nom*, for nominative, and since only tensed sentences take nominative subjects and tense is a feature of T, it is assumed that there is some feature under T relating to subjects. The issue then arises how this feature is checked. Now, if Case is a strong feature, then it will need to be checked in a more local relation than that between T and the DP *the dog* in (2).[5] Indeed, the very definition of subject relies on this structural position: the subject is defined as the element that is found in this position within TP. So far, we have used the terminology traditionally employed within Chomskyan theory: noun phrases are said to 'move' and leave behind a trace. However, in MP, it is assumed that a copy is made of the moved element, which is then merged higher in the tree. Under this view a copy of the element is left behind.

The distinction between copy and trace is not essential to us here, however (see Adger 2003: 145 for a discussion).

(3)

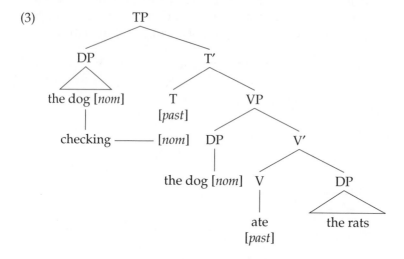

As noted in section 3, theories commonly espouse some principle of economy. As the name indicates, Minimalism is such a theory. Movement such as that illustrated here is assumed to be "expensive" and Minimalism's principle of economy rules overt movement out, unless this is the only way to make a derivation converge, that is to ensure that the resulting sentence is grammatical.

Before we turn from this brief description of the mechanics of the MP to an account of the fundamental properties of Lexical-Functional Grammar, MP's reliance on structure should be highlighted. Firstly, even though features appear to be the locus of information (both formal and semantic), given feature checking and the close relation between structure and features, tree structure is actually required to capture information. In order to have a past tense interpretation or to express perfective aspect, the structure of a sentence needs to contain a TP headed by a *past* feature or a PerfP headed by *perf*, respectively. Secondly, grammatical relations and semantic roles rely on structure for their definition and presence. For instance, in order for a noun phrase to have the grammatical relation subject, it must occur in a particular structural position in relation to a functional node T. We shall return to this issue below.

5.2   *Lexical-Functional Grammar*

Lexical-Functional Grammar, like all other theories mentioned above, except those in the Chomskyan tradition, is non-transformational. Within LFG, any linguistic element is assumed to have associated with it information of different types, e.g. phonetic information, information about categories and structure, and information about the functional aspects and the semantics of the string. The different types of information are represented in separate dimensions, e.g.

p(honetic)-structure, c(onstituent/ategory)-structure, f(unctional)-structure and s(emantic)-structure. LFG differs crucially from Chomskyan theory in that these dimensions of information are not related by transformations, but by so-called mapping relations, which allow non-one-to-one correspondence. This means that, say, one word in c-structure may be mapped to more than one feature in f-structure. LFG can then be described as a parallel correspondence theory: there are parallel representations of a linguistic element and the mapping relations ensure that there is appropriate correspondence between them.

Let's consider now the sentence in (4a) from an LFG perspective. In order to prepare the way for a comparison with MP, I will focus here on the c-structure, given in (4b), and the f-structure, as in (4c).

(4)　a.　The dog ate the rats.

　　b.

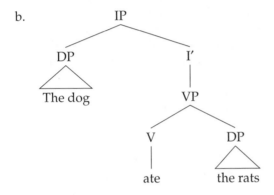

　　c.
$$\begin{bmatrix} \text{PRED} & \text{'eat'} \langle (\text{SUBJ}), (\text{OBJ}) \rangle \\ \text{SUBJ} & \begin{bmatrix} \text{PRED} & \text{'dog'} \\ \text{DEF} & + \\ \text{NUM} & sg \end{bmatrix} \\ \text{OBJ} & \begin{bmatrix} \text{PRED} & \text{'rat'} \\ \text{DEF} & + \\ \text{NUM} & pl \end{bmatrix} \\ \text{TENSE} & \text{past} \end{bmatrix}$$

In (4c), PRED is a semantic feature, which is the locus of subcategorization. The PRED feature for the verb states that the verb has the meaning 'eat' as a relation between the interpretation of the subject and the interpretation of the object. Hence in order for the f-structure to be complete, the structure must contain elements that can be mapped onto the subject and the object functions. Further semantic detail is captured in the s-structure, but is not of relevance to us here.

The c-structure in (4b) is based on assumptions different from those of (1b). Firstly, the number of functional categories is limited to three (C, I and D).[6]

A functional category is used when there is evidence that some functional feature is associated with a particular position. The presence of a functional feature is in itself not sufficient to motivate a functional category. The evidence for a functional category I in English comes from the special positional behavior of modal verbs and other auxiliaries. Secondly, even though there is an IP, parallel to TP in (1b), there is no head I. This is because within the rather unorthodox assumptions made about phrase structure within LFG, no node is obligatory unless required to be present by independent principles. IP and I' are in the tree because for English, the notion of subject is assumed to be defined structurally with respect to these two nodes. However, only certain verbs have the characteristics in English which associate them with I rather than V. These are the auxiliary verbs. Given that there is no auxiliary verb in this sentence and no independent principle which requires the presence of I, this node is simply pruned. Further crucial assumptions about phrase structure which are not illustrated in (4) can be illustrated by the data in (5) from Latin, which has a freer word order than English. Given the right information structural conditions, all word order permutations of (5a) are possible, and this would be represented as different versions of the tree in (5b) within LFG.

(5) a.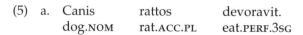

       Canis   rattos   devoravit.
       dog.NOM   rat.ACC.PL   eat.PERF.3SG

   b.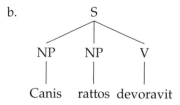

As (5b) illustrates, exocentric – or non-headed – categories are permitted within LFG. The S category in (5b) does not have a head in the way that the TP in (3) had a T head or the IP in (4b) had an I head. Neither the NP nor the VP daughter is of the same category as the mother. Even though functional information such as tense is represented on the verb, given the relatively free word order of Latin, it cannot be said to be associated with a particular structural position and hence there is no functional category I in (5b). Latin has no determiners and hence the argument can be extended to the D of noun phrases and hence they are labeled NP rather than DP. The Merge process in MP is defined to create only binary branching trees and the tree in (5b) would not be permitted. In LFG, on the other hand, c-structure is generated by phrase structure rules which do not contain an assumption that c-structure is limited to binary branching.

The mapping relations, which are at the heart of LFG, are mathematically well defined bi-directional functions, which means that the mapping relations involved in the analysis of the sentence in (4a) can either generate the c-structure if the f-structure is known, or the other way around. We will not go into the technical detail here, but in (4), as mentioned, the mapping is based on the structural position in c-structure. The subject is the DP which is the daughter of IP and sister of I′ and the object is the sister of V. Given what we have said about the free word order and the c-structure of Latin, on the other hand, the mapping cannot be based on the structural position. Instead it is based on the morphological case features of the noun phrases.[7] This is illustrated in (6), where in (6a), it is the specific position which provides the linguistic clue to which element is the subject, whereas in (6b) the case marking is the clue to subject status, regardless of where the noun phrase occurs. The corresponding sentences in English and Latin have the same f-structure, but this f-structure is mapped from different c-structures.

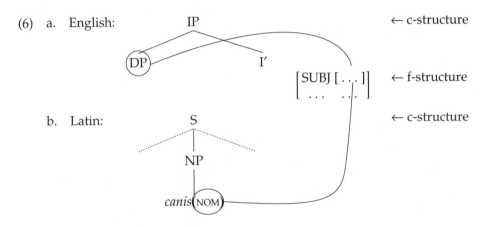

(6) a. English: IP   ← c-structure

                    DP   I′

                                              [SUBJ [...]]   ← f-structure
                                              [...   ...]

       b. Latin: S   ← c-structure

                                NP

                      canis NOM

5.3   *A comparison of MP and LFG*

A number of similarities and differences relating to assumptions about phrase structure between MP and LFG have been pointed out already. The analyses of English within MP and LFG share a number of properties. In particular, the grammatical relation of subject, and through that the relation to the semantic role agent, is defined through structure.

There are also crucial differences between the two theories. They differ for instance in the way in which elements select the phrases which must obligatorily accompany them. In Minimalism, a transitive verb like *eat* carries a categorial feature for its complement, namely N. The information that it is an object is derived from its structural position. In LFG, on the other hand, the selectional information is captured in terms of function, so that the verb requires an object. Language-specific restrictions on the relation between function and category are then stated separately, for instance if a language only permits noun phrases as subjects.

The two theories vary also in the extent to which the presence of certain features relies on the presence of structure. The word *has* in a sentence like *The dog has eaten the rats* captures two features, *perfect* and *present*. Within Minimalism, the checking procedure would require both of these features to be represented under separate nodes in the tree, giving rise to a PerfP and a TP. Within LFG, both features are mapped from the same word. In the case of English this word is found under one functional node, but in languages assumed not to have an I node, the word from which the same two features are mapped would be found under a lexical V node.

The main difference between the two approaches as far as the analysis of English is concerned can be said to reside in the centrality of structure in MP. In LFG, on the other hand, constituent structure is just one dimension of information, and is only used to capture that which is assumed to be truly structural on the basis of criteria like constituency tests. Still, anyone acquainting themselves with the two theories may feel that it does not make much difference whether functions are read directly off structure or whether they are associated with structure through a mapping algorithm. However, if we return to the Latin sentence in (5a), the differences appear more clearly. For a number of reasons, not least to make sure that the association with semantic roles is appropriate, i.e. to know 'which noun phrase eats which noun phrase,' one of the two noun phrases needs to be associated with the subject function. We saw that in an LFG analysis, this is done by direct mapping from the case marker, wherever it occurs in the c-structure, to the subject function in the f-structure. Within MP, on the other hand, the subject function is associated with a particular position within TP, which means that regardless of the word order, the subject noun phrase must at some stage of the derivation appear in that position. If it does not appear there in the surface structure, then it must have moved out of the position. Since elements can only move upwards in the tree under standard assumptions, this means that structure must be added above TP. Since overt movement is expensive in terms of the economy principle adopted within Minimalism and should be avoided unless necessary, these higher projections must contain strong features which motivate the movement. There is then a danger that these strong features appear to be purely diacritic – this is to say that the features seem to be there only to get the elements to appear in the right surface position. For the analysis to be convincing, the strong features should be independently motivated. For instance, with respect to word order in the clause, the appropriate features may be related to information structure.

The fundamental difference between MP and LFG is not so blatant when only English is considered. We have seen that in both frameworks, grammatical relations like subjects are defined by their position. This is of course not an accident. MP is heavily structure-based and English is a language which relies heavily on structure to signal grammatical information. The theoretical approaches that led to the development of MP were initially based almost exclusively on English. LFG, on the other hand, grew out of typological work and languages which appear not to rely on structure fed into the early development of the theory. There is now work within MP on a great number of different languages and some proponents of the theory have a very explicit interest in accounting for typological variation. However, this variation is now formally expressed exclusively as variation in types and strength of features.

Both theories also rely on some principle of economy, but its effect is radically different within the two theories. In MP, one economy effect that we have mentioned is the cost associated with overt movement. However, given that all languages are assumed to have the same underlying structure, and given that surface order varies substantially between languages, many languages will have substantial obligatory overt movement, motivated by strong features found under separate functional categories. In LFG, on the other hand, the economy principle militates against functional categories and structure which are not motivated by purely structural arguments.

5.4 *Optimality Theory (OT)*

Work within OT started little more than ten years ago and involves a radical departure from previous approaches. In this time it has gained ground particularly in phonology, where it is now the dominant theory, but also in syntax. The fact that OT aims to use the same theoretical framework to cover several areas of linguistics also makes it remarkable.

What makes OT's departure from traditional approaches to theory so radical is the way in which a grammatical sentence is assumed to have come about. As we have seen, in the traditional use of generative grammar, a grammar should generate all grammatical sentences of a language and no ungrammatical sentences. In OT in contrast, one part of the grammar component is assumed to generate a large – in fact infinite – number of potential expressions which compete to express the same underlying idea. These are referred to as output candidates. Another part of the grammar then adjudicates in this competition. It does so by applying a number of constraints which rule out certain properties. The constraints are such that any candidate is unlikely to satisfy them all, but the constraints are ranked, so that it becomes more important for a candidate to satisfy the highly ranked constraints. Which constraints are most highly ranked varies between languages. An example using the formalism should clarify.

The procedure in OT starts from an INPUT, that is the underlying form to be expressed. There is some variation as to what constitutes the input, but in phonology, it can be thought of as a phonemic underlying structure. In syntax, for a clause it can be assumed to be roughly the verb, its arguments and associated features. From this input, a set of output candidates are generated. This is done by a component called GEN. With regard to syntax, GEN generates structures like the ones we saw in 5.1 and 5.2 and exactly what type of rules

GEN contains will then depend on one's theoretical assumptions. As we have said, GEN produces a set of potential output candidates for each input and only one of these will be selected as the grammatical output. The core of OT is then a set of violable constraints, CON, against which the candidates are judged. The constraints are ranked so that there are some highly ranked constraints, the violation of which renders the output candidate ungrammatical. A lower ranked constraint can then be violated in order to satisfy a higher ranked one. Both GEN and CON are universal, so that language variation resides entirely in the ranking of the constraints within CON. To illustrate, let's consider two constraints: (1) states that an argument should occur in its canonical position, say next to its selecting verb, let's call it CANONICAL and (2) requires a *wh*-phrase to occur sentence initially, FRONT WH. If we imagine now an input containing the verb *eat*, a subject *the dog*, a future feature and the information that the object argument is questioned, we can express this informally as *eat* (*dog*[DEFINITE], WH) [FUTURE], i.e. a relation 'eat' holds between a definite 'dog' and a questioned element. GEN then takes this input and generates a large number of sentences. The exact words used will depend on the language of course, but I will use English words here. In order to get a feel for how the constraints in CON work, it is sufficient here to focus on two of the output candidates, namely the two which differ with respect to CANONICAL and FRONT WH, but which are identical in all other respects.[8] The constraints are displayed in the right-hand portion of a table, referred to as a tableau in OT, where the higher ranked constraints occur further to the left. The different output candidates are listed in columns on the left-hand side of the table with the actual input given above them. In the cells of the table, a star indicates a violation of that particular constraint and an exclamation mark indicates that the violation was fatal since there was a better candidate. Tableau 2.1 captures the constraint ranking for English; FRONT WH ranks above CANONICAL, and hence it is more important for the language to have *wh* phrases at the front of the clause than in their canonical position. In tableau 2.2, the opposite relation holds. As is customary in OT, a pointing hand is used to indicate the winning candidate.

The ranking in tableau 2.1 represents the situation in a language like English, which sacrifices the desire to have an object immediately following its verb in order to satisfy the constraint requiring fronting of a *wh*-word. Tableau 2.2, on

Tableau 2.1   FRONT *WH* ranked above CANONICAL

eat (*dog*[DEFINITE], WH) [FUTURE]	FRONT *WH*	CANONICAL
The dog will eat what	*!	
☞ What will the dog eat		*

Tableau 2.2   CANONICAL ranked above FRONT *WH*

eat (dog[DEFINITE], WH) [FUTURE]	CANONICAL	FRONT *WH*
☞ The dog will eat what		*
What will the dog eat	*!	
. . .		

the other hand, captures a language like Chinese, where *wh* words are left in their canonical position.[9]

Because OT in itself has nothing to say about the nature of GEN, this component receives different interpretations, in particular in syntactic applications of the theory. This also makes OT a meta-theory, rather than a theory, in that the shape of GEN and the formulation of the constraints depends on one's assumptions about syntactic theory. In the context of the two other theories we have considered here, there are syntactic OT analyses which can be described as MP-OT or LFG-OT depending on what assumptions underlie GEN and the constraints.[10]

6   Conclusion

One thing I hope this chapter has demonstrated is that the distinction between description and theory is by no means clear cut. It is difficult to conceive of any interesting linguistic description which does not make some abstract assumptions. Similarly, within theories analyses can be found which do little more than state the data the way a pre-theoretical description would, even though they use the terminology of a theoretical framework.

Criteria which have been suggested in the literature as being crucial in distinguishing a theory from a description, or to judge the quality of a theory, such as Chomsky's levels of adequacy or ontological parsimony, are difficult to apply. With respect to the latter, for instance, we have seen that principles of economy as applied to linguistic theories tend involve a trade-off; simplicity in one part of the analysis is paid for by complexity in another part.

The fact that there are a number of different theories for different areas of linguistics seems no bad thing, given that it is still a relatively speculative area of investigation. Terminology and mechanisms for explanation vary between theoretical frameworks. Consequently, the questions naturally asked, and the answers provided, will vary between theories. Variation between theories ensures breadth of coverage, and as long as researchers are literate in each other's terminology, there should be ample room for cross-fertilization between theories.

NOTES

1   For problems with the use of terms such as introspection and acceptability, see Meyer and Nelson (ch. 5, this volume).

2   There is also some variation within theories in technical details. Where this is the case, I have attempted to describe the approach most characteristic of the theory.

3   Case in Chomskyan theory is not the same as morphological case marking, but is an abstract feature capturing grammatical relations. In order to indicate this distinction it is always written with a capital C.

4   An additional category vP is usually assumed. This is not directly relevant here. Noun phrases are assumed to be headed by a determiner and are hence referred to as D(eterminer)P.

5   The situation is slightly more complicated and a feature specifically relating to subjects, often called the Extended Projection Principle (EPP) feature, is required.

6   C stands for complementizer and is also standardly assumed in Minimalism.

7   This involves a concrete interpretation of case as a feature marked by linguistic material, contrasting with the abstract Case of MP (cf. n. 3). The agreement marking on the verb also plays a role in the identification of the subject and in some languages this may be the only clue, in which case the mapping is from the agreement marking. We will, however, not illustrate this here.

8   In the example below, the issue of subject auxiliary inversion in English is ignored.

9   Of course the losing candidate in tableau 2.1 is grammatical in English, but not as an unmarked question.

10 There is of course also a very substantial body of work within both MP and LFG which does not assume an OT approach.

FURTHER READING

For description, I refer to the references provided in Meyer and Nelson (this volume). For the original statements on the Minimalism Program, I recommend Chomsky (1995), though these are not written for the beginner and should maybe only be tackled after an introductory text like Adger (2003). For LFG, apart from core texts such as (Bresnan, 2001), the proceedings of LFG conferences are published online at cslipublications.stanford.edu/hand/miscpubsonline.html, the most recent one at the time of writing being Butt and King (2005). There are some books which compare Chomskyan theory with non-transformational theory. However, none of these is up to date, the most recent one is Borsley (1999). A book that is more up to date and provides some limited comparison with LFG is Carnie (2001). For OT, there are a number of collections of articles, for instance Legendre et al. (2001) and Sells (2001). For those who are interested in the theoretical properties of different models, I suggest Croft (1995), or, for a more polemical approach, Lappin et al.

(2000) and the responses that followed in the same and the next volume of that journal.

Adger, David (2003) *Core syntax: a minimalist approach*. Oxford: Oxford University Press.

Borsley, Robert (1999) *Syntactic theory: a unified approach*. London: Edward Arnold.

Bresnan, Joan (2001) *Lexical-functional grammar*. Oxford: Blackwell Publishers.

Butt, Miriam and Tracy Holloway King (eds.) (2005) *The proceedings of the LFG05 conference*. Stanford, CA: CSLI Publications. cslipublications.stanford.edu/LFG/9/lfg05.html.

Carnie, Andrew (2001) *Syntax*. Oxford: Blackwell Publishers.

Chomsky, Noam (1995) *The minimalist program*. Cambridge, MA: MIT Press.

Croft, William (1995) Autonomy and functionalist linguistics. *Language* 71, 490–532.

Lappin, Shalom, Robert D. Levine, and David E. Johnson (2000) Topic . . . comment: the structure of unscientific revolutions. *Natural Language and Linguistic Theory* 18, 665–71.

Legendre, Géraldine, Jane Grimshaw, and Sten Vikner (eds.) (2001) *Optimality-theoretic syntax*. Cambridge, MA: MIT Press.

Sells, Peter (ed.) (2001) *Formal and empirical issues in optimality theoretic syntax*. Stanford, CA: CSLI Publications.

REFERENCES

Adger, David (2003) *Core syntax: a minimalist approach*. Oxford: Oxford University Press.

Biber, Douglas, Stig Johansson, Geoffrey Leech, Susan Conrad, and Edward Finegan (1999). *Longman grammar of spoken and written English*. Harlow: Longman.

Bresnan, Joan (2001) *Lexical-functional grammar*. Oxford: Blackwell Publishers.

Burridge, Kate and Jean Mulder (1998) *English in Australia and New Zealand: an introduction to its history, structure and use*. Oxford: Oxford University Press.

Chalmers, A. F. (1982) *What is this thing called science? An assessment of the nature and status*. Milton Keynes: Open University Press.

Chomsky, Noam (1957) *Syntactic structures*. Cambridge, MA: MIT Press.

Chomsky, Noam (1964) *Current issues in linguistic theory*. The Hague: Mouton.

Chomsky, Noam (1965) *Aspects of the theory of syntax*. Cambridge, MA: MIT Press.

Chomsky, Noam (1980) *Rules and representations*. New York: Columbia University Press.

Chomsky, Noam (1982) *Lectures on government and binding*. Series in Generative Grammar. Dordrecht: Foris.

Chomsky, Noam (1986) *Barriers*. Cambridge, MA: MIT Press.

Chomsky, Noam (1993) A minimalist program for linguistic theory. In *The view from Building 20: essays in linguistics in honor of Sylvain Bromberger*, eds. Ken Hale and Samuel Jay Keyser, 1–52. Cambridge, MA: MIT Press.

Chomsky, Noam (1995) *The minimalist program*. Cambridge, MA: MIT Press.

Dalrymple, Mary (2001) *Lexical functional grammar*. Syntax and Semantics 34. New York NY: Academic Press.

Falk, Yehuda (2001) *Lexical-functional grammar: an introduction to parallel constraint-based syntax*. Stanford, CA: CSLI Publications.

Gazdar, Gerald, Ewan Klein, Geoffrey K. Pullum, and Ivan A. Sag (1985)

Generalized Phrase Structure Grammar.
Oxford: Blackwell.

Huddleston, Rodney, and Geoffrey K.
Pullum (2002) *The Cambridge grammar
of the English language.* Cambridge:
Cambridge University Press.

Hudson, Richard A. (1984) *Word
grammar.* Oxford: Blackwell.

Hudson, Richard A. (1990) *English word
grammar.* Oxford: Blackwell.

Hughes, Arthur, and Peter Trudgill
(1980) *English accents and dialects: an
introduction to social and regional
varieties of British English.* London:
Edward Arnold.

Kager, René (1999) *Optimality theory.*
Cambridge: Cambridge University
Press.

Katz, Jerrold J. (ed.) (1985) *The philosophy
of linguistics.* Oxford: Oxford
University Press.

Lyons, John (1977) *Semantics.* 2 vols.
Cambridge: Cambridge University
Press.

McCarthy, John (2001) *A thematic guide to
optimality theory.* Cambridge:
Cambridge University Press.

Miller, Jim, and Regina Weinert (1998)
*Spontaneous spoken language: syntax
and discourse.* Oxford: Clarendon
Press.

Milroy, James, and Lesley Milroy (eds.)
(1993) *Real English: the grammar
of English dialects in the British Isles.*
London: Longman.

Pollard, Carl, and Ivan A. Sag (1994)
Head-driven phrase structure grammar.
Chicago: University of Chicago Press.

Prince, Alan, and Paul Smolensky (2004)
*Optimality theory: constraint interaction
in generative grammar.* Oxford:
Blackwell.

Quirk, Randolph, Sidney Greenbaum,
Geoffrey Leech, and Jan Svartvik
(1985) *A comprehensive grammar of
the English language.* London:
Longman.

Trask, Larry (2002) *Mind the gaffe: the
Penguin guide to common errors in
English.* London: Penguin.

Trudgill, Peter and Jean Hannah (2002)
International English, 4th edn. London:
Edward Arnold.

Van Valin, Robert D. Jr, and Randy La
Polla (1997) *Syntax. structure, meaning
and function.* Cambridge: Cambridge
University Press.

Wolfram, Walt, and Natalie Schilling-
Estes (1998) *American English: dialects
and variation.* Oxford: Blackwell.

Wood, Mary McGee (1993) *Categorial
grammar.* London: Routledge.

3 English Corpus Linguistics

TONY MCENERY AND COSTAS GABRIELATOS

1 Introduction

Since the 1960s, electronic corpora have come to prominence as a resource used by linguists. While their use remains a source of debate and controversy to this day (see for example Newmeyer 2003; Prodromou 1997; Seidlehofer 2003: 77–123; Widdowson 1991) their contribution to linguistics in general, and English linguistics in particular, as well as to language teaching, is now widely acknowledged. Corpus tools have not only strengthened the position of descriptive linguistics, but have also enhanced theoretically oriented linguistic research. This contribution has been felt most strongly in English linguistics, as it was pioneering work undertaken on English language corpora, such as the *Brown* corpus (Francis and Kučera 1964), which set the agenda for much of the work that has been undertaken using corpora since then. In this chapter we will examine the nature of corpus linguistics, review the general contribution of corpora to linguistic theory and then explore in more depth the contribution of corpora in four major areas:

- language description in general, and the production of reference resources in particular;
- lexicogrammar and the lexical approach to language analysis and description (lexical grammar);
- the teaching of English as a foreign language;
- the study of language change, with particular reference to the role that corpora have to play in theoretically informed accounts of language change.

2   The Nature of Corpus Linguistics

Introductory books on corpus linguistics are generally at pains to assert that corpus linguistics is not a branch of linguistics, nor a linguistic theory, but a methodology, one of the possible ways of 'doing' linguistics (e.g. Biber et al. 1998: 3–4; Kennedy 1998: 7; McEnery and Wilson 2001: 2; Meyer 2002: xi). For some, the term *corpus linguistics* is now synonymous with *empirical linguistics* (e.g. Sampson 2001: 6). However, it has been argued that, although it is not a linguistic theory in itself, corpus linguistics is more than just a methodology; rather, it is "a new research enterprise" and "a new philosophical approach to the subject" (Leech 1991: 106). It has also been proposed that corpus linguistics has a "theoretical status" (Tognini-Bonelli 2001: 1), in that observations of language facts lead to the formulation of hypotheses and generalizations, which are then unified in a theoretical statement; corpora need not simply be used to test existing theories, particularly ones formulated mainly on the basis of intuitions (2001: 2; see also section 3 below).

A point that all writers defining corpus linguistics agree upon is that corpus linguistics is empirical, in that it examines, and draws conclusions from, attested language use, rather than intuitions. This is not to say that intuitions play no role in corpus linguistics, but that they do not provide the data for analysis, nor do intuitions supersede the empirical evidence. Also, as a rule, corpus linguistics examines samples, however large, of language use, as it is typically impossible to capture the entirety of a language in a corpus. Yet corpus linguistics can examine entireties if, for example, the corpus content is limited in terms of one or more of the following: authorship, topic, and place and date of publication. For example, it is feasible to build corpora containing the entire work of a novelist, or the text of a newspaper over a period of time.

Another central characteristic of modern corpus linguistics is the use of computers; in fact, the term 'corpus linguistics' is now synonymous with 'computer corpus linguistics' (e.g. Leech 1992: 106). Hunston (2002: 20) makes explicit the dual function of computers in facilitating the collection and storage of large amounts of language data, and in enabling the development of the software that is used to access and analyze the corpus data. The pivotal role of computers in corpus linguistics is such that corpus linguistics has also been defined as a branch of computational linguistics (e.g. Oostdijk 1991: 2). The benefits of the use of computers in corpus linguistics are substantial. Computers and software programs have enabled researchers to collect, store and manage vast amounts of data relatively quickly and inexpensively. Data analysis and processing is fast and, in many instances, automated. The use of computers "gives us the ability to *comprehend*, and to account for, the contents of . . . corpora in a way which was not dreamed of in the pre-computational era of corpus linguistics" (Leech 1992: 106). Automated processes also allow for the replicability of studies, and the checking of the statistical reliability of results.

Although corpus linguistics does not downplay the importance of the qualitative interpretation of the data (e.g. Mair 1991), it does, nevertheless, have a strong focus on quantitative information, that is, frequency counts and statistical measures. The absolute and relative frequency of linguistic items features heavily in most, if not all, corpus studies. Statistical information based on the frequency of occurrence of language items is at the heart of probabilistic accounts of language (e.g. Halliday 1991). Statistical measures on the strength of lexical co-occurrence, which also take into account the relative frequency of the co-occurring items, play a central role in much of the research done within the neo-Firthian paradigm (e.g. Stubbs 2002).

3   Debates in Corpus Linguistics

It was mentioned in the previous section that corpus linguistics is viewed primarily as a methodology, not a theory. However, this should not be understood to imply that corpus linguistics is theory-free. The focus and method of research, as well as the type of corpus selected for a study, is influenced by the theoretical orientation of the researchers, explicit or implicit. Kennedy's statement that corpus linguistics has "a tendency sometimes to focus on lexis and lexical grammar rather than pure syntax" (1998: 8) is a case in point. Methodologically, corpus linguistics is equally diverse and encompasses different approaches to corpus building and use.[1] The main points of tension in corpus linguistics, which are interconnected, concern the relation between theory and data, the utility of corpus annotation,[2] and the role of intuitions.

These tensions have been formalized in the distinction between *corpus-based* and *corpus-driven* approaches to linguistics (e.g. Tognini-Bonelli 2001). This distinction is not acknowledged by all corpus linguists, and it has been felt by some to be overstated (Aarts 2002: 121), because "the worlds of the corpus-based and of the corpus-driven linguist may not be all that far apart as they are made out to be" (p. 123). However, since at the centre of this distinction lie the issues outlined above, the definitions of the corpus-based and corpus-driven approaches can serve as a springboard for the discussion of these issues.

In the corpus-based approach, the corpus is mainly used to "expound, test or exemplify theories and descriptions that were formulated before large corpora became available to inform language study" (Tognini-Bonelli 2001: 65). Although the intuitive basis of the theories being tested is seen as a weakness of this approach, it is not as much the target of criticism as the attitudes to, or techniques for, dealing with discrepancies between theoretical statements and corpus data that are supposed to characterize corpus-based linguists. Corpus annotation is a central feature of three techniques that are used. The first is to "insulate the data,"[3] that is, either to dismiss data that do not fit the theory, or to make the data fit the theory, for example, by annotating the corpus according to the theory (2001: 68–71). The second technique is to reduce the data to "a set of orderly categories which are tractable within existing descriptive systems" (2001: 68), again by annotating the corpus. The criticism here is two-pronged: the annotation scheme is based on a pre-conceived theory, and the manual annotation of the training corpus is influenced by both the theory and the annotator's intuitions. The third technique is "building the data into a system of abstract possibilities, a set of paradigmatic choices available at any point in the text" (2001: 74), and is strongly associated with Halliday's probabilistic view of grammar (e.g. 1991, 1992). This stance is criticized mainly on two related grounds: its focus is predominantly paradigmatic rather than syntagmatic, that is, it is concerned with grammar rather than lexis (Tognini-Bonelli 2001: 75–7), and, consequently, requires an annotated corpus, since "grammatical patterns . . . are not easily retrievable from a corpus unless it is annotated" (2001: 77).

The basic tenet of the corpus-driven approach is that any "theoretical statements are fully consistent with, and reflect directly, the evidence provided by the corpus" (2001: 84). Corpus-driven research aims at discovering facts about language free from the influence of existing theoretical frameworks, which are considered to be based on intuitions, and, therefore, are not comprehensive or reliable. Consequently, research is carried out on unannotated corpora, as annotation would impose a restrictive theoretical taxonomy on the data. A further characteristic of this approach is that it makes no distinction between lexis and grammar, as that, too, would require using existing distinctions, which may not be supported by the corpus data. Finally, in the corpus-driven approach the starting point of research is the patterning of orthographic words.[4] The remainder of this section will discuss views on the role of theory, intuitions, and annotation. As these issues are interrelated, their discussion will overlap to some extent.

As far as the role of theory in corpus linguistic research is concerned, it is more helpful to regard different approaches as falling between two end-points of a continuum, rather than belonging to one of two polar extremes. At one end, the corpus is used to find evidence for or against a given theory, or one or more theoretical frameworks are taken for granted;[5] at the other, the observed patterns in the corpus data are used as a basis from which to derive insights about language, independent of pre-existing theories and frameworks, with a view to developing a purely empirical theory. Of course this distinction begs the question of whether data observation and analysis can ever be atheoretical. It is interesting to note that the corpus-based approach, which is criticized in Tognini-Bonelli (2001), is associated with corpus research influenced by the work of Leech (e.g. 1991) or Halliday (e.g. 1991), and is presented as typically prioritizing "the information yielded by syntactic rather than lexical patterns" (Tognini-Bonelli 2001: 81), whereas the corpus-driven approach, which is proposed in Tognini-Bonelli (2001) , is associated with corpus research influenced by the work of Sinclair (e.g. 1991) and Firth's contextual theory of meaning, and favors a focus on lexical patterning. This indicates that the distinction is not only methodological, but also theoretical. Hunston and Francis (2000: 250), who have located their study of *pattern grammar* within the corpus-driven paradigm, state that their method "is indeed theory-driven," as "theories are, in a sense, constructed by methods."

Our view is that an atheoretical approach is not possible and hence the idea of corpus-driven approaches to language must be seen as an idealized extreme, because, as Stubbs (1996: 47) notes, "the concept of data-driven linguistics must confront the classic problem that there is no such thing as pure induction . . . The linguist always approaches data with hypotheses and hunches, however vague." Sampson (2001: 124) shifts the focus from the formulation of hypotheses to their testing:

> We do not care how a scientist dreams up the hypotheses he puts forward in the attempt to account for the facts – he will usually need to use imagination in formulating hypotheses, they will not emerge mechanically from scanning the data. What is crucial is that any hypothesis which is challenged should be *tested* against interpersonally observable, objective data.

The testing of hypotheses on corpus data is related to the use of intuitions and the annotation of corpora. Sinclair (2004a: 39) contrasts two attitudes in corpus linguistics research in a manner which reveals that, for those working within the corpus-driven paradigm, the use of annotation is seen as interconnected with the use of intuition:

> Some corpus linguists prefer to research using plain text, while others first prepare the texts by adding various analytic annotations. The former group express reservations about the reliability of intuitive "data," whereas the latter group, if obliged, will reject corpus evidence in favor of their intuitive responses.

One explanation for this connection is that adherence to a given theory is expected to have influenced the linguist to such an extent that the categories and structures recognized by the theory have become part of his/her intuitions. Sampson (2001: 135) highlights the role of schooling in the forming of intuitions: "Certainly we have opinions about language before we start doing linguistics . . . In some cases our pre-scientific opinions about language come from what we are taught in English lessons, or lessons on other languages, at school." Similarly, Sinclair (2004a: 40) sees intuition not as a "gut reaction to events, [but] educated in various ways, and sophisticated." It can be argued that the influence of education on intuitions about language is more pronounced in linguists whose education and training involves familiarization with a number of theories, and, not uncommonly, in-depth study of a specific theoretical framework.

Although the usefulness of intuitions in the forming of hypotheses has been challenged by corpus-driven linguists, there seems to be a consensus that intuitions are unavoidable in the interpretation of corpus data (e.g. Hunston 2002: 65). However, Sinclair (2004a: 47) has argued that there is a way for "keeping . . . intuition temporarily at bay." The technique seems to involve the decontextualization of the observed patterns and a temporary disassociation of form and meaning, and is aided by examining the vertical patterns of the key word in a concordance, or slotting in alternative words in a frame (e.g. *on the __ of*). Sinclair (2004a: 47–8) argues that:

> Since the essence of finding the meaning-creating mechanisms in corpora is the comparison of the patterns – as physical objects and quasi-linguistic units – with the meanings, it is valuable to be able at times to study one without the other. This takes a little skill and practice, but to my mind should be an essential part of the training of a corpus linguist.

One criticism of annotation is that it imposes the categories of a theoretical framework on the data, a practice which may interfere with finding evidence against the theory, or with discovering language features that the theory does not predict. There is also disagreement on whether annotation adds information, and therefore "value," to the corpus (Leech 1997a: 2), or whether it "loses information" (Sinclair 2004a: 52), because it assigns only one unalterable tag, when the word may not clearly belong to one existing category. Finally, reservations have been expressed regarding the degree to which corpus researchers are aware of the theoretical assumptions underlying different annotation schemes (e.g. Hunston 2002: 67; Sinclair 2004a: 55–6).

Leech (1997a: 6–8) outlines three "practical guidelines, or standards of good practice" (p. 6) for the annotation of corpora, and three further "maxims [applicable] both to the compilers and users of annotated corpora" (pp. 6–7), which partly address these reservations.

1   The raw corpus should be recoverable.
2   The annotation should be extricable.
3   The corpus user should have access to documentation providing information about the annotation scheme, the rationale behind it, the annotators, the place of annotation, and comments on the quality of annotation.
4   The annotation scheme "does not come with any 'gold standard' guarantee, but is offered as a matter of practical usefulness only" (p. 6).
5   The annotation scheme should be "based as far as possible on **consensual** or theory-neutral analyses of the data" (p. 7) [boldface in original].
6   "No one annotation scheme should claim authority as an absolute standard" (p. 7).

There is agreement on the necessity for the unannotated version of a corpus to be available to researchers (Leech 1997a: 6; Sinclair 2004a: 50–1). There also seems to be an area of consensus on the need for researchers to be aware of the theoretical principles behind the annotation scheme. Although Leech's point (3) above does not include the explicit statement of the theory informing the annotation, it can be argued that the theoretical framework should be inferable from the information given in the documentation.

The main point of concern, that of the imposition of a theory on the data, seems to be largely unresolved. Linguists of the corpus-driven persuasion would consider existing annotation schemes to be influenced by intuition-based theories, and, therefore, restricting. Proponents of annotation would see the annotated corpus as "a repository of linguistic information, because the information which was implicit in the plain text has been made explicit through concrete annotation" (McEnery and Wilson 2001: 32). However, some consensus, albeit implicit, regarding the categories used in annotation schemes seems to exist, as corpus-driven studies do make use of what might be called traditional categories, such as 'verb,' 'preposition,' 'object,' 'clause' and 'passive,' without a definition (e.g. Hunston and Francis 2000; Tognini-Bonelli 2001), which indicates that they are treated as given. Furthermore, if, as Sinclair (2004a: 47–8) proposes, it is feasible for linguists to distance themselves from their intuitions, it can be argued that it is also feasible to adopt an informed and critical approach towards the annotation. Finally, irrespective of the perceived usefulness of the annotated corpus as a product, the annotation process can reveal the strengths and limitations of the theory informing the annotation scheme and lead to its modification – a process which is consistent with an empirical approach. Aarts (2002: 122) argues that "the only way to test the correctness and coverage of an existing description is to formalize it into an annotation system and test it on a corpus . . . It is the annotation *process*, rather than its *result* (i.e. an annotated corpus) that matters" (see also Leech 1992: 112).

Although within the corpus-driven paradigm annotation is seen as counter-productive when the corpus is used for theoretically oriented research, it is deemed acceptable when the corpus is annotated with a view to being used in an "application" (Sinclair 2004a: 50–6), that is, "the use of language tools in order to achieve a result that is relevant outside the world of linguistics . . . [such as] a machine that will hold a telephone conversation, or a translating machine or even a dictionary" (p. 55). An argument that can be advanced on the basis of this view is that if applications relying on a corpus which has been annotated according to a theoretical framework are successful, then this can be regarded as an indication that the theory affords helpful insights into actual language use.

Undoubtedly, there are pitfalls and limitations in uncritically using an annotated corpus. However, the use of an unannotated corpus has its own pitfalls and limitations. An unannotated electronic corpus lends itself to the examination of forms and their patterns, as the software exists that will produce a concordance of a word-form for manual examination, or statistical measures of the strength of its collocation patterns, from an unannotated corpus.[6] However, an unannotated corpus is of little, if any, use if the research focus is upon grammatical categories, semantic notions or pragmatic functions. Tognini-Bonelli (2001: 89–90) concedes that "while collocation is instantly identifiable on the vertical axis of an alphabetical concordance, colligation represents a step in abstraction and is therefore less immediately recognizable unless the text is tagged with precisely the required grammatical information." Sampson (2001: 107) agrees that, "in general, more complex forms of investigation may only be possible if the computer has access to some form of detailed linguistic analysis of the text."

Also, the interpretation of concordance lines (e.g. Hunston 2002: 38–66), that is, the manual examination of concordances in order to identify patterns, which is a frequently used technique of corpus-driven linguists, is open to what we might call 'implicit annotation.' That is, while examining concordance lines, researchers may assign grammatical or semantic roles to words or configurations of words, either unwittingly, influenced by tradition or their education, or consciously, refraining from using established roles and patterns.

What becomes evident from the discussion of tensions in corpus linguistics is that theoretical and methodological issues are interconnected. Therefore, these issues will, inevitably, be revisited in the remainder of this chapter. In sum, when considered from specific theoretical or methodological viewpoints, different approaches to corpus linguistics appear to have merits, as well as problems and limitations. However, when considered from the viewpoint of linguistics in general, the current diversity in corpus research can only be seen as an indication of health, and should be welcomed. The next section examines in some detail the theoretical assumptions and methodological positions of what has been termed the lexical approach (or lexical grammar), and which lies behind the corpus-driven approach to linguistic research.

4   Lexicogrammar and Lexical Grammar

A major contribution to English corpus linguistics is the body of work related to lexicogrammar. This work will be covered at some length in this chapter, both because it has a salience in corpus linguistics and because it undoubtedly represents a unique contribution made by corpus linguists to linguistic theory. The idea of lexicogrammar stems from the tension caused by generating a strict distinction between the lexical and grammatical, and distinguishing between the syntagmatic and paradigmatic dimensions of language, what Sinclair (1991: 109–10) also terms the *slot and filler model* or the *open choice principle*. In this view of language, words are combined according to grammatical principles, that is, grammatical structures have grammatically defined 'slots' that can be filled by any semantically appropriate word fulfilling the grammatical criteria. This view was challenged by Firth through the concept of collocation, which concerns "syntagmatic relations between words as such, not between categories" (Stubbs 1996: 35). Sinclair (1991: 110) notes that "the open-choice principle does not provide substantial enough restraints on consecutive words. We would not produce normal text simply by operating the open-choice principle." It is unsurprising then that researchers have focused on breaking down this distinction.

Following Firth, Sinclair (1991) proposed the *idiom principle* to account for syntagmatic relations between words which cannot be explained in terms of grammar. His approach, which he terms *lexical grammar* (Sinclair 2004b: 164), is to discover generalizations about language by examining the interaction and patterning of lexis. In a sense, this entails approaching grammar via lexis, as evidence from large corpora "suggests that grammatical generalizations do not rest on a rigid foundation, but are the accumulation of the patterns of hundreds of individual words and phrases" (1991: 100; see also Halliday 1992: 64).

Halliday (1991, 1992) presents lexis and grammar as being "the same thing seen by different observers" (1992: 63) or "complementary perspectives" (1991: 32), and prefers the term *lexicogrammar*. He presents lexis and grammar as two ends of a continuum, with grammar being the "deeper" end. As examples of the 'lexis' end he cites sense relations, for example the different types of associations between the word *run* and the words *walk, hop,* and *jog* respectively. Examples of 'grammar' are polarity, mood, and transitivity, whereas prepositions and systems of modality occupy a middle position. In Halliday's words, one should keep in mind that "if you interrogate the system grammatically you will get grammar-like answers and if you interrogate it lexically you get lexis-like answers" (1992: 64).

At the root of this approach to lexical meaning and language description is Firth's notion of *meaning by collocation* (Firth 1951/1957). The notion of collocation, and its application to defining lexical meaning, as well as its use as the basis for a lexical description of English by a group of linguists often dubbed 'Neo-Firthians,' has had a profound influence, not only on the scope and focus of research in English linguistics, but also on the compilation of corpora and the use of corpus-based methodologies.

Firth (1951/1957: 194–6) introduced the term *collocation* to refer to one of the three "levels" of meaning he distinguished: "meaning by collocation," the "conceptual or idea approach to the meaning of words" and "contextual meaning." Later, Halliday (1966) and Sinclair (1966) took this idea further and, without abandoning collocation as defining meaning, introduced the notion that patterns of collocation can form the basis for a lexical analysis of language alternative to, and independent of, a grammatical analysis. In fact, they regarded the two levels of analysis as being complementary, with neither of the two being subsumed by the other. However, it is interesting to note that Halliday's and Sinclair's approaches take as their respective starting points the two ends of the lexicogrammar continuum. Halliday 'interrogates' language grammatically, aiming "to build the dictionary out of the grammar" (1992: 63); Sinclair 'interrogates' language lexically seeking to discover "facts . . . that cannot be got by grammatical analysis" (1966: 410). In fact, Sinclair (2004b: 164) distinguishes *lexicogrammar* from *lexical grammar*: "[lexicogrammar] is fundamentally grammar with a certain amount of attention to lexical patterns within the grammatical frameworks; it is not in any sense an attempt to build together a grammar and lexis on an equal basis."

But perhaps the contrast of lexis and grammar obscures more than it illuminates, as "lexical items do not contrast with each other in the same sense as grammatical classes contrast" (Sinclair 1966: 411). Stubbs explains that collocation, which is at the centre of a lexical description of language, is "a purely lexical relation, non-directional and probabilistic, which ignores any syntactic relation between the words" (2001: 64). Sinclair sees the lexical item "balanc[ing] syntagmatic and paradigmatic patterns, using the same descriptive categories to describe both dimensions" (1998: 23).

Firth (1968) defined *collocation* as a relation between words, and introduced the notion of *colligation* for relations at the grammatical level, that is the interrelation of "word and sentence classes or of similar categories" and not "between words as such" (1968). Sinclair (1991: 170) defined collocation as "the occurrence of two or more words within a short space of each other in a text," and proposed a span of four to five words on either side of the node (i.e. the word whose collocations are examined) (1968: 105–6, 121). From early on, collocation was understood in relation to the probability that two words will co-occur. Firth (1968: 181) stated that collocation is "an order of mutual expectancy" (see also Hoey 1991: 7; Sinclair 1966: 418; Stubbs 2001: 64). *Colligation* is now understood in a somehow less restricted sense than that defined by Firth (1968: 181), and may include the co-occurrence of lexis and grammatical categories (Stubbs 2001: 112), and in some cases it is understood as only the latter, that is "the grammatical company a word keeps" (Hoey 1997: 8). A third relation between words, also a feature of the idiom principle (Sinclair 1991: 110), is that of *semantic prosody*, defined as the "consistent aura of meaning with which a form is imbued by its collocates" (Louw 1993: 157; see also Sinclair 1991: 112). Stubbs (2001: 111–12) makes a finer distinction between *semantic preference*, the "relation between a lemma or word-form and a set of semantically related words," and *discourse prosody* (or *semantic prosody*), "a feature which extends over more than one unit in a linear string . . . Since they are evaluative, prosodies often express the speaker's reason for making the utterance, and therefore identify functional discourse units."

Underlying the lexical approach to the analysis of language are a series of requirements relating to research methodology. Firstly, and perhaps most importantly, the researcher's reliance on intuitions and traditional concepts and categories has to be minimized as much as possible, if it cannot be excluded altogether (see Phillips 1989: 5; Stubbs 1996: 22). Sinclair (1991: 39) sees a role for intuitions "in evaluating evidence rather than creating it." Consequently, as we saw in section 3 above, corpus annotation is treated with caution, if not viewed unfavorably, as it represents the imposition of categories and preconceptions on the part of the annotator or the programmer of the annotation software.[7] However, there are researchers within the Neo-Firthian paradigm who have adopted the view that, despite its perceived problems and limitations, there are cases when annotation may be acceptable (e.g. Hunston 2002: 80–94), or even desirable (e.g. Teubert 1999).

Intuitions can be sidestepped if the linguist consciously tries to suppress his/her intuitions when examining concordances (Sinclair 2004a: 47; see also section 3), or if the analysis is automatic and relies on the computation of statistical results (Sinclair 1966: 413). This notion has been taken as far as treating a text as "essentially a statistical phenomenon" (Phillips 1989: 17). The only phase of lexical research where intuitions, or rather "intentionality and human reasoning," are considered acceptable, or at least unavoidable, is in "the validation and interpretation of [the] processed data" (Teubert 1999; see also Firth 1957: 1, 29; Stubbs 1996: 47).

Secondly, any generalizations at the lexical level must be informed by the collocational patterns of lexical items (Sinclair 1991: 8). What is taken as the unit of corpus-based analysis is the orthographic word, rather than the lemma, as *a priori* lemmatization is seen as introducing the analyst's subjective intuitions (p. 41).[8] A further reason is that different forms of what is traditionally considered the same 'word' (i.e. lemma) have been observed to display different patterns. Sinclair (1991: 53–65, 154–6) examined the senses and syntactic patterns of the different forms of the lemma YIELD in a 7.3 million word corpus of written texts, and provided evidence of correlation between the different forms of YIELD, on the one hand, and meaning and syntactic patterns on the other.

Thirdly, corpora should contain whole texts, not samples. In Firthian and neo-Firthian linguistics, language is seen as a social phenomenon, which is observable in discourse and text. This consideration, coupled with findings indicating that different parts of a text demonstrate different patterning in terms of lexical and grammatical frequencies and relations (cf. Stubbs 1996: 32–4), points towards the building of corpora that contain whole texts rather than samples (e.g. Sinclair 1991: 19).

Finally, this approach favors very large corpora.[9] Since the basis of the analysis is words rather than categories, the researcher needs to examine a large number of instances of specific word-forms in order to be able to recognize patterns. The problem for lexis-based research is that the smaller the corpus, the higher the percentage of *hapax legomena*, that is, words which occur only once (e.g. Kennedy 1998: 100; Sinclair 1991: 18–19), or words with too low a frequency for dependable generalizations to be made. Table 3.1 summarizes the main characteristics of lexis-based language description and their implications for corpus building and corpus-based research methodology.

It may not be an overstatement to say that the main impetus, if not the driving force, behind much English corpus-based lexical research is the development of a description of language which takes as its basic units lexical items, rather than grammatical categories, such as noun or verb (Stubbs 1996: 35). In fact, some corpus linguists (e.g. Teubert 1999) have gone as far as to effectively equate corpus linguistics with collocation-based research on lexical description. This view is disputable, but what seems to be indisputable is that this approach to language description has prompted the use of lexis-based research methodologies, particularly those examining collocations and the behavior of different forms of the same root, by studies that do not intend to contribute to the lexis-based paradigm of linguistic research. For example, given the ease of exploring corpora lexically[10] and Halliday's views on language, many English corpus linguists have started to view language lexically in order to get 'lexis-like' answers to what have been traditionally treated as grammatical questions. The following section provides examples of a range of methodological and theoretical approaches to corpus linguistics.

Table 3.1   Characteristics of lexis-based approaches

Characteristics of lexis-based language description	Implications for corpus building and analysis
• Analysis needs to be as free as possible from introspective assumptions.	• No annotation. • No lemmatization: calculation of the collocations of orthographic words. • Reliance on (automatic) statistical analysis.
• Linguistic features do not normally show the same distribution across different sections of a text.	• Corpora should contain whole texts, not samples.
• A large number of occurrences of different words is needed for dependable analysis.	• Corpora should be as large as possible.

5   Corpus Studies

Corpus linguistics may be viewed as a methodology, but the methodological practices adopted by corpus linguists are not uniform. This was clearly indicated in the discussion of the distinction between corpus-based and corpus-driven approaches (section 3). It was also pointed out that this distinction, superficially a methodological one, is theoretically motivated. Consequently, theoretical and methodological decisions in corpus linguistics are interlinked, although, it has to be stressed, there is no clear one-to-one correspondence between theoretical orientation and methodology in corpus studies. Therefore, the discussion of studies in this section will inevitably involve both methodological and theoretical issues.

The neo-Firthian approach to language description, and the word-based research paradigm associated with it, have indeed influenced current corpus research. However, this does not entail that all word-based studies, or studies focusing on lexical patterning, aim to contribute to a lexical description of English. Increasingly, studies investigating a grammatical phenomenon rely on the morphology or semantics of the lexis involved, while studies which focus on the collocational behavior of specific lexical items also draw on their semantic and grammatical properties. In fact, in a number of cases, the same study can be described equally well as either a grammar-focused study taking into account lexical properties, or a lexis-focused study concentrating on the grammatical behavior of specific lexical items.[11] The discussion of studies in this section, therefore, should be read bearing in mind the indeterminacy and uncertain fusion of lexis and grammar. Corpus-based studies taking lexical items as their starting point draw on a number of theories and research approaches, and there is variation within what might, at first glance, be perceived as a single research paradigm.

Regardless of theoretical considerations, there are strong practical reasons for the appeal of word-based corpus research, even if the focus of the study is a grammatical construction. The reasons have to do with annotation. Word-based research can be carried out even with raw corpora, using software that picks out word-forms and presents the examples in a concordance (cf. Kennedy 1998: 8), although the lack of grammatical information will somehow limit the scope and effectiveness of the research. Category-based research needs, ideally, corpora annotated for grammatical structures and syntactical properties, which are time consuming to develop, or, at least, corpora annotated for the grammatical properties of words (e.g. parts of speech). However, even in a grammatically tagged corpus, it is much easier to derive concordances, say, of the verb *give* in all of its forms, than a concordance of all of the present perfect constructions. If a raw corpus is used, the former will be slightly more time consuming, but the latter will require a much bigger investment in time.[12] Halliday (1992: 64) summarizes the practical considerations of word-based and category-based research as follows:

> The lexicologist's data are relatively easy to observe: they are words, or lexical items of some kind, and . . . it is not forbiddingly difficult to parse them out. The grammarian's data are very much less accessible: I cannot even today ask the system to retrieve for me all clauses of mental process or marked circumstantial theme or high obligation modality.

A large number of corpus linguists seem to practice eclecticism in the research techniques they use, irrespective of whether they work within a specific theoretical framework, or within the research paradigm in which a given technique was first used or with which it is associated. In some respects, studies tend to adopt methodologies which demonstrate what Hunston terms a "synergy between word-based methods and category-based methods" (2002: 86).

The use of corpora in linguistic research can be placed on a cline between two points. One end treats the corpus as the sole object of study, with intuitions being excluded from all consideration as much as possible. This approach can be regarded as an extreme reaction to what Fillmore (1992) has described as "armchair linguistics," that is, the use of intuition and introspective examples as the only sources of data. The other end treats corpora as a convenient repository of instances of attested use, with the added benefit of word-and-category search and concordancing capabilities, from which the examples that fit a theory or support a point in a discussion can be selected should the user wish to do so. In the latter approach to using corpora, there is no attempt to make the results of an experiment totally accountable to corpus data – the corpus is simply a body of casually used examples.

Between the two extreme points lie studies which combine corpus evidence with intuitions and data drawn from elicitation experiments.[13] There are perils at either end or at any point along the continuum. Those who selectively use corpora can be accused of preferring data that fits their theory while ignoring inconvenient examples. Those linguists who renounce intuition are excluding from their research a possibly rich source of evidence. Furthermore, given that the use of intuitions in the examination of the data is inescapable, a purportedly intuition-free approach to the data will involve unwitting, and therefore, unchecked, use of intuitions. Between the two extremes a blend of these criticisms may apply. Yet, from the perspective of the authors of this chapter, an approach to corpus use that combines intuition with a systematic use of corpus evidence is increasingly becoming the established norm, echoing the sentiments of Johansson (1991: 6) who cautioned that "linguists who neglect corpora do so at their peril, but so do those who limit themselves to corpora." Linguists are increasingly limiting themselves exclusively neither to corpora nor to intuition. They are using both.

In terms of their main goal, studies may be theoretically oriented, some aiming at contributing, directly or indirectly, to a specific theoretical framework. For example, studies may locate themselves within the paradigm of lexico-grammar (e.g. Hunston and Francis 2000; Renouf 2001), probabilistic grammar (e.g. Carter and McCarthy, 1999), cognitive linguistics (e.g. Gilquin 2003; Gries 2003; Gries and Stefanowitch 2004; Schmidt 2000; Schonefeld 1999), or within paradigms not readily associated with corpus-based or corpus-driven methodologies (e.g. Di Sciullo et al. 1986; Paulillo 2000). Studies may also be predominantly descriptive, that is, studies which do not explicitly subscribe to a specific theory, with an aim to discovering lexicographical and language teaching applications (e.g. McEnery and Kifle 2001, Altenberg and Granger 2002; McEnery and Xiao 2004). In terms of their research focus, studies may, for example, aim to define and explore lexical meaning (e.g. Partington, 2004), concentrate on the phraseology of a word (e.g. Hunston 2001), investigate the behavior of multi-word lexical items (e.g. De Cock et al. 1998), explore lexicogrammar (Stubbs 1996: 36), focus on the syntactic properties of grammatical structures (e.g. Duffley 2003), or examine the distribution of grammatical categories (e.g. Biber 2001). Corpus-based methodologies are also being increasingly adopted in research within pragmatics and discourse analysis (e.g. Aijmer and Stentström 2004; Archer 2005; Partington et al. 2004; Vivanco 2005; Wang 2005), critical discourse analysis (e.g. Baker 2005; Baker and McEnery 2005; Hardt-Mautner 1995; Koller and Mautner 2004; McEnery 2005; Orpin 2005; Polovina-Vukovic 2004; Sotillo and Wang-Gempp 2004), metaphor (e.g. Charteris-Black 2004; Deignan 2005), and stylistics (e.g. Burrows 2002; Semino and Short 2004; Stubbs 2005).

Within the body of corpus research it is possible to distinguish different types of studies (e.g. see Stubbs 2002: 227, 238). One way in which the studies can be categorized is in terms of their research methodology; corpus studies can be categorized according to the extent that they rely on automatic statistical calculations or the manual examination and interpretation of concordances.[14] An example of a study that is mainly statistical would be the calculation of the frequency and strength of collocation patterns within a given span in an unannotated corpus. Although reliance on intuitions is unavoidable in the interpretation of statistical results, or the analysis of corpus examples, it can also be present in the annotation (explicit or implicit) of a corpus. A second distinction, directly related to the previous one, has to do with the size of the sample: if the study uses automatic analysis, then a large corpus can be used; if corpus examples are to be manually analyzed, then a smaller sample will have to be used.

The insights from corpus-based studies on specific areas of grammar, lexis, and their interface inform large-scale works which aim to offer a comprehensive view of the English grammar and lexicon. The next section will provide an overview of corpus-based reference grammars and dictionaries.

6   Reference Works

Corpora are now commonly used as the basis of reference grammars and dictionaries both for native speakers and learners of English. Although grammars and dictionaries are usually seen as being complementary, there has been a convergence of coverage between the two, mostly in the light of corpus evidence. Increasingly, grammars take lexical matters into account,[15] and dictionaries (usually for learners) include grammatical information in their entries. Like small-scale studies, reference works differ in the manner in, and extent to, which they make use of corpora, and the theoretical frameworks they operate in. In this section we will first discuss the impact of corpora on grammars of English before moving on to a fuller discussion of the impact of corpora on English lexicography.

Some grammars may draw their evidence and present examples from corpora only,[16] and consistently provide detailed (i.e. numerical) frequency and distributional information[17] either as part of a comprehensive grammar of English (e.g. Biber et al. 1999) or as part of a work focused on some aspect of English (e.g. the study of English verbs by Mindt 2000). Other grammars, while they take into account corpus evidence as well as findings from existing corpus-based studies, without necessarily restricting themselves to a single corpus,[18] may also draw data from elicitation experiments.[19] Such grammars provide a combination of attested and intuition-derived examples, and usually give information about frequency and distribution in more general terms (e.g. Quirk et al. 1985; Huddleston et al. 2002). Huddleston et al. (2002: 11) are quite explicit regarding their choice of data sources and their rationale for that choice:

> The evidence we use comes from several sources: our own intuitions as native speakers of the language; the reaction of other native speakers we consult when

we are in doubt; data from computer corpora . . . and data presented in dictionaries and other scholarly work on grammar. We alternate between different sources and cross-check them against each other, since intuition can be misleading and can contain errors.

There are also a number of pedagogical grammars for students of English, either general, such as *Collins COBUILD English grammar* (1990), or with a specific focus, for example *Collins COBUILD grammar patterns 1: Verbs* (1996), and Mindt (1995), which focuses on modal verbs.

Corpus-based grammars are relatively new.[20] Dictionaries, on the other hand, have long been based upon attested language use in the form of collections of citation slips or collections of texts, for example. Some of the collections of data used to construct pre-corpus dictionaries were impressive in size given that the compilation and analysis was done manually (see Landau 2001: chs. 2 and 6). Unlike grammar-focused studies, where relatively small corpora can afford enough linguistic evidence for the purposes of the study, truly large corpora are needed for lexicographical purposes as "many words and expressions do not occur frequently enough to provide the lexicographer with enough evidence in a sample corpus" (Landau, 2001: 287). It is not a coincidence that the Bank of English (or Birmingham Corpus, as it was called originally), which was built for the purpose of compiling a dictionary (Cowie 1999; Landau 2001), is a monitor corpus, that is, an ever-expanding one. However, a representative finite corpus can also afford useful lexicographic insights. If a large representative corpus does not include a lexical item "one can conclude that the lexical item, if it exists, either is extremely uncommon or it is used almost exclusively in a specialized field that the corpus does not cover" (Landau 2001: 297). Such a corpus can also provide information about the relative frequency and distribution of lexical items and their collocation patterns, as well as grammatical information (since most representative corpora are tagged).

Lexicography has benefited from electronic corpora and its attendant software in a number of ways related to both the content and the compilation process of dictionaries. The dictionaries that utilized computer corpora very early on were English learner dictionaries, the earliest one being the *Collins COBUILD English Language Dictionary*, published in 1987. Currently, all major English learner dictionaries,[21] and, increasingly, native-speaker dictionaries[22] are corpus based (Jackson 2002: 131).

The use of corpora in dictionary construction has not merely entailed replacing citation slips with corpora. Corpora have led dictionary compilers to base decisions about inclusion and the information about entries on corpus evidence, as opposed to the more subjective decisions relied upon by the compilers of citation slip based dictionaries (cf. Landau 2001: 191–3, 205, 302–5). What Ooi (1998: 48) calls "casual citation," that is, selecting attested examples in a less than rigorous way has been supplanted by a more rigorous corpus-based approach. Modern dictionaries tend to be corpus driven rather than compiler driven. In addition, dictionaries can now provide information about frequency, medium (written or spoken), distribution in different contexts of use, more detailed sense information, collocation patterns and grammatical properties, as a consequence of that data being available in corpora. Landau (2001: 304–5) gives an example of how a corpus can assist lexicography:

> Another perennial problem is deciding whether the present or past participle of a verb has acquired adjectival status and merits inclusion as a lemma in its own right. In the past lexicographers had no way to decide this. With a corpus that has been grammatically tagged, they do.

It must be stressed that Landau's example above should be understood as carrying the caveat that the annotation scheme, and the theoretical assumptions behind it, are known and accepted by the lexicographers involved.

Word frequencies may also be used as a criterion for including words in, or excluding words from, a dictionary. Space in a hard-copy edition of a dictionary is limited, and corpora can provide information on which to base decisions about which items to select for inclusion.[23] This is often important when compiling defining vocabularies for learner dictionaries of English. Learner dictionaries are also of interest because they are often based not only on native-speaker corpora, but also on learner corpora and on corpora comprising texts from language-teaching coursebooks. Insights from learner corpora enable dictionary compilers to provide a more detailed treatment of areas where learners seem to have problems. While corpora have contributed enormously to dictionary building, they have not replaced citation slips entirely. Corpora, particularly closed ones, cannot provide much help for dictionary makers in looking for new words. For this reason, dictionaries supplement corpus data with citations collected either manually or from the internet.

As was mentioned earlier, the availability of corpora and research tools has also provided a readily accessible testing ground for linguistic theories. In the case of dictionaries, the implications and applications of the research findings within different paradigms are helping to drive home the fact that dictionary-making is not a theory-free enterprise, and that the establishment, or influence, of different theoretical paradigms, in combination with corpus use and technological developments, will continue affecting the development of dictionaries, both in terms of the types of information dictionaries include, and the format of the dictionaries themselves. The addition of collocational and distributional information to the more traditional meanings and sense relations (usually synonymy and hyperonymy) is one of the latest developments. For example, Fillmore and Atkins (1994), working within Frame Semantics, investigated the use of the word *risk* in a corpus and compared their findings with the information given in ten monolingual dictionaries. They highlighted the following areas of difficulty: sense differentiation in the verb and noun, the distinction between 'run a risk' and 'take a risk,' and patterns of verb complementation (1994: 363), and concluded that:

> While in some cases the corpus material did suggest ways forward, more often than not it raised other more complex problems, a tough new fact to be understood and incorporated into our description of the word. It soon became apparent that the wealth of information which the corpus held could not be compressed into the format of a two-dimensional entry in a printed dictionary. The word was so complex that a multidimensional picture of it was required if we were to set out its full potential and its network of relationships within the language.   (1994: 365)

Given the confrontation with data that a corpus linguist engaged in lexico-graphic research faces, it is hardly surprising to discover that some linguists have looked at the interface between lexis and grammar in particular, and have started to doubt that a clear division between the two exists. It appears that lexis and grammar are entangled rather than linked. For this reason, in building corpora for the construction of dictionaries, lexicographers have developed approaches to language that challenge existing linguistic categories and approaches.

Dictionary research, grammar building and lexicogrammatical research have all, clearly, been major beneficiaries of work in English corpus linguistics. Yet another related area has also benefited immensely from the development of corpora – English language teaching (ELT). This will be the subject of the next section.

7   Language Teaching

Modern approaches to the teaching of English as a foreign language have been strongly influenced by both the lexicogrammar tradition and the corpus-based approach to dictionary and grammar construction. Yet corpus use contributes to language teaching in other ways, because, apart from research on native-speaker (L1) corpora, English language teaching also benefits from research on learner corpora and corpora of ELT coursebooks (cf. Aston 2000; Aston et al. 2004; Gabrielatos 2005; Granger et al. 2002; Leech 1997b; Sinclair 2004c).

Pedagogical materials and reference books for learners can now draw on the findings of an ever-increasing and diverse body of corpus-based research. Research on native-speaker corpora has yielded a more accurate and detailed description of English, which, in turn, informs the content of pedagogical grammars and dictionaries, as well as the design of syllabuses and coursebooks (cf. Hunston and Francis 1998; Kennedy 1992; Owen 1993; Römer 2005). Research on learner corpora affords insights into the ways that learners of English use the language, provides indications about language learning processes, and contributes to second language acquisition (SLA) research (e.g. Granger et al. 2002; Jones and Murphy 2005). The identification of frequent learner problems, particularly problems specific to learners of a given first language, can further facilitate the design of syllabuses and pedagogical materials (e.g. Nesselhauf 2005). Corpora of English language teaching coursebooks can provide a helpful

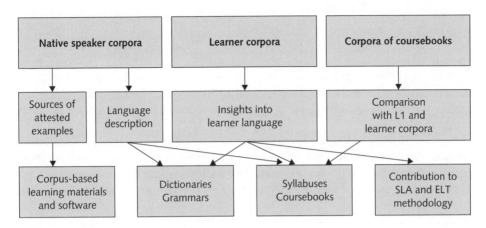

Figure 3.1   Corpora and language teaching

comparison between native language use in different contexts and the language that learners are exposed to in coursebooks (e.g Harwood 2005; Römer 2004). The analysis of discrepancies will provide a helpful guide as to the kinds of texts that should be included in pedagogical materials. Such corpora already guide decisions about the content and focus of dictionaries (e.g. the *Macmillan English Dictionary for Advanced Learners*, 2002).[24] The examination of corpora of coursebooks can also reveal whether, and to what extent, the language in coursebook texts influences the speech and writing of learners. Finally, language corpora can be used by learners and teachers as a source of attested language examples, with learners either having access to corpora and having been familiarized with corpus software, or working with printouts of concordances (e.g. Johns 1991; Aston 1997). Figure 3.1 (adapted from Gabrielatos 2003) provides an outline of the contribution of corpora and corpus research to language teaching, as summarized above, and shows the multiple connections between different types of corpora, and the insights that their analysis affords, and applications to language learning and teaching. The remainder of this section expands on the contribution of corpus linguistics to language teaching and learning.

Research on L1 corpora has yielded convincing evidence that traditional, intuition-based views on language are very often at odds with actual language use (e.g. Sinclair 1997: 32–4). Also, corpus-based research on general and specialized corpora has revealed patterns and uses that introspective accounts had previously failed to detect. This is pertinent to language teaching, as the information about English structure and use that is communicated to learners, either by pedagogical materials or teachers, is still, to a large extent, based on intuitions. As we have already mentioned, intuitions are useful, but not necessarily accurate. Having a native or good command of a language does not endow a language teacher with a conscious, clear and comprehensive picture of the language in all of its contexts of use. What is more, native speaker intuitions vary from user to user. A case in point is the published view of a native-speaker teacher that in English, "question tags, along with bowler hats, mostly belong to 1960s BBC broadcasts" (Bradford 2002: 13). This view is in sharp contrast with the corpus findings of Biber et al. (1999: 211), who report that "about every fourth question in conversation is a question tag." However, as was shown in section 6 above, a large number of pedagogical reference books which are informed by corpus studies are now available to English language learners.

Studies of learner language mainly compare learner use of specific features in different contexts with that of native-speakers in quantitative and qualitative terms, and engage with the examination and classification of learner errors. Error analysis seeks to identify frequent errors or error patterns with reference to one or more of the following factors: the learners' L1, level and age, the medium of production (speech or writing), the genre, and the context of use. Studies of learner language, usually based on written corpora, have also focused on learner use of a large variety of features of lexicogrammar, such as lexical chunks (De Cock et al. 1998), complement clauses (Biber and Reppen 1998), the progressive aspect and questions (Virtanen 1997, 1998), and the use of epistemic modality (McEnery and Kifle 2002), as well as discourse features, such as overstatement (Lorenz 1998), connectors (Altenberg and Tapper 1998), and speech-like elements in writing (Granger and Rayson 1998). Corpus-based research of learner language contributes to English language teaching in two respects. Research findings point towards the aspects of learner use which should be prioritized in language instruction and aid the compilation of pedagogical and reference materials at different levels of competence. The examination of learner language also affords insights into the process of language learning (e.g. Tono 2000).

Both native-speaker and learner corpora can be used directly in language teaching, either in class or for self-study. The former can provide exposure to language in use, whereas the latter can raise awareness of language problems common to a specific L1. Corpus-based approaches to language awareness can be distinguished according to two ways that a corpus is utilized (Leech 1997b: 10). In the first, the corpus is used as a source of attested language examples for the teacher or materials writer (e.g. Tribble and Jones 1990; Tribble 1997; Granger and Tribble 1998; Osbourne 2000). Johns (2002: 108–9) provides an example of the use of concordances in the classroom: learners are given ten groups of five concordance lines each where the key word (in this case a noun) is missing, as well as a list of the ten missing nouns (each corresponding to one group of concordance lines), and are asked to decide which noun completes each group. Teachers can manipulate the corpus examples by restricting them to a specific medium (writing/speech), genre, or text type. Of course, when using very small or selective corpus samples, teachers need to inform learners that no valid conclusions can be drawn about the actual or relative frequency of a language feature on the basis of the corpus examples. Teachers can also regulate the amount of text available to learners, from only a few words on either side of the key word to a sentence or a paragraph. In the second approach, learners work directly with corpora (cf. Aston 1996), either following instructions given by the teacher or contained within a CALL[25] program (e.g. Hughes 1997; Milton 1998), or working on areas of their own choice (e.g. Johns 1997). Bernardini (2002: 174–5) reports on an example of learners influencing the direction of a corpus-based lesson. The learners were investigating the phraseology of *high standards* in the BNC, using the concordance function to look for typical collocates. While examining verb collocates on the left-hand side, a learner noticed the intensifier *extremely*. This led the learner to query the phrase *extremely high* and investigate right-hand collocating nouns. The teacher used this opportunity to ask learners to investigate the distribution of *extremely high* in the subcorpora.

Corpus use in English language teaching is often associated with a "data-driven" approach to learning, which regards the learner as a researcher (Johns 1991). However, it should be pointed out that corpus use is not restricted to any single teaching methodology. It is compatible with all methodologies that accept an explicit focus on language structure and use, i.e. teaching approaches which see a role, central or marginal, for consciousness-raising through noticing (e.g. Sharwood Smith 1981; Lightbown 1985; Schmidt 1990), that is, encouraging and guiding learners to pay attention to language features and patterns and, not unlike corpus researchers, formulate and test generalizations themselves, rather than being given a rule. In other words, corpus use fits equally well within language-based and task-based approaches to language learning (cf. Nunan 1989; Fotos and Ellis 1991; Loschky and Bley-Vroman 1993; Skehan 1998).

The use of corpora in language teaching has provided new opportunities for learner independence. According to Johns (1997: 101), when using corpora or corpus-based materials, "students define their own tasks as they start noticing features of the data for themselves – at times features that had not previously been noticed by the teacher." Also, corpus use has given a new lease of life to the language lab, and has suggested a more flexible and learner-centered use for CALL materials (e.g. McEnery et al. 1997). The introduction of corpora to the language classroom has also challenged the traditional role of teachers, which does not mean that the teacher's role is diminished; rather, that it is enriched and diversified. The teacher is seen not so much as the provider of facts about language as a consultant or co-researcher.

Another benefit of working with corpus samples from representative corpora of different varieties (e.g. British or American English) and different genres (e.g. academic English, chatroom English) is that learners develop an awareness of different varieties of English in a number of contexts. This exposure is expected to facilitate their understanding and enrich their language use, but, more importantly, to drive home the fact that English is anything but uniform.

8   Language Change

So far, the discussion of the contribution of corpora to linguistic research has been concerned with issues relating to the description and analysis of modern English. However, the availability, and relative ease of construction, of corpora comprising texts from different periods of the development of English[26] makes it possible to investigate changes in different aspects of the English language. Renouf (1997: 185) points out that "historical text study has long been ripe for automation." Electronic corpora have made data collection more time-efficient and have enabled researchers to tackle areas hitherto made forbidding by the volume of materials that needed to be collected (Rissanen 1997: 6). Nevalainen and Raumolin-Brunberg (2003: 23) mention a further advantage of corpus-based diachronic studies, namely that the language is produced without the prompting, participation or presence of a researcher, which "may affect the linguistic choices people make."

Studies on the development of English usually examine four periods: Old, Middle, Early Modern and Modern English. In terms of what is compared, we can distinguish between (1) contrasting different historical periods; (2) contrasting one or more past periods and Modern English; and (3) given that computer corpora on Modern English now span more than forty years, tracking changes within recent decades. What follows is a brief review of studies providing a range of examples of the use of corpora in the study of long-term and recent language change.

Kytö (1996) compared the morphology of adjective comparison (inflectional, periphrastic, and double forms)[27] in Late Middle and Early Modern English using the Helsinki Corpus of English Texts. The results show a slight increase in the inflected forms, and a slight decrease in the periphrastic forms, with the changes being more pronounced in the case of the superlative, and only sporadic use of the double form. Lopez-Couso and Mendez-Naya (2001) examined the development of declarative complement clauses with *if* and *though* in Old, Middle and Early Modern English, using the diachronic part of the Helsinki Corpus of English Texts. According to their data, the frequency of *if* complements has increased since the Old English period, whereas *though* complements, although more frequent in Old English, became obsolete in the early seventeenth century.

Krug (2000) studied the development of the modal expressions *have got to/gotta, have to/hafta* and *want to/wanna* in a number of diachronic and contemporary corpora.[28] Apart from concluding that they all show signs of ongoing auxiliarization, that is, they now display more of the formal characteristics of modal auxiliaries, he also observed that "frequency seems to be a fundamental parameter in the genesis of the new category [i.e. the modal expressions *have got to/gotta, have to/hafta* and *want to/wanna*]" (2000: 251). Mair et al. (2003) compared the tag frequencies in two corpora, LOB (1961) and F-LOB (1991), to investigate whether English has become more 'nominal.' They found that nouns, particularly proper nouns, and adjectives were significantly more frequent in FLOB, as were 'noun + common noun' sequences. Leech (2003) and Smith (2003) examined a number of British and American English corpora from 1961 and 1991/2[29] and showed that there was a decline overall in the use of central modals, and an increase in the frequency of semi-modals.[30]

A new corpus developed by Bas Aarts and Sean Wallis at University College London is the *Diachronic Corpus of Present-day Spoken English* (DCPSE).[31] DCPSE contains spontaneous spoken British English, and comprises comparable categories from the *London-Lund Corpus* (1960–76) and the British English component of the *International Corpus of English* (ICE-GB, early 1990s). The DCPSE contains 800,000 words, and has been grammatically annotated (tagged and parsed), as well as annotated for features of interaction, such as speaker and turn overlaps, making it particularly suitable for diachronic research on spoken grammar.

Baayen and Renouf (1996) focused on neologisms and compared the productivity of two prefixes (*un-*, *in-*) and three affixes (*-ly*, *-ness*, *-ity*) in *The Times* database (1989–92, 80 mil. words) and in the COBUILD corpus (18 mil. words). One of their conclusions was that "word formation in the native stratum of the lexicon is much more productive than dictionaries would suggest" (1996: 92). Collier (1998) outlines a two-stage methodology for tracking changes in semantic relations, on the evidence of collocational profiles, in the section of UK newspapers in the ACRONYM corpus database system (Renouf 1996). Two databases of significant collocations are compared: the year in focus and the previous years. Collocational changes are tagged according to whether their significance has increased/decreased (termed *up/down* collocates), or whether they have appeared/disappeared (*new/gone* collocates). In the second stage, the significant collocates of the target word are extracted, but only those fulfilling certain criteria, say the *up* and *new* collocates, are considered. The *up* and *new* collocates are then treated as nodes and their collocates are calculated, but only those occurring more than once are retained. The common collocates-of-collocates are used to draw the semantic profile of the node, as their "collocate profiles overlap to a lesser or greater extent with that of the original target word" (Collier 1998: 264). It is interesting to note that using newspaper corpora enables the researchers to identify extremely short-term changes, albeit in a specific domain.

One facet of language change which lies on the lexicogrammatical interface is grammaticalization.[32] Grammaticalization can be seen diachronically as "a process whereby lexical items and constructions come in certain linguistic contexts to serve grammatical functions, and, once grammaticalized, continue to develop new grammatical functions" (Hopper and Traugott 1993: xv).

Rissanen (1997) traced the emergence and development of the pronominalization of *one* from Old to Modern English, and examined six types of pronominal uses, based mainly on the Helsinki Corpus.[33] According to his analysis, developments were more pronounced in Middle and Early Modern English. Rissanen (1997: 135) sees a connection between the pronominalization of *one* and the "loss of the inflectional endings of the language and the consequent collapse of the Old English case system." A study by Brems (2003), focussing on the syntactical properties of 'measure nouns' in *of*-phrases (e.g. 'a kilo of apples'), investigates one of the parameters defining grammaticalization, *coalescence*, "a syntactic criterion [which] concerns an increase in bondedness or syntactic cohesion of the elements that are in the process of grammaticalizing, i.e. what were formerly individually autonomous signs become more dependent on each other to the extent that they are increasingly interpreted as together constituting one "chunk," which as a whole expresses a (grammatical) meaning" (2003: 291). The study revealed that although some constructions, namely *bunch(es) of*, *heap(s) of* and *piles(s) of*, "have developed a quantifier use comparable to that of regular quantifiers," not all measure noun constructions show the same degree of grammaticalization (p. 309). A theoretically important observation was that the assessment of the structural status of measure nouns in these constructions was made difficult by the interdependence of their lexical and grammatical status (2003).

The examples of studies on language change presented here testify to the wealth of opportunities afforded by corpora to examine a very wide span of the history of English. Furthermore, the variety of theoretical approaches taken to the diachronic study of English is a further indication that, while the lexical approach is an important and major contribution to English corpus linguistics, it represents but one way to approach corpus data.

Conclusion

In this chapter we have not tried to present a comprehensive overview of English corpus linguistics, as the scope of corpus based studies of English is vast. What we have done instead is to outline the major impacts that corpora have had on the study of the English language. From changing the way in which basic reference resources relating to the English language have been developed through to the development of a critical, lexicogrammatical approach to establish theories and categorization of language, and beyond lexicogrammar to the study of English through the ages using a range of theoretically informed approaches, corpus data has changed the way the English language is studied. It has also changed the way that the language is taught. So while the term 'English corpus linguistics' will remain somewhat vague and inclusive, covering potentially any study of the English language which uses corpus data, this chapter has presented those changes to the study of English which it would be difficult to imagine occurring had English language corpora not been developed.

Appendix 1   Information on corpora mentioned in the chapter

ARCHER Corpus (A Representative Corpus of Historical English Registers)

Language variety	British and American English
Size	1.7 million words
Medium	Writing, including written representation of speech (e.g. drama)
Time period	Early Modern English (1650–1990)
Annotation	Unannotated
More information	Biber et al. (1994a, 1994b)

The Bank of English

Language variety	British English
Size	450 million words in January 2002
Medium	Writing
Time period	Mostly after 1990
Annotation	POS tagged
More information	User guide: www.titania.bham.ac.uk/docs/svenguide

The British National Corpus (BNC)

Language variety	British English
Size	100 million words
Medium	90% writing, 10% speech
Time period	Early 1990s
Annotation	Part of speech tagging using CLAWS 5
More information	Aston and Burnard (1998), BNC website: www.natcorp.ox.ac.uk

The Brown University Corpus (Brown)

Language variety	American English
Size	1 million words
Medium	Writing
Time period	1960
Annotation	Raw version and different annotated versions
More information	Francis and Kucera (1964), Manual: http://khnt.hit.uib.no/icame/manuals/brown/INDEX.HTM

The Freiburg–Brown Corpus of American English (Frown)

Language variety	American English
Size	1 million words
Medium	Writing
Time period	1991
Annotation	
More information	Hundt et al. (1999), http://khnt.hit.uib.no/icame/manuals/frown/INDEX.HTM

The Freiburg–LOB Corpus of British English (FLOB)

Language variety	British English
Size	1 million words
Medium	Writing
Time period	1991
Annotation	POS tagged using CLAWS 8
More information	Hundt et al. (1998), http://khnt.hit.uib.no/icame/manuals/flob/INDEX.HTM

The Helsinki Corpus (Diachronic Part)

Language variety	British English
Size	1.5 million words
Medium	Writing
Time period	Old, Middle and Early Modern English (c.750 to c.1700)
Annotation	Unannotated
More information	Kytö (1996)

The International Corpus of English, British English component (ICE–GB)

Language variety	British English
Size	1 million words
Medium	Writing and speech
Time period	1990–1998
Annotation	POS tagged and parsed
More information	Greenbaum (1996); www.ucl.ac.uk/english-usage/ice-gb/index

The Lancaster/Oslo–Bergen Corpus (LOB)

Language variety	British English
Size	1 million words
Medium	Writing
Time period	1961
Annotation	Raw version and POS tagged version using CLAWS 1
More information	Johansson et al. (1978) and Johansson et al. (1986)

The Survey of English Usage

Language variety	British English
Size	1 million words
Medium	Writing and speech
Time period	Between 1955 and 1985
Annotation	POS tagged
More information	www.ucl.ac.uk/english-usage/about/history

NOTES

1   See also Meyer and Nelson, ch. 5, this volume, for a discussion of data collection and corpus building.

2   Annotation is the manual or automatic process of adding information to a corpus. The information may refer to the grammatical, syntactical, semantic, or pragmatic properties of words, phrases, structures, sentences, or longer stretches of text. Grammatical annotation is also referred to as (grammatical or part-of-speech) *tagging*.

3   Perhaps 'to insulate the theory from the data' describes this practice more clearly.

4   See section 4, 'Lexicogrammar and lexical grammar,' for a more detailed treatment of this approach.

5   For example, Biber et al. (1999) make use of some frameworks used in Quirk et al. (1985), but they are also influenced by research in lexicogrammar (Biber et al. 1999: viii, 13).

6   For a discussion of statistical collocational analysis see Barnbrook (1996: ch. 5), Hunston (2002: ch. 4).

7   See McEnery (2003) for a further discussion of these criticisms of corpus annotation.

8   For example, Phillips (1989) lemmatizes on the basis of a preliminary investigation of collocation patterns.

9   The number of words that the term 'large corpus' denotes has been constantly increasing. The one-million-word Brown Corpus was considered large in the mid-1960s, whereas, forty years later, the Bank of English is almost half a billion words.

10 See section 5 for a brief discussion of the practical appeal of word-based research.

11 For example, Kennedy (1998: 121–54) presents within "grammatical studies centred on morphemes or words" (1998: 121) research focusing on the frequency of modal verbs, verb+particle combinations, prepositions, and conjunctions, together with research on tense-aspect marking, voice, and the subjunctive.

12 Note, however, that research into querying grammatically parsed corpora is developing apace; see, for example, Nelson et al. (2002).

13 For a discussion of data collection see Meyer and Nelson, ch. 5, this volume.

14 See Hunston (2002: chs. 3 and 4) for a discussion.

15 Biber et al. (1999: 13–14) make it explicit that they treat grammatical and lexico-grammatical patterns.

16 Biber et al. (1999) is based on a single corpus, the Longman Spoken and Written English Corpus (40 million words); Mindt (2000) is based on the British National Corpus (BNC) (Aston and Burnard 1998).

17 It is, of course, feasible to provide frequency and distributional information even when the book is based on studies carried out using different corpora, particularly when the corpora represent specialized domains. If different general corpora are used, this will assume that the corpora are comparable in terms of representativeness and size.

18 Huddleston and Pullum (2002) use the Brown Corpus, the Australian Corpus of English, the LOB corpus and the Wall Street Journal Corpus, as well as data from newspapers, plays, books, and film scripts (2002: 11, n. 3); Quirk et al. (1985) is informed by research using the Survey of English Usage, the Brown Corpus, and the LOB corpus (1985: 33).

19 For a discussion, see Meyer and Nelson, ch. 5, this volume.

20 Though there are grammars dating back some time which are clearly corpus based, most notably the grammar of Fries (1952).

21 *Cambridge Advanced Learner's Dictionary* (2003, 2nd edn.), *Collins COBUILD Advanced Learner's English Dictionary* (2003, 4th edn.), *Longman Dictionary of Contemporary English* (2003, 4th edn.), *Macmillan English Dictionary for Advanced Learners* (2002), *Oxford Advanced Learner's Dictionary* (2002, 6th edn.).

22 *Collins English Dictionary* (2003, 6th edn.), *Oxford Dictionary of English* (2003, 2nd edn.).

23 However, space in the CD-rom editions of dictionaries is much less restricted, and in online dictionaries space is almost unlimited.

24 The Macmillan Curriculum Corpus is "a 20 million-word corpus specially developed for the *Macmillan School Dictionary*. This unique corpus includes texts from coursebooks of different levels and school subjects, from countries where English is used as a second language, and from countries where English is the medium of instruction in schools" (www.macmillandictionary.com/ school/about/corpus).

25 Computer Assisted Language Learning.

26 Notably the diachronic component of the Helsinki Corpus (Kytö and Rissanen 1988).

27 Kytö (1988: 124) provides the example of *easy*, which, during the Middle and Early Modern English periods, appeared in all three forms: inflectional (*easier/easiest*), periphrastic (*more/most easy*), and double (*more easier/most easiest*).

28 The diachronic component of the Helsinki Corpus (Old to Early Modern English, pre-850 to ca. 1700), the ARCHER Corpus (1650–1990), as well as a corpus of Shakespeare's works, LOB/FLOB, Brown/Frown, BNC, and the *Guardian* CD-rom (1990–7).

29 Brown (1961), LOB (1961), FLOB (1991), Frown (1992), Survey of English Usage (1959–85), ICE-GB (1990–2).

30 See also Biber (2004); Mair and Leech (ch. 14, this volume).

31 www.ucl.ac.uk/english-usage/ diachronic/index.

32 See Lindquist and Mair (2004).

33 Rissanen (1997: 88) notes that "other corpora, concordances, dictionaries and primary texts have also been studied."

FURTHER READING

Introductory books

Barnbrook, G. (1996) *Language and computers: a practical introduction to the computer analysis of language*. Edinburgh: Edinburgh University Press.

Biber, D., Conrad, S., and Reppen, R. (1998) *Corpus linguistics: Investigating language structure and use*. Cambridge: Cambridge University Press.

Hunston, S. (2002) *Corpora in applied linguistics*. Cambridge: Cambridge University Press.

Kennedy, G. (1998) *An introduction to corpus linguistics*. London: Longman.

McEnery, T. and Wilson, A. (2001) *Corpus linguistics*, 2nd edn. Edinburgh: Edinburgh University Press.

Meyer, C. (2002) *English corpus linguistics: an introduction*. Cambridge: Cambridge University Press.

Partington, A. (1996) *Using corpora for English language research and teaching*. Amsterdam: John Benjamins.

Sampson, G. (2001) *Empirical linguistics*. London: Continuum.

Stubbs, M. (1996) *Text and corpus analysis: computer assisted studies of language and culture*. Oxford: Blackwell.

Stubbs, M. (2001) *Words and phrases: corpus studies of lexical semantics*. Oxford: Blackwell.

Tognini-Bonelli, E. (2001) *Corpus linguistics at work*. Amsterdam and Philadelphia: John Benjamins.

Edited volumes

Aijmer, K. and Altenberg, B. (eds.) (2004) *Advances in corpus linguistics*. Papers from the 23rd International Conference on English Language Research on Computerized Corpora (ICAME 23), Göteborg, May 22–6, 2002. Amsterdam: Rodopi.

Altenberg, B. and Granger, S. (eds.) (2002) *Lexis in contrast: corpus-based approaches*. Amsterdam: John Benjamins.

Botley, S., McEnery, T., and Wilson, A. (eds.) (2000) *Multilingual corpora in teaching and research*. Amsterdam: Rodopi.

Burnard, L. and McEnery, T. (eds.) (2000) *Rethinking language pedagogy from a corpus perspective*. Frankfurt am Main: Peter Lang.

Connor, U. and Upton, T. A. (eds.) (2004) *Applied corpus linguistics: a multidimensional perspective*. Amsterdam: Rodopi.

Garside, R., Leech, G., and McEnery, T. (eds.) (1997) *Corpus annotation: linguistic information from computer text corpora*. London; New York: Longman.

Granger, S., Hung, J., and Petch-Tyson, S. (eds.) (2002) *Computer learner corpora, second language acquisition and foreign language teaching*. Amsterdam: John Benjamins.

Granger, S. and Petch-Tyson, S. (eds.) (2003) *Extending the scope of corpus-based research: new applications, new challenges*. Amsterdam: Rodopi.

Ketteman, B. and Marko, G. (eds.) (2002) *Teaching and learning by doing corpus analysis*. Proceedings from the Fourth International Conference on Teaching and Language Corpora, Graz, July 19–24, 2000. Amsterdam: Rodopi.

Lindquist, H. and Mair, C. (2004) *Corpus approaches to grammaticalization in English*. Amsterdam: John Benjamins.

Leistyna, P. and Meyer, C. F. (eds.) (2003) *Corpus analysis: language structure and language use*. Amsterdam: Rodopi.

Mair, C. and Hundt, M. (eds.) (2000) *Corpus linguistics and linguistic theory* (ICAME 20) Amsterdam: Rodopi.

Renouf, A. (ed.) (1998) *Explorations in corpus linguistics.* Amsterdam: Rodopi.

Scott, M. and Thompson, G. (eds.) (2001) *Patterns of text: in honour of Michael Hoey.* Amsterdam and Philadelphia: John Benjamins.

Simpson, R. C. and Swales, J. M. (eds.) (2001) *Corpus linguistics in North America.* Ann Arbor: University of Michigan Press.

Lexical approach

Hoey, M. (1991) *Patterns of lexis in text.* Oxford: Oxford University Press.

Hunston, S. and Francis, G. (1999) *Pattern grammar.* Amsterdam: John Benjamins.

Sinclair, J. McH. (1991) *Corpus concordance collocation.* Oxford: Oxford University Press.

REFERENCES

Aarts, J. (2002) Review of E. Tognini-Bonelli, *Corpus linguistics at work.* *International Journal of Corpus Linguistics* 7 (1), 118–23.

Aijmer, K. and Altenberg, B. (eds.) (1991) *English corpus linguistics: studies in honour of Jan Svartvik.* London: Longman.

Aijmer, K. and Altenberg, B. (eds.) (2004) *Advances in corpus linguistics.* Papers from the 23rd International Conference on English Language Research on Computerized Corpora (ICAME 23), Göteborg, May 22–6, 2002. Amsterdam: Rodopi.

Aijmer, K. and Stenström, A.-B. (eds.) (2004) *Discourse patterns in spoken and written corpora.* Amsterdam: John Benjamins.

Alatis, J. (ed.) (1991) *Georgetown University round table on languages and linguistics 1991.* Washington, DC: Georgetown University Press.

Altenberg, B. and Granger, S. (eds.) (2002) *Lexis in contrast: corpus-based approaches.* Amsterdam: John Benjamins.

Altenberg, B. and Tapper, M. (1998) The use of adverbial connectors in advanced Swedish learners' written English. In Granger (ed.), 80–93.

Archer, D. (2005) *Questions and answers in the English courtroom (1640–1760:* *a sociopragmatic analysis.* Amsterdam: John Benjamins.

Aston, G. (1996) The British National Corpus as a language learner resource. Paper presented at the Second Conference on Teaching and Language Corpora, Lancaster University, UK, August 9–12. Also online: www.natcorp.ox.ac.uk/using/papers/aston96a.

Aston, G. (1997) Enriching the learning environment: corpora in ELT. In Wichmann et al. (eds.), 51–64.

Aston, G. (2000) Corpora and language teaching. In Burnard and McEnery (eds.), 7–17.

Aston, G. and Burnard, L. (1998) *The BNC handbook: exploring the British National Corpus with SARA.* Edinburgh: Edinburgh University Press.

Aston, G., Bernardini, S., and Stewart, D. (eds.) (2004) *Corpora and language barriers.* Amsterdam and Philadelphia: John Benjamins.

Atkins, B. T. S. and Zampolli, A. (eds.) (1994) *Computational approaches to the lexicon.* Oxford: Oxford University Press.

Baayen, R. H. and Renouf, A. (1996) Chronicling the times: productive lexical innovations in an English newspaper. *Language: Journal of the*

Linguistic Society of America 72 (1), 69–96.

Baker, M., Francis, G., and Tognini-Bonelli, E. (eds.) (1993) *Text and technology: in honour of John Sinclair.* Philadelphia and Amsterdam: John Benjamins.

Baker, P. (2005) *Public discourses of gay men.* London: Routledge.

Baker, P. and McEnery, T. (2005) A corpus-based approach to discourses of refugees and asylum seekers in UN and newspaper texts. *Language and Politics* 4 (2), 197–226.

Barnbrook, G. (1996) *Language and computers: a practical introduction to the computer analysis of language.* Edinburgh: Edinburgh University Press.

Bazell, C. E., Catford, J. C., Halliday, M. A. K., and Robins, R. H. (eds.) (1966) *In memory of F. R. Firth.* London: Longman.

Bernandini, S. (2002) Exploring new direction for discovery learning. In Ketteman and Marko (eds.), 165–82.

Biber, D. (2001) Using corpus-based methods to investigate grammar and use: some case studies on the use of verbs in English. In Simpson and Swales (eds.), 101–15.

Biber, D. (2004) Modal use across registers and time: an analysis based on the ARCHER corpus. In A. A. Curzan and K. Emmons (eds.), *Studies in the history of the English language II: unfolding conversations.* Berlin: Mouton de Gruyter, 189–216.

Biber, D., Finegan, E., and Atkinson, D. (1994a) ARCHER and its challenges: Compiling and exploring a representative corpus of historical English registers. In Fries et al. (eds.), 1–13.

Biber, D., Finegan, E., Atkinson, D., Beck, A., Burges, D., and Burges, J. (1994b) The design and analysis of the ARCHER Corpus: a progress report. In Kytö et al. (eds.), 3–6.

Biber, D., Conrad, S., and Reppen, R. (1998) *Corpus linguistics: investigating language structure and use.* Cambridge: Cambridge University Press.

Biber, D., Johansson, S., Leech, G., Conrad, S., and Finegan E. (1999) *Longman grammar of spoken and written English.* London: Longman.

Biber, D. and Reppen, R. (1998) Comparing native and learner perspectives on English grammar: a study of complement clauses. In Granger (ed.), 145–58.

Boswood, T. (ed.) (1997) *New ways of using computers in language teaching.* Alexandria, VA: TESOL.

Bradford, R. (2002) Grammar is by statisticians, language is by humans. *IATEFL Issues* 167, 13.

Brems, L. (2003) Measure noun constructions: an instance of semantically-driven grammaticalization. *International Journal of Corpus Linguistics* 8 (2), 283–312.

Burnard, L. and McEnery, T. (eds.) (2000) *Rethinking language pedagogy from a corpus perspective.* Papers from the third international conference on teaching and language corpora. Hamburg: Peter Lang.

Burrows, J. (2002) The Englishing of Juvenal: computational stylistics and translated texts. *Style* 36 (4), 677–9.

Cambridge advanced learner's dictionary (2003) 2nd edn. Cambridge: Cambridge University Press.

Carter, R. and McCarthy, M. (1999) The English get-passive in spoken discourse: description and implications for an interpersonal grammar. *English Language and Linguistics* 3 (1), 41–58.

Charteris-Black, J. (2004) *Corpus approaches to critical metaphor analysis.* Basingstoke: Palgrave-Macmillan.

Collier, A. (1998) Identifying diachronic change in semantic relations. In Renouf (ed.), 259–68.

Collins COBUILD Advanced learner's English dictionary (2003) 4th edn. London: Harper Collins.

Collins COBUILD English grammar (1990) London: Harper Collins.

Collins English dictionary (2003) 6th edn. London: Harper Collins.

Collins COBUILD Grammar patterns 1: verbs (1996) London: Harper Collins.

Cowie, A. P. (1999) *English dictionaries for foreign learners: a history*. Oxford: Oxford University Press.

Crookes, G. and Gass, S. M. (eds.) (1993) *Tasks and language learning: Integrating theory and practice*. Clevedon: Multilingual Matters.

De Cock, S., Granger, S., Leech, G., and McEnery, A. M. (1998) An automated approach to the phrasicon of EFL learners. In Granger (ed.), 67–79.

Deignan, A. (2005) Metaphor and corpus linguistics. *Converging Evidence in Language and Communication Research 6*. Amsterdam: John Benjamins.

Di Sciullo, A.-M.; Muysken, P., and Singh, R. (1986) Government and code-mixing. *Journal of Linguistics* 22 (1), 1–24.

Duffley, P. J. (2003) The gerund and the *to*-infinitive as subject. *Journal of English Linguistics* 31 (4), 324–52.

Facchineti, R. and Krug, M. (eds.) (2003) *Modality in contemporary English*. Berlin: Mouton de Gruyter.

Fillmore, C. J. (1992) "Corpus linguistics" or "Computer-aided armchair linguistics." In J. Svartvik (ed.), 35–60.

Fillmore, C. J. and Atkins, B. T. S. (1994) Starting where the dictionaries stop: The challenge of corpus lexicography. In Atkins and Zampolli (eds.), 349–93.

Firth, J. R. (1951/1957) Modes of meaning. In *Papers in Linguistics 1934–1951*. London: Oxford University Press.

Firth, J. R. (1968) A synopsis of linguistic theory. In Palmer (ed.), 168–205.

Flowerdew, J. (ed.) (2001) *Academic discourse*. London: Longman.

Fotos, S. and Ellis, R. (1991) Communicating about grammar: a task-based approach. *TESOL Quarterly* 25 (4), 605–28.

Francis, W. N. and Kučera, H. (1964) *A standard corpus of present-day edited American English*. Providence: Brown University.

Fries, C. (1952) *The structure of English*. New York: Harcourt Brace.

Fries, U., Tottie, G., and Schneider, P. (eds.) (1994) Creating and using English language corpora. Papers from the Fourteenth International Conference on English Language Research on Computerized Corpora, Zürich 1993. Amsterdam: Rodopi.

Gabrielatos, C. (2003) Corpora and ELT: Just a fling, or the real thing? Plenary address at INGED 2003 International Conference, Multiculturalism in ELT Practices: Unity and Diversity, organized jointly by BETA (Romania), ETAI (Israel), INGED (Turkey), and TESOL Greece, Baskent University, Ankara, Turkey, October 10–12, 2003.

Gabrielatos, C. (2005) Corpora and language teaching: just a fling or wedding bells? *TESL-EJ* 8 (4) www.tesl-ej.org/ej32/al.

Garside, R., Leech, G., and McEnery, T. (eds.) (1997) *Corpus annotation: linguistic information from computer text corpora*. London: Longman.

Gilquin, G. (2003) Causative *get* and *have*: so close, so different. *Journal of English Linguistics* 31 (2), 125–48.

Granger, S. (ed.) (1998) *Learner English on computer*. London: Addison Wesley Longman.

Granger, S. and Rayson, P. (1998) Automatic profiling of learner texts. In Granger (ed.), 119–31.

Granger, S. and Tribble, C. (1998) Learner corpus data in the foreign language classroom: form-focused instruction and data-driven learning. In Granger (ed.), 199–209.

Granger, S., Hung, J., and Petch-Tyson, S. (eds.) (2002) *Computer learner corpora, second language acquisition and foreign language teaching*. Amsterdam: John Benjamins.

Greenbaum, S. (ed.) (1996) *Comparing English worldwide: the International Corpus of English*. Oxford: Clarendon Press.

Gries, S. T. (2003) Towards a corpus based identification of prototypical instances of constructions. *Annual Review of Cognitive Linguistics* 1, 1–27.

Gries, S. T. and Stefanowitsch, A. (2004) Extending collostructional analysis: a corpus-based perspective on 'alternations.' *International Journal of Corpus Linguistics* 9 (1), 97–129.

Halliday, M. A. K. (1966) Lexis as a linguistic level. In Bazell et al. (eds.), 148–62.

Halliday, M. A. K. (1991) Corpus studies and probabilistic grammar. In Aijmer and Altenberg (eds.), 30–40.

Halliday, M. A. K. (1992) Language as system and language as instance: the corpus as a theoretical construct. In Svartvik (ed.), 61–77.

Hardt-Mautner, G. (1995) Only connect: critical discourse analysis and corpus linguistics. UCREL Technical Papers 6. Lancaster University.

Harwood, N. (2005) What do we want EAP teaching materials for? *Journal of English for Academic Purposes* 4 (2), 149–61.

Hoey, M. (1991) *Patterns of lexis in text*. Oxford: Oxford University Press.

Hoey, M. (1997) From concordance to text structure: new uses for computer corpora. In Lewandowska-Tomaszczyk and Melia (eds.), 2–23.

Hopper, P. J. and Traugott, E. C. (1993) *Grammaticalization*. Cambridge: Cambridge University Press.

Huddleston, R. and Pullum, G. K., et al. (2002) *The Cambridge grammar of the English language*. Cambridge: Cambridge University Press.

Hughes, G. (1997) Developing a computing infrastructure for corpus-based teaching. In Wichmann et al. (eds.), 292–307.

Hundt, M., Sand, A., and Siemund, R. (1998) *Manual of information to accompany the Freiburg-LOB Corpus of British English ('FLOB')* Freiburg: Englisches Seminar, Albert-Ludwigs-Universität Freiburg.

Hundt, M., Sand, A., and Skandera, P. (1999) *Manual of information to accompany the Freiburg-Brown Corpus of American English ('Frown')* Freiburg: Englisches Seminar, Albert-Ludwigs-Universität Freiburg.

Hunston, S. (2001) Colligation, lexis, pattern and text. In Scott and Thompson (eds.), 13–33.

Hunston, S. (2002) *Corpora in applied linguistics*. Cambridge: Cambridge University Press.

Hunston, S. and Francis, G. (1998) Verbs observed: a corpus-driven pedagogic grammar. *Applied Linguistics* 19 (1), 45–72.

Hunston, S. and Francis, G. (2000) *Pattern grammar*. Amsterdam: John Benjamins.

Hyltenstam, K. and Pienemann, M. (eds.) (1985) *Modelling and assessing second language acquisition*. Clevedon, North Somerset: Multilingual Matters.

Jackson, H. (2002) *Lexicography: an introduction*. London: Routledge.

Johansson, S. (1991) Computer corpora in English language research. In Johansson and Stenström (eds.), 3–6.

Johansson, S., Leech, G., and Goodluck, H. (1978) *Manual of information to accompany the Lancaster-Oslo/Bergen Corpus of British English, for use with digital computers*. Department of English, University of Oslo.

Johansson, S., Atwell, E., Garside, R., and Leech, G. (1986) *The tagged LOB Corpus: user's manual*. Norwegian Computing Centre for the Humanities, Bergen.

Johansson, S. and Stenström, A.-B. (eds.) (1991) *English computer corpora: selected papers and research guide*. Berlin: Mouton de Gruyter.

Johns, T. (1991) Should you be persuaded: two examples of data driven learning. In Johns and King (eds.), 1–16.

Johns, T. (1997) Contexts: the background, development and trialling of a concordance-based CALL program. In Wichmann et al. (eds.), 100–15.

Johns, T. (2002) Data-driven learning: the perpetual challenge. In Ketteman and Marko (eds.), 107–17.

Johns, T. and King, P. (eds.) (1991) Classroom concordancing. *ELR Journal* 4. University of Birmingham.

Jones, S. and Murphy, M. L. (2005) Using corpora to investigate antonym acquisition. *International Journal of Corpus Linguistics* 10 (3), 401–22.

Kennedy, G. (1998), *Introduction to corpus linguistics*. Harlow, Essex: Longman.

Kennedy, G. (1992) Preferred ways of putting things with implications for language teaching. In Svartvik (ed.), 335–78.

Ketteman, B. and Marko, G. (eds.) (2002) *Teaching and learning by doing corpus analysis*. Proceedings from the Fourth International Conference on Teaching and Language Corpora, Graz July 19–24, 2000. Amsterdam: Rodopi.

Koller, V. and Mautner, G. (2004) Computer applications in critical discourse analysis. In C. Coffin, A. Hewings, and K. O'Halloran (eds.), *Applying English grammar: functional and corpus approaches*. London: Hodder and Stoughton: 216–28.

Krug, M. (2000) *Emerging English modals: a corpus-based study of grammaticalization*. Berlin: Mouton de Gruyter.

Kytö, M. (1996) *Manual to the diachronic part of the Helsinki Corpus of English Texts*, 3rd edn. Helsinki: University of

Helsinki Press. http://khnt.hit.uib.no/icame/manuals/HC/INDEX.HTM

Kytö, M. (1996) "The best and most excellentest way": the rivalling forms of adjective comparison in Late Middle and Early Modern English. In Svartvik (ed.), 123–44.

Kytö, M. and Rissanen, M. (1988) The Helsinki Corpus of English texts: classifying and coding the diachronic part. In Kytö et al. (eds.), 169–79.

Kytö, M., Rissanen, M., and Wright, S. (eds.) (1994) *Corpora across the centuries*. Proceedings of the First International Colloquium on English Diachronic Corpora, St Catharine's College Cambridge, March 22–7, 1993. Amsterdam: Rodopi.

Kytö, M., Ihalainen, O., and Rissanen, M. (eds.) (1988) *Corpus linguistics, hard and soft*. Proceedings of the Eighth International Conference on English Language Research on Computerized Corpora. Amsterdam: Rodopi.

Lancashire, I., Meyer, C., and Carol, P. (eds.) (1996) Papers from English language research on computerized corpora (ICAME 16) Amsterdam: Rodopi.

Landau, I. L. (2001, 2nd edn.) *Dictionaries: the art and craft of lexicography*. Cambridge: Cambridge University Press.

Leech, G. (1991) The state of the art in corpus linguistics. In Aimer and Altenberg (eds.), 8–29.

Leech, G. (1992) Corpora and theories of linguistic performance. In Svartvik (ed.), 105–22.

Leech, G. (1997a) Introducing corpus annotation. In Garside et al. (eds.), 1–18.

Leech, G. (1997b) Teaching and language corpora: a convergence. In Wichmann et al. (eds.), 1–23.

Leech, G. (2003) Modality on the move: the English modal auxiliaries 1961–1992. In Facchineti and Krug (eds.), 223–40.

Lewandowska-Tomaszczyk, B. and Melia, P. J. (eds.) (1997) *Practical Applications in Language Corpora (PALC '97)* Łódź: Łódź University Press.

Lightbown, P. (1985) Can language acquisition be altered by instruction? In Hyltenstam and Pienemann (eds.), 101–12.

Lindquist, H. and Mair, C. (eds.) (2004) *Corpus approaches to grammaticalization in English.* Amsterdam: John Benjamins.

Ljung, M. (ed.) (1997) *Corpus-based studies in English.* Papers from the Seventeenth International Conference on English Language Research on Computerized Corpora (ICAME 17) Amsterdam: Rodopi.

Longman dictionary of contemporary English (2003) 4th edn. Harlow, Essex: Longman.

Lopez-Couso, M. J. and Mendez-Naya, B. (2001) On the history of *if-* and *though-* links with declarative complement clauses. *English Language and Linguistics* 5 (1), 93–107.

Lorenz, G. (1998) Overstatement in advanced learners' writing: Stylistic aspects of adjective intensification. In Granger (ed.), 53–66.

Loschky, L. and Bley-Vroman, R. (1993) Grammar and task-based methodology. In Crookes and Gass (eds.), 123–66.

Louw, B. (1993) Irony in the text or insincerity in the writer? The diagnostic potential of semantic prosodies. In Baker et al. (eds.), 157–76.

Macmillan English dictionary for advanced learners (2002) Basingstoke, Hampshire. Macmillan.

McEnery, A. M. (2003) Corpus linguistics. In Mitkov (ed.), 448–63.

McEnery, A. M. (2005) *Swearing in English: bad language, purity and power from 1586 to the present.* London: Routledge.

McEnery, A. M., Wilson, A., and Baker, J. P. (1997) Teaching grammar again after twenty years: corpus-based help for teaching grammar. *ReCALL Journal* 9 (2), 8–17.

McEnery, A. and Kifle, N. (2002) Epistemic modality in argumentative essays of second language writers. In Flowerdew (ed.), 182–95.

McEnery, T. and Wilson, A. (2001) 2nd edn. *Corpus linguistics.* Edinburgh: Edinburgh University Press.

McEnery, A. M. and Xiao, Z. (2004) Swearing in modern British English: the case of *fuck* in the BNC. *Language and Literature* 13 (3), 237–70.

Mair, C. (1991) Quantitative or qualitative corpus analysis? Infinitival complement clause in the Survey of English Usage corpus. In Johansson and Stenström (eds.), 67–80.

Mair, C., Hundt, M., Leech, G., and Smith, N. (2003) Short term diachronic shifts in part-of-speech frequencies: a comparison of the tagged LOB and F-LOB corpora. *International Journal of Corpus Linguistics* 7 (2), 245–64.

Meyer, C. F. (2002) *English corpus linguistics.* Cambridge: Cambridge University Press.

Milton, J. (1998) Exploiting L1 and interlanguage corpora in the design of an electronic language learning and production environment. In Granger (ed.), 186–98.

Mindt, D. (1995) *An empirical grammar of the English verb: modal verbs.* Berlin: Cornelsen Verlag.

Mindt, D. (2000) *An empirical grammar of the English verb system.* Berlin: Cornelsen.

Mitkov, R. (2003) *Handbook of computational linguistics.* Oxford: Oxford University Press.

Nelson, G., Wallis, S., and Aarts, B. (2002) *Exploring natural language: working with the British component of*

the International Corpus of English.
Amsterdam: John Benjamins.

Nesselhauf, N. (2005) Collocations in a learner corpus. *Studies in Corpus Linguistics 14.* Amsterdam: John Benjamins.

Nevalainen, T. and Kahlas-Tarkka, L. (eds.) (1997) *To explain the present: studies in the changing English language in honour of Matti Rissanen.* Mémoires de la Société Néophilologique de Helsinki. Helsinki: Société Néophilologique.

Nevalainen, T. and Raumolin-Brunberg, H. (2003) *Historical sociolinguistics.* London: Longman.

Newmeyer, F. J. (2003) Grammar is grammar and usage is usage. *Language* 79 (4), 682–707.

Nunan, D. (1989) *Designing tasks for the communicative classroom.* Cambridge: Cambridge University Press.

Ooi, V. B. Y. (1998) *Computer corpus lexicography.* Edinburgh Textbooks in Empirical Linguistics. Edinburgh: Edinburgh University Press.

Oostdijk, N. (1991) *Corpus linguistics and the automatic analysis of English.* Amsterdam: Rodopi.

Orpin, D. (2005) Corpus linguistics and critical discourse analysis: examining the ideology of sleaze. *International Journal of Corpus Linguistics* 10 (1), 37–61.

Osbourne, J. (2000) What can students learn from a corpus? Building bridges between data and explanation. In Burnard and McEnery (eds.), 193–205.

Owen, C. (1993) Corpus-based grammar and the Heineken effect: Lexico-grammatical description for language learners. *Applied Linguistics* 14 (2), 167–87.

Oxford advanced learner's dictionary (2002) 6th edn. Oxford: Oxford University Press.

Oxford dictionary of English (2003) 2nd edn. Oxford: Oxford University Press.

Palmer, F. R. (ed.) (1968) *Selected papers of J.R. Firth 1952–59.* London: Longmans.

Partington, A. (2004) "Utterly content in each other's company": semantic prosody and semantic preference. *International Journal of Corpus Linguistics* 9 (1), 131–56.

Partington, A. Morley, J., and Harman, L. (eds.) (2004) *Corpora and discourse.* Proceedings of CamConf 2002, Università degli Studi di Camerino, Centro Linguistico d'Ateneo, September 27–9. New York: Peter Lang.

Paulillo, J. C. (2000) Formalising formality: an analysis of register variation in Sinhala. *Journal of Linguistics* 36 (2), 215–59.

Phillips, M. (1989) *Lexical structure of text*: *discourse analysis monograph no. 12.* English Language Research, University of Birmingham.

Polovina-Vukovic, D. (204) The representation of social actors in the Globe and Mail during the break-up of the former Yugoslavia. In L. Young and C. Harrison (eds.), *Systemic functional linguistics and critical discourse analysis.* London and New York: Continuum, 155–72.

Prodromou, L. (1997) Corpora: the real thing? *English Teaching Professional* 5, 2–6.

Quirk, R., Greenbaum, S., Leech, G., and Svartvik, J. (1985) *A comprehensive grammar of the English language.* London: Longman.

Renouf, A. (1996) The ACRONYM Project: Discovering the textual thesaurus. In Lancashire et al. (eds.), 171–87.

Renouf, A. (1997) Tools for the diachronic study of historical corpora. In Nevalainen and Kahlas-Tarkka (eds.), 185–99.

Renouf, A. (ed.) (1998) *Explorations in corpus linguistics.* Amsterdam: Rodopi.

Renouf, A. (2001) Lexical signals of word relations. In Scott and Thompson (eds.), 35–54.

Rissanen, M. (1997) Introduction. In Rissanen et al. (eds.), 1–15.

Rissanen, M., Kytö, M., and Heikkonen, K. (eds.) (1997) *Grammaticalization at work: studies of long-term developments in English*. Berlin: Mouton de Gruyter.

Römer, U. (2004) Textbooks: a corpus-driven approach to modal auxiliaries and their didactics. In J. McH. Sinclair (ed.), *How to use corpora in language teaching*. Amsterdam: John Benjamins, 185–99.

Römer, U. (2005) *Progressives, patterns, pedagogy: a corpus-driven approach to progressive forms, functions, contexts and dialects*. Amsterdam: John Benjamins.

Sampson, G. (2001) *Empirical linguistics*. London: Continuum.

Schmid, H.-J. (2000) *English abstract nouns as conceptual shells: from corpus to cognition*. Berlin: Mouton de Gruyter.

Schmidt, R. W. (1990) The role of consciousness in second language learning. *Applied Linguistics* 11 (2), 129–58.

Schonefeld, D. (1999) Corpus linguistics and cognitivism. *International Journal of Corpus Linguistics* 4 (1), 137–71.

Scott, M. and Thompson, G. (eds.) (2001) *Patterns of text: in honour of Michael Hoey*. Amsterdam/Philadelphia: John Benjamins.

Seidlhofer, B. (ed.) (2003) *Controversies in applied linguistics*. Oxford: Oxford University Press.

Semino, A. and Short, M. H. (2004) *Corpus stylistics*. London: Longman.

Sharwood Smith, M. (1981) Consciousness-raising and the second language learner. *Applied Linguistics* 2, 159–69.

Simpson, R. C. and Swales, J. M. (eds.) (2001) *Corpus linguistics in North America*. Ann Arbor: University of Michigan Press.

Sinclair, J. McH. (1966) Beginning the Study of Lexis. In Bazell et al. (eds.), 410–31.

Sinclair, J. McH. (ed.) (1987) *Looking up: an account of the COBUILD Project in lexical computing*. London: Collins ELT.

Sinclair, J. McH. (1991) *Corpus concordance collocation*. Oxford: Oxford University Press.

Sinclair, J. McH. (1998) The lexical item. In Weigang (ed.), 1–24.

Sinclair, J. (2004a) Intuition and annotation: the discussion continues. In Aijmer and Altenberg (eds.), 39–59.

Sinclair, J. (2004b) *Trust the text: language, corpus and discourse*. London: Routledge.

Sinclair, J. McH. (ed.) (2004c) *How to use corpora in language teaching*. Amsterdam: John Benjamins.

Skehan, P. (1998) *A cognitive approach to language learning*. Oxford: Oxford University Press.

Smith, N. (2003) Changes in the modals and semi-modals of strong obligation and epistemic necessity in recent British English. In Facchineti and Krug (eds.), 241–66.

Sotillo, S. M. and Wang-Gempp, J. (2004) Using corpus linguistics to investigate class, ideology and discursive practices in online political discussions: pedagogical applications of corpora. In U. Conner and T. A. Upton (eds.), *Applied corpus linguistics*. Amsterdam: Rodopi, 91–122.

Stefanowitsch, A. (2005) The function of metaphor: developing a corpus-based perspective. *International Journal of Corpus Linguistics* 10 (2), 161–98.

Stubbs, M. (1996) *Text and corpus analysis: computer-assisted studies of language and culture*. Oxford: Blackwell.

Stubbs, M. (2001) *Words and phrases: corpus studies of lexical semantics*. Oxford: Blackwell.

Stubbs, M. (2002) Two quantitative methods of studying phraseology in English. *International Journal of Corpus Linguistics* 7 (2), 215–44.

Stubbs, M. (2005) Conrad in the computer: examples of quantitative stylistic methods. *Language and Literature* 14 (1), 5–24.

Svartvik, J. (1966) *On voice in the English verb*. The Hague: Mouton and Co.

Svartvik, J. (ed.) (1992) *Directions in corpus linguistics: proceedings of the Nobel Symposium 82, Stockholm, 4–8 August 1991*. Berlin: Mouton de Gruyter.

Svartvik, J. (ed.) (1996) *Words: proceedings of an international symposium, Lund, 25–26 August 1995*. Stockholm: Kungl. Vitterhets Historie och Antikvitets Akademien.

Teubert, W. (1999) Corpus linguistics: a partisan view. *TELRI Newsletter* April (8), 4–19.

Tognini-Bonelli, E. (2001) *Corpus linguistics at work*. Amsterdam: John Benjamins Publishing Company.

Tono, Y. (2000) A computer learner corpus based analysis of the acquisition order of English grammatical morphemes. In Burnard and McEnery (eds.), 123–32.

Tribble, C. (1997) Put a corpus in your classroom: using a computer in vocabulary development. In Boswood (ed.), 266–8.

Tribble, C. and Jones, G. (1990) *Concordances in the classroom*. London: London Group UK Limited.

Virtanen, T. (1997) The progressive in NS and NNS student compositions: evidence from the International Corpus of Learner English. In Ljung (ed.), 299–309.

Virtanen, T. (1998) Direct questions in argumentative student writing. In Granger (ed.), 94–106.

Vivanco, V. (2005) The absence of connectives and the maintenance of coherence in publicity texts. *Journal of Pragmatics* 37 (8), 1233–49.

Wang, S. (2005) Corpus-based approaches and discourse analysis in relation to reduplication and repetition. *Journal of Pragmatics* 37 (4), 505–40.

Weigang, E. (ed.) (1998) *Contrastive lexical semantics*. Amsterdam and Philadelphia: John Benjamins Publishing Company.

Wichmann, A., Fligelstone, S., McEnery, T., and Knowles, G. (1997) *Teaching and language corpora*. New York: Addison Wesley Longman.

Widdowson, H. G. (1991) The description and prescription of language. In Alatis (ed.), 11–24.

4   English Grammar Writing

ANDREW LINN

1   Grammar Books

Grammar writing constitutes the oldest continuous tradition of explicit language study in the history of western linguistics. We all think we know what a grammar is, but *grammar* is a label that has been used and abused in more ways than any other in linguistics. In the specific sense of a written presentation of the structuring principles of a language it has meant different things to different users at different times and in different places. The use of the name *grammar* for this type of text has come down to us from the Latin *Ars Grammatica*, a direct translation of the Greek τέκνή γραμματική, meaning 'skill in the use of letters.' The study of language has clearly come a long way since it amounted to little more than being able to read and write. Innumerable grammar books have passed through the hands of students and scholars alike in the course of the centuries, and grammar production has been as much of an industry for publishers and booksellers as it has for linguists.

Grammars, like dictionaries, form part of the familiar scenery of linguistics, and it is easy to forget that they carry enormous power. An individual grammar book can *be* the English language for millions of people, so it is essential to have a critical sense of why a grammar is as it is: what does it not say and what does it conceal? In the first half of the nineteenth century Lindley Murray's *English Grammar* of 1795 captured the mood of the time. It entered at least 65 British editions as well as many editions and reprints in the USA, Europe and the British Empire, not to mention offshoots and imitators (see the papers in Tieken-Boon van Ostade 1996). The authoritarian style and the 22 confident rules of syntax might not find favour with today's linguists, but its impact on the popular understanding of and attitudes towards English grammar is incalculable. The modern-day equivalent in terms of impact is maybe the Longman ELT machine, presided over by the dominant *Longman grammar of spoken and written English*, regarded as authoritative in Europe and America alike, and the more recent *Longman advanced learners' grammar* of 2003, but there are a number of other major publishers hard at work in this market too.

How best to present the grammatical system of English is certainly not a given, and a range of competing factors influence why a particular grammar book ends up taking its particular form. The factors involved in shaping an individual grammar book do not, however, form an undifferentiated bundle. Their relative importance will vary from one book to the next. Is it more important that the needs of the users be catered for or is it more important that a particular theoretical stance be taken? Is it more important to be exhaustive or to be simple? In Stockwell, Schachter, and Partee's 1973 study, *The major syntactic structures of English*, for example, the adoption of a particular theoretical framework (transformational-generative) was more important than other competing factors, which in their turn dominated other grammars from the same year, such as *A university grammar of English* from the Quirk, Greenbaum, Leech, and Svartvik stable and *A mathematical grammar of English* by George Hemphill. This is not the place to set out a theory for understanding grammar writing, but in the course of this overview our principal question will be why certain grammar books have been as they are and why particular approaches have, like Murray and the Longman grammars, been successful in particular contexts, and this has to be understood in terms of the competing factors underlying grammar-writing.

Individual grammar books may, then, be characterized by the interplay of differently prioritized variables in their construction, but we do nonetheless instinctively recognize a grammar book as opposed to some other sort of publication about language, so let us consider some of the features which make the genre recognizable. Around 1990 there was a flurry of activity considering the nature of grammars, specifically *reference grammars*. Gottfried Graustein and Gerhard Leitner suggest that grammar books in general have three essential properties, and we will accept these as at least some of the key stylistic features of the genre:

1 Grammars of a language are more or less comprehensive and systematic accounts of the major categories, structures, and functions of linguistic expressions found in the language under description [. . .]
2 Grammars of a language do not, and, perhaps, should not, aim to represent the totality of a language in its regional, social, stylistic or temporal extensions. They select relevant sections according to linguistic and user-related criteria [. . .]
3 Grammars of a language, like other types of reference materials, are not meant to be read from beginning to end but to be used wherever a need arises. They are to provide insights into the 'making and working' of a language and to answer very concrete questions, regardless of theoretical or other issues.   (Graustein and Leitner 1989: 5–15)

It has become standard practice in what some (e.g. Leitner 1984) have called 'grammaticology' (the study of grammar writing) to divide English grammar books into various functional categories. Thus the *school tradition* is distinguished from the *scholarly tradition*, and *teaching grammars* are distinguished from *reference grammars*. The 'scholarly tradition' and 'reference grammars' have received greatest attention from the grammaticologists, but in breadth of impact the other categories are more important, and we shall discuss grammars of all categories in what follows, treating the functions as part of a continuum, not as isolated types of "grammaticography." These distinctions are often unhelpful anyway, since many grammars have been written to serve one function and have come to serve another or have not differentiated, whether in how they were written or how they were used, between the different functions.

2   The First 300 Years

Grammars have been written in the west for over two millennia, and grammar-writing in the modern age carries its past with it. There is a burden of tradition on anyone writing a grammar, a body of expectation that discourages innovation. One of the truly pioneering grammars was *The Structure of English* of 1952 by Charles Carpenter Fries, the first to use recordings of live data as its corpus. Fries draws attention to the 'cultural lag' in grammar writing, and his reward for bringing English grammar writing into line with the usual practices of modern linguistics was a watery reception by the community of English language teachers. Gleason (1965) gives a fascinating account of what happened when English grammar writing and linguistics clashed in mid-twentieth-century America. Fries is an exception, and our history remains to a large extent one characterized by repetition and imitation.

The year 1586 is the annus mirabilis of English grammar writing, the year it all started. William Bullokar published his *Pamphlet for Grammar* that year with the express intention of showing that English grammar was rule-governed like Latin, something not generally assumed to be the case. To counteract this widely held view, Bullokar modeled his English grammar slavishly on the Latin grammar attributed to William Lily and prescribed for use in the schools by Henry VIII, and the subsequent history of English grammar writing was one of gradual and hard-won liberation from the shackles of Latin grammar.

Bullokar wrote in English, using his own reformed spelling system, but, moving into the seventeenth century, grammars of English still tended to be written in Latin, Christopher Cooper's of 1685 being the last of the Latin ones. The burden of tradition means that the history of grammar writing for most languages is characterized by a move forward, then several shuffles back before the initial move forward is attempted again. Caution is the watchword, and the history of linguistics is littered with failed reform attempts, which have withered only to bud and flower years later. For example, where Bullokar had listed paradigms for noun declension, stating quite categorically that 'A substantiue is declined with fiue cases in both numbers,' the polymath John Wallis in his 1653 *Grammatica Linguæ Anglicanæ*, thinking about the nature of the English language on its own terms and not filtered through Latin, was able to state equally categorically that 'substantives in English do not have different genders or cases.' This was not the end of the matter, and nearly a century and a half later Lindley Murray is still having to cite grammatical authorities to defend the fact that English does not exhibit the same case system as Latin and Ancient Greek.

The seventeenth century, as well as witnessing the emergence of the 'scholarly tradition' (if we continue to accept these different functional categories) in the work of Wallis, also saw the emergence of two closely related grammar-writing traditions, both inspired by the needs of the time, and both subsequently big business. Firstly, English became increasingly significant for commercial and diplomatic reasons, and this called for grammars of English as a foreign language. Between 1646 and 1686 English grammars were printed in Denmark, Germany, Hungary, The Netherlands, and Sweden. Secondly, grammars were now being written for non-learned native-speaker audiences too. Cooper published an English translation of his grammar in 1687 for 'Gentlemen, Ladies, Merchants, Tradesmen, Schools, and Strangers (that have so much knowledge of our English tongue as to understand the Rules).' Moving from the seventeenth to the eighteenth century, education became more widespread and there was a hunger for popular scientific presentations. In line with the mood of the time we find grammars like John Brightland's *A Grammar of the English tongue* of 1711 (now usually attributed to Charles Gildon et al.), intended for children, women and others without a Latin background, and James Greenwood's popular *Essay towards a practical English grammar* of the same year, also intended for children and the 'Fair Sex.' (See Vorlat 1975.) Both these types of grammar show the role market forces have played in grammar production, and a characteristic of both traditions has consequently been opportunism: responding to new audiences and new circumstances of use.

By the end of the eighteenth century over 270 grammatical works dealing with English had been published (Gneuss 1996: 28), and the figure for the next fifty years is getting on for 900 new grammars (Michael 1991: 12), the majority very much like the others. It was commonplace for a would-be grammarian to argue that local needs were subtly different to the needs of learners elsewhere or that the analysis of a particular grammatical point was erroneous in all competing grammar books, and so a new work was needed. Modern-language teaching in Europe until the very late nineteenth century was an ad hoc business, provided not as a matter of course but when there happened to be someone around offering to provide it (see the studies in Engler and Haas 2000). Even in the venerable European universities the modern languages tended to be taught by so-called *language masters*, who occupied a low status and were employed on a par with the teachers of other practical skills like fencing and dancing. Charles Julius Bertram was a good example of those entrepreneurs who flourished as English teachers and grammar-writers. He worked as an English teacher in Copenhagen and in 1753 published a substantial *Royal English–Danish grammar*, in which he claimed to have 'discovered many previously unknown and useful rules.' In reality he was simply responding to the publishing opportunities presented by a particular pedagogical circumstance (see Linn 1999). Local needs and opportunities have continued to fuel much English grammar writing. Staying in Denmark, although any country could probably be chosen, the prescribed grammars in the departments of English at the universities in recent years have tended to be those written by the presiding professor, being used for the duration of that professor's reign (Bent Preisler, *personal communication*). The fact that specific textbooks are written for specific situations is of course no surprise, but the point is that the teaching of English grammar and writing about it is more of a patchwork of local examples than a solid linear tradition.

English grammatical literature prior to 1800 has been charted quite fully, and the publication of Görlach (1998) is of great benefit to work on the nineteenth century. Görlach lists 21 'topics worthy of detailed study,' the majority of which are yet to be addressed, so there is plenty to do before we understand adequately how English grammar was approached, studied, and taught in that century, and Görlach's main bibliography contains 1,936 items. In line with what we have already established about English grammar writing, the principal factor motivating the majority of these publications is local pedagogical circumstances, and Edward Shelley's *The people's grammar; or English grammar without difficulties for 'the million,'* published in 1848 in Huddersfield, Yorkshire, is but one example, in this case aimed at 'the mechanic and hard-working youth, in their solitary struggles for the acquirement of knowledge.'

Utilitarian grammars in nineteenth-century America were not much different from their European counterparts, although, apart from Lindley Murray, there was little importation from Britain into the American market: 'English grammars suffered no sea change in their transatlantic migration' (Algeo 1986: 307). An important sea change in grammar-writing, and one affecting European and American practice alike, was however the move from a *word-based* to a *clause-based* framework for description. The traditional word-and-paradigm model of grammar-writing, inherited from the Latin tradition, aimed to show how words related to other words, while the new clause-based grammars sought to show how words related to grammatical units, and the clause-based approach remains the dominant one in English grammars today. It can be traced back to the German scholar, Karl Ferdinand Becker, whose analysis of syntactic relations rapidly gained influence outside Germany, thanks largely to an enthusiastic reception from language teachers. As with Murray (and indeed the Latin grammarian Donatus and others besides), it was the applicability of the system in the classroom that led to its success. Becker's *Schulgrammatik der deutschen Sprache* of 1848 appeared in England in English translation in 1855, and it was quickly adapted for the American teaching scene by Samuel Greene and others in the 1850s.

While Lindley Murray was popular in American schools, as the nineteenth century progressed that popularity diminished in direct proportion to the increase in popularity of the 1823 *Institutes of English grammar* by Goold Brown. Like Murray (and Becker), Brown was in no sense a professional linguist, and his primary concerns were moral rather than linguistic. He is contemptuous of other grammarians including Murray and contemptuous of innovation, whether in the language or in how it is taught and described: 'the nature of the subject almost entirely precludes invention,' he writes. The study of grammar is quite simply the inculcation of rules for the improvement of those who learn them. In both content and method this is a stern product of the previous century, and editions continued to appear until 1923, carrying the principles and methods of the eighteenth century on into the twentieth, aided and abetted by other popular schoolbooks. Brown did more than anyone, at least in America, to cement the popular association of grammar study with inviolable rules and, by association, with rules of propriety and morals. The final baroque indulgences of this tradition are to be found in Brown's 1851 *Grammar of English grammars*, over 1,000 pages of lessons in correct usage and the avoidance of error. Exhaustiveness triumphed over usefulness, but Brown's approach to grammar-writing should not be derided simply because it was archaic and confused description and prescription. It was what language users themselves wanted, and to this day it is parents, broadcasting agencies and legislators and not linguists who have the greatest power and the loudest voices in dictating the direction of grammar teaching.

A major factor motivating the writing of English grammars in the nineteenth century is improved teaching methods. Becker's system grew out of his interest in the universal "logic" of grammar, but other reformed methods were more directly inspired by pedagogical needs. A direct result of the move to clause-based presentations was the introduction around 1880 of the highly popular Reed and Kellogg diagrams (see figure 4.1), as found, for example, in *Higher lessons in English* of 1886 by Alonzo Reed and Brainerd Kellogg, horizontal branching trees showing the relationship between words in a sentence, and still used in American schoolbooks in the 1980s.

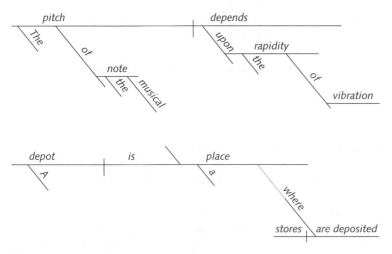

Figure 4.1 Examples of Reed and Kellogg diagrams
Source: Reed and Kellogg 1886: 42, 108

There has long been a close relationship between the study of grammar and the teaching of composition in America, much more so than in Europe, and this may go some way towards explaining the greater emphasis on the development of visual aids of this sort.

In the 1830s Franz Ahn and Heinrich Gottfried Ollendorff presented their new "practical" means of learning foreign languages, using what came to be called the *grammar-translation* method, supposedly to enable those without formal language training to master the given language quickly. Grammars, based on repeated practice of grammatical structures (hence 'practical'), using artificially constructed sentences, were immensely popular, and Ahn and Ollendorff spawned copious imitators, even for native speakers, as evidenced by R. B. Morgan's 1920 *Exercises in English grammar for junior forms*. By 1920, however, the tide had turned on this sort of grammar writing, and amongst those most vociferous in their attacks were Sweet and Jespersen, who we shall turn to next.

When we remember that the first half of the nineteenth century witnessed the appearance of nearly 900 new titles, summarizing grammar-writing up to this point in so few pages is clearly going to be hopelessly superficial. However, all that activity on the surface reflected a smaller number of currents underneath. These can be summarized as follows:

1   English grammatical practice to the mid-nineteenth century tended to be rather uniform, responding to local needs rather than reflecting real change in the understanding of English grammar.
2   Advances in practice, such as the use of English as the metalanguage and an analysis of the language on its own terms, happened only gradually, and, as in the process of language change, conservative and radical practice have always existed side-by-side.
3   Method was not addressed to any significant extent until the nineteenth century when there was a radical shift to "practical" and clause-based presentations.
4   Grammar writers did not differentiate systematically between "scholarly" grammars and "teaching" grammars. Instead, the form of individual grammar books tended to be dictated first and foremost by local needs.

3   'The European Scholarly Tradition'

The label *Great Tradition* was coined by the Dutch linguist Flor Aarts, and it corresponds to what Gleason, surveying the scene from the other side of the Atlantic, calls 'the European scholarly tradition.'

The study of modern languages was professionalized in the course of the nineteenth century. Modern languages entered both school and university curricula, and this called for proper studies of those languages, based on sound scientific principles, undertaken by scholars with sound scientific credentials.

English was studied by the early linguists of the historical-comparative school, but naturally this tended to be as part of a more general historical and comparative enterprise. The first of the "mighty monosyllables" of this school (the others being Grimm and Bopp), Rasmus Rask, wrote a grammar of English (the *Engelsk Formlære* of 1832), which had some pedagogical intent, but was really part of Rask's life's work to compare the structure of as many languages as possible. Jacob Grimm included Modern English in his *Deutsche Grammatik* (1822–37), which, despite the name, is a vast treasure-trove of forms from the Germanic languages, ancient and modern. None of this, although indicating that English grammar was taken seriously by the first generation of full-time linguists, contributed much to English grammaticography.

As the century progressed attention turned more systematically within linguistics to the spoken language, underpinned by the development of phonetic science and supported by the appearance of new specialist journals. By the final decades of the century there was an international community of English scholars, working together to advance understanding of the language's structure very rapidly, and there were now large numbers of university students, the majority training to be teachers of English, calling on the fruits of their investigations. The institutional and intellectual framework was at last in place for the production of large-scale English grammars at the confluence of the well-established historical work from earlier in the century and the "new philology" of the final decades.

The first out was Henry Sweet with *A new English grammar: logical and historical* which appeared in two parts, the first of 1892 embracing 'introduction, phonology, and accidence,' and the second of 1898 covering syntax. The similarity between its title and that of the great contemporary dictionary, *A New English dictionary on historical principles* (later known as the *OED*), is noteworthy. Sweet was for many years President of the Philological Society, whose brainchild the dictionary was.

Sweet opens the first volume by explaining his motivations:

> This work is intended to supply the want of a scientific English grammar, founded on an independent critical survey of the latest results of linguistic investigation as far as they bear, directly or indirectly, on the English language.

As with Fries, it is getting English grammar-writing au courant with contemporary linguistic theory and practice that is Sweet's principal motivating factor. A secondary factor is weaknesses in existing grammar books, specifically Maetzner's *Englische Grammatik* of 1860–65, which appeared in English translation as *An English grammar: methodical, analytical and historical* in 1874, and motivated Sweet's title. There are those who regard Eduard Adolf Maetzner as the pioneer of the *Great Tradition*. His English grammar was certainly comprehensive, covering over 1,700 pages, but it was concerned above all with the history of the language and comparison with related languages. It was archaic in other ways too, dealing with pronunciation in terms of letters rather than sounds and treating the syntax in notional rather than formal terms. Maetzner had an impact, however, and the fact that Sweet is using his work as a starting point three decades later does indicate that his work was not forgotten. The great strength of Sweet's grammar is that it presented the state of the art. The heart of the matter is contemporary spoken English, but sections on the history of language and on the history of English are to be found alongside articulatory phonetics.

Another successful British grammar of the period was Nesfield's *English grammar past and present*. Its success was due in large part to the range of students it aimed to appeal to. John Collinson Nesfield had worked for many years in India, and his grammar was written first for the Indian market. He notes that 'for England no less than for India it is best to assume that the average student does not know very much to start with.' He also takes into account the requirements of public exams in Britain and includes the questions on the history of the language from the London Matriculation Papers. Furthermore he hopes that 'this book may be of some use at Ladies' Colleges and any other institutions where Historical as well as Modern English is made an object of study.' If a distinction is maintained between "scholarly" and "teaching" grammars, Sweet is very much on the former side and Nesfield the latter, but in terms of approach they were both typical grammar-writers, tempering received methods and analyses with cautious innovation. H. E. Palmer's *Grammar of spoken English* of 1924, was firmly in the phonetic tradition of Sweet but went a stage further than Sweet in being dedicated entirely to the spoken language and so includes, for example, a full account of intonation patterns in English, and it went further than Nesfield in being dedicated entirely to the teaching and study of English as a foreign language. It has been argued that Palmer's grammar (while relatively brief) forms part of the *Great Tradition*. I wouldn't disagree, but the point does show how difficult it is to pigeon-hole English grammar-writing into neat, clearly quantifiable traditions.

The next two generations of authors of comprehensive English grammars were not native speakers. The Danish scholar Otto Jespersen visited Sweet in England and shared Sweet's commitment to the study and teaching of the spoken language. Both Sweet and Jespersen wrote a number of shorter grammars in addition to their major English grammars, and Jespersen's first foray into the field was while still an undergraduate. His major work was the seven-volume *Modern English grammar on historical principles*, whose title immediately reveals the lineage from Sweet, and in the preface to volume 2 Jespersen states that his 'debt to the Great New English Dictionary is conspicuous on many pages.' Like Sweet's grammar, its organizing principles are non-standard. From *Sounds and spellings* Jespersen, for personal reasons, moves on to syntax in volumes 2 through 5. By the time the morphology volume came to be written Jespersen was an elderly man and the volume was completed with the help of three research assistants. Volume 7 (back to syntax) was completed and published posthumously. In the preface to volume 1 Jespersen explains his key motivation in this grammar:

> It has been my endeavour in this work to represent English Grammar not as a set of stiff dogmatic precepts, according to which some things are correct and others absolutely wrong, but as something living and developing under continual fluctuations and undulations, something that is founded on the past and prepares the way for the future, something that is not always consistent or perfect, but progressing and perfectible – in one word, human.

Randolph Quirk in 1989 described it as 'a continual source of inspiration and value' (Juul and Nielsen 1989: viii), and Chomsky talks very positively of the value of Jespersen's work, noting how he and his circle 'rediscovered' Jespersen around 1960 after Jespersen had been out of fashion for a decade and a half (from Bas Aarts's interview with Chomsky at MIT, 9 February 1996). Jespersen is one of the few European grammarians to have been treated as authoritative in the United States as well as Europe. In 1933, the same year as Bloomfield's *Language*, Jespersen published a single-volume work, *Essentials of English grammar*, in which he set out his principal ideas about grammar, the most innovative being the grammatical categories of *rank*, *junction* and *nexus*. This way of analyzing the components of the sentence explicitly avoids reference to the word classes involved, instead seeing the relations in terms of (usually three) ranks which can combine to form nexuses (clauses).

The writing of comprehensive English grammars now passed to The Netherlands. Later Dutch scholars have been justifiably proud of this tradition, and the work of the three grammarians in question, Hendrik Poutsma, Etsko Kruisinga and Reinard Zandvoort has been well documented (see especially F. Aarts, 1986; see also Stuurman, 1993, for biographical treatments of Dutch scholars of English). English grammar has been an object of study in The Netherlands since the annus mirabilis of 1586, when a work entitled *The Coniugations in Englische and Netherdutche* was published at Leiden, so there was a long tradition to build upon.

The first Dutch grammar in the *Great Tradition* was Poutsma's *Grammar of late modern English* (1904–29). Its subtitle reads 'for the use of continental, especially Dutch, students,' and this, as well as its object of study, sets it apart from Sweet and Jespersen. Poutsma's grammar does not have an explicitly historical dimension, and so looks forward to later twentieth-century grammarwriting, but it is based on the language of literature and is in this way archaic vis-à-vis Sweet's emphasis on the "living language." *A grammar of late modern English* is reminiscent of the *Englische Philologie* (2nd edn., 1892/1896) by Johan Storm in thoroughly blurring the boundaries between *scholarly* and *teaching* grammars, and indeed Poutsma acknowledges his debt to Storm. In their size and detail Poutsma and Storm are clearly *scholarly*, but they are written for the teaching of (advanced-level) students of English as a foreign language. This shows why English grammaticography is best treated as a continuum of practice, where motivating factors are simply combined and prioritized according to context.

Untraditionally, although following the lead of earlier Dutch grammarians of English, Poutsma begins with the sentence and its elements before proceeding to the parts of speech, and the two volumes on the sentence later appeared in revised editions, taking into account more recent scholarship. Reading these volumes, one senses that Poutsma suffered for his art. He complains often of the difficulty of the labour, the unsatisfactory nature of its fruits, and at the end of it all of the relief 'now that it has been completed, and the strain of many a long year of strenuous work has been removed.' He is not the only grammarian of English to complain of the punishing nature of the work. It is unusual now to find single-authored grammars of English, and modern readers cannot fail to be impressed by the years of patient work, of unceasing observation and analysis that went into these monumental English grammars. But all those years of labour meant that Poutsma's grammar was in the end too indigestible for student use.

Although still a formidable 'scientific description of the Structure of Present [*sic*] English,' Etsko Kruisinga's *Handbook of present-day English* was much more what its name suggested. We earlier characterized the tradition of grammar-writing as advancing by steps forward and steps back. Kruisinga represents a step forward from Poutsma in his opening volume on *English sounds*, which (in the tradition of Storm, Sweet and Jespersen) includes a full exposition of general phonetics, including anatomical and acoustic diagrams. It is also quite free of any historical dimension. As Kruisinga tells us in the 1914 preface to the second edition:

> Bits of historical grammar interspersed in a book describing a particular stage, and especially the living stage, are not the proper introduction to a genuine historical study, nor do they help to understand the living language better.

I can't believe that evidence is still needed to show that it was not Saussure who somehow invented synchronic study in linguistics, but here is a bit just in case. The journey from historical to contemporary grammar-writing is now complete, but, given the nature of progress in grammar-writing, others were still making this journey (for example, an *English historical grammar* by M. K. Minkov was published in Sofia in 1955). However, with its traditional sounds → parts of speech → a final rather short section on sentence structure, Kruisinga's looks more early-nineteenth-century in its plan than Poutsma's. It should be said by way of mitigation that the 1941 abridgement, *An English grammar*, written in conjunction with P. A. Erades, dealt with the elements of the sentence first.

The third in this Dutch triumvirate is R. W. Zandvoort. His *Handbook of English grammar* shows that it is not length or detail that qualifies grammars for nomination to the *Great Tradition*. This really is a handbook in a way that Kruisinga's just wasn't. Grammarians learn from their predecessors. Storm and Jespersen and Poutsma had been treasure-troves of information, unwieldy and hard-to-use. Zandvoort's *Handbook*, with the benefit of the long-view, is a single-volume compendium of the tradition and, as Zandvoort puts it himself, a 'point of departure' into that tradition. It is not a strikingly original work, but none of the great landmark grammars of any language have been. They have been compendia. Zandvoort summarizes what had gone before in a clear and student-friendly way. It was last published in 1981 in its fifteenth edition, enjoying worldwide popularity in a crowded market, and by 1981 several new approaches to grammaticography had come along. F. Aarts (1986: 375) is right in his summary:

> If Sweet's *New English grammar* marks the transition from the nineteenth century school grammars to the scholarly grammars of the twentieth century, Zandvoort's *Handbook* may be said to represent the end-point of the scholarly grammatical tradition of the first half of the twentieth century.

4　The United States

Before moving on to English grammars of the most recent decades, we must stop to consider what had been going on in the United States. All the grammars we reviewed in the last section grew out of a specifically *European* way of doing language study, historical and then phonetic, data rather than theory oriented, although some advanced-level American grammars did feel their influence (M. M. Bryant's 1945 *Functional English grammar*, for example, was heavily influenced by Jespersen). While Gleason calls the tradition the 'European scholarly tradition,' there was one American grammar, which was firmly in it, *A grammar of the English language in three volumes* by George O. Curme. In the event there were only two volumes, *Syntax* (volume 3) in 1931 and *Parts of speech and accidence* (volume 2) in 1935. Volume 1, which was to cover *History of the English language, sounds and spellings, word-formation* and to be written by Hans Kurath, did not appear. In the manner we have become used to, there is a mixture of the old-fashioned and the pioneering here. Curme's data is primarily literary, and like other linguists of the late nineteenth and early twentieth centuries he treats all post-sixteenth-century literature as part of the living tradition of the language. His indebtedness to the European grammarians and to the *OED* is explicit and evident throughout, not least in the rich mine of data. This is truly a *Great Tradition* grammar for America, embracing American as well as British literary language, and, in a way that is still quite novel in the early 1930s, 'considerable attention has been given also to colloquial speech, which in its place is as good English as the literary language is in its place' (p. viii). Curme was aware that the scholarly market and the college market did not have the same demands, so he, like his European colleagues, produced a range of briefer presentations of English grammar along the same lines (e.g. *English grammar*, 1947).

We have already mentioned Fries and his radical move to use a proper corpus. Algeo (1991: 126) describes Fries as 'the greatest American English grammarian of the twentieth century,' and, if we gauge greatness by indications of influence, so he was. Curme's grammar, although much more substantial than any of Fries's studies, belonged to a previous generation. Fries was firmly Structuralist, born the same year as Bloomfield, and he was not the only English grammarian working within this framework. Major contributions to English grammaticography from the post-Bloomfieldian era include the 1951 *Outline of English structure* by George L. Trager and Henry Lee Smith, Jr. This is typical of the earlier post-Bloomfieldians in being predominantly dedicated to phonology with only a few tentative pages on syntax. It is also noteworthy that, while the Europeans heaped praise and gratitude on their predecessors, here a clean break with the past is intended: 'no discussion is given of previous work or of differing analyses and conclusions' (p. 7). Towards the end of the 1950s other books appeared with the same aim of breaking with what their authors regarded as an unscientific past and of putting the study and teaching of English grammar on a new, sound (post-Bloomfieldian) footing, but now properly Structuralist, showing the architecture of interrelated structures *from sound to sentence in English*, in the words of the subtitle of Archibald Hill's *Introduction to linguistic structures* from 1958. A particularly good example of American grammars of English from this period, destroying its past, explicitly borrowing the title of Robert Lowth's prescriptive grammar of 1762 as it seeks to move on from the tradition of English grammar teaching spawned by Lowth, is James Sledd's 1959 *Short introduction to English grammar*. Sledd's comprehensive litany of acknowledgements to other linguists is very striking: not one of them is based outside the United States and not one predates Bloomfield. Syntax did get a proper treatment in 1960 with Eugene A. Nida's *Synopsis of English syntax*, using immediate constituent analysis, but this was a reprint of Nida's 1943 University of Michigan doctoral dissertation, and, while the focus within American linguistics was now turning from phonology to syntax, the dominant analytical framework had also moved on.

With the move in the 1960s from a descriptive, data-oriented bias in the study of English grammar to a theory-oriented bias, there was no longer an appetite for traditional grammar-writing. There was too much of a whiff of mothballs about it. It is not altogether clear why a theory-driven linguistics should have been incompatible with grammar-writing of the sort we have been discussing. However, grammar-writing had been descriptive and pedagogically oriented for too long, and grammar-writing is, as we know, a conservative craft, so maybe the fortress was just too solid for post-Chomskyan linguistics to storm. In any case, while the period up to the 1970s was dramatic for general linguistics, the *Great Tradition* of English grammar foundered until 1972 and the publication of *A grammar of contemporary English*. The transformational-generative school and its offshoots has preferred to address specific aspects of English grammar, and indeed *grammar* has come to mean something quite different in this tradition. When Paul Roberts wrote in his grammar book of 1962 that 'grammar is something that produces sentences of a language,' he meant something very different to Curme only 15 years earlier. Even works with quite traditional-sounding titles, such as *English transformational grammar* (R. A. Jacobs and P. S. Rosenbaum 1968) or *Introductory transformational grammar of English* (M. Lester 1971), are very limited in their scope compared with Hill or Sledd, never mind Sweet or Jespersen. R. B. Long's 1961 *The sentence and its parts: a grammar of contemporary English* is something of an isolated beacon. Norman C. Stageberg's 1965 *Introductory English grammar* is interesting in this respect. It is essentially a classic Structuralist account of the shape of the English language and an overtly pedagogical one at that, including exercises. However, it has a very brief appendix by Ralph Goodman entitled *Transformational grammar*, 'presented primarily as a pedagogical not a theoretical work.' It proved to be a step too far. There have of course been "scholarly" English grammars since then with other primary theoretical motivations (J. Muir's 1972 *A modern approach to English grammar: an introduction to systemic grammar*, and R. M. W. Dixon's 1991 *A new approach to English grammar, on semantic principles*, to name but two at random), and their scope has perforce been similarly limited. When the exercise of a theoretical model dominates all other factors in a would-be grammar book, a traditional English grammar is not, it seems, possible (see, however, the papers in Graustein and Leitner, 1989, for an attempt at greater integration).

5   The Period since the 1970s

Those mourning the passing of the *Great Tradition* felt it had risen again in 1972 with the publication of *A grammar of contemporary English* (*GCE*) by Randolph Quirk, Sidney Greenbaum, Geoffrey Leech, and Jan Svartvik. In common with its predecessors in this tradition it is substantial, only one volume, but at 1,120 pages this isn't something for a student to put in her pocket. As with its predecessors the goal of comprehensiveness is the highest ranked factor in its production, and it was certainly the most thorough account of the structuring principles of English to date, since, unlike its predecessors and for obvious historical reasons, it sought to account for the structure of English worldwide: 'our field is no less than the grammar of educated English current in the second half of the twentieth century in the world's major English-speaking communities' (p. v). It is also unlike, for example, Sweet and Jespersen in that it is limited to the traditional heart of grammar, syntax, and inflectional morphology. The margins of the language have been rubbed away with the passing of the twentieth century. Derivational morphology and suprasegmental phonology are relegated to appendices and, in this respect, *GCE* is less comprehensive than some of its predecessors.

Bearing in mind that it was published in 1972, it is remarkably theoretically eclectic and neutral. American theoretical linguistics of the day was temperamentally unsuited to the production of a full-scale grammar. What was needed was the heavily diluted theoretical mix of four Europeans, just one of them working in the United States. Gone are the days of the single-authored grand grammar book, and gone is the possibility of one person reading himself to an exhaustive knowledge of the English language or a variety of it. Most striking of all the superlative things about *GCE* is that it is the first European example of the genre to be produced by (mostly) native speakers since Sweet's *New English grammar* in the previous century.

   GCE would prove to be a productive patriarch over the following decades. The first two offspring recognized the fact that different types of reader required different approaches. Greenbaum explained that *GCE* and its 1985 successor (see below) were:

> addressed not only to scholars in English linguistics and theoretical linguistics, but also to those from other disciplines who wish to refer to points in English grammar, for example literary critics or researchers in informational [*sic*] technology. We also wanted to make it accessible to nonspecialist readers. (Greenbaum 1986: 8)

Reviewers were more sceptical, wondering whether they might in fact only appeal to other grammarians of English (see Svartvik 1986). (The *Collins cobuild grammar* is also rare in making the bold claim that it is 'for anyone who is interested in the English language and how it works.') In 1975 Leech and Svartvik oversaw *A communicative grammar of English*, geared towards learners of English as a foreign language, which focused on function rather than form, and this has been immensely successful (a second edition appeared in 1994). Two years earlier in 1973 Quirk and Greenbaum produced a version intended more for university-level students, which took the same form as the parent volume but in less detail. The intended readers in these two versions were higher ranked as factors in their production than was comprehensiveness. The parent volume entered a second edition in 1985, but to indicate the extent of its revision (now standing at 1,779 pages) and the greater ambition of the project, it now bore a new title, *A comprehensive grammar of the English language* (*CGEL*). This has also spawned little versions of itself, notably the 1990 *Student's grammar of the English language* by Greenbaum and Quirk. Leech (with Margaret Deuchar and Robert Hoogenraad) has also addressed the needs of native-speakers at a lower level in the educational system with the *English grammar for today* (1982), and this remains popular with native-speaker students of the English language.

   It is fair to say that *CGEL* is still universally accepted as the first port of call for information about English grammar. But grammar-writing has not stood still in its wake. Two large-scale multi-authored grammars of English have appeared since then, namely the *Longman grammar of spoken and written English* (1999) and the *Cambridge grammar of the English language* (2002). It is rather soon to gauge the impact of the latter, but the list of contributors to it is enough to indicate its quality (see B. Aarts, 2004, for a review). A glance along the shelves of a well-stocked library or a flick through the catalog of one of the major academic publishers reveals a mind-boggling amount of activity, largely because of the call worldwide for resources to teach and study English as a foreign language/as a second language/for special purposes. Many such grammars are written, as throughout our history, in response to local needs, or in response to the needs of particular English-language examinations, and the major international grammars are often reissued for local markets. The highly successful *English grammar in use* volumes by Raymond Murphy (CUP) are available in Italian, French, Spanish, German, and Thai editions, and under different titles for the North American market. They also come in a range of formats, with CD-rom or cassette, with or without exercises. The move towards enhanced *flexibility* in grammar books for learners of English is also evidenced by the provision for different levels of student. Oxford University Press series (such as *Grammar sense*) have responded to this need particularly effectively, and their encyclopedia of problematic constructions and usages (*Practical English usage* by Michael Swan) seems to have struck a particular chord with learners. Grammars for the teaching of English as a foreign language tend to take a *contextual* approach: grammar is taught and practiced via communicational contexts, as in, to take only one of countless examples, *Exploring grammar in context* by Ronald Carter, Rebecca Hughes, and Michael McCarthy (2000).

Communication is now firmly at the heart of English grammars for non-native and native speakers alike at all levels. This way of dealing with grammar has filtered down from Leech and Svartvik (1975), and ultimately from the systemic-functional approach to grammar associated with Halliday and his collaborators. Bent Preisler's *Handbook of English grammar on functional principles*, Talmy Givón's *English grammar: a function-based introduction*, Angela Downing and Philip Locke's *A University course in English grammar*, all from 1992, and Graham Lock's *Functional English grammar* of 1996 are explicitly in this tradition. They are all of different national origins, but exemplify the fact that, in so far as any theory has penetrated English grammars, it is very definitely that of communicative functions derived from Halliday (although not all these grammarians would necessarily see themsleves as Hallidayan in outlook).

Surveying the contemporary scene in a wide-ranging article like this is never going to be anything more than sketchy and at worst it will just degenerate into a list. There are some clear tendencies in English grammar-writing today, and, as we said of the nineteenth century, all that activity on the surface reflects a smaller number of currents underneath. We have left out a huge amount of surface activity, and by concentrating on Europe and North America, we have omitted, for example, the theoretically eclectic approach of grammarians working in Australia and writing for native-speaker students, notably Rodney Huddleston (in various grammars), succeeded by Peter Collins and Carmella Hollo in their 2000 *English grammar: an introduction*. Not to mention the brief 1968 *English grammar* of F. S. Scott, C. C. Bowley, C. S. Brockett, J. G. Brown, and P. R. Goddard, written initially for use in New Zealand.

There is one generalization that we can make with absolute confidence. After half a millennium, and despite the decline in the formal study of English grammar in British and American schools, the writing of English grammars has never been more vigorous than it is now. English linguistics is only around

150 years old, and much of its theory and practice disappears overnight, touching very few. Grammar-writing by contrast is an activity which touches countless numbers from professors to language learners the world over.

NOTE

I am indebted to the following for the benefit of their knowledge of English grammars in a range of contexts: Mark Amsler, Gibson Ferguson, Sheena Gardner, Werner Hüllen, Arne Juul, Natascia Leonardi[†], Bent Preisler, and Richard Smith.

FURTHER READING

Howatt, A. P. R. (1984) *A history of English language teaching*. Oxford: Oxford University Press.

Howatt, A. P. R. and Smith, R. C. (2002) *Modern language teaching: the reform movement*. London and New York: Routledge.

Michael, I. (1987) *The teaching of English from the sixteenth century to 1870*. Cambridge: Cambridge University Press.

Robins, R. H. (1997) *A short history of linguistics*, 4th edn. London and New York: Longman.

Primary references

Bertram, C. J. (1753) *The Royal English– Danish grammar eller grundig Anvisning til det Engelske Sprogs Kundskab*. Copenhagen: Trykt paa Auctoris Bekostning af A. H. G[odiche] og L. H. L[illie].

Biber, D., Johansson, S., Leech, G., Conrad, S., and Finegan, E. (1999) *Longman grammar of spoken and written English*. London and New York: Longman.

Brown, G. (1823) *The institutes of English grammar, methodically arranged; with forms of parsing and correcting, examples for parsing, questions for examination, false syntax for correction, exercises for writing, observations for the advanced student, five methods of analysis, and a key to the oral exercises: to which are added four appendixes*. New York: Samuel S. and William Wood. (Reprinted with an introduction by Charlotte Downey, 1982. Delmar, NY: Scholars' Facsimiles and Reprints.)

Brown, G. (1851) *The Grammar of English grammars with an introduction, historical and critical; the whole methodically arranged and amply illustrated; with forms of correcting and of parsing, improprieties for correction, examples for parsing, questions for examination, exercises for writing, observations for the advanced student, decisions and proofs for the settlement of disputed points, occasional strictures and defences, and exhibition of the several methods of analysis, and a key to the oral exercises: to which are added four appendixes, pertaining separately to the four parts of grammar*. London: Delf and Trübner.

Bryant, M. M. (1945) *A functional English grammar*. Boston: Heath.

Bullokar, W. (1586) *Pamphlet for Grammar*. London: Henry Denham.

Carter, R., Hughes, R., and McCarthy, M. (2000) *Exploring grammar in context: grammar reference and practice, upper-intermediate and advanced*. Cambridge: Cambridge University Press.

Collins, P. and Hollo, C. (2000) *English grammar: an introduction*. London: Macmillan.

Cooper, C. (1685) *Grammatica Linguæ Anglicanæ*. London: Benj. Tooke.

Curme, G. O. (1931/1935) *A grammar of the English language in three volumes*. 2 vols. Boston, New York, Chicago, Atlanta, San Francisco, Dallas, London: D. C. Heath and Company.

Curme, G. O. (1947) *English grammar*. New York: Barnes & Noble, Inc.

Dixon, R. M. W. (1991) *A new approach to English grammar, on semantic principles*. Oxford: Clarendon Press.

Downing, A. and Locke, P. (1992) *A university course in English grammar*. London and New York: Routledge (2nd edn, 2002).

Foley, M. and Hall, D. (2003) *Longman advanced learners' grammar: a self-study reference & practice book with answers*. London and New York: Longman.

Fries, C. C. (1952) *The structure of English: an introduction to the construction of English sentences*. New York: Harcourt, Brace & Company; London: Longmans, Green & Company, 1957.

Givón, T. (1992) *English grammar: a function-based introduction*, 2 vols. Amsterdam and Philadelphia: John Benjamins.

Greenbaum, S. and Quirk, R. (1990) *A student's grammar of the English language*. London: Longman.

Grimm, J. (1822–37) *Deutsche Grammatik*, 2nd edn. Göttingen: Dietrich.

Hemphill, G. (1973) *A mathematical grammar of English*. The Hague and Paris: Mouton.

Hill, A. A. (1958) *Introduction to linguistic structures: from sound to sentence in English*. New York: Harcourt Brace and Company.

Huddleston, R. and Pullum, G. K. (2002) *The Cambridge grammar of the English language*. Cambridge: Cambridge University Press.

Jacobs, R. A. and Rosenbaum, P. S. (1968) *English transformational grammar*. Waltham, Mass., Toronto, London: Blaisdell Publishing Company.

Jespersen, O. (1909–49) *A modern English grammar on historical principles*. 7 vols. Copenhagen: Ejnar Munksgaard; Heidelberg: Carl Winters Universitätsbuchhandlung; London: George Allen & Unwin Ltd.

Jespersen. O. (1933) *Essentials of English grammar*. London: George Allen & Unwin Ltd.

Kruisinga, E. (1909–32) *A Handbook of present-day English*, 4 vols. Utrecht: Kemink en zoon; Groningen: P. Noordhoff.

Kruisinga, E. and Erades, P. A. (1941) *An English grammar*, 1 vol., 2 parts. Groningen: P. Noordhoff.

Leech, G. and Svartvik, J. (1975) *A communicative grammar of English*. London: Longman (2nd edn. 1994).

Leech, G., Deuchar, M., and Hoogenraad, R. (1982) *English grammar for today: a new introduction*. London: Macmillan.

Lester, M. (1971) *Introductory transformational grammar of English*. New York, Chicago, San Francisco, Atlanta, Dallas, Montreal, Toronto, London, Sydney: Holt, Rinehart & Winston, Inc.

Lock, Graham (1996) *Functional English grammar: an introduction for second language teachers*. Cambridge: Cambridge University Press.

Long, R. B. (1961) *The sentence and its parts: a grammar of contemporary English*. Chicago: University of Chicago Press.

Maetzner, E. A. (1860–5) *Englische Grammatik*, 2 parts, 3 vols. Berlin: Weidmann.

Maetzner, E. A. (1874) *An English grammar: methodical, analytical and historical.* 3 vols. Trans. by C. J. Grece. London: John Murray.

Morgan, R. B. (1920) *Exercises in English grammar for junior forms.* London: John Murray.

Muir, J. (1972) *A modern approach to English grammar: an introduction to systemic grammar.* London: B. T. Batsford Ltd.

Murphy, R. (1987) *English grammar in use: a reference and practice book for intermediate students.* Cambridge: Cambridge University Press.

Nesfield, J. C. (1898) *English grammar past and present in three parts.* London: Macmillan.

Nida, E. A. (1960) *A synopsis of English syntax.* Norman, OK: Summer Institute of Linguistics.

Palmer, H. E. (1924) *A grammar of spoken English, on a strictly phonetic basis.* Cambridge: W. Heffer & Sons Ltd.

Poutsma, H. (1904–29) *A grammar of late modern English,* 5 vols. Groningen: P. Noordhoff.

Preisler, B. (1992) *A handbook of English grammar on functional principles.* Århus: Aarhus University Press.

Quirk, R., Greenbaum, S., Leech, G., and Svartvik, J. (1972) *A grammar of contemporary English.* London: Longman.

Quirk, R. and Greenbaum, S. (1973) *A university grammar of English.* London: Longman.

Quirk, R., Greenbaum, S., Leech, G., and Svartvik, J. (1985) *A comprehensive grammar of the English language.* London: Longman.

Rask, R. (1832) *Engelsk Formlære.* Copenhagen: Gyldendal.

Reed, A. and Kellogg, B. (1886) *Higher lessons in English. A work on English grammar and composition, in which the science of the language is made tributary to the art of expression. A course of practical lessons carefully graded, and adapted to everyday use in the school-room.* New York: Clark & Maynard.

Roberts, P. (1962) *English sentences.* New York, Chicago, San Francisco, Atlanta, Dallas: Harcourt, Brace & World, Inc.

Scott, F. S., Bowley, C. C., Brockett, C. S., Brown, J. G., and Goddard, P. R. (1968) *English grammar: a linguistic study of its classes and structures.* London, Edinburgh, Melbourne, Auckland, Toronto, Hong Kong, Singapore, Kuala Lumpur, Ibadan, Nairobi, Johannesburg, Lusaka, New Delhi: Heinemann Educational Books Ltd.

Shelley, E. (1848) *The people's grammar: or English grammar without difficulties for 'the million.'* Huddersfield: Bond & Hardy.

Sinclair, J. (ed. in chief) (1990) *Collins cobuild English grammar.* London: HarperCollins.

Sledd, James (1959) *A short introduction to English grammar.* Glenview, IL: Scott, Foresman and Company.

Stageberg, N. C. (1965) *An introductory English grammar: with a chapter on transformational grammar by Ralph Goodman.* New York, Chicago, San Francisco, Toronto, and London: Holt, Rinehart & Winston, Inc.

Stockwell, R. P., Schachter, P., and Partee, B. H. (1973) *The major syntactic structures of English.* New York, Chicago, San Francisco, Atlanta, Dallas, Montreal, Toronto, London, and Sydney: Holt, Rinehart & Winston.

Swan, M. (1995) *Practical English usage,* 2nd edn. Oxford: Oxford University Press.

Sweet, H. (1892) *A new English grammar: logical and historical. Part I: introduction, phonology, and accidence.* Oxford: Clarendon Press.

Sweet, H. (1898) *A new English grammar: logical and historical, part II: syntax.* Oxford: Clarendon Press.

Trager, G. L. and Smith, Jr., H. L. (1951) *An outline of English structure.* Washington: American Council of Learned Societies.

Zandvoort, R. W. (1945) *A handbook of English grammar.* Groningen: Wolters-Noordhoff.

Biographical dates

Franz Ahn (1796–1865)
Karl Ferdinand Becker (1775–1849)
Charles Julius Bertram (1723–1765)
Goold Brown (1791–1857)
William Bullokar (ca. 1531–1609)
Christopher Cooper (ca. 1646–1698)
George O. Curme (1860–1948)
Charles Carpenter Fries (1887–1967)
Samuel Greene (1810–1883)
Jacob Grimm (1785–1863)
Otto Jespersen (1860–1943)
Brainerd Kellogg (fl. 1866–1914)
Etsko Kruisinga (1875–1944)

Hans Kurath (1891–1992)
William Lily (1468?–1522)
Eduard Adolf Maetzner (1805–1892)
John Collinson Nesfield (fl. 1885–1949)
Heinrich Gottfried Ollendorff (1803–1865)
H. E. Palmer (1877–1949)
Hendrik Poutsma (1856–1937)
Rasmus Rask (1787–1832)
Alonzo Reed (d. 1899)
Henry Lee Smith, Jr (1913–1972)
Johan Storm (1836–1920)
Henry Sweet (1845–1912)
George L. Trager (1906–1992)
John Wallis (1616–1703)
Reinard Zandvoort (1894–1990)

REFERENCES

Aarts, B. (2004) Review of *The Cambridge grammar of the English language. Journal of Linguistics* 40 (2), 365–82.

Aarts, F. (1986) English grammars and the Dutch contribution. In Leitner (1986), 363–86.

Algeo, J. (1986) A grammatical dialectic. In Leitner (1986), 307–33.

Algeo, J. (1991) American English grammars in the twentieth century. In Leitner (1991a), 113–38.

Engler, B. and Haas, R. (eds.) (2000) *European English studies: contributions towards the history of a discipline.* Published for the European Society for the Study of English by the English Association.

Gleason, Jr., H. A. (1965) *Linguistics and English grammar.* New York, Chicago, San Francisco, Toronto, and London: Holt, Rinehart and Winston.

Gneuss, H. (1996) *English language scholarship: a survey and bibliography from the beginnings to the end of the nineteenth century.* Binghamton, NY: Center for Medieval and Early Renaissance Studies.

Görlach, M. (1998) *An annotated bibliography of nineteenth-century grammars of English.* Amsterdam and Philadelphia: John Benjamins.

Graustein, G. and Leitner, G. (eds.) (1989) *Reference grammars and modern linguistic theory.* Tübingen: Max Niemeyer Verlag. (Linguistische Arbeiten, 226.)

Greenbaum, S. (1986) *The grammar of contemporary English* and the *Comprehensive grammar of the English language.* In Leitner (1986), 6–14.

Juul, A. and Nielsen, H. F. (eds.) (1989) *Otto Jespersen: facets of his life and work.* Amsterdam and Philadelphia: John Benjamins.

Leitner, G. (1984) English grammaticology. *International Review of Applied Linguistics in Language Teaching* 23, 199–215.

Leitner, G. (ed.) (1986) *The English reference grammar: language and linguistics, writers and readers.* Tübingen: Max Niemeyer Verlag.

Leitner, G. (ed.) (1991a) *English traditional grammars: an international perspective.* Amsterdam and Philadelphia: John Benjamins.

Leitner, G. (1991b) Eduard Adolf Maetzner (1805–1902). In Leitner (1991a), 233–55.

Linn, A. R. (1999) Charles Bertram's *Royal English–Danish grammar*: the linguistic work of an eighteenth-century fraud. In D. Cram, A. Linn, and E. Nowak (eds.), *History of linguistics 1996, vol. 2: From classical to contemporary linguistics*. Amsterdam and Philadelphia: John Benjamins, 183–91.

Michael, I. (1991) More than enough English grammars. In Leitner (1991a), 11–26.

Stuurman, F. (1993) *Dutch masters and their era. English language studies by the Dutch, from the last century into the present. A retrospective collection of biographical texts*. Preface by Sir Randolph Quirk. Amsterdam: Amsterdam University Press.

Svartvik, J. (1986) *A communicative grammar of English*. In Leitner (1986), 15–24.

Tieken-Boon van Ostade, I. (ed.) (1996) *Two hundred years of Lindley Murray*. Münster: Nodus Publikationen.

Vorlat, E. (1975) *The Development of English grammatical theory 1586–1737 with special reference to the theory of parts of speech*. Leuven: Leuven University Press.

5 Data Collection

CHARLES F. MEYER AND
GERALD NELSON

1 Introduction

Data collection has been a neglected methodological concern within linguistics. This situation has arisen, Schütze (1996) argues, because many linguists have not taken data collection seriously. Generative linguists have relied almost exclusively on 'introspection' for data – a process whereby the linguist uses his or her intuitions to invent examples and make grammaticality judgments.[1] This methodology has resulted in what Schütze (1996: xi) characterizes as 'grammars of intuition' that have little bearing on 'everyday production or comprehension of language.' Other linguists have turned to experimentation to obtain data, but these linguists, Schütze (1996: xi) notes, often fail to employ 'standard experimental controls,' leading to questionable analyses because the data being used have been tainted by the 'pseudoexperimental procedure' used to collect it.

   If data collection is viewed as a methodological issue, it becomes incumbent upon the linguist to understand not just *how* data are collected but *why* certain ways of collecting data are better suited to some analyses than others. Chafe (1992: 82–9) provides a useful overview of the types of data that exist and the ways that data can be collected. He observes that data can be 'artificial' or 'natural' and collected through processes that are either 'behavioral' or 'introspective' (1992: 84). Data collected by experimentation are artificial because any experimental situation (e.g. asking individuals to rate a series of sentences as acceptable or unacceptable) is divorced from the natural contexts in which language is used. In contrast, data obtained from an actual corpus of language (e.g. a transcribed collection of spontaneous conversations) are natural because a corpus contains instances of real language usage. Both types of data collection are behavioral because when conducting an experiment or examining a corpus, linguists are observing how language is used. But when linguists use their intuitions as a source of data, they are creating the data themselves and thus collecting it through a process that is introspective.

Each of these methods of data collection has individual strengths and weaknesses, making one method better for a particular analysis than another. For instance, in investigating the structure of newspaper editorials, it makes little sense to gather data through introspection, since one analyst's perceptions of the structure of editorials might be quite different from another analyst's perceptions, and there is really no way to prove which analyst is correct. In a case like this, it would be much more desirable to collect samples of actual newspaper editorials and analyze the types of linguistic structures that they contain. Such an analysis would be based on a real dataset of newspaper editorials and could be confirmed or disconfirmed by any other analyst examining the same dataset.

But while a corpus might be the most appropriate source of data for a study of newspaper editorials, for other kinds of analyses, a corpus will not produce the necessary linguistic information. As Chomsky (1962a) has observed, whatever one finds in a corpus is restricted to what is in the corpus and is not representative of the entire potential of a given language. A corpus contains a record of structures that speakers or writers actually use; it does not contain all the structures that they might potentially use. For instance, coordinate constructions containing 'gapped' constituents have been the subject of much linguistic inquiry. A gapped construction contains missing constituents in the second clause, such as the verb *ordered* in example (1) below:

(1)   I ordered fish and my son [ ] a hamburger

Johnson (2000) notes that objects as well as verbs can be gapped (example 2), and, following McCawley (1993), observes that on some occasions not just the verb is gapped but the determiner preceding the subject noun phrase in the second clause (example 3):

(2)   Some consider him honest and others ~~consider him~~ pleasant.
      (Johnson 2000: 95)

(3)   Too many Irish setters are named Kelly and ~~too many~~ German shepherds ~~are named~~ Fritz.   (Johnson 2000: 104)

However, in a one million word corpus of speech and writing, Tao and Meyer (2005) found ten examples such as (2), but no examples such as (3). Instead, gapping in Tao and Meyer's corpus was restricted most frequently to either an auxiliary verb (example 4) or copular *be* (example 5):

(4)   I was mowing the lawn and my son [ ] trimming the hedges.

(5)   The pianist was quite good and the oboe player [ ] somewhat average.

Had studies of gapping been restricted to examples occurring only in corpora, linguists would never have been able to uncover the entire range of constructions to which this process applies. Consequently, in a case such as this, introspection is crucial to isolating all potential constructions subject to the particular linguistic process being investigated.

The examples above provide a brief introduction to the types of data that can be used in linguistic analyses, and the methodological issues that the use of particular datasets raise. In the remainder of this chapter, we wish to explore these issues in greater detail, focusing our discussion on data obtained through introspection, experimentation, and the collection of spoken and written texts.

2   Introspection

Even though introspection has been the dominant way of collecting data within generative linguistics since the 1950s, within linguistics in general, it is a relatively new methodology. Most linguistic analyses prior to this period were based on naturally occurring data. For instance, Fillmore (1992: 36–8) describes his experiences in 1957 deciding what kind of dissertation he would write. He could have taken the traditional route. This would have required him to spend over a year recording and transcribing a corpus of speech, and once this was done devoting additional time doing a detailed phonetic/phonemic analysis of the data, an endeavor that would have resulted in 'some practical guidelines on how large a corpus of spoken language needs to be for it to be considered an adequate reservoir of the phonological phenomena of the language' (Fillmore 1992: 36).

But Fillmore rejected this kind of analysis because during the period in question the 'empiricism' of the American structuralist model of language was losing favor to the more 'mentalist' views of the generative model. For Chomsky, language was a product of the mind. As a consequence, it was no longer necessary – indeed it was wrongheaded – to follow 'a set of analytic procedures for the discovery of linguistic elements such as phonemes or morphemes' that ultimately produce little more than 'the inventory of these elements' (Chomsky 1962b: 537–8). Such a 'discovery procedure,' Chomsky argued, resulted in only a 'performance grammar,' a listing of what speakers of a language actually produce. And this list would have included utterances containing mistakes, hesitations, and stammers: 'performance errors' that reveal little about the native speaker's knowledge of his or her language. Of greater importance, Chomsky claimed, is the creation of a 'competence grammar,' a grammar reflecting 'the fluent native speaker's knowledge of the language' (Radford 1988: 3). And obtaining data for writing a competence grammar required the linguist to rely only on his or her intuitions about language.[2]

Within generative grammar, introspection produced two types of data. Many linguistic analyses consisted of sentences created by the analyst to support the particular linguistic argument being advanced. For instance, Lobeck (1999: 100–5) uses introspective data to discuss similarities and differences between

VP-Ellipsis, gapping, and pseudo-gapping. She notes that each of these types of ellipsis involves the deletion of some kind of constituent: a lexical verb and (if present) its complements. Thus, in (6a), an instance of VP-Ellipsis, the entire predication in the second clause (*wants to buy a skateboard*) is ellipted; in (6b), a verb (*wants*) and its complement (*to buy*) is gapped in the second clause; and in (6c), even though it would be possible to gap both the auxiliary and lexical verb (*will buy*), only the lexical verb (*buy*) is ellipted, producing an instance of pseudo-gapping:

(6)   a.   Mary wants to buy a skateboard and Sam does [*e*] too.
      b.   Mary wants to buy a skateboard and Sam [*e*] a bicycle.
      c.   Mary will buy a skateboard and Sam will [*e*] a bicycle.
           (Lobeck 1999: 101)

In addition to inventing sentences to develop her argument, Lobeck also uses her intuitions to make grammaticality judgments so as to develop a linguistic argument by introducing data that is grammatical and ungrammatical. She notes, for instance, that while all three types of ellipsis can occur in coordinated clauses, only VP-Ellipsis can be found in subordinate clauses. To support this generalization, she includes each ellipsis-type in a subordinate clause following the verb *think*. According to Lobeck's intuitions, the example containing VP-Ellipsis (7a) is clearly grammatical, while the examples illustrating gapping (7b) and pseudo-gapping (7c) are quite ungrammatical:

(7)   a.   Mary bought a skateboard and she thinks that Sam should [*e*] too.
      b.   *Mary bought a skateboard and she thinks that Sam [*e*] a bicycle.
      c.   *Mary will buy a skateboard and she thinks that Sam should [*e*] a
           bicycle.   (Lobeck 1999: 101)

Thus we see that Lobeck (1999: 99) uses introspective data not just to describe the differences between the three types of construction but to make a larger theoretical point: that while gapping and pseudo-gapping are true instances of ellipsis (termed 'PF deletion' in Minimalist Theory), VP-Ellipsis is more like pronominalization. The missing verb and complement in a sentence such as (7a) are better analyzed as a single empty pronominal.

   The reliance in generative grammar on introspective data reflects not just an anti-empiricist bias but the greater emphasis in this theory on 'explanatory adequacy' rather than 'observational' or 'descriptive' adequacy. Many linguists would be content to simply observe that a sentence such as (7b) is ungrammatical or describe the constraints that make (7a) grammatical and (7b) and (7c) ungrammatical. But Chomsky has always argued that 'the goals of linguistic theory can be set much higher than this' (Chomsky 1966: 20); that is, that a linguistic description should do more than simply describe a language such as English but 'provide an implicit definition of the notion "human language"' (Chomsky 1972: 21). Thus, in her analysis, Lobeck (1999) uses the introspective data from English that she cites to demonstrate how it sheds light on well established linguistic categories in Minimalist Theory (e.g. PF Deletion or empty pronominals). These categories go beyond English and describe processes common in all languages.

The priority attached in generative grammar to explanatory adequacy has minimized the need for developing a more rigorous methodology for collecting data. As Chomsky (1965: 20) has noted, 'sharpening of the data by more objective tests is a matter of small importance for the problems at hand.' If linguists are engaged in the development of competence grammars, they need only use their intuitions to gain access to linguistic competence and reach judgments about the grammaticality of the data they use to develop their theories. Many, however, have questioned this assumption. Schütze (1996: 19–36) surveys the work of many linguists who claim that it is impossible to gain access to the native speaker's linguistic competence, and he ultimately concludes:

> in principle, there might someday be an operational criterion for grammaticality, but it would have to be based on direct study of the brain, not on human behavior, if it turns out to be possible to discern properties of the mind (e.g., the precise features of the grammar) from physical properties of the brain. (Schütze 1996: 26)

Thus, when linguists use their intuitions to produce data, they are in essence making acceptability judgments about the data, not grammaticality judgments.[3] And because acceptability is within the realm of performance, linguists who rely only on their own intuitions for data often produce theories of language that are reflective of their own idiolects – their own personal views of what is acceptable or unacceptable.

Because acceptability judgments can be idiosyncratic, it is not uncommon to find linguists who will reject a linguistic analysis simply because they disagree about the acceptability of the data upon which the analysis is based. In a methodological discussion of the use of grammaticality judgments in generative analyses, Wasow (2002: 158) comments that he coined the terms 'strong' and 'weak' crossover (cf. Wasow 1972) to reflect differences he had with Postal (1971) concerning the acceptability of sentences (8b) and (9b).

(8)   a.   Which teachers$_i$ did Pat say thought the students disliked them$_i$?
       b.   *Which teachers$_i$ did Pat say they$_i$ thought the students disliked?

(9)   a.   Which teachers$_i$ criticized the students who disliked them$_i$?
       b.   ?Which teachers$_i$ did the students who disliked them$_i$ criticize?

'Crossover' constraints predict which NPs in *Wh*-questions can be coreferential. For Postal (1971), (8b) and (9b) are equally unacceptable and as a result are subject to a single crossover constraint. However, for Wasow (2002), (9b) is less unacceptable than (8b), a difference in acceptability that leads him to posit two types of crossover constraints. And to further support this distinction,

Wasow (2002: 158) notes that in his 1972 study he included 'examples of weak crossover sentences taken from novels by respected writers.'

Manning (2003) finds similar problems in a study of verb subcategorization that he conducted. He comments that many treatments of verb subcategorization make erroneous claims because the data introduced reflect the intuitions of the analysts, which differ significantly from the facts of language usage. For instance, Manning (2003: 299) notes that Pollard and Sag (1994) claim that the verb *consider* can be followed by predicative complements (example 9) but not *as*-complements (example 10):

(9)   We consider Kim to be an acceptable candidate.

(10)   *We consider Kim as an acceptable candidate.

However, in an analysis of texts in the *New York Times*, Manning (2003: 299) found many examples (such as 11) where *consider* could take an *as*-complement.

(11)   The boys consider her as family and she participates in everything we do.

Manning (2003: 299) comments that if counterexamples such as (11) were anomalous, then 'Pollard and Sag got that one particular fact wrong.' But his analysis found many additional instances where Pollard and Sag's (1994) data were simply wrong, casting serious doubts on the legitimacy of the theoretical points they were making.

The problems in data collection that Wasow (2002) and Manning (2003) document point to two key limitations of introspection. First, data collected introspectively is decontextualized: it exists in the linguist's mind, not in any real communicative context. However, 'with richer content and context,' as Manning (2003: 300) notes, what might sound awkward and ungrammatical out of context can become quite grammatical in context. Thus, it is not surprising that many linguistic analyses can be brought into question when the constraints that are proposed are tested in a broader linguistic context. This consideration points to a more fundamental flaw of introspection: even though, as Chomsky has argued, introspection allows the analyst to work with data that might not easily be found in corpus, at the same time, by not consulting a corpus, the analyst might never discover data that are key to the analysis being conducted. In other words, introspection blinds the analyst to the realities of language usage.

Chomskyan linguists might counter this criticism by acknowledging that this is indeed true: that the 'probabilistic information drawn from corpora is of the utmost value for many aspects of linguistic inquiry' (Newmeyer 2003: 698). But because the study of usage patterns in corpora is more within the realm of performance than competence, information on these patterns 'is all but useless for providing insights into the grammar of any individual speaker' (2003). However, as was noted earlier, competence is really impossible to gain direct access to: our only gateway to it is through performance. And even though Chomskyan linguists make a clear distinction between competence and performance, many linguists have argued that performance is more closely related to competence than some have claimed. Leech (1992: 108), for instance, argues that 'the putative gulf between competence and performance has been over-emphasized . . . since the latter is a product of the former.' Others have advocated the creation of 'usage-based grammars' (cf. Langacker 2000): theoretical models of languages based on actual language usage.

Introspection will always be a useful tool for linguists, but to rely solely on it for data creates, as we have noted in this section, a limited and potentially misleading dataset upon which to conduct linguistic analyses. For this reason, many linguists have turned their attention to other means of collecting data – experimentation and the creation of linguistic corpora – topics we will discuss in the next two sections.

3 Experimentation

To ensure that the data used in a linguistic analysis reflects more than a single analyst's intuitions about language, some linguists have designed various kinds of experiments intended to elicit grammaticality judgments from groups of speakers of English. Cowart (1997: 64) describes a number of different experimental designs for eliciting judgments from subjects. Experiments can be written or spoken. For instance, subjects can be given printed questionnaires in which they are asked to either judge the acceptability of sentences or perform various operations. Alternatively, experiments can be presented in spoken form. For instance, the experimenter can meet with subjects individually or in groups and present material to them orally. Such experiments can also be recorded and presented without the experimenter present.[4]

As Cowart (1997) notes, each type of experiment has advantages and disadvantages. If experimenters conduct the experiments in person, their physical presence during the experiment might prejudice the responses obtained. If the experiment is presented in written form, subjects may apply standards of formal written English in arriving at judgments, not the standards they would apply in casual spoken English. But despite the problems that written questionnaires have, because they are relatively 'easy to prepare and administer' (Cowart 1997: 64), they have become a common way to present experimental data to subjects.

Greenbaum and Quirk (1970: 3) describe a number of elicitation tests that can be administered using questionnaires. Their tests fall into two main categories: 'performance' tests and 'judgment' tests. Performance tests require individuals to manipulate the structure of a particular sentence. For instance, if the experimenter wished to test the claim that speakers of American English prefer singular verbs with collective noun phrases, he/she could give a group of subjects the sentence *The committee met on a regular basis* and ask them to

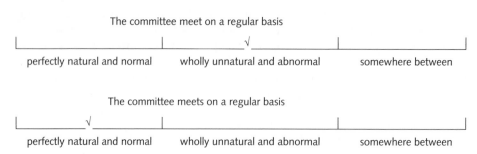

The committee meet on a regular basis

perfectly natural and normal   wholly unnatural and abnormal   somewhere between

The committee meets on a regular basis

perfectly natural and normal   wholly unnatural and abnormal   somewhere between

Figure 5.1   Judgment test for subject-verb agreement with collective nouns

rewrite it, making *met* a present tense verb. This type of 'selection' test, as Greenbaum and Quirk (1970: 4) note, requires subjects to choose 'between two or more variant forms.' In rewriting the sentence, subjects will need to select either a singular or plural verb form, since the past tense form is unmarked for number. And whichever form they choose will provide evidence of whether they prefer a singular or plural verb with collective nouns.

Judgment tests, in contrast, require subjects to express opinions about the acceptability or unacceptability of a sentence. For instance, in figure 5.1, subjects are given the two sentences together and are asked to rate their relative acceptability by placing a check-mark in one of the boxes below each sentence.

This type of 'preference' test (Greenbaum and Quirk 1970: 5) can provide evidence as to whether subjects prefer singular vs. plural verbs with collective noun phrases, or whether they find both constructions of equal acceptability.

Each of these tests has advantages and disadvantages. By directly asking individuals whether they prefer singular or plural verbs, the linguistic issue at hand will be immediately apparent. As a consequence, many individuals might not give a natural response, but try to determine what they might have been taught in school about subject-verb agreement. In cases such as this, one can never be entirely sure whether the responses are genuine or not. On the other hand, if the individuals are asked to rewrite the sentences, the issue of using a singular or plural verb will not be directly presented to them. However, because of the open-ended nature of this type of experiment, some individuals may not give a relevant response. For instance, subjects might not follow instructions and provide additional revisions to a sentence not specified in the instructions. They could completely revise the original sentence and produce a new version (e.g. *The members of the committee meet on a regular basis*) that contains a singular verb but that, at best, provides only indirect evidence of their preference for singular verbs with plural nouns.

As experiments are constructed, there are a host of additional concerns that need to be considered, ranging from deciding exactly what population of English speakers should be tested to determining how sentences being presented in an experiment are best ordered. We describe considerations such as these below.

3.1 Subjects

Selecting participants for an experiment involves determining which population of speakers should participate in the experiment and from this population how many speakers are necessary to yield valid results.

In determining who the target population for an experiment should be, it is first of all important to understand that research has shown that more linguistically informed individuals have markedly different intuitions about language than less linguistically informed individuals. For instance, Snow and Meijer (1977: 172–3) conducted an experiment in which they asked two groups of native speakers of Dutch to evaluate a series of sentences exhibiting variations of word order in Dutch. One group had considerable experience in linguistics; the other group did not. The biggest difference between the groups was that the linguists were not only more consistent in their judgments but 'showed greater agreement with one another as well . . .' (Snow and Meijer 1977: 172). This finding led Snow and Meijer (1977: 176) to conjecture that in making grammaticality judgments, linguists might be failing to notice small semantic differences between sentences, or they might be producing biased judgments by allowing 'their linguistic theory [to] determine their judgments of unclear cases.' Whatever the reason, Snow and Meijer (1977) argue that it is necessary to incorporate the judgments of non-linguists in any data being used for linguistic analysis (cf. Schütze 1996: 114–15 for a survey of other viewpoints on this topic).

In selecting subjects for an experiment, it is useful to draw upon research done in sociology that uses mathematical formulas to determine how many individuals from a given 'sampling frame' are needed to produce a 'representative' and therefore 'valid' sample. The most reliable and valid way to select participants is to use a 'random sample': from a given population, mathematical formulae are used to randomly select a subset of that population. However, since random samples often require very large numbers of participants, linguists have typically used less rigorous sampling procedures, such as 'haphazard, convenience, or accidental sampling' (i.e. using whatever population is available for participating in an experiment) (Kalton 1983: 90), or 'judgment, purposive, or expert choice sampling' (i.e. deciding before an experiment is given who would be the best population to participate in the experiment) (Kalton 1983: 91).

Although convenience and judgment sampling are less desirable than random sampling (cf. Kretzschmar and Schneider 1996: 33), they are often the only sampling types available, since logistical constraints will limit many individuals to administering experiments in academic contexts. However, Cowart (1997) provides evidence that it is possible to obtain valid and useful experimental results from testing students attending classes in university settings. One experiment involved testing the *that-* trace effect (Chomsky and Lasnik 1977) with differing verbs in the main clause:

(12)   a.   Who do you suppose invited Ann to the circus?
     b.   Who do you suppose Ann invited to the circus?
     c.   Who do you suppose that invited Ann to the circus?
     d.   Who do you suppose that Ann invited to the circus?
       (Cowart 1997: 25)

As Cowart (1997: 18) notes, 'there is a certain subject-object asymmetry' in constructions such as (12) when *that* is either present or absent. Without *that*, subject (12a) and object (12b) extraction is possible; with *that*, only object extraction (12d) is possible: subject extraction (12c) is not possible. Cowart wished to determine whether the type of verb used in the main clause affected the acceptability of sentences such as those in (12). He used four verbs: *suppose* (as in 12), *hear*, *wish*, and *feel*.

A total of 332 undergraduates at three different universities in the United States were given sets of sentences containing the four verbs listed above in the four different contexts illustrated in (12), and were asked to rate the acceptability of each sentence on a five-point scale from 'fully normal, and understandable' to 'very odd, awkward, or difficult . . . to understand' (Cowart 1997: 71). The results from the three universities were very systematic, with each group of students rating the sentences with subjects extracted with *that* (12c) much lower in acceptability than the other three sentences (Cowart 1997: 27).

Even though Cowart (1997) found very similar responses across different groups of speakers, as Schütze (1996: 77–81) notes, there will always be inter- and intrasubject variation in the responses that people give to very similar sentences. Groups of individuals will rate the same sentences differently, and a given individual may respond slightly differently to sentences with identical syntactic structures but different lexical items. A certain amount of 'variance,' as Cowart (1997: 40–1) terms it, is not necessarily bad, 'provided that some of this variability is under the experimenter's control.' If an experimenter finds, for instance, that males and females respond differently to a given linguistic construction, before interpreting the results, the experimenter will want to be sure that this difference is truly a difference in how males and females feel about the construction, not a difference that is attributable to a faulty experimental design. Thus, Cowart (1997: 44) is quite correct that 'the art of experiment[al] design consists in controlling variance,' since the better the design of an experiment, the more confidence one can have in the results that are obtained.

3.2   Experimental design

Even though experimentation is not widely done in mainstream linguistic research, considerable research has been devoted to discussing how to design experiments that are valid and that will yield reliable results (cf. Quirk and Svartvik 1966; Greenbaum and Quirk 1970; Schütze 1996; and Cowart 1997).

This research has isolated a number of areas that are keys to an effective experiment: the wording of instructions given to subjects, the manner in which the sentences to be judged are presented, and the types of acceptability judgments that subjects are asked to make.

3.2.1   Instructions

When eliciting linguistic judgments from linguistically naïve subjects, it is impossible to avoid the 'observer's paradox' (Labov 1972: 209): the methodological quandary that as soon as subjects realize that their linguistic behavior is being 'observed,' many will change the way that they speak, no longer producing natural speech but speech that conforms, for instance, to perceived prescriptive norms. Even though it is impossible to avoid the fact that an experiment is an unnatural context in which to study language behavior, it is possible to minimize the effects of the observer's paradox by giving subjects explicit instructions outlining precisely which kinds of judgments the experimenter wishes them to give. In a sense, as Meyer (2002: 57) notes, subjects need to be told what is stressed over and over again in any introductory linguistics class: that no linguistic form is more 'correct' than any other linguistic form, and that when linguists study language, they are interested not in what individuals may have been taught about correct or incorrect usage in school, but in how they naturally feel about a given linguistic construction.

The best way to convey this information is by giving subjects very explicit information about the purpose of the experiment they are taking part in and the kinds of judgments about the data that the experimenter wishes them to make. Schütze (1996: 188) comments that many experiments have failed because the tasks that subjects have been instructed to perform were explained 'too briefly and vaguely.' He argues that instructions should:

- be specific, explaining how sentences should be judged, and listing the considerations (e.g. prescriptive norms) that should not be used in making judgments.
- allow for subjects to 'say sentences out loud' in addition to reading them 'to overcome some prescriptive compunctions associated with written norms.'
- contain examples of good and bad sentences (not illustrating the point being tested) with discussion of why the sentences are good and bad.
- be of a 'reasonable length' so that subjects are not burdened with excessive detail.

Even though the experimenter can go to great lengths to ensure that instructions provide specific guidance for subjects, ultimately it can never be truly known whether subjects are giving genuine responses to sentences. Cowart (1997: 56–9) conducted an experiment in which he gave two groups of subjects the same set of sentences but different instructions for evaluating them: a set of 'intuitive' instructions asking for neutral assessments of the sentences, and a set of 'prescriptive' instructions eliciting more prescriptively based judgments of the sentences. Both groups evaluated the sentences very similarly, leading Cowart (1997: 58) to conclude 'that subjects have very little ability to deliberately adjust the criteria they apply in giving judgments.' Because of the small size and scale of this experiment, its results must be interpreted carefully. But the results do indicate how little is actually known about the nature of judgments that individuals give sentences, and the methodological complexities involved in attempting to get test subjects to provide the kinds of judgments that the experimenter is seeking.

3.2.2   *The presentation of sentences*

In addition to deciding which sentences to include in an experiment, the experimenter needs to be concerned with the order in which sentences are presented.

Any linguistic experiment will contain a series of sentences intended to test various hypotheses. Greenbaum (1977) describes a series of experiments that he conducted to test such hypotheses as whether subjects thought sentences in the active voice were more frequent and acceptable than sentences in the passive voice and whether subjects (all speakers of American English) judged *might not* (to express possibility) as more frequent and acceptable than *may not*. To test claims such as these, Greenbaum (1977: 84–5) constructed test booklets containing contrasting pairs of sentences. Figure 5.2 contains an example of what a page eliciting frequency judgments looked like.

A second page was created for each distinction being tested using different lexical content to test the same syntactic distinction (e.g. *Bruce called Jane* was compared with *Jane was called by Bruce*).

Subjects were given test booklets in which the data were presented in various different orders. Pages were randomized for each test booklet, and half the subjects received the sentence pairs in one order (e.g. active sentence first, then the passive sentence), the other half in the reverse order (e.g. passive, then active). Random ordering like this is important because if all subjects received test pages in the same order, for instance, there is a chance that sentences on adjoining pages might influence the judgments that subjects give (cf. Schütze 1996: 134–5 and Cowart 1997: 98–102 for more details on order effects in

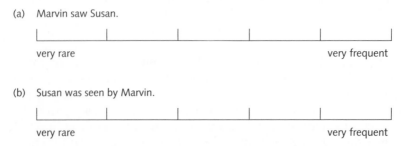

Figure 5.2   Sample booklet page testing perceived frequency of actives and passives

experiments). Cowart (1997: 51–2) also advises that test booklets contain 'filler sentences': sentences containing linguistic constructions unrelated to the hypotheses being tested. Filler sentences help prevent subjects from being habituated to the same linguistic constructions. Greenbaum's (1977) experiment did not contain any filler sentences probably because he was testing so many different linguistic points that subjects would not become habituated to any one type of linguistic construction.

In his experiment, Greenbaum had subjects rate the frequency and acceptability of sentence pairs on a five-point scale, from 'vary rare' to 'very frequent.' Greenbaum could have just as easily had subjects directly evaluate each pair, asking them to state whether each (a) sentence was more frequent or acceptable than each (b) sentence, whether each (b) sentence was more frequent and acceptable than each (a) sentence, or whether the two sentences were equally frequent or acceptable. There is some evidence to suggest that the scalar method of evaluation that Greenbaum (1977) employed is preferable. Schütze (1996: 62–70) provides a comprehensive survey of the many studies that have argued for the view that grammaticality judgments are not either/or choices but on a continuum.

4   Corpus Building

Despite Chomsky's objections to the corpus-based approach, the compilation and analysis of corpora has developed exponentially since the 1908s. McEnery and Wilson (2001: 2) make an important distinction between 'early' corpus linguistics, and the form that it now takes. In using the term 'early' corpus linguistics, they refer to various corpus-based enterprises which were undertaken from the 1950s to the 1970s, that is, before large-scale computerization. Among these enterprises was Fries' work, based on a corpus of around 250,000 words of recorded telephone conversations. The corpus was not computerized, and had to be transcribed and analyzed entirely by hand, which was obviously very labour-intensive, time-consuming, and expensive. The corpus formed the basis of Fries' influential work, *The Structure of English* (1952). The sheer amount of human effort (and potential human error) involved in enterprises such as this simply provided further ammunition for observers who were fundamentally opposed to the methodology.

The major breakthrough came in the early 1980s with the availability of relatively inexpensive computer hardware and software. The computer has made available to linguists data-processing capabilities which have hitherto been unknown, and has revolutionized both data collection and data analysis. The key factors in the computer revolution have been speed of processing and the sheer amount of data that can be analyzed. Since the 1980s, corpus linguists have been compiling ever-larger databases of machine-readable data. Corpora of one million words were considered large in the early 1980s, but corpus linguists now regularly use corpora of 100 million words, such as the British

National Corpus (Burnard and Aston 1998), and even 500 million words, such as the Cobuild Bank of English (Sinclair 1987). It is likely that even larger corpora than these will become the norm in the near future.

The computer revolution has brought about a revival in corpus linguistics, but the availability of ever-increasing processing power and ever-larger corpora have not in themselves answered the objections raised by critics such as Chomsky. The basis of Chomsky's criticism was that we can never generalize from the findings in a (necessarily finite) corpus to the language as a whole. Since the set of all possible sentences in a language is unbounded, any sample of that language, no matter how large, will always be skewed or unrepresentative.[5] The point is a valid one, though it could be said to apply to all probabilistic sampling techniques, and indeed the sampling techniques adopted by modern corpus linguists are widely used in many disciplines, notably in the social and natural sciences. Kretzschmar, Meyer, and Ingegneri (1997) explore the use of sampling procedures in corpus linguistics, and show the parallels between this methodology and those used in conducting political opinion polls. Opinion polls use probability sampling in an effort to predict how an entire voting population will vote. By adopting a principled sampling procedure to ensure maximal representativeness, they are able to generalize their findings beyond their necessarily finite sample to the population as a whole, always building into their calculations a tolerable margin of error. In the same way, the corpus builder must adopt a rigorous sampling technique during the data collection phase, to ensure that the corpus is maximally representative of the language used by the population under review. In the broadest terms, the role of the corpus builder is to construct a 'scale model' of the language (or a well-defined subset of the language) according to rigorous sampling principles. If the corpus is truly to scale, the linguist can be confident that his findings based on that corpus can be 'scaled up' or generalized to the language as a whole, always bearing in mind that a statistical margin of error operates in all sampling procedures.

This is the general principle underlying the design of a representative corpus, though as Kretzschmar, Meyer, and Ingegneri (1997: 168–9) show, the application of this principle in practice is fraught with logistical difficulties. They consider what kind of corpus would be required to be truly representative of American English in the 1990s. As they point out, many important decisions would have to be made, given the size of the population (about 250 million), and its ethnic and regional diversity. Should all ethnic groups be included, and if so, in what proportions? Should all regions be sampled? Should the corpus include non-native speakers as well as native speakers? These are just some of the many questions which every corpus builder must address at the very beginning of a corpus project. Even if they can be answered satisfactorily, it still remains for the corpus builder to contact and record an enormous number of speakers over a vast geographical area. Logistical problems such as these are not confined to spoken corpora. Using one of Kalton's (1983: 82) formulas for calculating necessary sample size, Kretzschmar, Meyer, and

Ingegneri (1997: 173) estimate that in order to provide a representative sample of the 49,276 books printed in the United States in 1992, samples from around 2,200 books would have to be included. Taking 2,000-word extracts from each of these, a corpus of around 4.4 million words would be required.

We should not conclude from this that a representative corpus of American English is impossible to build, but it does provide a salutory reminder that building a statistically representative corpus is logistically very difficult and (in many cases) prohibitively expensive. It also strongly suggests that corpora such as the one-million-word Brown corpus are far too small to be statistically reliable. Such a corpus is 'reflective' rather than 'representative' of American English (Kretzschmar, Meyer, and Ingegneri 1997: 168).

In recent years a great deal of attention has been paid to the problem of representativeness, and to corpus design as a whole (Atkins, Clear, and Ostler 1992; Quirk 1992; Biber 1993). Biber (1993) provides the most comprehensive discussion. Central to Biber's argument is that corpus building should be a cyclical process. The corpus builder should begin by identifying the population and the range of text types to be included. A provisional corpus design can then be put in place, and a small 'pilot corpus' can be built. The pilot corpus should then be empirically tested, to check, for example, whether it contains adequate coverage in terms of linguistic variability. The results of this testing will indicate how the provisional design needs to be modified. In this way, the design can be repeatedly modified in an "almost continuous" cycle (Biber 1993: 256).

According to Biber, the corpus builder must initially produce a very clear, principled definition of the target population that the corpus is intended to sample. This includes two aspects: (1) a definition of the boundaries of the population – what texts will be included or excluded, and (2) a definition of the hierarchical organization of the population to be included, i.e., what text categories are included in the population (Biber 1993: 243). Central to the sampling procedure is the use of a sampling frame. A sampling frame may be defined as a complete, comprehensive inventory of the population of texts from which the samples will be selected. In practice, sampling frames for written data are usually reference books such as *Books in Print* or the *British National Bibliography*, or library catalogues. In compiling the LOB corpus, for example, periodicals and newspapers were selected from those listed in *Willing's Press Guide* (1961) (Johansson et al. 1978). Provided that the sampling frame is genuinely comprehensive, its use ensures that all texts have an equal chance of being selected for inclusion in the corpus. The selection of texts from within the sampling frame can be carried out either by random sampling, or by what Biber (1993: 244) calls 'stratified sampling,' that is, by first identifying sub-genres or 'strata' within the population of texts as a whole, and then by sampling within each sub-genre.

Sampling frames are used extensively in designing written corpora, but cannot be applied to most kinds of spoken data. Instead, demographic sampling is used. Crowdy (1993) describes how demographic sampling was used in the process of collecting spoken data for the British National Corpus. This is essentially different from using a sampling frame, in that it selects informants (speakers) rather than texts. The selection is made on the basis of social variables such as age, sex, education, and regional background. As pointed out earlier, demographic sampling in corpus building has parallels in other disciplines, such as the social sciences, where researchers attempt to define a representative cross-section of the entire population. In sampling language use, however, there is a crucial difference; namely, that not all people have equal opportunity to produce all types of discourse. While all speakers can provide conversational data for the linguist, only elected members of parliament can provide parliamentary debates, and only members of the legal profession can provide legal discourse, and so on. Furthermore, strict demographic sampling according to sex, for example, may not always reflect the realities of language use. In building the ICE-GB corpus (Greenbaum 1996), Nelson (1996) observed that if a corpus is to accurately reflect the population from which it is drawn, it must inevitably mirror at least some of the social inequalities which exist in that society. For example, while as a general principle the ICE-GB corpus attempted to sample both male and female speakers equally, it was quickly discovered that in many areas of British society males and females are not in any sense equally represented. In both politics and the legal profession, to cite just two areas, females are very significantly under-represented. In these two domains – politics and law – a direct application of demographic sampling would be inappropriate, since it fails to reflect language use. To take account of realities such as these, strict demographic sampling must be supplemented with a context-based approach (Crowdy 1993). In the context-based approach, specific types of discourse, such as parliamentary debates, are specifically targeted for inclusion in the corpus.

McEnery and Wilson (2001: 80) summarize the use of statistical sampling methods as follows: 'the constant application of strict statistical procedures should ensure that the corpus is as representative as possible of the larger population, within the limits imposed by practicality.' The use of statistical procedures at the corpus building stage is crucially important, and it is equally important at the stage of corpus analysis. A great deal of attention has been paid to this issue in recent years. Oakes (1998) provides the first full-length study of statistical techniques which can be applied by the corpus linguist, including clustering, multivariate analysis, and measures of collocation strength. Kilgarriff (1996) considers the use of the standard chi-square test for statistical significance, and explores the limitations of the test when applied to language data. The issue is taken up by Rayson and Garside (2000), who propose the use of Log-likelihood statistics as a more appropriate method of measuring distributional variation across corpora or subcorpora. The use of statistics in corpus analysis is also examined in detail in Dunning (1993), Biber, Conrad, and Reppen (1998), Kilgarriff and Rose (1998), and Nelson, Wallis, and Aarts (2002).

The advantages of the 'modern' corpus-based approach have long been recognized (Chafe 1992; Fillmore 1992; Leech 1992). A corpus contains authentic examples of naturally occurring patterns of language use, which frequently contradict even native-speaker intuitions. Furthermore, these examples always occur in a wider context, since corpora, especially those used for syntactic research, always consist of running text. In many areas of linguistic research, this context is crucially important to the interpretation of the data, and it is typically not available in data derived from either introspection or elicitation. A corpus also offers the advantage of scale: the ability to examine very large amounts of data with speed and accuracy. Related to the concept of scale is the concept of variety. Aarts (1999) reflects on what has been called the Great Tradition of English grammars – Kruisinga, Poutsma, Jespersen, Quirk, et al. – and observes that what they describe 'is in reality the description of only one variety of the language: one dialect, one sociolect, one medium' (Aarts 1999: 3–4). Specifically, traditional grammars were restricted for the most part to 'standard,' 'educated,' written, British English. See also Linn (ch. 4, this volume). According to Aarts, what the mega-corpora have brought about is a much greater awareness of the immense variety of language in use. The availability of large electronic corpora forces us to devise new descriptive models for language in general and for specific languages in particular.

The various methods of collecting linguistic data that we have discussed in this chapter have their supporters and their critics. However, recent thinking on the issue tends to see these methods – ideally at least – as complementary (Chafe 1992; Svartvik 1992). Chafe (1992: 96), in particular, looks forward to the day when linguists of all types – introspective linguists, experimental linguists, and corpus linguists – will be more versatile in their approaches, and will freely use a variety of methodologies and techniques.

NOTES

1 The term 'introspection' is problematic when used to describe the kinds of judgments that individuals make when they use their intuitions to rate the grammaticality of sentences. As Schütze (1996: 48–52) notes, 'introspection' has its origins in psychology, where it was used to describe experiments in which 'The idea was to describe internal experience in terms of elementary sensation. That is, rather than saying that one sees a book, one should relate the colors, shapes, etc. that are perceived.' However, 'introspection' is such a commonly used term in linguistics that we will continue to use it in this chapter, even though it does not accurately describe what individuals do when they make linguistic judgments.

2 The exception, of course, are cases where linguists are working with languages that they themselves do not speak. In these situations, it is common to consult native speakers of these languages to elicit judgments of grammaticality.

3 Schütze (1996: 19–27) documents how inconsistently the terms 'grammaticality judgment' and 'acceptability judgment' have been

used in the literature. He ultimately rejects any distinction between the terms, deciding to regard *'grammaticality judgment* and *acceptability judgment* as synonyms, with the understanding that the former is unquestionably a misnomer, and only the latter is a sensible notion' (Schütze 1996: 26–7, emphasis in original).

4   Sociolinguists have developed other ways of collecting data, including dialect surveys, interviews, and what Starks and McRobbie-Utasi (2001) label 'polling techniques': questionnaires sent out by mail or email or administered over the telephone. However, these techniques are more useful for studying lexical or phonological variation, not the kinds of syntactic/semantic/pragmatic preferences described in this section.

5   Even this objection, however, may be mitigated to some extent with the development of 'open-ended' corpora or 'monitor' corpora. Sinclair (1991) has pioneered the use of monitor corpora, that is, machine-readable collections of texts which are continually being increased in size by the addition of new data. As such, they are not a 'synchronic snapshot' (McEnery and Wilson 2002: 22) of the language, in the way a finite corpus is, but a constantly changing data collection. The use of a monitor corpus now means that we no longer have to rely entirely on 'core' corpora, however large. We can now supplement them with much larger monitor corpora, against which 'core' corpora can be continually compared and validated.

FURTHER READING

Chomsky, N. (1962) Explanatory models in linguistics. In E. Nagel, P. Suppes, and A. Tarski (eds.), *Logic, methodology and philosophy of science: proceedings of the 1960 International Congress for Logic, Methodology and Philosophy of Science.* Stanford: Stanford University Press, 528–50.

Cowart, Wayne (1997) *Experimental syntax: applying objective methods to sentence judgments.* Thousand Oaks, CA: Sage.

Greenbaum, S. and Randolph Quirk (1970) *Elicitation experiments in English.* London: Longman.

Leech, G. (1992) Corpora and theories of linguistic performance. In Svartvik (ed.), 105–22.

Manning, Christopher (2003) Probabilistic syntax. In Bod, Rens, Jennifer Hay, and Stefanie Jannedy (eds.), *Probabilistic linguistics.* Cambridge, MA: MIT Press, 289–341.

Schütze, Carson T. (1996) *The empirical base of linguistics.* Chicago: University of Chicago Press.

Wasow, T. (2002) *Postverbal behavior.* Stanford, CA: CSLI Publications.

REFERENCES

Aarts, Jan (1999) The description of language use. In Hasselgard, Hilde, and Signe Oksefjell (eds.), *Out of corpora: studies in honour of Stig Johansson*. Amsterdam: Rodopi, 3–20.

Abercrombie, D. (1965) *Studies in phonetics and linguistics*. Oxford: Oxford University Press.

Atkins, S., J. Clear, and N. Ostler (1992) Corpus design criteria. *Literary and Linguistic Computing* 7, 1–16.

Biber, Douglas (1993) Representativeness in corpus design. *Literary and Linguistic Computing* 8 (2), 243–57.

Biber, Douglas, Susan Conrad, and Randi Reppen (1998) *Corpus linguistics: investigating language structure and use*. Cambridge and New York: Cambridge University Press.

Burnard, Lou and Guy Aston (1998) *The BNC handbook: exploring the British National Corpus with SARA*. Edinburgh: Edinburgh University Press.

Chafe, Wallace (1992) The importance of corpus linguistics to understanding the nature of language. In Jan Svartvik (ed.), *Directions in corpus linguistics*. Berlin: Mouton de Gruyter, 79–97.

Chomsky, Noam (1962a) A transformational approach to syntax. In Archibald Hill (ed.), *Proceedings of the third Texas conference on problems of linguistic analysis in English*. Austin: University of Texas, 124–58.

Chomsky, Noam (1962b) Explanatory models in linguistics. In Ernest Nagel, Patrick Suppes, and Alfred Tarski (eds.), *Logic, methodology, and philosophy of science*. Stanford: Stanford University Press, 528–50.

Chomsky, Noam (1965) *Aspects of the theory of syntax*. Cambridge, MA: MIT Press.

Chomsky, Noam (1966) *Topics in the theory of generative grammar*. The Hague: Mouton.

Chomsky, Noam (1992) Corpora and theories of linguistic performance. In Svartvik (ed.), 105–22.

Chomsky, Noam and Howard Lasnik (1977) Filters and control. *Linguistic Inquiry* 8, 425–504.

Cowart, Wayne (1997) Experimental syntax: applying objective methods to sentence judgments. Thousand Oaks, CA: Sage.

Crowdy, Steve (1993) Spoken corpus design. *Literary and Linguistic Computing* 8 (2), 259–65.

Dunning, Ted (1993) Accurate methods for the statistics of surprise and coincidence. *Computatonal Linguistics* 19 (1), 61–74.

Fillmore, Charles (1992) "Corpus linguistics" or "computer-aided armchair linguistics." In Jan Svartvik (ed.), *Directions in corpus linguistics*. Berlin: Mouton de Gruyter, 35–60.

Greenbaum, Sidney (1977) Judgments of syntactic acceptability and frequency. *Studia Linguistica* 31, 83–105.

Greenbaum, Sidney (1996) *Comparing English worldwide: the International Corpus of English*. Oxford: Clarendon Press.

Greenbaum, Sidney and Randolph Quirk (1970) *Elicitation experiments in English*. London: Longman.

Johansson, Stig, Geoffrey Leech, and H. Goodluck (1978) Manual of information to accompany the Lancaster–Oslo/Bergen Corpus of British English, for use with digital computers. Oslo: Department of English, University of Oslo.

Johnson, Kyle (2000) Gapping determiners. In K. Schwabe and N. Zhang (eds.), *Ellipsis in conjunction*. Tübingen: Max Niemeyer Verglag, 95–115.

Kalton, Graham (1983) *Introduction to survey sampling*. Beverly Hills, CA: Sage.

Kilgarriff, Adam (1996) Why chi-square doesn't work, and an improved LOB-Brown comparison. ALLC-ACH Conference, June, Bergen, Norway.

Kilgarriff, Adam and T. Rose (1998) Measures for corpus similarity and homogeneity. Proceedings of the Third Conference on Empirical Methods in Natural Language Processing, Granada, Spain, 46–52.

Kretzschmar, William A., Charles F. Meyer, and Dominique Ingegneri (1997) Uses of inferential statistics in corpus studies. In Magnus Ljung (ed.), *Corpus-based studies in English*. Amsterdam: Rodopi, 167–77.

Kretzschmar, William A. and Edgar Schneider (1996) *Introduction to quantitative analysis of linguistic survey data*. Thousand Oaks, CA: Sage.

Labov, William (1972) *Sociolinguistic patterns*. Philadelphia: University of Pennsylvania Press.

Langacker, Ronald (2000) A dynamic usage-based model. In Michael Barlow and Suzanne Kemmer (eds.), *Usage-based models of language*. Stanford: Stanford University Press, 1–63.

Leech, Geoffrey (1991) The state of the art in corpus linguistics. In Karin Aijmer and Bengt Altenberg (eds.), *English corpus linguistics*. London: Longman, pp. 8–29.

Lobek, Anne (1999) VP ellipsis and the minimalist program: some speculations and proposals. In Shalom Lappin and Elabbas Benmamoun (eds.), *Fragments: studies in ellipsis and gapping*. New York: Oxford University Press, 98–123.

Manning, Christopher (2003) Probabilistic syntax. In Bod, Rens, Jennifer Hay, and Stefanie Jannedy (eds.), *Probabilistic linguistics*. Cambridge, MA: MIT Press, 289–341.

McCawley, James D. (1993) Gapping with shared operators. In *Berkeley Linguistics Society*, Berkeley, CA, 245–53.

McEnery, Tony and Andrew Wilson (2001) *Corpus linguistics*, 2nd edn. Edinburgh: Edinburgh University Press.

Meyer, Charles F. (2002) *English corpus linguistics: an introduction*. Cambridge: Cambridge University Press.

Meyer, Charles F. and Hongyin Tao (2004) Gapped coordinations in English discourse and grammar. Paper presented at the Fifth North American Symposium on Corpus Linguistics, Montclair, NJ.

Nelson, Gerald (1996) The design of the corpus. In Sidney Greenbaum (ed.), *Comparing English worldwide: the International Corpus of English*. Oxford: Clarendon Press, 27–35.

Nelson, Gerald, Sean Wallis, and Bas Aarts (2002) *Exploring natural language: working with the British component of the International Corpus of English*. Amsterdam: John Benjamins.

Newmeyer, Frederick (2003) Grammar is grammar and usage is usage. *Language* 79, 682–707.

Oakes, Michael P. (1998) *Statistics for corpus linguistics*. Edinburgh: Edinburgh University Press.

Pollard, C. and I. A. Sag (1994) *Head-driven phrase structure grammar*. Chicago, IL: University of Chicago Press.

Postal, Paul (1971) *Cross-over phenomena*. New York: Holt, Rinehart, & Winston.

Quirk, Randolph (1992) On corpus principles and design. In Jan Svartvik (ed.), *Directions in corpus linguistics*. Berlin: Mouton de Gruyter, 457–69.

Quirk, Randolph and Jan Svartvik (1966) *Investigating linguistic acceptability*. The Hague: Mouton.

Radford, A. (1988) *Transformational grammar*. Cambridge: Cambridge University Press.

Rayson, Paul and Roger Garside (2000) Comparing corpora using frequency profiling. Proceedings of the workshop on comparing corpora, held in conjunction with the 38th annual meeting of the Association for Computational Linguistics (ACL 2000), October 1–8, Hong Kong, 1–6.

Schütze, Carson T. (1996) *The empirical base of linguistics*. Chicago: University of Chicago Press.

Sinclair, John (1987) *Looking up: an account of the Cobuild project in lexical computing*. London: Collins ELT.

Sinclair, John (1991) *Corpus, concordance, collocation*. Oxford: Oxford University Press.

Snow, Catherine and Guus Meijer (1977) On the secondary nature of syntactic intuitions. In Sidney Greenbaum (ed.), *Acceptability in language*. The Hague: Mouton, 163–77.

Starks, Donna and Zita McRobbie-Utasi (2001) Collecting sociolinguistic data: some typical and some not so typical approaches, *New Zealand Journal of Sociology* 16, 79–92.

Svartvik, Jan (ed.) (1992) *Directions in corpus linguistics*. Berlin: Mouton de Gruyter.

Svartvik, Jan (1992) Corpus linguistics comes of Age. In Jan Svartvik (ed.), *Directions in corpus linguistics*. Berlin: Mouton de Gruyter, 7–13.

Tao, Hongin and Meyer, Charles, F. (2005) Gapped coordinations in English: form, usage and implications for linguistic theory. Unpublished manuscript.

Wasow, T. (1972) Anaphoric relations in English. Doctoral dissertation, MIT.

Wasow, T. (2002) *Postverbal behavior*. Stanford, CA: CSLI Publications.

Part II   Syntax

6 English Word Classes and Phrases

BAS AARTS AND LILIANE HAEGEMAN

1 Introduction: Aims and Scope

In this chapter we introduce two concepts which are essential for the description of the grammar of a language: *word classes* and *phrases*. In the first part of the chapter (section 2), we examine the classification of words into categories and we highlight some of the many problems that may arise. Among other things, we will outline some of the solutions proposed for dealing with words that seem to have properties of different categories. In the second part of the chapter we turn to the grouping of words into phrases, and we examine in particular the constituency of what is referred to as the 'verb phrase' (sections 3–4). We will integrate our conclusions into a representation of the structure of clauses (section 5). Section 6 is a brief summary of the chapter.

2 Word Classes

2.1 *Definitions*

Word classes (also known as *parts of speech*) are essential for any grammatical description, even though we can never really be entirely sure what their nature is. The reason for this uncertainty is that word classes are not tangible three-dimensional entities, but mental concepts, i.e. they 'exist' only in our minds. Word classes can be viewed as abstractions over sets of words displaying some common property or properties. In this section we will be looking at a number of approaches to word classes, asking in particular how we can define them, and whether they have sharp boundaries.

For English, most linguists agree on the need to recognize at least the following word classes: *noun, verb, adjective, preposition, adverb, determinative* and *conjunction*. Each of these word classes is illustrated in the sentence below:

(1)   [determinative The] [noun chairman] [preposition of] [determinative the] [noun committee] [conjunction and] [determinative the] [adjective loquacious] [noun politician] [verb clashed] [conjunction when] [determinative the] [noun meeting] [verb started]

Each member of the word classes can be the head of an associated *phrasal projection*, e.g. a noun can be the head of a *noun phrase*, an adjective can be the head of an *adjective phrase*, verbs head *verb phrases*, prepositions head *prepositional phrases*, etc.[1] Phrases will be discussed in greater detail in sections 2 and 3. Sections 4 and 5 consider the way phrases are combined to form clauses.

The question arises how to define word classes. The oldest way to go about this is by appealing to so-called *notional definitions*, an approach familiar from school grammars. In this tradition, a noun is defined as 'a word that denotes a person place or thing,' and a verb is an 'action word.' While perhaps useful in certain pedagogical settings, notional definitions are not adequate. For nouns, the definition clearly fails, for example in the case of abstract words like *freedom*, *intelligence* and *rudeness*. As far as verbs are concerned, there are many words that do not refer to actions, but which we would nevertheless want to call verbs, e.g. *sleep, think, concentrate, seem, please*, etc. Moreover, in spite of their denotation, the words *action* and *activity* are nouns and not verbs.

A variant of this semantic approach to defining word classes is to argue that word classes should be defined in terms of more abstract semantic criteria. Thus for Langacker (1987: 189) word classes are 'symbolic units' whose semantics determines the category the elements belong to. For example, a noun is a symbolic unit that semantically instantiates a schema referred to as [THING]. Verbs designate processes, while adjectives and adverbs designate atemporal relations (Langacker 1987: 189; see also Taylor 2002: 341ff). Other linguists stress that the definitions of word classes should make reference to the *discourse roles* of words. For Hopper and Thompson "the basic categories N and V are to be viewed as universal lexicalizations of the prototypical discourse functions of 'discourse-manipulable participant' and 'reported event'" (1984: 703).

To supplement these meaning-based definitions (or even to replace them), we can try to define word classes in terms of their morphosyntactic properties, i.e. by using inflectional and distributional properties. Under this view, nouns are words that can typically be associated with plural and genitive morphology,[2] and which can occur in the position of X in the frame 'determinative-adjective-X.' Following this line of thinking, the word *cat* is a noun because it has a plural form *cats* and a genitive form *cat's*, and because it occurs in a sequence such as *a beautiful cat*. The word *cheerfully* is not a noun because it lacks a genitive and a plural, and because the string **the beautiful cheerfully* is illicit. Verbs are words that can take tense inflections and that can occur to the immediate right of a modal auxiliary; thus *arrive* is a verb because it has a past tense form *arrived* and because it can occur in a string such as *he will arrive tonight*.[3] In English, there are many words that can be assigned to different categories depending on their different syntactic environments. An often cited example is *round*, which can be a noun (*this is your round, John*), an adjective (*a* *round surface*), a verb (*they rounded the corner*), or a preposition (*round the clock*). (See also note 8.)

In the vast majority of cases we can assign words to word classes without much difficulty, but there are words about which linguists disagree as to what might be the best way to classify them. We will discuss a few such problematic cases in the next section. In section 2.3 we deal with the issue of words whose properties would justify simultaneously assigning them to distinct classes.

2.2 Some problematic cases: determinatives

Consider first the noun phrases in (2):

(2)   a politician/the politician

The question arises to which word class we should assign words like *a* and *the*. At first sight, there are at least three possibilities:

* *a* and *the* are adjectives
* *a* and *the* are articles
* *a* and *the* are determinatives

The representation in (1) reveals which analysis we prefer, but we may ask ourselves whether there is any supporting evidence for this preference. Consider first the alternative possibility that *the* is an adjective. If this were indeed the case, it would be difficult to explain the contrasts shown in (3) and (4).

(3)   a.   loquacious, boring politicians
      b.   politicians are loquacious
      c.   very loquacious politicians

(4)   a.   *the a politician
      b.   *politician is a/the
      c.   *very a/the politician

The data in (3) and (4) show that words like *a* and *the* are more restricted in their distribution than adjectives: while we can combine ('stack') adjectives to the left of the noun, as in (3a), we cannot combine *a* and *the*, as (4a) shows. Also, while adjectives can be positioned to the right of a verb like *be* (cf. (3b)), this is not possible for *a* and *the* (cf. (4b)). Finally, while adjectives can be preceded by intensifying words like *very* (cf. (3c)), words like *a* and *the* cannot (cf. (4c)).[4] Notice also that while words like *loquacious* and *boring* have clear descriptive (or 'lexical') meaning, words like *a* and *the* do not have such lexical meaning. All they contribute, meaningwise, to the phrases in which they occur is 'indefiniteness' or 'definiteness' (hence the more specific labels *indefinite article* and *definite article*).[5] Clearly, then, we have some arguments to assign *a* and *the* to a word class distinct from that of adjectives because their distributional and semantic properties are sufficiently different from those of adjectives.

One way to separate *a* and *the* from adjectives would be to classify *a* and *the* as 'articles.' The traditional class of articles is usually taken to comprise just these two words, and no others. This is problematic, however, because there are a number of other words which behave very much like *a* and *the*. For instance, *this, that, these* and *those* (traditionally called *demonstrative pronouns*) are distributionally similar to the articles in that they can also immediately precede nouns. Like *the*, the demonstratives encode that the noun phrases they introduce are definite.

(5) a.   this/that politician
     b.   these/those politicians

Demonstratives differ from the definite article in that they also signal that the referent of the associated noun phrase is *proximal* ('nearby') or *distal* ('far away')[6] and, unlike the definite article, the demonstratives have number inflection: *this/that* are singular in number, while *these/those* are plural. What is of interest to us, though, is the parallel distribution of *a/the* and the demonstratives.

Given the above considerations, it seems that to accommodate all these words we need a class that is wider than the two-member class of articles. In recent discussions this more comprehensive class has been labeled the class of *determinatives* (Huddleston 1984; Huddleston and Pullum et al. 2002; see also n. 7).

The case of words like *a* and *the* is relatively straightforward, and most present-day grammarians would agree that calling such elements adjectives is misguided. However, there are a number of other words, some with quite distinct properties, which have more controversially been claimed to belong to this class of determinatives. Quirk et al. (1985: 253ff) in fact distinguish three sub-classes of determinatives: *predeterminatives, central determinatives* and *postdeterminatives*.[7] Here are some examples from each of these classes:

Predeterminatives: *all, both, half, double, such,* etc.
Central determinatives: *a, the, this, that, these, those, my, his,* etc.
Postdeterminatives: *two, three, second, third, last, next, few, many,* etc.

The three labels aim to reflect the distributional properties of the words belonging to the class. Quirk et al. claim that if there is more than one determinative only the order *predeterminative – central determinative – postdeterminative* is allowed. What is more, in any one noun phrase there can only be one item from the class of central determinatives and one item from the class of predeterminatives. Multiple postdeterminatives are possible. Thus, for example *all the many questions*, with one item from each of the determinative classes shown above, is fine, but **all both books* with two predeterminatives is not permitted, and neither is **my this book*. On the other hand, *the last two days*, which contains a central determinative and two postdeterminatives, is licit.

While the classification above offers a neat descriptive taxonomy of the determinatives and captures some of their distributional (linear precedence) properties, there are problems with it. For example, why is it that we cannot select more than one element from the predeterminative and central determinative classes, while there is no such restriction in the case of postdeterminatives? And what about problematic examples such as the following:

(6)   a.   many a good book
      b.   these many good books

In (6a) the word *many* seems to be a predeterminative as it precedes a central determinative, while in (6b) *many* follows a central determinative, and hence is arguably best classified as a postdeterminative. How do we solve this problem? Let's consider some more data. Consider (7) and (8) below:

(7)   very many books

(8)   many books, more books, most books

The fact that an intensifying element can precede *many* and that *many* itself has comparative and superlative forms suggests that perhaps *many* ought to be regarded as an adjective, not as a determinative, because adjectives generally allow intensification and the occurrence of comparative and superlative forms. But then, what about (6a)? Surely this example shows that *many* cannot possibly be an adjective? This objection to classifying *many* as an adjective would be valid *only* if adjectives could never occupy the position occupied by *many* in (6a), but this is not the case, as the following example shows:

(9)   Seldom have I seen *so magnificent a palace*!

On the other hand, the word *many* is not quite like other adjectives either: in (10a) *many* is followed by a PP *of the books*; a similar pattern is not possible with the adjective *nice* (10b):

(10) a.   many of the books
      b.   *nice of the students

Given its contradictory properties, *many* has received different analyses in the literature. Taking (10) as core evidence, Huddleston and Pullum et al. (2002: 539ff) analyze *many* as a determinative, but obviously this leaves questions as to how to account for its adjectival properties. In a generative framework, Kayne (2002) takes the view that *many* is adjectival and accounts for its determinative properties by assuming that it moves to a determinative position.

Consider next the behavior of *such*, a similarly contentious word that is regarded by some grammarians as a determinative (cf. Quirk et al. 1985: 257), while others regard it as an adjective, cf. Huddleston et al. (2002: 435) and Spinillo (2003).

(11)   such a nice day

(12)   no such thing

(13)   the next such event

In Quirk et al.'s approach, a word like *such* would again have to be regarded as anomalous because it can occur in the position occupied by predeterminatives, as well as in the position occupied by postdeterminatives. If we regard *such* as an adjective this problem does not arise: in (12) and in (13) the word would have the position typical of adjectives, in (11) it could have been fronted to a position to the left of the determinative. A third alternative is proposed in Biber et al. (1999: 280ff), who analyze *such* as a *semi-determiner* to reflect its intermediate status between determiners and adjectives. For a recent transformational analysis of *such*, which appeals to movement to account for its distribution, see Wood (2002).

The discussion above does not pretend to be exhaustive and many other similar problems could be raised for the classification above. The discussion only serves to show that it is not always obvious how to classify specific words.

2.3   *Word class boundaries and gradience*

The problematic cases discussed in the previous section raise the more general question whether the boundaries between the word classes can really be sharply delimited. Readers will have noticed that in assigning our problem words to word classes we systematically made an *either-or* choice. That is to say, we assumed that words like *many* and *such* belonged *either* to the class of determinatives *or* to the class of adjectives. Although we did conceive of the possibility that in one use a word may belong to one category, and in another use it may belong to another category, crucially, we did not envisage a situation in which in a particular use one word would simultaneously belong to more than one category. We also did not envisage that a word could partially belong to one category and partially to another. Such a procedure is very much in keeping with a very dominant line of thinking in linguistic categorization that goes back to Aristotle. Aristotle held that as far as membership of categories is concerned a particular element A either belongs to a category α or to a category β, but not to both categories at the same time. In addition, he held that all members of a category are equal members, so that it is not possible to be a member of a category to a certain degree. The main attraction of the Aristotelian approach to categorization is that a grammar that has neatly delimited categories is less 'messy' than a grammar that doesn't, and arguably it is necessary to impose such an abstraction (an 'idealization') onto the facts of language in order to be able to even begin to make sense of the often complex and intricate facts of natural languages.

Formal approaches to linguistics (e.g. Noam Chomsky's theory of language) have adopted a fairly strictly Aristotelian approach to categorization.[8] This view was countered by other schools of linguistics whose thinking was influenced by the philosopher Ludwig Wittgenstein. In thinking about the notion 'game,' Wittgenstein had noticed that the concept is difficult to define: there are many activities which we would call games, but which are nevertheless quite different. For instance, skipping is a game and it is something you can do by yourself, while football is a game played by two teams. Wittgenstein's solution to this classificatory problem was to say that all games bear a *family resemblance* to each other, in the same way that members of a family do.

Wittgenstein influenced work in psychology by Eleanor Rosch and her collaborators who did experiments which involved showing subjects a large number of pictures of animals and objects, e.g. birds and chairs (cf. Rosch 1978). The subjects were then asked if a particular picture showed a good or bad example of the animal or object in question. The results revealed that subjects perceived particular instances of animals or objects as more prototypical than others. For example, a sparrow was perceived as a more typical example of a bird than a penguin. This type of work in *Prototype Theory* influenced cognitive linguists who refused to accept what we might call the categorial straitjacket, and strove to build the concept of prototypes into their theories. In such frameworks, there have been proposals to conceptualize grammatical categories in terms of prototypes. How would this work? One way to do this is to examine the syntactic behavior of a particular word, say a verb, in a given context, to compare it to the behavior of another such word, and to decide on the basis of that comparison which is the more typical verb. For example, if we compare the distributional potential of the word *must* with that of *eat* we find that the former cannot occur on its own, and always has to precede a verb (e.g. *I must go to London* but not **I must to London*). Furthermore, *must* lacks a third person singular ending (**musts*) and a past tense form (**musted*). The word *eat* is not constrained in the same way: it can occur without an accompanying verb (e.g. *I eat bagels every day*), it has a third person ending (e.g. *He eats bagels every day*), and it has a past tense form (e.g. *He ate bagels every day*). On the basis of such data we might wish to introduce gradience: we could say that both *must* and *eat* are verbs but that *eat* is a more prototypical verb than *must* (see also notes 24 and 29). This approach leads to postulating what is called *Subsective Gradience*: grammatical categories involve a categorial *core* (the prototypes) as well as a *periphery* which consists of a number of less prototypical members. Note that if no gradience is allowed, there are two options. One might say that modals such as *must* are auxiliary verbs which are obligatorily tensed (and hence have a restricted distribution) or, alternatively, one could say that given their particular morphological and distributional properties modals are not verbs at all.

Another dimension of gradience, which we will call *Intersective Gradience* (IG) involves categories resembling each other to varying degrees. The so-called gerund in English is a good example. Consider the examples below:

(14)   I'm so tired of [this builder incompetently *plastering* the walls].

(15)   [The builder's incompetent *plastering* of the walls] was a frustratingly slow process.

Both examples contain the word *plastering*, and in both cases this word has verb-like properties, as well as noun-like properties. In (14) the verbal properties are that *plastering* ends in *-ing*, a typical verbal inflection. In addition, this word appears to take a noun phrase as its subject (*this builder*) and as its complement (*the walls*), and is modified by a manner adverb (*incompetently*). In (15) *plastering* is preceded by a genitival noun phrase (i.e. *the builder's*, cf. *the builder's van*) and by an adjective phrase (*incompetent*), and is followed by a prepositional phrase (i.e. *of the walls*, cf. *the color of the walls*). These are all properties of nouns. Conversely, in (15) *plastering* cannot be preceded by an adverb (**incompetently plastering of the walls*). In conclusion, it seems that *plastering* in (14) is more verb-like than *plastering* in (15).

We can now approach these examples in at least three ways. Firstly, we could say that verbs and nouns are on a *cline* or *gradient*, such that these word classes shade into each other gradually.[9] Another possibility is to say that *plastering* in these two examples is a hybrid element and belongs to the classes of verb and noun at the same time. This strategy is adopted in cognitive approaches to grammar. It is also proposed in Hudson (2003). Notice that both these strategies would mean abandoning the strict Aristotelian separation of the categories. A third possible strategy would be to retain the sharp boundaries between the verb and noun classes, and say that although *plastering* in (14) has verbal as well as nominal properties, the verbal ones (for instance taking an NP object and having an adverbial modifier) outweigh the nominal ones, and for that reason *plastering* is a verb. In (15) the converse situation obtains: here the nominal features (e.g. being modified by a genitival NP and by an adjective phrase) are more numerous than the verbal features, and we therefore conclude that *plastering* is a noun. We will say that the classes of verbs and nouns *converge* upon each other, and that this is manifested by the possibility of elements displaying verbal and nominal features at the same time in different proportions.[10]

3   From Word to Phrase

3.1   *Grouping words*

Having discussed words as units of grammar, we now turn to phrases, which we regard as 'expansions' or 'projections' of words. Consider sentence (16a), which consists of eight words. It is uncontroversial that these words are grouped into strings that form units, both in terms of form and in terms of meaning. For instance, in (16b) it is generally agreed that the determinative *the* and the noun *students* form a unit. It is also agreed that the core of this constituent is the noun *students*, hence the string *the students* is referred to as a noun phrase.[11] In the same vein, the string *just recently* is labeled an adverb phrase.

(16) a. [det The] [N students] [V have] [V completed] [det the] [N assignments] [Adv just] [Adv recently]
      b. [NP [det The] [N students]] [V have] [V completed] [NP [det the] [N assignments]] [AdvP [Adv just] [Adv recently]][12]

The structural grouping of the words in a sentence is represented either by a so-called labeled bracketing or by means of tree diagrams, a format that has been popular since the emergence of generative grammar in the 1960s and which we will turn to presently.

Informally, one might define a noun phrase as a unit or a constituent whose most important element is a noun. This definition implies that NPs in fact need not contain more than just a noun:

(17) [NP [N Children]] bring [NP [N happiness]]

The definition will obviously have to be adapted to include NPs without a nominal head. To mention a few examples, consider the phrases *the rich* and *the poor* in (18a) and the bracketed constituents in (18b) which contain a determinative element but lack a head noun.

(18) a. [NP The rich] do not understand [NP the miseries of [NP the poor]]
      b. The students have chosen their texts. [NP These three] have been selected by [NP many][13]

Typically, noun phrases can be replaced by pronouns: in (19), from Quirk et al. (1985: 76), the pronoun *he* replaces *the man* and the pronoun *her* replaces *the little Swedish girl.*

(19) The man invited the little Swedish girl because he liked her.

An NP functioning as a predicate may be replaced by *so*:

(20) Mary is [NP an excellent teacher] and *so* is her sister

There also seems to be agreement that the italicized strings in the following sentences are NPs:

(21) a. *The discovery of the wreck* caused consternation
      b. What we need is *a careful examination of all the details*
      c. We need *a quick reappraisal of the situation*

By analogy with the definition of NPs above, we can say that an adjective phrase (AP) is a constituent whose core element is an adjective. The italicized strings in (22) are APs.

(22)   a.   John is *very envious of his sister.*
       b.   Mary is *afraid of the consequences of this decision.*

It is possible to substitute the AP by means of *so*:

(23)   a.   John is [_{AP} very envious of his sister] and *so* is Bill.
       b.   Mary is [_{AP} worried about the consequences of this decision] and *so* am I.

Prepositional phrases are constituents with a preposition as their core, as illustrated by the bracketed strings in (24):

(24)   a.   Mary is [_{PP} *in London*].
       b.   Mary arrived [_{PP} *on Tuesday*].

And once again, these strings can be replaced, this time by pro-forms like *there* or *then*:

(25)   a.   John is *there* too.
       b.   John arrived *then* too.

In (24a) the PP can also be replaced by *so*:

(26)   Mary is [_{PP} in London] and *so* is John.

3.2   *The verb phrase*

Identifying noun phrases, adjective phrases and prepositional phrases is usually fairly straightforward. We turn now to verb phrases, which require more extensive discussion. Analyzing the grouping of words around verbs has led to many sharply different analyses, two of which we will compare in this section. We will provide arguments for one of these analyses and against the other.[14]

3.2.1   *The problem: two approaches to the verb phrase*

In the representation in (16) above, repeated here for the reader's convenience as (27), the affiliation (if any) of the verbal elements *have* and *completed* is left open. In fact, in the literature there is an interesting split in how such units are treated and in how the overall structure of clauses is elaborated. In one line of thinking *have* and *completed* are taken to form a constituent (labeled VP, for instance); in another, the string *completed their assignments just recently* would be one constituent (VP) of the clause, and the auxiliary is represened as a separate constituent of the clause. The first approach is represented by (27b) based on Quirk et al. (1985: 39); the other is represented by (27c). In (27b) the label 'auxiliary' is used to signal that the node dominates an element belonging to the class of auxiliaries. In (27c) the label 'Aux' is provisionally introduced to signal a specific structural position in the clause which is occupied in our example by the finite auxiliary.[15]

(27) a. [$_{NP}$ [$_{det}$ The] [$_N$ students]] [$_V$ have] [$_V$ completed] [$_{NP}$ [$_{Det}$ their]] [$_N$ assignments]] [$_{AdvP}$ [$_{Adv}$ just] [$_{Adv}$ recently]]

   b.

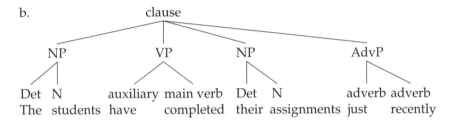

   c.

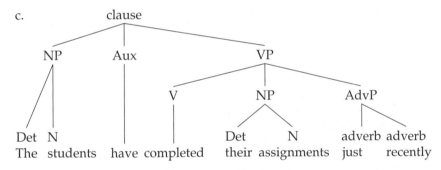

These two analyses of the verb phrase have consequences for the overall structural relations in clauses. In (27b) the subject NP, the VP complement and the VP adjunct are on the same hierarchical level; they are all immediate constituents of the clause. In (27c) the subject NP is a privileged constituent of the clause: it is hierarchically more 'prominent' in that it is an immediate constituent of the clause, while the complement of the verb, the NP *their assignments*, is an immediate constituent of VP, itself an immediate constituent of the clause.[16]

   In the next sections we show that structure (27c) is preferable to structure (27b). We will see that a closer look at some data reveals that postulating a VP along the lines of (27b) is in conflict with the assumptions about structure elaborated in section 3.1.

   Representation (27b) is similar to those adopted in earlier transformational approaches (Chomsky 1957, 1955/1975), while representations along the lines of (27c) have been adopted in more recent versions of generative syntax.

Interestingly, the two major comprehensive grammars of English also differ to some extent in terms of the structure they adopt, with Quirk et al. endorsing an approach along the lines of (27b) and Huddleston and Pullum et al. adopting a variant of (27c). For a more general discussion of the different status of the two representations see also Leech (2004).

In fact, Quirk et al. (1985: 79) seem to assume something like the structure in (27c) – in addition to (27b) – when they introduce the category of 'predicate,' and provide a structure as in (28):

(28)

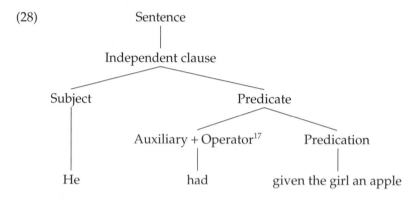

Quirk et al. (1985: 90) discuss the co-existence of the two representations. They say:

> There are occasions, however, when such alternative analyses seem to be needed, on the grounds that some of the generalizations that have to be made require one analysis, and some require another. It is for this reason that we have presented, in this chapter, two ways of analysing a clause: one analysis in terms of the elements S,V,O,C, and A,[18] and the other in terms of subject and predicate, the predicate being subdivided into operator and predication.

Given that their grammar remains relatively informal, these authors do not spell out in detail how the two analyses are formally related, or which of the two is more basic. But see also Leech (2004). In section 5 we actually integrate (27c) into a representation like that in (28).

3.2.2   *The relation of the complement to the verb*

Consider again the examples of the uncontroversial phrases discussed in section 3.1. The italicized strings in (29a), (29b), (29c) illustrate NPs, those in (29d), (29e) APs, and those in (29f), (29g) PPs:

(29) a. *The discovery of the wreck* caused consternation.
       b. What we need is *a careful examination of all the details*.
       c. We need *a quick reappraisal of the situation*.
       d. John is *very envious of his sister*.

    e.   Mary is *afraid of the consequences of this decision.*
    f.   This chapter is *about categories and structure.*
    g.   Mary arrived *on Tuesday.*

In each of these examples the complement of the head of the construction is taken to be part of the phrase. Thus, for instance, the complement of the N *discovery* is the string *of the wreck*, which is taken to be part of the NP. This is corroborated by the fact that the string *the discovery of the wreck* can be replaced by the pronoun *it.* Similarly, *of his sister*, the complement of the adjective *envious* in (29), is taken to be part of the AP, etc. With respect to NP and AP, the discussion in Quirk et al. (1985: 62ff) is fully compatible with such an analysis.

When we turn to VPs, though, things are different. According to the approach in (27b) the complement of the verb, whether it is a predicate, a direct object NP or a subcategorized PP, is not part of the VP. Rather, the verb and the auxiliaries form a constituent separate from the verb's complement and from its adjunct. Quirk et al. (1985: 39) and many others use the label VP for this sequence of one or more auxiliaries and the lexical verb taken together; others use a different label but the implications for the structure are similar.[19]

3.2.3   Medial adjuncts

One consequence of assuming that the verb phrase consists of just auxiliaries and the main verb is that very often the VP will have to be taken to be discontinuous. In the attested examples in (30) we find non-verbal material intervening between the auxiliaries and the verb.

(30) a.   This has *very much repeatedly* been the story of staphyloccocus aureus. (*The Guardian*, 12.7.02, p. 6, col. 7)
      b.   The result is a hobbled place, where working for public services can *only with difficulty* make you proud.   (*The Guardian*, 1.29.03, p. 8, col. 6)
      c.   The former Treasury minister, Geoffrey Robinson, was *last night publicly* upbraided for "self-indulgence" and playing "personality politics" . . .   (*The Guardian*, 10.16.00, p. 2, col. 1)

We either have to say that the VP in such examples contains verbal elements, as well as any intervening (non-verbal) adverb phrase(s), PP(s) and NP(s), or else we have to say that the VP is discontinuous and that the italicized segments are somehow 'outside' the VP. Observe that the assumption implicit in the traditional literature is that constituents such as NP, PP etc. are not routinely discontinuous. Discontinuous NPs, for instance, are usually accounted for in terms of extraposition.

Suppose we assume that VPs conceived of as in (27b) are not normally discontinuous and that therefore the italicized adjuncts in (30a)–(30c) are part of the VP. If this is true then, according to (27b), the manner adjunct *very carefully* will be part of the VP in (31b) but not in (31a), which is surprising, to say the least.

(31)   a.   Jack will examine the evidence *very carefully*.
     b.   Jack will *very carefully* examine the evidence.

3.2.4   *Substitution*

In the literature there seems to be a consensus that proforms typically replace constituents, even though this assumption is not always made fully explicit. Thus, for instance NPs can be replaced by pronouns (see Quirk et al. 1985: 76), while predicative NPs, APs, and PPs can be replaced by *so*, as we have seen. Let us explicitly adopt the assumption that a proform replaces a constituent, which may be a word or a phrase. This assumption will lead us to the conclusion that the verb and its complement[20] must be a constituent. This is shown by the examples in (32):

(32)   a.   John has left the office, and *so* has Mary.
     b.   The evenings have turned very cold, and *so* have the mornings.
     c.   John has left for another job, and *so* has Mary.
     d.   John has passed the new information to the police, and *so* has Bill.

In each of the above examples *so* substitutes for the verb and its complement. If substitution is structure-dependent, then the substitution data above are clearly much more compatible with the structure in (27c) than with that in (27b). These data also suggest that the inflected auxiliary is *not* included in the VP.

The same conclusion also seems to follow from the following observation in Quirk et al. (1985: 76): "But *so* has a more important function in modern usage, namely to substitute – along with the 'pro-verb' DO – for a main verb *and whatever follows it in the clause*" (our italics). The following attested examples illustrate how a verb + its complements (italicized here) can be replaced by *do* (see Miller 2002).

(33)   a.   [Linley] said: 'Why do you *keep the cellar door locked*? Have you always done'?   (Elizabeth George, *Missing Joseph*, Bantam Books, 1993, p. 272)
     b.   If I had wanted to *hurt someone*, believe me, I would have done. (Elizabeth George, *Missing Joseph*, Bantam Books, 1993, p. 172)
     c.   If Sir Alex wants to *sign somebody* he can do.   (*The Guardian*, 12.31.02, p. 14, col. 1)
     d.   There was page upon page of tribute to "The Man who saved The Mirror," some of it from people who should have *known better*, and indeed had done a few years earlier.   (*The Guardian*, G2, 11.5.01, p. 2, col. 3)

Again, if substitution is structure-dependent, then these data conflict with (27b), which treats the VP as a string of auxiliaries + a lexical verb. Once again, the tensed auxiliary is not affected by the substitution process.

3.2.5   *Movement*

It is generally assumed that constituents have a canonical position in the clause, and that they may be moved from that position for particular communicative effects. For instance, in (34a), (34b), (34c) an NP is fronted, in (34d) an AP is fronted:

(34)   a.   *Everything that doesn't sell* we give to Goodwill.   (*The Guardian*, 1.3.03, p. 5, col. 1)
   b.   *The news,* when it comes, he seems to take well enough.   (*The Guardian*, G2, 7.26.02, p. 2, col. 1)
   c.   *A lot of the elements that surround you in the job*, you sometimes think are just a vast conspiracy to divorce you from ordinary life.   (*The Guardian*, 4.26.02, G2, p. 6 col. 4)
   d.   Our dustmen arrive too early for me to check, but our fishmonger and his staff in Petersfield all wear ties (Letters, October 22) and *very smart* they look too.   (Letters to the Editor, *The Guardian*, 10.23.02, p. 9, col. 5)

We assume that fronting a constituent is structure-dependent. (35a) shows that the verb is fronted *with* its complement, whereas simply fronting a verb without its complement is not possible (cf. 35b). Again this is unexpected under (27b) but it follows naturally from (27c).

(35)   a.   "But I couldn't rewind time, I just had to get over it." And *get over it*, she did.   (*The Guardian*, 9.6.01, p. 15, col. 8)
   b.   *And *get*, she did over it.

Consider also the following sentences from which we can draw the same conclusion:

(36)   a.   Pete says he will call his bank manager, and *call his bank manager* he will –.
   b.   *Pete says he will call his bank manager, and *will call his bank manager* he –.

(37)   a.   *Clear their debts* though they must –, this isn't going to be easy for them.
   b.   *Must clear their debts* though they –, this isn't going to be easy for them.

In (35a), (36a), and (37a) verb + complement combinations are fronted, while the dummy auxiliary *do* in (35a) and the modal auxiliaries *will* and *must* in (36a) and (37a) stay behind. See Aarts (2001) for discussion.

Patterns referred to as 'predicate inversion' and illustrated by the attested example in (38) also offer support for (27c). Here again, the lexical verb is fronted with its complement, leading to inversion of *be* around the subject. It is not clear how such patterns could be derived by movement on the basis of the structure in (27b).

(38) *Competing with him* are Jack Nicholson, who would set a record of four Oscars if he won for his portrayal of a retired widower in *About Schmidt*, Daniel Day-Lewis, who plays a ferocious, knife-wielding butcher in *Gangs of New York*; Nicolas Cage in *Adaptation*, and Adrien Brody, of *The Pianist*, the only one of the five not nominated previously.   (*The Guardian*, 2.12.03. p. 5, col. 2)

3.2.6   Coordination

Once constituents are formed they may be coordinated. We reproduce the following extract from Quirk et al. (1985: 46):

[T]wo or more units of the same status on the grammatical hierarchy may constitute a single unit of the same kind. This type of construction is termed COORDINATION, and, like subordination, is typically signalled by a link-word termed a conjunction: in this case a COORDINATING conjunction. The most common coordinating conjunctions are *and, or* and *but*.

COORDINATION OF CLAUSES
a.   [[$_S$ It was Christmas Day] and [$_S$ the snow lay thick on the ground]]

COORDINATION OF PREPOSITIONAL PHRASES
b.   You can go [[$_{PP}$ by air] or [$_{PP}$ by rail]]

COORDINATION OF NOUNS
c.   His [[$_N$ son] and [$_N$ daughter]] live in Buenos Aires

When we turn to coordinations involving verbs, it becomes clear that the coordinated segments containing a verb correspond more to the VP as represented in structure (27c) than to the VP as represented in (27b). Quirk et al. (1985: 949) give (39a), while (39b) is attested. Observe that in both these examples the complements of the verbs (and some adjuncts in (39b)) participate in the coordination.

(39) a.   You must *take the course* and *pass the examination.*
      b.   Word spreads rapidly through a telephone tree, she said, which has *galvanized activists in the West Yorkshire valley* and *already filled six Calderdale buses for next Saturday's London demonstration.* (*The Guardian*, 2.8.03, p. 4, col. 4)

If coordination implies the linking of two constituents, then the data in (39) again tend to favor representation (27c).[21]

From the discussion above we tentatively conclude that a structure like that in (27b), in which a VP does not include the complement(s) of the verb, is not compatible with a conception in which constituents are units of structure and units of sense. We therefore adopt the structure in (27c). In the next section we elaborate the structure of clauses in terms of such a view of the VP.

4   Clause Structure

Before we can integrate the type of VP we postulate here (cf. (27c)) into the representation of the complete clause, we need to address two points. What happens when there is more than one auxiliary in a clause? What happens when there is no auxiliary at all?

4.1   *Stacked auxiliaries*

Consider the following example:[22]

(40)   This student might have been writing a letter.

On the basis of *so*-substitution in (41) and coordination in (42) we conclude that the string *writing a letter* is a constituent, a VP, as shown in (43):

(41)   Mary thinks this student might have been [writing a letter], and *so* he might have been.

(42)   This student might have been [writing a letter] or [watching TV].

(43)   This student might have been [$_{VP}$ writing a letter].

The question arises how to deal with the sequence of auxiliaries *might have been*. Morphologically and distributionally, the aspectual auxiliaries *have* and *been* share properties of verbs: they can be finite or nonfinite, and when finite they may show agreement morphology:

(44)   a.   He has/had been writing a letter.
       b.   Having been writing letters all day . . .

(45)   a.   He is/was writing a letter.
       b.   To be writing letters all day would be terrible.

If *have* and *be* are verbs, then they should be able to head verb phrases. We will say that unlike lexical verbs the aspectual auxiliaries select a VP as their complement.

The examples in (46) provide evidence that the string *been writing a letter* in (40) is a constituent: in (46) *so* substitutes for *been writing a letter* and in (46) the string *been writing a letter* is coordinated with the string *been watching TV*.[23] In the attested (46c), (46d), the coordinated VPs include a non-finite auxiliary. In (47), *so* substitution and coordination show that the string *have been writing a letter* is also a constituent.

(46) a.   Mary thinks the student might have *been writing a letter,* and *so* he might have.
     b.   The student might have *been writing a letter* or *been watching TV.*
     c.   He had *claimed asylum in 1998* and *been refused in 2001.*   (*The Guardian,* 1.16.03, p. 1, col. 4)
     d.   Determining precisely how much money has *made it to New York* and *actually been distributed* is difficult.   (*The New York Times,* 12.30.02, p. B4, col. 1)

(47) a.   Mary thinks the student might *have been writing a letter* and *so* he might.
     b.   The student might *have been writing a letter* or *have been watching TV.*

Data such as those in (46)–(47) show that while the verb, its complement(s) and adjuncts form a constituent, the finite auxiliary can remain outside the VP. (But see also section 5.) Observe that modals remain *in situ* when verb+ complement combinations are displaced. The modal auxiliaries are inflected for tense; they are formally always either present or past. On the basis of these observations, we propose the provisional structure in (48):

(48)

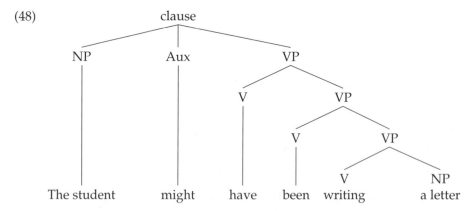

The core VP is *writing a letter,* which expresses the kind of event denoted by the clause. The merger of the core VP with the auxiliary *been* creates another VP and adds progressive aspect to the event; the merger of *have* with the resulting VP adds perfectivity. The stacked structure in (48) manages both to express constituency relations and to encode the scopal relations of the auxiliaries.

For clauses with one or more aspectual auxiliaries, but without a modal auxiliary, such as (49a), we maintain the structure in (48) as a starting point, but in addition we assume that in such cases the finite aspectual auxiliary, which, as shown above, originates as the head of a VP, moves into the auxiliary slot (see Emonds 1970, 1976, 1987; Pollock 1989, 1997; Haegeman and Guéron 1999; Aarts 2001). We will account for this movement in section 4.2.[24]

(49) a. The student has been writing a letter.

b.

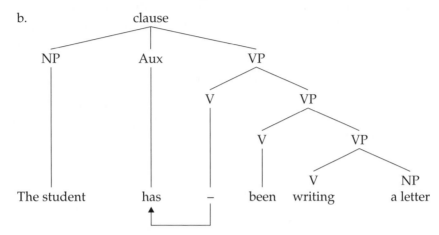

Infinitival clauses such as the bracketed constituent in (50a) can be analyzed with *to* occupying the position 'Aux,' as in (50b):

(50) a. I expect [my students to have been writing numerous protest letters].

b.

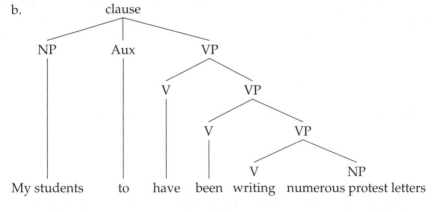

In the representations above, clauses systematically contain three basic constituents: a subject, an Aux position (containing an auxiliary or the infinitive marker *to*) and a VP. This constituency has an intuitive semantic appeal to it: a clause could be seen as the application of a particular event/state of affairs to a referent, and the element occupying the Aux position serves to qualify the linking in terms of time, probability, etc.[25] The representation singles out the subject as the most prominent NP in the clause: the subject is an immediate constituent of the clause. This is a positive result since we know that all finite clauses have subjects, even when the subject lacks semantic content,[26] in which case impersonal *it* and *there* are inserted. In addition, the structural prominence of the subject can be related to a number of properties which single it out, for instance the fact that the subject is the most accessible to syntactic processes such as relativization (cf. Keenan and Comrie 1977), and the observation that subjects are often privileged antecedents for reflexives and anaphoric pronouns (Halmari 1994).

4.2   *Clauses without auxiliaries*

The question arises what happens if a clause does not contain any auxiliaries. One might propose that in the absence of auxiliaries a clause such as (51a) consists simply of a subject NP and a VP, as represented in (51b).

(51)   a.   The student wrote a letter

   b.

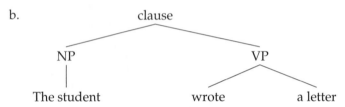

With respect to the informal semantics outlined above this is unattractive. In structure (48) there are three major components: (i) a predicate (the VP) as applied to the (ii) subject (NP), and (iii) the linking element in the position labeled 'Aux.' The element in the Aux position qualifies the subject-VP link in terms of modality or time. In (51b) there is no longer a linking position available.

   If we consider how (51a) behaves with respect to the various diagnostics for structure applied in the preceding sections, it is also not clear that the tense morpheme of the verb should be an integral part of the VP. Observe, for instance, that if we replace the VP by *so*, then the tense morpheme is stranded and realized on the auxiliary *do*:

(52)   The student wrote a letter and so *did* the professor.

Similarly, if we front the VP, then we do not actually move the tense morpheme of the verb along, as shown by example (35a) repeated here as (53):

(53)   "But I couldn't rewind time, I just had to get over it." And get over it, she did.   (*The Guardian*, 9.6.01, p. 15, col. 8)

Furthermore, in negative clauses without aspectual or modal auxiliaries the tense of a lexical verb is not realized on the verb itself but it is realized separately on *do*:

(54)   The students *did* not write any letters.

These data suggest that the tense morpheme should have some independence with respect to the VP. When there is no aspectual or modal auxiliary in the clause, tense serves to link the subject and the predicate and locates that link in time. In clauses without auxiliaries, we will separate the tense structurally from the VP and locate it in the position previously labeled 'Aux'. By adopting this analysis, we can generalize the ternary structure elaborated above and assume that all clauses consist of a predicate as applied to a subject, and that the link is encoded in a particular position, and that it can be qualified by a separate unit, realized by an auxiliary, by *to* or by the tense morpheme.

The auxiliaries that were shown to occupy the linking position (originally labeled 'Aux') are inflected for tense. We can postulate that the crucial feature of this linking position is its inflectional nature, and we will relabel the position 'Aux' as 'I' for 'inflection.' 'I' is an abstract *functional head*, which carries inflectional and agreement features, and hosts (modal) auxiliaries in finite clauses, as well as the element *to* in non-finite clauses.[27] We represent (51) as in (55):

(55)

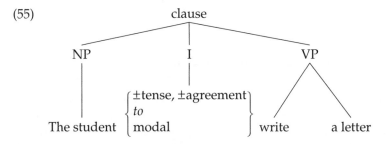

As discussed in section 4.1, a finite aspectual auxiliary is inserted as the head of a VP and moves up to the position 'I,' previously labeled 'Aux' (see (49b)). We can make sense of this movement now: the aspectual auxiliary moves up to 'I' in order to pick up its finite inflection in 'I.' In (56), a more accurate representation of (49), *have* moves to 'I,' and picks up the third person singular inflection, resulting in *has:*

(56)

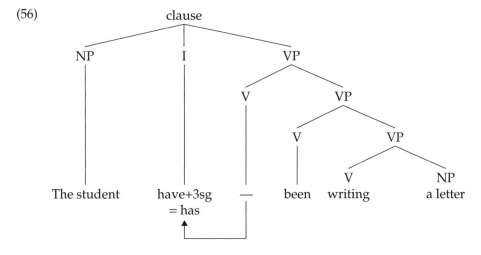

In case there is only a tense morpheme in the clause, this is either affixed to the verb,[28] or it is spelt out by means of the auxiliary *do*. The latter arises in negative or interrogative clauses.[29]

One context in which the tense morpheme in the 'I'-node in (55) is not affixed to V concerns clauses with so called emphatic *do*, when the actual validation of the link between subject and predicate is focused on: (57) contains some such examples:

(57) a. The student did write the letter.
      b. I'm probably more benevolent towards Mr Livingstone than a lot of people and I actually do think he's very brave in trying congestion charging.   (*The Guardian*, 1.3.03, p. 3, col. 4)
      c. People close to Senate leader Tom Daschle say he should be considered a possible candidate, but many Democrats say they would be surprised if he does run.   (*Atlanta Journal Constitution*, 12.1.02, p. A6, col. 5)

5   Rethinking the Structure of the Clause

Structure (27c) displays ternary branching. We have consistently used such ternary branching structures in this chapter. However, there is an intuition that sentences are essentially organized on a binary scheme in that a subject combines with a predicate. This intuition is reflected in representation (28), which we reproduced from Quirk et al. (1985: 79). The two proposals can be combined into one structure.

A potential counterexample to the ternary branching structure in (27c), and evidence for a binary branching structure along the lines of (28) is the following type of example:[30]

(58)   The Smiths will have arrived and should have read their mail.

We could address this point in two ways. One option would be to posit an ellipted subject (coreferential with *the Smiths*) before *should*:

(59)   [$_{coordination}$ [$_{clause}$ The Smiths will have arrived] and [$_{clause}$ Ø should have read their mail]]

This isn't entirely satisfactory, however, as we might then also posit ellipsis in cases like (39). Moreover, an ellipsis analysis becomes harder to maintain in view of data such as (60). The ellipted constituent in representation (60) could not be said to be 'coreferential' with *no one*, since *no one* does not refer to a particular entity.

(60)   a.   No one could understand it or would take the trouble to read it.
    b.   [coordination [clause No one could understand it] or [clause Ø would take the trouble to read it.]][31]

Alternatively, pursuing developments in generative grammar (see Haegeman 1997), we could adapt our structure (27c) in the spirit of the binary branching format of (28), using a particular formalism in generative grammar.

(61)

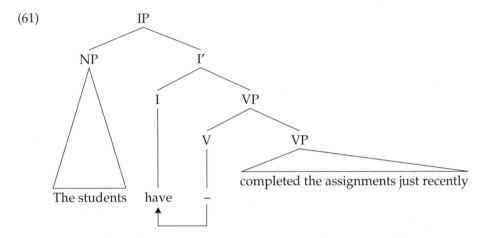

According to (61), a clause is a projection of 'I', or an 'Inflection Phrase' (IP). I' ('I-bar') is a constituent consisting of the inflection node 'I' and the VP. I' corresponds to Quirk *et al*'s 'Predicate' in (28). The subject NP combines with I' to form IP.

Under this hypothesis, (58) is derived by coordinating two constituents of the type I', each consisting of the modal in 'I' and the VP:

(62)   [IP The Smiths [coordination [I' will have arrived] and [I' should have read their mail]]

For more details on the implementation of this type of structure, the interested reader is referred to the literature, see e.g. Kayne (1984) and Haegeman and Guéron (1999) for an application to English.

6   Conclusion

In this chapter we discussed the issue of how to classify words into categories ('word classes'), and how words are combined into larger units (phrases).

We discussed a number of problems that arise with respect to classifying words into categories. In particular, we have raised the possibility of gradience in categorizing words.

In the discussion of phrases, one phrase type, the VP, was singled out. We argued for a conception of the VP as containing a lexical verb together with any complement(s) and adjunct(s). This account is shown to be preferable to one in which the VP contains merely auxiliaries (if present) and the main verb.

We also propose that each clause contains a specific position, labeled 'I,' which hosts inflectional properties. In the final section of the chapter we show how the proposed structure can accommodate the traditional conception of sentences in terms of a combination of a subject and a predicate.

NOTES

Our thanks are due to Peter Collins and Rodney Huddleston for reading an earlier draft of this chapter.

1 Following the generative tradition, a phrase headed by a subordinating conjunction could be argued to be a clause (see Haegeman and Guéron 1999: ch. 10).

2 Obviously plural endings are restricted to countable nouns.

3 In general terms, morphosyntactic definitions are valid cross-linguistically, but the specific inflectional or distributional properties will be determined by the language in question.

4 Observe that not all adjectives have all the properties listed here: some cannot precede nouns (*an afraid cat*), others cannot function as predicates (*the point is main; cf. the main point*). Non-gradable adjectives cannot be modified by degree words (*a very nuclear war*), but while adjectives will have at least a subset of the properties, the articles do not have any of them.

5 For some discussion of the semantics of the articles see, among others, Hawkins (1978) and Lyons (1999).

6 See also Cornish (2001) and the references in n. 5 above.

7 In fact Quirk et al. (1985) use the labels *predeterminer, central determiner* and *postdeterminer*. They use the label *determiner* as a form label and *determinative* as a function label. In this chapter we follow Huddleston and Pullum (2002) in using *determinative* as a form label, and *determiner* as a function label. Quirk et al.'s labels have been adjusted in accordance with this practice.

8 It should be noted that in recent years there have been various attempts to elaborate a more refined conception of categorization. One approach tries to deal with what seem to be intermediate categories. See for instance Biber et al. (1999), Corver and Van Riemsdijk (2001), and Aarts (2004a, 2004b) for discussion.

The approach referred to as Distributed Morphology proposes that categories such as nouns or verbs are not specified in the lexicon. Rather, categorially underspecified roots such as *round* are inserted in different positions in the structure and these positions will determine a particular nominal or verbal behavior. We will not elaborate on this approach here (for discussion see Halle and Marantz 1993).

9 On clines and gradients see Bolinger (1961), Halliday (1961) and Quirk et al. (1985).

10   For further details of this approach, see Aarts (2004a, 2004b, forthcoming). For a selection of papers on linguistic indeterminacy, see Aarts et al. (2004). For a generative approach to nominalization see Fu, Roeper and Borer (2001) and the literature cited there. See also n. 14.

11   Since Abney (1987) it has been assumed in generative approaches that the head of the noun phrase is in fact the determinative (the DP-hypothesis).

  (i)   [$_{DP}$ [$_{det}$ The] [$_{NP}$ youngest children]] bought [$_{DP}$ [$_{det}$ a] [$_{NP}$ book of fairy tales]]

We refer to the literature for that discussion. For an introduction see Aarts (2001) and Haegeman and Guéron (1999).

12   The bracketing in (16b) is incomplete as we have not indicated any VP. We return to this point in section 3.2.

13   As Peter Collins (p.c.) points out, the examples in (18) are subtly different, in that in (18a) *the rich* and *the poor* do not require an understood head to be available in the context.

  A question arises whether the NPs in (17) have a zero determinative:

  (i)   [$_{NP}$ [$_{det}$ Ø] [$_{N}$ Children]] bring [$_{NP}$ [$_{det}$ Ø] [$_{N}$ happiness]]

Similarly, one might think of postulating a zero noun in (18):

  (ii)   a.   [$_{NP}$ The rich Ø] do not understand [$_{NP}$ the miseries of [$_{NP}$ the poor Ø]].
       b.   [$_{NP}$ These three Ø] have been selected by [$_{NP}$ many Ø]

We won't pursue these issues here, as it would lead us too far astray.

14   Gerunds pose an additional problem for the labeling of phrases. To accommodate the nominal and verbal properties of phrases whose head is a gerund, it has been proposed that in such cases the head of a phrase may, as a marked option, be of a different category from that of the phrase itself. Pullum (1991), for instance, argues (against Abney 1987) that the head of a gerund in English may be of the category V, while the containing phrase may be nominal. This 'hybrid' status of the projection would account for the fact that the internal structure of the gerund in (i) is clausal, with a verb taking a nominal complement (*pieces of paper*) and being associated with adverbial modifiers such as *often*, while its external distribution is like that of an NP.

  (i)   [John often throwing pieces of paper during class] bothered the teacher.

15   As will become clearer later, the position labeled Aux hosts finite auxiliaries, the finite form of the copula *be*, the infinitive marker *to*, and the finite inflection of the verb. See section 4.2.

16   Observe that an alternative representation could be one in which auxiliary and verb form a constituent which is the head of the predicate, which also contains complement(s) and adjunct(s).

  (i)   [$_{S}$ The students [$_{predicate}$ [have completed] their exams just recently]]

As will become clear below, the arguments in favor of (27c) suggest that the finite auxiliary should be separated from VP. This is not compatible with (i).

17   The class of *operators* includes all
     the auxiliary verbs, but in e.g. *Is
     John here?* and *Have you any idea how
     old he is?* both *is* and *have* are also
     operators.
18   This would correspond to (27b).
19   Bache and Davidsen-Nielsen (1997:
     38) use the term 'predicator,' for
     instance.
20   And indeed at least some adjuncts.
     A stacked structure internal to the
     VP will allow the distinction
     between complements and adjuncts
     to be made. For reasons of space we
     cannot go into this here.
21   Rodney Huddleston notes (p.c.) that
     data like (i) could be argued to favor
     the analysis in (27b):

     (i)   I [have read] and [may
            recommend] Kim's new
            textbook.

     However, this example involves a
     process that is called *Right Node
     Raising*, such that the verb *read*
     shares its (right-raised) direct object
     with *recommend*:

     (ii)   I [have read – $_i$] and [may
            recommend – $_i$] [Kim's new
            textbook]$_i$.

     See Huddleston and Pullum et al.
     (2002: 1343ff) who call this
     phenomenon *Delayed Right
     Constituent Coordination*.
22   The data are based on Radford
     (1988: 162–4).
23   Quirk et al. (1985: 949) provide the
     examples in (i) and (ii):

     (i)   Most people will have read
            the book or have seen the film.
     (ii)   Most people will have read
            the book or seen the film.

     They seem to suggest that these
     coordinations result from some

kind of left-peripheral ellipsis in
the clause. They do not make the
structural basis for this claim
explicit, but note that by simply
assuming coordination of VPs we
can generate the patterns in (i) and
(ii) without an additional appeal to
ellipsis. See also section 5 on ellipsis
and coordination.

24   It is not clear whether we should
     propose that like aspectual
     auxiliaries, English modals are
     inserted under a node V and move
     to Aux. The rationale for the
     analysis of aspectual auxiliaries in
     (49b) is that these auxiliaries may also
     appear in nonfinite forms, in which
     case they follow a modal or another
     auxiliary. But modals themselves are
     always tensed, and they lack
     nonfinite forms. See also n. 29.
25   Interestingly, despite their
     conception of the verb phrase as in
     (27b), Quirk et al. (1985: 121) also
     suggest an analysis of sentences
     containing sequences of auxiliaries
     which is very similar to (50), one
     in which each auxiliary selects a
     predication consisting of the next
     auxiliary combined with another
     predication. Thus the sentence *He
     might have been being questioned by the
     police* is analyzed as in (i):

     (i)   [$_S$ [$_{Subject}$ He] [$_{Predicate}$ might
            [$_{Pred.1}$ have [$_{Pred.2}$ been [$_{Pred.3}$
            being [$_{Pred.4}$ questioned by the
            police]]]]]]

     Using the binary branching
     format discussed in section 5,
     (i) can straightforwardly be made
     compatible with the hypothesis
     concerning VP structure that we
     endorse.
26   "A subject is obligatory in finite
     clauses except in imperative clauses,
     where it is normally absent but
     implied" (Quirk et al. 1985: 725).

27 For reasons of space we cannot elaborate the proposed structure in more detail. See Haegeman and Guéron (1999) and Aarts (2001) for further discussion. For more technical discussion in terms of the generative framework see Pollock (1989) and (1997). In the generative literature it has been proposed that the ternary structure be reinterpreted in terms of binary branching (Kayne 1984). For an introduction see Haegeman and Guéron (1999). See also section 5.

28 In the earlier generative literature this process was referred to as 'Affix hopping.' See Haegeman and Guéron (1999) for further discussion of why the inflection moves onto lexical verbs.

29 With respect to the status of modals discussed in n. 24 above, we might say that they are verbs/auxiliaries, and that they differ from aspectual auxiliaries in that they are necessarily finite.

30 As pointed out by Peter Collins (p.c.)

31 Thanks to Rodney Huddleston (p.c.) for the example.

FURTHER READING

Aarts, Bas and Meyer, Charles F. (1995) *The verb in contemporary English: theory and description*. Cambridge: Cambridge University Press.

Haegeman, Liliane (1994) *Introduction to government and binding theory*, 2nd edn. Oxford: Blackwell Publishers.

Haegeman, Liliane (1997) *Elements of grammar*. Dordrecht: Kluwer.

Lakoff, George (1987a) *Women, fire and dangerous things: what categories reveal about the mind*. Chicago and London: University of Chicago Press. (Chs. 1 and 2 are reprinted in Aarts et al. 2004.)

Langacker, Ronald W. (1987) *Foundations of cognitive grammar*, vol. 1: *Theoretical prerequisites*. Stanford: Stanford University Press.

Langacker, Ronald W. (1991) *Foundations of cognitive grammar*, vol. 2: *Descriptive application*. Stanford: Stanford University Press.

Newmeyer, Frederick J. (1998) *Language form and language function*. Cambridge, MA: MIT Press.

Taylor, John (2004) *Linguistic categorization*, 3rd edn. Oxford: Oxford University Press.

REFERENCES

Aarts, Bas (2001) *English syntax and argumentation*, 2nd edn. Basingstoke: Palgrave Macmillan.

Aarts, Bas (2004a) Conceptions of gradience in the history of linguistics. *Language Sciences* 26, 343–89.

Aarts, Bas (2004b) Modelling linguistic gradience. *Studies in Language* 28 (1), 1–49.

Aarts, Bas (forthcoming) *Syntactic gradience*.

Aarts, Bas, Denison, David, Keizer, Evelien, and Popova, Gergana (eds.) (2004) *Fuzzy grammar: a reader*. Oxford: Oxford University Press.

Abney, Steven (1987) The English noun phrase in its sentential aspect. Ph.D. dissertation MIT.

Bache, Carl and Nielsen, Niels Davidsen (1997) *Mastering English*. Berlin and New York: Mouton de Gruyter.

Biber, Douglas, Johansson, Stig, Leech, Geoffrey, Conrad, Susan, and Finegan, Edward (1999) *Longman grammar of spoken and written English*. Harlow: Longman.

Bolinger, Dwight L. (1961) *Generality, gradience and the all-or-none*. The Hague: Mouton. (Chs. 1 and 2 are reprinted in Aarts et al. 2004.)

Chomsky, Noam (1955/1975). *The logical structure of linguistic theory*. New York: Plenum.

Chomsky, Noam (1957) *Syntactic structures*. The Hague: Mouton.

Cornish, F. (2001) Modal *that* as determiner and pronoun: the primacy of the cognitive-interactive dimension. *English Language and Linguistics* 5, 297–317.

Corver, Norbert and Henk van Riemsdijk (eds.) (2001) *Semi-lexical categories: the function of content words and the content of function words*. Berlin: Mouton de Gruyter.

Emonds, Joseph (1970) Root and structure preserving transformations. Cambridge, MA: MIT dissertation, distributed by Indiana University Linguistics Club.

Emonds, Joseph (1976) *A transformational approach to English syntax*. New York: Academic Press.

Emonds, Joseph (1978) The verbal complex V'-V in French, *Linguistic Inquiry* 9, 151–75.

Fu, Jingqi, Thomas Roeper, and Hagit Borer (2001) The VP within process nominals: evidence from adverbs and the VP anaphor *do so*. *Natural Language and Linguistic Theory* 19, 549–82.

Haegeman, Liliane and Jacqueline Guéron (1999) *English grammar: a generative perspective*. Oxford: Blackwell.

Halmari, Helena (1994) On accessibility and coreference. *Nordic Journal of Linguistics* 17, 35–60.

Hawkins, John A. (1978) *Definiteness and indefiniteness: a study in reference and grammaticality prediction*. London: Croom Helm.

Halle, Morris and Marantz, Alec (1993) Distributed morphology and the pieces of inflection. In: Jay Keyser and Ken Hale (eds.), *The view from building 20*. Cambridge, MA: MIT Press.

Halliday, M. A. K. (1961) Categories of the theory of grammar. *Word* 17, 241–92. (Reprinted in Halliday 2002: 37–94.)

Halliday, M. A. K. (2002) *On grammar*. Volume 1 of the collected works of M. A. K. Halliday, ed. Jonathan Webster. London and New York: Continuum.

Hopper, Paul J. and Thompson, Sandra A. (1984) The discourse basis for lexical categories in Universal Grammar, *Language* 60, 703–52. (Reprinted in Aarts et al. 2004.)

Huddleston, Rodney (1984) *An introduction to the grammar of English*. Cambridge: Cambridge University Press.

Huddleston, Rodney and Pullum, Geoffrey K. et al. (2002) *The Cambridge Grammar of the English Language*. Cambridge: Cambridge University Press.

Hudson, Richard (2003) Gerunds without phrase structure. *Natural Language and Linguistic Theory* 21 (3), 579–615.

Kayne, Richard (1984) *Connectedness and binary branching*. Dordrecht: Foris.

Kayne, Richard (2002) On the syntax of quantity in English. Ms New York University

Keenan, Ed and Comrie, Bernard (1977) Noun phrase accessibility and universal grammar. *Linguistic Inquiry*, 8, 63–99.

Langacker, Ronald W. (1987) *Foundations of cognitive grammar*, vol. 1: *Theoretical prerequisites*. Stanford: Stanford University Press.

Leech, Geoffrey (2004) A new Gray's Anatomy of English grammar. *English Language and Linguistics* 8, 121–47.

Lyons, Christopher (1999) *Definiteness*. Cambridge: Cambridge University Press.

Miller, Philip (2002) Les emplois non finis de *do* auxiliaire. In Claude Delmas (ed.), *Construire et reconstruire en linguistique anglaise: syntaxe et sémantique*. CIEREC: Travaux 107. Publications de l'Université de Saint-Etienne, 185–98.

Pollock, Jean-Yves (1989) Verb movement, UG and the structure of IP. *Linguistic Inquiry* 20, 365–425.

Pollock, Jean-Yves (1997) Notes on clause structure. In Liliane Haegeman (ed.), *Elements of grammar*. Dordrecht: Kluwer, 237–80.

Pullum, Geoffrey K. (1991) English nominal gerund phrases as noun phrases with verb phrase heads. *Linguistics* 29, 763–99.

Quirk, Randolph, Greenbaum, Sydney, Leech, Geoffrey, and Svartvik, Jan (1985) *A comprehensive grammar of the English language*. London: Longman.

Radford, Andrew (1988) *Transformational grammar*. Cambridge: Cambridge University Press.

Rosch Eleanor (1978) Principles of categorization. In Eleanor Rosch and Barbara B. Lloyd (eds.), *Cognition and categorization*. Hillsdale, NJ: Lawrence Erlbaum, 27–48. (Reprinted in Aarts et al. 2004.)

Spinillo, Mariangela (2003) On *such*. *English Language and Linguistics* 7 (2), 195–210.

Taylor, John R. (2002) *Cognitive grammar*. Oxford: Oxford University Press.

Wood, J. L. (2002) Much about *such*. *Studia Linguistica* 56, 91–116.

7 Verbs and their Satellites

D. J. ALLERTON

1 Introduction

Verbs is the name given to a particular class of words sharing certain grammatical and semantic characteristics. Since no two languages are grammatically identical, verbs as a class must differ from language to language, but they have enough common grammatical features across languages to merit the shared label.[1] These shared features are of various kinds, and different ones are highlighted by different grammarians. In the valency approach being adopted here, the most important syntactic feature is that an independently operating verb shapes the syntactic structure of the clause in which it appears. In the English sentences (1)–(4) the words *stumbled*, *seemed*, *damaged*, and *thrust* are classified as verbs, and as such they each require the core part of the clause to have a particular structure:

(1) The child stumbled.

(2) The child seemed unhappy.

(3) The child damaged the key.

(4) The child thrust the key into the lock.

As a result, sequences like the following must be regarded as ungrammatical:

(5) *The child stumbled the key.

(6) *The child seemed.

(7) *The child thrust (the key).

On the other hand, replacing *the child* in sentences (1)–(4) with, for example, *the rabbit* or *the professor*, will not affect the viability of the sentences, and even replacing it with, for example, *the rose* or *the stone*, will produce a sentence that merely sounds semantically odd. The noun at the core of what is traditionally called the subject therefore lacks the ability to shape the rest of the sentence in the way the verb does. This capacity a verb has for requiring a particular sentence structure is often referred to as the VALENCY (or VALENCE), or alternatively as the ARGUMENT STRUCTURE of the verb.

Verbs in our examples (1)–(4) share another feature: they all appear in a form, normally referred to as its tense, that is distinctively 'past' in meaning, typically referring to an event or state – let us say, more simply, an "eventuality"[2] – in the past. If we change the verb form to the present (giving the forms *stumbles, seems, damages* and *thrusts*), we find that each sentence retains broadly the same meaning, except that it now refers to a period of time that includes the present moment. The majority of verbs (represented in our initial examples by *stumble, damage* and *thrust*) refer to events rather than states, and when they occur in the simple present tense, they normally[3] involve a repeated eventuality. When we want to refer to a single present event, we usually have to use the so-called progressive aspect (e.g. *is stumbling*), though not in the case of sentence (2), which refers to a state rather than an event. This all means that the selection of frequency adverbials (like *always*) or of time adverbials (like *last night*) is dependent on the choice of features in the verb itself, such as TENSE (i.e. present vs past) and ASPECT (such as progressive vs non-progressive). These features are in principle applicable to any verb.

Apart from valency and tense/aspect, there is another set of elements that are strongly influenced by the main verb in a sentence: these are adverbials of manner, method and degree. Consider now these two expanded versions of our original set of four sentences:

(1a)   The child suddenly stumbled.

(2a)   The child suddenly seemed unhappy.

(3a)   The child suddenly damaged the key.

(4a)   The child suddenly thrust the key into the lock.

(1b)   The child really stumbled.

(2b)   The child really seemed unhappy.

(3b)   The child really damaged the key.

(4b)   The child really thrust the key into the lock.

In the (a) set of sentences we find the adverb *suddenly* preceding the verb; it could also have occurred in final position, where it would usually be unstressed. In either case it gives us information about the manner in which the eventuality arose, but it is unusual in being able to occur with such a wide range of verbs and verb valency structures. Most manner adverbs are limited by the individual choice of verb: *awkwardly*, for instance, would be possible in (1), (3), and (4) but not in (2); *eagerly* and *slowly* only seem likely in (4). In the (b) set of sentences *really* emphasizes the substantial degree of the verbal action or state. (In sentence-initial position *really* would have the different value of a sentence adverbial meaning 'in reality, not just apparently.') But here again some adverbs of this type are more limited in their combinability with individual verbs: *badly* would only be possible with (1) and (3); the same applies to *slightly* (which can also appear in final position), although it can occur before the adjective *unhappy*; and *fully* could only occur in (4), except that it seems even more likely before the phrase *into the lock*. Such adverbials of manner or degree, which we can call LEXICAL VERB MODIFIERS, provide epithets which describe the individual type of verbal action or state but in a general way.

We have thus seen that satellites or dependents of a lexical verb like *stumble, seem, damage* or *thrust* are of three kinds, each of which develops one of the essential characteristics of verbs: the valency of a verb determines the number and types of elaborators[4] (or "arguments") it requires or permits; the "Aktionsart" of a verb determines the way it interacts with time, occasion and timing; the individual type of eventuality it refers to regulates its lexical adverbials.

Of these three characteristics of verbs, the first and the third are partly shared with adjectives. In English, adjectives, like verbs, can demand to be accompanied by certain companion elements, as in *dependent (on something), independent (of something), free (from something), angry (with/at someone about/over something)*; but whereas every standard format English sentence[5] includes a verb, it does not necessarily include an adjective. On the third point, adverbial modification is similar for verbs and adjectives, with both word classes allowing modification with a similar range of aspect, method, manner and degree adverbials, although there are minor differences, such as that *very* is only used with adjectives, and *greatly* is only used with verbs. It is the second point, however, that really distinguishes verbs and adjectives most clearly: in languages like English only verbs are inflected for tense and thus include a marker of time.

So far we have seen verbs as a single class or category, with subclassification necessary to allow for valency differences; but there is another group of verbs that lies outside this subclassification, namely auxiliary verbs. Under the heading of tense and aspect we noted above that three of our four original verbs (all except *seemed*) allowed present progressive forms like *is stumbling*; they also allow past progressive forms like *was stumbling*, as well as perfect forms like *has stumbled* and *had stumbled*. These complex verb forms are sequences of words,[6] each of which is a verb, in the sense that it has a potential for a tense distinction, but only the first word in each sequence is actually "tensed." Thus the form *is stumbling* contrasts with *was stumbling* as present as against past, in a similar way to that in which *stumbles* constrasts with *stumbled*. In these complex verb forms the last verb is always a normal verb with a lexical meaning (i.e. a LEXICAL VERB) that gives the verb form its valency requirements, while the preceding verbs have the auxiliary function (hence: AUXILIARY verbs) of supplying the lexical verb with meanings like tense, aspect and modal meanings like likelihood and obligation. Thus in a complex form like:

(8)   would have been stumbling

would is tensed (past/hypothetical as opposed to present *will*) and thus can appear in a finite clause, while *have* and *been* are non-tensed and thus limited to non-finite clauses; on the other hand, *would, have* and *been* are all auxiliary verbs, while *stumbling* is the sole lexical verb. With the exception of the modal *must*, which is mainly limited to present use) all auxiliary verbs have the possibility of being tensed (although they are idiosyncratic on the question of which tense meanings – time, remoteness of conditional clause, distancing of reporter in reported speech – they permit), and they are semantically linked to temporal and modal adverbials (such as *last night* or *possibly*), but they do not contract direct valency relationships (with subjects, objects and the like) in the usual way. They can therefore be regarded either as a very special subclass of verb (i.e. as auxiliary verbs) or as an independent category closely related to verbs (i.e. as verbal auxiliaries).

2   Theoretical Approaches to Verb Subcategorization

Auxiliaries are not the only items that are a matter of controversy: the way verb subclassification is treated and the terminology used to describe it very much depends on the theoretical approach adopted. In traditional grammars and dictionaries an oversimplified division was made into transitive and in-transitive verbs on the basis of whether they had an object or not; thus *stumble* and *seem* were both simply treated as intransitive, while *damage* and *thrust* were both treated as transitive. In the field of teaching English as a foreign language in the 1920s and 1930s H. E. Palmer and A. S. Hornby developed a much finer classification of verb patterns, and in the 1940s and 1950s C. Fries and Z. S. Harris presented schemes in an American structuralist framework. The influential Quirk et al. grammars of 1972 and 1985 carried on these tradi-tions, while incorporating insights from newer approaches: they referred to this field as "verb complementation" and made a detailed division of verbs into subclasses, so that *stumble* would be "intransitive" (in a narrower sense), *seem* would be "intensive" (a term borrowed from M. A. K. Halliday and in 1985 replaced with "copular"), *damage* would be "monotransitive" and *thrust* would be "transitive" with a compulsory "adjunct," while *make* in *make her happy* would be "complex transitive."

Since 1950 a range of different theoretical approaches has been developed, many of them influenced by N. Chomsky. In Chomsky's *Aspects of the theory of syntax* (1965) verbs were seen as being subcategorized for potential syntactic contexts directly, in that a simple transitive verb, for instance, was given the feature [— NP]. Since the 1970s, however, verb subcategorization has been described in terms of the "argument" structure of predicates (this terminology deriving from mathematical logic). At the most abstract level of analysis objects and similar elements are dependents of the verb, and each of these is associated, for a given verb, with a particular "thematic relation" (or θ-role) i.e. a semantic role relative to the eventuality referred to by the verb. This analysis is integrated into a syntactic theory (the "X-bar analysis") that assumes that every phrase has a head (such as a verb) that gives the phrase its basic character, and two kinds of dependent, complements (which are "licensed" by individual verbs) and specifiers (which are more generally available). This approach thus highlights the similarities between, on the one hand, verb phrases (with verbs at their core, generally available auxiliaries, and objects and other "complements" according to the individual verb) and on the other hand, for instance, noun phrases (with nouns at their core, generally available determiners, and prepositional complements of nouns according to the individual noun)[7].

Generalized Phrase Structure Grammar operates in a broadly similar way to transformational-generative grammar, except that, in an attempt to achieve a more economical descriptive system, it rejects "transformational" rules and decomposes subclass labels into syntactic features. *Head-Driven Phrase Structure Grammar* (Pollard and Sag 1994) stresses the key role of a lexical head in determining the grammatical properties of the phrase it is at the heart of; these include its structure in terms of word classes, the kinds of dependent elements involved and their semantic relationships.

Categorial grammar aims to achieve economy of a different kind: it seeks a minimal number of primitive categories, defining all other categories in terms of these. In the standard case the only categories are noun and sentence, so that the predicate (or verb phrase) can be defined as the category that converts a noun (phrase) into a sentence, and transitive verb is the category that converts a noun phrase into a predicate. This means that, unlike most other theories, categorial grammar interprets verbs as a derived class, rather than a primary one.

One of the chief problems for any grammatical theory is how to account for different clause structures that are possible for the same verb, the classic case being the active and passive clause structures that typical transitive verbs permit. Whereas the different models of Transformational Grammar have all used rules that move noun phrases from one position to another, *Lexical Functional Grammar* (Horn 1983, Bresnan 2001) has a level of "functional structure" to mediate between the valency of the verb and the different syntactic structures (active and passive) in which the verb appears. Other functional models of grammar (Halliday's *Systemic Functional Grammar*, Dik's *Functional Grammar*,

Starosta's *Lexicase*, Perlmutter and Postal's *Relational Grammar*, Tesnière's *Valency Grammar*) go further in that they admit subject, object, etc. as primitive notions.

A model of grammar that describes everything in terms of constituency is in one sense simpler, but it has the disadvantage that constituency descriptions have to be very complex to account for differences that are otherwise described as functional differences. For instance, copular verbs like *seem* and transitive verbs like *damage* both take a following noun phrase, as in (2) and (3) above, and if the clause types are not distinguished through the functions of the noun phrases, some kind of constituency distinction may have to be contrived. Hale and Keyser (2002: 9), for instance, describe *(the leaves) turn red* as involving a "composite" structure, and it is true that *the leaves turn* is possible without the adjective phrase *red*, which might be seen as a so-called small clause (Aarts 1992); but such a solution cannot be so readily applied to *(the leaves) become dry* or *(her cheeks) turn red*.

Within constituency models of grammar it is often insisted that all construc- tions are binary, i.e. that they have two constituents (Kayne 1984). Yet verbs that require complementation with two phrases, for instance verbs like *give*, which take an indirect object besides a direct one, or verbs like *thrust*, which require a (direct) object and an adverbial specifying place, apparently form constructions with three elements [verb + direct object + indirect object/place specification]. If so-called "binary branching" is required, the two elements that complement that verb have to added as separate layers, an inner one (usually the direct object) and an outer one (the other element). This binary approach places a severe limitation on the nature of syntactic structure, and although it should always be asked, for any three-element construction, whether any two of the elements form a closer bond, it is not necessary to assume that this will always be the case.

A non-binary model of grammar permits (but does not require) us to regard a sequence of [subject + verb + object] as, in some sense, a single construction. The subcategorization of verbs can then take account of subjects, and this is done in Valency Grammar, for instance. In a language like English, in which every clause compulsorily has a subject, this may seem a pointless luxury, although it is necessary at some stage to specify the semantic role of the subject for a given verb, to make clear, for instance, that the verbs *please* and *like* have subjects and objects with virtually obverse semantic roles. In a lan- guage like German we find subjectless sentences like *Mir ist kalt* 'To-me is cold'; in such languages it is obviously essential to specify a verb's capacity for taking a subject.

In the following account of verbs and their satellites, it will not be assumed that constructions are binary; so that we shall be able to say that *thrust the key in the lock* is a verb phrase (or predicate) with three constituents. On the issue of just how much grammatical information is located in the syntactic structure of a sentence, how much resides in syntactic functions, and how much in the lexical characteristics of individual verbs, we shall aim for a model that provides the clearest and simplest description of all the facts. A further principle will be that English needs to be described in its own right, although it shares grammatical features with other languages and a description that brings out these common features is helpful.

3   The Semantic Nature of Verbs

Syntactically verbs determine the number and kind of co-constituents they have; semantically they give a label to the kind of eventuality they represent, be this a state, an action or some other kind of process. Semantically, there is a big difference, for example, between the process of giving, which involves three participating entities (a giver, a receiver, and a thing given), and the process of snowing, which involves no other entities outside the snow(ing) itself.

We have also seen that the eventualities which verbs refer to are usually located in time: an eventuality may be momentary, as when lightning strikes, or it may have duration, as when it snows; and eventualities that have duration may have different phases, as when a journey is seen as a sequence of departing, traveling and arriving. The terms "Aktionsart" and "verbal aspect" are used to indicate the different ways the event denoted by the verb phrase is mapped on to the dimension of time. It is possible to envisage three levels of description:

(i)   an underlying **semantic** level, where the states, processes, etc. of the world of our experience are described;
(ii)   a **lexical** level, at which lexical items are selected, each with its individual "aspectual character" (Lyons 1977: 706) or Aktionsart e.g. "durative";
(iii) a **morphosyntactic** level, covering the various ways, derivational, inflectional, and periphrastic, in which a lexeme (group) can be modified to express the appropriate duration or timing: thus a verb (phrase) can be put into the "perfective," "perfect," "progressive" etc., this being the dimension of verbal aspect.

Semantic contrasts of the kind described at level (i) can thus be produced in various ways: at level (ii) by changing the lexical verb (e.g. *travel* vs *arrive*), by changing the verbal construction (e.g. *tire* vs *tire out, attack* vs *be on the attack*), or at level (iii) by changing the derivational, inflectional or periphrastic grammar of the verb.

Mostly we talk about single events, but sometimes we group similar events together as repetitions or habitual actions. This obviously complicates the question of the duration of events, since an event that has no real duration can acquire some when it is repeated, so that, for instance, while a cough is momentary, a bout of coughing clearly lasts through time.

Although verbs are usually thought of as primarily designating actions or processes, some of the most frequently used verbs designate STATES, i.e. internally unchanging CONDITIONS (such as *be (out of touch), feel (unhappy), have (blue eyes), like (bananas), lack (help)*) or static POSITIONS (such as *be at home, stay away, live abroad*), in which an entity finds itself. Both types of state are compatible with duration adverbials like *for two weeks*, even when they refer to one specific occasion, cf.:

(9)   On one occasion the child felt unhappy for ages.

(10)   Once Martin lived abroad for two years.

Both conditions and positions are thus static eventuality types in that they have endured though time and are unchanging during this period. They answer questions like *What was the situation like?* or *What state, condition or position was* SUBJECT *in?*, whereas all other eventuality-types are "happenings" and answer questions *What did* SUBJECT *do?* or *What happened?*.

One kind of happening gives us our second eventuality-type, PROCESSES, which (like states) can persist through time but (unlike states) are "dynamic," in the sense that they involve change through time. They can be interpreted as including not only natural processes, as expressed by verbs like *grow, rust, leak, float* but also agent-controlled processes like *walk, read, play, meditate*, which would normally be described as "activities." Both of these kinds of process can cooccur with standard duration adverbials, cf.:

(11)   On that occasion the ship leaked for two months.

(12)   That time the child played for two hours.

Both kinds of process, natural and agent-controlled, are obviously happenings involving the subject.

The happenings we have just considered all have duration, and this duration can be specified, or queried with a question like *For how long . . . ?/How long . . . for?*. Some combinations of verb with object or other elaborator specify a limited amount of the process or activity, so that the verb elaboration structure names a complex eventuality-type, e.g. *grow six inches, age ten years, play a match*. Such verb phrases are not combinable with normal duration adverbials, but they can be used with an *in*-phrase of duration, cf.:

(13a)   *The child grew six inches for two years.
(13b)   The child grew six inches in two years.

This is presumably because the scope of the process (or activity) has already been limited by a frame, making a duration adverbial *for* inappropriate, but one with *in* natural. Such eventualities can be referred to as "frame-limited" processes or activities.

Regardless of whether they are frame-limited or not, processes agree with states in having duration but differ from them in being dynamic, i.e. constituting happenings. The third major class of eventuality-types, which is also dynamic, differs from both states and processes in having no duration, i.e. being punctual, at least in the eyes of the language user. The labels given to this group include the rather misleading "achievements" (Vendler 1967; Dowty 1979) and "punctual changes" (Egg 1995); but to emphasize their suddenness and their capacity for being agent-controlled in some cases but not in others, we can call them simply STROKES (Allerton 2002).[8] The three major types of eventuality are therefore differentiated thus:

STATES	static = unchanging	with duration
PROCESSES	dynamic = changing	with duration
STROKES	dynamic = changing	without duration

Strokes are therefore momentary happenings, such as the unplanned *blink, have an accident, occur to me, notice the time* and the planned *wink, climb (a hill), throw a ball, note the time*. Strokes of both types are of course very natural with punctual time adverbials like *at three o'clock* or *after the meeting* but are incompatible with duration adverbials, unless they are given an iterative or habitual interpretation, as in:

(14)   Sophie blinked/winked for ten minutes.

Both of these sentences have to be interpreted with the V-*ed* word meaning 'kept on V-ing.'

Within the class of strokes there are two groups of verb meanings that, while referring to a momentary or punctual event, locate this at one end of a resulting state or process, at the beginning in the case of INCEPTIONS (as in *launch a boat, set out for home*), at the end in the case of TERMINATIONS (as in *close a meeting, arrive home*). Inceptions and terminations respectively imply a later or earlier process: for instance, both igniting and extinguishing normally imply burning. But both inceptions and terminations can be regarded as subvarieties of strokes.

Apart from the three basic eventuality types (states, processes and strokes) and their variants (inceptions, terminations), there are some compound eventuality types composed of combinations of these. The best known of these is often referred to (following Vendler and Dowty) as "accomplishments," and can be viewed as a combination of a process (or activity) and an ensuing termination. Verbs or verb phrases that denote processes which come to a climax as their end-point, belong to this category, some being uncontrolled events, like *leak out, mature, develop a cold*, others being agent-directed, like *build a house, catch up (with somebody), learn a poem*. Since, however, the term "accomplishment" suggests an agent, we can use the term CULMINATIONS, as a more neutral term, reserving "accomplishment" for the agent-directed subvariety. Because they simultaneously refer to the process and its climax, culminations allow apparently contradictory sentences like:

(15)   The tree is (in the process of) maturing, but hasn't actually matured yet.

(16)   They've been building the house for two years but haven't quite built it yet.

Such sentences are not possible with frame-limited processes, because the frame limit measures the extent of the process or activity without referring to an end-point as the climax. But culminations share with frame-limited processes like those of (13b) the possibility of combining with duration adverbials with *in*, cf.:

(16b)   They built the house in a year.

For such duration adverbials no climax is needed; all that is needed is an activity with clear limits.

There is a second type of (relatively unexplored) compound eventuality, which can be seen as the reverse of culminations; we can term them EXERTIONS. They involve a combination of an inception and a process or state, such that the verb elaboration structure refers both to the initial action of taking up the process or state and to the continuation of it. Verb patterns like *stand up*, *remember (something)* and *take aim* all seem to have this double value, so that we can find the (a) uses that are typical of a stroke (or "achievement") and the (b) uses that are typical of a state or process:

(17a)   At that moment the child suddenly stood up.
(17b)   The child stood up for ten minutes.
(17c)   The child's standing up lasted ten minutes.

(18a)   At that moment the child suddenly remembered the name.
(18b)   The child remembered the name for ten minutes (but then forgot it again).
(18c)   The child's remembering of the name lasted for ten minutes.

The (c) sentences are particularly interesting, in that they are strictly ambiguous between an interpretation referring to the inception part of the exertion, i.e. the act of taking up the required state or process and the more natural one, in which it is the following state or process that lasts for the time referred to. Exertion verbs refer to a process or state that, once started, can thus be kept going for some time, with the same verb phrase referring both to the starting and the continuation of the process.

Culminations and exertions are two clear cases of compound eventuality types, but there is possibly a third. Some strokes and processes seem to imply a physical change of state for the entity affected, the so-called "patient" (regardless of whether human or not); indeed this apparently applies to all cases where there is a physical effect on the entity denoted by the object, so that the past participle of the verb also appears naturally as a premodifer of a noun, cf.:

(19)   The child noticed the window. [cf. *the noticed window]

(20)   The child cleaned the window. [cf. the cleaned window]

The eventuality type found in the examples of (20) might be called "treatments" or "strokes/processes with result," but they can be regarded as a special case of a stroke or process respectively.

   "Aktionsarten" are linked to verbal aspect, which for English chiefly means the progressive and the perfect. These periphrastic forms are in principle possible with all verb lexemes, but in fact the progressive is only natural with verbs denoting processes, because its primary meaning is that a process is or was in progress at a particular point in time. Sentences like those of (21) with a process verb or verb phrase in the progressive:

(21)   The crowd was applauding the captain.

are thus perfectly natural. Stative verbs, however, do not naturally occur in the progressive, cf.:

(22)   *The results are depending on the methods of analysis.

Verbs that are punctual in meaning, i.e. those that refer to strokes, are often reinterpreted in the progressive to refer (not to an event in progress but) to an event about to happen. This is particularly true of inceptions and terminations, as in (23a) and (23b) respectively:

(23)   a.   The president was interrupted as she was opening the meeting.
       b.   The athlete collapsed as he was reaching the finishing line.

The most likely interpretation of these sentences is that the meeting was not actually opened or that the finishing was not actually reached. For further discussion of the notions of aspect and Aktionsart, see Binnick (ch. 11, this volume).

4   The Semantic Nature of Verb Elaborators

The close association (through tense, aspect, etc.) with time and timing was our second major feature of verbs; but now it is time to return to the first, i.e. their ability to shape the syntactic structure of the sentence or clause in which they appear. On the basis of the examples *snow* and *give* we noted that the semantic nature of a verb is bound up with the number of elaborators (or "arguments," e.g. subject, object) that it permits or requires. These elaborators are syntactic items that also have a clear semantic role, but this depends in part on the meaning of the verb. We therefore need to ask just what semantic roles such elements can have, bearing in mind that the discussion of them has a long history, ranging from the grammarians of Ancient India and Greece, through late nineteenth-century and early twentieth-century philologists (H. Paul, O. Jespersen) and twentieth-century theorists (L. Tesnière, C. J. Fillmore) to recent practitioners of transformational grammar with their θ-roles.

The basic meaning of all elaborators, whether subject, object or some other syntactic function, is something like 'involved item.' If there is only one elaborator, this will most commonly be the subject, with its precise semantic value being determined by the individual verb: thus *deteriorate* and *prosper* denote a (change in the) condition of someone or something, and their subject will naturally be the entity that is in that condition; *cough* and *whistle*, on the other hand, denote an activity, and their subjects will therefore naturally refer to the entities that carry out that activity. Most intentional human activity, on the other hand, is goal-directed, targeted either towards other human beings or towards other aspects of their environment, which means that there will be at least two participants, the one being the goal and the other being the human agent. But we need to consider the different types of eventuality individually.

States, with their subvarieties conditions and positions, imply an item that is in that state. A condition can be permanent (i.e. a permanent characteristic) or temporary, but in either case it must be attributed to something, which we might term the CHARACTERIZED item. For instance, a child might be brown-eyed or strong on a relatively permanent basis, but angry or ill for a limited time; either way, these would be conditions. Such states can be expressed either by simple verbs (e.g. *grieve*) or by combinations of a copular verb plus adjective phrase or noun phrase (e.g. *be/feel sad; be/feel foolish/a fool*); in the latter case the state is one of the elaborators of the verb. In the case of positions (or locations) there is a POSITIONED (or LOCATED) item that is (situated) or lives or stands, etc. in a particular place. Grammatically they normally involve a subject referring to the positioned item, a locative verb (which in English can be the verb *be*) and an adverbial indicating the position. Thus characterizational (or "ascriptive") *be* is elaborated with a state (*be foolish/a fool*), and locational *be* with a position (*be at home*). But there is a third possibility, exemplified by *be the author of the book*: this is what Halliday (1985/2003) terms an IDENTIFIER, and *be* here has an identificatory (or specificatory) function.

Turning next to happenings, and firstly to processes, we usually find an affected entity or PATIENT, which is subjected to it: for instance, *improve* (in its intransitive use) and *deteriorate* have a patient as subject.

(24)   The results improved.

(25)   The results deteriorated.

Processes can also have a causer, something or (more commonly), someone who is in some sense responsible. This is commonly referred to as the AGENT, but whether it is actually the performer and whether it intends the action, varies from case to case, cf.

(26)   The children washed their hands.

(27)   The children grew their hair.

(28)   The children slipped on the ice.

(29)   The children fainted.

(30)   The children liked the game.

In other words the notion of 'agent' is rather a diffuse one: in (27) *the children* permitted rather than caused their hair to grow; in (28) and even more in (29), *the children* are unintentional performers and could just as well be regarded as a 'patient,' although in a sense they still did something. In (30) *the children* is an EXPERIENCER or 'mental processor' who is stimulated into liking by the object *the game*. Alternatively all of the subjects of (26)–(30) could be seen as some kind of 'performer.'

When a verb involves an agent and a patient, these normally fill subject and object positions respectively. Thus (24) corresponds to (31):

(31)   The manager improved the results.

(32)   *The manager deteriorated the results.

but, as (32) shows, some verbs, like *deteriorate*, are purely intransitive and thus do not allow mention of an agent.

In object position, too, a range of meanings is possible:

(33)   The child altered the poem.

(34)   The child wrote the poem.

(35)   The child saw the poem.

The verb *altered* in (33) gives its object a 'patient' meaning, i.e. a pre-existing entity is changed in some way as a result of the verbal process; in other words it is a so-called "affected object." In (34), on the other hand, after the verb *wrote*, we find an "effected object," or object of RESULT, in the sense that the entity designated by the object comes into existence as a result of the verbal process. The object of (35) is different again, in that it refers to something that is neither patient nor result but is rather the MENTAL FOCUS or stimulus of the perceiver, cf. also (30) above. A further possibility of (spatial) RANGE is found in verb elaboration structures like *climb the mountain, run a marathon.* Or again all the examples just discussed could be seen as subvarieties of 'goal' (cf. further Schlesinger 1995).

Similar problems of demarcation are found amongst the semantic roles of indirect and direct objects, as illustrated by:

(36) The teacher gave some books to the child.

(36′) The teacher gave the child some books.

(37) The teacher supplied the child with books.

(38) The child received some books from the teacher.

The classic indirect object construction of (36) and (36′) has the RECIPIENT in indirect object position, either with a preposition[9] (36) or without one (36′); but verbs like *supply*, as in (37), have a recipient in direct object position; and a verb such as *receive*, as in (38), can even have the recipient in subject position. Once again we see how a verb's meaning can shape the range of elaborators and their semantic contribution. The case of recipients is made even more complex by the fact that it is difficult to draw a clear line between a recipient and a BENEFICIARY. In principle, a recipient receives some goods or services, and a beneficiary receives some benefit from an action by others, but there is clearly an overlap, as the examples of (39) show:

(39) The grandparents sent a/the bicycle for the child.
      The grandparents bought a/the bicycle for the child.
      The grandparents made a/the bicycle for the child.
      The grandparents repaired a/the bicycle for the child.

In the corresponding prepositionless construction (. . . *sent the child a/the bicycle*, etc.) the sentences are in descending order of acceptability, and the variant with the definite article is less likely than the one with the indefinite article (Allerton 1978; cf. also Givón 1984; Larson 1988; Hudson 1992).

Various circumstantial semantic roles play a role in verb valency, of which the most important is INSTRUMENT. Such a meaning is most usually conveyed with adverbial phrases introduced by *with, by means of* or *using*; but after verbs such as *use, utilize* it can occupy object position. In sentences like (40) it can be found in subject position:

(40) The key opened the door.

although such sentences have an implied meaning 'agent who is trying to use the instrument.' Other circumstantial meanings, such as TIME and PLACE can be found in:

(41)   Tomorrow is (the day of) the concert.

(42)   The room holds fifty people.

although both subjects could also be regarded as cases of a 'characterized entity.' Again such possibilities are strongly limited by the choice of verb.

5   The Syntactic Identification of Verb Elaborators

So far we have taken syntactic functions like subject and object for granted, but they can no more be presupposed than verbs can. Like "verb" itself they are labels for categories in individual languages that have similarities and differences relative to comparable categories in other languages. They therefore need to be defined autonomously for English.

Transitive verbs like *damage* or *thrust* may be used either in the active, as in (3) and (4), now renumbered as (43a)/(43b), or in the passive, as in (44a)/(44b):

(43)   a.   The child damaged the key.
       b.   The child thrust the key into the lock.

(44)   a.   The key was damaged by the child.
       b.   The key was thrust into the lock by the child.

It is generally agreed that the active use of the transitive verbs constitutes the basic or "unmarked" use, and certainly it is the use that is more comparable to the patterns of intransitive verbs. In identifying functional categories, therefore, we need a set of criteria that gives clear results for simple active sentences but also for the superficial form of the other structures. In other words, we need criteria for identifying subjects, objects, etc. that will tell us which phrases have which surface functions in any kind of sentence. When we later compare active sentences with passive and other "transformed" sentences, we shall need to set up deeper, more abstract categories to explain the links between elaborators in the different structures.

Assuming that the lexical Verb (**V**) with its potential for tense, etc., presents no problems of identification, we can begin our surface functional categories with the Subject (**S**), which we can identify in English through the following criteria:

(i)   position. The subject is the noun phrase in a declarative sentence that either immediately precedes the lexical verb or precedes it with only auxiliaries and certain adverbials (but no noun phrases) coming between the two. Cf. *Michael is always making a fuss.*

(ii)   LACK OF PREPOSITION. The subject (like the object) always appears as a noun phrase without a preposition, whereas prepositional objects, for instance, have a preposition. Cf. *Martin introduced me to Prunella.*

(iii)   CASE. The subject is the noun phrase that, when represented by a simplex (non-coordinated) pronoun, invariably appears in the nominative case (*I*, etc.), whereas the object, and even the predicative (or "descriptor," see below) occurs in the oblique form. Cf. *She dislikes him/He dislikes her/It is him (not her),* etc.

(iv)   CONCORD. The subject is the only noun phrase that (in clauses without a modal auxiliary) determines the number of the verb in a finite clause, where this is possible (i.e. in present and past tenses for the verb *be*, but only in the present tense for all other verbs). Cf. *She is making a complaint/complaints / They are making a complaint/complaints / He likes them.*

(v)   OBLIGATORINESS. The subject is obligatory in all declarative and interrogative sentences, whereas the obligatoriness or even the permissibility of objects, etc. depends on the valency of the individual verb. In an individual case, therefore, either there will be only one obligatory noun phrase, viz. the subject, or there will be more than one, in which case reference needs to be made to criteria (i) to (iv). Cf. *The professor is teaching (the new class).* Additionally, the subject is the noun phrase that is ellipted in a standard imperative sentence. Cf. *Teach the new class.*

Further criteria for identifying the subject could be added, such as the fact that it is the subject which transposes its position relative to the finite auxiliaries in *yes/no*-questions and other patterns, or that it is the subject that is retained in pronominal form in question tags (like . . . *didn't they?*). But even on the basis of the five criteria listed, the subject can be unequivocally identified in most English clauses. Existential sentences like *There are two books on the table (aren't there?)* present more complex problems of identification, but they are perhaps best described separately.

Turning to the OBJECT (**O**), we can begin by noting that it has already been partly distinguished from the surface subject on the basis of criteria (i), (iii), (iv), and (v) above. The first criterion, position, is obviously critically important in English. Although a surface object can appear before the subject, for instance in a clause with "object-fronting," or in relative clauses with a relative pronoun as object, as in (45) and (46) respectively, the object never appears as the noun phrase that immediately precedes the lexical verb and its auxiliaries; this position is reserved for the surface subject:

(45)   Prunella he quite likes.

(46)   (The book) which he quite likes (is . . .).

This means that the surface object is a prepositionless noun phrase that either immediately precedes the subject, as in (45) and (46), or, more normally, immediately follows the lexical verb, with only the possibility of certain adverbials intervening between verb and object, and these only in formal English when the object noun phrase is long or complex, as in (47):

(47)   We completed yesterday a building that even the Prince of Wales admires.

There is one important exception to this rule for the normal position of the object: verbs with three elaborators like *give, offer* or *tell* allow an INDIRECT OBJECT (**IO**) in its prepositionless form to appear before the (direct) object, as in (48):

(48)   He gave the child a book.

The fact that this is a marked word order is demonstrated by the fact that this constituent order is impossible when the direct object is an unstressed pronoun,[10] cf.:

(48a)   *He gave the child it.

These proposed positional criteria for identifying the surface object, together with the criterion of case, actually pick out the broader category of "(prepositionless) non-subject noun phrase" or "object-like noun phrase" rather than solely object. To distinguish surface objects from other non-subject noun phrases, we can consider the following:

(49)   The piano damaged a/the carpet.

(50)   The piano resembled a/the pianola.

(51)   The piano weighed a ton.

(52)   The piano had a stool.

(53)   The piano seemed an antique.

Sentence (49) contains a noun phrase (*a/the carpet*) that certainly counts as an object. The other sentences, however, contain a post-verb noun phrase that is best regarded as belonging to a slightly different category. It is true that all the sentences share certain features: for instance, they freely allow an adverb like *obviously* to intervene between the subject and the verb, but not between the verb and the following noun phrase; and they allow the post-verb noun phrase to be fronted to pre-subject position. But their post-verb noun phrases also differ.

The noun phrase of (53), *an antique*, stands out as most different from the others. In traditional grammar such noun phrases are referred to as "complements," and this usage is retained by Quirk et al. (1985), although the term "complement" is used by Halliday (1985) for all of the non-subject noun phrases of (49)–(53), including objects. Many other grammarians use the term "predicate nominal,"[11] for which there then has to be a corresponding term "predicate adjectival," to cover the possibility of something like *(very) ancient* replacing *an antique* in (53), to give:

(54)   The piano seemed (very) ancient.

Jespersen's (1933: 124–31) term for both nominal and adjectival possibilities, "predicative," is adopted in Allerton (1982) but lacks distinctiveness. The term used here, DESCRIPTOR (symbolized as "D"), which is already used in computer technology, is taken over from Allerton (2002). These can be subdivided into NOMINAL DESCRIPTORS (= "ND") and ADJECTIVAL DESCRIPTORS (= "AD"). A further subclass of descriptor needs to be recognized to describe the post-verb phrase in sentences like:

(55)   The piano seemed in good condition.

Such preposition phrases (i.e. combinations of preposition and noun phrase) are certainly not adverbial in function and were identified by Jespersen as "predicative." They clearly have the function of complementing verbs like *seem* and *be*, though, as we shall see shortly, they cannot be regarded as "prepositional objects" either. The verb *seem* in general is not permitted to occur without a suitable element to satisfy its valency, but obviously this can be a suitable preposition phrase, just as well as an adjective phrase or noun phrase. All three possibilities make equally good answers to questions like *What was the piano like?* or *What state was the piano in?* We shall simply call such phrases PREPOSITIONAL DESCRIPTORS (or "predicatives") and abbreviate them as "PD." Further examples (with appropriate subjects) would be *in good health, out of condition, in a bad mood.*

The capacity for being replaced by equivalent adjective phrases (or pre-position phrases) is thus a distinguishing feature of nominal descriptors, compared with other non-subject noun phrases. A second criterion for recognizing them is their inability to be the focus of a cleft sentence, cf.:

(53c)   *It was an *antique* that the piano seemed (not a wreck).

The differentness of the descriptors of (53)–(55) compared with the object-like noun phrases of (49)–(52) is, of course, related to the fact that semantically the latter refer to independent entities, while descriptors refer to a quality or attribute of the subject itself. They do this not only in the structures we have been considering (with verbs like *be, remain, become, seem*) but also in more complex structures of the form **S + v + O + ND/AD/PD**, such as *make the antique saleable, keep the antique in good condition.*[12]

The non-subject noun phrases of (50) to (53) are not themselves all identical. Although they may all be regarded as "object-like," only (49) has an OBJECT in the narrow sense of a noun phrase that is a potential subject of a passive sentence, cf.:

(49p)   A/The carpet was damaged by the piano.

What is more, only true objects allow a so-called "*tough*-movement" sentence like:

(49t)   A/The carpet was difficult to damage (in those days).

Since, therefore, noun phrases like *a pianola, a ton* and *a stool* in (50), (51), and (52) respectively have some but not all of the characteristics of objects, we shall call them OBJOIDS (abbreviation "Ö"). The examples given actually represent three different subtypes of objoid[13] (Allerton, 1982: 83–5).

"True" objects then correspond to a passive subject. Verbs like *give* and *offer* take two such objects, because they allow either of two noun phrases to occur in the object position, as in

(56)   The new piano offered an opportunity to us.

(57)   The new piano offered us an opportunity.

This means that two different passive sentences are possible:

(58)   We were offered an opportunity by the new piano.

(59)   An opportunity was offered (to) us by the new piano.

We shall follow traditional practice (as opposed to that of some modern grammarians) by referring both to noun phrases like *us* in (56) and to preposition phrases like *to us* in (57) as INDIRECT OBJECTS, but only in so far as the proposed candidate may appear *both* after the normal object in the form of a preposition phrase *and* before the normal object as a noun phrase.[14]

Two further categories should be mentioned for the sake of completeness: the first is that of INDIRECT OBJOID (**IÖ**) as it appears in sentences with two object-like noun phrases that lack the potential for being a passive subject, i.e. they have an indirect objoid as well as a (direct) objoid after the verb (cf. *The new piano cost me five pounds*); the second is that of OBLIQUE OBJECT (**OO**) as it appears in sentences with two full objects (with passivization potential), the second of which may have a preposition (*for*) but can drop it without changing its position vis-à-vis the direct object (cf. *He envied me (for) my new piano.*)

We have already met preposition phrases in a predicative function after verbs like *seem*; but they also have other functions in relation to a lexical verb. Consider the following examples:

(60)   The new piano interfered with the view.

(61)   The new piano differed from the pianola.

(62)   The new piano stood beside the bookcase.

(63)   The new piano deteriorated in the conservatory.

The preposition phrases of (60) and (61) clearly differ from those of (62) and (63) on at least two counts. The prepositions in (60) and (61) are each fixed with no possible alternative (e.g. *to*, *in*), while in (62) and (63) any semantically appropriate preposition could be substituted, e.g. *behind*, *against*, *near* in (62), and *outside*, *under*, *near* in (63). Moreover, the whole preposition phrases of (62) and (63) can be reduced to *there*, without a substantial change of sense, and can be elicited using the question word *where*; whereas the preposition phrases of (60) and (61) cannot be reduced to *there*, and are most naturally elicited using questions of the form *What . . . with/from/etc.?* This makes it plain that while the preposition phrases of (62) and (63) can be described as adverbial phrases of place, those of (60) and (61), having a preposition selected by the verb, and being nominal enough in nature to be elicited by a *what*-question, can be regarded as object-like elaborators of the verb. The preposition phrases of (60) and (61) are, however, not grammatically identical. They seem to display a similar difference to that we noted above between objects and objoids, i.e. that only (60) has a natural passive transform; cf.:

(60p)   The view was interfered with by the new piano.

(61p)   *The pianola was differed from by the new piano.

We can refer to items like *with the view* in (60) and *from the pianola* in (61) as PREPOSITIONAL OBJECTS and PREPOSITIONAL OBJOIDS respectively (abbreviations **PO** and **PÖ**).

The adverbial phrases of (62) and (63) are not quite identical either. Whereas *in the conservatory* in (63) is a free modifier adverbial (abbreviated as **Avl**) of the type that can appear in any sentence, *beside the bookcase* in (62) has a special link to the lexical verb *stand*, which belongs to a set of verbs (including also *stand*, *lie*, *live*, *reside*, *last*, etc.) that are incomplete without a following adverbial of the category appropriate for the individual verb (a place adverbial for *stand*, a duration adverbial for *last*, etc.). These adverbials belong to the valency of the verb as an ADVERBIAL ELABORATOR (abbreviated as **AE**).

Some single word adverbials, i.e. adverbs, have an even stronger link with the verb, so that the combination of verb-plus-adverb has a semantic unity; these are the well-known "phrasal verbs." For example, in the sentences:

(64)   The new piano played up.

(65)   The new pianist hung about.

The adverbs *up* and *about* cannot be contrasted with other adverbs of the same type (e.g. *down, nearby*) in the usual way, and the overall meaning of the verb-plus-adverb combination is at least partly unpredictable: *play up* does not mean 'engage in games in a higher position' but rather 'act awkwardly'; *hang about* does not mean 'remain suspended in the vicinity' but rather 'stay too long in a place.' We can refer to the adverbs in these combinations as LIMITER ADVERBS, and record them simply as "L," a phrasal verb appearing as "V-L." Combinations of a similar kind occur with transitive verbs and an object in sentences like:

(66)   The traffic held the pianist up.

(67)   The pianist turned the offer down.

In patterns of this kind the sequence of **v + O + L** represents the primary pattern, which is also available when the object is converted to a pronoun, e.g. *the pianist* in (66) or *the offer* in (67) can be pronominalized to *her/him* or *it*, respectively. There is a variant of this pattern in which the **L** particle precedes the object (e.g. *make up the story*) but this is only available when the object is a full lexical noun phrase or a stressed pronoun.

   Some verbs take an embedded sentence, i.e. some sort of clause rather than a phrase as an elaborator. The required clause may be a full finite clause (most commonly a *that*-clause) or it may be a non-finite clause based on an infinitive or a gerund, cf.:

(68)   The pianist said that live music had a great appeal.

(69)   The pianist offered to play for nothing.

(70)   The pianist enjoyed disturbing the neighbours.

We can describe this aspect of the valency of the verbs *say, offer* and *enjoy* as involving elaboration with a FINITE clause (= **F**), with an INFINITIVE structure (= **I**), or a GERUND structure (= **G**) respectively. Since the clause is embedded in the place where an object (e.g. *something*) would occur, it can be seen as replacing an object, and could actually be represented as $\{F\}^O$, etc.

   When the infinitive or the gerund is preceded by its own independent subject, the latter must be mentioned: this pattern can be represented as **S-I** (i.e. as infinitive preceded by its own subject) or as **S-fI** (i.e. as infinitive preceded by its own subject preceded by *for*) in cases like (71)–(73) below, or as **S-G** (i.e. as gerund preceded by its own subject) in cases like (74). In the case of infinitives the subject noun phrase is unaccompanied in British English, except when the preceding verb takes a prepositional object with *for*, whereas in American English *for* is used more generally: ·

(71)   The pianist caused her to sing a wrong note.

(72)   The pianist wanted (*AmEng.* for) her to sing a wrong note.

(73)   The director arranged for her to sing a wrong note. (cf. arrange for the singing)

(74)   The pianist anticipated her singing a wrong note.

Although in (71) the whole sequence of *her to sing* is understood semantically as the object of the verb *cause*, this sequence is not an acceptable subject for a passive sentence; but the noun phrase *her* alone can be extracted from its clause to become a passive subject, as in (71p), a process sometimes referred to as "raising":[15]

(71p)   She was caused (by the pianist) to sing a wrong note.

In (74) the gerund preceded by its own independent subject only takes a preceding preposition following a prepositional verb, in which case the original preposition is retained:

(75)   The pianist objected to her singing a wrong note. (cf. object to the singing)

In such cases usage differs as to whether *her* corresponds to an object pronoun (= *Mary*) or a possessive pronoun (*Mary's*).[16]

Grammatically versatile verbs like *want* or *intend* can either occur (like *decide*) with a directly following infinitive, or (like *cause*) with its own independent subject before the infinitive. On the other hand, *enjoy* in (70) is impossible with the infinitive but natural with a gerund construction; and the verb *show* is impossible with both infinitive and gerund but does occur with a finite clause like *say* in (68) above. Verbs need to be lexically specified for the types of embedded pattern they accept. Some verbs, moreover, are restricted to clausal complementation: the verb *condescend*, for instance, always requires a following infinitive.

In a sentence like:

(76)   The pianist persuaded her to open the door.

we see a structure that looks like the **S-I** pattern of (71) but differs from it, because passivization of *her to open the door* is impossible. The word *her* in (76) is not simply the subject of the infinitive *to open*; it is primarily the object of the verb *persuade*. It therefore needs to be regarded as a case of **O + I**. Yet another structure appears in (77), which is like (71) except that it involves the bare infinitive (without *to*), which contrasts with gerunds in terms of progressivity:

(77)   The pianist saw her sing/singing an aria.

Passivization of ... *her sing/singing an aria* to ... *an aria (be) sung/being sung by her* is would give the wrong meaning, because, as in example (76), *her* alone is the object of the main verb (*saw*), giving us the pattern $S + v + O + \{I_0/G\}^{AE}$, in which I_0 marks the bare infinitive (without *to*).

A further complication involves the precise status of the subject of the finite verb. Consider the examples:

(78)   The pianist hoped to entertain the audience.

(79)   The pianist happened to entertain the audience.

Sentence (78) is similar to (though not identical to) (69), but (79) is rather different in that, although according to our tests the subject of the verb *happen* is simply *the pianist*, it seems semantically more appropriate to identify the subject as the whole discontinuous infinitive clause *the pianist ... to entertain the audience* (cf. the sentence *It happened that the pianist entertained the audience*). We can indicate this as $\{S\}^S + v + [\text{-}I]$. Alternatively, as proposed for instance in Huddleston and Pullum (2002: 1194–8), such sentences can be described as having a "raised" subject, in the sense that the phrase *the pianist* is apparently extracted out of its position of subject of the non-finite verb *entertain* and superficially promoted to the level of subject of the main clause verb *happen*.[17]

Something similar is found in the following:

(80)   It seems/seemed that the pianist entertained the audience.

On the face of it such a sentence looks like a case of extraposition, i.e. a structure formed when a clausal subject is replaced by *it* and postponed till the end of the sentence (as in *It annoyed me that he left early*). But an "unextraposed" version of this sentence is ungrammatical:

(81)   *That the pianist entertained the audience seemed.

Sentences like (80) may therefore have to be regarded as an additional sentence pattern, requiring an empty *it* subject and an obligatory *that*-clause, in other words as $S_\emptyset + v + F$. The subject is empty in the sense that it cannot be replaced by a full noun phrase, such as *the situation*. Empty *it*-subjects of a different kind are required anyway for "meteorological verbs":

(82)   It/*The weather snowed all morning.

This *it* is a true subject (by the tests we started from) but, unlike the *it* of *It is snowy*, etc. (cf. Bolinger 1977) it is irreplaceable and therefore empty of semantic content. We can therefore mark it as $S_\emptyset$.

Finally, returning briefly to passive sentences like (44a) and (44b) above, we recall that they may include a *by*-phrase (*by the child*) that corresponds to the active subject. According to our criteria for surface categories, this can be neither a subject nor an object; but nor is it a freely available adverbial (**Adv**). Later we can compare active sentences with passive and other "transformed" sentences, and try to explain the links between elaborators in the different structures. But in the surface passive sentence the passive correlate of the active subject appears as what in Allerton (1982: 43) is termed "perject" (**J**). This *by*-phrase has never been satisfactorily labelled by grammarians: some refer to it using the semantic label "agent phrase," but like the valency subject it represents, it has a value that goes well beyond this; others talk simply of a *by*-phrase, but this fails to make clear that it is not a freely occurring adverbial (or adjunct), since it only occurs in passive sentences, where it remains part of the valency elaboration of the lexical verb.

6   The Verb Elaboration Structures

Having established the range of elements that occur as verb elaborators, we can now ask what structures they form with the verb. As we have seen, a subject is a required constituent of every sentence, even with meteorological verbs. Depending on its valency requirements, a **v** also adopts none, one, two or three of the elements **O, IO, Ö, ND, AD, PD, PO, PÖ, AE, L, F, I** or **G**. (If it is passive, it must have a different **S** derived from the original **O, IO, OO** or **PO** and may also include a **J** in place of the original **S**.) But not all combinations are possible. We can see the range of verb valency structures found in English in table 7.1.

Since noun phrases and adjective phrases can appear as part of verb valency, nominal and adjectival complements may become part of the elaboration of a verb, though at a secondary level; in other words the noun phrase or adjective phrase is "licensed" by the verb, and then in turn has the power to "license" its own complementation. This means, for instance, that adjective phrases like the following may appear as a descriptor (= predicative complement) after copular verbs, like *be* or *seem*: *able to speak French, capable of speaking French, confident that she could speak French; a tendency to speak French, a habit of speaking French, the fact that she spoke French.*

7   Obligatory and Optional Elaborators

Although such functional categories as object are necessary to define a particular verb elaboration structure, this does not mean that they are always obligatorily present. For instance, we need to make a distinction between intransitive verbs (which do not permit an object) and those transitive verbs that may leave out their object. There is moreover more than one kind of optionality. But, starting

Table 7.1 English verb valency patterns

---

1 Without an embedded clause

Structure	Example of structure
MONO-VALENT	
S + v	*The child rested.*
S$_\varnothing$ + v	*It rained.*
BI-VALENT	
S + v + O	*The child saw me.*
S + v + O$_\varnothing$	*The child enjoyed itself.*
S + v + Ö	*The child resembled me.*
S + v + ND	*The child became a fanatic.*
S + v + AD	*The child became very angry.*
S$_\varnothing$ + v + AD	*It was/got late.*
S + v + PD	*The child got into a bad mood.*
S + v + PO	*The child relied on me.*
S + v + PÖ	*The child differed from me.*
S + v + AE	*The child sat in front of me.*
S + v + L	*The child broke down.*
TRI-VALENT	
S + v + O + IO	*The child gave the toy to me.*
	The child gave me the toy.
S + v + O + OO	*She envied the child (for) her beauty.*
S + v + IÖ + Ö	*The child cost me ninety euros.*
S + v + O + ND	*The child made me a fanatic.*
S + v + O + AD	*The child made/got me very angry.*
S + v + O + PD	*The child got me into a bad mood.*
S + v + O + PO	*The child kept an eye on me.*
S + v + O + PÖ	*The child deprived me of sleep.*
S + v + O$_\varnothing$ + PÖ	*The child absented him/herself from school.*
S + v + O + AE	*The child led me upstairs.*
S + v + O + L	*The child answered me back.*
S + v + O$_\varnothing$ + L	*The child pulled itself together.*
S + v + L + PO	*The child put up with me.*
S + v + L + PÖ	*The child stood out from the others.*
S + v + L + AE	*The child came over badly.*
S + v + PO + PÖ	*The child applied to me for permission.*
S + v + PO + PD	*The child looked on me as an expert.*
S + v + ND + PÖ	*The child looked a genius to me.*
S + v + AD + PÖ	*The child looked brilliant to me.*

Table 7.1 (*continued*)

Structure	Example of Structure
TETRA-VALENT	
S + v + O + IO + PÖ	*The child paid a large sum to me for it.*
	The child paid me a large sum for it.
S + v + O + AE + AE	*The child moved it from here to there.*
S + v + O + L + AE	*The child put the message over well.*
S + v + O + L + IO	*The child typed out the article for me.*
S + v + O + L + PÖ	*The child played me off against them.*

2   *With an embedded clause*

Structure	Example of structure
S + v + {I}^{O}	*The child offered to vanish.*
S + v + {G}^{O}	*The child enjoyed vanishing.*
S + v + {S-I}^{O}	*The child caused me to vanish.*
S + v + {f-S-I}^{O}	*The child arranged for me to vanish.*
S + v + {S-G}^{O}	*The child criticized me/my vanishing.*
S + v + P + {S-G}^{O}	*The child objected to me/my vanishing.*
S + v + O + {I}^{PÖ}	*The child persuaded me to vanish.*
S + v + O + {P-G}^{PÖ}	*The child dissuaded me from vanishing.*
S + v + O + {I°/G}^{AD}	*The child saw me vanish/vanishing.*
S + v + {F}^{O}	*The child said that I had vanished.*
S$_ø$ + v + {F}^{O}	*It seemed that the child had vanished.*
{S-}^{S} + v + [-I]	*The child seemed to vanish.*

with obligatory elaborators, it is easy to find examples of verbs that require their object to be present on all occasions, e.g. *catch, damage, dread, find*. This means that sequences such as **Mary caught* are normally unacceptable as sentences in any context. We can describe the object (or prepositional object, etc.) of such verbs as OBLIGATORILY PRESENT and speak of PROHIBITED OMISSION.

Turning to optional elaborators, we find one kind of omissibility of objects with the verb *watch*. Sentences like *Mary's watching* do occur, but only when the speaker has reasons for believing that the listener will be able to identify the object being watched, e.g. *us, that television program*. Whenever verbs like *watch* (or *choose, enter, hurt, pull*, etc.) are used without an overt object, the listener feels obliged to reconstruct a definite specific one from the surrounding linguistic and situational context. The verbs in question have a DEFINITE object that is prone to CONTEXT-BOUND OMISSION or is ELLIPTABLE.

When, however, the speaker utters a sentence like *Mary's reading*, there is no question of the listener being required to reconstruct the thing being read. The speaker has omitted the object not because it is obvious from the context (though it could be); rather, the speaker sees the thing being read as unimportant or even irrelevant to the message. In practical terms the speaker abstains from mentioning the nature of the object of the verb *read*, and the listener simply ignores it; indeed the verb is being used as though it were intransitive. Verbs which allow their objects to be omitted in a similar way include *clean, dig, draw, paint*. We can say that the verbs in question have an INDEFINITE object that is prone to CONTEXT-FREE OMISSION or is SUPPRESSIBLE.

There are groups of verbs that have a fuller structure (with an object etc.) and a shorter structure (without one), but where the relationship between them is not just one of (not) including certain information. This is the case, for example, with verbs like *shrug (one's) shoulders, nod (one's head)*. Since verbs like *shrug* and *nod* imply one particular kind of object, the inclusion of that object adds no extra information. The object can in such cases be regarded as a REDUNDANT object that is prone to ECONOMICAL DELETION or is DISPENSABLE. Some verbs allow omission of their object when it is understood as being co-referential with the subject: verbs like *dress, scratch* or *shave* behave like this, and can be said to be prone to REFLEXIVE DROPPING. Yet other verbs, whenever they appear with a plural (coordinated) subject, allow omission of their object when it is understood as involving a two-way relationship with the subject, so that the subject performs the action on the object and the latter reciprocates: verbs like *meet, kiss*, and (in one use) *marry* behave like this, and can be said to involve RECIPROCAL DROPPING.

Some verbs are used in two different valency structures that have a more complex relationship that goes beyond merely leaving out an object etc. These are verbs denoting a change in state or position, such as *bend, cook, fill* or *roll*, which either mention the patient alone in subject position, or alternatively mention both the patient in object position and the agent-causer in subject position, as in:

(83)   The fork bent.

(84)   The child bent the fork.

These sentences illustrate two different verb elaboration structures for the same verb, and we could say that such verbs are grammatically versatile (in the same way that a single noun can have countable and uncountable uses). But these are not exceptional irregular facts about particular words; there are indeed hundreds of verbs in English which allow these two structures with precisely the same semantic relationship. They have been variously described as "ergative" (because ergative-nominative languages would use the ergative case for the agent, but the nominative for the patient in both structures) or "middle" (because the intransitive structure exemplified by (83) has a crypto-reflexive sense, like the Ancient Greek middle voice). This ERGATIVE-MIDDLE set of verbs thus needs to be recognized as a separate verb class, which participates in two different verb valency structures, giving them a kind of compound or multiple valency. As we noted in examples (24)–(25) and (31)–(32) above concerning the verbs *improve* and *deteriorate*, not all intransitive verbs with this change of state/position meaning allow both structures: while *bend* and *improve* are ergative-middle, *lessen* and *deteriorate* are intransitive only, and *find* and *destroy* are transitive only, cf.:

(85)   The child found/destroyed the book.

(86)   *The book found/destroyed.

Some transitive verbs allow a middle use with certain adverbs, where the meaning is something like 'allow itself to be *v*-ed easily,' as in:

(87)   The book sold easily/quickly.

but this can be regarded as a special construction. Discussion of these verbs takes us into the general question of the precise relationship between the different structures in which a verb can occur.

8   Transformationally and Quasi-transformationally Related Structures

The possibility of a verb being associated with two different structures can arise through that verb having a kind of double potential (as in the case of ergative-middle verbs). It can also arise because a grammatical structure has two different formats or two different structures have a precise transformational relationship.

The case of indirect objects was discussed above for examples (36) and (39), reproduced for convenience as (88) and (89):

(88)   The teacher gave some books to the child.

(88′)   The teacher gave the child some books.

(89)   The grandparents bought the bicycle for the child.

(89′)   The grandparents bought the child the bicycle.

We found that true indirect object verbs regularly occur with both patterns, although the prepositionless pattern is excluded when the indirect object is an unstresssed definite pronoun. For the reasons given there it is reasonable to regard (88′) and (89′) as an alternative format for this construction. A prepositionless construction without any change in word order is also possible in the case of the construction of a verb with object and oblique object, as in:

(90)   The teacher envied the pupil (for) her good memory.

Again two formats are possible for the same construction but this time with less of a difference between them.

We now come to the important question of the analysis of passive sentences, for which the following examples will be relevant:

(91)   The child saw the mouse.

(92)   The mouse was seen by the child.

(93)   The mouse came into view.

Judging by the criteria proposed for examples (43) and (44) earlier, *the child* is the subject in (91), while *the mouse* is the surface subject in (92) and (93). When comparing active and passive sentences like (91) and (92), however, we noted a correspondence on the one hand between the passive subject and the active object (*the mouse*) and on the other between the passive "perject" and the active subject (*(by) the child*). This has prompted grammarians to speak of "deep," "underlying" or "valency" subjects and objects when referring to the correlates of passive functions in the more basic active structures. Although these more abstract categories may seem to be just a matter of the semantic role of the elements, a comparison of the surface subject (*the mouse*) in (92) and (93) shows that they have the same semantic role ('stimulus') but that at the deeper valency level the former is an object (of the verb *see*) while the latter is a subject (of the verb *come*).

Since the "deep" valency level of description is independent of both the surface level and the semantic level, it is possible to find contrasting sets like:

(94)   The public enjoyed the speech.

(95)   The speech was enjoyed by the public.

(96)   The speech pleased the public.

(97)   The public was pleased by the speech.

The noun phrases and preposition phrases of the sentences can be described as follows:

(94)   SURFACE SUBJECT   +   SURFACE OBJECT
       valency subject   +   valency object
       'experiencer'   +   'stimulus'

(95)   SURFACE SUBJECT   +   SURFACE PERJECT
      valency object   +   valency subject
      'stimulus'   +   'experiencer'

(96)   SURFACE SUBJECT   +   SURFACE OBJECT
      valency subject   +   valency object
      'stimulus'   +   'experiencer'

(97)   SURFACE SUBJECT   +   SURFACE PERJECT
      valency object   +   valency subject
      'experiencer'   +   'stimulus.'

But it is important to emphasize that, although the connections between semantic roles and valency functions are to some extent arbitrary, the correspondences involved in the transformational relationship between active and passive structures are perfectly regular ones. Leaving aside the semantic roles (which in any case are determined by the individual lexical verb), we could represent the relationship between active and passive sentences by marking surface functions with the capital letters used already (**S, O,** etc.) and by attaching to every superficial descriptive category an oblique stroke (or "slash") followed by a lower case letter indicating the corresponding element in an equivalent active simple verb structure. Elements which have no correlate in the simple verb structure being labelled as ... /ø. Sentences (94) and (95) could thus be represented at a valency level as (96) and (97) respectively:

(98)   The public enjoyed the speech.

    S/s + V/v + O/o

(99)   The speech was enjoyed by the public.

    S/o + *be*/**ø + V-***en*/**v + J/s**

Structures with other regular transformational relationships, such as so-called *tough*-movement sentences, could be represented in a similar way:

(100)   The speech was easy to like.

    S/o + *be*/**ø + AD/ø + I/v (Ø/s)**

This brings out the fact that the adjective *easy* requires the subject of which it is predicated to be interpreted as the object of the verb in its complementation.

As well as regular transformational relations, languages seem to have less regular quasi-transformational patterns of correspondence. Of special relevance to us here are what are referred to in Allerton (2002) as "stretched verb constructions." We can begin with (99), which is semantically quite close to (98), but structurally might possibly be represented as follows:

(101)   The public derived enjoyment from the speech.

$$S/s + V/ø + O/v + PÖ/o$$

The collocation *derive enjoyment from* has a meaning that is not essentially different from *enjoy*, so that semantically such correspondences obtain. But grammatically, even at the deeper valency level, *derive* is a verb and *enjoyment* is a noun. Such quasi-transformational relationships between "kindred" constructions are therefore semantic in nature but need to be recognized, because they often give the speaker a wide choice between different verbal construction types to express broadly the same meaning, as these examples show:

(102)   The child helped the teacher.

(103)   The child was helpful to the teacher.

(104)   The child was a helper of the teacher.

(105)   The child was a help to the teacher.

(106)   The child was of help to the teacher.

(107)   The child came to the help of the teacher.

(108)   The child gave help to the teacher.

Choosing a particular structure out of such a possible range clearly affects the grammatical structure of the whole sentence, but what all stretched verb constructions share is the way the process of helping is signaled by an adjective or noun rather than the verb.[18] The verb in such constructions has been variously described as a *light* or *thin* verb, or as a *support* verb, because its semantic contribution is so weak.

Verbs can thus range in their semantic contribution from full lexical verbs through light verbs to auxiliary verbs. But the main lexical verb lies at the heart of a sentence and determines its basic network of relationships in that sentence. As Humpty Dumpty puts it when talking to Alice (in *Through the looking glass*) about words:

They've a temper some of them – particularly verbs, they're the proudest – adjectives you can do anything with, but not verbs.

This is what Tesnière (1959: 15), one of the founders of dependency and valency grammar, meant by referring to the main verb as the "node of nodes" ('nœud des nœuds'), cf. also Allerton (1995). Using another metaphor, we could say that a verb is like a planet with or without a number of satellites.

NOTES

I would like to express sincere thanks to Bas Aarts, Geoffrey Leech and an anonymous reader for their constructive criticism and helpful comments.

1   On the definition of word classes, see Aarts and Haegeman, ch. 6, this volume.

2   Some linguists, following Lyons (1977: 483ff), use the term "situation" as an overall term, but this has the disadvantage of suggesting a state rather than an event.

3   An exception is to be found in the genre of commentaries, e.g. *Smith thrusts his arms out in despair at missing that one.*

4   In this account the term ELABORATOR in the sense of 'phrase which is selected by the individual verb to elaborate its meaning' will be preferred to "argument," which (apart from its ambiguity) suggests a limitation to noun-like elements.

5   Sentences of a non-standard format can be verbless; they include elliptical sentences (e.g. *Probably*) and minor sentences following arthaic patterns (e.g. *The more the merrier, Down with strong drink!*).

6   In a more abstract analysis such word sequences can be seen as a combination of lexical verb with one or more auxiliaries in the abstract "formatives": thus *had stumbled* can be seen as *stumble* + PAST + *has* − -*ed/-en*.

7   A more recent suggestion, stemming from S. P. Abney is the so-called "DP analysis," i.e. that a noun phrase has a determiner (rather than a noun) as its "head" (or core element) so that it should rather be called a determiner phrase (= DP).

8   The more neutral term "stroke" is preferred to the commonly used term "achievement," because the latter too strongly suggests an eventuality aimed at by an agent, something that clearly does not apply to examples like *blink, have an accident.*

9   See discussion of examples (56)–(59) below.

10   In some regional forms of English, in northern England for instance, a prepositionless pronominal indirect object is found after the direct object (as in *He gave it me*). This can be seen as further evidence of the differentness of indirect object verbs. See also the discussion of example (89') below.

11   This term has the disadvantage of apparently referring to any nominal element in the predicate (e.g. objects) but it does not.

12   It is a complex matter distinguishing descriptors (following an object) from adverbials of the subject adjunct type (Aarts 1995), but sequences like *eat the vegetables raw* ('eat the vegetables when they are raw') need to treated as having an adjective phrase in the role of optional free adverbial rather than an elaborator of the verb.

13   The three different types of objoid can be termed "match" (as with *resemble, match,* etc.), "measure" (as with *weigh, cost,* etc.) and "possession" (as with *have, lack,* etc.). The identificatory use of *be* discussed above (as in *be the author of the book*) can be regarded as involving a match objoid.

14   Some grammarians depart from the traditional view of indirect objects by insisting that only the form without a preposition, as in (36'), is a true indirect object. They then have to say that *give* and all verbs like it (*lend, offer, send, show,* etc.) can take either an indirect object or a

prepositional object (although the two patterns are synonymous), while verbs like *return, demonstrate, explain* can only take a prepositional object. At least for the sake of non-native learners (who notoriously confuse them) it seems useful to keep the two verb types apart with different labels for their elaborators.

15 See also below, p. 168.

16 In traditional grammar and in the approach of some modern grammarians this is tantamount to saying that the noun phrase can be construed as accusative or genitive.

17 One problem with this analysis is that it seems to assume that the embedded clause *the pianist to entertain the audience* would naturally occur in a position after the main verb *happen*, which is not the typical position for a subject, even when it is a clause. Another approach is to see (79) as involving a kind of compound verb *happen to see*, in which *see* is the semantic head, but *happen* is the syntactic main verb.

18 This change in the expression of the verbal eventuality so that it appears not as a verb but as a noun or adjective can be seen as a grammatical kind of methaphor; see Simon-Vandenbergen et al. (2003).

FURTHER READING

Aarts and Meyer (1995); Allerton (1982); Allerton (2002); Bache (1997); Dahl (1985); Frawley (1992); Huddleston and Pullum (2002); Quirk et al. (1985).

REFERENCES

Aarts, B. (1992) *Small clauses in English: the non-verbal types.* Berlin and New York: Mouton de Gruyter.

Aarts, B. (1995) Secondary predicates in English. In Aarts and Meyer 1995: 75–101.

Aarts, B. and Meyer, C. F. (1995) *The verb in contemporary English: theory and description.* Cambridge: Cambridge University Press.

Allerton, D. J. (1978) Generating indirect object constructions in English. *Journal of Linguistics* 14, 21–33.

Allerton, D. J. (1982) *Valency and the English verb.* London: Academic Press.

Allerton, D. J. (1995) La délimitation des "régissants" et des "subordonnés" chez Tesnière. In Madray-Lesigne, F. and Richard-Zappella, J. (eds.) *Lucien Tesnière aujourd'hui.* Louvain and Paris: Peeters, 249–55.

Allerton, D. J. (2002) *Stretched verb constructions in English.* London: Routledge.

Bache, C. (1997) *The study of aspect, tense and action: towards a theory of the semantics of grammatical analysis,* 2nd edn. (1st edn. 1995). Frankfurt: Lang.

Bolinger, D. L. (1977) *Meaning and form.* London: Longman.

Bresnan, J. (2001) *Lexical-functional syntax.* Oxford: Blackwell.

Brown, E. K. and Miller, J. E. (1996) *Concise encyclopedia of syntactic theories.* Oxford: Pergamon.

Chomsky, N. (1965) *Aspects of the theory of syntax.* Cambridge, MA: MIT Press.

Dahl, Ö. (1985) *Tense and aspect systems.* Oxford: Blackwell.

Dik, S. (1978) *Functional grammar.* Amsterdam: North Holland.

Dowty, D. (1979) *Word meaning and Montague grammar.* Dordrecht: Reidel.

Egg, M. (1995) The intergressive as a new category of verbal Aktionsart. *Journal of Semantics* 12, 311–56.

Fillmore, C. J. (1977) The case for case re-opened. In Cole, P. and Sadock, J. M. (eds.), *Syntax and semantics: grammatical relations.* New York: Academic Press, 59–81.

Frawley, W. (1992) *Linguistic semantics.* Hillsdale, NJ: Lawrence Erlbaum.

Fries, C. C. (1952) *The structure of English: an introduction to the structure of English sentences.* New York: Harcourt Brace.

Givon, T. (1984) Direct object and dative shifting: semantic and pragmatic case. In F. Plank (ed.), *Objects: towards a theory of grammatical relations.* London: Academic Press, 151–82.

Hale, K. and Keyser, S. J. (2002) *Prologomenon to a theory of argument structure.* Cambridge, MA: MIT Press.

Halliday, M. A. K. (2003) *An introduction to functional grammar,* 3rd edn. London: Edward Arnold (1st edn. 1985).

Harris, Z. S. (1951) *Methods in structural linguistics.* Chicago: University of Chicago Press.

Horn, G. M. (1983) *Lexical-functional grammar.* Berlin: Mouton de Gruyter.

Hornby, A. P. (1954) *A guide to patterns and usage in English.* London: Oxford University Press.

Huddleston, R. and Pullum, G. K. (2002) *The Cambridge grammar of the English language.* Cambridge: Cambridge University Press.

Hudson, R. A. (1992) So-called "double objects" and grammatical relations. *Language* 68, 251–76.

Jespersen, O. (1933) *Essentials of English grammar.* London: Allen and Unwin.

Kayne, R. (1984) *Connectedness and binary branching.* Dordrecht: Foris.

Larson, R. (1988) On the double object construction. *Linguistic Inquiry* 19, 335–91.

Lyons, J. (1977) *Semantics.* Cambridge: Cambridge University Press.

Palmer, H. E. (1939) *A grammar of spoken English,* 2nd edn. (1st edn. 1924). Cambridge: Heffer.

Paul, H. (1909) *Prinzipien der Sprachgeschichte.* Halle: Niemeyer.

Perlmutter, D. M. (ed.) (1983) *Studies in relational grammar.* Chicago: University of Chicago Press.

Pollard, C. and Sag, I. A. (1994) *Head-driven phrase structure grammar.* Chicago: University of Chicago Press and Stanford: CSLI Publications.

Quirk, R., Greenbaum, S., Leech, G., and Svartvik, J. (1972) *A grammar of contemporary English.* London: Longman.

Quirk, R., Greenbaum, S., Leech, G., and Svartvik, J. (1985) *A comprehensive grammar of the English language.* London: Longman.

Simon-Vandenbergen, A. M., Taverniers, M., and Ravelli, Louise (eds.) (2003) *Grammatical metaphor: views from systemic functional linguistics.* Amsterdam: John Benjamins.

Schlesinger, I. M. (1995) 'On the semantics of the object.' In: Aarts and Meyer 1995: 54–74.

Starosta, S. (1988) *The case of Lexicase.* London: Pinter.

Tesnière, L. (1959) *Éléments de syntaxe structurale.* Paris: Klincksieck.

Vendler, Z. (1967) Verbs and times. In Vendler, Z., *Linguistics in philosophy.* New York: Cornell University Press, 97–121.

8   Clause Types

PETER COLLINS

1   Introduction

Clause type is the technical term referring to the syntactic categories of declarative, interrogative, imperative and exclamative, each of which is associated with a characteristic use, as illustrated below:

Clause type	Example	Characteristic meaning/use
Declarative	*She is sensible*	Statement
Interrogative	*Is she sensible?*	Question
Imperative	*Be sensible!*	Directive
Exclamative	*How sensible she is!*	Exclamatory statement

Declarative is the 'unmarked' or 'default' type, lacking the distinctive properties of the other types (such as subject-auxiliary inversion in the case of interrogatives) Directive is a general term covering orders, requests, instructions, and the like (the term *command*, as commonly used in traditional grammars, being too specific to capture the range of uses associated with imperative clauses). Following Huddleston (1984: 352) *exclamatory statement* is preferred over the more familiar term *exclamation*, which fails to distinguish the characteristic use of exclamative clauses from the exclamatory realization of other use categories (e.g. *Who the hell are you?* as an exclamatory question representing the interrogative clause type).

Some grammars (e.g. Quirk et al. 1985) use the term *sentence type*, but the grammatical system in question strictly belongs to the clause rather than the sentence. One piece of evidence for this claim is that the clause type categories may be applied, except for imperatives, to subordinate clauses as well as to main clauses (the underlined clauses in *I suppose <u>that she is sensible</u>, I doubt <u>whether she is sensible</u>, I realize <u>how sensible she is</u>* are respectively declarative, interrogative, and exclamative). Another piece of evidence is the impossibility of applying a type category to a whole sentence in which there is a coordination of clauses of different types (as in *Have another glass of champagne, or would* *you prefer wine?* [imperative + interrogative]; *What an excellent meal we had, and it only cost $30!* [exclamative + declarative]).

The syntactic categories of clause type represent the mutually exclusive terms of a grammatical system. This claim is not undermined by the possibility of sentences ambiguous between an exclamative and interrogative structure (e.g. *What excellent products are sold there*), insofar as such sentences can only be interpreted as one or the other in a particular context. It is the criterion of mutual exclusiveness that obliges us to exclude echo questions from the clause type system. Echo questions are formed by questioning some element of what the previous speaker has said (which McCawley 1988: 720 calls the *stimulus*), they may be overlaid on any of the clause types and are not mutually exclusive with them. For instance the echo question uttered by Speaker B in the following exchange *A It's very annoying. B It's very what?* belongs to the declarative clause type, that in *A Go to Kakadu. B Go where?* to the imperative clause type.

The four-term system of clause type presented above is that found standardly in descriptive grammars of English (e.g. Quirk et al. 1985; Biber et al. 1999) However Huddleston (1994) argues for a five-term system in which *closed interrogatives* (e.g. *Is she sensible?*) are distinguished from *open interrogatives* (e.g. *How sensible is she?*) on the grounds that, despite their being similarly used to ask questions, they have distinct syntactic properties. Whereas closed interrogatives always exhibit subject-auxiliary inversion, this is merely a secondary feature of open interrogatives, triggered by the fronting of a non-subject interrogative phrase. The most distinctive syntactic property of open interrogatives is thus not subject-auxiliary inversion, as in closed interrogatives, but, rather, the invariable presence of an interrogative phrase involving a *wh*-word. The presence of inversion would not in any case be sufficient grounds to treat closed and open interrogatives as subclasses of a single larger class, because inversion is found in various other constructions as well (such as declaratives with a fronted negative e.g. *Never had I seen such a spectacle!* and some exclamatives e.g. *How hard have I tried to please them!*). It follows that the interrogatives *Is Tom the treasurer?* and *Who is the treasurer?* do not share any syntactic property which differentiates them from the declarative *Tom is the treasurer.*

2   Syntax vs. Semantics vs. Pragmatics

The clause type system raises vexing issues concerning the interrelationship between syntax and semantics/pragmatics. Consider the relationship between the declarative clause *Tina is sensible* and the interrogative *Is Tina sensible?*. Semantically, they are partly alike and partly different. What they share is a common propositional meaning: both express the proposition 'Tina is sensible.' Where they differ most is in their non-propositional meaning, more specifically in their illocutionary force: a typical utterance of the declarative would be a statement, used to assert the proposition, but a typical utterance of the interrogative would be a question, used to question the proposition. Statements, questions, and directives are in essence pragmatic categories. Each represents a very general class of speech acts which embraces a range of more specific categories; e.g. assertions and predictions as types of statement; orders, requests and invitations as types of directive (see Huddleston and Pullum 2002: 858; Quirk et al. 1985: 804). Beyond these there are a vast number of illocutionary categories that are not subsumed under any of the general categories, such as promises, congratulations, bets, wishes, and the like.

While clause type is an important determinant of illocutionary force, it is not the only one. For instance, if a declarative such as *Maria is Spanish* is uttered with rising intonation, this will typically have the effect of making what would otherwise be a statement into a question. One special device of relevance here is the *performative* use of verbs that denote illocutionary acts (e.g. *admit, swear, urge, apologize, warn, suggest*); that is, their use to effect the performance of the very acts they denote. Performative utterances are characterized by a precise specification of illocutionary force, which is identified in their propositional content (thus the warning force of *I warn you to leave* is identifiable in the proposition it expresses, but the statement force of *I warned you to leave* is not similarly identified in its propositional content).

Unlike the syntactic categories of clause type, illocutionary categories are not mutually exclusive. Where an utterance has more than one illocutionary force, as Huddleston and Pullum (2002: 859) observe, one will be primary or salient and the other secondary. For example, in a typical utterance of *I advise you to make an appointment* the advice force is primary and the statement force secondary (the statement simply being the means by which the advice is issued), as reflected in the greater likelihood that the utterance would be reported as *You advised me to make an appointment* rather than *You said you advised me to make an appointment*).

When the illocutionary force of an utterance is different from that normally conveyed by the clause type concerned, we have what is generally referred to as an *indirect speech act* (e.g. a typical utterance of the imperative clause *Have a nice holiday!* will have the (indirect) force of a wish rather than a directive, insofar as having a nice holiday is not normally considered to be within the addressee's control; similarly, the closed interrogative *Do you have a cigarette?* is often used as an indirect request for a cigarette, and in this case the question about the addressee's possession of a cigarette is of secondary importance to the indirect request. Indirect speech acts have varying degrees of indirectness. Compare for instance a mother's *It's getting late*, uttered with the intention of directing her child to go to bed, where there is a considerable discrepancy between the indirect directive meaning 'Go to bed' and the proposition directly expressed by the declarative 'It is getting late,' with a job applicant's *I wish to apply for the position advertised*, where the applicant will be readily understood to have performed the illocutionary act of applying for the position in question, rather than merely wishing to do so, insofar as the wish is satisfied simply by the submission of the application.

Indirect illocutionary force may be signaled in various ways. For instance the exclamatory statement force of the interrogative *Gee, is he strong!* is reinforced by the non-propositional marker *gee* and by the likely selection of a falling intonation terminal, rather than the rising terminal typically associated with closed questions). Often used as an indicator of indirect illocutionary force is the conventional use of certain expressions, e.g. the use of the modal *can* and the adverb *please* in a request such as *Can you pass the salt, please?*, where by contrast *Are you able to pass the salt?* is unlikely (unless there is actual doubt as to the addressee's ability to perform the desired activity).

3   A Semantic Level?

In some grammatical accounts of clause type it is suggested that a distinction between the three levels of syntax, semantics, and pragmatics can be consistently maintained. For instance Quirk et al. (1985: 804) describe the four general illocutionary categories presented above (statements, questions, directives, and exclamative statements) as 'semantic' classes, distinguishing them from the more specific 'pragmatic' categories associated with each. Their justification is the possibility of mismatches occurring both between the semantic and pragmatic categories (what Quirk et al. define as indirect speech acts) and between the syntactic and semantic categories. An example of the former is said to be *I think you'd better leave at once* – a (pragmatic) request made by a (semantic) statement rather than by a (semantic) directive; an example of the latter is *I'd love a cup of tea* – a (semantic) directive in the form of a (syntactic) declarative rather than in the form of a (syntactic) imperative. The problem with this, as pointed out by Huddleston (1988), is that both types of mismatch are standardly treated in the pragmatics literature as types of indirect speech act, and if there is no principled basis for distinguishing the two types of mismatch then neither is there for distinguishing the semantic and pragmatic levels. There is however one important qualification to be made here: as demonstrated by Huddleston (1994) it is necessary, in the case of interrogative clauses, to distinguish between these levels (which he does by invoking a distinction between the semantic concept of *question* and the pragmatic concept of *inquiry*: see section 5 below).

4   Declaratives and Statements

Declarative is, as noted above, the unmarked clause type, with respect to which the other three syntactic classes can be defined in terms of their special properties. A declarative is typically used to make a statement, an utterance which expresses a proposition assessable as true or false. However there are (as Huddleston 1984: 358 observes) at least three types of linguistic factor that may disrupt this correlation between declarative clause type and the illocutionary force of statement. Firstly, when illocutionary verbs such as *forgive, promise, testify, offer,* and *congratulate* are used performatively the statement force is relegated to secondary status. Thus when the declarative clause

I congratulate you is used by the speaker to congratulate the addressee, it has the primary illocutionary force of a congratulation rather than a statement (as reflected in the likelihood of its being reported as *You congratulated me* rather than *You said you congratulated me*). Secondly, rising intonation (or a question-mark in writing) can be used to signal that a declarative is being used as a question rather than a statement (albeit a conducive question: *You've seen the Grand Canyon?* predisposes the speaker to accept a positive answer, whereas *Have you seen the Grand Canyon?* is neutral). That *You've seen the Grand Canyon?* is in fact syntactically declarative rather than interrogative is suggested by its resistance to non-affirmative items such as *ever* (**You've ever seen the Grand Canyon?*; compare *Have you ever seen the Grand Canyon?*). Thirdly, a declarative can be endowed with indirect directive force by various additional means, such as the selection of a modal used deontically (e.g. *You will/must be here by five*), or an expression of the speaker's wishes (e.g. *I would like you to accompany me*).

5   Interrogatives, Questions, and Inquiries

The distinguishing property of questions, as a semantic category, is their capacity to define a set of answers. For example for the question *Did you enjoy it?* there are just two possible answers, one positive and one negative (each expressible in a variety of ways, but each of these understood to constitute the same answer: *I enjoyed it*; *I did*; *Yes*; *Yes I did*, etc.; versus *I did not enjoy it*; *I didn't*; *No*; *No I didn't*, etc.). Notice that it is possible to make a response to a question (where *response* is a pragmatic category) without providing an answer to it. For instance, if upon being asked *Did you enjoy it?* I reply *Maybe* or *It's none of your business* then my response is one that fails to answer the question. Even a response such as *You know that I did* fails to qualify technically as an answer, because even though it entails *Yes* it is not logically equivalent to *Yes*.

Pragmatically, questions are prototypically associated with the illocutionary category of inquiry (as in the question *What's your name?* asked by a speaker who does not know the addressee's name and wants to know what it is). However not all questions are used to make inquiries. For example a teacher who asks her students *What was the name of Australia's first Prime Minister?* will presumably know the answer to the question and be seeking to test the students' knowledge. Or a question such as *Did they?*, prompted by the observation *They really enjoyed the concert*, is not used to make an inquiry (insofar as the answer has already been provided), but rather merely to provide an attentive response.

Questions may be cross-classified on a number of dimensions. The most widely known is that based on the different types of possible answers: between what are commonly called *yes/no-questions*, *alternative questions*, and *wh-questions*.

(1) Yes/no-questions have two possible answers, positive and negative. The question itself provides the propositional content for one of the answers, while the other answer has the reverse polarity (e.g. Q *Has he left?* A *He has left* or *He hasn't left*; Q *Hasn't he left?* A *He hasn't left* or *He has left*).

(2) Alternative questions have a set of alternatives as answers which can be derived directly from the question, the propositional content being logically equivalent to a disjunction of propositions. For example the answers to the alternative question *Is his light on or off?*, namely *His light is on* and *His light is off*, correspond to each of the disjoined propositions in "His light is on or his light is off." More than two alternatives may be expressed: *Would you like tea, coffee, or neither?* Syntactically, alternative questions are distinguished by the obligatory presence of *or* (which cannot be paired with *either*) Whereas yes/no-questions usually have the form of a (single) closed interrogative clause, alternative questions may have the form of one or more than one interrogative clause (e.g. *Is his light on or off?* Versus *Is his light on or is it off?*).

Yes/no-questions are sometimes analyzed (e.g. by Karttunen 1977: 5) as being derived from alternative questions. However, while an alternative question such as *Is he coming or not?* may be logically equivalent to the yes/no-question *Is he coming?*, they differ in that the propositional content of both the positive and negative answers is expressed in the former, but not the latter. And, as noted by Huddleston (1994: 417) there are distributional differences involving embedding constructions (compare *I doubt whether he is coming* versus **I doubt whether he is coming or not*; **I'm going, whether he is coming* versus *I'm going, whether he is coming or not*). Pragmatically, too, the alternative question differs from the yes/no-question in foregrounding the exhaustiveness of the alternatives, in a way that may give rise to an emotive overlay of aggressiveness or impatience.

(3) *Wh*-questions (sometimes also referred to as *special*, *open*, and *variable* questions) express a proposition containing a variable, the answer being arrived at by the substitution of a value for the variable. Thus the propositional content of *What did she buy?* can be represented as 'You bought x' and the answers are arrived at by supplying different values for the variable x: *She bought a dress*; *She bought a coat*; *She bought a hat*; etc. *wh*-questions may be multi-variable, as in *Who wants what?* and *Who gave what to whom?* (for a detailed account see Comorovski 1996, who labels these *multiple constituent questions*).

Wh-questions have the form of an open interrogative clause in which a non-subject interrogative phrase is usually fronted, triggering subject-auxiliary inversion. There has been extensive discussion of this process in the generative literature, where it is generally referred to as *wh-movement*. Amongst other things, it has been noted that there are restrictions on the application of *wh*-movement where the interrogative word originates from a position within an embedded clause: the embedded clause cannot, for instance be a relative clause (compare *He noticed a woman who was painting something* and **What did he notice a woman who was painting?*). It is possible for an open interrogative clause to be reduced to the interrogative phrase alone (e.g. *A We're going on a* *holiday. B When?*), or the interrogative phrase plus a stranded preposition (e.g. *A Loosen the nuts first. B What with?*).

Limitations of space here preclude detailed discussion of the range of additional question types in English which any comprehensive account must address (see, e.g., Quirk et al. 1985: 810–16, 825–6; Huddleston and Pullum 2002: 876–97). These include: *deliberative* questions, which differ from typical information-oriented questions in that answers to them have the force of directives rather than statements (e.g. *Shall we follow you?*; *Where will I put it?*); *conducive* questions, which are biased towards one particular answer (e.g. *Doesn't he look handsome?* is biased towards the positive answer *He looks handsome*); and questions with interrogative tags, where the tags are formed via reduction of a closed interrogative clause, and typically change both the polarity and illocutionary force of the utterance (e.g. *She's very tall, isn't she?*; *She isn't very tall, is she?*).

Let us, finally, revisit the issue of distinguishing three levels in the analysis of questions. It is immediately apparent that there cannot be an exact correspondence between the syntactic and semantic levels, insofar as we have identified two clause types – closed and open interrogatives – at the syntactic level, but three question types at the semantic level. One category involving a syntactic–semantic mismatch to which reference has already been made, is that of so-called *declarative questions* (i.e. yes/no-questions or alternative questions with declarative syntax where the question meaning is signaled via prosody or punctuation, as in *He has left?* and *You're physically unable to help, or you're simply feeling off colour?*). Another, noted by Morgan (1978) and Huddleston (1994), is that of conventionalized expressions whose original question meaning has been lost in the process of developing a new force. For example a salutation such as *How do you do* and a rebuke such as *How dare you interrupt me* no longer serve to define a set of answers in English (e.g. *I do well; I dare bravely*). Yet another category is the echo-question, a special type of construction – usually yes/no or *wh* – which, as we have already noted, may be associated with any clause type. Consider the range of yes/no-echoes and wh-echoes in the following exchanges: *A He invited Sally. B He invited Sally/who?* [declarative]; *A Did he invite Sally? B Did he invite Sally/who?* [closed interrogative]; *A Who invited Sally? B Who invited Sally/who?* [open interrogative]; *A Invite Sally! B Invite Sally/who?* [imperative]; *A How lucky Sally is! B How lucky Sally/who is?* [exclamative]. In fact, the stimulus may (as noted by McCawley 1988: 722) be non-clausal, which is confirmation that this type of question is not related to clause type (e.g. *A Good morning, Dear! B Good morning who?*).

Non-isomorphism is also in evidence between the semantic and pragmatic levels. While questions are prototypically used with the illocutionary force of inquiries, as we have already noted exceptions are commonplace. A question may be used to indirectly convey, inter alia, a suggestion (e.g. *Why don't you take out a loan?*), a request (e.g. *Could I please borrow your car?*), an exclamatory statement (e.g. *Boy, is he clumsy!*), or an order (e.g. *Will you be quiet?*). Conversely, an inquiry may be conveyed indirectly by a statement (e.g. *I would like to know when the movie starts*), rather than directly by a question (e.g. *When does the movie start?*).

6 Imperatives and Directives

Whereas a statement – the illocutionary act characteristically performed by the utterance of a declarative clause – can be assessed as either true or false, a directive – the illocutionary act characteristically performed by the utterance of an imperative clause – cannot (for discussion of the problems associated with truth-conditional semantic accounts of imperatives, see Aarts 1989). Rather, the proposition expressed by an imperative clause represents a potential situation, one which may or may not be complied with (Davies 1986: 48). In much of the literature, especially the philosophical literature, the term *imperative* is used ambivalently to refer to both clause type and speech act (e.g. Hamblin 1987; Merin 1991). Contemporary reference grammarians (e.g. Quirk et al. 1985; Biber et al. 1999; Huddleston and Pullum 2002) are generally more careful to restrict *imperative* to clause type, and most use *directive* as a technical term covering a broad range of speech acts. These embrace a continuum extending from, at one end, acts for which there is a strong expectation of addressee-compliance (e.g. orders and commands, such as *Get your feet off the coffee table!* and *Surrender your weapons!*, which typically invoke institutionalized authority and may involve penalties for non-compliance) to, at the other end, those where the expectation is weaker (e.g. suggestions and recommendations, such as *Prune your roses in August* and *Have faith in your own abilities*, where compliance is understood to be in the addressee's interests). The set includes requests such as *Please give me a hand with the dishes* (which are like orders in deriving from the speaker's will, but unlike them in offering the addressee the option of not complying), instructions such as *Rotate the filter anti-clockwise* (where compliance will enable a certain goal to be achieved), invitations such as *Call me whenever you like* (where the future action is something that the addressee will not necessarily benefit from, but rather find pleasing), and permission-granting as in *Feel free to take photographs* (which involves the removal by the speaker of potential impediments to the action).

Directives may be conveyed indirectly. For example, interrogatives are commonly used to make requests, where an imperative might otherwise appear too blunt or impolite, especially between non-intimates. Typically the speaker will question the addressee's ability to perform the desired action (e.g. *Can you help me?*; *Would it be possible for you to arrive by 7 p.m.?*), or the addressee's willingness to do so (e.g. *Would you mind helping me with the dishes?*). Declaratives can also have indirect directive force, the indirectness in many such cases not serving the interests of politeness (e.g. *You will/must stop that now*; *Trespassing is forbidden*).

Imperative clauses can be subclassified syntactically into two types: the central kind which Huddleston and Pullum (2002: 924) call *ordinary imperatives*;

and those containing *let* (the special grammaticalized *let*, that is, which can only occur in imperatives of this type), which Huddleston and Pullum call *let-imperatives*, Davies (1986) the *let-construction*. We shall begin by discussing the properties of the major type which, for convenience, will be referred to simply as *imperatives*. These properties are generally considered to demarcate imperatives sharply from the other clause types (Culicover 1976: 152, describes the imperative as "an idiosyncratic construction in most languages," while for Schmerling 1982: 203, imperative clauses are "formally primitive relative to indicative clauses"). However, the case has been made by some that imperatives have largely unexceptional syntax; e.g. by Beukema and Coopmans (1989), working within a Government-Binding framework, and by Potsdam (1998) within the Principles and Parameters framework.

Although imperatives typically occur without a subject, they can normally be interpreted as if they had *you* as subject (as evidenced by the use of 2nd person reflexive pronouns, as in *Behave yourself/*you*, and the appearance of *you* in tags, as in *Behave, will you?*. If a subject is present it will be either *you* (as in *You behave yourself*) or a 3rd person subject representing the addressee(s) or a subset of the addressees (e.g. *Somebody answer that phone*; *Everyone whose surname begins with 'A' stand up*). In negative imperatives the subject will follow *don't*, as in *Don't you be cheeky!*; *Don't anyone stop!*. When *you* is retained as subject in imperatives the motivation is sometimes to signal a contrast, as in *You go this way and I'll go that way*, sometimes to provide an emotive reinforcement of the speaker's authority (e.g. *You watch your manners*; *You just rest your weary legs here*). The distinction between subject and vocative in imperatives, where both functions are optional and addressee-referential, is less pronounced than it is with declaratives. This is especially so in final position (e.g. *Clap your hands everyone*), where the prosodic separation normally associated with a clause-initial vocative may be less determinate.

A distinctive structural property of imperatives is the categorical requirement of the dummy auxiliary *do* in negatives (specifically, those where it is the verb that is negated; e.g. *Don't admit anything* rather than *Admit nothing*) *Do* is not, as it is in other clause types, mutually exclusive here with other auxiliaries (e.g. *Don't be browbeaten*; *Don't be eating when they arrive*). Similarly, in emphatic positive imperatives *do* is required invariably, and not just in the absence of another auxiliary (e.g. *Do come along*).

Imperatives display a strong preference for dynamic VPs (not surprisingly, in that directives prototypically seek some type of action from the addressee). However it is certainly not the case, as some have claimed (e.g. Stockwell et al. 1973) that stative VPs are excluded altogether. As Davies (1986: 13) notes, while *Understand the answer* and *Hope it rains* sound odd, *Just understand this – I never meant to hurt you* and *Stop moaning and hope for the best* are fine. Davies suggests that the differences relate to the possibility of the state or event being within the addressee's control, noting that this criterion also serves to explain the unacceptability of imperatives with a dynamic VP, such as *Inherit a million*. A property of the imperative construction is its capacity to assign an agentive role to the subject where it wouldn't have such a role in the corresponding declarative (e.g. *Sue is polite* describes a state, but *Be polite* enjoins the addressee to engage in a certain type of activity, the exercising of good manners). This property also appears in passive imperatives, where again the construction can assign to the (understood) subject an agentive role that it wouldn't have in a comparable declarative, particularly in negatives (compare *Don't be caught* with *You weren't caught*).

There are some cases where the agentive interpretation normally associated with imperatives is blocked – or at least strongly diminished – by their conventional use as indirect speech acts. For example *Have a nice holiday* and *Enjoy your meal* convey wishes rather than directives, insofar as having a nice holiday and enjoying a meal are situations that would not usually be considered as being under someone's control. Imperatives with a non-agentive interpretation are also found in coordinations such as *Annoy us again and you'll be in trouble*, where the imperative appearing as the first clause has a conditional implication ('If you annoy us again you'll be in trouble'). In fact such clauses display a number of properties not conventionally associated with imperatives: ready tolerance of stative predicates (e.g. *Know the answer and you'll get an A*); compatibility with negative polarity items such as *any* and *ever* (e.g. *Say anything else and there'll be trouble*); the possibility of a non-2nd person subject interpretation (e.g. *Call myself Lord Bowen-James and everyone thinks I'm putting on airs*); and the possibility of a past interpretation (e.g. *Take a holiday in those days and you would be roundly criticized*). Differences such as these have prompted some (e.g. Bolinger 1977) to propose that such clauses be derived from conditional clauses. However there are a number of problems with this suggestion, including the availability of conditional clauses for which there is no corresponding imperative (e.g. *If you are the owner of this dog you are in trouble*; compare **Be the owner of this dog*), and the use of *do* in the formation of verbal negatives (e.g. *Don't be on her doorstep with flowers every week and she gets moody*; compare *If you *don't be/aren't . . .*).

A further distinctive grammatical feature of imperatives is their reliance on a quite different set of grammatical principles in the formation of interrogative tags than those that apply in the case of declarative (and exclamative) clauses. Sadock (1970) suggests that they should be treated as being derived by ellipsis from those interrogatives which convey an indirect directive force matching the direct force of the imperative, what he terms 'whimperatives.' For example the most likely tags for the request *Give me a hand* would be the positive *will you?* and the negative *won't you?* (but further possibilities exist, including *could you?*, *would you?*, *can you?*, and *can't you?*). *Will you?* is construable as an elliptical version of *Will you give me a hand?* and *won't you?* of *Won't you give me a hand?* (both of which may have indirect request force). By contrast, a negative imperative such as *Don't spend too much money* will take only a positive tag (*will you?*), as we might predict from the availability of *Will you not spend too much money?* as a negative directive, but not of *Won't you spend too much money?*. The normal tag for *let's*-imperatives is *shall we?*, as in *Let's have a swim*, *shall we?*. Undoubtedly there is some truth in Schmerling's (1982: 214) claim that imperative tags are "frozen expressions," but the conventionalization is not absolute. As the discussion above suggests, the tag must at least be pragmatically compatible with the imperative clause: *must you?* and *should you?* are never possible (as noted by Bouton 1990).

Imperative clauses are further distinguishable from the other clause types by the unavailability of subordinate counterparts. The subordinate subjunctive clause in mandative constructions of the type *It is essential that you be there* has certain semantic affinities with main clause imperatives. However, as Huddleston (1984: 359) argues, apart from the occurrence of a base form as their first verb, these are grammatically quite different from (main clause) imperatives in that many have no imperative analogue (as can readily be seen if we change the subjunctive clause in the last example into *that he be there* or *that there be consensus*: witness the unacceptability of **He be there* and **There be consensus*). A similar argument could be used to reject infinitival clauses as in *She told him to be there* as subordinate imperatives.

Our final topic in this section is *let*-imperatives, the term we are using for imperatives containing a grammatically and semantically specialized use of *let* that is distinguishable from its normal use with the meaning 'allow.' The latter may be used in ordinary 2nd person imperatives such us *(Somebody) please let us (come) in, won't you?* There are two types of *let*-imperative. In the first type exemplified by *Let's have a party*, *let* is always followed by *us*, which is usually contracted to *'s* and whose reference normally includes the addressee(s) as well as the speaker. These are called *let's constructions* by Clark (1993), and *1st person inclusive let-imperatives* by Huddleston and Pullum (2002). The second type normally has 3rd person reference, as in *Let there be light* and *Let that be a lesson to them*, but also allows 1st and 2nd person reference, as in *Let me/us/ you be punished for this terrible oversight*. These are called *let-constructions* by Clark (1993), and *open let-imperatives* by Huddleston and Pullum (2002).

The contractibilty of *us* in the 1st person inclusive construction is grammatically distinctive: in no other English construction is *us* contractible. Opinions are divided as to whether *us/'s* should be analyzed as object (Huddleston and Pullum 2002: 934; Davies 1986: 242) – note for example that nominative *we* cannot replace *us* (**Let's we have a party*); or as subject (Quirk et al. 1985: 829; Potsdam 1998: 297) – note for example the appearance of *we* in the interrogative tags that may occur with this construction (*Let's have a party, shall we?*). The reference of *us/'s* may, particularly in informal contexts, not be 1st person inclusive but rather 2nd person, as in Biber et al.'s (1999: 1117) example of a teacher saying to her class *Let's do it please*, or 1st person exclusive, as in Biber et al's example of a medical specialist saying to his patient *Let's have a look at your tongue*). Manifestations of the 1st person inclusive construction are subject to a good deal of dialectal variation, associated with the differing degrees of grammaticalization that *let* has undergone in the usage of various speakers. For example, many speakers allow sentences such as the following (the examples are from Potsdam 1998: 267): *Let's you and me be roommates next year;*

Let's US go instead; Let's us and them challenge the winners; Let's all of us go; Let's everyone try and behave; Let's no one forget to turn off the lights. In these perhaps marginally standard examples the contraction is obligatory and the NP following *let's* unambiguously the subject, suggesting that *let's* is a single word functioning simply as an imperative marker. A similar analysis for *let's* is suggested by the negative construction with *don't* following *let's*, as in *Let's don't forget* (which is fairly uncommon, and described as as "esp. AmE" by Quirk et al. 1985: 830).

Let-imperatives of the second type are syntactically similar to ordinary imperatives, except that they do not allow an interrogative tag or the insertion of *you* as subject (?*You don't let there be light, will you*). The main differences are pragmatic, the construction typically having an optative and/or hortatory force, calling for some future activity to occur but not necessarily seeking the compliance of any specific addressee(s) in effecting it (as exemplified by the possibility of having existential *there* or dummy *it* as the NP following *let*; e.g. *Let there be a re-trial; Let it be known that I will seek revenge*). Nevertheless, even pragmatically it is often difficult to draw the line between imperatives with causative *let* and those with hortatory/optative *let*, especially with conventionalized forms of expression which resist the kinds of syntactic manipulation (adding a tag, inserting *you*, etc.) which might facilitate classification. Consider for example *Let the games begin* and *Let 'x' represent the first variable*. Here, even though *you* or a *will you* tag are not permitted, *let* conveys the sense 'allow,' serving as more than merely an illocutionary marker. And, even though there is no specific addressee, it is understood that the involvement of the addressee(s) is required.

7 Exclamatives and Exclamatory Statements

Exclamative clauses feature the fronting of a *wh*-phrase (more specifically, a *wh*-phrase with *how* or *what*, these being the only *wh*-items that can express degree), except when the *wh*-phrase is subject and therefore already in initial position. In this respect exclamative clauses are structurally similar to open interrogatives, giving rise to the possibility of ambiguity in abstraction from relevant intonational or punctuational indicators (e.g. *What fun lies in store for us* meaning either 'An exceptional amount of fun lies in store for us!' or 'What is the amount of fun that lies in store for us?'). As in interrogatives the *wh*-phrase in exclamatives can derive from a subordinate clause (e.g. *How stupid we thought he looked!*) and it can be a PP (e.g. *For how long did she put up with his drunken behavior!*, though more commonly the preposition is stranded as in *How long did she put up with his drunken behavior for!*). A further similarity is the possibility of reduction to just the wh-phrase, as in *What a day!* and *How odd!*.

Like exclamative *how*, interrogative *how* can be used as a degree modifier. However, its semantic role within open interrogative clauses is different from that of its exclamative counterpart: in the exclamative *How clever he is!* we understand that the degree of his cleverness is extraordinary; in the interrogative *How clever is he?* we understand that his cleverness is simply to be located at some point on a scale of cleverness (precisely where, the speaker anticipates, will be indicated in the answer). Exclamative *how* is distinctive in two further respects: unlike interrogative *how* it can modify another degree modifier (compare *How very clever he is!* with **How very clever is he?*); and as an adjunct expressing degree (e.g *How they pursued him!*) it contrasts with interrogative *how* which usually expresses manner (e.g. *How did they pursue him?*). Exclamative *what* and interrogative *what* are similar in their grammatical functions, as either head of an NP (e.g. *What he has achieved!*; *What has he achieved?*) or determiner (e.g. *What parties they throw!*; *What parties do they throw?*), but differ in that exclamative *what* is always concerned with degree, interrogative *what* with identity.

A significant grammatical difference between main clause exclamatives and open interrogatives is that subject-auxiliary inversion occurs obligatorily with the fronting of the *wh*-phrase in interrogatives, but typically not with that in exclamatives. When it does occur in exclamatives subject-auxiliary inversion tends to have a rhetorical or literary flavor, as in *How bitterly did he regret his decision!*, and structural ambiguity is possible ('How bitterly he regretted his decision!' versus 'To what degree did he bitterly regret his decision?'). Ambiguity is perhaps even more likely in subordinate clauses, with the subject normally preceding the predicator in both open interrogatives and exclamatives, and the prosodic/punctuational differences that generally block one or the other reading in the case of main clauses here tending to be less salient or even absent. Thus *He knows how slow the ferry is* is ambiguous, interpretable as either 'He knows that the ferry is extraordinarily slow' or 'He knows the answer to the question "How slow is the ferry?".' There may even be, in some contexts, a pragmatic similarity between the two possible interpretations, making it difficult to determine which is the intended or most appropriate one. For instance the indirect complaint force of *How many times have I had to save your skin!* relates on one reading to its question force as an interrogative at the direct level (albeit a rhetorical question, to which only an uncooperative addressee would be tempted to supply an answer), and on another to its exclamatory force as an exclamative at the direct level (the speaker's disapproval stemming from the assessment that the number of times the addressee has had to be assisted is extraordinary).

There is good deal of disagreement in the literature over the delimitation of the exclamative class. While there is consensus that sentences introduced by *what* and *how* such as *How handsome he is!* and *What a handsome man he is!* are exclamative clauses, some writers also accept sentences such as *Is syntax easy!* (e.g. McCawley 1973; Jacobson 1987), *It is such a nice day!* (e.g. Elliott 1974; Michaelis and Lambrecht 1996), and NPs such as *The things he eats!* (Zanuttini and Portner 2003). However, we shall argue that while these represent constructions which can convey similar illocutionary force to exclamative clauses, they can do so only indirectly, for it is only in 'true' exclamatives that the exclamatory statement force has been grammaticalized.

Despite the exclamative force of *Is syntax easy!* (which McCawley 1973 labels an *exclamatory-inversion sentence*), syntactically it is a closed interrogative, and semantically a question (insofar as it has a set of possible answers, even though it differs from an inquiry in not inviting the addressee to supply any answer). According to McCawley, exclamatory-inversion sentences are distinguishable from ordinary yes/no-questions on a number of grounds, including their compatibility with interjections such as *boy* and *wow*, and their requirement of a definite subject (**Is something easy!*). However, as Huddleston (1993) observes, this merely suggests that not all yes/no-questions can be used to make exclamatory assertions (just as not all yes/no-questions can be used as directives; e.g. *Would you please sit down?* but not *Did they sit down?*).

As for declarative sentences with *such* and *so*, it is undeniable that there are grammatical parallels between these items and *what* and *how* (*What/Such a great holiday it was!*; *How/So much is not understood!*). However *such* and *so* cannot be regarded as markers of the exclamative clause type insofar as they are not obligatorily clause-initial, and they can occur also in interrogatives (e.g. *Why is he such a bore?*) and imperatives (e.g. *Don't be so defensive!*). Furthermore, *It is such a nice day!* differs from a 'true' exclamative in its ability to serve as complement to a non-factive verb such as *think* (*I think it's such a shame*; compare **I think what a shame it is*).

The things he eats! and *The money he spends on clothes!* are examples of what Huddleston and Pullum (2002: 923) refer to as *extraposable NPs*: they can appear in extraposed subject position after predicates such as *amazing*, as in *It's amazing the things he eats!*). As mere NPs they cannot, of course, represent a clause type. Furthermore the extraposed-subject sentences with which they may be associated, which are treated by some (e.g. Michaelis and Lambrecht 1996) as exclamatives, differ from direct exclamatory statements in asserting rather than merely implicating the speaker's judgment (see further below for discussion of this implicature).

Consider finally the semantic and pragmatic properties of exclamatives. Exclamative clauses normally have the force of what Huddleston (1984: 374) calls an *exclamatory statement*, a statement overlaid by an emotive element. Compare for instance the exclamative *What a strong performance she gave!* with its declarative counterpart *She gave a strong performance*: the former is provided with an attitudinal component by the implicature that the performance is to be located at an extreme point on a scale. Semantically, there is a close semantic parallel with *She gave such a strong performance!*. But there is also a difference: the declarative sentence with *such* asserts, rather than presupposes, that 'She gave a strong performance.' Consequently it could more readily serve as a response to a question such as *How was the concert?* (whereas *What a strong performance she gave!* would sound decidedly odd because of the presupposed status of the proposition that supplies the answer).

Exclamatives typically do not serve to advance a discourse informationally, but rather to express the speaker's affective stance or attitude towards some event or state of affairs. The event or state in question is expressed in the form of a presupposed open proposition, and thus is backgrounded as uncontroversial information by the speaker. That this is so is suggested, as Huddleston and Pullum (2002: 922) observe, by the use of interrogative tags with exclamatives. It is possible to have a reversed polarity acknowledgement-seeking tag (with falling intonation), as in *What a strong performance she gave, didn't she!*, where the acknowledgement relates not just to the proposition that she gave a strong performance but also to the attitudinal stance (that the strength of the performance was remarkable). However, a constant polarity tag would sound odd, as in *What a strong performance she gave, did she!*, because it would seek acknowledgement of the proposition, and incongruously so in view of its presupposed status.

The claim that the propositional component of exclamative clauses is backgrounded is supported by further evidence. For one thing, they are incompatible with 'non-factive' verbs (compare *I recall what a strong performance she gave*; **I believe what a strong performance she gave*), a restriction referred to as *factivity* by Zanuttini and Portner (2003), who ascribe it to the presupposed open proposition expressed by exclamatives. For another, exclamative clauses are unable to serve as answers to questions, because the information which provides the answer to a question will normally be asserted rather than presupposed: *What a strong performance she gave!* is not an answer to the question *Did she give a strong performance?*

We have already mentioned the scalar implicature associated with exclamatives, the implicature that "the degree of the scalar property in question is unusually high," as Michaelis and Lambrecht (1996: 384) put it. The value of the variable expressed by the exclamative phrase is not specified, but simply interpretable as extraordinary. Thus *How smart he is!* implicates that the property of smartness denoted by the exclamative phrase lies at the extreme end of some contextually given scale, that it is greater than any alternatives that one might consider. In some cases it may not be clear which end of the scale is relevant, as in *What a performance he gave!* It is from this scalar implicature that the affective stance associated with exclamative utterances derives. Some writers are uncautiously specific in describing this stance as, for example, one of 'surprise' or 'unexpectedness.' As Zanuttini and Portner (2003: 54) observe, however, in exclaiming *What a delicious dinner you've made!* a speaker "doesn't mean to imply that he or she didn't expect a good dinner (. . .) Rather, the speaker implies that the tastiness of the dinner exceeds the range of possibilities previously under consideration, presumably something like the range of tastiness the speaker has experienced at other people's houses. It doesn't need to imply that the speaker expected anything less at this house."

8   Conclusion

We have seen that clause type in English is standardly treated as a four-term system, with each term associated with a characteristic illocutionary force.

However, this correspondence may be overridden – in indirect speech acts – by a variety of factors, including prosody and the performative use of speech act verbs. The system of clause type raises challenging questions as to the relationship between syntax, semantics, and pragmatics. The syntactic category of interrogatives is argued to be distinguishable both from the semantic category of questions (classifiable on one important dimension into wh-questions, yes/no-questions, and alternative questions), and the pragmatic category of inquiries (embracing queries, suggestions, requests, and the like). Imperative clauses typically have directive force, but directives are also commonly conveyed by the other clause types (e.g. by an interrogative such as *Would you mind helping me?* or a declarative such as *You must not touch it*). A distinction is posited between ordinary imperatives and *let*-imperatives. One important consideration in the analysis of the latter is the varying degrees of grammaticalization that *let* has undergone with different English speakers. The delimitation of the exclamative clause type has been the subject of some disagreement. In this chapter it is maintained that the class is limited to clauses introduced by an exclamative phrase with *what* or *how*, and excludes structures such as *Isn't syntax easy!* and *Syntax is so easy!*: only in the former is the illocutionary force of exclamatory statement grammaticalized.

NOTE

I wish to thank Geoffrey Leech, Rodney Huddleston, and Bas Aarts for helpful comments on this chapter.

FURTHER READING

Davies, E. (1986) *The English imperative.* London: Croom Helm.

Elliott, D. (1974) Toward a grammar of exclamations. *Foundations of Language* 11, 231–46.

Huddleston, R. D. (1994) The contrast between interrogatives and questions. *Journal of Linguistics* 30, 411–39.

Huddleston, R. D. and Pullum, G. K. (2002) *The Cambridge grammar of the English language.* Cambridge: Cambridge University Press.

Potsdam, Eric. (1998) *Syntactic issues in the English imperative.* New York: Garland Publishing, Inc.

Quirk, R., Greenbaum, S., Leech, G., and Svartvik, J. (1985) *A comprehensive grammar of the English language.* London: Longman.

Zanuttini, R. and Portner, P. (2003) Exclamative clauses: at the syntax–semantics interface. *Language* 79, 39–81.

REFERENCES

Aarts, F. (1989) Imperative sentences in English: semantics and pragmatics. *Studia Linguistica* 43, 119–34.

Beukema, F. and Coopmans, P. (1989) A government-binding perspective on the imperative in English. *Journal of Linguistics* 25, 417–36.

Biber, D., Johansson, J., Leech, G., Conrad S., and Finegan, E. (1999) *Longman grammar of spoken and written English*. London: Longman.

Bolinger, D. (1977) *Meaning and form*. London: Longman.

Bouton, L. F. (1990) The imperative tag: a thing apart. *World Englishes* 9, 37–51.

Clark, B. (1993) *Let* and *let's*: procedural encoding and explicature. *Lingua* 90, 173–200.

Comorovski, I. (1996) *Interrogative phrases and the syntax–semantics interface*. Dordrecht: Kluwer.

Culicover, P. (1976) *Syntax*. New York: Academic Press.

Davies, E. (1986) *The English imperative*. London: Croom Helm.

Elliott, D. (1974) Toward a grammar of exclamations. *Foundations of Language* 11, 231–46.

Hamblin, C. L. (1987) *Imperatives*. Oxford: Blackwell.

Huddleston, R. D. (1984) *Introduction to the grammar of English*. Cambridge: Cambridge University Press.

Huddleston, R. D. (1988) Review of R. Quirk et al., *A comprehensive grammar of the English language*. *Language* 64, 345–54.

Huddleston, R. D. (1993) On exclamatory-inversion sentences. *Lingua* 90, 259–69.

Huddleston, R. D. (1994) The contrast between interrogatives and questions. *Journal of Linguistics* 30, 411–39.

Huddleston, R. D. and Pullum, G. K., et al. (2002) *The Cambridge grammar of the English language*. Cambridge: Cambridge University Press.

Jacobsen, S. (1987) Is *Am I Happy!* an exclamatory question. *Studier I Modern Språkvetenskap* 8, 42–5.

Karttunen, L. (1977) Syntax and semantics of questions. *Linguistics and Philosophy* 1, 3–44.

McCawley, J. D. (1988) *The syntactic phenomena of English*. Chicago: University of Chicago Press.

McCawley, N. (1973) Boy! Is syntax easy? *Papers from the Ninth Regional Meeting of the Chicago Linguistic Society*. Chicago: Chicago Linguistic Society, 366–77.

Merin, A. (1991) Imperatives: linguistics vs. philosophy. *Linguistics* 29, 669–702.

Michaelis, L. and Lambrecht, K. (1996) The exclamative sentence type in English. In A. E. Goldberg (ed.), *Conceptual structure, discourse and language*. Stanford, CA: CSLI, 375–89.

Morgan, J. L. (1978) Two types of convention in indirect speech acts. In P. Cole (ed.), *Syntax and semantics 9: pragmatics*. New York: Academic Press, 261–80.

Potsdam, E. (1998) *Syntactic issues in the English imperative*. New York: Garland Publishing, Inc.

Quirk, R., Greenbaum, S., Leech, G., and Svartvik, J. (1985) *A comprehensive grammar of the English language*. London: Longman.

Tregidgo, P. S. (1982) *Let* and *let's*. *ELT Journal* 36, 186–8.

Sadock, J. M. (1970) Whimperatives. In J. M. Sadock and A. L. Vanek (eds.), *Studies presented to R. B. Lees by his students*. Edmonton: Linguistic Research Inc., 223–5.

Schmerling, S. F. (1982) How imperatives are special, and how they aren't. In

R. Schneider (ed.), *Papers from the parasession on nondeclaratives*. Chicago: Chicago Linguistic Society, University of Chicago, 202–18.

Stockwell, R. P., Schachter, P., and Partee, B. H. (1973) *The major syntactic structures of English*. New York: Holt, Rinehart & Winston.

Zanuttini, R. and Portner, P. (2003) Exclamative clauses: at the syntax–semantics interface. *Language 79*, 39–81.

9 Coordination and Subordination

RODNEY HUDDLESTON AND GEOFFREY K. PULLUM

0 Introduction

Where a sentence contains two or more clauses they are generally related syntactically in one of two ways, coordination or subordination, as illustrated in (1):

(1) i COORDINATION   [*My sister is a lawyer*] [*and my brother is a doctor*].
     ii SUBORDINATION   [*They forgot* [*that my brother is a doctor*]].

In (i) the two clauses are of equal syntactic status: they are not functionally distinguishable, each being **coordinate** with the other. In (ii), by contrast, they are of unequal status, with one (*that my brother is a doctor*) **subordinate** to the other, the **superordinate** clause.

In traditional grammar, where the concept of constituent structure played a much less significant role than it does in most modern theories of syntax, the superordinate clause in (1ii) is just *they forgot* (see, for example, Curme 1931: 174–5; Onions 1971: sections 20, 22.8; also Trask 1993: 'main clause'; Richards et al. 1985: 'dependent clause'). Modern grammars, however, mostly take the superordinate clause in such examples to be co-extensive with the whole sentence, so that the subordinate clause is **embedded** within, i.e. a constituent of, the superordinate clause, as indicated by our bracketing above. More particularly, it has a **dependent** function within it: it is a complement of the **head** verb *forgot*.

Our initial examples illustrate different relations between **clauses**. The relation of coordination, however, holds not just between clauses but also between smaller units. In *They invited* _my daughter and her husband_ the underlined sequence is a coordination of NPs, in *They invited my* _father and mother_ we have a coordination of nouns, and so on. For some scholars the same applies to the relation of subordination. Matthews (1997: 360), for example, gives the primary sense of subordination as '= dependency,' which covers the relation between modifiers, complements, etc. and the head of the construction. In *He has long* *hair*, for example, *long* is a dependent (modifier) of *hair* and hence, in this usage, subordinate to it, while *long hair* is a dependent (object) of *has* and hence again subordinate to it.

In traditional grammar, however, the term 'subordination' (when understood in a grammatical sense) is normally restricted to clauses. A distinction is drawn between **subordinate clauses** and **main clauses** (= nonsubordinate clauses), whereas no parallel distinction is drawn for phrases and words. Similarly **subordinating conjunctions** are words which introduce clauses whereas **coordinating conjunctions** are not limited to the function of joining clauses. Numerous modern scholars retain this traditional restricted sense of 'subordination.' Trask (1993: 268), for example, defines it as the 'phenomenon by which one clause . . . forms a constituent of another clause, the **matrix clause**' (where 'matrix clause' is another term for 'superordinate clause'). Descriptive grammars which define or use subordination in the traditional sense include Quirk et al. (1985: 44) and Sinclair (1990: 342–3); see also such student texts as Hurford (1994), which has an entry for 'subordinate clause' but not for 'subordination.'

In this chapter we adopt the traditional, more restrictive sense of subordination. For the more general sense we use the term 'dependency': in the above *He has long hair*, for example, we continue to treat *long* as a dependent of *hair* but we will not say that *long* is subordinate to *hair*, and similarly for other cases of dependency in this example. We likewise take 'embedding' to be applicable quite generally: just as *that my brother is a doctor* is embedded within the larger clause in (1ii), so in *the father of the bride* the NP *the bride* is embedded within the larger NP. But we do not say that it is subordinate to the larger NP. These constructions thus fall outside the scope of this chapter. Section 1 accordingly deals with coordination as it applies to units of any size, while section 2 deals with the subordination of clauses. Our account draws extensively on *The Cambridge Grammar of the English Language* (Huddleston and Pullum et al. 2002), referred to henceforth as *CGEL*.

1   Coordination

Coordination, we have said, is a relation holding between two or more elements of equal syntactic status. None is a dependent of any other, and none is a head – coordination is a non-headed construction. We call the elements or parts **coordinates**. This is a functional term, contrasting with heads and dependents in headed constructions. The words that mark the relation – most commonly the words *and* and *or* – are called **coordinators**.

1.1   Terminology

'Coordination' is a familiar traditional term. 'Coordinate' and 'coordinator' are transparent terms for the parts and markers respectively, which we take from Matthews (1981: 197).

Most work in formal grammar uses the term 'conjunction' in place of 'coordination,' and thence 'conjunct' in place of 'coordinate.' It is a puzzle why 'conjunction' was introduced to replace a perfectly satisfactory existing term, especially as it is potentially confusing because of its other well-established senses. First, it conflicts with the traditional use of 'conjunction' as the name of a part of speech used to mark either coordination or subordination. And second, there is a conflict with usage in logic: for example, while *Kim overslept and the bus was late* and *Kim overslept or the bus was late* are both coordinations, the first expresses logical conjunction and the second logical disjunction.

1.2   The category status of coordinations

In our earlier example *my daughter and her husband*, the coordinates (*my daughter* and *her husband*) are NPs, and the usual practice in formal grammar is to analyze the whole coordination as an NP too. More generally, for any category α a coordination of α constituents is itself taken to be an α (see, e.g., the entry in Trask 1993 under 'coordinate structure'). A compelling objection to this approach, however, is that – as is well known – coordinates do not always belong to the same category. Subject to general constraints that we take up below, constituents of different categories can be coordinated, as in the examples given in (2) (see *CGEL*: 1326–9 for a larger sample):

(2)   i   *He is* [*an entrepreneur* and *extremely wealthy*]. (NP + AdjP)
      ii   *The article was* [*very long* and *of little relevance*]. (AdjP + PP)
      iii *I can't remember* [*the cost* or *where I bought it*]. (NP + Clause)
      iv   *The University provides an opportunity* [*for adventures of the mind* and *to make friendships that will last a lifetime*]. (PP + Clause)
      v   *They replaced it* [*immediately* and *at no extra cost*]. (AdvP + PP)
      vi   *She found an inconsistency between the* [*state* and *federal laws*]. (N + Adj)

The underlined coordinates in (i) are respectively an NP and an AdjP, but the coordination as a whole clearly belongs to neither of these categories. Analogously for the other examples.

For this reason we take 'coordination' itself as a category term. Thus whereas in *He is an entrepreneur* the predicative complement belongs to the category NP, in (2i) it belongs to the category coordination. And the same will hold for *He is* [*an entrepreneur* and *an extremely wealthy man*]. Whether a particular member of the coordination category is admissible at a given place in sentence structure will of course depend on what the coordinates are, as discussed in section 1.3.2 below, where we present an account slightly modified from the one in *CGEL*.

1.3   Distinctive syntactic properties of coordination

In this section we outline the most important syntactic properties that distinguish coordination from other constructions.

1.3.1 No grammatical limit to the number of coordinates

All the coordinations cited so far consist of just two coordinates, but there can be any number: three in *You can have [pork, beef or lamb]*; four in *I was [tired, hungry, cold and very depressed]*; five in *Meetings are held in [March, May, July, September, and November]*; and so on, without any limit set by the grammar.

1.3.2 The requirement of syntactic likeness

We have said that coordinates are of 'equal syntactic status,' which implies that they are syntactically alike. In most cases they belong to the same category; but we interpret the data in (2) as indicating that in fact it is **functional** likeness rather than **categorial** likeness that is crucial.[1] As a first approximation, we could state the condition on the admissibility of a coordination of two elements α and β as in (3), with illustrations given in (4):

(3)   A coordination of α and β is admissible at a given place in sentence structure if and only if each of α and β is individually admissible at that place with the same function.

(4)   i   a.   *We invited [the manager and several staff members].*
           b.   *We invited the manager.*
           c.   *We invited several staff members.*
      ii   a.   *The article was [very long and of little relevance].* (= (2i))
           b.   *The article was very long.*
           c.   *The article was of little relevance.*
      iii a.   **He left [the country and this morning].*
           b.   *He left the country.*
           c.   *He left this morning.*

The simplest case is illustrated in (4i): the coordination in (a) is admissible as object of *invited* because each coordinate can occur on its own with that function, as in (b–c). Set (ii) covers the coordination of expressions of unlike category: *very long* is an AdjP while *of little relevance* is a PP but each can occur on its own here with the function of predicative complement, and hence the coordination of the two is admissible. Set (iii) illustrates the ungrammaticality resulting from a failure to satisfy condition (3). Although each coordinate can occur in the position of the coordination – and although they both belong to the category NP – they do not have the same function, *the country* in (b) being object while *this morning* in (c) is adjunct.

Condition (3) is, as we say, only a first approximation. This generalization covers the default case, but special provision needs to be made to handle various kinds of exception. Some of these are illustrated in (5) (again, *CGEL* gives a fuller discussion, in pp. 1323–6):

(5)   i   *[The toaster and the electric kettle] don't work any more.*
      ii   *%They've arranged for [your father and I] to see her.*

iii   *[To delay any longer and letting your son get involved] would be unwise.*
iv   *[One or other] of them will have to resign.*

- In (i) the coordinates would be admissible on their own only if we change *don't* to *doesn't*: **agreement** features may need to be adjusted.
- Many speakers use nominative forms of personal pronouns (especially 1st person singular *I*) in coordinations in contexts where the accusative form would be required if the pronoun occurred on its own.
- Example (iii) illustrates a special case where categorial likeness is required in addition to functional likeness: an **infinitival** cannot normally be coordinated with a **gerund-participial** (as we call the construction headed by a verb with the suffix *·ing*).
- In (iv) *one* could occur in place of the coordination but *other* could not: **other of them* is not a well-formed NP. *One or other* is an example of a fixed phrase with the form of a coordination.

1.3.3   The marking of coordination

Coordination is usually but not invariably marked by one or more coordinators. Three patterns to be distinguished are shown in (6):

(6)   i   SIMPLE SYNDETIC   *You need [celery, apples, walnuts, and grapes].*
      ii   POLYSYNDETIC   *You need [celery and apples and walnuts and grapes].*
      iii   ASYNDETIC   *You need [celery, apples, walnuts, grapes].*

The major contrast is between **syndetic** coordination, which contains at least one coordinator, and **asyndetic** coordination, which does not. In constructions with more than two coordinates there is a further contrast within syndetic coordination between the default **simple syndetic**, which has a single coordinator marking the final coordinate, and **polysyndetic**, where all non-initial coordinates are marked by a coordinator (which must be the same for all of them). The coordinator forms a constituent with the coordinate which follows: we refer to expressions like *and grapes* as an **expanded coordinate**, with *grapes* itself a **bare coordinate**.

The two most central coordinators are *and* and *or*. *But* is also uncontroversially a coordinator in examples like *I tried to phone her but there was no answer* (and uncontroversially a preposition in *It causes nothing but trouble*), but is subject to various restrictions that do not apply to *and* and *or*. Most importantly, it is restricted to binary coordinations: compare **He was old but healthy but rich*.[2]

Nor combines negation with *or*: *He didn't have enough money for a deposit nor any prospect of obtaining a loan*. Some other items showing similarities with coordinators – e.g. *so, yet, as well as, plus* – are discussed in *CGEL* (pp. 1313–23).

The initial coordinate is not, in English, marked in the same way as the others. Instead it can be marked by *both, either,* or *neither,* which are paired with *and, or,* and *nor* respectively: *both young and healthy, either young or healthy, neither young nor healthy*.[3] Examples of this kind involve **correlative** coordination.

Both, either and *neither* also function as **determiner** in NP structure: *both parents, either parent, neither parent.* For this reason we classify them as **determinatives** – along with *the, a, this, that, some, any,* etc.[4] They differ from coordinators in that they are not invariably positioned immediately before the coordinate, but may be 'displaced,' as in (7):

(7)   i   *They will <u>either</u> have to <u>increase taxes</u> <u>or</u> <u>reduce spending</u>.*
     ii   *Usually he <u>was</u> <u>either</u> <u>too busy to get away</u> <u>or</u> <u>couldn't summon up the energy for the trip</u>.*

Prescriptive manuals tend to advise against such displacement, but this is a matter of stylistic preference, not the avoidance of ungrammaticality (see **either (3)** in Merriam-Webster 1994: 385).

1.3.4   *No fronting of coordinator + coordinate*
An expanded coordinate can never be fronted, as constituents with a dependent function commonly can. Compare, for example:

(8)   i   a.   *She recommended a holiday, <u>although I had my thesis to finish</u>.*
         b.   *<u>Although I had my thesis to finish</u>, she recommended a holiday.*
     ii   a.   *She recommended a holiday, <u>but I had my thesis to finish</u>.*
         b.   **<u>But I had my thesis to finish</u>, she recommended a holiday.*

The underlined constituent in (ia) is a dependent (an adjunct), and can be placed at the front of the whole construction, as in (ib). The underlined element in (iia), however, is coordinate, not dependent, and hence cannot be placed at the front, as we see from (iib) (interpreted as a reordering of (iia)). Note that the meanings of (ia) and (iia) are similar, but the grammatical difference is very sharp.

1.3.5   *'Across the board' application of syntactic processes*
Related to the requirement of syntactic likeness between coordinates is the requirement that such syntactic processes as relativization apply **across the board**, i.e. to all coordinates. Again this provides a useful contrast with non-coordinate constructions. Compare:

(9)   i   a.   *<u>He has lots of experience</u> but <u>he hasn't got a degree</u>.*
         b.   *I appointed a guy [<u>who has lots of experience</u> but <u>who hasn't got a degree</u>].*
     ii   a.   *<u>He has lots of experience</u> though <u>he hasn't got a degree</u>.*
         b.   **I appointed a guy [<u>who has lots of experience</u> though <u>who hasn't got a degree</u>].*

In (ia) the underlined clauses are coordinate, and when we relativize the process applies to both coordinates, so that *he* is replaced by *who* in both of them (thus preserving their syntactic likeness). But in (iia) they are not coordinate: the second is within a dependent (an adjunct) introduced by *though*. Relativization cannot apply to both clauses here; it applies to just the superordinate one, giving *I appointed a guy who has lots of experience though he hasn't got a degree.*

1.4   Order of coordinates

In the simplest and most prototypical cases the order of coordinates is free, so that reversing them has no significant effect on acceptability or interpretation. But there are also many cases where coordinates are not freely reversible in this way:

(10)   i   a.   *I live in Paris and work in a bank.*
          b.   *I work in a bank and live in Paris.*
    ii   a.   *I went home and had a bath.*
          b.   *I had a bath and went home.*
   iii   a.   *first and foremost*
          b.   **foremost and first*

The VP coordinates in (i) illustrate the free reversibility cases; this kind of coordination is commonly called **symmetric**. By contrast, (ii–iii) illustrate **asymmetric** coordination. In (ii) both versions are perfectly acceptable, but would normally be interpreted differently, with the order of coordinates matching the temporal order of events: in (a) I went home first and had a bath when I got home, whereas in (b) I had a bath before going home. One special case of asymmetric coordination involves **lexicalized** expressions, such as (iiia).

In some cases of asymmetrical coordination the across-the-board requirement is relaxed, as in *Here are some flowers which I've just been down the road and bought for you.* Here *which* relates to the second coordinate but not the first: compare non-relative *I've just been down the road and bought some flowers for you.*

1.5   Main-clause and lower-level coordination

We have noted that coordination can apply to a large range of constituents of varying categories (nouns, verbs, adjectives, etc.) and levels (words, phrases, clauses). The major distinction we draw is between **main-clause** coordination and **lower-level** coordination, coordination within the structure of some main clause. Compare:

(11)   MAIN-CLAUSE COORDINATION   LOWER-LEVEL COORDINATION
   i   a.   *Where is he and*   b.   *I don't know [what he wants*
        what does he want?   *or where he is].*
  ii   a.   *I invited him, but*   b.   *I invited [the doctor and*
        he couldn't come.   *the priest].*
 iii   a.   *I'd better go now or I'll be late.*   b.   *No one [got up and complained].*

In many cases lower-level coordination is logically equivalent to corresponding clausal coordination. For example, (11iib) is equivalent to *I invited the doctor and I invited the priest*. There are, however, numerous cases where no such equivalence holds between the two levels of coordination. A typical example is (11iiib). This is clearly not equivalent to *No one got up and no one complained*, which could be false where (11iiib) was true (if someone rose without complaining, or grumbled while seated).

1.6 *Distributive vs. joint coordination*

Related to the issue of equivalence between the two levels of coordination is the distinction between **joint** and **distributive** coordination illustrated in (12):

(12) DISTRIBUTIVE COORDINATION JOINT COORDINATION

  i a. [*Kim* and *Pat*] are dishonest. b. [*Kim* and *Pat*] are a pair of crooks.

  ii a. [*Kim* and *Pat*] signed on yesterday. b. [*Kim* and *Pat*] met yesterday.

The coordination in (ia) is distributive in that the property of dishonesty is predicated of Kim and Pat individually: each was dishonest. The property of being a pair of crooks, by contrast, can only apply to them jointly: each was a crook, but neither was a pair of crooks. Similarly, the predicate in (iia) applies to Kim and Pat individually: they each signed on. But (iib) means that they met each other, something that they can only do jointly.

The distinction is reflected grammatically in certain ways. For example, joint coordination (at least for most speakers) excludes correlative coordination: thus we could add *both* before *Kim* in (ia/iia) but not in (ib/iib). Note then that *Kim and Pat are crooks* counts as distributive, the distinction between plural *crooks* and singular *a crook* being disregarded; here *both* can readily be added.

1.7 *Non-basic coordination*

We have confined our attention so far to the syntactically simplest kinds of coordination, which we call **basic** coordination. Here the coordinates occur one after the other, alone or accompanied by a marker (coordinator or determinative), and are found as constituents in comparable non-coordinate constructions. To conclude our survey we review summarily various more complex, or **non-basic**, constructions.

1.7.1 *Expansion of coordinates by modifiers*

(13) *This will benefit [your father and of course your mother as well].*

Here the second coordinate is accompanied not just by the coordinator *and*, but by the modifiers *of course* and *as well*.

1.7.2   Gapping, or gapped coordination

(14)   *One of them is likely to get a distinction and the other a credit*.

The middle part of the second coordinate is missing: we understand "the other is likely to get a credit."

1.7.3   Right nonce-constituent coordination (a.k.a. non-constituent coordination)

(15)   *She worked [in London for two years and in Paris for three]*.

The coordinates do not occur elsewhere as constituents: in *She worked in London for two years*, for example, *in London for two years* is not a single constituent. In (15), however, it is a constituent: it acquires the status of constituent for the nonce, as it were, by virtue of the coordination. In this construction the nonce-constituents occur on the right and must be of like structure (cf. *She worked [in London for two years and in Paris at the Louvre]*).

1.7.4   Delayed right constituent coordination (a.k.a. right node raising)

(16)   *He quickly [noticed and took advantage of these weaknesses]*.

This corresponds to the basic coordination *He quickly noticed these weaknesses and took advantage of them*. The element understood in (16) as object of *noticed*, i.e. as right constituent of the first coordinate, is delayed to the end of the coordination and related also to the second coordinate. At least one of the coordinates in this construction is not a constituent in the corresponding basic coordination.

1.7.5   End-attachment coordination

(17)   *We gave [Sue] a second chance, [but not her brother]*.

Here, the second coordinate is not adjacent to the first, but is attached at the end of the clause.

2   Subordination

As indicated at the beginning of the chapter, we are taking 'subordination' in the more restrictive of the two senses it has in the grammatical literature, that where it applies to the subordination of clauses.

2.1 Subordinate clause and main clause as syntactic categories

The reason why traditional grammar singles out clauses for special treatment is that there are important differences of internal form between **subordinate clauses** and non-subordinate ones, i.e. **main clauses**. Compare:

(18) MAIN CLAUSE SUBORDINATE CLAUSE
i a. *She is ill.* b. *I realize that she is ill.*
ii a. *Has she arrived yet?* b. *I wonder whether she has arrived yet.*
iii a. *She is late.* b. *It's unusual for her to be late.*

- In (i) the subordinate clause is distinguished from the main clause by the subordinator *that*.
- In (ii) it is distinguished by the subordinator *whether* + subject–predicator order.
- In (iii) it is distinguished by the subordinator *for*, the infinitival marker *to*, the accusative case of the subject pronoun and the form of the verb.

Subordinate clause and main clause thus have the status of syntactic **categories**. Note, by contrast, that even those works that use 'subordination' in the more general sense of dependency do not make a comparable subcategory distinction between subordinate and main within other categories, such as NPs, PPs, AdjPs, etc. – or nouns, prepositions, adjectives, etc.

A subordinate clause is generally defined (in modern works) as an embedded clause, a clause functioning as a dependent within the structure of some larger clause (see, e.g., Matthews 1997: 360; Trask 1993: 268; Hurford 1994: 232). It is important, however, to distinguish between two kinds of definition. A **language-particular** definition of some grammatical term provides criteria for determining which expressions are covered by that term in the particular language under investigation. A **general** definition provides a principled basis for applying the same term in different languages.[5] We need this distinction because clauses that are standardly classified as subordinate do not invariably function as dependent within a larger clause.

To see this, note first the following examples from Quirk et al. (1985: 840–1):

(19) i *That you could ever want to marry such a man!*
ii *To think that I was once a millionaire!*
iii *What to do in an emergency.*

The first two stand as (exclamatory) sentences on their own, while the third is used as a title or heading over a text that tells you what to do in an emergency. We follow Quirk et al. in treating these as exceptional uses of subordinate clauses, not exceptional forms of main clauses.

Second, note that there are strong grounds for recognizing a type of construction distinct from both dependency and coordination: the construction we call **supplementation**.[6] A **supplement** is an element that is loosely attached rather than being tightly integrated into the structure; it can take numerous different forms, including both subordinate and main clauses, as in (20):

(20)   i   *We've offered the job to Sue (<u>who has easily the best qualifications</u>), but I don't think she'll accept.*
       ii *We've offered the job to Sue (<u>she has easily the best qualifications</u>), but I don't think she'll accept.*

The underlined supplement in (i) is a subordinate clause, marked as such by the relative pronoun, while that in (ii) is a main clause. They differ in form but not in function.

For these two reasons we do not think the textbook definition of subordinate clause cited above thus provides rigorous enough criteria for determining whether or not an English clause is subordinate. Modified slightly, however, it will serve as a general definition: we can say that a language can be said to have subordinate clauses when it has a grammatically distinct subcategory of clause whose most prototypical members characteristically function as dependent within the structure of a larger clause.[7] It is not possible to give a language-particular definition of comparable brevity: the distinctive properties of subordinate clauses in English will emerge from a detailed description of the various subclasses of subordinate clause. In view of the limitations of space, the account given below will inevitably be incomplete.

2.2   *Finiteness*

In languages generally, the concept of finiteness normally applies in the first instance to verbs, and then derivatively to clauses, a clause being finite or non-finite according as the verb is finite or non-finite. In traditional grammars a finite verb is one that is inflected for person and number – and is therefore 'limited' (hence 'finite') with respect to the kinds of subject it can combine with (see, e.g., the definition in the *OED*). Modern grammars, based on a wider range of languages, tend to define a finite verb as one that can occur as the verb of a main clause (or a declarative main clause), the connection with the traditional definition being that it is the verbs of main clauses that characteristically exhibit the maximum amount of inflectional marking for person, number, tense, and other verbal categories (see Matthews 1997: 129; Trask 1993: 103–4)

Historical change in English has reduced the number of inflectionally distinct verb-forms in such a way that the distinction between finite and non-finite clauses can no longer be satisfactorily defined purely in terms of verb inflection. Consider the underlined clauses in (21):

(21)   i   <u>*Be patient.*</u>   [imperative clause]
        ii   *It is essential <u>that he be patient.</u>*   [subjunctive clause]
       iii   *It is essential <u>for him to be patient.</u>*   [infinitival clause]

Both traditional and modern grammars analyze (i–ii) as finite and (iii) as non-finite, yet they all contain the same form of the verb. No verb in English has morphologically distinct forms in these constructions, and there is accordingly no justification for saying (as traditional grammar does) that they contain different inflectional verb-forms. In particular, there is no justification for saying that the *be* of (i–ii) differs from that of (iii) in being a present tense form. Note in this connection that the *be* of (ii) can occur in contexts that do not accept genuine present tense forms, as in *I demanded that he <u>be</u> reinstated immediately, but of course he wasn't* (cf. **I hoped that he <u>is</u> reinstated immediately, but of course he wasn't*). As far as Present-day English is concerned, the terms 'imperative,' 'subjunctive' and 'infinitival' apply to clause constructions, not to verb inflection. The verb in all three is in what we call the **plain form** – it is morphologically identical to the lexical base.[8]

Prototypical finite clauses are those with a tensed verb (a preterite or present tense verb), but there are sound reasons for including imperatives and subjunctives with the finites even though the verb is non-tensed.

- Imperatives are like clauses with tensed verbs in that they take the dummy auxiliary **do** in verbal negation (compare *They don't talk to him*; *Don't talk to him*). This **do** does not occur in non-finite clauses. Imperatives also differ from the latter in that they are restricted (or virtually restricted) to main clauses.
- Leaving aside fixed phrases or formulae (*So be it*; *Long live . . .* , etc.) subjunctives occur only as subordinate clauses; they are nevertheless best classified as finite along with tensed clauses in that they take the same subordinator, *that* (compare (21ii) with *I hope <u>that he is patient</u>*), and nominative case for personal pronoun subjects – contrast *for* and *him* in non-finite (21iii). For many speakers at least, moreover, the verb in subjunctives can be replaced by a present-tense form as a stylistic variant.

Granted then that the imperative and subjunctive clauses in (21) are correctly classified as finite and the infinitival as non-finite, it follows that for English finiteness is not fully definable in terms of verb inflection. In particular, a finite clause cannot be defined as one containing a tensed verb.

Non-finiteness is a marker of subordination: finite clauses may be main or subordinate, but non-finite ones are always subordinate (though not invariably embedded, as illustrated in (19ii–iii)). Non-finite subordinate clauses differ structurally from main clauses more radically than do finite subordinate clauses.

In the remainder of the chapter we look first at finite subordinate clauses, and then, more briefly, at non-finites.

2.3   Finite subordinate clauses

We distinguish three major subcategories of finite subordinate clause – **relative**, **comparative** and **content** clauses. We consider these in turn and then compare this classification with more familiar ones from traditional or modern grammars.

2.3.1   Relative clauses

The prototypical relative clause functions as modifier within NP structure, as in:

(22)   i   *We consulted* [*the woman <u>who first suggested this solution</u>*].
    ii   *I followed* [*the advice <u>which you gave me</u>*].

They are called relative clauses because they are grammatically related to an antecedent: in these examples, *woman* and *advice*, the heads of the NPs, are the antecedents for the relative pronouns *who* and *which* respectively.

The underlined clauses in (22) are ***wh* relatives**: they contain one of the relative words *who, whom, whose, which*, etc., as (or within) the initial constituent and anaphorically linked to an antecedent. The relative word may have a variety of functions within the relative clause: in (22i) it is subject, in (ii) it is object, and in *I couldn't find* [*the text <u>to which she had referred</u>*] it is complement of a preposition, and so on.

Non-*wh* relatives lack a relative word, but there is nevertheless a covert element whose interpretation is determined by the antecedent, just as that of the relative words is. Compare (22ii) with the two subtypes of non-*wh* relative clause shown in (23):

(23)   i   *I followed the advice <u>that you gave me</u>.*   [*that* relative]
    ii   *I followed the advice <u>you gave me</u>.*   [bare relative]

In both there is a missing object of *gave* reconstructible from the antecedent: we understand that you gave me some advice. *That* relatives are introduced by the subordinator *that*, as in (23i), whereas bare relatives like (ii) lack it.[9] The bare relative is not normally admissible when the gap is in subject function. Thus we can replace the NP in (22i) by *the woman that first suggested this solution*, but here the *that* is not omissible.

On a dimension that is partly but not wholly independent of this contrast between the *wh* and non-*wh* constructions, we can classify relative clauses on the basis of their function. The major distinction here is between **integrated** and **supplementary** relative clauses, traditionally called 'restrictive' and 'non-restrictive' respectively:

(24)   i   *Politicians <u>who make extravagant promises</u> aren't trusted.*   [integrated]
    ii   *Politicians, <u>who make extravagant promises</u>, aren't trusted.*
                                                    [supplementary]

Integrated relatives are tightly integrated into the larger construction containing them, both prosodically and informationally, whereas supplementary relatives are more loosely attached: they are set apart prosodically (and usually marked off punctuationally), and the information they express is presented as supplementary rather than an integral part of the larger message.

The examples given in (24) were chosen as ones where the traditional labels work well enough. The relative clause in (i) is semantically restrictive in that it picks out a subset of politicians: the implication is that some politicians make extravagant promises whereas others do not, and it is the former subset that aren't trusted. Example (ii), by contrast, is semantically non-restrictive: it says that politicians in general aren't trusted, and the relative clause gives the additional information that politicians in general make extravagant promises.

We have not retained the traditional terms because integrated relatives do not in fact need to be semantically restrictive in this way. Consider the following example from a Dick Francis novel:

(25) *The father <u>who had planned my life to the point of my unsought arrival in Brighton</u> took it for granted that in the last three weeks of his legal guardianship I would still act as he directed.*

The relative clause is integrated (it clearly would not be read as a separate intonation unit), but it does not serve to distinguish one father from another: the narrator obviously had only one father. The reason why the information it expresses is presented as an integral part of the message is that it is essential to understanding why the person in question took it for granted that the narrator would act as he directed. The semantic restrictiveness illustrated in (24i) provides one common reason for presenting the informational content of the relative clause as integral to the larger message, but it is certainly not the only reason, and it is accordingly potentially misleading to apply the term 'restrictive' to all integrated relative clauses.[10]

The most common type of integrated relative functions as modifier to a preceding noun, as in (22–23), (24i), (25). But two further constructions involving integrated relatives deserve mention:

(26) i   *It's Kim <u>that I can't stand</u>.*   [cleft relative]
      ii *I'll eat <u>what's left</u>.*   [fused relative]

Example (i) is a cleft counterpart of the more elementary clause *I can't stand Kim*: it serves to foreground *Kim* and background the rest, by putting it in an embedded clause, a **cleft relative**. *Kim* is antecedent for the understood object of *stand*, but the relative clause does not modify *Kim*: *Kim that I can't stand* is not an NP. The range of functions for the covert relativized element is considerably larger in cleft relatives than in modifying relative clauses. For example, we have *It was with a knife <u>that he cut it</u>* with covert instrumental adjunct, but not **This is the knife <u>that he cut it</u>*.

What's left in (26ii) is a **fused relative** in that *what* represents a fusion of the head in NP structure and the subject of the relative clause – compare the non-fused (and somewhat formal) construction *that which is left*. Likewise for *whoever* in <u>*Whoever is responsible for the accident*</u> *should be charged*, where again we may compare with non-fused *the person who is responsible for the accident*. It is important to emphasize that *what's left* and *whoever is responsible for the accident* are NPs, not (or at least, not at the highest level of structure) clauses. Clauses denote abstract entities such as propositions, not things that can be eaten, or people who should be charged.

2.3.2   Comparative clauses

These clauses function as complement of *than*, *as* or (in informal style) *like* in comparative constructions:

(27) i   *The pool was a good deal longer than <u>she'd said it was</u>.*
      ii *The pool was about twice as long as <u>it was wide</u>.*
      iii *You didn't meet us at the airport, like <u>you promised</u>.*

The syntactically distinctive property of comparative clauses is that they are structurally reduced relative to non-elliptical main clauses. Thus in (i) the predicative complement of *was* is not overtly expressed, and similarly in (iii) the complement of *promised* is left implicit. The reduction is less obvious in (ii) but nonetheless important: there is an unexpressed degree modifier of *wide*. The comparison is between HOW long the pool was and HOW wide it was, and just as there is an overt degree modifier of *long* (*twice as*), so there is a covert degree modifier of *wide* – which is why it is inadmissible to add an overt one (**The pool was about twice as long as it was three meters wide*). All comparative clauses involve some obligatory reduction, but typically they involve some optional reduction too; note, for example, that we could add *you would* in (iii). Reduction may result in a non-finite or even verbless clause: *She arrived earlier than <u>expected</u>* (compare finite *than we had expected*), *She didn't stay as long as <u>usual</u>* (compare *as it is usual for her to stay*).

2.3.3   Content clauses

The default subcategory of finite subordinate clauses is the **content** clauses, which lack the special features of relative and comparative clauses. The system of clause type, contrasting declarative, interrogative, etc. applies to this subclass of subordinate clauses as well as to main clauses, except that the imperative type is not found in content clauses.[11] Compare:

(28)		MAIN CLAUSE	CONTENT CLAUSE
i	DECLARATIVE	<u>*She is right.*</u>	*I know <u>that she is right</u>.*
ii	CLOSED INTERROGATIVE	<u>*Is she right?*</u>	*I wonder <u>whether she is right</u>.*
iii	OPEN INTERROGATIVE	<u>*What did they say?*</u>	*Tell me <u>what they said</u>.*
iv	EXCLAMATIVE	<u>*What a fuss he made!*</u>	*Tell her <u>what a fuss he made</u>.*

One further subcategory is the subordinate subjunctive, as in (21ii) above.

That and *whether* in (28i–ii) are subordinators: their function is to mark the subordination of declaratives and closed interrogatives respectively. Declarative is the default clause type, and its marker *that* is very often omissible (as in *I know <u>she is right</u>*). In closed interrogatives a marker is required, to distinguish them from declaratives – either *whether* or *if* (in its non-conditional use: *I wonder <u>if she is right</u>*).

Subordinators are traditionally analyzed as 'subordinating conjunctions,' but that traditional category also embraces numerous words such as *after, although, because, before,* conditional *if, unless, until,* etc., which are syntactically and semantically very different from subordinators. Compare *that* and *whether* in (28i–ii) with, for example, *before* and *although* in (29):

(29) i *We left the meeting <u>before the vote was taken</u>.*
      ii *We set out <u>although it was raining</u>.*

That and *whether* are grammatical markers of subordination, so that *that she is right* and *whether she is right* are simply the subordinate counterparts of the main clauses *she is right* and *is she right?* and make essentially the same semantic contributions. *Before* and *although* in (29), by contrast, have lexical meaning which makes the underlined constituents adjuncts of time and concession respectively. In this respect they are like the prepositions *before* and *despite* in (30):

(30) i *We left <u>before the vote</u>.*
      ii *We set out <u>despite the rain</u>.*

We therefore take *before* and *although* in (29) as heads taking clauses as complement, just as *before* and *despite* in (30) are heads taking NPs as complement. It is then not the underlined sequences themselves in (29) that are subordinate clauses but the sequences following the head: *the vote was taken* and *it was raining*. These are, more specifically, content clauses.

The similarity between examples like (29) and (30) was noted many years ago by Jespersen (1924: 89), who argued that the heads in both cases should be analyzed as prepositions. There is no more reason to assign *before* to two different categories because of the different categories of its complements than there is to do the same with *believe*, which can similarly take either an NP or a clause as complement. And there is no more reason to distinguish *although* from *despite* categorially than there is to distinguish, say, *complain* and *use*. Jespersen's proposal that prepositions have a wider range of possible complements than just NP has been generally adopted in formal grammar, particularly with respect to uniting intransitive prepositions like *away* and *back* with transitive ones like *at* and *with* (see, e.g., Emonds 1972; Jackendoff 1973, 1977; McCawley 1998: 195–6). We argue further for it in *CGEL* (pp. 1011–14), and stress the extension to allowing clause complements of prepositions.[12]

2.3.4   *The classification of finite subordinate clauses*

The above three-way classification into relative, comparative and content clauses differs quite radically from the classification of finite subordinate clauses found in traditional and indeed also in most modern grammars.

What traditional grammars say is that there are three kinds of subordinate clause, named after three of the parts of speech: 'noun clauses,' 'adjective clauses,' and 'adverb clauses.' The idea is that the clauses are functionally like words of the corresponding categories. Compare, for example:

(31)		WORD	'SUBORDINATE CLAUSE'
i	NOUN	*Victory is certain.*	*That we'll win is certain.*
ii	ADJECTIVE	*the sleepy child*	*the child who was sleeping*
iii	ADVERB	*We left early.*	*We left before the vote was taken.*

In (i) both underlined expressions function as subject, in (ii) as modifier of a noun and in (iii) as time adjunct. This traditional analysis is very deeply ingrained, but we find it untenable for three reasons.

(a)   First, a high proportion of so-called adverb clauses are far better analyzed as PPs, as we have just seen (in connection with *before the vote was taken*). The clause functioning as complement within the PP would be a noun clause in the traditional scheme.

(b)   Second, those adverb clauses that remain when we remove the PPs are systematically identical with noun clauses. Compare:

(32)	'ADVERB CLAUSE'	'NOUN CLAUSE'
i a.	*It was so hot that we stayed indoors.*	b. *I remember that we stayed indoors.*
ii a.	*I'm going whether you like it or not.*	b. *I don't care whether you like it or not.*

It is a mistake to assign the subordinate clauses in (a) and (b) to separate **categories**: they simply differ in **function**. The case is entirely parallel to that of a pair like *She died last Monday in hospital* and *She spent last Monday in hospital*: no one would dream of suggesting that *Monday* belongs to different categories here, though it is head of an adjunct in the former and head of an object in the latter.

(c)   Thirdly, the distribution of noun and adjective clauses is in fact very different from that of the corresponding word classes. Compare, for example, (33):

(33)	NOUN	'NOUN CLAUSE'
i a.	*We expect victory.*	b. *We expect that we will win.*
ii a.	**his surprise her resignation*	b. *his surprise that she had resigned.*
iii a.	**She is confident success.*	b. *She is confident that she will succeed.*

While 'noun clauses' are like nouns in that both can function as complement to verbs, they differ importantly from nouns in that they, but not nouns, can also function as complement to nouns and adjectives, as illustrated for *surprise* and *confident* in (ii–iii). Similarly with adjective clauses and adjectives. 'Adjective clause' is a traditional name for relative clauses (Matthews 1997: 8). While relative clauses are like adjectives in functioning as modifier to nouns in the core integrated construction shown in (31ii), they have a range of other non-adjective-like functions. There is nothing adjective-like about a cleft relative as in (26i). The supplement function illustrated in (24ii) is distinct from modification and can be filled by a wide range of categories, not merely (or even characteristically) adjectives. And relative clauses, unlike adjectives, can modify superlative adjectives and adverbs, as in *He's the fattest he's ever been* and *She ran the fastest that she had ever run*.

We conclude that the distribution of subordinate clauses should be described directly, not as parasitic on that of nouns, adjectives, and adverbs. (For fuller discussion of this issue see Huddleston and Pullum 2004.)

Modern theoretically informed works abandon the categories 'noun clause' and 'adjective clause,' but many still seem to accept adverb clauses (e.g., Trask 1993: 10; Hurford 1994: 232). The terms we find instead of 'noun clause' and 'adjective clause' are 'complement clause' and 'relative clause,' respectively. But the former term fails to recognize that while the clauses in question usually function as complement of one kind or another they are also found as adjuncts, as in:

(34) i *What do the basic laws of physics care about life and consciousness that they should conspire to make a hospitable universe?*
  ii *He'll resign, whether he is found guilty or innocent.*

The subordinate clauses here are not in complement function. But again, that is no reason for assigning them to a different category than in *It's odd that they should conspire to make a hospitable universe* and *I don't care whether he is found guilty or innocent.*[13]

Notice, moreover, that the comparative clauses of (27) do have complement function, but differ in significant ways from so-called 'complement clauses.'

2.4 *Non-finite clauses*

There are three major types of non-finite clause: (1) infinitival, (2) gerund-participial, and (3) past-participial. Two subtypes of infinitival clause are distinguished by the presence or absence of *to*:

(35) i INFINITIVAL   (a) *I want to repaint the kitchen.* [*to*-infinitival]
          (b) *I helped repaint the kitchen.* [bare infinitival]
  ii GERUND-PARTICIPIAL *Inviting the Smiths was a mistake.*
  iii PAST-PARTICIPIAL *Their son was among those arrested for drunkenness.*

Subjects of *to*-infinitivals are preceded by *for*: *For him to lose his temper like that is most unusual*. Historically, this derives from the preposition *for*, but synchronically it is a clause subordinator, like *that*, *whether* and *if* in content clauses.

Gerund-participials contain the verb-form marked by the suffix ·*ing*. Traditional grammars distinguish two inflectional forms with this suffix: a gerund, like the *inviting* of (35ii), and a present participle, as in *I won't be inviting the Smiths again*. But no verb in English shows any correlated morphological distinction. The syntactic distinction between gerunds and present participles is traditionally based on functional analogies with nouns and adjectives, but again such analogies do not provide a satisfactory basis for classification (see *CGEL*: 1220–2).

Past-participials may be either passive, as in (35iii), or perfect, as in *They have arrested him for drunkenness*. Note that we take an auxiliary verb to be the head of its clause, not a dependent of a following 'main verb.' *Have* here thus takes a past-participial clause as its complement – and similarly progressive *be* takes a gerund-participial clause as complement, and so on (*CGEL*: 1209–20).

The great majority of non-finite clauses, including those in (35), contain no subject, but the interpretation involves an 'understood subject,' and a great deal of work has been devoted to investigating this phenomenon. Three major cases can be distinguished:

(36)   i   a.   *Liz tried to warn you.*   b.   *I persuaded Liz*
                                                       to accept the offer.   [control]

       ii a.   *Liz seems to respect you.*   b.   *I expected Liz*
                                                       to accept the offer.   [raising]

       iii a.   *It was foolish*   b.   *Liz admitted it had been*
                to invite him.   *foolish to invite him.* [non-syntactic]

In (i) the understood subordinate-clause subject is generally described as **controlled**: the interpretation is fixed by reference to an element with a certain syntactic function in the matrix clause – the matrix subject in (a), the object in (b) (*Liz* is understood to be subject of *warn*, and of *accept*). The relevance of a certain specific syntactic function does not imply that semantics is of no relevance here; it has been persuasively argued (Sag and Pollard 1991; Culicover and Jackendoff 2003) that control is very much a semantic matter, and can operate across sentence boundaries (e.g., *John made Susan a promise. It was to take care of himself/*herself*). But although the fact that the direct object is the controller in (36ib) has much to do with the fact that the meaning of the sentence specifies Liz as the target of persuasion, and hence as the one whose acceptance is sought, that does not mean that there is any alternative to having the matrix object control the interpretation in constructions of that kind. Syntax is involved in the generalization too.

The examples in (ii) are different in that *Liz* here bears no semantic relation to the matrix verb. The sentences are equivalent respectively to *You seem to be respected by Liz* and *I expected the offer to be accepted by Liz*. The NP *Liz* belongs semantically in the subordinate clause, but is located syntactically in the matrix. It is accordingly described as a **raised** complement (a raised subject in (a), a raised object in (b)). Finally, in (iii) the interpretation of the missing subject is not determined by either syntax or semantic rule, but depends on context and inference: the understood subject of *invite* will be whoever it is reasonable to think, in the discourse or conversational context, might have been the source of the invitation.

NOTES

1 Sag et al. (1985) take a different tack, analyzing such facts purely in terms of categories, not functions. Their account makes use of underspecification: a coordination of (say) AdjP and NP belongs to a category that is neutral between the two, and can appear only where either AdjP or NP would be permitted, e.g., as complement to the copula. The approach taken by Sag et al. appears to us to be unable to cover the full range of possibilities for coordination of unlike categories dealt with in *CGEL*.

2 The attested sentence *It's meant to be a comedy, but it's not funny, but it's compulsive viewing* is not a counterexample to this claim, for it contains internal bracketing: the first two clauses are coordinated to form a coordination which, as a whole, is coordinated with the third clause. We thus have two coordinations each with two coordinates, not one coordination with three coordinates.

3 *Neither* is also occasionally paired with *or*: *neither young or healthy*.

4 Note that (following Huddleston 1984: 97–8) we use 'determin<u>er</u>' as the name of a **function** (compare 'modifi<u>er</u>') and 'determina<u>tive</u>' as the name of a **category** (compare 'adjec<u>tive</u>'). The determiner can be realized by other expressions besides determinatives, such as genitive and interrogative NPs, as in *the boy's shoes* and *what size shoes*. Similarly, most determinatives can occur in other functions besides determiner: *this* and *no*, for example, are modifiers in *this tall* and *no better*, while *both*, *either* and *neither* are markers of coordination in the examples under consideration here.

5 This distinction, which derives, essentially, from Lyons 1966, is discussed in *CGEL*: 28–33 and invoked extensively throughout that work.

6 See *CGEL*, pp. 1350–62, for a discussion of supplementation that owes a great deal to joint work with John Payne.

7 It should be noted that not every language has subordinate clauses. For example, many Amazonian languages appear not to have any subordinate clauses.

8 We thus restrict the subjunctive to traditional grammar's 'present subjunctive,' arguing in *CGEL*: 85–8 that pairs like (*if it*) *be* and (*if it*) *were* are not different tenses of a single mood. We take this *were* to be an isolated relic from an earlier inflectional system; we call it an irrealis mood-form.

9   Arguments for taking *that* as a subordinator rather than a pronoun are given in *CGEL*: 1056–7.

10   We should note that many modern grammars use the term 'appositive' in place of the traditional 'non-restrictive.' This is unsatisfactory, because the contrast between integrated and supplementary applies to standard cases of apposition as well as to relative clauses. Thus we have integrated apposition in *I was referring to W. S. Allen the applied linguist*, and supplementary apposition in *Let me introduce Kim Jones, our new neighbour*. For fuller discussion of the integrated vs supplementary distinction, see *CGEL*: 1058–66.

11   We have taken the term 'content clause' from Jespersen (1909–49, III: 23–4), but extended it to cover non-declaratives as well as declaratives.

12   The same argument applies to comparatives *than*, *as*, and *like*; this is why they are not included in the subordinate clauses in (27).

13   This is also one reason why we drop the widespread use of the term 'complementizer' and call *that* and *whether* 'subordinators.' Another reason is that *that* can also introduce relative clauses, as in (23i).

FURTHER READING

Biber, D., Johansson, S., Leech, G., Conrad, S., and Finegan, E. (1999) *Longman grammar of spoken and written English*. Harlow: Pearson Education (section D).

Borsley, R.D. (2003) Against ConjP. *Lingua* 115, 461–82.

Gazdar, G. (1981) Unbounded dependencies and coordinate structure. *Linguistic Inquiry* 12, 155–84.

Grover, C. (1994) Coordination. In R. E. Asher (ed.-in-chief), *The encyclopedia of language and linguistics*. Oxford: Pergamon Press, 762–8.

Huddleston, R. and Pullum, G. K., et al. (2002) *The Cambridge grammar of the English language*. Cambridge: Cambridge University Press, chs. 11–15.

McCawley, J. D. (1998) *The syntactic phenomena of English*, 2nd edn. Chicago: University of Chicago Press, chs. 9, 13, 20.

Quirk, R., Greenbaum, S., Leech, G., and Svartvik, J. (1985) *A comprehensive grammar of the English language*. London: Longman, chs. 13–17.

Shopen, T. (ed.) (1985) *Language typology and syntactic description, vol. II: Complex constructions*. Cambridge: Cambridge University Press (2nd edn., 2006).

Vincent, N. (1994) Subordination and complementation. In R. E. Asher (ed.-in-chief), *The encyclopedia of language and linguistics*. Oxford: Pergamon Press, 4391–6.

REFERENCES

Culicover, P. W. and Jackendoff, R. S. (2003) The semantic basis of control in English. *Language* 79, 517–56.

Curme, G. O. (1931) *Syntax*. Boston: D.C. Heath.

Emonds, J. E. (1972) Evidence that indirect object movement is a structure-preserving rule. *Foundations of Language* 8, 546–61.

Huddleston, R. (1984) *Introduction to the grammar of English*. Cambridge: Cambridge University Press.

Huddleston, R., Pullum, G. K., et al. (2002) *The Cambridge grammar of the English language*. Cambridge: Cambridge University Press.

Huddleston, R. and Pullum, G. K. (2004) The classification of finite subordinate clauses. In G. Bergh, J. Herriman, and M. Mobärg (eds.), *An international master of syntax & semantics: papers presented to Aimo Seppänen on the occasion of his 75th birthday*. Göteborg: Acta Universitatis Gothoburgensis, 103–16.

Hurford, J. R. (1994) *Grammar: a student's guide*. Cambridge: Cambridge University Press.

Jackendoff, R. S. (1973) The base rules for prepositional phrases. In S. R. Anderson and P. Kiparsky (eds.), *A festschrift for Morris Halle*. New York: Holt, Rinehart, & Winston, 345–56.

Jackendoff, R. S. (1977) *X̄ Syntax*. Cambridge, MA: MIT Press.

Jespersen, O. (1924) *The philosophy of grammar*. London: Allen & Unwin. New York: Holt.

Lyons, J. (1966) Towards a 'notional' theory of the 'parts of speech.' *Journal of Linguistics* 2, 209–36. Reprinted, with additional material, in J. Lyons, *Natural language and universal grammar* (1991), 110–45. Cambridge: Cambridge University Press.

Matthews, P. H. (1981) *Syntax*. Cambridge: Cambridge University Press.

Matthews, P. H. (1997) *The concise Oxford dictionary of linguistics*. Oxford: Oxford University Press.

McCawley, J. D. (1998) *The syntactic phenomena of English*, 2nd edn. Chicago: University of Chicago Press.

Merriam-Webster's dictionary of contemporary English usage (1994) Springfield, MA: Merriam-Webster.

Onions, C. T. (1971) *Modern English syntax*, ed. B. D. H. Miller. London: Routledge & Kegan Paul.

Quirk, R., Greenbaum, S., Leech, G., and Svartvik, J. (1985) *A comprehensive grammar of the English language*, London: Longman.

Richards, J., Platt, J., and Webber, H. (1985) *Longman dictionary of applied linguistics*. Harlow: Longman.

Sag, I. A., Gazdar, G., Wasow, T., and Weisler, S. (1985) Coordination and how to distinguish categories. *Natural Language & Linguistic Theory* 3, 117–71.

Sag, I. A. and Pollard, C. J. (1991) An integrated theory of complement control. *Language* 67, 63–113.

Sinclair, J. (ed.-in-chief) (1990) *Collins COBUILD English grammar*. London: Collins.

Trask, R. L. (1993) *A dictionary of grammatical terms in linguistics*. London: Routledge.

10 Tense in English

LAURA A. MICHAELIS

1 Introduction

Humans conceive of time in terms of space, as shown by the language that we use to talk about temporal relations: we habitually speak of *stretching out* or *compressing* an activity, *heading toward* the future, *returning to* the past and so on (Whorf 1956; Lakoff and Johnson 1980; Binnick 1991: ch (1)). When describing the meanings of the tenses, linguists have relied on a specific instance of the space–time analogy: the TIMELINE. The timeline is a line (or, equivalently, an ordered set of points) that is unbounded at both ends and segmented into three parts: the past, the present, and the future. The points on the timeline may be times by themselves or times paired with events. While we can describe various relations among points on the timeline, only one type of relation counts as a tense relation: that which includes the time at which the linguistic act is occurring. As Lyons states (1977: 682), "the crucial fact about tense [. . .] is that it is a deictic category. A tensed proposition, therefore, will not merely be time-bound [. . .] it will contain a reference to some point or period of time which cannot be identified except in terms of the zero-point of the utterance."

The relationship between utterance time and the time of the situation described may be direct, as in the case of ABSOLUTE TENSES like the past tense, or indirect, as in the case of RELATIVE TENSES like the future perfect (e.g., *I will have left [by the time you read this letter]*), in which the leaving event is represented as in the past relative to a point that is in the future relative to utterance time (the point at which the letter is read). Like other linguistic reference points that are anchored in the 'here and now,' the temporal zero-point can, under the appropriate conditions, be identified with times other than the time of speaking or writing. One such case is that in which a writer uses the time of message interpretation, rather than the time of message construction, as the zero-point (Declerck 1991: 15). For example, a note writer may choose the formulation *I'm across the hall* rather than *I will be across the hall*. The shifting of the temporal zero-point also occurs in subordinate clauses, both temporal and conditional, as in, e.g., *When/if you have finished your test, [raise your hand]*. Here, a present-perfect predication is used despite the fact that its reference point is located in a (hypothetical) future rather than at the time of speaking (McCawley 1981).

When we talk about the 'location' of the temporal zero-point we are of course making use of the space–time analogy. But if the zero-point is a temporal landmark, what is being located relative to it? Comrie (1985: 14) tells us that "tenses locate situations either at the same time as the present moment [. . .], or prior to the present moment, or subsequent to the present moment." This definition appears transparent, in that it partakes of the logic of the space–time analogy, but in fact there is reason to question whether tense "locates situations." If the situation in question is an event, then it is certainly true, for example, that a past-tense sentence like (1a) locates the cab ride prior to the time of speech, but do past-tense STATE predications, as in (1b), localize the situations that they denote in a similar way?

(1) a. I took a cab back to the hotel.
     b. The cab driver was Latvian.

If a speaker makes the assertion in (1b) following that in (1a), no sensible hearer will respond by asking whether the cab driver is still Latvian now. This is presumably because the cab driver's Latvian identity is highly unlikely to desist following the cab ride. Why then has the speaker of (1b) chosen to 'locate' the cab driver's Latvian identity in the past? The answer, which the German logician Hans Reichenbach provided over fifty years ago, is that tenses do not express the relationship between the temporal zero-point and the time of the state of affairs described. Rather, tenses express the relationship between speech time and another interval of interest, which Reichenbach (1947) referred to as REFERENCE TIME (R). Reference time is in principle distinct from either the time of the utterance (which Reichenbach refers to as SPEECH TIME, or S) or the time of the situation that the speaker is describing (which Reichenbach refers to as EVENT TIME, or E). Reference time, according to Klein (1992: 535), is "the time for which, on some occasion, a claim is made." In (1a), for example, R is a specific past time that both the speaker and hearer can identify, while in (1b) R is the time established by (1a): the time of the cab ride. What (1b) shows us is that when a speaker makes a past-tense stative assertion, she or he may vouch only for that portion of the state's tenure that coincides with the mutually relevant interval. In the following section, we will further explore the concept of reference time, its role in relative tenses like the past perfect, and the manner in which it relates to the two fundamental situation types, events and states.

The foregoing discussion has touched upon yet another questionable assumption about tense – that one can analyze it without reference to aspect. Certainly, as Comrie (1985: 6–7) observes, the two notions are conceptually separable: aspect involves the internal temporal structure of a situation (e.g., whether or not it includes transitions) rather than its placement on the timeline relative to speech time. The view that tense and aspect are semantically distinct is a basic premise of compositional models of English verb morphology, like that of Klein (1992). Such accounts assume that each component of semantic inter-pretation is associated with a distinct component of morphology or syntax. For example, periphrastic forms like the present progressive are analyzed as having a tense component (expressed by the finite auxiliary verb) and an aspect component (expressed by the present participial complement). The separability of tense and aspect is assumed as well in logical approaches to temporal relations like that of Herweg (1991), in which tenses are represented as operators that have scope over aspectual operators like the progressive, and aspectual oper-ators in turn have scope over predicate-argument complexes or, equivalently, tenseless propositions, e.g., *I take- a cab back to the hotel* in (1). However, as we have seen, states and events relate in distinct ways to the reference times for which they are asserted, and this fact alone suggests that tense and aspect "are [. . .] intimately related, and interact quite extensively" (Hornstein 1991: 9).

One such interaction is observed by Comrie (1985: 7): "many languages have forms that include specification both of location in time and of internal temporal contour; thus Spanish *hablé* is both perfective aspect and past tense." Here Comrie is illustrating the phenomenon of ASPECTUAL SENSITIVITY, as described by De Swart (1998): tenses may select for specific aspectual classes, as the Spanish perfective past invokes the class of events and processes. While aspectual sensitivity is generally illustrated by reference to the imperfective and perfective past tenses of the Romance languages, aspectually sensitive tenses can be found in English as well. In particular, we will see that the English present tense is an aspectual-class selector, and that many of its uses can be ascribed to this property. As observed by Langacker (1991: 259–60), Smith (1997: 110–12) and others, the present (or – in Langacker's formulation – the event of speaking), is construed as a single moment. Events have hetero-geneous internal structure (i.e., distinct subphases), and for this reason they take time. Accordingly, one cannot confirm that an event of a given type has occurred if one has access only to a single moment in the time course of that event. By contrast, states are effectively atemporal (Bach 1986): they can be verified on the basis of a single momentaneous sample. This entails that the present tense is semantically compatible only with state predications. This account, however, appears to leave us with no explanation of the fact that event verbs do indeed appear with present inflection, as in (2–3):

(2)   The flight arrives at noon.

(3)   My sister walks to work.

Certainly, neither the flight's arrival nor an episode of my sister walking to work must overlap the time of speech in order for (2) or (3) to be truthful assertions. Therefore, these examples suggest that the present tense has func-tions beyond that of reporting situations ongoing at speech time; the majority of scholars of English tense indeed assume this to be the case (see Kučera 1978; Binnick 1991: 247–51; and Dahl 1995 for discussion). However, as we will see in section 3, there is a way to analyze the functions exemplified in (2–3) that is highly compatible with the assumption that the present tense selects for the class of states. According to this view, both 'scheduled future' present predications like (2) and generic present predications like (3) are the products of COERCION, or, equivalently, implicit type shifting (De Swart 1998; Jackendoff 1999). Coercion can be illustrated in its application to the grammar of English nominal expressions. English determiners like the indefinite article select for nouns that denote countable entities, as in *an apple*. However, when the indefinite article is combined with a nominal that denotes a mass rather than a bounded entity, it forces an interpretation of that entity as a bounded quantity, as in, e.g., *a wine*, which denotes a portion or variety of wine. Here, as in the case at hand, the semantic requirements of the grammatical marker cause it to override intrinsic semantic features of the word with which it combines, resulting in a shift in what the word designates. Similarly, the present tense, as a state selector, can impose stative readings on any dynamic verb with which it combines, thereby resolving semantic conflict between the verb and the inflection that is attached to it. We will see that future and generic readings of present-tense predications can be analyzed as the products of this coercion mechanism.

In addition to interacting semantically, within a given grammatical construction, exponents of tense and aspect also interact within the system of time reference in English: aspectual constructions can express the same basic temporal relations that tense inflections do. These overlaps will be discussed in section 4. The English present perfect construction, e.g., *We've lost our lease*, is a notorious case of such a functional overlap. Theorists are not in agreement concerning the appropriate treatment of the English perfect construction; it has been analyzed as both a tense and an aspect (see Fenn 1987; Declerck 1991: 10–13; Klein 1992; and Binnick, this volume, section 3.1, for discussion). However, as we will see, there are good reasons to regard the perfect as an aspectual construction, and in particular as a stativizing construction (Herweg 1991). This function reflects its history: it emerged in Old English as a resultative construction containing a passive participle in agreement with the direct object. Through subsequent reanalysis, the participle came to be construed as predicating an action of the individual to whom the subject refers (Bybee et al. 1994; Hopper and Traugott 1993: 57–8). It is at this point that the present perfect and simple past tense come to be synonyms: as McCawley (1981) points out, it makes sense to refer to the past perfect as a 'past in past' form, but it makes much less sense to refer to the present perfect as a 'past in present,' since this is exactly what the simple past is. By the same token, we cannot appropriately refer to the perfect as a relative tense, because the present perfect encodes the same temporal relation that the simple past does: anteriority of the denoted event to speech time. Thus, the simple past and the present perfect do not appear to be distinguishable at the level of semantics. Instead, as both

Slobin (1994) and Michaelis (1998: ch. 5) argue, the two forms of past-time reference are distinguished by their use conditions. The development of this discourse-pragmatic division of labor served to differentiate the two converging constructions.

Additional evidence that an aspectual construction may function as a tense without losing its aspectual properties is provided by the so-called future tense of English, a periphrastic construction whose head is the modal verb *will*. A number of scholars, including Binnick (1991: 251–2) and Hornstein (1991: 19–20), have argued that the modal future of English does not have future reference but rather present-time reference, as indicated by patterns of adverbial co-occurrence. This will lead us to conclude that modal-future sentences are in fact present-tense stative predications. As we will see in section 4, this analysis of the English modal future, combined with the analysis of the present tense developed in section 3, has a significant implication for our description of the tense system of English: this system, rather than being based upon a past–nonpast division, as many scholars (e.g., Comrie 1985; Van Valin and LaPolla 1997) have assumed, is in fact based upon the opposition between past and present.

2   Reference Time

The primary insight behind Reichenbach's (1947) model of tense is that the meaning of every tense can be represented as a sequence of the three time points mentioned above: E, R and S. In Reichenbach representations, these points are separated either by a line, which is used to indicate that the left hand point precedes the right hand point, or by a comma, which is used to indicate that the two points are identical (i.e., not ordered with respect to one another). In the case of the simple tenses – past, present, and future – R and E are identical: the time referred to is also the time of the state of affairs denoted by the sentence. By contrast, in the case of the relative tenses, e.g., the past perfect, E and R are distinct: the time that the speaker is referring to is a time that either precedes or follows the time of the state of affairs denoted by the sentence. Reichenbach's representations of the simple tenses and the three perfect 'tenses' are given in (4a–f). For each tense representation, an example sentence is given, along with specification of the R point (which may or may not be overtly referred to by a subordinate clause or adverbial expression):

(4)   a.   **Present**: E,R,S (e.g., *She's at home right now*; R = right now)
      b.   **Past**: E,R_S (e.g., *She was at home yesterday*; R = yesterday)
      c.   **Future**: S_E,R (e.g., *She will be home this evening*; R = this evening)
      d.   **Present perfect**: E_S,R (e.g., *The crowd has now moved to plaza*; R = now)
      e.   **Past perfect**: E_R_S (e.g., *The crowd had moved to the plaza when the police showed up*; R = the time at which the police arrived)

f. **Future perfect**: S_E_R (e.g., *The crowd will have moved to the plaza by the time you call the police*; R = the time at which the police are called) or E_S_R (e.g., *That's Harry at the door; he will have bought wine*; R = the time of answering the door)

Hornstein (1991) extends the Reichenbach framework in order to account for constraints on DERIVED TENSE STRUCTURES, which result either from adverbial modification or clause combining. According to Hornstein (1991: 15), derived tense structure (DTS) must preserve the tense structure of the input sentence, which he refers to as the basic tense structure (BTS). He states two conditions under which BTS may be preserved:

(5) a. No points are associated in DTS that are not associated in BTS.
   b. The linear order of points in DTS is the same as that in BTS.
      (Hornstein 1991: 15, (13))

Hornstein proposes (1991: 17) that adverbial modification is a function that maps a BTS into a DTS that is identical to the BTS of the particular adverbial expression. For example, the BTS of the adverb *yesterday* is E,R_S, while that of *tomorrow* is S_E,R. Accordingly, the DTS of (6a) obeys (5) while that of (6b) violates (5):

(6) a. Harry arrived yesterday.
   b. *Harry left tomorrow.

In (6a′) and (6b′) we see the BTS-DTS mappings that produce (6a) and (6b), respectively:

(6′) a.   yesterday

$$E,R\_S \;\rightarrow\; E,R\_S$$
$$|$$
$$\text{yesterday}$$

   b.   tomorrow

$$E,R\_S \;\overset{*}{\rightarrow}\; S\_E,R$$
$$|$$
$$\text{tomorrow}$$

Sentence (6a) is well formed because the adverb *yesterday* does not create associations that are not already present in the BTS of the base sentence (*Harry arrived*), nor does it alter the linear association of points within this BTS. By contrast, (6b′) violates (5b): the adverb *tomorrow* alters the linear association of points within the BTS of *Harry left*: while this BTS places S after E and R, modification by *tomorrow* requires that S precede these two points.

Crucially, as Hornstein demonstrates (1991: ch. 2), the constraints on temporal modification given in (5) scale up to more complex constructions, in particular those that contain finite subordinate clauses headed by temporal connectives like *when*, *while*, *after* and *before*. In describing such constructions, Hornstein capitalizes on the basic insight, mentioned above, that "S may be anchored to times other than the moment of utterance" (Hornstein 1991: 126). The particular constraint on temporal embedding that he proposes is as follows: "a sentence that modifies another sentence [must] share its S point and its R point" (Hornstein 1991: 44). The linking of the respective S and R points must preserve the BTS of both the subordinate and main clause. In (7a–b) we see two examples of complex clauses, the first of which obeys (5) and the second of which violates it:

(7)   a.   Harry will leave when Sam has arrived.
      b.   *Harry will leave when Sam arrived.

The grammaticality contrast in (7a–b) is explained according to the representations of these sentences in (7a′–b′), respectively. In these representations, the respective S and R points of the main and subordinate clauses have been associated.

(7′)   a. $S_1\_R_1, E_1$ (Main clause: *Harry will leave*)

                $E_2\_S_2\_R_2$ (Subordinate clause: *Sam has arrived*)

      b. $S_1\_R_1, E_1$ (Main clause: *Harry will leave*)

                $R_2\_E_2\_S_2$ (Subordinate clause: *Sam arrived*)

Hornstein assumes that the linking of S_2 to S_1 occurs first, followed by the linking of R_2 to R_1 (1991: 43). He thus states the constraint on clause combination as follows (ibid.): "The movement of R_2 to a position associated with R_1 must obey [the constraints stated in (5)]." Thus, once S_1 and S_2 are associated in (7a′), R_1 and R_2 can be associated without requiring reorderings in either of the two input representations. (Notice that while the association of R_1 and R_2 requires breaking of the association between R_2 and S_2, neither clause of (5) prevents this.) By contrast, once S_1 and S_2 are associated in (7a′), the association of R_1 and R_2 can occur only if the order of R_1 relative to R_2 is altered as shown. Since this reordering would violate (5b), Hornstein correctly predicts that (7b) is semantically anomalous.

It is not clear, however, that the constraints on derived tense structures also apply to MODAL uses of absolute and relative tenses, in which tenses are used to express speakers' judgments, either about the degree of likelihood or the factuality status of an event denoted by the subordinate clause of a conditional sentence (Fleischman 1989). These examples include those in which the present tense, the past tense and the past perfect appear in the subordinate clauses of future, hypothetical and counterfactual sentences, respectively:

(8) a. If she **arrives** before midnight, she will catch the shuttle.
     b. If she **arrived** before midnight, she would catch the shuttle.
     c. If she **had arrived** before midnight, she would have caught the shuttle.

In (8a), present tense is used in the subordinate clause to denote a future event; in (8b), past tense is used to denote a future event that is presumed by the speaker to be relatively unlikely; and in (8c), the past perfect is used to denote an event that is presumed by the speaker not to have occurred. Clearly, these subordinate tenses do not denote the relationship between E and S, or E and R, that is shown in the representations in (4). Hornstein argues (1991: 73–9) that while the constraints on derived tense structures do not predict the particular tense uses in (8), they do not rule them out either. All such sentences meet the conditions on derived tense structures "on the assumption that simple modals are in the present tense, whereas *modal + have* are past-tense forms" (p. 77). We will return to the question of why the modal or *will* future is generally barred from the subordinate clauses of futurate conditionals like (8a) in section 4 below.

Another problem of clause embedding that is widely discussed in the literature on tense is that of SEQUENCE OF TENSE (Comrie 1986; Enç 1987; Declerck 1991: 157–91, Hornstein 1991: ch. 4). Sequence of tense phenomena involve the BACKSHIFTING of the tense of a present, past-tense or future predication when that predication is the complement of a past-tense verb of speaking or thinking. Examples involving indirect speech are given in (9); the sentences in parentheses beside each example show the direct-speech counterparts of each embedded clause:

(9) a. Debra said she **liked** the wine. ("I like the wine")
     b. Debra said she **had brought** a bottle of wine. ("I brought a bottle of wine")
     c. Debra said she **would bring** some wine. ("I will bring some wine")

The tenses in the embedded clauses of such sentences are relative tenses, because they do not relate the situation denoted (e.g., Debra's liking the wine or having brought a bottle of wine) directly to speech time; instead the S point of the embedded clause is identified with the event time of the matrix clause – the time of the event of speaking. To model sequence of tense, Hornstein proposes a SOT (sequence-of-tense) rule, which shifts the S of the embedded clause and associates it with E of the matrix clause (Hornstein 1991: 137). The position of the E and R points of the embedded representation relative to S of the matrix clause in the derived tense structure predicts the form of the backshifted tense in the embedded clause. An example of the application of the SOT rule, as applied to (9b), is given in (10):

(10) E_1, R_S_1 SOT E_1, R_S_1
                $\rightarrow$ |
      E_2, R_S_2 E_2, R_S_2

In the derived tense structure that is output by the SOT rule, shown on the right side of the arrow, the association of the embedded clause's S point with the matrix clause's E point has caused the embedded clause's E point to precede both the matrix R point and the matrix S point. Since, as shown in (4e), the schema E_R_S corresponds to the past perfect, the SOT rule correctly predicts that the backshifted form of the past tense will be the past perfect. At the same time, however, not all theorists of tense presume the existence of a backshifting rule for sequence of tense. Declerck (1991, 1995) and Declerck and Depraetere (1995) argue that sentences like (9a) simply illustrate two distinct uses of the past tense: the verb *said* illustrates the absolute use, in which the past tense indicates anteriority of R to S, while the verb *liked* illustrates a relative use, in which the past tense indicates simultaneity of the situation to a reference time that is in the past relative to S. This analysis is based on the observation that the use of the past tense to indicate simultaneity is attested independently of SOT contexts – for example, in coordinate sentences like *I danced and my sister played the recorder*. Here, the first sentence establishes a past reference time and the second an activity that overlaps this past reference time (see Binnick, this volume, section 6, for discussion of rhetorical relations in temporal discourse).

Thus far we have seen some of the properties of Reichenbach's framework that are responsible for its enduring appeal: it not only provides an elegant way of representing the meanings of the tenses, but can also be used to capture constraints on the embedding of one tensed clause in another. Several failings of the Reichenbach framework, including its inability to distinguish between events and states and its overly restrictive view of temporal-adverb reference, are discussed by Declerck (1991: 224–32). An additional problem, recognized by a number of discourse theorists starting in the 1980s, is that Reichenbach's conception of R is static; he argues, for example, that assertions in a narrative must share a reference point (Reichenbach 1947: 293). This view is difficult to square with the fact that narratives depict a time course. We now turn to attempts by discourse theorists to expand the Reichenbach conception of reference time in order to describe the temporal sequencing of events in narrative.

In the prototypical case, a narrative is a sequence of past-tense assertions. For this reason we will focus here on the semantic representation of such assertions. Logical accounts of the meaning of the English past tense can be divided into two general types. In both types of accounts, the past-tense marker is viewed as an operator, e.g., *Past*, that has scope over a tenseless proposition. The truth of the resulting proposition is evaluated at speech time. The first type of account, associated with Prior (1967), is that in which a proposition of the form *Past* (*A*) is judged to be true if and only if the tenseless proposition *A* is true at a time *t-1* earlier than speech time, *t*. In the second type of account, advocated by Reichenbach (1947), a past-tense sentence is interpretable as true or false only relative to a specific past interval, reference time. Partee (1984) observes that under Prior's view, the truth of an assertion in the simple past depends on the truth of the base sentence at SOME point in the past, whereas under Reichenbach's view, the truth of a past-tense assertion depends on the truth of the base sentence at THAT time in the past. Most modern accounts of past-time reference follow Reichenbach's view rather than that of Prior. One reason for this is that there is evidence to suggest that reference-time specification must be part of the truth conditions of past-tense sentences. For example, a speaker who makes the assertion *I took out the garbage* will be viewed as lying if he completed the denoted action merely at *some* point in the past (say, a month ago) rather than at the time that he knows the hearer has in mind, say, this morning.

The idea that R is an interval that is mutually identifiable to speaker and hearer underlies Partee's (1984) claim that past tense sentences 'refer back' to an already established reference time, as in the narrative passage in (11):

(11)   Police have arrested a suspect in last week's string of convenience store robberies. They apprehended the suspect as he left a downtown Denver nightclub. He was taken into custody without incident.

In (11), the present-perfect 'lead sentence' establishes a past reference time (the time of the arrest), while the two following past-tense sentences evoke that same past interval as they elaborate the circumstances of the arrest. It is in this sense that we may say that the two past-tense sentences in (10) are anaphoric: like pronouns, they rely on the interpreter's ability to recover the identity of a discourse-active entity, in this case, a past interval. However, as Partee (1984) and Hinrichs (1986) point out, past-tense sentences need not receive the anaphoric interpretation that they have in (11). As described by Binnick (this volume, section 6), there is another narrative mode, which Dowty (1986) refers to as TEMPORAL DISCOURSE, in which the sequence of sentences in the narrative matches the real-time structure of the world that is being described. The passage in (12) provides an example of temporal discourse:

(12)   Sue began to walk out. She paused for a moment and then turned around to face her accusers once again. The room was silent except for the ticking of the wall clock. She began to speak, shook her head and hurriedly exited.

In (12), for example, the time at which Sue paused is not the same interval as that during which she began to walk out of the room; the latter interval follows the former. Thus, the past-tense sentence *She paused for a moment* does not 'refer back' to the reference time of the prior past-tense sentence (*Sue began to walk out*); rather, it refers to a time *R+1*. This means that in a temporal discourse like (12) there must be some procedure for updating R during the course of the narrative (Partee 1984; Hinrichs 1986; Dowty 1986). Approaches to this problem within formal semantics have typically relied on some version of Discourse Representation Theory (Kamp and Reyle 1993). Whether formal or informal, however, models of tense use in texts must acknowledge the central role played by sentence aspect in the identification of reference time.

To see this, let us return to the passage in (12). Here, we can notice that while the event assertion *[Sue] turned around to face her accusers* induces us to advance R, the state assertion *The room was silent* does not. Rather, we interpret the state of silence as holding at the same point that Sue turned around to face her accusers.

There is, however, another reading of the predication *The room was silent* in which silence was a consequence of Sue's action. This reading clearly does require updating of R: the room's silence began at a reference time following that of the sentence *[Sue] turned around*. On this latter reading, in fact, the assertion *The room was silent* denotes not a state but an event – the event of the room's becoming silent. Partee (1984) captures these two distinct interpretations by means of the following generalization: if the situation denoted is an event, R includes the event, and elapses with its cessation; if the situation denoted is a state, R is included within that state, and does not elapse (i.e., it remains the reference time for the next assertion). Dowty's (1986) Temporal Discourse Interpretation principle is a similar generalization, although Dowty assumes, contra Partee (1984), that state predications, like event predications, move reference time forward in temporal discourse. Dowty (1986) proposes that pragmatic inferences concerning possible overlap relations determine whether the situation denoted is interpreted as holding at both the new reference time and prior reference times. He argues (1986: 48) that

> the inferences we draw in a narrative about which events or states overlap with others in the narrative [are] not really a consequence of the times sentences are *asserted* to be true, but rather also in part a consequence of the times at which we *assume* that states or events actually obtain or transpire in the real world, intervals of time which may in some cases be greater than the intervals of time for which they are simply asserted.

Dowty goes on to point out that since a state assertion may be true for an interval that includes the interval for which the actual assertion is made, state predications can always be understood to extend 'backwards' in the time line of the text to include previously invoked reference times. In making this observation, however, Dowty has implicitly acknowledged that direction of inclusion is not a contextual implication but a semantic property of state predications. It is in fact the same property that leads Comrie (1976) Langacker (1986) and Smith (1997), among others, to the observation that perfective aspect, as in (13a), encodes an 'external viewpoint' while imperfective aspect, as in (13b), encodes an 'internal viewpoint' (see Binnick, this volume, section 3):

(13) a.   Sue went home at noon.
      b.   Sue was home at noon.

In (13a), noon is interpreted as an interval during which the act of Sue's going home occurred. In (13b), by contrast, noon is interpreted as a point within the span of time that Sue was at home. By assuming that state predications include their references times, we can also account for the fact that the situations denoted by stative predications are always temporally extensible: a stative assertion that is true at a given reference time may also be true at a superinterval that includes that reference time (Herweg 1991). This means that one can always follow an assertion like (13b) with a 'proviso' that suspends the inference that (13b) invites:

(14)　In fact, she is still home now.

Sentence (13b) triggers the inference that Sue was not home during any intervals that include noon; had she been, the reasoning goes, the speaker would have made a stronger assertion, involving that larger interval. The fact that this inference, which is based upon Grice's first maxim of quantity ('Say as much as you can'), can be preempted indicates that states are unconfined by the reference times for which they are asserted; they are, as Bach (1986) says, temporally ill founded. Direction of inclusion can also be used to account for ambiguities that arise in adverbially modified predications containing state verbs, as in (15):

(15)　Sue was in Cleveland yesterday.

Sentence (15) has both a stative interpretation and an episodic (event) interpretation. In the former case, the reference time named by *yesterday* is included within the time that Sue was in Cleveland. In the latter case, the daylong interval exhausts Sue's stay in Cleveland. What this shows is that aspectual construal does not depend on the inherent aspectual semantics of the verb, but rather on the direction of inclusion selected by the interpreter.

The mere fact that past-tense predications like (15) are ambiguous between state and event readings provides evidence against the traditional model of the English past tense, in which it "express[es] an explicit temporal relation, that the narrated events occurred before the moment of speech" (Bybee et al. (1994: 152). Such definitions are sufficient for past-tense *event* predications, but it is only by examining past-tense *state* predications as well that we can arrive at a sufficiently general definition of the past tense. As we have seen, the past tense merely locates R before S; it is the aspect of a predication that determines whether it denotes a situation that ended prior to speech time. In the next section, we will examine another tense–aspect interaction, which occurs when reference time and speech time coincide.

3　The Present Tense as State Selector

The present tense, according to Bybee et al. (1994: 152), "carries no explicit meaning at all; it refers to the default situation from which other tenses represent deviations." Because of its neutral semantics, they argue, the present tense can "absorb the meaning inherent to normal social and physical phenomena, and this meaning if described and broken down explicitly, consists of habitual occurrence and behavior as well as ongoing states" (ibid.). The analysis raises more questions than it answers. First, why should ongoing states be more "normal" than ongoing events? Second, why should a meaningless construction require a disjunctive definition, involving both ongoing states and habituals? But even leaving these concerns aside, it is apparent that one could not describe the aspectual constraints that the present tense exhibits, or the coercion effects that it triggers, if one did not view it as meaning something. As discussed in the Introduction, the present tense can be viewed as an aspectually sensitive tense operator that selects for the class of states. As we saw, this selection behavior comes from the logical relationship between time depth and the conditions of verification upon event reports. It is this selection behavior that yields habitual and gnomic construals of sentences that combine present-tense inflection with an intrinsically dynamic verb like *smoke* or *float*, as in (16–17), respectively:

(16)   Ally smokes.

(17)   Oil floats on water.

Many aspectual theorists, including Krifka et al. (1995), conflate habitual and gnomic sentences (statements of general principles) under the general rubric of GENERIC sentences. In accordance with Krifka et al. (1995) and Bybee et al. (1994: 152), we will assume that the differences between habitual sentences (which Krifka et al. refer to as CHARACTERIZING SENTENCES) and gnomic sentences (which Krifka et al. refer to as REFERENCE TO TYPES) can be traced to characteristic properties of nominal reference. Nominal expressions in gnomic sentences have attributive reference, leading to contingency readings. For example, one can paraphrase (17) by means of a conditional sentence: if there is something that counts as oil, it will float on whatever substance qualifies as water. Habitual sentences like (16) do not have contingency readings, since they attribute properties to specific individuals. However, habitual and generic sentences both differ from episodic sentences in that they entail iteration of the denoted event and express nonincidental facts about the world.

In a typological survey of the generic-episodic distinction, Dahl (1995) suggests that although all languages use grammatical markers to distinguish between generic and episodic sentences, no language dedicates grammatical resources exclusively to this function (p. 425). One can reach an even stronger conclusion when considering English data, because in English there does not appear to be *any* grammatical marking of the generic-episodic distinction. Dahl has assumed that there is a single marker of genericity in each of the languages in his study, taking the present tense to be the 'generic marker' for English. This appears to be a mistake, however, as generic statements can be expressed by a number of other tense–aspect combinations. These include the simple past and past progressive, as exemplified in (18–19), respectively:

(18)   Dogs chased cars in those days,

(19)   During that summer parents were keeping their children indoors.

These examples show, as Langacker observes (1996: 292), that generic predications can denote situations which hold "for either a bounded or an unbounded span of time, i.e., their validity has a temporal *scope*" [emphasis in original]. Therefore, we cannot define generic sentences as either a class of state sentences or a class of present-tense sentences: as shown in (18–19), past-tense sentences and progressive sentences can also be used to make generic assertions. However, we can say that generic sentences are highly likely to be expressed by the present tense, and that speakers are highly likely to use the present tense when called upon to produce a generic sentence. This correlation suggests that genericity is not only a contextual inference but also one that is based upon a semantic prototype. The generic-episodic distinction is a contextual one because it hinges on inferences about the size of the relevant time scales. If the intervals separating instances of the iterated event are judged to be small, as in (20), the predication will be judged as episodic; if the iterated events are judged to be widely dispersed through time, as in (21), the predication will be judged generic:

(20)   The light flashed

(21)   The Catholic mass was recited in Latin.

But there is still a sense in which (21) is not a 'true' generic sentence, because the situation reported is not ongoing at speech time. It is this intuition that leads us to conclude that genericity is a prototype-based concept. The best examples of generic sentences not only invoke large time scales but also denote situations that hold at speech time. Why should this be? When a situation is reported as including the reference time, as states are, nothing preempts the inference that this situation also holds at times prior to and subsequent to the reference time. An interpreter who is placed 'inside' a situation in this way is therefore free to conclude that the situation is a fact about the world rather than merely incidental. Now, certainly (21) could be construed as a state sentence, since the situation that it denotes could be understood to include an already evoked reference time (e.g., the sixteenth century). However, (21) also has a 'closed,' episodic interpretation in which, e.g., the Catholic mass was recited in Latin only prior to the Second Vatican Council. This is because the past tense is aspectually neutral: as seen in the previous section, past-tense sentences may be ambiguous between event and state readings. Sentence (15), repeated here as (22), is a past-tense sentence that is ambiguous in exactly this way:

(22)   Sue was in Cleveland yesterday.

The present tense, however, is not aspectually neutral. Present-tense sentences are intrinsically state sentences, and for this reason the present tense is more strongly correlated with the generic construal than is the past tense. Observe, for example, that (23) has only a generic construal:

(23)   The Catholic mass is recited in Latin.

As mentioned, generic sentences describe multiple instances of a given event, e.g., recitation of the Catholic mass. But how can a present-tense sentence denote an event, repeated or otherwise, when, as we saw above, present-tense sentences denote states? Certainly, a repeated event does not necessarily qualify as a state: iterated-event sentences like (20) are event sentences rather than state sentences. The problem can be framed as follows: if the present tense is a state selector, it must find a state within the semantic representation of the tenseless proposition with which it combines. In the case of (23), for example, this tenseless proposition is *The Catholic mass be- recited in Latin*. The semantic representation of this proposition does in fact contain selectable states: an event sequence must, by definition, contain periods of stasis, or, equivalently, RESTS, which hold between adjacent subevents (Michaelis 2004). This is equivalent to saying that every transition has both an anterior, onset, phase and a posterior, offset, phase (Bickel 1994). The present tense, as a state selector, can select that rest which includes the reference time (i.e., speech time).

Of course, every event, whether iterated or not, has both an anterior state (the state that holds before the event occurs) and posterior state (the state that holds after the event has occurred). This observation leads naturally to a coercion-based account of the so-called futurate present in English. This construction is exemplified in (3), repeated here as (24):

(24)   The flight arrives at noon.

Since arrival has an extended temporal profile that cannot fit inside the present moment, that event must be 'flipped' onto either one side or the other of the present partition in order for the semantic conflict between the tense inflection and the verb to be resolved. Thus (24) denotes the state that lasted until the event of arrival. While in many languages the equivalent of (24) can be interpreted as a perfect predication (via selection of the state phase *following* the denoted event), in English, as a matter of linguistic convention, coercion selects the state phase that *precedes* the denoted event. These observations point to the conclusion that the specific coercion effects triggered by a given aspectually sensitive form, e.g., the present tense, may vary from language to language, while the aspectual-selection properties of that form do not.

By viewing the present tense as a state selector, we can address a long-standing puzzle concerning temporal reference in English: why isn't the

English present tense used for event reporting? Notice, for example, that (25–26) are ungrammatical if construed as reports of events ongoing at speech time:

(25)   *Look! Harry runs by the house!

(26)   *They finally fix the sidewalk!

As evidence that the ungrammaticality of (25–26) is due to the impossibility of overlap with the moment of speech, consider that similar effects occur in reported speech, in which, as described in section 2 above, a matrix verb of cognition or speech provides a surrogate speech time for the subordinate-clause predication. If the subordinate clause contains a stative verb, the sentence is ambiguous: we do not know whether the speech act reported upon was originally in the present tense or past tense (Declerck 1991: 26–7, 1995). Sentence (27) exemplifies this ambiguity:

(27)   Sue said that she preferred white wine.

If Sue's speech act is to be reconstructed as a stative predication, i.e., *I prefer white wine*, it includes the time at which she uttered it. If, alternatively, Sue's speech act is to be reconstructed as an event predication, i.e., *I preferred white wine*, the situation described by Sue must precede the time of her speech act. Notice, however, that if we were to replace the subordinate-clause verb *preferred* with an event verb, e.g., *drank*, Sue's original speech act could only be reconstructed as a past-tense predication. In other words, an event cannot be construed as overlapping speech time, whether speech time is the time at which the speaker is speaking or a surrogate speech time – the time at which someone is depicted as speaking.

Cooper (1986) argues that the English Present is "exotic" in requiring a higher degree of coincidence between speech time and situation time than does present-tense inflection in other languages: "the semantic location of the present in other languages requires the discourse [time] to temporally overlap the event [time] rather than be identical with it" (p. 29). However, it appears that what makes the English present tense idiosyncratic in comparison to the present tenses of other languages (e.g., the Romance languages) is that it is not a general-purpose stativizer. Those type shifts which the English present tense fails to perform are those which are performed by periphrastic stativizing constructions – specifically, the perfect and progressive constructions. The emergence of these two constructions, via possessive and a locative periphrases, respectively, increased the overall transparency of the type-shifting system in English, but contrary to what we might expect, these newly developed stativizers did not merely narrow the functional range of the present tense. When the perfect obtained a continuative meaning in Early Middle English, as exemplified in (28), it in fact took over a function previously performed by the PAST tense, exemplified in (29–30):

(28) Ant ye, mine leove sustren, **habbeth** moni dei **icravet** on me after riwle.
      'And you, my beloved sisters, have for many days desired a rule from
      me.' (*Ancrene Wisse*, ca. 1220)

(29) A Ic wite **wonn** minra wraecsitha.
      'Always I [have] suffered the torment of my exiles.' (*The Wife's Lament*,
      ca. 970)

(30) For that sothe **stod** a than writen hu hit is iwurthen.
      'For that truth [has] remained always in writing, about how it
      happened.' (Layamon's *Brut*, ca. 1200)

Unlike the perfect, whose current use conditions were largely in place by the
thirteenth century (Carey 1994), the progressive is a relatively recent innovation (Joos 1964). As of Shakespeare's time, the alternation between the present
tense and the present progressive was apparently conditioned only by metrical
considerations (Dorodnikh 1989: 107), as when the present tense is used to
convey progressive meaning in Romeo's question *What light through yonder
window breaks?*. According to Joos (1964: 146) the progressive attained its current
usage only in the nineteenth century, when it came to be used in passive
predications, e.g., *The lamps were being lighted*, as against the earlier middle
form, *The lamps were lighting*. Again, however, it would be shortsighted to
analyze this development as having occurred at the expense of the present
tense alone, as when Bybee, et al. (1994: 144) state that "the Progressive appears
to have been taking over some of the functions of the Present for several
centuries." Indeed, as we saw in (25–26), simple present-tense predications
in English, unlike those in, e.g., French, lack progressive readings, but so do
simple PAST-TENSE sentences, as shown by (31):

(31) When I entered the church, they recited the mass in Latin.

Sentence (31) does not have a reading in which the recitation of the mass was
ongoing prior to my entering the church. In order to achieve this 'overlap'
interpretation, the past progressive (i.e., *They were reciting the mass in Latin*)
would be required. Thus, we can hypothesize that the introduction of the
progressive construction in English narrowed the functional range of BOTH the
present and past tenses, and not merely the present tense. The progressive
replaced tense-based coercion as the means of denoting overlap between an
event and the currently active reference time.

4   Functional Overlaps between Aspect and Tense

While the preceding section concerned implicit type-shifting, or coercion, an
interpretive process through which the meaning of a verb is shifted in order to

resolve semantic conflict between a verb and its grammatical context, the present section will concern EXPLICIT type-shifting, in which verbal aspect is shifted through grammatical means, in particular through the use of periphrastic, auxiliary-headed constructions (Herweg 1991). Several of these constructions have meanings that are indistinguishable from those of specific tenses, and this is why they are of interest to us here. In type-shifting constructions, the auxiliary verb denotes the output type (a state) while the nonfinite complement denotes the input type (an event). In English, these constructions include the perfect, the progressive and the modal (or 'will') future. These constructions are not uniformly viewed as stativizers in the literature, and so it is worthwhile to look at the evidence that they are. One line of evidence comes from stativity tests like Vlach's (1981) *when*-test: if the situation denoted by the main clause can be construed as overlapping an event denoted by a temporal clause introduced by *when*, it is a state. If, alternatively, the main-clause situation cannot be construed as overlapping the *when*-clause event, but must instead be construed as following that event, it is an event. Using this test, we can show that progressive sentences are state sentences. In (32–34), the verbs whose aspectual properties are being diagnosed are shown in boldface:

(32) **State**: When Harry met Sue, she **preferred** white wine.

(33) **Event**: When Harry met Sue, she **drank** a glass of white wine.

(34) **Progressive state**: When Harry met Sue, she was **drinking** a glass of white wine.

In (32), just as in (34), we see that the main-clause situations (Sue's preferring white wine, Sue's drinking a glass of white wine) overlap the event of Harry's meeting Sue. That is, the progressive predication in (34) has the same overlap interpretation as the stative predication in (32), indicating that progressive predications are appropriately viewed as state predications. Together, (32) and (34) contrast with (33), in which the main-clause situation (Sue's drinking a glass of white wine) cannot be construed as overlapping the event of meeting. What type of state is the progressive state? According to Michaelis (2004), it is a state derived via selection of an intermediate state or 'rest' between two transition points in the temporal representation of an activity. In the case of the progressive predication in (34), this intermediate state might be the period of stasis between two swallows of wine. By viewing the progressive as an intermediate-state selector, we can account for the fact that progressive predications report upon events that are ongoing at R. Analogous observations can be made about the perfect aspect:

(35) **State**: When Harry met Sue, she **preferred** white wine.

(36) **Event**: When Harry met Sue, she **drank** a glass of white wine.

(37)   **Perfect state**: When Harry met Sue, she had **drunk** a glass of white wine.

The application of the *when*-test in (37) is somewhat less straightforward than that in (34), so some further explanation is required. In (37), we construe the event of Sue's drinking a glass of white wine as having preceded the event in which Harry met her. What does precedence have to do with overlap? The two notions amount to the same thing in the case of the perfect construction, since perfect predications can be said to denote a state of aftermath following the occurrence of that event denoted by the participial complement (Herweg 1991). It is this state of aftermath which overlaps the event denoted by the subordinate clause in (37). Thus, while perfect predications, e.g., *The Eagle has landed*, are state predications, they also count as event reports, since they assert a past event by means of asserting its resultant state (see Binnick, this volume, section 3.3 for discussion of the various uses of the perfect aspect). It is therefore no surprise that a periphrastic present-perfect construction may take over the functions formerly served by a morphological past-tense construction, as in modern spoken French. In English, however, the opposite development appears to have occurred: the present perfect currently has more restrictive use conditions than the past tense. These conditions, described by Fenn 1987 and Michaelis 1998, among others, include the prohibition against specification of event time (38), and against use of the present perfect in information questions that presuppose the occurrence of a unique past event, as in (39):

(38)   *I have woken up at dawn this morning.

(39)   *When have you woken up?

As Comrie (1976) observes, there is no reason in principle that (38) could not be used as a response to a question like 'Why do you look so tired?' Certainly, in such a context the present-perfect predication would describe a state of aftermath, as required by its semantic analysis. Nor is there any logical reason that (39) could not be used as an inquiry into the time of rising of someone who is currently awake. The constraints illustrated in (38–39) instead appear to be consequences of the development of a discourse–pragmatic opposition between two nearly synonymous forms of past-time reference, one a tense construction, the past tense, and the other an aspectual (stativizing) construction, the present perfect (Slobin 1994). According to Michaelis (1998: ch. 5), this opposition involves temporal anaphora: while the present perfect establishes a reference time, the past tense, as described in section 2, either establishes or evokes a previously established reference time.

   The degree of functional overlap between exponents of tense and aspect becomes particularly clear when one considers the English modal future. Unlike other languages, English has no morphological future tense, but only a periphrastic construction containing the auxiliary *will*, a form derived via semantic bleaching from a stative verb meaning 'want.' While this construction is a stativizer, that function is somewhat more difficult to establish by means of the *when*-test than were the stativizing functions of the progressive and perfect constructions. The reason is that *will* has no unambiguous past tense: the past-tense forms of modals, e.g., *would*, have subjunctive functions rather than unambiguous past-time reference (Fleischman 1989; Langacker 1991: ch. 6). There are, however, other ways of establishing that a clause denotes a state, one of which involves temporal reference. Present-time adverbials, including *now* and *at this moment* are compatible only with stative predications, for the reasons outlined in section 3: the present is conceived as a moment, and only states are verifiable on the basis of a single momentaneous 'sample.' Given the fact that present-time adverbials are compatible with modal-future predications, as exemplified in (40–41), we have reason to conclude that modal-future predications are in fact state predications:

(40)   My daughter will now play the clarinet for you.

(41)   I will fill out the form right now.

The state denoted by modal-future predications is an anterior state, i.e., the 'preparatory phase' preceding an event. The behavior of morphological future tenses, in those languages which have them, is very much different. As pointed out by Hornstein (1991: 19–20), for example, French future-tense predications are not compatible with present-time adverbial reference:

(42)   *Je donnerai   une conférence maintenant.
       I   give:1SG:FUT a   lecture   now
       'I will now give a lecture.'

If the English modal future in fact has present-time reference – that is, if its temporal representation is not S_E,R, as shown in (4c), but S,R_E, the mirror image of the present-perfect representation given in (4d) – we have a potential explanation for the tendency for subordinate futurate clauses, as in (43), to lack the modal:

(43)   a.   *When the Prime Minister will arrive, they will play the national anthem.
       b.   When the Prime Minister arrives, they will play the national anthem.

Nieuwint (1986) proposes that the modal future in English expresses a prediction, and therefore that sentences like *They will play the national anthem* predicate a state of the present time (e.g., that the appropriate preparatory conditions for the event in question exist). On this understanding, sentences like (43a) are semantically anomalous: they appear to reverse the order of events intended by the speaker. If the playing of the national anthem occurs during the time when the Prime Minister is about to arrive, then the playing precedes his arrival rather than following it. On Nieuwint's account, therefore, the preemption of the modal future in subordinate-clause contexts like that in (43b) follows from the fact that the English modal future associates S and R. See Declerck and Depraetere (1995) for an alternative proposal.

While many scholars, including Hornstein, have observed that English lacks a true future tense like that of French, there is disagreement about the implications of this fact for the tense system of English. Many, including Comrie (1985), view English as having a past–nonpast tense distinction. The rationale for this analysis comes from the supposition that the English present tense does not denote present time, since it is also used to express future events and temporally unbounded situations, in particular generic ones. However, as we saw in Section 3, both futurate present and generic predications can be seen as the products of stative coercion triggered by the aspectual selection properties of the present tense. It is therefore reasonable to conclude that the English tense system is based instead upon a past–present distinction: English lacks a future tense but has both a past tense and a present tense. Each of these tenses can combine with the auxiliary head of a periphrastic aspectual construction, including the progressive, the perfect and the modal future. In specific grammatical contexts, as we have seen, each of these constructions may stand in for a tense: the progressive replaces the present tense when an event is being reported as ongoing at speech time, the past tense replaces the perfect when the speaker is referring to a specific past interval, and the present tense replaces the modal future in the subordinate clause of a futurate conditional sentence. These interactions need not, however, be taken to imply that the perfect, progressive and modal-future constructions are tenses. As we have seen, tenses fix the location of R with respect to S, while the periphrastic constructions that we have looked at in this section do not: their auxiliary verbs, when finite, can be inflected either for present tense or past tense.

5   Conclusion

In this brief survey of English tense, we have discussed a number of misconceptions about tense. One of these is that tense locates situations. In fact, as we have seen, tense merely locates reference time, while aspect determines the manner in which the denoted situation relates to reference time. Another misconception about tense is that the present tense is meaningless or, at the very least, identifies a far broader interval than the present interval alone. This view is based upon the observation that the present tense combines with both state verbs and event verbs. As we have seen, however, the ability of the present tense to combine with event verbs need not be viewed as evidence of its lack of semantic restrictions; such combinatory freedom can instead be viewed as evidence of the aspectual sensitivity of the English present tense and its consequent ability to shift the aspectual type of verbs with which it combines. As a state selector, the present tense is capable of selecting state phases within the temporal representations of events. The importance of aspect to an understanding of the English tense system is underscored by the fact that, as we have seen, certain auxiliary-verb constructions with tense-like functions, e.g., the perfect construction, also function as stativizers. In such constructions, the state denoted by the tensed auxiliary verb is ordered relative to the event denoted by its complement in a way that resembles the ordering relations encoded by tense, and for this reason type-shifting constructions like the perfect aspect are often functionally indistinguishable from tense constructions like the past tense.

Throughout this survey, we have gained insight into the semantics of tense by examining the interaction of tense and aspect, both within a given grammatical construction and within the system of temporal reference in English. The depth of these interactions should not, however, be taken as evidence that tense and aspect are inextricable at the level of semantics. Rather, it is only by carefully distinguishing the functions of tense markers from those of aspectual markers that we can say anything rigorous about the interplay between the two systems.

FURTHER READING

Binnick, Robert I. (1991) *Time and the verb*. Oxford: Oxford University Press.

Bybee, Joan, Revere Perkins, and William Pagliuca (1994) *The evolution of grammar*. Chicago: University of Chicago Press.

Comrie, Bernard (1985) *Tense*. Cambridge: Cambridge University Press.

Declerck, Renaat (1991) *Tense in English: its structure and use in discourse*. London: Routledge.

Dowty, David (1986) The effects of aspectual class on the interpretation of temporal discourse: semantics or pragmatics? *Linguistics and Philosophy* 9, 37–61.

Fleischman, Suzanne (1989) Temporal distance: a basic linguistic metaphor. *Studies in Language* 13, 1–50.

Hornstein, Norbert (1991) *As time goes by*. Cambridge, MA: MIT Press.

Klein, Wolfgang (1994) *Time in language*. London: Routledge.

Partee, Barbara (1984) Nominal and temporal anaphora. *Linguistics and Philosophy* 7, 243–86.

Reichenbach, Hans (1947) *Elements of symbolic logic*. New York: Macmillan.

Smith, Carlota S. (1997) *The parameter of aspect*. Dordrecht: Kluwer Academic Publishers.

Smith, Carlota S. (2003) *Modes of discourse: the local structure of texts*. Cambridge: Cambridge University Press.

REFERENCES

Bach, Emmon (1986) The algebra of events. *Linguistics and Philosophy* 9, 5–16.

Bickel, Balthasar (1997) Aspectual scope and the difference between logical and semantic representation. *Lingua* 102, 115–31.

Binnick, Robert I. (1991) *Time and the verb*. Oxford: Oxford University Press.

Bybee, Joan, Revere Perkins, and William Pagliuca (1994) *The evolution of grammar*. Chicago: University of Chicago Press.

Carey, Kathleen (1994) Pragmatics, subjectification and the grammaticalization of the English perfect. Unpublished doctoral thesis, University of California, San Diego.

Comrie, Bernard (1976) *Aspect*. Cambridge: Cambridge University Press.

Comrie, Bernard (1985) *Tense*. Cambridge: Cambridge University Press.

Comrie, Bernard (1986) Tense in indirect speech. *Folia Linguistica* 20, 265–96.

Cooper, Robin (1986) Tense and discourse location in situation semantics. *Linguistics and Philosophy* 9, 17–36.

Dahl, Östen (1995) The marking of the episodic/generic distinction in tense-aspect systems. In G. Carlson and F. Pelletier (eds.), *The generic book*. Chicago: University of Chicago Press, 412–25.

Declerck, Renaat (1991) *Tense in English: its structure and use in discourse*. London: Routledge.

Declerck, Renaat (1995) Is there a relative past tense in English? *Lingua* 97, 1–36.

Declerck, Renaat and Ilse Depraetere (1995) The double system of tense forms referring to future time in English. *Journal of Semantics* 12, 269–310.

De Swart, Henriette (1998) Aspect shift and coercion. *Natural Language and Linguistic Theory* 16, 347–85.

Dorodnikh, Anatolij (1989) The English progressive and other verb forms in a historical perspective. *Folia Linguistica Historica* 9, 105–16.

Dowty, David (1986) The effects of aspectual class on the interpretation of temporal discourse: semantics or pragmatics? *Linguistics and Philosophy* 9, 37–61.

Enç, Murvet (1987) Anchoring conditions for tense. *Linguistic Inquiry* 18, 633–57.

Fenn, Peter (1987) *A semantic and pragmatic examination of the English perfect*. Tübingen: Gunter Narr Verlag.

Fleischman, Suzanne (1989) Temporal distance: a basic linguistic metaphor. *Studies in Language* 13, 1–50.

Herweg, Michael (1991) Perfective and imperfective aspect and the theory of events and States. *Linguistics* 29, 969–1010.

Hinrichs, Erhard (1986) Temporal anaphora in discourses of English. *Linguistics and Philosophy* 9, 63–82.

Hopper, Paul J. and Elizabeth Closs Traugott (1993) *Grammaticalization*. Cambridge: Cambridge University Press.

Hornstein, Norbert (1991) *As time goes by*. Cambridge, MA: MIT Press.

Jackendoff, Ray (1999) *The architecture of the language faculty*. Cambridge, MA: MIT Press.

Joos, Martin (1964) *The English verb: form and meaning*. Madison: University of Wisconsin Press.

Kamp, Hans and Uwe Reyle (1993) *From discourse to logic: an introduction to model-theoretic semantics of natural language, formal logic and discourse representation theory*. Dordrecht: Kluwer.

Klein, Wolfgang (1992) The present perfect puzzle. *Language* 68, 525–52.

Krifka, Manfred, Francis Jeffry Pelletier, Gregory N. Carlson, Alice ter Meulen, Godehard Link, and Gennaro Chierchia (1995) Genericity: an introduction. In G. Carlson and F. Pelletier (eds.), *The generic book*. Chicago: University of Chicago Press, 1–124.

Kučera, Henry (1978) Some aspects of aspect in Czech and English. *Folia Slavica* 2, 196–210.

Lakoff, George and Mark Johnson (1980) *Metaphors we live by*. Chicago: University of Chicago Press.

Langacker, Ronald W. (1986) *Foundations of cognitive grammar*, vol (1. Stanford: Stanford University Press.

Langacker, Ronald W. (1991) *Foundations of cognitive grammar*, vol. 2. Stanford: Stanford University Press.

Langacker, Ronald W. (1996) A constraint on progressive generics. In A. Goldberg (ed.), *Conceptual structure: discourse and language*. Stanford: CSLI Publications, 289–302.

Lyons, John (1977) *Semantics*, vol. 2. Cambridge: Cambridge University Press.

McCawley, James D. (1981) Notes on the English Perfect. *Australian Journal of Linguistics* 1, 81–90.

Michaelis, Laura A. (1998) *Aspectual grammar and past-time reference*. London: Routledge.

Michaelis, Laura A. (2004) Type shifting in construction grammar: an integrated approach to aspectual coercion. *Cognitive Linguistics* 15, 1–67.

Nieuwint, Pieter (1986) Present and future in conditional protases. *Linguistics* 24, 371–92.

Partee, Barbara (1984) Nominal and temporal anaphora. *Linguistics and Philosophy* 7, 243–86.

Prior, Arthur (1967) *Past, present and future*. Oxford: Oxford University Press.

Reichenbach, Hans (1947) *Elements of symbolic logic*. New York: Macmillan.

Slobin, Dan I. (1994) Talking perfectly: discourse origins of the present perfect. In W. Pagliuca (ed.), *Perspectives on grammaticalization*. Amsterdam: John Benjamins, 119–33.

Smith, Carlota (1997) *The parameter of aspect*. Dordrecht: Kluwer Academic Publishers.

Van Valin, Robert D., and Randy J. LaPolla (1997) *Syntax*. Cambridge; Cambridge University Press.

Vlach, Frank (1981) The semantics of the progressive. In P. Tedeschi and A. Zaenen (eds.), *Syntax and semantics*, vol. 14. New York: Academic Press, Inc., 415–34.

Whorf, Benjamin Lee (1956) *Language, thought, and reality*. Ed. John B. Carroll. Cambridge, MA: MIT Press.

11   Aspect and Aspectuality

ROBERT I. BINNICK

1   Introduction

The term *aspect* refers to *situation aspect* (section 2), *viewpoint aspect* (section 3), and *phasic aspect* (section 4). Some scholars (e.g., Verkuyl 1996) call aspectual phenomena in general *aspectuality*, as opposed to *aspects*, the specific aspectual categories. Some (Dik 1997) use *aspectuality* as a cover term for situation and viewpoint aspect.

2   Situation Aspect

2.1   *The types of eventualities*

Situation aspect (Smith 1983, 1986, 1991), *lexical aspect*, or *Aktionsart* 'kind of action,' concerns the classification of *eventualities* (Bach 1981, 1986) or *situations* (Mourelatos 1978), that is, states of affairs or occurrences, in terms of their temporal properties, and, secondarily, the classification of the types of expressions referring to them in particular languages.

States, denoted by *stative* expressions such as the verb *exist*, contrast with *events*, denoted by *eventive* expressions such as *arrive*. Many scholars recognize a third aspectual class, the *process* (Mourelatos 1978) or *activity* (Vendler 1957), denoted by a *processual* expression such as *run*. Vendler (1957) distinguishes expressions denoting momentary events, *achievements* (e.g., *win a race*), from those for events extending over time, *accomplishments* (e.g., *draw a picture*). *Point* (Miller and Johnson-Laird 1976) or *semelfactive* (Smith 1991) processes like blinking once may similarly be distinguished from extended processes like running. A *serial* expression (*whimper* in (1)) denotes a *series*, a sequence of recurring eventualities of a uniform type (Freed 1979).

(1)   The puppy whimpered all night.

Although the well known classificatory scheme of Vendler (1957) categorizes verbs and phrases (*reach the top*), Verkuyl (1972) shows that the relevant linguistic level is that of the clause or proposition, since aspectual classification may be affected by any of the various expressions accompanying the verb, including the subject (Dowty 1979; Platzack 1979; Carlson 1981). Thus *swam* is processual, and *swam across the pool* eventive, but whereas (2) refers to an event, (3) refers to a series.

(2)   One of the applicants swam across the pool.

(3)   All of the applicants swam across the pool.

States are properties of times, whereas events and processes occur at times (Davidson 1967; Parsons 1990). But, unlike events, processes are not individual, countable things that can be referred to (Bach 1981; Krifka 1989), though an *episode*, the occurrence of a process or state over a *bounded* or closed interval (period) of time, is event-like (4).

(4)   I was extremely ill only once, but it lasted for weeks.

Expressions belonging to the various aspectual classes differ in their semantic and grammatical properties. For example, they interact differently with adverbials (section 2.2) and with the viewpoint aspects (section 3.4).

The grammatical and semantic properties of the various types of expressions have been hypothesized to reflect the semantic structures of those expressions, composed of basic semantic elements which underlie the lexical components (morphemes) comprising the expressions (Pustejovsky 1990; Tenny 1994; Jackendoff 1996; Levin and Rappaport Hovav 1999).

2.2   *The temporal properties of eventualities*

The various classes of eventualities are distinguished by the temporal properties of *stativity*, *telicity*, and *durativity*, and also differ as to *cumulativity* and *partitivity*.

States are *stative*: they are uniform and lack both internal structure and development. Non-states may consist of different parts or *phases* (section 2.3), and show development over time.

States tend to endure, and so are normally *durative*, holding of intervals of time. Events and processes may be durative (accomplishments like climbing a mountain, processes like ageing), or non-durative and momentary (achievements such as spotting a coin on the pavement, point processes such as blinking once). Series are inherently durative.

Since an event is the transition from an *initial state* to a *result* or *consequent state*, it is *telic* (Garey 1957), containing an inherent *end-point* or *terminal bound*, the *point of culmination* (Moens and Steedman 1987, 1988), beyond which the event cannot be said to progress. States, processes, and series are *atelic*.

However, an event may be represented as incomplete (5), as not having reached its terminal point, and accordingly as lacking an actual end-point or *final bound*. On the other hand, a non-event may be assigned a final bound, as in (6).

(5)   John was reading *Hamlet* (when Susan came in).

(6)   The puppy {was lonely/dozed/barked repeatedly} until his owners returned.

Because of their different temporal properties, the types of eventualities differ as to the types of adverbials they co-occur with (Dowty 1979). A *frame adverbial* (*in a minute*) normally combines with an eventive expression, and with a non-eventive expression (7), triggers an *ingressive* or *inchoative* interpretation, as the initiation respectively of the process or state in question. Conversely, an *adverbial of duration* (*for a while*) normally combines with an atelic expression, and triggers a processual interpretation of an eventive expression (8).

(7)   In a minute, John saw what he had to do.

(8)   Susan read the book for a while.

Non-events are *cumulative* (Krifka 1989); two consecutive eventualities con-stitute an eventuality of the same type, so that (9) and (10) jointly entail (11). They are also *partitive* (Carlson 1981): portions of such an eventuality extending over intervals are themselves eventualities of the same type, so (11) entails both (9) and (10). States have the *subinterval property*: if the state s expressed by an expression e holds over an interval of time I, s holds over any time I', even a point, within I (Bennett and Partee 1978). Events are neither cumulative nor partitive. Thus (12) entails (13), but (14) contradicts (15).

 (9)   John {was ill/ran/coughed repeatedly} from noon to 3 in the afternoon.

(10)   John {was ill/ran/coughed repeatedly} from 3 to 5 in the afternoon.

(11)   John {was ill/ran/coughed repeatedly} from noon to 5 in the afternoon.

(12)   Susan read for five hours.

(13)   Susan read for three hours.

(14)   Susan read the book within five hours.

(15)   Susan read the book within three hours.

2.3   *The phasic structures of eventualities*

Eventualities consist, in general, of sequences of parts or *phases*. The various types of eventualities differ as to what phases they contain.

The model of Moens and Steedman (1987, 1988) is one that has been widely followed. States and processes consist of unitary phases.

An achievement consists solely of a point of transition; this may be the culmination of an implicit process (*arrive*), or the transition into a state (*appear*) or process (*break into song*). An accomplishment consists of a *preparatory phase*, a durative process (such as the activity of climbing a mountain), and an achievement (the point at which the top of the mountain is reached), the *event* proper. Moens and Steedman (1987, 1988) include the consequent state in the *event nucleus*, along with the preparatory process and culmination point; this accounts for narrative advance (section 6). Any of these phases may itself be complex (Steedman 2001: 11).

The preparatory phase may be designated, as in (16), by the progressive aspect (section 3.2). However, the progressive is also used with achievements (17), which lack preparatory phases. In such cases, it designates an analogous *preliminary phase* (Freed 1979; Johnson 1981), which Moens and Steedman (1987, 1988) identify with the initial state preceding an event. (For an alternative analysis of the progressive with eventive expressions, see section 5.3.)

(16)   Mr. Blandings was building his dream house.

(17)   The train was arriving at the station.

On the role of phase in *phasic* theories of aspect, see section 5.3.

Stages such as the beginning or middle of an occurrence are also called *phases* and their marking, *phasic aspect* (section 4).

3   Viewpoint Aspect

3.1   *Defining the viewpoint aspects*

Viewpoint aspect (Smith 1983, 1986, 1991), *verbal aspect*, or *grammatical aspect*, is a widespread grammatical category, but may not be found in all languages (Dahl 2001).

Viewpoint aspect involves the marking of "different ways of viewing the internal temporal constituency of a situation" (Comrie 1976: 3). Aspectual markers, unlike tense markers, do not indicate objective differences, and the same eventuality can be represented in different ways, as in (18, 19).

(18)   Susan built kayaks.

(19)   Susan was building kayaks.

Many grammarians follow Comrie (1976) in distinguishing *perfective aspect*, which provides an "external" view of the eventuality as a single, complete whole, from *imperfective aspect*, which gives a partial, "internal" view; and, further, in recognizing two varieties of the imperfective: *habitual aspect*, which represents the eventuality as a series (section 2.1), and *continuous aspect*, which represents it as in its course, and hence incomplete.

Theorists differ on whether, in the absence of an overt aspectual marker, the simple tenses mark aspect. The default aspectual interpretation of such a sentence depends on its aspectual class. An eventive expression normally is interpreted as representing a complete eventuality (20), while an atelic expression such as a process (21) or state (22) is interpreted as representing an incomplete one.

(20)   Mr. Blandings built his dream house.

(21)   The children played.

(22)   John was hungry.

For this reason, the tenses are seen by some as aspectually indifferent (Hatcher 1951; Comrie 1976: 25), and in phasic theories of aspect (section 5.3), aspect is accordingly optional. In boundedness (section 5.1) and relational (section 5.2) theories, however, aspect is obligatory, the simple tenses marking aspect as well as tense. Smith (1991) proposes that the simple tenses mark *neutral aspect*, which includes the *initial bound* and at least a portion of the interior of the eventuality. Alternatively, the tenses may be viewed as perfective, in boundedness theories because they include both initial and final bounds of the actual occurrence, in relational theories because the eventuality fills its referential frame.

Habitual aspect may be marked by *used to* (23) or the modal *will/would* (24). That the situation marked by *used to* no longer holds is not part of the meaning of the marker, but a cancelable implicature (interpretation in context), as shown by the tag "and he still does" in (23). Habitual aspect is also an interpretation of a non-stative expression in a simple tense (25). Expressions receiving an habitual interpretation generally may receive a *generic* interpretation as well (26), as characterizing a period of time but not referring to specific occurrences, nor, often, to specific subjects. Consequently some refer to *generic aspect* (Dahl 1985).

(23)   John used to swim every day, and he still does.

(24)   Every now and then, John {will/would} suddenly burst into song.

(25)   Susan {swam/ate an apple/built kayaks} (regularly/once in a while).

(26)   The cat catches mice.

Continuous aspect represents the eventuality as in its course, and hence incomplete. Some see the *progressive* form in English, which consists of the auxiliary verb *be* and the progressive participle (*was sleeping* in 27) as simply marking continuous aspect, while others (e.g., Comrie 1976) define *progressive aspect* as a variety of continuous aspect, in which the eventuality is represented as non-stative or *dynamic*, i.e., in the course of development (28). (On the meaning and use of the progressive form, see section 3.2.)

(27)   Susan was sleeping.

(28)   Mr. Blandings was building his dream house.

In addition to progressive aspect, most grammarians since Dillon (1973), consider English to have *perfect aspect*, marked by the *perfect form*, structurally similar to the progressive form, consisting of an auxiliary verb (*have*) and the perfect participle (*swum* in (29)). Trager and Smith (1951), Joos (1964), and Palmer (1987), however, call the perfect *phase*, and Bauer (1970), *status*. Fenn (1987: 247) argues against perfect aspect on the ground that the perfect form can combine with a marker of aspect, the progressive (30), without causing a contradiction. Peculiarities of the present perfect tense that are not shared by the other perfect tenses, such as its inability to combine with definite past time adverbials (31, 32), have been seen as arguing against its simply combining present tense with perfect aspect (McCawley 1971; Michaelis 1994). (On the meaning and use of the perfect form, see section 3.3.)

(29)   John has swum across the pool.

(30)   John has been swimming all afternoon.

(31)   *John has swum yesterday.

(32)   John had swum the day before.

The perfect represents an anterior eventuality as viewed from the perspective of a *reference time* (Michaelis, ch. 10, this volume, section 2). Expressions such as *be to* and *be going to* (33) similarly represent a posterior eventuality as viewed from a reference time, and hence, according to some grammarians (Comrie 1976), mark *prospective aspect*. The *futurate* (relatively future) interpretation of the simple and progressive present tenses (*performs, is performing* in 33) is also considered by some (Lewis 1986) to constitute prospective aspect. These various expressions presuppose different grounds for the prediction of future events (Binnick 1974; Smith 1981; Goldsmith and Woisetschlaeger 1982; Prince 1982): the futurate tenses and *is to* (33) a planned or scheduled eventuality; *is about to* (34), a reasonable expectation; and *is going to* either of these (33, 34) or an intention (35).

(33)   Next Tuesday, Susan {performs/is performing/is to perform/is going to perform} before the Queen.

(34)   Watch out, it's {about to/going to} blow!

(35)   Susan says that she's going to run for public office.

On the interaction of situation aspect and viewpoint aspect, see section 3.4.

3.2   *Progressive aspect*

Traditionally, progressive aspect is defined in terms of temporal properties, namely *durativity*, *unboundedness*, and *dynamicity*.

The progressive aspect represents an eventuality as durative, while the perfective represents an eventuality as a durationless atom. Hence adverbials referring to points in time are restricted in the perfective to the initial (36) or final (37) bound of an event, while the progressive allows them to refer – and representing the eventuality as unbounded, without end-points, it restricts them to referring – to points falling within the event (38).

(36)   At noon, Susan ran out of the room.

(37)   At noon, Susan won the marathon.

(38)   At noon, Susan was {running out of the room/winning the marathon}.

The progressive represents the eventuality as dynamic and developing (Marchand 1955); the perfective represents it as static and unchanging. This may explain why the progressive is incompatible with stative expressions (39) (Leech 1971: 20ff; Comrie, 1976: 35). However, the progressive can be used for temporary states (40) (Leech 1971: 22ff), states in which there is a change of intensity (41), or ones which result from the actions of an agent (42).

(39)   *Paris is being between London and Berlin.

(40)   I'm feeling tired.

(41)   They're believing in God more and more.

(42)   The children are being difficult.

It poses a challenge for theories of the progressive that there are many types of sentences in which the progressive and perfective differ little in meaning, if at all, e.g., (43–46) (Hatcher 1951; Comrie 1976: 37).

(43)   {You're looking/you look} good.

(44) They {just said/were just saying} that . . .

(45) {We hereby inform/we are hereby informing} you that . . .

(46) {They have played/they have been playing} cards now for ten hours.

For the analysis of progressive aspect in modern theories of aspect, see sections 5.1–5.3.

3.3 *Perfect aspect*

The perfect has four principal uses (Comrie 1976: 56ff), the *resultative, experiential, continuative* perfects, and *perfect of recent past*. McCawley (1971) calls these the *stative, existential, universal*, and *hot news* perfects respectively. The continuative perfect has also been called the *inclusive perfect*, or *perfect of persistent situation*. With the exception of the hot news perfect, all these uses co-occur with the various tenses, though for reason of simplicity, only present tense examples are presented below.

The resultative perfect represents a state of affairs resulting from a prior event (47). It allows adverbials of recency (*just, recently*).

(47) Mother has just gone to the store.

The experiential perfect indicates the previous occurrence of an eventuality on at least one occasion (48), and its repeatability (49) (McCawley 1971; Leech 1971: 33). Leech (1971: 32) calls the present perfect an indefinite past tense, since it allows indefinite time adverbials of frequency (*often*) or quantity (*ever, never, twice*) (48).

(48) Mother has been to a World's Fair twice.

(49) Woody Allen has directed {#*Annie Hall*/an Oscar-winning film}.

The continuative perfect indicates an eventuality, previously begun, which continues at the reference time (50). It occurs with adverbials of duration (*for an hour, since yesterday*). The major use of the perfect progressive is for processes in the continuative perfect, though the perfect may be used by itself (51).

(50) The children have been outside all morning.

(51) Susan has {walked/been walking} for three hours now.

The perfect of recent past (52) reports an event that is presupposed to have happened recently. It allows adverbials of recency.

(52) The council has just voted to raise taxes.

In American English, the past tense often replaces the present perfect (53 = 54), but cannot substitute for its continuative use (55).

(53)   Mother went to the store (and is still there).

(54)   Mother has gone to the store (and is still there).

(55)   *Susan {walked/was walking} for three hours now.

The various uses of the perfect are considered by some to be predictable contextual interpretations (Bauer 1970; McCoard 1978; Fenn 1987), dependent on the types of adverbials co-occurring with the sundry aspectual classes, and not distinct meanings of the perfect itself, though Michaelis (1998) argues to the contrary. The continuative interpretation occurs when a non-eventive expression combines explicitly or implicitly with an adverbial of duration (56). The progressive allows the continuative perfect with events by rendering an eventive expression non-eventive (57). Eventive expressions otherwise receive either a resultative interpretation, triggered by an explicit or implicit adverbial of recency (58), or an experiential interpretation, triggered by an implicit or explicit adverbial of frequency or quantity (59). Because the relevant adverbial need not be contained in the sentence itself, nor even explicit, it is possible for the perfect to receive more than one interpretation, even in context (60 could be resultative or experiential). Michaelis (1998) cites (61), which plays on this "ambiguity."

(56)   Susan has been at the fair for an hour.

(57)   Susan has been reading *Hamlet* for an hour.

(58)   Susan has {just/recently} built a kayak in her garage.

(59)   Susan has {never/only once/often} built a kayak in her garage.

(60)   Susan has built a kayak.

(61)   I've had a wonderful evening, but this wasn't it.   (Groucho Marx)

McCoard (1978) identifies four types of theories of the perfect. In *current relevance theory* the perfect presupposes "current relevance [at the reference time]," which is subject to a number of complicated conditions. For example, current relevance generally (62), but not invariably (63), requires that the subject be alive. In *indefinite past theory* the perfect represents an anterior event occurring at a non-specific time. *Extended now theory* proposes that the perfect is used for events occurring in an interval of time whose upper bound is the reference time, thus allowing definite time adverbials referring to intervals containing the reference time itself (64). *Embedded past theory* sees the perfect as simply a past-tense embedded within the scope of another tense, as if (65) means 'it is the case that Susan went to the fair.' None of these theories has won acceptance by a majority of scholars.

(62) {#Melville/Amy Tan} has never written a novel about voles.

(63) Shakespeare has never been more highly regarded than today.

(64) Susan has been to the store {today/this morning}.

(65) Susan has gone to the fair.

Because the perfect represents the view of an occurrence from a later time, and not a view of the "internal temporal constituency" of the occurrence itself, it poses a challenge for boundedness theories of aspect (section 5.1). Relational theories of aspect (section 5.2) and phasic aspect theories (section 5.3), however, define the aspects uniformly.

3.4 *Situation aspect in relation to viewpoint aspect*

Situation aspect interacts with viewpoint aspect in all the aspects.

Sentences in the present tense are generally interpreted as referring to current eventualities only with stative expressions (66), including the progressive (67) and perfect (68). With eventive and processual expressions, the present tense has only habitual (69) or generic (70) interpretations, though there are exceptions, including reportative (71) and performative utterances (72).

(66) John {was/is/will be} tall.

(67) Susan {was/is/will be} visiting her mother.

(68) Susan {had/has/will have} visited her mother.

(69) Susan visits her mother.

(70) Lions eat meat.

(71) We now mix the ingredients together, like so.

(72) I agree.

The other tenses act similarly when their reference times (Michaelis, this volume, section 2) are momentary (73) or the sentence represents an act of speech (74) or thought (75).

(73)   When John opened the door, Susan {#chewed gum/was chewing gum}.

(74)   Susan denied that she {#chewed/was chewing} gum.

(75)   Napoleon was thrilled. Grouchy {#arrived/was arriving}!

The progressive, in contrast, normally cannot be used with stative expressions, though there are exceptions (section 3.2).

From the progressive with eventive expressions there arises the *imperfective paradox* (Dowty 1977, 1979). Sentences like (76) refer to events that may never occur and objects that may never exist; (76) entails neither (77) nor (78).

(76)   Susan was building a kayak.

(77)   Susan built a kayak.

(78)   There was a kayak, which Susan built.

Dowty (1979, 1986) proposes a solution in terms of possible future histories, that is, possible outcomes, and possible objects, but Parsons (1989, 1990) rejects this in favor of a solution which involves partial events and partial objects (Vlach 1981; Hinrichs 1983; Cooper 1985; Ter Meulen 1985, 1987). In phasic aspect theories (section 5.3), however, sentences like (76) are considered not to refer to accomplishments, but rather to their preparatory phases.

The habitual aspect is interpreted differently depending on aspectual class. *Used to* with stative expressions (79) does not receive an habitual interpretation. Similarly, with *will/would* or the simple tenses, an expression for an unbounded process (80) or state (81) is interpreted as an ingressive or inchoative event.

(79)   John used to be {president of the club/ill/heavier than he is now}.

(80)   Whenever Susan smiled, John {would frown/frowned}.

(81)   Susan {would understand/understood} complicated explanations in no time.

In the prospective aspect, too, expressions for states (82) and unbounded processes (83) receive inchoative and ingressive interpretations respectively.

(82)   If it's the last thing I do, I'm going to be (= 'become') wealthy some day.

(83)   John's about to play (= 'start playing') with the other children.

The interpretation of sentences in the perfect aspect likewise depends on the aspectual class of the expressions the marker is added to (section 3.3).

4   Phasic Aspect

Phasic aspect concerns reference to one or more stages (*phases*) of an eventuality, for example its beginning (84) or its end (85). Phasic aspect may be explicitly marked by an *aspectualizer* (aspectualizing verb) such as *begin* (84) or *stop* (85), or may be a contextual interpretation, such as inchoation (86).

(84)   John began to run.

(85)   John stopped running.

(86)   At that instant, John finally understood what he had to do.

Eventualities may be divided into *initial*, *medial* (*cursus, course*), and *final* phases, defined respectively by the aspectualizing verbs (*aspectualizers*) *begin/start, continue/keep/keep on*, and *stop/cease* (Freed 1979).

Freed (1979) argues that the aspectualizer *finish* refers to a *terminal* phase, preceding the point of culmination. This phase follows the final phase and is excluded by *stop*; thus (87) does not entail (88), though (88) entails (87).

(87)   Mr. Blandings stopped building his dream house.

(88)   Mr. Blandings finished building his dream house.

5   Theories of aspect

5.1   *Boundedness theories of aspect*

Comrie's definition of aspect as a "view of the internal constituency of an eventuality" (section 3.1) has been interpreted in different ways. Smith (1991) defines the aspects in terms of how much of the eventuality they include. Thus the perfective includes the entire eventuality, including initial and final bounds, while the imperfective excludes these and represents the eventuality as its internal portion only. Hence we may call hers a *boundedness* theory of aspect.

The perfect and prospective do not represent views of the eventuality itself, but rather the eventuality as viewed from the perspective of a reference time (Reichenbach 1947; Michaelis, ch. 10, this volume, section 2). As a result, those who subscribe to boundedness theories of aspect generally do not recognize perfect and prospective aspects, or follow Comrie (1976) in defining them in quite a different way from the progressive and perfective.

In theories such as Smith's (1986, 1991), the interactions of the aspectual classes (situation aspect) with the perfective and imperfective (viewpoint) aspects come about because the aspects include or exclude one or both bounds, whereas the various types of eventualities differ in boundedness. For example, the progressive renders an event incomplete by excluding its bounds (Smith 1986, 1991), while the perfective represents it as a completed whole by including them (Blansitt 1975). But the interactions of the aspectual classes with the perfect and the prospective (section 3.4), which are not defined in terms of boundedness, cannot be accounted for in the same way.

5.2   Relational aspect theories

Relational aspect theories such as that of Johnson (1981) define the aspects in terms of temporal relationships holding between the reference time R (also called the *frame of reference* or *temporal frame*) and the time E of the eventuality, rather than temporal properties of the eventualities themselves. Klein (1994) proposes that in the imperfective, the reference time is a *proper subinterval* of the time of the eventuality, that is, R falls entirely within E (89), whereas in the perfective the reverse is the case, and E is a subinterval of R. E may, however, either fall entirely within R (90) or be identical to R (E = R) and thus fill its frame (91). This accounts for the intuition that the perfective represents an external view of the eventuality, while the imperfective represents an internal view.

(89)   At noon, Susan was driving home.

(90)   Yesterday, Susan saw a shooting star.

(91)   While Susan sat reading, John listened to the radio.

Relational aspect theories provide a unified account of the aspects, since the perfect and the prospective are also defined in terms of temporal relationships, albeit ones of precedence rather than inclusion. In the perfect the eventuality E precedes the reference time R and in the prospective the reverse is the case, R preceding E. Thus relational aspect theories define four possible aspects.

Because theories such as Klein's define perfectivity in terms of inclusion of the eventuality in the frame, their accounts of the interaction of situation aspect and viewpoint aspect are similar to those of boundedness theories (section 5.1), and they have a similar difficulty in accounting for the interactions of situation aspect with the perfect and the prospective (section 3.4).

5.3   Phasic aspect theories

Unlike the other types of theories, phasic theories of aspect (Moens and Steedman 1987, 1988; De Swart and Verkuyl 1999; De Swart 2004) do not treat situation and viewpoint aspect as distinct, since both have to do with the temporal structures of eventualities. Situation aspect concerns their inherent typology (section 2.1), while the role of the aspectual markers, as well as aspectualizers (92) and bounding expressions such as *for half an hour* (De Swart 1998) (93), is to modify expressions, thereby transforming one aspectual class into another (De Swart 2004).

(92) Susan finished {*being happy/!running/*driving trucks for a living/ building the kayak}.

(93) John swam for half an hour.

This transformation or *type coercion* may be explicitly marked, but may be implicit, forced by the mismatch between the expected and actual types of an expression. For example, the resultative and experiential perfects normally refer to the result state following an event (94). With a stative or processual expression (95), the situation following the eventuality is interpreted as the result state of an event.

(94) Susan has eaten a worm.

(95) Susan has been a teaching assistant.

Because the progressive refers to the preparatory phase of an eventuality (section 2.3), it excludes stative expressions, since states lack such phases. The progressive transforms an accomplishment expression into one for a process (96), and forces coercion of an achievement expression into one for an accomplishment (97), which contains such a phase. Moens and Steedman (1987) view such a process as a dynamic state.

(96) They were climbing the mountain.

(97) They were reaching the summit of the mountain.

It is because the perfective involves no aspectual modification, and hence represents all phases of the eventuality, that with events (98), which are telic, it conveys a sense of completion, but not with atelics (99).

(98) They reached the summit of the mountain.

(99) Susan was asleep.

The perfect is likewise a stativizer, transforming eventive expressions into those for their result states, so that (100) and (101) entail one another (Moens and Steedman 1987). Accordingly, the perfect forces an eventive interpretation of an atelic expression (as in 102), either inchoative/ingressive (the continuative perfect), in which case the course of the eventuality itself becomes the result state, or episodic (the existential perfect), with the situation following the cessation of the eventuality as the result state.

(100) The windows have broken.

(101) The windows are broken.

(102)   John has run for over an hour.

The prospective similarly transforms eventive expressions into those for their preliminary phases, that is, initial states (103). The prospective differs from the future tense in referring to an eventuality which, although it will continue and possibly finish in future, has in a sense already begun. As with the perfect, an atelic is coerced into an eventive expression (104). (Michaelis, ch. 10, this volume, section 4, however, analyzes the future similarly as the "mirror image" of the perfect, and ascribes the futurate use of the present tenses to a type coercion.)

(103)   They're bringing out your puppy next.

(104)   They're playing (= 'starting to play') with your puppy next.

De Swart and Verkuyl (De Swart and Verkuyl 1999: 116; De Swart 2004) attempt to account for the properties of series by arguing that habitual sentences in the simple tenses (105) result from coercion of eventive expressions into atelic ones. It may be that "habitual" *will/would* and *used to* are best understood as marking similar type coercions.

(105)   Susan usually falls asleep while watching the telly.

The effect of the markers of viewpoint aspect is to transform basic types of aspectual classes into derived types that can perform different discourse functions. For example, the subsidiary, *background* material in a narrative discourse, which accompanies the *foreground* events (Hopper 1979), consists primarily of stative sentences (*he was hungry* in 106). The progressive and perfect aspects transform sentences into stative ones that can serve such a function, as in (107), in which the eventive expressions *slaughter his guards* and *escape*, and the processual *march north*, are transformed into stative, non-perfective expressions. The role of aspect in discourse is the subject of section 6.

(106)   John looked for a place to eat. He was hungry.

(107)   News came. Kornilov's faithful *Tekhintsi* had slaughtered his guards at Bykhov, and he had escaped. Kaledin was marching north . . . (Reed, *Ten Days that Shook the World*)

5.4   *Tenses as aspectual selectors*

In phasic theories of aspect (section 5.3), the function of viewpoint aspects is to transform the aspectual class of an expression. Recently it has been suggested that alongside such type transformers there are type *selectors*, which are sensitive to, and select, certain aspectual classes (de Swart 1998; de Swart and Verkuyl 1999).

Michaelis (ch. 10, this volume, section 3) proposes that the present tense is a state selector, occurring only with stative sentences, either basic (108) or derived by type coercion (109). In the case of the habitual or generic interpretation of eventive expressions (110), she argues that the tense selects the periods of stasis, the *rests*, between sequenced subevents. She further proposes that the futurate present (111) reflects the same kind of forced sequentiality we see in sentences like (112), as opposed to those like (113), in which a stative predicate allows simultaneity of the eventualities.

(108)   Susan is tall.

(109)   John is eating.

(110)   Susan swims.

(111)   John sings tomorrow.

(112)   When Susan entered, John leapt up.

(113)   When Susan entered, John was leaping up.

6   Aspect in Discourse

An explanatory account of aspect depends on understanding the function of aspect in discourse. The *textual function* (Fleischman 1990, 1991; Waugh 1991) is to create and maintain the coherence of the discourse at global and local levels of structure.

Global structure depends on the genre of the discourse. *Narrative* genres, for example fiction, contrast with genres of *discourse* (Benveniste 1959) or *commentary* (Weinrich 1964), such as conversation or reportage, both in structure and the use of tense and aspect. Narrative has a *foreground* (Hopper 1979) or main narrative line consisting normally of a chain of eventive clauses in the simple past tense (114). Tense use is *anaphoric*, linking the reference time of each clause to a specific time introduced by another clause in the narrative. The *background* of narrative (Hopper 1979) consists of non-eventive sentences (the second sentence in 115) and/or ones in non-perfective aspects (the third sentence in 115).

(114)   I came, I saw, I conquered. (Caesar, *Gallic Wars*)

(115)   Tom looked for a restaurant. He was hungry. He hadn't eaten for hours.

Genres of commentary are associated with non-eventive sentences (116). Tense use is *deictic*, the times of the eventualities relating directly to the *deictic center*, which is usually the time of utterance, and not to one another. In (117), unlike (115), there is no temporal relationship between the sentences.

(116)   Formic acid can be obtained from a colourless fluid secreted by ants . . .
It is a strong irritant. Commercially it is obtained from sodium formate
. . .   (*Pears Cyclopaedia*)

(117)   . . . before his name became widely known with the publication of *Justine*,
Durrell had the support of a vigorous minority . . . Henry Miller was
the first to speak out for him.   (Moore, *The world of Lawrence Durrell*)

In the local structuring of discourse, aspect serves to maintain coherence on three levels, the *linguistic, intentional*, and *attentional* (Grosz et al. 1995).

On the linguistic level, discourse coherence has to do with temporal relationships, with the *binding* or *anchoring* of the reference point of each clause by some time referred to in the preceding discourse. The binding time may be denoted by an expression such as a time adverbial (118) or noun phrase (119), or by a clause (120).

(118)   For the next few days the temperature was pleasant.

(119)   The war years were hard on Tom's family.

(120)   John entered the room. Jane was standing by the window.

In a narrative discourse, however, the reference points of linked clauses are not identical, but characteristically form a sequence in which each is slightly later than the preceding one (121); non-eventive, background clauses, however, do not in general trigger such *narrative advance* (122) (Kamp 1979; Dry 1981, 1983; Kamp and Rohrer 1983; Partee 1984; Hinrichs 1986).

(121)   Tom came in. Sue held up the newspaper.

(122)   Tom came in. Sue was holding up the newspaper.

Phasic aspect theories (section 5.3) account for narrative advance by assuming that foreground clauses take as their reference times the time introduced by the immediately preceding clause in the narrative sequence, including its result state, which is later than the reference time of the anchoring clause (Moens and Steedman 1988). No narrative advance occurs with backgrounded non-events (123) because they lack result states.

(123)   Susan was unhappy. John decided to help her.

Since the aspectual class of the sentence may be modified by aspectual markers (Moens and Steedman 1987, 1988; Boogaart 1999: section 3.3), viewpoint aspect plays a central role in discourse coherence on the linguistic level.

Temporal sequence is only one relationship that can hold between the events expressed by a sequence of eventive clauses. An event may precede (124), or form part of (125), the eventuality in the preceding clause. Sequences with non-eventive clauses (126, 127) likewise define various temporal relations, including temporal sequence (127) (examples from De Swart and Verkuyl 1999: 157).

(124)   The ship sank on its maiden voyage. The crew ran it into an iceberg.

(125)   John wrote a *roman à clef*. He wrote Susan into chapter 4.

(126)   Hilary entered the room. Phil was reading in his chair.

(127)   Hilary entered the room. Phil was happy to see her.

Temporal relations in discourse depend on *rhetorical relations* (Lascarides and Asher 1991, 1993; Lascarides and Oberlander 1993), also called *coherence, discourse* or *topical relations* (Hobbs 1979, 1985; Polanyi 1985; Thompson and Mann 1987; Mann and Thompson 1988; Scha and Polanyi 1988), which hold between segments of the discourse. Each of these relations defines a temporal relationship. *Narration* or *sequence* (128) and *consequence* (129) define temporal sequence; *explanation, precedence* (124); and *elaboration,* inclusion (125). When such a rhetorical relation is absent (130), temporal sequence does not suffice to assure discourse coherence (Caenepeel 1995).

(128)   A car came slowly down the street. It stopped in front of Harry's house.

(129)   A car stopped in the car park. A dog barked.

(130)   A car stopped in the car park. Anna sliced some radishes.

On the intentional level, local discourse coherence is a matter of the logic of the discourse, and consists precisely in attaching each clause to some segment of the preceding discourse by such a rhetorical relation.

On the attentional level, coherence is a matter of topical relevance, so discourse coherence is maintained by attaching each clause to a preceding segment of discourse, in narrative an episode with a common line of events, and in non-narrative a *thread*, a set of statements sharing a common topic (Grosz et al. 1995). Rhetorical relations structure discourse on the attentional level by coordinating or subordinating material to the immediately preceding segment of discourse (Hobbs 1985; Lascarides and Asher 1993; Caenepeel and Moens 1994; Spejewsky 1996), thereby either maintaining the current segment or creating secondary narrative lines (131) or subordinate threads (132).

(131)   Tom got home late and was very tired. He had worked a long, hard day and had had a frustrating drive home through dense traffic.

(132)   I told Frank about my meeting with Ira. We had talked about ordering a Butterfly. (based on Webber 1988)

Coordinating rhetorical relations, typically marked by perfective aspect, include *narration* (133) and *listing* (134). Subordinating rhetorical relations include explanation (135), *elaboration* (136), and *consequence* (137).

(133)   Bill sang a song. Jane thanked him on behalf of the audience.

(134)   Bill sang a song. Jane played the piano.

(135)   The waste bin burst into flame. Someone threw a lighted match into it.

(136)   Susan visited her aunt Martha. They had tea on the verandah.

(137)   The waste bin burst into flame. Someone grabbed the fire extinguisher.

Perfective aspect tends to maintain the segment, while a non-perfective often marks a shift into a subordinate thread. Thus (138) is ambiguous, while in (139) the past perfect unambiguously marks the second sentence as belonging to a subsidiary thread (Webber 1988).

(138)   I told Frank about my meeting with Ira. We talked about ordering a Butterfly.

(139)   I told Frank about my meeting with Ira. We had talked about ordering a Butterfly.

In secondary narrative lines, such as extended flashbacks, we may find non-perfective tenses that are not normally associated with narrative, such as the past perfect (140) (Kamp and Rohrer 1983; Comrie 1986).

(140)   He had not been known to them as a boy; but . . . Sir Walter had sought the acquaintance, and though his overtures had not been met with any warmth, he had persevered in seeking it.   (Austen, *Persuasion*)

Discourse subordination is often associated with *focalization*, that is, a change in perspective or viewpoint. Subordinate structures often indicate such focalization. In (141) (Kamp and Rohrer 1983), the past perfect *had eaten* indicates the viewpoint of Mme Dupont, the perfective *ate* in (142) that of the narrator.

(141)   The telephone rang. It was Mme Dupont. Her husband had eaten too many oysters. The doctor recommended a change in lifestyle.

(142) The telephone rang. It was Mme Dupont. Her husband ate too many oysters. The doctor recommended a change in lifestyle.

In *free indirect discourse*, part of a subordinate narrative line or thread takes the form of a structure, such as an independent clause, typical of independent, superordinate units. Free indirect discourse is focalized, and deictic elements take as their deictic center the reference time of their frame (i.e., the implicit act of thought or speech in which they occur). Tenses normally deictic are anaphoric in their use; in (143) *now* means 'then' ('at that time'), and the past tense *was* is present relative to the reference time of its frame.

(143) As his foot touched the deck his will, his purpose he had been hurrying to save, died out within. It had been nothing less than getting the schooner under-way, letting her vanish silently in the night from amongst these sleeping ships. And now he was certain he could not do it.   (Conrad, *Within the tides*)

Summary

Situation aspect classifies occurrences and situations into events, processes, states, and series, depending on their inherent temporal structures. Viewpoint aspect explicitly marks different ways of viewing the temporal structures of eventualities. Phasic aspect refers to stages of occurrences or situations. Situation aspect interacts with viewpoint aspect. Older theories of viewpoint aspect define the aspects in terms of which end-points of occurrences or situations, if any, they include, or in terms of the temporal relationship holding between the situation or occurrence and its frame of reference. More recent theories treat a viewpoint aspect as transforming one type of occurrences or situations into another. Amongst the functions served by aspect in discourse is to maintain the coherence of the discourse.

NOTE

I would like to thank Bas Aarts, Bernard Comrie, Laura Michaelis, an anonymous reviewer, and my colleague Deborah James for their comments on this chapter.

FURTHER READING

A comprehensive bibliography may be found at: www.utsc.utoronto.ca/~binnick/TENSE/. On the progressive: Scheffer (1975); Williams (2001). On phasic aspect: Woisetschlaeger (1977); Brinton (1988).

On aspect in discourse: Sperber
and Wilson (1986); Ehrlich (1990);
Kamp and Reyle (1993); Ter Meulen

(1995); Lascarides and Asher (2003).
On temporal adverbials: Rathert
(2004).

REFERENCES

Bach, E. (1981) On time, tense,
and aspects: an essay in English
metaphysics. In Cole, P. (ed.),
Radical pragmatics. New York:
Academic Press, 63–81.

Bach, E. (1986) The algebra of events.
Linguistics and Philosophy 9, 5–16.

Bauer, G. (1970) The English 'perfect'
reconsidered. *Journal of Linguistics* 6,
189–98.

Bennett, M. and Partee, B. H. (1978)
*Toward the logic of tense and aspect in
English*. Bloomington: Indiana
University Linguistics Club.

Benveniste, E. (1959) Les relations de
temps dans le verbe français. *Bulletin
de la Société de Linguistique de Paris* 54,
69–82.

Binnick, R. I. (1974) Will and be going to
I, II. In W. Bauer et al. (eds.), *Studien
zur generativen Semantik*. Frankfurt:
Athenaion 118–37.

Blansitt, E. (1975) Progressive aspect.
Working Papers on Language Universals
18, 1–34.

Boogaart, R. (1999) *Aspect and temporal
ordering*. The Hague: Holland
Academic Graphics.

Brinton, L. (1988) *The development of
English aspectual systems: aspectualizers
and post-verbal particles*. Cambridge:
Cambridge University Press.

Caenepeel, M. (1995) Aspect and
text structure. *Linguistics* 33,
213–53.

Caenepeel, M. and Moens, M. (1994)
Temporal structure and discourse
structure. In C. Vet and C. Vetter
(eds.), *Tense and aspect in discourse*.
Berlin: de Gruyter, 5–20.

Carlson, L. (1981) Aspect and
quantification. *Syntax and Semantics*
14, 31–64.

Comrie, B. (1976) *Aspect*. Cambridge:
Cambridge University Press.

Comrie, B. (1986) Tense and time
reference: from meaning to
interpretation in the chronological
structure of a text. *Journal of Literary
Semantics* 15, 12–22.

Cooper, R. (1985) *Aspectual classes in
situation semantics*. Stanford: Center
for the Study of Language and
Information, Stanford University.

Dahl, Ö. (2001) Languages without
tense and aspect. In K. H. Ebert
and F. Zúñiga (eds.), *Aktionsart and
aspectotemporality in non-European
languages*. Zürich: Seminar für
Allgemeine Sprachwissenschaft,
159–73.

Davidson, D. (1967) The logical form
of action sentences. In N. Rescher
(ed.), *The logic of decision and action*.
Pittsburgh: University of Pittsburgh
Press, 81–95.

De Swart, H. (1998) Aspectual shift as
type coercion. *Natural Language and
Linguistic Theory* 16, 347–85.

De Swart, H. (2004) Type, tense and
coercion in a cross-linguistic
perspective. In E. Francis and
L. Michaelis (eds.), *Mismatch:
form-function incongruity and the
architecture of grammar*. Stanford:
CSLI Publications, 231–58.

De Swart, H. and Verkuyl, H. (1999)
Tense and aspect in sentence and
discourse: lecture notes of the 11th
European Summer School in Logic,

Language, and Information. Utrecht: Utrecht Institute of Linguistics OTS. On-line publication (www.folli.uva.nl/CD/1999/library/pdf/hhh.pdf).

Dik, S. (1997) *The theory of functional grammar*. Berlin: Mouton de Gruyter.

Dillon, G. L. (1973) Perfect and other aspects in a case grammar of English. *Journal of Linguistics* 9, 271–9.

Dowty, D. (1977) Toward a semantic analysis of verb aspect and the English 'imperfective' progressive. *Linguistics and Philosophy* 1, 45–78.

Dowty, D. (1979) *Word meaning and Montague grammar*. Dordrecht: Reidel.

Dowty, D. (1986) The effects of aspectual class on the temporal structure of discourse: semantics or pragmatics? *Linguistics and Philosophy* 9, 37–61.

Dry, H. (1981) Sentence aspect and the movement of narrative time. *Text* 1, 233–40.

Dry, H. (1983) The movement of narrative time. *Journal of Literary Semantics* 12, 19–53.

Ehrlich, S. (1990) *Point of view: a linguistic analysis of literary style*. London: Routledge.

Fenn, P. (1987) *A semantic and pragmatic examination of the English perfect*. Tübingen: Gunter Narr Verlag.

Fleischman, S. (1990) *Tense and narrativity: from medieval performance to modern fiction*. Austin: University of Texas Press.

Fleischman, S. (1991) Toward a theory of tense-aspect in narrative discourse. In J. Gvozdanovic and T. A. J. M. Janssen (eds.), *The function of tense in texts*. Amsterdam: North-Holland, 75–97.

Freed, A. (1979) The *semantics of English aspectual complementation*. Dordrecht: Reidel.

Garey, H. (1957) Verbal aspect in French. *Language* 33, 91–110.

Goldsmith, J. and Woisetschlaeger, E. (1982) The logic of the English progressive. *Linguistic Inquiry* 13, 79–89.

Grosz, B. J., Joshi, A. K., and Weinstein, S. (1995) Centering: a framework for modelling the local coherence of discourse. *Computational Linguistics* 21, 203–25.

Hatcher, A. (1951) The use of the progressive form in English. *Language* 27, 254–80.

Hinrichs, E. (1983) The semantics of the English progressive: a study in situation semantics. *Proceedings of the regional meeting, Chicago Linguistic Society* 19, 171–82.

Hinrichs, E. (1986) Temporal anaphora in discourses in English. *Linguistics and Philosophy* 9, 63–82.

Hobbs, J. (1979) Coherence and coreference. *Cognitive Science* 3, 67–90.

Hobbs, J. (1985) *On the coherence and structure of discourse*. Stanford: Stanford University, Center for the Study of Language and Information.

Hopper, P. (1979) Aspect and foregrounding in discourse. *Syntax and Semantics* 12, 213–41.

Jackendoff, R. (1996) The proper treatment of measuring out, telicity, and perhaps even quantification in English. *Natural Language and Linguistic Theory* 14, 305–54.

Johnson, M. (1981) A unified temporal theory of tense and aspect. *Syntax and Semantics* 14, 145–71.

Joos, M. (1964) *The English verb: form and meanings*. Madison: University of Wisconsin Press.

Kamp, H. (1979) Events, instants, and temporal reference. In R. Bäuerle, (ed.), *Semantics from different points of view*. Berlin: Springer Verlag, 376–417.

Kamp, H. and Reyle, U. (1993) *From discourse to logic*. Dordrecht: Kluwer.

Kamp, H. and Rohrer, C. (1983) Tense in texts. In R. Bäuerle et al. (eds.), *Meaning, use, and interpretation of language*. Berlin: Walter de Gruyter, 250–69.

Klein, W. (1994) *Time in language*. London: Routledge.

Krifka, M. (1989) Nominal reference, temporal constitution and quantification in event semantics. In R. Bartsch et al. (eds.), *Semantics and contextual expressions*. Dordrecht: Foris, 75–115.

Lascarides, A. and Asher, N. (1991) Discourse relations and defeasible knowledge. In *Proceedings of the 20th annual meeting of the Association for Computational Linguistics*. Berkeley: University of California, 55–62.

Lascarides, A. and Asher, N. (1993) Temporal interpretation, discourse relations and common sense entailment. *Linguistics and Philosophy* 16, 437–93.

Lascarides, A. and Asher, N. (2003) *Logics of conversation*. Cambridge: Cambridge University Press.

Lascarides, A. and Oberlander, J. (1993) Temporal coherence and defeasible knowledge. *Theoretical Linguistics* 19, 1–37.

Leech, G. (1971) *Meaning and the English verb*. London: Longmans.

Levin, B. and Rappaport Hovav, M. (1999) Two structures for compositionally derived events. In T. Matthews and D. Strolovitch (eds.), *Proceedings of Semantics and Linguistic Theory IX*. Ithaca, NY: CLC Publications, 199–223.

Lewis, M. (1986) *The English verb: an explanation of structure and meaning*. London: Language Teaching Publication.

McCawley, J. (1971) Tense and time reference in English. In C. Fillmore and D. Langendoen (eds.), *Studies in linguistic semantics*. New York: Holt, Rinehart, & Winston, 97–113.

McCoard, R. (1978) *The English perfect: tense-choice and pragmatic inferences*. Amsterdam: North-Holland.

Mann, W. and Thompson, S. (1988) Rhetorical structure theory: toward a functional theory of text organization. *Text* 8, 243–81.

Marchand, H. (1955) On a question of aspect: a comparison between the progressive form in English and that in Italian and Spanish. *Studia Linguistica* 9, 45–52.

Michaelis, L. (1994) The ambiguity of the English present perfect. *Journal of Linguistics*, 30, 111–57.

Michaelis, L. (1998) *Aspectual grammar and past-time reference*. London: Routledge.

Miller, G. and Johnson-Laird, P. (1976) *Language and perception*. Cambridge: Cambridge University Press.

Moens, M. and Steedman, M. (1987) Temporal ontology in natural language. In *Proceedings of the 25th annual meeting of the Association for Computational Linguistics*. Stanford: Stanford University, 1–7.

Moens, M. and Steedman, M. (1988) Temporal ontology and temporal reference. *Journal of Computational Linguistics* 14, 15–28.

Mourelatos, A. (1978) Events, processes, and states. *Linguistics and Philosophy* 2, 415–34.

Palmer, F. (1987) *The English verb*. London: Longmans.

Parsons, T. (1989) The progressive in English. *Linguistics and Philosophy* 12, 213–41.

Parsons, T. (1990) *Events in the semantics of English*. Cambridge, MA: MIT Press.

Partee, B. (1984) Nominal and temporal anaphora. *Linguistics and Philosophy* 7, 243–86.

Pianesi, F. and Varzi, A. (1996) Events, topology, and temporal relations. *The Monist* 79, 89–115.

Platzack, C. (1979) *The semantic interpretation of aspect and Aktionsarten: a study of internal time reference in Swedish*. Dordrecht: Foris.

Polanyi, L. (1985) A theory of discourse structure and discourse coherence. In P. Eilfort, et al. (eds.), *Papers from the general session at the 21st Regional*

Meeting of the Chicago Linguistics Society. Chicago: Chicago Linguistics Society, 25–7.

Prince, E. (1982) The simple futurate: not simply progressive futurate minus progressive. *Proceedings of the Regional Meeting, Chicago Linguistic Society* 18, 453–65.

Pustejovsky, J. (1990) Semantic function and lexical decomposition. In U. Schmitz, R. Schutz, and A. Kunz (eds.), *Linguistic approaches to artificial intelligence.* Frankfurt am Main: Peter Lang, 243–303.

Rathert, M. (2004) *Textures of time.* Berlin: Akademie Verlag.

Reichenbach, H. (1947) *Elements of symbolic logic.* London: Macmillan.

Scha, R. and Polanyi, L. (1988) An augmented context free grammar. In *Proceedings of the 12th International Conference on Computational Linguistics.* Budapest, 573–7.

Scheffer, J. (1975) *The progressive in English.* Amsterdam: North-Holland.

Smith, C. (1981) The futurate progressive: not simply future + progressive. *Proceedings of the Regional Meeting, Chicago Linguistic Society* 17, 369–82.

Smith, C. (1983) A theory of aspectual choice. *Language* 59, 479–501.

Smith, C. (1986) A speaker-based approach to aspect. *Linguistics and Philosophy* 9, 97–115.

Smith, C. (1991) *The parameter of aspect.* Dordrecht: Kluwer.

Spejewsky, B. (1996) Temporal subordination and the English perfect. In T. Galloway and J. Spence (eds.), *Proceedings of Semantics and Linguistic Theory VI.* Ithaca: Cornell University Press, 261–78.

Sperber, D. and Wilson, D. (1986) *Relevance: communication and cognition.* Oxford: Blackwell.

Steedman, M. (2001) *The productions of time.* Dept. of Computer & Information Science, University of Pennsylvania.

On-line publication (ftp.cogsci.ed.ac.uk/pub/steedman/temporality/temporality.pdf).

Tenny, C. (1994) *Aspectual roles and the syntax–semantics interface.* Dordrecht: Kluwer.

Ter Meulen, A. (1985) Progressives without possible worlds. *Proceedings of the Regional Meeting, Chicago Linguistic Society* 21, 408–23.

Ter Meulen, A. (1987) Incomplete events. In J. Groenendijk et al. (eds.), *Proceedings of the Sixth Amsterdam Colloquium.* Amsterdam: Instituut voor Taal, Logica en Informatie.

Ter Meulen, A. (1995) *Representing time in natural language: the dynamic interpretation of tense and aspect.* Cambridge, MA: MIT Press.

Thompson, S. and Mann, W. (1987) Rhetorical structure theory: a framework for the analysis of texts. *IPRA Papers in Pragmatics* 1, 79–105.

Trager, G. and Smith, H. (1951) *An outline of English structure.* Washington, DC: ACLS.

Vendler, Z. (1957) Verbs and times. *Philosophical Review* 66, 143–60. Reprinted, 1967, in Vendler, Z., *Linguistics in philosophy.* Ithaca: Cornell University Press, 97–121.

Verkuyl, H. (1972) *On the compositional nature of the aspects.* Dordrecht: Reidel.

Verkuyl, H. (1996) *A theory of aspectuality: the interaction between temporal and atemporal structure.* Cambridge: Cambridge University Press.

Vlach, F. (1981) The semantics of the progressive. *Syntax and Semantics* 14, 271–92.

Waugh, L. (1991) Tense-aspect and hierarchy of meanings: pragmatic, textual, modal, discourse, expressive, referential. Waugh, L. and Rudy, S. (eds.), *New vistas in grammar: invariance and variation.* Amsterdam: John Benjamins, 242–59.

Webber, B. (1988) Tense as discourse anaphor. *Computational Linguistics* 14, 61–73.

Weinrich, H. (1964) *Tempus: besprochene und erzählte Welt*. Stuttgart: Kohlhammer.

Williams, C. (2001) *Non-progressive and progressive aspect in English*. Fasano di Puglia: Schena Editore.

Woisetschlaeger, E. (1977) *A semantic theory of the English auxiliary system*. Bloomington: Indiana University Linguistics Club.

12 Mood and Modality in English

ILSE DEPRAETERE AND SUSAN REED

1 Introduction

The term 'modality' is a cover term for a range of semantic notions such as ability, possibility, hypotheticality, obligation, and imperative meaning. This is a serviceable definition for practical purposes. If, however, we wish to provide a more theoretically useful definition, we need to find what it is that all modal utterances have in common. This turns out to be by no means evident (cf. e.g. Krug 2000: 39–43). What, for example, does the imperative mood, whose prototypical function is to convey a command, have in common with the auxiliary verb *can* in its meaning of 'ability,' or the auxiliary verb *might* when it expresses a type of possibility meaning, as in *You might be right about that*? What does the hypothetical meaning of a sentence like *If the dog lost a bit of weight it could use the cat-flap* have in common with the obligation meaning of *You have to pay to get in*?

One feature that is common to all modal utterances is that they do not represent situations as straightforward facts (cf. e.g. Zandvoort 1964: 395; Bache and Davidsen-Nielsen 1997: 316). However, the wealth of literature on modality would seem to suggest that linguists intuitively feel that modality is something semantically far richer than 'lack of factuality.' We can get nearer to a positive characterization of modality if we say that modal meaning crucially involves the notions of necessity and possibility (Larreya 1984; Van der Auwera and Plungian 1998; Huddleston and Pullum et al. 2002: 173), or rather, involves a speaker's judgment that a proposition is possibly or necessarily true or that the actualization of a situation is necessary or possible. But more semantically precise links between such meanings as we mention above are not forthcoming.

In what follows, we shall work on the basis that all modal utterances are non-factual, in that they do not assert that the situations they describe are facts, and all involve the speaker's comment on the necessity or possibility of the truth of a proposition or the actualization of a situation. We will return to the discussion of theoretical problems concerning modality in section 4.3.

Modality may be coded in various ways, including verbal inflections, auxiliary verbs, adverbs, and particles. The grammatical coding of modal meaning in verb inflections is known as mood. English makes relatively little use of inflectional systems to express modal meanings: the imperative mood is common in English, and there is limited use of the subjunctive mood, but modality in English is primarily expressed by non-inflectional items. These include a variety of elements, including adverbials like *perhaps, in all probability* etc., and 'hedges' like *I would think (that)* (cf. e.g. Hoye 1997; Krug 2000; Huddleston and Pullum et al. 2002: 173–5). The principal means of expressing modality in English, however, is the set of modal auxiliary verbs. Given the centrality of modal auxiliaries to modality in English,[1] a considerable part of this chapter will be concerned with the meanings expressed by these auxiliaries. We will begin, however, with a brief look at mood in English.

2   Inflectional Moods

In English, there are usually said to be three inflectional moods: the imperative, the subjunctive, and the indicative. The meanings they respectively communicate are captured quite nicely by the labels used by Jespersen (1958: 632): 'will-mood,' 'thought-mood,' and 'fact-mood.' Here we will chiefly be concerned, after a glance at the imperative, with the subjunctive mood.

The unmarked function of an *imperative* utterance is to signal that the speaker wants a certain state of affairs to be brought about (i.e. considers it necessary), and directs the addressee to bring it about:

(1)   *Come* here!

(2)   *Have* some more cake!

The imperative is not marked for tense, being formally realized by the base form of the verb.[2]

The subjunctive mood creates an intensional domain in the sense that there is reference to a state of affairs that is the case in a possible world, but the speaker does not assert that the state of affairs holds (or held, or will hold) in the actual world.

The traditional labels *present subjunctive* and *past subjunctive* (the latter only existing for the verb *be*) refer more to form than to meaning. The form of the present subjunctive is the base form of the verb, i.e. the same form as is normally used for most persons in the present tense. The past subjunctive is only distinct from the past indicative for first and third persons singular, which are realized by the form *were*.[3] The terms *present subjunctive* and *past subjunctive* should not be taken to refer to the time reference of the forms in question. The present subjunctive can be embedded in a clause with present, past or future time reference (cf. (5c)). The past subjunctive always refers either to a hypothetical (or 'tentative' – cf. Declerck and Reed (2001)) situation or to a counterfactual situation, but the hypothetical or counterfactual situation may be located in the present, the past or the future:

(3) Jimmie wishes/wished/will wish his girlfriend *were* with him.

The present subjunctive is used in formulaic expressions (cf. (4)), in more or less fixed phrases functioning as conditional clauses (cf. (5a), (5b)) and after expressions (verbs, adjectives, and nouns) that express volition (cf. (5c)), the so-called mandative subjunctive. In the latter case, *should* + infinitive is a less formal alternative:

(4) a. God *save* the Queen
    b. If that's how you feel, so *be* it.
    c. *Perish* the thought.

(5) a. You can refer to this at a later date, if need *be*. (Cobuild, ukmags)[4]
    b. If truth *be* told, it all sounds a bit earnest. (Cobuild, ukmags)
    c. The board desires/ordered/will request that changes *be* (*should be*) made to the plans.

The past subjunctive is used productively in hypothetical (cf. (6a)) and counterfactual (cf. (6b)) conditional clauses and after the verb *wish* (cf. (6c)), but is not used as a mandative subjunctive:

(6) a. What would you say if I *were* to refuse to go?
    b. If she *were* living closer, I'd visit her more often.
    c. I wish I *were* in Phoenix now.

The indicative normally represents situations as facts, but the indicative past tense and past perfect can also be used modally, in specific structures, to represent situations as non-factual or counterfactual:

(7) It would be great if it *rained* tonight.

(8) If only Meg *was/had been coming* with us.

(9) I wish/wished he *had told* me about it.

The past form and the past perfect used with modal meaning do not have past time reference as part of their meaning (though the situations they refer to may be interpreted as located in the past). The past perfect still normally expresses anteriority with respect to a situation, but not necessarily to a past time situation; more importantly, the modal past perfect signals that the situation it refers to did not actualize, i.e. is counterfactual.

As pointed out in the introduction, modality in English is overwhelmingly expressed by non-inflectional means, i.e. modal auxiliaries. This observation has led Huddleston (1984) to expand the category of purely inflectional mood to what he calls *analytic mood*, i.e. non-inflectional verbal forms that establish modal meaning. While *mood* in this way becomes an extremely broad category, this proposal has the advantage of effectively encompassing all the possible verb forms involved in establishing modal meaning.

Although most authors on modality agree that both moods and modal auxiliaries should be included within modality as expressing the possible and the necessary rather than facts, there is no tradition of treating mood and modal auxiliaries together, nor a practice of describing the function they share by means of a common stock of descriptive categories. It is perhaps due to the very large range of forms and meanings involved once the two categories are united that they tend to be dealt with separately. In everyday practice, modality in English is most commonly linked with modal auxiliaries, given the important role, noted above, played by modals in the expression of modality in English. Accordingly, in the next section, we will list the formal characteristics of English modal auxiliaries before we go on to look in section 4 at the meanings that they can express and at ways of categorising modality in English, focusing on what Huddleston calls analytic mood.

3   Analytic Mood: Formal Properties of Modal Auxiliaries

Traditionally, a distinction is made between central modals (*can, could, may, might, shall, should, will, would, must*) and peripheral or marginal modals (*dare, need, ought*). In addition, we find a group of verbs referred to as semi-modals, quasi-modals or periphrastic modals. This somewhat open-ended category includes *have to, be able to, be going to*, but can also include a variety of other verbs such as *be supposed to, be about to* and *be bound to*.

The central modals have all the 'NICE' properties that are criterial to the classification of a form as an auxiliary verb. (cf. e.g. Palmer 1987: 14–21). That is, they have a negative form consisting of the auxiliary followed by *not*, they can precede the subject in subject–verb inversion (for example in interrogatives), they can occur in 'code,' i.e. they can be used instead of a full lexical verb which has occurred in the context (for example *She will help and so will I*), and they can be used in emphatic affirmation (*She probably won't help, but she MIGHT (do).*). This means that unlike lexical verbs they do not require the use of *do* in such contexts. In addition, unlike lexical verbs the central modals are invariable for person and number – they have no third person singular -*s* form – and have no non-finite forms.

Peripheral modals differ from central modals, in the case of *dare* and *need* because these auxiliaries only occur in non-assertive contexts and in the case of *ought* principally because it takes a *to*-infinitive. The semi-modals, being generally composed of *be* X *to*, generally have the NICE properties in respect of the *be* part of their form, but unlike the central and peripheral modals they

Table 12.1   Formal characteristics of modals

	Central modals	Peripheral modals	Semi-modals
do required in NICE (*Negation, Inversion, Code, Emphasis*) contexts	–	–[5]	–[6]
-s for third person singular	–	–	+
non-finite forms	–	–	+

do inflect for person and number and they have nonfinite forms. In addition, they can co-occur with the central modal auxiliaries (cp. *She may be able to help* vs **She may can help*). *Have to* is frequently included with the semi-modals on the basis of its semantics, and we shall follow this tradition here. On the formal level, however, it must be acknowledged that there is little justification for its inclusion, as *have to* requires *do*-support in NICE contexts (cf. Huddleston and Pullum et al. 2002: 112). Table 12.1 summarizes the formal basis on which the distinctions are principally drawn (cf. e.g. Quirk et al. 1985: 136–48; Westney 1995; Biber et al. 1999: 483–6; Huddleston and Pullum et al. 2002: 106–14).

For reasons of space, we cannot explore in detail the formal behavior of the different sets of verbs systematically. It is, however, important to add that while the central modals *can*, *may*, *shall* and *will* (but not the marginal modals) all have past forms, the latter do not necessarily indicate past time (cf. e.g. (14), (19)). It is often the case that periphrastic forms have to be used to refer to the past (e.g. *He managed to get (* could get) to the station in time*), and/or that the past form of the modal can only be used with past time reference in a restricted number of contexts (e.g. *He could swim at the age of six*: reference to a state vs. *He is the only one who did not drown: he was able to swim (* could swim) across the lake*: reference to an actualized event). Likewise, the location of modal meaning in the future presupposes the use of a periphrastic form (e.g. *He will be able to read when he's six*) (cf. 5.2). Issues of this type are covered in e.g. Declerck (1991a); Hewings (1999); Biber et al. (1999).

4   Categorizations of Modal Meanings Expressed by Analytic Mood

4.1   *Epistemic vs. non-epistemic (or root) meaning*

In English analytic modality, we can make an initial distinction between epistemic and nonepistemic, or root modality. Both types of modality have as their basis the notions of necessity and possibility, but the former deals with the necessity or possibility of the truth (or non-truth) of propositions while the latter deals with the necessity or possibility of the actualization of situations. *Epistemic* modality reflects the speaker's judgment of the likelihood that the proposition underlying the utterance is true, the epistemic scale of likelihood ranging from weak epistemic possibility (*That may be John*) to epistemic necessity (*That must be John* = 'it is necessary that [that is John] is true' and *That can't be John* = 'it is necessary that [that is not John] is true').

Root modality reflects the speaker's judgments about factors influencing the actualization of the situation referred to in the utterance. Within root modality we find root possibility, root necessity and two categories that are normally treated separately within root modality, namely ability and volition. Cutting across the root necessity and root possibility categorization is the category of deontic modality, which includes obligation – a type of root necessity – and permission – a type of root possibility. *Deontic* modality typically refers to 'the necessity or possibility of acts performed by morally responsible agents' (Lyons 1977: 823). Deontic modality also implies an authority, or 'deontic source' – which may be a person, a set of rules, or something as vague as a social norm – responsible for imposing the necessity (obligation) or granting the possibility (permission). Thus *John must go home* means, on a deontic (obligation) reading, something like 'it is necessary for John to go home' plus, for example, 'I oblige John to go home,' and *John can go home* means, on a deontic (permission) reading, 'it is possible for John to go home' and, for example, 'the rules permit John to go home.'

Non-deontic root possibility (sometimes simply referred to as 'root possibility') (*You can get coffee from this machine.*) and non-deontic root necessity (*The fish have to be fed every day*) concern possibility and necessity that arise, not via a particular authority but due to circumstances in general. They can be paraphrased simply 'it is possible (for . . .) to' (cf. (10), (16)) and, for necessity, 'it is necessary (for . . .) to' (cf. (23)) or even just 'it is important to' (cf. (32)).[7] Note that non-deontic root possibility differs on the one hand from epistemic possibility and on the other hand (though more arguably) from ability. It differs from epistemic possibility in that it does not imply a speaker's evaluation of how possible it is that some proposition is true but rather refers to the effect of circumstances on the possibility of actualization of some situation; it differs from ability in that it refers to possibility arising out of enabling or disabling circumstances outside the subject referent, as opposed to enabling or disabling factors that are entirely internal to the subject referent (see below). The non-deontic root possibility meaning of *Can you come tomorrow?* can thus be paraphrased by 'is it possible for you to come tomorrow?' plus 'are there any external circumstances preventing you/do external circumstances allow you to do so?'.

Finally, we come to ability and volition. These modalities, too, combine the meaning of possibility with the notion of specific factors affecting that possibility. The ability meaning of *Can you climb over that wall?*, can be paraphrased by 'is it possible for you to climb over that wall?' plus 'do you have the physical (and perhaps mental) abilities and/or skills to make it possible?'. The volition meaning of *I'll help you* can be paraphrased by 'It is possible for me to help you' and 'I am willing and intend to do so.'

4.2   *Meanings expressed by the central modals*

Each of the central modal auxiliaries can be used with more than one meaning. In the survey below, we provide a list of the principal meanings expressed by the central modals.

Can

(10)   [The fact that] John Major *can* become Prime Minister [is] proof enough that class is no longer a barrier. (ICE-GB, S2B-036) (root possibility)

(11)   "*Can* I hold you and kiss you, here and now? I can't stand this!" "No, my darling, no." (Cobuild, UK books) (permission)

(12)   *Can* you speak any East European languages? (ICE-GB, S1A-014) (ability)

Could

(13)   For example, with the simple digging of a well a large amount of pasture *could* be reclaimed but they had no organizational features to allow for this. (ICE-GB, W1A-012) (root possibility)

(14)   There has been recurring speculation that Futura *could* be planning a full-scale bid for Headlam and the latter's directors repeated last October's statement that they have not been informed of Futura's intentions. (epistemic possibility) (ICE-GB, W2C-012)

May

(15)   You never know, I *may* eventually get a full-time job. (ICE-GB, W1B) (epistemic possibility)

(16)   Epilepsy causes movements, sensations and behavior of many sorts. The fit *may* be limited to an area of the brain and its functions partial epilepsy) or *may* be generalized. (Cobuild, UK books) (root possibility)

(17)   *May* I sit down for a minute? (ICE-GB, W2F-018) (permission)

(18)   NO BOOK OR OTHER LIBRARY MATERIAL *MAY* BE TAKEN FROM THE LIBRARY'S PREMISES. (ICE-GB, W2D-006) (permission)

Might

(19) I suspect that you *might* be seeking a room in a house of young women in want of nocturnal company. (ICE-GB, W1B-015) (epistemic possibility)

(20) You said to me once you *might* come to London to visit. (ICE-GB, W1B-008) (epistemic possibility)

Must

(21) With all the bits of work you've done over the years, your CV *must* be pretty full? (ICE-GB, W1B-001) (epistemic necessity)

(22) You *must* tell DVLA as soon as you buy a used vehicle. (ICE-GB, W2D-010) (root necessity)

(23) To track environmental change the gene pool *must* be able to: (a) maintain and continuously update an adequate reserve of variants [. . .]; also (b) switch between alternative forms of phenotypic expression (. . .) or flexible phenotypic responses (. . .). (ICE-GB, W1A-009) (root necessity)

Will

(24) The main proposals of the White Paper *will* come into operation in April 1991. (ICE-GB, W2A-013) (epistemic)

(25) Anyone who has flown over the tropics *will* have seen the persistent pall of smoke which all too often signifies forests on the wane. (ICE-GB, W2B-028) (epistemic necessity)

(26) Why *won't* anyone believe them? (www) (volition)

Would

(27) Colubus Columba then prophesied that he *would* become a beggar and that his son *would* run from house to house with a half empty bag and that he *would* die in the trench of a threshing-floor. (ICE-GB, W1A-002) (epistemic)

(28) *Would* you get the Fairground Attraction album (on CD) for me? (ICE-GB, W1B-002) (volition)

Shall

(29) We *shall* be away on holiday for a fortnight from Wednesday 29 August. (ICE-GB, W1B-027) (epistemic)

(30)   Rightly, the Government's policy is that the pound *shall* not be taken from our pockets against the will of the people. (ICE-GB, W2E-001) (root necessity)

Should

(31)   You *should* just about get this letter by the time I get home. (ICE-GB, W1B-011) (epistemic necessity)

(32)   Did you know that smiling might make you feel better? Read our article on why you *should* smile to find out even more interesting facts! (www) (root necessity)

Three things should be mentioned here. Anticipating the discussion in section 4.3 somewhat, it should be pointed out that *will* and *shall* (and *would* and *should*) used for prediction (examples (24), (27), (29), and (31)) do not fit as comfortably in the paradigm of 'either possibility or necessity of the truth of a proposition.' Prediction does involve some judgment of likelihood, but it is not clear whether a prediction says that something is 'necessarily' or, rather, 'possibly' the case. As will be pointed out in 4.3, it is a matter of debate whether these uses of *shall* and *will* are modal: the fact that it is hard to describe them in terms of the traditional modal labels is already indicative of their uniqueness. Second, the examples given do not exhaust the range of modal meanings that each auxiliary can express. Thirdly, and relatedly, it will be evident from this list that the relationship between modal auxiliaries and modal meanings in English is many-to-many (cf. e.g. Coates 1983: 26): each auxiliary has a range of modal meanings, and a given modal meaning can generally be expressed by more than one of the modal auxiliaries, albeit sometimes with varying shades of meaning or with varying acceptability in certain registers. In section 5, we will return to the question of the multiplicity of meanings expressed by modals and explore in more detail the way in which temporal information is communicated by modals. For detailed discussion of the various meanings of modal auxiliaries, we refer the reader to the in-depth treatments mentioned in note 9.

4.3   Approaches to the classification of modal meanings

Partly due to the fact that, in classifying modal meanings, it is possible to use various parameters as criterial to their classification, there exists in the literature a fairly diverse assortment of classifications of modal meaning. Below we outline a few of the recent approaches to classifying modality in English.

Coates' (1983) analysis of English modal auxiliaries leads her to a basic two-way split between epistemic modality and root modality. Her examination of corpus examples shows that root modals taken as a whole differ from epistemic modals in systematic ways: root modals have shared semantico-syntactic features, typically, for example, having animate and agentive subjects, and they are linked by similarities in intonation patterns which distinguish them from epistemic modals (cf. Coates 1983: 21 *et passim*). However, Coates does not merely argue that root modalities are in important ways homogeneous in their difference from epistemic modalities, but also that the various types of root modality should not be grouped into subcategories such as 'deontic' modality (cf. above). Such subcategorization, she argues, would obscure the fact that there exist deontic and non-deontic meanings of a single modal auxiliary which form a single spectrum of meaning, rather than being discrete meanings (cf. 5.1).

Quirk et al. (1985) distinguish between intrinsic and extrinsic modality. This classification cuts across the root-epistemic division. *Extrinsic* modality involves 'human judgment of what is or is not likely to happen' (1985: 219) and covers (epistemic and non-deontic root) possibility, (epistemic and non-deontic root) necessity and prediction, whilst *intrinsic* modality involves 'some kind of intrinsic human control over events' (*ibid.*). Deontic modality and volition are categorized together as intrinsic modality. As for ability, the authors note: 'The "ability" meaning of *can* is considered extrinsic, even though ability typically involves human control over an action' (1985: 221). For Quirk et al., an assertion or question about a being's ability to do something implies some sort of judgment about the likelihood of actualization of the situation, and it is this aspect of ability meaning that informs their categorization of ability as extrinsic.

For Bybee and Fleischman (1995, based on Bybee 1985) (whose approach, in fact, is a broad cross-linguistic one, rather than one concerned purely with English modality), the division used in Coates' (1983) analysis is essentially the correct one, based on their observation that markers of obligation, desire, ability, permission and non-deontic root possibility 'predicate conditions on an agent with regard to the completion of an action referred to by the main predicate' (1995: 6). In contrast, epistemic modality, as Bybee and Fleischman point out, concerns the truth of the proposition as a whole, and rather than relating an agent to an action, it deals with the speaker's commitment to the truth of the proposition. The group of modalities referred to by Coates as 'root' modality are referred to by Bybee and Fleischman as *agent-oriented* modality, in order to reflect the shared semantic feature on which their categorization is based.[8]

Palmer (2001) distinguishes between *propositional* modality, which is concerned with 'the speaker's attitude to the truth-value or factual status of the proposition,' and *event* modality, which is concerned with whether or not the event referred to in the utterance can or must be realized. Propositional modality subsumes *evidential* and *epistemic* modality, the essential difference between these being that 'with epistemic modality speakers express their judgments about the factual status of the proposition [*John may/must/will be in his office*], whereas with evidential modality they indicate the evidence they have for its factual status' (Palmer 2001: 8). Within event modality, Palmer distinguishes between *dynamic* modality, which covers ability and volition, and *deontic* modality, which, as usual, accounts for permission and obligation. Dynamic modality 'comes from the individual concerned,' whilst deontic modality comes 'from an external source' (2001: 10). Thus, most of the 'root' modality meanings are categorized not only according to their semantic role vis à vis the situation referred to rather than the proposition expressed, but also according to whether the modality always affects the subject referent or whether it always affects a discourse participant. (The two may of course coincide – a first person subject referent is also the speaker.) Palmer also points out that ability sometimes has to 'be interpreted more widely,' in the sense that the circumstances that affect the subject's physical and mental powers also need to be taken into account. The effect of circumstances in general upon the possibility or not of a situation's actualising is accounted for by Coates (cf. above) as non-deontic root possibility rather than as part of ability, on the basis of the fact that such circumstance-affected possibility is not associated with many of the semantic and syntactic features which are associated with ability meaning. However, non-deontic root possibility is not recognized as a distinct area of meaning by Palmer.

Huddleston and Pullum et al. (2002), like Palmer (1990), make a three-fold distinction between epistemic, deontic and dynamic modality. The category of dynamic modality covers ability, volition and non-deontic root modality. Huddleston and Pullum et al.'s categorization differs from Palmer (2001) in having no superordinate category (equivalent to 'root') that includes dynamic and deontic modality. In other words, non-deontic root possibility, ability, and volition are not presented as (nontrivially) more closely related to permission and obligation than they are to epistemic modality.

In Van der Auwera and Plungian (1998), whose aim is to provide a general account of modal meaning across languages, modal meaning is restricted to those 'semantic domains that involve possibility and necessity as paradigmatic variants' (1998: 80). Their account places willingness (and non-inferential evidentiality, as in German *Er soll krank sein (He is said to be ill)*) outside the range of what is meant by 'modality.' The authors start from the distinction between modal meaning that has scope over the whole proposition and modal meaning that concerns 'aspects internal to the state of affairs that the proposition reflects' (1998: 82). The basic distinction is thus one between epistemic and non-epistemic modality, the latter category consisting of participant-internal and participant-external modality. Participant-internal modality involves possibility and necessity that 'is internal to a participant engaged in the state of affairs' (1998: 80); it covers what is called *ability* (with human or non-human subjects), *dynamic possibility*, and *capacity* by others. Participant-external modality implies reference to circumstances external to the 'participant engaged in the state of affairs and that make the state of affairs either possible or necessary.' Non-deontic root possibility and deontic modality (since 'circumstances' can also concern the will of another person or a norm (1998: 81)) are covered by participant-external modality. Table 12.2 provides a (slightly simplified) summary of the classifications discussed above.

Table 12.2 Classification of (analytical) modal meaning

epistemic modality	*root necessity*	*root possibility*	*ability*	*obligation*	*permission*	*willingness or volition*	
epistemic	root modality						Coates (1983)
extrinsic				intrinsic			Quirk et al. (1985)
epistemic	n/a	agent-oriented					Bybee and Fleischman (1985)
propositional modality — evidential / epistemic; event modality	n/a		dynamic	deontic		dynamic	Palmer (2001)
epistemic	dynamic			deontic		dynamic	Huddleston and Pullum et al. (2002)
epistemic / non-epistemic	participant-internal	participant-external — non-deontic		participant-internal	participant-external — deontic	n/a	Van der Auwera and Plungian (1998)

4.3 Theoretical problems regarding modality and the classification of modal meaning

Modal auxiliaries (including peripheral modals and semi-modals) in English are notably susceptible to evolution, both in terms of their meaning (cf. e.g. Sweetser 1990; Coates 1995; Myhill 1997; Nordlinger and Traugott 1997), and in terms of their grammatical behavior, which may affect the approximation of peripheral or semi-modals to the status of central modal (cf. Krug 2000). This variability across time requires care in handling corpus material in the analysis of a given modal. In addition, the semantic diversity of the meanings that have been classed as modal (cf. section 1) and the somewhat fuzzy boundaries of modality naturally bring some difficulties of analysis with them. Questions arise about, on the one hand, which modal verbs, in which uses, count semantically as modal, and on the other hand, which meanings themselves count as modal. We mention below two of the most common issues regarding the classification of English modal auxiliaries and their meanings.

One well-known debate concerns the question of whether *will* can always be said to be a modal auxiliary or whether in its most frequent use it is no longer modal, with a basic meaning of intention or willingness, but purely a marker of future tense (cf. (24)) (see e.g. Declerck 1991b: 8–13; Huddleston 1995; Larreya 2000). Another English modal which provides ground for debate is the auxiliary *can*, in various of its uses, most obviously, its ability use.

One use of ability *can* is essentially suppletive to the English aspectual paradigm (cf. e.g. Leech 1987: 25). In the absence of an acceptable progressive form of verbs of inert perception such as *hear, see, smell* – *I am hearing the sea* – and certain uses of state cognition verbs such as *understand*, English uses *can* plus infinitive instead. Thus, what is literally a statement of ability, *I can hear the sea*, is interpreted more or less directly as equivalent to a progressive interpretation of *I hear the sea*. This use of *can* is often argued to be non-modal.

More controversial is the normal use of *can* with ability meaning. A sentence such as *Tommy can reach the door handles now* may be seen not so much as giving a speaker's judgment about the likelihood of a situation actualizing as making a factual statement about Tommy's ability. Palmer (2001: 179) comments: 'Dynamic ability is less central to modality than deontic permission in that it does not involve the speaker's attitude to the factuality or actualization of the situation.' Indeed, Steele (1975: 38, cited in Palmer (1990)) claims that ability *can* is not a modal because it only describes "the potential" of the subject referent rather than the likelihood of the situation (cf. also e.g. Palmer 1986: 102; Bache and Davidsen-Nielsen 1997: 325; Hoye 1997: 44). However, Quirk et al.'s classification of ability meaning alongside meanings reflecting 'human judgment of what is or is not likely to happen' (cf. 4.2) gives us a clue to an alternative analysis, one in which asserting or questioning someone's ability to do X is equivalent to an (asserted or questioned) assessment of the likelihood that X will happen. It is arguable that if I say *Tommy can reach the door handles now*, this amounts to a judgment about the likelihood of the subject referent's carrying out the action referred to in the VP: if Tommy *can* reach the door handles then the likelihood is that he *will* reach the door handles at the next opportunity.

5   Further Issues in the Meaning of Modal Auxiliaries

Having defined the categories of modality, we can now return to the multiplicity of meanings of modal auxiliaries, more in particular to the question whether modals are ambiguous or vague with respect to the meaning(s) they communicate. In 5.2, we will focus on the way in which temporal information is communicated by sentences with modal verbs.

5.1   Polysemy vs. monosemy

It has become clear in the course of the discussion that most modals can express both epistemic and root meaning: for instance, *must* can be used for epistemic necessity (*You must be cold*) and (deontic and non-deontic) root necessity (*You must stay in*); *may* can express epistemic possibility (*You may be right*) and root possibility, for example permission (*You may come in*). Apart from this, modals also express a variety of meanings in another way: any random corpus of examples containing a particular modal auxiliary (e.g. *must*) used in a particular meaning (e.g. obligation) reveals differences in shades of meaning communicated. In the case of obligation *must*, for instance, obligation may be weak (e.g. 'mere' advice given by the speaker) or strong (e.g. an order imposed by the speaker) (cf. e.g. Coates 1983: 34, 39; Huddleston and Pullum et al. 2002: 175–7, 181, 186). The following examples, as far as one can judge them without taking a greater context into consideration, exhibit an increase in strength of the necessity:

(33)   (a)   You *must* come and visit us as soon as you can. (ICE-GB, W1B-004)
     (b)   I *must* go back to work now. (ICE-GB, W1B-001)
     (c)   (mother to child) You *must* take your swimming costume tomorrow, because you have swimming lessons on Wednesday.
     (d)   When sons marry fathers *must* give them a proportion of his herd. (ICE-GB, W1A-011)
     (e)   You *must* be ordinarily resident in Great Britain (England, Scotland and Wales) and present there at the date of your claim. (ICE-GB, W2D-005)

In fact, corpus examples reveal a great deal of indeterminacy: it is often difficult to pin down the 'meaning' communicated by the modal unequivocally. For the example in (34), for instance, it makes little, if any difference whether we paraphrase this by 'it is possible to double the dose,' functioning as a suggestion, or by 'it is permitted to double the dose':

(34)   [The] dose *can* be doubled to last through the night or for long car journeys. (Cobuild, sunnow)

Two questions follow from these observations: (a) Do modals have a core meaning which is present in all their uses (the monosemy analysis) or are the different meanings sufficiently (semantically) independent to allow us to say that a modal is polysemous? (b) For each of the modal meanings communicated by a particular modal, what are its necessary and/or prototypical characteristics? While the two questions are not unrelated, for reasons of space we will have to limit ourselves to a few remarks on the question of polysemy, and refer the reader to the references in note 9 for detailed descriptions of the modal meanings communicated by particular modals.[9]

Many linguists defend the idea that modals are polysemous, with at least a sense distinction between root and epistemic meanings of a given modal. (cf. e.g. Lyons 1977; Traugott 1989; Bybee and Fleischman 1995; Palmer 2001; Huddleston and Pullum et al. 2002). Ambiguous examples constitute major evidence to that effect: in the examples in (35), for instance, it is impossible to decide – out of context – whether the modal has root or epistemic meaning:[10]

(35)   (a)   At the same time he *must* remember one of the principal lessons of Vietnam: that wars cannot be successfully pursued without strong public support. (ICE-GB, W2E-004)
         (b)   You *must* live near the university.
         (c)   You *may* have a car. (Hoye 1997: 42)

Since both interpretations cannot co-exist, one has to decide what meaning is intended before the sentence can be understood. This observation is taken to be evidence for the fact that root and epistemic meanings are semantically distinct. Other criteria that are used to justify the semantic difference between root and epistemic meanings are: (a) each of them is associated with a number of clear syntactic and semantic criteria (e.g. scope of negation cf. 5.2.1); (b) they have different paraphrases (e.g. root possibility: *it is possible for p*, epistemic possibility: *it is possible that p*).

Indeterminate examples are not always ambiguous: in (36) below, for example, the meanings of epistemic necessity and root necessity are mutually compatible, and this is what Coates calls an instance of *merger*. There are clearly two separate meanings (epistemic and root necessity) involved, but the distinction is 'neutralized' (Coates 1983: 17):

(36)   A: Newcastle Brown is a jolly good beer.
         B: Is it?
         A: Well it *ought to be* at that price. (Coates 1983: 17)

The fact that indeterminate examples of the kind shown in (34) and in (36) are numerous and do not cause a breakdown in communication is used by 'monosemists' to make their case: they argue that each modal has a core meaning, and that it is the contexts in which it is used that determine how it is interpreted, i.e. each modal has one invariant meaning with different contextual uses (cf. e.g. Ehrman 1966; Tregidgo 1982; Haegeman 1983; Klinge 1993; Groefsema 1995; Papafragou 2000).

Most linguists (e.g. Leech and Coates 1980) argue for a semantic distinction between root and epistemic readings, but do not go as far as claiming that all the meanings communicated by one particular auxiliary are semantically distinct. If one argues for a unitary treatment of meaning, the unitary meaning will provide a relatively small base which needs to be considerably enriched so as to find ways of explaining how the multiple interpretations are pragmatically derived. While the polysemy/monosemy question is obviously important, in the end, one is basically pursuing the same aim: that of setting up a taxonomy into which all the meanings find their place, the difference being that the semantics/pragmatics dividing line is drawn at different points.

5.2   Composition of a modal utterance

5.2.1

Although the phraseology is not always the same, there is general agreement that a sentence with a modal consists of two parts: P and M, i.e. a proposition[11] which represents a particular situation and a modal meaning. *You may be right about that* can be paraphrased as *It is possible* (M) *that you are right* (P). In a similar way, *You can park in front of the garage* is made up of *It is possible* (M) *for you to park in front of the garage* (P). A first consequence of this composition is that negation may bear either on the proposition (*You may/not be right about that*) or on the modal meaning expressed (*You cannot/park your car in front of the garage*) (cf. e.g. Palmer 1995).

5.2.2

This basic insight is also needed to describe accurately the temporal information that is contained in a modal utterance. A distinction should be made between on the one hand, the temporal location of the modal meaning, for instance, in the case of obligation one might ask, is the obligation located in the past, the present or the future? (cf. *She had to be back by ten* vs. *She has to be back by ten* vs. *She will have to be back by 10*), and, on the other hand, the temporal relation between the modal meaning communicated and the situation referred to, i.e. is there a relationship of anteriority, simultaneity or posteriority between the modal meaning and the situation? (cf. *She may be in her room* (simultaneity: there is a present possibility that she is in her room at present)), *She may be back by ten* (posteriority: there is a present possibility that she will be back by ten), *He may have missed his train* (anteriority: there is a present possibility that at some time in the past he missed his train). Although this observation has not gone unnoticed (cf. e.g. Larreya 1984; Leech 1987: 94–9; Declerck 1991a), it sometimes lies at the basis of inaccurate wording (what is actually a temporal relation between the modal meaning and the situation is referred to as the temporal location of the modal meaning (cf. e.g. Huddleston and Pullum et al. 2002: 182) and a systematic, comprehensive description of the system of temporal location and temporal relations appears to be lacking. To give an idea of the variety of combinations of temporal relations that are possible, we offer table 12.3 for the meaning 'necessity' in English.

Three general observations may be made concerning this survey. First, as pointed out in 3, not all modals have a past form that locates the modal meaning in the past sector. For example, *must* cannot be used with the meaning past obligation in direct speech. In such cases, other modals, or periphrastic modals, may supply semantic gaps (cf. e.g. He *had to be* back by 10).

A second observation is that certain modal meanings are inherently incompatible with particular temporal relationships. For example, deontic modality expressed by *must* implies a relationship of simultaneity or posteriority; this means that there is no example of deontic root necessity with anterior P since it is pragmatically impossible to give someone permission or oblige someone to do something in the past. (cf. e.g. Lyons 1977: 824; Declerck 1991a: 383).

A third, related, observation is that particular modal meanings cannot be located in particular time sectors in direct speech. Epistemic modality by definition entails the making of a judgment about the likelihood that it is true that something is the case. This means that the modality itself must be located at the time of the judgment – either speech time or some implicitly or explicitly evoked speech (or thought) time. This explains why the table has gaps for (direct speech) epistemic modality located in the past or the future. Epistemic modality can be located in the past provided the source of the judgment is some sort of reported speaker (or thinker), that is, provided the sentence is part of some kind of indirect (including free indirect) reported speech or thought. For example *Long John had to have hidden the treasure somewhere* expresses a past epistemic judgment about an anterior situation – the judgment belongs to an implicitly evoked thinker, presented as thinking something like '*Long John must have hidden the treasure somewhere.*' Similarly, epistemic modality can only be located in the future when it is explicitly embedded in a future speech-situation and is clearly 'present modality' for the reported speaker or thinker, for example: *Hilda will say/think that you must be mad.* In other words, while it is possible to formulate epistemic necessity in the past or in the future, it always features in a context of indirect or free indirect speech.

6 Conclusion

We have seen that the range of meanings covered by the term 'modality' is functionally very wide. 'Modality' includes meanings such as ability and

Table 12.3 Root and epistemic necessity: forms used to express temporal reference and temporal relations

Time reference of modality	Type of modality (root/epistemic)	Temporal relation of P to M	Form	Example
present time	root	anteriority	/	/
		simultaneity	/	/
		posteriority	*must* (etc.) + present inf.	You *must be* back by 10.
	epistemic	anteriority	*must* + perfect inf.	There's a smell of tobacco in here. Someone *must have been smoking.*
		simultaneity	*must* + present inf.	He *must be* stuck in a traffic jam.
		posteriority	*be bound to* / *should* + present inf.	The truth *is bound to come* out. The parcel *should reach* her tomorrow.
past time (direct speech)	root	anteriority	/	/
		simultaneity	*had to* + present inf.	His mum was a teacher and he was her pupil when he was 10. He *had to call* his mum 'teacher' at school, just like the other kids.
		posteriority	*had to* + present inf.	He *had to be* back by 10.
	epistemic	anteriority	/	/
		simultaneity	/	/
		posteriority	/	/
future time (direct speech)	root	anteriority	/	/
		simultaneity	*will have to* + present infinitive	Once you are at Eton, you *will have to obey* your tutor's orders.
		posteriority	*will have to* + present infinitive	You *will have to be* back by 10.
	epistemic	anteriority	/	/
		simultaneity	/	/
		posteriority	/	/

volition, which tend to characterize the subject referent, permission, and obligation, which predicate compelling or permitting external conditions of the subject referent, epistemic possibility and epistemic necessity, which involve a speaker's confidence (or lack of it) in the truth of a proposition, the subjunctive, which creates possible worlds and the imperative, which functions directly as a means of attempting to influence the addressee's actions.

Nevertheless, these categories have enough in common for linguists in general to treat the field as a unified one. As far as English modality in particular is concerned, a clause containing a modal auxiliary becomes twin-faceted, providing complex possibilities for the temporal location and/or the negation of the modality and of the proposition. The area of temporal interpretation of modal utterances in English is one which is yet to be fully researched. Above all, the modal auxiliaries display a suppleness and breadth of meaning and a never-ceasing development that provides an absorbing challenge for current and future analysts.

NOTES

We would like to thank Bert Cappelle, Renaat Declerck, Liliane Haegeman, Raphael Salkie, and Johan Van der Auwera for exchanging their points of view on particular questions of modality. We are also extremely grateful to Jennifer Coates, Renaat Declerck, and Paul Larreya for taking the time to comment on an earlier, longer draft of our text. Thanks are due, too, to Bas Aarts for his very helpful and detailed advice. The text has also benefited from the remarks of one anonymous referee. We are, of course, solely responsible for any shortcomings in the final version.

1   The variety of English referred to throughout in this chapter is standard British English.

2   Huddeston and Pullum et al. (2002: 89–90) point out that although the form used in the imperative construction is never tensed, there are grounds for considering an imperative clause to be more like a finite clause than it is like a nonfinite clause.

3   In this view of the past subjunctive, we follow Quirk et al. (1985). However, both the extent and the existence of the past subjunctive in current English are open to debate. See, for example, the different approach taken in Huddeston and Pullum et al. (2002: 86–8).

4   Original examples come either from the Cobuild corpus, the ICE-GB (International Corpus of English, British English component) corpus, or the world wide web, and are marked accordingly. Note that disfluencies in the corpus examples have been removed to facilitate reading.

5   Note that *ought* occasionally combines with *do*. (cf. Quirk et al. 1985: 139–40).

6   Note that *have to*, unlike the semi-modals constructed with *be*, requires *do*-support in NICE contexts.

7   Whilst the dividing line between deontic and non-deontic root possibility appears to cause few problems, it seems to us that the

dividing line between deontic and non-deontic root necessity is considerably more problematic. For example: *The Franks did make great efforts to try and govern Brittany, so it must be asked what stood in the way of preventing their rule, what were the limiting factors to Frankish control?* (ICE-GB, W1A-003). Here there is no authority insisting on the asking, and yet a suitable paraphrase would not be 'so it is necessary to ask what stood in the way of preventing their rule' but rather 'so we are obliged to ask . . .' or 'this (circumstance) obliges us to ask . . .'

8   Bybee and Fleischman also refer to 'speaker-oriented' modality, which is expressed by inflectional forms that mark directives, such as the imperative form in English.

9   Coates (1983) remains the most solid descriptive analysis of the meanings of the modal auxiliaries in English. She adopts a so-called 'fuzzy set' approach to describe the meanings of the modals, whereby a *core* is surrounded by a *skirt* whose outer edge is the *periphery*. The core represents examples that have all the prototypical features associated with a particular meaning. As we move away from the core, we come across examples that share fewer

and fewer of these prototypical characteristics. As Coates' corpus-based analysis shows, prototypical examples are relatively few in number, most examples in the corpus she explored belonging to the skirt. Cf. also Larreya (1984: 262–346), Quirk et al. (1985: 219–39), Declerck (1991a: 360–446), Huddleston and Pullum et al. (2002: 175–212). For detailed descriptive analyses of particular modals, cf. e.g. Boyd and Thorne (1969), Palmer (1990), Tregidgo (1982), Haegeman (1983), Bolinger (1989), Tanaka (1990), Groefsema (1995), Myhill (1997).

10   Note that these examples differ from that in (34), which is indeterminate between permission and possibility without any suggestion of ambiguity. Cf. Larreya (1984: 25–6) for a very good description of different kinds of indeterminacy.

11   As is for instance pointed out by Leech and Coates (1980: 86), P either refers to the proposition (in the case of e.g. epistemic necessity or epistemic possibility) or to the event indicated by the predicate (in the case of e.g. permission). Cf. also Huddleston (1984: 167), Larreya and Rivière (2005: 83).

FURTHER READING

Coates (1983) is the most comprehensive corpus study of English modals available today. Larreya's book (1984) is also a very rich, corpus-based introduction to modal meaning and modals in English. In note 9, we have listed some investigations into particular modals that are less broad in scope. Palmer's

books on modals (1990), (2001) – the latter being concerned with modality from a cross-linguistic perspective – belong to the core literature on modals, as do Bybee and Fleischman (1985) and Van der Auwera and Plungian (1998), similarly cross-linguistic studies.

REFERENCES

Bache, C. and Davidsen-Nielsen, N. (1997) *Mastering English*. Berlin and New York: Mouton de Gruyter.

Biber, D., Johansson, S., Leech, G., Conrad, S., and Finegan, E. (1999) *Longman grammar of spoken and written English*. London: Longman.

Bolinger, D. (1989) Extrinsic possibility and and intrinsic potentiality: 7 on *may* and *can* + 1. *Journal of Pragmatics* 13 (1), 1–23.

Boyd, J. and Thorne, J. (1969) The semantics of modal verbs. *Journal of Linguistics* 5, 57–74.

Bybee, J. L. (1985) *Morphology: a study of the relation between meaning and form*. Amsterdam and Philadelphia: John Benjamins.

Bybee, J. L. and Fleischman, S. (1995) Modality in grammar and discourse: an introductory essay. In J. L. Bybee and S. Fleischman (eds.), *Modality in grammar and discourse*. Amsterdam and Philadelphia: John Benjamins, 1–14.

Coates, J. (1983) *The semantics of the modal auxiliaries*. London and Canberra: Croom Helm.

Coates, J. (1995) The expression of root and epistemic possibility in English. In J. L. Bybee and S. Fleischman (eds.), *Modality in grammar and discourse*. Amsterdam and Philadelphia: John Benjamins, 55–66.

Declerck, R. (1991a) *A Comprehensive descriptive grammar of English*. Tokyo: Kaitakusho.

Declerck, R. (1991b) *Tense in English: its structure and use in discourse*. London: Routledge.

Declerck, R. and Reed, S. (2001) *Conditionals: a comprehensive empirical analysis*. Berlin: Mouton de Gruyter.

Ehrman, M. (1966) *The meanings of the modals in present-day American English*. The Hague: Mouton and Co.

Groefsema, M. (1995) *Can, may, must* and *should*: a relevance theoretic account. *Journal of Linguistics* 31, 53–79.

Haegeman, L. (1983) *The semantics of 'will' in present-day British English: a unified account*. Brussels: Paleis der Academiën.

Hewings, M. (1999) *Advanced grammar in use*. Cambridge: Cambridge University Press.

Hoye, L. (1997) *Adverbs and modality in English*. London and New York: Longman.

Huddleston. R. (1984) *English grammar: an outline*. Cambridge: Cambridge University Press.

Huddleston, R. (1995) The case against a future tense in English. *Studies in Language* 19, 399–446.

Huddleston, R., Pullum, G. K., et al. (eds.) (2002) *Cambridge grammar of the English language*. Cambridge: Cambridge University Press.

Jespersen, O. (1958) (1914) *A modern English grammar on historical principles VII. Syntax*, vol. 1. London: Allen and Unwin, Copenhagen: Ejnar Munksgaard.

Klinge, A. (1993) The English modal auxiliaries: from lexical semantics to utterance interpretation. *Journal of Linguistics* 29, 315–57.

Krug, M. G. (2000) *Emerging English modals*. Berlin: Mouton de Gruyter.

Larreya, P. (1984) *Le possible et le nécessaire*. Poitiers: Nathan-recherche.

Larreya, P. (2000) Modal verbs and the expression of futurity in English, French and Italian. In J. van der Auwera and P. Dendale (eds.), *Modal verbs in Germanic and Romance Languages* (= *Belgian Journal of Linguistics* 14). Amsterdam: John Benjamins, 115–29.

Larreya, P. and Rivière, C. (2005) *Grammaire explicative de l'anglais*, 3rd edn. Paris: Pearson Longman.

Leech, G. N. (1987) *Meaning and the English verb*. Burnt Mill, Harlow: Longman.

Leech, G. N. and Coates, J. (1980) Semantic indeterminacy and the modals. In S. Greenbaum et al. (eds.), *Studies in English linguistics*. The Hague: Mouton, 79–90.

Lyons, J. (1977) *Semantics*. Cambridge: Cambridge University Press.

Myhill, J. (1997) *Should* and *ought*: the rise of individually oriented modality in American English. *English Language and Linguistics* 1, 3–23.

Nordlinger, R. and Traugott, E. C. (1997) Scope and the development of epistemic modality: evidence from *ought to*. *English Language and Linguistics* 1, 295–317.

Palmer, F. R. (1986) *Mood and modality*. Cambridge: Cambridge University Press.

Palmer, F. R. (1987) *The English verb*, 2nd edn. London: Longman.

Palmer, F. R. (1990) *Modality and the English modals*, 2nd edn. London and New York: Longman.

Palmer, F. R. (1995) Negation and the modals of possibility and necessity. In J. L. Bybee and S. Fleischman (eds.), *Modality in grammar and discourse*. Amsterdam and Philadelphia: John Benjamins, 453–71, 308–11.

Palmer, F. R. (2001) *Mood and modality*, 2nd edn. Cambridge: Cambridge University Press.

Papafragou, A. (2000) *Modality: issues in the semantics–pragmatics interface*. Amsterdam and New York: Elsevier Science.

Quirk, R., Greenbaum, S., Leech, G., and Svartvik, J. (1985) *A comprehensive grammar of the English language*. London and New York: Longman.

Steele, S. (1975) Past and irrealis: just what does it all mean? *International Journal of American Linguistics* 41, 200–17.

Sweetser, E. (1990) *From etymology to pragmatics*. Cambridge: Cambridge University Press.

Tanaka, T. (1990) Semantic changes of *can* and *may*: differentiation and implication. *Journal of Linguistics* 266, 89–123.

Traugott, E. C. (1989) On the rise of epistemic meanings in English: an example of subjectification in semantic change. *Language* 65 (1), 31–55.

Tregidgo, P. (1982) MUST and MAY: demand and permission. *Lingua* 56, 75–92.

Van der Auwera, J. and Plungian, V. A. (1998) Modality's semantic map. *Linguistic Typology* 2, 79–124.

Westney, P. (1995) *Modals and periphrastics in English*. Tubingen: Niemeyer.

Zandvoort, R. W. (1964) *A handbook of English grammar*. Groningen: J. B. Wolters.

13 Information Structure

BETTY J. BIRNER AND
GREGORY WARD

1 Introduction

In this chapter we examine the way in which noncanonical syntactic constructions contribute to an orderly presentation of information in a discourse. Ever since the early contributions of Halliday and the Prague School (e.g., Halliday 1967; Halliday and Hasan 1976; Firbas 1966), it has been a linguistic truism that human languages tend to structure discourse on the basis of a 'given before new' principle – that is, in any particular sentence, information that is assumed to be familiar, or GIVEN, tends to be placed before that which is assumed to be NEW. One way of ensuring that this flow of information is preserved is through the use of noncanonical constructions, i.e. syntactic structures in which the canonical order of elements (in English, subject-verb-object) is rearranged. Chafe (1976) uses the term 'packaging' to refer to this use of syntactic structuring to serve pragmatic functions, noting that by choosing to package information using one structure rather than another, a speaker accommodates his or her speech to various "states of the addressee's mind."

Because different noncanonical constructions impose constraints on the familiarity of their constituents, a speaker's choice of syntactic construction can signal the constituents' assumed familiarity level, which in turn can assist the hearer in constructing a coherent discourse model. In this way, the constraints on the information status of the constituents within a noncanonical construction are directly tied to that construction's discourse function – i.e., the function for which a speaker uses that construction.

Various individual constructions serve distinct discourse functions relating to the structuring of information within the discourse, and these functions work together to create generalized patterns of information structure. For example, Prince (1981) and Horn (1986) posit a "conspiracy of syntactic constructions'" preventing NPs representing relatively unfamiliar information from occupying subject position (see also Kuno 1971, inter alia). For example, Horn (1986) argues that leftward movement in general serves to prepose "thematic" or familiar information, whereas rightward movement serves to postpose non-thematic or unfamiliar information. Dichotomies such as theme/rheme, topic/comment, and focus/ground have all been proposed by researchers attempting to account for the well-grounded intuition that given information tends to precede new information.

What these previous approaches have in common is a general approach based on the degree to which information is assumed to be available to the hearer prior to its evocation in the current utterance. However, extensive research has shown that constraints on information structure do not apply to all noncanonical constructions in the same way. Certain of these constructions have been shown to be sensitive to the information status of entire clauses; others have been shown to be sensitive to the information status of individual constituents and their position within the clause. In some cases, the information status of such constituents is tied to their standing within the discourse, i.e., whether the information conveyed by those constituents has been previously evoked or can be plausibly inferred from something that has been previously evoked; alternatively, the information status of these constituents can be tied to their standing vis à vis the hearer, i.e., whether the speaker believes the information already constitutes part of the hearer's knowledge store (Prince 1992). For those constructions sensitive to the information status of entire clauses, these clauses represent information that is salient in the discourse, with some sub-portion serving as the FOCUS, or new information, of the utterance. We begin our survey with a discussion of information structuring at the clausal level.

2   Open Propositions

A proposition rarely consists entirely of information all of which has the same information status. Rather, propositions include both given and new information, sometimes in complex arrangements, with certain constructions reserved for particular orderings of clausal elements with different information statuses. In this section, we examine one information-structuring device – the open proposition – and show how a number of unrelated constructions make use of this structure.

Chomsky (1971) argues that certain aspects of semantic interpretation are determined by the syntax (at the level of surface structure), with FOCUS being such a notion. The focused constituent both contains and is determined by the INTONATION CENTER, while the presupposition is obtained by replacing the focus with a variable. The structuring of information into a focus and a presupposition directly affects what constitutes a well-formed conversational exchange, as illustrated in (1):

(1)   a.   Is it JOHN who writes poetry?
      b.   It isn't JOHN who writes poetry.
      c.   No, it is BILL who writes poetry.   (= Chomsky 1971, exx. (38), (39))

Chomsky notes that "[u]nder normal intonation the capitalized word receives main stress and serves as the point of maximal inflection of the pitch contour" (1971:199). In the semantic representations of (1a) and (1b), *John* is the focus of the sentence (realized as the intonation center), and *someone writes poetry* is the presupposition (the result of replacing the focus with a variable). In (1c), a natural response to (1a) or (1b), the presupposition remains the same, while the focus changes to *Bill*. An appropriate response, then, is simply one sharing the presupposition of the question.

Jackendoff (1972) agrees that "intuitively, it makes sense to speak of a discourse as 'natural' if successive sentences share presuppositions" (1972: 230). He defines the focus of a sentence as "the information in the sentence that is assumed by the speaker not to be shared by him and the hearer," and the presupposition as "the information in the sentence that is assumed by the speaker to be shared by him and the hearer" (1972: 16). Jackendoff posits a focus marker F, which is ultimately realized as stress, such that "if a phrase P is chosen as the focus of a sentence S, the highest stress in S will be on the syllable of P that is assigned highest stress by the regular stress rules" (Jackendoff 1972: 58).

Following in this tradition, Prince (1986) identifies a class of noncanonical syntactic constructions that are sensitive to the focus-presupposition division. Corresponding to Chomsky's and Jackendoff's notion of presupposition is Prince's notion of an OPEN PROPOSITION (OP), which, like presuppositions, serves to mark presumed shared knowledge in discourse. An open proposition contains one or more variables and represents what the speaker assumes to be salient or inferrable in the discourse at the time of utterance. The OP required for the felicity of a given utterance is derived by replacing its tonically stressed constituent with a variable whose instantiation corresponds to the focus of the utterance (see also Rochemont 1978; Gazdar 1979; Karttunen and Peters 1979; Wilson and Sperber 1979; Prince 1981b; Ward 1988; Välimaa-Blum 1988; Vallduví 1992; Lambrecht 1994).

Prince classifies a host of constructions, including preposings, clefts, and inversions, as marking an OP as salient in the discourse. A preposing, for example, consists of two parts: the open proposition (containing one or more variables) and the focus. The instantiation of a variable in an OP constitutes an utterance's focus, represents new information, and is realized prosodically with a pitch accent. Consider, for example, the focus preposing in (2):

(2)   Yeah we did it. *Two or three times we did it.*
      (*Come Back to the 5 & Dime, Jimmy Dean Jimmy Dean*)
      OP: WE DID IT X TIMES (where X is a member of the set of numbers).

Here, the open proposition may be paraphrased informally as 'we did it some number of times.' This OP is clearly salient in the discourse, given the previous utterance *Yeah we did it*. The focus itself, *two or three times*, has not been evoked in the prior discourse and is therefore not part of the open proposition;

however, it stands in a salient set (entity-attribute) relationship with information evoked in the previous utterance. In what follows, we survey a number of constructions that are sensitive to the presence of a contextually salient open proposition.

2.1   Clefts

The noncanonical constructions most associated with open propositions are CLEFT SENTENCES, of which there are two principal subtypes, IT-CLEFTS and WH-CLEFTS (Prince 1978; Ward, Birner, and Huddleston 2002). *Wh*-clefts may be further classified into two types based on constituent order: REVERSED and NON-REVERSED, resulting in the three types illustrated in (3):

(3)   a.   I bought a red wool sweater. [non-cleft]
      b.   It was a red wool sweater that I bought. [*it*-cleft]
      c.   What I bought was a red wool sweater. [non-reversed *wh*-cleft]
      d.   A red wool sweater was what I bought. [reversed *wh*-cleft]

The reason clefts are so closely associated with open propositions is that they wear their information structure on their sleeves. Clefts consist of two parts: the open proposition, corresponding to the presupposition of the utterance, and the focus. For the clefts in (3b–d), the OP may be derived by replacing the focused constituent with a variable, resulting in the OP "I BOUGHT X." This OP must constitute presupposed shared knowledge in order for the cleft to be felicitous; that is, each of the examples (3b–d) presupposes that the speaker bought something. The focus, *a red wool sweater*, is the instantiation of the variable and represents new information.

   In addition, the use of a cleft implicates that the instantiation of the variable is both exhaustive and exclusive. Thus, the speaker's use of any of the clefts in (3) implicates that a red wool sweater constitutes the sum total of the purchase, i.e. that the speaker didn't (on the occasion in question) buy anything else. Note that this implicature is absent from the non-cleft (3a), which is consistent with the speaker's having bought additional items.

   It-clefts may also be classified into two types; however, this distinction is not based on formal criteria, but rather on whether the information represented by the presupposition is discourse-old or discourse-new (Prince 1992). Consider first the discourse-old presupposition associated with the clefts in (4):

(4)   a.   A: Did you turn the air-conditioning off?
           B: No, *it was Kim.*
      b.   Inexperienced dancers often have difficulty in ending the Natural Turn in the correct alignment . . . *It is usually the man who is at fault.*
      c.   John only did the illustrations for the book. *It was Mary who wrote the story.*   (= Ward, Birner, and Huddleston 2002, exx. (33i–iii))

The context for (4a) is one in which it is known that someone turned the air-conditioning off; B's response takes the form of a truncated *it*-cleft, a construction that permits the omission of discourse-old information. In (4b), the presupposition that someone is at fault follows from what has just been said. In (4c) the existence of the book suggests that someone wrote the story.

The other type of *it*-cleft involves an OP that is discourse-new, exemplified in (5):

(5) a. It was 50 years ago that the first real computer was built in Philadelphia.
    b. It is with great pleasure that I now declare this Exhibition open.
    c. The Indians were helpful in many ways. It was they who taught the settlers how to plant and harvest crops successfully in the New World. (= Ward, Birner, and Huddleston 2002, exx. (34i–iii))

In such examples, most of the new information is conveyed by the relative clause. As with the first type, however, the information in the relative clause is presented as a presupposition, i.e. as factual and uncontroversial. The concept of presupposition is thus distinct from that of old information: information does not have to be given to be presupposed (see also Abbott 2000). The focused element in this second type of *it*-cleft may be an adjunct, as in (5a–b), or an argument, as in (5c).[1]

2.2 *Gapping*

As demonstrated by Levin and Prince (1986), gapping also requires a contextually salient open proposition for felicity. Consider the gapped sentence in (6):

(6) Ross studied law and Norris history. (= Levin and Prince 1986, ex. (1))

In the case of gapping, the OP contains at least two variables. For (6), the required OP is (7):

(7) X STUDIED Y (WHERE X IS A MEMBER OF SOME SALIENT SET OF PEOPLE AND Y IS A MEMBER OF THE SET OF ACADEMIC SUBJECTS).

As with clefts, the instantiations of these variables receive nuclear stress. It is this open proposition (i.e., that someone studied something) that must be contextually salient at the time of the gapping; indeed, felicitous gapping requires the presupposed portion of the OP to have been explicitly evoked in the prior utterance. The new information (i.e., the instantiations of the OP variables) corresponds to the two focal constituents, *Norris* and *history* in (6). Notice also that these foci stand in a salient set relationship with previously known or inferrable information; that is, part of the OP that must be salient is the fact that the instantiation of X will be drawn from some salient set of people, while the instantiation of Y will be drawn from the set of academic subjects.

Thus far, we have examined two constructions – clefts and gapping – that are clear cases of open proposition constructions. We now turn to a number of other constructions whose information structure is not quite so transparent, but which are nonetheless cases of open proposition constructions, as we will see in the following sections.

2.3   *Preposing*

A number of previous studies (Prince 1981b; Ward 1988; Birner and Ward 1998; inter alia) have shown that certain types of preposing constructions also require a salient or inferrable open proposition within the current discourse. Preposings can be classified into two major types on the basis of their prosodic and information structure: FOCUS PREPOSING and TOPICALIZATION. As we saw above in (2), repeated below for convenience, the preposed constituent of a focus preposing contains the focus of the utterance and receives nuclear accent; the rest of the clause is typically deaccented:[2]

(8)   Yeah we did it. *Two or three times we did it.*
      (*Come Back to the 5 & Dime, Jimmy Dean Jimmy Dean*)
      OP: WE DID IT X TIMES.

Here, the preposed constituent, *two or three times*, bears the nuclear accent, which identifies it as the focus of the utterance. The OP is given in (8), which we can gloss informally as "We did it some number of times." This OP is clearly salient in context: in the immediately prior utterance, the speaker mentions that they had 'done it,' licensing the inference that they had done it some number of times. As shown in (8), the focus itself, *two or three times*, is not part of the open proposition; however, it stands in a salient set relationship with the previous utterance.

The preposed constituent of a topicalization, on the other hand, does **not** contain the focus but it does bear one or more pitch accents since it typically is contained within its own INTONATIONAL PHRASE (Pierrehumbert 1980). Intonationally, preposings of this type contain multiple accented syllables: (at least) one occurs within the constituent that contains the focus and (at least) one occurs within the preposed constituent. Although not the focus, the preposed constituent in a topicalization is constrained to represent a member of a contextually salient set (Prince 1981b; Ward 1988; Birner and Ward 1998). The focus of a topicalization occurs elsewhere in the clause and, as with all focus-sensitive constructions, receives nuclear accent. Of course for both topicalization and focus preposing, other constituents may bear pitch accents. Intonationally speaking, the difference between focus preposing and topicalization is that only the former requires that the nuclear accent be on the preposed constituent.[3] Consider (9):

(9)   [context: A and B are discussing which film to see]
   A: Ok, our choices are "Star Struck" playing on Sansom Street and either "The Return of Martin Guerre" or "L'Etoile du Nord," both playing at the Ritz.
   B: I vote for "Star Struck." *The OTHER ones you have to go all the way down to Second and WALNUT to see.*
   (conversation)

Here, the preposed constituent *the other ones* (i.e., the two movies playing at the Ritz) is not the focus; rather, it is the location of those movies that represents the focus of the utterance (with *Walnut* being the intonational center of the phrase *all the way down to Second and Walnut*). However, the preposed constituent does represent a member of the set {movie choices} evoked by A's utterance, and it is this set that links B's utterance to A's proposal.[4]

The OP for a topicalization is determined in much the same way as for focus preposing, except that the set member represented by the preposed constituent is replaced in the OP by the full set, as in (10):

(10)   a.   OP = You have to go to X location to see {movies}.
       b.   Focus = all the way down to Second and Walnut.

In (10a), the OP includes the variable corresponding to the focus (10b), but note that the preposed constituent *the other ones* has been replaced by the set {movies}, i.e. the set that includes both the preposed constituent and the other relevant members of that set. In other words, the OP that is salient in (9) is not that one has to travel to Second and Walnut to see the movies playing at the Ritz, but rather that there is some distance that one must travel to see any movie, as indicated in (10a).[5]

Thus, both types of preposing require the presence of a salient or inferrable OP at the time of utterance for felicity.[6] The focus of the preposing may appear either in preposed position (as in the case of focus movement), or in canonical position (as in the case of topicalization). However, in both cases the preposed constituent serves as the link to the preceding discourse via a salient set relation.

2.4   Inversion

An inversion is a sentence in which the logical subject appears in postverbal position while some other, canonically postverbal, constituent appears in preverbal position (see Birner 1994, 1996). The following are representative examples:

(11)   a.   There are huge cartons and tins of nuts, vanilla, honey, peanut butter. Varieties of herb tea are visible. *On the counter are loaves – whole wheat, cinnamon raisin, oatmeal, rye, soy sunflower, corn meal.*   (S. Terkel, *Working*, NY: Avon, 1974, p. 607)

b. *Immediately recognizable here is the basic, profoundly false tenet of Movie Philosophy 101, as it has been handed down from "Auntie Mame" and "Harold and Maude"*: Nonconformism, the more radical the better, is the only sure route to human happiness and self-fulfillment. (= Ward, Birner, and Huddleston 2002, ex. (34ii))

c. She's a nice woman, isn't she? *Also a nice woman is our next guest* ...   (= Ward, Birner, and Huddleston 2002, ex. (11iii))

d. Two CBS crewmen were wounded by shrapnel yesterday in Souk el Gharb during a Druse rocket attack on Lebanese troops. They were the 5th and 6th television-news crewmen to be wounded in Lebanon this month. One television reporter, Clark Todd of Canada, was killed earlier this month. *Wounded yesterday were cameraman Alain Debos, 45, and soundman Nick Follows, 24.*   (*Philadelphia Inquirer*, 9/24/83)

As with preposing, any phrasal constituent can be fronted via inversion. While they differ in terms of the type of constituent being fronted, what all of the examples in (11) have in common is that some canonically postverbal, lexically governed constituent appears in preverbal position, while the logical subject appears in postverbal position. For convenience, we will refer to these as the PREPOSED and POSTPOSED constituents, respectively.[7]

As with clefts, gapping, and preposing, felicitous inversion is also sensitive to the presence of a salient OP. Associated with each inversion in (11) is an OP that is required to be salient in the context in order for the inversion to be felicitous. What this OP is for any given inversion can be determined in the same way as for preposing: the preposed constituent is replaced with the relevant set of which it is a member and the focused item is replaced with a variable. In the case of (11d), this process results in (12):

(12) a. OP = X WAS WOUNDED AT {TIME}.
      b. Focus = cameraman Alain Debos, 45, and soundman Nick Follows, 24.

Again, we see that the OP includes the set of which the preposed constituent is a member. Thus, the OP is not simply that "X was wounded yesterday," but rather the more abstract proposition that X was wounded at some time. It is this OP that must be salient or inferrable in the discourse context for the inversion to be felicitous. Consider the same utterance in a context in which the OP is not licensed:

(13) Several CBS crewmen arrived in Souk el Gharb last week to cover the latest peace talks. *#Wounded yesterday were cameraman Alain Debos, 45, and soundman Nick Follows, 24.*

Here, the context does not license the OP required for this inversion to be felicitous. Thus, inversion involves the same sorts of OPs that have been shown to be relevant for preposing and clefts.[8]

The requirement of an open proposition is not limited to noncanonical syntactic constructions. In what follows, we take a brief look at two constructions that involve canonical word order, yet are sensitive to the presence of a contextually salient OP, namely deferred equatives and epistemic *would*.

2.5   *Deferred equatives*

Deferred reference (Nunberg 1977, 1979, 1995) is a type of non-literal language involving the metonymic use of an expression to refer to an entity related to, but not denoted by, the conventional meaning of that expression. Consider Nunberg's classic 'ham sandwich' example in (14):

(14)   [server to co-worker in deli]
       The ham sandwich is at table 7.   (= Nunberg 1995, ex. (19))

In (14), the speaker's reference is 'deferred' in the sense that she is referring indirectly to the person who ordered the ham sandwich via the ham sandwich itself. Various types of deferred reference – and the various linguistic mechanisms available for such reference – have been identified and discussed in the literature. One of these mechanisms is the so-called EQUATIVE SENTENCE or IDENTITY STATEMENT – a copular sentence of the form NP-*be*-NP – as illustrated in (15):

(15)   a.   [customer to server holding tray full of dinner orders at a Thai restaurant]
            I'm the Pad Thai.   (conversation, 8/10/02)
       b.   Samir Abd al-Aziz al-Najim is the four of clubs.   (*Chicago Tribune*, 4/19/03)
       c.   [physician assigning interns to patients] You and you are shortness of breath. You and you take vertigo. And last but not least, knee pain.   (*ER*, 4/24/03)

In each of the equative sentences in (15), the speaker equates the referents of the two NPs, thereby conveying a correspondence between them. In (15a), for example, the speaker identifies himself with his lunch order to convey indirectly that he is the person at the table who ordered the Pad Thai.

Ward (2004) has observed that such deferred equative sentences crucially involve an open proposition. As with gapping, the OP of a deferred equative contains two variables, corresponding to the two sets from which the instantiations of these variables are drawn. Consider (15a), repeated below in (16):

(16)   a.   I'm the Pad Thai.
       b.   OP: X MAPS ONTO Y (where X is a member of the set of customers and Y is a member of the set of orders).
       c.   Foci: I, the Pad Thai.

In the context of a server distributing various lunch orders to a group of diners, the fact that there is a correspondence between customers and their orders is highly salient. We can represent the relevant OP as in (16b). The OP corresponding to (16a) is determined in the usual way by replacing both of the foci (*I, the Pad Thai*) with variables. The instantiation of the variables must be drawn from the two sets involved in the mapping – in this case, the set of customers and the set of meal orders. In other words, for (16) we might gloss the instantiation informally as: "I, a member of the set of customers, correspond to the Pad Thai, a member of the set of orders." What makes the utterance in (16a) 'deferred' is not a transfer of sense or reference from either of the NPs in the equative; rather, it is the coercion of *be* to *map onto* as represented in the OP.

In fact, it is precisely this coercion of the copula's meaning that requires the presence of a salient OP. Note that if the OP in (16b) is not salient, the deferred equative is infelicitous, as seen in (17):

(17)   A: How was your meal?
        B: Good. #I was the Pad Thai.

Here, the OP in (16b) – that various customers correspond to various orders – is not salient, and the deferred equative is correspondingly infelicitous. Note that the infelicity of B's utterance in (17) is not the result of one's answering the question "How was your meal?" with a description of what one ate, nor is it the result of referring to one's lunch order with a definite article, as long as that order is uniquely identifiable in context.[9] As seen in (18), the corresponding non-deferred reference is felicitous:

(18)   A: How was your meal?
        B: Good. I had the Pad Thai.

Rather, the infelicity of the deferred equative in (17) can be attributed to the absence of a contextually salient double-variable OP. It is crucial that there be two variables; as (19) shows, a single-variable OP is insufficient to guarantee felicity:

(19)   A: Sorry you had to have lunch all by yourself. What did you have?
        B: #I was the Pad Thai. [cf. I had the Pad Thai.]

Here, the single-variable OP 'I HAD X FOR LUNCH' is insufficient to license the deferred reference. Note that non-deferred equatives, illustrated in (20), are not subject to the requirement of a contextually salient OP:

(20)   a.   I think that guy over there is my next-door neighbor.
        b.   Hello. I'm the Chair of the Linguistics Department. I'm calling to see if . . .
        c.   George Bush is the President of the United States.

None of these equatives requires that any particular OP be salient in order to ensure felicity.

2.6   *Epistemic* **would**

Another canonical-word-order construction sensitive to the presence of a contextually salient open proposition is the epistemic *would* construction, as analyzed in Birner, Kaplan, and Ward 2003. This construction, illustrated in (21), consists of a referential subject (typically but not necessarily a demonstrative), the epistemic modal *would*, and the equative copula *be*.[10]

(21)   This is just a storage area. [pointing] *That would be our pile of stuff on the left.*   (tour of stable facilities by one of many resident trainers, each of whom is allocated space for storage, etc., 7/30/02)

The use of the modal here is epistemic in the sense that the speaker is using it to convey his assessment of the truth of the proposition expressed. That is, in (21) he conveys his confidence in the proposition that the pile of stuff in question belongs to him. Crucial to the felicity of the construction is the salience of the OP in (22):

(22)   OP: THAT PILE OF STUFF ON THE LEFT IS X.

In the context of the speaker providing a tour of the facilities, this OP is salient; that is, on a tour, one expects that various items will be identified. In this way, the speaker's use of the epistemic *would* construction serves to instantiate the variable of the OP, and in this case he does so with the identity of the pile of stuff. Consider the same utterance if produced in a context in which the identity of the pile is not at issue:

(23)   a.   Hi. Have a seat; I'll get you a cup of coffee. Careful where you sit in this mess, though. #*That would be our pile of stuff on the left.*
       b.   Hi. Have a seat; I'll get you a cup of coffee. Careful where you sit in this mess, though. *That's our pile of stuff on the left.*

Where the identification of the pile is not salient prior to the utterance, use of epistemic *would* is infelicitous (as in 23a), while the corresponding utterance without a modal (as in 23b) is fine.

The referent of the subject of epistemic *would* can either be a discourse-old entity (as with the pile in (21) above), or else the variable of the OP, as in (24) below (as shown in Ward, Kaplan, and Birner (to appear)):

(24)   A: [Hotel guest] To get to the early opening for Epcot, do you take a tram or a boat?
       B: [Concierge] *That would be the boat, Ms. Birner.*   (telephone conversation, 9/97)

OP: You take X to get to the early opening for Epcot (where X is a member of the set of transportation options).

In (24), the demonstrative subject lacks a plausible antecedent in the discourse; instead, *that* in this example must be interpreted as anaphoric to the variable in the OP. In fact, in Ward et al. (to appear), we note that the possibility of variable reference for the subject NP is but one of a number of similarities that the epistemic *would* construction shares with *that*-clefts (Jenkins 1975; Ball 1977, 1978; Wirth 1978; Hedberg 1990).

3   Information Status

As we have shown, the salient OP required by constructions like epistemic *would* and preposings constitutes information that is already familiar in the discourse context. And, as we have seen, a wide range of constructions are sensitive to this sort of familiarity, i.e. the familiarity of a proposition minus one of its constituents. Another type of familiarity to which a construction can be sensitive is what we will call *information status*. We will define information status as the degree of familiarity of some sub-propositional element – that is, an element which is a part of a larger proposition. This subpropositional element may be expressed as any part of speech; the examples in (25) illustrate cases of preposing that place an NP, a PP, and a VP in fronted position, respectively:

(25)   a.   I work on the 6th floor of a building. I know some of the elevator riders well. *Others I have only that nodding acquaintance with and some are total strangers.*   (*Philadelphia Inquirer*, 9/5/83)
   b.   Consume they did–not only 15 kegs of beer, which they guzzled like soda pop, but also the free Coors posters which they seized as works of art to adorn their dorm walls. *For their heads, they were given free Coors hats and for their cars free Coors bumper stickers.*   (*Philadelphia Inquirer*, 10/7/83)
   c.   "I enjoyed the practice of law, but it wasn't my highest priority," said Aronson, who retired in 1999 at age 55. "Law has a certain sense of propriety. Magic and entertainers inherently break that down. I always wanted to play."
       And play he did. Larry Gray, who still works at the firm, said Aronson was one of the brightest lawyers he's ever known, but he recalls seeing the hobbyist magician break out card tricks after completing big real-estate deals, or using magic to break the ice with new clients.   (*Chicago Tribune*, 8/24/03)

In each of the examples in (25) the information represented by the preposed constituent stands in a set relationship to information evoked in the prior discourse. In (25a), *others* stands in a set relationship with the previously mentioned *some of the elevator riders*; both represent subsets of the set of elevator riders. In (25b), the evoked heads and cars are members of the set of potential recipients of the Coors freebies. And in (25c), *play* stands in an identity relation with the previously evoked *play*; that is, playing has been evoked in the prior sentence, and since every singleton set is still a set, every element stands in a set relationship with itself. The relationship between preposed information and the prior context will be discussed more fully below; what is important to note at the outset is that the noncanonical placement of a subpropositional element is reliably correlated with a constraint on its contextual distribution.

Although we have said that information status involves the status of subpropositional elements, such an element may itself be an entire proposition embedded within another proposition; in this case it is a closed, rather than an open, proposition, and it is the status of the entire embedded proposition (rather than any focus/presuppositional structure within it) that is relevant for its information status, as illustrated in (26):

(26)   Philip knew Mary loved him. *That she was also jealous of him* he had never guessed.

Here, the preposed constituent is *that she was also jealous of him*, representing an entire proposition. And as expected, this proposition stands in a set relationship with the previously evoked *Mary loved him*, i.e., the set of attitudes Mary has toward Philip. Thus, although *that she was also jealous of him* represents a proposition, it is also a subpropositional constituent within a larger proposition, which itself is expressed via a noncanonical syntactic construction – and in that capacity, this subpropositional proposition is subject to the same contextual constraint as any other preposed constituent.

In English, information status is based on the interaction of three distinct dichotomies: old vs. new status, relative vs. absolute status, and discourse vs. hearer status. Broad generalizations can be drawn regarding the first two; that is, for a wide range of noncanonical constructions in English, one can predict from the form of the construction whether it will require a given constituent to be old or new, and whether the constraint will be a relative or an absolute one. The third dimension, however, appears to be assigned more or less arbitrarily to linguistic forms; although more of the constructions we will consider here require a particular discourse status than a particular hearer status, there does not seem to be any principled way of predicting for a given form whether it will be sensitive to discourse or hearer status.

3.1   *The information-status matrix*

As shown in Birner and Ward 1998, noncanonical constructions in English are used in consistent and characteristic ways to structure information in discourse, and significant cross-construction generalizations apply to families of related constructions. Below we will address some of these generalizations.

As noted above, it is well known that English tends to structure information within a sentence such that given information precedes new (e.g., Halliday 1967; Halliday and Hasan 1976). Since the early Prague School work on syntax and discourse function (e.g., Firbas 1966), researchers have amassed evidence for this correlation between sentence position and givenness in the discourse. How to define 'given' and 'new,' however, has been a matter of some debate. Moreover, it is not the **actual** status of some informational element that is relevant for the felicitous use of a construction, but rather the speaker's and hearer's beliefs regarding each other's beliefs (Prince 1981a). Thus, my use of a definite such as *the pizza* in reference to some object does not depend for its felicity on there being a single unique pizza present in the context, or even on whether either or both discourse participants have such an entity in their discourse model, but rather on each interlocutor's belief regarding the other's beliefs. Hence, an utterance such as *the pizza is coming* will be felicitous in reference to a nonexistent pizza we mutually (and falsely) believe is being delivered soon, whereas it will be infelicitous if we do not believe we share such a mutual belief (even if such a pizza does exist – e.g., if one of us has ordered it without the other's knowledge). Prince 1981a adopts the term ASSUMED FAMILIARITY to reflect the fact that only an omniscient observer can know what knowledge exists in the interlocutors' discourse models, while actual language users must operate on the basis of what they *assume* constitutes shared knowledge between them and their interlocutors (or can be accommodated as such by a cooperative hearer).

Prince 1992 distinguishes three basic notions of given vs. new information. The first is focus/presupposition structure, as discussed above with respect to constructions requiring a contextually salient open proposition. This is a propositional-level constraint.

The remaining two distinctions constrain the status of subpropositional constituents; these are the distinctions between, on the one hand, discourse-old and discourse-new information and, on the other hand, hearer-old and hearer-new information. Discourse-old information is that which has been evoked in the prior discourse, whereas discourse-new information is that which has not been previously evoked. Hearer-old information is that which, regardless of whether it has been evoked in the current discourse, is assumed to be known to the hearer, while hearer-new information is assumed to be new to the hearer. Combining these two dichotomies results in four possible information statuses as shown in table 13.1.

Thus, consider (27):

(27) Gov. Rod Blagojevich, while scaling back a massive capital program, said Friday he would endorse a $3.6 billion state construction budget that includes new money to build schools and millions of dollars for legislative pork-barrel projects. (*Chicago Tribune*, 8/23/03)

Table 13.1 Hearer-Status vs. Discourse-Status

	Hearer-old	*Hearer-new*
Discourse-old	Previously evoked in the discourse	(non-occurring)
Discourse-new	Assumed to be known, but not yet evoked in the discourse	Assumed to be new to both discourse and hearer

Source: Adapted from Prince 1992

Here, *Gov. Rod Blagojevich* constitutes information that is discourse-new but hearer-old; that is, one can assume that the readers of a Chicago newspaper are likely to know of the state's governor (rendering Blagojevich hearer-old), but he has not been mentioned in the current discourse (rendering him discourse-new). The pronoun *he*, however, is the second evocation of Blagojevich; hence, it represents information that is now both hearer-old and discourse-old, having been mentioned previously in the discourse. Finally, *a $3.6 billion state construction budget* represents information that not only has not been previously evoked in the discourse, but also can be assumed to be new to the hearer; thus, this information is both discourse-new and hearer-new. The fourth category, information that is discourse-old but hearer-new, is assumed by Prince to be non-occurring, given that a speaker typically assumes that the hearer is attending to the discourse, and thus that anything that has been evoked in the discourse is also known to the hearer. Notice that while Prince uses these terms primarily with respect to the information status of an entity, we will use them more broadly for not only entities but also attributes, relations, and propositions – any category of information that may be known or unknown to a language user.

We have said above that broad generalizations can be stated regarding the correlation of form and function in English noncanonical syntactic constructions. These correlations moreover corroborate the longstanding observation of a given-before-new ordering of information within noncanonical clauses in English. In what follows, we will show that preposing constructions (that is, those that place canonically postverbal constituents in preverbal position) mark the preposed information as given in some sense, while postposing constructions (those that place canonically preverbal constituents in postverbal position) mark the postposed information as new in some sense (i.e., either to the discourse or to the hearer). Finally, constructions that reverse the canonical ordering of two constituents (placing a canonically preverbal constituent in postverbal position while placing a canonically postverbal constituent in preverbal position) mark the preposed information as being at least as familiar within the discourse as is the postposed information (Birner and Ward 1998). In sum:

Table 13.2   Information status by number and location of noncanonically positioned arguments

Positioning of noncanonical argument(s):	*Information status:*
Single preposed argument	(Discourse- or Hearer-) Old
Single postposed argument	(Discourse- or Hearer-) New
Two arguments reversed	Preposed no newer than postposed

Source: Adapted from Ward and Birner 1998

Contextual constraint on noncanonical word order in English

- Preposed elements represent given information, and postposed elements represent new information.
- The above constraint is absolute in the case of a single noncanonically positioned constituent and relative in the case of two noncanonically positioned constituents.
- Whether it is discourse or hearer status that is relevant is arbitrarily associated with any given construction.

That is to say, whether a constituent is constrained to represent old or new information correlates with whether it is being preposed or postposed, and whether the constraint is absolute or relative correlates with, respectively, whether a single constituent appears in noncanonical position or two constituents appear noncanonically positioned with respect to each other. Thus, we find the situation shown in table 13.2.[11]

We will discuss each of the three above-listed categories of noncanonical constructions in turn.

3.2   *Single preposed argument*

Although argument reversal involves the preposing of a constituent (in combination with the postposing of another constituent), the term *preposing* is typically reserved for cases in which a single argument is preposed. Preposings in this sense are discussed above and illustrated in (25), repeated here in (28) with the associated canonical-word-order (CWO) variants:

(28) a. *Others I have only that nodding acquaintance with.*
          CWO: I have only that nodding acquaintance with others.
      b. *For their heads, they were given free Coors hats and for their cars free Coors bumper stickers.*

CWO: They were given free Coors hats for their heads and free Coors bumper stickers for their cars.

c. *And play he did.*
CWO: And he did play.

The contextual constraint presented above correctly predicts that a single preposed constituent, as in these examples, is required to represent information that is, in some sense, given. And as shown in Birner and Ward 1998, drawing on Ward 1988, the relevant sense of givenness is discourse-old status. As shown in Birner 1994 and Birner and Ward 1998, however, discourse-old status includes not only information that has been explicitly evoked in the prior discourse, as in (28c), but also information that can be inferred based on its relationship (typically a set-based relationship) to information evoked in the prior discourse. Thus, our earlier observation that in each case the preposed constituent stands in a set relationship to previously evoked information is directly tied to the requirement that this constituent represent discourse-old information.

As demonstrated in section 2 above, felicitous preposing also requires a contextually salient open proposition, and preposings can be divided into two types – topicalization and focus-movement – depending on whether the focus of the OP is (within) the preposed constituent or some other element. Nonetheless, in both types the preposed constituent is constrained to represent information that is discourse-old, in the sense of being either explicitly evoked in the prior discourse or inferrable based on previously evoked information (Birner 1994; Birner and Ward 1998):

(29) a. They send us casualties; *everything else they run OUT of.* (*M*A*S*H*)
   b. I saw Shakespeare last night. *MacBETH it was.* (*Educating Rita*)

Example (29a) is a topicalization, in that the focus of the utterance is the tonically stressed constituent *run out of.* Nonetheless, the preposed constituent *everything else* stands in a set relationship with the previously evoked *casualties.* Example (29b) is a focus-movement, because the preposed *Macbeth* is the focus of the utterance, and here again it stands in a set relationship with the set of Shakespearean plays, evoked by the utterance *I saw Shakespeare last night.* Notice that the construction itself cues the hearer to try to establish such a relationship between the preposed constituent and the prior context:

(30) They send us casualties; *food they run out of.*

Here, the hearer will take *food* and *casualties* to constitute fellow members of a salient set, perhaps of items one might find in a military hospital. However, when no such relationship can plausibly be constructed, the preposing is infelicitous:

(31) I saw Shakespeare last night. #*Long it was.*

Here, there is no plausible salient set that contains both *Shakespeare* and *long*, nor any obvious inference leading from the former to the latter. Instead, *long* represents discourse-new information; hence, the utterance is infelicitous.

Notice also that this constraint does not apply in the case of a referential pronoun appearing in the position canonically held by the fronted constituent, as with left-dislocation:

(32)   Gray admitted it was an unusual moment in the world of high-powered law but the act went off like a charm.

.   "There are some things they did that you just couldn't believe," he said. *"People who hadn't seen things he does in the past, they were just amazed."*   (*Chicago Tribune*, 8/24/03)

Here, the fronted NP *people who hadn't seen things he does in the past* represents information that is new not only to the discourse but also, presumably, to the hearer. The coreferential pronoun *they* is in subject position, a position disfavored for information that is both discourse-new and hearer-new. The left-dislocation allows the people in question to be introduced prior to the utterance of the subject, preventing the subject from representing brand-new information (see Prince 1997). Thus, left-dislocation differs from preposing not only syntactically, in the presence of the referential pronoun, but also functionally, and for this reason we do not include left-dislocations in the category of preposing constructions. Hence, it remains the case that in all instances of true preposing – where the 'moved' constituent's canonical position remains empty – the preposed constituent represents discourse-old information.

3.3   Single postposed constituent

This category includes both existential and presentational *there*-sentences, illustrated in (33a–b), respectively:

(33)   a.   Some Democratic district and county leaders are reported trying to induce State Controller Arthur Levitt of Brooklyn to oppose Mr. Wagner for the Mayoral nomination in the Sept 7 Democratic primary. These contend *there is a serious question as to whether Mr. Wagner has the confidence of the Democratic rank and file in the city.* (Brown Corpus, subcorpus A)

   b.   He lived and breathed for the mining company. No man could have reached his spot nor held it without being ruthless, and Hague had made a virtue of ruthlessness all of his life. *There came a ghost of noise at the office door* and Hague swung to see Kodyke in the entrance from the outer room.   (Brown Corpus, subcorpus N)

Existential *there* occurs with main-verb *be*, as in (33a), while presentational *there* occurs with other verbs, such as *came* in (33b). In (33a), *a serious question . . .* is postposed from its canonical subject position to the end of the clause, and in

(33b), *a ghost of noise* is similarly postposed. Note that although each of these constructions involves the placement of a dummy *there* in subject position, this *there* is nonreferential, and therefore the contextual constraint presented above applies. Thus, the question in (33a) and the ghost of noise in (33b) both constitute new information. However, the two constructions are sensitive to slightly different constraints: Both satisfy the expected requirement that the postposed information be new, but in the case of existential *there*, as in (33a), it is hearer-new status that is relevant, and in the case of presentational *there*, as in (33b), it is discourse status that is relevant. To see this, consider (34):

(34)   a.   The aldermen were the first group to march in the Fourth of July parade. #*Behind them there was the mayor*, and then came the marching bands.
       b.   The aldermen were the first group to march in the Fourth of July parade. *Behind them there came the mayor*, and then came the marching bands.

In (34a), the main verb is *be*, making this an instance of existential *there*. And as predicted, a postverbal NP that is discourse-new but hearer-old (*the mayor*) is infelicitous, because existential *there* requires its postverbal NP to represent hearer-new information. In the case of presentational *there* in (34b), however, the same NP is felicitous postverbally, because the construction requires only that the postverbal NP represent discourse-new information, regardless of its hearer status.

Again, notice that when a referential pronoun appears in subject position, the postposed constituent is not constrained to represent new information:

(35)   Fred (thought balloon): Just look at Jock doing his tricks . . .
       Onlooker: Well, I never.
       Fred: *He's a good little performer, Jock . . .* very talented. ("Fred Basset" comic strip, 6/11/95)

This is an instance of right-dislocation, in which the postposed *Jock* is coreferential with the subject pronoun *he*. And here, the constraint on postposed information does not apply, as evidenced by the felicity of the postposed *Jock* in the context of its prior evocation in the first line. Thus, right-dislocation, with its referential pronoun in the postposed constituent's canonical position, is not subject to the constraint. As we saw above with fronted constituents, we see here again that the constraint applies if and only if no referential element appears in the postposed constituent's canonical position.

3.4   Two arguments reversed

As with preposing and postposing, this category includes two major constructions: passivization and inversion. However, unlike the subtypes of preposing and postposing, these two constructions have not traditionally been thought of as related. Nonetheless, in both cases, two constituents appear in noncanonical position (we are here considering only passives containing *by*-phrases), and both are subject to the constraint presented above, i.e. that the preposed constituent not represent less familiar information within the discourse than does the postposed constituent (Birner 1994, 1996).

First, consider inversion, illustrated in (36):

(36)   a.   New York is still No. 1, but Los Angeles – the western-most anchor of the fast-growing Sun Belt – has officially replaced Chicago as the nation's second-largest city, the Census Bureau reported yesterday. *Also official yesterday was the change in rank of Philadelphia from fourth-largest city to fifth.* (*Philadelphia Inquirer*, 4/8/84)

   b.   The congregation of a church in Tulsa, Okla., recently took out bank loans and donated cars, jewelry, houses and cash to raise $1.5 million for a new church auditorium . . . *Among the automobiles donated was a restored 1957 Thunderbird and a vintage 1952 pickup.* (*Philadelphia Inquirer*, 9/19/83)

   c.   Dear Ann Landers: Our Phi Beta Kappa son, age 22, is living at home and working in a department store until he decides on further schooling. "Neil" is a pleasure to have around. He's a son any parent would be proud of. *Also working in the store is a 29-year-old woman who has an 8-month-old child.* (*Chicago Tribune*, 1/18/90)

Like preposing, inversion permits a variety of constituent types in fronted position, as evidenced by the preposed AdjP, PP, and VP in (36a–c), respectively. In all of the examples in (36), the preposed information is discourse-old, having been evoked in the prior discourse: *official* is evoked by *officially* in (36a), *the automobiles donated* is evoked by *donated cars* in (36b), and *working in the store* is evoked by *working in a department store* in (36c). And in each case, the information represented by the postposed constituent – Philadelphia's change in rank, the Thunderbird and pickup, and the 29-year-old woman – is discourse-new. Notice, however, that the constraints on the preposed and postposed constituents are not absolute; the preposed constituent is not required to always be discourse-old, nor must the postposed constituent always be discourse-new:

(37)   a.   His French began to yield to his Arabic as he struggled through the neighborhood's one-way streets and broken pavement. *Scrawled boldly on the blotched stone facade of a yellowish apartment house were the words MITTERRAND DEHORS.* (C. Potok, *The Gift of Asher Lev*, NY: Knopf, 1990, p. 224)

   b.   White voters approved by a large margin a new constitution that for the first time extends political rights to other races, final returns showed yesterday. [. . .]

> *Approving the constitution were 1,360,223 voters* and rejecting it were 691,577, a ratio of nearly 2-1.　(*Philadelphia Inquirer*, 11/4/83)

In (37a), the preposed constituent is discourse-new; however, notice that the postposed constituent is also discourse-new. Similarly, in (37b), the postposed voters are discourse-old – the same set of white voters evoked in the first sentence – but the constitution mentioned in the preposed constituent is also discourse-old.[12] Therefore, it is not the case that the preposed constituent must be discourse-old or the postposed constituent discourse-new. Instead, what is required is that the preposed constituent not represent discourse-new information when the postposed constituent represents discourse-old information, as in (38):

(38)　Everywhere he walked in the neighborhood, he saw signs bearing the words MITTERRAND DEHORS. #*Scrawled boldly on the blotched stone facade of a yellowish apartment house were these words.*

Thus, as shown in Birner 1994, the constraint on inversion is a relative one; the preposed constituent is constrained to represent information that is at least as familiar as that represented by the postposed constituent.

Birner 1996 shows that the same constraint applies to passives containing *by*-phrases, as in (39):

(39)　Sam Caldwell, State Highway Department public relations director, resigned Tuesday to work for Lt. Gov. Garland Byrd's campaign. Caldwell's resignation had been expected for some time. *He will be succeeded by Rob Ledford of Gainesville, who has been an assistant more than three years.*　(Brown Corpus, subcorpus A)

Here, the preposed *he* represents the discourse-old Caldwell, while the postposed *Rob Ledford of Gainesville* is discourse-new. Again, however, it is not the case that the preposed constituent is required in any absolute sense to be discourse-old, or the postposed constituent to be discourse-new; consider, for example, (40):

(40)　*Appointment of William S. Pfaff Jr., 41, as promotion manager of The Times-Picayune Publishing Company was announced Saturday by John F. Tims, president of the company.* Pfaff succeeds Martin Burke, who resigned. *The new promotion manager has been employed by the company since January, 1946, as a commercial artist in the advertising department.*　(Brown Corpus, subcorpus A)

Notice here that there are two passives. In the first, the preposed and postposed constituents are both discourse-new – i.e., in this (discourse-initial) context, neither the appointment nor John F. Tims has been previously evoked in the discourse. In the second, the preposed and postposed constituents are both discourse-old: The preposed NP *the new promotion manager* represents the previously mentioned Pfaff, whereas the postposed NP *the company* represents the previously mentioned Times-Picayune Publishing Company. Thus, neither discourse-new information in preposed position nor discourse-old information in postposed position is disallowed. What is disallowed is the appearance of preposed discourse-new information in the context of postposed discourse-old information, as in (41):

(41)   Appointment of William Pfaff Jr., 41, as promotion manager of The Times-Picayune Publishing Company was announced Saturday. #*Martin Burke, who resigned, is succeeded by Pfaff.*

Here, the preposed *Martin Burke* represents discourse-new information, while the postposed *Pfaff* represents discourse-old information, and the passive is therefore infelicitous.

When the *by*-phrase is absent, of course, it is impossible to judge the familiarity of the information contained therein. Such clauses are frequently used when the speaker does not know, or prefers not to identify, the agent, or when none exists:

(42)   Stacy Lynn Allen and Eric Anthony Schlabach were united in holy matrimony on Saturday, September 20, 2003, at First Methodist Church in Dandridge, Tennessee. (*The Gypsum Advocate*, 4/22/04, p. B6)

Here, the absence of a *by*-phrase gives the writer a way of omitting mention of who performed the ceremony – i.e., who did the uniting. Interestingly, in these cases the preverbal NP is not constrained to represent discourse-old information; that is to say, it is not subject to the constraint on a single noncanonical constituent. (Indeed, in (42) that NP is discourse-new.) Instead, the constraint on the full passive is rendered moot by the absence of the second noncanonically positioned constituent, and the speaker is able to use this sentence-type to avoid including the canonical subject, while simultaneously being unconstrained with respect to the discourse status of the remaining argument.

4   Conclusion

The structuring of information in English is a complex issue, but as we have shown, broad generalizations can nonetheless be made regarding both the types of givenness and newness to which noncanonical constructions may be sensitive, and the specific constraints that are likely to apply to a particular construction type. We have surveyed a range of syntactic constructions that require an open proposition to be salient in the discourse at the time of utterance, as well as a range of constructions that are sensitive to either the hearer status or the discourse status of some subpropositional constituent. In some cases, as with preposing, both types of constraint may apply; that is, a felicitous preposing requires not only that the appropriate open proposition be salient in the discourse context, but also that the preposed constituent represent discourse-old information (whether or not it is the focus of the open proposition). Finally, we have shown that functions are not randomly correlated with forms in English; consistent cross-constructional correlations hold between a noncanonically positioned constituent's placement and the constraint on its information status, and between the number of noncanonically positioned constituents and the relative or absolute nature of the constraints on their placement. However, not all aspects of the constraints to which a particular construction is sensitive are predictable on the basis of that construction's formal properties. As evidenced by the difference between existential and presentational *there*-sentences, whether a construction is sensitive to hearer status or discourse status appears to be a fact that is arbitrarily associated with each construction. Thus, the correlation of form and function in English is not entirely predictable, but as we have shown, it is subject to strong and reliable correlations that hold across a wide range of construction types.

NOTES

For helpful discussions of the topics covered in this chapter, we are indebted to Barbara Abbott, Larry Horn, Jeff Kaplan, Andy Kehler, and Ellen Prince. We also thank Bas Aarts and an anonymous reviewer for many detailed comments on an earlier draft.

1 Note that the same type of information structuring that we see in clefts can also be achieved with canonical word order through prosodic means alone. Thus in the context of (c) MARY *wrote the story* can convey the same information as *It was Mary who wrote the story*.

2 By 'accent,' we mean 'intonational prominence' in the sense of Terken and Hirschberg 1994: "a conspicuous pitch change in or near the lexically stressed syllable of the word" (1994:126); see also Pierrehumbert 1980.

3 See Birner and Ward 1998 for more information on the distribution of pitch accents in noncanonical syntactic constructions.

4 Note that the preposed constituent bears an accent in (9) not because it is the focus but because it occurs in a separate intonational phrase.

5 In Ward 1983, another – highly constrained – type of topicalization is identified and described, involving a preposed constituent that represents the epitome of a salient attribute. Such preposing, termed EPITOMIZATION, is often used for ironic effect, as illustrated in (i):

(i)   [context: Reporter is interviewing Jack Black, whose idea of haute cuisine is a double cheeseburger with fries] Charlie Trotter, this guy ain't. (*Chicago Tribune*, 9/21/03, pp. 7–18)

Here, the relevant attribute – gastronomic sophistication – is epitomized by Charlie Trotter, the internationally renowned restaurateur. The preposed constituent of epitomization serves to link the epitomized attribute to the prior discourse. In the case of (i), the attribute is being ironically contrasted with the low-brow eating habits of Jack Black, widely known for his boorish behavior. (See Birner and Ward 1998 for more discussion of this and other types of preposing constructions.)

6   As noted in Ward 1988 and Birner and Ward 1998, there is one preposing construction – LOCATIVE PREPOSING – that does not require a salient OP but does require a locative element in preposed position.

7   Note that the syntax of inversion remains controversial (see Kuno 1971; Green 1985; Safir 1985; Bresnan and Kanerva 1989; Coopmans 1989; Hoekstra and Mulder 1990; Rochemont and Culicover 1990; Bresnan 1994; inter alia), and the use of these terms is not meant to be taken as an endorsement of any particular syntactic account.

8   As with preposing (see note 6), there is one inversion construction – LOCATIVE INVERSION – that does not require a salient OP for felicity. See Birner and Ward 1998 for discussion.

9   For a discussion of the pragmatic constraints on the definite article, see Kadmon 1990; Hawkins 1991; Gundel et al. 1993; Birner and Ward 1994; Lambrecht 1994; Roberts 2003; Abbott (to appear); inter alia.

10   In addition to the copula *be*, a small set of intransitive verbs are also possible with this construction.

11   This correlation applies to a range of constructions in English that involve the noncanonical placement of one or more constituents whose canonical position is not filled by a referential element (such as an anaphoric pronoun). It is traditional to think of such constructions as involving the 'movement' of the preposed or postposed constituents from their canonical positions (hence the absence of a referential constituent in that position), but we take no position on how these constructions are best analyzed syntactically. Our interest is in their functional properties, and specifically in their use by speakers for the purpose of structuring information in a discourse.

12   In these instances it might appear that the function of the inversion could not be to place relatively familiar information before relatively unfamiliar information, given that both the preposed and postposed constituents have the same status. Birner 1994 shows, however, that in these cases there is a more subtle sort of relative familiarity at play: When both constituents represent discourse-old information, it is consistently the more recently mentioned information that is placed in initial position, whereas when both constituents represent discourse-new information, it is the postposed constituent that typically provides the topic of the next clause; the preposed constituent in such a situation generally describes the setting, the details of which are relatively unimportant in the discourse and which is therefore not taken up as the topic of the subsequent discourse.

FURTHER READING

To learn more about the general approach to information structure taken in this chapter, see Birner and Ward 1998; Prince 1981a, 1986, 1992; and Ward, Birner, and Huddleston 2002. For more information regarding proposed constraints on individual constructions, see Birner 1994, 1996; Bresnan 1994; Coopmans 1989; Green 1980, 1985; Hedberg 1990, 2000; Jenkins 1975; Kuno 1971; Levin and Prince 1986; Nunberg 1995; Prince 1978, 1981b, 1997; Ward 1983, 1988, 2004; and Wirth 1978. For background information on issues of discourse structure and function, see Firbas 1966; Gazdar 1979; Halliday 1967; Halliday and Hasan 1976; Lambrecht 1994; and Vallduví 1992.

REFERENCES

Abbott, Barbara (2000) Presuppositions as nonassertions. *Journal of Pragmatics* 32, 1419–37.

Abbott, Barbara (2004) Definiteness and indefiniteness. In L. R. Horn and G. Ward (eds.), *The handbook of pragmatics*. Oxford: Blackwell, 122–49.

Ball, Catherine N. (1977) *Th*-clefts. In C. Ball and P. Price (eds.), *Penn Review of Linguistics* 2 (2), 57–64.

Ball, Catherine N. (1978) *It*-clefts and *th*-clefts. Paper presented at the Summer Meeting of the Linguistic Society of America, Champaign-Urbana, IL.

Birner, Betty J. (1994) Information status and word order: an analysis of English inversion. *Language* 70, 233–59.

Birner, Betty J. (1996) Form and function in English *by*-phrase passives. *Chicago Linguistic Society* 32, 23–31.

Birner, Betty J., Jeffrey P. Kaplan, and Gregory Ward (2003) Epistemic modals and temporal reference. Paper presented at the Annual Meeting of the Linguistic Society of America, Atlanta, Georgia.

Birner, Betty J. and Gregory Ward (1994) Uniqueness, familiarity, and the definite article in English. *Berkeley Linguistics Society* 20, 93–102.

Birner, Betty J. and Gregory Ward (1998) *Information status and noncanonical word order in English*. Amsterdam and Philadelphia: John Benjamins.

Bresnan, Joan (1994) Locative inversion and the architecture of Universal Grammar. *Language* 70, 72–131.

Bresnan, Joan and Jonni Kanerva (1989) Locative inversion in Chichewa: a case study of factorization in grammar. *Linguistic Inquiry* 20, 1–50.

Chafe, Wallace (1976) Givenness, contrastiveness, definiteness, subjects, topics, and point of view. In C. Li (ed.), *Subject and topic*. New York: Academic Press, 25–55.

Chomsky, Noam (1971) Deep structure, surface structure, and semantic interpretation. In D. Steinberg and L. Jakobovits (eds.), *Semantics: an interdisciplinary reader in philosophy, linguistics, and psychology*. Cambridge: Cambridge University Press, 183–216.

Coopmans, Peter (1989) Where stylistic and syntactic processes meet: locative inversion in English. *Language* 65, 728–51.

Firbas, Jan (1966) Non-thematic subjects in contemporary English. *Travaux Linguistiques de Prague* 2, 239–56.

Gazdar, Gerald (1979) *Pragmatics: implicature, presupposition, and logical form.* New York: Academic Press.

Green, Georgia (1980) Some wherefores of English inversions. *Language* 56, 582–601.

Green, Georgia (1985) The description of inversions in Generalized Phrase Structure Grammar. *Berkeley Linguistics Society* 11, 117–46.

Gundel, Jeanette, Nancy Hedberg, and Ron Zacharski (1993) Cognitive status and the form of referring expressions in discourse. *Language* 69, 274–307.

Halliday, Michael A. K. (1967) Notes on transitivity and theme in English, Part 2. *Journal of Linguistics* 3, 199–244.

Halliday, Michael A. K. and Ruqaiya Hasan (1976) *Cohesion in English.* London: Longman.

Hawkins, John A. (1991) On (in)definite articles: implicatures and (un)grammaticality prediction. *Journal of Linguistics* 27, 405–42.

Hedberg, Nancy (1990) Discourse pragmatics and cleft sentences in English. Ph.D. dissertation, University of Minnesota.

Hedberg, Nancy (2000) The referential status of clefts. *Language* 76, 891–920.

Hoekstra, Teun and René Mulder (1990) Unergatives as copular verbs: locational and existential predication. *Linguistic Review* 7, 1–79.

Horn Laurence R. (1986) Presupposition, theme and variations. *Papers from the Parasession on Pragmatics and Grammatical Theory. Chicago Linguistics Society* 22, 168–92.

Jackendoff, Ray (1972) *Semantic interpretation in generative grammar.* Cambridge, MA: MIT Press.

Jenkins, Lyle (1975) *The English existential.* Tübingen: Niemeyer.

Kadmon, Nirit (1990) Uniqueness. *Linguistics and Philosophy* 13, 273–324.

Karttunen, Lauri and Stanley Peters (1979) Conventional implicature. In C.-K. Oh and D. Dinneen (eds.),

Syntax and semantics 11: Presupposition. New York: Academic Press, 1–56.

Kuno, Susumu (1971) The position of locatives in existential sentences. *Linguistic Inquiry* 2, 333–78.

Lambrecht, Knud (1994) *Information structure and sentence form.* Cambridge: Cambridge University Press.

Levin, Nancy S. and Ellen F. Prince (1986) Gapping and causal implicature. *Papers in Linguistics* 19 (3), 351–64.

Nunberg, Geoffrey (1977) The pragmatics of reference. Ph.D. dissertation, City University of New York.

Nunberg, Geoffrey (1979) The non-uniqueness of semantic solutions: polysemy. *Linguistics and Philosophy* 3, 143–84.

Nunberg, Geoffrey (1995) Transfers of meaning. *Journal of Semantics* 12, 109–32.

Pierrehumbert, Janet (1980) The phonology and phonetics of English intonation. Ph.D. dissertation, MIT.

Prince, Ellen F. (1978) A comparison of *wh*-clefts and *it*-clefts in discourse. *Language* 54, 883–906.

Prince, Ellen F. (1981a) Toward a taxonomy of given/new information. In P. Cole (ed.), *Radical pragmatics.* New York: Academic Press, 223–54.

Prince, Ellen F. (1981b) Topicalization, focus-movement, and Yiddish-movement: A pragmatic differentiation. *Berkeley Linguistics Society* 7, 249–64.

Prince, Ellen F. (1986) On the syntactic marking of presupposed open propositions. *Papers from the Parasession on Pragmatics and Grammatical Theory, Chicago Linguistic Society* 22, 208–22.

Prince, Ellen F. (1992) The ZPG letter: subjects, definiteness, and information-status. In S. Thompson and W. Mann (eds.), *Discourse description: diverse analyses of a fundraising text.* Amsterdam and Philadelphia: John Benjamins, 295–325.

Prince, Ellen F. (1997) On the functions of left-dislocation in English discourse. In A. Kamio (ed.), *Directions in functional linguistics*. Amsterdam and Philadelphia: John Benjamins, 117–43.

Roberts, Craige (2003) Uniqueness in definite noun phrases. *Linguistics and Philosophy* 26, 287–350.

Rochemont, Michael (1978) A theory of stylistic rules in English. Ph.D. dissertation, University of Massachusetts at Amherst.

Rochemont, Michael and Peter Culicover (1990) *English focus constructions and the theory of grammar*. Cambridge: Cambridge University Press.

Safir, Kenneth (1985) *Syntactic chains*. Cambridge: Cambridge University Press.

Terken, Jacques and Julia Hirschberg (1994) Deaccentuation and words representing 'given' information: effects of persistence of grammatical function and surface position. *Language and Speech* 37 (2), 125–45.

Välimaa-Blum, Riitta (1988) Finnish existential clauses: their syntax, pragmatics and intonation. Ph.D. dissertation, The Ohio State University.

Vallduví, Enric (1992) *The informational component*. New York: Garland.

Ward, Gregory (1983) A pragmatic analysis of Epitomization: Topicalization it's not. *Papers in Linguistics* 17, 145–61.

Ward, Gregory (1988) *The semantics and pragmatics of preposing*. New York: Garland.

Ward, Gregory (2004) Equatives and deferred reference. *Language* 80, 262–89.

Ward, Gregory, Betty Birner, and Rodney Huddleston (2002) Information packaging. In Geoffrey K. Pullum and Rodney Huddleston et al. *The Cambridge grammar of the English language*. Cambridge: Cambridge University Press, ch. 16, 1363–1447.

Ward, Gregory, Jeffrey P. Kaplan, and Betty J. Birner. To appear. Epistemic *would*, open propositions, and truncated clefts. In N. Hedberg and R. Zacharski (eds), *Topics on the grammar-pragmatics interface: Papers in honor of Jeanette K. Gundel*. Amsterdam and Philadelphia: John Benjamins.

Wilson, Deirdre and Dan Sperber (1979) Ordered entailments: an alternative to presuppositional theories. In C.-K. Oh and D. Dinneen (eds.), *Syntax and semantics 11: Presupposition*. New York: Academic Press, 299–323.

Wirth, Jessica (1978) The derivation of cleft sentences in English. *Glossa* 12, 58–81.

14   Current Changes in English Syntax

CHRISTIAN MAIR AND GEOFFREY LEECH

1   Introduction

Syntactic change differs from lexical change in at least two important ways. First, it generally unfolds much more slowly, sometimes taking hundreds of years to run its course to completion, and secondly, it tends to proceed below the threshold of speakers' conscious awareness, which makes impressionistic or introspection-based statements on ongoing changes in English grammar notoriously unreliable. A third difficulty in pinning down syntactic change in present-day English is that a rather small number of alleged syntactic innovations are strongly stigmatized. This has biased discussion in favor of such high-profile issues at the expense of developments which are, arguably, more comprehensive and far-reaching in the long run. Examples which come to mind include the use of *like* as a conjunction (as in *And it looks like we could even lose John*) or the use of *hopefully* as a sentence adverb (*Hopefully, they'll go back and set it up*).[1] Such shibboleths have aroused an inordinate amount of expert and lay comment, while developments which appear to be systematically if gradually transforming the grammatical core of standard English, such as the continuing increase in the frequency of the progressive aspect or the spread of gerundial complements at the expense of infinitival ones (see section 4 below), tend to go largely unnoticed.

We define "current" changes in English as those developments for which there has been a major diachronic dynamic since the beginning of the twentieth century. For practical reasons, we focus largely on the written standard forms of English in Britain and the United States, fully aware that this strategy will prevent us from including some cutting-edge innovations in contemporary spoken English which are likely to be incorporated into the standard in the long run.

When it comes to analysing syntactic change, there are two approaches. Where the focus is on the diachronic development of grammars as decontextualized linguistic systems, syntactic change is often seen as an abrupt or discrete alteration of structures, rules, and constraints (e.g. in the generativist tradition embodied in the work of David Lightfoot – from Lightfoot 1979 to Lightfoot 1999). But where the starting point for the analysis of historical change is the study of recorded performance data in their linguistic and social context – as, for example, in grammaticalization theory (Hopper and Traugott 2003) or the budding field of historical sociolinguistics (cf. Nevalainen and Raumolin-Brunberg 2003) – the picture that emerges is one of gradual evolution rather than abrupt change. Syntactic changes are seen as embedded in a context where semantic, pragmatic, and sociolinguistic factors assume roles as determinants of change. However, even those scholars who conceive of syntactic change in terms of discrete steps will agree that the spread of linguistic innovations throughout the community (or conversely, the dying out of obsolescent forms) is a gradual phenomenon. It is understandable, then, that in the time-span of the one century that is the focus of this chapter, we are unlikely to see any one change run out its full course, from inception in particular genres, registers or discourse communities, to full establishment in the core standard grammar. What we are able to note, though, are shifting frequencies of use for competing variants which – over the course of a century – may well build up into impressive statistical trends.

Not only will a change proceed gradually (if one looks at the language as a whole), but it will also proceed at differential speeds in different regional varieties of English and different styles and textual genres. This is why, after a necessarily brief review of the literature on ongoing grammatical change in present-day English, the present chapter will largely be corpus-based, focusing on the examination of substantial samples of different varieties of writing at different times. As a point of departure we will take mid-twentieth-century standard American and British written English as documented in two widely known and widely used matching reference corpora, namely the Brown and LOB corpora. To cover developments towards the end of the twentieth century, we will also use the Frown and F-LOB corpora, which were built to match Brown and LOB as closely as possible in size and composition but contain texts published not in 1961, as the originals do, but in 1992 and 1991 respectively.[2] The four equivalent corpora are available in untagged and tagged versions,[3] making it feasible to study changes in textual frequency in terms of not only individual words and word sequences but also of grammatical categories.[4] Beyond the limitations of the written medium and the thirty-year period spanned by these corpora, we will where necessary extend our evidential base by making use of other electronic text resources, such as small collections of spoken data[5] and the corpus formed from OED quotations.

2   Some Important Previous Studies

The popular literature on ongoing changes in the English language (see Barber 1964 and Potter 1975 for two typical examples) tends to focus on phonetic and lexical rather than grammatical change. Among grammatical changes the emphasis is on cases which have aroused the concern of prescriptivists. A typical list of changes suspected to be going on in present-day standard English is the following one, which is largely based on Barber (1964: 130–44):

a. a tendency to regularize irregular morphology (e.g. *dreamt* → *dreamed*)
b. revival of the "mandative" subjunctive, probably inspired by formal US usage (*we demand that she take part in the meeting*)
c. elimination of *shall* as a future marker in the first person
d. development of new, auxiliary-like uses of certain lexical verbs (e.g. *get, want* – cf., e.g., *The way you look, you **wanna**/**want to** see a doctor soon*)[6]
e. extension of the progressive to new constructions, e.g. modal, present perfect and past perfect passive progressive (*the road **would** not **be being built**/ **has** not **been being built**/ **had** not **been being built** before the general elections*)
f. increase in the number and types of multi-word verbs (phrasal verbs, *have/take/give a ride*, etc.)
g. placement of frequency adverbs before auxiliary verbs (even if no emphasis is intended – *I never have said so*)
h. *do*-support for *have* (*have you any money?* and *no, I haven't any money* → *do you have/ have you got any money?* and *no, I don't have any money/ haven't got any money*)
i. demise of the inflected form *whom*
j. increasing use of *less* instead of *fewer* with countable nouns (e.g. *less people*)
k. spread of the s-genitive to non-human nouns (*the book's cover*)
l. omission of the definite article in certain environments (e.g. *renowned Nobel laureate Derek Walcott*)
m. "singular" *they* (*everybody came in their car*)
n. *like, same as,* and *immediately* used as conjunctions
o. a tendency towards analytical comparatives and superlatives (*politer* → *more polite*)

Of these, a–h belong to the sphere of the verb phrase, while i–m belong to the sphere of the noun phrase (n–o belong to neither). Certain of these supposed changes do have support from corpus evidence – b, c, d, e, h, i, l, m – although in some cases the focus of change as listed above is misleading. Thus *shall* (item c) has been undergoing a general decline, not restricted to the first person. Similarly, the s-genitive (item k) has been showing a general increase, not specific to non-human nouns.

Note that defining many of these changes as "current" or "ongoing" means stretching the concepts somewhat. *Whom*, for example, has been optionally replaceable by *who* in many common uses since the Early Modern English period. By the nineteenth century, it was a marker of formal style, really obligatory only if preceded by a preposition. This is very much the situation today, and so any report that *whom* is on its deathbed is, to say the least, premature (see 3 below). Similarly, most of the truly recent change in the comparison of disyllabic adjectives (item o) has not been in the direction of more analyticity but of reducing the variability of forms for individual adjectives (Bauer 1994: 80).

Some recent work on ongoing change has combined the corpus-based approach with other methods in detailed studies of lexicogrammatical phenomena. Rickford et al. (1995), for example, traced the recent emergence of the topic-introducing preposition *as far as* (e.g. "as far as my situation, I am less than optimistic . . ."), which they see as having been derived from clauses of the type *as far as X is concerned* through a process of grammaticalization. Some time before that, and without mentioning the technical term "grammaticalization" – the heading under which such processes would almost certainly be subsumed in current work on syntactic change – Olofsson (1990) traced a similar development, namely the emergence of prepositional uses of *following*, splitting off from the mainstream use of the form as a participle in nonfinite clauses. The emergence of (*be*) *like* as a quotation-introducing form in some spoken registers of American English (and increasingly in British English) is the focus of a study by Romaine and Lange (1991). Such studies, while valuable in themselves, say little about the language as a whole. It is difficult to generalize from their results, and an investigation of such cases will probably not direct the linguist to those parts of the grammatical core which are undergoing potentially far-reaching change.

Among recent work on current grammatical change, two publications deserve special mention because they aim to meet higher methodological standards than the rest: Bauer (1994) stands out in seeking to support all statements he makes with textual evidence, and Denison (1998) offers a magisterial survey of developments in English grammar since 1776 that is unrivalled in its comprehensiveness. Denison, who as a contributor to volume IV of the *Cambridge History of the English Language* covers the period from 1776 to 1997, focuses on the nineteenth and early twentieth centuries and on continuities with the preceding Early Modern English period treated in volume III of the same work, rather than on recent and current change. Nevertheless, for our purpose, Denison's work goes beyond that of others in providing a list of suspected changes in twentieth-century English which is based on a systematic sifting of the available evidence rather than on anecdotal observations and narrow prescriptive concerns.

3   The Role of Corpora in Investigating Current Changes

One important role of corpora in the study of ongoing grammatical change is "negative": they can provide evidence that some suspected change has not actually been proceeding in the assumed direction in a given period of time. For an example we return to the "demise" of *whom* – widely assumed to be

Table 14.1   *Whom* in four matching corpora

	1961	1991/2	Difference (% age of 1961)
British English (LOB/F-LOB)	219	177	−19.4
American English (Brown/Frown)	146	166	+13.4

inevitable ever since Sapir put the case for it in his classic *Language* (1921: 166–74), but clearly not substantiated by later corpus findings. In the four corpora (LOB, Brown, F-LOB and Frown) providing the evidential database for the present chapter the figures shown in table 14.1 are obtained.

If anything, such figures show that there is fluctuation, or even convergence between the two major regional standards, rather than an overall decrease.[7] Synchronic results for the late twentieth century based on the one-hundred-million-word *British National Corpus* (BNC) are also instructive. With a total raw frequency of 12,596, or ca. 129 occurrences per million words, *whom* cannot exactly be called a rare word. Its function as a style marker, however, becomes obvious once one looks at the frequencies in different textual genres: 141 instances per million for written English (with outliers beyond 200 in the more formal genres) contrasts with 26 per million overall for spoken English, and as little as 5 per million in the spontaneous dialogue of conversation.

The most valuable role of corpora in the study of syntactic change, however, is not the "negative" one of refuting wrong hypotheses, but their "positive" role, which manifests itself either in a differentiated confirmation of an existing assumption or – even more valuable – in the discovery of ongoing changes which have not even been noticed by observers so far.

The following sections 4 to 6 will give such "positive" corpus evidence for the recent development of grammatical constructions, for many of which Denison's 1998 survey has noted a pronounced diachronic dynamic since the late eighteenth century. It is likely, therefore, that these changes are still with us today, and can be considered truly current. With some of them, such as the *get*-passive or the *going-to* future, the crucial structural changes had already taken place before the year 1776, Denison's starting point, so that any statistical increase in material from ca. 1900 is likely to represent a spread of these innovations – for example, from less formal into more formal registers and styles (see, e.g., Hundt 2001 or Mair 1997). However, some other structures (for example certain new progressives, on which see 4.1. below) represent genuine recent innovations in the sense that they were not firmly established in any style before the twentieth century.

Although the spotlight tends to fall on innovatory changes and their diffusion, corpora also provide evidence of changes in the direction of attenuation and loss. For example, the four corpora show a declining frequency in the use of many modal auxiliaries and of *wh*-relative pronouns. We will examine these, together with gains in apparently competing categories – so-called semi-modals like *going to*, and *that-* and zero relativization – in sections 4 and 5.

4   The Changing Verb Phrase

4.1   *Progressive aspect*

Although our four one-million-word corpora are too small to yield definitive findings for rare grammatical constructions, they are more than sufficient in size to investigate major current trends in the tense, modality, aspect, and voice systems of English, in particular the continuing spread of the progressive form. Here two different phenomena need to be distinguished:

*   an increase in the frequency of occurrence of progressives in general, and
*   the establishment of the progressive in a few remaining niches of the verbal paradigm in which it was not current until the twentieth century.

Both phenomena represent direct twentieth-century continuations of well-established long-term trends. The fairly dramatic increase in the frequency of the progressive from late Middle English onwards has been confirmed, for example, by Jespersen (1909–49: IV, 177), who used Bible translations from various periods as parallel historical corpora.[8] Today's filling of structural gaps in the verbal paradigm also builds on such previous episodes, for example the emergence of the progressive passive (*dinner was being prepared*) approximately 200 years ago, superseding "passival" *dinner was preparing* (on which see Denison 1998: 148ff). In a manual analysis of all progressive forms in the press sections (A–C, ca. 176,000 words each) of the four corpora, Mair and Hundt (1995) have obtained the figures shown in table 14.2.

As can be seen, the increases observed are statistically significant both in the British and the American data, which is not the case for the regional contrasts to be observed between British and American English at any one time. Further research on the tagged versions of the entire two British corpora was carried out by Nicholas Smith (2002), who noted a highly significant

Table 14.2   Progressive forms in the press sections (A–C) of the four reference corpora

	1961	1991/92	*Difference (% age of 1961)*
British English (LOB/F-LOB)	606	716	+18.2
American English (Brown/Frown)	593	663	+11.8

Significances: LOB-F-LOB $p < 0.01$, Brown-Frown $p < 0.05$; LOB-Brown and F-LOB-Frown $p > 0.05$.

increase of 28.9 percent – from 980 to 1,263 – for the present active progressive. Smith's equivalent provisional figures for Brown and Frown show a very similar trend (an increase of 31.8 percent from 996 to 1,316).[9] However, the growth in progressive usage is patchy: the comparison between LOB and F-LOB shows a particularly high increase in the modal progressive – e.g. *should be leaving* – (29.3 percent) and in the passive progressive – e.g. *is being held* – (31.3 percent), while the past progressive actually shows a decrease of 9.0 percent. Moreover, the steep increases in the modal and passive progressive in the British corpora are not matched by similar increases in the American corpora.

However, that there has been a general and significant increase in the frequency of progressives in the course of the twentieth century seems beyond doubt. What is more difficult to provide is a convincing explanation. Are we dealing with an instance of grammatical change directly, or are we seeing one grammatical symptom of a more general stylistic change, in which the norms of written English have moved closer to spoken usage, where the progressive has presumably always been more common than in writing? (See, for example, the findings in Biber et al. 1999: 461–3.) There is little sign of the progressive extending its territory by combination with 'non-progressive' verbs like the stative *know* and *wish*. Even where in particular cases such uses can be shown to be recent, they are far too rare to play a role in accounting for the statistical increase which is documented in the corpora.[10] On the other hand, one use of the progressive seems to be a genuinely new development: its so-called interpretative use (see Huddleston and Pullum 2002: 165) in such contexts as:

(1)   I can only add that when Paul Gascoigne says he will not be happy until he stops playing football, he **is talking** rot.   (F-LOB, A 09: 81ff)

(2)   When he speaks of apocalypse, however, he **is not speaking** of it in the literal and popular sense.   (Frown, D 02: 120ff)

In (1), the two predications 'says he will not be happy . . .' and 'is talking rot' must refer to precisely coterminous situations, since the second is merely a more abstract interpretation of the first. There is apparently no reason why one should be treated as imperfective against the background of the other. But what we seem to have here is a further extension of the basic uses of the progressive, namely seeing a situation 'from the inside' (Comrie 1976: 4), to the metacommunicative level. As Huddleston and Pullum put it, "the internal (imperfective) view is appropriate to the explanatory function of the clause – in emphasising duration, the progressive metaphorically slows down or extends the situation in order to be able to focus on clarifying its nature" (2002: 165). Example (2) is similar: here it is sufficient to note that the progressive (*is . . . speaking*) and non-progressive (*speaks*) could by no means be interchanged.

Another semantic extension of the progressive, to a 'future as a matter of course' interpretation (see Leech 2004: 67), appears to account for much of the increase observed between LOB and F-LOB in the modal progressive, especially with *will* (see Smith 2003a):

(3)   He **will be standing down** at the next general election.   (F-LOB, B 20: 30)

(4)   Why, you **will be asking** me to bomb Essen next.   (F-LOB, F 24: 142)

Here the 'in-progress' meaning of the progressive applies, not to the action of 'standing down' or 'asking' itself, but to the circumstances already set in train and leading up to that action, which is assumed to take place in the not-too-distant future. One possible motive for using *will* + progressive, rather than the non-progressive *will stand down*, is that *will* + V can imply that the action will be actuated by the volition of the speaker or the subject referent. By using the progressive, the speaker disclaims or at least backgrounds that implication.

A more radical grammatical change is at stake in the second phenomenon mentioned above, the establishment of progressives in those few remaining niches of the verbal paradigm from which they were excluded up to the twentieth century. With these constructions, the four corpora prove too small to yield conclusive results. The present perfect progressive passive is attested in none of them. The British data yield three instances of modalized passive progressives, two from LOB and one from F-LOB:

(5)   To ridicule them only pushes them farther into themselves, so that they become unable to speak about it to anybody and the seeds of any amount of trouble are sown, the harvest of which **may still be being reaped** at forty or fifty.   (LOB, D6: 16ff)

(6)   We have also to notice that while the entropy of our given system will increase with external or given time, this relation is not reciprocal, for, if we first choose our time, a rare state in our stationary process **will just as likely be being approached** as **being departed from**.   (LOB, J18: 197ff)

(7)   So the news that a second park-and-ride route **could be being introduced** for a trial period at Clifton Moor north of the city should be welcomed, especially as Christmas is approaching.   (F-LOB, B18: 109ff)

The first thing to note about these examples is that the progressive is not obligatory yet in such constructions, a sign of their recentness. Secondly, the yield of examples from the four corpora, while clearly not conclusive in itself, is not fortuitous. Modal forms of the type represented by examples (5) to (7) are easy to find in the 100,000,000-word *British National Corpus* (with textual data from the late twentieth century). The present perfect passive progressive, on the other hand, is attested just once:

(8)   That er, er, little action has been taken in the last thirty forty years since this **has been being discussed**, erm, I think the first international conference erm, produced their own report in nineteen sixty.   (BNC, JJG 542)

Significantly, this example is from a transcription of spontaneous speech. Again, as in (5) to (7) above, the use of the progressive is not yet obligatory. Summarising the corpus data, we can say that the complex forms in question can be attested if the database is sufficient, and that their spread seems to take place more easily in the modal environments (*be being*) than in the present perfect (*been being*).

Another former lacuna in the use of the progressive was the progressive form of the copula – a use which can be traced back for about 200 years but probably was not fully established until late in the nineteenth century (Jespersen 1909–49: IV, 225f.). Here, the four corpora suggest that this construction (although still rare) has grown in frequency in written English between 1961 and 1991/2. There is an increase from 3 to 20 instances of the progressive copula from Brown to Frown, and from 8 to 17 from LOB to F-LOB.

4.2   Modality: modal auxiliaries, so-called semi-modals, and the subjunctive

It is well known that the class of modal auxiliaries emerged as a separate syntactic category around the beginning of the Early Modern English period, and that in the later modern period, there has been an ongoing grammaticalization of some verbal constructions called "semi-modals" such as *have to* and *be going to*, which in function and behavior overlap with these modals. The semi-modals are a rather loosely-defined grouping of verbal idioms, which are much more frequent in spoken than in written English – indeed, some of them have acquired reduced pronunciations, reflected popularly in written forms such as *gotta* and *gonna*. In addition, the lexical verb *want* shows early signs of auxiliation/grammaticalization, including phonetic erosion in *wanna* (Krug 2000: 117–66); this is why, though not an established semi-modal yet, it is included in the list in table 14.4 below.

It has remained an open question how far the rise of these semi-modals has encroached on the use of modal auxiliaries. However, a study of the modals in our four corpora leaves no doubt that there is a decline in their use during the later twentieth century, as shown in table 14.3. The counts include verb and negative contractions: e.g., under *will* are counted *won't* and *'ll*.

In table 14.3, the modals are listed in order of frequency in the LOB corpus, an ordering which varies comparatively little in the four corpora. There are, however, some big differences in the steepness of the fall in frequency. The least frequent modals – *shall*, *ought to*, and *need* (in auxiliary construction) – have plummeted, and the mid-frequency modals *must* and *may* have also declined drastically. On the other hand, the most common modals *will*, *can* and *would* have maintained their position robustly.

Table 14.3 Decline in the use of the modal auxiliaries in the four reference corpora

	British English		Log likhd[a]	Diff (%)[b]		American English		Log likhd	Diff (%)
	LOB	F-LOB				Brown	Frown		
Would	3,028	2,694	20.4	−11.0	*Would*	3,053	2,868	5.6	−6.1
Will	2,798	2,723	1.2	−2.7	*Will*	2,702	2,402	17.3	−11.1
Can	1,997	2,041	0.4	+2.2	*Can*	2,193	2,160	0.2	−1.5
Could	1,740	1,782	2.4	+2.4	*Could*	1,776	1,655	4.1	−6.8
May	1,333	1,101	22.8	−17.4	*May*	1,298	878	81.1	−32.4
Should	1,301	1,147	10.1	−11.8	*Should*	910	787	8.8	−13.5
Must	1,147	814	57.7	−29.0	*Must*	1,018	668	72.8	−34.4
Might	777	660	9.9	−15.1	*Might*	635	635	0.7	−4.5
Shall	355	200	44.3	−43.7	*Shall*	267	150	33.1	−43.8
Ought (*to*)	104	58	13.4	−44.2	*Ought* (*to*)	70	49	3.7	−30.0
Need + V	87	52	9.0	−40.2	*Need*	40	35	0.3	−12.5
Total	14,667	13,272	73.6	−9.5	Total	13,962	12,287	68.0	−12.2

[a] Log likelihood is a measure of statistical significance: a value of 3.84 or more equates with chi-square values > 0.05; a value of 6.63 or more equates with chi-square values > 0.01.
[b] The column headed Diff (%) gives the increase (+) or decrease (−) in occurrences as a percentage of the frequency in the 1961 corpora.

While BrE and AmE have been developing along broadly parallel lines (over-all loss of frequency by around 10 percent in both sets of corpora), it is nevertheless interesting to note that figures for AmE were already slightly lower in 1961, and the decline has been a little sharper in AmE since. This looks like a follow-my-leader situation, in which BrE is following in the track of AmE. Less clear trends are seen with the representatively varied set of semi-modals listed in table 14.4. There is a rise in the over-all frequency of this class in BrE and AmE, but this is mainly due to the increases for *need to*, *want to*, and – in AmE – *be going to*. For other forms, there is stability, and in one case (*be to*) even a significant decline (table 14.4).

Perhaps what is most striking is that the semi-modals in aggregate are so much less frequent than the modals: added together they are less frequent than the single modal *will*! From this evidence it is obviously difficult to mount a general argument that the semi-modals are increasing *at the expense of* the core modals. On the other hand, going beyond the evidence of tables 14.3 and 14.4 to look at spoken data, there are two good reasons for seeing at least some link between the fall of the modals and the rise of the semi-modals. One reason is that the evidence from spoken corpora,[11] covering much the same period, shows a steeper fall for the modals and rise for the semi-modals

Table 14.4   Increase in the use of semi-modals in the four reference corpora

BrE	LOB	F-LOB	Log likhd	Diff (%)	AmE	Brown	Frown	Log likhd	Diff (%)
BE *going to*[a]	248	245	0.0	−1.2	BE *going to*[a]	219	332	23.5	+51.6
BE *to*	454	376	7.6	−17.2	BE *to*	349	209	35.3	−40.1
(*Had*) *better*	50	37	2.0	−26.0	(*Had*) *better*	41	34	0.7	−17.1
(HAVE) *got to*[a]	41	27	2.9	−34.1	(HAVE) *got to*[a]	45	52	0.5	+15.6
HAVE *to*	757	825	2.7	+9.0	HAVE *to*	627	643	0.1	+1.1
NEED *to*	54	198	83.0	+249.1	NEED *to*	69	154	33.3	+123.2
BE *supposed to*	22	47	9.2	+113.6	BE *supposed to*	48	51	0.1	+6.3
Used to	86	97	0.6	+12.8	*Used to*	51	74	4.3	+45.1
WANT *to*[a]	357	423	5.4	+18.5	WANT *to*[a]	323	552	60.9	+70.9
Total	2,069	2,275	9.2	+10.0	Total	1,772	2,101	28.4	+18.6

[a] Forms spelt *gonna, gotta* and *wanna* are counted under *be going to, have got to,* and *want to.*

respectively. In the comparison between the two small spoken corpora, modals fall −17.3 percent and semi-modals rise +36.1 percent, in contrast with the figures for LOB and F-LOB of −9.5 percent and +10.0 percent respectively. It has been impossible to make such a comparison for AmE, for which no such comparable corpora exist. However, a second striking result was arrived at by comparing overall frequency of modals and of semi-modals in a ca. 4-million-word corpus of AmE conversation.[12] Compared with a ratio of 1:5.9 (semi-modals: modals) for both F-LOB and Frown, the AmE corpus of conversation yielded a ratio of 1:1.6. Another way of putting this is to estimate that in current spontaneous dialogue among American speakers, semi-modals are 62.5 percent as frequent as core modals (counting core modal frequency as 100 percent and using the lists of modals and semi-modals in Tables 3 and 4). This is vastly different from the picture we get from the written corpora of the 1990s, both American and British, where the comparable figure is only 17 percent. It suggests that, as is often suspected, the spoken American variety of the language is the main driving-force of change in this area, as presumably in others, and places the encroachment of semi-modals on the territory of the modals in AmE speech, in frequency terms, beyond doubt. This has its most forthright demonstration in the fact that in the American conversational corpus mentioned above, HAVE (*got*) *to* is more than 10 times as frequent as *must*.[13]

In diametric contrast to the semi-modals, the subjunctive in English is a historical relic, more characteristic of formal written style than of the spoken language. Only two forms of it survive with any degree of currency, and even these are not morphologically distinctive, and can usually only be identified following singular subjects. These are the mandative subjunctive occurring in *that*-clauses following certain controlling items such as the verb *suggest* (10) and the so-called *were*-subjunctive signalling hypothetical meaning (11):

(10)   Yesterday, he had suggested that he **sleep** in the spare room from now on. (F-LOB, K 22: 19ff)

(11)   It felt as if she **were** alone in the world.   (LOB, P 16: 79ff)

In the early to mid-twentieth century, it was imagined that the English subjunctive was reaching the end of its long road of decline.[14] But for the later twentieth century, the four corpora show a fascinating picture: whereas a gradual decline of the mandative subjunctive seems to continue in AmE, it has seen a modest revival, from a very low ebb, in British English – apparently under the influence of American English, where this form shows greater currency.[15] The *were*-subjunctive, on the other hand, shows a continuing decline in BrE – from 95 occurrences to 41 in LOB and F-LOB.

4.3   *Nonfinite verbal forms*

Nonfinite verbal forms – infinitives, gerunds and participles – are another grammatical category which has become more functionally prominent, and correspondingly more frequent in discourse, since the Middle English period. In spite of the relative lack of attention that these forms have received in the literature on current change in English, there is no indication that the diachronic dynamic that characterized these forms in Early Modern English has abated in the recent past. Infinitival clauses with an explicit notional subject introduced by *for* (e.g. constructions such *as it is easy for common ground to be forgotten in disputes over methods* or *they arranged for us to be met at the station*) are clearly on the increase – from 294 instances in LOB to 332 in F-LOB[16] –, and so are gerundial complement clauses.

For example, it is striking to see how recent the apparently rock-solid semantic contrast between infinitives and gerunds is after the verb *remember*. Since individual matrix verbs governing nonfinite complement clauses are usually not frequent enough to draw conclusions from the attestations in the four matching corpora, the data this time is provided by the quotation base of the *OED* (2nd edition on CD-rom), and the time frame is extended to three centuries – from 1700 to the present. Three constructional types are distinguished: (a) prospective *to*, as in the current *I must remember to fill in the form*, (b) retrospective *-ing*, as in *I remember filling in the form*, and (c) the now defunct retrospective construction with the infinitive, as in *I remember to have filled in the form*. Since the number of quotations available for the three centuries under review varies, frequencies (in table 14.5) are given as "*n* occurrences/10,000 quotations."

Table 14.5 reveals fluctuation – and structural stability – for prospective *to*, but a clear reversal of preferences for the retrospective uses, with the late

Table 14.5 Gerunds and infinitives after *remember* in the OED quotation base – normalized frequencies ("n/10,000 quotes," rounded to the first decimal), with absolute frequencies in brackets

	(a) prospective to	(b) retrospective -ing	(c) retrospective to
eighteenth century	5.5 (15)	1.8 (5)	4.8 (13)
nineteenth century	2.2 (17)	4.1 (31)	2.1 (16)
twentieth century	5.8 (28)	12.0 (58)	0.8 (4)

Table 14.6 *To*-infinitives : V-*ing* after *begin* in the four reference corpora

	1961	1991/2
British English (LOB/F-LOB)	260:23	204:20
American English (Brown/Frown)	230:53	202:95

BrE vs. AmE 1961 p < 0.001; BrE vs. AmE 1991/92 p < 0.001, BrE diachr. not significant, AmE diachr. p < 0.001).

nineteenth century acting as the pivotal period of transition. Note in particular that the gerund increases to an extent greater than would have been necessary merely to compensate for the declining retrospective infinitive.

There is one matrix verb for which a growing popularity of the gerund is attested clearly even in the four matching corpora, namely *begin* as shown in table 14.6. The increase seems to be restricted to American English so far.

Close analysis of the data (Mair 2002) reveals that, as expected, the diachronic development documented in the table is just one strand in a complex fabric of factors, including grammatical context, the partly contrasting semantic import of the gerundial and infinitival complement types, text-type specific preferences, and the regional origin of a speaker/writer.

A final example, which is included chiefly because it shows British English diverging from US usage in the course of the twentieth century, is provided by *prevent*. Well into the recent past (c. 1900), this verb was variously used with or without the preposition *from* before the gerund in both British and American English (cf., e.g., the relevant entries in the *OED* or *Websters 3rd* and Aarts 1992: 90–111 for a discussion of the theoretical aspects of this change). In the course of the twentieth century, however, the *from*-less variant was eliminated from American English, whereas it became increasingly common in British English, as is illustrated in table 14.7.

Table 14.7 From : "zero" after *prevent* NP in the four reference corpora

	1961	*1991/2*
British English (LOB/F-LOB)	34:7[a]	24:24
American English (Brown/Frown)	47:0	36:1[b]

BrE diachr. p < 0.01; all other contrasts not significant.

[a] One of the seven instances of *prevent NP V-ing* in LOB has *her* as the notional subject of the gerund and could thus have been excluded as representing the "archaic" type (*prevent my leaving*) disregarded here.
[b] The sole American attestation of the "British" pattern (in Frown) is from a work of military history dealing with, significantly, the Battle of Britain.

4.4   The colloquialization of written English: passives and contractions

Factors of genre, register and style are essential for the study of any grammatical change in progress as they promote or constrain the spread of an innovation throughout the language and the community. The phenomena dealt with in this section provide a particularly compelling illustration of this point, as they show that fairly dramatic changes can be documented in written corpora long after the actual forms under consideration have become established in the grammar. The canonical *be* passive has been declining in frequency according to the evidence of the four written corpora, shown in table 14.8.

The picture this gives of the passive is remarkably similar to that given of the modals above, although the percentage loss of 12.4 percent for BrE and 20.1 percent for AmE is somewhat more dramatic. The passive is one of the foremost grammatical indicators of textual genre, and most common by far in academic writing (category J in the four corpora). Over the last two decades, prescriptive recommendations concerning its use have changed, with many style guides now advising against the use of passives in academic writing, especially in the United States. In a genre-differentiated analysis, Hundt and Mair accordingly noted a particularly pronounced decline in the frequency of passives in the Frown J-category, but were able to point out that the trend was

Table 14.8 Decline in frequency of use of the *be* passive in the four reference corpora

	1961	*1991/92*	*Log lkhd*	*Diff. (%)*
British English (LOB/F-LOB)	13,331	11,708	109.8	−12.4
American English (Brown/Frown)	11,650	9,329	263.7	−20.1

Table 14.9 Rise in frequency of the use of *get* passives in the four reference corpora

	1961	1991/2
British English (LOB/F-LOB)	34	53
American English (Brown/Frown)	35	64

Significances: LOB-F-LOB $p < 0.05$, Brown: Frown $p < 0.01$; LOB-Brown and F-LOB-Frown $p > 0.05$.

significant in British English and in further textual genres (e.g. press), as well (1999: 231–2).

In theory, *be*-passives need not necessarily be replaced by active paraphrases, but could be being displaced by a rival construction, such as the *get*-passive. As table 14.9 shows, this argument is impossible to defend. While the *get* passive has increased significantly, both in British and in American English, the increase is infinitesimal in terms of absolute figures and cannot compensate for the drop in *be*-passives (see table 14.9).

Certainly not the *be* passive, and not even the younger *get* passive, have been involved in any direct grammatical changes in the past century. Rather, the drop in *be* passives and the increase in *get* passives is a discourse phenomenon, pointing to the fact that in the course of the past century written English has moved closer to the norms of spoken usage. The *be* passive is comparatively rare in speech and is strongly associated with the written medium (particularly with academic writing – see, for example, Biber et al. 1999: 476). In the current social climate, demands for writing to be more accessible and readable affect writing practice in many fields – from journalism and academia to the design of official forms, and because of this a decrease in the frequency of the passive is to be expected. In those cases in which writers wish to use a passive, on the other hand, resistance to a traditionally spoken and informal form such as the *get* passive will be minimized.

Another striking case of written language progressively adopting norms of spoken language is the marked increase in the use of contracted forms evidenced in the four corpora. This applies both to verb contractions (as in *it's*, *I'll*) and to negative contractions (*-n't*) – see table 14.10.

The shift towards contracted forms is much more dramatic in AmE, but is also strong in BrE. As was the case with the passive, it could be argued that writers are not entirely free in their choice of form but influenced by prescriptive recommendations or, in the case of journalists, by even stricter conventions of house-style. But even a change in house-style in this case would just be a belated reflection of actual change in community preferences, and support the argument for a growing tendency towards the colloquialization of written English.

Table 14.10 Verb and negative contractions in the four corpora

		1961	*1991/92*	*Log Lkhd*	*Diff. (%)*
BrE (LOB/ F-LOB)	verb contractions	3,143	3,898	79.1	+23.7
	negative contractions	1,950	2,482	62.6	+26.9
AmE (Brown/ Frown)	verb contractions	2,822	5,073	644.6	+79.3
	negative contractions	2,098	2,983	152.5	+41.8

5   The Changing Noun Phrase

Preliminary analysis of some aspects of noun phrase structure in the four corpora has shown changes in frequency of use just as impressive as those we have reported for verb constructions. The most mysterious of these is an increase in BrE of over 5 percent for nouns[17] (with a slightly lower figure of over 4 percent for AmE). So high is the frequency of nouns, particularly in prototypically written styles of English (e.g. news and academic prose – see Biber et al. 1999: 609–11) that this increase, though apparently small, is statistically highly significant (with a log likelihood of 350). Moreover, it seems to run contrary to the assumption – also defended in 4.4. above – that written English is being influenced by the spoken variety (where nouns are much less frequent). There is a corresponding increase in adjectives, together with a significant decrease in pronouns, articles and other determiners, which suggests that, instead of an increase in the number of noun phrases, the increase in nouns is due to a greater density of nouns and adjectives per noun phrase. Further analysis has shown, as part of the explanation for the reduction of article frequency, that the increase of nouns is partly due to an increase of proper nouns, especially the acronymic variety illustrated by *IBM*. Also, there has been a highly significant increase, in both AmE and BrE, of noun + noun sequences (e.g. *union leader*, *campaign coordinator*, *committee chairman*), as table 14.11 shows.

The second row of the table indicates an even larger and more significant increase if the count excludes what the tagger regards as proper nouns in second position – in effect, excluding complex names such as *Kansas City*. This narrows down the nature of the change to common-noun compounding expressions, suggesting a resurgence of the Germanic preference for noun + noun sequences over the more Romance-favored prepositional phrase as a means of elaborating the content of noun phrases. This hypothesis is given some support from a decline (in LOB → F-LOB) of 2.9 percent for prepositions, and a greater decline of 4.7 percent for *of*-phrases in particular.

The above findings support recent work by Biber and Clark (2002), who have also noted that noun modification by clauses has been giving way to

Table 14.11   Noun + noun sequences: increasing frequency from LOB to F-LOB

	LOB: frequency	F-LOB: frequency	Log likelihood	Difference (%)
All noun + noun sequences	32,201	38,016	466.3	+17.7
Noun + common noun only	20,761	26,539	691.9	+27.5

Frequency counts derived from unedited computer output.

non-clausal modification strategies such as the use of premodifying nouns or post-modifying prepositional groups. Functionally, these structural trends suggest that noun phrases in written English are becoming somewhat denser and more compact in their presentation of information. This clearly goes against the tendency towards the informal and colloquial which was noted in many verb-phrase phenomena. Without going too far into detail, we would like to suggest one obvious way of resolving this apparent paradox. A comprehensive trend towards colloquialization affecting all relevant grammatical markers of written style "across-the-board," as it were, is highly unlikely because it would represent a clearly dysfunctional development, making it difficult for the written language to fulfil one of its primary functions, which is the compression of information.

A more compact, premodifying style of noun phrase elaboration is also promoted by the increasing use of another Germanic form, the *s*-genitive. The comparisons of LOB with F-LOB and Brown with Frown show an increase of the s-genitive of 24.1 percent and 41.9 percent respectively, which certainly helps explain a decrease in the frequency of *of*-phrases. Inevitably, because the *of*-phrase is much more frequent and versatile than the s-genitive, the decline of *of*-phrases does not match the increase of s-genitives in percentage terms. But the competing relation between the two constructions shows up more sharply if the count is restricted to *of*-phrases which are semantically interchangeable with s-genitives. A provisional analysis of a small 2 percent sample of the four corpora on this basis showed a decline of s-genitive-matched *of*-phrases of 23.4 percent (BrE) and 24.2 (AmE).

As for postmodification in the noun phrase, the most intriguing category to study from the point of view of recent change is the relative clause. Briefly, relativization with *wh*-relative pronouns is giving way to relativization using *that* or zero. As *wh*-relativization is strongly associated with prototypical written registers (e.g. news and academic prose), this has to count as another instance of the colloquialization of the written medium. A further parameter – closely connected with this – is the choice between the 'pied piping' construction with a preposed preposition (*the project on which I'm working*, etc.) and the preposition-stranding construction (*the project I'm working on*, etc.), where the preposition typically occurs in final position in the clause. Again, the tendency is to move away from preposing and toward stranding – perhaps another case where a more learned Romance overlay on English syntax is being undermined by a native Germanic construction more at home in the spoken language.[18]

Our frequency analysis of relativization has so far had to rely on sample counts and (in the case of AmE) on tagging approximations with built-in correction factors (see note 9). In particular, the bracketed frequency figures in table 14.12 lack the reliability of other tables. Nevertheless, it is unlikely that further confirmatory checks will change the general picture.

In BrE, there has been a general decline in *wh*-relative pronouns, whereas in AmE it is the single pronoun *which* that has suffered extreme disfavor. This change is presumably due to a well-known interdict, in American style guides, against *which* as an introducer of restrictive relative clauses, and clearly *that* is the beneficiary of this ban. Since the texts in Frown were published (in 1992), the switch from *which* to *that* will no doubt have gone further, as a result of the widespread incorporation of the anti-*which* 'rule' in grammar checkers and word processors.[19]

Before leaving the noun phrase, we should add a final word on pronouns, which provide one notable exception to the rule that syntactic change takes place below the threshold of conscious control. In 1961 the so-called 'generic' use of *he* for both male and female reference was well established, and hardly under threat. Conscious efforts inspired by the women's movement of the 1970s and 1980s, however, ensured that by 1991/2, generic *he* was declining fast, and various alternatives were jostling to fill the semantic gap left by

Table 14.12 Change in the use of relativization devices

BrE	LOB	F-LOB	Log likhd	Diff. (%)	AmE	Brown	Frown	Log likhd	Diff. (%)
Which	4,406	3,997	21.0	−9.5	Which	3,516	2,256	261.7	−34.9
Who	2,095	2,013	1.9	−4.2	Who	2,164	2,223	0.6	+2.4
Whom[a]	214	170	5.2	−20.6	Whom[a]	133	154	1.5	+15.5
Whose	293	244	4.6	−17.0	Whose	246	255	0.1	+3.4
That[b]	(1,353)	(1,479)	(5.2)	(+9.0)	That[b]	(1,829)	(2,710)	(173.0)	(+48.3)
zero[c]	(253)	(297)	(3.4)	(+17.1)	zero[c]	(191)	(235)	(4.6)	(+23.1)
pied-piping	1,401	1,168	21.9	−16.9%	pied-piping	1,153	972	15.9	+15.9
preposition stranding[c]	(18)	(74)	(36.4)	(+310.0)	preposition stranding[c]	(91)	(109)	(1.6)	(+19.5)

[a] Since we are counting relative *whom* only in this table, the counts are smaller than those which occur in table 14.1, where both interrogative and relative *whom*s are counted.
[b] The count of *that*-relatives is approximate: it depends on automatic tagging, and a margin of error is to be allowed for.
[c] These counts are based on sampling.

its fall. Although the frequencies are low compared with third-person pronouns in general, the four corpora show the predictable changes. A sample of approximately 500 instances of *he/him/his/himself* from each corpus showed a decline of gender-neutral use from 32 (LOB) to 4 (F-LOB), and from 20 (Brown) to 7 (Frown). Oppositely, a comparable sample of *they* and its variants showed a rise in the use of singular *they* from 0 (LOB) to 9 (F-LOB), and from 7 (Brown) to 9 (Frown). Although rare in all four corpora, the gender-neutral coordinated pronouns *he or she* rose in frequency for the entire corpora from 11 to 37 (LOB → F-LOB) and from 9 to 56 (Brown → Frown). Ultimately, the need to plug the gap left by the demise of gender-neutral *himself* may lead to the establishment of a new pronoun *themself* – perhaps the clearest example of true grammatical innovation in standard English in our period.[20]

(11)   You won't be the first or last man or woman who gets **themself** involved in a holiday romance.   (BNC: K4D 386)

6   Conclusion

Although this survey of current change in English syntax has been necessarily selective, we have tried to achieve a reasonable coverage of core aspects of syntax by focusing on major categories in the verb phrase and noun phrase.

Before concluding it will be as well to consider very briefly what factors have been influencing the changes we have noted. One factor intrinsic to the functioning of any language at any time is grammaticalization – which, as we saw in the cases of the progressive and the semi-modals, may take centuries to come to full fruition. A second factor is socio-cultural, and hence more specific to the social context of English in the twentieth century: colloquialization, or the tendency for written language to adopt features associated with spoken language. There are strong indications that such a process has been at work in the written language for centuries (see Biber and Finegan 1989), and in this chapter we have noted such diverse cases as the increasing use of the progressive and semi-modals; the decline of *wh*-relative pronouns and the rise in the use of *that* and zero relative clauses; the growing use of contractions in written texts; the use of singular *they*. In written British English, a third factor – Americanization – intermingles with the other two. We have looked at one case – the apparent revival of the mandative subjunctive – where American influence seems to override colloquialization, but often these two socio-cultural processes work together – for example, in the increasing use of semi-modals and the declining use of *be* passives. A fourth factor was touched on at the end of the last section – an ideological motivation (avoidance of sexual inequality) for replacing an older pronoun usage by a newer one. Such conscious movements for the change of language are rare, or at least are rarely successful. Hence there is something particularly unusual about this case, not least in the short time period that it took to produce a high-profile syntactic reform of language behavior. Feminist recommendations in this case were clearly helped by the fact that singular *they*, which has a long history in the language, did not need to be promoted as a new form but was merely allowed to resurface in the standard after it had been proscribed by eighteenth and nineteenth century prescriptivists.

Although it may be fairly uncontroversial to say that such influences have been at work, it is virtually impossible to disentangle them, and to build a predictive model to account for kinds and degrees of frequency change taking place during a particular period. Processes such as colloquialization and Americanization are patchy and unpredictable in their results. One important linguistic factor to bear in mind is the competing relation between a spreading syntactic phenomenon and an alternative means of conveying the same meaning. In almost all the changes we have discussed, it is possible to name one (or more) competing construction(s):

LOSING GROUND		GAINING GROUND
modal auxiliary	v.	semi-modal
infinitive complement	v.	gerundial complement
be-passive	v.	*get*-passive
of-phrase	v.	s-genitive
wh-relative	v.	*that* or zero relativization
gender-neutral *he*	v.	singular *they* or coordinated pronouns (*he or she*, etc.)

But the frequency picture rarely gives unequivocal support to the hypothesis that one form is being ousted or superseded by the other. The semantic and pragmatic parameters of linguistic choice are usually too complex to allow a simple inverse correlation to be observed of the kind "more of X means less of Y." In the longer term, such factors must be closely investigated if we are to develop more adequate models of syntactic change taking full account of changes in frequency or preference.

This chapter has demonstrated that there has been noticeable change in the past century even in a rigidly codified language variety such as written standard English, and that the spread of individual innovations can be documented in language corpora. Further, we have shown that those accounts of ongoing grammatical change that are based on anecdotal or impressionistic observation are generally unreliable. They can err in three ways: (1) suspecting change where there is stable long-term variability; (2) over-emphasizing the importance of a small number of often marginal shibboleths important to prescriptivists; and (3) failing to notice the ever present groundswell of linguistic change, apparent in long-term developments in the core grammar. Further studies will have to account for the trends sketched here in the context of contemporary synchronic variation, in particular text-type variation and regional variation in standard Englishes worldwide.

NOTES

We thank Bas Aarts, co-editor of this volume, and two anonymous readers for their valuable comments on a draft of this chapter. Thanks are also due to Nicholas Smith, who undertook most of the automatic corpus processing and a considerable amount of the manual analysis. We also gratefully acknowledge the support of the Arts and Humanities Research Board (AHRB) and the British Academy (Leech) and Deutsche Forschungsgemeinschaft (Mair), who provided research funding.

1   It is only the second case which represents a genuine innovation – with a first OED attestation from 1932 (s.v. *hopefully*, adv. 2); the use of *like* as a conjunction can be documented from the Early Modern English period onwards, and the only new thing about it in the twentieth century is that it is losing the stigma attaching to it in the eyes of many writers.

2   The four corpora each contain about a million words of running text, sampled in 500 chunks of ca. 2,000 words each and covering a range of fifteen written genres. They are available from ICAME, the International Computer Archive of Modern and Medieval English, in Bergen, Norway, whose homepage contains further relevant information. See www.hit.uib.no/corpora.

3   By a tagged corpus, we mean a corpus in which each word token is supplied with a grammatical label specifying its part of speech – see Mair et al. (2002) for further details.

4   Much of the corpus-based research reported here, particularly that based on the LOB, F-LOB, Brown and Frown corpora, has been carried out collaboratively by the authors, their colleagues and researchers at the Universities of Freiburg and Lancaster.

5   See n. 10 for further details of the spoken corpora used. Corpus-based real-time studies of changes in the grammar of the spoken language will be encouraged by the creation of "a parsed and searchable diachronic corpus of present-day spoken English," which is under way at the Survey of English Usage (University College London); see www.ucl.ac.uk/english-usage/diachronic.index for details.

6   While it is not referred to as such in the literature aimed at wider audiences, this is an obvious case of grammaticalization: the gradual incorporation of lexical material into the grammar of the language.

7   This goes against previous research based on other corpora, in which results did point towards a decline in the discourse frequency of *whom* in spoken and written English in the late twentieth century (Aarts and Aarts 2002: 128).

8   Jespersen's way of making his point is obvious and elegant. More fine-grained and differentiated statistical evidence is provided by Nehls (1988), among others.

9   Although the Brown and Frown corpora have been part-of-speech tagged, this has been done automatically, so far without manual post-editing, so that a tagging error rate of ca. 2 percent currently remains in the corpora. This means that these figures for Brown and Frown, in particular, are likely to need some minor correction when the necessary editing work has been done. The broad trends shown in this and other tables in

this chapter are, however, very unlikely to be affected by such changes. It is in the nature of corpus linguistic research that some revision of the quantitative data will arise from further scrutiny and analysis of the same data. All our figures are in this sense provisional.

10 The phenomenon of the "stative progressive" tends to be curiously overrated in the literature on recent changes. In many cases apparent exceptional or innovative uses are the result of polysemy. Thus, *forget* in its sense of *neglect* (*you're forgetting your mother*) is clearly compatible with the progressive. In others, they can be easily handled as contextually licenced rule-breaking for communicative-rhetorical effect (as in *are you seeing what I am seeing?* – in which the point is that visual perception, which is normally subconscious, is made the subject of conscious reflection. See Visser (1973: 1973–86) for a rich compilation of relevant data.

11 With the permission and help of Bas Aarts and Gerry Nelson at the Survey of English Usage (University College London) Leech was able to make a frequency analysis of (semi-)modals in two very small (80,000 words) but roughly comparable corpora of spoken BrE of approximately the early 1960s and the early 1990s. These are from corpora collected by the Survey: the SEU corpus and the ICE-GB corpus. Further details are given in Leech (2003, 2004).

12 We are grateful to Della Summers, of Pearson Education, for permission to use this corpus, the Longman Corpus of Spoken American English. It was collected in the late 1990s on demographic principles, and consists largely of impromptu conversation.

13 The argument presented here is generally compatible with the corpus-based findings in Biber et al., who also establish that semi-modals are more common in speech than writing and that two of them, namely *have to* and *be going to*, are particularly frequent in American English. However, they also point out that the trend is not unbroken and that *have got to* and *had better* are more usual in British English (1999: 487).

14 Serpollet (2001: 531) quotes this statement from Harsh (1968): "the inflected subjunctive, though hardly in a state of robust health, has been taking a long time to die. But that it is still dying [. . .] can hardly be denied."

15 Serpollet (2001: 541) gives the following provisional frequency data for the mandative subjunctive from the four corpora: LOB 14 → F-LOB 33 occurrences; Brown 91 → Frown 78 occurrences. Hundt (1998: 163, 173), following a slightly different methodology, gets: LOB 12 → F-LOB 44. See further data on the British revival of the mandative subjunctive in Övergaard (1995).

16 This includes all uses of this functionally very versatile constructional pattern, which, in addition to the noun-clause uses illustrated, also functions as postmodification in noun phrases (*a tendency for job satisfaction to decrease with age*) or as adverbial clause (*for the plan to be successful, we need money and manpower*), among others.

17 For this and other changes in frequency of word classes between LOB and F-LOB, see Mair et al. (2002).

18 Altenberg (1982: 302), in a study of seventeenth-century genitives and *of*-phrases, surmises that "the drift

away from [the genitive] that had begun in late Old English seems to have reached its peak in the seventeenth century." If so, this trend appears to be now undergoing some reversal.

19   Such minor computer-driven changes in writing norms are, of course, merely the tip of an iceberg. The internet/world wide Web and the various forms of computer-mediated communication associated with it have already become a powerful force in language change on many levels – from lexical innovation to changes in discourse conventions.

20   *Themself* is too rare in written English to appear in any of our four corpora. According to Huddleston and Pullum (2002: 494) it has been attested in standard English since the 1970s. The OED, which does not have an entry for *themself*, lists 41 mostly Middle English and Early Modern English occurrences in its quotation base, many of them with a distinctly nonstandard ring.

FURTHER READING

Aitchison, J. (1991) *Language change: progress or decay*, 2nd edn. Cambridge: Cambridge University Press.

Bauer, L. (1994) *Watching English change: an introduction to the study of linguistic change in standard Englishes in the twentieth century*. London: Longman.

Barber, Ch. (1964) *Linguistic change in present-day English*. London and Edinburgh: Oliver & Boyd.

Bybee, J. and Hopper, P. (eds.) (2001) *Frequency and the emergence of linguistic structure*. Amsterdam: John Benjamins.

Croft, W. (2000) *Explaining language change: an evolutionary approach*. London: Longman.

Crystal, D. (2001) *Language and the internet*. Cambridge: Cambridge University Press.

Denison, D. (1998) Syntax. In S. Romaine (ed.), *The Cambridge history of the English language*, vol. IV: *1776–1997*. Cambridge: Cambridge University Press, 92–329.

Krug, M. (2000) *Emerging English modals: a corpus-based study of grammaticalization*. Berlin and New York: Mouton de Gruyter.

Leech, G. (2003) Modality on the move: the English modal auxiliaries 1961–1992. In R. Facchinetti, M. Krug, and F. Palmer (eds.), *Modality in contemporary English*. Berlin and New York: Mouton de Gruyter, 223–40.

Potter, S. (1975) *Changing English*, 2nd edn. London: Deutsch.

REFERENCES

Aarts, B. (1992) *Small clauses in English: the non-verbal types*. Berlin and New York: Mouton de Gruyter.

Aarts, F. and Aarts, B. (2002) Relative *whom*: 'a mischief-maker.' In A. Fischer, G. Tottie, and H.-M. Lehmann (eds.), *Text types and corpora*. Tübingen: Narr, 123–30.

Altenberg, B. (1982) *The genitive v. the of-construction: a study of syntactic* variation in 17th century English. Lund Studies in English 62. Lund: CWK Gleerup.

Barber, Ch. (1964) *Linguistic change in present-day English*. London and Edinburgh: Oliver & Boyd.

Bauer, L. (1994) *Watching English change: an introduction to the study of linguistic change in standard Englishes in the twentieth century*. London: Longman.

Biber, D. and Finegan, E. (1989) Drift and the evolution of English style: a history of three genres. *Language* 65, 487–517.

Biber, D., Johansson, S., Leech, G., Conrad, S., and Finegan, E. (1999) *The Longman grammar of spoken and written English*. London: Longman.

Biber, D. and Clark, V. (2002) Historical shifts in modification patterns with complex noun phrase structures. In T. Fanego et al. (eds.), *English historical syntax and morphology: selected papers from 11 ICEHL, Santiago de Compostela, 7–11 September 2000*. Amsterdam: John Benjamins, 43–66.

Comrie, B. (1976) *Aspect*. Cambridge: Cambridge University Press.

Denison, D. (1998) Syntax. In S. Romaine (ed.), *The Cambridge history of the English language*, vol. IV: *1776–1997*. Cambridge: Cambridge University Press, 92–329.

Harsh, W. (1968) *The subjunctive in English*. Tuscaloosa, AL: University of Alabama Press.

Hopper, P. and Traugott, E. (2003) *Grammaticalization*, 2nd edn. Cambridge: Cambridge University Press.

Huddleston, R. and Pullum, G. K. (2002) *The Cambridge grammar of the English language*. Cambridge: Cambridge University Press.

Hundt, M. (1998) *It is important that this study (should) be based on the analysis of parallel corpora*: on the use of the mandative subjunctive in four major varieties of English. In H. Lindquist et al. (eds.), *The major varieties of English: papers from MAVEN 97, Växjö 20–22 November 1997*. Växjö: Växjö University Press, 159–73.

Hundt, M. (2001) What corpora tell us about the grammaticalization of voice in *get*-constructions. *Studies in Language* 25, 49–87.

Hundt, M. and Mair, Ch. (1999) 'Agile' and 'uptight' genres: the corpus-based approach to language-change in progress. *International Journal of Corpus Linguistics* 4, 221–42.

Jespersen, O. (1909–49) *A modern English grammar on historical principles*. 7 vols. Copenhagen: Munksgaard.

Leech, G. (2004) *Meaning and the English verb*, 3rd edn. London: Longman.

Leech, G. (2003) Modality on the move: the English modal auxiliaries 1961–1992. In R. Facchinetti, M. Krug, and F. Palmer (eds.), *Modality in contemporary English*. Berlin and New York: Mouton de Gruyter, 223–40.

Leech, G. (2004) Recent grammatical change in English: data, description, theory. In B. Altenberg and K. Aijmer (eds.), *Advances in corpus linguistics: proceedings of the 23rd ICAME Conference, Gothenburg, 2002*. Amsterdam: Rodopi, 61–81.

Lightfoot, D. (1979) *Principles of diachronic syntax*. Cambridge: Cambridge University Press.

Lightfoot, D. (1999) *The development of language: acquisition, change, and evolution*. Malden, MA: Blackwell.

Mair, Ch. and Hundt, M. (1995) Why is the progressive becoming more frequent in English? A corpus-based investigation of language change in progress. *Zeitschrift für Anglistik und Amerikanistik* 43, 111–22.

Mair, Ch. (1997) The spread of the *going-to*-future in written English: a corpus-based investigation into language change in progress. In R. Hickey and St. Puppel (eds.), *Language history and linguistic modelling: a festschrift for Jacek Fisiak on his 60th birthday*. Berlin: Mouton de Gruyter, 1537–43.

Mair, Ch. (2002) Three changing patterns of verb complementation in Late Modern English: a real-time study based on matching text corpora. *English Language and Linguistics* 6, 105–31.

Mair, Ch., Hundt, M., Leech, G., and Smith, N. (2002) Short term diachronic shifts in part-of-speech frequencies: a comparison of the tagged LOB and F-LOB corpora. *International Journal of Corpus Linguistics* 7, 245–64.

Nehls, D. (1988) On the development of the grammatical category of verbal aspect in English. In J. Klegraf and D. Nehls (eds.), *Essays on the English language and applied linguistics on the occasion of Gerhard Nickel's 60th birthday*. Heidelberg: Groos, 173–98.

Nevalainen, T. and Raumolin-Brunberg, H. (2003) *Historical sociolinguistics: language change in Tudor and Stuart England*. London: Longman.

Olofsson, A. (1990) A participle caught in the act: on the prepositional use of *following*. *Studia Neophilologica* 62, 23–35, 129–49.

Övergaard, G. (1995) *The mandative subjunctive in American and British English in the 20th century*. Stockholm: Almqvist & Wiksell International.

Rickford, J., Mendoza-Denton, N., Wasow, T., and Espinosa, J. (1995) Syntactic variation and change in progress: loss of the verbal coda in topic restricting *as far as* constructions. *Language* 71, 102–31.

Romaine, S. and Lange, D. (1991) The use of *like* as a marker of reported speech and thought: a case of grammaticalization in progress. *American Speech* 66, 227–79.

Sapir, E. (1921) *Language: an introduction to the study of speech*. New York: Harcourt, Brace & Co.

Serpollet, N. (2001) The mandative subjunctive in British English seems to be alive and kicking . . . Is this due to the influence of American English? In P. Rayson, A. Wilson, T. McEnery, A. Hardie, and S. Khoja (eds.), *Proceedings of the Corpus Linguistics 2001 Conference*. Lancaster University: UCREL Technical Papers, vol. 13, 531–42.

Smith, N. (2002) Ever moving on? The progressive in recent British English. In P. Peters, P. Collins and A. Smith (eds.), *New frontiers of corpus research: papers from the twenty first International Conference on English Language Research on Computerized Corpora, Sydney 2000*. Amsterdam: Rodopi, 317–30.

Smith, N. (2003a) A quirky progressive? A corpus-based exploration of the *will + be + -ing* construction in recent and present day British English. In D. Archer, P. Rayson, A. Wilson, and T. McEnery (eds.), *Proceedings of the Corpus Linguistics 2003 Conference*. Lancaster University: UCREL Technical Papers, vol. 16, 714–23.

Smith, N. (2003b) Changes in the modals and semi-modals of strong obligation and epistemic necessity in recent British English. In R. Facchinetti, M. Krug, and F. Palmer (eds.), *Modality in contemporary English*. Berlin/New York: Mouton de Gruyter, 241–66.

Visser, F. Th. (1973) *An historical syntax of the English language*, vol. 3, part 2. Leiden: Brill.

15   English Constructions

ADELE E. GOLDBERG AND
DEVIN CASENHISER

0   Introduction

Constructions have been defined variously in the literature, but the traditional use of the term corresponds to a conventional pairing of form with (semantic or discourse) function. This article provides examples of uncontroversial instances of constructions, clarifies some of the debates surrounding the term currently, and also briefly explores a broad-based range of constructionist theories that have converged on the basic idea that traditional constructions play a central theoretical role in language.

1   A Brief History of "Constructions"

It was the Roman orator, Cicero, who in the first century BCE, provided our first known application of the word *constructio* (from which English derives the word 'construction') to a grouping of words. Half a century later, Priscian (ca. 500 CE), began using the word *constructio* as a grammatical term, and the Medieval Linguists known as the Modistae (twelfth century) spent much of their time considering the nature of the construction itself. Their work centered on defining the construction as 'an ordering of words that agree and express a complete meaning.' Their basic criterion for a construction was that it consisted of at least two words in which one of the words was said to 'govern' or 'require' the other word or words. This notion of construction must be both grammatically well-formed and express a meaningful sentiment. *The crowd run*, would have been rejected on syntactic grounds (subject-verb agreement), and *Colorless green ideas sleep furiously* would have been rejected as a construction on the grounds that it is semantically vacuous. In short, the Modistae believed that constructions were not defined simply on the basis of form (i.e., syntax), but also on function (i.e., semantics).

As in the twelfth century, it is still debated what exactly counts as a construction, but in general, the term *construction* refers to *classes* of actual expressions, that is to grammatical patterns. This use of *construction* has a long tradition within descriptive grammars, being used to characterize, for example, relative clauses, passives, topicalization, and so on. On this view, a construction is any systematic phrasal pattern of form and function.

2   Approaches to Constructions

Linguists vary in their approaches to constructions. Nonetheless, the majority of linguists are willing to apply the term 'construction' to certain grammatical patterns that have unusual quirks in either their formal properties or their semantic interpretation (or both) that make them ill suited for universal status. That is, these cases do not follow completely from any general principles and so their patterns can not be predicted; they must be learned piecemeal. Notice, however, that it is not the case that these are simple idioms to be learned as individual chunks. They are in fact phrasal *patterns* with identifiable and definable generalizations.

As an example of a clear case of an English construction, consider the TIME-*AWAY* CONSTRUCTION as in the sentence *Sam slept the whole trip away*. The syntax of the construction can not be accounted for by the rules of English, nor by generative theory (Jackendoff 1997). Furthermore, the meaning of the utterance is not obvious from just considering the meaning of the words in the sentence. What does it mean, for example, to '*sleep a trip*'? Indeed, the meaning only becomes clear when we compare utterances with the same construction (e.g., *They danced the night away, John knitted the entire weekend away*). That is, the construction indicates that the specified time was vigorously spent/wasted while engaged in the action specified by the main verb.

Another example of a clear case of an English construction is the INCREDULITY CONSTRUCTION (e.g., *Him, a trapeze artist?!*). This construction is used to express an attitude towards a proposition, one of incredulity. The speaker in the example above expresses incredulity that the person in question is a trapeze artist. The form of the construction does not obey general rules of English. For one thing, there is no verb and yet the expression stands alone as a full utterance and conveys an entire proposition. In addition, the accusative case marking is normally used for objects, and yet the initial NP would seem to act as a subject or topic argument (cf. *He's a trapeze artist?!*) (e.g., Lambrecht 1990).

The COVARIATIONAL CONDITIONAL CONSTRUCTION (e.g., *The more the merrier*) is another example of an unusual construction. The construction is interpreted as involving an independent variable (identified by the first phrase) and a dependent variable (identified by the second phrase). The word *the* normally occurs at the beginning of a phrase headed by a noun. But in this construction it requires a comparative phrase. The two major phrases of the construction resist classification as either noun phrases or clauses. The requirement that

Table 15.1 Productive or semi-productive constructions that are unusual cross-linguistically

TIME *AWAY* CONSTRUCTION	*sleeping the days away.*
INCREDULITY CONSTRUCTION	*Him, a trapeze artist?!*
COVARIATIONAL CONDITIONAL CONSTRUCTION	*The more chips you eat, the more you want.*
PURELY BENEFACTIVE DITRANSITIVE WITH NON-REFLEXIVE PRONOUN (informal; regional variation)	*I think I'm gonna make me a sandwich.*
WHAT'S X DOING Y?	*What are your shoes doing on the table?*
Stranded preposition construction	*What did you put it on?*
NPN CONSTRUCTION	*day after day*
TO N CONSTRUCTION	*to school; to camp; to hospital (British English)*

two phrases of this type be juxtaposed without conjunction is another non-predictable aspect of the pattern. Because the pattern is not strictly predictable, a construction is posited that specifies the particular form and semantic function involved (Fillmore, Kay, and O'Connor 1988; Culicover and Jackendoff 1999).

In any given language, there are a very large number of such constructions. Table 15.1 provides a few additional examples. Some theorists have argued that such constructions are epiphenomenal, apparent only because of an interacting set of universal, fixed principles with parameters selected on a language-particular basis (Chomsky 2000). In the principles and parameters framework, grammatical constructions are "taxonomic artifacts, useful for informal description perhaps but with no theoretical standing" (Chomsky 2000). This idea is motivated by the view that "the [apparent] diversity and complexity [of languages] can be no more than superficial appearance" (Chomsky 2000) because this is thought to be the only way language could be learnable, given the impoverished input children are exposed to. Most generative grammarians thus conclude, with Chomsky, that "the search for explanatory adequacy requires that language structure must be invariant, except at the margins" (Chomsky 2000).

These researchers accordingly attempt to predict the properties of patterns such as are found in table 15.1 on the basis of general, universal principles. If such attempts are unsuccessful in this endeavor, the pattern is relegated to the "periphery" or "residue" of language. As such, it is determined to be an uninteresting bit of a language that is not subject to the same cognitive principles at work in the 'core' grammar of a language.

3   Constructionist Approaches to Syntax

Over the past two decades, a new theoretical approach to language has emerged that treats constructions as central. Many linguists with varying backgrounds have converged on several key insights that have given rise to a family of *constructionist* approaches (Lakoff 1987; Langacker 1987; Fillmore et al. 1988; Langacker 1991; Gleitman 1994; Goldberg 1995; Michaelis and Lambrecht 1996; Culicover 1999; Kay and Fillmore 1999; Croft 2001; Diessel 2001; Jackendoff, 2002; Tomasello 2003; Fillmore, Kay, Michaelis, and Sag in progress; Culicover and Jackendoff 2005; Goldberg 2006). Constructionist approaches embrace the traditional view that patterns such as passive, topicalization and relative clauses are conventional pairings of form and (semantic or discourse) function – *constructions*.

Generative linguists point to such patterns (the passive, the relative clause, or the interrogative) and reason that they involve formal universals in need of an explanation. The constructionist approach, on the other hand, takes a somewhat different view of what is universal. We acknowledge that the associated functions are (near) universal, but attribute their ubiquity to their functions: it is quite useful to be able to deemphasize the normally most prominent argument (passive); modify nominal referents with propositions (relative clauses) and ask questions (interrogatives). Other types of cross-linguistic generalizations are sought by appealing not to language universals, but to general cognitive, pragmatic and processing factors (e.g., Croft 2003; Goldberg 2004, 2006).

At the same time, constructionists generally emphasize that except in cases of shared diachronic history or language contact, constructions in different languages often differ in subtle aspects of their forms and/or functions (e.g., see Dixon 1984; Lambrecht 1994; Dryer 1997; Zhang 1998; Kim and Maling 1999). As Tomasello (2003) notes, what is truly remarkable is the degree to which human languages differ from one another, given that all languages need to express roughly the same types of messages. Constructional approaches anticipate such wide variability across languages (Van Valin and LaPolla 1997; Croft 2001; Garry and Rubino 2001).

One issue that arises is the question of explanatory adequacy. Language researchers are generally in agreement that a theory is only explanatorily adequate if we can ultimately account for how languages can be learned from the initial state on the basis of the input. The approaches differ, however, both in what each theory believes it is necessary to account for, and in each theory's view of the richness of the initial state. As mentioned, generative linguists often relegate constructions such as the INCREDULITY CONSTRUCTION to the periphery of the theory. As such, they have no reason to account for the way in which they are learned. Moreover, more prolific constructions such as the PASSIVE are considered to exist in many languages and as such may be universal and part of the genetic language component. Constructionists hold neither of these views and therefore believe that a theory of language learning must necessarily account for how all constructions are learned. Typically, constructionist theories of learning claim that language input is in fact rather rich, not impoverished, and that language learners bring to the task a host of pragmatic and cognitive abilities which they employ to great effect in the task of language learning (these include the ability to make statistical generalizations, and the ability to use semantics and pragmatics to help guide interpretation and generalization) (see, e.g., Tomasello 1999, 2003).

In spite of these important differences, constructionist approaches share certain foundational ideas with the mainstream generative approach that has held sway for the past several decades. Both general approaches agree that it is essential to consider language as a cognitive (mental) system; both approaches acknowledge that there must be a way to combine structures to create novel utterances, and both approaches recognize that a non-trivial theory of language learning is needed.

4   Why Constructions?

Constructionists generally apply the term 'construction' to patterns that systematically combine any morphological or phrasal elements, allowing for compositional phrasal constructions. On this view, even basic sentence patterns of a language, such as transitive, intransitive and ditransitive – not just usual patterns such as those presented in table 15.1 – can be understood to involve constructions (Goldberg 1995; Jackendoff 1997). The alternative is to assume that the form and general interpretation of basic sentence patterns of a language are determined by semantic and/or syntactic information specified by the main verb. The sentence patterns given in (1) and (2) indeed appear to be determined by the specifications of *give* and *put* respectively:

(1)   Mike gave her a pencil.

(2)   Laura put her book on the shelf.

Give is a three argument verb. An act of giving requires three participants: a giver (or 'agent'), a recipient, and something given (or 'theme'). It is therefore expected to appear with three phrases corresponding to these three roles. In (1), for instance, *Mike* is agent, *her* is recipient, and *a pencil* is theme. *Put*, another three argument verb, requires an agent, a theme (object that undergoes the change of location) and a repository of the theme's motion. It appears with the corresponding three arguments in (2).

Although the main verb may appear to determine the form of the constructions in (1) and (2), the form of the sentence patterns of a language are generally not determined by independent specifications of the main verb. For example, it is implausible to claim that *sneeze* has a three argument sense, and yet it can appear in (3). The patterns in (4)–(6) are likewise not naturally determined by the main verbs:

(3)   *He sneezed his tooth right across town.*   (R. Munsch, *Andrew's loose tooth*)

(4)   *She smiled herself an upgrade.*   (D. Adams, *Hitchhiker's guide to the galaxy*)

(5)   *We laughed our conversation to an end.*   (J. Hart, *Sin*)

(6)   *They could easily co-pay a family to death.*   (NYT, 1/14/02)

If, however, basic sentence patterns can involve constructions (as constructionists believe), then verbs can be understood to combine with argument structure constructions to account for such data. Consider the verb *slice* and the various constructions in which it can appear (labeled in parentheses):

(7)   a.   He sliced the bread.   (transitive)
      b.   Pat sliced the carrots into the salad.   (caused motion)
      c.   Pat sliced Chris a piece of pie.   (ditransitive)
      d.   Emeril sliced and diced his way to stardom.   (*way* construction)
      e.   Pat sliced the box open.   (resultative)

In all of these expressions *slice* means 'to cut with a sharp instrument.' The specific interpretation of the word, however changes depending on the argument structure with which the verb is used. (7a) suggests something acting on something else, (7b) suggests something causing something else to move, (7c) shows someone intending to cause someone to receive something, (7d) someone moving somewhere, and (7e) someone causing something to change state (Goldberg 1995, 2006). Constructionists suggest that it is the argument structure construction that provides the direct link between surface form and general aspects of the interpretation. Accordingly, while most linguists agree that constructions are required for unusual patterns, constructionists invoke constructions for the basic, regular patterns of language as well.

In order to capture differences in meaning or discourse properties between surface forms, constructionist theories do not derive one construction from another, as is typically done in mainstream generative theory. An actual expression typically involves the combination of a dozen different constructions beginning with the individual words themselves. For example, the construct in (8) involves the list of constructions given in (9a–f):

(8)   What did Chris buy her mother?

(9)   a.   *Chris, buy, her, mother, what, did* constructions (i.e., words)
      b.   DITRANSITIVE CONSTRUCTION (instantiated by the combination of *what* and *Chris buy her mother*)

c. INTERROGATIVE CONSTRUCTION (formed by combining initial *wh-word* with the SUBJECT-AUXILIARY CONSTRUCTION and clause with a "missing" argument)

d. SUBJECT-AUXILIARY INVERSION CONSTRUCTION (instantiated by *did Chris*)

e. VP CONSTRUCTION (instantiated by [*buy her mother*])

f. NP CONSTRUCTION (instantiated by *What, Chris,* and *her mother*)

Note that "surface form" need not specify a particular word order, nor even particular grammatical categories, although there are constructions that do specify these features. For example, the ditransitive construction in (9) and discussed above is characterized in terms of a set of argument types. The overt order of arguments in (9) is determined by a combination of a VERB PHRASE CONSTRUCTION with the INTERROGATIVE CONSTRUCTION, the latter of which allows for the "theme" argument (represented by *What*) to appear sentence-initially.

5 What Counts as a Construction?

The majority of constructionists argue that not only are phrasal grammatical patterns constructions, but grammatical patterns that combine two or more morphemes lexically are also constructions. Still other theorists emphasize the parallels between morphemes, words, idioms and larger phrasal patterns by applying the term "construction" to any conventional pairing of form and function, including *individual* morphemes and root words along with idioms, partially lexically filled and fully general linguistic patterns. Examples of each of these types are given in table 15.2 from lexical to phrasal.

According to the more inclusive use of the term construction, any linguistic pattern is recognized as a construction as long as some aspect of its form or function is not strictly predictable from its component parts or from other constructions recognized to exist. In addition, many researchers observe that there exists linguistic and psycholinguistic evidence that patterns are stored even if they are fully predictable as long as they occur with sufficient frequency (Bybee 1995; Barlow and Kemmer 2000; Tomasello 2003). Thus these highly frequent expressions, even if fully compositional, are sometimes labeled "constructions" as well. As a result of such varying theoretical views, researchers have different ideas about what kinds of utterances count as constructions (figure 15.1).

Different surface forms are typically associated with slightly different semantic or discourse functions. Take for example, the DITRANSITIVE CONSTRUCTION, which involves the form, Subj V Obj1 Obj2 (e.g., (1), (10b), (11b)).

(10) a. Liza bought a book for Zach.
      b. Liza bought Zach a book.

Table 15.2 Examples of constructions, varying in size and complexity; form and function are specified if not readily transparent

ROOT WORDS	e.g., *book, dog, or*	
COMBINATION OF MORPHEMES	e.g., *un*-V	
IDIOM (FILLED)	e.g., *Going great guns*	
IDIOM (PARTIALLY FILLED)	e.g., *jog* <someone's> *memory*	
DITRANSITIVE (DOUBLE OBJECT) CONSTRUCTION	Form: Subj [V Obj1 Obj2] (e.g., *Mike gave her a book; He baked her a carrot cake.*)	Meaning: transfer (intended or actual); see text.
PASSIVE	Form: Subj aux VPpp (PP$_{by}$) (e.g., *The house was hit by lightening*)	Discourse function: to make undergoer topical and/or actor non-topical

(11) a.   Liza sent a book to storage.
     b.   Liza sent Stan a book.
     c.   ??Liza sent storage a book.

The ditransitive form evokes the notion of transfer or "giving." This is in contrast to possible paraphrases. For example, while (10a) can be used to mean that Liza bought a book for a third party because Zach was too busy to buy it himself, (10b) can only mean that Liza intended to give Zach the book. Similarly while (11a) can be used to entail caused motion to a location (the book is caused to go to storage), the ditransitive pattern requires that the goal argument be an animate being, capable of receiving the transferred item (cf. 11b, 11c). As is clear from considering the paraphrases, the implication of transfer is not an independent fact about the words involved. Rather, the implication of transfer comes from the ditransitive construction itself.

Constructions are combined freely to form actual expressions as long as they are not in conflict. For example, the specification of the ditransitive construction that requires an animate recipient argument conflicts with the meaning of *storage* in (11c) resulting in unacceptability. The observation that language has an infinitely creative potential is accounted for, then, by the free combination of constructions.

Oftentimes, the difference between two seemingly synonymous constructions is due not to semantic generalization, but to generalizations about *information structure* properties of the construction. Information structure has to do with the way in which a speaker's assumptions about the hearer's state of knowledge and consciousness at the time of speaking is reflected in surface form (see

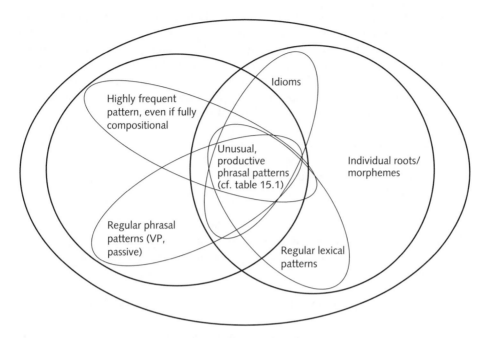

Figure 15.1 Possible conceptions of what should count as a construction

Ward and Birner, ch. 13, this volume). In particular, there is a reliable statistical tendency for the recipient argument in ditransitives to have already been mentioned in the discourse (often encoded by a pronoun) as compared to prepositional paraphrases (Erteschik-Shir 1979; Thompson 1990; Arnold, Wasow, Losongco, and Ginstrom 2000).

Consider the LEFT-DISLOCATION and TOPICALIZATION CONSTRUCTIONS in English. At first (12) and (13) seem to be synonymous:

(12) Jazz, she loves it.   Left-dislocation

(13) Jazz, she loves.   Topicalization

However, using the parsed version of the Switchboard Corpus, Gregory and Michaelis (2001) document subtle distinctions between them. The majority of the referents of the fronted NP in topicalizations are previously mentioned and yet do not persist as topics. The opposite holds for left dislocations. Thus, the LEFT-DISLOCATION CONSTRUCTION is TOPIC ESTABLISHING, whereas the TOPICALIZATION CONSTRUCTION tends to be used for MORIBUND TOPICS.

Along these same lines, it has been claimed that languages typically have special constructions that allow for noncanonical packaging of information. To take another example, Lambrecht (1994) defines SENTENCE FOCUS (SF) CONSTRUCTIONS as constructions that are formally marked as expressing a pragmatically structured proposition in which both the subject and the predicate are in focus. He goes on to describe several properties of SF constructions. The function of SF constructions is presentational – namely, to present an entity or an event into the discourse (cf. also Sasse's (1987) entity-central vs. event-central thetic sentences). An English SF construction that introduces an event into the discourse is characterized by having pitch accent only on the logical subject, and not on the predicate phrase, as in (14).

(14)   Context: What happened?
    a. Her BROTHER is sick.
    b. Her HONDA broke down.
    c. PETER called you.

The subject in this construction is not topical and cannot be pronominal. For example, (15) can only be interpreted with a narrow focus on the subject argument (an ARGUMENT FOCUS reading) and does not permit a sentence focus interpretation:

(15)   HE is sick.   (possible context: A: Is she sick? B: No, HE is sick)

The predicate in the SF construction typically has semantics that are compatible with presentation, with SF constructions cross-linguistically favoring certain unaccusative verbs such as *arrive, come, die,* and *disappear.* The same function, indicated in English by sentence accent, is marked by different formal means in other languages. The need for a full range of expressive power motivates the existence of marked construction types such as the SF construction.

Facts about the use of entire constructions, including register (e.g., formal or informal), dialect variation, etc. may be stated as part of the construction as well. Constructionist approaches provide a direct way of accounting for these facts, since constructions specify a surface form and a corresponding function.

6   Constructions in Generative Grammar

Certain current generative frameworks share the basic idea that some type of meaning is directly associated with some type of form, independently of particular lexical items (e.g., Borer 1994; Marantz 1997; Hale and Keyser 1998; Borer 2001). To the extent that syntax plays a role in contentful meaning, these other approaches are "constructional," and they are occasionally referred to that way in the literature.

However, these approaches are fundamentally different from the type of constructional approaches outlined above. In particular, these generative accounts do not adopt a non-derivational (monostratal) approach to syntax, as other constructionist approaches do. They also do not emphasize speaker construals of situations; the emphasis is rather on rough paraphrases. "Constructions" are assumed to be pairings of underlying form and coarse meaning, instead of surface form and detailed function. Only certain syntactic patterns are viewed as instances of constructions; words or morphemes are assumed to be stored in a separate component, and most syntactic generalizations are assumed to make no reference to semantics or function. Another critical difference is that constructions are assumed to be universal and part of Universal Grammar. Finally, constructions are assumed to be compatible with Minimalist architecture and assumptions, instead of providing an alternative way to view our knowledge of grammar. See Goldberg (2006: ch. 3) for a review of these approaches and comparison with the type of constructionist approaches outlined in earlier sections.

7   Conclusion

As with the medieval Modistae, linguists today have varying notions about what types of utterances count as constructions. It is safe to say, however, that in essence a construction is a pattern in the formal properties of a language (i.e., in its form) that is associated with a particular function. While various theories may choose to interpret this definition broadly or more narrowly, the basic notion of a construction as a pattern of form and function remains the same.

FURTHER READING

Croft, W. (2001) *Radical construction grammar*. Oxford: Oxford University Press.

Culicover, P. W. and Jackendoff, R. (2005) *Simpler syntax*. Oxford: Oxford University Press.

Fillmore, C. J., Kay, P., and O'Connor, M. C. (1988) Regularity and idiomaticity in grammatical constructions: The case of *Let Alone*. *Language* 64, 501–38.

Goldberg, A. E. (1995) *Constructions: a construction grammar approach to argument structure*. Chicago: Chicago University Press.

Goldberg, A. E. (2006) *Constructions at work: the nature of generalizations in language*. Oxford: Oxford University Press.

Lakoff, G. (1987) *Women, fire, and dangerous things: what categories reveal about the mind*. Chicago: University of Chicago Press.

Lambrecht, K. (1994) *Information structure and sentence form*. Cambridge: Cambridge University Press.

Langacker, R. W. (1987) *Foundations of cognitive grammar*, vol. 1. Stanford, CA: Stanford University Press.

Tomasello, M. (2003) *Constructing a language: a usage-based theory of language acquisition*. Cambridge, MA: Harvard University Press.

REFERENCES

Afarli, T. (1987) Non-subject pro-drop in Norwegian, *Linguistic Inquiry* 18, 339–45.

Arnold, J. E., Wasow, T., Losongco, A., and Ginstrom, R. (2000) Heaviness vs newness: the effects of structural complexity and discourse status on constituent ordering. *Language* 76, 28–55.

Barlow, M. and Kemmer, S. (2000) *Usage based models of grammar.* Stanford, CA: CSLI Publications.

Borer, H. (1994) The projection of arguments. In J. Runner (ed.), *University of Massachusetts Occasional Papers in Linguistics* 17, 19–47.

Borer, H. (2001) *Exo-skeletal vs endo-skeletal explanations: syntactic projections and the lexicon.*

Bybee, J. L. (1995) Regular morphology and the lexicon. *Language and Cognitive Processes* 10, 425–55.

Chomsky, N. (1965) *Aspects of the theory of syntax.* Cambridge, MA: MIT Press.

Chomsky, N. (1981) *Lectures on government and binding.* Dordrecht: Foris Publications.

Chomsky, N. (1995) *The minimalist program.* Cambridge, MA: MIT Press.

Chomsky, N. (2000) *New horizons in the study of language and mind.* Cambridge: Cambridge University Press.

Croft, W. (2001) *Radical construction grammar.* Oxford: Oxford University Press.

Croft, W. (2003) *Typology and universals,* 2nd edn. Cambridge: Cambridge University Press.

Culicover, P. W. (1999) *Syntactic nuts: hard cases, syntactic theory and language acquisition.* Oxford: Oxford University Press.

Culicover, P. W. and Jackendoff, R. (1999) The view from the periphery: the English correlative conditions. *Linguistic Inquiry* 30, 543–71.

Culicover, P. W. and Jackendoff, R. (2005) *Simpler syntax.* Oxford: Oxford University Press.

Diessel, H. (2001) *The development of complex sentence constructions in English: a sage-based approach.* Leipzig: University of Leipzig.

Dixon, R. M. W. (1984) The semantic basis of syntactic properties. *Berkeley Linguistic Society* (583–95) Berkeley.

Dryer, M. S. (1997) Are grammatical relations universal? In S. A. Thompson (ed.), *Essays on language function and language type.* Amsterdam: John Benjamins, 115–43.

Erteschik-Shir, N. (1979) Discourse constraints on dative movement. In G. Sankoff (ed.), *Syntax and semantics,* vol. 12. New York: Academic Press, 441–67.

Fillmore, C. J., Kay, P., Michaelis, L., and Sag, I. (in progress) *Construction grammar.* Stanford: CSLI.

Fillmore, C. J., Kay, P., and O'Connor, M. C. (1988) Regularity and idiomaticity in grammatical constructions: the case of *Let Alone. Language* 64, 501–38.

Garry, J. and Rubino, C. (2001) *Facts about the world's languages: an encyclopedia of the world's major languags past and present.* New York: H.W. Wilson.

Gleitman, L. (1994) The structural sources of verb meanings. In P. Bloom (ed.), *Language acquisition: core readings.* Cambridge, MA: MIT Press.

Goldberg, A. E. (1995) *Constructions: a construction grammar approach to argument structure.* Chicago: Chicago University Press.

Goldberg, A. E. (2004) But do we need Universal Grammar? A comment on Lidz et al. (2003), *Cognition.*

Goldberg, A. E. (2005) Argument realization: the role of constructions, lexical semantics and discourse factors. In J.-O. Östman (ed.), *Construction grammar(s): cognitive and cross-language dimension*. Amsterdam: John Benjamins.

Goldberg, A. E. (2006) *Constructions at work: the nature of generalization in language*. Oxford: Oxford University Press.

Gregory, M. L. and Michaelis, L. A. (2001) Topicalization and left dislocation: a functional opposition revisited. *Journal of Pragmatics 33*, 1665–706.

Hale, K. and Keyser, J. (1998) On the complex nature of simple predicators. In W. Geuder (ed.), *The projection of arguments*. Stanford, CA: CSLI.

Jackendoff, R. (1997) Twistin' the night away. *Language 73 (3)*, 534–59.

Jackendoff, R. (2002) *Foundations of language*. Oxford: Oxford University Press.

Kay, P. and Fillmore, C. J. (1999) Grammatical constructions and linguistic generalizations: The What's X doing Y? construction. *Language 75*, 1–34.

Kim, S. and Maling, J. (1999) Resultatives: the view from abroad, Ms., Brandeis University.

Lakoff, G. (1987) *Women, fire, and dangerous things: what categories reveal about the mind*. Chicago: University of Chicago Press.

Lambrecht, Knud (1990) "What, me worry?" *Mad Magazine* sentences revisited. *Proceedings of the 16th Annual Meeting of the Berkeley Linguistics Society*. Berkeley, California, 215–28.

Lambrecht, K. (1994) *Information structure and sentence form*. Cambridge: Cambridge University Press.

Langacker, R. W. (1987) *Foundations of cognitive grammar*, vol. 1. Stanford, CA: Stanford University Press.

Langacker, R. W. (1991) *Foundations of cognitive grammar*, vol. 2. Stanford, CA: Stanford University Press.

Marantz, A. (1997) No escape from syntax: don't try morphological analysis in the privacy of your own lexicon. In L. Siegel (ed.), *University of Pennsylvania Working Papers in Linguistics 4 (2)*, 201–25. Philadelphia.

Michaelis, L. A. and Lambrecht, K. (1996) Toward a construction-based model of language function: the case of nominal extraposition. *Language 72*, 215–47.

Sasse, Hans-Jürgen (1987) The thetic/categorical distinction revisited. *Linguistics 25*, 511–80.

Thompson, S. A. (1990) Information flow and dative shift in English discourse. In P. Mühlhäusler (ed.), *Development and diversity: linguistic variation across time and space*. Summer Institute of Linguistics.

Tomasello, M. (1999) *The cultural origins of human cognition*. Cambridge, MA: Harvard University Press.

Tomasello, M. (2003) *Constructing a language: a usage-based theory of language acquisition*. Cambridge: Harvard University Press.

Van Valin, R. D. J. and LaPolla, R. J. (1997) *Syntax: structure, meaning and function*. Cambridge: Cambridge University Press.

Zhang, N. (1998) The interactions between construction meaning and lexical meaning. *Linguistics 36*, 957–80.

Part III   Phonetics and Phonology

16 English Phonetics

MICHAEL K. C. MACMAHON

1 Types of Phonetics

Phonetics, often described as the 'scientific study of speech production,' is concerned with (a) the processes that generate an air-stream which carries linguistic content (ARTICULATORY PHONETICS), (b) the physical characteristics of the resulting sound waves that pass between the speaker's VOCAL TRACT and the listener's ears (ACOUSTIC PHONETICS), and (c) the processes whereby the mechanical movements of the ear-drum, created by the action of the sound waves, are transmitted into the middle and inner ear and perceived at a cortical level as sound (AUDITORY PHONETICS). Much of phonetic theory and description relates to articulatory phonetics; EXPERIMENTAL PHONETICS (occasionally still called INSTRUMENTAL PHONETICS) refers to the study of phonetic data by means of instrumentation for the study of postures and movements of the speech organs (e.g. medical instrumentation, especially MRI) and the resulting acoustic patterns (e.g. software for acoustic analysis). For details of the philosophy and instrumentation of experimental phonetics, see e.g. Stone (1997), Docherty and Foulkes (1999), Hayward (2000), Gick et al. (2002).

The discipline which underpins the description of the articulatory aspect of the sounds of all languages is GENERAL PHONETICS. The term ENGLISH PHONETICS refers to the description of the sounds encountered in English as a world-wide language. English is spoken in a wide variety of ACCENTS (i.e. modes of pronunciation), some based on regional, some on social, some on idiosyncratic criteria. In the UK, the most fully described accent is Received Pronunciation (RP), even though it is spoken by a minority of people. Conversely, in the USA, the majority pronunciation is General American (GA), the most fully described accent.

2   Phonetics and Phonology

Phonetics differs from phonology in that it focuses on the mechanics of sound production and transmission, irrespective of how the sounds may operate as part of a language system; phonology focuses on the 'function,' or 'organization,' or 'patterning' of the sounds (see also ch. 17, this volume, 'English Phonology and Morphology', and ch. 18, this volume, 'Prosodic Phonology').

3   The Production of Sounds

3.1   *The speech organs*

In general, speech sounds in English are produced by the interaction of the respiratory mechanism, the laryngeal mechanism and the oral and nasal mechanisms – the exceptions are the so-called GLOTTALIC and VELARIC airstream mechanisms (see below). Figure 16.1 shows a mid-line (SAGITTAL) view of the head and neck, with the major anatomical landmarks relevant for phonetic study marked: these constitute the SPEECH ORGANS within the VOCAL TRACT.

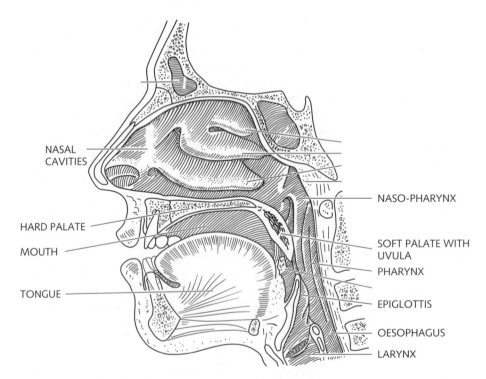

Figure 16.1   Sagittal section of the nose, mouth, pharynx, and larynx
Source: Armstrong 1939

For most sounds in English, an air-stream, generated by the lungs, passes up the trachea where it may be modified by the action of the vocal and ven-tricular folds (see below) before passing into the pharynx. Depending on the position of the soft palate, which may be raised against the posterior wall of the pharynx to create a relatively air-tight seal, or lowered by varying degrees away from the posterior wall, air will flow either into the nasal cavities or continue into the mouth. More recently, studies have re-examined the disposi-tion of the soft palate *vis-à-vis* the posterior pharyngeal wall in the production of various speech-sounds. Kuehn and Moon (1998), for example, identified certain differences dependent on the type of vowel, the state of the glottis, and the sex of the speaker.

For descriptive purposes, it is often assumed that any differences between individual speakers' vocal tracts – e.g. the size and shape of the oral cavity – can be discounted. Yet the structure of the vocal tract can vary somewhat, depending on age, sex, and individual factors, and thus differences of head and neck anatomy may need to be taken into account when assessing phonetic data. The male larynx is generally larger than the female, and so too is the pharynx. There can be variation in the length, width, and curvature of the roof of the mouth, as well as the style of dentition. For further discussion, see Catford (1977: 21–3), and especially Mackenzie Beck (1997).

The tongue is traditionally viewed as consisting of six different areas: the TIP, BLADE, FRONT (sometimes referred to as MIDDLE), BACK, ROOT, and RIMS (or SIDES).

The actions of the tongue and/or the lips in relation to different parts of the roof of the mouth modify the air-stream such that a large variety of different sounds are produced: all can be classified into one of two categories, CON-SONANT and VOWEL. These terms do not necessarily coincide with the same expressions as used in any discussion of alphabetic letters. A phonetic VOWEL is a sound in which there is no obstruction to the air-stream – for example the sound of the word <ah>. A phonetic CONSONANT is a sound in which there is an obstruction of some sort to the air-stream – for example the first and last sounds in the word <mat>. VOWELS and CONSONANTS are often referred to as SEGMENTS of speech: even so, they are not the only aspects of speech which come within the province of phonetics. A series of phonetic activities accom-pany the production of the segments. Known variously as SUPRASEGMENTALS, SUPRASEGMENTAL FEATURES, NON-SEGMENTAL FEATURES, and PROSODIC FEATURES (see ch. 19, this volume, 'Intonation') they include the emphasis given to par-ticular parts of words by additional respiratory activity (STRESS) and the action of the vocal folds (INTONATION), and the TEMPO and RHYTHM of speech. A speaker's combination of the segmental and suprasegmental features used in his/her speech creates a particular VOCAL PROFILE. Some of this may be rela-tively unchanging, and act as a form of audible 'background' (VOICE QUALITY) which aids in identifying a speaker (cf. Nolan (1983); and see below section 9).

Much of phonetic terminology is Latinate in character (e.g. 'bilabial,' 'fricative,' 'supraglottal') – simply because of the discipline's long history.

THE INTERNATIONAL PHONETIC ALPHABET (revised to 1993)

CONSONANTS (PULMONIC)

	Bilabial	Labiodental	Dental	Alveolar	Postalveolar	Retroflex	Palatal	Velar	Uvular	Pharyngeal	Glottal
Plosive	p b			t d		ʈ ɖ	c ɟ	k ɡ	q ɢ		ʔ
Nasal	m	ɱ		n		ɳ	ɲ	ŋ	N		
Trill	ʙ			r					ʀ		
Tap or Flap				ɾ		ɽ					
Fricative	ɸ β	f v	θ ð	s z	ʃ ʒ	ʂ ʐ	ç ʝ	x ɣ	χ ʁ	ħ ʕ	h ɦ
Lateral fricative				ɬ ɮ							
Approximant		ʋ		ɹ		ɻ	j	ɰ			
Lateral approximant				l		ɭ	ʎ	L			

Where symbols appear in pairs, the one to the right represents a voiced consonant. Shaded areas denote articulations judged impossible.

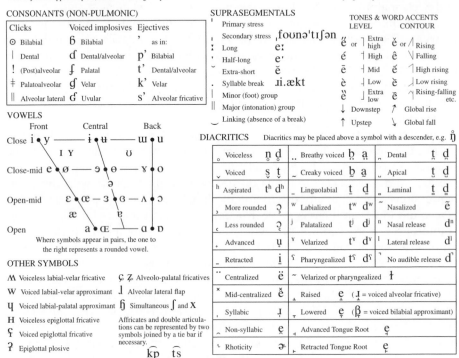

CONSONANTS (NON-PULMONIC)

Clicks	Voiced implosives	Ejectives
ʘ Bilabial	ɓ Bilabial	' as in:
ǀ Dental	ɗ Dental/alveolar	p' Bilabial
ǃ (Post)alveolar	ʄ Palatal	t' Dental/alveolar
ǂ Palatoalveolar	ɠ Velar	k' Velar
ǁ Alveolar lateral	ʛ Uvular	s' Alveolar fricative

SUPRASEGMENTALS

ˈ Primary stress	ˌfoʊnəˈtɪʃən
ˌ Secondary stress	
ː Long	eː
ˑ Half-long	eˑ
˘ Extra-short	ĕ
. Syllable break	ɹi.ækt
ǀ Minor (foot) group	
ǁ Major (intonation) group	
‿ Linking (absence of a break)	

TONES & WORD ACCENTS

LEVEL		CONTOUR	
e̋ or ˥	Extra high	ě or ˩˥	Rising
é ˦	High	ê ˥˩	Falling
ē ˧	Mid	e᷄ ˦˥	High rising
è ˨	Low	e᷅ ˩˨	Low rising
ȅ ˩	Extra low	e᷈ ˧˩˧	Rising-falling etc.
↓ Downstep		↗ Global rise	
↑ Upstep		↘ Global fall	

VOWELS

Front Central Back

Close   i • y ——— ɨ • ʉ ——— ɯ • u

Close-mid   e • ø ——— ɘ • ɵ ——— ɤ • o

Open-mid   ɛ • œ — ɜ • ɞ — ʌ • ɔ

Open   a • ɶ ——— ɑ • ɒ

Where symbols appear in pairs, the one to the right represents a rounded vowel.

(ɪ ʏ, ʊ, ə, æ, ɐ positioned on chart)

OTHER SYMBOLS

ʍ Voiceless labial-velar fricative	ɕ ʑ Alveolo-palatal fricatives
w Voiced labial-velar approximant	ɺ Alveolar lateral flap
ɥ Voiced labial-palatal approximant	ɧ Simultaneous ʃ and X
ʜ Voiceless epiglottal fricative	Affricates and double articula-
ʢ Voiced epiglottal fricative	tions can be represented by two symbols joined by a tie bar if necessary.
ʡ Epiglottal plosive	k͡p t͡s

DIACRITICS   Diacritics may be placed above a symbol with a descender, e.g. ŋ̊

̥ Voiceless	n̥ d̥	̤ Breathy voiced	b̤ a̤	̪ Dental	t̪ d̪
̬ Voiced	s̬ t̬	̰ Creaky voiced	b̰ a̰	̺ Apical	t̺ d̺
ʰ Aspirated	tʰ dʰ	̼ Linguolabial	t̼ d̼	̻ Laminal	t̻ d̻
̹ More rounded	ɔ̹	ʷ Labialized	tʷ dʷ	̃ Nasalized	ẽ
̜ Less rounded	ɔ̜	ʲ Palatalized	tʲ dʲ	ⁿ Nasal release	dⁿ
̟ Advanced	u̟	ˠ Velarized	tˠ dˠ	ˡ Lateral release	dˡ
̠ Retracted	i̠	̴ Pharyngealized	tˤ dˤ	̚ No audible release	d̚
̈ Centralized	ë	̴ Velarized or pharyngealized	ɫ		
̽ Mid-centralized	e̽	̝ Raised	e̝ (ɹ̝ = voiced alveolar fricative)		
̩ Syllabic	n̩	̞ Lowered	e̞ (β̞ = voiced bilabial approximant)		
̯ Non-syllabic	e̯	̘ Advanced Tongue Root	e̘		
˞ Rhoticity	ɚ	̙ Retracted Tongue Root	e̙		

Figure 16.2 The International Phonetic Alphabet
Source: www.arts.gla.ac.uk/ipa/fullchart; and International Phonetic Association 1999

Categories of description and classification generally follow the conventions of the International Phonetic Association (cf. International Phonetic Association (1999); for a criticism, see Roach (1987); see also Ladefoged and Everett (1996), Picard (1997)). Phonetic notation, with some specific exceptions, is that of the International Phonetic Alphabet (see figure 16.2, and downloadable from www.arts.gla.ac.uk/IPA/ipa; cf. International Phonetic Association 1999). For the description, classification and notation of a variety of non-standard sounds used in pathological speech forms, there is the Extended IPA alphabet (International Phonetic Association (1999: 186–93), and downloadable from www.arts.gla.ac.uk/IPA/ipa). Square brackets [ ] are used to indicate sounds, forward slashes // to indicate phonological units (see ch. 17, this volume, 'English Phonology and Morphology').

Many of the symbols in the IPA's Alphabet (the 'IPA Chart') are based on the roman alphabet: this does not mean necessarily that their sound values will be those of such letters in the roman alphabet itself. Thus, the [c] symbol, for a voiceless palatal plosive, is not used in a phonemic transcription of English. The word <cat> would be written in IPA not with a [c] as its first sound, but with a [k]. (The symbol [c] is however sometimes needed when transcribing the speech of young children or certain speech pathologies or some adult pronunciations of /k/ and /g/ before front close vowels, e.g. in KEEN, GEESE.) In phonemic notations, it is usual practice to choose as the representative of the phoneme the most appropriate symbol: thus for the /r/ phoneme in English, despite [r], a voiced alveolar trill, being a relatively infrequent realization of the phoneme, the choice of the phoneme symbol is dictated by the ease with which the [r] symbol is associated with the particular phoneme by dint of the orthographic conventions of <r> in English. Angle brackets < > enclose normal orthographic forms in the roman alphabet.

3.2   Air-stream mechanisms

For speech to be audible, an air-stream must be generated. For English, the commonest air-stream mechanism is the PULMONIC, using the lungs, rib-cage and associated muscle groups. The direction of air-flow is occasionally INGRESS-IVE, rather than EGRESSIVE – for example when counting to oneself (cf. Catford (1977: 68); cf. also Van Buuren (1988: 28)). For comparison, in Tohono O'odham, a language spoken along the Mexico/Arizona border, women use pulmonic ingressive speech to express conversational intimacy (Hill and Zepeda 1999). The VELARIC air-stream mechanism, in which a small pocket of air is trapped in the mouth and moved ingressively at the same time as an articulatory movement takes place, is used in for example the 'tut-tut!' exclamation: an alveolar CLICK or two alveolar clicks. If the air-stream is egressive, but is generated by an upwards action of the larynx instead of pressure from the lungs, an EJECTIVE sound is produced. The occurrence of ejectives in English has been noted informally for many years – especially in some Northern English and Scottish accents in certain word-final positions as the realization of /p, t, k/ – but to date a full-scale sociolinguistic study of their occurrence is lacking (cf. Ashby and Maidment 2005: 107). If the larynx is depressed at the same time as an articulation is made, the resulting sound is an IMPLOSIVE, or, with simultaneous vibration of the vocal folds, a VOICED IMPLOSIVE. Such sounds are restricted to certain pathological forms of speech, e.g. types of dysfluency. On clinical phonetics, see e.g. Ball and Duckworth (1996).

3.3   *Laryngeal modifications to the air-stream*

The vocal folds lie approximately horizontally in the larynx, and can move into a variety of positions by the action of the air-stream beneath them (SUBGLOTTAL pressure), as well as the innervation patterns of the muscles within the folds. For an understanding of how the sounds [s] and [z] differ in words like <fussy> and <fuzzy>, it is sufficient to appreciate that in the first sound the vocal folds remain relatively wide apart, whereas in the second they come close together and vibrate. (The vibration can be felt by touching the thyroid cartilage with the finger.) The [s] of <fussy> is VOICELESS, the [z] of <fuzzy> VOICED. These two possibilities are STATES OF THE GLOTTIS – but see below on PHONATION types. The acoustic consequences (especially spectral tilt) of the anatomical differences between the vocal folds of males and females have been discussed recently by Chuang and Hanson (1999); for recent work on modeling the aerodynamics and acoustics of phonation, see Zhang et al. (2002).

In the production of the 'GLOTTAL STOP' (more accurately, the GLOTTAL PLOSIVE), the vocal folds are the means whereby the air-stream is completely obstructed – they come together totally and momentarily block the air-stream. As a result, they cannot be used in this particular context to participate in a phonemic distinction between voiced and voiceless. (For details of the use of the glottal plosive in English, see below section 4.3.)

3.4   *Phonation types*

A variety of different settings of the vocal folds are possible, far more than is suggested by the descriptions above of 'voiceless' and 'voiced.' The term PHONATION TYPES (sometimes described as VOICE QUALITIES, but see section 9) is used to designate these various possibilities: see Catford (1977) for details. CREAK (sometimes called VOCAL FRY) is the slow irregular vibration of the front end of the vocal folds, and is extremely common in many accents of English world-wide, both in male and female speakers. WHISPER results from a narrowing of the vocal folds. BREATH involves the vocal folds being relatively wide apart, with a relatively high volume-velocity of air. Various combinations of these, with a range of values, are used in English: e.g. a voice that is moderately creaky, but also slightly whispery and slightly breathy. The VENTRICULAR FOLDS, which lie above the vocal folds and the laryngeal ventricles, create what can best be described as a 'rasping' sound. They are used in certain specific contexts – e.g. a sudden shout of anger. For a fuller discussion of phonation types and their uses, in both 'normal' and 'emotional' speech, see Laver (1980), Nolan (1983), Klatt and Klatt (1990), Gobl and Ní Chasaide (2003).

The larynx can move vertically within the neck. Some speakers habitually keep it in a relatively high position, others, conversely, in a relatively low position; and yet others have it in approximately a mid-point position. The particular SETTING of the larynx plays a part in creating a speaker's VOICE QUALITY: see below, section 9. Certain vertical and forward-tilting movements of the larynx, usually more noticeable in male than female speakers, derive from necessary adjustments to the air-flow associated with the pitch (F0) of a sound (Honda et al. (1999)).

4   Consonant Sounds

All consonant sounds involve some degree of obstruction or obstructions to the air-stream. The obstruction is specified by MANNER OF ARTICULATION (the type of obstruction) and the PLACE OF ARTICULATION (the location of the obstruction within the vocal tract. For example, the initial sounds in the words <mat>, <bat>, <sat>, <yes> illustrate different types of manner: NASAL, PLOSIVE, FRICATIVE, APPROXIMANT respectively. Other manners are: AFFRICATE <chase> and LATERAL <let>. For some speakers of English, the <r> of <rat> is a TAP or a TRILL. For an extended discussion of the taxonomies of consonant sounds, which reaches conclusions, some of which are different from those of the IPA, see Laver (1994: 119–58).

4.1   *Places of articulation*

On the IPA Chart, there are altogether 16 places of articulation, of which at least 8 are used in accents of English. Some accents do not use RETROFLEX and/or UVULAR sounds, and LABIAL-PALATAL, ALVEOLO-PALATAL, PHARYNGEAL, and EPIGLOTTAL sounds are not found in English – except sometimes in the speech of young children or certain types of speech pathology.

Examples

- BILABIAL (= using both lips): <pan>, <ban>, <man>
- LABIODENTAL (= using the lower lip and upper central incisor teeth): <fish>, <living>, <red> (for some speakers)
- DENTAL (= using the upper central incisor teeth): <thigh>, <thy>
- ALVEOLAR (= using the alveolar ridge): <ten>, <den>, <Len>, <send>, <Zen>, <net>, (for some speakers) <red>
- POSTALVEOLAR (= using the rear edge of the alveolar ridge): (for some speakers) <red>
- PALATOALVEOLAR (= using the rear edge of the alveolar ridge and the front part of the hard palate): <chain>, <Jane>; cf. with the postalveolar articulation of (for some speakers) <train> and <drain>
- RETROFLEX (= using the tongue tip and blade curled back underneath the hard palate): (for some speakers) <red>, <first>
- PALATAL (= using the hard palate): <yes>, <queue>
- VELAR (= using the soft palate): <cat>, <get>, <sing>
- UVULAR (= using the rear part of the soft palate and the uvula): (for some speakers) <price>, <bring>

- GLOTTAL (= using the vocal folds as the two articulators): (for most speakers) <u>h</u>elp>, (for some speakers) <tha<u>t</u>>, <i<u>t</u> is>
- LABIAL-VELAR (= using two places of articulation simultaneously: bilabial and velar): <<u>w</u>eather>, <<u>wh</u>at>

4.2   Primary and secondary articulations

The lateral sound in the word <let> involves the tip and/or blade of the tongue touching the alveolar ridge (or close by), with one or both rims lowered, such that the air-stream exits from the mouth over the rims, not the mid-line, of the tongue. Such a description captures only one, albeit a major, part of the configuration of the tongue's surface. The front of the tongue might, for example, be simultaneously raised towards the hard palate. An additional positioning of, in this case, part of the tongue constitutes a SECONDARY ARTICU-LATION. The term PRIMARY ARTICULATION refers to the place and manner of articulation of a consonant sound. Secondary articulations are discussed below.

4.3   Plosives

A plosive sound involves a momentary complete obstruction to the air-stream, which concludes with an 'explosive' element: cf. the [p], [t] and [k] sounds in <<u>p</u>in>, <<u>t</u>in>, <<u>k</u>in>. There are six plosive phonemes in English, although the number of sounds which realize the six runs to well over twenty. The three plosives /p/, /t/, and /k/ share certain characteristics – apart from the fact that they are all voiceless – namely the way in which the pressurized air-stream created by the total obstruction is released. (An aerodynamic model of how a bilabial plosive is made is discussed in Pelorson et al. 1997). In many accents of English, the word <pepper> /'pɛpə(r)/, with emphasis on the initial syllable, is pronounced with different [p] sounds: the first /p/ is ASPIRATED, the second UNASPIRATED. The difference lies in the timing of the onset of voicing in the following vowel sound. After the first [p], there is a discernible delay, during which air continues to flow from the vocal tract before the voicing of the vowel sound begins; in the second [p] there is no, or hardly any, delay. The first [p] is said to have a VOICE-ONSET TIME (VOT) of roughly 100 milliseconds (i.e. a tenth of a second). The IPA diacritic for aspiration, [ʰ], reveals nothing about the type of VOT. A more informative articulatory/phonatory notation of the first /p/ in <pepper> would be [pɛ̥].

Various studies have been conducted into VOT values in particular accents of English. For British English, the major one is Docherty (1992), which examines in detail the VOT values of plosives and fricatives of several male speakers of English English. A preliminary study of adult American English speakers classified according to racial type and gender reveals durational differences of VOT (Ryalls et al. 1997). More recently, attention has begun to focus on VOT patterns in children's speech according to age and sex: see e.g. Koenig (2000), Whiteside and Marshall (2001). A consequence of some adult speakers of

English having relatively short VOT values in their accents is that they may regard the second sound in a word like <spin> to be a [b], not a [p]: i.e. [sbɪn]; similarly, [sdɪk] <stick> and [sguːl] <school>. A minimal pair like <discussed/ disgust> may therefore be neutralized or almost neutralized.

Aspiration of the voiced plosives /b, d, g/ is rare, and when it occurs its duration is usually only about 10 milliseconds – which is scarcely perceptible auditorily. Instead, it is the DEVOICING of these plosives which claims attention. In certain contexts, e.g. utterance-initial and utterance-final position, the phonemes may not be fully voiced. In a word such as <big>, said in isolation, the /b/ may have a positive VOT; in the /g/, the voicing may end before the articulators have separated. The retention acoustically and perceptually of the distinction between words such as <pick> and <pig> will depend on the interplay of other factors, especially the amount of respiratory effort expended in their production, and the lengths of the sounds and the vowel sounds immediately preceding them.

These examples above illustrate what is technically POST-ASPIRATION, i.e. the onset of voicing after a specific time-interval. The opposite phenomenon, PRE-ASPIRATION, is the cessation of voicing in a vowel preceding a plosive (and sometimes other sounds, e.g. fricatives): for example, the word <cat> pronounced in such a way that the /a/ is not voiced throughout. Accents of English traditionally associated by geography with Celtic languages (e.g. Irish) often reflect this phonetic feature. Indeed, a word like <cat> might be pronounced as [ka̯a̯t] (= [kʰaʰt]) with post-aspiration and pre-aspiration in the same word. Studies so far have shown that pre-aspiration of voiceless plosives is more widespread in the UK than had previously been assumed: it occurs with some speakers from at least Newcastle, Middlesborough, and Hull – see e.g. Docherty and Foulkes (1999). In certain cases, the speaker's sex and age will determine the amount of pre-aspiration.

A relatively slow release of a plosive, especially a voiceless one (/p, t, k/), produces a brief, and sometimes weak, fricative at the end of the sound. The word <time> for example may be pronounced with an initial [tˢ] – where the superscript [s] indicates a short [s] sound immediately following the release of the [t]. AFFRICATION (see also under AFFRICATE below) is heard in many accents of English, but especially those of the South East of England. Here a continuum can be set up, extending from marked affrication in Cockney, through moderate in Estuary English, and relatively slight in other regional accents of the South East, to minimal in RP.

When two plosives occur in sequence (e.g. the /pt/ sequence in <wrapped> /rapt/, or the /gd/ sequence in <bagged> /bagd/), the first of the two is very likely to be released either just before the second, or simultaneously with it: this constitutes DELAYED or MASKED RELEASE. In a word like <midnight>, said at a normal conversational speed, the end of the /d/ anticipates the required lowering of the soft palate for the following nasal [n] sound, and the pressurized air-stream leaves the vocal tract through the nasal cavities, not the mouth: NASAL RELEASE. Nasal release occurs across word-boundaries too: e.g.

mark>. It also occurs in utterance-final position in certain styles of speaking: for example, in informal speech an utterance ending with a voiceless plosive (e.g. the /k/ in the word <mark>) may have a nasally released sound: in this particular case, [kⁿ] rather than simply [k].

/t/ and /d/, when followed directly by /l/, are usually released LATER-ALLY: i.e. the pressurized air exits over the rims of the tongue – in anticipation of the following /l/. Examples are: <that light> and <bad light>. However, if syllable-final /t/ is pronounced as the glottal plosive [ʔ], there is no possibility of lateral release. The use of /tl/ and/dl/ for syllable-initial /kl/ and /gl/, as in the phrase <clean gloves> (pronounced as though it were written <tlean dloves>) is now very rare.

The places of articulation associated with the plosives are traditionally BILABIAL, ALVEOLAR, and VELAR. There are, however, several subtleties. For example, the /p/ in <cupful> may be LABIODENTAL (= using the lower lip and upper front teeth); the /t/ in <eighth> (/eɪtθ/) and the /d/ of <width> may be DENTAL (= using the upper front teeth); the /t/ and /d/ in <try> and <dry> may be POSTALVEOLAR (= using the very back of the alveolar ridge where it merges with the hard palate). Intervocalic and syllable-final /t/ in certain accents tends in informal speech at least to be GLOTTAL (see also next paragraph). The /k/ and /g/ of <keen> and <geese> may be PALATAL, compared with the /k/ of <corn> and the /g/ of <got>.

GLOTTALLING and (PRE-)GLOTTALIZATION need to be distinguished. The former is the use of the glottal plosive in place of, typically, post-vocalic /t/ (e.g. <what it is> pronounced as [wɒʔ ɪʔ ɪz]) but also, for some speakers, post-vocalic /p/ and /k/ (e.g. <rap music>). (PRE-)GLOTTALIZATION is the insertion of a glottal plosive in front of another sound, sometimes for emphasis: cf. [ʔtɛn] *versus* [tɛn], [ðaʔt] *versus* [ðaʔ] and [ðat], [ʔəʊ] *versus* [əʊ]. A series of studies over the last 15 years has highlighted the intricate sociolinguistic and stylistic factors determining glottalling and pre-glottalization in several accents of British English: Aberdeenshire (Marshall 2003), Bolton (Shorrocks 1988), Cardiff (Mees 1987, Mees and Collins 1999), Glasgow (Stuart-Smith 1999), Middlesborough (Llamas 2000), RP in general (Fabricius 2002a), Tyneside (Trousdale 2002). A study of the same in non-specific American English is Dilley et al. (1996). In some Yorkshire varieties of English, the glottal plosive is also used as a realization of the definite article <the> (Jones 2002).

4.4 *Fricatives*

A FRICATIVE is a sound in which there is audible friction or turbulence: for example the /s/ in the word <sat> or the /v/ in <living>. The number of fricative phonemes varies between 6 and 11, depending on the accent. The 'full' set consists of: /f/ <fine>, /v/ <vine>, /θ/ <thigh>, /ð/ <thy>, /s/ <loose>, /z/ <lose>, /ʃ/ <fission>, /ʒ/ <vision>, /x/ <loch> (cf. <lock>), /ʍ/ <whine> (cf. <wine>), /h/ <head>. Speakers of English English are unlikely to have the last two, /x/ and /ʍ/, whereas many (but not all) Scottish English and Irish English speakers will. Some accents of English English, together with some individual speakers regardless of their linguistic origin, rarely use /θ/ and /ð/: the classic example is Cockney English English (cf. Wells 1982: 328). Most speakers of English in Ireland maintain a distinction between e.g. <thigh> and <tie>, <thy> and <die/dye>, but the 'fricatives' may be dental plosives (contrasting with alveolar plosives). The intervocalic /t/in a word like <later> in some accents (particularly certain forms of Irish English) is realized as a voiceless alveolar approximant (sometimes described as a voiceless alveolar slit fricative), and symbolized in various ways, usually as [ṯ] or [ṭ] (cf. Wells 1982: 429).

The type of stricture, i.e. spatial relationship between the articulators, in /f/ and /v/can vary depending on the speaker's dentition: for some, there is a small gap between the lower lip and upper teeth; for others, the friction is created by air passing through any small interstices (gaps) between the upper teeth. The /s/ phoneme can be described as a voiceless alveolar fricative, but there are a number of variables which determine the precise type of sound used, especially the position, length, depth, and angle of the narrow air-channel between the articulators, and the possibility of the air-stream, once it has passed the alveolar stricture, being deflected to some degree by the central incisors (both upper and lower) and/or the lower lip. The traditional distinction between a 'dorsal' [s] (with the tongue-tip behind the lower front teeth) and an 'apical' [s] (with the tongue-tip behind the upper front teeth) is inadequate to characterize the sometimes subtle differences between types of /s/ in English. Studies, such as those by Stuart-Smith et al. (2003), have focused attention on the precise articulatory configurations of different forms of /s/, together with sociolinguistic explanations for the differences.

The POSTALVEOLAR (in pre-1989 IPA terminology, PALATOALVEOLAR) fricatives /ʃ/ and /ʒ/ are similar to /s/ and /z/ in that their place of articulation can vary, together with any accompanying LABIALIZATION (= lip-rounding, or lip-protrusion) or PALATALIZATION (= raising of the front of the tongue towards the hard palate) (two types of SECONDARY ARTICULATION): cf. Catford 1988: 89–90, 2001: 85–6.

The voiceless velar fricative /x/ occurs mainly in non-English British English accents, e.g. Scottish English and Irish English, in words such as <loch>, <dreich> and <ach>, and in names – e.g. <Achray>. The precise place of articulation can vary: it is usually further forward (PRE-VELAR or even PALATAL) in <dreich>, but further back, sometimes UVULAR, in <loch>.

The traditional, and IPA, designation of /h/ is that it is a voiceless glottal fricative. The degree of friction is variable: for many speakers the sound is an approximant and equivalent to a voiceless vowel sound whose tongue-shape anticipates that of the following voiced vowel. The word <hand>, for example, though phonemically /hand/, is more realistically notated phonetically as [ḁand]. Different allophones of /h/ will therefore occur: cf. the different types of /h/ in <ʜand>, <ʜeat>, <ʜoot>. Intervocalically, /h/ is sometimes a breathy voiced version of the following vowel sound: cf. <beʜind> with <ʜind>, <perʜaps> with <ʜappen>.

The only fricative which uses two simultaneous places of articulation is /ʍ/, a so-called voiceless LABIAL-VELAR sound. Variants occur: a voiceless velarized bilabial fricative [ɸˠ] and a voiceless labialized velar fricative [xʷ].

4.5   Affricates

An AFFRICATE is a plosive followed immediately by a fricative at the same place of articulation. In the words <chess> and <Jack>, the initial consonants are postalveolar plosives and postalveolar fricatives. Note that the IPA symbolization [ʧ] and [ʤ] obscures the fact that both plosive elements are postalveolar, not alveolar; for this reason, some phoneticians use non-IPA [č] and [ǰ] for these sounds.

4.6   Taps, flaps, and trills

In many American pronunciations of a word like <later>, the intervocalic /t/ is an alveolar TAP: a sound in which the tip and/or blade of the tongue makes a very brief and loose contact with the alveolar ridge. Some British and Irish accents use the same, or a similar, tap realization of /t/ in this intervocalic context. A series of taps constitutes a TRILL. Though not used as extensively as the tap, it can be heard for example in some Scottish accents as the realization of /r/ in certain phonological contexts. A FLAP differs from a tap in that the movement of the tongue does not involve the tongue returning to its starting-point (as in a tap). The retroflex flap can be heard, for example in a word like <bring> or <rain>, in some accents of British English which are influenced by particular Indian languages (e.g. Hindi).

4.7   Approximants

If the gap between the articulators in a fricative sound is increased slightly, the turbulence ('friction') gives way to a LAMINAR (= smooth) air-stream. The /j/ of <yet> and the /w/ of <wet> are typical APPROXIMANTS. Like /h/ (see above), they are best considered, from the point of view of their production, to be vowel sounds, involving a *brief* trajectory movement from a vowel ([ɪ] in the case of <yes> and [ʊ] in the case of <wet>) to the following vowel: hence [ɪɛt] and [ʊɛt]. They differ from vowels proper primarily in length: the duration of the /w/ of <wet> and the /j/ of <yet> is approximately one-third that of the /ɛ/ vowel. Some realizations of these two approximants are fricative: cf. /j/ in <queue> with /j/ in <you>; and /w/ in <quick> with /w/ in <wick>. /w/, though classified as labial-velar, usually involve a degree of labialization: hence, more accurately, LABIALIZED LABIAL-VELAR.

4.8   Lateral

The lateral phoneme /l/ can be classified as a type of approximant (hence LATERAL APPROXIMANT) or, more traditionally, simply as a LATERAL. In English, there is only one lateral phoneme, but there are a variety of realizations. For many speakers, the sound is a voiced alveolar lateral approximant [l] – at least in syllable-initial position, although a voiced alveolar lateral TAP is sometimes heard. As the second element in a syllable, in e.g. the word <clean>, the realization may be an approximant (sometimes voiceless, then becoming voiced) or a brief voiceless lateral fricative [ɬ] becoming a voiced lateral approximant, or a voiceless, then voiced, lateral tap. Not surprisingly, as these examples show, there is considerable variation in the precise phonetic qualities of /l/ in different accents of English. The insertion of an /l/ in a word ('intrusive /l/') comparable to the insertion of an /r/ ('intrusive /r/') is heard in some accents of southern Pennsylvania: e.g. <drawing> pronounced as if it were spelled <drawling> (Gick 2002).

Word-medially and/or syllable-finally (e.g in <silly> and <hill>), the lateral approximant may have a degree of secondary articulation: either VELARIZATION (= raising of the back of the tongue towards the soft palate) or PHARYN-GEALIZATION (= retraction of the root of the tongue towards the pharynx). Both types are traditionally described as 'dark' [l]'s. For some speakers, syllable-final /l/ is PALATALIZED (= with the front of the tongue raised towards the hard palate; 'clear' [l]). For others, the sound is not a lateral approximant in this position, but a vowel sound – as a result of L-VOCALIZATION. The precise quality may vary somewhat from speaker to speaker, but a realization near to a back close-mid unrounded vowel is typical; see in particular the discussion in Tollfree (1999: 174–175). Foulkes and Docherty (1999) provides information about recent findings on L-VOCALIZATION in British and Irish English accents. See also ch. 27, this volume, 'Phonological Vairiation: A Global Perspective.'

4.9   Nasals

For most speakers of English, there are three nasal phonemes: /m/, /n/ and /ŋ/. Some accents in the north-west of England, whilst using the [ŋ] sound as an allophone of /n/, have only two nasal phonemes: such speakers pronounce <sin> as [sɪn] and <sing> as [sɪŋg]. Voiceless or partially voiceless, rather than voiced, allophones can sometimes be heard after /s/: cf. <smile> and <mile>, <snow> and <no/know>. The labiodental nasal occurs, for some speakers, in the environment of labiodental fricatives: e.g. <symphony>, <brimful>. A dental nasal is often used before a dental fricative: e.g. <tenth>, <run then>.

4.10   The sounds of /r/

The consonant phoneme which exhibits the most degree of phonetic variation is /r/. (The *distribution* of /r/ is a matter of phonology: those accents which permit only prevocalic /r/ (e.g. many accents of English English, Australasian English and South African English) are NON-RHOTIC. The others, which permit pre-vocalic, pre-consonantal, and pre-pausal /r/, are RHOTIC. The term RHOTIC, however, is sometimes used in a different sense, as a cover-term for any type of 'r' sound.) The phonetic possibilities for /r/, depending on the speaker and the context in which /r/ occurs, include: voiced labiodental approximant [ʋ], voiced alveolar tap [ɾ], voiced alveolar trill [r], voiced postalveolar approximant [ɹ], voiced postalveolar fricative [ɹ], voiceless postalveolar fricative [ɹ̥], voiced retroflex approximant [ɻ], voiced retroflex flap [ɽ], voiced uvular fricative [ʁ], and voiceless uvular fricative [χ]. Of these, the commonest are the voiced postalveolar approximant [ɹ] and the voiced alveolar tap [ɾ]. The insertion of an /r/ into the pronunciation of a word, though not justified historically by the orthography, is now very common in many accents of non-rhotic British English. Examples of INTRUSIVE /r/ include <idea(r) of it>, <Ma(r) and Pa>, <law(r) and order>. There are only particular phonological contexts in which this can occur, namely after syllable-final /ə/, /ɑː/ and /ɔː/. Occasionally intrusive /r/ can be heard in rhotic accents: e.g. Scottish English <idea(r)>.

5   Vowel Sounds

5.1   *Describing vowel sounds*

By definition, a vowel sound, unlike a consonant sound, should offer no obstruction to the air-stream. As far back as the mid-nineteenth century, phoneticians have held to the view that two parameters govern the production of a vowel sound: the configuration of the tongue surface and the position and shaping of the lips. Due to the tongue's mobility and the fact that in almost all vowel sounds the tongue's upper surface assumes a convex shape, it has normally been found sufficient to plot the position of the highest part of the tongue along two axes: the horizontal and the vertical. The possible trajectories of the tongue in the production of vowel sounds then lead to the establishment of the so-called VOWEL-SPACE beneath the hard and soft palates, whose outer limits are represented in the CARDINAL VOWEL diagram. The latter provides not only a schema of the vowel-space, but also a set of auditory and articulatory *reference* points along those outer limits, similar to the principle of the cardinal points of a compass. There are 18 Cardinal Vowels, set up in the early 1900s by the English phonetician Daniel Jones. However, normally four additional vowels, as well as a set of non-Cardinal vowels, are added to the set (see the IPA Chart).

For descriptive purposes, and without reference to any instrumental data, it can be sufficient to consider vowels as having a consistently convex tongue shape, but imaging evidence (e.g. MRIs) sometimes reveals a flat, even a concave, shape to the tongue's surface, especially with more open vowels. Additionally, the traditional perspective of a mid-line sagittal view of the vocal tract when describing the tongue's shape in the production of vowels conceals the part played by the configuration of the tongue surface in the lateral dimension. Current research, using primarily MRI data, is adjusting this traditional two-dimensional concept of vowel production and vowel description: one such study, with speakers of Swedish but relevant for an understanding of vowel production in English, is Engwall (2003).

5.2   Categories of vowels

Vowel sounds are categorized as either monophthongal (= produced with no tongue and/or lip movement within the same syllable) or diphthongal (= produced with some tongue and/or lip movement within the same syllable). Examples of each are: the [a] of <h<u>a</u>t> and the [aɪ] of <h<u>eigh</u>t>. Two symbols, as in [aɪ], signal that the sound is diphthongal. Further classifications of diphthongs can be established, based on the direction in which the tongue moves (e.g. FRONT CLOSING as in [haɪt] (<height>), CENTERING as in [hɪə] (<hear>, <here>), etc. A third possibility, a triphthongal pronunciation, is found in e.g. pronunciations of the <i> of <fire> (/faɪə/) of various non-rhotic accents.

5.3   Other aspects of vowels

Traditionally, vowels have been described as being either short, half-long or long: for example, short in SIT [sɪt], half-long in SID [sɪˑd], and long in SEED [siːd]. Instrumental studies have provided the physical evidence (expressed in milliseconds) on which such perceptions are based, but have revealed, unsurprisingly, a far greater range of vowel lengths than the traditional threefold distinction suggests. The association of vowel-length with particular phonological and morphological features (e.g. the SCOTTISH VOWEL-LENGTH RULE) is dealt with elsewhere (ch. 17, this volume, 'English Phonology and Morphology').

   Accompanying a vowel sound may be NASALIZATION (= lowering of the soft palate such that the air-stream flows simultaneously through the nasal cavities and mouth): cf. the vowel sound in <m<u>a</u>n> with that in <b<u>a</u>d>. The former vowel is likely to have a perceptible degree of nasalization because of its position between two nasal consonants. Nasalization can also be a feature of VOICE QUALITY (see section 9).

   Standard textbooks on English phonetics (e.g. Cruttenden, 2001: 105–43) provide illustrations of vowel locations on the Cardinal Vowel chart, and show that there are few areas of the VOWEL-SPACE that are not used in at least one major accent of English. To coin a phrase, there are no 'deaf-spots.' This is borne out, too, by acoustic plots of the first two formants of vowels (F1 and F2), broadly equivalent to tongue location in the articulatory/auditory vowel-space. Indeed, the availability of software for acoustic analysis, especially for F1/F2 plots, has now made the accurate calculation of the relative position of vowels within the vowel-space considerably easier to achieve than by using the traditional articulatory-auditory comparison of a vowel sound with its nearest Cardinal Vowel reference-point(s). Even so, much recent work on English pronunciation in which vowels have been the focus of attention has been concerned mainly with phonological questions, especially phonemic systems and the nature of phonetic change over time, rather than with precise details of realization: see e.g. Foulkes and Docherty (1999); see also ch. 27, this volume, 'Phonological Variation in English: A Global Perspective.'

6   Acoustic Phonetics

The orientation and terminology of acoustic phonetics is quite different from that of articulatory phonetics, and derives from classical physics. However, studying the relationships between acoustic and articulatory/phonatory data is one of the expected tasks of the phonetician. The task has been made much easier in recent years by the development of various pieces of appropriate software.

Sound is the audible patterned movement of millions of air molecules. The resulting SOUND WAVES can be of different types. Comparing the sound waves of the vowel sound [a] and the consonant sound [t], one can establish three significant ways in which they can differ: PERIODICITY, FREQUENCY, and AMPLITUDE. In [a] there is a PERIODIC, i.e. regular, repetition of the pattern of airflow through the larynx and the rest of the vocal tract; in [t], the release of the air in a sudden burst is not repeated, and hence the production of [t] creates an APERIODIC sound wave. In [a], but not [t], the sound wave repeats itself many times, even though a listener will hear it as a single, unbroken sound. [a] repeats itself at a certain FREQUENCY, i.e. so many times per second. Thirdly, [a] is louder than [t] – the result of the greater pressure generated by the air molecules: the AMPLITUDE of [a] is therefore greater than that of [t]. Frequency correlates well, if not always precisely, with the PITCH of a sound; amplitude with LOUDNESS.

Most repetitive sounds are COMPLEX, in that they are made up of a series of waves which are inherently regular in terms of frequency and amplitude – SINE waves: for example, the sound [a]. Some simple arithmetic, however, reveals the relationships between the sine waves: a complex wave is created by a series of sine waves. The sine wave with the lowest frequency is called the FUNDAMENTAL FREQUENCY, and the frequencies of the other sine waves are whole-number multiples of the fundamental. Thus, if the fundamental frequency of a complex wave is 100 Hz (i.e. the wave repeats itself 100 times a second), the other sine waves will be 200 Hz, 300 Hz, 400 Hz, etc. Particularly in male speech, there can be upwards of 50 identifiable sine waves making up a complex wave. The individual waves within the complex wave are the HARMONICS. Identifying the constituent sine waves of a complex wave is carried out by FOURIER ANALYSIS. Software reveals relatively easily the results of this process in the form of SOUND SPECTROGRAMS.

The fundamental frequency is generated by the vocal folds: for example, if they vibrate 200 times a second, then the frequency value of the resulting wave-form will also be 200 Hz. However, due to the shape and length of the vocal tract between the vocal folds and the lips and/or nostrils, certain parts of the complex wave will have their amplitudes increased (or decreased) by the principle of RESONANCE. The FORMANTS of, principally, vowel-sounds are the areas within the range of frequency where resonance has increased the amplitudes of the sound-waves. For practical purposes, one can envisage a direct connection between the shaping of the vocal tract for e.g. vowel sounds, and the occurrence of formants. In vowels where the tongue body effectively divides the vocal tract into two cavities, F_1, the first formant, is associated with the pharynx; F_2, the second formant, with the forward part of the mouth. Thereafter, the relationship is less obvious with the remaining formants – and in vowels there can be up to five. Numerical values for formants (usually in Hz) should be interpreted with caution: they normally refer to the point in a sound where the speech organs have achieved a (near-)stationary point; the remaining parts of the sound, where the speech organs modify their position towards and thereafter away from this point, create a changing series of numerical values.

Consonant sounds generally vary from vowels in their acoustic composition. Plosives are characterized not by formants but by a period of silence, followed by a NOISE-BURST. Taps, flaps, and trills reveal a similar type of pattern. Different fricatives have specific areas of increased amplitude at particular frequencies. Approximants (including lateral approximants) and nasals share with vowels the occurrence of formants.

Expositions of the main features of acoustic phonetics for English can be found in Fry (1979), Ladefoged (1962; 2nd edn. 1996), Olive et al. (1993), Stevens (1998).

7 Stress and Accentuation

The words <billow> and <below> have emphasis on the first and second syllables respectively; in other respects, their pronunciation is very similar. The source of the emphasis is a combination of activities, particularly an increase in the amount of respiratory effort expended on the syllable, and the choice of pitch pattern. Restricting the word STRESS to an increase in respiratory effort, we can say that the stressed syllable is different in the two words. ACCENTUATION refers more broadly to the various factors, especially the choice of intonation pattern, that cause a syllable (like the <bi-> or the <low> in the example above) to 'stand out' for a listener. See further ch. 19, this volume, 'Intonation.'

7.1 Pitch

In most cases, pitch is the perceptual equivalent of the speed at which the vocal folds vibrate, and can be expressed in terms of Hz (or an alternative numerical scale). Thus, if the vocal folds vibrate 150 times a second (150 Hz) and then vibrate 190 times a second, the pitch will be heard as having risen. All speakers operate within a particular personal pitch-range (sometimes called a TESSITURA), with adult male speakers having generally lower Hz values than adult female speakers. Changes of pitch can be displayed visually by software. Alternative methods are the use of musical values (e.g. by setting up a nominal pitch range of 12 semitones and noting the alterations in pitch within that scale), or describing impressionistically the alterations in pitch, usually syllable by syllable. See further ch. 19, this volume, 'Intonation.'

8 Rhythm

The study of speech rhythm has been a relatively neglected area – except in the context of metrics and poetry (but cf. Roach 2003). Rhythm may be considered to be the temporal organization of accented and unaccented syllables, based on the lengths of the syllables and the occurrence of an isochronous or near-isochronous pulse or beat. Thus, a sentence like <When did they say they'd come> could be said with a variety of rhythmical patterns (with emphasis on <When>, <they> and <come>, or on <When> and <say>, or on <did>, <say>, <come>, etc. The lengths of the individual syllables can be calculated, either using musical conventions (e.g. crotchets/quarter-notes, etc.) or instrumental means (see next paragraph), or impressionistically according to three possible syllable-lengths: short, medium, and long. A classic example of a rhythmical contrast in RP and some other accents of British English is the phrase /teɪkgreɪtələʌndən/. Depending on the lengths of the syllables /greɪ/ and /tə/, the meaning is either <Take Grey to London> or <Take Greater London>.

A considerably more sophisticated method of analysis is to measure the lengths of syllables in milliseconds, and, by focusing on the differences in duration of contiguous syllables, to apply a variability index to compute at least something of what native listeners regard as the rhythmic patterns of speech. For example, a study of Singaporean English and British English speakers (Deterding 2001) found significant differences between the two varieties, which can be associated to a limited extent with the traditional distinction between syllable-timed rhythm in Singaporean English and stress-timed rhythm in British English.

9 Voice Qualities

Every speaker uses a systematized set of phonological and phonetic choices, but all are dependent on a series of particular long-term SETTINGS of his/her vocal tract – the source of the speaker's VOICE QUALITY. (This use of the term should be distinguished from 'voice quality' in the sense of 'phonation type.') The settings may be associated with a particular regional and/or social accent of English, or else, as far as one can tell, be idiosyncratic. Thus, for some speakers, the tongue is typically 'anchored' further forward in the mouth; for others further back. For some speakers, the lips are normally unrounded, and, even when a rounded segment is required by the phonology, the result may not be a fully rounded articulation. For some speakers, the vocal folds always generate an element of creak when the person is speaking; for others, there may be no creak, but perhaps some breathiness, or some other phonatory activity. The tendency for the various muscle groups which control the position and movements of the speech organs to operate within a specific set of limits lies at the basis of the settings. In general, the analysis of voice qualities is a relatively new area of phonetic enquiry, having developed significantly only since the early 1980s. For a detailed description of settings in relation to voice qualities, see Laver (1980), Nolan (1983).

The vertical position of the larynx and the typical settings of the vocal folds (and sometimes the ventricular folds too) contribute to a speaker's voice quality. The position of the soft palate might be thought to be an either/or choice dependent on the phonology (NASAL consonant /m/ versus ORAL consonant /b/, etc.). In fact, for some speakers, an oral phoneme might always be realized with some degree of nasalization; the converse applies too: a nasal phoneme being realized with limited nasal air-flow due to the near-closure of the soft palate against the posterior wall of the pharynx. The settings of the tongue in relation to a nominal 'neutral' position are various: for example DENTALIZED (= with the tongue habitually anchored further forward towards the lower front teeth), VELARIZED (= with the center of gravity of the tongue further back, and further up towards the soft palate), etc. There are several general positions or ranges of movement for the lips: from spread, with little vertical distance between them, to fully rounded and with a relatively large vertical gap between them. Finally, the position of the LOWER JAW, the MANDIBLE, can affect a person's voice quality: the jaw might be typically lowered or raised, fronted or backed.

Examples of the descriptive conventions applied to the analysis of different speakers include: *Speaker A* – 'moderately tense, slightly lowered larynx, extremely nasal, extremely creaky voice'; Speaker B – 'slightly raised larynx, slightly denasal, slightly whispery voice, with slight labiodentalization, slightly protruded open rounding and intermittent creak' (Laver 1980). Unfortunately, our present state of knowledge of voice qualities across accents of English does not permit wide-ranging generalizations to be made, based on regional, social, age, gender, and other factors. Thus, the study of voice qualities lags behind sociophonetic studies of segmental and, to a lesser extent, other non-segmental features.

10   Phonetics since the 1950s

A comparison since the 1950s of the state of phonetic knowledge about English and the theoretical and instrumental bases on which that knowledge rests shows the remarkable progress that has been achieved. In the 1950s, the standard study of British English phonetics was Daniel Jones' *Outline of English Phonetics* (Jones 1956). The work, orginally published in 1918, focuses almost exclusively on RP – though without being over-prescriptive; and some instrumental data is quoted. In the 1960s, the publication of Gimson's *Introduction to the Pronunciation of English* (1st edn. 1962) signaled a change of direction: a firmer theoretical basis (phonology *versus* phonetics), the introduction of some acoustic data, a slightly wider sociolinguistic viewpoint, and some consideration of historical periods of English in phonological and phonetic terms. The intervening years have seen a much wider sociolinguistic perspective being applied to the study of English phonetics, signaled for example by the major three-volume publication by Wells (1982) on accents of English worldwide. Furthermore, there has been an acceleration in the use of experimental phonetic techniques, especially those for acoustic, aerodynamic, and imaging purposes, leading to much more detailed phonetic observations than was ever possible in earlier years. Finally, a considerable amount of information about phonetics is available on the www.

FURTHER READING

Since the 1990s, a number of introductory textbooks on phonetics (both general phonetics and the phonetics of English) have appeared. All cover essentially the same ground, but with slightly different emphases. In reverse chronological order, they include:

Ashby, Michael and Maidment, John (2005) *Introducing phonetic science.* Cambridge: Cambridge University Press.

Ladefoged, Peter (2004) *Vowels and consonants: an introduction to the sounds of language*, 2nd edn. Oxford: Blackwell Publishers (1st edn., 2001).

Collins, Beverley and Mees, Inger M. (2003) *Practical phonetics and phonology: a resource book for students.* London and New York: Routledge.

Catford, John C. (1988; 2001) *A practical introduction to phonetics*, 2nd edn. Oxford: Clarendon Press. Oxford: Oxford University Press (1st edn., 1988).

Ladefoged, Peter (2001) *A course in phonetics*, 4th edn. Fort Worth: Harcourt College Publishers (previous edns.: 1975, 1982, 1993).

Roach, Peter (2001) *Phonetics.* Oxford: Oxford University Press.

Ball, Martin J. and Rahilly, Joan (1999) *Phonetics: the science of speech.* London: Arnold.

Carr, Philip (1999) *English phonetics and phonology: an introduction.* Oxford: Blackwell.

Clark, John, and Yallop, Colin. (1995) *An introduction to phonetics and phonology*, 2nd edn. Oxford: Blackwell.

Compilations of more advanced studies on several aspects of phonetics are:

Hardcastle, William J. and Laver, John (1997) *The handbook of the phonetic sciences.* Oxford: Blackwell Publishers.

Windsor Lewis, Jack (ed.) (1995) *Studies in general and English phonetics: essays in honour of Professor J.D. O'Connor.* London and New York: Routledge.

Laver, John (1991) *The gift of speech: papers in the analysis of speech and voice.* Edinburgh: Edinburgh University Press.

Ramsaran, Susan (ed.) (1990) *Studies in the pronunciation of English: a commemorative volume in honour of A.C. Gimson.* London: Routledge.

Of the pronouncing dictionaries which use IPA, the following are recommended:

Wells, John C. (1990) *Longman pronunciation dictionary.* Harlow: Longman Group.

Upton, Clive, Kretzschmar, William A. Jr., and Konopka, Rafal (2001) *Oxford dictionary of pronunciation for current English.* Oxford: Oxford University Press.

Jones, Daniel, Roach, Peter, Hartman, James and Setter, Jane (2004) *English pronouncing dictionary* (with CD-rom). Cambridge: Cambridge University Press.

REFERENCES

Armstrong, Katherine F. (1939) *Aids to anatomy and physiology for nurses.* Ondon: Bailliere, Tindall, and Cox.

Ashby, Michael and Maidment, John (2005) *Introducing phonetic science.* Cambridge: Cambridge University Press.

Ball, Martin J. and Duckworth, Martin (1996) *Advances in clinical phonetics.* Amsterdam and Philadelphia: John Benjamins.

Catford, John C. (1977) *Fundamental problems in phonetics.* Edinburgh: Edinburgh University Press.

Catford, John C. (1988; 2001) *A practical introduction to phonetics*, 2nd edn. Oxford: Clarendon Press. Oxford: Oxford University Press (1st edn., 1988).

Chuang, Erika S. and Hanson, Helen M. (1999) Glottal characteristics of male speakers: acoustic correlates and comparison with female data. *Journal of the Acoustical Society of America* 106 (2), 1064–77.

Cruttenden, Alan (ed.) (2001) *Gimson's pronunciation of English*, 6th edn. London: Arnold; New York: Oxford University Press.

Deterding, David (2001) The measurement of rhythm: a comparison of Singapore and British English. *Journal of Phonetics* 29, 217–30.

Dilley, Laura, Shattuck-Hufnagel, Stefanie, and Ostendorff, Mari (1996) Glottalization of word-initial vowels as a function of prosodic structure. *Journal of Phonetics* 24 (4), 423–44.

Docherty, Gerard J. (1992) *Timing of voicing in British English obstruents.* Berlin: Foris Publications.

Docherty, Gerard J. and Foulkes, Paul (1999) Derby and Newcastle: instrumental phonetics and variationist studies. In Foulkes and Docherty (eds.), 47–71.

Engwall, Olov (2003) Combining MRI, EMA and EPG measurements in a three-dimensional tongue model. *Speech Communication* 41 (2–3), 303–29.

Fabricius, Anne (2002a) Ongoing change in modern RP: evidence from the disappearing stigma of t-glottalling. *English World-Wide* 23 (1), 115–36.

Fabricius, Anne (2002b) Weak vowels in modern RP: an acoustic study of happY-tensing and KIT/schwa shift. *Language Variation and Change* 14 (2), 211–38.

Foulkes, Paul and Docherty, Gerard (eds.) (1999) *Urban voices: Accent studies in the British Isles.* London: Arnold.

Fry, Dennis (1979) *The physics of speech.* Cambridge: Cambridge University Press.

Gick, Bryan (2002) The American intrusive /l/. *American Speech* 77 (2), 167–83.

Gick, Bryan, Minkang, A., and Whalen, Douglas H. (2002) MRI evidence for commonality in the post-oral articulations of English vowels and liquids. *Journal of Phonetics* 30 (3), 357–71.

Gimson, A. C. (2001) See Cruttenden (2001).

Gobl, Christer and Ní Chasaide, Ailbhe (2003) The role of voice quality in communicating emotion, mood and attitude. *Speech Communication* 40 (1–2), 189–212.

Hardcastle, William J. and Laver, John. (1997) *The handbook of the phonetic sciences.* Oxford: Blackwell Publishers.

Hayward, Katrina (2000) *Experimental phonetics.* Harlow: Pearson Education Limited.

Hill, Jane H. and Zepeda, Ofelia (1999) Language, gender and biology: pulmonic ingressive airstream in women's speech in Tohono O'odham. *Southwest Journal of Linguistics* 18 (1), 15–40.

Honda, Kiyoshi, Hiral, Hiroyuki, Masaki, Shinobu, and Shimada Yasuhiro (1999) Role of vertical larynx movement and cervical lordosis in F0 control. *Language & Speech* 42 (4), 401–11.

Hughes, Arthur and Trudgill, Peter (1979; 1987) *English accents and dialects: an introduction to social and regional varieties of British English.* London: Edward Arnold.

International Phonetic Association (1999) *Handbook of the International Phonetic Association: a guide to the use of the International Phonetic Alphabet.* Cambridge: Cambridge University Press.

Jones, Daniel (1956) *An outline of English phonetics,* 8th edn. Cambridge: W. Heffer & Sons Ltd.

Jones, Mark J. (2002) The origin of Definite Article Reduction in northern English dialects: evidence from dialect allomorphy. *English Language & Linguistics* 6 (2), 325–45.

Klatt, Laura C. and Klatt, Dennis H. (1990) Analysis, synthesis, and perception of voice quality variations among female and male talkers. *Journal of the Acoustical Society of America* 87 (2), 820–57.

Koening, Laura L. (2000) Laryngeal factors in voiceless consonant production in men, women and 5-year olds. *Journal of Speech, Language, and Hearing Research* 43 (5), 1211–22.

Kuehn, David P. and Moon, Jerald B. (1998) Velopharyngeal closure force and *levator veli palatini* activation levels in varying phonetic contexts. *Journal of Speech, Language, and Hearing Research* 41 (1), 51–62.

Ladefoged, Peter (1962; 1996) *Elements of acoustic phonetics,* 1st edn. Edinburgh: Edinburgh University Press. Chicago and London: University of Chicago Press (2nd edn., 1996).

Ladefoged, Peter and Everett, David (1996) The status of phonetic rareties. *Language* 72, 4, 794–800.

Laver, John (1980) *The phonetic description of voice quality.* Cambridge: Cambridge University Press.

Laver, John (1994) *Principles of phonetics.* Cambridge: Cambridge University Press.

Llamas, Carmen (2000) Middlesborough English: convergent and divergent trends in a "part of Britain with no identity." *Leeds Working Papers in Linguistics and Phonetics* 8, 123–48.

MacKenzie Beck, Janet (1997) Organic variation of the vocal apparatus. In Hardcastle and Laver (1997), 256–97.

Marshall, Jonathan (2003) The changing sociolinguistic status of the glottal stop in northeast Scottish English. *English World-Wide* 24 (1), 89–108.

Mees, Inger (1987) Glottal stop as a prestigious feature in Cardiff English. *English World-Wide* 8 (1), 25–39.

Mees, Inger and Collins, Beverley (1999) Cardiff: a real-time study of glottalisation. In Foulkes and Docherty, 185–202.

Nolan, Francis (1983) *The phonetic bases of speaker recognition.* Cambridge: Cambridge University Press.

Olive, Joseph P., Greenwood, Alice, and Coleman, John S. (1993) *Acoustics of American English speech: a dynamic approach.* New York: Springer.

Pelorson, Xavier, Hofmans, G. C. J., Ranucci, Massimo, and Bosch, R. C. M. (1997) On the fluid mechanics of bilabial plosives. *Speech Communication* 22 (2–3), 155–72.

Picard, Marc (1997) English flapping and the feature [vibrant]. *English Language & Linguistics* 1 (2), 285–94.

Roach, Peter (1987) Rethinking phonetic taxonomy. *Transactions of the Philological Society* 24–37.

Roach, Peter (ed.) (2003) *A bibliography of timing and rhythm in speech* [updated to 2 April 2003]: www.personal. rdg.ac.uk/~llsroach/peter.

Ryalls, John, Zipprer, Allison, and Baldauff, Penelope (1997) A preliminary investigation of the effects of gender and race on voice onset time. *Journal of Speech, Language, and Hearing Research* 40 (3), 642–5.

Shorrocks, Graham (1988) Glottalization and gemination in an English urban dialect. *Canadian Journal of Linguistics* 33 (1), 59–64.

Stevens, Kenneth N. (1998) *Acoustic phonetics.* Cambridge, MA and London: MIT Press.

Stone, Maureen (1997) Laboratory techniques for investigating speech articulation. In Hardcastle and Laver (1997), 11–32.

Stuart-Smith, Jane (1999) Glasgow: accent and voice quality. In Foulkes and Docherty, 203–22.

Stuart-Smith, Jane, Timmins, Claire, and Wrench, Alan (2003) Sex and gender in /s/ in Glaswegian. *Proceedings of the 14th International Congress of Phonetic Sciences*, Barcelona, 1851–4.

Tollfree, Laura (1999) South east London English: discrete *versus* continuous modelling of consonantal reduction. In Foulkes and Docherty, 163–84.

Trousdale, Graeme (2002) Variable ambisyllabicity. *English Language and Linguistics* 6 (2), 267–82.

Van Buuren, Luc (1988) Margaret Thatcher's pronunciation: an exercise in ear-training. *Journal of the International Phonetic Association* 18 (2), 26–38.

Wells, John C. (1982) *Accents of English.* 3 vols. Cambridge: Cambridge University Press.

Whiteside, S. P. and Marshall, J. (2001) Developmental trends in voice onset time: some evidence for sex differences. *Phonetica* 58 (3), 196–210.

Zhang, Cheng, Zhao, Wei, Frankel, Steven H., and Mongeau, Luc (2002) Computational aeroacoustics of phonation, Part II: effects of flow parameters and ventricular folds. *Journal of the Acoustical Society of America* 112 (5), 2147–54.

17 English Phonology and Morphology

RICARDO BERMÚDEZ-OTERO AND APRIL MCMAHON

1 Introduction

The title of this chapter poses a daunting challenge, since the morphophonology of present-day English is one of the most intensively studied areas in the whole of morphology and phonology. Indeed, as key innovations in phonological and morphological theory have been introduced, they have frequently been illustrated by means of case-studies from English: this is true not only for classical rule-based generative phonology (Chomsky and Halle 1968; henceforth *SPE*), but more recently for connectionist and dual-route approaches to inflection (Rumelhart and McClelland 1986; Pinker and Prince 1988) and for output-output correspondence within Optimality Theory (OT) (Benua 1995, 1997). It follows that we must define our aims somewhat narrowly.

First, then, this chapter focuses on interactions between phonology and morphology in present-day English and their implications for the shape of the morphology–phonology interface in natural language. Perforce, we disregard phonology–syntax interactions, although clearly some key facts and concepts in morphophonology have close phonosyntactic analogues. Our data are drawn from both British and American dialects, standard and vernacular, though obviously no variety is exhaustively described. We focus on facts that have figured prominently in the wider theoretical debate, but also pay some attention to phenomena that seem peculiar to English. Even the latter, however, underscore points of general relevance: as we shall see in section 3.5, for example, some of the idiosyncrasies of present-day English morphophonology are the product of historical contingencies; this illustrates how, when contending with the effects of diachrony, morphophonological theory routinely encounters historically conditioned facts that it can note but not explain.

From a theoretical viewpoint, we concentrate on major conceptions of the morphology–phonology interface, abstracting away from other dimensions of variation between theories. Wherever possible, therefore, our presentation is neutral between rule-based and constraint-based systems, with 'rule' simply meaning 'symbolic generalization' unless otherwise stated or required by context. We accordingly ignore the differences between rule-based Lexical Phonology and Morphology (LPM: e.g. Kaisse and Shaw 1985; Kiparsky 1982b, 1985) and Stratal OT (Bermúdez-Otero 1999, forthcoming; Kiparsky 1998, 2000; Orgun 1996), except where the choice of model has affected the demarcation of phonology, morphology, and the lexicon (section 2) or the application of concepts such as cyclicity and level segregation (section 3). The general aim of the chapter is to sift through the intricate debate (often highly esoteric and theory-internal) that surrounds English morphophonology and to identify key concepts and issues that deserve our continued attention, regardless of major shifts in the theoretical landscape.

2   The Division of Labour between Phonology, Morphology, and the Lexicon

2.1   The problem

We have thus far identified our main concern as being the interaction of morphology and phonology in present-day English, but the problem can only be formulated if we can first distinguish between (1) computations performed in the phonology, (2) computations performed in the morphology, and (3) lexical storage.

Here, however, the spectrum of opinion is extraordinarily wide. *SPE* did not countenance an independent morphological module and envisaged lexical storage as maximally economical, with all alternations derived via phonological rules. On the other hand, in connectionist and so-called cognitive approaches (Rumelhart and McClelland 1986; Bybee 1995, 2001) the lexicon is highly concrete and massively redundant: all grammatical knowledge, whether phonological or morphological, is taken to inhere in the network of associations between items stored in long-term memory, so that, in effect, the lexicon *is* the grammar.

2.2   Testing the boundaries

Most practitioners would assume intermediate positions between these two extremes; but, again, this raises the difficulty of formulating explicit criteria for drawing boundaries between the phonology, morphology, and lexicon. The typical approach here has been to propose tests to identify genuine phonological rules. Below we review a number of these tests, although our list is not exhaustive.

- *SPE* allowed unlimited phonological opacity: such restrictions as it imposed emerged during acquisition from (relatively ill-defined) provisions in the evaluation measure. In contrast, [Bybee-]Hooper's (1976) True Generalization Condition requires genuine phonological rules to be *transparent*, and therefore not to be contradicted by surface evidence. Although this work has been influential, the proposal seems too strong: more recent research usually acknowledges that phonological rules may be opaque, but proposes grammatical architectures that impose severe formal restrictions upon the complexity of phonological opacity effects, over and above learnability considerations (see e.g. Bermúdez-Otero 2003: section 2).

- Phonological *naturalness* has often been seen as a hallmark of genuine phonological rules, although 'naturalness' has variously been defined formally (e.g. genuine phonological rules operate over features, which define natural classes of segments, rather than random segment lists), or functionally (e.g. genuine phonological rules are phonetically grounded), or typologically. In OT, whether mono- or poly-stratal, naturalness is a key criterion, as every genuine phonological process must be the best solution to the problem posed by a given ranking of phonological markedness and faithfulness constraints. Definitions overlap here, since the notion of markedness in OT is intrinsically typological, but can be given both formal and functional readings, as in the recent controversy over the grounding of constraints (Bermúdez-Otero and Börjars 2006; Hale and Reiss 2000; Hayes 1999a; Hayes et al. 2004).

- In Kiparsky's (1994: 16) reading, Ford and Singh (1983) and Spencer (1991: section 4.4) claim that all rules subject to *morphological conditioning* are morphological. A more nuanced version of this approach is advanced by Anderson (1992), who asserts that genuine phonological rules (as opposed to 'word-formation,' i.e. morphological, rules) can be circumscribed to a morphologically defined domain, but cannot refer to specific morphemes or morphological/syntactic features. This claim is explicitly endorsed in Stratal OT by Orgun (1996) and, *modulo* alignment constraints, by Bermúdez-Otero (forthcoming: ch. 2). The cost of this strategy may be a proliferation of cophonologies (but see section 4 for some interesting applications). Monostratal OT, in contrast, tacitly reverts to the *SPE* position that all morphological information is available to the phonology (see Bermúdez-Otero forthcoming: ch. 2; Orgun and Inkelas 2002: 116).

- Kiparsky (1994) asserts that morphological rules can be distinguished from phonological rules (both lexical and postlexical) by the cluster of *formal properties* in (1):

(1) a. Phonological rules	b. Morphological rules
General	item-specific
manipulate single phonological units	manipulate phonologically arbitrary strings
observe phonological locality conditions	observe morphological locality conditions
follow all morphological rules in the same cycle	precede all phonological rules in the same cycle

The properties in (1a) are clearly related to the criteria of transparency and naturalness: any transparent phonological rule will *ipso facto* be general and follow all morphological operations in the same cycle, while any natural phonological rule will *ipso facto* manipulate nonarbitrary phonological constituents and observe phonological locality conditions. However, it should be clear that (1a) falls far short of requiring absolute transparency or naturalness. In consequence, Kiparsky's (1994) proposal can easily be adopted in post-*SPE* rule-based frameworks, where opacity is formally unlimited and naturalness criteria are defined formally rather than functionally; but it will not work in theories with strong transparency and naturalness requirements – including, interestingly, Kiparsky's own (1998, 2000) stratal version of OT.

- More recent work in Stratal OT seeks to derive the typical life-cycle of phonological rules (Harris 1989; McMahon 2000) from properties of the phonological learning algorithm. From this viewpoint, Bermúdez-Otero (2003, forthcoming) suggests that phonological alternations triggered by an *independent phonotactic requirement* are easier to acquire, and therefore more resistant to morphologization and lexicalization, than phonological alternations lacking in phonotactic motivation. The evidence of Berko's (1958) classic *wug* test supports this claim: Berko found that, by age five, children acquiring English know that the plural noun suffix is an alveolar fricative, i.e. /-S/; however, when selecting among its surface allomorphs, i.e. [-z ~ -s ~ -ɪz], children perform best when the choice is phonotactically determined (e.g. [wʌg-z], [bɪk-s]), slightly worse when the choice requires knowledge of the underlying voice specification of the suffix (e.g. [lʌn-z], though *[lʌn-s] is phonotactically fine), and worst of all when there is competition between several potential repair strategies (e.g. [tæs-ɪz] with epenthesis vs *[tæs] with coalescence).

- Finally, in their *dual-route approach to morphology* Pinker and Prince (1988) have produced detailed and fairly explicit criteria for distinguishing between lexical storage and morphological computation, at least for inflection. These criteria turn out to be relevant to the distinction between lexicon and phonology, although their applicability is limited. First, if a morphological item is (or can be) constructed online, the logic of the theory requires that all phonological alternations associated with that construction should also be computable online. Thus, since the past tense and past participle suffix /-d/ is added to verb stems by a genuine morphological rule, it follows that the [-d ~ -t ~ -ɪd] alternation must also be generated by a (phonological) rule. As it happens, this rule is independently required to capture robust word-level phonotactic constraints, which provide further evidence for it. However, this argument does not work in the opposite direction: a phonological pattern may be enforced by a discrete symbolic generalization represented in the grammar even if it does not trigger alternations associated with regular morphological processes. An extreme case would be that of productive phonotactic patterns in isolating languages, which do not cause alternations but are shown to be grammatically active in, for instance, the nativization of loans (Yip 1993, 1996).

2.3   Do the criteria converge?

If the theory of grammar is to have nontrivial empirical content, one should aim to draw the boundaries between phonology, morphology, and the lexicon by means of a set of logically independent but empirically convergent criteria. As we have seen, however, some of the criteria reviewed in the previous section are mutually incompatible: for example, if phonological rules must be typologically or phonetically natural, then the scope of phonological computation will be considerably narrower than if the status of an alternation depends only on its form and locality properties, as suggested by Kiparsky (1994). Finding a set of convergent criteria has in fact proved to be rather hard. In this section we shall illustrate these difficulties by considering the possible involvement of a phonological process of vowel shift in the alternations found in strong verbs (e.g. *eat~ate*) and in irregular weak verbs (e.g. *keep~kept*).

As is well-known, present-day English has a number of vowel alternations triggered by morphologically sensitive processes of shortening and lengthening (see e.g. *SPE*: 178ff; Myers 1987). Their morphological conditioning is discussed in section 3 below.

- In stressed antepenultimate syllables followed by a stressless penult, long vowels are subject to so-called 'trisyllabic shortening': e.g. *sāne~sănity*, *serēne~serĕnity*. This can be regarded as the result of trochaic shortening under final syllable extrametricality: i.e. (*săni*)<*ty*>, *se*(*rĕni*)<*ty*> (Hayes 1995: section 6.1.5). Trochaic shortening also applies in penultimate syllables before the suffix *-ic*: e.g. *cyclōne~cyclŏnic*, *Hellēne~Hellĕnic* (see section 4 below).
- Long vowels undergo shortening in closed syllables, assuming word-final consonants to be extrasyllabic: e.g. *dēe*<*p*>*~dĕp*<*th*>, *fī*<*ve*>*~fĭfty*.
- Finally, short vowels undergo lengthening when immediately followed by C*i*V sequences: e.g. *comĕdy~comēdian*, *harmŏny~harmōnious*.

In *SPE*, the qualitative aspect of these alternations is handled by means of a rule of long vowel shift, which largely recapitulates traditional accounts of the diachronic evolution of long vowels in Early Modern English:

(2)   *Long vowel shift in* SPE

		sane	*sanity*
a.			
	UR	/æː/	/æː/
	Trisyllabic shortening	–	æ
	Long vowel shift	eː	–
b.		*cyclone*	*cyclonic*
	UR	/ɔː/	/ɔː/
	Trochaic shortening	–	ɔ
	Long vowel shift	oː	–

c.

	deep	*depth*
UR	/eː/	/eː/
Closed syllable shortening	–	e
Long vowel shift	iː	–

d.

	comedy	*comedian*
UR	/e/	/e/
C*i*V lengthening	–	eː
Long vowel shift	–	iː

Consider now the vowel alternations found in strong verbs such as *eat~ate*, *dig~dug*, and *fly~flew*, extensively discussed in Halle and Mohanan (1985). Halle and Mohanan's analysis is ostensibly within LPM, but wears the restrictions inherent in the architecture of that model very lightly; in fact, it approximates in abstractness the *SPE* description on which it is based (see McMahon 2000). Following the programmatic assumptions of *SPE*, Halle and Mohanan seek to derive these vowel alternations by rule, whilst positing the smallest possible number of rules and maximizing the application of each rule (i.e. its 'functional yield'). To achieve this end, Halle and Mohanan formulate a number of (essentially morphological) processes of ablaut, and allow their output to take a free ride on long vowel shift. The alternations are thus factored out into a morphological and a phonological component.

(3) *Strong verb alternations in Halle and Mohanan (1985)*

	eat	*ate*
UR	/eː/	/eː/
Lowering ablaut	–	æː
Long vowel shift	iː	eː

If we assume that strong past tense and past participle forms are irregular and therefore stored in long-term memory, as convincingly argued in Pinker and Prince (1988) and related work, it becomes unnecessary to divide vowel alternations such as *eat~ate* into a morphological and a phonological component. In consequence, even if one countenances a synchronic phonological rule of vowel shift (and this is a big 'if,' on which see below), vowel shift will not need to be involved in strong verb morphology. Taking advantage of this result, McMahon (1990, 2000) replaces Halle and Mohanan's single word-level rule of long vowel shift by two stem-level rules of long vowel shift and short vowel shift; these two rules apply only in derived environments created by the previous application of a shortening or lengthening rule (on the blocking of stem-level rules in nonderived environments, see section 3.3 below).

(4) *Vowel alternations in McMahon (1990)*

a.

	eat	*ate*
UR	/iː/	/eː/
Long vowel shift	blocked	blocked

b.

	sane	sanity
UR	/eː/	/eː/
Trisyllabic shortening	–	e
Short vowel shift	–	æ
Long vowel shift	blocked	–

c.

	comedy	comedian
UR	/e/	/e/
CiV lengthening	–	eː
Short vowel shift	blocked	–
Long vowel shift	–	iː

By doing away with problematic free rides, McMahon's analysis represents a clear improvement on Halle and Mohanan's in terms of concreteness and learnability. Admittedly, Pinker and Prince's approach to strong verb morphology does not necessarily prevent one from factoring out alternations such as *eat~ate* into a lexically listed part and a part derived by a free ride through an *SPE*-style word-level rule of long vowel shift; but it is hard to see why this should be a desirable option unless one is wedded to the notions of maximal lexical economy and maximal rule utilization – in which case one would not accept the premises of Pinker and Prince's model in the first place. In this example, therefore, a measure of convergence is achieved: applying Pinker and Prince's dual-route model of morphology results in considerable gains in terms of the generality, transparency, and learnability of phonological rules.

Let us now turn to irregular weak verbs such as *keep~kept*, *sleep~slept*, *bite~bit*, or *light~lit*. As we saw above, the vowel alternations found in these verbs are replicated in many other constructions; in this sense, they fulfill Kiparsky's generality criterion for genuine phonological processes (see (1)). By Pinker and Prince's criteria, however, they are always associated with irregular (nondefault) morphology: e.g. *-t* against default *-d*, *-th* against default *-ness*. Therefore, if Pinker and Prince are right, then both *keep* and *kept* will have to be stored in long-term memory; the question is whether *kept* will be listed as /kiːp-t/ or as /kep-t/.

In the light of section 2.2, there are good *prima facie* arguments for handling the length component of the *keep~kept* alternation by means of a phonological rule of closed syllable shortening: this process is natural (and indeed phonetically grounded), largely transparent, and blind to morphology within its domain (on the notion of domain, see section 3.2 below). Closed syllable shortening is also required independently to handle robust phonotactic constraints on morphologically underived items. In turn, the qualitative dimension of the alternation could be analyzed using McMahon's (1990, 2000) stem-level rule of short vowel shift. In contrast with closed syllable shortening, however, vowel shift is still somewhat problematic: e.g. it has no independent phonotactic motivation, involves Greek-letter variables (or, in OT terms, contrived versions of faithfulness), and has a messy penumbra of (un)gliding and (un)rounding rules.

In the case of the irregular weak verbs, therefore, we are confronted with an instance of nonconvergence between demarcation criteria. If the naturalness of closed syllable shortening persuades us to derive the alternating vowels from a single underlier, then we are also committed to computing the far less natural qualitative component of the alternation. But, paradoxically, this would imply that naturalness and transparency (which led us to consider closed syllable shortening as a plausible phonological rule in the first place) are not reliable criteria for distinguishing between lexicalized patterns and genuine phonological generalizations after all.

2.4 Cutting the Gordian knot

How, then, can one solve this impasse? There seem to be two possibilities.

First, we might propose that, at least at the highest grammatical level, phonological generalizations are not constrained by naturalness: they may be pure inductive generalizations, and therefore less markedness-driven than history-driven (in the sense that they simply encapsulate the synchronic outcome of processes that were once natural and transparent). If so, the criterion for the psychological reality of a phonological rule at the stem level will just be whether the rule can be acquired by induction: this may to a large extent be determined by the rule's transparency, but naturalness clearly has nothing to do with it. The question then arises as to whether this type of purely inductive rule is essentially different from a morphological rule in the style of the word-formation processes of Anderson's (1992) a-morphous morphology. If they are broadly the same kind of entity, there may be no reason beyond familiarity of convention to write vowel shift in a feature-based format, with Greek letter variables and the like, instead of employing notation roughly like that in (5).

(5) /iː/ alternates with /e/
     /eɪ/ alternates with /æ/   etc.

Of course, this option brings us back to the earlier problem of distinguishing between morphological and phonological processes. Those not wishing to take this direction might retreat to the middle-way position defined by Kiparsky (1994), where genuine phonological rules need not be natural in a typological or phonetic sense, but only in the purely formal sense of referring to phonological categories and obeying phonological locality conditions. This, however, will not be a possibility in frameworks where all phonological levels are optimality-theoretic.

Alternatively, we may choose to list *kept* as /kep-t/, thereby dispensing with vowel shift as a phonological rule. Here, the perceived difference between closed syllable shortening and vowel shift in terms of typological and phonetic naturalness, transparency, and independent phonotactic motivation is directly reflected in their grammatical status: shortening becomes a static phonological generalization over stem-level domains, while vowel shift is reduced to a pattern of relationships among stored lexical entries. Interestingly, this implies that the output of every stem-level computation is stored in long-term memory (for related arguments, see Kiparsky 1982b; Giegerich 1988, 1999). In turn, this result has significant implications: in section 3.4 we show that, given certain plausible assumptions about blocking, storing every stem-level output as a lexical entry produces results which resemble stratum-internal cyclicity. Cyclicity and the related concepts of domain and level, however, are the topic of the next section.

3   Misapplication

3.1   *The problem*

Once phonology, morphology, and the lexicon have been appropriately demarcated, the theory of grammar must account for their interactions. In particular, the setup of the morphology–phonology interface must explain how morphological structures can cause phonological generalizations to misapply. Present-day English abounds in instances of such misapplication.

Underapplication is said to occur when a phonological process *p* fails to apply even though a morphological (or syntactic) construction *m*, or a phonological process triggered by *m*, creates the conditioning environment of *p*. In certain varieties of Northern Irish English, for example, the coronal noncontinuants /t, d, n, l/, usually realized as alveolar, become dental when followed by [r] or [ɚr] (Harris 1989: 40). This process of dentalization applies normally when its structural description is met within a single morpheme (6a) or within a form derived by class-I suffixation (6b), but it fails when its conditioning environment is created by class-II suffixation (6c), compounding (6d), or syntactic concatenation (6e). For the terms 'class I' and 'class II,' see Siegel (1974) and much subsequent work.

(6)   *Dentalization (Northern Irish dialects)*
    a. [t̪]*rain*, [d̪]*rain*, *ma*[t̪]*er*, *la*[d̪]*er*, *spa*[n̪]*er*, *pi*[l̪]*ar*
    b. *sani*[t̪]*ary*, *eleme*[n̪t̪]*ary*
    c. *shou*[t]*er*, *ru*[n]*er*   (agentive *-er*)
       la[t]*er*, *fi*[n]*er*   (comparative *-er*)
    d. *foo*[t]*rest*, *su*[n]*roof*
    e. *goo*[d] *riddance*, *ca*[l] *Rose*

The absence of dentalization in (6d) and (6e) can conceivably be explained in purely phonological terms; the process may simply be blocked by prosodic word boundaries: e.g. [ω[ω *foot*][ω*rest*]], [φ[ω*good*][ω*riddance*]]. In (6c), however, the cause of underapplication is clearly morphological.

Other phonological processes that underapply in the presence of class-II suffixes include trochaic shortening and closed syllable shortening, discussed in section 2.3: e.g. *prov*[əʊ]*ke*, *prov*[ɒ]*c-ative*, but *prov*[əʊ]*k-ing-ness*; *d*[iː]*p*, *d*[e]*p-th*, but *d*[iː]*p-ness*. However, Northern Irish dentalization is special in that it is a purely allophonic process, as the alveolar and dental realizations of the coronal noncontinuants are in complementary distribution; see section 3.3 for the theoretical implications of this fact.

In cases of overapplication, a phonological process *p* applies even though its conditioning environment is destroyed by a morphological (or syntactic) construction *m*, or by another phonological process triggered by *m*. In Canadian English, for example, the diphthongs /aɪ/ and /aʊ/ undergo raising to [əi] and [ʌʊ] when immediately followed within the same prosodic word by a voiceless obstruent that does not belong to a syllable with stronger stress (Chambers 1973). Like Northern Irish dentalization, this process is allophonic, in that the surface distribution of the raised and unraised diphthongs is entirely predictable. As observed in Bermúdez-Otero (2003: section 5.1), however, Canadian raising underapplies in the presence of class-II suffixes: e.g. [aɪfʊl] *eyeful*; cf. [əifəl] *Eiffel* (*Tower*), [nəitreɪt] *nitrate*. More famously, raising overapplies before a /t/ that becomes voiced through flapping (Joos 1942):

(7) *Canadian raising*
   normal application   overapplication
                               b. [rəiɾər] *writer*
   a. [rəit] *write*
                               c. [rəiɾ oʊdz] *write odes*

In (7b) and (7c), the phonological environment created by, respectively, class-II suffixation and syntactic concatenation triggers flapping. By causing /t/ to become voiced, however, flapping removes the conditions for diphthong raising, which nonetheless applies; cf. (7a).

3.2   Domains, cycles, levels

Rule-based LPM and Stratal OT provide derivational (i.e. serial) accounts of morphologically induced misapplication. In both theories the design of the morphology–phonology (and syntax–phonology) interface is based upon three key concepts: domains, cycles, and levels.

Let us use the symbol $\mathcal{P}$ to denote any phonological function associating a phonological input with its corresponding output representation. In rule-based theory, $\mathcal{P}$ is defined by means of a battery of extrinsically ordered transformations; in OT, it consists of a pass through GEN and EVAL, i.e. $\mathcal{P}(x) = $ EVAL(GEN(x)). A phonological domain can now be defined as the input to any single application of $\mathcal{P}$. In LPM and Stratal OT, it is assumed that the morphological and syntactic structure of a linguistic expression creates a nested hierarchy of phonological domains. Consequently, a single application of $\mathcal{P}$ may take scope over a unit smaller than the utterance (e.g. a stem or a word).

Domain structure, however, is usually taken to be impoverished in relation to morphological and syntactic structure: every phonological domain is associated with some morphological or syntactic construction, but not every morphological or syntactic construction creates a phonological domain (Bermúdez-Otero forthcoming: ch. 2; though cf. Orgun 1996). Within this domain structure, the phonological function $\mathcal{P}$ applies cyclically from the smallest, most deeply embedded, to the largest, most inclusive domain. If, for example, an expression e has the domain structure $[[x][[y]z]]$, the claim is that $\mathcal{P}(e) = \mathcal{P}(\mathcal{P}(x), \mathcal{P}(\mathcal{P}(y), z))$.

In LPM and Stratal OT, however, the phonology of a language does not consist of a single function $\mathcal{P}$, but of a set of distinct functions $\{\mathcal{P}_1, \mathcal{P}_2, \ldots, \mathcal{P}_n\}$, conventionally known as 'levels' or 'strata.' Different grammatical units (e.g. stems, words, phrases) create phonological domains of different types, each calling for the appropriate function (e.g. the stem-level, word-level, or phrase-level function). In present-day English it is generally acknowledged that three levels suffice to describe the relevant morphology–phonology and syntax–phonology interactions (Booij and Rubach 1987: section 5; Borowsky 1993; but cf. Halle and Mohanan 1985); we shall henceforth continue to designate these levels with the labels 'stem level,' 'word level,' and 'phrase level.' Within the confines of the grammatical word, morphological operations may idiosyncratically create either stem-level or word-level domains: so-called class-I affixes trigger the application of the stem-level function, whereas class II-affixes invoke the word-level function. *Pace* Siegel (1974), the stem and word levels are not mutually ordered: word-level domains have been argued to occur inside stem-level domains (Aronoff and Sridhar 1983; Fabb 1988). In general, though, the classification of English word-formation processes as stem-level or word-level is uncontroversial (though see Giegerich, 1999). In contrast, section 3.3 below shows that the traditional stratal allocation of certain lexical (i.e. word-bound) phonological generalizations is untenable.

Given the grammatical resources just described, one can explain the under-application of Northern Irish dentalization in (6c) as follows. Consider the phonological domain structure of *finer*, ignoring the phrase level:

(8)   [word-level [stem-level faɪn] ɚr]

In (8), the conditions for dentalization are not fulfilled within the stem-level domain, but only within the word-level domain created by the class-II comparative suffix *-er*. Suppose now that dentalization is a stem-level phonological process (see section 3.3 for further discussion). If so, it will not apply in the larger domain: in serial terms, the addition of the suffix counterfeeds dentalization.

Interestingly, stratification and cyclicity can account for instances of phonological misapplication that are not directly caused by morphological or syntactic operations. Consider, for example, the derivation of the word *mitre* in Canadian English:

(9)   *mitre*
   UR   /maɪtər/
   Raising   məɪtər
   Flapping   məɪɾər

Here, flapping counterbleeds raising, just as in (7b) and (7c) above, even though the structural description of flapping is met within a single morpheme. Assume, however, that the morpheme MITRE can only occur legally as (part of) a morphologically well-formed word in a syntactically well-formed phrase – even if it is a phrase consisting of a single unaffixed word. If so, expressions containing MITRE will always have the following phonological domain structure:

(10) [$_{\text{phrase-level}}$ (. . .) [$_{\text{word-level}}$ (. . .) [$_{\text{stem-level}}$ maɪtər] (. . .)] (. . .)]

In section 3.1, however, we saw that raising is a stem-level process, since its domain excludes word-level (class-II) suffixes; flapping, in contrast, is phrase-level, as its environment can be created by syntactic concatenation (see (7c)). It therefore follows that /maɪtər/ must undergo raising in the stem cycle, followed by flapping in the phrase cycle. Thus, the stratal account of paradigmatic misapplication in (7b,c) also deals with the nonparadigmatic opacity effect in (9) without further stipulation.

In fact, the proponents of Stratal OT claim that all instances of opacity can be explained in this way: misapplication, they assert, always arises from the serial interaction between cycles (e.g. Bermúdez-Otero 1999, 2003, forthcoming; Kiparsky 1998, 2000). In this respect, Stratal OT is more falsifiable and typologically restrictive than rule-based LPM, which allows extrinsic rule ordering within cycles. If borne out by extensive empirical testing, this claim would therefore constitute a genuine explanatory advance. According to Bermúdez-Otero (2003, forthcoming), moreover, using cyclicity and stratification to account for both paradigmatic and nonparadigmatic opacity can enhance learnability. The acquisition procedure he proposes enables learners to use information from alternations in order to recognize departures from input-output identity in nonalternating items and to discover their correct underlying representation. In this view, alternations such as (11a) and (11b) alert English learners to the flapping of input /t/ and /d/ in (11c) and (11d), even though, in the latter, the flap does not alternate:

(11) a. /raɪt ~ raɪt oʊdz/   b. /raɪd ~ raɪd ʌphɪl/
       [rəɪt ~ rəɪɾ oʊdz]   [raɪd ~ raɪɾ ʌphɪl]
       write ~ write odes   *ride ~ ride uphill*
    c. /maɪtər/   d. /spaɪdər/
       [məɪɾər]   [spaɪɾər]
       mitre   *spider*

Incidentally, note that psycholinguistic evidence from repetition priming experiments supports the existence of abstract underlying representations such as /maɪtər/ and /spaɪdər/ (Luce et al. 1999).

3.3   *What level?*

In the preceding section we said that Northern Irish dentalization must be a stem-level process because its domain excludes word-level (class-II) affixes. In classical LPM, however, the rule has typically been assigned to the word level (e.g. Borowsky 1993: 209–10; but cf. Harris 1989). This counterintuitive move is motivated by a desire to uphold the principle of Structure Preservation. Though the precise formulation of this condition on rule application has been hotly debated, the statement in (12) will suffice for our purposes (see e.g. Kiparsky 1985: 92; Kaisse and Shaw 1985: section 2.4):

(12)   *Structure Preservation*
        The application of stem-level phonological rules must not violate morpheme structure constraints.

Here, the term 'morpheme structure constraints' refers to constraints on underlying representations. Rule-based LPM usually assumes some form of underspecification (typically, radical underspecification: e.g. Kiparsky 1982a, b; Archangeli, 1988); though cf. McMahon (2000: ch. 5). Accordingly, predictable features are banned from underlying representations. The intent of (12), in this context, is to prevent stem-level phonological rules from generating underlyingly noncontrastive segments. In Northern Irish English, however, [t, d, n, l] and [t̪, d̪, n̪, l̪] are in perfect complementary distribution; as noted in section 3.1, the occurrence of the dental allophones is fully predictable. This means, however, that, if (12) is correct, dentalization cannot apply at the stem level. Thus, LPM faces a contradiction: the domain criterion and Structure Preservation assign Northern Irish dentalization to different levels.

There is good evidence, however, that the fault lies with Structure Preservation. First, the principle has never been successfully defined in formal terms. The statement in (12), for example, conflicts with Kiparsky's (1982a: 167–8; 1982b: section 3.2) own solution of the Duplication Problem (Clayton 1976), which arises over the fact that stem-level phonological rules often conspire to bring class-I derivatives in line with morpheme structure constraints. Kiparsky (1982a, b) suggested that morpheme structure constraints could be eliminated, since restrictions on nonderived lexical items could be captured by the stem-level rules applying in structure-building mode to radically underspecified underlying representations; but, paradoxically, the formulation of Structure Preservation in (12) seems to make crucial reference to morpheme structure constraints. There has also been disagreement as to whether or not feature spreading may evade Structure Preservation (e.g. MacFarland and Pierrehumbert 1991; Kaisse and Hargus 1994).

Secondly, if dentalization is assigned to the word level, then one must find some means of blocking its application before class-II suffixes, but all the expedients available for this purpose weaken the empirical content of LPM in patently undesirable ways. One possibility would be to stipulate that the rule is blocked by morpheme boundaries (notated in rule-based LPM as ']'). As Harris (1989, note 2) observes, however, this solution undermines the principle that phonological generalizations do not refer to morphological information except insofar as their domain may be morphologically defined (see sections 2.2 and 3.2 above). More drastically, Borowsky (1993) prevents *all* word-level rules from applying across morpheme boundaries by ordering word-level phonology *before*, rather than *after*, word-level morphology. Empirically, however, this proposal finds counterexamples both in present-day English and in other languages: see section 3.5 below, though cf. Borowsky (1993: n. 15). Theoretically, it subverts the very concept of domain laid out in section 3.2.

The obvious solution, then, is to abandon Structure Preservation and to assign Northern Irish dentalization to the stem level. But the case of dentalization is not unique: Canadian raising violates Structure Preservation in the intended sense too (see sections 3.1 and 3.2). Present-day English has a surprisingly wide array of allophonic processes whose application is restricted to stem-level domains (see Harris 1990). In section 3.5 we return to this topic, as we reflect on why so much of present-day English phonology is transacted at the stem level.

From a theoretical viewpoint, it is interesting to note that the issue of Structure Preservation does not arise in Stratal OT. In accordance with the optimality-theoretic principle of Richness of the Base (see e.g. McCarthy 2002: section 3.1.2), the theory does not permit language-particular restrictions to be directly imposed upon underlying representations. Rather, a phonological feature is underlyingly contrastive if a faithfulness constraint ranked high in the stem-level hierarchy shields it from the neutralizing pressure of markedness; otherwise, it is predictable (allophonic). Accordingly, stem-level rankings control the content of underlying representations (via Lexicon Optimization), and not the other way around (see Bermúdez-Otero 1999: 124; Bermúdez-Otero forthcoming: ch. 3).

There are clear advantages to relying on the evidence of domains as the sole criterion for assigning phonological generalizations to their respective levels. First, this enables one to maintain the highly restrictive approach to opacity outlined in section 3.2, whereby the relative ordering of phonological processes is entirely determined by the size of their domains. Secondly, a strict correlation between stratal ascription and domain of application aids learnability since, to determine whether a ranking r holds in the constraint hierarchy of level l, the learner need only consider whether r is true (applies normally) in l-domains; the constraint ranking algorithm need not include provisions to deal with morphologically induced misapplication (Bermúdez-Otero 2003, forthcoming; cf. Hayes 1999b: section 8).

Classical LPM incorporates another principle of rule application that interferes with the establishment of a one-to-one correspondence between levels and domain types: the Strict Cycle Condition. There is a vast literature on this principle (see e.g. Mascaró 1976; Kiparsky 1982a: 154), but, again, the statement in (13) will suffice for our purposes:

(13)   *Strict Cycle Condition*
       Stem-level rules can apply in structure-changing mode only to representations derived in the same cycle.

According to (13), a stem-level rule can change structure (e.g. replace or delete, rather than merely add, features) only in derived environments, i.e. only when the rule's structural description is met by virtue of the previous application of a morphological or phonological process in the same cycle. In other words, blocking in nonderived environments would be a property of stem-level phonological rules. The somewhat opaque label 'Strict Cycle Condition' refers to the classical assumption that the stem level is internally cyclic (for discussion of this idea, see section 3.4 below).

Together with Structure Preservation, the Strict Cycle Condition shaped the standard treatment of vowel shift in rule-based LPM. Vowel shift (*if* countenanced as a synchronic phonological phenomenon at all) should be stem-level, since all the vowel length processes that feed it, such as trochaic shortening and closed syllable shortening, are blind to word-level affixes (see section 2.3). Yet, ignoring the fact that vowel shift alternations are confined to stem-level domains, classical LPM analyses of English morphophonology place the vowel shift rule in the word level (e.g. Halle and Mohanan 1985). This is motivated by the desire to retain an abstract *SPE*-style approach to the English vowel inventory, which requires nonderived lexical items to take a free ride on long vowel shift: since the Strict Cycle Condition bans free rides on stem-level rules, long vowel shift had to be assigned to the word level. As we saw in section 2.3, McMahon (2000: ch. 3) reconciles the Strict Cycle Condition with the domain criterion by formulating two derived-environment-only stem-level rules of long vowel shift and short vowel shift. Note, however, that Kiparsky (1993) gives up the Strict Cycle Condition on empirical grounds and treats blocking in nonderived environments as a property that may or may not hold for any rule at any level.

3.4   *Is the stem level internally cyclic?*

We have just seen that, in classical LPM, the stem level is assumed to be internally cyclic. In essence, this means that stem-level morphological operations generate a particularly rich phonological domain structure: *every* stem-level morphological construction – not just the *outermost* – constitutes a phonological domain.

(14)   *Stem-level phonological domain structure in* originality
    a.   *if the stem level is internally noncyclic*
        [stem-level originality]
    b.   *if the stem level is internally cyclic*
        [stem-level [stem-level [stem-level origin]al]ity]

In the case of English, this assumption is primarily motivated by stress-related facts, which were already adduced as evidence for the cycle in *SPE*. A good example is the misapplication of pretonic secondary stress assignment in class-I derivatives (see e.g. Hammond, 1989). The monomorphemic items in (15) show that English has 'polar rhythm' (van der Hulst, 1984): in a pretonic sequence of light syllables, secondary stress is assigned by building trochees from left to right, not from right to left. In words with three pretonic light syllables, this results in a characteristic dactylic sequence: ὸσσ.

(15)   **(àbra)ca**(dábra)
       (dèli)ca(tésse)n
       (pèri)pa(téti)c

In words derived by class-I suffixation, however, polar secondary stress often misapplies:

(16)   *(dìvi)si(bíli)ty   di(vìsi)(bíli)ty   cf. di(vísi)ble
       *(òri)gi(náli)ty   o(rìgi)(náli)ty   cf. o(rígi)nal
       *(Èli)za(bé)than   E(lìza)(bé)than   cf. E(líza)beth

If the stem level is cyclic, the facts can be interpreted as showing that the primary stress assigned to the base in the inner cycle is preserved as secondary stress in the derivative during the outer cycle, blocking polar rhythm:

(17)   *domain structure*   [[Elizabeth]an]
       inner cycle   E(líza)beth
       outer cycle   E(lìza)(bé)than

Though apparently well-motivated, however, this postulate of classical LPM again distorts the correlation between levels and domain types. Consider, for example, the English phonotactic constraint that forbids clusters of nasal consonants in the coda. Its precise formulation need not concern us here; let us simply call it 'nasal cluster simplification.' This constraint must clearly be active at the stem level, since it overapplies before word-level affixes: e.g. [dæmɪŋ] *damn-ing*, not *[dæm.nɪŋ]; cf. [dæm.neɪ.ʃn] *damn-ation*. However, if nasal cluster simplification applies cyclically at the stem level, we have a problem:

(18)   *domain structure*   [[dæmn]eɪʃn]
       inner cycle   dæm   by nasal cluster simplification
       outer cycle   *dəmeɪʃn

Note that it would do no good, either, to assume that the Strict Cycle Condition blocks nasal cluster simplification in the inner cycle, for in that case input [_word-level_ [_stem-level_ dæmn]ɪŋ] would incorrectly be realized as *[dæm.nɪŋ]. Unsurprisingly, Borowsky (1993: 202) assigns nasal cluster simplification to the word level, but at the same high cost as Northern Irish dentalization (see section 3.3). For their part, Halle and Mohanan (1985) set up an extra phonological level (level 2 in their system), which is internally noncyclic but precedes inflectional suffixation.

Interestingly, the problem disappears if one assumes that all stem-level outputs are listed in long-term memory (section 2.4), so that stem-level phonological rules essentially work like 'lexical redundancy rules' (Jackendoff 1975): they express static phonotactic generalizations over stem-level domains, and they capture the relationship between stem-level derivatives and their bases in a purely redundant fashion. Let us assume, on this premise, that there are stored in the English lexicon the following three items: (1) a bound root /_root_ dæmn/, (2) a free noun stem /_N_ dæm/, and (3) a derived noun stem /_N_ dæmneɪʃn/. The relationship between /_root_ dæmn/ and /_N_ dæm/ will be redundantly captured by a stem-level morphological process of root-to-stem conversion, plus the stem-level phonological constraint of nasal cluster simplification, which encodes the fact that well-formed stems do not contain clusters of nasal consonants in the coda. Similarly, a stem-level morphological rule of *-ation* suffixation will redundantly express the relationship between /_root_ dæmn/ and /_N_ dæmneɪʃn/. The following question now arises: what prevents this suffixation rule from applying to the listed stem /_N_ dæm/, giving */_N_ dæm-eɪʃn/→[_N_ dəmeɪʃn]? The answer is quite simple: blocking, i.e. the independently motivated principle whereby the existence of a listed lexical entry prevents word-formation processes from generating a competing form (see e.g. Aronoff and Anshen 1998: section 1.1). In this view, /_N_ dæmneɪʃn/ blocks */_N_ dæm-eɪʃn/ in the same way that *went* blocks **goed*. The absence of */_N_ dæm-eɪʃn/ is entirely contingent on the presence of /_N_ dæmneɪʃn/, for */_N_ dæm-eɪʃn/ violates no grammatical principle or rule other than blocking: the rule of *-ation* suffixation, for example, does not subcategorize for bound roots only (cf. e.g. *sum ~ summation*).

As suggested in Borowsky (1993: 220), listing all stem-level outputs provides a viable alternative to stratum-internal cyclicity as the explanation for the misapplication of secondary stress assignment in (16). Assume, first, that English lexical entries are allowed to contain metrical information. This assumption is clearly justified by stress contrasts such as *A(méri)ca* vs *ba(nána)*. Given Richness of the Base (see section 3.3), a Stratal OT analysis must preserve such underlying oppositions whilst simultaneously excluding impossible stress patterns such as **ci(tý)* or **(cítro)nella*. This could be done by setting up ranking (19) in the stem-level constraint hierarchy:

(19)   FTBIN, *LAPSE » MAX-FootHead » NONFIN
   a.   FTBIN
        Feet must be binary at some level of analysis (μ, σ).

b. *LAPSE
A prosodic word must not contain two adjacent unfooted syllables.
c. MAX-FootHead
The output correspondent of an input foot head must be a foot head.
d. NONFIN
The final syllable of a prosodic word must not be footed.

Example (20) illustrates the operation of this ranking; for the sake of simplicity, we only consider candidates where primary stress is realized on the rightmost foot. As desired, the constraint hierarchy preserves the underlying contrast between *A(méri)ca* and *ba(nána)*, but rules out hypothetical *ci(tý)* or *(cítro)nella*.

(20)

Stem Level		FTBIN	*LAPSE	MAX-FootHead	NONFIN
/ba(nána)/	(bána)na			*!	
	ba(nána) ☞				*
/A(méri)ca/	(Àme)(ríca)			*!	*
	A(méri)ca ☞				
/(cítro)nella/	(cítro)nella		*!		
	ci(tróne)lla			*!	
	citro(nélla)		*!	*	*
	(cìtro)(nélla) ☞				*
ci(tý)	ci(tý)	*!			*
	(cíty) ☞			*	*

There is therefore no obstacle to assuming that the noun *Elízabeth* is specified in its lexical entry as bearing stress on the antepenultimate syllable. Given input /N E(líza)beth/, the stem-level constraint hierarchy simply acts as a static checking device, redundantly expressing the well-formedness of its metrical structure. We can now turn to *Elìzabéthan*. Since *ex hypothesi* the base *Elízabeth* is underlyingly stressed on the second syllable, one can just state that the position of the pretonic stress in the derived form is a consequence of faithfulness to input specifications overriding polar rhythm. In our rudimentary Stratal OT analysis we could simply posit the ranking MAX-FootHead » ALIGN(ω,L;Σ,L), whereby the preservation of underlying foot heads takes precedence over the preference for prosodic words that begin with a foot.

(21)

/E(líza)beth-an/	MAX-FootHead	ALIGN(ω,L;Σ,L)
(Èli)za(bé)than	*!	
E(lìza)(bé)than ☞		*

Of course, the logic of the analysis requires *Elìzabéthan* itself to be stored in long-term memory: the stem-level stress rules (as well as the relevant word-formation processes) express its relatedness to *Elízabeth* in a static and redundant fashion. Strikingly, however, the assumption that polar rhythm can be overriden by underlyingly specified foot heads correctly predicts that, when so specified, monomorphemic items may exceptionally fail to show the expected initial dactyl: e.g. *apòtheósis*, *egàlitárian*, *Epàminóndas*, etc. Finally, the proposed account also predicts that stem-level morphological constructions can subcategorize for bases with certain stress profiles: the noun-forming suffix *-al*, for example, only attaches to end-stressed verbs, e.g. *remóv-al* but **depósit-al* (Marchand 1969: 236–7). This is a classic argument for the interleaving of morphology and phonology in the lexicon (e.g. Kaisse and Shaw 1985: 18; cf. Odden 1993); in the current approach, however, the stress profile of the base is simply visible in its underlying representation.

At this stage one begins to notice a remarkable consilience of results. Sections 3.2 and 3.3 showed that the falsifiability, restrictiveness, and learnability of stratified grammars improves dramatically when the stratal ascription of phonological processes is determined solely by domain size. In the pursuit of this goal, we were forced in section 3.3 to challenge the LPM principles of Structure Preservation and Strict Cyclicity, which turned out to be problematic for independent reasons. In this section, we have gone on to question the assumption that the stem level is internally cyclic, suggesting instead that stem-level phonological rules behave like lexical redundancy rules in the sense of Jackendoff (1975). In section 2.4, however, we saw that, by assuming stem-level outputs to be lexically listed, it is possible to decouple the quantitative and qualitative aspects of alternations such as *keep~kept*, and thereby to uphold strong naturalness as a demarcation criterion for genuine phonological rules, as required by Stratal OT. These convergent results indicate that stratification and cyclicity remain fruitful tools for the analysis of the morphology–phonology (and syntax–phonology) interface, and that a more strict understanding of the notion of domain than previously adopted can lend new life to stratal-cyclic theories of grammar.

3.5   *Why is the word-level phonology of English so permissive?*

Sections 3.3 and 3.4 have shown that, in present-day English, several phonological generalizations traditionally thought to hold at the word level actually belong in the stem level; this includes allophonic rules such as Northern Irish dentalization and Canadian raising, as well as neutralizing processes such as nasal cluster simplification, trochaic shortening, closed syllable shortening, and (if phonological at all) vowel shift. In fact, English phonotactic constraints seem oddly lax at the word level, compared with the stem level. Burzio (2002) couches this observation in terms of output–output correspondence in OT (henceforth, OO-correspondence; see section 3.6 below). Markedness constraints, he observes, appear to be highly ranked for class-I forms, which are as a result forced to alternate with their bases: e.g *órigin ~ orígin-al, k*[i:]*p ~ k*[e]*p-t, eleme*[nt] *~ eleme*[n̪t]*-ary*. In contrast, class-II forms seem compelled to violate markedness constraints in order to avoid alternations: there is thus no stress reassignment in *éffort-less-ness* (cf. *éffort*), no closed syllable shortening in *s*[i:]*p-ed* (cf. *s*[i:]*p*), no dentalization in *ru*[n]*-er* (cf. *ru*[n]).

Burzio takes both Stratal OT and standard implementations of OO-correspondence to task for not explaining this fact. Nonetheless, there are reasons to believe that it is not up to Universal Grammar to provide an explanation. First, the word-level phonology of English is not entirely inert: thus, although the inflectional suffixes /-d/ and /-z/ do not trigger closed syllable shortening, they do undergo alternations driven by constraints against geminates and against clusters of obstruents that disagree in voicing. Secondly, word-level constraints are far more stringent in other languages. In Spanish, for example, there is a neutralizing stem-level process whereby stressed /we/ alternates with unstressed /o/: e.g. *buén-o* 'good' ~ *bon-dád* 'goodness.' In present-day colloquial Spanish, the domain of this neutralization process excludes the superlative suffix *-ísim(o)*, which must therefore attach at the word level: *buén-o* 'good' ~ *buen-ísim-o* 'best.' Unlike English word-level suffixes, however, *-ísim(o)* does affect the location of stress.

In fact, the idiosyncratic permissiveness of English word-level phonology seems to be a historical accident. There is, for example, a good diachronic explanation for the fact that present-day English assigns primary word-stress at the stem level. In OE, primary stress was assigned by aligning a moraic trochee with the *left* edge of the domain; in consequence, the OE ancestors of present-day class-II suffixes (e.g. *-dom*, *-less*, *-ness*) were neutral with respect to primary stress. In Latin, however, the rules for primary stress targeted the *right* edge of their domain, which included derivational and inflectional material; as a result, the Latin and Romance ancestors of present-day class-I suffixes were stress-affecting. For this reason, when English learners reinterpreted stress assignment as proceeding from right to left, they had to exclude class-II suffixes from its domain; hence, the new stress rule was placed in the stem level with the class-I suffixes.

Similarly, the contrast between the stem-level inflectional ending /-t/, as in *dr*[e]*m-t*, and word-level /-d/, as in *s*[iː]*m-ed*, arose through a chronological fluke (see e.g. Lass 1992: 125–30). Both suffixes originate in a Germanic ancestor that attached to the verb root by means of a thematic vowel. Present-day English /-t/ reflects tokens of this Germanic suffix in long-stemmed class-1 weak verbs, where the thematic vowel became subject to syncope already in prehistoric OE; the output of syncope then fed closed syllable shortening in lOE or eME: e.g. Gmc *keːp-i-ð-ɑ > OE keːp-t-e > eME kep-t-ə 'kept.' In contrast, present-day English /-d/ goes back to tokens of the same Gmc suffix in class-2 and short-stemmed class-1 weak verbs, which only lost the thematic vowel in lME, too late to undergo closed syllable shortening.

Finally, allophonic processes such as Northern Irish dentalization and Canadian raising have ended up in the stem level through analogical change. This fact is hardly surprising, for in their ordinary life-cycle phonological processes typically climb from lower to higher grammatical strata (e.g. Bermúdez-Otero 1999: 98–104; Bermúdez-Otero forthcoming; Harris 1989; McMahon 2000: ch. 4).

3.6   OO-correspondence

So far, we have analyzed morphologically induced misapplication in present-day English in terms of domains, cycles, and levels. In OT, however, OO-correspondence (Benua 1997) has lately become an increasingly popular alternative. This theory posits constraints that require the output representation of a morphologically derived form to be identical with its correspondent in the output representation of the base. Stratal distinctions are handled by indexing OO-correspondence constraints to particular affix classes: in English, for example, class-I and class-II forms would be evaluated by OO_I- and OO_{II}-constraints, respectively.

As an illustration, consider again Northern Irish dentalization. In Benua's (1997: section 5.3.1) analysis, normal applications of dentalization are triggered by the following constraint hierarchy:

(22)   *ALV-RHOTIC » *DENT » IO-IDENT[±distributed]

The context-free constraint *DENT favours alveolar as the unmarked place of articulation for coronal noncontinuants; before rhotics, however, context-sensitive *ALV-RHOTIC requires dentals. To block dentalization in *ru*[n]*-er*, Benua ranks *ALV-RHOTIC below OO_{II}-IDENT[±distributed], which prevents any segment in a class-II derivative from disagreeing in distributedness with its correspondent in the base: cf. *ru*[n]. In contrast, *ALV-RHOTIC dominates OO$_I$-IDENT[±distributed], thereby forcing dentalization in class-I *eleme*[n̪t]-*ary*; cf. *eleme*[nt].

(23)

		OO$_{II}$-IDENT[±distributed]	*ALV-RHOTIC	OO$_I$-IDENT[±distributed]	*DENT
runner base: *ru*[n]	*ru*[n̪]*er*	*!			*
	ru[n]*er* ☞		*		
elementary base: *eleme*[nt]	*eleme*[n̪t]*ary* ☞			*	*
	eleme[nt]*ary*		*!		

In this approach, the relative phonotactic laxity of the word level compared with the stem level is reflected in the high ranking of OO$_{II}$-constraints and the low ranking of OO$_I$-constraints (see section 3.5).

The theory of OO-correspondence has been severely criticized on both empirical and theoretical grounds (Orgun 1996; Bermúdez-Otero 1999; Kiparsky 1998, 2000). Its opponents highlight problems in the selection of surface base-forms and adduce cases where there is no transparent output form that can act as the source of misapplication. In turn, the advocates of OO-correspondence have searched for instances of misapplication that resist analysis in terms of stratification and cyclicity. At first blush, the Withgott effect looks like a good candidate. In American English, flapping appears to overapply in derived forms such as *càpi*[ɾ]*alístic* (from *cápi*[ɾ]*al*); cf. words with the same stress profile such as derived *mìli*[t]*arístic* (from *míli*[t]*àry*) and nonderived *Nàvra*[t]*ilóva* (Withgott 1982). One could argue that *càpi*[ɾ]*alístic* gets its flap through OO-correspondence with *cápi*[ɾ]*al* (Steriade 2000). For a stratal approach, in contrast, the facts may at first seem problematic: flapping is a phrase-level process and should therefore be blind to morphological structure (see sections 3.1 and 3.2). As shown in Jensen (2000: 208–11) and Bermúdez-Otero (forthcoming: ch. 2), however, flapping does not really overapply, but is simply sensitive to differences in foot structure: the underlying /t/ in *càpi*/t/*alístic* surfaces in foot-medial position, whereas it is foot-initial in *mìli*/t/*arístic* and *Nàvra*/t/*ilóva* (see also Davis 2005).

(24)   (cápital)-istic   →   (càpita)(lístic)
                                                     ↓
                                                    [ɾ]

    cf.

            (míli)(tàry)-istic   →   (mìli)(ta(rístic))
                                                     ↓
                                                    [t]

            Navrati(lóva)   →   (Nàvra)(ti(lóva))
                                                     ↓
                                                    [t]

It is thus foot construction, rather than flapping, that misapplies, but this is entirely expected, as foot construction takes place at the stem level (see sections 3.4 and 3.5).

4   The Emergence of Morphology

Up to now, we have managed to describe morphology–phonology interactions in present-day English without allowing the phonology access to any morphological information other than domain structure (see section 2.2). This approach, however, faces a severe challenge from instances of phonological nonuniformity among stem-level affixes, particularly in relation to stress assignment (Pater 2000; Raffelsiefen 1999; Zamma 2005). Most class-I adjective-forming suffixes, for example, render the final syllable extrametrical (25a), but -*ic* triggers mere consonant extrasyllabicity (25b):

(25)   a.   (ómi)<**nous**>, o(rígi)<**nal**>, (tóle)<**rant**>
        b.   a(tómi)<**c**>, Ger(máni)<**c**>, pro(phéti)<**c**>

One could handle the idiosyncratic behavior of -*ic* by specifying its underlying representation with some *ad hoc* phonological diacritic, such as an empty vowel: i.e. /-ɪkØ/. However, this strategy for dealing with phonological nonuniformity is unlikely to succeed in the general case. Consider, for example, the opposition between suffixes inducing 'weak retraction' (e.g. adjectival -*oid*) and suffixes inducing 'strong retraction' (e.g. verbal -*ate*); see Liberman and Prince (1977: 274–6). What underlying phonological property can cause -*oid* to place primary stress upon a preceding heavy syllable, whilst -*ate* throws it upon the antepenult regardless of the weight of the penult?

(26)   a.   *Weak retraction*:   ellípsòid, mollúscòid, cylíndròid
        b.   *Strong retraction*:   désignàte, législàte, cóntemplàte

It would seem that we need an approach to these facts that captures their morphological nature more directly.

    Anttila's (2002) optimality-theoretic research into cophonologies has lately opened up a promising line of attack on this problem. Let us consider (25) in the light of his work. First, one may characterize the stem-level phonology of present-day English in terms of a partial ordering of constraints; following Inkelas and Zoll (2003), we call this 'the master hierarchy.' The master hierarchy will include rankings that prohibit degenerate feet, stress lapses, and so forth (see section 3.4), but it will not specify whether or not the last syllable in the domain is footed. This can be achieved simply by leaving the constraints for syllable extrametricality (NonFin; see (19d) above) and for exhaustive footing (Parse-σ) mutually unordered. Now, according to Anttila's concept of 'the emergence of morphology,' stem-level morphological constructions can exploit the areas of phonological indeterminacy allowed by the master hierarchy. Thus, most class-I adjective-forming suffixes invoke a stem-level cophonology that demands syllable extrametricality (NonFin » Parse-σ); *-ic*, however, invokes a stem-level ranking that forces the final syllable to be footed (Parse-σ » NonFin).

(27)   *The emergence of morphology at the stem level*
    a.   *The master hierarchy*:
       FtBin » NonFin   (cíty), *not* *(cí)ty
       {NonFin, Parse-σ}
    b.   *Cophonology A*:
       FtBin » NonFin » Parse-σ   o(rígi)<nal>
    c.   *Cophonology B*:
       FtBin » NonFin
       Parse-σ » NonFin   a(tómi)<c>

In this approach, the master hierarchy captures the core phonotactic generalizations that hold across stem-level domains, thereby setting limits to phonological nonuniformity. Trochaic shortening, for example, applies to all stem-level forms, whether they are subject to cophonology A (e.g. nouns, ordinary suffixed adjectives) or cophonology B (e.g. verbs, nonderived adjectives, *-ic* adjectives):

(28)   *Trochaic shortening*
    a.   *In cophonology A*:   A(mĕri)<ca>
                        sin(cĕri)<**ty**>   cf. sincēre
                        (nătu)<**ral**>   cf. nāture
    b.   *In cophonology B*:   de(vĕlo)<p>
                        de(crĕpi)<t>
                        cy(clŏni)<c>   cf. cyclōne

This follows automatically if the ranking for trochaic shortening (RhHrm » Max-μ; see Prince and Smolensky, 1993: 59–60) is part of the master hierarchy.

5   Conclusion

Close analysis of the relationship between phonology, morphology, and the lexicon in present-day English continues to yield new insights into the nature and organization of grammars. Theories based on stratification and cyclicity dominated the field during the 1980s. Today, the stratal approach faces tough competition, but is still fostering new advances in our understanding of the morphology–phonology interface.

FURTHER READING

Many of the works referred to above address relatively specific aspects of English phonology and morphology, but for an accessible introductory overview see Giegerich (1992); Jensen (1993) is similar in scope, but slightly more demanding. Introductions to Optimality Theory can be found in Archangeli and Langendoen (1997) and Kager (1999): the former, though somewhat out of date, offers a particularly approachable statement of the basic ideas of OT; the latter includes a chapter on output-output correspondence. Giegerich (1999) and McMahon (2000) include surveys of Lexical Phonology and Morphology, and discuss its application to several synchronic and diachronic problems in English morphophonology. Bermúdez-Otero (forthcoming) will provide a book-length study of Stratal Optimality Theory, also including applications to English. Readers interested in the study of sound change in Optimality Theory should consult Holt (2003) or Bermúdez-Otero (2006).

Archangeli, Diana and D. Terence Langendoen (eds.) (1997) *Optimality*
theory: an overview. Oxford: Blackwell.

Bermúdez-Otero, R. (2006) Phonological change in optimality theory. In Keith Brown (ed.), *Encyclopedia of language and linguistics,* 2nd edn. Oxford: Elsevier, vol. 9, 497–505.

Bermúdez-Otero, R. (forthcoming) *Stratal optimality theory.* Oxford: Oxford University Press.

Giegerich, Heinz J. (1992) *English phonology: an introduction.* Cambridge: Cambridge University Press.

Giegerich, Heinz J. (1999) *Lexical strata in English: morphological causes, phonological effects.* Cambridge: Cambridge University Press.

Holt, D. Eric (ed.) (2003) *Optimality theory and language change.* Dordrecht: Kluwer.

Jensen, John T. (1993) *English phonology.* Amsterdam: John Benjamins.

Kager, René (1999) *Optimality theory.* Cambridge: Cambridge University Press.

McMahon, April (2000) *Lexical phonology and the history of English.* Cambridge: Cambridge University Press.

REFERENCES

Anderson, S. (1992) *A-morphous morphology.* Cambridge: Cambridge University Press.

Anttila, A. (2002) Morphologically conditioned phonological alternations. *Natural Language and Linguistic Theory* 20, 1–41.

Archangeli, D. (1988) Aspects of underspecification theory. *Phonology* 5, 183–208.

Aronoff, M. and Anshen, F. (1998) Morphology and the lexicon: lexicalization and productivity. In A. Spencer and A. M. Zwicky (eds.),

The handbook of morphology. Oxford: Blackwell, 237–47.

Aronoff, M. and Sridhar, S. N. (1983) Morphological levels in English and Kannada; or, Atarizing Reagan. In J. Richardson, M. Marks, and A. Chukerman (eds.), *Chicago Linguistic Society 19: parasession on the interplay of phonology, morphology, and syntax*. Chicago: Chicago Linguistic Society, 3–16.

Benua, L. (1995) Identity effects in morphological truncation. In J. Beckman, L. Walsh Dickey, and S. Urbanczyk (eds.), *University of Massachusetts occasional papers in linguistics*, vol. 18: *Papers in optimality theory*. Amherst: GLSA, 77–136.

Benua, L. (1997) Transderivational identity: phonological relations between words. Doctoral dissertation, University of Massachusetts, Amherst. Available at ROA 259, Rutgers Optimality Archive, http://roa.rutgers.edu/.

Berko, J. (1958) The child's learning of English morphology. *Word* 14, 150–77.

Bermúdez-Otero, R. (1999) Constraint interaction in language change / Opacity and globality in phonological change. Doctoral dissertation, University of Manchester / Universidad de Santiago de Compostela.

Bermúdez-Otero, R. (2003) The acquisition of phonological opacity. In J. Spenader, A. Eriksson, and Ö. Dahl (eds.),*Variation within Optimality Theory: Proceedings of the Stockholm Workshop on 'Variation within Optimality Theory.'* Stockholm: Department of Linguistics, Stockholm University, 25–36. Expanded version available at ROA 593, Rutgers Optimality Archive, http://roa.rutgers.edu/.

Bermúdez-Otero, R. (forthcoming) *Stratal optimality theory*. Oxford: Oxford University Press.

Bermúdez-Otero, R. and Börjars, K. (2006) Markedness in phonology and in syntax: the problem of grounding. In P. Honeybone and R. Bermúdez-Otero (eds.), *Linguistic knowledge: perspectives from phonology and from syntax*. Special issue of *Lingua* 116 (5).

Booij, G. and Rubach, J. (1987) Postcyclic versus postlexical rules in lexical phonology. *Linguistic Inquiry* 18, 1–44.

Borowsky, T. (1993) On the word level. In S. Hargus and E. M. Kaisse (eds.), *Studies in lexical phonology*. San Diego: Academic Press, 199–234.

Burzio, L. (2002) Surface-to-surface morphology: when your representations turn into constraints. In P. Boucher (ed.), *Many morphologies*. Somerville, MA: Cascadilla Press, 142–77.

[Bybee-]Hooper, J. (1976) *An introduction to natural generative phonology*. New York: Academic Press.

Bybee, J. (1995) Regular morphology and the lexicon. *Language and Cognitive Processes* 10, 425–55.

Bybee, J. (2001) *Phonology and language use*. Cambridge: Cambridge University Press.

Chambers, J. K. (1973) Canadian raising. *Canadian Journal of Linguistics* 18, 113–35.

Chomsky, N. and Halle, M. (1968) *The sound pattern of English*. New York: Harper and Row.

Clayton, M. L. (1976) The redundance of underlying morpheme-structure conditions. *Language* 52, 295–313.

Davis, S. (2005) 'Capitalistic' vs 'militaristic': the paradigm uniformity effect reconsidered. In L. Downing, T. A. Hall, and R. Raffelsieffen (eds.), *Paradigms in phonological theory*. Oxford: Oxford University Press.

Fabb, N. (1988) English suffixation is constrained only by selectional restrictions. *Natural Language and Linguistic Theory* 6, 527–39.

Ford, A. and Singh, R. (1983) On the status of morphophonology.

In J. Richardson, M. Marks, and A. Chukerman (eds.), *Chicago Linguistic Society 19: Parasession on the interplay of phonology, morphology, and syntax*. Chicago: Chicago Linguistic Society, 63–78.

Giegerich, H. J. (1988) Strict cyclicity and elsewhere. *Lingua* 75, 125–34.

Giegerich, H. J. (1999) *Lexical strata in English: morphological causes, phonological effects*. Cambridge: Cambridge University Press.

Hale, M. and Reiss, C. (2000) Phonology as cognition. In N. Burton-Roberts, P. Carr, and G. Docherty (eds.), *Phonological knowledge: conceptual and empirical issues*. Oxford: Oxford University Press, 161–84.

Halle, M. and Mohanan, K. P. (1985) Segmental phonology of Modern English. *Linguistic Inquiry* 16, 57–116.

Hammond, M. (1989) Cyclic stress and accent in English. *Proceedings of the West Coast Conference on Formal Linguistics* 8, 139–53.

Harris, J. (1989) Towards a lexical analysis of sound change in progress. *Journal of Linguistics* 25, 35–56.

Harris, J. (1990) Derived phonological contrasts. In S. Ramsaran (ed.), *Studies in the pronunciation of English: a commemorative volume in honour of A. C. Gimson*. London: Routledge, 87–105.

Hayes, B. (1995) *Metrical stress theory: principles and case studies*. Chicago: University of Chicago Press.

Hayes, B. (1999a) Phonetically-driven phonology: the role of Optimality Theory and inductive grounding. In M. Darnell, E. Moravcsik, F. J. Newmeyer, M. Noonan, and K. Wheatley (eds.), *Functionalism and formalism in linguistics*, vol. I: *General papers*. Amsterdam: John Benjamins, 243–85.

Hayes, B. (1999b) Phonological acquisition in Optimality Theory: the early stages. ROA 327, Rutgers Optimality Archive, http://

roa.rutgers.edu/. Revised version published (2004) in R. Kager, J. Pater, and W. Zonneveld (eds.), *Fixing priorities: constraints in phonological acquisition*. Cambridge: Cambridge University Press.

Hayes, B., Kirchner, R., and Steriade, D. (2004) *Phonetically based phonology*. Cambridge: Cambridge University Press.

Hulst, H. van der (1984) *Syllable structure and stress in Dutch*. Dordrecht: Foris.

Inkelas, S. and Zoll, C. (2003) Is Grammar Dependence real? ROA-587, Rutgers Optimality Archive, http:// roa.rutgers.edu/.

Jackendoff, R. S. (1975) Morphological and semantic regularities in the lexicon. *Language* 51, 639–71.

Jensen, J. T. (2000) Against ambisyllabicity. *Phonology*, 17, 187–235.

Joos, M. (1942) A phonological dilemma in Canadian English. *Language* 18, 141–4.

Kaisse, E. M. and Shaw, P. A. (1985) On the theory of lexical phonology. *Phonology Yearbook* 2, 1–30.

Kaisse, E. M. and Hargus, S. (1994) When do linked structures evade Structure Preservation? In R. Wiese (ed.), *Recent developments in lexical phonology*. Düsseldorf: Heinrich Heine Universität, 185–204.

Kiparsky, P. (1982a) From cyclic phonology to lexical phonology. In H. van der Hulst and N. Smith (eds.), *The structure of phonological representations*, vol. 1. Dordrecht: Foris, 131–75.

Kiparsky, Paul (1982b) Lexical morphology and phonology. In I.-S. Yang (ed.), *Linguistics in the morning calm: selected papers from SICOL-1981*. Seoul: Hanshin, 3–91.

Kiparsky, P. (1985) Some consequences of lexical phonology. *Phonology Yearbook* 2, 85–138.

Kiparsky, P. (1993) Blocking in nonderived environments. In S. Hargus and E. M. Kaisse (eds.),

Studies in lexical phonology. San Diego: Academic Press, 277–313.

Kiparsky, P. (1994) Allomorphy or morphophonology? In R. Singh with R. Desrochers (eds.), *Trubetzkoy's orphan. Proceedings of the Montréal Roundtable "Morphonology: contemporary responses" (Montréal, September 30– October 2, 1994).* Amsterdam: John Benjamins, 13–31.

Kiparsky, P. (1998) Paradigm effects and opacity. Ms., Stanford University.

Kiparsky, P. (2000) Opacity and cyclicity. In N. A. Ritter (ed.), *A review of optimality theory*, 351–65. Special Issue of *The Linguistic Review*, 17, 2–4.

Lass, R. (1992) Phonology and morphology. In N. Blake (ed.), *The Cambridge history of the English language*, vol. 2: *1066–1476.* Cambridge: Cambridge University Press, 23–155.

Liberman, M. and Prince, A. (1977) On stress and linguistic rhythm. *Linguistic Inquiry* 8, 249–336.

Luce, P. A., Charles-Luce, J., and McLennan, C. (1999) Representational specificity of lexical form in the production and perception of spoken words. *Proceedings of the 14th International Congress of Phonetic Sciences (ICPhS99)*, San Francisco, August, 1999, 1889–92.

MacFarland, T. and Pierrehumbert, J. (1991) On ich-Laut, ach-Laut and Structure Preservation. *Phonology* 8, 171–80.

Marchand, H. (1969) *The categories and types of English word-formation*, 2nd edn. Munich: C. H. Beck'sche Verlagsbuchhandlung.

Mascaró, J. (1976) Catalan phonology and the phonological cycle. Doctoral dissertation, MIT.

McCarthy, J. J. (2002) *A thematic guide to optimality theory.* Cambridge: Cambridge University Press.

McMahon, A. M. S. (1990) Vowel shift, free rides and strict cyclicity. *Lingua* 80, 197–225.

McMahon, A. M. S. (2000) *Lexical phonology and the history of English.* Cambridge: Cambridge University Press.

Myers, S. (1987) Vowel shortening in English. *Natural Language and Linguistic Theory* 5, 485–518.

Odden, D. (1993) Interaction between modules in Lexical Phonology. In S. Hargus and E. M. Kaisse (eds.), *Studies in lexical phonology.* San Diego: Academic Press, 111–44.

Orgun, C. O. (1996) Sign-based morphology and phonology, with special attention to optimality theory. Doctoral dissertation, University of California, Berkeley. Available at ROA 171, Rutgers Optimality Archive, http://roa.rutgers.edu/.

Orgun, C. O. and Inkelas, S. (2002) Reconsidering bracket erasure. In G. Booij and J. van Marle (eds.), *Yearbook of morphology 2001.* Dordrecht: Kluwer, 115–46.

Pater, J. (2000) Non-uniformity in English secondary stress: the role of ranked and lexically specific constraints. *Phonology* 17, 237–74.

Pinker, S. and Prince, A. (1988) On language and connectionism: analysis of a parallel distributed processing model of language acquisition. *Cognition* 28, 73–193.

Prince, A. and Smolensky, P. (1993) *Optimality theory: constraint interaction in generative grammar.* Report no. RuCCS-TR-2. New Brunswick, NJ: Rutgers University Center for Cognitive Science. Revised August 2002: ROA 537, Rutgers Optimality Archive, http://roa.rutgers.edu/.

Raffelsiefen, R. (1999) Phonological constraints on English word formation. In G. Booij and J. van Marle (eds.), *Yearbook of morphology 1998.* Dordrecht: Kluwer, 225–87.

Rumelhart, D. E. and McClelland, J. L. (1986) On learning the past tenses of English verbs. In D. E. Rumelhart,

J. L. McClelland, and the PDP
Research Group (eds.), *Parallel
distributed processing: explorations in
the microstructure of cognition*, vol. 2.
Cambridge, MA: MIT Press,
216–71.

Siegel, D. (1974) Topics in English
morphology. Doctoral dissertation,
MIT.

Spencer, A. (1991) *Morphological theory.*
Oxford: Blackwell.

Steriade, D. (2000) Paradigm uniformity
and the phonetics-phonology
boundary. In M. B. Broe and
J. B. Pierrehumbert (eds.), *Papers in
laboratory phonology V: Acquisition and
the lexicon.* Cambridge: Cambridge
University Press, 313–34.

Withgott, M. M. (1982) Segmental
evidence for phonological constituents.
Doctoral dissertation, University of
Texas, Austin.

Yip, M. (1993) Cantonese loanword
phonology and optimality theory.
Journal of East Asian Linguistics 2,
261–91.

Yip, M. (1996) Lexicon optimization in
languages without alternations. In
J. Durand and B. Laks (eds.), *Current
trends in phonology: models and methods*,
vol. 2. Salford: European Studies
Research Institute, University of
Salford, 759–90.

Zamma, H. (2005) Predicting varieties:
partial orderings in English stress
assignment. Ms., Kobe City University
of Foreign Studies / University
College London. Available at
ROA-712-0205, Rutgers Optimality
Archive: http://roa.rutgers.edu.

18 Prosodic Phonology

MICHAEL HAMMOND

1 Introduction

Chomsky and Halle (1968) inaugurated generative phonology with a spectacular analysis of English. The linchpin of this analysis was their treatment of the vowel shift (as reflected in synchronic alternations like: *opaque* – *opacity* [òpʰék]-[òpʰǽsəɾi], *convene* – *convention* [kʰənvín]-[kʰənvɛ́nʃən], *line* – *linear* [lájn]-[líniər], etc.). Their analysis suggested, in fact, that the vowel shift was probably the defining property of English phonology.

While the vowel shift was certainly a cataclysmic event in the history of English, subsequent work has drawn into question whether it can be taken as a central organizing aspect of synchronic English phonology. First, synchronic alternations based on vowel shift are quite limited in scope, only occurring with certain suffixes. In addition, the contexts where we expect to find these alternations are rife with exceptions. Moreover, there is a whole body of literature showing that vowel shift alternations do not extend readily to neologisms or new words.

In addition, there has been increased attention paid to the prosodic aspects of English phonology – syllable and foot structure – and it has become clear that English enjoys a remarkable prosodic organization that plays a role in virtually every aspect of its phonological system.

In this chapter, we review the evidence for the prosodic underpinnings of English phonology. We start with the syllable, first reviewing the extralinguistic evidence for this unit and then the classical arguments for syllable structure in English. We then turn to the more controversial aspects of English syllable structure, e.g. final clusters, ambisyllabicity, and timing units.

We next turn to higher-level foot structure. Again, the exposition begins with a discussion of the extralinguistic evidence for this unit, followed by the classical evidence in English. We then turn to the controversial aspects of foot structure, e.g. ternarity, quantity-sensitivity, and predictability.

2   Structure in Phonology

What is prosody generally? Here, we take prosody to be the organization of phonological material into phonologically motivated sequences. It can thus be opposed to the simultaneous grouping of features or feature-like elements into segments, but also opposed to the sequential grouping of segments into morphemes (since these are not phonologically motivated sequences).

There are two clear prosodic units that can be motivated in English on the basis of both intuitive and linguistic arguments: the syllable and foot. For example, English-speaking subjects will readily agree on the number of syllables in words like *hat* [hæt], *candy* [kʰændi], *potato* [pʰətʰéɾo], and *Minnesota* [mìnəsóɾə]: one, two, three, and four respectively. As a first approximation, we can characterize the syllable as a vowel plus surrounding consonants. We might syllabify the words above as follows (using a period or full stop to mark syllable edges):

.hat.   .can.dy.   .po.ta.to.   .Mi.nne.so.ta.

The foot is a higher-level unit that groups syllables together. Interestingly, as we'll discuss further in section 4 below, foot structure is not so accessible to conscious intuition, but we can find compelling evidence from a variety of sources to posit feet as follows for the words above (using curly brackets to mark the edges of feet): {hát}, {cándy}, po{táto}, and {Mìnne}{sóta}. Basically, a foot is composed of a stressed syllable along with some number of adjacent stressless syllables.

In sections 3 and 4, we consider the evidence for and precise structure of these two units.

3   Syllables

What is a *syllable*? The standard definition has it that a syllable is a peak of sonority, where sonority refers to the intrinsic "loudness" of sounds.[1] For example, the first syllable of *candy*, [kʰæn], has the high-sonority element [æ] as its peak and two less-sonorous consonants as peripheral elements. This definition is both too general and too specific, but we can start with it as a first approximation.

3.1   Extralinguistic evidence for the syllable

Evidence that there is such a grouping comes from a variety of sources. Consider first the extralinguistic evidence for the syllable.

One source of evidence is poetry. There are several poetic traditions in English where the number of syllables is regulated. For example, in iambic pentameter, each line must have ten syllables.[2] Shakespeare's famous eighteenth sonnet is a fine example.

> Shall I compare thee to a summer's day?
> Thou art more lovely and more temperate:
> Rough winds do shake the darling buds of May,
> And summer's lease hath all too short a date:
> . . .

Language games also provide evidence for the syllable. For example, the language game *Geta* involves inserting the sequence -*idig*- [ɪɾɪg] into each syllable. For example, a word like *Minnesota* would be pronounced in Geta as [mɪɾɪgìnɪɾɪgəsɪɾɪgótʰɪɾɪgə]. Another game with similar properties is *Op*, where the sequence [ap] is inserted into each syllable, e.g. [mapìnapəsapórapə]. In both cases, the game is best described in terms of the unit syllable.

Another argument for the syllable in English comes from hyphenation, the principles which govern how orthographic words can be split up to accommodate line breaks. For example, a word like *Minnesota* can be hyphenated in certain places, but not others, e.g. *Min-ne-so-ta*. These potential hyphenaton positions are controlled by several factors: morphology, spelling, and syllabification. Morphology plays a role in that hyphens are preferentially placed at a morpheme boundaries, e.g. *unable* [ənébəl] is better hyphenated as *un-able*, rather than *u-nable*. Spelling also plays a role. For example, double letters are better split by a hyphen than not, e.g. *at-test* [ətʰést] is much better than *att-est* or *a-ttest*. Finally, the relevant fact in the present context is that syllabification plays a role. There must be at least a syllable on each side of the hyphen. For example, one cannot hyphenate *four-th* [fórθ], even though the morphemic criterion is met. In addition, all else being equal, hyphens prefer to go at syllable junctures, e.g. *ca-vort* [kʰəvórt], not *cav-ort*.[3]

Yet another argument for syllables comes from their conscious accessibility; as noted at the beginning of this chapter, English-speaking subjects can readily identify the number of syllables in most words.

Interestingly, there are problematic cases, e.g. *flower* vs. *flour* [flawər]/[fláwr] or *towel* vs. *cowl* [tʰáwəl]/[kʰáwl]. In cases like these, subjects seem perhaps unduly influenced by the spelling. In addition, one can argue that these ambiguities are a consequence of there being "too much" material for one syllable.[4]

Intuitions are also rather confused about the precise boundaries between syllables. For example, when asked what the syllables of a word like *about* [əbáwt] are, subjects will consistently divide the syllables before the [b]. On the other hand, a word like *any* [éni] is far less clearly divided. It turns out that the conditions under which this ambiguity occurs are rather clear. First, when the second syllable is stressless, an intervocalic consonant is more likely to be affiliated to the left. Second, the more sonorous the intervocalic consonant, the more likely it is to affiliate to the left. Third, an intervocalic consonant is more likely to affiliate to the left if the preceding vowel is lax.[5]

3.2   *Linguistic evidence for the syllable*

The simplest linguistic argument for the syllable in English comes from the distribution of segments. If we assume that all syllables in English are composed of a vowel with some number of surrounding consonants and we assume that words are exhaustively broken up into syllables, it then follows that all word-internal consonant sequences must be decomposable into a syllable-final sequence followed by a syllable-initial sequence. This makes the empirical prediction that the set of medial clusters can be *predicted* from the set of word-initial and word-final clusters.

For example, we expect to find words like *hamster* [hǽmstər] because we have words that end in [m] and words that begin in [st], e.g. *seem* [sím] and *store* [stór]. On the other hand, we do not expect to find words like *[bǽdvdə] since there is no division of [dvd] that results in both a possible word-final and a possible word-initial sequence.

word-final	word-initial	word-final	word-initial
dvd	Ø	**none**	apple
dv	d	**none**	door
d	vd	bad	**none**
Ø	dvd	spa	**none**

Interestingly, this argument should apply biconditionally, but it does not. Thus, there are no medial clusters that cannot be decomposed into at least one instance of a legal word-final cluster followed by a legal word-initial cluster. On the other hand, there are quite a few examples of clusters that can be constructed from legal word-final sequences followed by word-initial sequences that do not occur, e.g. [s-ʃ], [kst-str], [ŋks-fr], etc.[6] Some of these gaps follow from linear restrictions on the distribution of English sounds, for example [s-ʃ]; others have yet to be explained satisfactorily.

Another argument for the syllable in English comes from the distribution of stress. (We return to this in more detail in section 4 below.) Basically, the distribution of stress in English depends on the syllabic analysis of a string. For example, unsuffixed verbs and adjectives are generally stressed on one of the last two syllables of the word.

penult	ultima
edit [ɛ́rɪt]	acquiesce [æ̀kwiɛ́s]
abandon [əbǽndən]	appertain [æ̀pərtʰén]
abolish [əbálɪʃ]	cajole [kʰədʒól]
alter [óltər]	careen [kʰərín]
deliver [dəlívər]	harass [hərǽs]

If the generalization is best stated in terms of the syllable, then this constitutes an argument for the syllable.

Unsuffixed nouns are generally stressed on one of the last *three* syllables of the word.

ultima	penult	antepenult
affair [əfér]	abbot [ǽbət]	abacus [ǽbəkəs]
bazaar [bəzár]	bagel [bégəl]	banister [bǽnɪstər]
parade [pʰəréd]	carat [kʰǽrət]	caramel [kʰǽrəməl]
pecan [pʰəkʰán]	fuchsia [fjúʃə]	emerald [émərəld]
saloon [səlún]	hundred [hándrəd]	hyacinth [hájəsɪnθ]

Again, if the generalization is best stated in terms of the syllable, then this constitutes an argument for the syllable.

The arguments just given from stress are not as compelling as one might hope when given in this form. The problem is that the generalizations as given could equally well be stated in terms of *vowels*, rather than syllables per se. We can, however, refine the argument so that reference to syllables cannot be replaced with reference to vowels.

We can do this by considering the distribution of stress with respect to syllable *weight*.[7] The basic observation is that the rightmost stress in English nouns can only occur three syllables from the right (on the antepenult) if one of three conditions hold:

1   The penultimate syllable isn't closed by a consonant, e.g. *abacus* [ǽbəkəs]
2   The noun is suffixed, e.g. *humbleness* [hámbəlnəs]
3   The final syllable is [ər] or [i], e.g. *carpenter* [kʰárpəntər]

In the latter two cases, the penult *may* be closed by a consonant.[8]

The argument for an account in terms of syllables comes from a consideration of what it means empirically to be "closed by a consonant." Specifically, if the penultimate vowel is followed by some number of consonants that can begin a word (and thus begin a syllable) then the antepenult can be stressed. On the other hand, if the penult is followed by some sequence of consonants that cannot begin a word – and thus cannot begin a syllable – then the word cannot have stress on the antepenult.

Thus a word like *agenda* [ədʒéndə] cannot bear stress on its antepenult because [nd] cannot begin a word in English. The fact that it cannot begin a word means that it cannot be a syllable onset[9] and that it must therefore be split into two syllables when it occurs medially, i.e. [.ə.dʒén.də.]. On the other hand, the consonant sequence that occurs in the same position in a word like *algebra* [ǽldʒəbrə] can occur word-initially – for example in *brew* [brú] – and therefore does not need to be split into two separate syllables.

The same point applies to larger clusters, e.g. the contrast between *conundrum* [kʰənándrəm] and *orchestra* [órkəstrə]. The word *conundrum* cannot bear antepenultimate stress because the cluster [ndr] cannot occur at the beginning of a word and at least one consonant must occur in the penultimate syllable. On the other hand, the [str] cluster in *orchestra* can begin a word (as in *string* [stríŋ]) and therefore need not close the penultimate syllable.

Summarizing thus far, we have presented evidence of several sorts in favor of incorporating syllables into the analysis of English words.

3.3   *The formal representation of the syllable*

To accommodate this evidence, we can suppose that words are organized into syllables. There is a bit of a paradox, however. We can write rules or principles that can predict how words are syllabified. Under normal generative assumptions, this would imply that underlying or input forms are not syllabified and that syllables are added in the course of the phonological derivation.[10]

One problem with this view is that there is psycholinguistic evidence that the lexicon is organized in terms of prosody. That is, various experiments involving lexical access suggest that the mental lexicon contains information about the syllabification (and stress) of words. Some analyses have taken these facts to heart and posited input representations with prosodic structure already encoded, e.g. Golston (1996).

Setting aside the question of when words are syllabified, consider first *how* they are syllabified. Let us represent syllables with Greek σ and affiliation of segments to syllables with association lines. As a first approximation, we can represent the syllabification of *agenda* as follows.

This is not explicit enough as it does not indicate the affiliation of individual elements. The following diagram adds this additional detail.

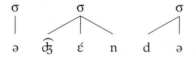

This includes the same information as the "dot" notation that we used above, but more directly captures the intuition we've been working with: syllables are hierarchically organized segmental structure, not pseudo-segmental boundary elements, like "dot."

The structures above are only one possible way of grouping the segments of *agenda* together. Focusing just on the [nd] cluster, there are three possible divisions: [.nd], [n.d], and [nd.]. The first, we have ruled out on the grounds that [nd] is impossible word-initially. Nothing we have said so far would distinguish between the representation above and the following one.

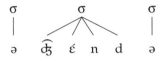

There is, in fact, a huge debate on how such ambiguous clusters are partitioned: the most orthodox position holds that ambiguous consonants are affiliated as onsets. This is termed the *Maximal Onset Principle* and has the effect of preferring [.ə.d͡ʒέn.də.] over other alternatives (Kahn 1980).

There is clear evidence for something like the Maximal Onset Principle from a number of languages, but the facts in English are quite ambiguous. Kahn argues that syllabification in English depends at least partially on the distribution of stress. The facts come from the distribution of aspiration and flapping in English. First, voiceless stops and affricates are aspirated when they occur at the beginning of a word.

pan [pʰǽn]   tan [tʰǽn]   can [kʰǽn]   Chan [t͡ʃʰǽn]

This aspiration is usually notated as devoicing of the following segment, when the voiceless stop occurs first in a cluster.

ply [pl̥áj]   pry [pr̥áj]   cry [kr̥áj]

Voiceless stops are not aspirated when they occur after an [s] in a word-initial cluster.

span [spǽn]   stan [stǽn]   scan [skǽn]

Word-final stops are unreleased:

nap [næp̚]   gnat [næt̚]   nack [næk̚]

From what we have seen so far, we can say that voiceless stops and affricates are aspirated word-initially. It is also possible to characterize this in terms of syllables: syllable-initial voiceless stops and affricates are aspirated. However, the facts presented so far do not require this.

Let's now consider word-internal examples. An intervocalic voiceless stop is aspirated if the following vowel is stressed, regardless whether the preceding vowel is stressed or stressless.

unstressed-stressed	stressed-stressed
appeal [əpʰíl]	topaz [tʰópʰæz]
attack [ətʰǽk]	atoll [ǽtʰɔl]
accost [əkʰɔ́st]	recap [ríkʰæp]
mature [məʧʰúr]	recharge [riʧʰárʤ]

On the other hand, if the following vowel is stressless, then the consonant is unaspirated. In some dialects, if it is coronal, then it is flapped.

stressed-unstressed	unstressed-unstressed
happy [hǽpi]	canopy [kʰǽnəpi]
pity [pʰíɾi]	vanity [vǽnəɾi]
tacky [tʰǽki]	comical [kʰáməkəl]
catchy [kʰǽʧi]	literature [líɾərəʧ͡ər]

These facts show that a simple word-based analysis won't suffice: the consonant can be aspirated word-medially, in addition to word-initially. On the other hand, a simple syllable-based approach won't work either.

To accommodate these additional facts, Kahn proposes that syllabification in English depends on stress. Specifically, when the following vowel is stressed, an intervocalic consonant affiliates as an onset; when the following vowel is stressless, the consonant affiliates of *both* syllables. This results in the following representations for the relevant portions of *pan*, *appeal*, and *happy*.

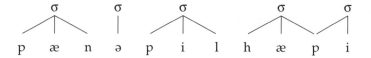

Aspiration occurs when a voiceless stop occurs at the left edge of a syllable. This groups together initial cases like *pan* and medial pre-stress cases like *appeal*.

There are a number of complications that result when consonant clusters are considered (Kahn 1980), but also with morphologically complex items. For example, Withgott (1982) cites the opposition between *militaristic* [mìlətʰərístɪk] and *capitalistic* [kʰæpərəlístɪk] as evidence that the morphological structure of an item can affect the likelihood of aspiration/flapping. Stress-based resyllabification is a controversial question to this day and we return to it in section 4 below.

Another classic argument for the syllable in English comes from *Closed Syllable Shortening* (Myers 1987). Vowels are shortened when they occur in what we can think of as a closed syllable. Here are some medial alternations.

retain [rìtʰén]   retention [rìtʰɛ́nʃən]
abstain [ǽbstén]   abstention [ǽbstɛ́nʃən]
conceive [kʰənsív]   conception [kʰənsɛ́pʃən]
redeem [rìdím]   redemption [rìdɛ́mpʃən]

There are also examples in final position.

five [fájv]   fifth [fífθ]
wide [wájd]   width [wítθ]
leap [líp]   leapt [lépt]
mean [mín]   meant [mént]
dream [drím]   dreamt [drémt]
kneel [níl]   knelt [nélt]
keep [kʰíp]   kept [kʰépt]
clean [kl̥ín]   cleanse [kl̥énz]

This phenomenon is complicated by several factors. First, the length alternation is mediated by vowel shift; thus vowels are not paired in the intuitively
obvious way, but through the various changes introduced by vowel shift. The
second complication is that there are lots of exceptions. For example:

change [ʧʰénʤ]   reaped [rípt]   child [ʧʰájld]
seemed [símd]   quaint [kwént]   steeped [stípt]
eighth [éθ]   ninth [nájnθ]

The main problem with this argument is that it requires a more complex
notion of what constitutes a closed syllable. Specifically, medially, a single
consonant is sufficient to close a syllable, but word-finally, two consonants are
required to close a syllable. Thus, there is shortening in *retention* [rìtʰɛ́nʃən]
because the relevant syllable is closed by [n]. In *wide* [wájd], the single consonant [d] is insufficient to trigger shortening and it only applies when a
second consonant is added: *width* [wídθ].

In fact, there is good reason to believe that final syllables are to be treated
differently from medial syllables in other regards. For example, Harris (1994)
argues that while syllables like text [tʰékst] are possible in final position, they
are disallowed medially. Final syllables allow more final consonants than
medial syllables. This fact – and the preceding one about closed syllable
shortening – can both be accommodated if we revise the claim that words
are exhaustively parsed into syllables. Following Harris, let us suppose that
a word can be construed as a sequence of syllables followed by a lone consonantal position. This will allow for extra consonants word-finally and also
allow for a simpler characterization of closed syllable shortening. Syllables are
shortened when they are closed by a single consonant. The reason why a word
like *wide* doesn't undergo shortening is because the final consonant can be
accommodated in the extra word-final consonantal position.[11]

3.4   Summary

We have seen that there is clear evidence for syllables in English. This evidence allows us to conclude that English words are parsed into units organized in terms of sonority.

We have also seen that English phonology is sensitive to syllable weight, but we have left open precisely how this weight might be encoded.[12]

Finally, we have seen that the affiliation of intervocalic consonants is unclear. It can be argued that intervocalic consonants might be preferentially affiliated with stressed syllables (or preferentially not affiliated with stressless syllables), but other analyses are possible as we will see in section 4.

4   Feet

Another unit of word-level prosody is the *foot*. The foot groups a stressed syllable together with some number of adjacent stressless syllables. There is extensive evidence for such a unit from a number of sources.

4.1   Extralinguistic evidence for the foot

The main extralinguistic evidence for the foot comes from poetry. For example, a line of iambic pentameter can be characterized as a sequence of five "iambic" feet. The effect of this characterization is that the even-numbered positions can readily support a lexically stressed syllable (a syllable that would be marked as stressed in a dictionary); odd-numbered positions do so only under duress. The former have been dubbed "strong" positions, the latter "weak" positions. For example, the first line in the sonnet cited above has lexical stresses on the fourth, eighth, and tenth syllables. The same lines cited above are repeated below with all lexical stresses marked with acute accents. In addition, lexical stresses that occur in odd-numbered positions have been underlined.

> Shall I compáre thee to a súmmer's dáy?
> Thou art more lóvely and more témperate:
> <u>Róugh</u> wínds do sháke the dárling búds of Máy,
> And súmmer's léase hath all too shórt a dáte:
> . . .

Relatively few stresses occur in odd positions; the only case in this example is a line-initial monosyllabic word adjacent to another lexical stress: "Rough winds . . ." This is fairly typical of the English metrical tradition (Hammond 1991; Hanson and Kiparsky 1997; Hayes 1983, 1989b; Kiparsky 1977).

This force of the current argument comes from viewing each line as a sequence of five binary units, rather than ten syllable-sized units. This follows from the typological observation that "strong" metrical positions typically alternate with "weak" positions. The existence of triple meters, e.g. anapestic (wws), dactylic (sww), or amphibrachic (wsw), undercuts this argument in obvious ways.

Notice too that this argument does not address the "grouping" aspect of feet; it does not give a direct rationale for why any particular medial syllable should be grouped either to the left or to the right. For example, consider a string of three syllable positions in the middle of some line alternating from strong to weak and to strong. The only reason to group the weak syllable with the following strong one is to insure the full parsing of the line into feet:

{w s} {w s} {w s} {w s} {w s}

Were we to group them the other way – grouping the weak positions with the preceding strong positions – we would not achieve a complete parsing of the string:

w {s w} {s w} {s w} {s w} s

This is an argument for feet in general, but not an overpowering one. It is built purely on the alternating distribution of strong and weak positions.

A more compelling argument for the foot in English comes from the "Name Game" (Hammond 1990). This language game is played by fitting different names to a particular template. For example, here is how the game is played with the name *Joey* [d͡ʒói].

Joey, Joey, bo-boey	[d͡ʒoi d͡ʒoi bo boi]
banana fana fo-foey	[bənænə fænə fo foi]
me my mo-moey	[mi maj mo moi]
Jo-ey	[d͡ʒo i]

The game comes from a popular song by the same name from 1965 by Shirley Ellis. The game is still played by children who've never heard the original song.

There are two interesting aspects to the game. First, notice how the game involves substituting various consonants for the initial consonant(s) of the name. It turns out that this substitution is for the entire string of onset consonants, not just the first consonant. This is confirmed by the pattern with a name like *Brenda* [brɛ́ndə].

Brenda, Brenda, bo-benda	[brɛndə brɛndə bo bɛndə]
banana fana fo-fenda	[bənænə fænə fo fɛndə]
me my mo-menda	[mi maj mo mɛndə]
Bren-da	[brɛn də]

This pattern of substitution has interesting implications for the nature of English onsets and rhymes, but we won't pursue this here (Hammond 1990).

The foot-related restriction on the game is that it can be played with only certain types of names. For example, it can be played with any monosyllabic name, but with only certain polysyllabic ones. With disyllabic names, the game can only be played with names with a single stress on the first syllable (like those in the first column below); all other stress patterns are unacceptable in the game.

óσ	σó	óὸ	ὸó
Joey	Annette	Anton	Diane
Larry	Ramon	Omar	Danielle
Mona	Jerome	Gertrude	Tyrone
Bridget	Marie	Carmine	Eugene

For example, with a name like *Annette* [ənέt], subjects will either refuse to play or convert the name to an acceptable stress pattern, e.g. [ǽnət] or [nέt]. The facts presented so far would suggest that a stressed syllable followed by a stressless syllable forms a special unit in English: a trochaic foot.

This is confirmed by the behavior of longer words which generally eschew the game. Names composed of a stressed syllable followed by two stressless syllables are, however, marginally capable of undergoing the game, e.g. names like *Christopher* [krístəfər], etc. These suggest that perhaps a three-syllable unit might be more apropos, but we return to this issue below.

4.2   Linguistic evidence for the foot

We now consider more traditional linguistic evidence for the foot in English. The most compelling evidence comes from *Expletive Infixation* (McCarthy 1982; Hammond 1997, 1999). In certain dialects of English, the expletive *fuckin'*, *bloody*, or *damn* can be infixed into another word, e.g. as in *Minne-fuckin'-sota* [mìnəfʌ́kɪnsóɾə]. (To accommodate the faint-hearted, we will notate the infix as *f** in subsequent untranscribed examples.)

What is important in the present context is that (1) not all word types can undergo this infixation, and (2) the locus of infixation is strictly limited. Moreover, while not all dialects of English exhibit this phenomenon, speakers readily learn the construction. Strikingly, these adult learners of the construction exhibit the same restrictions as those speakers for whom the construction is native.

The restrictions are as follows. To allow infixation at all, a candidate word must exhibit more than one stress. In addition, the primary stress of the domain cannot be the first stress. The first restriction distinguishes ungrammatical *ba-f*-nana* [bəfʌ́kɪnnǽnə] from grammatical *ban-f*-dana* [bǽnfʌ́kɪndǽnə]. The second restriction distinguishes ungrammatical *anec-f*-dote* [ǽnəkfʌ́kɪndòt] from grammatical *Tenne-f*-ssee* [tʰὲnəfʌ́kɪnsí].

Confining our attention to words with these properties, the infix can only go in certain positions. First, it must occur before the main stress. This accounts for the position of the infix in *bandana*: [bænfʌkɪndǽnə], rather than *[bændǽfʌkɪnnə]. Likewise, in a word like *formaldehyde*, the infix must go before the primary stress, rather than after it, e.g. [fòrfʌkɪnmæ̀ldəhàyd], rather than *[fòrmæ̀ldəfʌkɪnhàjd].[13]

Second, if there is a single stressless syllable, then the infix must go to the right of that syllable. Thus, in a word with adjacent stresses, the infix goes between the stresses, e.g. *robust* [ròfʌkɪnbʌ́st]. This allows for multiple infixation sites if there is more than one stress before the primary stress, e.g. *Timbuktu* [tʰìmfʌkɪnbʌ̀ktʰú] or [tʰìmbʌ̀kfʌkɪntʰú]. When there is a single stressless syllable between stresses, the infix must go after the stressless syllable. Thus *Tennessee* is infixed as [tʰɛ̀nəfʌkɪnsí], rather than *[tʰɛ̀fʌkɪnnəsí]. Likewise, *Minnesota* must be infixed as [mìnəfʌkɪnsórə], rather than as *[mìfʌkɪnnəsórə].

Finally, if there are two stressless syllables between the stresses, then the infix must follow the first stressless syllable, but may follow the second as well. For example, a word like *Winnepesaukee* can undergo infixation to [wìnəfʌkɪnpəsɔ́ki] or [wìnəpəfʌkɪnsɔ́ki].

These facts suggest – like the Name Game – that there is a privileged grouping of a stressed syllable with a following stressless syllable. The locus of infixation can thereby be defined as occurring between two feet.

Notice that, as with the Name Game facts, that there is some unclarity about whether there is a ternary foot. One possible characterization of the possibility of infixation after two stressless syllables in a form like [wìnəpəfʌkɪnsɔ́ki] is that the first *three* syllables comprise a foot. We return to this below.

The central argument for the foot in English, however, has been the distribution of stress. The basic empirical observation has been that stresses in English are distributed in an alternating fashion from right to left and that this alternation can most effectively be captured with trochaic feet built from the right edge of the word.

Recall the distribution of stress presented in the charts in section 3.2 above. There we saw that with unsuffixed verbs stress must fall on one of the last two syllables; with unsuffixed nouns, stress must fall on one of the last three syllables. Stresses further to the left are subject to a similar restriction, not specific to lexical category: there can be no more than two stressless syllables intervening between stresses. In addition, a word cannot begin with more than one stressless syllable.

These restrictions interact in very complex ways with syllable weight (Chomsky and Halle 1968; Hammond 1999; Pater 2000) and a full treatment of the effect of syllable weight on pretonic stress is far beyond the scope of this chapter. The two restrictions above, however, are true regardless of syllable weight.

We now go through the basic cases to see that this is so. A single syllable before a stressed syllable can be stressed or stressless.

stressed	stressless
caffeine [kʰæ̀fín]	platoon [pḷətʰún]
tattoo [tʰæ̀tʰú]	canal [kʰənǽl]
bamboo [bæ̀mbú]	confetti [kʰənféɾi]
vendetta [vèndéɾə]	obsidian [əbsíɾiən]

Two syllables before a stressed syllable can exhibit every combination of stresses, except both stressless.

ò̀ó̀	chimpanzee [ʧʰìmpʰæ̀nzí]
	Timbuktu [tʰìmbʌ̀ktʰú]
	Istanbul [ìstànbúl]
ò̀σ	Alexander [æ̀ləgzǽndər]
	magazine [mæ̀gəzín]
	Minnesota [mìnəsóɾə]
σò̀	electricity [əlèktɹ̩ísəɾi]
	employee [əmpḷɔ́jí]

With longer spans, there are far fewer relevant cases and – though the restrictions we've posited are indeed satisfied – there are unexplained gaps. With three syllables preceding the main stress we get these patterns:

ò̀σσó	marionette	[mæ̀ɹiənét]
	Indianapolis	[ìndiənǽpəlɪs]
	Kilimanjaro	[kʰìləmənʤáro]
σò̀σó	aperitif	[əpʰɛ̀ɹətʰíf]
	Louisiana	[ləwìziǽnə]
	Scheherazade	[ʃəhɛ̀ɹəzád]
ò̀ò̀σó	phantasmagoria	[fæ̀ntʰæ̀zməgóɹiə]
	alcaptonuria	[æ̀lkʰæ̀ptənúɹiə]
ò̀σò̀ó	daffodowndilly	[dæ̀fədàwndíli]
	Halicarnassus	[hæ̀ləkʰàrnǽsəs]
	Buenaventura	[bwènəvèntʰúɾə]

Even when we include rather obscure words and names, we are still missing two patterns: σò̀ò̀ó and ò̀ò̀ò̀ó.[14]

The key generalizations still hold however. Moreover, they can be used to argue that there is a unit foot that organizes English syllables into words. Recall that the generalizations governing monomorphemic words were (1) that there cannot be three stressless syllables in a row, and (2) that a word cannot begin with two stressless syllables. If we assume that a foot in English is composed of a stressed syllable followed by at most a single stressless syllable, then the generalizations given can be captured by assuming that words are

well-formed when unfooted syllables cannot occur next to each other. There is
no way to foot a word that begins with two stressless syllables without violating either the definition of the foot or this restriction. Likewise, a word with
three stressless syllables next to each other would also have to violate one of
these restrictions. These ideas are shown diagrammatically in the following
examples. (As before, feet are indicated with curly braces.) First, we see that a
medial span of three stressless syllables is unparsable.

Canton	. . . ó } { ó . . .
Minnesota	. . . ó σ } { ó . . .
Winnepesaukee	. . . ó σ } σ { ó . . .
IMPOSSIBLE	. . . ó σ } σ σ { ó . . .

Then we see that an initial span of two stressless syllables is also unparsable.

hat	{ ó . . .
cavort	σ { ó . . .
IMPOSSIBLE	σ σ { ó . . .

Notice that an account of these distributional regularities in terms of a
ternary foot would not fare so well. The basic idea would presumably be to
adopt a foot where a stressed syllable can be followed by at most *two* stressless
syllables. To account for the fact that no more than two stressless syllables
can occur in sequence, we would say that a word must be exhaustively parsed
into these ternary feet. A stressless three-syllable span would then necessarily
involve at least one unparsed syllable.

Canton	. . . ó } { ó . . .
Minnesota	. . . ó σ } { ó . . .
Winnepesaukee	. . . ó σ σ } { ó . . .
IMPOSSIBLE	. . . ó σ σ } σ { ó . . .

The problem is that the ternary account would then stumble with the prohibition against two stressless syllables word-initially. The absence of these would
seem to suggest that at most one unfooted syllable can occur at the beginning
of a word, not two. That, however, doesn't gibe with the assumption that there
can be no unfooted syllables medially. We would be left saying that medially
there can be no unfooted syllables, but initially there can be at most one.

hat	{ ó . . .
cavort or IMPOSSIBLE?	σ { ó . . .
IMPOSSIBLE	σ σ { ó . . .

The distributional facts then argue that English words are organized into
feet. Those feet are trochaic: composed of a stressed syllable followed by at
most one unstressed syllable. Moreover, unlike with syllabic parsing, parsing by
feet need not be exhaustive. A single syllable may be skipped between feet.[15]

Confirming evidence for a trochaic foot in English comes from syncope (Hammond 1999: 165–6). A stressless syllable may be elided in certain circumstances in English. For example, a word like *parade*, normally pronounced [pʰəréd], may be pronounced as [pṛéd] in more casual or rapid speech. There are a number of interesting segmental and lexical restrictions on when this can occur, but what is relevant in the present context are the syllabic and stress-based restrictions.

First, an initial stressless syllable can be syncopated:

parade	[pʰəréd]	[pṛéd]
Toronto	[tʰəránto]	[tṛánto]
Marina	[mərínə]	[mrínə]
Canadian	[kʰənériən]	[kṇériən]

Second, a medial stressless syllable can syncopate after a stress and before a stressless syllable:

opera	[ápərə]	[áprə]
general	[ʤénərəl]	[ʤénrəl]
chocolate	[ʧʰákələt]	[ʧʰáklət]

Third, when two stressless syllables occur between two stressed syllables, either can syncopate:[16]

respiratory	[réspərətʰòri]	[résprətʰòri]	[réspərtʰòri]
glorification	[glòrəfəkʰéʃən]	[glòrfəkʰéʃən]	[glòrəfkʰéʃən]

Strikingly, syncope cannot occur when the stressless syllable occurs directly between two stresses. The following pairs of words can be compared.

syncopates	doesn't syncopate
opera	operatic [àpərǽrɪk]
general	generality [ʤènərǽləri]
glorification	glorify [glórəfàj]
respiratory	respirate [réspərèt]

The environment for syncope can be expressed very simply on the assumption that feet are trochaic: syncopate when it would result in more complete parsing of the word. The following chart shows how in each case, syncope results in a better parse.[17]

	before syncope	after syncope
opera	{ápə}rə	{áprə}
parade	pʰə{réd}	{pṛéd}
respiratory	{réspə}rə{tʰòri}	{résprə}{tʰòri}

5   Syllables and Feet

Syllabification and footing interact in several interesting ways. In this section, we consider two: quantity sensitivity and flapping.

We have seen that the location of the rightmost stress in English is contingent on syllable weight. There are two principal analyses of these facts. One view has it that feet do not count syllables, but instead count *moras*: Hayes (1995).[18] On this view, feet contain precisely two moras and sensitivity to syllable weight follows from this restriction. The other view has it that stress can be attracted to heavy syllables directly, via the *Weight-to-Stress* (WSP) principle (Prince and Smolensky 1993).

Consider a word like *aroma* [ərómə], with a heavy bimoraic penultimate syllable. Under the bimoraic foot approach, the penultimate syllable gets stress because, after skipping the rightmost syllable, the foot must be built as close to the right as possible.[19] Since the penult is bimoraic and the foot must contain precisely two moras, the foot settles on the penult: a{ro}ma. Were the stress to settle on the antepenult, the foot would have to be trimoraic: *{aro}ma.

Under the WSP approach, the final syllable is skipped as well. The left-headed foot must also be built on the right edge, all else being equal, placing stress on the antepenult. The WSP forces stress on the penult instead: a{ro}ma.

The two approaches thus make the same predictions for nouns with heavy penults. They also make the same predictions for words with light antepenults and penults, e.g. *Canada* [kʰǽnəɾə] {Cána}da. They make different predictions, however, for words with a heavy antepenult, e.g. *fantasy* [fǽntəsi]. The bimoraic foot places stress on the antepenult, but does not include the penult: {fan}tasy. The WSP analysis also places stress on the antepenult, but includes the penultimate syllable: {fanta}sy.

Hayes argues the virtues of the bimoraic foot for its typological implications and Mester (1994) argues its virtues for its consequences with respect to the lexical phonology of English, it fails to describe the facts of syncope and expletive infixation as described above. If, for example, feet can contain only two moras, then a word like *candelabra* [kʰæ̀ndəlábrə] should be footed as follows: {can}de{labra}. This, in turn, predicts that expletive infixation should be possible after the first or second syllable, yet it is only possible after the second: *cande-f*-labra*, **can-f*-delabra*. In addition, this would predict that the second syllable of such a form should be able to undergo syncope, yet it cannot: *[kʰæ̀ndlábrə]. Thus, the evidence from English prosodic phonology is that quantity sensitivity should be effected by direct constraints on quantity (the WSP), rather than on foot size per se.

Another argument that supports this conclusion is that syllables with three moras are arguably possible in English. For example, Hammond (1999) argues that the difference between well-formed sequences like *bike* [bajk] and ill-formed sequences like *[bawk] follows from a trimoraic maximum on English syllable structure. If this is so, then this poses a challenge to a theory of footing predicated on a two-mora foot maximum.

The other domain where syllables and feet interact is stress-conditioned allophony like aspiration and flapping. In section 3.3 above, we showed how Kahn proposes a theory of resyllabification that depends on stress. His proposal then accounts for the distribution of aspiration (and flapping in relevant dialects) based on syllable structure.

Kiparsky (1979) proposes a different analysis of those facts where aspiration depends directly on foot structure. The basic idea is that foot-medial obstruents become "lax." This laxity prevents aspiration. In relevant dialects, a lax intervocalic coronal will undergo flapping. The issue is quite complex, but the facts we have cited above would argue against a foot-based analysis. Specifically, the possibility of flapping between two stressless syllables, as, for example, in *vanity* [vǽnəɾi], is accounted for directly under the syllable-based analysis, but requires some reorganization of foot structure to be accommodated under the foot-based analysis, since the final syllable is unfooted.[20]

Both accounts require some readjustment of prosodic structures to accommodate the distribution of aspiration. The syllable-based analysis requires some form of resyllabification and the foot-based account requires various sorts of syllable adjunction. Another argument in favor of the syllable-based analysis is that intuitions about syllabic affiliation of unaspirated intervocalic stops are somewhat ambiguous (Treiman and Danis 1988; Treiman and Zukowski 1990). On the other hand, there does not appear to be intuitional support for the required syllable adjunctions on the foot-based approach.

5.1   Summary

We have seen that there is evidence of a variety of sorts for trochaic feet in English. A trochaic foot is composed of a stressed syllable followed by at most one stressless syllable. In addition, feet are subject to the restriction that at most one unfooted syllable may occur in a row.

A number of controversial issues have been touched on. The foremost is how to treat syllable weight. The stress pattern of a word is clearly a function of syllable weight, but, as argued above, precisely how to accommodate this is a matter of some debate (Harris 1994; Hayes 1995; Hammond 1999; Pater 2000).

Another important issue that we have only scratched the surface of is the degree to which the stress pattern of English is *predictable*. There are many examples where we simply cannot predict which stress pattern might occur, e.g. *banana* [bənǽnə] vs. *Canada* [kʰǽnəɾə]. Researchers have taken a number of positions on how to treat these cases (Halle and Vergnaud 1987; Hammond 1999; Pater 2000).

As noted above, a third controversial issue is the treatment of aspiration (and flapping).

Finally, the size and nature of feet is a controversial question. We've already discussed the *moraic trochee* proposal (Hayes 1995), but there are other approaches to foot structure as well (Burzio 1994).

6 Conclusion

In this chapter, we have considered the arguments and nature of prosodic organization in English words. There is clear evidence that words should not be construed simply as a string of segments, but that those segments are further organized into syllables and feet.

There are higher-level prosodic structures as well, governing the combination of words into phrases. For example, there are structures encoding phonological cliticization, phrasal timing, and intonational structure.[21]

There are many controversial aspects of these structures, but there are quite clear points as well. For example, syllabification before a stressed syllable is sharp, but syllabification before a stressless syllable is subject to different interpretations. Feet are generally trochaic, though one might be able to argue for dactylic feet in at least some circumstances.

The central conclusion is that one cannot hope to understand the organization of sounds into words in English without attending to the prosodic grouping that we have discussed.

NOTES

Thanks to Heidi Harley, April McMahon, and several anonymous reviewers for useful feedback. All errors are my own.

1 See Chomsky and Halle (1968) for this definition and further discussion. See Hooper (1972) for an early characterization in generative phonology.
2 There are additional restrictions on the stress patterns of lines that are discussed in section 4.
3 In general, orthographic systems provide a compelling extralinguistic argument for syllables as syllable-based writing systems are widespread. The English orthographic system is, of course, alphabetic, and so the argument

from English is more subtle (Kessler and Treiman 1997).
4 We return to this question below.
5 See Treiman and Danis (1988) and Treiman and Zukowski (1990) for discussion of the experimental evidence for these factors and Hammond (1999) for how these factors can be modeled linguistically.
6 All of these can occur in morphologically complex items like compounds; we confine our attention here to monomorphemic examples, which are more restricted.
7 The basic facts here were first brought up in Chomsky and Halle (1968); the import of these facts for syllabification was first published in

Hayes (1981), though the idea had been circulated several years earlier in a widely cited, but never published manuscript: Halle and Vergnaud (1977).

8 Note that this generalization applies to the rightmost stress, whether it is the strongest stress in the word or not. Thus a form like *mackintosh* [mǽkənt^{h}àʃ] does not constitute an exception because of the final secondary stress.

9 The term "onset" refers to the consonantal material that occurs on the left side of a syllable; the term "rhyme" refers to the syllable peak and all the material to the right.

10 We can remain agnostic about the precise nature of that derivation, whether it proceeds in a multi-step rule-based fashion or in a single step with constraints.

11 Precisely what this position is and how it is to be treated theoretically is a controversial question. See Harris (1994) and Hammond (1999) for discussion.

12 See Hayes (1981), Levin (1985), Kaye and Lowenstamm (1984), and Hayes (1989a) for discussion.

13 This latter position is possible only if the base form is altered so that the primary stress falls on the last syllable: *[fòrmǽldəfʌ́kɪnhájd].

14 Some speakers distinguish among stresses I have marked as secondary; I leave these distinctions aside here.

15 See Hayes (1995) for a proposal of this sort on general typological grounds.

16 Note that *respiratory* is not a relevant case in some dialects of English where there is no secondary stress.

17 One alternative account has it that syncopation occurs unless that results in adjacent stresses. This accounts for many of the cases presented, but incorrectly predicts that syncope should be possible in trochaic words like *coda* [k^{h}óɾə], *[k^{h}ód].

18 The classical definition of the mora, due to McCawley (1968), maintains simply that a light syllable has one mora and a heavy syllable has two.

19 The rightmost syllable of nouns is generally unfooted if short; this is due to "Extrametricality" or NONFINALITY (Hayes 1981; Hammond 1999).

20 See Hammond (1982, 1999) and Jensen (2000) for more discussion.

21 See Nespor and Vogel (1986) and Hayes (1989b) for discussion.

FURTHER READING

The classic straw man for prosodic phonology is Chomsky and Halle (1968), who propose a completely linear/ segmental treatment of English phonology.

Kahn (1980) offers the first treatment of English syllable structure in generative phonology.

Liberman and Prince (1977) offer the first treatment of English stress in terms of hierarchical structure. Hayes (1981) offers the first use of "feet" in the treatment of English stress.

Recent treatments of English prosodic phonology include Harris (1994) and Hammond (1999).

REFERENCES

Burzio, L. (1994). *Principles of English stress*. Cambridge: Cambridge University Press.

Chomsky, N. and Halle, M. (1968). *The sound pattern of English*. New York: Harper & Row.

Golston, C. (1996). Direct Optimality Theory: representation as pure markedness. *Language* 72, 713–48.

Halle, M. and Vergnaud, J.-R. (1977). Metrical structures in phonology: a fragment of a draft, MIT manuscript.

Halle, M. and Vergnaud, J.-R. (1987). *An essay on stress*. Cambridge: MIT Press.

Hammond, M. (1982). Foot-domain rules and metrical locality. In *WCCFL*, vol. 1, 207–18.

Hammond, M. (1990). The Name Game and onset simplification. *Phonology* 7, 159–62.

Hammond, M. (1991). Poetic meter and the arboreal grid. *Language* 67, 240–59.

Hammond, M. (1997). Vowel quantity and syllabification in English. *Language* 73, 1–17.

Hammond, M. (1999). *The phonology of English*. Oxford: Oxford University Press.

Hanson, K. and Kiparsky, P. (1997). A parametric theory of poetic meter. *Language* 72, 287–335.

Harris, J. (1994). *English sound structure*. Oxford: Blackwell.

Hayes, B. (1981). *A metrical theory of stress rules*. New York: Garland (1980 MIT doctoral dissertation).

Hayes, B. (1983). A grid-based theory of English meter. *Linguistic Inquiry* 14, 357–94.

Hayes, B. (1989a). Compensatory lengthening in moraic phonology. *Linguistic Inquiry* 20, 253–306.

Hayes, B. (1989b). The prosodic hierarchy in poetic meter. In P. Kiparsky and G. Youmans (eds.),

Rhythm and meter. San Diego: Academic Press, 201–60.

Hayes, B. (1995). *Metrical stress theory*. Chicago: University of Chicago Press.

Hooper, J. (1972). The syllable in phonological theory. *Language* 48, 525–40.

Jensen, J. T. (2000). Against ambisyllabicity. *Phonology* 17, 187–236.

Kahn, D. (1980). *Syllable-based generalizations in English phonology*. New York: Garland (1976 MIT doctoral dissertation).

Kaye, J. and Lowenstamm, J. (1984). De la syllabicité. In F. Dell, D. Hirst, and J.-R. Vergnaud (eds.), *Form sonore du language*. Paris: Hermann, 123–59.

Kessler, B. and Treiman, R. (1997). Syllable structure and the distribution of phonemes in English syllables. *Journal of Memory and Language* 37, 295–311.

Kiparsky, P. (1977). The rhythmic structure of English verse. *Linguistic Inquiry* 8, 189–247.

Kiparsky, P. (1979). Metrical structure is cyclic. *Linguistic Inquiry* 8, 421–42.

Levin, J. (1985). A metrical theory of syllabicity. Ph.D. thesis, MIT.

Liberman, M. and Prince, A. (1977). On stress and linguistic rhythm. *Linguistic Inquiry* 8, 249–336.

McCarthy, J. (1982). Prosodic structure and expletive infixation. *Language* 58, 574–90.

McCawley, J. (1968). *The phonological component of a grammar of Japanese*. The Hague: Mouton.

Mester, A. (1994). The quantitative trochee in Latin. *Natural Language and Linguistic Theory* 12, 1–61.

Myers, S. (1987). Vowel shortening in English. *Natural Language and Linguistic Theory* 5, 485–518.

Nespor, M. and Vogel, I. (1986). *Prosodic phonology*. Dordrecht: Foris.

Pater, J. (2000). Non-uniformity in English secondary stress: the role of ranked and lexically specific constraints. *Phonology* 17, 237–74.

Prince, A. and Smolensky, P. (1993). *Optimality Theory*. University of Massachusetts and University of Colorado.

Treiman, R. and Danis, C. (1988). Syllabification of intervocalic consonants. *Memory and Language* 27, 87–104.

Treiman, R. and Zukowski, A. (1990). Toward an understanding of English syllabification. *Memory and Language* 29, 66–85.

Withgott, M. (1982). Segmental evidence for phonological constituents. Ph.D. thesis, University of Texas, Austin.

19 Intonation

FRANCIS NOLAN

1 Introduction

The term intonation refers to a means for conveying information in speech which is independent of the words and their sounds. Central to intonation is the modulation of pitch, and intonation is often thought of as the use of pitch over the domain of the utterance. However, the patterning of pitch in speech is so closely bound to patterns of timing and loudness, and sometimes voice quality, that we cannot consider pitch in isolation from these other dimensions. The interaction of intonation and stress – the patterns of relative prominence which characterize an utterance – is particularly close in many languages, including English. For those who prefer to reserve 'intonation' for pitch effects in speech, the word 'prosody' is convenient as a more general term to include patterns of pitch, timing, loudness, and (sometimes) voice quality. In this chapter, however, intonation will be used to refer to the collaboration of all these dimensions, and, where necessary, the term 'melody' will be used to refer specifically to the pitch-based component.

Intonation is used to carry a variety of different kinds of information. It signals grammatical structure, though not in a one-to-one way; whilst the end of a complete intonation pattern will normally coincide with the end of a grammatical structure such as a sentence or clause, even quite major grammatical boundaries may lack intonational marking, particularly if the speech is fast. Intonation can reflect the information structure of an utterance, highlighting constituents of importance. Intonation can indicate discourse function; for instance most people are aware that saying 'This is the Leeds train' with one intonation constitutes a statement, but, with another, a question. Intonation can be used by a speaker to convey an attitude such as friendliness, enthusiasm, or hostility; and listeners can use intonation-related phenomena in the voice to make inferences about a speaker's state, including excitement, depression, and tiredness. Intonation can also, for instance, help to regulate turn-taking in conversation, since there are intonational mechanisms speakers can use to indicate that they have had their say, or, conversely, that they are in full flow and don't want to be interrupted.

Intonation is not the only linguistic device for which pitch is recruited by languages; many languages use pitch to distinguish words. In languages around the world as diverse as Thai, Hausa (Nigeria), and Mixtec (Mexico), words are distinguished not only by vowels and consonants but also by the use of one of a limited set of distinctive pitch patterns or heights on each syllable. Such languages are called tone languages. A number of other languages, such as Swedish and Japanese, make a more limited use of pitch to distinguish words. These languages might best be called lexical accent languages. All tone languages and lexical accent languages also have intonation, but in general the greater a language's use of pitch for distinguishing words, the less scope it has to develop an elaborate intonation system. English, on the other hand, is not a tone language or lexical accent language, and is generally agreed to have relatively complex intonation.

This chapter is set out as follows. Section 2 gives an introduction to what intonation consists of, and how we can visualize it and analyze it phonologically. It also draws attention to the aspects of prosody which are characteristic of English. Section 3 gives some examples of the kinds of information which intonation can carry and the intonational forms which are used in English. Section 4 looks at the variation in intonation to be found in dialects[1] of English. Section 5 concludes the chapter with some general observations. In no respect does this chapter attempt to give a comprehensive account, which would be impossible within its scope; rather it samples the phenomena of English intonation to provide an overview. Readers who want more comprehensive accounts, both of English intonation and intonational theory, can follow up references in the 'Further Reading' Section as well as specific references cited in the text.

The examples of intonation patterns given in the Chapter assume, unless otherwise stated, a variety of pronunciation which has sometimes been termed 'standard Southern British English' (SBE) – the prestige variety of the south east of England which also serves in varying degrees as a prestige norm elsewhere in the British Isles. However the patterns used for examples will be similar to patterns in General American, and so the examples should be accessible not only to the large number of speakers of those two varieties but also to the much larger population of English speakers who have passive knowledge of those pronunciations.

2   What Is Intonation Made of, and How Can We Represent It?

2.1   *The acoustics of intonation*

Figure 19.1 shows two acoustic analyses of the utterance 'But Melanie's never been *near* the manuscript', spoken as a sharp retort to someone who might have said for instance 'Melanie doesn't think the manuscript's genuine'. The top analysis is a spectrogram, showing how the resonances and other acoustic components of speech evolve and change over time. A phonetic transcription has been added to show roughly which parts of the signal correspond to which linguistic elements. The bottom analysis shows a plot of the fundamental frequency, the acoustic consequence of the rate at which the vocal cords are vibrating in voiced speech. The fundamental frequency contour is more or less what we hear as the changing pitch of the speech. The contour is not continuous because voiceless sounds inevitably interrupt it; and furthermore whenever the vocal tract is obstructed the fundamental frequency is perturbed. However the general trend of the pitch is clear. The utterance starts mid-low on 'But', goes low on 'Mel(anie)', rises to a peak on 'near', and falls sharply and thereafter stays low and level. This of course is not the only way the sentence could be said, but it is one appropriate way given the context described above.

Remember that intonational pitch works hand in hand with other prosodic dimensions, notably duration. It is clear from the spectrogram that the most prominent syllable in the utterance 'near' takes up a disproportionate time compared to other syllables. Other durational correlates of prominence are less straightforward, since they interact with segmental determinants of duration (e.g. phonological vowel length); but it can be seen for instance that the unstressed vowel of 'the' is shorter than the immediately following vowel, that of 'man(uscript)'. Note too that the trisyllable 'manuscript' is more than 50 percent longer than 'Melanie', also trisyllabic; this is partly as a result of the former's more complex syllable structure, but also because a lengthening of sounds (a *rallentando*) is found at the end of an intonation pattern.

2.2   General characteristics of English prosody

All languages have ways of making given linguistic elements stand out in the stream of speech, of making them 'prominent'. One or more syllables in a word may be stressed ('di<u>ver</u>sifi<u>ca</u>tion'); and some words in an utterance will be more prominent than others ('I <u>told</u> you to go <u>home</u>'). Languages differ, however, in what might be termed their 'prominence gradient', the steepness of change between prominent and non-prominent elements. At the syllabic level, English is characterized by a steep prominence gradient. Prominent syllables have full vowels, i.e. vowels which are not schwa or unstressed /ɪ/ (as in the first and last syllables of 'decided' in those dialects where schwa is not used in this context), and have relatively long durations. Non-prominent syllables often have reduced vowels (most commonly schwa). By contrast in French, for example, the average gradient between a prominent and a non-prominent syllable is less steep; French unstressed vowels are generally not reduced, and stressed syllables are less salient.

The fact that English is characterized by a steep prominence gradient is central to its intonation. One of the few things on which there has been a consensus among intonation analysts is that, put simply, interesting things

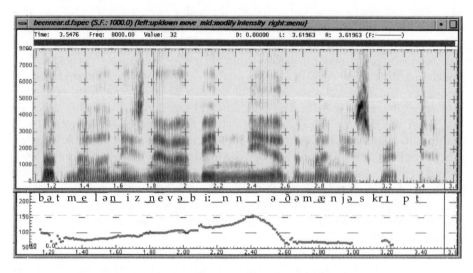

Figure 19.1   Acoustic representations of 'But Melanie's never been near the manuscript'. Top, spectrogram revealing segmental timing information; and bottom, time-aligned fundamental frequency contour

happen to the pitch around prominent syllables; such syllables are associated with a pitch *landmark*. This is seen most clearly in figure 19.1 in the case of the word 'near', which coincides with a high point, a *peak*, after which the pitch drops sharply over the whole range used in the utterance. 'Mel(anie)' coincides with a low point, a *trough*, after which the pitch climbs steadily to the peak. Could we look at prominence the other way round, and say 'these syllables are prominent *because* they are associated with pitch landmarks'? The factor which breaks the circularity is that the prominence pattern of a word is independent of pitch. A word's stress pattern, or metrical prominence pattern, is often predictable from its phonological and morphological structure; and it is also realized, mainly through timing relations, even when spoken without a pitch accent. The word 'manuscript' in figure 19.1 has no pitch landmark associated with it (it's low and level), but it is still apparent from the rhythm that the syllable *man-* is the stressed syllable (we will return in section 3 to why this word should be accentually neglected in this way). In fact, if we were to resynthesize the utterance on a monotone, the prominence relations would still be completely clear. In describing English intonation, the 'association' of a pitch landmark with a particular stressed syllable is crucial; it is termed a *pitch accent* (or often just *accent*). The melody of an utterance consists to a large extent of the sequence of its pitch accents, and the description and classification of these landmarks forms a central part of current models of intonation.

English, then, is a language in which there is a relatively sharp difference between prosodically prominent events and those which lack prosodic prominence. The melodic part of intonation involves tonal events associated with points of prosodic prominence, and additionally with boundaries of intonational phrases.

2.3   *The phonology of intonation*

Using the term 'phonology' with respect to intonation implies that there are discrete, contrastive linguistic units[2] underlying the continuously variable melody of speech, and that these units do not have meaning (any more than a phoneme has a meaning), but can function in context, singly and in combination, to convey meaning. These implications are now widely accepted.

In (1) below there are two alternative phonological (or 'intonological') analyses of the intonation of the utterance in figure 19.1, the melody of which is now represented as a stylized pitch curve[3]:

(1)   But ↗   MElanie's · never been\NEAR the · manuscript

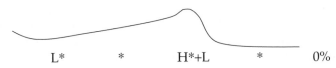

L*   *   H*+L   *   0%

Embedded in the sequence of words (in which small capitals indicate pitch accents) are symbols from an analysis within what has become known as the British tradition, developed in works such as Palmer (1922), Kingdon (1958), O'Connor and Arnold (1961/1973), and Crystal (1969). The intonational elements are shown by the diacritics before the stressed syllables of words (the symbols used vary from author to author, but the ones chosen here illustrate the general point). Before 'near', for instance, there is a sloping line which indicates a fall. The fall is specifically the *nucleus*, that is, the accent which occurs last and often constitutes the most salient point of the utterance. The stressed syllable of 'Melanie' initiates a pre-nuclear rise, represented by the diagonal up-arrow. The elements of the system, then, are generally pitch movements; the exception in this example being the dots before 'nev(er)' and 'man(uscript)' which mark a stressed syllable within an existing pitch trend (here rising and low level respectively).

Below the stylized pitch curve is an equivalent 'autosegmental-metrical' (AM) analysis (for the term AM, see Ladd 1996: 2–4). AM descriptions take as their atoms the H (high) and L (low) tones of autosegmental phonology, originally applied to tone languages, combining these tones when needed into 'bitonal' (or potentially larger) elements. The Hs and Ls constitute pitch targets, and pitch movements arise from interpolating between ('joining up') these targets. The 'metrical' part of the name arises because, crucially, certain tones are tied to metrically prominent events in the utterance (in effect stressed syllables) as noted in 2.2 above; this is represented in the notation by adding an asterisk to the tone. Thus the syllable 'near' in the example is stressed and associated specifically with the high tone of the H*+L bitonal pitch accent. Metrically strong syllables without a pitch accent are not marked in most AM transcription systems, but logically could be shown as here by an asterisk.

The AM framework became the dominant paradigm in intonational research under the influence of Pierrehumbert (1980) and subsequent work, for instance Beckman and Pierrehumbert (1986) (for an introduction to AM and a critique see Ladd 1996). A modified version of Pierrehumbert's (1980) description is expressed in the ToBI transcription system which was agreed on as a unified set of conventions for transcribing American English, particularly in work on speech corpora (see Silverman et al. 1992; Beckman 1999); and a number of language-specific adaptations such as G-ToBI for German (Baumann, Grice, and Benzmüller 2001) and ToDI for Dutch (Gussenhoven, Rietveld, and Terken 1999). The particular variant of the AM class of descriptions used here is the IViE system (the acronym standing for Intonational Variation in English) which was developed as part of a research project[4] into the intonation of a number of urban centers in the British Isles.

Superficially the British and AM analyses look very different, but there is a high degree of compatibility. Most of the intonational phenomena which can be expressed in one can be expressed in the other, and some of the differences between specific analyses in the two traditions are incidental. One essential difference, however, concerns the boundary of an intonation unit, or *intonational phrase* (IP) as it is now commonly known. An essential task in making an intonation analysis is to divide the speech into intonational phrases. These may be separated by pauses, but more often in fluent speech the end of an intonational phrase will be marked (if at all) only by a degree of slowing (pre-boundary lengthening), and the real essence of an intonational phrase is its internal coherence in terms of intonation pattern (rather in the way that we don't expect to find a gap between syllables, but rely for their demarcation on their internal coherence in terms of lawful combinations of sounds). AM models assume that an intonational phrase boundary may (or in most versions must) have a *boundary tone* associated with it. We can illustrate this if we imagine a reply to 'But Melanie's never been near the manuscript' consisting of an incredulous 'Never?!' with an overall falling-rising contour. A 'British' analysis would classify this as a fall-rise pitch accent. IViE would regard it as H*+L H%, with the final H% indicating a tone 'belonging' to the intonational phrase boundary. On the face of it these seem equivalent, but if we add more material to the response while keeping the pattern equivalent, and leaving the main stress on 'Never', we will find that the rising part of the fall-rise is delayed to the end:

(2)   NEver?!   She's NEver seen the manuscript?!

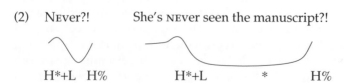

H*+L H%   H*+L   *   H%

Phenomena like this suggest that intonational equivalence is captured more transparently through the use of boundary tones. However it is still useful to recognize the coherence of patterns such as H*+L H%, and the combination can be called a (nuclear) *tune*.

Although IViE acknowledges the importance of boundary tones, it allows IP-final boundaries to be tonally unspecified (0%) when there is no pitch movement in the immediate vicinity, unlike most AM models which require H% or L% to be specified. In doing this, it merely extends and makes explicit the practice in other models of not specifying tone on many IP-initial boundaries. Henceforth in this chapter examples will be presented and discussed in terms of the IViE transcription system, albeit a somewhat simplified version. For the full IViE inventory of pitch accents, boundary tones, and intonational processes see for instance Grabe, Nolan, and Farrar (1998), and Grabe (2001).

2.4 Non-phonological components of intonation

Not all intonational effects lend themselves to analysis in terms of discrete categories such as pitch accents and boundary tones. Other intonational effects are communicative in the sense that the speaker has a choice, but are essentially gradient. For instance each of the following ways of saying an utterance conveys progressively greater involvement (whether or not this is the speaker's true feeling):

(3) I'd LOVE to meet him   I'd LOVE to meet him   I'd LOVE to meet him

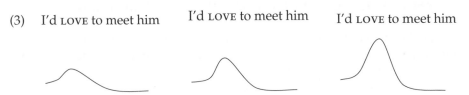

but identifying three gradations (rather than four, or seven, or more) is arbitrary; *pitch range* here behaves as a continuum.

This non-categorical aspect of intonation probably provides a link to the origin of intonation in very basic physical and physiological phenomena. In order to explain certain universal tendencies in the use of pitch Gussenhoven (2002), building on earlier work by Ohala (e.g. 1983, 1984), proposes three *biological codes*: the *frequency code*, the *effort code*, and the *production code* (which I will rename the *respiratory code*). For instance, small objects or animals produce high frequencies, and so high pitch is a natural way to signal submissiveness in the animal kingdom, and by (metaphorical) extension politeness or uncertainty (among other things) in human interaction – the frequency code. Greater physical effort, resulting from physiological arousal, will produce more energetic movements, and more dramatic pitch change, and by extension can naturally signal involvement (as in (3)) or linguistic emphasis – the effort code. And as vocalization proceeds, air is used up, subglottal pressure drops, and the natural tendency is for pitch to get lower in the course of a vocalization, so it may be natural to signal newness by high pitch and older information by lower pitch – the respiratory code. Quite possibly the categories of intonational phonology represent in some measure the *grammaticalization* of these codes; it is tempting to see the use of H% in (some) questions as arising from the frequency code. We shall see in section 3 that the task of intonational signaling in English is shared between a discrete, clearly phonological resource and a gradient component.

Relatively little attention has been paid to systematizing the description of the non-categorical part of English intonation (though Crystal (1969) does discuss many relevant phenomena). A useful prerequisite to understanding those aspects involving pitch range (best used as a 'catch all' term) is a clear set of terminology. We can distinguish the following: *speaking tessitura*, a given speaker's range of comfortable speaking pitch; *pitch level*, the overall placement of an utterance within a speaker's tessitura; *pitch span*, the general distance between highs and lows in an utterance; *pitch excursion*, a local high–low distance, e.g. associated with a pitch accent; and *downtrend*, the lowering of pitch over the course of an utterance. In these terms the degrees of involvement in (3) are signaled by changes in pitch span (manifested in the excursion of a single pitch accent, but if the utterance were longer the changes would affect the whole of the utterance).

3   Functions and Forms of English Intonation

Section 2 introduced some of the general concepts required for understanding intonation. This section exemplifies how English intonation carries a number of different kinds of information.

3.1   *Grammatical structure*

An important role of intonation is as the 'punctuation' of spoken languages, marking the division between grammatical units and more generally helping the listener to follow the utterance. The function is brought sharply into focus on occasion when the words used allow more than one grammatical parse, for instance 'While eating my dog my cat and I watched television'. In writing we would use a comma; after 'dog' for the more unsavoury interpretation, and after 'eating' (and probably another comma separating 'my dog' and 'my cat') for the pleasanter interpretation. An intonational equivalent of this comma in these two positions is transcribed in (4) and (5) respectively – a falling pitch accent followed, crucially, by a high boundary tone, along with a slowing down before the boundary:

(4)   While EATing my D O G   my CAT and I WATChed TELevision

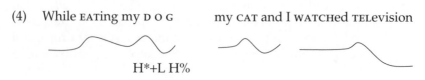

H*+L H%

(5)   While ᴇᴀᴛ i n g   my ᴅᴏɢ my ᴄᴀᴛ and I ᴡᴀᴛᴄʜed ᴛᴇʟᴇvision

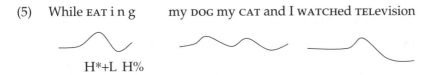

H*+L H%

Note, however, that the relation between grammatical units and intonational units is not one-to-one. It is possible to phrase the following sentence intonationally in at least two ways:

(6)   If you're ʀᴇᴀᴅy   we'll ɢ ᴏ   If you're ʀᴇᴀᴅy we'll ɢ ᴏ

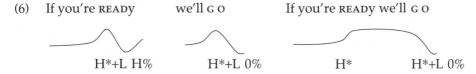

H*+L H%   H*+L 0%   H*   H*+L 0%

without there being any corresponding change in grammatical structure. We might regard the change as a kind of 'connected speech process' like segmental assimilation, correlated with – but not directly determined by – speech rate. In general, then, we can regard grammatical structure as determining the point at which intonational phrase boundaries can occur, but whether they do or not depends on performance factors such as speech rate. The slower and more careful the speech, the more explicitly will grammatical structure be signaled in intonational phrasing.

In some cases intonation can guide the listener to grammatical structure which is not directly to do with phrasing. For instance the intonation of the words 'The Norwegians who are rich enjoy life to the full' can signal whether the relative clause is restrictive, meaning that, specifically, rich Norwegians enjoy life to the full:

(7)   The Norwᴇɢians who are ʀ ɪ ᴄʜ   enjᴏy life to the ꜰ ᴜ ʟʟ

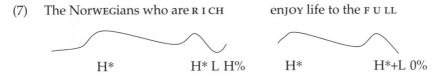

H*   H* L H%   H*   H*+L 0%

or whether the relative clause is non-restrictive, implying that all Norwegians are rich, and having a status more like a parenthetical remark (e.g. '. . . and they're rich . . .'):

(8)   The Norwᴇɢians   who are ʀɪᴄʜ   enjᴏy life to the ꜰ ᴜ ʟʟ
                          and they're ʀɪᴄʜ

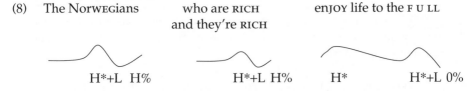

H*+L H%   H*+L H%   H*   H*+L 0%

Whilst cases of intonational disambiguation such as the ones above are useful for illustrative purposes, intonation provides guidance to the grammatical structure of all speech.

3.2   *Information structure*

Another thing which intonation does is to highlight points of high informational importance in the utterance. Each word in the lexicon has a stressed syllable, or, perhaps better, a 'stressable' syllable. This means that this syllable has the potential to be the site of prosodic prominence in an utterance. The prominence is usually manifested as greater duration, greater intensity (the primary physical correlate of loudness), and in the majority of cases a pitch accent. In the word 'about' it is the second syllable which is stressable. If we cite 'about' in isolation (9), the second syllable will carry a pitch accent – often H*+L. If however we say the word as part of the utterance 'I'll be at the station about five,' there will be by default no prominence on the second syllable of 'about' beyond what may be perceived as a result of the 'full vowel' (in this case a diphthong) it contains and its rhythmic context. But if, again, the specified time is already present in the discourse, and the speaker wants to focus on the approximation implied by the preposition 'about' ('no, don't buy tickets for the 5.02, it's too risky'), then that word can carry a pitch accent (rightmost example in (9)).

(9)   ABOUT   I'll BE there about FIVE   I'll BE there ABOUT five

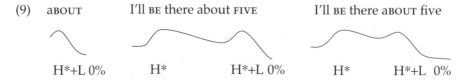

   H*+L 0%   H*   H*+L 0%   H*   H*+L 0%

This exemplifies an important principle, that the speaker adjusts prominence according to communicational need. In the citation utterance there is no redundancy (i.e. predictability), and no word which is more important than 'about'. In the sentence uttered when the specified time is new information, 'five' is more important, and the presence of a temporal preposition is predictable from the rest of the sentence. It would be most unnatural to speak a sentence putting a pitch accent on every word, and as a first rule of thumb we can expect content words to have a pitch accent and grammatical words to lack one.

In fact at the same time as associating 'about' with a pitch accent the speaker has robbed 'five' of the prominence it had the first time round. This kind of adjustment of prominence is a crucial feature of English intonation, often called *deaccenting*[5]. By deaccenting 'five', focus has been placed on 'about'; and 'five', which is *given* information, is relegated to a lower level of salience. Deaccenting happens when a word is given by virtue of being repeated (10) or being substituted by a hypernym (11):

(10)   I OFFERED her a COFFEE but it TURNS out she doesn't DRINK coffee

(11)   I OFFERED her a BEER but it TURNS out she doesn't DRINK alcohol

In such examples it is intonationally ill-formed in English[6] – and will give rise to a perceptual double-take on the part of the listener – if the given item carries prominence equal to that of its first occurrence. In contrast many languages, such as Italian and Romanian (Ladd 1996: 176–7), do not typically have deaccenting of given information. Absence of deaccenting in a language, however, does not necessarily mean that givenness goes unsignaled. In Icelandic, which does not deaccent given information (Nolan and Jónsdóttir, 2001), it seems that the information structure is reflected in gradient prominence levels, and deaccenting may just be a grammaticalization of a very general reflex of the effort code.

So far the use of intonational pitch accents in English seems rather logical; informationally rich items are made to stand out and other information is backgrounded by deaccenting. But it has long been remarked that the relation between information and accent is not always so transparent, as in cases such as the following:

(12)   Look OUT! That CHAIR's broken

In the context of someone about to sit down, 'chair' is contextually given, and being broken is the unexpected, crucial information. Yet, perversely at first sight, 'chair' gets the main accent. But this kind of accentuation is probably the intonational equivalent of pointing; first make sure the listener looks at the chair, because then the problem will be perceived directly.

Also initially opaque is the kind of contrast between the following utterances:

(13)
The DEER was shot by JOHN   the BUTCHer   The DEER was shot by JOHN   the butcher

H*+L 0% H*+L 0%   H*+L 0%   *   0%

In the first version 'butcher' is in apposition, and explains that John is the butcher. It's rather like a reduced non-restrictive relative clause. The pitch accent on the item in apposition ('butcher') usually echoes the pitch accent on the word to which it is in apposition ('John'), but with a less extensive pitch excursion. In the second version on the other hand 'butcher' is an evaluative epithet, a metaphorical application of the word expressing (here) the speaker's disapproval of John's recreational pursuits. It carries a rhythmic stress, indicated here by the asterisk, but no pitch accent. This deaccenting is conventional, but not easy to explain. Conceivably it is a grammaticalized form of the reduced pitch span which often accompanies parenthetical expressions, including expressions of opinion, as in 'John – and I think he's a butcher because of it – is the one who shot the deer'.

A comprehensive account of the relation of intonation to information structure would be too lengthy for the scope of this chapter, but as a final, very specific case, consider the following:

(14)   Eᴍᴍa doesn't dance with ᴀɴʏone   Eᴍᴍa doesn't dance with ᴀɴʏone

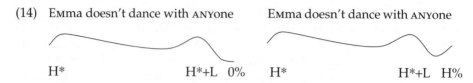

   H*   H*+L 0%   H*   H*+L H%

In reply to 'why didn't she dance with Wayne?' the first version, with a low boundary tone, means that Emma will refuse all men who ask her to dance without exception. The second, with a high boundary tone, means that Emma is selective; she doesn't accept just *any* offer. The difference may arise from two broad categories of intonational meaning that have been associated with boundary tones. Low endings are thought of as assertive and non-continuative, for which Cruttenden (1997: 163) has proposed the term *closed*, and high endings as non-assertive and continuative, or *open*. Thus the high boundary tone in the second version leaves it open for the speaker to express, or the listener to infer, a qualification, e.g. ' – but she'll say yes if the man looks rich'.

3.3   Discourse function

The best known fact about intonation is that questions rise. Like most well known facts it is a considerable oversimplification. Counterexamples are easy to find. English 'Wh-' questions in particular are more often falling at the end than rising:

(15)   Wʜᴀᴛ are you ᴅoing on Sᴀᴛurday?   How oʟᴅ is he?

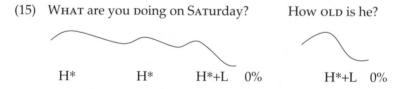

   H*   H*   H*+L   0%   H*+L   0%

Nonetheless the popular belief that the voice goes up in questions has some basis in truth. 'Yes-no' (or 'general') questions can rise:

(16)   Have you ғɪɴɪsʜᴇᴅ the ᴀʀᴛicle?   OR   Have you ғɪɴished the ᴀʀᴛicle?

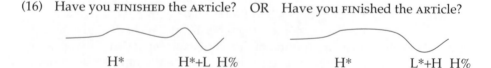

   H*   H*+L H%   H*   L*+H H%

These two versions are both common; the first has a falling rising pattern on the last word, and the second steps down to the final word but then rises to the end[7]. Ending high is in keeping with the *open–closed* distinction mentioned above, and Gussenhoven's *frequency code* and *respiratory code* (section 2). The questioner perhaps metaphorically submits to the greater knowledge of the hearer, and leaves it open to the listener to provide completive information. However it is still perfectly well-formed to say:

(17)   Have you FINished the ARTicle?

One might nonetheless assume that if there is nothing in the words to indicate that an utterance is a question (a 'morphosyntactically unmarked question') then the phonological choice of a high boundary tone would be obligatory; nevertheless the second utterance below will be interpreted as a question:

(18)   She's FINished the ARTicle   OR   She's FINished the ARTicle?

The question is marked by gradient aspects of pitch range; the *downtrend* is less steep, and the *pitch excursion* of the nuclear accent is greater. In tone languages, where local pitch movements are determined lexically, intonation will rely heavily on such pitch range effects. In English there is a rich and to some extent complementary interplay in the signaling of discourse function between morphosyntactic marking, discrete intonational marking, and gradient intonational marking.

3.4   Attitude and the speaker's state

From the brief survey above concerning questions it can be seen very clearly that there is no one-to-one mapping between discourse function and intonation pattern. Some of the reason for this is that intonation is also doing other, less linguistic, work, conveying information for instance about the speaker's attitude. The example (17) of a question ending in a fall is unambiguously a question (because of the syntax), but a rather less genial, more demanding one than those in (16). Furthermore although we have tacitly assumed that statements are *closed* and are associated with low endings, not every statement ends low. Most famously, the spread through many varieties of English of the 'high rising terminal' (see e.g. Fletcher, Wales, Stirling, and Mushin 2002) – the trend to end intonational phrases on a high and rising pitch – has made rising intonation on non-question utterances commonplace, as for instance in examples like the following (where !H* indicates a lowered or *downstepped* high accent):

(19)   MY name's JOHN SMITH.   I've got an appOINTment with Dr SANDerson.

The speaker is not asking for information, but is more probably using a signal for non-assertiveness (the *frequency code*) as a politeness strategy.

There is no denying the role of intonation in conveying attitude, as witness both the common observation that the problem was 'not what he said but the way that he said it', and the large amount of attention devoted to the attitudinal function of intonation in books tutoring learners of English. However with attitude we are entering particularly difficult territory. Not only is someone's attitude hard to describe (much harder, say, than the linguistic description of an utterance as a declarative consisting of two clauses and functioning as a question), but also a person's attitude shades into their psychological state. Whilst choosing a 'polite' or 'informal' intonation is primarily a matter of attitude, a person whose intonation might be described as 'angry' may be genuinely experiencing that emotion and expressing it unchecked, may be trying with only partial success to hide it, or may be feigning anger to signal that the matter in hand is one which deserves condemnation. There is a large body of work on how speech is affected by actual emotions and psychological states (see e.g. Scherer, 2001), but these non-linguistic determinants lie outside the scope of this chapter.

As we have seen in (16–17) and (19), categorical choices are available in English to convey attitude. But as we would expect from the link between attitude and psychological state, the deliberate communication of attitude also employs devices which directly reflect Gussenhoven's (2002) *biological codes*. The gradations of *pitch span* in (3) on the words 'I'd love to meet him' directly mimic (or indeed are) the effects of physiological arousal, and convey progressively greater involvement. It is tempting to say 'greater enthusiasm', but we must beware of attributing specific meanings to intonational effects; if we impose a similar continuum of increasing pitch spans on the reply 'I'd rather *not* meet him', the strength of feeling is mapped in a similar way, but we can no longer label it enthusiasm.

One aspect of attitude is *accommodation*, the degree to which a speaker matches the speech of an interlocutor. Undoubtedly prosodic accommodation occurs widely. For instance if one person uses whispery phonation and a reduced pitch span, their interlocutor may well do the same. Failure to accommodate pitch span, for instance, can lead to ill-formed exchanges; if the intention of the third utterance in (20) is genuinely to congratulate, the response is appropriate to an utterance in the manner of the first, both in terms of phonological choices and pitch span, but not the second, against which it will sound somewhat grudging:

(20)
I've JUST been proMOTed   I've JUST been pro M O T ed   CONGRAtuLAtions

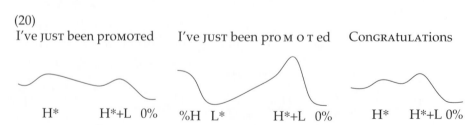

H*   H*+L 0%   %H L*   H*+L 0%   H*   H*+L 0%

3.5 *Discourse regulation*

In a successful conversation *turn-taking* by the speakers happens smoothly. Depending on the type and degree of formality of the interaction, interruptions may be appropriate, but they will be recognizable as such by the participants, as will the point at which a speaker has finished what he or she has to say. The 'traffic signals' which regulate a well-formed interaction are mainly intonational.

End-of-turn markers include low pitch, reduced loudness, and rallentando (lengthening of turn-final elements). The low ending and lengthening (indicated by the stretched spacing of the text) in the first utterance in (21) give it an air of finality. This does not preclude further comment on the topic (e.g. a question about it from the listener), but it does open the floor to another speaker. On the other hand the lack of slowing (or even accelerando) in the second utterance, combined with sustained final high pitch often used in listing items, indicates that more is to come and the speaker is not willing to yield the floor.

(21)

... then we went to the SHOPP i n g c e n t e r   ... then we went to the SHOPping center

Again we can relate this intonational use of pitch to Gussenhoven's (2002) biological codes. The *respiratory code* ('production code' in his terms) links low pitch and finality by virtue of the reduction in subglottal pressure as air is used up in speaking, and this link could be extended metaphorically to a conversational turn. Conversely attempts to wrest the floor from the speaker will be characterized by high pitch and loudness.

4 Intonational Variation

Varieties of languages are marked not only by their vowels and consonants but also by their prosody. The intonation of some varieties is often remarked on by outsiders using terms such as 'sing-songy' or 'flat'. One of the most distinctive dialects of English from the intonational point of view is Northern Irish English (NIE), which 'always goes up at the end'. The truth is a little more complex, as shown in (22).

(22)

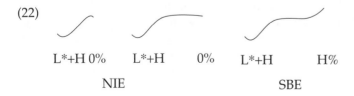

L*+H 0%   L*+H   0%   L*+H   H%

NIE   SBE

The first and second patterns show the commonest nuclear 'tune' of NIE. The first pattern shows what happens on short (usually monosyllabic) phonetic material, such as the answer 'three' to the question 'how many?'. It looks and sounds pretty much like a rise; but as soon as the phonetic material becomes longer (e.g. 'three of them') as in the second pattern, it becomes clear that the 'underlying' pattern is a 'rise-plateau'. This nuclear tune can be analyzed within the IViE system as L*+H 0%. This is a pattern which seems not to occur in Southern British English (SBE), or most other dialects; as shown in the third schema a nuclear rise co-occurs in SBE only with a high boundary tone (and the tune functions as a question, not a statement).

Here we have what appears to be a phonological difference between dialects, specifically a difference – similar to a segmental phonotactic difference – determining the permissible combination of phonological elements or possible *tunes*. It is also possible in NIE to drop sharply at the end of the plateau to an L% boundary, again yielding a tune which is not available in SBE or most other dialects.

There are (at least) two other ways in which dialects can manifest a difference in their intonational phonology. First, dialects can differ in terms of what intonological elements they have in their inventory, just as a dialect may lack a phoneme (SBE does not have the voiceless labial-velar which distinguishes 'what' from 'watt,' while Scottish does, for instance). The intonational inventory will, of course, depend on analytic assumptions; one could dispose of the segmental difference just mentioned by treating the voiceless labial-velar as the combination of /h/ and /w/. Within the IViE framework, which assumes that an intonational phrase boundary tone T% will be manifested by pitch movement directly adjacent to the boundary, it seems that SBE lacks an L% boundary in its inventory. Nuclear falls are accounted for as H*+L, reflecting the fact that as material is added after the nuclear syllable, the low pitch is still attained shortly after the accented syllable and not at the boundary, as in (23). There are no cases where a fall can be associated unambiguously with the boundary and not with a prominent syllable, contrary to the NIE pattern discussed above.

(23)   JOHN   JONathan was the name of that man I was thinking of

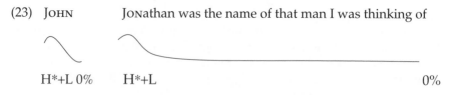

H*+L 0%   H*+L   0%

Second, the association of intonational elements with functions and meanings shows considerable variation between dialects. Grabe and Post (2002) examined read statements and inversion questions in the IViE corpus and found the distribution of nuclear tunes (last pitch accent and boundary tone) shown in figure 19.2 for SBE (Cambridge) and NIE (Belfast). It can be seen that Belfast uses predominantly the rise-plateau L*+H 0% pattern in statements,

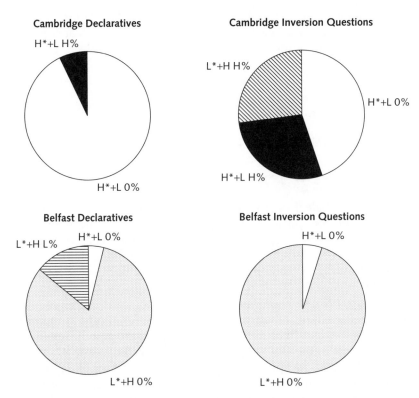

Figure 19.2 Distribution of patterns between statements and inversion questions
Source: After Grabe and Post 2002

and overwhelmingly in questions, revealing that these utterance types are generally not phonologically distinct. In Cambridge, statements mostly have a falling nucleus – a straightforward difference in usage. Almost half of the inversion questions also have this pattern, but the option exists to use a rise (L*+H H%) or a fall-rise (H*+L H%). As an aside, informal polling of students in Cambridge by the author, involving presenting a polite inversion question with each of these two patterns and asking 'which is more old-fashioned', has consistently shown the rise to be perceived as the 'old-fashioned' alternative. The subtlety of intonational variation is underlined by Ladd (1996: 122) who notes that the fall–rise nuclear tune H*+L H% on a request such as 'Can I have the BILL please?', which is perfectly polite in British English, may be heard as condescending or peremptory by a speaker of American English.

So far we have looked at intonational variation that can be analyzed in terms of discrete phonological categories. There are also differences which are a matter of phonetic realization. One such is the way a dialect behaves under 'tonal crowding', that is, when there is only a very short time, because of limited phonetic material, to achieve several intonational targets (Hs and Ls).

Idealizing somewhat, there are two possibilities: to 'compress', and try to squeeze all the targets into the available time; or to 'truncate', and give up on achieving one or more targets. These strategies are schematized in (24):

(24)   NINE   SIX   NINE   SIX

H*+L   H*+L   H*+L   H*+L

        compressing   truncating

The compressing dialect on the left attempts to realize the full fall despite the very short vocalic nucleus of 'six' (short because of the phonologically lax vowel, and pre-fortis clipping) by making the pitch change steeper. The truncating dialect on the right does not alter the rate of pitch change, and 'runs out of road' leaving an incomplete fall[8]. Hungarian has been described as a 'truncating' language (Ladd 1996: 132–6), while English is thought of as 'compressing'. Grabe (1998) showed that German truncates falls but compresses rises.

Table 19.1 summarizes results in Grabe, Post, Nolan, and Farrar (2000) for four dialects of English (with German added for comparison). It can be seen that SBE conforms to the stereotype of English as a compressing language, as does Newcastle. Leeds, despite being similar to SBE in terms of its intonational phonology, is truncating when it comes to realization, as is Belfast (which as we have seen is phonologically unusual, and lacks the rises on which to test this parameter).

Another source of realizational differences is the way in which intonational targets align with segmental material. In the extreme, alignment differences pretty much oblige us to recognize a phonological difference, as in the case schematized in figure 19.3 of Connaught and Donegal Irish (Gaelic) reported by Dalton and Ní Chasaide (2003). It is tempting, and probably realistic, to

Table 19.1 Summary of truncation and compression of nuclear pitch accents in four English dialects

	Rise	*Fall*
SBE	compresses	compresses
Newcastle	compresses	compresses
German	*compresses*	*truncates*
Leeds	truncates	truncates
Belfast	truncates	–

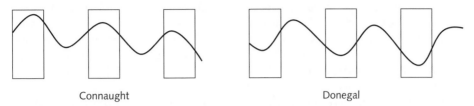

Connaught   Donegal

Figure 19.3 Schematic representation of the alignment of intonational pitch relative to prominent syllables (shown as boxes) in two dialects of Irish (Gaelic). The rectangles indicate the alignment of accented syllables

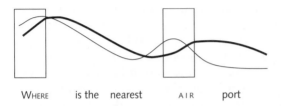

W<small>HERE</small>   is the   nearest   A I R   port

Figure 19.4 Schematic comparison of lagged peaks (heavy line) as in Scottish English and aligned peaks. The rectangles indicate the alignment of accented syllables

speculate that the Donegal pattern might have developed as a result of a progressive historic drift rightwards of the intonational targets relative to the segments; but within our current intonational models it would be stretching credulity to do other than recognize Connaught as having H* accents and Donegal as having L* accents.

On the other hand, take the comparison schematized in figure 19.4 between SBE and the Scottish dialect of Anstruther, Fife (based on Aufterbeck 2003). In SBE (thin line), peaks are aligned with the accented syllables. In Fife, the peaks lag, and the accented syllable itself manifests a perceptually salient upglide. After the nuclear peak, the pitch also declines more gradually than in SBE. This impressionistic description captures the difference, but is the difference phonological (as we decided Donegal vs. Connaught Irish had to be), or realizational?[9] Aufterbeck argues that the difference here is realizational, and, in effect, that both dialects are associating prominent syllables with high rather than low pitch. This view is in keeping with Farrar and Nolan (1999) who demonstrated that (utterance initial) H* peaks in SBE were not tightly tied to the accented syllable, being allowed to lag when there were no utterance-initial unstressed syllables – a case of tonal 'allophony'. Recognizing SBE allophonically lagged peaks as H* opened the way to treating more severely lagged peaks in other dialects, such as Newcastle, as H* despite relatively low pitch on the accented syllable.

Acknowledging that a substantial amount of intonational variation is realizational rather than a difference of phonological system may explain why there is relatively good between-dialect comprehension of intonation –

occasional misinterpretation of affect notwithstanding. As we move from varieties of English which are historically indigenous to the British Isles to those which have emerged world wide, however, we find cases of fundamental prosodic differences influenced by substratum languages. These may give rise to comprehension difficulties. I will focus on one, potentially interrelated, cluster of prosodic differences.

It has long been recognized that languages can differ in terms of rhythm, and this is sometimes discussed in terms of *syllable-timing* and *stress-timing* (cf. Abercrombie 1967: 96–8). In the ideal syllable-timed language, each syllable would take up the same amount of time, or be *isochronous*, whereas in the ideal stress-timed language, it is the *stress-foot* which would be isochronous (the stress-foot consists of a stressed syllable plus any unstressed syllables which intervene before the next stress). According to this view French is a good example of syllable-timing, and English is a good example of stress-timing. In reality, however, experimental phonetics has failed to support either isochrony in any strict sense or a polar division of languages into two types. Nevertheless the impression which these terms sought to capture is real, and can be quantified. Recently progress has been made using a number of measures including the Pairwise Variability Index (PVI). The PVI simply expresses the average difference between successive pairs of phonetic units – in duration, intensity, or vowel quality. It turns out, for instance, that as expected French has a lower durational PVI value for vowels and consonants than English (Grabe and Low 2002), reflecting more evenly timed syllables (well short of isochrony, of course).

The first application of the PVI was in fact to dialects of English, in a comparison of SBE and Singapore English – the latter of which has been described as 'syllable-timed'. Low (1998) and Low, Grabe, and Nolan (2000) showed that, compared to SBE, Singapore English had less pairwise variability in vowel duration[10], vowel intensity, and vowel spectral dispersion (how peripheral a vowel is in the acoustic vowel space). To a large extent this reflects the fact that Singapore English is much more reluctant than SBE to reduce unstressed vowels to schwa. Singapore English could be said to have on average a less steep *prominence gradient* between syllables than SBE.

Separately, Low (1998) demonstrated that speakers of Singapore English do not deaccent given information (see section 3); they are quite happy to say things like *I* offered *her* coffee *but she doesn't* drink coffee, with a full accent on the second occurrence of 'coffee'. The strategy of backgrounding less important parts of the utterance by intonational means seems not to be grammaticalized. It is intriguing to speculate that at the level of pitch accents, too, Singapore English has a less steep prominence gradient; there may be a scaling of pitch accents according to information, but radical reduction (to zero) is not an option. It remains to be investigated whether there really is a systematic scaling of pitch accents according to information structure (short of deaccenting), or whether this kind of intonational signaling of informational value is simply absent. What is clear is that the lack of vowel reduction and the lack of deaccenting conspire to make Singapore prosodically radically different from (e.g.) SBE, and create problems for speakers of SBE in lexical access and comprehension. Deterding (1994: 71) notes that the British model of intonation 'is inappropriate for [Singapore English], because there is no clear nucleus acting as the focus of information or anchor for information within each intonational phrase', and 'it is almost certain that other world varieties of English will pose a similar challenge to our ingrained assumptions about English intonation'.

5   Conclusion

One of the 'design features' of speech is that pitch is variable independently of the sounds being produced. This is possible because the rate of vibration of the larynx does not have to match a resonant frequency of the vocal tract (unlike a brass player's lips, the vibration of which is coupled to a resonance of the tube which makes up the instrument). As a consequence pitch can be recruited to carry information over and above that borne by the vowels and consonants of language, functioning (as we saw in section 1) either as lexically significant tone, or non-lexically as intonation. In doing so, pitch operates in tandem with durational factors and loudness.

Intonation, as an information channel independent of the words chosen, carries a number of quite distinct strands of information. We have seen that the ways in which it does so include signals mirroring physiologically determined changes in pitch, on the one hand, and abstract phonological categories on the other. The latter may originally derive from grammaticalization of biologically determined frequency effects, but the status of phonological intonational categories as members of an abstract linguistic system means that their relationship to information is potentially arbitrary.

This arbitrariness should lead us to expect variation across languages and dialects, and section 4 discussed such variation between dialects. Even those intonational effects whose basis in biology is more transparent are highly conventionalized, and so can vary. Intonation, then, is just as significant a component of a dialect as the pronunciation of its vowels and consonants.

English is generally regarded as having a complex intonation system. English, of course, is not a tone language and so intonational categories can flourish without competition for the resource of pitch variation. But even among non-tone languages English seems to rely rather heavily on intonation for signaling. Schubiger (1965) compares English to German, which often uses pragmatic particles where English uses intonation. For instance, she cites 'rejoinders with the connotation "by the way you talk (or act) one would think you didn't know (or were ignorant of the circumstances)"', which in German naturally include the particle 'doch', for instance 'Ich bin doch eben erst aufgestanden' ('I've only just got up'). 'Doch' does not readily translate lexically, but the connotation is achieved in English by a low pre-nuclear accent:

(25)   I've ONLY just got U P

    L*   H*+L 0%

It may seem to be stretching a point to claim unusual complexity for English intonation from this one little corner of information signaling, but whether or not the claim that English is unusual in the richness of its intonation can be proved there is no doubt that English intonation remains a highly elaborate and flexible communicative resource. This chapter has sought to give an overview of some of the ways English intonation is used to convey a wide variety of information.

NOTES

1   It would strictly be more accurate here to say 'accents of English,' since not all varieties to be considered differ greatly beyond pronunciation; but since in this Chapter 'accent' is used crucially as a prosodic term, it is convenient to use 'dialect' for any variety.

2   Admittedly with intonation the concept of phonological opposition (or contrast) is more problematic than in segmental phonetics; there is no straightforward equivalent to the 'minimal pair' question, since judgments on whether two utterances are 'the same' in terms of intonation are less clear-cut than a decision about whether two utterances represent the same word. Nonetheless all systematic analyses of intonation make phonological assumptions, for instance that there are variant events which count as the same (cf. allophones), and that events which change meaning don't count as the same.

3   Such stylized pitch curves have no theoretical status, but will be used throughout this article as a convenient way to convey the shape of the melody of utterances.

4   'English Intonation in the British Isles' funded by ESRC grant R000237145; www.phon.ox.ac.uk/~esther/ivyweb.

5   We have already seen an example of this: the word 'manuscript' in figure 19.1 is deaccented.

6   But see section 4 for dialects to which this doesn't apply.

7   Evidence that the nuclear accent is L*+H rather than L*, which might appear to model this utterance, would come if we extended the unaccented material after the nucleus – for instance '. . . the article you were writing' – in which case the rise would be likely to plateau out after 'article' followed by a final short rise at the boundary.

8   Then why not regard 'six' here are carrying just H* rather than H*+L? The main reason is that this would create the curious situation whereby the intonation pattern chosen was determined by the phonetic content of the word selected. Better to allow a degree of abstractness in the

analysis, and treat the pattern always as H*+L underlyingly.

9   The fact that the quandry arises at all may suggest that we are wrong to think in terms of discrete phonological categories rather than gradiently variable patterns, but as in all levels of linguistic analysis the abstract categories allow us to model linguistic equivalence in the face of contextual variation.

10   Note though that Grabe and Low (2002) show that Singapore English is still much nearer rhythmically to SBE than to a canonically syllable-timed language such as French.

FURTHER READING

For an accessible and wide-ranging all-round introduction to the forms and functions of intonation, focusing on English, see Cruttenden (1997), while Ladd (1996) provides an objective overview and critique of the autosegmental-metrical approach to intonational phonology, and explores several problematic areas in the description of intonation including the definition and use of pitch range.

Gussenhoven (2004) deals with the tonal and intonational use of pitch across languages and discusses what is universal or language specific, and Hirst and Di Cristo (1998) offers a compendium of descriptions of the intonation of a large selection of languages.

A classic (and highly detailed) analysis of the prosody of British English within the 'British' descriptive framework is to be found in Crystal (1969), while more pedagogically oriented descriptions within the same tradition are provided by O'Connor and Arnold (1961/1973) and Couper-Kuhlen (1986).

Pierrehumbert (1980) is pivotal in theoretical terms, marking as it does the first comprehensive application of autosegmental mechanisms to the description of English intonation. It also provides wide overview of patterns found in American English. The ToBI transcription system, based on Pierrehumbert (1980), and information about its adaptation to other languages can be accessed on the web at www.ling.ohio-state.edu/~tobi. Information about IViE, a further adaptation aimed for English dialect intonation, and references to work on intonational variation in the British Isles, can be found at www.phon.ox.ac.uk/~esther/ivyweb.

REFERENCES

Abercrombie, D. (1967) *Elements of general phonetics.* Edinburgh: Edinburgh University Press.

Aufterbeck, M. (2003) Scottish English intonation: a phonetic analysis of a Fife dialect. Doctoral dissertation, University in Cambridge.

Baumann, S., Grice, M., and Benzmüller, R. (2001) GToBI: a phonological system for the transcription of German intonation. In Puppel, S. and Demenko, G. (eds), *Prosody 2000: speech recognition and synthesis.* Poznan: Adam Mickiewicz University, pp. 21–8.

Beckman, M. (1999) *ToBI*.
www.ling.ohio-state.edu/~tobi.

Beckman, M. and Pierrehumbert, J.
(1986) Intonational structure in English
and Japanese. *Phonology Yearbook* 3,
255–309.

Couper-Kuhlen, E. (1986) *An introduction
to English prosody*. Tübingen:
Niemeyer.

Crystal, D. (1969) *Prosodic systems
and intonation in English*. London:
Cambridge University Press.

Cruttenden, A. (1997) *Intonation*,
2nd edn. Cambridge: Cambridge
University Press.

Dalton, M. and Ní Chasaide, A. (2003)
Modelling intonation in three Irish
dialects. *Proceedings of the 15th
International Congress of Phonetic
Sciences*, Barcelona, 1073–6.

Deterding, D. (1994) The intonation
of Singapore English. *Journal of the
International Phonetic Association* 24,
61–72.

Farrar, K. and Nolan, F. (1999) Timing
of F0 peaks and peak lag. *Proceedings
of the 14th International Congress of
Phonetic Sciences*, San Francisco, 961–4.

Fletcher, J., Wales, R., Stirling, L., and
Mushin, I. (2002) A dialogue act
analysis of rises in Australian English
map task dialogues. *Proceedings of
Speech Prosody 2002*, Aix-en-Provence,
299–302.

Grabe, E. (1998) Comparative
Intonational Phonology: English
and German. Doctoral dissertation,
MPI Series in Psycholinguistics 7.
Nijmegen: Max Planck Institute for
Psycholinguistics.

Grabe, E. (2001) The IViE labelling
guide, version 3. www.phon.ox.ac.uk/
~esther/ivyweb/guide.html.

Grabe, E., Nolan, F., and Farrar, K.
(1998) IViE: A comparative
transcription system for intonational
variation in English. *Proceedings of the
5th International Conference on Spoken
Language Processing*, Sydney, Australia.

Grabe, E., Post, B., Nolan, F., and Farrar,
K. (2000) Pitch accent realisation in
four varieties of British English. *Journal
of Phonetics* 28, 161–85.

Grabe, E. and Low, E.-L. (2002)
Durational variability in speech
and the rhythm class hypothesis.
In Gussenhoven, C. and Warner, N.
(eds.), *Papers in laboratory phonology 7*.
Berlin: Mouton de Gruyter, 515–46.

Grabe, E. and Post, B. (2002) Intonational
variation in the British Isles.
Proceedings of Speech Prosody 2002,
Aix-en-Provence, 343–46.

Gussenhoven, C. (2002) Intonation and
interpretation: phonetics and
phonology. *Proceedings of Speech
Prosody 2002*, Aix-en-Provence, 47–57.

Gussenhoven, C. (2004) *The phonology of
tone and intonation*. Cambridge:
Cambridge University Press.

Gussenhoven, C., Rietveld, T., and
Terken, J. (1999) *ToDI: transcription of
Dutch intonation*. http://
lands.let.kun.nl/todi/todi/home.htm.

Hirst, D. and Di Cristo, A. (eds.) (1998)
*Intonation systems: a survey of twenty
languages*. Cambridge: Cambridge
University Press.

Kingdon, R. (1958) *The groundwork of
English intonation*. London: Longman.

Ladd, D. R. (1996) *Intonational phonology*.
Cambridge: Cambridge University
Press.

Low, E.-L., Grabe, E., and Nolan, F.
(2000) Quantitative characterizations
of speech rhythm: syllable-timing in
Singapore English. *Language and Speech*
43, 377–401.

Nolan, F. and Jónsdóttir, H. (2001)
Accentuation patterns in Icelandic. In
van Dommelen, W. A. and Fretheim,
T. (eds), *Nordic Prosody: Proceedings of
the Eighth Conference, Trondheim 2000*.
Frankfurt-am-Main: Lang, 187–98.

O'Connor, J. D. and Arnold, G. F.
(1961/1973) *Intonation of colloquial
English*. London: Longman (2nd edn.,
1973).

Ohala, J. J. (1983) Cross-language use of pitch: an ethological view. *Phonetica* 40, 1–18.

Ohala, J. J. (1984) An ethological perspective on common cross-language utilization of F0 in voice. *Phonetica* 41, 1–16.

Palmer, H. E. (1922) *English intonation, with systematic exercises.* Cambridge: Heffer.

Pierrehumbert, J. B. (1980) The phonology and phonetics of English intonation. Ph.D. dissertation, MIT. Published 1988 by Indiana University Linguistics Club.

Scherer, K. (2001) Vocal communication of emotion: a review of research paradigms. *Speech Communication* 40, 227–56.

Schubiger, M. (1965) English intonation and German modal particles: a comparative study. *Phonetica* 12, 65–84.

Silverman, K., Beckman, M. E., Pitrelli, J., Ostendorf, M., Wightman, C., Price, P., Pierrehumbert, J., and Hirschberg, J. (1992) ToBI: a standard for labeling English prosody. *Proceedings of the Second International Conference on Spoken Language Processing*, Banff, Canada, 867–70.

Part IV   Lexis and Morphology

20 English Words

DONKA MINKOVA AND ROBERT STOCKWELL

"English Words" is an umbrella topic; it can be addressed from the point of view of sound structure, morphological composition, syntactic type and function, meaning, collocational possibilities, regional, social, and stylistic variation, and many other angles. Our goal in taking up this topic will be limited to a description of the vocabulary of English in terms of size, type and token frequency. We will also discuss the evolution of the lexicon with reference to its historical sources. The chapter ends with a brief survey of some recent patterns of vocabulary enrichment.

1 Estimating the Size of the English Vocabulary

It is often remarked that English has an impressively large lexicon. This is undoubtedly true, but it is difficult to offer objective counts and comparisons regarding the size of the lexicon. On the one hand, the vocabulary reflects the political, economic, cultural, and social events in the histories of its speakers. Extensive contacts with other languages have contributed to the buildup of a very sizeable and etymologically diverse word-stock. On the other hand, constant fluctuation makes measuring the size of the lexicon of any language problematic. No single dictionary can record both archaic words and recent neologisms, all the dialect and slang words, or all the words used in specialized fields: biology, computer science, genetics, chemistry, law, religion, and so on. The potential of deriving transparent new words from existing roots and affixes is practically unlimited; words such as *Beetlehood*, *Chaplinesque*, *deejaying*, *emeritude*, *moronize*, *tennisracketology*, *trimetallic*, *schmooseaholic*, *usurpress*, are easily produced and understood, but they are not likely to make it into a dictionary. Moreover, it is difficult to decide when a word has become "naturalized"; dictionaries commonly record borrowed words, even when they continue to be perceived as phonologically or morphologically foreign. Therefore it is an open question whether words like *Blitzkrieg* (German), *divan* (Arabic), *nabob* (Urdu), *tsunami* (Japanese), *glasnost* (Russian), *kukumakranka* (Khoikhoin) should be included in the counts of the English word-stock or not, though they may certainly be familiar to many speakers of English, and all of them are entries in the *Oxford English Dictionary* (OED).[1]

With these disclaimers in mind, it is still possible to offer some idea of what the inventory of the English lexicon looks like. The estimated number of entries in the so called "unabridged" dictionaries of English ranges between 300,000–450,000 entries; the latter figure is based on the approximate count in *Webster's Third New International Dictionary of the English Language* of 1961. According to the OED *Dictionary Facts*, the 20 volumes of the Second Edition include 291,500 entries, of which 12,200 are for "non-naturalized words." The *Preface* states further that "in addition to the headwords of main entries, the Dictionary contains 157,000 combinations and derivatives in bold type, and 169,000 phrases and combinations in bold italic type, making a total of 617,500 word-forms." The number of OED entries and the citation database are continually expanding. In 1997, after the appearance of the Additions Series (1993, 1997), the work on the *OED Online* project began. Judging from the rate of addition of new entries to the first range of newly revised and updated entries (running from the letter *M* to the word *mahurat*, 286 new entries for the range of 1045 main entries in the second edition), one can calculate, crudely, that the new version of the OED will have over 75,000 new main entries. Evidently, the definition of what counts as a single dictionary entry is fluid and allows for very wide margins; any attempt at further precision is impossible because of the unlimited potential for compounding and derivation. The OED policy on compounds and derivatives is indicative of how blurred the line between a "headword" and a compound or a derivative can be:

> Compounds are frequently collected together in a section or group of sections at or near the end of an entry. They are followed by a quotation paragraph in which examples of each compound are presented in alphabetical order of the compound. *Some major compounds are entered as headwords in their own right.*
>
> Derivatives . . . are typically entered as the final section of an entry. *Many derivatives are included as headwords in their own right.* They are followed by a quotation paragraph illustrating examples of usage. (*Guide to OED Entries*, emphases ours)

Clearly, the size of the dictionary records exceeds by far the vocabulary of an individual speaker. The vocabulary used by Shakespeare in his plays and sonnets, a countable set, amounts to just over 29,000 different words, out of a total of 884,647 words of running text.[2] This is somewhat misleading, because inflectional forms (*work, working, worked*) are counted as separate words. A more narrowly defined count will bring that number down to only about 21,000.

Counting the words used and known by an average speaker of English is beset with the same obstacles that prevent us from calibrating the vocabulary of the language as a whole. In addition, age, gender, education, occupation, ethnic and geographic factors, personal history, and so on, are variables that make the picture extremely unstable. Still, estimates of the word-command of an adult educated speaker exist, placing the counts in the 10,000–60,000 words range. The passive vocabulary exceeds the active vocabulary by about 25 percent, raising the number of lexemes recognized by a user to approximately 75,000.[3] The words we use or recognize are not all of the same order of structural importance or frequency; the following section addresses the layering of the English lexicon.

2   Core and Periphery

Among the parameters that characterize each lexical item in the language are its frequency, grammatical type, meaning, etymology, and phonological structure. The most frequent words form the *core* of the vocabulary, shared by all adult speakers; outward from that core lie layers of words of decreasing frequency and familiarity. Here is how the editors of the *OED* describe the situation:

> The vast aggregate of words and phrases which constitutes the vocabulary of English-speaking people presents . . . the aspect of one of those nebulous masses familiar to the astronomer, in which a clear and unmistakable nucleus shades off on all sides, through zones of decreasing brightness. The English vocabulary contains a nucleus or central mass of many thousand words whose 'Anglicity' is unquestioned; . . . but they are linked on every side with other words which are less and less entitled to this appellation and which pertain ever more and more distinctly to the domain of local dialect, of slang, . . . of the peculiar technicalities of trades and processes, of the scientific terminology common to all civilized nations, and of the actual languages of other lands and peoples.   (*OED*, 2nd edn., p. xxiv)

Graphically, the core–periphery distribution of the vocabulary can be represented as a series of concentric circles, where the "nucleus" is composed of the absolutely essential words without which sentence composition or basic communication would be unthinkable (figure 20.1).

The core vocabulary is composed of items of high frequency: in figure 20.1 the innermost circle represents the one thousand most frequent words in the language, the second layer – the next one thousand, and so on. The numerical tags are arbitrary, of course, and the placement of a particular lexeme in one of the layers will depend on the type of text investigated. The core includes lexemes which form the structural backbone of syntax, namely articles, conjunctions, prepositions, auxiliaries, pronouns, quantifiers, determiners. Invariably, such items rank highest in frequency studies: all but five of the top fifty items in the Rank List in Francis and Kučera (1982: 465) are function words. That list ranks 6,000 words extracted from the Brown Corpus, a data base of 1,014,000 words from 500 samples of texts from a very broad range of genres. The frequency ranking is headed, understandably, by function words: *the, be,*

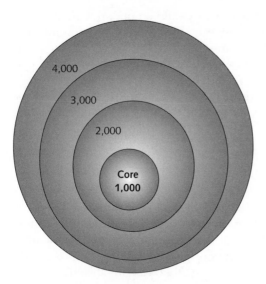

Figure 20.1   The core–periphery layering of the lexicon

of, and, a, in. Among the most frequent open-class lexemes (frequency ranking in parentheses) are: (33) *say*, (40) *make*, (44) *man*, (46) *time*, (47) *go*, (54) *year*, (56) *new*, etc. A frequency analysis based on a corpus of British English texts (the Lancaster-Oslo/Bergen (LOB) Corpus), comparable in size (a million words) and number of text samples (500) to the Brown Corpus, makes the point even more dramatically: *all* of the fifty most frequent words in the LOB Corpus are function words (Johansson and Hofland 1989: 19–20).

Like estimates of vocabulary size, the estimate of a word's frequency will vary depending on the size of the corpus, the types of material included (spoken or written), the range of text types (informative vs. imaginative), and further subcategories within those groups. The decisions involving grammatical tagging, a refinement which was initiated by the compilers of the LOB Corpus, and which is an important component of lexical studies today, can also affect the frequency ranking of a word. All of these finer distinctions are taken into consideration in the most recent full-scale study of the lexicon by Leech, Rayson, and Wilson (2001). Their corpus – the British National Corpus (BNC) – is a hundred times larger than the Brown and the LOB corpora, and it draws on more recent material, dating mainly from 1985 to 1994. Their specialized frequency lists reveal considerable differences between spoken and written English, as well as differences within the varieties of spoken and written English. A sample of their listings illustrating these differences is given in table 20.1; frequencies are rounded per million word tokens.

Such data enriches the picture of frequency layering of the lexicon, and it also makes it imperative that generalizations about frequency should be treated only as approximations: there can be no absolute ranking because even within

Table 20.1 Rank and Frequency in the British National Corpus

Rank	Word	Frequency in speech	Frequency in writing
1.	the	39,605	64,420
2.	I	29,448	6,494
3.	you	25,957	4,755
⋮	⋮	⋮	⋮
31.	know	5,550	734
32.	well	5,310	634
⋮	⋮	⋮	⋮
51.	then	3,474	1,378
52.	get	3,464	709
⋮	⋮	⋮	⋮
715.	education	115	277
716.	social	115	458

Source: Based on Leech, Rayson and Wilson (2001: 144–5)

the very center of the metaphorical concentric circles the range of variation may be significant. Nevertheless, what we know intuitively about "basic" words is confirmed statistically: the one thousand lexeme types, or about 2 percent of the total graphic words[4] that occur more than a hundred times in the LOB Corpus, account for more than two-thirds (68.5 percent) of all the word tokens in that corpus (Johansson and Hofland 1989: 21). This is largely due to the concentration of function words in the core. Thus, in spite of fluctuations within the core, the broad association between the notion of core and the frequency of the items residing there remains valid.

The notions of core and periphery are useful because they are correlated not only with frequency of usage, but also with the parameters of grammatical type, meaning, etymology, and syllable structure. The core vocabulary is made up of functionally and semantically indispensable words. These words are also etymologically near-homogeneous and morphologically simple, while the outer circles present a more diverse picture, both in terms of word origins and in terms of morphological complexity.

Etymologically, the core vocabulary is predominantly Germanic: only four of the top-ranked one hundred words in the Brown Corpus are of "foreign" origin, and as the first recorded dates in the OED show, they are very early loans. These are (64) *state*, n. (c. 1225), (81) *use*, v. (1240), (93) *people* (1292), (100) *just*, adv. (1382). In the LOB Corpus only *very* (ca. 1250) and *people* make it into the first one hundred words, ranked (81) and (99) respectively. For comparison, among the top-ranked items in the spoken English portion of the BNC there are only three non-Germanic items: (74) *very*, (85) *people*, and (98) *really*

(c. 1430). For the written portion of the BNC the first loanword is (86) *people*, followed by (91) *very*, and (94) *just*.[5] It is a commonplace observation that in everyday conversation, the basic *bread-water-food-kitchen-eat-sleep-dream-wake-run* type of discourse covered by the 1,000 most frequent words in the language, up to 83 percent of the items are descendants of Old English words. The situation is not static, however. In a recent study Hughes (2000: 392–4) points out that the composition of the core vocabulary has been changing in favor of borrowings. In his estimate of the "kernel" of 600 words, taken from a body of 5,000 words, about half are of non-Anglo-Saxon origin, including, e.g., *society, class, company, energy, machine, system, program, science*, and excluding, e.g., *heaven, hell, foul, evil*.

The concentration of Germanic words drops dramatically in the 2,000 word layer. A spot-check of the items in the frequency range 1,490–1,500 shows that half of the words in the spoken portion of the BNC (*responsible, catch, population, property, huge*), and half of the words in its written section (*treated, legislation, previously, ministers, materials*) are non-Germanic. The proportion of native words decreases further in the 3,000-word layer. As noted above, word frequency counts are multiply variable. Nevertheless, large-scale vocabulary studies can be informative about the etymological composition of English in relation to the relative frequency of words. Table 20.2 shows the results of one such study, based on more than fifteen million running words, over half of which were recorded in business and personal correspondence reflecting ordinary everyday activities.[6]

The percentages in the first row of table 20.2 bear out the assertion that even beyond the first one hundred items, the core lexicon, which includes function words and common words such as *water* and *food, go, sleep, wake, sister* and *brother, green* and *yellow*, is predominantly native in origin. Lexemes covering more complex and abstract notions: *autonomy, capitalism, cognition, delight,*

Table 20.2   Sources of the most frequent 10,000 words of English

Frequency	English (%)	French (%)	Latin (%)	Norse (%)	Other (%)
1,000	83	11	2	2	2
2,000	34	46	11	2	7
3,000	29	46	14	1	10
4,000	27	45	17	1	10
5,000	27	47	17	1	8
6,000	27	42	19	2	10
7,000	23	45	17	2	13
8,000	26	41	18	2	13
9,000	25	41	17	2	15
10,000	25	42	18	1	14

discretion, elegant, psychoanalysis, supreme, reverberate, telethon, which are spread over the outer frequency layers, are loanwords. Words from the realm of ideas, art, science and technology, and specialized discourse generally, reside in the more peripheral layers. There, the proportion of borrowed words increases. A very significant drop of the native component occurs in the second row: only 34 percent of those words have survived directly from Old English. In that same frequency range, the 1,000 to 2,000 range, the proportion of combined French and Latin words jumps from 13 percent in the first 1,000 to an impressive 57 percent. After that, the proportion of native words goes down more slowly, and remains approximately steady at 25 percent in the last four rows. The share of French and Latin remains remarkably stable in the outer layers. Starting with the 2,000 band, the proportion of 'other' sources is on the rise. The largest contributors to that group are Dutch and Greek, but it also includes Italian, Spanish, German, and many other sources, including words of uncertain and unknown etymologies.

Another common denominator for the items designated as core and periphery lexicon is their syllable structure: ninety-three of the first one hundred words in the Brown Corpus are monosyllabic words and the remaining seven have two syllables: *only, about, other, also, many, even, people.* At the other end of the frequency ranking, at the metaphorical periphery, function words which are typically mono- or disyllabic disappear completely; the items are all major class words. Predictably, the majority of the entries here are derived or polysyllabic words. Some examples from the same corpus are: (5,943) *hierarchy,* (5,955) *thoroughly,* (5,962) *subordinate n.,* (5,977) *attachment,* (5,980) *interpreter,* (5,981) *inclination,* (5,994) *paramount.* The proportion of monosyllabic words in the peripheral layers is relatively low; this corresponds to the commonly made association between "learned" vocabulary and morphological and phonological complexity, the latter including polysyllabicity and stress-shifting in the Latinate portion of these outer layers.[7]

3 The Paths and Perils of Borrowing Words

The data in table 20.2 allows us to average the frequencies in the various etymological categories. Based on that source, the origin of the 10,000 most frequent words in the language breaks down like this (in percentages):

Old English	31.8
French	45
Latin (post-OE)	16.7
Other Germanic languages	4.2
Other languages	2.3

This distribution is reflected in figure 20.2. The vocabulary of English is thus a blend of indigenous words and loanwords; the affixes used to form new

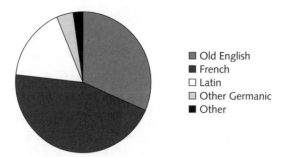

Figure 20.2   Vocabulary distribution according to etymology (PDE)

words are also of mixed origin. This section will look closer into the ways in which new and borrowed words intersect and interact with the pre-existing word-stock.

The most straightforward case of borrowing brings in a completely new form and meaning, e.g. *panther* (1220), *athlete* (1528), *tsar* (1555), *giraffe* (1594) *condor* (1604), *volcano* (1613), *kumquat* (1699), *kiwi* (1835) and the names of numerous "exotic" animals and birds), *tobacco* (1588), *mahogany* (1660), *maraschino* (1791), *yoga* (1820), *tsunami* (1897), *bolshevik* (1917), *mah-jong* (1922). Such words enter the language as mono-morphemic items, irrespective of their compositionality in the source language. Apart from metaphoric extension of the literal meanings (sit on a *volcano*, drug *tsar*, etc.), the interaction between these items and the native word-stock is primarily phonological. When such borrowings violate some native phonotactic constraint, they are subject to changes which bring them in line with the native phonology: vowel shift in *athlete* and *volcano*, cluster simplification in *tsar*, *maraschino*, vowel insertion in *athlete*, affrication in *giraffe*, stress shift and loss of palatal [l] in *bolshevik*. Apart from phonological assimilation, however, such borrowings tend to preserve their formal and semantic identity and independence.

A somewhat different mode of borrowing duplicates the native lexicon at least partially. The duplicate can correspond to the pre-existing word etymologically, semantically, or quite commonly, both etymologically and semantically. The degree of overlap between the earliest known form and meaning, the *etymon*, and the current form and meaning is largely unpredictable: *work* and *erg* are not too far apart in meaning, but the same root, Indo-European (IE) **werg-* 'to do' appears in *allergy, bulwark, energy, metallurgy, playwright, organ*, etc. IE **wed-* surfaces as *water, wet, wash, winter, otter*, all going back to Old English, but the same root gives us *hydro-* (Greek), *inundate, undulate* (Latin), *whiskey* (Gaelic), *vodka* (Russian). The fact that all of these items are cognates is an etymological curiosity; beyond that they are unremarkable and the naïve speaker may be unaware of their common origin. Recognition of the *formal* relationship of words going back to the same IE root

Table 20.3 Recognition of cognates based on the First Consonant Shift

Consonant class	IE	Germanic	Latin	Greek	Examples
Voiceless stops	p	f	p	p	fee, fellow, pecuniary
	t	θ	t	t	thin, tender, hypotenuse
	k	h	c	k	behest, cite, kinetic
Voiced stops	b	p	b	b	lap, labile, labor
	d	t	d	d	ten, December, decade
	g	k	g	g	cram, agora, category
Voiced aspirated stops	bʰ	b	f	ph	balk, fulcrum, phalanx
	dʰ	d	f	th	deed, fact, thesis
	gʰ	g	h	kh	girdle, cohort, chorus

rests most commonly on the set of consonantal correspondences in items in two phonological shapes: Germanic vs. non-Germanic, the latter primarily Latin, French, or Greek. The most frequent correspondences are summarized on table 20.2.

Very large numbers of such cognates in PDE are related in this way. Although the historical depth of the correspondences renders the semantic relationships obscure, the regularity of the consonantal pairings is such that it has led scholars to the formulation of the notions "sound law" and "regularity of sound change." The borrowed versions of the shared original etymon can appear in phonological forms which correlate both with the constraints in the donor language (penultimate stress in *December, decorum, veranda*), and with native processes (vowel shift in *labor, decade, thesis*, stress shift in *category*).

Phonological and semantic variability is not restricted to pairs of Germanic and Classical or French words. It can arise also when two Germanic languages come in contact, as was the case with Old English and Old Norse during the latter part of the Old English period. Pairs such as *kirk-church, dike–ditch, skirt-shirt* are the result of such borrowing. The genetic closeness of the donor language to English and the historical depth of the borrowing guaranteed the essentially Germanic nature of the items related in this way. The Old Norse members of such pairs share root-initial stress and their phonotactics, though historically divergent, have become part of the overall set of phonotactic constraints in PDE. Here are some examples (figure 20.3) of the phonological and semantic divergence of lexemes derived from the same etymon in two different Germanic languages:

Different phonological shapes of the same etymological input can sometimes be due entirely to differences within the non-Germanic donor languages, as in the pairs *debt-debit, frail-fragile*. Almost always, the members of such pairs

Source: PDE

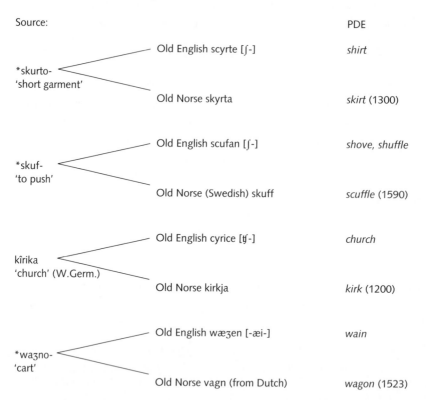

Figure 20.3   Cognates based on early contact with other Germanic languages

were borrowed at different dates, and intuitive awareness of the relationships had ceased to exist. Thus words that had already been borrowed from French in Middle English (ME) were sometimes re-borrowed from Latin, resulting in duplication of the original meaning and noticeable similarity of form. Here are some examples (table 20.4); the dates in parentheses are the first attestations of the words in the OED.

More examples of that type are the pairs *garner-granary; poor-pauper; purvey-provide; sever-separate; spice-species; strait-strict; sure-secure*, see further Serjeantson (1961: 262). The Latin adjectives for "kingly" and "lawful" have even given rise to triplets; in the forms *real, royal,* and *regal* and *leal, loyal,* and *legal,* they were imported first from Anglo-Norman, then from Old French, and last directly from Latin.

Yet another mode of vocabulary change is the duplication of meaning: if the language has a word for a particular notion already, and a new word is added which has a similar meaning, but a completely different shape, the resulting pair or set of words will be partial synonyms. Again, the words can come from

Table 20.4   Re-borrowing of the same lexical item from French and Latin

ME loanword	EModE loanword	Source
count (1325)	*compute* (1634)	L. *computare*, OFr. *Cunter*
cross, v. (1391)	*cruise* (1651)	L. *cruc-em*, OFr. *Croiz*
debt (1225)	*debit* (1682)	Lat. *debitum*, OFr *dete, dette*
frail (1382)	*fragile* (1513)	L. *fragilis*, OFr *fraile, frele*
ray (13–)	*radius* (1597)	L. *radius*, OFr. *rai, ray*

different daughters of Germanic, as is the case with *heaven–sky* (OE *heofon* 'heaven, the clouds. atmosphere' and ON *sky*, 'cloud, firmament'), *field–veld* (1785) (OE *feld* 'earth, open land' and Dutch *veldt*, Afrikaans *veld* 'the unenclosed country or open pasture-land'); similarly *shrub–scrub, ditch–dike, draw–drawl*. The most typical case, however, is the expansion of a semantic set by the historical addition of Romance loanwords which duplicate meanings already covered by existing Germanic lexemes. This is what happened in the case of *swine–pork, freedom–liberty*, and hundreds of other pairs or clusters of words, e.g. *feed–nourish* (ca. 1290), *white–blank* (c. 1325), *manly–virile* (1490)–*macho* (1928), *red–rouge* (1485)–*rubid* (1656), *climb–ascend* (1382), *top–summit* (1470)–*apex* (1603). In these sets the first word goes back to Old English. The later borrowings have the same meaning as the English word in the source languages, but they have developed new shades of meanings or different stylistic values within English.

4 The History of Vocabulary Expansion in English

The size and the etymological composition of the English lexicon have changed in harmony with the demographic and cultural history of its speakers. When we turn to the very early history of the English vocabulary, the problem of counting entries is compounded by the nature of the records. The extant body of texts gives us access only to a very limited portion of the language spoken outside the scriptoria where the texts were created. Moreover, the survival of texts is often a matter of historical accident – the records we draw on may be a small portion of what was actually written, but got randomly destroyed. Considering that the great literary figures of Anglo-Saxon England, people such as Ælfric (ca. 955–ca. 1010) and Wulfstan (d. 1023) were fluent in Latin, and wrote in both languages, it is probably the case that their total individual lexicons were as big as those of highly educated modern English speakers. They were linguistically, and lexically, extremely sophisticated. We just can't prove it with word lists that are comparable to the modern "unabridged" dictionaries. With that preamble in mind, it is still logical to assume that language contact and the historical progress in every sphere of human activity has indeed resulted in vocabulary "growth" from OE to PDE.

The Dictionary of Old English, currently under preparation at the Center for Medieval Studies at the University of Toronto,[8] is based on a corpus of 3,037 texts.[9] They represent a complete record of surviving Old English except for some variant manuscripts of individual texts. The number of words attested in Old English is estimated, conservatively, and prior to the completion of the *Dictionary*, at roughly 23,000–24,000 items.[10] Only about 3 percent of these are of non-Germanic origin. The vocabulary of Old English can therefore be described as etymologically homogeneous. The lexicon reflects the nature of the texts: the surviving materials are religious, didactic, legal, or stylized poetic compositions. We have no way of recovering all of the everyday words that must have been used in the various dialects, but never went on record. Manuscript production was a highly specialized activity in a pre-literate society; nevertheless, the words found in the monolingual OE texts are overwhelmingly of Germanic descent. This uniformity of lineage is in sharp contrast with the heterogeneous character of the PDE lexicon as shown in figure 20.2 and table 20.2.

When talking about vocabulary expansion, it is important to note that 65 percent to 85 percent of the Old English vocabulary has been "lost" – some words became obsolete (*fain* 'with pleasure,' *hight* 'is called,' *lorg* 'weaver's beam,' *shaw* 'a thicket, a small grove'), or restricted to dialectal use (*atter* 'poison,' *emmet* 'ant,' *mere* 'marsh, fen,' *losel* 'worthless person, a profligate, rake, scoundrel'). Sometimes the notions these words covered were no longer needed, as is the case with *hidegild* 'a fine paid in lieu of a flogging,' *fleam* 'a surgical instrument for letting blood,' *thane* 'a military attendant, follower, or retainer,' *heriot* 'feudal service/military equipment.' Lexical loss can be induced also by borrowing, primarily from Latin or French. Here (table 20.5) is a sample of words which did not compete successfully with the corresponding loanword and fell into disuse.

Table 20.5   The replacement of Old English lexemes by loan synonyms

Old English	Latest OED quote	Replacement	Earliest OED quote
bede 'prayer'	1554	prayer (OF. preiere)	1300
blee 'color'	1460[11]	color (OF. color)	1290
dight 'to ordain'	1558	ordain (AFr. ordeiner)	1300
ferd 'army'	1350	army (F. armée)	1386
glad 'to rejoice'	1622	rejoice (OF. rejoiss-)	1303
rede 'advice'	1599[12]	advice (OFr. avis)	1297

Later borrowing could lead to the loss of only some, but not all of the meanings of the original OE word, as in *craft*, originally also 'art,' *cynn* 'kin,' originally also 'species,' *haven*, originally also 'harbor,' *gast* 'ghost,' originally also 'spirit.' All of these "losses" were obviously offset by the adoption of the Romance words with overlapping meaning.

We now turn to a survey of the etymological composition of the English lexicon in chronological sequence, starting with the words borrowed by Germanic speakers from Latin before Germanic was "exported" to the British Isles.

4.1   Latin influence on Continental Germanic

Proto-Germanic was spoken from around 500–200 BC to the beginning of the Christian era or later. The Germanic-speaking tribes of that period are believed to have formed a generally unified linguistic community, distributed over a broad geographic area in northwestern and central Europe. Various dialects must have existed, of course, but they must have been mutually intelligible. Some time after the beginning of the Christian era, perhaps around the second or third century AD, the first major split of Germanic occurred: between East Germanic, with the Goths migrating to southeast Europe, and Northwest Germanic. The split between North and West Germanic is dated roughly between ca. 300–600 AD.

The early borrowing of Latin words into the widening stream that became Old English must be considered at two dates and under two quite different circumstances: the Continental period, and the settlement period. Borrowing into Germanic on the continent was quite extensive: some 400 words from Latin had already made their way north, though only a small fraction of them made their way onward to Britain with the fifth-century settlers. These are the earliest loanwords coming from Latin into Germanic. Semantically, because of the nature of the trade-contact between the Romans and the residents of Germania, they tend to be connected with bartering, agriculture, construction, and warfare: e.g. OE: *ceap* 'cheap,' *ynce* 'inch,' *mynet* 'coin,' *win* 'wine,' *butere* 'butter,' *ciese* 'cheese,' *pipor* 'pepper,' *cealc* 'chalk,' *weall* 'wall,' *stræt* 'street,' *mile, sock, candle, pound, toll, copper, pillow*. Except for the First Consonant Shift, the prosodic and segmental shape of these words is thoroughly Germanic: they have initial stress, and their phonotactics are unexceptional. Their foreignness is of interest only to etymologists.

4.2   Celtic and Roman Britain

Prior to the arrival of Germanic-speaking settlers in Britain in the middle of the fifth century, the British Isles were inhabited by Celtic-speaking people. The Celts may have settled in Britain as early as ca. 2000 BC but not later than the sixth to the first century BC. From 43 AD to 410 AD, Britain was a province of the Roman Empire. The Roman occupation of Britain has left a great deal of archeological evidence; however, the contacts between the indigenous Celts and the Romans in Britain have left but marginal traces on the language which subsequently became the dominant language of the British Isles, namely Old English.

During the 350 years prior to the departure of the Romans the superstrate language, at least in the southern part of the country, was Latin. The local substrate language(s) continued to be spoken, but the substrate speakers had to acquire some measure of competence in the superstrate language. Briefly, the Celts in Britain when the Germani arrived were speakers of both Celtic and Latin. After the middle of the fifth century the new superstrate language became the variety of West Germanic that developed into Old English. The Latin words that came into Old English could have been from contacts made with the continent after the Germanic settlement of Britain, or from newly arriving settlers over a considerable span of time, or from Celtic speakers of Latin, at least in the early settlement years. Words of this sort include *ancor* 'anchor,' *ele* 'oil,' *forca* 'fork,' *cest* 'chest,' *pail, pott* 'pot,' *tunne* 'tun, cask' (possibly just a Celtic word not derived from Latin); *cæster* 'camp,' *catte* 'cat,' *cocc* or *kokke* 'rooster,' *Læden* 'Latin.'

Given the long contact beween the Celts and the settlers from Germania, and given that Old English had become the superstrate and local Celtic languages the substrate, the linguistic situation was extremely complex. In essence, Celtic was two substrate layers down (Old English the superstrate, some sort of Latin the upper substrate, Celtic the lower substrate), so it is not surprising that very few Celtic words made their way into early English. The only common Celtic elements are in place names; place names have the advantage and the prestige of having been there first, and their transfer into the invading language is predictable. Examples of such names with Latin pieces inside them, or that are entirely Latin in origin, are *Thames* (Lat. *Temesa*), *Yorkshire, Devonshire, Canterbury, Dorchester, Davenport, Manchester, Lancaster, Winchester, Exeter, Gloucester, London*. Among the place-name elements borrowed from the Celts are *-combe* 'valley' and *-torr* 'rock, peak.' Real Celtic loanwords into English (not Latin words transmitted through Celtic, such as *cross* and *ancor* 'hermit') are extremely few. Among the common nouns that have survived into PDE are: *bin, brat* 'cloth, cloak,' *cradle, dun, crag, curse, loch*.

The adoption and spread of Christianity at the end of the sixth century promoted the learning of Latin and the translation of many religious and scholastic texts from Latin into Old English. Religion thus became the channel through which the first significant number of learned Latin words came into the language. Latin words related to the introduction of Christianity (some of these words go back to Greek prototypes) are: *apostle, cleric, bishop, candle, anthem, devil, monastery, monk*. Scholarly words adopted through translations of Latin learned (medical, biological), and literary texts are: *paper, school, verse, cancer, fever, paralysis, plaster, camel, elephant, tiger, plant, elm, lily, pine, beet, oyster, radish*. It was in Old English that the first loan-translations, or *calques*, appear on record: Lat. *Lunæ dies* 'day of the moon' → OE *Monan-dæg*, 'Monday';

Lat. *Martis dies* 'day of Mars,' O.E. *Tiwes-dæg* 'Tuesday' (*Tiw* was the Anglo-Saxon of the Norse god of war corresponding to the Roman god of war *Mars*), Lat. *evangelicum* 'good news,' O.E. *godspell* 'good tidings,' ME *evangely* 'gospel'.[13]

4.3 Early North Germanic additions

The most profound and lasting influence on the vocabulary of English that can be traced back to another branch of Germanic is associated with the continuous presence of the Vikings, speakers of Old Norse, in Anglo-Saxon England from the middle of the ninth century onwards. The Viking Age in Europe is dated ca. 750–1050. During that time Old Norse was spoken not just in present-day Scandinavia, but also in Iceland, Greenland, the Faroe Islands, the islands off the coast of Scotland and in parts of Ireland, Scotland, England, Northern France (Normandy), and Russia.

The Viking incursions and their permanent settlements into large parts of eastern England became a source of lexicon diversification. The ninth-century establishment of a territory northeast of the Thames which came to be called the Danelaw, legitimized the presence of the northern strand of Germanic in the country and created conditions for permanence, and possibly peaceful integration of the two "cousin" languages. Once the attacks and the warring had subsided, the two languages, Old English and Old Norse, were on an equal linguistic footing. The conditions for linguistic integration peaked in the first half of the eleventh century when the country was under Danish rule (1017–1042).

It is estimated that about one thousand words were adopted from Old Norse between the end of the eighth and the middle of the eleventh century. Most of these items are common everyday words: *bank, bull, call, fellow, guess, leg, loan, score, skill, sister, skin, sky.* Very significantly, Scandinavian is the source of some important function words: *they, them, their,* possibly also *she* and *are, till* and *though.* Old Norse also contributed extensively to the formation of place-names in England: there are about 600 of them today ending in *-by,* 'settlement, town,' *-thwaite* 'a plot of land,' *-thorp(e)* 'village,' etc. Phonologically, the addition of a number of words with root-initial /sk-/ from Old Norse enriched the range of possible root-initial clusters in English. The influence of Scandinavian is attested also in the pronunciation of words such as *get* (*OE gietan*), *give* (*OE giefan*), in which the boldfaced sounds would have been pronounced [j-], had it not been for the ON [g-] pronunciation.

4.4 The Norman Conquest and its effect on the composition of the lexicon

The borrowings discussed so far did not affect the etymological homogeneity of the English lexicon. Early Latin borrowings were limited in number; they were also generally restricted to specific registers of language. The historic event which put the vocabulary of English onto a non-Germanic track was the Norman Conquest of 1066. The cultural and linguistic consequences of the eleventh-century occupation of Britain by speakers of Norman French were far-reaching. The demographic minority spoke little or no English and maintained strong cultural and linguistic ties to Normandy for at least a century and a half. The political and cultural ties to France continued throughout Middle English. Although after the beginning of the thirteenth century the Anglo-Norman nobility gradually became more and more "English," the relationship between English and the two other languages dominating the administrative and legal scene, Latin and Anglo-Norman/Old French, continued to be that of a universally spoken substrate (English) to two culturally dominant languages (Latin and French).

Before we present the remainder of a chronological account of the evolution of the English lexicon, some comments are needed on how the massive borrowing of French words into English came about. As Thomason and Kaufman (1988: 263–331) have convincingly argued, it was not a simple superstrate-hand-down-to-substrate transfer because there were never many speakers of French in England, especially after the thirteenth century. Few English speakers learned French between 1066 and 1250, after which date there was no need to, and the largest portion of the new lexicon came at a time (1200–1400) when there were practically no competent French speakers for an Englishman to talk to. Moreover, Thomason and Kaufman (1988: 329) point out that the linguistic influence of French on Middle English folk speech was normal for coastal Northwestern Europe. Thus, the French influence on English was through cultural superiority, and English was not very exceptional among the languages of Europe in this regard. Words were borrowed from all spheres of cultural contact characteristic of the higher social status of the French-speaking nobility: lexicon from literature, religion, government, law, warfare, architecture, art, science, medicine, was rapidly absorbed into English. The new rulers brought with them legal, administrative, military, and political terms which often paralleled existing English words: *liberty, assembly, council, guard(ian), parliament, record, tax, army, defense, navy, soldier.* In the areas of literature, art, science, medicine, English borrowed words such as *beauty, color, romance, music, poet, physician, surgeon, grammar, logic, study,* etc. Along with that, many core words were also borrowed: *air, beast, city, close, dangerous, diet, feast, flower, glue, haste, jealous, journey, judge, liquor, mountain, noble, oil, part, peace, pork, river, servant, soil, story, tender, very,* etc. All in all, approximately 10,000 words were borrowed from Anglo-Norman and continental French into ME (1066–1476).[14] Seventy-five percent of these borrowings are still in use.

Among the long-term consequences of the increased presence of Romance vocabulary in the Middle English lexicon were changes of the phonemic inventory, greater frequency of individual phonemes, and the introduction of new prosodic patterns. (For word-formation influences, see chs. 21 and 23, this volume.) Borrowed /v/-initial words (e.g. *vapor* (1390), *valentine* (1400), *vagrant* (1444)), and /z/-initial words (e.g. *zephyr* (c. 1386), *zodiac* (ca. 1392), *zone* (1394)) contributed to the phonemicization of the voiced velar spirants /v/ and /z/. A later, seventeenth-century change affecting the phonemic inventory, the palatalization of <-s + -ion, -ure> to [-ʒ], in e.g. *derision, occasion, measure,* and the identification of this new consonant with the French [ʒ] as in e.g. *beige, rouge,* led to the addition of the voiced palatal fricative /ʒ/ to the phonemic inventory of English. The Romance vocabulary also contributed to the higher frequency of the palatal fricative /ʃ/ and the affricates /tʃ/ and /dʒ/. Words borrowed with palatal consonants, or phonological sequences that later developed naturally into palatals, include (before 1200) *chancellor, chapel, passion, catch, cheer, gentle, charity, large, chasten, ginger, fresh.* In the thirteenth century the borrowings of palatals or incipient palatals are even more common: *burgess, physician, preacher, judge, chasten, creche, scourge, dangerous, devotion, jealous, patience, adventure, special, change, exchequer.* In the fourteenth century the numbers are overwhelming and can only be minimally sampled: *merchant, official, page, nation, archer, kerchief, rage, stature, touch, precious.* It is worth noting that all of these loans were early enough to feel completely "naturalized" today.

The effect of the newly adopted Romance lexicon on the prosodic structure of Middle English is of special interest. For disyllabic words borrowed early, stress on the initial syllable of the word became the default: *fortune, language, mammon, minus, mercy, moral, mountain, novel, pagan, palate, primer, sentence, sermon, solid.* This is fully in line with the Germanic pattern of root-initial stress. Words which were borrowed as trisyllabic followed the Latin stress rule: if the penultimate syllable was light (or "short" in the Latinist literature), the antepenultimate was stressed: *melody, mystery, regimen, patient, Samuel, violent.* Such words also fit the native model of word-initial main stress. These two types did not affect the native prosodic system. However, the nativization of French borrowings with heavy suffixes such as *-ance/-ence, -esse, -(i)er, -io(u)n, -ité(e), -y(e), -ment, -ous* was a more complex process. Initially, within English, they developed a second stress two syllables back from the main stress: *àrgumént, èloquénce, iàlousé, pàrlemént,* etc. Such loans provided important evidence against root-initial stress in English, a prosodic innovation which was bolstered by the influx of Latinate vocabulary during the Renaissance. Word-types responsible for the establishment of a competing, weight-based pattern of stress in English were trisyllabic words with a heavy penultimate syllable (*aroma* (1100), *asylum* (1430)), (though compare *calendar* (1205), *discipline* (1382), *sinister* (1411))), and words derived from non-stress-neutral suffixes: *avaricious, Chinese, metricality, pathetic.*

4.5 The Renaissance and after

The two centuries following the introduction of the printing press in England in 1476 stand out as the period of most rapid vocabulary growth in the history of the language. Even as the nationalistic spirit was rising and with it the respect for the vernacular, Latin and Greek continued to dominate the class-rooms as obligatory components of good education. Some 4,500 new words were recorded in English during each decade between 1500 and 1700. Over 20,000 words borrowed from the Classical languages between 1500 and 1700 have survived to this day.[15] Unlike the first wave of influence from the classical languages, mostly mediated by French, the Renaissance classical borrowings entered the language largely in their original form. Some words borrowed from Latin during that period are *alumnus, contend, curriculum, exclusive, investigate, relate, sporadic, transcendental.* From the fields of mathematics and geometry, botany, biology, geography, medicine are: *abdomen, antenna, calculus, cerebellum, codex, commensurable, compute, evaporate, lacuna, larva, radius, recipe, species.* A substantial number of everyday words were also adopted; they probably started out as specialized words, but quickly became part of the common vocabulary: *frequency, parental, plus, invitation, offensive, virus.* Affixes were also borrowed from Latin, e.g. the suffixes *-ence, -ancy, -ency, -y*, and the prefixes *ante-, post-, sub-, super-*. It was this second wave of Latinate lexicon that produced a new set of weight- and affix-sensitive constraints on stress placement in PDE.

Greek words which came through Latin, and possibly through French, are words such as *atheism, atmosphere, chaos, dogma, economy, ecstasy, drama, irony, pneumonia, scheme, syllable.* Direct borrowings from Greek are *asterisk, catastrophe, crypt, criterion, dialysis, lexicon, polyglot, rhythm, syllabus.* In addition to the introduction of novel principles of stress assignment for the Latinate vocabulary, these neo-classical loanwords brought new minor morphological patterns into the system, as in the plurals *larvae, calculi, cornua, hiatus.*

The non-classical portion of the loan vocabulary recorded in early Modern English and after is diverse in origin. Some examples of borrowings from Italian include: *artichoke* (1531), *bazaar* (1599), *gondola* (1549), *vermicelli* (1669), *squadron,* (1562), *balcony* (1619), *fresco* (1598), *opera* (1644), *rotunda* (1687), *stanza* (1588), seventeenth- and eighteenth-century musical loan-words, e.g. *duet, maestro, tempo, soprano* etc. Early loans from Dutch are *drill,* v. (1622), *foist,* v. (1545) *knapsack* (1603), *pickle,* v. (1552) *smuggle,* v. (1687), *rant,* v. (1598), *trigger* (1621), *yacht* (1557), *bully* (1710). Among the Renaissance borrowings from Spanish are: *buoy* (1596), *cargo* (1602), *guava* (1555), *hammock* (1555), *masquerade* (1654), *mestizo* (1588), *negro* (1555), *potato* (1565), *siesta* (1655).

The eighteenth and nineteenth centuries are also marked by rapid increase of the vocabulary. The leading foreign source for that period is French, followed by Spanish (Algeo 1998: 78), though neo-Classical vocabulary continued to be created through the flourishing of scientific inquiry and the opening of new fields of knowledge: *electromotive* (1806), *invertebrate* (1826), *agglomerate* (1830) *pterodactyl* (1830). Once again, gauging the size and growth of the lexicon is a difficult task because of the incompleteness of the documentation. Algeo (1998: 63) cites, very cautiously, post-1776 rates of increase between 63 percent and 34 percent.

5 Recent Acquisitions: Second Half of the Twentieth Century

Over the last century, the proportion of borrowed words has decreased considerably, in spite of active international contacts: obviously the flow is from English to other languages. That of course does not stop English from borrowing words when needed, as it always has. Algeo (1998: 85) estimates the proportion of loanwords to other types of new words in six twentieth-century sources as ranging between 4.3 percent and 18.8 percent. New words coming into English, borrowing as well as new creations of all types, have been carefully charted in a single source, Cannon (1987). The summary below is drawn from there. The time-line of the survey is limited to 1963 through 1981. Any extrapolation to longer-term trends would be reckless.

Based on a sharply delineated set of sources,[16] Cannon provides an exhaustive analysis of his 13,683 word corpus. Borrowings constitute only 7.5 percent of the total of new words. In earlier times, Latin was the most common source. Now French loans are the most common: 254 items, followed by 80 Japanese, 80 Spanish, 75 Italian, and so on down to 5 each from Bengali, Danish, Indonesian, Korean, and Persian.

But borrowing is not our only source of new words. New technologies sometimes bring an avalanche of new words. In the second half of the twentieth century the fields of biotechnology and computer science exploded with new lexicon, as aeronautics did in the first half and aerospace along with computer science in the second half. In the seven-year period between the first and second editions of *The Cambridge Encyclopedia of the English Language*, David Crystal (2002) had to add an entire chapter to accommodate the growth of internet-based words such as *flaming* 'shouting via capitalization,' *offline* 'privately,' *firmware, freeware, groupware, wetware* 'the brain,' *webonomics, webzine, netiquette, geekification*. The internet has generated an endless list of new abbreviations, of which these are but a sample: *URL* 'Uniform Resource Locator,' *DDS* 'Digital Data Storage,' *HTML* 'HyperText Markup Language,' *IAP* 'Internet Access Provider,' *PDF* 'Portable Document Format,' and very many more – and it is impossible to say how many are ephemeral; a lot, one would guess. Cannon (1987: 148) lists 2,480 items within the shortening category – 18 percent of his total. There can be no question, however, that such items constitute the fastest growing and most volatile part of the vocabulary: there are 400,000 such entries in the 11th edition of *Acronyms, Initialisms & Abbreviations Dictionary* (Gale Research Company, 1987).

Under the category of additions (suffixes and prefixes, derivational morphology in general), Cannon lists 3,313 items, 24 percent of his corpus. The extremely high productivity of the sciences, especially chemistry and pharmacology, accounts for most of this naming activity. Quite similar numbers emerge from the same sources in compounding: 3,591 noun compounds, for example.

All composites taken together, combining by affixation and by compounding, come to 53.7 percent of his data (3,313 affixations and 4,040 compounds).

One may conclude from this survey, somewhat sweepingly, if not rashly, that English has turned inward to its own resources for new words and new readings. As it is the Latin of the twenty-first century, required in all fields of science, required worldwide in travel, politics, and global communication, perhaps this inner-directed expansion is to be expected.

NOTES

1   All references in this chapter are to the *OED Online* (http://dictionary.oed.com/), based on the 2nd edn. of 1989 and updated quarterly with about 1000 new and revised entries. Copyright © Oxford University Press 2004.

2   These figures are based on Spevack, Marvin (1968–80), *A Complete and Systematic Concordance to the Works of Shakespeare*. Hildesheim: Georg Olms, cited in Crystal (1995: 123).

3   These figures are based on the information in Crystal (1995: 123). We think that the upper ranges of the estimate are unrealistic.

4   The definition of "graphic word" includes not only lexical items, but also any other sequence of alphanumeric characters surrounded by spaces, see Hofland and Johansson (1982: 7, 39).

5   See Leech et al. (2001: 144, 180).

6   The original results of the investigation were published in *A Statistical Linguistic Analysis of American English* by A. Hood Roberts, The Hague: Mouton, 1965, pp. 35–8. The tabulation of the results used here is from Williams (1975: 67).

7   The layers referred to here are not coextensive with the affixation strata in lexical phonology; both core and periphery items are "lexical" in the lexical phonology sense.

8   The 2005 progress report http://www.doe.utoronto.ca/report/report.html states that the DOE online is under development. Web access to the materials up to and including G is expected in 2006. The drafting of entries for H, I/Y and L is progressing well.

9   For comparison, the first edition of the OED (1884–1928) used citations from 2700 authors; the number of works represented in quotations in it was 4,500 (http://dictionary.oed.com/about/facts.html). There is no comparable data on OED 2 (1989), but for that edition the number of quotations is given as 2,436,600.

10   These estimates are cited in Kastovsky (1992: 293).

11   Two further isolated entries, 1623 and 1850, are obvious and deliberate archaisms.

12   The word is used only until the beginning of the seventeenth century. After that date it is rarely found until revived in archaic and poetic diction in the nineteenth century (OED).

13   A more recent example of a *calque* is the expression 'that goes without saying,' a loan-translation of the French expression *cela va sans dire*, or the twentieth-century introduction of *ivory tower* from the French *tour d'ivoire*.

14 The estimate is based on a word's first appearance as recorded by the *Oxford English Dictionary*, see Baugh and Cable (1993: 174).

15 For these figures see Stockwell and Minkova (2001: 41–3). For an excellent survey of the lexical changes in early Modern English, see Nevalainen (1999), especially at pp. 336–76.

16 *The Barnhart Dictionary of New English since 1963* (1973), *The Second Barnhart Dictionary of New English* (1980), and Merriam's 1981 Addenda Section to *Webster's Third New International Dictionary of the English Language* (1961), providing a data base of 13,683 documented and dated new entries into the language.

FURTHER READING

Algeo, J. (1998) Vocabulary. In Suzanne Romaine (ed.), *The Cambridge history of the English language, vol. I: 1776–1997*. Cambridge: Cambridge University Press, 57–92.

Algeo, J. (ed.) (1991) *Fifty years among the new words*. Cambridge: Cambridge University Press.

Burnley, David (1992) Lexis and semantics. In Norman Blake (ed.), *The Cambridge history of the English language, vol. II: 1066–1476*. Cambridge: Cambridge University Press, 409–500.

Cannon, G. H. (1987) *Historical change and English word-formation: Recent vocabulary*. New York: P. Lang.

Hughes, G. (2000) *A history of English words*. Oxford: Blackwell.

Kastovsky, D. (1992) Semantics and vocabulary. In Richard Hogg (ed.), *The Cambridge history of the English language, vol. I: the beginnings to 1066*. Cambridge: Cambridge University Press, 290–407.

Katamba, Francis X. (2004) *English words: Structure, history, usage*. London: Routledge.

Marchard, Hans (1975) *Categories and types of present-day English word formation*, 2nd edn. München: C. H. Beck.

Nevalainen, T. (1999) Early Modern English lexis and semantics. In Roger Lass (ed.), *The Cambridge history of the English language, vol. III: 1476–1776*. Cambridge: Cambridge University Press, 332–459.

Serjeantson, M. S. (1935; 1961) *A history of foreign words in English*. London: Routledge and Kegan Paul.

REFERENCES

Algeo, J. (1998) Vocabulary. In Suzanne Romaine (ed.), *The Cambridge history of the English language, vol. IV: 1776–1997*. Cambridge: Cambridge University Press, 57–92.

Barnhart dictionary companion, The (ca. 1982-current). Cold Spring, NY: Lexik House Publishers.

Baugh, A. C. and Th. Cable (1993) *A history of the English language*, Englewood Cliffs, NJ: Prentice Hall.

Cannon, G. H. (1987) *Historical change and English word-formation: Recent vocabulary*. New York: P. Lang.

Crystal, D. (1995; 2002) *The Cambridge encyclopedia of the English language*.

Cambridge: Cambridge University Press.

Francis, W. N. and H. Kučera (1982) *Frequency analysis of English usage: Lexicon and grammar.* With the assistance of Andrew W. Mackie. Boston: Houghton Mifflin.

Hofland, K. and S. Johansson (1982) *Word frequencies in British and American English.* Bergen: Norwegian Computing Center for the Humanities; Harlow: Longman.

Hughes, G. (2000) *A history of English words.* Oxford: Blackwell.

Johansson, S. and K. Hofland (1989) *Frequency analysis of English vocabulary and grammar,* 2 vols. Oxford: Clarendon Press.

Kastovsky, D. (1992) Semantics and vocabulary. In Richard Hogg (ed.), *The Cambridge history of the English language, vol. I: The beginnings to 1066.* Cambridge: Cambridge University Press, 290–407.

Leech, G., P. Rayson, and A. Wilson (2001) *Word frequencies in written and spoken English: Based on the British National Corpus.* London: Longman.

Nevalainen, T. (1999) Early Modern English lexis and semantics. In Roger Lass (ed.), *The Cambridge history of the English language, vol. III: 1476–1776.* Cambridge: Cambridge University Press, 332–459

Serjeantson, M. S. (1961) [1935]. *A history of foreign words in English.* London: Routledge and Kegan Paul.

Stockwell, R. and D. Minkova (2001) *English words: history and structure.* Cambridge: Cambridge University Press.

Thomason, S. G. and T. Kaufman (1988) *Language contact, creolization, and genetic linguistics.* Berkeley and Los Angeles: University of California Press.

Williams, J. M. (1975) *Origins of the English language: A social and linguistic history.* New York: Free Press.

21 Compounds and Minor Word-formation Types

LAURIE BAUER

1 Introduction

Most word-formation in English (independent of whether 'word-formation' is taken to include or exclude inflectional morphology) is done through the three processes of prefixation, suffixation, and compounding. Some internal modification (umlaut, ablaut) is generally seen as supporting inflectional affixation, while other sub-types (stress-shift, consonantal change) are seen as supporting derivational morphology. Two other types, back-formation and conversion (also known as zero-derivation, functional shift) are seen as closely related to derivational affixation, and are best dealt with as extensions to that category. This chapter deals first with the compounds, and then with other minor-types of word-formation which are not clearly morphological in nature.

The processes dealt with here may thus be united as non-affixal instances of word-formation in English. These are all extremely frequently used methods of forming new lexical items in modern English. Interestingly, it is often difficult to draw a firm line between the different types, the borders tending to be fuzzy rather than clear-cut. At the same time, there are differences between compounds and these minor word-formation types. The most obvious one is the regularity which is usually attributed to compounding, as opposed to the formal irregularity which is often seen as characterizing the minor word-formation types. This is sometimes characterized as a distinction between the productivity of compounding (implying rule-governed behavior; see Bauer 2001) as opposed to the creativity of other types (implying the predominance of analogy and other processes which are not rule-governed).

The central question in this chapter will be one of definition. Just what is a compound, and how much does the category cover? How reliable a criterion is stress? Where does compounding stop and blending begin?

1.1   *Productivity and lexicalization*

One problem which recurs in any discussion of word-formation is the matter of productivity. Although the term PRODUCTIVE is used in various ways in morphology (see Bauer 2001), we can fundamentally say that a process is productive while and to the extent it used in the coinage of new forms. Purely syntactic processes are usually assumed to be totally productive: they are assumed not to have lexical exceptions, not to be restricted by factors related to etymology, the word-classes involved, or demands for euphony. Any of these may have an effect in word-formation. On the other hand, the lexicon of English contains many words whose precise form or meaning could not be predicted on the basis of the current state of the language. In some instances, the process has simply ceased being productive. We have a word like *dread-nought*, but cannot create a new parallel like **fearterrorist*. In other cases, an existing word has acquired particular connotations or meanings which make it non-compositional or idiomatic. For example, a frogman is not a person who happens to have bulging eyes or a long tongue, nor yet a man who collects, eats or sells frogs. The meaning of *frogman* is fixed. Such patterns or examples are said to be LEXICALIZED.

1.2   *Words*

If you were learning English, and you learnt *protrude, protrudes, protruding, protruded*, how many words would you have learnt? If you answer 'four,' you are taking *word* in the sense WORD-FORM, and if you answer 'one' you are taking *word* in the sense of LEXEME. The lexeme subsumes the different inflected forms illustrated for *protrude*. In this particular example, the BASE is *protrude*, and the other word-forms are produced from that base. (On inflection, see further, ch. 22, this volume.) Word-formation is about the formation of lexemes rather than about the formation of word-forms.

There is another, related, term which must be distinguished from lexeme, and that is lexical item (sometimes called listeme). A LEXICAL ITEM is anything which must be listed in a speaker's mental dictionary. This includes lexemes, may include smaller items such as suffixes, but also includes items made up of more than one lexeme such as *red herring, bark up the wrong tree, put up with*, and so on.

2   Compounds

2.1   *Preliminaries*

Compounds are frequently given a slightly paradoxical definition as words which are made up of two words. We can be slightly more precise than that, even if the delimitation of compounds will be a question to which we shall have reason to return. First, we must understand that *word* in the loose definition given above is to be understood in the sense of 'lexeme.' Compounds are lexemes in the sense that they have – in appropriate word-classes – the ability and requirement to inflect just like lexemes which do not have a complex internal structure. Compounds are distinguished from other lexemes in that their internal structure shows two or more lexemic bases (which we will call the ELEMENTS of the compound) – forms which in other places in the language inflect independently and can on their own act as the heads of relevant phrases. In compounds it is typically the case (though we shall come back to whether this is always the case) that only one of these lexemic bases, in English typically the right-hand one, can show overt inflection. Moreover, we generally restrict the term 'compound' to those multi-lexemic lexical items which do not arise through the lexicalization of syntactic structure. *Love-in-a-mist* and *forget-me-not*, while they are undoubtedly lexical items of English, are, by this criterion, not compounds. *Namby-pamby* and *shilly-shally* are equally not compounds, because they fail to meet the part of the definition which states that a compound must contain bases of two independent lexemes.

Not only is it the case that only the final element in an English compound can usually inflect, it is also the case that in a very large number of cases the final element in isolation denotes a hyperonym or superordinate term for what is denoted by the compound as a whole. *Windmill* denotes a type of mill, *dive* is a superordinate of *sky-dive*, *sky-blue* is a hyponym of *blue*. In such instances, the final element determines not only an important part of the meaning of the compound, it determines the word-class of the compound and, in most cases, the inflectional class of the compound (*flittermouse* makes its plural in the same way that *mouse* does; *understand* makes its past tense in the same way that *stand* does). Inflection is typically marked on the final element of the compound, whether it is regular or irregular. In such cases we may talk of this final element as being the HEAD of the compound. We shall return below to extensions to this notion of headedness, and to some problems and exceptions.

In calling a compound a lexeme, I made specific reference to the notion of an item which takes a global inflection. But there is a common perception that a 'word' of English (of whatever type) corresponds in some way to an ORTHOGRAPHIC WORD, the word as delimited by spaces on the page. We must, therefore, state at the outset that any such definition of the compound in English is totally impracticable. First, large numbers of English compounds can be found with different spellings in different dictionaries. We might, for instance, find *coffee pot*, *coffee-pot* or *coffeepot*, depending on the dictionary we care to consult. When even dictionaries fail to agree, we can be sure that actual usage provides a bewildering amount of variation. Second, we must note that there is a principle of English spelling whereby any item consisting of more than one orthographic word is hyphenated (and thus presumably turned into 'one word' orthographically) when it occurs in attributive position. Thus the phrasal *false advertising* appears to become a single orthographic words in *false-advertising laws*. It is not clear that such examples are meaningfully analyzed as compounds rather than as rank-shifted syntax. Worse, in actual usage this gives us such attested examples as *to fill AB social class-type jobs* and the *ex-vice queen of Hollywood* (Bauer and Renouf 2001) which create orthographic units which appear to run counter to fundamental constituent analysis. Even greater nonsense is generated by examples such as *the New York–Los Angeles flight*, which appears to contain *York–Los* as a single orthographic word. For reasons such as this, the compound needs to be defined independently of the ortho-graphic word.[1]

Compounds are classified and cross-classified in a number of different ways. We have traces of a classification designed for Sanskrit compounds remaining in terms like *bahuvrihi* and *dvandva* (see below); we have structuralist analyses of various types, traces of which remain in terms like *endocentric* and *exocentric*; we have transformationally based analyses which see sentential relations persisting in the relationships between elements in compounds. Perhaps the classification which makes the fewest assumptions and which is easiest to apply is a fundamental division between compounds functioning as different word-classes in a sentence. Using this system we talk about COMPOUND NOUNS, ADJECTIVES, VERB, PREPOSITIONS, etc. While other classifications will be required, this is the one we shall take as basic here.

With compounding, as with other instances of word-formation (in par-ticular conversion), we need to distinguish in principle between the final result of the word-formation process and the process by which a particular form was coined. Take *baby-sit* as an example. On the surface, this is a compound verb: it is used as a verb in sentences such as *I have been asked to baby-sit for the Smiths*, and it contains two lexemic bases, and is inflected according to the pattern of the word-final element (*My aunt baby-sat for us last night*). But it did not come into being by taking *baby* and *sit* and putting them together into a new compound verb. The verb *baby-sit* is formed from the earlier form *baby-sitter*. *Baby-sitter* is formed in much the same way as other compounds such as *train-driver*. But while *baby-sit* has become a verb, we do not say **He train-drives for SNCF in Paris*. In terms of the final form or *Wortgebildetheit*, *baby-sit* is a compound; in terms of the process by which it was formed or *Wortbildung*, it is an instance of back-formation. This distinction has led to some confusion in the past.

In what has been said above, a compound has been defined as a form. There is another definition of compound current in the literature, according to which a compound is defined less by its form (although it must still contain two lexemic bases) as by its status as a lexical item. *Windmill* is accepted as a compound because it is well established in the community, but if we were to read that a particular author 'has become a veritable book-mill, churning out two novels a year every year,' *book-mill* would not count as a compound because it is a new and ad hoc formation. In contradistinction to that position, it is here argued that the process of becoming well-known and semantically specialized is independent of any structural properties. Sentences such as *How do you do?* become fixed and specialized in meaning, but they are still examples of the same structures they were before they became fixed in meaning. The same is true of compounds. They are always compounds, but some of them are well-known and specialized in meaning, others are less well-known. The label 'compound' has nothing to do with how often a particular expression is used, so that both *windmill* and *book-mill* are compounds.

Precisely where the border between compounding as a lexical process and premodification as a syntactic process might run is currently a matter of some controversy, and cannot be solved here. The discussion above tends to favor viewing compounding as lexical rather than syntactic, but for wider discussion see e.g. Bauer (1998), Giegerich (2004), Levi (1978), Munat (2003), and Olsen (2000).

2.2 The phonology of compounds

Whereas the phrase *black bird* takes its major stress on the right-hand element, *blackbird* is stressed on the left-hand element. This stress difference is often taken to be a defining one in terms of English compounds (see e.g. Chomsky and Halle 1968). The argument is rarely made explicitly (though see Bauer 2004), but presumably depends on the orthographic unity of *blackbird* and the fact that words typically have a single stress while *black bird* has the possibility of two stresses if it does not carry the intonational nucleus.[2] This stress-based division has been challenged in the literature, so we need to consider it carefully here.

There is a semantic difference between *black bird* and *blackbird* which appears to be an important part of the distinction: while *black birds* provides a description of a set of birds, *blackbirds* provides a classification of birds. We can see the difference in that *a brown black bird* is nonsensical, while *a brown blackbird* is not, *a very black bird* makes sense while *a very blackbird* is probably not even grammatical. In *black bird*, then, *black* is a gradable adjective (an EPITHET in one terminology), while in *blackbird*, *black* is non-gradable (a CLASSIFIER). In every instance where we get an adjective-noun construction with COMPOUND STRESS (forestress, left-hand stress) we find this classificatory meaning. But the reverse is not true. Where we get the classificatory meaning, we do not necessarily get compound stress. Contrast 'blackbird, 'blue-tit and 'whitefly on the one hand with black 'fly, black 'robin, blue 'fox, red 'cardinal, red 'mullet, red 'squirrel, white 'ant and white 'gold on the other. The differences appear to be purely in terms of stress pattern, not in terms of the semantics (or, following from the semantics, the syntactic patterns in which each can occur). If we say *I saw a very black robin*, we are no longer talking about the species of robin which is the black robin and *a brown red squirrel* is not necessarily a contradiction in terms. That being the case it is not clear why stress should be taken to be criterial for compounding: the construction type appears to be independent of stress; the stress seems to be an extra marker which is not necessarily present, possibly a marker of degree of lexicalization rather than anything else.[3] This notion is developed in Bauer (2004), where it is shown that on average items displaying compound stress are more frequent than those without it.

When we consider noun-noun compounds, the role of stress becomes even more difficult to distinguish. First, although we can find some examples where the stress does seem to be predictable, there are many others where it is not. Lees (1963) seems to have been the first to point out that '*apple cake* contrasts with *apple* '*pie* and that '*Madison Street* contrasts with *Madison* '*Avenue* in terms of stress. This observation appears to be robust, and indicates that stress is not (or is not always) a correlate of semantic structure. On the other hand, a distinction between a '*toy factory* ('a factory in which toys are made') and a *toy* '*factory* ('a factory which is itself a toy'), between a '*concrete factory* ('a factory in which concrete is produced') and a *concrete* '*factory* ('a factory built of concrete') seems to imply that stress is not only contrastive in noun-noun constructions, but does correlate (or does sometimes correlate) with meaning. When we look away from these series of compounds we find less agreement. Not only do dictionaries and pronunciation guides often give conflicting patterns for individual collocations, individual speakers do not seem to be able to assign a consistent stress pattern to known lexical items, and speakers vary in the assignation of stress patterns in actual speech (Bauer 1983a). We seem a long way from the received phonological wisdom of two discrete classes.

When we look beyond nouns, the pattern does not get clearer. Compound adjectives like *sky-blue* take phrasal stress in predicative position, but compound stress in attributive position, thus behaving according to the rules of iambic reversal (sometimes termed stress shift). The same is true of other compound adjectives like *lead-free* or *machine-readable*. Here stress appears to be determined by principles which are separate from the status of the relevant construction.

Compound verbs derived by backformation (like *baby-sit*) or by conversion (like *to carbon-copy*) retain the stress of the words from which they are derived. Adjective-verb constructions (which may also be formed by backformation or conversion), where the adjective is usually interpreted with adverbial force, seem to show final stress: *fine-tune*, *soft-land*. Particle-verb constructions like *over-achieve* again show final-element stress. While some compound verbs like *freeze-dry* do, or do sometimes, show compound stress, compound stress does not seem to be a feature of compound verbs.

All things considered, although we often find first-element stress in things we wish to call compounds, there is little evidence that first-element stress is a necessary or even consistent correlate of compound structure. We still lack a good theory of how stress is assigned to compound items, although some mixture of lexical conditioning (including here lexicalization) and semantic patterning seems likely, with a large admixture of influence from the immediately surrounding context. In our present state of ignorance it seems dangerous to equate first-element stress with compound structure. See Olsen (2000) and Giegerich (2004) for further contrasting views on the subject.

2.3   The lexical structure of compounds

There is no known lexical restriction of the words which can be compounded. Indeed, many scholars have commented that any sequence of noun and noun, for instance, can be given an interpretation as a compound. While such a statement may be a little over-enthusiastic (*'tree-oak* is difficult to assign a meaning to, and we should recall Jespersen's (1942: 140) claim that Carlyle's *mischief-joy* is foreign to the genius of the language), nonetheless it shows the generally accepted position. The claim in Bauer (1983b: 206) that only an etymologically-defined subset of adjectives (primarily Germanic ones) enter into adjective-noun compounds is falsified by examples such as *dra'matic society*, *'musical box*, *'primary school*, *'solar system* and many others. It is sometimes claimed that nominalizations do not compound easily with each other. This seems to be the result of the fact that only in very restricted situations are compounds such as *knowledge expansion* required, rather than a strong restriction.

2.4   The grammatical structure of compounds

In the default cases, compounds in English have the structure lexemic-base + lexemic-base (+ inflection). Specifically, this excludes inflections from positions which are compound-internal. This is related by many to the principles of lexicalism, principles which seem rather more threatened by the fact that phrases can apparently be used in the first element of compounds, as in *He . . . gave . . . me a don't-mess-with-me look*,[4] *give-me-the-money-or-I'll-blow-your-brains-out scenarios*,[5] and so on. There are a number of places where this view of what comprises a compound is challenged by apparently parallel and synonymous constructions which break with this expected structure in a number of ways. Some of these will be considered below.

Briefly, though, it should first be pointed out that although compounds with more than two elements have been admitted in the definitions given here, no such examples have been provided. It seems that longer compounds such as *railway timetable* can virtually always be broken down into nested compounds, each of which shows binary branching. Incidentally, where orthography shows apparent structure in these instances, as in *[railway] [timetable]*, it appears to provide accurate information. The exceptions to binary branching are DVANDVA compounds such as *Rank-Hovis-McDougal* where the ability to assign a binary structure to the tree can arise only through knowledge of history (the rather specialized history of business mergers) rather than linguistic knowledge.

2.4.1   Internal plurals

The general rule with English compounds is that the modifying (left-hand) element occurs in the stem form. However, some things which otherwise look like compounds have the modifying element marked as plural. The term *teeth-ridge*, for example, is a standard part of linguistic terminology, and *teeth* is a plural form. It is often claimed that this kind of structure arises only when the plural form is irregular, as is the case with *teeth*, and thus presumably independently listed in the lexicon. *Mice-infested*, we are told, is acceptable English, *rats-infested* is not.

Acceptability is rather slippery in this area. While *mice-infested* is undoubtedly accepted and used by some speakers,[6] it seems that most speakers still prefer to stick to the stem-form modifier and say *mouse-infested*. At the same time, there are sufficient examples like *suggestions box* for it to be clear that there is no simple ban on plurals (regular or not) in modifying position. Rastall (1993) suggests that plurals are used where the sense demands them, but this seems too strong a claim. Consider examples such as *a two-man boat* where even the numeral *two* fails to call forth a plural marker – compare also *all-party talks*. The general preference for singulars (or, perhaps more accurately, unmarked forms) is not the only way in which the modifying noun in such constructions is constrained.

It is not usual for the modifying noun to be submodified by an adjective. Given a compound like *library book*, a *white library book* is usually interpreted as a white book from a library rather than as a book from a white library.[7] There are exceptions, such as *blue-sky research*, *hot-air balloon*, *red letter day* (but note that *air balloon* etc. are not established as compounds) and *black market prices*, but a reading where any adjective modifies the head of a N + N construction (or the construction as a whole) is clearly the default. It is hard to tell how far this is a matter of grammar and how far it is a matter of pragmatics, but further constraints suggest that it may be grammar.

If a single adjective modifying the first noun is rare, conjoined adjectives modifying the first noun seem to be virtually impossible. *Green and yellow bruise treatment*, for instance, is odd, perhaps because of the rarity of appropriate opportunities for such constructions.

Post-modification of the modifying noun also seems to be awkward though real examples are found such as *the health and safety in employment act*; but relative clauses appear not to occur (perhaps because a plural noun would frequently be required, as in **a students who attend this university demonstration*).

In the continental Germanic languages such as Dutch, German, and Swedish there is a tendency to use an *-s* (which in German and Swedish might be interpreted as a genitive rather than a plural) to mark constituent structure in an [[A B] C] construction, separating the B element from the C element (Josefsson 1997: 60; Krott et al. 2004). It is not clear how far any such tendency can be found in English, largely because textual examples of the relevant structures are extremely rare. However, the author has attested a distinction between *[British Council] [job file]* and *[British Council jobs] [file]* which suggests that such an option may be open in English. If it is, it may be used in constructions like *Human Rights Commission* to show when a premodifying adjective modifies only the left-hand element of the compound.

Both Rastall (1993) and Pinker (1999) suggests that the difference between *suggestion box* and *suggestions box* is that in the former an N is used in the modifying position while in the latter it is an entire NP, introduced in much the same way as the much longer phrases illustrated earlier. If this were the case, we might expect to find that those instances where an NP occurs are similar to those in which other phrasal categories, including sentences, occur: that is the phrase is cited as whole and is often, though not always, idiomatic, and we might expect to find all kinds of NP occurring freely in modifying position. That appears not to be true, though a detailed corpus study would be useful in this area.

2.4.2 Internal possessives

Alongside internal plurals we also find things that look like compounds except that they have internal possessives: *cat's-cradle, cat's-eye, cat's-paw, cat's-tail* alongside compounds like *cat door, cat-gut, catnap, cat-walk,* etc. We should note that while these things are written as possessives, all we can strictly say about them is that they contain a linking -*s*-, which in some cases could also be interpreted as plural. Alternatively we could accept these as lexicalized syntactic structures like the *love-in-a-mist* examples cited earlier, and thus not as genuine compounds at all.

There is some evidence that these should be taken as genuine possessives (at least in origin). First, we find things like *wolf's-bane* (not **wolves-bane*). Second, we should note that possessives marked by -*'s* are more usual with humans and animates than with inanimates. If we look at a number of first elements and the number of possessives which are found in constructions where they would be feasible (a *witch-hunt* could not be a *witch's hunt* because the meaning would be different), we find the figures given in table 21.1 (based on the entries in *The Chambers Dictionary* – Schwartz 1994). It is quite clear that possessive forms are most common with humans and then with higher animals and least so with inanimates.

Table 21.1 Comparative numbers of possessive first elements

First element	Number with -'s	Number with non-possessive form
Dog	16	47
Frog	3	4
Hand	2	45
Lion	3	2
Table	0	29
Widow	7	1
Witch	7	2
Wolf	3	6

Source: Schwartz 1994

If we accept these things as genuine possessives, it is still not clear how they should be dealt with grammatically. They are usually just seen as syntactic structures, not lexical ones, and if we can add that they have become idiomatized or lexicalized, that seems appropriate. In terms of defining compounds, though, we are again in the situation where things that are lexicalized seem to be very like compounds.

2.4.3 Non-predicate adjectives

There is a series of adjectives in English which Levi (1978) calls NON-PREDICATE ADJECTIVES, since they do not normally occur in predicative position. These adjectives are often derived from nouns and are not gradable. When they occur in attributive position, they sometimes have a function equivalent to that of the related noun. So, for example, *atomic bomb* and *atom bomb* denote the same thing, as do *language instruction* and *linguistic instruction, tooth decay* and *dental decay*, and so on. Levi (1978) argues that these two constructions are equivalent constructions, to be dealt with in the grammar in the same way. In most instances, if there is an attributive adjective, it is used and a noun is used in those cases where no attributive adjective can be found. While things are not quite that simple (*bovine lick* and *bovine parsley* would not be good replacements for *cow-lick* and *cow-parsley*) there is enough here to raise interesting possibilities, especially since some of the mis-matches can be explained in terms of style, connotations, lexicalization and the like. The lack of a compound like *operation mis-management* (noted above in 2.3) can be explained by the possibility of *operational mis-management*, and the fact that *theatre management* does not mean the same as *theatrical management* can be explained by the fact that *theatrical* has gained certain overtones (of the excessively dramatic, for example, which has made it become a gradable adjective) in the course of its history. *Library book* and *book-shop* are fine because there are no established adjectives corresponding precisely to *library* and to *book*, but *electricity power* and *cranium damage* are odd because we have the possibility of *electric power* and *cranial damage*. Although there is much to be worked out in the detail here, the idea is appealing in part because it explains how our learned Romance and neo-latinate vocabulary interacts with our native Germanic vocabulary, with compounding being predominantly a Germanic phenomenon.

2.4.4 Headedness

For most compound nouns and verbs, the notion of headedness in compounds is uncontroversial. A *money belt* refers to a type of belt not a type of money, *freeze-dry* denotes a type of drying. Such compounds are clearly right-headed. However, there are a set of compounds where these rules do not apply so easily.

The first of these types carries the Sanskrit name of BAHUVRIHI. These are compounds like *red-head* and *hatchback* which denote neither a type of head nor a type of back respectively. Rather they denote a person who has a red head (in that it is covered with red hair) and a car which has a back which opens upwards like a hatch. Because they denote something which has the named feature, these are sometimes termed POSSESSIVE compounds. In Bloomfield's terminology, these are termed EXOCENTRIC compounds: that is, their head is missing and is external to the compound itself. This is misleading. In *red-head* it is quite clear that whatever the compound as a whole denotes, the element *red* still modifies the element *head*. So these compounds do have a grammatical head, although it does not always determine the inflection class of the compound as a whole (for example, *The Oxford English Dictionary* gives *arsefeet* 'bird sp.' but *pussyfoots* 'stealthy person'; Bauer 2003). These heads show only some of the typical features of heads. We might call them SEMI-HEADS.

Next consider the series of nouns like *shoot-out*, *put-down*, etc. The final form of these words is a compound noun made up of a verb and a particle. But unlike most compound nouns they have no heads (except possibly in that the second element carries the inflection: *put-downs*, **puts-down*). This is probably due to the method of formation, which is a nominalization of a phrasal verb with a typical verb-to-noun stress-shift (compare [im'port]$_v$ → ['import]$_N$). Other lexemes which might appear to be compound in form but which were not historically formed by a compounding process may also lack the typical right-hand head of the English compound: *attorneys general*; *mothers-in-law*. Even things like *passers-by* may be seen as a nominalization from a phrasal verb (albeit a different type of nominalization).

The Romance type illustrated by *pick-pocket* (now probably no longer productive) is not regularly right-headed, either. It does not denote a type of pocket.

There are a few compounds which are left-headed. Forms such as *whomever* (inflected on the left-hand element), *Model T* (a type of model, not a type of T).

When we come to compound adjectives, it is difficult to discuss their headedness at all. There are, to be sure, forms like *sky-blue* which appear right-headed, and which are clearly adjectival. But there are large numbers of items, apparently compound in form, used as premodifiers to nouns for which word-class appears to be irrelevant. Consider, for example, *pass-fail test*, *kick-arse attitude*, *before-tax profits*, *chuckaway item*, *quick-change artiste*, *no-drug behaviors*, *oestrogen-only pill* (Bauer and Renouf 2001). Rather than setting up a whole series of different types of exocentric compound adjectives, it is probably better to see items like these as complex compounds. We know that compound nouns with two elements allow a range of word-classes in modifying position: adjective in *blackbird*, noun in *computer screen*, verb in *call-girl*, preposition in *downtime*, whole phrase/clause/sentence in *a don't-mess-with-me look*. In the three-term items cited above, it is probably best to say that this flexibility is being exploited by the use of constituents of any type and from any level of analysis being taken up to fill the slot. That being the case, we can keep the label of compound adjective for those formations which clearly have an independent existence outside the longer compound construction. *Sky-blue* can occur in many constructions as an adjectival head, but *pass-fail* is restricted to a premodifier in the kind of construction illustrated above.

2.4.5   Neo-classical compounding

Neo-classical compounding is the formation of words like *coprolith, genocide, psychology* which are created in modern times using elements from the classical languages Latin and Greek. There are a number of questions about neo-classical compounds in English (and other modern European languages) none of which has received a thoroughly satisfactory answer at this stage.

First, although they are termed compounds, and there is some justification for this in their headedness and the variable semantic relationship between the elements (see below 2.5.1), it is not altogether clear that they should be treated alongside compounds rather than as a separate type of word-formation. Nevertheless, they appear to mirror some of the relationships we find in native compound traditions. So alongside native compounds like *redfish* we find neo-classical compounds like *rhododendron*, alongside those like *wolf-spider* we find *lycanthrope*, alongside *headache* we find *cephalgia*, alongside *cheese-lover* we find *philosopher*, and alongside *saber-tooth* we find *mastodon*. This parallelism is itself suggestive, if no more.

Next, the boundaries of the type are not clear. Do words such as *psycholinguistics* and *Kremlinology* count as neo-classical compounds or as derivatives? The implications of a decision have not been fully worked out.

Next, are there rules for the formations in English, and if so are they different from the rules in the classical languages? In Greek, for instance, it seems clear that the medial *-o-* is a linking element which belongs to neither element; in English that is less clear. Moreover, it is not clear whether there is a fixed set of morphophonemic adjustments that must today be made when these elements are juxtaposed, or whether the morphophonemics simply reflect those in the classical languages. For some discussion see Bauer and Huddleston (2002).

2.5   *The semantics of compounding*

2.5.1   Endocentric compound nouns

Where compounds contain an element whose base is verbal, there is increasing evidence that this verb plays a large part in determining the semantics of the compound as a whole. For example, in *deer hunting*, where *hunting* is a word containing a verbal base, *deer* is an argument of the verb. In *deer hunter*, not only is deer an argument of the verb, but the subject of the verb is also present in the *-er* suffix. In *nose-bleed*[8] and *call-girl*, the nominal element which co-occurs with the verb is an argument of the verb. In *alcohol-dependent, alcohol* is again an argument of the verb *depend*. So the interpretation of the compound is determined, to some extent, by the grammatical pattern available for the verb.

However, this is not always true. In *town crier, sky-diving, color-code, free-associate* the interpretation of the noun does not appear to be constrained by the syntactic possibilities of the verb. Rather the relationship between the elements appears to be much freer. For instance, a *city surveyor* could be a person who surveys cities (meaning determined by the verb) or a surveyor

Table 21.2 Levi's twelve possible meanings of compounds

Relationship	Examples
CAUSE (first element subject of *cause*)	*drug death; viral infection*
CAUSE (first element object of *cause*)	*tear gas; mortal blow*
HAVE (first element subject of *have*)	*lemon peel; feminine intuition*
HAVE (first element object of *have*)	*picture book; industrial area*
MAKE (first element subject of *make*)	*daisy chain; consonantal pattern*
MAKE (first element object of *make*)	*honeybee; sebaceous glands*
USE (instrumental)	*steam iron; solar generator*
BE	*soldier ant; consonantal segment*
IN	*field mouse; marital sex*
FOR	*horse doctor; avian sanctuary*
FROM	*olive oil; solar energy*
ABOUT	*abortion vote; criminal policy*

Source: Based on Levy 1978: 76–7

who works for a city (meaning independent of the verb). The relationship is seen to be freest when no verb is found in the compound, so that noun-noun compounds have been discussed particularly in terms of the meaning relationships that may hold between the elements.

For some scholars there is a finite list of relationships which may hold in those instances where there is no verb constraining the relationship. For example, Levi (1978) lists twelve, illustrated in table 21.2. Others suggest that no such list can capture all the possible relationships between the elements of compounds. For example, it is not clear where *spaghetti western* or *wisdom tooth* would fit into table 21.2. We might also object that it is often not clear which meaning a particular compound illustrates: is *horse blanket* an instance of HAVE or an instance of FOR, for example.

If an exhaustive listing of meanings is possible, as Levi suggests, then we have to account for the fact that apparently contrastive elements (or meanings) are deleted between the deep structure formulation of the compound and its surface structure. Levi was writing in a period and within a model where this seemed less objectionable than it seems today. If we have no exhaustive list of meanings, we have to account for the fact that at least the range of meanings established by Levi may be read into the relationships between the elements of noun-noun compounds. I would suggest that this can be achieved by understanding the relationship between the elements to be 'A type of element-2 efficiently brought to mind by mention of element-1.' The relationship between the two elements is usually treated in compounds as positive, non-modal, and inherent or permanent. (*Picture book* from Table 21.2 could not mean 'a book without pictures,' 'a book which may contain pictures,' or 'a book which

Table 21.3   Subtypes of coordinative compound

DVANDVA:	*Alsace-Lorraine, Hewlett-Packard.*
APPOSITIONAL:	*poet-playwright, secretary-treasurer, fighter-bomber, washer-drier.*
TRANSLATIVE:	*a **Greek–English** dictionary, the **London–Paris** flight.*
PARTICIPATIVE:	***German–American** cooperation, the **Australia–New Zealand** trade deal.*

contains pictures just today.') While such a meaning relationship is considerably more abstract than any envisaged by Levi, it has the advantage of being applicable to all compounds of this type, and thus of being assignable to the construction. Such a solution cuts across much of the dispute there has been about the semantics of compounding for the last century or more, and provides a unified solution which we may term the MNEMONIC THEORY of compounding.

2.5.2   Coordinative compounds

The class of dvandva compounds in Sanskrit is made up of compounds which denote the unity made up of the two distinct items named in the elements of the compound. English has very few compounds which fit this model precisely: a couple of geographic names (*Alsace-Lorraine, Schleswig-Holstein*) and rather more names of businesses formed by mergers (*Time-Warner, Goodman-Fielder, Hewlett-Packard*, etc.). Frequently, however, the label has been misleadingly applied to any compound which can be glossed by inserting the word *and* between the elements of the compound. If there is any unity here it is much better captured by the label COORDINATIVE COMPOUND. Several types of coordinative compound can be found in English, including the true dvandvas. The types and their suggested labels (some of them well-established, some of them novel) are given in table 21.3.

2.6   The pragmatics of compounding

Compounds are compact. This is what makes them suitable in headlines, and what makes them appear semantically incomplete. It is what makes them useful for showing subcategorization, and it also makes them useful as a mechanism for referring back to some past discussion by providing a neat summary of it.

. . . the one with the woman in the orange coat . . .
(22 lines)

The **orange-coat lady**, now in grey with pearls, was the driver.[9]
   I saw a woman standing in the lighted kitchen, leaning back against a counter. In her left hand was a bottle of tequila . . .
(101 pages)

The **tequila woman** almost certainly lived in the house.[10]

While it seems unlikely that this is a major function of compounds, it is one of the uses to which compounds are well suited by virtue of their structure.

2.7 The word-classes of compounds

As we have seen, compound nouns are common, in many guises, and there are at least some clear examples of compound adjectives. Compound prepositions are usually ignored in discussions of compounding, but *into, onto* are certainly treated as orthographic compounds, and *because of, off of, owing to* could be treated as compounds despite the fact that their historical origin in syntax is clear. Compound verbs are of interest in that some authorities deny there are any (Marchand 1969: 100). This represents a failure to distinguish between process of formation and final form. But it seems likely that even in terms of process of formation, there are instances of verbal compounding in English, although it is often impossible to show that the past participle has not been used before the infinitive. At least the type in Hamlet's *out-Herod Herod* seems productive today, especially with proper-names in the base (Bauer and Renouf 2001).

2.8 Conclusion

More questions have been raised in this section than have been answered. We can finish the section with yet another: How far is compounding a part of lexis? It is assumed by most people that since compounds are lexemes, their formation must be lexical. Yet they have been seen as syntactic formations at least since Lees (1963), and Kuiper (1999) argues that they should still be seen in that way. This may take us back to the question of definition with which we began. Can we create lexemes by syntax? Or is lexeme-creation the lexicalization of syntactic output? But whether compounds are fundamentally syntactic or morphological structures, their fascination remains. They are lexical items with obvious structure whose ultimate status and unity is still not entirely clear.

3 Minor Word-formation Types

3.1 Introduction

Taxonomists are always seeking a classification and terminology which will allow us to distinguish the various types of structure that are found in a language like English. While we can do this, once we start looking at minor word-formation types there are many formations which do not fit neatly into any predetermined category. Accordingly, any classification does no more than label some (perhaps rather vague) prototypical categories, and we can find examples which appear to straddle the boundaries of the categories. Here fairly traditional categories are provided, and some of the borderlines are explored. It is not clear that the fuzziness has any theoretical implications beyond the suggestion that we may not be operating with the best possible categories. It is not clear that any major predictions depend upon which of these categories a particular example belongs to.

3.2   *Word-manufacture*

The term WORD-MANUFACTURE is used to refer to the creation of words as nothing more than a sequence of letters or phonemes. The letters or phonemes must (with a certain amount of freedom which is hard to quantify) form patterns which are permitted within English, but otherwise there is no requirement of internal structure, and indeed, we would expect internal morphological structure to be absent. Word-manufacture is used most obvious in the formation of new trade names like *Kodak* and *Exxon*,[11] but also occurs in the rest of the vocabulary. Words such as *barf* 'vomit,' *blurb*, *boff* 'have sexual intercourse with,' *quark*,[12] *scag* are probably (it is often difficult to tell with certainty) instances of word-manufacture.

It seems that word-manufacture is not as easy as it might seem. People are probably reluctant simply to generate random strings of letters/phonemes which match English patterns to the requisite degree. Partly this is because unmotivated formation is such an unnatural thing to do. Partly it is because randomly-generated strings may nevertheless have resonances with existing English words which may be distracting or undesirable. Examples such as *nylon* show the problem, though. Consider the formation of the word *nylon*, often quoted as an instance of word-manufacture. By the time *nylon* was first used in 1938, *rayon* had been in use for fourteen years, and both of them seem also to resonate with *cotton* (1300) and *chiffon* (1765). Although it seems unlikely that any resonance with words like *arson*, *bison*, *lemon*, *moron* was intended, there may nevertheless have been some from what were, at the time, relatively new scientific terms like *ergon* (1873), *proton* (1893), *argon* (1898), and *photon* (1916). Certainly, by the time we get to *Orlon* (1948), *Dacron* (1951), and *Dralon* (1955) we must suspect that the final *-on* is no longer a random set of letters/phonemes, but a semi-meaningful element, somewhere between a phonaestheme and a morph.

While it may be difficult to discern an instance of word-manufacture, in principle it is clear that word-manufacture is the creation of words without any influence from meaningful sub-parts of the word.

3.3   *Clipping*

Clipping refers to the shortening of some word while the original meaning is retained. Clipping does not create lexemes with new meanings, but lexemes with a new stylistic value. Examples are *coon* (< *racoon*), *deb* (< *debutante*), *flu* (< *influenza*), *jumbo* (< *jumbo jet*), *mike* (< *microphone*), *phone* (< *telephone*), *perm* (< *permanent wave*), *shrink* (< *head shrinker*), *stash* (< *moustache*) which show that

(1) the material which is removed may come from the beginning of the word, the end, or both, (2) that it is not always the semantic head of the word which is retained, (3) that it is not always the stressed syllable in the word which is retained and (4) that a compound or phrase may be clipped to provide a single clipping. In the instances dealt with under (1), we may distinguish terminologically between FORECLIPPINGS, BACK-CLIPPINGS and AMBICLIPPINGS.

While clippings seem to arise through a desire to have more compact lexemes (and we might postulate a preferred length of one or two syllables, based on the few examples given above), clippings are frequently given additional suffixal material, which has the effect of lengthening them again. These EMBELLISHED CLIPPINGS (Bauer and Huddleston 2002) are regionally variable in their productivity, Australian English being perhaps particularly open to their use. Examples are *barbie* (< *barbecue*), *garbo* (< *garbage collector*), *preggers* (< *pregnant*), *rellie* (< *relative* = 'family member'). In instances like *cardie* (< *cardigan*) or *pollie* (< *politician*) it may not be clear whether the clipping is embellished or not.

These embellished clippings are reminiscent of HYPOCORISTICS or pet names. *Liz* might be a clipping from *Elizabeth*, and then *Lizzy* an embellished clipping, and similarly with *Fred* and *Freddie* from *Frederick*. Hypocoristics, though, show a bewildering array of variation, no doubt because of the persistence of hypocoristics as independent names, the persistence of nursery pronunciations, and the vagaries of historical change. *Nell* from *Helen* and *Ned* from *Edward*, may seem perverse, and *Harry* and *Hal* from *Henry* are inexplicable in modern terms, as is *Chuck* from *Charles*. The sheer range of hypocoristics from *Elizabeth* and *Margaret* is in itself astonishing. Surprisingly, speakers of English keep inventing new ways to make up hypocoristics. A relatively recent one gives us *Bazza* (< Barry) and *Shazza* (< Sharon) (incidentally showing a relationship between /r/ and /z/ not seen in English since the time when the relationship between *was* and *were* was transparent in a way it no longer is). It seems likely that hypocoristics form something of an elephant's graveyard of cast-off clippings and embellished clippings.

Clippings may be compounded with each other to give CLIPPING COMPOUNDS such as *hazchem* (< *hazardous chemical*), *humint* (< *human intelligence*) *kidvid* (< *kid's video*), *nicad* (< *nickel cadmium*) *psy ops* (< *psychological operations*), *spag bol* (< *spaghetti bolognese*). The term may also be taken to include compounds which have just one of the elements clipped, such as *autochanger* (< *automatic record changer*), *op art*, *slomo* (< *slow motion*), *teletext*. Note that some of these examples may look just like instances of affixation or neo-classical compounding: some etymology is necessary to distinguish between *teletext* (< *television text*) and *telephone* (a neo-classical compound).

3.4   *Alphabet soup*

There is a whole range of letter-based word-formation patterns, many of which merge imperceptibly into one another. Unfortunately the terminology in this area is not altogether stable. I shall use the term ALPHABETISM as a superordinate term for this set of formations.

An INITIALISM is one type of alphabetism. In an initialism, the initial letters of the words in a phrase are taken to replace the phrase. These letters are pronounced as a sequence of letters. Thus we find examples such as *CPI* (< *Consumer Price Index*), *DUI* (< *driving under the influence* [of alcohol]), *mia* (< *missing in action*, pronounced /ɛm aɪ eɪ/), *fob* (< *free on board*), *FBI* (< *Federal Bureau of Investigation*), *LGM* (< *Little Green Men*), *MIT* (< *Massachusetts Institute of Technology*), *PC* (< *politically correct* or *personal computer* or *police constable*), *UN* (< *United Nations*), and so on. Let us call the phrase which underlies the initialism the ORIGINAL. It can be seen from the examples above that not every word of the original has to be represented in the initialism, letters representing grammatical words being easily dropped.

In some cases, the initialism has the same distribution as the original, so that *mia* can occur predicatively but not attributively, just as is the case with the original. In other cases, the distribution is subtly different. Thus it is not clear why we talk about *the FBI* but not about **the MIT*.

Where the initial letters of an original are such as to provide something which can be pronounced as a word, and this option is taken, we have an acronym. An ACRONYM is an initialism which is pronounced according to ordinary grapheme-phoneme conversion rules. *Aids* (< *acquired immune deficiency syndrome*, pronounced /eɪdz/), *BASIC* (< *Basic All-purpose Symbolic Instruction Code*), *Eftpos* (< *electronic funds transfer at point of sale*), *laser* (< *light amplification by stimulated emission of radiation*), *SALT* (< *Strategic Arms Limitation Talks*), *scuba* (< *self-contained underwater breathing apparatus*), *TESOL* /ˈtiːsɒl/ (< *Teaching of English to Speakers of Other Languages*), *UNESCO* (< *United Nations Educational, Scientific and Cultural Organization*) are acronyms. As with initialisms, it can be seen that not all the initial letters of the original are inevitably used in the acronym. It can also be seen that the orthography of acronyms is inconsistent, with the most familiar terms which are not names of organizations tending towards the use of lower case.

While it might seem clear that *FBI* could not be an acronym, because English syllable structure does not allow an initial /fb/ cluster, the choice between an initialism and an acronym is on occasions an open one. *MIT* could have been pronounced as an acronym /mɪt/ but happens to be pronounced as an initialism. There are many such examples. Given the pressure for an acronym, which leads to the creation of potential originals from suitable letter-sequences (as in *ASH* (< *Action on Smoking and Health*)), why acronyms should be avoided in some cases is a mystery.

It will be noted that initialisms and acronyms function as nouns and adjectives. They do not appear to be used as verbs (although subsequent conversion of an initialism cannot be ruled out) and they are not used as prepositions.

Although these definitions of initialism and acronym are clear-cut, the reality of alphabetic formations is far less so. There are several ways in which actual forms can diverge from these prototypes.

First of all, the letters that appear in the alphabetism may not (all) be initial letters. For example *TB* comes from *TuBerculosis*, where the <B> is not initial to anything. In *ddI* (< *DiDeoxyInosine*) the letters are, if anything, morpheme-initial. In *mifepristone* (< *aMInoPHenol-PRopyne-oeSTradIol-one*) the letters are not only not initial, they are in the wrong order: at this point we have to ask whether this is an alphabetism or just word-manufacture – at least up to the point where the recognizable suffix *-one* is added. In *ID*, the letters are contiguous in the original *IDentity*, so that we might want to see this as a clipping rather than an initialism. The boundaries start to become vague.

We find examples where only one element in the word is reduced to an alphabetism, which is thus likely to be a single letter: (*e-mail, e-commerce*). At this point it may not be clear whether we should analyze such items as clipping compounds or as alphabetisms.

We find examples which look like initialisms but where the initial letter does not stand for any meaningful original (*the A-list, OK*[13]). If an alphabetism is defined in terms of its process of derivation from an original, such examples are problematic.

We find examples which are pronounced as acronyms, but where the pronunciation is not derivable from the set of letters in the original. An FBI agent may be called a *fibbie*, where the origin of the first <i> or /ɪ/ is unclear (why is it not *febbie* or an *effbie*?). *SCSI* (< *Small Computer System Interface*) is pronounced /skʌzi/, as if an acronym, but it might equally well, or better, have been /skɒzi/. Note, moreover, that if *SCSI* can be pronounced as a well-formed word, there is no reason why *DUI* should not become /d(j)uːi/ (contrast *GUI* [< *Graphical User Interface*] which is pronounced /guːi/).

In the face of so much variation, the ordinary language term ABBREVIATION is often as much use as anything else.

3.5 *Blending*

BLENDS, or portmanteau words as Humpty Dumpty called them, are lexemes made out of a phonological parts of two (rarely more) other words, with the parts which remain from the originals being determined purely phonologically without any reference to morphs. Examples are *motel* (< *motor hotel*), *sexploitation* (*sex+exploitation*), *smog* (< *smoke+fog*). In some cases, there may be some part of the blend which is common to the two words of the original (as in *sexploitation*) but this is not a requirement for a blend.

In some ways, blends look like clipping compounds, and, indeed, the two are often treated as a single phenomenon. However, we can make a distinction by definition. In a clipping compound, the first part of both words in the original is represented in the new form; in a blend the first part of the first word in the original and the last part of the second word in the original are represented in the new form. Thus *sitcom* (< *situational comedy*) is a clipping compound, while *monergy* (< *money+energy*) is a blend.

Semantically or in terms of origin, we can distinguish two fundamental types of blend. There are those like *smog* where the words in the original, *smoke* and *fog*, are in paradigmatic relationship with each other, and those like *motel*, where the two words in the original, *motor* and *hotel*, are in a syntagmatic relationship to each other (see Dressler 2000). We may term these, respectively, PARADIGMATIC ORIGIN BLENDS and SYNTAGMATIC ORIGIN BLENDS. In some instances, such as *monergy*, it may not be clear at first glance which category a particular blend fits into, but a little etymological research may be sufficient to make matters clear (according to Tulloch 1991, this – now outdated – term meant money spent on energy, not something which was simultaneously money and energy, and so it is syntagmatic).

Various attempts have been made to try to explain the structure of blends. None has yet been totally successful. It is not clear whether the description would be easier if syntagmatic and paradigmatic origin blends were distinguished, or whether precisely the same rules of formation affect both. It seems likely that in at least one respect, they do not.

In syntagmatic origin blends, the order of the elements is determined by the original. A *motor hotel* cannot be a *hotel motor* (because of the headedness rules determining the structure of compounds), and so **hotor* is an impossible blend with this meaning. With *smoke* and *fog*, on the other hand, the ordering of elements in the blend appears to be governed by some independent set of constraints. Given *ballute* from *balloon* and *parachute*, why is it not *paraloon*? We might postulate that *foke* is blocked as the outcome of *fog+smoke* because of homonymy with *folk*, but even if that is true, there are many instances where either order might seem possible in principle.

Kelly (1998) argues that in paradigmatic origin blends (which he terms CONJUNCTIVE) the first element is (a) higher in frequency than the second, (b) shorter than the second (in terms of number of syllables) and (c) a more prototypical member of its set than the second. Where these constraints are not obviously met (as in *brunch* < *breakfast+lunch*), it may be the case that there are one-off extraneous factors which over-rule the constraints (such as the temporal ordering of breakfast and lunch in this particular example).

Tendencies can also be found in the point in the blend at which the switch from the first word of the original to the second takes place. For example, where there is phonological overlap between the two words, that overlap defines the switch point (and accordingly, it becomes difficult to determine whether the /eks/ which remains in *sexploitation* comes from the *sex(ual)* or from the *exploitation*. But where there is no shared material, Kelly (1998) suggest that speakers prefer to retain consonant clusters, and will keep syllable rimes together more often that onset + peak sequences. While we might expect this area to be one of interest for writers within Optimality Theory, I am not aware of any postulated constraint tableau to account for English blend structure, though it must be assumed that some such constraint ranking is involved. (See Bat-El 2000 on blends in Hebrew and Gries 2004 on English for studies which show how this kind of approach might work.) It should be noted, however, that it sometimes appears that the overlap between words is orthographic rather than phonological, and that blends have some kind of basis in the written language, despite the fact that most speakers are relatively unfazed about forming blends without reference to the orthography. This orthographic link seems to tie blends in with alphabetisms as formations parasitic upon the written structure of the language, despite the fact that phonological rules may be so useful in describing the structure of so many of them.

Occasionally, repeated blends with a particular word can give rise to a recurrent SPLINTER, which may later be accepted as a full-blown word-forming unit. For instance, the element *-scape* in *starscape* is a splinter arising originally from a blend of *sea* and *landscape* and then more following the same pattern. Other splinters are *-(et)eria*, *-(a)nomics*.

3.6   Echo words

As was pointed out in section 2.1, words like *namby-pamby* and *shilly-shally* do not meet the definition of compounds, though they are frequently called RHYME-MOTIVATED and ABLAUT-MOTIVATED COMPOUNDS, respectively, with the term ECHO WORD being a less technical label. There are some complete reduplicates like *booboo* 'mistake,' *gee-gee* 'horse.' Minkova (2002) deals with the ablaut cases in an Optimality Theoretic framework. The interest with such cases is on the degree to which the onset consonant in the rhyming cases and the vowel alternation in the ablaut cases is predictable from general principles, and why the attested alternations should be preferred. Minkova points out that these formations are less productive now than they once were, but we do still find a lot of compounds whose creations is partly motivated by rhyme: things like *dead-head*, *Dream Machine*, *fag hag*, *gang-bang*.

3.7   Conclusion

Although these minor types of word-formation may not be linguistically very important, arising as they do, at the point where system gives way to random creativity, they are nonetheless of increasing importance in the lexicon of modern English in terms of the sheer number of new forms created by them. Many of these new forms are ephemeral, extremely localized or rather slangy in tone; but so are many words formed by more established word-formation processes. These should not be reasons for dismissing them.

4   Future study

Although we know a lot about compounds and minor word-formation types, it can be seen that even the taxonomy is not particularly robust. Optimality Theory is providing new ways of looking at the minor word-formation types, and may create new classes if it can be shown that the old categories are simply different superficial results of the same underlying processes, which does not seem unlikely. An application of Optimality Theory to neo-classical compounds might also prove rewarding. Where compounds are concerned, the major problem is still a definitional one: can any lexical process of compounding be distinguished from apparently similar syntactic processes? Such a problem is not necessarily confined to English, though it is a vital one for English. In going forward, we probably need to take care to deal with productive processes separately from lexicalized ones, and to look more carefully at corpus data.

NOTES

1   In corpus linguistics, where 'words' have to be derived from the printed text without any preliminary grammatical analysis, there is often no alternative to an orthographic criterion for wordhood. This does not make such a definition desirable or valid; it just makes it the best possible definition. Many corpus linguists forced to adopt such a criterion are well aware of the problems that this gives rise to. Since even spoken corpora are usually transcribed for analysis, the problem may even arise there.

2   If it does carry the intonational nucleus, the stress will fall on the right-hand element in non-contrastive environments, which is not what we find with *blackbird*. However, we must not confuse stress phenomena with intonational phenomena.

3   We occasionally observe items passing from one class to another. *Cold drink* has started to get first-element stress within my lifetime.

4   Lawrence Sanders, *McNally's Puzzle* (London: Hodder & Stoughton, 1996: 9).

5   Stephen Solmita, *Force of Nature* (New York: Putnam, 1989: 24).

6   *Mice manure* occurs in Tony Hillerman, *The First Eagle* (London: HarperCollins, 1999: 61).

7   Consider, for example, Robert Campbell, *The Lion's Share* (New York: The Mysterious Press, 1996: 79): 'Then his little wife ran off with a foreign motor mechanic . . . that is, a mechanic who repaired foreign cars.' The preferred reading is deliberately overridden, showing that either reading can be found, but that in some instances we have to work to get the marked reading.

8   *Nose-bleed* is an unusual compound for a number of reasons, one of which is that it does not seem to be headed. *Bleed* is not a synchronically available nominal form (in the way that, for instance, *desire* is, corresponding to the verb *desire*). There is nothing in the etymology of the word to explain its rather odd form. The pattern appears not to be productive, perhaps because in words like *nosedive* the *dive* is interpreted as a noun rather than as a verbal stem.

9   Dick Francis, *Comeback* (London: Michael Joseph, 1991: 103).

10 Richard Laymon, *Night in the Lonesome October* (London: Headline, 2001: 51, 152).

11 Note the <xx> spelling which is not found elsewhere in English, though the pronunciation /ɛksɒn/ is consistent with English structures.

12 Although *quark* comes from a line by James Joyce, and so is not strictly word-manufacture when applied to a sub-atomic particle, it was presumably invented *de novo* by Joyce.

13 Although various etymologies of this expression have been suggested, there still seems to be some doubt as to what the origin really was, and in any case it is hard in the current state of the language to reconstruct anything meaningful here.

FURTHER READING

General introductions to English word-formation (often including minor types) are provided by Adams (1973, 2001), Bauer (1983), Marchand (1969), Plag (2003). Of these, Marchand's is the classic work, Adams tends to be taxonomic and have a lot of good examples, Bauer and especially Plag are rather more theoretical, with Bauer now theoretically rather old-fashioned. A recent survey is in Bauer and Huddleston (2002). On compounds in particular, the most recent work is Ryder (1994), though it is not a general study of compounding in English. For a wider view of compounds, looking beyond English, see Bauer (2001).

Adams, Valerie (1973) *An Introduction to modern English word formation*. London: Longman.

Adams, Valerie (2001) *Complex words in English*. Harlow: Longman.

Bauer, Laurie (1983) *English word-formation*. Cambridge: Cambridge University Press.

Bauer, Laurie (2001) Compounding. In Martin Haspelmath, Ekkehard König, Wulf Oesterreicher and Wolfgang Raible (eds.), *Language universals and language typology*. Berlin and New York: de Gruyter, 695–707.

Bauer, Laurie and Rodney Huddleston (2002) Lexical word-formation. In Rodney Huddleston and Geoffrey K. Pullum (eds.), *The Cambridge grammar of the English language*, Cambridge: Cambridge University Press, 1621–1721.

Marchand, Hans (1969) *The categories and types of present-day English word-formation*, 2nd edn. Munich: Beck.

Plag, Ingo (2003) *Word-formation in English*. Cambridge: Cambridge University Press.

Ryder, Mary Ellen (1994) *Ordered chaos: The interpretation of English noun-noun compounds*. Berkeley: University of California Press.

REFERENCES

Bat-El, Outi (2000) The grammaticality of 'extragrammatical' morphology. In Ursula Doleschal and Anna M. Thornton (eds.), *Extragrammatical and marginal morphology*, Munich: LINCOM, 61–81.

Bauer, Laurie (1983a) Stress in compounds: a rejoinder. *English Studies* 64, 47–53.

Bauer, Laurie (1983b) *English word-formation*. Cambridge: Cambridge University Press.

Bauer, Laurie (1998) When is a sequence of two nouns a compound in English? *English Language and Linguistics* 2, 65–86.

Bauer, Laurie (2001) *Morphological productivity*. Cambridge: Cambridge University Press.

Bauer, Laurie (2003) Review of Martin Haspelmath, *Understanding Morphology* (London: Arnold, 2002) *Journal of Linguistics* 39, 424–7.

Bauer, Laurie (2004) Adjectives, compounds and words. *Nordic Journal of English Studies* 3, 7–22.

Bauer, Laurie and Rodney Huddleston (2002) Lexical word-formation. In Rodney Huddleston and Geoffrey K. Pullum (eds.), *The Cambridge grammar of the English language*, Cambridge: Cambridge University Press, 1621–1721.

Bauer, Laurie and Antoinette Renouf (2001) A corpus-based study of compounding in English. *Journal of English Linguistics* 29, 101–23.

Chomsky, Noam and Morris Halle (1968) *The sound pattern of English*. New York: Harper and Row.

Dressler, Wolfgang U. (2000) Extragrammatical vs. marginal morphology. In Ursula Doleschal and Anna M. Thornton (eds.), *Extragrammatical and marginal morphology*, Munich: LINCOM, 1–10.

Giegerich, Heinz J. (2004) Compound or phrase? English noun-plus-noun constructions and the stress criterion. *English Language and Linguistics* 8, 1–24.

Gries, Stefan Th. (2004) Shouldn't it be *breakfunch*? A quantitative analysis of blend structure in English. *Linguistics* 42, 639–67.

Jespersen, Otto (1942) *A modern English grammar on historical principles. Part VI: Morphology*. London: Allen and Unwin and Copenhagen: Munksgaard.

Josefsson, Gunlög (1997) *On the principles of word formation in Swedish*. Lund: Lund University Press.

Kelly, Michael H. (1998) To 'brunch' or to 'brench': some aspects of blend structure, *Linguistics* 36, 579–90.

Knowles, Elizabeth (ed.) (1997) *The Oxford dictionary of new words*. Oxford: Oxford University Press.

Krott, Andrea, Gary Libben, Gonia Jarema, Wolfgang Dressler, Robert Schreuder, and Harald Baayen (2004) Probability in the grammar of German and Dutch: interfixation in triconstituent compounds. *Language and Speech* 47, 83–106.

Kuiper, Koenraad (1999) Compounding by adjunction and its empirical consequences. *Language Sciences* 21, 407–22.

Lees, Robert B. (1963) *The grammar of English nominalizations*. Bloomington: Indiana University and The Hague: Mouton.

Levi, Judith N. (1978) *The syntax and semantics of complex nominals*. New York: Academic Press.

Marchand, Hans (1969) *The categories and types of present-day English word-formation*, 2nd edn. Munich: Beck.

Minkova, Donka (2002) Ablaut reduplication in English: the criss-crossing of prosody and verbal art. *English Language and Linguistics* 6, 133–69.

Munat, Judith E. (2003) When is a noun string a phraseological unit? *Ranam* 36, 31–47.

Olsen, Susan (2000) Compounding and stress in English: a closer look at the boundary between morphology and syntax. *Linguistische Berichte* 181, 55–69.

Pinker, Steven (1999) *Words and rules*. London: Weidenfeld & Nicolson.

Rastall, Paul (1993) On the attributive noun in English. *IRAL* 31, 309–13.

Schwartz, Catherine (ed.) (1994) *The Chambers dictionary*. Edinburgh: Chambers.

Tulloch, Sara (ed.) (1991) *The Oxford dictionary of new words*. Oxford: Oxford University Press.

22   English Inflection and Derivation

JAMES P. BLEVINS

1   Introduction

Modern English approaches the ideal of an isolating language. Open-class items have comparatively few forms, so that many inflectional categories either remain unmarked, or are expressed periphrastically. The inflectional system is particularly simple, even by the standards of a West Germanic language. Regular paradigms contain at most four forms, and the inflectional exponents that distinguish these forms do not show much variation, apart from some phonologically conditioned allomorphy. English retains a number of 'strong' noun and verb forms, along with a few other irregular formations. These residual patterns do occasionally recruit a historically weak item, as in the case of *dove* or *snuck*, which, for many North American speakers, may replace the weak preterites *dived* and *sneaked* (Taylor 1994). However, the creation of new strong forms is so rare and sporadic that one cannot regard the strong patterns as productive inflection classes in any useful sense.

The derivational system is considerably richer and more varied. In addition to compounding processes and 'minor' word formation processes, which are covered in greater length in chapter 21 of this volume, English has various prefixal and suffixal strategies for forming new lexemes. As with inflectional patterns, it is important to distinguish productive from non-productive patterns, in order to avoid overstating the complexity of the derivational system. Mixing synchronic and historical patterns leads to the idea that English contains separate Latinate and Germanic sublexicons, and that a given derivational exponent may occur either with Latinate or Germanic bases. Chomsky and Halle (1968) distinguish between 'primary' and 'secondary' affixes, whereas Aronoff (1976) introduces a feature [±Latinate], which allows affixes to 'select' bases from a particular sublexicon. However, the productivity of Latinate formations is open to question, given that Latinate bases comprise an essentially closed class and Latinate exponents induce idiosyncratic phonological changes. Hence it is highly plausible that the affixes that co-occur with these bases are likewise frozen, and, hence, that no productive derivational exponent in English selects a particular sublexicon.

The limited exponent inventory of English determines a correspondingly simple word structure. The few clearly inflectional exponents in English are suffixal, and at most one inflectional suffix may occur in any word. Derivational exponents are more numerous and may cooccur within a stem. Derivational prefixes tend to be category-preserving markers of morphosemantic lexeme-formation processes, and are commonly analyzed as attaching before derivational suffixes, which characteristically mark category-changing processes. Given that the historical ablauting process that gave rise to strong noun and verb forms is no longer active, as noted above, the productive morphological processes in English are predominantly affixal, and, indeed, concatenative.

From a typological perspective, the limited form variation within the English morphological system is of somewhat less interest than the way that functions are distributed over available forms. Noun paradigms have two forms: a stem form, which realizes the singular, and a plural form, usually marked by *-s* (/z/). Possession may be marked by the 'phrasal affix' *-s* (Anderson 1992), but the morphological categories of Case and Gender are not distinctive for common nouns. A number of forms that once expressed case contrasts survive in pronominal paradigms, but with subtly different functions. The former nominatives occur as simple subjects of finite verbs, whereas historically accusative or dative forms function as independent or 'default' forms (Hockett 1947).

The paradigms of regular verbs contain just four distinct forms: a stem form, an '*s*-form,' an '*ing*-form,' and an '*ed*-form.' The stem form expresses a range of functions, including imperative mood and 'non-3sg' present. Present participles and gerunds are realized by the *-ing* form, while regular preterites, and perfect and passive participles are all realized by the *-ed*. Strong verbs tend to retain a contrast between preterites and perfect/passive participles, yielding five forms.

Although forms in *-s* are often classified as '3sg present' forms, both the tense and agreement properties of these forms are anomalous. Forms in *-s* are arguably better described as 'impersonal' (in one of the many senses of this term, cf. Blevins 2003a), i.e., as marking 'anti-agreement.' Like '3sg' forms in other languages, forms in *-s* occur with expletives, with sentential and prepositional subjects, and, in fact, with any subject that does not bear a 'marked' person or number feature. The 'present' interpretation of forms in *-s* is also anomalous. Forms in *-s* or, like 'non-3sg' stem forms, cannot be used for punctual events (where the progressive is required instead), but can be freely used to express a future meaning, or even to give immediacy to the narration of past events.

Periphrastic strategies largely compensate for the shortage of synthetic verb forms. It is sometimes said that English has no future tense, though what is usually meant is just that the language lacks a synthetic future verb form. The future is hardly unusual in this regard, as English also lacks synthetic passive, perfect and progressive forms. Instead, future tense, passive voice, and perfect, and progressive aspect are all expressed by periphrastic constructions consisting of a modal or auxiliary and a participle or infinitive. These 'compound tenses' present a longstanding descriptive challenge, as they appear to straddle the boundary between syntax and morphology. The fact that periphrastic constructions express a single morphosyntactic property leads one tradition to treat them as analytic forms of a single lexeme (Curme 1935; Ackerman and Stump 2004; Lieb 2003). Yet within the post-Bloomfieldian tradition, the syntactic independence exhibited by auxiliaries and 'main' verbs has been regarded as evidence that periphrastic constructions are syntactic combinations.

To provide a more detailed description of the English morphological system, it is useful to follow the traditional practice of separating 'lexeme-preserving' or 'paradigmatic' processes, which define new forms of a lexeme, from the 'word-formation' processes that create new lexemes. In what follows, the first type of processes are designated as 'inflectional' and the second type as 'derivational.' There are, of course, other ways in which the terms 'inflection' and 'derivation' can be understood and applied to morphological patterns in English. In some cases, these differences determine slightly different analyses, such as the treatment of a class-changing exponent such as *-ly* as 'inflectional' (Haspelmath 1996). In other cases, the differences lead to more radical variation, such as the treatment of plural as a derivational category (Beard 1995). Depending on how precisely inflection and derivation are demarcated, there may also be phenomena that resist a clear classification. For the most part, these differences reflect a lack of consensus about the meaning of the terms 'inflection' and 'derivation,' rather than substantive disagreements about the analysis of individual constructions. Although any of the established interpretations of 'inflection' and 'derivation' would be suitable for the purposes of the present chapter, a traditional view is adopted for the sake of familiarity.

2 Inflection

The inflectional system of English comprises a large regular subsystem and a few highly circumscribed irregular patterns. The regular system contains a small number of general formations, which incorporate an even smaller number of exponents. This system is summarized in its entirety in (1).

(1)

Word Class	Form	Exponent	Examples
Noun	plural	-s (/z/)	mugs, spas, books, buses
Verb	'3sg present'		sells, walks, sees, pushes
	preterite	-ed (/d/)	quelled, talked, skied, swatted
	'past' participle		
	'present' participle	-ing (/ɪŋ/)	eating, being, squealing, walking
	gerund		
Adjective	comparative	-er (/əɹ/)	faster, older, milder, yellower
	superlative	-est (/əst/)	fastest, oldest, mildest, yellowest

As the chart in (1) indicates, there are at most five productive inflectional exponents in English. The morph that marks noun plurals, which is represented orthographically by *-s* and phonemically as /z/, is the same **form** as the morph that marks 3sg verbs. Preterites and past participles are likewise marked by the morph *-ed* (/d/), while present participles and gerunds are marked by the morph *-ing* (/ŋ/). The small exponent inventory of English leads to various cases of inflectional syncretism. Descriptions of English must confront the problem of determining which cases of identity in form reflect the neutralization of contrastive morphosyntactic properties and which cases are merely due to the fact that English lacks the morphotactic resources to 'spell out' certain contrastive properties. Only nouns and verbs retain a significant number of irregular formations, as the irregularity in the adjectival system is restricted to the suppletion in *good–better–best* and *bad–worse–worst*. Forms in *-ing* are completely regular, as are non-auxiliary verb forms in *-s*. The irregularity in the noun and verb systems is thus largely confined to noun plurals and verbal preterites and past participles. Irregular noun and verb forms can be assigned to 'classes,' such as those in (3) and (9), which exhibit the residue of once-productive patterns. However, these classes typically have few members in modern English – well below the threshold required to recruit new members on more than a sporadic basis – and thus exert a very limited influence on the inflection of new nouns or verbs.

Sections 2.1 and 2.2 summarize the inflectional patterns within the nominal and verbal systems, and highlight some features of particular interest within each system. Section 2.3 turns to adjectives and then to gerundive and participial forms, which appear to straddle word classes in English.

2.1   *Nouns*

As noted in the introduction, English nouns inflect for number, but not case or gender. The misalignment of prosodic and grammatical structure in English sometimes leads descriptions to treat the possessive marker -'s in *Eloise's book* as a genitive inflection. Zwicky (1987) and Stump (2001) develop a variant of this analysis in which the marker -'s is treated as an 'edge inflection.' Yet most accounts follow Hockett (1947: 142) and Wells (1947: 193) in treating -'s as an element that attaches to the right edge of a noun **phrase**. On this analysis, possessive phrases have the left-branching structure in (2).

(2)   a.   [NP Eloise]'s book
      b.   [NP [NP Eloise]'s sister]'s book
      c.   [NP the director of personnel]'s office

The element -'s may attach to *Eloise* in (2a) and (2b) because proper names have the distribution of noun phrases. In (2b), -'s also attaches to the noun phrase *Eloise's sister*, not to the common noun *sister*. Hence the sequence *sister's* may be a prosodic unit, though it is not a grammatical unit. The phrasal character of -'s is confirmed by patterns like (2c), in which -'s clearly attaches to the noun phrase *director of personnel* and not to *personnel*, which just occurs at the right edge of the phrase.

2.1.1   *Number*

Noun plurals in English can be assigned to the three broad categories in (3). Regular plurals are marked by the exponent -*s* (/z/), which has the phonologically-conditioned variants [z], [s] and [əz]. In addition, English contains a number of irregular formations. Some of these plurals have no exponent, others retain ablaut patterns, and a couple of nouns preserve the historically weak ending -*en*. The third class contains nouns whose plural forms have been borrowed with their singulars.

(3)

Type	Exponent	Examples
Regular	-s	mugs ([z]), spas ([z]), books ([s]), buses ([əz])
Irregular	Ø	sheep, fish, deer, etc.
	ablaut	man – men, foot – feet, goose – geese, mouse – mice
	-en	child – children, ox – oxen
Foreign	-on – -a	criterion – criteria, phenomenon – phenomena
	-is – -es	analysis – analyses, crisis – crises, thesis – theses
	-ix – -ices	matrix – matrices, index – indices, appendix – appendices

The vast majority of English nouns follow the regular pattern, as do virtually all new nouns. Apart from the odd whimsical extension of irregular formations, such as the use of *vaxen* as the plural of the computer system *vax*, irregular patterns are not extended to new nouns. The surviving strong plural forms are relatively stable, but there is some speaker variation regarding nouns such as *roof*, whose plurals may either conform to the irregular voicing pattern, and end in [vz], or follow the regular pattern, and end in [fs]. Speakers are, naturally, aware of the remaining strong patterns, and these patterns sometimes inhibit the formation of regular plurals like *mongooses*, even though speakers show an even more general reluctance to extend the irregular ablaut pattern to these cases.

Some frequently occurring foreign formations have been nativized in Modern English, while others remain confined to particular registers. Whereas *crises* is securely established as the plural of *crisis*, forms such as *phenomena* are often used in the singular, even by some educated speakers. The use of *data* as the plural of *datum* is largely restricted to academic contexts; elsewhere *data* is more commonly encountered as a mass noun. Singulars in *-ix* often have alternative regular plurals in [əz]. Pairs of alternative plural forms may acquire different meanings, as in the case of *appendices*, which refers to material at the end of a printed work, and *appendixes*, which refers to body parts.

A number of forms, such as *children* or *agendas*, are occasionally described as 'double plurals.' These examples represent cases in which a historically plural form has been reanalyzed as a singular, and thus provided a base for the addition of 'another' plural marker. In the case of *children*, the *-r* reflects the strong Germanic plural (retained in the German cognate *Kinder*), while the final *-en* reflects the weak plural marker, added when *-r* was no longer a transparent plural marker. In Latin, the form *agenda* is likewise the plural of *agendum*. Although some speakers are aware of this paradigmatic relationship, *agenda* is most frequently used as a singular, whose plural is formed with the regular exponent *-s*. In short, English 'double plurals' do not involve what Matthews (1991) terms 'extended exponence,' as the property 'plural' is not multiply marked at any synchronic stage.

The historically strong ablauted plurals and weak plurals in *-en* tend to occur more freely in compounds and derivational formations than do regular or foreign plurals. For example, many speakers perceive a contrast between *oxen cart* and **dogs cart*, between *lice-infested* and **fleas-infested*, and between *teeth cleaner* and **hands cleaner*. These contrasts are sometimes interpreted as evidence that irregular plural forms represent a type of 'unproductive' (Anderson 1992: 128) or 'inherent' (Booij 1996) inflection that may feed derivation, or, alternatively, as evidence that these form are number-neutral 'second stems' (cf. Aronoff 1994) that underlie plurals and compounds.

There is, however, a comparatively large number of counterexamples to the generalization that *s*-plurals do not occur in compounds. Interestingly, many of these cases involve collective plurals, like those in (4), which follow the pattern of *brother–brethren* rather than *brother–brothers*.

(4)

Singular	Collective Plural	Compound
saving	savings	savings bank
arm	arms	arms race
system	systems	systems analyst
custom	customs	customs union
admission	admissions	admissions office

There is a waning prescriptive pressure to pluralize the first element of Latinate compounds such as *attorney general*, *sergeant major* or *notary public*. This is, however, very much a learned pattern, and plurals like *attorneys general*, *sergeants major* or *notaries public* are almost never encountered in spontaneous speech. Some nominalized forms of phrasal verbs follow a similar pattern, exhibiting head inflection (Stump 1995). Thus the agentive nominal *passer-by*, derived from the phrasal verb *pass by*, has the plural *passers-by*, not **passer-bys*. However, the placement of the plural marker appears to be influenced by the nominal character of the marker *-er*. In cases where a peripheral nominalizing marker is available, the plural reverts to edge inflection. In the colloquial language, a transitive phrasal verb such as *pick up* has the agentive nominal *picker uper*, where the first occurrence of *-er* attaches to the lexical verb *pick* and the second attaches to the phrasal verb *pick up*. The plural of this nominal is then *picker upers*, with a peripheral *-s*, not **pickers uper* (or **pickers upers*).

2.1.2   The case of pronouns

Descriptions of personal pronouns in English traditionally recognize at least a binary case contrast. Jespersen (1933: 132) states that 'In some pronouns, but no other word-class, we find a distinction between the two "cases" **nominative** and **objective**,' and suggests the analysis in (5).

(5)	Nominative	I	we	he	she	they	who
	Objective	me	us	him	her	them	whom

Quirk et al. (1985: 346) similarly distinguish 'subjective' from 'objective' pronouns in (6).

(6)

		Personal		Possessive		
Pers	Num	Subjective	Objective	Determinative	Independent	Reflexive
1st	Sg	I	me	my	mine	myself
	Pl	we	us	out	ours	ourselves
2nd	Sg	you	you	your	yours	yourself
	Pl	you	you	your	yours	yourselves
3rd	Sg	he	him	his	his	himself
		she	her	her	hers	herself
	Pl	they	them	their	theirs	themselves

Yet, as the 'scare quotes' in the passage from Jespersen indicate, even traditional analysts harboured doubts about the status of case oppositions in Modern English. Post-Bloomfieldians expressed their reservations more forcefully, and clearly regarded traditional treatments as anachronistic. The objections that Hockett (1947: 241–2) raises remain equally relevant today.

At least in certain dialects, the morphs *I* and *me* (and similarly *we* and *us*, *he* and *him*, etc.) are in non-contrastive distribution; in some dialects, indeed, the complementation is probably complete. We may suspect that if it were not for the Latinizing school tradition, the complementation would be complete for most speakers: *I* initially, except in isolation, *me* directly after a verb or a preposition and in isolation. Actual exceptions to this are either on the Latin pattern (*It's I*, or *Who's there? – I*, instead of *Me*), or are overcorrections (*between you and I*) . . . There is no longer any justification for speaking of case in English; for the distinction between subjective and objective 'cases' (under whatever name) disappears as soon as *I* and *me*, etc., are shown to belong to the same morpheme.

For most if not all English speakers, expressions such as *It's I*, or *Who's there? – I*, are archaisms, perhaps learned at some point in school, but unusable outside the classroom. Similar remarks apply to comparative and coordinate environments. Educated speakers of standard English may come to accept – and, perhaps, even prefer – nominative objects of comparison in examples such as *He is faster than I*. However, less frequently drilled patterns, such as *They are faster than we*, remain anomalous for many speakers. The use of forms such as *I* and *we* in coordinate environments also bears the mark of the prescriptive school tradition. Pupils are often taught explicitly to use nominative pronouns in coordinate subjects, and even to place a 1sg pronoun last in a coordinate subject. Hence a coordinate subject such as *me or him*, which is common in children's speech and even in many colloquial registers, is deprecated in literary registers, where it is replaced by *he or I*.

It is instructive to contrast these expressions with their counterparts in modern German, which retains a more robust case system. In examples such as *Wer ist da? – Ich* 'Who is there – I,' or *Sie sind schneller als wir* 'They are faster than we,' the first person nominative pronouns *ich* and *wir* are required, and alternatives such as accusative *mich* and *uns* are unacceptable. In coordinate subjects such as *er oder ich* 'he or I,' the pronouns are likewise obligatorily nominative.

Moreover, even within literary registers of standard English, coordinated nominatives like *he or I* exhibit properties suggestive of an inculcated pattern. Speakers are especially prone to 'hypercorrect' in coordinate environments and use nominative pronouns as direct objects or as prepositional objects, as in Hockett's example *between you and I*. This type of error tends to be symptomatic of instructed patterns, where speakers are attempting to conform to a model of 'correct' usage. It is also noteworthy that English lacks any grammatical strategy for determining the agreement properties of coordinate pronouns. The agreement properties of coordinate subjects in languages such as German or Russian are often attributed to a process of 'principled resolution' which, for example, assigns 1st person priority over 2nd person, and assigns 2nd person priority over 3rd person (Corbett 1991). Discussions of coordinate structures, such as Sag et al. (1985) or Hudson (1995) provide no evidence of a comparable strategy in English. Instead, speakers confronted with the task of selecting a present tense verb in the frame '*He or I* . . .' may choose an invariant modal, adopt a salvage strategy of selecting a verb form that agrees with the nearest conjunct, or simply resort to circumlocution.

Taken together, these considerations indicate that case is no longer a distinctive category in modern English, even within the pronominal system. Hudson (1995) reaches much the same conclusion, on different grounds. As proposed by Jespersen (1933) and Quirk et al. (1985), the personal pronoun system in English is divided into one set of default or 'elsewhere' forms, and another set of 'special-purpose' forms with a more restricted distribution. However, this split does not pattern with the division between nominative and 'objective' cases in Old English or modern German, but rather with the contrast between preverbal subject clitics and independent pronouns in a language like French. Former nominative pronouns such as *I* and *he* correspond to the French preverbal subject clitics *je* and *il*, which occur solely as simple subjects, and cannot occur in isolation or in coordinate or comparative environments. Forms such as *me* and *us* likewise correspond to the 'emphatic' forms *moi* or *lui*, which occupy all other syntactic positions. The reclassification of English personal pronouns in terms of 'subject' and 'general' forms is set out in (7).

(7)

	1sg	*1pl*	*2nd*	*3sg*			*3pl*
Subject	I	we	we	he	she	it	they
General	me	us	us	him	her	it	them

2.2   *Verbs*

Noun and verb paradigms in English both exhibit 'word-inflection' in the sense of Bloomfield (1933: 225). A noun stem may stand alone as a singular noun. A verb stem, which provides a base for the other forms in (8), may stand alone as an infinite, imperative or general present form.

(8)

Form	*Regular*	*Strong*
Stem	walk	eat
Present Participle	walking	eating
Past Participle	walked	eaten
Preterite	walked	ate
3sg Present	walks	eats

Regular verb paradigms contain three forms based on the stem: a form in
-ing that functions as a present participle and gerund, a form in *-ed* that functions as a preterite and past participle, and a '3sg' present form in *-s*. Irregular
main verbs also have stem-based forms in *-ing* and *-s*, but exhibit distinctive
patterns of preterite and participial suppletion. A partial list of patterns is
given in (9). Quirk et al. (1985: 115ff) can be consulted for a more comprehensive list and detailed discussion.

(9)

Pattern	Stem	Preterite	Past Participle
Regular	walk	walked	walked
No Syncretism	sing	sang	sung
	eat	ate	eaten
No Variation	cut	cut	cut
	hit	hit	hit
Preterite = Past Participle	meet	met	met
	seek	sought	sought
Preterite = Stem	beat	beat	beaten
Stem = Past Participle	come	came	come

Due to their frequency, the irregular verbs are of importance to the learner
of English, and are prominent in pedagogical descriptions. However, the classes
exhibit essentially frozen patterns, and do not recruit formerly weak verbs,
or apply to new verbs with any regularity. The psycholinguistic studies summarized in Clahsen (1999) indicate that native speakers of English memorize
irregular conjugational forms, and do not 'derive' them synchronically from
the stem form.

The conjugational system of English is very simple in certain respects. Regular
paradigms contain four morphotactically simple forms, and irregular paradigms
may add a fifth. Each form is either based on the stem and a regular suffix
(*-ing*, *-ed* or *-s*), or follows one of a small number of suppletive patterns. Hence,
the main descriptive challenge for a description of English arises in determining the number of **entries** that are realized by these forms, particularly by the
'past participle,' the '3sg present' and the 'present participle.' Some approaches
to this challenge are outlined briefly below.

2.2.1   Compound tenses

The pre-Bloomfieldian English tradition tends to recognize a large number of 'compound tenses,' which are 'formed by the use of a present or a past tense of an auxiliary in connection with a participle or an infinitive' (Curme 1935: 319). The individual compound tenses are summarized in (10).

(10)

Tense/Aspect/Voice	Auxiliary	Main Verb
Progressive	be	Present Participle
Passive		Past Participle
Perfect	have	
Future	will	Stem

This type of analysis nicely captures the way that periphrastic formations express morphosyntactic properties through distinctive combinations of forms. For example, passive voice is not uniquely associated with the auxiliary *be*, which may also occur in the progressive, nor with the past participle, which may also occur in the perfect. Rather, passive voice is expressed by the distinctive **combination** of a general auxiliary *be* and a 'past' participle. Perfect aspect is similarly expressed by a past participle and form of *have*, as proposed in Ackerman and Webelhuth (1998) and Spencer (2001). The progressive is likewise expressed by *be* and a 'present participle' (Lee 2004).

The traditional conception of compound tenses is implicitly 'construction-based' in essentially the sense of Kay and Filmore (1999). Properties such as passive, perfect and progressive are not 'assembled' in a bottom-up fashion from the meanings assigned to individual auxiliaries and participles. Instead, a traditional account proceeds in a top-down fashion from a properties to the particular combinations of auxiliaries and participles that spell them out. The meanings of auxiliaries and participles are preserved in a compound tense, but the meaning of the compound tense is more than just the sum of the meanings of its parts. The interpretation of the present perfect provides a useful illustration. The English present perfect is grammatically a present construction, as Klein (1992) confirms. The use of this construction to refer to past events reflects the implication that an event that is completed in the present must have occurred in the past. In an example such as *has arrived*, the present auxiliary *has* contributes the present tense meaning, the participle *arrived* contributes the lexical meaning of *arrive*, and the combination of *has* and *arrived* express perfective aspect.

The fact that the auxiliaries in passive, perfect and progressive tenses may themselves have compound forms introduces a limited degree of 'recursion' within the system of complex tenses. An example such as (11a) illustrates the full expansion of this system. Working outward from the passive *be observed*, one can construct the progressive *be being observed*, the perfect *have been being observed*, and finally the future *will have been being observed*. Although none of these properties are obligatorily present, they are always realized in the fixed order in (11b) when they are expressed.

(11)   a.   They surely will have been being observed.
       b.   Future < Perfect < Progressive < Passive

The 'expansions' of the auxiliary system thus involve a finite – indeed quite small – number of elements, with highly restricted combinations. There are plausible explanations for some restrictions, while others are less well understood. The innermost placement of the passive can be attributed to the claim that the passive is a derivational, stem-forming, process (Bresnan 1982; Blevins 2003a). Conversely, the outermost placement of the future *will* reflects the fact that *will* is a finite modal, and that verbs in English do not subcategorize for finite verb phrase complements. Yet the ordering of the perfect and progressive is not attributable to any general considerations of this nature.

Within the post-Bloomfieldian tradition that originates with Harris (1951) and Chomsky (1957, 1975), these patterns have usually been treated as syntactic. The main disagreement within this literature concerns whether auxiliaries should be regarded as verbs in their own right (Ross 1969), as 'specifiers' of main verbs (Chomsky 1970), or as a type of 'functional' category (Chomsky 1995). On the other hand, the morphosyntactic coherence of these expansions, and the limited combinations that they allow, have led a number of recent accounts (notably Börjars et al. (1997) and Ackerman and Stump (2004)) to rehabilitate a traditional perspective and treat them as morphological.

2.2.2   Agreement or anti-agreement?

Apart from the auxiliaries *be* and *have*, all verbs in English have a single preterite form, which does not vary according to form of its subject. The future auxiliary *will* is also invariant, though some speakers retain a contrast between first and second person *shall* and third person *will*. The opposition between stem forms and forms in *-s* thus represents the only regular agreement pattern within the conjugational system of English. Although there is no question about the number of forms in a regular present paradigm, there is again some dispute about the number of present entries.

One traditional answer is supplied by Curme (1935), who proposes the six entries in (12): a 3sg entry *walks* and five homophonous entries, one for each person-number combination realized by *walk*. Most contemporary descriptions regard this analysis as unsatisfactory, since there is no motivation within the verb system for recognizing five distinct stem entries.

(12)

Person	Singular	Plural
1st	walk	walk
2nd	walk	walk
3rd	**walks**	walk

Much of the syncretism in (12) can be eliminated by adopting the Bloomfieldian idea that the verb paradigm with the largest number of forms determines the number of cells for all paradigms. Since the present paradigm of *be* has three distinct forms: 1sg *am*, 3sg *is* and a general form *are*, this entails that regular verbs also have the three entries in (13): a 3sg entry in *-s*, a 1sg stem entry, and a general stem entry.

(13)

Form	Person	Number
walks	3	sg
walk	1	sg
walk	–	–

By treating *am* as an isolated entry within the irregular paradigm of *be*, Huddleston (1984) and Quirk et al. (1985) reduce regular paradigms to the limit of two entries: a stem form and an *s*-form. Significantly, Huddleston (1984) and Quirk et al. (1985) agree in treating the stem form as a general present form, and the *s*-form as a dedicated 3sg form. The analyses in (14) illustrate the most straightforward interpretation of this proposal, on which forms like *walks* are assigned the features [3] and [sg], while general forms like *walk* are unspecified (or partly specified) for person and number.

(14)

Form	Person	Number
walks	3	sg
walk	–	–

An intuitively appealing feature of this proposal is that the stem form is clearly the **morphotactically** unmarked form in the present paradigm. Nevertheless, it is much less clear is that this form is also **morphosyntactically** unmarked. As in many other languages, '3sg' forms in English occur in contexts where the syntactic subject is an inappropriate agreement 'controller.' Although syntactic subjects are generally obligatory in English, a variety of subject types – including expletives, clauses, infinitives and prepositional phrases – are not appropriate agreement controllers. For example, the sentences in (15) contain sentential and infinitival subjects, which lack person and number features and thus cannot enter into agreement relations with personal verb forms. In these environments, forms in *-s* are obligatory, and the ostensibly general stem forms are disallowed.

(15)　a.　[$_S$ That Max drives at night] alarms/*alarm his friends.
　　　b.　[$_{VP}$ To neglect to vote] is/*are highly irresponsible.
　　　c.　[$_S$ That Max drives at night] tends/*tend to alarm his friends.
　　　d.　[$_{VP}$ To neglect to vote] seems/*seem (to be) highly irresponsible.

The fact that forms in *-s* are required in contexts where there is no agreement controller suggests that the stem form is not, in fact, unmarked for agreement properties. This pattern also suggests that the exponent *-s* does not mark agreement with a 3sg subject, but rather signals **non-agreement** with a personal subject. The correct generalization for standard English appears to be that an *s*-form may **not** cooccur with any subject that bears the marked person features [1] or [2] or the marked number feature [pl]. Since 3sg NPs and non-NPs both lack marked features, the *s*-form occurs with these subjects, but not with any plural or 1st or 2nd person subject. The present stem form is then not a general form *tout court*, but a general personal form, which requires a personal subject.

A simple contrast between personal and non-personal entries will capture the binary structure of regular verb paradigms in English. This contrast cannot be expressed directly in terms of person or number features alone, since a personal entry may have a marked value for either feature. However, the contrast can be expressed in terms of a binary feature, such as 'Agr' in (16), given an appropriate correspondence between Agr and the Person and Number properties of nominal subjects.

(16)

Form	*Agr*
walks	–
walk	+

If the property '[Agr +]' is implied by any marked Person or Number feature (i.e., by 1st or 2nd person or by plural number), English personal pronouns will have the Agr values in (17). Singular NPs will pattern with 3sg pronouns, and plural NPs with 3pl pronouns. Subject-verb agreement is then wholly determined by Agr properties: a subject and verb agree if they have compatible Agr features, and fail to agree otherwise. Since person and number properties are not distinctive for regular verbs, the verbal entries in (16) are not specified for these features. Person and number features do, of course, distinguish pronominal forms, and are specified in the entries in (17).

(17)

Form	Person	Number	Agr
we	1	pl	+
I	1		+
you	2		+
they		pl	+
he/she/it			−

It is the use of 'Agr' as a feature 'interface' between verb and noun entries that permits the simple verb paradigms in (16). Person and number properties remain relevant within the pronominal system, but do not enter into agreement relations, or influence the structure of regular verb paradigms, as they do in the traditional analysis in (12). Instead, the person and number features of nominals imply Agr features, which determine compatibility with regular verb forms. Nominals with a [1], [2] or [pl] feature will be positively specified for Agr and thus combine with the stem form of a regular verb. Conversely, nominals that lack marked features will combine with the *s*-form.

2.2.3   Minor patterns and innovations

The traditional division of verbs into 'main' and 'helping' classes is largely based on distributional criteria, as 'helping' verbs may undergo 'inversion,' cooccur with negative elements and occur in a variety of other environments that disallow main verbs. The subsequent division of helping verbs into modal and auxiliary subclasses is principally morphological. Whereas auxiliaries tend to have full inflectional paradigms, modal paradigms are defective, and usually consist of a single form.

Modal and auxiliary verbs exhibit a few distinctive morphological patterns, though none of these patterns can be described as productive, given that modals and auxiliaries form a small, closed class. Finite forms of the auxiliaries *be*, *have* and *do* have negative forms in -*n't*, as do many modals. These formations are historically contractions with the negative adverb *not*, and the term 'negative contraction' is still applied to them. However, as Zwicky and Pullum (1983) show, forms in *-n't* are inflected forms in modern English, not reductions of syntactic constructions containing *not*. The negative forms of modals and auxiliaries are not always predictable from the affirmative form, as in the case of *will–won't*, *must* [mʌsnt]–*mustn't* [mʌsnt] or *do* [du]–*don't* [downt]. Once these irregular patterns have been listed, it is not clear how much work remains for a synchronic contraction rule.

The status of 'weak' auxiliaries is somewhat less settled. Some descriptions treat contractions such as *I'm*, *we'll* or *she's* as reductions of the corresponding strong forms *I am*, *we will* and *she has/is*, whereas others recognize parallel inventories of strong and weak auxiliaries. Whether or not one regards this entire class as incipient morphology, there are at least some instances that pattern with morphological formations. The reduction of auxiliary *have* to [əv] and thence to [ə] has produced a new class of contracted forms colloquially represented as *woulda*, *couldn'ta*, etc. The morphological character of this pattern is suggested by the fact that it extends [ə] to contexts that do not allow the unreduced auxiliary, at least in standard varieties of English. Forms such as *hadda* and *hadn'ta* are often acceptable to speakers who do not accept the ostensible sources **had have* and **hadn't have*.

2.3   Adjectives, participles, and gerunds

Adjectives do not inflect for agreement properties, and, apart from a few isolated examples like *lone–alone*, do not vary in form between attributive and predicative functions. Most monosyllabic adjectives and many disyllabic adjectives have synthetic comparatives in *-er*, and superlatives in *-est*, as illustrated by *old–older–oldest* and *yellow–yellower–yellowest*. The majority of adjectives with two syllables, and nearly all with three or more, form analytic comparatives with *more*, and superlatives with *most*, as in *foolish–more foolish– most foolish* or *precocious–more precocious–most precocious*. A number of disyllabic adjectives may follow either pattern; thus *narrow–narrow–narrowest*, alongside *narrow–more narrow–most narrow*. A few monosyllables lack synthetic forms, and follow the analytic pattern, as in *right–more right–most right* or *tan–more tan–most tan*.

Traditional descriptions tend to classify synthetic comparatives and superlatives as inflectional, on the grounds that they pattern more like forms of an adjective than as independent adjectives in their own right. Although positive, comparative and superlative forms can be consolidated into a single adjectival paradigm, these forms may participate in processes that are traditionally classified as derivational. In particular, comparative and superlative forms may occur in some of the same types of compounds as the corresponding positive forms. Thus *older-seeming* patterns with *old-seeming* and *faster-growing* with *fast-growing*. Some accounts interpret the fact that comparatives and superlatives may 'feed' compounding as evidence that these forms are cases of 'inherent' inflection (Booij 1996), much like the strong noun plurals discussed in section 2.1.1. However, the distribution of comparative and superlative forms can also be taken as evidence that the distinction between lexeme-preserving paradigmatic processes and lexeme-creating processes is orthogonal to the contrast between 'word-forming' inflection and 'stem-forming' derivation (Blevins 2001).

2.3.1   Verbal participles

Present and past participles are usually included in the inflectional paradigm of English verbs, in large part because of the role that they play in the formation of periphrastic verbal constructions. The adjectives that correspond to these participles are, on the other hand, often regarded as falling outside the verbal paradigm. Adjectives may sometimes correspond to a perfect participle (or to the perfect 'use' of a past participle), as in the case of *a matriculated student*, the counterpart of *the student has matriculated*. However, adjectives corresponding to present and passive participles (or to passive 'uses' of the past participle) represent a much more common pattern. Nearly any intransitive present participle may function as an attributive modifier, as in *a sleeping child*, *the charging boar*, etc. Passive participles of transitive verbs may likewise serve an attributive function, as in *a lost handbag*, *the neglected evidence*, etc. Whereas traditional accounts characteristically refer to adjectival or attributive 'uses' of verbal participles, contemporary approaches tend to regard participial adjectives as separate elements, derived by a process of 'transposition' (Haspelmath 1996; Spencer 1999) or 'zero conversion' (Bresnan 1982, 2001). Yet a peculiar aspect of many conversion-based approaches is that the participial 'input' to a conversion rule is already implicitly adjectival, in that the term 'participle' is merely a designation for a verbal form with adjectival properties.

The traditional view that participles are latently adjectival can be recast formally by treating adjectives as neutral for whatever features are taken to distinguish verbs from adjectives. In the X-bar model of Chomsky (1970), the feature is [±N], so that participles will be lexically unspecified for [N], as van Riemsdijk (1983) proposes. Underspecification can then be resolved within a disambiguating syntactic or morphological context, along the lines originally suggested in Chomsky (1970). An underspecified participle will be resolved to an adjective when it combines with an adjectival exponent, or when it occurs with a predicate that selects an adjectival complement, or when it is introduced in an attributive context that requires an adjective. A participle will be resolved to a verb when it occurs with a verbal exponent, or is introduced in a periphrastic construction or in any other environment that selects a verb. The implementation of this analysis is fairly straightforward, and is set out in more detail in Blevins (2005). However, the main virtue of this type of analysis is the way that it reconciles the traditional view that a participle is a single item with multiple 'uses' with the fact that a participle functions unambiguously as a verb or adjective in any particular use.

2.3.2 *Gerunds*

The use of categorial neutrality to express the traditional notion of 'an X used as Y' suggests a similar solution to the problem posed by 'gerunds' in English. In addition to functioning as present participles and attributive adjectives, forms in *-ing* also head 'gerundive nominal' and regular 'derived nominals' (Chomsky 1970). Examples of each type of gerundive construction are given in (18).

(18)   a.   [$_{NP}$ their [$_{V'}$ [$_V$ renewing] the lease]]
       b.   [$_{NP}$ the [$_{N'}$ [$_N$ renewing] of the lease]]
       c.   [$_{NP}$ the [$_{N'}$ [$_N$ renewal] of the lease]]

The gerundive nominal in (18a) exhibits the structure proposed in Pullum (1991), in which the form in *-ing* heads a verbal phrase within a larger noun phrase. In the regular derived nominal in (18b), the form in *-ing* functions as a noun within a fully nominal construction. The irregular derived nominal in (18c) has the same structure as (18b), but is headed by the deverbal noun *renewal*. Contemporary analyses of forms in *-ing* tend to divide up these forms in one of two ways. One approach groups gerundive nominals with derived nominals as instances of a general 'nominalization' process that excludes present participles (Jackendoff 1977). Another group gerundive nominals with present participles, as verbal constructions that are categorially distinct from derived nominals (Huddleston 1984; Pullum 1991). However, there is really no need to split up the class of forms in *-ing* in either way. As with participles, one may assume, adapting the proposal of Chomsky (1970: 22), that these items 'appear in the lexicon with fixed selectional and strict subcategorization features, but with a choice as to the features associated with the lexical categories noun, verb, adjective.' The neutrality of an underspecified entry for *renewing* can again be resolved in a disambiguating syntagmatic context. The entry for *renewing* is resolved to a noun when it is combined with a category-specific exponent, such as plural *-s*, or when it is introduced into the nominal context in (18b). Yet when introduced into the verbal context in (18a), *renewing* is resolved to a verb. This context-dependence again captures the traditional treatment of *-ing* forms as single items with multiple 'uses.' In contrast, the entry for a deverbal noun such as *renewal* in (18b) has a fully determinate category ([+N, −V] in X-bar terms), and is only compatible with a nominal context.

3   Derivation

The strategies for creating new lexemes in English are more numerous and considerably more varied than those available for inflecting existing lexemes. Moreover, whereas inflectional processes are generally regarded as productive (and sometimes even defined in terms of productivity, as in Haspelmath 1996), the processes that create new lexemes differ greatly in generality and regularity.

The class of morphotactic processes such as 'clipping,' acronym formation or 'blending,' can be dealt with briefly here, as they are discussed at greater length elsewhere in the volume. Each of these processes define new forms, either with no change, or no predictable change in meaning or grammatical properties. The output of clipping may correspond to an initial element of a longer word, as in *prep* for *preparatory*, a final element, as in *phone* for *telephone*, or even a medial sequence, as in *flu* for *influenza*. Although recent clippings may be marked by an apostrophe, as in *'flu*, and initially perceived as colloquial, over time they come to establish an identity separate from their historical base. The same independence is characteristic of acronyms. Thus the acronym *OPEC* functions as a proper name, without a preceding article, whereas *Organization of Petroleum Exporting Countries* shows the distribution of a common noun phrase. Blending is a similarly sporadic process, which combines parts of existing words to form new words, such as *smog* from *smoke* and *fog*, or *eurocrat*, from *European* and *bureaucrat*. Cases of 'word manufacture' are often assigned to classes according to the relation between 'source' items and manufactured 'outputs'; e.g., whether an output corresponds to an initial, final or medial part of an original item. Yet this classification is essentially taxonomic, and does not interact significantly with other grammatical processes.

English also contains a variety of processes that induce a change in grammatical and/or semantic properties, which may – though need not – be accompanied by a change in form. These processes are sometimes taken to define a 'derivational paradigm,' which contains the members of different word or valence classes that can be derived from a given lexeme. The following outline of the English derivational subsystem begins by distinguishing the processes that alter valence or meaning in section 3.1 from those that change word class in section 3.2. Sections 3.3 and 3.4 then consider the role of analogical processes and interactions between derivational and inflectional processes.

3.1   *Category-preserving processes*

Although English verbs exhibit valence alternations, valence classes are not marked morphologically. As discussed in section 2.2.1, the contrast between active and passive voice is not marked on participles in English, reflecting the general pattern in West Germanic (Blevins 2003b). Alternations between what are sometimes termed 'causative' and 'inchoative' entries are similarly unmarked in English, so that forms such as *break*, *open* or *sink* may function either as transitive or as (unaccusative) intransitive verbs. As in many languages, transitive verbs may be used intransitively, and intransitives may occur with a 'cognate object,' but neither usage involves a change in verb form.

English contains a number of suffixal exponents that change the meaning or subclass of a noun. Productive examples include *-dom*, *-ship*, and *-monger* in (19), as well as the more recent *-gate*. Some of these formations show an affinity with compounds, and Marchand (1966: 290) classifies *-monger*, in particular, among the 'semi-suffixes' that 'stand midway between suffixes and full words.'

(19)

Suffix	Meaning	Examples
-dom	'territory, domain'	kingdom, martyrdom, fandom, hackerdom
-ship	'state or condition'	courtship, editorship, friendship, marksmanship
-monger	'promoting' (disparaging)	scandalmonger, scaremonger, warmonger

However, category-preserving processes are predominantly prefixal in English. These processes may express logical notions such as negation or *Aktionsart* meanings such as repetition, as well as a variety of other lexical semantic notions. Some examples of prefixal patterns are given in (20).

(20)

Prefix	Category	Meaning	Status	Examples
anti-	N	'against'	productive	anti-slavery, anti-vivisection, anti-war
ante-	N	'preceding'	lexicalized	antecedent, antechamber, antedate
un-	V	'reversal'	productive	unpack, unravel, unwind, unzip
un-	A	'not'	productive	uncertain, un-English, unkind, unwise
in-	A	'not'	lexicalized	ineligible, immaterial, irrelevant
dis-	A	'not'	lexicalized	dishonest, disloyal, dispassionate
re-	V	'again'	productive	reread, retell, reheat, re-cover
re-	V	'back'	lexicalized	recline, recuperate, recover, return

Some prefixal elements within borrowings have never been established as separate morphs in English. This is clearly the case for *re-* in *recline* in (20), or *pre-* in *prescribe*, which contrast with *re-* in *reread* and *pre-* in *pre-heat*. The relation between adjectival *un-* and *in-* parallels the relation between suffix pairs such as *-ness* and *-ity*, which are discussed in section 3.2 below. Whereas *un-* applies to an open class of adjectives, including participial adjectives, *in-* occurs in Latinate formations, where it is sometimes described as 'assimilating in place to a following consonant.' Given the restricted distribution of *in-*, the 'assimilation' illustrated by *immaterial* and *irrelevant* in (20) is best regarded as a historical process. The negative prefix *dis-* shows a similarly restricted distribution, and, as Marchand (1966: 112) notes, 'does not in general combine with non-Romance elements.'

3.2   *Category-changing processes*

A notable property of Modern English is the lack of any consistent marking of word class or subclass. The basic stems of nouns, verbs and adjectives do not exhibit any characteristic pattern, so that the 'conversion' or 'coercion' of an item from one class to another is indicated by its cooccurrence with inflectional or derivational exponents, or by its use in a particular syntagmatic context. Just about any noun can be 'verbed,' so to speak; that is, used as a verb that denotes an activity conventionally related to the noun meaning. A similar process may apply to adjectives as well, yielding a characteristically causative interpretation. However, as illustrated by 'verbed,' the conversion to a verb is not marked by a change in the form of the item, but is instead signaled by the verbal inflection *-ed*.

Adjectives may also assume a nominal function with no change in form, though this usage is somewhat less common than in other Germanic languages. Frequently occurring examples, such as *the rich* or *the innocent*, often have a conventionalized character. This strategy can be extended to new adjectives, such as *the stubborn* or *the naturalized*, which are clearly perceived as neologisms.

A number of noun-verb pairs are distinguished by stress patterns. These pairs are often listed in pedagogical descriptions, and there is no evidence that the alternation reflects a synchronically active process in English. The nouns *áddress*, *cónvict*, *súbject* and *tórment* normally have initial stress, while the corresponding verbs: *addréss*, *convíct*, *subjéct* and *tormént* are usually produced with final stress. A few verb-noun pairs exhibit vowel and voicing differences, as in the case of the noun *bath* ([baθ]) and the verb *bathe* ([beɪð]), but this pattern is again not productive. Back formation may yield verbs that differ from the substantives on which they are based. Thus the final vowel [aɪ] in *televize* and *opine* contrasts with the penultimate [ɪ] in *television* and *opinion*.

As noted in connection with the derived nominal constructions in section 2.3.2, English retains a class of irregular deverbal nouns, sometimes termed 'action nominalizations.' Unlike productive forms in *-ing*, the form of these deverbal action nominals is not in general predictable from the form of the corresponding verb. Moreover, none of these irregular patterns are extended to new verbs, and most occur only with existing Latinate stems. The examples in (21) all retain the meaning 'act of V*ing*,' but many have also acquired stative or lexicalized abstract noun meanings.

(21)

Effect	Suffix	Examples
V → N	-age	breakage, coverage, shrinkage, spoilage
	-al	arrival, approval, refusal, survival, withdrawal
	-ance/-ence	acceptance, attendance, emergence, resistance
	-ion	destruction, instruction, production, reduction
	-ment	appeasement, confinement, improvement

English also contains a number of highly productive category-changing processes, including the strategies for forming deverbal adjectives and deadjectival verbs in (22).

(22)

Effect	Suffix	Stems	Examples
V → A	-able	any	approachable, believable, breakable, livable, readable
A → V	-ize	any	civilize, legalize, tenderize, westernize, winterize

Various other derivational processes come in productive and non-productive pairs. For example, English contains the two strategies for forming agentive nominals illustrated in (23). Nominals in *-er* can be formed from nearly any verb in English, including the phrasal verbs *pass by* and *pick up* mentioned in section 2.1.1, which have the nominals *passer-by* and *picker-upper*. A few agentive nominals have no corresponding verbs, as in the case of *butcher*. The suffix *-ant* also marks agentive nominals, though, like the suffixes in (21), *-ant* occurs only with a closed class of Latinate stems.

(23)

Effect	Suffix	Stems	Examples
V → N	-er	any	baker, complainer, manager, receiver
	-ant/-ent	Latinate	attendant, contestant, dependent, inhabitant
A → N	-ness	any	fairness, redness, tenderness, strangeness
	-ity	Latinate	agility, gravity, insanity, reality, curiosity

The strategies for forming abstract deadjectival nouns in (23) exhibit a parallel contrast. Nouns in *-ity* are confined to Latinate formations, as Aronoff (1976) notes, and exhibit what is sometimes termed 'trisyllabic shortening' (Chomsky and Halle 1968). This is illustrated by the pair *agile–agility*, as the long final vowel [ai] in *agile* corresponds to the short penultimate vowel [ɪ] in *agility*. In contrast, nouns in *-ness* are formed from an open class of stems and do not induce a change in their base. To distinguish *-ity* from *-ness*, Chomsky and Halle (1968) assign *-ity* to a class of 'primary' affixes that combine with their base before 'secondary' affixes such as *-ness*. Aronoff (1976) likewise introduces the lexical features [±Latinate] to allow *-ity* to 'select' bases from a Latinate sublexicon. Models that incorporate a notion of 'level ordering' (Kiparsky 1982) impose a parallel classification by treating *-ity* as 'level 1' suffix that attaches before the 'level 11' prefix *un-*.

3.3   Productivity and analogy

These contrasts between exponents, levels, and 'sublexicons' serve essentially to reinstate a distinction between productive and nonproductive exponents, which is thoroughly obscured in Chomsky and Halle (1968). A 'secondary' exponent such as *-ness* marks a productive nominalization process, which may apply to new adjectives. A 'primary' affix, such as *-ity* or *-ant*, on the other hand, is largely encapsulated in existing forms. The sole productive use of *-ity* is in combination with *-able*, where it is encapsulated in a complex exponent *-ability*. Existing forms in *-ity* or *-ant* may provide a basis for analogical extensions, though analogized forms need not be morphologically transparent. A traditional four-part proportional analogy (Hock 1991: 172) provides a means of generalizing forms in *-ity*, *-ant*, *-ion*, etc. The basic schema in (24a) takes a morphological relationship between a pair of forms *a* and *b* as the basis for deducing a form *X* from an established form *c*. For example, the relationship between the adjective *grammatical* and the noun *grammaticality* can serve as the basis for deducing a nominal counterpart of *ungrammatical*. This deduction is set out in (24b), which asserts that *grammatical* is to *grammaticality* as *ungrammatical* is to **ungrammaticality**.

(24)　Analogical extensions
　　a.　$a : b = c : X$
　　b.　*grammatical : grammaticality = ungrammatical : X*
　　c.　$X =$ *ungrammaticality*

Similar deductions can account for the generalization of other nonproduct-ive exponents. The correspondence between *complete* and *completion* and the existence of the form *incomplete* permit the extension of *-ion* in the form *incom-pletion*, understood in the sense of an 'incomplete forward pass' in American football. In this way, the traditional process of analogical deduction extends the use of exponents that do not freely combine with new bases. However, the resulting forms often resist the sort of 'compositional' analyses that can usually be assigned to productive formations. On first exposure, analogized formations may even have something of a neologistic character, though the intended interpretation is usually salient, and comes to be associated with the new term.

The contrast between *ungrammaticality* and *ungrammaticalness* highlights a key difference between analogized back-formations and productive formations (irrespective of whether productive forms are attributed to 'word-building' rules or to productive analogical principles of the sort proposed in Paul 1968 [1880]). The analysis of *ungrammaticalness* is given in (25). The adjective *grammatical* provides a base for the derived adjective *ungrammatical*, which underlies the nominalization *ungrammaticalness*. The structure in (25) also corresponds transparently to the interpretation of un*grammaticalness*, which is normally understood as 'the state or property of being ungrammatical,' rather than as the negation of 'the state or property of being grammatical.'

(25)　$[_N [_A$ un $[_A$ grammatical$]]$ ness$]$

The analysis of *ungrammaticality* is much less straightforward, as any structure that combines *-ity* and *un-* with the base *grammatical* will tend to violate the distributional restrictions on one of these exponents. The analyses in (26) exhibit the two possible orders for combining *-ity* and *un-*.

(26)　Derivational bracketing 'paradoxes'
　　a.　$[_N$ un $[_N [_A$ grammatical$]$ ity$]]$
　　b.　$[_N [_A$ un $[_A$ grammatical$]]$ ity$]$

Models that treat Latinate exponents as productive usually classify *-ity* is a primary or 'level 1' suffix and *un-* as a secondary or 'level 11' prefix. This dictates the structure in (26a), in which *-ity* combines with *grammatical*, yield-ing the nominal *grammaticality*, to which *un-* then attaches. This structure is motivated by the assumption that level affixes may induce stress shift, from grammátical to grammaticálity in this case. Yet this structure clearly violates the distributional constraints on *un-*, which otherwise attaches to adjectives, not nouns. The alternative in (26b) observes the constraints on *un-*, by combining *un-* first with the adjective *grammatical*, and then attaching *-ity*. This analysis also corresponds more transparently to the semantic analysis. But (26b) violates the generalization that level affixes attach before level affixes. The fact that the distributional requirements of -*ity* and *un*- are not mutually satisfiable leads to an impasse – or a 'paradox' – if one assumes that both exponents combine with *grammatical* to form *ungrammaticality*. It does not really matter whether one thinks of the analyses in (26) as representing a part-whole structure, as in Lieber (1992), or whether one regards the analyses as representing the order in which word formation rules are applied to *grammatical*, as in Anderson (1992) or Stump (2001). The introduction of -*ity* in these analyses is problematic, whether the exponent is assigned to an entry or associated with a rule. An analogical analysis avoids this problem, by treating *ungrammaticality* as a type of back formation in which -*ity* is not an immediate exponent. This analysis represents a trivial extension of the general account of bracketing paradoxes in Spencer (1988). The traditional schema in (24a) is a more general form of the 'proportional analogy' that Spencer (1988: 675) proposes as 'a general principle of English word formation operating over entries in the permanent lexicon.' As Spencer (1988) shows, this principle sanctions a wide range of cases, from truncations, such as *psycholinguist*, derived from the pair *linguistics–linguist* and the established form *psycholinguistics*, to compounds, such as *baroque flautist*, from the pair *flute–flautist* and the established form *baroque flute*. Hence, extensions of nonproductive exponents and the existence of various classes of bracketing paradoxes in English can both be understood 'if we don't treat [them] as the result of morphological derivation, but rather as a kind of back-formation licensed by existing lexical entries' (Spencer 1988: 675).

Bracketing paradoxes have attracted considerable attention in the morphological literature (see, e.g., Williams 1981; Stump 1991; Sproat 1992), and various strategies have been proposed for segregating demands that appear not to be satisfiable in a single structure. Yet if established lexical forms play the role that Spencer (1988) proposes, it may be that many apparent 'paradoxes' are just a symptom of misapplying a productive analysis on analogized patterns. This suggests in turn that much of the complexity attributed to the English derivational system – from levels and sublexicons through mechanisms for resolving bracketing paradoxes – compensates for the reluctance to distinguish productive from nonproductive processes in Chomsky and Halle (1968). Productivity has since become more of an active research topic, and the large and growing literature concerned with the productivity of derivational formations includes Baayen (1992), Plag (1999), and Bauer (2001).

3.4   *Organization of derivational and inflectional processes*

Overall, the morphological system of English exhibits a simple organization, which is mirrored to some degree by the simple morphotactic structure of non-compound words. English retains a stock of native Germanic stems, along with a sizeable collection of borrowings, many of Latinate origin. In some cases, sub-units within these items have become established as independent stems or derivational exponents. However, the morphotactic patterns exhibited by many Latinate formations, although transparent in varying degrees to the speaker or analyst, are not extended beyond an original stock of forms. Descriptive strategies designed to restrict particular exponents to a Latinate 'sublexicon' implicitly concede the point that these elements do not have the status of independent units in English. Similar remarks apply to any elements restricted to a Germanic 'sublexicon.'

Word forms are often assigned a relatively uniform structure in English. Lexical roots are usually assumed to be modified by the category-preserving processes in section 3.1, which are chiefly prefixal, and by category-changing processes in section 3.2, which are exclusively suffixal. The output of these derivational processes provides a base for the few remaining inflectional suffixes of English. As noted in section 2, neither verbs nor adjectives retain personal agreement markers. The one regular verbal agreement exponent, -*s*, is more accurately described as marking non-agreement. The plural marker -*s* is the sole productive noun inflection, as case is no longer distinctive even for pronouns.

FURTHER READING

Detailed descriptions of the English morphological system can be found in the two comprehensive grammars of modern English, Quirk et al. (1985) and Huddleston and Pullum et al. (2002). Aspects of the English system are also covered in many general introductions to morphological theory, including Bauer (1988), Spencer (1991) and Haspelmath (2002). Other general works, including Matthews (1991), Carstairs-McCarthy (1992), and Spencer and Zwicky (1998), provide further discussion of some of the theoretical and methodological issues that arise in descriptions of the English system.

REFERENCES

Ackerman, F. and Stump, G. (2004) Paradigms and periphrastic expression: a study in realization-based lexicalism. In A. Spencer and L. Sadler (eds.), *Projecting morphology*. Stanford: CSLI Publications, 111–58.

Ackerman, F. and Webelhuth, G. (1998) *A theory of predicates*. Stanford: CSLI Publications.

Anderson, S. R. (1992) *A-morphous morphology*. Cambridge: Cambridge University Press.

Aronoff, M. (1976) *Word formation in generative grammar*. Cambridge, MA: MIT Press.

Aronoff, M. (1994) *Morphology by itself: stems and inflectional classes*. Cambridge, MA: MIT Press.

Baayen, R. H. (1992) Quantitative aspects of morphological productivity. In G. Booij and J. van Marle (eds.), *Yearbook of morphology 1991*. Dordrecht: Kluwer, 109–50.

Bauer, L. (1988) *Introducing linguistic morphology*. Edinburgh: Edinburgh University Press.

Bauer, L. (2001) *Morphological productivity*. Cambridge: Cambridge University Press.

Beard, R. (1995) *Lexeme-morpheme base morphology: a general theory of inflection and word formation*. Albany, NY: SUNY Press.

Blevins, J. P. (2001) Paradigmatic derivation. *Transactions of the Philological Society* 99, 211–22.

Blevins, J. P. (2003a) Passives and impersonals. *Journal of Linguistics* 39, 473–520.

Blevins, J. P. (2003b) Stems and paradigms. *Language* 79, 737–67.

Blevins, J. P. (2005) Remarks on gerunds. In C. O. Orgun and P. Sells (eds.), *Morphology and the web of grammar: essays In memory of Steven G. Lapointe*. Stanford: CSLI Publications, 25–47.

Bloomfield, L. (1933) *Language*. Chicago: University of Chicago Press.

Booij, G. (1996) Inherent verses contextual inflection and the split morphology hypothesis. G. Booij and J. van Marle (eds.), *Yearbook of morphology 1995*. Dordrecht: Kluwer, 1–16.

Börjars, K., Vincent, N., and Chapman, C. (1997) Paradigms, pronominal inflection and periphrasis. In G. Booij and J. van Marle (eds.), *Yearbook of morphology 1996*. Dordrecht: Kluwer, 155–80.

Bresnan, J. (1982) The passive in lexical theory. In J. Bresnan (ed.), *The mental representation of grammatical relations*. Cambridge, MA: MIT Press, 3–86.

Bresnan, J. (2001) *Lexical-functional syntax*. Oxford: Blackwell.

Carstairs-McCarthy, A. (1992) *Current morphology*. London: Routledge.

Chomsky, N. (1957) *Syntactic structures*. The Hague: Mouton.

Chomsky, N. (1970) Remarks on nominalization. In R. A. Jacobs and P. S. Rosenbaum (eds.), *Readings in English transformational grammar*. Waltham: Ginn and Company, 232–86. Reprinted in *Studies on semantics in generative grammar*. The Hague: Mouton, 1–61.

Chomsky, N. (1975) *The logical structure of linguistic theory*. Chicago: University of Chicago Press.

Chomsky, N. (1995) *The minimalist program*. Cambridge, MA: MIT Press.

Chomsky, N. and Halle, M. (1968) *The sound pattern of English*. New York: Harper & Row.

Clahsen, H. (1999) Lexical entries and rules of language: a multidisciplinary study of German inflection. *Behavioral and Brain Sciences* 22, 991–1013.

Corbett, G. (1991) *Gender*. Cambridge: Cambridge University Press.

Curme, G. O. (1935) *A grammar of the English language*, vol. 1: *Parts of speech and accidence*. Boston: Heath.

Harris, Z. S. (1951) *Methods in structural linguistics*. Chicago: University of Chicago Press.

Haspelmath, M. (1996) Word-class-changing inflection and morphological theory. In G. Booij and J. van Marle (eds.), *Yearbook of morphology 1995*. Dordrecht: Kluwer, 43–66.

Haspelmath, M. (2002) *Understanding morphology*. London: Arnold.

Hock, H. H. (1991) *Principles of historical linguistics*, 2nd edn. Berlin: Mouton de Gruyter.

Hockett, C. F. (1947) Problems of morphemic analysis. *Language* 23, 321–43. Reprinted in Joos (1957), 229–42.

Huddleston, R. D. (1984) *Introduction to the grammar of English*. Cambridge: Cambridge University Press.

Huddleston, R. D., Pullum, G. K., et al. (2002) *The Cambridge grammar of the English language*. Cambridge: Cambridge University Press.

Hudson, R. (1995) Does English really have case? *Journal of Linguistics* 375–92.

Jackendoff, R. (1977) *X-syntax*. Cambridge, MA: MIT Press.

Jespersen, O. (1933) *Essentials of English grammar*. London: Allen and Unwin.

Joos, M. (ed.) (1957) *Readings in linguistics*, vol. I. Chicago: University of Chicago Press.

Kay, P. and Filmore, C. J. (1999) Grammatical constructions and linguistic generalizations: The *what's X doing Y?* construction. *Language* 75, 1–33.

Kiparsky, P. (1982) Lexical phonology and morphology. In *Linguistics in the morning calm*. Seoul: Hanshin, 3–91.

Klein, W. (1992) The present perfect puzzle. *Language* 68, 535–52.

Lee, S.-A. (2004) Progressive and aspectual verb constructions in English. Ph.D. thesis, University of Cambridge.

Lieb, H.-H. (2003) Notions of paradigm in grammar. In D. A. Cruse (ed.), *Lexikologie/Lexicology*. (Handbücher zur Sprach- und Kommunikationswissenschaft) Berlin: Mouton de Gruyter.

Lieber, R. (1992) *Deconstructing morphology*. Chicago: University of Chicago Press.

Marchand, H. (1966) *The categories and types of present-day English word-formation: a synchronic-diachronic approach*. University of Alabama Press.

Matthews, P. H. (1991) *Morphology*. Cambridge: Cambridge University Press.

Paul, H. (1968) *Prinzipien der Sprachgeschichte*. Tübingen: Max Niemayer Verlag.

Plag, I. (1999) *Morphological productivity: structural constraints in English derivation*. Berlin: Mouton de Gruyter.

Pullum, G. K. (1991) English nominal gerund phrases as noun phrases with verb-phrase heads. *Linguistics* 763–99.

Quirk, R., Greenbaum, S., Leech, G., and Svartvik, J. (1985) *A comprehensive grammar of the English language*. London: Longman.

van Riemsdijk, H. (1983) The case of German adjectives. In F. Heny and B. Richards (eds.), *Linguistic categories: auxiliaries and related puzzles*. Dordrecht: Reidel, 223–52.

Ross, J. R. (1969) Auxiliaries as main verbs. *Journal of Philosophical Linguistics* 1, 77–102.

Sag, I. A., Gazdar, G., Wasow, T., and Weisler, S. (1985) Coordination and how to distinguish categories. *Natural Language and Linguistic Theory*, 117–71.

Spencer, A. (1988) Bracketing paradoxes and the English lexicon. *Language* 64, 663–82.

Spencer, A. (1991) *Morphological theory*. Oxford: Blackwell.

Spencer, A. (1999) Transpositions and argument structure. In G. Booij and J. van Marle (eds.), *Yearbook of morphology 1998*. Dordrecht: Foris, 79–102.

Spencer, A. (2001) The paradigm-based model of morphosyntax. *Transactions of the Philological Society* 99, 279–313.

Spencer, A. and Zwicky, A. M. (eds.) (1998) *Handbook of morphology*. Oxford: Blackwell.

Sproat, R. (1992) *Unhappier* is not a bracketing paradox. *Linguistic Inquiry* 23, 347–52.

Stump, G. T. (1995) The uniformity of head marking in morphological theory. In G. Booij and J. van Marle (eds.), *Yearbook of morphology 1994*. Dordrecht: Kluwer, 245–96.

Stump, G. T. (1991) A paradigm-based theory of morphological mismatches. *Language* 67, 675–725.

Stump, G. T. (2001) *Inflectional morphology: a theory of paradigm structure*. Cambridge: Cambridge University Press.

Taylor, A. (1994) Variation in past tense formation in the history of English. In *University of Pennsylvania Working Papers in Linguistics 1*. Philadelphia, 143–59.

Wells, R. (1947) Immediate constituents. *Language* 23, 81–117. Reprinted in Joos (1957), 186–207.

Williams, E. (1981) On the notions "lexically related" and "head of a word." *Linguistic Inquiry* 12, 245–74.

Zwicky, A. M. (1987) Suppressing the Zs. *Journal of Linguistics* 23, 133–48.

Zwicky, A. M. and Pullum, G. K. (1983) Cliticization vs. inflection: English *n't*. *Language* 59, 502–13.

23   Productivity

INGO PLAG

1   Introduction

Speakers of English (and of course also of other languages) can coin new words on the basis of other words or word-forming elements. For example, we can turn the adjective *cute* into a noun *cuteness* by adding the suffix *-ness*, or we can form a new compound by joining two existing words, as in *train connection*. A closer analysis of such word-formation processes reveals that much of what happens in this domain is rule-governed, in the sense that there are predictable form-meaning relationships among similar morphologically complex words. For example, we can say that adjectives regularly can take the suffix *-ness* and that *-ness* derivatives regularly express a meaning that can be paraphrased as 'the property of being X,' with 'X' standing for the meaning of the base.

Assuming the existence of such morphological rules, patterns or processes according to which complex words are formed, one can easily observe that some rules (or affixes) are quite often used to create new words, whereas others are less often used, or not used at all for this purpose. For example, it seems that no new verb can be formed in Modern English with the help of the prefix *en-* (as in *enlist, enroll, enshrine*, etc.), while the verbal suffix *-ize* happily adjoins to adjectives or nouns to make up new verbs (as in *peripheralize*, first attested 1987 and *Clintonize*, first attested 1992, both according to the *OED*).

In this sense, some morphological rules can be called productive and other rules unproductive or less productive. A number of interesting questions arise from this fact. What makes a given rule productive or unproductive? How can we measure the productivity of a given rule and which mechanisms are responsible for the variability in the productivity of morphological processes?

Another important theoretical problem is whether productivity should be regarded as a theoretical primitive, i.e. a non-derivable property of word formation rules, or an epiphenomenon, i.e. a property that results from other properties of the rule in question or some yet-to-be-detected mechanisms. It is clear, for example, that the productivity of a rule is never unrestricted in the sense that any given word may serve as its base. In particular, there can be phonological, morphological, syntactic, and semantic conditions on possible bases, or on the derivatives themselves, which may limit the productivity of the process.

The notion of productivity is relevant also for the common distinction between inflection and derivation (see ch. 22). It is commonly assumed (e.g. Haspelmath, 2002: 75) that inflectional processes are fully productive, whereas derivational processes are characterized by varying degrees of productivity, with the majority not being fully productive. In other words, inflectional processes apply to all words of a given word class, which is not the case for derivational processes. For example, all verbs in English can take the past tense morpheme, but not all verbs take the adjectivizing suffix *-ive* (*invent* – *invented* – *inventive, associate* – *associated* – *associative,* but *call* – *called* – **callive, cite* – *cited* – **citive*). Though intuitively appealing, there are some problems with the idea that inflection is fully productive. For example, one could argue that though fully productive as a category, the *regular* past tense affix {*-ed*} (with its three allomorphs [d], [t] and [əd]) is not fully productive, since there are quite a number of verbs which do not take one of these allomorphs, but use ablaut (e.g. *sang, dug*), change their stems (e.g. *brought*), take no overt suffix (e.g. *put*), or use a combination of different coding strategies (e.g. *kept*). Such ill-behaved verbs are of course well known as 'irregular verbs,' and, in order to save productivity as a distinguishing criterion between inflection and derivation, we could simply say that all *regular* inflection is fully productive while derivational morphology is not. This would, however, create the problem that regular derivational processes could be said to be fully productive. Hence, productivity is an issue that seems not only relevant in word-formation but also in inflection. For reasons of space, we will confine our discussion of productivity in this chapter to derivational morphology.

Most of the more recent discussion on the nature of productivity has focused on English and empirical studies of productivity in other languages are still scarce. The reason for this state of affairs lies primarily in the availability of modern analytical tools, such as large electronic text corpora, lexical data bases and electronic dictionaries. English happens to be the language for which the these tools were readily available for the first time. It seems, however, that the findings and concepts developed using English as the sample language can be easily extended and applied to other languages, provided that the necessary methodological tools are available (cf. e.g. Evert and Lüdeling 2001 on German; Gaeta and Ricca 2003 on Italian).

2   Qualitative and Quantitative Aspects of Productivity

One important theoretical question concerning the nature of productivity is whether productivity is a quantitative or a qualitative notion. If productivity is of a qualitative nature, a process or affix could be said to either have this property or not. Alternatively, it has frequently been argued that productivity is a gradual phenomenon, which means that morphological processes are either more or less productive than others, and that completely unproductive or fully productive processes only mark the end-points of a scale. In the following subsection I will lay out the qualitative concept of productivity, which will be followed in section 2.2. by a discussion of approaches that have attempted to devise quantitative measures of productivity.

2.1 *Qualitative approaches*

Definitions of productivity can be found in any standard morphology textbook. Adams (1973: 197), for example, uses "the epithet 'productive' to describe a pattern, meaning that when occasion demands, the pattern may be used as a model for new items." Bauer (1983: 18) says that a word formation process is productive "if it can be used synchronically in the production of new forms," Spencer (1991: 49) considers a rule productive if it is "regularly and actively used in the creation of totally new words," and Plag (2003: 44) defines productivity as "[t]he property of an affix to be used to coin new complex words." These definitions may suggest that productivity is an all-or-nothing property of morphological processes. In one of the most recent monographs on productivity, Bauer (2001) explicitly advocates the all-or-nothing view, when, drawing on earlier work by Corbin (1987), he divides productivity into two distinct phenomena, one of them qualitative, the other quantitative in nature: availability and profitability. A morphological process is defined as available if it can be used to produce new words. "Availability is a yes/no question: either a process is available or it is not." (Bauer 2001: 205). Profitability, on the other hand, is the extent to which a morphological process may be employed to create new pertinent forms. This is a quantitative notion, and we will postpone the discussion of profitability until later.

The most problematic point concerning availability is the notion of 'morphological process' (or often called 'word formation rule') itself. Given a set of seemingly related words, on which grounds can one assume the existence of a word-formation rule as being responsible for the creation of these words? In general one would say that we can speak of a rule if there is a sufficient number of regular form-meaning correspondences of individual items, i.e. a recognizable pattern. The theoretical status of such patterns is however controversial. Some scholars believe that what has been traditionally called 'rule' or 'process' is just a larger set of words that are related to one another by the very general mechanism of analogy (e.g. Becker 1990; or, more recently, Skousen et al. 2002). And this analogical mechanism can also be used to coin words on an individual, idiosyncratic basis, which is what earlier, or more traditional, accounts of analogy are more concerned with. The problem now is that in a purely qualitative approach to productivity, an unproductive process would not be able to give rise to new formations at all. Empirically, however, we find that supposedly unproductive processes sometimes do yield new formations, because speakers use existing derivatives to form new words by way of pro-portional analogy. If this only happens once or twice, we might still say this is an unproductive rule, but where would we draw the line between productive and unproductive processes, if more words are coined? Would we say a process is productive after we have found two, three, five, ten, or twenty new analogical forms?

These considerations lead to the conclusion that even in a qualitative approach to productivity one has to assume the existence of three types of processes: Those that are clearly unproductive (with not even occasional analogical coin-ages), those that are clearly productive, and those processes that are not easily classified as either productive or unproductive. This is also acknowledged by Bauer, when he writes that "there might be cases of uncertainty" (2001: 205) with regard to the availability of a word-formation process.

In view of these problems, many researchers have abandoned the idea of a qualitative notion of productivity and have turned to the exact determination of what was introduced above as 'profitability.' These researchers have sought measures by which the productivity (here: profitability) of processes can be assessed, to the effect that totally unproductive and fully productive processes are conceptualized as end-points on a scale.

2.2   *Quantitative approaches*

A good starting point for quantitative measures of productivity is the definition by Bolinger (1948), which is based on the idea that productivity can be seen as a kind of probability. In his words, productivity is "the statistical readiness with which an element enters into new combinations" (1948: 18). Since the formulation of this definition more than half a century ago, a number of pro-ductivity measures have been proposed that try to model the insight behind this definition.

One prominent definition says that the productivity of an affix can be measured by counting the number of attested types (i.e. different words) with that affix at a given point in time, for example by counting the number of pertinent forms in an unabridged dictionary. The problem with this measure is that there can be many words with a given affix, but nevertheless speakers will not use the suffix very often to make up new words. In other words, the fact that the language has already many words with a given affix indicates that the suffix must have been productive at some period in the past. For example, many words with the nominalizing suffix *-ment* (*entertainment*, *punishment*, etc.) can be found, but the suffix was mainly productive between the mid-sixteenth and the mid-nineteenth century (e.g. Bauer 2001: 181). Similarly, the verbalizing suffix *-en* (as in *blacken*) is attested in numerous words, but hardly any of them was coined after 1900 (e.g. Plag 1999: 98).

Aronoff (1976) suggests a different productivity measure, the ratio of actual to possible words. 'Actual word' refers to existing established words with a given affix, while 'possible word' (or 'potential word') refers to words which could in principle be formed with that affix. The higher this ratio, the higher the productivity of a given rule. Largely ignored by later authors, this measure had already been proposed earlier by Berschin, who labeled it "Besetzungsgrad" ('degree of exhaustion,' 1971: 44–5). Anshen and Aronoff (1981: 64) point out the main weakness of this proposal: for extremely productive and for completely unproductive processes it makes wrong predictions. Thus, with highly productive affixes like *-ness* the number of potential words is, in principle, infinite, which necessarily leads to a comparatively low productivity index. With unproductive rules like *-th* nominalization it is unclear how the ratio of actual to possible words should be calculated. If one considers all actual words with this suffix as possible words, the ratio equals 1, which is the highest possible score and therefore counterintuitive. If, however, the number of possible words with this suffix is considered zero, the index cannot be computed at all.

Another, more general problem of Berschin's and Aronoff's proposals is how to actually count the number of possible words, since the number of possible formations on the basis of a productive rule is, in principle, uncountable, because new potential base words (e.g. new adjectives as bases for *-ness*) may enter the language any time. How can one quantify something that is, in principle, uncountable?

Coming back to the idea of counting the number of derivatives, one can say that this may still be a fruitful way of determining the productivity of an affix, namely if one does not count all derivatives with a certain affix in use at a given point in time, but only those derivatives that were newly coined in a given period, the so-called neologisms. In doing this, one can show that, for instance, an affix may have given rise to many neologisms in the eighteenth century but not in the twentieth century. The number of neologisms in a given period is usually determined with the help of historical dictionaries like the *OED*, which aims at giving thorough and complete information on all words of the language. For example, for the period from 1900 through 1985 we find 284 new verbs in *-ize* (Plag 1999: ch. 5) in the *OED*, which shows that this is a productive suffix. The power of the *OED* as a tool for measuring productivity should however not be overestimated, because quite a number of new words escape the eyes of the *OED* lexicographers. For instance, the number of *-ness* neologisms listed in the *OED* for the twentieth century (N = 279, Plag 1999: 98) roughly equals the number of *-ize* neologisms, although it is clear from many studies that *-ness* is much more productive than *-ize* (e.g. Plag et al. 1999; Hay and Baayen 2002).

Thus, in those cases where the *OED* does not list many neologisms it may be true that the affix is unproductive, but it is also possible that the pertinent neologisms simply have been overlooked (or not included for some other, unknown reason). Only in those cases where the *OED* lists many neologisms can we be sure that the affix in question must be productive. Given these problems involved with dictionary-based measures (even if a superb dictionary like the *OED* is available), one should also look for other, and perhaps more reliable measures of productivity.

Harald Baayen and his collaborators (1993ff) have developed some corpus-based productivity measures, which all rely on the availability of very large electronic text corpora. Such corpora are, for example, the British National Corpus (BNC) or the Cobuild Corpus, the former containing c. 100 million word tokens, the latter originally containing c. 18 million words, now having been turned into the ever-increasing Bank of English. The word lists that can be extracted from such corpora are the basis for corpus-based productivity research.

The first corpus-based measure to be mentioned here is the number of types, i.e. different words with a given affix. This measure, also known as the type-frequency *V*, has been discussed above, only that it is calculated here not on the basis of a dictionary, but on the basis of a representative language sample.

Two other measures proposed by Baayen rely heavily on the notion of hapax legomenon. Hapax legomena (or 'hapaxes' for short) are words that occur only once in a corpus. Such words are crucial for the determination of the productivity of a morphological process because in very large corpora hapaxes tend to be words that are unlikely to be familiar to the hearer or reader. Complex unknown words can be understood at least in those cases where an available word-formation rule allows the decomposition of the newly encountered word into its constituent morphemes and thus the computation of the meaning on the basis of the meaning of the parts. The word-formation rule in the mental lexicon guarantees that even complex words with extremely low frequency can be understood. Thus, with regard to productive processes, we expect large numbers of low frequency words and small numbers of high frequency words, with the former keeping the rule alive. In contrast, unproductive morphological categories will be characterized by a preponderance of words with rather high frequencies and by a small number of words with low frequencies.

The crucial point now is that, even if not all of the hapaxes with a given affix may be neologisms, we can be confident that it is among the hapaxes (as against words that have a higher frequency) that we find the highest proportion of neologisms (see, for example, Baayen and Renouf 1996; Plag 2003, for discussion). Given that the number of hapaxes of a given morphological category should correlate with the number of neologisms of that category, the number of hapaxes can be seen as an indicator of productivity. Note that it is not claimed that a hapax legomenon *is* a neologism. A hapax legomenon is defined with respect to a given corpus, and could therefore simply be a rare word of the language (instead of a newly coined derivative) or some weird ad-hoc invention by an imaginative speaker, as sometimes found in poetry or advertisement. The latter kinds of coinages are, however, extremely rare and can be easily weeded out.

The size of the corpus plays an important role in determining the nature of hapaxes. When the corpus is small, most hapax legomena will indeed be well-known words of the language. However, as the corpus size increases, the proportion of neologisms among the hapax legomena increases, and it is precisely among the hapax legomena that the greatest number of neologisms appear. The number of hapaxes is therefore an important measure for estimating the productivity of a morphological process.

There are, of course, methodological problems that need to be considered. First, as already mentioned, there is the question of corpus size. Small corpora like the 1 million word Wellington Corpus of Written New Zealand English are certainly too small for this kind of approach (cf. Bauer 2001: 150ff). Furthermore, there seem to be some rare cases of morphological categories where the proportion of neologisms among the hapaxes is unexpectedly low (see Plag 1999: 112ff). Other methodological problems concern the determination of pertinent word forms, involving sometimes empirically and theoretically problematic decisions. For example, it is not so easy to develop consistent criteria for or against the inclusion of words such as *entity*, *quantity*, *celebrity* as *-ity* derivatives. Such forms occur in abundance in English especially because this language has borrowed a large stock of its vocabulary from other languages (e.g. French, Latin, Greek). Often such words were morphologically complex in the donor languages but were not necessarily decomposed in the borrowing process. If many words with the same affix were borrowed, however, this may have eventually led to the reanalysis of most words of the category and even to a more or less productive derivational process in English, but with a residue of words, whose status as complex words remained questionable (see Dalton-Puffer 1996 for some discussion). In general, the so-called Latinate affixes seem less productive than native affixes (e.g. Plag 2003: chs. 4 and 7). Apart from borrowing, problems of classification can also arise through lexicalization, a process in which a complex word can adopt new and idiosyncratic senses which are no longer identical with the general meaning of the morphological category. For example, *curiosity* has the predictable meaning of 'property of being curious,' but it has also lexicalized the rather idiosyncratic meaning 'curious thing.'

In general the above-mentioned problems of classification are inherent in all work on derivational morphology and not restricted to a particular language or to corpus-based investigations (see Plag 1999: ch. 5; or Bauer 2001: section 5.3, for more discussion).

Coming back to the idea of estimating the probability with which new words are coined, we turn to Baayen's 'productivity in the narrow sense.' This measure calculates the ratio of the number of hapaxes with a given affix and the number of all tokens containing that affix. Metaphorically speaking, when calculating this measure we are going through all attested tokens with a given affix and picking out all words that we encounter only once. If we then divide the number of these words (i.e. the number of hapaxes) by the number of all tokens with that affix, we arrive at the probability of finding a hitherto unattested word (i.e. 'new' in terms of the corpus) among all the words of that category. This probability can be expressed by the following formula, where

P stands for 'productivity in the narrow sense,' n_1^{aff} for the number of hapaxes with a given affix and N^{aff} stands for the number of all tokens with that affix.

(1) $P = \dfrac{n_1^{\text{aff}}}{N^{\text{aff}}}$

P can be interpreted in such a way that a large number of hapaxes leads to a high value of *P*, thus indicating a productive morphological process. Conversely, large numbers of high frequency items lead to a high value of N^{aff}, hence to a decrease of *P*, indicating low productivity.

To summarize our review of different productivity measures, we can distinguish between the following methods:

- Using a text corpus or a large dictionary, productivity can be measured by counting the number of attested different words with a particular affix (i.e. the type-frequency *V*). The greater the type-frequency, the higher the productivity of the affix. This measure is, however, indicative of past, rather than present productivity.
- Productivity can be measured by counting the number of neologisms in a given period, using, for instance, a large historical dictionary. The greater the number of neologisms in that period, the higher the productivity of a given affix in that period.
- Productivity can be measured by counting the number of hapaxes with a given affix (n_1) in a large corpus. The higher the number of hapaxes, the greater the productivity.
- Finally, by dividing the number of hapaxes with a given affix by the number of tokens with that affix, we arrive at *P*, which indicates the probability of finding new words among all the tokens of a particular morphological category.

For illustration and discussion of the different productivity measures, let us look at some suffixes for which these measures are readily available, *-ion, -ist, -ity, -ish, -less, -ness* and *wise* (from Plag et al. 1999; Plag 2002; based on data from BNC and *OED*). Table 23.1 raises the question of which suffix is most productive. Let us first regroup the table according to each measure in the descending order of their values.

Table 23.2 reveals that each measure establishes a different productivity ranking, such that the different measures seem to contradict each other. However, as we will shortly see, this is not the case, since the different measures highlight different aspects of productivity.

The adverb-forming suffix *-wise* seems to be the most extreme case. While of highest productivity according to *P* it is of extremely low productivity according to the other measures. How can this paradox be solved? The low rank of *-wise* in terms of *V* and n_1 is an indication of the fact that it is a suffix that is used comparatively rarely. Not very many derivatives are used nor are

Table 23.1 Productivity measures and token frequencies of some affixes in the BNC and OED

	V	N^{aff}	n_1^{aff}	P	OED neologisms
-ion	2,392	1,369,116	524	0.00038	625
-ish	491	7,745	262	0.0338	101
-ist	1,207	98,823	354	0.0036	552
-ity	1,372	371,747	341	0.00092	487
-less	681	28,340	272	0.0096	103
-ness	2,466	106,957	943	0.0088	279
-wise	183	2,091	128	0.061	12

Table 23.2 Ranking of suffixes according to different measures of productivity

Rank	V		N		n_1		P		OED neologisms	
1	-ness	2,466	-ion	1,369,116	-ness	943	-wise	0.061	-ion	625
2	-ion	2,392	-ity	371,747	-ion	524	-ish	0.0338	-ist	552
3	-ity	1,372	-ness	106,957	-ist	354	-ness	0.0096	-ity	487
4	-ist	1,207	-ist	98,823	-ity	341	-less	0.0088	-ness	279
5	-less	681	-less	28,340	-less	272	-ist	0.0036	-less	103
6	-ish	491	-ish	7,745	-ish	262	-ity	0.00092	-ish	101
7	-wise	183	-wise	2,091	-wise	128	-ion	0.00038	-wise	12

very many newly coined. However, the high value of P shows that among all types with the suffix -wise the number of new coinages is quite high, such that the proportion of unknown words among all the -wise derivatives is high, indicating the suffix's potential to be easily used for the coinage of new forms, if need be. A look at some forms attested in the BNC supports this impression (cited from Dalton-Puffer and Plag 2000: 237):

(2) a. Bridhe lifted the baby, slipped a magic coral and rowan-berry necklace over his head and walked **sun-wise** round the bed three times for good fortune.

    b. They make no special demands **food-wise**, and tolerate a wide pH range.

The *OED* ranking reflects the fact that -*wise* words are, though easily derivable, not often used. The suffix -*ish* is very similar to -*wise* in this respect.

Turning to -*ion*, -*ity*, -*ist*, and -*less*, we can state that according to type-frequency, number of hapaxes and number of neologisms the suffixes -*ion*, -*ity*, and -*ist* must be regarded as quite productive, whereas the suffix -*less* is less productive. However, according to the *P* measure, the situation is exactly the opposite: -*less* must be regarded as more productive, and the suffixes -*ion*, -*ity*, and -*ist* as ranking very low on the scale. This apparent contradiction can be solved in the following way. The suffix -*less* does not occur in very many different words, and these words are also not so frequently used, hence the lower *V* and *N* figures, and the comparatively small number of hapaxes and *OED* neologisms. If we, however, only consider the words within this morphological category, we find that the *proportion* of hapaxes among all tokens is very high, which means that there is a high probability of finding new forms among all the words with -*less*. And this high probability is expressed by a high *P* measure. In less technical terms, the apparent contradiction can be explained by saying that we obviously don't use -*less* words a lot, but it is very easy to coin new ones. The opposite is the case for the categories of -*ion*, -*ity*, and -*ist* words. Each of these categories contains many different words, but these are on average of comparatively high frequency, and the chance of finding a newly coined word among all tokens of one of these categories is comparatively low. In other words, these suffixes are very often used with existing words, but in comparison to the many words we use, we do not so often coin new ones.

Finally, -*ness* scores high in terms of type-frequency and neologisms, but due to the high number of tokens (many -*ness* words are quite frequent, e.g. *happiness*) *P* is lower than that of -*wise* and -*less*. Taking all the different aspects together, -*ness* is the most productive suffix of all. It has a relatively high productivity in the narrow sense and is at the same time also used in a great number of derivatives. The comparatively low number of *OED* neologisms is indicative of the problematic data collection method mentioned already above.

In sum, we can say that researchers have a number of different measures at their disposal to assess the productivity of word-formation processes. Each measure highlights different aspects of productivity and brings with it special methodological problems of data sampling and data analysis. In order to make sound statements about 'the' productivity of a given affix different measures should be taken into account and be interpreted carefully in the light of the methodological problems involved in their computation.

Having clarified the notion of productivity and how productivity can be measured, we may now turn to the problem of how speakers know whether they can use a given affix for the creation of new words. As we will shortly see, this has to do with the question mentioned above whether the productivity of a rule is an inherent, primitive part of that rule or a property derivable on the basis of other properties. We will deal with these issues in the next section.

3   Psycholinguistic Aspects: Productivity and the Mental Lexicon

How can speakers know that a given affix can be used to coin new words? What do productive processes have in common that unproductive processes do not have? Which properties of affixes give rise to different degrees of productivity? In this (and also in the next) section, we will try to answer these questions, making reference to recent psycholinguistic research.

In the previous section we introduced productivity measures that make crucial reference to the frequency of lexical items. The basic reasoning behind the use of frequency in computing productivity is that the frequency of complex words significantly influences the way in which we process and store them. In most current models of morphological processing, access to morphologically complex words in the mental lexicon works in two ways: by direct access to the whole word representation (the so-called 'whole word route') and by access to the decomposed elements (the so-called 'decomposition route') (see McQueen and Cutler 1998 for an overview). This means that each incoming complex word is simultaneously processed in two ways, with one way of access finally succeeding. On the decomposition route it is decomposed in its parts and the parts are being looked up individually, on the whole word route the word is looked up as a whole in the mental lexicon. The two routes are schematically shown in (3):

(3)

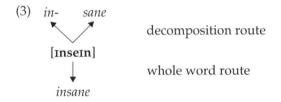

How does frequency come in here? According to Hay (2000, 2001), the degree of decomposability of a given word depends crucially on the relative frequency of the derived word and its base. Relative frequency is defined as the ratio of the frequency of the derived word to the frequency of the base and measures how frequent the derivative is with respect to its base:

(4) $f_{\text{relative}} = \dfrac{f_{\text{derivative}}}{f_{\text{base}}}$

With most complex words, the base is more frequent than the derived word, so that the relative frequency is smaller than unity. In psycholinguistic terms, the base has a stronger representation, or higher 'resting activation,' in the mental lexicon than the derived word. This leads to a preponderance of the decomposed route, since due to its high resting activation, the base will be accessed each time the derivative enters the system. In the opposite case, when the derived word is more frequent than the base, there is a whole word bias in parsing, because the resting activation of the base is lower than the resting activation of the derivative. For example, *business* is much more frequent than its base *busy* (35,141 vs. 4,879 occurrences in the BNC), so that *business* will have a whole word bias in access. Note that *business* (in the sense of 'company,' 'economic transactions' and related meanings) is also semantically and phonologically opaque, which is often the case with derivatives that have strong, i.e. lexicalized, whole word representations. Conversely, *blueness* has a base that is much more frequent than the derived form (10,059 vs. 39 in the BNC), so that there will be a strong advantage for the decomposed route. In general, the higher the frequency of the derived word in relation to the base word, the less likely is decomposition. Alternatively, the lower the frequency of the derived word in relation to the base word, the more likely is decomposition.

Hay shows that relative frequency also patterns with other properties of morphological categories: low relative frequency correlates with high productivity and low relative frequency correlates with high semantic transparency. These correlations do not come as a surprise. As already discussed in the previous section, productive morphological processes are characterized by a high number of low frequency words (i.e. many hapaxes, if we speak in terms of corpora). The lower the frequencies of derived words the lower their relative frequencies (holding the frequency of the base constant). Thus productive processes have a preponderance of words with low relative frequencies, whereas less productive morphological categories are characterized by a preponderance of words with higher relative frequencies. In a detailed study of the relation between parsing and productivity involving 80 affixes of English, Hay, and Baayen (2002) demonstrate that the more morphologically decomposable forms containing a given affix are in the lexicon, the more productive that affix will be. Thus, there is a strong relationship between relative frequency, parsing in perception and morphological productivity. Increased rates of parsing lead straightforwardly to increased productivity.

The fact that productive morphological categories are characterized by a high proportion of decomposable words is also responsible for the fact that productive processes exhibit a preponderance of semantically and phonologically transparent formations. This correlation between transparency and productivity has been established in many earlier publications (e.g. Aronoff and Schvaneveldt 1978; Anshen and Aronoff 1981; Cutler 1981).

We can now see that productive categories are semantically transparent as a consequence of processing, since productive processes favor the decomposed route, and decomposed storage strengthens the individual semantic representations of the constituent morphemes. Decomposition and individual storage of the constituent morphemes thus leaves little room for semantic drift and opacity, which arise easily under whole word access and storage, where the meanings of the parts are less likely to be activated. Hence semantic opacity and low productivity go hand in hand with high relative frequencies.

The relationship between phonological transparency and productivity is further substantiated in Hay and Baayen (2003), who investigate the role of junctural phonotactics with the 80 affixes from the earlier study. The term 'junctural phonotactics' refers to the possible combination of sounds that straddle a morphological boundary or juncture, as for example /n-a/ in the word *combin-ation*. Hay and Baayen (in press) start out from the assumption that speakers rely on phonotactics for the (pre-)processing of morphologically complex words. In pre-lexical processing, speakers posit morphological boundaries inside phoneme transitions that are unlikely to occur inside mono-morphemic words (see, e.g., Saffran et al. 1996a, 1996b, McQueen 1998). For example, the phoneme transition /pf/ (as in *cup-ful*) never occurs inside mono-morphemic English words and will therefore strongly facilitate decomposition in speech perception, while the transition /tɪ/ (as in *product-ive*) has a much higher probability of occurring morpheme-internally and will therefore not facilitate decomposition. Hay and Baayen now argue that decomposition in speech perception leads to decomposed forms in the lexicon. And, if, as stated above, decomposed forms in the lexicon lead to productivity, it can be predicted that there is a relationship between the junctural phonotactics associated with an affix, and that affix's productivity. This prediction is borne out by the facts. Hay and Baayen find a significant correlation between the kind of junctural phonotactics of an affix and that affix's productivity. Roughly speaking, the more illegal the phonemic transitions created by an affix are, the more pro-ductive that affix tends to be. Thus, phonotactics contributes probabilistically to the likelihood of decomposition and therefore to the degree of productivity.

To summarize, we can say that, psycholinguistically, productivity can be explained as a syndrome of properties, with parsability, relative frequency, semantic and phonological transparency as important factors. With regard to the question whether productivity is a derived notion or a theoretical prim-itive, we have seen that the productivity of an affix results in a complex fashion from the above-mentioned processing factors. Among these factors, semantic and phonological transparency are not only psycholinguistically, but also structurally determined in that it is the semantic and phonological structure of affixes and their derivatives that co-determine processing and storage of these forms. In the following, we will see that there are many more structural factors that play a significant role in influencing – and constraining – productivity. It is these factors that are responsible for the fact that Hay and Baayen's findings are not exceptionless principles but strong probabilistic tendencies, which are sometimes overruled by structural restrictions (see Plag 2002 for discussion).

4   Productivity Restrictions

One important factor restricting the productivity is of course the usefulness of a newly coined word for the speakers of the language. No matter which function a particular derivative serves in a particular situation, intended usefulness is a necessary prerequisite for the emergence of productively formed derivatives. But not all potentially useful words are actually created and used, which means that there must be certain restrictions at work. We must distinguish between, on the one hand, the general possibility to apply a word-formation rule to form a new word and, on the other hand, the opportunity to use such newly coined derivatives in speech. Both aspects are subject to different kinds of restriction, namely those restrictions that originate in problems of language use (so-called pragmatic restrictions) and those restrictions that originate in problems of language structure (so-called structural restrictions). We will discuss each type of restriction in turn.

4.1   *Pragmatic restrictions*

One of the most obvious usage-based factors influencing productivity is fashion. The rise and fall of affixes like *mega-*, *giga-*, *mini-* or *-nik* is an example of the result of extra-linguistic developments in society which make certain words or morphological elements desirable to use and therefore productive.

Another pragmatic requirement new lexemes must meet is that they denote something nameable. Although the nameability requirement is rather ill-defined, it captures a significant insight: the concepts encoded by derivational categories tend to be rather simple and general (e.g. adjectival *un-* 'not X,' verbal *-en* 'make X,' etc.) and may not be highly specific or complex, as illustrated in the example of an unlikely denominal verb forming category given by Rose (1973: 516): "grasp NOUN in the left hand and shake vigorously while standing on the right foot in a 2.5 gallon galvanized pail of corn-meal-mush." This does not mean, however, that more complex notions cannot be encoded by affixes, but that this requirement seems to be language-specific and is a mere tendency.

The problem with pragmatic restrictions is that, given a seemingly impossible new formation, it is not clear whether it is ruled out on structural grounds or on the basis of pragmatic considerations. Before claiming that a certain form is impossible due to pragmatic restrictions, it is therefore necessary to take a closer look at the structural restrictions involved, which often reveal that a form is impossible because it violates pertinent phonological, morphological, syntactic, or semantic restrictions.

4.2   *Structural restrictions*

Structural restrictions (or constraints) in word-formation may concern the traditional levels of linguistic analysis, i.e. phonology, morphology, syntax, and semantics. A general question that arises from the study of such restrictions is which of these should be considered peculiar to the particular word-formation rule in question and which restrictions are of a more general kind that operate on all (or at least some classes of) morphological processes (see

Plag 1999: ch. 3; or Bauer 2001: 126–43 for a detailed discussion of both kinds of restrictions).

Rule-specific constraints may concern the properties of the base or of the derived word. Let us start with phonological constraints, which can make reference to individual sounds or to prosodic phenomena such as syllable structure or stress. For example, suffixation of verbal *-en* (as in *blacken*) is subject to the segmental restriction that it only attaches to base-final obstruents (cf., e.g., *blacken* vs. **finen*) and to the prosodic restriction that it does not take bases that have more than one syllable.

Apart from being sensitive to phonological constraints, affixation may depend on the morphological structure of the pertinent base words. An example of such a morphological constraint is the suffix combination *-ize-ation*. Virtually every word ending in the suffix *-ize* can be turned into a noun only by adding *-ation*. Other conceivable deverbal nominal suffixes, such as *-ment*, *-al*, *-age*, etc., are systematically ruled out by this morphological restriction imposed on *-ize* derivatives (cf., for example, *colonization* vs. **colonizement*, **colonizal* or **colonizage*).

The suffix *-ee* (as in *employee*) illustrates a semantic restriction. Derivatives with that suffix must denote sentient entities, as shown, for example, by the impossibility to use *amputee* to refer to an amputated limb (see Barker 1998 for detailed discussion).

Finally, productivity restrictions can make reference to syntactic properties. One of the most commonly mentioned ones is the restriction of word-formation rules to members of a certain syntactic category. An example would be the adjectival suffix *-able* which normally attaches to verbs (as in *readable*), or the adjectival suffix *-al*, which attaches to nouns (as in *circumstantial*).

Let us now look at one productivity restriction that is of a more principled kind, blocking. The term 'blocking' has been used in various senses in the literature. Our discussion will be restricted to two kinds of synonymy blocking, token-blocking and type-blocking (Rainer 1988). Token-blocking involves the blocking of a potential regular form by an already existing synonymous word, an example of which is the blocking of **arrivement* by *arrival* or **stealer* by *thief*. In contrast, type-blocking concerns the blocking of the application of one rule by another rival rule (for example *-ness* and *-ity* suffixation).

Token-blocking is a relatively uncontroversial notion and will therefore not be discussed in great detail. One important aspect of token-blocking deserves mentioning, however, namely that it crucially depends on frequency. Contrary to earlier assumptions, Rainer (1988) shows that not only idiosyncratic or simplex words (like *thief*) can block productive formations (such as **stealer*), but that stored words in general can do so. As already discussed above, the storage of words is largely dependent on their frequency. Now, in order to be able to block a potential synonymous formation, the blocking word must be sufficiently frequent. In Rainer's experiment, the higher the frequency of a given word, the more likely it was that the word blocked a rival formation. Both idiosyncratic words and regular complex words are able to block other forms, provided that the blocking word is stored.

That such an account of blocking is on the right track is corroborated by the fact that occasionally really synonymous doublets do occur (which may later develop different meanings, e.g. *passivate/passivize*). Plank (1981: 181–2) already notes that blocking of a newly derived form does not occur in those cases where the speaker fails to activate the already existing alternative form. The likelihood of failing to activate a stored form is negatively correlated to the frequency of the form to be accessed. In other words, the less frequent the stored word is the more likely it is that the speaker will fail to access it (and apply the regular rule instead), and the more frequent the stored word is the more likely it is that the speaker will successfully retrieve it, and the more likely it is, therefore, that it will block the formation of a rival word. With frequency and storage being the decisive factors for token-blocking, the theory can naturally account for the occasional occurrence even of synonymous doublets.

We may now move on to the notion of type-blocking, which has been said to occur when a certain affix blocks the application of another affix (e.g. Aronoff 1976). The example *decency* vs. *decentness* would be a case in point. The crucial idea underlying the notion of type-blocking is that rival suffixes (such as *-ness*, *-ity*, and *-cy*) are organized in such a way that each suffix can be applied to a certain domain. In many cases one can distinguish between affixes with an unrestricted domain, the so-called general case (e.g. *-ness* suffixation, which may apply to practically any adjective), and affixes with restricted domains, the so-called special cases (for example *-ity* or *-cy* suffixation). The latter are characterized by the fact that certain constraints limit the applicability of the suffixes to a lexically, phonologically, morphologically, semantically or otherwise governed set of bases. Type-blocking would occur when the more special affix precludes the application of the more general affix.

The problem with this idea of type-blocking is that it cannot account for the patterning of the data. For example, Aronoff (1976: 53) regards formations involving nominal *-ness* as ill-formed in all those cases where the base adjective ends in *-ate*, *-ent* or *-ant*, hence the contrast between *decency* and what he considers an illegal form *decentness*. In his view, the systematic special case *-cy* (*decency*) precludes the general case *-ness*. There are, however, a number of problems with this kind of analysis. The first one is that, on closer inspection, *-ness* and its putative rivals *-ity* or *-cy* are not really synonymous, so that blocking could – if at all – only occur in those cases where the meaning differences would be neutralized. Riddle (1985) shows that there is in fact a slight but consistent meaning difference observable between rival *-ness* and *-ity* derivatives. Consider, for example, the pair in (5) (from Riddle 1985: 438):

(5)   a.   The lanterns demonstrated the *ethnicity* of the restaurant.
      b.   The lanterns demonstrated the *ethnicness* of the restaurant.

In (10a) the lanterns show to which ethnic group the restaurant belongs, whereas in (10b) the lanterns show that the restaurant has an ethnic appeal (as opposed to a non-ethnic appeal). In general, -*ness* formations tend to denote an embodied attribute, property or trait, whereas -*ity* formations refer to an abstract or concrete entity. Hence -*ity* and -*ness* are not completely synonymous, which would be a prerequisite for type-blocking. The second problem of the notion of type-blocking concerns the status of forms like *decentness*, which are in fact attested (a search on the internet yielded 279 occurrences, www.google.com, 08/28/2003) and even listed in dictionaries, hence not at all morphologically ill-formed. Furthermore, the occurrence of many attested doublets rather indicates that the domain of the general case -*ness* is not systematically curtailed by -*ity* or -*cy*: *destructiveness – destructivity, discoursiveness – discoursivity, exclusiveness – exclusivity, impracticalness – impracticality, inventibleness – inventability, naiveness – naivity, ovalness – ovality, prescriptiveness – prescriptivity* (all from the *OED*). The final problem with putative cases of type-blocking is to distinguish them from token-blocking. Thus, putative avoidance of *decentness* could equally well be a case of token-blocking, since one can assume that, for many speakers, the word *decency* is part of their lexicon, and is therefore capable of token-blocking (for a detailed discussion of affixal rivalry, see also Plag, 1999: ch. 8).

To summarize our discussion of blocking, we have seen that type-blocking as a general factor constraining productivity is problematic, while token-blocking restricts the productivity of affixes by preventing the formation of complex rival synonymous forms.

5 Conclusion

In this chapter we have looked at what it means when we say that a word-formation process is productive. The productivity of a given affix can be seen as its general potential to be used to create new words and as the degree to which this potential is exploited by the speakers. This degree can be assessed by various measures, both corpus-based and dictionary-based. We then discussed how complex words are stored and accessed in the mental lexicon, which is crucial for an understanding of the notion of productivity in word-formation. Productivity has been shown to be a derived notion. It emerges from the mental lexicon as the result of different properties, such as parsability, relative frequency, semantic and phonological transparency. Differences in productivity between affixes also raise the question of productivity restrictions. We have seen that apart from constraints on processing and usage, structural constraints also play an important role in restricting productivity. Possible words of a given morphological category need to conform to very specific phonological, morphological, semantic, and syntactic requirements. These requirements restrict the set of potential complex words, thus limiting productivity. Finally, token-blocking was discussed, which is a general psycholinguistic mechanism which prevents complex forms from being formed if a synonymous word is already available in the speaker's mental lexicon.

NOTE

I would like to thank Maria Braun, Sabine Lappe, Mareile Schramm, two anonymous readers and April McMahon for helpful comments on earlier drafts of this paper.

FURTHER READING

An accessible introduction to morphological productivity and the mental lexicon can be found in Plag (2003: ch. 3). Storage of and access to complex words in the lexicon are explained in more detail in Baayen (1993), Frauenfelder and Schreuder (1992). For corpus-based studies of the productivity of English affixes see Baayen and Lieber (1991), Baayen and Renouf (1996), Plag (1999: ch. 5), or Plag et al. (1999). Cowie (1999) and Scherer (2005) are diachronic studies of the productivity of some word-formation processes in English and German, respectively. The methodological problems involved in corpus-based analyses of derivational morphology are discussed in considerable detail in Plag (1999: chapter 5). Book-length studies of mainly structural aspects of productivity are Plag (1999) and Bauer (2001), which also contain useful summaries of the pertinent literature. For further elaboration of the psycholinguistic aspects of productivity, see Hay (2001), and Hay and Baayen (2002), (2003).

Baayen, H. (1993) On frequency, transparency and productivity. In G. Booij and J. van Marle (eds.), *Yearbook of morphology 1992*. Dordrecht, Boston, and London: Kluwer, 181–208.

Baayen, H. and Lieber, R. (1991) Productivity and English word-formation: a corpus-based study. *Linguistics* 29, 801–43.

Baayen, H. and Renouf, A. (1996) Chronicling *The Times*: productive lexical innovations in an English newspaper. *Language* 72, 69–96.

Bauer, L. (2001) *Morphological productivity*. Cambridge: Cambridge University Press.

Cowie, C. S. (1999) Diachronic word formation: a corpus-based study of derived nominalizations in the history of English. Ph.D. thesis, Cambridge University.

Frauenfelder, U. and Schreuder, R. (1992) Constraining psycholinguistic models of morphological processing and representation: the role of productivity. In G. Booij and J. van Marle (eds.), *Yearbook of morphology 1991*. Dordrecht, Boston, and London: Kluwer, 165–83.

Hay, J. (2001) Lexical frequency in morphology: Is everything relative? *Linguistics* 39 (4), 1041–70.

Hay, J. and Baayen, H. (2002) Parsing and productivity. In G. Booij and J. van Marle (eds.), *Yearbook of morphology 2001*. Dordrecht, Boston, and London: Kluwer, 203–35.

Hay, J. and Baayen, H. (2003) Phonotactics, parsing and productivity. *Rivista di Linguistica*.

Plag, I. (1999) *Morphological productivity: structural constraints in English derivation*. Berlin, New York: Mouton de Gruyter.

Plag, I. (2003) *Word-formation in English.* Cambridge: Cambridge University Press.

Plag, I., Dalton-Puffer, C., and Baayen, H. (1999) Morphological productivity across speech and writing. *English Language and Linguistics* 3, 209–28.

Scherer, C. (2005) *Wortbildungswandel und Produktivität: Eine empirische Studie zur nominalen -er-Derivation im Deutschen.* Tübingen: Niemeyer.

REFERENCES

Adams, V. (1973) *An introduction to English word-formation.* London: Longman.

Anshen, F. and Aronoff, M. (1981) Morphological productivity and phonological transparency. *Canadian Journal of Linguistics* 26, 63–72.

Aronoff, M. (1976) *Word formation in generative grammar.* Cambridge: MIT Press.

Aronoff, M. and Schvanefeldt, R. (1978) Testing morphological productivity. *Annals of the New York Academy of Science*: Papers in Anthropology and Linguistics 318, 106–14.

Baayen, H. (1993) On frequency, transparency and productivity. In G. Booij and J. van Marle (eds.), *Yearbook of morphology 1992.* Dordrecht, Boston, and London: Kluwer, 181–208.

Baayen, H. and Renouf, A. (1996) Chronicling *The Times*: Productive lexical innovations in an English newspaper. *Language* 72, 69–96.

Barker, C. (1998) Episodic *-ee* in English: A thematic role constraint on a new word formation. *Language* 74, 695–727.

Bauer, L. (1983) *English word-formation.* Cambridge: Cambridge University Press.

Bauer, L. (2001) *Morphological productivity.* Cambridge: Cambridge University Press.

Becker, T. (1990) *Analogie und morphologische Theorie.* Munich Wilhelm Fink.

Berschin, H. (1971) Sprachsystem und Sprachnorm bei spanischen lexikalischen Einheiten der Struktur KKVKV. *Linguistische Berichte* 12, 39–46.

Bolinger, D. (1948) On defining the morpheme. *Word,* 4, 18–23.

Booij, G. E. (1977) *Dutch morphology: a study of word formation in generative grammar.* Lisse: de Ridder.

Corbin, D. (1987) *Morphologie dérivationelle et structuration du lexique* (2 vols.). (*Derivational morphology and the structuring of vocabulary*). Tübingen: Niemeyer.

Cutler, A. (1981) Degrees of transparency in word formation. *Canadian Journal of Linguistics* 26, 73–7.

Dalton-Puffer, C. (1996) *The French influence on Middle English morphology: a corpus-based study of derivation.* Berlin, New York: Mouton de Gruyter.

Dalton-Puffer, C. and Plag, I. (2000) Categorywise, some compound-type morphemes seem to be rather suffix-like: On the status of *-ful*, *-type*, and *-wise* in present day English. *Folia Linguistica* 34, 225–44.

Evert, S. and Lüdeling, A. (2001) Measuring morphological productivity: Is automatic preprocessing sufficient? In P. Rayson, A. Wilson, T. McEnery, A. H., and S. Khoja (eds.), *Proceedings of the Corpus Linguistics 2001 Conference.* Lancaster: University Center for Computer Research on Language, 167–75.

Gaeta, L. and Ricca, D. (2003) Frequency and productivity in Italian derivation: A comparison between corpus-based and lexico-graphical data. *Rivista di Linguistica*, 15 (1).

Haspelmath, M. (2002) *Understanding morphology*. London: Arnold.

Hay, J. (2000) Causes and consequences of word structure. Ph.D. thesis, Northwestern University.

Hay, J. (2001) Lexical frequency in morphology: Is everything relative? *Linguistics* 39 (4), 1041–70.

Hay, J. and Baayen, H. (2002) Parsing and productivity. In G. Booij and J. van Marle (eds.), *Yearbook of morphology 2001*. Dordrecht, Boston, and London: Kluwer, 203–35.

Hay, J. and Baayen, H. (2003) Phonotactics, parsing and productivity. *Rivista di Linguistica*, 15 (1), 99–130.

McQueen, J. M. (1998) Segmentation of continuous speech using phonotactics. *Journal of Memory and Language*, 39, 21–46.

McQueen, J. M. and Cutler, A. (1998) Morphology in word recognition. In A. Spencer and A. Zwicky (eds.), *The handbook of morphology*. Oxford: Blackwell, 406–27.

Plag, I. (1999) *Morphological productivity: Structural constraints in English derivation*. Berlin, New York: Mouton de Gruyter.

Plag, I. (2002) The role of selectional restrictions, phonotactics and parsing in constraining suffix ordering in English. In G. Booij and J. van Marle (eds.), *Yearbook of morphology 2001*. Dordrecht: Kluwer, 285–314.

Plag, I. (2003) *Word-formation in English*. Cambridge: Cambridge University Press.

Plag, I., Dalton-Puffer, C., and Baayen, H. (1999) Morphological productivity across speech and writing. *English Language and Linguistics* 3, 209–28.

Plank, F. (1981) *Morphologische (Ir-)Regularitäten: Aspekte der Wortstrukturtheorie*. Tübingen: Narr.

Rainer, F. (1988) Towards a theory of blocking. In G. Booij and J. van Marle (eds.), *Yearbook of morphology 1987*. Dordrecht, Boston, and London: Kluwer, 155–85.

Riddle, E. (1985) A historical perspective on the productivity of the suffixes *-ness* and *-ity*. In J. Fisiak (ed.), *Historical semantics, historical word-formation*. Berlin: Mouton de Gruyter, 435–61.

Rose, J. H. (1973) Principled limitations on productivity in denominal verbs. *Foundations of Language* 10, 509–26.

Saffran, J. R., Newport, E. L., and Aslin, R. N. (1996a) Statistical learning by 8-month old infants. *Science*, 274, 1926–198.

Saffran, J. R., Newport, E. L., and Aslin, R. N. (1996b) Word segmentation: The role of distributional cues. *Journal of Memory and Language* 35, 606–21.

Schneider, K. P. (2003) *Diminutives in English*. Tübingen: Niemeyer.

Spencer, A. (1991) *Morphological theory: an introduction to word structure in generative grammar*. Cambridge: Cambridge University Press.

Skousen, R., Lonsdale, D., and Parkinson, D. B. (eds.) (2002) *Analogical modeling of language*. Amsterdam: Benjamins.

24 Lexical Semantics

KATE KEARNS

1 Introduction

The term *lexical semantics* is commonly used in contrast with *formal semantics* to refer to the study of *content words*, which have descriptive content specifying what kinds of entities and events they denote.[1] This chapter focuses on the main categorematic words, nouns, verbs, and adjectives. Sections 2 to 4 review main ideas in approaches to word meaning shaped by structuralism. Section 2 outlines lexical semantic fields, which reflect Saussure's view that word meanings are largely determined by their contrasts with the meanings of other words. Lexical relations, relations of affinity and contrast among words including synonymy, antonymy, hyponymy and meronymy, are discussed in section 3.

The major lexical relations, and relations among words in a classical lexical field are *paradigmatic* – they hold among words of the same distributional class, which in principle may be substituted for each other in a given context. *Syntagmatic* relations hold among words in construction, such as verb-object, or adjective-noun modification. Syntagmatic relations reflect internal aspects of sense which are generally captured by analyzing the sense of a word in terms of sense components. Sense components are reviewed in section 4. Section 5 turns to issues of sense variation, homonymy, polysemy and underspecification. The chapter closes with a few remarks on possible future directions in lexical semantics.

2 Semantic Fields

The simplest kind of semantic field is illustrated by the set of basic color terms in a language, such as English *blue, red, yellow, green, purple, brown, black, white, grey, pink*. Although normally sighted humans perceive the same colors, different languages lexicalize the color space differently (Berlin and Kay 1969), with more or fewer terms to cover the whole color space. For example, the space covered by English *blue* and *green* may be covered by a single term in another language. This term would be used to translate English *green*, but would actually have a different sense because it does not contrast with a distinct term for 'blue.' The sense of each word in a semantic field of this type is determined by the contrasts among the words in the set, which are all mutually exclusive in denotation.[2] The relation of mutual exclusion is not itself sufficient to determine that two words belong in a common semantic field, as words from different fields are also commonly incompatible (cf. *albatross, lipstick*). The identification of a field depends on a fixed domain, usually named by a single term such as *color*. In turn, the significance of the field for the senses of its terms depends on exhaustive lexicalization of the field.

An alternative view of semantic fields (see Lehrer 1974; Grandy 1992 for discussion), based on lexical relations such as hyponymy (see section 5.1) and specified contrast, is illustrated in the following diagram:

(1)

sheep			horse			human		
ram	ewe	lamb	stallion	mare	foal	man	woman	child

The field is based on the characteristic contrast relations of maturity and gender among hyponyms of a species term, rather than by a fixed domain: there is no basic domain comprising humans and (some) domestic animals. The cells structured by the characteristic contrast relations reveal lexical gaps. Juveniles are further distinguished by gender only for horses and humans. The set *bull, cow, calf* also belongs here, but in many dialects lacks a single species term in the sense 'cattle beast.'

3   Lexical Relations

3.1   *Synonymy*

Three main kinds of meaning relation fall under the rubric of *synonymy*.

The strictest notion of synonymy, which I shall call *absolute synonymy*, requires absolute identity of all aspects of meaning (including connotation, style and register) for two terms to be classed as synonyms. The sign of absolute identity is complete interchangeability: 'Absolute synonyms would be able to be substituted one for the other in any context in which their common sense is denoted with no change to truth value, communicative effect, or "meaning" (however "meaning" is defined)' (Edmonds and Hirst 2002: 107). Absolute synonymy is generally agreed to be extremely rare, if not non-existent, although candidates for absolute synonymy, such as *everybody/everyone* and *anyhow/ anyway*, are noted occasionally. Clark (1983) attributes the rarity of synonymy to a Principle of Contrast, 'Every two forms contrast in meaning,'[3] which guides language acquisition. The Principle of Contrast is seen at work in instances of language change where apparent synonymies disappear over time, either by the loss of one term or by changes in the sense of at least one term. For example, Norman English contained both native and French terms for domestic animals such as *sheep/mouton* and *pig/porc*. The French terms came to refer exclusively to the flesh as food rather than to the animal.

Given the Principle of Contrast, the main issue with synonymy is how apparent synonyms actually differ. Theoretical linguistics makes a cut between non-denotational and denotational differences. The central notion of synonymy in theoretical linguistics is Quine's (1951/1980: 27) *cognitive synonymy* (see also Cruse 1986: 88, 270ff), where 'the synonymy of two linguistic forms consists simply in their interchangeability in all contexts without change of truth value' (this includes absolute synonymy). Cognitive synonyms commonly illustrate differences in style, register and various modes of connotation. For example, *die, kick the bucket*, and *pass away* differ in style; connotations of evaluative coloring are illustrated in the 'conjugations' game (I'm *firm*, you're *stubborn*, she's *pig-headed*), and cultural association connotations include *Monday* connoting 'returning to work or school after the weekend break,' hence *Mondayitis* referring to the associated blues. Slight differences in denotational meaning distinguish what Cruse (1986: 285) calls *plesionyms*, such as *misty* and *foggy*, which differ in degree with a fuzzy boundary, and *swamp, fen, bog* and *marsh*.

From the point of view of lexicography, *near-synonyms* which might be confused and require careful discrimination include both plesionyms and cognitive synonyms. Eighteenth-century compilations of synonyms aimed to provide distinctions among words so similar in sense as to be easily confused, such as *austerity, severity*, and *rigor*. The words discussed in such works overlapped with the more obviously different words in word-finder lists such as *money, bullion, capital, cash, property, specie*, etc., which were chosen on the basis of looser similarities of sense and topic. A fusion of the two types of work led to a broadening of the notion of synonymy to include looser similarity (see Egan 1942 for a lively discussion), and *synonym* is still widely used informally in this broader sense.

Investigating computational treatments of near-synonymy, particularly machine translation, Edmonds (1999) observes that near-synonymy is a matter of degree, depending on the level of detail or fineness of grain used in defining word senses. For example, if words such as *pine* and *fir* are coarsely specified only as denoting conifer trees, they are in effect treated as absolute synonyms. A consistent identification of near-synonyms depends on a principle for establishing the grain level above which non-synonyms are distinguished, and below which near-synonyms are distinguished. Edmonds proposes a three-level model of lexical meaning: the top level consists of a single concept to which a cluster of near-synonyms are linked at the second level. The concept provides the core content shared by the near-synonyms. Near-synonyms are distinguished at the second level by semantic, stylistic and expressive distinctions, and at the third level by syntactic properties. Edmonds adopts a proposal from work by Graeme Hirst and others that top-level concepts may be operationally identified as language-independent: a concept which is lexicalized in a range of languages is likely to be a top-level concept. Near-synonyms, on the other hand, are found to be highly variable across languages. For example, the top-level concept 'Generic-Error' is linked to non-corresponding sets of near-synonyms in different languages: English *error, blunder, slip, mistake, lapse, howler*, etc.; French *faute, erreur, faux pas, bévue, bêtise, bavure, impair*, etc.; and German *Irrtum, Fehler, Mißgriff, Versehen, Schnitzer*, etc.

3.2   *Antonymy*

The term *antonym* is used both in a broad sense equivalent to 'opposite,' and in a restricted sense covering contrary adjectives (see below). I shall use the term in the broad sense.

Given the Principle of Contrast, antonymy, unlike absolute synonymy, is a natural and extremely common relation (see Jones (2002) and references cited there for discussion). It is the only relation for which many languages have a non-technical term (e.g. English *opposite*), and appears in child language – rhetorical devices based on antonym pairs appear before 3 years of age (Murphy and Jones 2003). Direct antonyms evoke a recognition sensation which Egan (1942: xxxi) calls 'the clash that gives so much savor to the antonym.'[4]

Despite the psychological prominence of antonymy, theoretical accounts have not found a single definition to cover all cases, and subdivide oppositions into a number of different types. Three main types (contrary, complementary, converse) are outlined here; for further discussion see Cruse (1986).

The central type (for which Lyons 1968: 450 and Cruse 1986: 88 reserve the term *antonym*) comprises *contrary adjectives* such as *long/short, good/bad* and *fast/slow*. These antonyms denote opposite poles on a property scale. The characteristic contrary entailments are, for example, *The rope is long* entails *The rope is not short*, and *The rope is short* entails *The rope is not long*.[5] The scale has a neutral middle ground covered by neither term, and *The rope is neither long nor short* may be true. Contrary adjectives are *gradable*, in that they may be modified for degree (*The rope is fairly long/very long*) and form comparatives (*This rope is longer than that one*).

The second major type of antonymy comprises *complementary adjectives* such as *true/false, dead/alive, open/closed*. These are contradictory, dividing a dimension into two spaces, so that, in addition to the entailments characteristic of contrariety, a negated complementary entails its antonym: for example, *The door is not closed* entails *The door is open*, and *The door is not open* entails *The door is closed*.

Complementary antonyms may be gradable or non-gradable. *True/false* and *alive/dead* are strictly non-gradable in their basic senses, although comparative and degree modified forms may be used figuratively (*What you say is very true*;

He's more dead than alive). Gradable complementaries generally have a *privative* member denoting the absence of a feature, with the other term denoting its presence: *clean* denotes the absence of dirt, and *dirty* its presence; *dry* denotes the absence of moisture and *wet* its presence; *safe* denotes the absence of danger and *unsafe* its presence, and so on. See Rusiecki (1985) and Horn (1989) for discussion.

Gradable antonyms usually have a *marked and unmarked member* (see Lehrer 1985 for discussion). The unmarked adjective is used in uncommitted degree questions, as in *How long is the ladder?*, which expresses no commitment that the ladder is long, in contrast with *How short is the ladder?*, which expresses a supposition that the ladder is short. The unmarked adjective may be morphologically related to a neutral noun denoting the property scale (uncommitted *length*, cf. committed *shortness*; also *width, height*), and may appear in measure phrases such as *three feet long, twice as long*, compared with *three feet short* which must be interpreted as 'three feet too short,' and # *twice as short*, which can only be interpreted as 'too short by twice as much.' The unmarked member denotes the positive pole of a scale, which may correlate with 'more' of a property (*long* denotes greater linear extent than *short*), although this does not apply with gradable antonyms where the positive, unmarked member denotes the 'absence of feature' value (*clean* denotes the absence of dirt; *How clean is it?* is uncommitted; *cleanness* is less committed than *dirtiness*). The positive member may also correlate with positive evaluation (*good* is unmarked, cf. marked *bad*), and markedness may also correlate with morphology, where the marked, negative antonym is derived by negative prefixation (*unhappy* is marked, cf. unmarked *happy*).

Although contrary and complementary antonyms are mainly adjectives, similar entailment patterns are found with some noun and verb antonyms. *Friend* and *foe/enemy* are contrary: *x is an enemy of y* entails *x is not a friend of y*, *x is a friend of y* entails *x is not an enemy of y*, and *x is neither a friend nor an enemy of y* may be true. The same relation holds for *insult/compliment*. Cruse (1986: 200–2) also notes verbal complementaries such as *win/lose, hit/miss*, and *pass/fail*.

Converse antonyms (also called *relational opposites*) are related by an entailment of the general form A(x,y) ↔ B(y,x). Converses include comparative adjectives (*x is warmer than y* entails and is entailed by *y is cooler than x*), prepositions (*x is before y ↔ y is after x*), verbs (*x precedes y ↔ y follows x; x sells y to z ↔ z buys y from x*), and nouns (*x is a parent of y ↔ y is an offspring of x*).

Although lexical sense relations are classed as paradigmatic, antonymy is also argued to be syntagmatic, because numerous rhetorical devices are based on antonym pairs. Charles and Miller (1989) found in experimental studies that antonym pairs frequently co-occur in sentences (e.g. *Strong hands act; weak hands react*). Justeson and Katz (1992) found that high-frequency adjectives co-occur with their antonyms in the same sentence at a rate much higher than chance, and propose that antonymy should be defined partly in terms of textual co-occurrence. Jones (2002) classifies different types of antonymy in terms of the rhetorical function of antonyms in context. The two major types he discusses are ancillary and coordinated antonymy. In ancillary antonymy, the contrast between the two antonyms is not the main contrast expressed by the sentence, but signals that two other terms are to be contrasted. For example, in *It is meeting public need, not private greed*, the antonymy *public/private* is ancillary to the main contrast of the message between *need* and *greed*. Coordinated antonyms signal exhaustiveness or inclusiveness of scale, as in *Today, the pressure to make hay while the sun fitfully shines has led to a massive slump in both public and private standards*, where coordinated *public* and *private* signal exhaustiveness – a slump in all standards. Like Justeson and Katz, Jones concludes that antonymy should be defined partly in terms of cooccurrence.

3.3   Hyponymy and hyperonymy

Hyponyms and *hyperonyms* (also called *subordinates* and *superordinates*) express relations of sense inclusion among nouns, corresponding to the relations of class inclusion structuring a taxonomy. For example, the class of cats is a subclass of the class of mammals, and the word *cat* is a hyponym (subordinate) of the word *mammal*. Conversely, the class of mammals properly includes the class of cats, and the word *mammal* is a hyperonym (superordinate) of the word *cat*. Broadly, a word entails its hyperonym, as in *Toby is a cat* entails *Toby is a mammal*, and the relation is transitive: given that *cat* is a hyponym of *mammal*, and *mammal* is a hyponym of *animal*, *Toby is a cat* also entails *Toby is an animal*.

Fellbaum and Miller (1990; see also Fellbaum 1998) identify a kind of sense inclusion relation for verbs dubbed *troponymy* (from Greek *tropos* 'manner'). To stroll is to walk in some manner, so *stroll* is a troponym of *walk*.

3.4   Meronymy and holonymy

Meronymy (also called *partonymy*) expresses a 'part-of' relation between the denotations of related nouns – for example, *trunk* and *branch* are meronyms of *tree*, and conversely, *tree* is a *holonym* of *trunk* and *branch*. Meronymy, identified as the part-whole relation, is defined as transitive in logic and mathematics, but linguistic studies have found considerable variation in transitivity. Lyons (1977: 313) pointed out that meronymy is transitive for the series *cuff, sleeve, jacket* (*The jacket has sleeves*, *The sleeves have cuffs*, *The jacket has cuffs*), but not for the series *handle, door, house* (*The house has a door*, *The door has a handle*, # *The house has a handle*). Cruse (1986: 165–6) suggests that the difference lies in the functional type of the different parts. A cuff is a decorative part of both the sleeve and the jacket, and so the relationship 'is a decorative part of' is transitive. A door-handle, on the other hand, has a functional relationship with the door ('manipulate the handle to open the door') that it does not have with the house, so the relation is not transitive.

The variable transitivity of meronymy has led to division into several subtypes of meronymy, although different authors offer different classifications of meronyms and use different criteria to identify them. Cruse (1986) argues that meronymy requires the acceptability of both a *part of* sentence and a *has* sentence, as in the pair *A finger is part of a hand* and *A hand has fingers*, showing that either sentence frame used alone can also apply to word pairs other than meronym/hyponym pairs. Other investigators take conceptual part-whole relations as criterial, rather than test sentence frames, and propose a range of 4–6 main subtypes of meronym. For example, in addition to the central type 'component of integral object,' Winston et al. (1987) add member-collection (*tree-forest*, *card-deck*), portion-mass (*slice-pie*, *grain-salt*), stuff-object (*gin-martini*, *steel-bicycle*), feature-activity (*paying-shopping*, *dating-adolescence*), and place-area (*oasis-desert*, *Everglades-Florida*): see also Chaffin et al. (1988) for numerous further subtypes of the part-whole relation.

4   Semantic Components

Almost all lexical semantic theories employ some form of *lexical decomposition* (also called *componential analysis*), analysing the sense of a word in terms of smaller sense components.[6] In practice, the type of components and structures proposed differ considerably for different lexical classes, particularly nouns and verbs, which have received the most attention. I shall consider nouns and verbs separately in the following discussion.

4.1   *Nouns*

A highly formalized analysis of noun senses as sets of semantic features comes from European structuralism, chiefly Hjelmslev and Jakobsen (see Lyons 1977: 317–35 and Löbner 2002: ch. 7 for discussion), who proposed that semantic features should have the same properties as phonological features: they should be (1) primitive, not analyzeable into smaller units, (2) universal, found across languages, and (3) binary, having a positive (marked) and negative (unmarked) value for each feature. The full feature inventory should have sufficient coverage to exhaustively define the sense of any word. The approach is illustrated in (2) below.

(2)		–JUVENILE		+JUVENILE	
		–FEMALE	+FEMALE	–FEMALE	+FEMALE
	sheep	ram	ewe	lamb	
	horse	stallion	mare	colt	filly
	pig			piglet	
	human			boy	girl

The features [±FEMALE] and [±JUVENILE] are possible candidates for universal, primitive, binary features. They are found in similar vocabulary sets across languages and express values in a two-way contrast. The general identification of 'female' as the marked value might be defended on the grounds of morphological patterns: in pairs such as *actor*/*actress* the feminine noun is marked. The markedness of 'juvenile' is suggested by the pair *pig*/*piglet*, and by the fact that many species nouns do not have a specific juvenile term. These features, however, leave residues of meaning, such as 'equine' in the *horse* set, which are not plausibly analyzed in terms of classical features. On the one hand, the content 'equine' is not easily analyzed into further components, and might be treated as a primitive [EQUINE]; similarly for [OVINE], [PORCINE], [HUMAN]. But on the other hand, these components are not in binary contrast (contrasting with each other and other species terms), nor are the animal components universal – a feature [EQUINE] would not appear in the language of a people unacquainted with horses.

The strong claim that all word senses can be exhaustively decomposed into universal atomic sense components has been largely abandoned, although a notable exception is the work of Anna Wierzbicka, who has developed an extensive system of reductive paraphrase using a basic vocabulary of about 60 terms, comprising the Natural Semantic Metalanguage (NSM). Wierzbicka claims that exhaustive sense definitions can be given in NSM. Her theory differs from componential analysis in that the terms of NSM are actual words in the language to be analyzed, rather than abstract cross-linguistic sense atoms – see Wierzbicka (1996), and for an accessible introduction see Goddard (1998).

The study of concrete noun senses is most strongly influenced by theories of object concepts (or mental categories) in cognitive psychology. In the classical view of concepts, attributed originally to Aristotle, a concept consists of a set of individually necessary and jointly sufficient features or attributes. As illustration, a possible classical analysis for FISH is shown below.

(3)   FISH   1.   living creature
             2.   lives in water
             3.   cold-blooded
             4.   breathes with gills
             5.   swims with fins and tail
             6.   has scales covering its skin
             7.   female lays eggs

The listed features are individually necessary: for any species, if it is a kind of fish then it has all the listed features. The features are jointly sufficient: if any species has all the listed features, then it is a kind of fish.

Serious problems for the classical theory of concepts and word senses were pointed out by Wittgenstein (1953/1958: paras 66–75), and later explored in detail by cognitive psychologists. Wittgenstein raised the issue of words like *game*, for which a classical feature set seems impossible to construct. The only features common to all games (and thus necessary) are such vague descriptors as 'activity,' which do not characterize games in particular. Features which characterize some games (and thus in combination with other features might form a jointly sufficient set) are absent from others: solitaire lacks competition, children's games may lack rules, gambling games may lack skill, and so on. Wittgenstein suggested that the unity of such concepts depends on *family resemblance*, in which every member of a family shares some features with some other members, but there may be no features shared by all members.

The second major criticism of classical concepts is based on evidence of *typicality effects* (also called *prototypicality effects*), first reported by Rips, Shoben and Smith (1973) and Rosch (1973), and studied in depth in a series of ground-breaking experiments by Rosch and her colleagues (see particularly Rosch 1975; Rosch and Mervis 1975; Rosch et al. 1976). The central finding is that different members of a category are not equally good exemplars of the category – for example, robins and sparrows are better examples (i.e. more typical) of BIRD than hawks and eagles, which are in turn better examples than chickens and penguins. The problem for the classical theory of concepts is that a list of necessary and sufficient features can only be the basis for classifying an object as a bird or a non-bird, and cannot provide a basis for judging different kinds of bird as more or less typical.

The significance of typicality effects for concept structures has been interpreted in a number of ways, and is still under debate. Only a brief outline of selected points in response to Rosch's findings is possible here – see Smith and Medin (1981) and Murphy (2002) for excellent detailed discussion of the issues.

One of the responses is *prototype theory*, in which a concept is structured as a space centered on a prototype. A prototype is an abstraction of maximal typicality for the category: for example, the BIRD prototype is about the size of a robin, is dullish brown or grey, flies and sings. Actual members of the category are located in the concept space at varying distances from the prototype, according to similarity. The closer a member is to the prototype, the more typical it is.

The prototype model has been widely adopted in *cognitive linguistics*, as a theory of linguistic concepts in general (see Taylor 1989/1995/2003), and as a theory of word meaning, particularly for polysemy. (A polysemous word has two or more distinct but related senses; see section 5 for discussion.) The subsenses of a polysemous word are described as more or less central, or prototypical. For example, Lakoff (1987) describes the sense of *mother* as a prototype (or in his terms, *radial category*), centered on the individual who is the genetic and birth mother of a child, raises the child and is a housewife. More peripheral members of the category include adoptive mothers, step-mothers, birth mothers of adopted children, surrogate mothers, and so on. Taking a prototype structure to represent polysemy, Geeraerts (1997) analyzes certain semantic changes in Dutch as shifts in the prototype center: semantic change occurs when a peripheral subsense of a polysemous word becomes central, and the original core sense becomes peripheral.

Research on object concepts including the work of Rosch has also established two main kinds of discrimination among concept attributes, which are still widely used. First (see also Miller and Johnson-Laird 1976), attributes are divided into (1) perceptual attributes such as size, color and shape (expressed by modifying adjectives), (2) structural parts (expressed by meronyms), and (3) functional attributes, including what an object does and how humans interact with it (expressed by commonly collocating verbs). Second, significant attributes for a concept (that is, attributes volunteered by subjects earlier than other attributes, volunteered by a majority of subjects, etc.) include many that are not essential for the concept, such as 'has four legs' for CHAIR or TABLE. Smith, Rips and Shoben (1974) proposed a distinction between characteristic features and defining features underlying different stages of classificatory judg-ments.[7] Quick and easy judgments, such as the falsity of *A robin is a car*, may rest on a comparison of any type of features, while slower and more difficult judgments such as *A chicken is a bird* must appeal to defining features. The classification, ranking or weighting of features according to their diagnostic value for membership in a concept is handled in a range of ways in different theories of concepts – see Smith and Medin (1981) and Murphy (2002) for discussion.

Although the developments reviewed here concern psychological concepts rather than word meanings directly, they are significant to lexical semantics to the extent that the senses of nouns are assumed to be the object concepts representing a noun's denotation.

4.2   *Verbs*

Research in the lexical semantics of verbs is dominated by studies in the syntax-semantics interface, a major concern in current syntactic theory. Selected main points are outlined here.

The central issue in the interface between verb senses and syntax is the *linking* or syntactic projection of the semantic arguments of a verb, which in many approaches are classified into broad types of event participant, called *thematic roles, thematic relations*, or *participant roles*. Thematic roles (or the informa-tion they encode) are components of verb meaning. Theories of thematic roles are developed to account for regularities in the syntactic realization of arguments. For example, with a verb that denotes an action done by one entity to another (*Jones folded the letter, Jones ate the pie, Jones stroked the cat*), the entity which does the action is expressed as (linked to, projected as) the subject of an active voice sentence, and the entity the action is done to is expressed as the direct object. Although there is considerable variation in the inventories of roles in use, their definitions, and proposed hierarchical relations among them, the roles described below are most commonly cited.[8]

Actor and *patient* are macroroles – they express very abstract content which may be combined with other roles. The actor is the performer of an action, or the source of energy in the event, may be sentient and act volitionally, and may cause change to occur to the patient. The patient is the undergoer of an action or change, is the 'energy sink' in the event, and is not volitionally involved.

Spatial or *localist roles*, originating with Gruber (1965) and developed by Jackendoff (1972), may be combined with the macroroles. Localist roles refer to location or movement in physical or metaphorical space. The entity which moves or is located in a state or location is the *theme*, the entity from which movement departs is the *source*, and the entity at which movement terminates is the *goal*. Where movement takes place in the field of possession, the goal is a *recipient*. For example, in *Jones threw the ball to the boundary*, *Jones* is actor and source, *the ball* is patient and theme, and *the boundary* is goal. In *Emily gave Keeper a bone*, *Keeper* is recipient. Verbs which express translocation of a theme select a *path*. A path may contain a goal: in *Jones threw the ball to the boundary*, *the boundary* is the goal, as above, and *to the boundary* is the path. A path may also lack an expressed end, as in *Harry wandered along the riverbank*.

Verbs of perception and emotion have the roles *experiencer*, the sentient being perceiving or experiencing emotion, and *stimulus*, the percept or cause of emotion. For example, *Jones* is the experiencer and *the article* is the stimulus in *Jones saw the article* and *The article delighted Jones*. The entity expressed in an instrumental *with*-phrase is an *instrument* (*Jones broke the lock with a hammer*), and some authors also use the *locative* role from the original Gruber–Jackendoff system for the relatum of a static location, such as *the garden* in *Jones was in the garden*.

For many researchers, thematic roles are useful expository devices but have no theoretical status as primitives. The information they encode is contained in partial representations of verb meaning called lexical conceptual structures (LCS), based largely on Dowty's (1979) analysis of central classes of verbal predicate, using primitive operators BECOME, CAUSE and DO, as illustrated below.

(4) a. LCS for adjective *dry*:   dry(y)
     b. The towel is dry.   dry(the towel)
(5) a. LCS for intransitive verb *dry*: BECOME[dry(y)]
     b. The towel dried.   BECOME[dry(the towel)]
(6) a. LCS for transitive (agentive) verb *dry*:
        DO(x, [do(x)] CAUSE [BECOME[dry(y)]]])[9]
     b. Jones dried the towel.
        DO(j, [do(j)] CAUSE [BECOME[dry(the towel)]]])

Dowty proposed his theory as an aspectual calculus, aiming to define the aspectual predicate classes, or *aktionsarten*. However, the predicate classes he defines are more thematic than aspectual: DO defines agentive verbs, BECOME defines inchoative verbs and CAUSE defines lexical causatives. In defining major verb classes, the primitive operators DO, BECOME and CAUSE are likely candidates for universal primitives, and are widely used in theories of LCS.[10]

Rappaport and Levin (1988) argued that thematic role lists in a verb's lexical entry are redundant, as the LCS contains the information that thematic roles encode. For example, the arguments classed as theme, and therefore linked to the direct object position, are defined by the LCS substructures '. . . [x come to be in LOCATION] . . .' and '. . . [x come to be in STATE] . . . ,' where 'come to be' is equivalent to Dowty's BECOME. Along similar lines, *agent* may be replaced by (or defined as) *x* in 'DO(x, . . .),' and *goal* by *z* in 'BECOME[at(y,z)].'

The most fully developed theory using similar structures is Jackendoff's (1983, 1990) theory of Conceptual Structural Representation (CSR). Jackendoff also employs a function-argument formalism, but covers a wider range of phenomena, has a richer range of functions, and has several classes of arguments that functions may select, including Thing, Place, Path, Event, and State. In contrast to lexical conceptual structures, which are explicitly linguistic, Jackendoff's conceptual structures are general cognitive structures.

5   Sense Variation

5.1   *Homonymy, polysemy, and underspecification*

There are three main types of variability in associating wordforms and meanings, homonymy, polysemy, and underspecification.

Two words A and B are *homonyms* if they have the same form F – conversely, a wordform F is *ambiguous* if it is shared by (at least) two different words A and B. For example, the wordform *calf* is shared by two words, the first meaning 'fleshy part of the lower leg,' and apparently derived from Old Norse *kálfi*, the second meaning 'young of a large mammal, especially cattle,' derived from Old West Saxon *cealf*. Changes over time in what were two distinct form-meaning pairs have produced a coincidental identity of form.

Polysemy is the property of a single word having distinguishable but related subsenses. For example, the verb *groom* has the distinct but related senses 'make (a person or animal) physically clean and neat' and 'prepare a person mentally for a career or position.'

Underspecification (also called *vagueness, generality*, and *indeterminacy*) is the property of having a general, inclusive sense which is compatible with different kinds of denotation. For example, the word *aunt* might be glossed as 'a female in a sibling-like relationship to one's parent,' which includes father's sister, mother's sister, father's brother's wife, and mother's brother's wife. Although kinship terminologies may distinguish between maternal and paternal connections, and between blood relations and relations by marriage, the word *aunt* is simply unspecified on these dimensions.

The three patterns are diagrammed in (7) below.

(7)   different words   same word

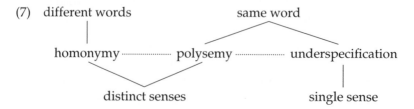

The boundaries separating polysemy from homonymy and underspecification are fuzzy (see Geeraerts 1993; Tuggy 1993 for discussion). Polysemous subsenses frequently drift apart over time until the relation between them is not easily apparent, and they appear homonymous. The two senses of *character*, for example, 'written symbol' and 'personality' are related through a common source, but would strike many speakers as unrelated. The boundary between polysemy and underspecification depends on criteria for identifying distinct senses, which do not always give clear results.

5.2 Criteria for sense differentiation

The three main signs of sense differentiation are (1) independent truth conditions, (2) identity of sense under anaphora and coordination, and (3) the possibility of a unified definition for all the putative senses.

Two senses of a word are shown to have independent truth conditions if the word can be both predicated and denied of the same entity without contradiction. So, for example, given the two senses of *light*, one can say truly that a dark-colored feather is $light_1$ (of low weight) but not $light_2$ (pale in color).

Identity of sense under anaphora is shown in a range of linguistic tests, including anaphoric proforms and VP deletion. Terms like *aunt*, which are underspecified for different types of denotation (maternal or paternal, by blood or by marriage), support anaphora which crosses the types, as in *Leo has three aunts and so does Paula, Leo visited his favorite aunt and Paula visited hers*, and *Leonie would like to be an aunt and so would Paula*, where any combination of different types of aunt may be the case. Co-ordination, as in *Paula and Leonie are both aunts*, also allows for Paula and Leonie to be different types of aunt. Combining two distinct senses of a word in an identity-of-sense construction results in an anomaly called *zeugma*, where the two distinct senses are simultaneously presented and cannot be united – Cruse (2000: 31) likens this to the visual Necker's cube effect. Geeraerts (1993: 229) gives the example *At midnight the ship passed the port and so did the bartender*, showing the 'bad pun' effect typical of zeugma, due here to the distinct senses of *port* as a harbour for ships or a type of wine. The polysemous senses of *follow* 'go after' and 'understand' are shown to be distinct in *John followed Mary and so did Bill*, which can mean that John and Bill both went after Mary, or both understood her, but not that John went after her and Bill understood her.

The criterion of a general unified definition as a sign of underspecification rather than polysemy is attributed to Aristotle. Underspecified *aunt* can be glossed as above 'a female in a sibling-like relationship to one's parent,' which is entailed for all and only the distinct types of aunt. Homonyms of *port*, on the other hand, ('harbour,' 'type of wine,' 'left side of sea-vessel') have no exhaustive superordinate sense. The canonical test results are summarized below in (8).

(8)

	x is A but not A is contradictory	zeugma	superordinate sense
underspecification	+	–	+
distinct senses	–	+	–

5.3   Problems for sense differentiation criteria

A number of writers (see Tuggy 1993; Geeraerts 1993, among others) point out cases where the tests reviewed above are inconsistent.

Many species terms such as *dog* and *lion* have one hyponym marked for gender, here the female terms *bitch* and *lioness*. The unmarked term *dog* has become an *autohyponym* (a hyponym of itself) with a distinct sense 'male dog' – this sense appears in the expression *dog fox*, opposed to *vixen*. The lack of contradiction in *Lady is a dog alright, but she isn't a dog* suggests that the senses 'canine' and 'male dog' are distinct, but the presence of the superordinate sense ('canine') suggests that *dog* is always unspecified for maleness. (In comparison, the general term *lion* seems to lack an established sense 'male lion,' as shown by the contradictoriness of *Elsa is a lioness but she isn't a lion*.) The zeugma test is uninformative – zeugma doesn't arise with *Lady is a dog and so is Fido* because the superordinate sense is available. In general, where an autohyponym is sufficiently established to be contrasted with its marked co-hyponym without contradiction, the test of independent truth conditions will clash with the other two tests.

Cruse (2000) argues that *knife* denotes a cluster of distinct subsenses, rather than a general superordinate sense, roughly 'handheld implement with a handle and blade, used for cutting.' A particular subsense of *knife* is activated by a given context, and the superordinate sense is not salient. Cruse writes that *Arthur bought a knife and so did Wilma* is understood as referring to the same kind of knife for both purchasers and not, for example, that Wilma bought a pruning knife and Arthur a carving knife. Cruse argues that a child sitting at the dining table with a penknife in his pocket, fingering his food, may answer truly *No* when asked *Haven't you got a knife?*, showing that the context-activated subsense 'table knife' is truth-conditionally independent from the superordinate sense. Tuggy (1993) discusses a similar pattern with the verb *paint*, which may denote a range of quite different actions including painting a portrait in oils, painting a wall during interior decorating, painting stripes on a roadway with a paint-spraying vehicle, applying iodine to skin or makeup to one's face, and so on. All these senses seem to fall under some superordinate sense along the lines of 'apply a colored liquid to a surface,' which suggests that *paint* is underspecified, but the other tests may indicate polysemy, depending on how different the relevant subsenses are. For example, *Jane has been painting and so have I* is non-zeugmatic if, for example, I have been painting the walls a plain color and Jane has been painting a freehand ornamental frieze on the wall, but zeugmatic if I have been painting stripes on the road or applying makeup.[11] In short, the general sense of an underspecified common term may be non-salient, displaced by a specific subsense activated by the context. Where this occurs, the activated subsense shows signs of distinctness from other subsenses and from the general sense, so the general sense criterion clashes with the criteria of independent truth conditions and identity of sense constructions.

A third kind of polysemy arises with terms for complex objects which belong simultaneously to different ontological types. For example, a book is both a physical object or tome, having as parts pages, cover and a jacket, and physical properties of weight, size, and color, and at the same time an abstract text object with parts such as chapters, sub-types such as novel, research report or reference work, and expressive properties such as sadness or comedy, clarity or turgidity. Cruse (2000: 39) argues that the tome and text sense have independent truth conditions in such contrasts as *Do you like the book? No, it's terribly badly written/Yes, it's beautifully produced.* The distinct senses are also separately selected by different modifiers, as in *a shabby secondhand book* (tome) and *a clever but rather sad book* (text), which may be zeugmatic when coordinated, as in *a sad secondhand book.*[12] In addition, there seems to be no general superordinate sense which unifies the text and tome senses. On the other hand, the unified nature of the text-tome complex supports non-zeugmatic anaphoric cross-reference in *I'm really enjoying this book but I wish it had larger print*, or *John picked up the book, opened it, and was soon lost in its intriguing surreal world.* The text/tome pattern occurs generally with words such as *novel, report, CD, letter,* and so on. Pustejovsky's Generative Lexicon theory (1995) formally represents complex objects of the text-tome type as *dot objects*, with 'dotted' variables $x \cdot y$, where the component variables x and y represent the separate text and tome components. The simultaneous involvement of both text and tome in *Jones read the book*, represented *read(e, j, x·y)*, is shown by the dotted variable $x \cdot y$.

Nunberg (1979) correlates the complex object phenomenon with other regular patterns of polysemy. He argues that many recurrent patterns of variable denotation, found across languages, are produced by pragmatic inference and should not be treated as established word senses. Such regular patterns of polysemy include *chicken* to denote the bird or its meat, *newspaper* to denote the publication or its publisher, the name *Yeats* to denote the poet or his work, the name *France* to denote the geographical region or the political entity, and so on. Some of these polysemies resemble the text/tome complex in (1) occurring productively with other similar nouns (e.g. the name of any artist to refer to his or her work, as in *I love Turner/Patrick White/the Coen brothers*), (2) denoting different ontological types, and (3) supporting non-zeugmatic anaphoric cross-reference, as in *Yeats did not enjoy hearing himself read aloud.*

However, not all types of regular polysemy support non-zeugmatic cross-reference. The test requires the two senses to be realized in the word without changes in syntactic behavior, which excludes the animal/meat polysemy of *chicken*, and other regular sense shifts associated with count/mass alternations. For example, the anomaly of *I fed chicken and then cooked it for dinner* stems from the selectional clash between *feed*, requiring the 'animal' sense of *chicken* which occurs with the count form, and the mass form which has only the 'meat' sense.[13] Nunberg also mentions the regular pattern illustrated in *Vanity is a vice/His vanity surprised me*, where the second occurrence of *vanity* is interpreted as 'the large extent of his vanity.' This pattern, also found with *height*, is zeugmatic with crossed readings, as in *His height was six foot three and surprised me*. It appears that dot objects constitute a proper subtype of regular polysemy.

5.4   Representing polysemy

In traditional lexicography, polysemous senses of what is considered to be the same word are listed under a single headword – this is the listing or enumerative approach to polysemy. Generative approaches to polysemy are more prominent in linguistic theory, especially given the increased emphasis on the contribution of context and pragmatics to the sense of a word in a particular use. Different solutions are offered depending in part on the kind of contextual contribution to be considered.

The 'prevailing topic' problem raised by Cruses's example of *knife* and Tuggy's *paint*, discussed above, is also illustrated by Blutner's (2002: 27) example *The tones sounded impure because the hem was torn*, which we cannot really understand until we know that a set of bagpipes is under discussion, and can then make the otherwise unavailable connection between sewn cloth and sound production. Here the linguistic context does not supply the necessary information. This kind of phenomenon, among others, supports a strong view that word senses cannot be specified in sufficient detail to allow for utterance understanding, and that an attempt to model a mental lexicon listing words and all their fully determinate senses is misguided. On the strongest version of this view, the linguistic semantic information contained in the mental lexicon covers only those components relevant to syntax and morphology, such as gender or the count/mass distinction. Beyond this, word-forms are linked directly to conceptual structures in the 'encyclopedia,' or store of general knowledge. Peeters (2000) gives detailed discussion of the dictionary vs. encyclopedia debate.

For regular patterns of polysemy (count/mass *pet lamb, roast lamb*; container/containee *break a bottle, drink a bottle*; figure/ground *break the window, paint the window*; product/producer *read the paper, sue the paper*; plant/food *prune the fig, eat the fig*; etc.), inferential rules are proposed to generate additional senses.[14] Pustejovsky (1995) proposes that each polysemy pattern instantiates a *lexical conceptual paradigm* in the lexicon which automatically generates the sense variations of its instances.

Pustejovsky (1995) also provides a detailed computational account of polysemy arising from different collocations. Elaborated lexical entries for nouns include information coded under four *qualia*: the *formal quale* specifies what kind of object the noun denotes, the *constitutive quale* specifies what it is made of, the *telic quale* specifies what it is typically used for, and the *agentive quale* specifies how it is typically created. Interacting with these elaborated noun structures are three compositional mechanisms. In *type coercion*, a verb coerces a noun phrase to denote the kind of argument the verb selects. For example, the verb *enjoy* selects an event as its internal semantic argument. In *enjoy the novel* and *enjoy the pie*, the verb coerces the generally object-denoting noun phrase to denote an event type, specifically the kind of event coded in the head noun's telic quale (what the thing is used for). This gives the interpretations 'enjoy reading the novel' and 'enjoy eating the pie.' *Co-composition* produces the interpretation of *bake a cake* as 'make a cake' (in contrast to *bake a potato* = 'cook a potato by applying heat'). Under co-composition, the verb *bake* is identified as the predicate in the agentive quale for *cake*, specifying the typical provenance of a cake – a cake is made by baking. *Selective binding* accounts for the different interpretations of *fast* in *fast typist* and *fast boat*. The adjective *fast* must modify a process, and in construction with a nominal argument, it selectively binds the process represented in the telic quale of the modified noun. Accordingly, in *fast typist* the adjective modifies 'a typist types' and in *fast boat* it modifies 'one travels in a boat.'

Certain regular patterns of polysemy with verbs correlate with changes in the syntactic projection of their arguments, termed *verb alternations* or *verbal diathesis*, the focus of considerable research in syntactic theory (for verbal alternations see Levin 1993; Levin and Rappaport Hovav 1995). Rappaport and Levin (1988) propose regular word formation rules acting on lexical conceptual structures to generate some of the extended uses of alternating verbs. For example, the 'fill' sense of *load* in *John loaded the truck with furniture*, entailing that the truck was filled with furniture, is derived from the 'put' sense in *John loaded furniture onto the truck*. The 'fill' sense is assigned an LCS which may be glossed 'x cause y to come to be filled/covered by means of x cause z to come to be at y,' derived by rule from the embedded 'put' sense 'x cause z to come to be at y.' Unlike the regular polysemies discussed above, these rules appear to be explicitly linguistic rather than pragmatic, given their correlation with syntactic variation. The word-formation approach to verbal alternation assumes a basic lexical entry for a verb from which others are derived for different polysemous senses of the verb. Thus a polysemous verb is assigned multiple sense specifications.

Fillmore's frame semantics presents an alternative view, in which a common frame representing the sense of a word subsumes the individual schemata which encode polysemous subsenses and their associated syntactic constructions. For example, Fillmore and Atkins (1994) propose a frame for RISK underlying different uses of *risk* as a noun or verb. *Take a risk*, in contrast to *run a risk*, indicates that the protagonist has taken a decision to act in a way which exposes him or her to the possibility of harm. The complement to the verb *risk* may denote (1) an action exposing one to the possibility of harm (*She wouldn't risk entering the cage*), (2) a harmful consequence (*She risked being mauled*), or (3) something valued which one might lose as a consequence of some action (*She risked her life*). The RISK frame contains all these elements and is unspecified for the differences among the specific schemata, each of which is a subset of the frame. Developed from frame theory, Construction Grammar (see Goldberg 1995 and ch. 15, this volume, and the references cited there) also assigns an underspecified interpretation to alternating verbs, and locates the specific components of the subsenses in the associated syntactic frames, or constructions.

The choice between underspecified verb meanings and constructional meaning on the one hand, or polysemous verbs with associated subcategorization patterns on the other, is a central issue in current research on verb syntax and semantics, concerning not only argument projection but also aspectual interpretation (see Tenny and Pustejovsky 2000).

6   Future Directions

Insights from lexicography and cognitive psychology have already made great contributions to the study of word meaning. Perhaps the most significant recent directions in lexical semantics are computational approaches to issues in these fields.

Classical lexicography has long been based on actual data collected from corpora, but before the computer age there were considerable practical limitations on what could be achieved. Computer applications now allow the rapid examination of large corpora, which can reveal subtle aspects of the meaning of a word not readily available to introspection, particularly in patterns of word co-occurrence. For example, Stubbs (2001) found that *cause* has strongly negative connotations revealed by its most common immediate collocates including *problem*, *damage*, *death*, *disease*, *concern*, *cancer*, *pain*, and *trouble*. Computational analysis of slightly wider word contexts, such as within the same sentence, may reveal patterns of rhetorical combination (cf. antonymy above), and still wider contexts reveal tendencies of particular words to be used together in discourses on particular topics. We may expect computational corpus studies in the future to reveal a great deal more about the semantic behavior of words in context.

Progress in artificial intelligence, particularly the design of integrated lexicons and knowledge bases for natural language processing, is likely to have an increasing influence on theories of the mental lexicon and theories of conceptual structure.

NOTES

I wish to thank Lynne Murphy, Paul Buitelaar, and Bas Aarts, whose careful reading and valuable comments were a great help in improving this chapter. Any remaining errors or infelicities are my own.

1   Content words (nouns, verbs, adjectives, and adverbs) are distinguished from *functional words* (e.g. articles, particles, most prepositions). Other terms for the same distinction are *open class* and *closed class* words, or *categorematic* and *syncategorematic* words.

2   Color terms are vague or 'fuzzy' at their boundaries. For example, blue and green shade together in a region we call *blue-green*, which is not exactly blue and not exactly green. But the terms are mutually exclusive in application to focal colors: focal or 'true' blue is not referred to by the word *green*. However, if a language has one word for the whole green + blue color space, a single word refers to both focal blue and focal green.

3   For discussion of similar observations see also Clark (1993: 69–83).

4   Direct antonyms are 'good' antonyms that clash full force, compared with indirect antonyms such as *plentiful/meagre*, *warm/cold*, *rigid/pliable*, and so on. Indirect antonyms are of at least two main kinds. First, terms may be indirectly opposed because they do not cover corresponding parts of a scale, as in the indirect opposition between *warm* and *cold*. *Warm* and *cold* are opposed as falling in the positive and negative parts respectively of the temperature scale, but they are only indirectly opposed because they are not equidistant from the

neutral midpoint of the scale: the direct oppositions are *warm/cool* and *hot/cold* (see Lehrer and Lehrer 1982). Second, the oppositions between terms may be mediated by a direct opposition holding between near-synonyms of the indirect antonyms (see Gross et al. 1989). For example, *rigid* and *pliable* are opposed in being broad near-synonyms of the more basic terms *hard* and *soft*. Subjectively perceived 'goodness' of antonymy may also be related to word frequency, as well-established antonyms tend to be high-frequency words.

5   The entailments 'A entails not B' and 'B entails not A' strictly express only mutual exclusion, and also hold among terms from different semantic fields (including non-antonyms), as noted in section 2. In the context of a linear property scale, however, contraries form a binary opposition which constitutes antonymy.

6   A notable exception is Fodor's (1975) claim that concepts, hence word meanings, are noncompositional and innate.

7   The distinction resembles Aristotle's distinction between essential and accidental properties of entities (see Yablo 1998). An important difference is that Aristotle's properties are borne by entities themselves, while concept attributes are components of human psychology.

8   As a system of broad semantic classification of arguments, corresponding to particular linguistic forms, thematic roles theory resembles and draws on earlier work. The Sanskrit grammarian Pānini in the fifth

century BC developed a similar system (see Kiparsky & Staal 1988 for discussion). A recent forerunner of thematic roles theory is Fillmore's (1968) theory of deep case. For general discussion of thematic roles theory see Jackendoff (1987) and Dowty (1991).

9   Here I have adopted Foley and van Valin's (1984) distinction between the agentivity operator DO and the dummy predicate *do*, representing an unspecified (potentially nonagentive) action.

10   CAUSE and BECOME were first proposed in McCawley's famous (1968) analysis of *kill* as 'cause to become not alive.' In later Role and Reference Grammar (van Valin and La Polla 1997), based on Dowty 1979, BECOME is used for gradual change, distinct from INCH (inchoative) representing instantaneous change. Jackendoff (1990: 91–5) uses GO instead of BECOME, and also has a separate INCH function.

11   A relevant point here which Tuggy does not raise is that the test example contains intransitive *paint*, which is more restricted than transitive uses. In my judgment, *I have been painting* cannot appropriately be used to refer to painting stripes on the road or applying makeup.

12   The zeugma test is sensitive to rhetorical effects. Norrick (1981: 115) cites the naturalness of *Judy's dissertation is still thought-provoking though yellowed with age*, compared with the somewhat zeugmatic *Judy's dissertation is thought-provoking and yellowed with age*. Note that the rhetorical frame of the acceptable sentence signals a contrast between the age of the text (not the tome) and its thought-provokingness, weakening the zeugma. Judgments in this area are variable: Nunberg (1979: 150) offers as normal *John's dissertation, which weighs five pounds, has been refuted*, which I find somewhat anomalous.

13   Nunberg (1979) argues that pragmatic specification of a word's sense is also demonstrated in deferred ostension, as when one points to a copy of a newspaper and says *That was bought by Hearst last week*, using ostension of the publication object to refer to the publisher. This also appears to fail with *chicken*. If one points to a chicken and says *I'm having that for dinner tonight*, the interpretation is that the particular bird is to be killed and eaten.

14   But see Lehrer (1990) for discussion of the limited productivity of pragmatic sense extension rules. Unpredictable productivity is problematic for a generative account.

FURTHER READING

The main text contains a number of recommendations for further reading on particular issues, in the form 'see author (year).' For general introductions to lexical semantics, I also recommend:

Aitchison, J. (2002) *Words in the mind: an introduction to the mental lexicon*, 3rd edn. Oxford: Blackwell, chs. 4–8.

Allan, K. (2001) *Natural language semantics*. Oxford: Blackwell, chs. 3, 5, 9, and 10.

Croft, W. and Cruse, D. A. (2004)
Cognitive linguistics. Cambridge:
Cambridge University Press, chs. 5–8.

Cruse, D. A. (2000) *Meaning in language:
an introduction to semantics and
pragmatics*. Oxford: Oxford University
Press, chs. 5–13.

Saeed, J. I. (1997) *Semantics*. Oxford:
Blackwell, chs. 3 and 9.

For current developments in
computational lexical semantics, I also
recommend two web pages. The
web page for SIGLEX (a Special
Interest Group on the Lexicon of
the Association for Computational
Linguistics), which includes links to
related research groups, corpora, and
online proceedings from SIGLEX
meetings, is at www.siglex.org. The
web page for WordNet, including
links to numerous downloadable
research papers, is at http://
wordnet.princeton.edu/.

REFERENCES

Berlin, B. and Kay, P. (1969) *Basic color
terms: their universality and evolution*.
Berkeley: University of Los Angeles
Press.

Blutner, R. (2002) Lexical semantics and
pragmatics. *Linguistiche Berichte* 10,
27–58.

Chaffin, R., Herrman, D. J., and Winston,
M. E. (1988) An empirical taxonomy
of part-whole relations: effects of
part-whole relation type on relation
identification. *Language and Cognitive
Processes* 3, 17–48.

Charles, W. and Miller, G. A. (1989)
Contexts of antonymous adjectives.
Applied Psycholinguistics 10, 357–75.

Clark, E. (1983) Meanings and concepts.
In J. H. Flavell and E. M. Markman
(eds.), *Cognitive development*, 4th edn.
Volume 3 of P. H. Mussen (ed.),
Handbook of child psychology.
New York: Wiley, 787–840.

Clark, E. (1993) *The lexicon in acquisition*.
Cambridge: Cambridge University
Press.

Croft, W. and Cruse, D. A. (2004)
Cognitive linguistics. Cambridge:
Cambridge University Press.

Cruse, D. A. (1986) *Lexical semantics*.
Cambridge: Cambridge University
Press.

Cruse, D. A. (2000) Aspects of the
micro-structure of word meanings.
In Y. Ravin and C. Leacock (eds.),
*Polysemy: Theoretical and computational
approaches*. Oxford: Oxford University
Press, 30–51.

Dowty, D. (1979) *Word meaning and
Montague Grammar*. Dordrecht:
Kluwer.

Dowty, D. (1991) Thematic proto-roles
and argument selection. *Language* 67,
547–619.

Edmonds, P. (1999) Semantic
representations of near-synonyms
for automatic lexical choice. Ph.D.
dissertation, University of Toronto.
(Available at www.cs.toronto.edu/
compling/Publications/Abstracts/
Theses/EdmondsPhD-thabs.)

Edmonds, P. and Hirst, G. (2002)
Near-synonymy and lexical choice.
Computational Linguistics 28,
105–44.

Egan, R. F. (1942) Survey of the history
of English synonymy. In W. A.
Neilson and J. P. Bethel (eds.),
Webster's dictionary of synonyms. G.
and C. Merriam Company, vii–xxxiii.

Fellbaum, Christiane (ed.) (1998)
WordNet: an electronic lexical database.
Cambridge, MA: MIT Press.

Fellbaum, C. and Miller, G. A. (1990) Folk psychology or semantic entailment? Comments on Rips and Conrad (1989) *Psychological Review* 97, 565–70.

Fillmore, C. (1968) The case for case. In E. Bach and R. Harms (eds.), *Universals in linguistic theory*. New York: Holt, Rinehart & Winston, 1–88.

Fillmore, C. and Atkins, B. (1994) Starting where the dictionaries stop: the challenge of corpus lexicography. In B. T. S. Atkins and A. Zampolli (eds.), *Computational approaches to the lexicon*. Oxford: Clarendon Press, 349–93.

Fodor, J. A. (1975) *The language of thought*. Hassocks: Harvester Press.

Foley, W. A. and van Valin, R. (1984) *Functional syntax and universal grammar*. Cambridge: Cambridge University Press.

Geeraerts, D. (1993) Vagueness's puzzles, polysemy's vagaries. *Cognitive Linguistics* 4, 223–72.

Geeraerts, D. (1997*) Diachronic prototype semantics*. Oxford: Clarendon Press.

Goddard, C. (1998) *Semantic analysis: a practical introduction*. Oxford: Oxford University Press.

Goldberg, A. (1995) *Constructions: a construction grammar approach to argument structure*. Chicago and London: University of Chicago Press.

Grandy, R. (1992) Semantic fields, prototypes, and the lexicon. In A. Lehrer and E. F. Kittay (eds.), *Frames, fields and contrasts*. Hillsdale, NJ: Lawrence Erlbaum, 103–22.

Gross, D., Fischer, U., and Miller, G. A. (1989) Antonymy and the representation of adjectival meanings. *Journal of Memory and Language* 28: 92–106.

Gruber, J. (1965) Studies in lexical relations. Ph.D. dissertation, MIT.

Horn, L. (1989) *A natural history of negation*. Chicago: University of Chicago Press.

Jackendoff, R. (1972) *Semantic interpretation in generative grammar*. Cambridge, MA: MIT Press.

Jackendoff, R. (1983) *Semantics and cognition*. Cambridge, MA: MIT Press.

Jackendoff, Ray (1987) The status of thematic relations in linguistic theory. *Linguistic Inquiry* 18, 369–411.

Jackendoff, R. (1990) *Semantic structures*. Cambridge, MA: MIT Press.

Jones, S. (2002) *Antonymy: a corpus-based perspective*. London and New York: Routledge.

Justeson, J. S. and Katz, S. M. (1992) Redefining antonymy: the textual structure of a semantic relation. *Literary and Linguistic Computing* 7, 176–84.

Kiparsky, P. and Staal, F. (1988) Syntactic and semantic relations in Pānini. In F. Staal (ed.), *Universals: studies in Indian logic and linguistics*. Chicago: University of Chicago Press, 184–218.

Lakoff, G. (1973) Hedges: a study in meaning criteria and the logic of fuzzy concepts. *Journal of Philosophical Logic* 2, 458–508.

Lakoff, G. (1987) *Women, fire, and dangerous things*. Chicago: University of Chicago Press.

Lehrer, A. (1974) *Semantic fields and lexical structure*. Amsterdam and London: North-Holland.

Lehrer, A. (1985) Markedness and antonymy. *Journal of Linguistics* 21, 397–429.

Lehrer, A. (1990) Polysemy, conventionality, and the structure of the lexicon. *Cognitive Linguistics* 1, 207–46.

Lehrer, A. and Lehrer, K. (1982) Antonymy. *Linguistics and Philosophy* 5, 483–501.

Levin, B. (1993) *English verb classes and alternations: a preliminary investigation*. Chicago: Chicago University Press.

Levin, B. and Rappaport Hovav, M. (1995) *Unaccusativity: at the syntax-*

lexical semantics interface. Cambridge, MA: MIT Press.

Löbner, S. (2002) *Understanding semantics*. London: Arnold.

Lyons, J. (1968) *Introduction to theoretical linguistics*. Cambridge: Cambridge University Press.

Lyons, J. (1977) *Semantics*. Cambridge: Cambridge University Press.

McCawley, J. D. (1968) Lexical insertion in a transformational grammar without deep structure. *CLS* 4, 71–80.

Miller, G. A. and Johnson-Laird, P. N. (1976) *Language and perception*. Cambridge, MA: Harvard University Press.

Murphy, G. L. (2002) *The big book of concepts*. Cambridge, MA: MIT Press.

Murphy, M. L. (2003) *Semantic relations and the lexicon*. Cambridge: Cambridge University Press.

Murphy, M. L. and Jones, S. (2003) Antonymy in children's and child-directed speech. Sussex Working Papers in Linguistics and English Language. (Available at www.sussex.ac.uk/linguistics/1-4-1.)

Norrick, N. (1981) *Semiotic principles in semantic theory*. Amsterdam: John Benjamins.

Nunberg, G. (1979) The non-uniqueness of semantic solutions: polysemy. *Linguistics and Philosophy* 3, 143–84.

Peeters, B. (ed.) (2000) *The lexicon-encyclopedia interface*. Oxford: Elsevier Science.

Pustejovsky, J. (1995) *The generative lexicon*. Cambridge, MA: MIT Press.

Quine, W. van O. (1951; 1980) Two dogmas of empiricism. In W. van O. Quine, *From a logical point of view*, 2nd edn. Cambridge, MA: Harvard University Press, 20–46.

Rappaport, M. and Levin, B. (1988) What to do with θ-roles. In Wendy Wilkins (ed.), *Thematic relations (Syntax and Semantics*, vol. 21). New York: Academic Press, 7–36.

Rips, L. J., Shoben, E. J., and Smith, E. E. (1973) Semantic distance and the verification of semantic relations. *Journal of Verbal Learning and Verbal Behavior*, 12, 1–20.

Rosch, E. (1973) On the internal structure of perceptual and semantic categories. In T. E. Moore (ed.), *Cognitive development and the acquisition of language*. New York and London: Academic Press, 111–14.

Rosch, E. (1975) Cognitive representation of semantic categories. *Journal of Experimental Psychology: General* 104, 192–233.

Rosch, E. and Mervis, C. B. (1975) Family resemblances: studies in the internal structure of categories. *Cognitive Psychology* 7, 573–605.

Rosch, E., Mervis, C. B., Gray, W. D., Johnson, D. M., and Boyes-Braem, P. (1976) Basic objects in natural categories. *Cognitive Psychology* 8, 382–439.

Rusiecki, J. (1985) *Adjectives and comparison in English: a semantic study*. Essex: Longman.

Smith, E. E. and Medin, D. L. (1981) *Categories and concepts*. Cambridge, MA: Harvard University Press.

Smith, E. E., Rips, L. J., and Shoben, E. J. (1974) Semantic memory and psychological semantics. *The psychology of learning and motivation* 8, 1–45.

Stubbs, M. (2001) *Words and phrases: corpus studies of lexical semantics*. Oxford: Blackwell.

Taylor, J. (1989; 1995; 2003) *Linguistic categorization: prototypes in linguistic theory*. Oxford: Clarendon Press.

Tenny, C. and Pustejovsky, J. (2000) *Events as grammatical objects*. Stanford, CA: CSLI.

Tuggy, D. (1993) Ambiguity, polysemy and vagueness. *Cognitive Linguistics* 4, 273–90.

Ungerer, F. and Schmid, H.-J. (1996) *An introduction to cognitive linguistics*. Essex: Longman.

Van Valin, R. D. and LaPolla, R. J. (1997) *Syntax: structure, meaning and function.* Cambridge: Cambridge University Press.

Wierzbicka, A. (1996) *Semantics, primes, and universals.* Oxford: Oxford University Press.

Winston, M. E., Chaffin, R., and Herrmann, D. (1987) A taxonomy of part-whole relations. *Cognitive Science* 11, 417–44.

Wittgenstein, L. (1953/1958) *Philosophical investigations.* London: Macmillan.

Yablo, S. (1998) Essentialism. In E. Craig (ed.), *Routledge encyclopedia of philosophy*, vol. 3. London and New York: Routledge.

25 Lexicography

JULIE COLEMAN

1 Introduction

A number of separate areas of scholarly activity are linked under the label *lexicography*. The central and original use of the term is with reference to the writing of dictionaries. It is also used to refer to the study of dictionaries and of their use, more precisely called *dictionary research, academic lexicography*, or *metalexicography*. This chapter will discuss current research and recent developments in the closely related fields of lexicography and dictionary research.

2 Definitions: Dictionary Typology

It is difficult to talk about lexicography, in either sense, without first considering what a dictionary is. An internet search for publications from 2003 with *dictionary* in the title found dictionaries of human rights, the Middle Ages, African-American architects, nuclear engineering, dreams, birds, love, and medical quotations, among many others. This demonstrates that to the publisher, and to the public, *dictionary* can mean merely 'an alphabetically arranged reference work,' and that it suggests clear explanation, authority and exhaustiveness. In reality, *encyclopaedia* is often used in the same way: for each of these dictionaries it was possible to find an encyclopaedia of the same or a closely related area, which presumably would, in most cases, have contained similar material. *Dictionary* may have the edge over *encyclopaedia* in commercial publishing merely because there is no necessity to choose between spelling variants.

A major endeavor of any field of research is to define and classify the object of study. Lexicography is no different: dictionary typology is a growing area of concern. Several scholars have attempted to provide a way of classifying dictionaries based on their structure, content, use, size, information categories included, languages covered, and so on, but none has yet succeeded in covering all the possibilities (see Hartmann 2001: 68–79).

To the lexicographer, *dictionary* tends to mean 'a reference work dealing with words,' thus often including thesauruses, but usually excluding encyclopaedias. In this category, then, we might include dictionaries of catchphrases, proverbs, idioms, etymology, new words, and personal and place names, all also published during 2003. We can also categorize dictionaries according to their intended users. During 2003 many bilingual and monolingual dictionaries were published, aimed at foreign and second language learners at various levels. There were college dictionaries, school dictionaries, beginners', elementary, intermediate and advanced dictionaries, illustrated dictionaries, and picture dictionaries. Some dictionaries aim for a particular use rather than type of user, such as rhyming dictionaries, crossword dictionaries, and so on. Others are restricted in terms of the area of vocabulary that they cover: dictionaries of slang and euphemism, dictionaries of synonyms and antonyms, dictionaries of British, American, Australian (etc.) English. Dictionaries are sometimes grouped by size, which is indicated in a number of ways: they can be for the desk or the pocket, they can be mini, super-mini, concise, compact, or unabridged. Some are aimed at a narrow scholarly audience, others at a mass market.

3 Dictionary Research

In short, there is a bewildering array of publications that describe themselves as dictionaries. Which of these are of interest to dictionary researchers? The answer is, in theory, most of those that are not encyclopaedic, but in practice very few. In reality, dictionary researchers have tended, in the main, to concentrate on dictionaries published before 1830, the *Oxford English Dictionary* (*OED*), and modern monolingual learners' dictionaries (but see Liberman, 2002).

3.1 Dictionary history

An early area of dictionary research was the history of the English dictionary. No one has yet produced anything to rival Starnes and Noyes's (1946) masterly account of the early history of the English dictionary, but several recent publications have supplemented it, including Hüllen's (1999) account of early thesauruses, Cowie's (1999) examination of learners' dictionaries, and Gotti's (1999) and Coleman's (2004a, 2004b) studies of slang and cant dictionaries. Useful studies of individual dictionaries include Reddick (1996) on Johnson's dictionary, Micklethwait (2000) and Morton (1994), on Noah Webster's *American Dictionary of the English Language*, and Mugglestone (2000) and Willinsky (1994), on the *OED*.

Dictionary researchers are also broadening the scope of their field chronologically and textually. Studies of manuscript dictionaries have challenged preconceptions about the history of the English dictionary, which has tended to focus on later printed works (Stein 1995; Cooke 1997a, 1997b; Lancashire forthcoming). Textually, historical dictionary studies are developing their understanding of the relationships between early monolingual and bilingual dictionaries (Takeda 1998).

3.2 Learners' dictionaries

Bilingual dictionaries have a longer history than monolingual English dictionaries, dating back to the Old English period, but dictionary research has suggested that monolingual learners' dictionaries are more useful to users, because they can provide more and better targeted information about the language to be learned (Leban 2002: 185; but see Stein 2002: 17 for a defence of bilingual dictionaries). There has been a consequent development of interest in the history of modern learners' dictionaries (Stein 2002: 70–100). Cowie (1999) identifies three generations of monolingual learners' dictionaries. The first generation was influenced by the vocabulary control movement, which sought to define English words using a restricted range of vocabulary (Longman EFL dictionaries still use this approach). The second generation was marked by its interest in phraseology, and the third by the use of computer technology. Heuberger (2000) brings this study up to date with an account of the current situation with regard to monolingual learners' dictionaries. In monolingual dictionaries the easy option of providing a translation equivalent for a term such as *pulley* or *hide-and-seek* is not available, and many use illustrations instead of lengthy definitions (Stein 2002: 125–58, 169–203).

The major learners' dictionaries are under constant revision, and details can most usefully be found at their websites, which are listed below. See Nichols (2003) for a discussion of British dominance in the monolingual learners' dictionary market.

3.2.1 User-perspective

The interests of the dictionary-user have also become an important focus in recent dictionary research (Atkins 1998). It is only through an understanding of how dictionaries are actually used that lexicographers can strive to improve them. Fraser (1997), for example, argues that in dictionaries aimed at native-speakers, pronunciation guides are most usefully given in the form of non-phonemic respellings (e.g. jep-pa-dize for *jeopardize*) rather than in the more commonly used International Phonetic Alphabet (IPA). Many user-perspective dictionary studies have concentrated on learners' dictionaries, both bilingual and monolingual. They consider how and why learners of English consult dictionaries, and how the dictionaries should be designed to ensure that their users can locate the information contained within them (Herbst and Popp 1999; Nesi 2000; Tono 2001). For example, a learner using a dictionary for translation would want to be able to locate the correct sense as quickly as possible, while one consulting a dictionary for the purposes of language production would be more likely to want extra information about grammar, syntax, pronunciation, and so on (Atkins and Varantola 1997; Otani 2002).

3.2.2   Computer corpora

Advancements in IT have played a large part in the development of learners' dictionaries, and also in the imaginings of dictionary researchers for their future (Fontenelle 1997; Kumar 1998; Nesi 1999). Ooi (1998: ch. 2) makes a useful distinction between computational linguistics (the building of lexicons for natural language processing), computational lexicography (the production or use of machine-readable dictionaries), and computer corpus linguistics (the principles and practice of compiling bodies of electronic texts of actual language). The use of language corpora has revolutionized the production of dictionaries like the Collins COBUILD and Longman learners' dictionaries: instead of beginning with a word-list, the compilers collect texts and recordings of English in use to ensure that they reflect actual usage rather than lexicographers' preconceptions or linguistic history. This inevitably raises new questions for researchers to explore (e.g. Atkins and Levin 1995; Kilgariff 1997). For example, if senses are ordered according to frequency of usage, does this provide users with the best way of understanding relationships between literal and figurative senses of the same word? (van der Meer 1999, 2002).

3.3   Dictionaries as cultural products

Under the influence of developments in literary, cultural, and historical studies, scholars in this field are now acutely aware that dictionaries are and always have been cultural products and political tools (e.g. Lara 1995; Stark 1999). Cultural biases in dictionaries are evident in their selection of headwords, usage labels, and citations, in the wording of definitions and ordering of senses, and even in their willingness to give etymologies from particular language sources (Algeo 1995; Görlach 1995: 82–127; Osselton 1995: 41; Whitcut 1995; Chardonnens 1997; Murphy 1998; Nakamoto 1998). An example of a dictionary serving a political purpose is Thomas Spence's *Grand Repository of the English Language*, published in 1775, which proposed a reformed alphabet that would enable the lower classes to achieve sufficient literacy to become politically aware (Beal 1999: 4). A more modern example is the production of dictionaries of Canadian English, which, Lilles (2000) argues, have been important in defining a sense of national as well as linguistic identity.

3.4   Dictionaries and the internet

By far the greatest shock to lexicographers' understanding of what a dictionary is has come from developments in the internet. There have always been non-scholarly dictionaries, some self-published, but there has been nothing to compare with the explosion in online dictionaries. A dictionary need no longer have a fixed form. The online version of the *OED*, for example, adds new and revised entries four times a year (http://dictionary.oed.com/). Although readers were encouraged to submit material to the *OED* for inclusion in the dictionary even when it was being edited on paper, online sites make this process easier and more immediate (e.g. www.peevish.co.uk/slang). Some online dictionaries do not edit the material submitted by their users at all, which changes entirely the relationship between dictionary-maker and dictionary-user (e.g. www.urbandictionary.com). Some sites allow the consultation of several online dictionaries simultaneously (e.g. www.onelook.com). Dictionary entries can be reordered or searched according to the user's needs, whether they are trying to understand a document (e.g. http://english.voycabulary.com/ [sic]), struggling to complete a crossword (e.g. wordplays.com), or attempting to write a poem (e.g. www.rhymer.com).

The internet has also facilitated the publication of research materials that would not otherwise have been economically viable. Ian Lancashire's Early Modern English Dictionaries Database (EMEDD) (www.chass.utoronto.ca/english/emed/emedd.html) is a prime example of this.

3.5   *The profession of lexicography*

A relatively recent development in the discipline, perhaps as a result of the increasing use of IT, is the establishment of training programmes and degree courses for lexicographers. Hartmann (2001: 7) notes that in the past 'people drifted into and out of dictionary making from such diverse occupations as theology and education . . . literature . . . philology . . . medicine . . . and music . . .' In contrast, Masters degrees in lexicography are now available at several universities, and many undergraduate linguistics programmes also include courses on lexicography. There are dictionary research centers at universities throughout the world. The websites of professional associations for dictionary researchers are a useful way of keeping up with activity in this area, and are listed below.

Interrelated with the establishment of these training programmes and professional organizations has been the gradual evolution of well-defined lexicographic theories:

> Lexicography, often misconceived as a branch of linguistics, is *sui generis*, a field whose endeavours are informed by the theories and practices of information science, literature, publishing, philosophy, and historical, comparative, and applied linguistics. Sister disciplines, such as terminology, lexicology, encyclopedia work, bibliography, terminography, indexing, information technology, librarianship, media studies, translation and teaching, as well as the neighbouring disciplines of history, education and anthropology, provide the wider setting within which lexicographers have defined and developed their field.   (Hartmann and James 2001: vii)

Publications in this area include manuals for lexicographers (e.g. Svensén 1993; Bergenholtz and Tarp 1995), accounts of developments in lexicographic practice (Béjoint 1995; Shcherba 1995), and textbooks for teachers, researchers, and students (Hartmann 2001; Jackson 2002). Gusun (1998), on the other hand, casts doubt both on the notion that lexicography is a discipline in its own right, and also on the idea that practising lexicographers are able to formulate theories for what they do.

It should come as no surprise that this field is well supplied with reference works. Kabdebo and Armstrong (1997) list dictionaries of various subjects. McGill (1996) provides the contact details and research interests of EURALEX members. Hartmann and James (2001) explain terms used in lexicography and dictionary research.

3.5.1   *Historical lexicography: current and recent projects*

Several major historical dictionary projects are currently underway, all making extensive use of computers, but none losing sight of the long traditions on which they build. These include the third edition of the *OED* (cited above), the *Dictionary of Old English* (www.doe.utoronto.ca), the *Historical thesaurus of English* (see Kay and Wotherspoon 2002) and the ninth edition of Partridge's *Dictionary of slang and unconventional English* (www.partridge-slang.com/what.html). Recently completed historical dictionary projects include the *Thesaurus of Old English* (TOE) (Roberts and Kay 1995; see also Hideki 2002), the *Dictionary of South African English on historical principles* (DSAE) (Silva, 1996), and the *Middle English dictionary* (MED) (Lewis 2001). The MED is also available online as part of the *Middle English Compendium* (http://ets.umdl.umich.edu/m/mec/).

4   Dictionary Content

Having talked about what a dictionary is, and what dictionary-researchers do, let us look more closely at what lexicographers do: at the contents of dictionaries. We will begin by comparing various dictionaries' entries for the word *dictionary*, starting with two relatively early English examples. Edward Phillips published his *New world of English words* in 1658:

> *Dictionary*, (lat.) called in Greek a Lexicon, a Book wherein hard words and names are mentioned and unfolded.

Samuel Johnson's dictionary appeared in 1755, and provided much more information:

> Dɪ'ᴄᴛɪᴏɴᴀʀʏ. *n.s.* [*dictionarium*, Latin.] A book containing the words of any language in alphabetical order, with explanations of their meaning; a lexicon; a vocabulary; a word-book.
>
> Some have delivered the polity of spirits, and left an account that they stand in awe of charms, spells, and conjurations; that they are afraid of letters and characters, notes and dashes, which, set together, do signify nothing; and not only in the *dictionary* of man, but in the subtler vocabulary of satan.   *Brown's* [sic] *Vulgar Errours, b.* i. *c.* 10. [other citations omitted]

In writing his dictionary, Johnson built on the work of his predecessors, taking the best features of previously published dictionaries, and adding new features to them. Here we can see that he gives the source form as well as language, while Phillips gives only the source language. Johnson offers synonyms as well as a definition, and he provides citations to illustrate the use of the word in context.

The dictionary that was to supersede Johnson's, the *OED*, provides, as might be expected, the longest entry:

> **dictionary** (dɪkʃənəɹɪ) [ad. med.L. *dictionarium* or *dictionarius* (sc. *liber*) lit. 'a repertory of *dictiones*, phrases or words' (see <u>DICTION</u>) in F. *dictionnaire* (R. Estienne 1539), It. *dizionario*, Sp. *diccionario*.]
>
> **1. a.** A book dealing with the individual words of a language (or certain specified classes of them), so as to set forth their orthography, pronunciation, signification, and use, their synonyms, derivation, and history, or at least some of these facts: for convenience of reference, the words are arranged in some stated order, now, in most languages, alphabetical; and in larger dictionaries the information given is illustrated by quotations from literature; a word-book, vocabulary, or lexicon.
>
> Dictionaries proper are of two kinds: those in which the meanings of the words of one language or dialect are given in another (or, in a polyglot dictionary, in two or more languages), and those in which the words of a language are treated and illustrated in this language itself. The former were the earlier.

This is followed by an account of the earliest uses of *dictionarius/dictionarium*, and related terms, concluding:

> Dictionaries (so entitled) of English and various modern languages appeared in England from 1547 onward; in the seventeenth century the name was gradually extended to works explaining English words, only 'hard words' being admitted into the earliest English Dictionaries.
>
> *Vocabulary* is now generally limited to a smaller and less comprehensive collection of words, or to a word-book of technical, or specific terms. *Lexicon* is the name usually given to dictionaries of Greek, Hebrew, Arabic, Syriac, Ethiopic, and some other literary languages. **1526** *Pilgr. Perf.* (W. de W. 1531) 233 And so Peter Bercharius in his dictionary describeth it. [. . .]

The *OED* offers dated citations for all senses (I have included only the first as an example), usually aiming for one citation per century of use, though online publication has reduced the emphasis on economy of citation in new entries. Several other definitions follow, arranged chronologically, where possible, each illustrated by its own citations (omitted here):

> † **b.** *fig.* The vocabulary or whole list of words used or admitted by any one. *Obs.* [1579, 1646, 1727]
>
> **c.** Colloq. phr. *to have swallowed the* (or *a*) *dictionary*: to use long or recondite words. [1934, 1966]
>
> **d.** An ordered list stored in and used by a computer; *spec.* (*a*) a list of contents, e.g. of a database; (*b*) a list of words acceptable to a word-processing program,

against which each word of text is checked. [1957, 1964, 1969, 1975, 1975, 1980, 1984]

The sense 'an alphabetical reference work' is treated separately:

2. a. By extension: A book of information or reference on any subject or branch of knowledge, the items of which are arranged in alphabetical order; an alphabetical encyclopædia: as a Dictionary of *Architecture, Biography, Geography*, of *the Bible*, of *Christian Antiquities*, of *Dates*, etc.

(Here the essential sense 'word-book' is supplanted by the accidental one of 'reference book in alphabetical order' arising out of the alphabetical arrangement used in modern word-books.) [1631, 1712, 1871]

b. *fig.* A person or thing regarded as a repository of knowledge, convenient for consultation. [1774, 1837, 1849, 1893]

3. *attrib.* and *Comb.*, as **dictionary English, meaning, order, phraseology, word, work; dictionary-maker, -making, -writer, -writing; dictionary-tutored** adj.; **dictionary-monger**, one who deals much with dictionaries; **dictionary-proof** *a.*, proof against the informing influence of a dictionary. [. . .]

Hence **dictionaryless** *a.*, without a dictionary. [1854]

The *OED* concludes by providing examples of compounds and derivatives. Note that it defines non-standard usages as well as those that are obsolete.

Chamber's English dictionary (Landau and Ramson 1990), boasting 265,000 definitions for 190,000 references, is rather briefer:

dictionary *dikshən-ə-ri, n.* book containing the words of a language alphabetically arranged, with their meanings, etymology, etc.: a lexicon: a work containing information on any department of knowledge, alphabetically arranged. [L.L. *dɪkʃənərɪ*; see **diction**.]

Chambers *Mini Dictionary* (Anderson, Higgleton, and Rennie 2002), with 45,000 definitions for 35,000 references, pares this entry down:

dictionary *noun.* (*plural* **dictionaries**) **1** a book giving the words of a language in alphabetical order, together with their meanings **2** any alphabetically ordered reference book.

The *Collins COBUILD English language dictionary* (Sinclair 1992), with 'over 70,000 references' is slightly fuller:

dictionary /dɪkʃənərɪ/, **dictionaries.** A **dictionary** is **1** a book in which the words of the language are listed alphabetically and their meanings are explained. **2** a book in which words in one language are listed alphabetically and are followed by words which have the same meaning in another language. EG . . . *an English-French dictionary.* **3.** any alphabetically ordered reference book on one particular subject or limited group of subjects. EG . . . *the Dictionary of National Biography.*

Note that citations here are unattributed: they are provided merely to illustrate the use of the term rather than to tell us anything about its history.

Harraps French-English/Anglais-Français Shorter English Dictionary (Goldie 1991), boasting 235,000 references and 460,000 translations, is obviously intended for a different purpose, indeed, it corresponds with COBUILD sense 2:

> **dictionary** ['dɪkʃən(ə)rɪ] *n* dictionnaire *m*; **English-French d.**, dictionnaire anglais-français; **d. of quotations**, dictionnaire de citations.

The entry in Partridge's *Dictionary of slang and unconventional English* (1967) is shorter yet and, it should be noted, does not define *dictionary* at all:

> **dictionary, up to.** Learned: coll.: C. 19.

Another specialist dictionary, Hartmann and James (2001), defines *dictionary* thus:

> **dictionary** A type of REFERENCE WORK which presents the vocabulary of a language in alphabetical order, usually with explanations of meanings.
>
> Since the sixteenth century the TITLE *dictionary* has been used for an increasingly wider range of alphabetic (but also thematic), general (but also specialized), monolingual (but also bilingual and multilingual) reference works, from the polyglot to the historical and the pedagogical dictionary. At the same time there has been a tendency for other terms to be used as designations for more specialized dictionary genres, e.g. THESAURUS, ENCYCLOPEDIA and TERMINOLOGY. To describe and evaluate the structural components of dictionaries, terms like MACROSTRUCTURE (the overall WORD-LIST and its organization) and MICROSTRUCTURE (the information categories presented inside entries) have been developed in the literature. [further references to entries within the dictionary and to further reading omitted]

Hartmann and James list 55 compounds and phrases beginning with *dictionary*, each as a separate headword. Writing for a specialized audience, they provide numerous cross-references to other specialist terms in small capitals.

4.1   Coverage of senses

Clearly, even with a relatively straightforward word to define, lexicographers make different choices about which senses to include. These are based on the perceived needs of the dictionary's intended users and on practical constraints such as the projected size and cost of the dictionary. The uses of *dictionary* listed in these works can be tabulated as shown in table 25.1.

All but Partridge, whose dictionary lists only non-standard uses, include the first sense, although Phillips' definition assumes that only difficult words would be listed, as was the case in early dictionaries of English. Most of the modern

Table 25.1   Definitions of *dictionary*

	word-book	bilingual word-book	vocabulary	list of words stored in a computer	alphabetical reference work	knowledgeable person	compounds & derivatives	phrases
Phillips	y	n	n	n	n	n	n	n
Johnson	y	n	n	n	n	n	n	n
OED	y	y	y	y	y	y	y	y
Chambers	y	n	n	n	y	n	n	n
Chambers mini	y	n	n	n	y	n	n	n
COBUILD	y	y	n	n	y	n	n	n
Harraps	y	y	n	n	y	n	n	n
Partridge	n	n	n	n	n	n	n	y
Hartmann & James	y	y	n	n	y	n	y	n

dictionaries recognize the bilingual dictionary as a distinctly different type of reference work, to the extent, in some cases, of providing it with a separate, numbered definition. The *OED* lists several senses that none of the other dictionaries include, largely because they are rare or obsolete. Partridge lists only one use, which none of the other dictionaries has: his purpose is to record slang, no matter how obscure. Although *dictionary* was used with the wider sense 'an alphabetical reference work' when Phillips and Johnson were compiling their dictionaries, they both choose not to include that meaning, presumably considering the first sense to be more correct. Both Hartmann and James and the *OED* have discursive paragraphs on the history and typology of the dictionary and distinguish *dictionary* from closely related terms.

Because the *OED* is a historical dictionary, it tends to order its senses chronologically. Learners' dictionaries now sometimes order senses by frequency, so that the most commonly used sense of a word, and therefore the one most often looked up, will come first.

These definitions reveal an interesting feature of historical dictionary study. While admitting that there is a limited range of ways in which a single word can be defined, there is a marked similarity between the Chambers definition and Johnson's. Chambers has been publishing dictionaries of English since at least the 1860s, and it is possible that the first compiler would have turned to the most authoritative dictionary then available. Later editors of the dictionary, and of offshoots such as the *Mini dictionary*, will have been editing Johnson's definition (itself perhaps derived from earlier dictionaries) ever since.

4.2   Dictionary entries

There is more to analyzing a dictionary's contents than merely counting up the number of senses given for each term, however. The structure of the dictionary entry can also be broken down into its constituent elements (table 25.2).

Based only on this sample, which may not be representative, the dictionaries provide a wide range of different types of information about the words they list. The only feature they all share is the headword. Five indicate how the word is pronounced, although Johnson shows only stress. Grammatical information also seems to be nonessential, though the dictionaries that do not indicate part of speech explicitly imply it in their definitions. Even though *dictionary* is entirely regular in forming its plural with *-ies*, two of these dictionaries list the plural form: both presumably aimed at learners. Etymologies, a feature important enough to some of these lexicographers to be included in their definition of *dictionary*, are excluded from most of the modern works, particularly those aimed at learners or providing restricted coverage. Even definitions are not essential: Harraps and Partridge instead provide a synonym in French or standard English. Phillips joins them in this, and for the purpose of improving our general knowledge, gives us a synonym in Greek. The inclusion of usage dates is a defining characteristic of historical dictionaries. Partridge gives only an indication of period, while the *OED* provides specific dates. Partridge and the *OED* both also provide usage labels within these entries, a common feature in any dictionary covering a variety of registers.

4.2.1   Citations

The three dictionaries in this selection that include illustrative citations did so for very different reasons and collected them in ways that illuminate changes in the practice of lexicography. Johnson used earlier dictionaries as the foundation for his work, as lexicographers had done for centuries (Reddick 1996: 50–1). Unlike earlier lexicographers, however, he systematically illustrated his entries with citations showing the words in use. These citations were largely selected from Johnson's own reading, and reflect his interests and outlook:

Table 25.2   Elements of dictionary entries for *dictionary*

	headword	pronunciation	part of speech	plural form	cross-reference	usage labels	numbered senses	definition	equivalent in another language	citation	usage dates	etymology	cognates
Phillips	y	n	n	n	n	n	n	y	y	n	n	y	n
Johnson	y	(y)	y	n	n	n	n	y	n	y	n	y	n
OED	y	y	n	n	y	y	y	y	n	y	y	y	y
Chambers	y	y	y	n	y	n	n	y	n	n	n	y	n
Chambers mini	y	n	y	y	n	n	y	y	n	n	n	n	n
COBUILD	y	y	n	y	n	n	y	y	n	y	n	n	n
Harraps	y	y	y	n	n	n	n	n	y	n	n	n	n
Partridge	y	n	n	n	n	y	n	n	(y)	n	y	n	n
Hartmann & James	y	n	n	n	y	n	n	y	n	n	n	n	n

the most that Johnson could do without violating his basic intention to provide a legitimate lexical work was to provide a stream of reminders spread throughout the text, consistent in their defense of orthodox Anglicanism and its establishment in, but independence from, the State. He could, however, develop a persistent rhetoric whereby he tied language, through a combination of definition and exemplification, to politico-theological argument.   (Reddick 1996: 164)

Johnson's is an example of a prescriptive dictionary: one that tells its users how the language should be used. His citations serve this end: the correct use of words by eminent writers sets an example to the dictionary-user. The *OED*, on the other hand, set out to be descriptive: to show how the language actually is used. To this end, Murray, the editor between 1879 and 1915, encouraged interested members of the public to send him citations from their own reading. Some noted down the odd word when a usage struck them as interesting.

A few read and excerpted systematically, ploughing through the works of individual authors. Others were called upon for their expertise in particular fields. An estimated five million citations from this reading programme found their way into the first edition of the *OED*. Within individual entries they were selected to show chronological coverage, and common connotations (shades of meaning) and collocations (co-occurrence with specific words or phrases).

There are a number of criticisms of the *OED*'s use of citations (see especially Schäfer (1980)), a few of which are reflected in the later development of dictionaries, including the *OED* itself. Murray's appeals to readers often emphasize the importance of recording common usages as well as the unusual, but with a large-scale reading programme using untrained readers, it is inevitable that interesting examples of uninteresting words will be passed over. There is also no guarantee against readers' ad hoc censorship of offensive or 'incorrect' usage. The use of vast databanks, like that of Collins COBUILD, overcomes these problems to some extent (see above). Lexicographers no longer piece together their entries from snippets of text selected for the purpose: they now have access to examples of words in use in thousands of entire works at the touch of a button.

The selection of texts is another way in which preconceptions and preferences can result in biased coverage of the language. The *OED* is based primarily on particular types of texts: literature, the Bible, academic writings. The third edition makes use of a wider range of text types, particularly newspapers and magazines. It is still largely based on written English however, so it can only reflect how the language is spoken in so far as spoken language is represented in written texts. Dictionaries like those from Collins COBUILD, aimed at learners of English, include transcriptions of spoken English in their language banks, and, as we have seen, use their citations to an entirely different end.

5   Market Forces

We should not forget that most dictionaries are commercial products, and have to meet market demand. An example of the clash between firmly held lexicographic theory and customers' wishes came with the publication of the third edition of Webster's dictionary of American English. The dictionary-makers sought, as dictionary-makers now generally do, to reflect the way English is used; the dictionary-buyers expected to be told what was right and wrong – and more to the point, they did not want to see usages that they regarded as wrong legitimized by inclusion (Stein 2002: 34–5). How can we tell our children that *ain't* is wrong, if they can retort that it is in 'the dictionary'? In fact, although lexicographers shy away from prescriptive pronouncements, publishers still provide this area of the market, in the shape of numerous usage guides and dictionaries of hard words (e.g. Schur 1989; Howard 1993; Miller and Swift 1995). Even these are less authoritarian than they used to be, for example:

> **enormity** (1) Great wickedness (of something)...; a serious offence...
> (2) Enormousness. • Sense (2) is common, but is regarded by many people
> as incorrect. (Weiner, Delahunty, and Whitcut 1994)

These two principles also clash in the treatment of offensive vocabulary in EFL
dictionaries. Modern lexicographers are very reluctant to use prescriptive labels
(e.g. *bad*, *vulgar*, *base*), but not to indicate the social connotations attached to
swear-words, racist, sexist, and homophobic vocabulary, would be to do a
disservice to their buyers (Stein 2002: 159–68).

6 Summary

Lexicography and dictionary research are exciting areas to work in. Both
are undergoing major changes, largely because of developments in IT. For
dictionary-makers as well as dictionary-users, computers, and particularly the
internet, offer previously unimaginable possibilities. At the same time, the
market for dictionaries of English in book-form continues to grow. Dictionary
researchers' work in reviewing these works and in studying how they are
used feeds back into the next generation of dictionaries, and it is likely that, as
a result, the dictionary market will specialize still further. Meanwhile, those
undertaking historical dictionary research are reopening questions about the
development of the English dictionary that were previously thought to have
been authoritatively settled.

PROFESSIONAL ASSOCIATIONS FOR DICTIONARY RESEARCHERS

AFRILEX: African Association for
Lexicography www.up.ac.za/
academic/libarts/afrilang/
homelex.html

ASIALEX: Asian Association for
Lexicography http://
tonolab.meikai.ac.jp/~tono/
asialex/

DSNA: Dictionary Society of North
America http://polyglot.lss.wisc.edu/
dsna/index.html

EURALEX: European Association
for Lexicography www.ims.uni-
stuttgart.de/euralex

ISHLL: International Society for
Historical Lexicography and
Lexicology www.le.ac.uk/ee/
jmc21/ishll.html

SIGLEX: A special interest group of
the Association for Computational
Linguistics www.cis.upenn.edu/
~mpalmer/siglex2.html

ONLINE DICTIONARIES

A dictionary of slang:
   www.peevish.co.uk/slang
DOE: www.doe.utoronto.ca
EMEDD: www.chass.utoronto.ca/
   english/emed/emedd.html
MED: http://ets.umdl.umich.edu/m/
   mec/
OED: http://dictionary.oed.com/
one-look dictionary search:
   www.onelook.com

Partridge's dictionary: www.partridge-
   slang.com/what.html
urban dictionary:
   www.urbandictionary.com
VoyCabulary: http://english.
   voycabulary.com/
wordplays:wordplays.com
WriteExpress online rhyming dictionary:
   www.rhymer.com

LEARNERS' DICTIONARY WEBSITES

Cambridge (http://
   dictionary.cambridge.org/)
Chambers (www.chambersharrap.co.uk/
   chambers/index.php)
Collins COBUILD (www.collins.co.uk/
   books.aspx?group=140)

Longman (www.longman.com/
   dictionaries/international.html)
Oxford (www.oup.com/elt/?cc=gb)

FURTHER READING

Apresjan, Juri (2000) *Systematic lexicography*. Trans. Kevin Windle. Oxford: Oxford University Press.

Berry, H. (2001) Rethinking politeness in eighteenth-century England: Moll King's coffee house and the significance of 'flash talk.' *Transactions of the Royal Historical Society* 11, 65–81.

Carr, M. (1997) Internet dictionaries and lexicography. *International Journal of Lexicography* 10, 209–21.

Considine, J. (1997) Etymology and the *Oxford English Dictionary*: a response. *International Journal of Lexicography* 10, 234–6.

Considine, J. (2001) Narrative and persuasion in early modern English dictionaries. *Review of English Studies* 52, 2, 195–206.

Fowler, R. (1998) Robert Browning in the *Oxford English Dictionary*: a new approach. *Studies in Philology* 95, 333–50.

Landau, Sidney I. (1984) *Dictionaries: the art and craft of lexicography*. New York: Charles Scribner's Sons.

Lundbladh, C.-E. (1997) Etymology and the historical principles of *OED*. *International Journal of Lexicography* 10, 231–3.

McArthur, T. (1999) *Living words: language, lexicography and the knowledge revolution*. Exeter: University of Exeter Press.

Mugglestone, L. (1999) Balance and bias in dictionaries. *English Review* 9 (4), 13–15.

Murphy, M. L. (1999) Racing for definitions in South Africa. *Verbatim* 24 (2), 10–13.

Murray, K. M. Elizabeth (1977) *Caught in the web of words: James Murray and the Oxford English Dictionary.* New Haven, CN: Yale University Press.

Nakao, K. (1998) The state of bilingual lexicography in Japan: learners' English–Japanese/Japanese–English dictionaries. *International Journal of Lexicography* 11, 35–50.

Nishimura, T. (2002) Japanese learners' problems in using English-Japanese dictionaries. In H. Gottlieb, J. E. Mogensen, and A. Zettersten (eds.), *Symposium on lexicography X: Proceedings of the Tenth International Symposium on Lexicography May 4–6, 2000 at the University of Copenhagen.* Tübingen: Niemeyer, 243–51.

Prechter, S. (1999) Women's rights – children's games: sexism in learners' dictionaries of English. *Multilingua* 18, 47–68.

Rundell, M. (1999) Dictionary use in production. *International Journal of Lexicography* 12, 35–53.

Scholfield, P. (1999) Dictionary use in reception. *International Journal of Lexicography* 12, 13–34.

Simpson, J. and Weiner, E. (2000) An online *OED. English* 16 (3), 12–19.

Stein, G. (1985) *The English dictionary before Cawdrey.* Tübingen: Niemeyer.

Stein, G. (2002) *Better words: evaluating EFL dictionaries.* Exeter: Exeter University Press.

Van Sterkenburg, P. (2003) *A practical guide to lexicography.* Amsterdam: John Benjamins.

Watanabe, H. (1998) Quotations from linguists and philologists in *OED*: Several problems as they stand in the present form of the dictionary as an electronic database. In A. Zettersten, V. H. Pedersen, and J. E. Mogensen (eds.), *Symposium on lexicography VIII: Proceedings of the Eighth International Symposium on Lexicography May 2–4, 1996, at the University of Copenhagen.* Tübingen: Niemeyer, 299–306.

Yamada, S. and Komuro, Y. (1998) English lexicography in Japan: its history, innovations, and impact. In T. McArthur and I. Kernerman (eds.), *Lexicography in Asia: selected papers from the Dictionaries in Asia Conference, Hong Kong and other papers.* Tel Aviv: Password Publishers Ltd., 149–66.

Zettersten, A. and Lauridsen, H. (2002) From projection to reception – on the process of bilingual dictionary making. In H. Gottlieb, J. E. Mogensen, and A. Zettersten (eds.), *Symposium on lexicography X: Proceedings of the Tenth International Symposium on Lexicography May 4–6, 2000 at the University of Copenhagen.* Tübingen: Niemeyer, 325–30.

REFERENCES

Algeo, J. (1995) British and American biases in English dictionaries. In B. B. Kachru and H. Kahane (eds.), *Cultures, ideologies, and the dictionary: studies in honor of Ladislav Zgusta.* Tübingen: Niemeyer, 205–12.

Anderson, S., Higgleton, E., and Rennie, S. (eds.) (2002) *Chambers mini dictionary.* Edinburgh: Harraps.

Atkins, B. T. S. and Levin, B. (1995) Building on a corpus: a linguistic and lexicographical look at some near synonyms. *International Journal of Lexicography* 8, 85–114.

Atkins, B. T. S. and Varantola, K. (1997) Monitoring dictionary use. *International Journal of Lexicography* 10, 1–45.

Atkins, B. T. S. (1998) *Using dictionaries: studies of dictionary use by language learners and translators.* Tübingen: Niemeyer.

Beal, J. (1999) *English pronunciation in the eighteenth century: Thomas Spence's 'Grand Repository of the English Language.'* Oxford: Oxford University Press.

Béjoint, Henri. (1995) *Tradition and innovation in modern English dictionaries.* Oxford: Clarendon.

Bergenholtz, H. and Tarp, S. (1995) *Manual of specialised lexicography: the preparation of specialised dictionaries.* Amsterdam: John Benjamins.

Chardonnens, L. S. (1997) Familiarity breeds contempt: on the use of *well-known* in *OED. Notes and Queries* 242 (2), 171–2.

Coleman, J. (2004a) *A history of cant and slang dictionaries,* vol. 1: *1567–1784.* Oxford: Oxford University Press.

Coleman, J. (2004b) *A history of cant and slang dictionaries,* vol. 2: *1785–1858.* Oxford: Oxford University Press.

Cooke, J. (1997a) Problems of method in early English lexicography: the case of the Harley glossary. *Neuphilologische Mitteilungen* 158 (3), 241–51.

Cooke, J. (1997b) Worcester books and scholars, and the making of the Harley glossary (British Library MS. Harley 3376). *Anglia* 115, 441–68.

Cowie, A. P. (1999) *English dictionaries for foreign learners: a history.* Oxford: Oxford University Press.

Fraser, H. (1997) Dictionary pronunciation guides for English. *International Journal of Lexicography* 10, 181–208.

Fontenelle, T. (1997) *Turning a bilingual dictionary into a lexical-semantic database.* Tübingen: Niemeyer.

Goldie, J. (1991) *Harraps French-English/ Anglais-Français shorter English dictionary.* London and Paris: Harraps.

Görlach, M. (1995) *New studies in the history of English.* Heidelberg: Universitätsverlag C. Winter.

Gotti, M. (1999) *The language of thieves and vagabonds: 17th and 18th century canting lexicography in England.* Tübingen: Niemeyer.

Gusun, L. (1998) Traditionality and creativity in lexicography. In T. McArthur and I. Kernerman (eds.), *Lexicography in Asia: selected papers from the Dictionaries in Asia Conference, Hong Kong and other papers.* Tel Aviv: Password Publishers Ltd., 21–31.

Hartmann, R. R. K. and James, G. (2001; 1998) *Dictionary of lexicography.* London: Routledge.

Hartmann, R. R. K. (2001) *Teaching and researching lexicography.* Harlow: Longman.

Herbst, T. and Popp, K. (eds.) (1999) *The perfect learners' dictionary (?).* Tübingen: Niemeyer.

Heuberger, R. (2000) *Monolingual dictionaries for foreign learners of English: a constructive evaluation of state-of-the-art reference works in book form and on CD-ROM.* Vienna: Braumüller.

Hideki, W. (2002) A thesaurus of old English revisited. In H. Gottlieb, J. E. Mogensen, and A. Zettersten (eds.), *Symposium on lexicography X: Proceedings of the Tenth International Symposium on Lexicography May 4–6, 2000 at the University of Copenhagen.* Tübingen: Niemeyer, 313–24.

Howard, G. (1993) *The good English guide.* London: Pan Macmillan.

Hüllen, W. (1999) *English dictionaries 800–1700: the topical tradition.* Oxford: Oxford University Press.

Jackson, H. (2002) *Lexicography: an introduction.* London: Routledge.

Johnson, S. (1755) *A dictionary of the English language.* London: W. Strahan (etc.).

Kabdebo, T. and Armstrong, N. (1997) *Dictionary of dictionaries*, 2nd edn. London: Bowker Saur.

Kay, C. J. and Wotherspoon, A. W. (2002) Turning the dictionary inside out: some issues in the compilation of a historical thesaurus. In J. E. Díaz Vera (ed.), *A changing world of words: studies in English historical lexicography, lexicology and semantics*. Amsterdam/New York: Rodopi, 109–35.

Kilgariff, A. (1997) Putting frequencies in the dictionary. *International Journal of Lexicography* 10, 135–55.

Kumar, A. (1998) The societal contexts of Sanskrit, English and Hindi thesauruses, and the multilingual possibilities of the computer age. In T. McArthur and I. Kernerman (eds.), *Lexicography in Asia: selected papers from the Dictionaries in Asia Conference, Hong Kong and other papers*. Tel Aviv: Password Publishers Ltd., 41–59.

Lancashire, I. (2004) Lexicography in the early modern period: The manuscript record. In J. Coleman and A. McDermott (eds.), *Historical dictionaries and historical dictionary research: papers from the First International Conference on Historical Lexicography and Lexicology, at the University of Leicester, 2002*. Tübingen: Niemeyer, 19–30.

Landau, S. I. and Ramson, W. S. (1990) *Chambers English dictionary*. Edinburgh: Chambers.

Lara, L. F. (1995) Towards a theory of the cultural dictionary. In B. B. Kachru and H. Kahane (eds.), *Cultures, ideologies, and the dictionary: studies in honor of Ladislav Zgusta*. Tübingen: Niemeyer, 41–51.

Leban, K. (2002) Towards a Slovene-English false-friend dictionary. In H. Gottlieb, J. E. Mogensen, and A. Zettersten (eds.), *Symposium on lexicography X: Proceedings of the Tenth International Symposium on Lexicography May 4–6, 2000 at the University of Copenhagen*. Tübingen: Niemeyer, 185–97.

Lewis, R. E. (2001) *Middle English dictionary*. Ann Arbor: University of Michigan Press.

Liberman, A. (2002) The length and breadth of an entry in an etymological dictionary. In H. Gottlieb, J. E. Mogensen, and A. Zettersten (eds.), *Symposium on lexicography X: Proceedings of the Tenth International Symposium on Lexicography May 4–6, 2000 at the University of Copenhagen*. Tübingen: Niemeyer, 199–209.

Lilles, J. (2000) The myth of Canadian English. *English* 16 (2), 3–9.

McGill, S. (1996) *Who's who in lexicography*. Exeter: Dictionary Research Centre, University of Exeter.

Micklethwait, D. (2000) *Noah Webster and the American dictionary*. Jefferson, North Carolina: MacFarland & Company.

Miller, C. and Swift, K. (1995; 1980) *The handbook of non-sexist writing*. London: The Women's Press.

Morton, H. C. (1994) *The story of Webster's third*. Cambridge: Cambridge University Press.

Mugglestone, L. (ed.) (2000) *Lexicography and the OED: pioneers in the untrodden forest*. Oxford: Oxford University Press.

Murphy, M. L. (1998) Defining people: race and ethnicity in South African English dictionaries. *International Journal of Lexicography* 11, 1–33.

Nakamoto, K. (1998) From which perspective does the definer define the definiendum: anthropocentric or referent-based? *International Journal of Lexicography* 11, 205–18.

Nesi, H. (1999) A user's guide to electronic dictionaries for language learners. *International Journal of Lexicography* 12, 55–66.

Nesi, H. (2000) *The use and abuse of EFL dictionaries: how learners of English as a foreign language read and interpret dictionary entries*. Tübingen: Niemeyer.

Nichols, W. (2003) English dictionary making in America today. *Kernerman Dictionary News* 11, 6–9.

Ooi, V. B. Y. (1998) *Computer corpus lexicography*. Edinburgh: Edinburgh University Press.

Osselton, N. E. (1995) *Chosen words: past and present problems for dictionary makers*. Exeter: University of Exeter Press.

Otani, Y. (2002) Who uses English-Japanese dictionaries and when? Their bidirectional working. In H. Gottlieb, J. E. Mogensen, and A. Zettersten (eds.), *Symposium on lexicography X: Proceedings of the Tenth International Symposium on Lexicography May 4–6, 2000 at the University of Copenhagen*. Tübingen: Niemeyer, 267–72.

Partridge, E. (1967) (1937) *A dictionary of slang and unconventional English*. 5th edn. London: Routledge & Kegan Paul.

Phillips, E. (1658) *The new world of English words*. London: Printed by E. Tyler for Nath. Brooke.

Reddick, A. (1990) *The making of Johnson's dictionary 1746–1773*. Cambridge: Cambridge University Press.

Roberts, J., and Kay, C., with Grundy, L. (1995) *A thesaurus of Old English*. London: King's College London Centre for Late Antique and Medieval Studies.

Schäfer, J. (1980) *Documentation in the O.E.D.: Shakespeare and Nashe as test cases*. Oxford: Clarendon Press.

Shcherba, L. V. (1995) Towards a general theory of lexicography. *International Journal of Lexicography* 8, 314–50.

Schur, N. W. (1989; 1987) *A dictionary of challenging words*. London: Penguin.

Silva, P. (ed.) (1996) *A dictionary of South African English on historical principles*. Oxford: Oxford University Press in association with the Dictionary Unit for South African English.

Sinclair, J. (1992; 1987) *Collins COBUILD English language dictionary*. London and Glasgow: Collins.

Stark, M. (1999) *Encyclopedic learners' dictionaries: a study of their design features from the user perspective*. Tübingen: Niemeyer.

Starnes, De Witt T. and Noyes, G. E. (1946) *The English dictionary from Cawdrey to Johnson 1604–1755*. Chapel Hill: University of North Carolina Press.

Stein, G. (1995) Chaucer and Lydgate in Palgrave's *Lesclarcissement*. In B. B. Kachru and H. Kahane (eds.), *Cultures, ideologies, and the dictionary: Studies in honor of Ladislav Zgusta*. Tübingen: Niemeyer, 127–39.

Stein, G. (2002) *Better words: evaluating EFL dictionaries*. Exeter: University of Exeter Press.

Svensén, B. (1993) *Practical lexicography: principles and methods of dictionary-making*. Trans. John Sykes and Kerstin Schofield. Oxford: Oxford University Press.

Takeda, R. (1998) A radical change of direction: English lexicography in the fifteenth century. In T. McArthur and I. Kernerman (eds.), *Lexicography in Asia: selected papers from the Dictionaries in Asia Conference, Hong Kong and other papers*. Tel Aviv: Password Publishers Ltd., 177–87.

Tono, Y. (2001) *Research on dictionary use in the context of foreign language learning*. Tübingen: Niemeyer.

van der Meer, G. (1999) Metaphors and dictionaries: the morass of meaning, or how to get two ideas for one. *International Journal of Lexicography* 12, 195–208.

van der Meer, G. (2002) Metaphors: how do dictionaries scramble out of this morass of meaning? In H. Gottlieb, J. E. Mogensen, and A. Zettersten (eds.), *Symposium on lexicography X: Proceedings of the Tenth International Symposium on Lexicography May 4–6,*

2000 at the University of Copenhagen. Tübingen: Niemeyer, 231–42.

Weiner, E. S. C., Delahunty, A., and Whitcut, J. (1994) *The little Oxford guide to English usage.* Oxford: Clarendon Press.

Whitcut, J. (1995) Taking it for granted: some cultural preconceptions in English dictionaries. In B. B. Kachru and H. Kahane (eds.), *Cultures, ideologies, and the dictionary: studies in honor of Ladislav Zgusta.* Tübingen: Niemeyer, 253–7.

Willinsky, J. (1994) *Empire of words: the reign of the OED.* Princeton, New Jersey: Princeton University Press.

Part V   Variation, Discourse, Stylistics, and Usage

26 Syntactic Variation in English: A Global Perspective

BERND KORTMANN

1 Introduction

Compared with the study of phonological variation, much less is known about syntactic variation in English, especially among non-standard (or vernacular) varieties, which will stand at the center of this chapter. For one thing, significantly more data are necessary to identify interesting instances and, above all, larger patterns of syntactic variation. Many differences between varieties, especially between the national (written) standard varieties, are not categorical (such that one variety has a certain grammatical element or syntactic construction which another has not). Rather the vast majority of differences are quantitative in nature (see chapter 15), i.e. a given construction may be preferred in one variety but used distinctly less frequently in another. Only once a critical mass of data is available can the semantic/pragmatic patterns underlying such marked differences in text frequency be identified. For non-standard varieties, we are only at the very beginning of large-scale quantitative studies using the toolkit of corpus linguistics.

Since the 1990s, computerized corpora (based on transcribed recordings of oral-history interviews or conversations among dialect speakers from the 1970s or later) have been or are currently being compiled for a growing number of non-standard varieties (e.g. the Freiburg English Dialect Corpus (FRED), the Newcastle Electronic Corpus of Tyneside English (NECTE), the Northern Ireland Transcribed Corpus of Speech (NITCS)), even if they cannot rival in size the megacorpora for the national standard varieties of English (see chapters 4 and 15). At the same time, we simply know much more about syntactic variation in non-standard varieties now than we did since the early 1980s (cf. e.g. Edwards et al. 1984) due to an increased number of relevant studies. The majority of these deal with individual phenomena in individual dialects or dialect areas, as compiled for example in such a milestone collection as Trudgill and Chambers (1991), but there are also excellent structural surveys for regional and non-regional varieties of English, such as those provided in Milroy and Milroy (1993) for the British Isles and in Kortmann et al. (2004) on a world scale. The wealth of data and information in the new corpora, new questionnaire-based fieldwork, and the constantly growing body of relevant research on syntactic variation puts us in the privileged position that, for the first time, it will soon be possible to systematically explore syntactic variation across (regional or social) non-standard varieties in, and ultimately even across, different parts of the English-speaking world (for the British Isles, see for example the cross-varietal corpus-based studies in Kortmann et al. 2004).

It is exactly in this spirit that this chapter has been written. It is a first attempt at providing an overview of syntactic variation in English on a global scale. As for the varieties included, its focus will be on non-standard varieties of English (including English-based pidgins and creoles) and spontaneous spoken varieties of standard English. It is notoriously hard to define Standard English (cf. Trudgill 1999b) and even more so what a spoken standard is (cf. Cheshire 1999; see also chapter 28). Neither of them is a uniform concept, nor is it always possible to draw a sharp distinction between written and spoken Standard English, on the one hand, and standard and non-standard spoken English, on the other hand. If we follow Trudgill's characterization of Standard English as a social dialect "which is distinguished from other dialects of the language by its *grammatical* forms" (1999b: 125), the fact must be acknowledged that nevertheless, even in the written language, there is (at times quite considerable) variation across the national standards like British, American, Irish, or Australian English. However, variation across (formal) written standard varieties, especially between British and American English, will be largely left aside in this chapter (but see chapter 15, this volume). Also what will not be discussed here are a range of grammatical features which are widely known as typical of spontaneous conversational English, especially among young speakers (e.g. special reporting constructions with *go, all, like*, or *all like*), or characteristics of spoken language in general (e.g. ellipsis, run-on sentences, fragmented syntax), as described in chapter 28, Miller and Weinert (1998) and Biber et al. (1999).

In sections 2–6 an overview of the syntactic (and, marginally, morphological) variation in the following major grammatical subsystems will be given: the noun phrase, tense and aspect, mood and modality, negation, agreement, and subordination. For each of these grammatical subsystems, what will be identified and illustrated are (1) the most pervasive tendencies and distinctive patterns across (at least larger parts of) the English-speaking world and (2) properties of individual non-standard varieties which are striking from a cross-linguistic point of view. The examples used are all genuine and for the most part taken from the handbook volume by Kortmann et al. (2004), which is also the major source for statements on the (degree of) geographical pervasiveness or restrictedness of individual grammatical features. The focus of these five sections will be on form, i.e. on the coding devices which are available for the individual grammatical subsystems across the non-standard varieties of

English. Functional variation, i.e. the variation which can be found in the frequency and the ways in which these coding devices are put to use in individual varieties, will be touched upon only occasionally. Major conclusions to be drawn from these largely descriptive accounts will be discussed in section 7. Among the issues addressed will be the following: What can the syntax of non-standard varieties tell us about the standard English(es) of tomorrow? What can current linguistic theories learn from syntactic variation within individual languages? The answers to these and other far-reaching questions will show that the study of syntactic variation, and grammatical variation in general, is a budding and most exciting field in English linguistics, with many discoveries still to be made and holding many promises for anyone interested in language variation, language change, language comparison, and linguistic theory.

2   The Noun Phrase

2.1   *Pronouns, pronoun exchange, pronominal gender*

Apart from what is going on in relative clauses, which will be discussed in section 6.1, the most interesting and pervasive instances of morphosyntactic variation in the noun phrase can be observed for pronouns. Here are the most widespread tendencies in (varieties of) spontaneous spoken English across the world:

(P1)   *Them* instead of demonstrative *those* (e.g. *in them days . . . , one of them things . . .*).

(P2)   Special forms or phrases for the second person plural pronoun (different from the second person singular *you*. For example, *youse* (Irish English, Northumberland/Tyneside), *y'all* (Southern US), *aay, yufela*, or phrases like *you . . . together* (East Anglia), *all of you, you ones/'uns, you guys, you people*.

(P3)   A regularized reflexives-paradigm which extends the formation method 'possessive pronoun + *-self/selves*' to all persons, thus *hisself* and *theirselves*, partly combined with the independent regularization tendency of using *-self* for singular and plural (e.g. *theirself, ourself*) as long as the possessive pronoun indicates number (thus *yourself* = singular, *yourselves* = plural).

(P4)   *she/her* used for inanimate referents (e.g. *Here she comes: Timber!*, *She was burning good* [about a house], *See that roof? We finished her yesterday*) or without clear referents (e.g. in fixed expressions like *she's fine, she's cool, she'll be joe*, all meaning 'it doesn't matter' in Australian and New Zealand English); by contrast only few varieties invariably use generic *he* (e.g. Gullah and Fiji English).

The following phenomena can be observed relatively frequently, partly even in spoken Standard English (P5). All of them relate to the marking of grammatical functions (subject, different kinds of objects) by unusual pronominal forms:

(P5)   *myself / meself* in a non-reflexive function, as a kind of avoidance strategy for subject *I / me* or object *me* (e.g. *my / me husband and myself*, *This is myself with a cow*, *The mail can have connections with myself*).

(P6)   *me* instead of *I* in coordinate subjects (e.g. *Me and my brother / My brother and me were late for school*); this is also found for other persons, e.g. *them* in colloquial American English, as in *When are Julie and them gonna go pick her up?* It seems that in the non-standard varieties of English, the subject form of a pronoun is used only when it is the single subject of a verb (Peter Trudgill, p.c.).

(P7)   In several varieties *us* can be used in at least one of the following functions: as a possessive marker (e.g. *Us George was a nice one*, *We like us town*), as a (mostly indirect) object form in the singular (e.g. *Show us 'me' them boots*), or as a subject: typically when followed by a nominal apposition, as in *Us kids used to pinch the sweets like hell*, more rarely by itself, as in *Us'll do it*.

2.2   Absence of plural marking, plural and genitive marking on noun phrases, article use

Outside the domains of pronominal usage and relativization, the following fairly widespread phenomena of syntactic variation within the noun phrase come to mind.

(NP1)   The most pervasive of these is the absence of plural marking after measure nouns (e.g. *three yard*, *four pound*, *five year*), which for some nouns is also regular usage in the standard (as in *She's five foot four*).

(NP2)   Group plurals (e.g. *That President has two Secretary of States*).

(NP3)   Group genitives (e.g. *The man I met's girlfriend is a real beauty*).

(NP4)   More varied is the use of articles, for which so far it seems impossible to come up with a pattern underlying the observable variation. This involves either the omission of a definite article (e.g. *Father rented the farm under Squire*, *Take them to market*) or an indefinite article (e.g. *I had nice garden*, *They had awful job*), or their insertion (e.g. *about a three fields*, *about a seven inches square on a board*, *I left the school in early age*, *Do they keep the goats?*). Another option found in the same or other varieties is the use of the definite article where Standard English uses the indefinite article (e.g. Irish English *I had the toothache*, *He's the wise boy*).

2.3   Comparison of adjectives

(NP5)   Double comparatives and superlatives (e.g. *Sometimes that is so much more easier to follow*, *She's got the most loveliest clothes*) can be found in varieties of English in all parts of the world (e.g. spontaneous spoken American English, New Zealand English, dialects of northern England).

(NP6)   Regularized comparison strategies. Independently of double compar-
        atives/superlatives, or in combination with them, many non-standard
        varieties use the inflectional comparison strategy (e.g. in *He is the
        regularest kind a guy I know*) along with the analytic one (e.g. in *one of
        the most pretty sunsets*) where Standard English allows only one of the
        two strategies for the relevant adjective (cf. Murray and Simon 2004).

3   The Verb Phrase

In the verb phrase, the most interesting syntactic and morphological variation
can be observed in the domain of tense and, especially, aspect. Many non-
standard varieties, pidgins and creoles in particular, have richer aspectual
systems than Standard English has. Among the most pervasive tendencies are
the first three:

3.1   Tense and aspect

(T1)   A wider range of uses of the Progressive. This involves not only a
        higher text frequency due to the use of the Progressive as a marker of
        informality and speaker involvement. It is also due to its use with a
        wider range of verbs (i.e. stative verbs) than in Standard English (e.g.
        I'm liking this, *So what are you wanting from me*?). Indeed, the Progress-
        ive in non-standard and spontaneous spoken English seems to be well
        on its way towards an Imperfective (cf. also Gachelin 1997).

(T2)   A much more important role of habitual marking. The marking of
        habitual aspect is much more strongly grammaticalized in many
        varieties than it is in Standard British or American English. The most
        widespread habitual markers are *be* (invariant as in African American
        Vernacular English *He be sick*, or inflected as in Irish English *He be's
        at home*), *does/doz* (in practically all pidgins and creoles, e.g. Barbados
        He does catch fish pretty), or combinations of the two (e.g. Irish English
        There does be a meeting of the company every Tuesday). *Be* or *do be* are often
        also combined with the Progressive in marking habituality (e.g. African
        American Vernacular English *I always be playing ball* or Irish English
        They do be shooting there a couple of times a week).

(T3)   A weakening or loss of the strict division between the Present Perfect
        and the Simple Past. The division of tasks known from (written)
        Standard British English is quite an exception among the varieties of
        English (cf. Miller 2004). This distinction is increasingly getting blurred,
        especially in the non-standard varieties. Either the two tense forms are
        encroaching onto each others' territories, e.g. *just* + Simple Past for
        recent past (*Sorry, Bill's not in. He just went out*), Simple Past for the
        experiential perfect (*Were you ever in London?*), or Present Perfect with
        definite past time adverbials (*Some of us have been to New York years
        ago*), or a different tense form is used for at least some of the traditional

functions of the Present Perfect (e.g. the Simple Present in Irish English for the continuative perfect in *I know him since my schooldays*). The dominant pattern across varieties of English, including the standard varieties, clearly is the Simple Past (increasingly) doing service for all major uses of the Present Perfect apart from the continuative perfect.

(T4)   *Be* as a perfect auxiliary. Some varieties, notably Irish English, have retained the older Germanic pattern of a *be*-perfect (e.g. *They're not left school yet*) along with the *have*-perfect, the former being used with verbs of motion and change like *come, go, change, improve, die.*

(T5)   *Do* as a tense and aspect marker. In non-standard varieties of English, especially in pidgins and creoles, *do* is primarily used for the marking of aspect, notably as a habitual marker (typically *does/doz*, exceptionally *did* as in *We've been up milking at 6 o'clock in the morning, and then we did go on haymaking*) and a completive/perfective marker (*done/don*; see (T6)), only rarely as a progressive marker. In the domain of tense, two uses stand out: unstressed *do(es)/did* as a simple analytic tense carrier for Present and Past Tense in the English Southwest (*This man what do own this, I thought you did mean a rubber*) and the Anterior *did* in many pidgins and creoles, as in Panamanian Creole *Wen ai did smaal tiŋ woz chiyp* (cf. Kortmann 2004a).

(T6)   Completive/perfect *done* 'finish/stop, have already V-ed.' This is a pervasive feature of American non-standard varieties and English-based pidgins and creoles (e.g. *He done go fishing, You don ate what I has sent you?*).

(T7)   Past tense/anterior marker *been.* The use of this marker, as in *I been cut the bread*, is found in several varieties spoken in North America and the Caribbean (e.g. Newfoundland English, Gullah, Urban African American Vernacular English, Eastern Caribbean English) but is considerably rarer than the relevant forms of *do.*

(T8)   Loosening of sequence of tenses rule. An example is *I noticed the van I came in* (instead of: *had come in*) *was not really a painter's van.* This phenomenon, and even more so (T9), are very common in spontaneous spoken English.

(T9)   *Would* in if-clauses. An example is *If I would/I'd be you, . . . , If they wouldn't have made a scrap of slate, . . .*

(T10) *Was sit/stood* with progressive meaning. Sometimes also discussed under the heading of 'pseudo-passive,' this phenomenon (e.g. *when you're stood 'are standing' there you can see the flames*) seems to be restricted to varieties spoken in England, there increasingly also in the spoken standard (cf. Cheshire et al. 1993: 70–1; Klemola 2002: 52–5).

3.2   *Modal verbs*

(M1)   Different paradigms of modal verbs. Almost all spontaneous spoken varieties, least so perhaps in Britain, have largely abandoned, or are in the process of doing so, the use of *shall* (at least as a pure future time marker), *should* (at least for the marking of mere hypotheticality) and *ought* (*to*), closely followed by *may* (especially in the permission sense). On the other hand, a number of new modals can be seen to emerge (see chapter 15), notably *gonna* (as a neutral predictive future marker), *wanna* ('should,' as in *You wanna see a doctor*), *gotta* (epistemic 'must'), and *let's* (adhortative, as in *Let's you and him jump*).

(M2)   Double (or: multiple) modals. These constructions are a distinctive feature of Scottish and Tyneside English, but are used most frequently in many varieties spoken in the Southern states of the US (cf. e.g. Nagle 2003). There seem to exist a number of restrictions on possible sequences of double modal constructions: e.g. in Scottish and Tyneside English, *may* or *might* are usually found in initial position (roughly meaning 'maybe'), *can* or *could* in second position. The low frequency of double modals in everyday speech seems to be due to their restriction to certain pragmatically governed contexts, notably one-on-one conversations (very often in the form of negotiations), and potentially face-threatening situations. Typical examples are *I tell you what we might should do*, *You might could try a thousand K*, *Could you might possibly use a teller machine?*

(M3)   Epistemic *mustn't*. In a number of varieties (e.g. spontaneous spoken American English) *mustn't* can be used or is even exclusively used (Scottish English, Northumbria/Tyneside) as an epistemic modal meaning 'can't, it is concluded that . . . not,' as in *This mustn't be true*, *This mustn't be the place*, *The lift mustn't be working*.

3.3   *Verb morphology*

(VP1)   Regularization (e.g. *draw-drawed-drawed*) and/or reduction of irregular verb paradigms. Either past tense and past participle verb forms are identical (with the past tense form doing service for both, as in *I've ate the apple*, or the past participle, as in *I seen one the other day*), or the base form also serves as past tense and past participle (e.g. *She give me that one the other night*, *She learnt cheese making here and I come here to live*).

(VP2)   A-prefixing on *ing*-forms. This archaic feature, as in *They wasn't a-doin' nothin' wrong*, can be observed especially in many varieties in North America (e.g. spontaneous spoken American English, African American Vernacular English, Appalachian English), but also in British Creole and the dialect of East Anglia.

3.4   *Adverbs*

(VP3)   Adverbs have the same form as adjectives (e.g. *Come quick, He treated her wrong right from the start, He done good*). This is a truly universal property of spontaneous spoken and non-standard varieties of English. In many varieties it also applies to adverbs which are used as degree modifiers (e.g. *a high technical job, That's real good, This pie is awful good*).

4   Negation

In the domain of negation the two negation features most widely known to occur in all non-standard varieties are multiple negation (or negative concord) and invariant *ain't*. But there are other negators, notably invariant *don't* and especially preverbal *never*, which are almost equally frequent. The other two negation features presented below are used in considerably fewer non-standard varieties:

(N1)   Multiple negation / negative concord (e.g. *He won't do no harm, I couldn't say nothing about them, I've never been to market to buy no heifers*). The frequency with which multiple negation is used in individual non-standard varieties may vary greatly. In white dialects of American English, for example, frequencies have been found to vary between 50 and 80 per cent (Schneider 2000: 219). A striking pattern Anderwald (2002: 109–14 and unpublished work) has found in corpus-based studies of England, Scotland, and Wales is a south–north cline, with rough proportions of multiple negation usage of 40 to 45 per cent in the South of England, 30 per cent in the Midlands, and around 10 per cent in the North of England, Scotland and Wales. Interesting variation can also be found for syntactic and lexical constraints on multiple negation in different varieties (e.g. in African American Vernacular English multiple negation crosses clause boundaries, indefinite constituents of embedded clauses being marked negatively because the predicate of the super-ordinate clause is marked negatively; Schneider 2000: 219).

(N2)   *Ain't.* Invariant *ain't* in present tense declaratives, questions, and tags represents a neutralization in the negative between *be* (e.g. *I ain't going out tomorrow, They're all in there ain't they?*) and (auxiliary) *have* (e.g. *I ain't had a look at them yet, Gotta be lucky at something, ain't you love?*), as well as a neutralization of person distinctions of Standard English. In some varieties, especially pidgins and creoles, there is a tendency to extend the use of *ain't* to full verb *have* (e.g. *Ain't you trouble with your car?*). In fact, in African American Vernacular English *ain't* is also used as a full verb negator equivalent to *don't/doesn't* and, especially, *didn't* (e.g. *sumpin' I ain't know about, You ain't expect to find her over here, did you?*; Schneider 2000: 214–15). In some pidgins and creoles, *ain't* (or: *in/en/eh*) has even acquired the function of a general (i.e. tense-independent) preverbal negator (e.g. Trinidadian English *The girl eh lie* 'The girl didn't lie') as further described in (N5).

(N3)   Invariant *don't* for all persons in the present tense (e.g. *He don't like me*; for its history and current distribution in the British Isles, see Anderwald 2002: 151–70).

(N4)   Equally widespread as multiple negation is *never* as (preverbal) past tense negator referring to single occasions or unspecified stretches of time in the past, equivalent to Standard English *didn't* (e.g. *He never came, I never found the berries till it was time to come home, Did you hit him? No, I never*). *Never* in these contexts is typically unstressed. According to Cheshire et al. (1993: 67), this use of *never* is frequent even in formal written (British) English.

(N5) *No* used as a preverbal negator "... is a feature which is practically universal in English-related pidgins ... and creoles" (Schneider 2000: 211), e.g. *me no iit brekfus* (Guyana) or *I no bin nget a breakfas dis-day* (Pitcairn). The negator *no* (instead of *not*) is of course also known from Scotland and closely related varieties (Orkney and Shetland, marginally Northumbria) where it is the default negator with *be*, *will* and *have* (e.g. *She's no leaving, That's miles away, is it no?, A'm no ready yet*).

(N6) *Was–weren't* split. For *be* in the Past Tense, many non-standard varieties across the world generalize either *was* or *were* for all persons in the singular and plural, in positive as well as negative sentences (for instance, the dialects of Southeast England exhibit a pervasive *was-wasn't* pattern; see also (A6) in section 5). In a considerable number of varieties, however, for instance in some Southern US vernaculars and dialects in England (see Anderwald 2002: 171–93), there is a mixed system: *was* is generalized for all persons in singular and plural only in affirmatives, while *were*, or rather *weren't*, is used for all persons in singular and plural in negative sentences, as in *The boys was interested, but Mary weren't*. At least in England, this mixed system is the most frequent one among *was/were*-generalizing dialects. What has happened in these varieties can be interpreted as a process of remorphologization (Wolfram and Schilling-Estes 1996) or exaptation: the number distinction for the *was/were* choice, which has become largely redundant in Standard English, has been replaced by a polarity distinction. Interestingly, the second possible type of mixed system among *was/were*-generalizing varieties of English, namely *were* in positive and *wasn't* in negative sentences, is not attested beyond idiolectal usage.

(N7) Invariant question tag *isn't it/in't it/innit* (e.g. *They are quite a couple, innit?, They had them in their hair, isn't it?, But they make dustbins big enough now, in't it?, You can go with your Mum then, innit?*). Typical of London adolescent speech (*innit*) and Welsh English (*isn't it*), this tag is spreading in England and in other parts of the world. For adults in England, *innit* is still largely used as the non-standard variant of *isn't it* (i.e. only following *is* in the main clause).

5 Agreement

There is a pervasive tendency in non-standard and spontaneous spoken varieties of English to do away with or at least considerably weaken subject-verb agreement. For affirmative sentences this is illustrated in (A1–7), for negative sentences in (A8).

(A1)   Invariant present tense forms due to zero marking for the third person singular (e.g. *So he show up and say, What's up?*).

(A2)   Invariant present tense forms due to generalization of third person singular *-s* for all persons (e.g. *I sees the house*); in several varieties (e.g. in Southeast England, where this feature is recessive though) this involves *does* used for all persons (e.g. *You doesn't look too good*) and even full verb *has* for all persons (e.g. *I has no money*).

(A3)   *There's, there is, there was* in existential/presentational sentences with plural subjects (e.g. *There's/There is/There was two men waiting in the hall, There's cars outside the church*). This pattern is firmly established in spontaneous spoken English (cf. also section 7.2).

(A4)   Deletion of *be* (e.g. *She___ smart, We___ going as soon as possible*).

(A5)   Deletion of auxiliary *have* (e.g. *I ___ eaten my lunch*).

(A6)   *Was/were*-generalization. As mentioned under (N6) in section 3, many non-standard varieties have abandoned the *was/were* distinction known from Standard English. Alternatively, they either generalize *was* or *were*. Anderwald (2002) found, that in negated sentences this generalization of a Past Tense form of *be* is three times as likely as in non-negated sentences, with generalized *weren't* being much preferred over *wasn't* in negated sentences, while generalized *was* is preferred over *were* in positive sentences. *Was*-generalization is discussed by various authors, together with the pattern in (N6), under the heading of *default singulars* (e.g. Chambers 2004) or *singular concord* (Henry 1995, 2002). A special case of this non-agreement pattern is (A7).

(A7)   The so-called Northern Subject Rule (NSR). In the dialects of (especially Northern) Ireland, Scotland and the North of England the following variant of the (non-)agreement pattern in (A6) can be found (cf. Klemola 2002; Pietsch 2004): every verb in the present tense can take an *s*-ending unless its subject is an immediately adjacent simple pronoun. (Third person singular verbs always take the *s*-ending, as in Standard English.) In other words, the NSR involves a type-of-subject constraint (pronoun vs. common/proper noun) and a position constraint (+/− immediate adjacency of pronominal subject to verb). Thus, in NSR-varieties we get examples like the following: *I sing* (vs. **I sings*), *Birds sings, I sing and dances.*

(A8)   Loss of subject-verb agreement in negative sentences as illustrated in section 5, i.e. through invariant *ain't* (N2), *don't* (N4) and either *wasn't* or *weren't* generalization (N6).

Taking all these points together one must agree with Hudson (1999: 205) that English dialects seem to be on their way towards a system lacking subject-verb agreement, as we know it from the continental Scandinavian languages (cf. also section 7.4).

6   Subordination

Of the three major types of subordinate clauses, relative clauses and relativization strategies are by far the best investigated ones for non-standard varieties of English (cf. most recently Herrmann 2004 for six dialect areas in England). Much less research has been done for complement clauses, and almost none for adverbial clauses (with the exception of Häcker 1999 for Scottish English). This is why relative clauses will take center stage in this section. For relative clauses, there is a pervasive tendency in the non-standard and spontaneous spoken varieties of English to strongly prefer relative particles (i.e. invariant relativizers) over the case-marked relative pronouns (*who, whose, whom*), or to use relative particles exclusively (see R1–R4). These relative particles are typically used for inanimate and non-personal antecedents, but can also be used for animate and personal antecedents (e.g. for *which*: *and the boy which I was at school with . . .* ; see Herrmann 2004).

(R1)   Relative particle *that*. The use of *that* for animate referents in restrictive relative clauses, as in *The man that painted the house . . .* , is part of the standard (especially in American English). In many non-standard varieties, however, *that* is additionally used in non-restrictive relative clauses (e.g. *My daughter, that lives in London, . . .*).

(R2)   Relative particle *what*. In many non-standard varieties, the relative particle *that* is rivalled in frequency only by *what* (e.g. *This is the man what painted my house, people what got families . . .* , *It were Aggie what done the trouble*). *What* as a relative particle is quite a newcomer and has, for example, significantly spread in England since the 1950s (see Herrmann 2004).

(R3)   Other relative particles used include *as* (e.g. *He was a chap as got a living anyhow, one chap as lived next door to us . . .*) and *at* (possibly just a phonological variant of *that* due to *th*-dropping) in Appalachian English and several varieties spoken in the British Isles. At least in the British Isles, both options are strongly receding however.

(R4)   Use of analytic *that his/that's* or *what his/what's* (rarely: *at's, as'*) instead of *whose*, as in *The man what's wife has died, The chap what's house got burnt down*.

(R5)   Gapping (or: zero-relativization) in subject position. In Standard English, the omission of a relativizer is possible only for the object position (as in *The man ___ I saw . . .* , *The man ___ I gave the book to*). In non-standard varieties and spontaneous spoken English, gapping is possible in the subject position, too, especially in existential/ presentational *there*-sentences (e.g. *There's a lot more children___ go these days, There was one or two people ___ made their living by this*), it-clefts (e.g. *I'll not say it was myself ___ was cause of this, It was the Common Market ___ done it*) and with definite head noun phrases (e.g. *The man ___ lives there is a nice chap, He was the boy ___ could have opened her up*). But this strategy is certainly not restricted to these three syntactic environments, as the following example shows: *And he had a lot of wooden traps ___ was set with a string.* Gapping in subject position can safely be considered a universal relativization strategy of non-standard and spontaneous spoken English.

(R6)   Resumptive (or: shadow) pronouns (e.g. *This is the house which I painted it yesterday, they'd put a couple in the old anchor boat what we weren't using it*): Resumptive pronouns seem to be used especially in complex relative clauses like *They sold this and some at Cary and I jumped in and bought this, which I were lucky in a way to get it* (Southwest England).

In the domain of complementation, only the following two fairly widespread tendencies can be observed:

(C1)   Inverted word order in indirect questions, i.e. the same word order in embedded and non-embedded interrogatives (e.g. *I'm wondering what are you gonna do, He asked me had I seen his daughter, I asked would there be a party*). This is typical for the Celtic Englishes, Orkney and Shetland English, but also for a considerable number of varieties of English in other parts of the world (e.g. Newfoundland English, Urban African American Vernacular English, Surinamese Creole, South African English, Pakistani English) and spontaneous spoken English in general.

(C2)   In infinitival purpose clauses ('in order to'), a number of varieties (especially the Celtic Englishes) use unsplit *for to*, as in *We always had gutters in the winter time for to drain the water away.*

All other instances of syntactic variation within the domains of complementation and adverbial subordination hold only for individual varieties or very small sets of varieties, like the use of a complementizer derived from the verb *to say* in several pidgins and creoles (e.g. Gullah, Bislama, British Creole), complementation patterns for individual verbs different from Standard English (e.g. a wider range of verbs which can be followed by a bare infinitive, as in Irish English *She allowed him stay out late*), or the special use of prepositions and/or subordinators in adverbial clauses (e.g. *till* '(in order) to,' *from* 'since,' *whenever* 'when (punctual),' *the time (that)* 'when' in Irish English, or *while* meaning 'until' in the Central and Northern dialects of England).

7   General Patterns and Tendencies

In this section the grammatical phenomena described above will be looked at and interpreted from different perspectives. Each perspective by itself and, certainly, all perspectives taken together will show what makes syntactic variation so fascinating to study, and what it can contribute to a wide range of central issues in the study of language and the development of linguistic theory.

7.1 Conservativeness vs. innovation: non-standard features spreading to the standard

The study of syntactic variation in non-standard varieties offers at the same time a look at the past and the future. On the one hand, non-standard varieties exhibit conservative features as found only in earlier periods of the English language and no longer in present-day Standard English. Examples include many morphological forms (e.g. irregular verb forms (VP1), *a*-prefixing (VP2), pronouns like *thou, thee, thy*), the *be*-perfect along with the *have*-perfect (T4), unsplit *for to* (C2), or the so-called Northern Subject Rule (A7), which can be traced back to the thirteenth and fourteenth centuries and whose regional distribution in present-day England is largely the same as in Late Middle English. In many cases, of course, the relevant features are not used exactly in the same way as they were in previous periods; from their historical sources they developed their own life and developed in new directions. This is characteristic especially of contact varieties and transplanted Englishes. Many pertinent examples could be given from pidgins and creoles (for instance, from the tense and aspect domain, as illustrated for *do* (T5) and (T6) in section 3) which in the course of their development have often expanded the syntax of their non-standard founder varieties (cf. Schneider 2000 on the role of diffusion and, especially, selection in the evolution of New Englishes).

So even where existing features of non-standard syntax and morphosyntax can be traced to earlier periods, there is often an element of innovation involved (cf. also Klemola 2002). It is the innovative aspects of non-standard syntax, i.e. where we can observe innovations not observable in earlier and, especially, the present-day standard varieties, that will be addressed in the present section. More exactly, the focus will be on the question which, or rather what kinds of, grammatical features stand a chance to spread from the non-standard to the standard in the future (spreading first to the spoken, ultimately perhaps to the written standard; see also chs. 15 and 28). As is well known in historical linguistics, spoken language is the motor of language change. Roughly, four broad classes of very widespread features of non-standard syntax may be distinguished (for details cf. Kortmann 2004b).

(A) pervasive features on a global scale, operating below consciousness (i.e. with a relatively broad social acceptance, at least in informal/spontaneous spoken English): e.g. development of the Progressive into an Imperfective (T1), use of would in *if*-conditionals (T9), weakening and ultimately disappearance of the grammaticalized opposition between the Present Perfect and the Simple Past (T3), *never* as past tense negator (N4), *there's* + plural noun phrase (A3), further spread of *that* as relativizer (R1), non-reflexive *myself* (P5), *she/her* used for inanimate referents (P4), possibly even the reintroduction of a distinct second person plural pronoun (P2).

(B) pervasive features on a global scale, operating above consciousness (i.e. with some stigma associated with them): e.g. multiple negation (N1), *ain't* (N2), relativizer *what* (R2), copula deletion (A4), and most of the phenomena leading to the loss of subject-verb agreement described in section 5.

(C) supraregional features (within individual parts of the English-speaking world), operating below consciousness: e.g. for the British Isles *was stood/sat* for the Progressive 'was standing/sitting' (see T 10), marked word order in double object constructions involving two pronominal NPs (*Give me it, please*; cf. Cheshire et al. 1993: 73–5); invariant tag *isn't it* or *innit* (N7).

(D) supraregional features (within individual parts of the English-speaking world), operating above consciousness: e.g. completive or perfective *done* (North America; see T6).

Of these four classes, A and C stand the greatest chance of providing candidates for a future (at least spoken) standard, at least in a given part of the English-speaking world. These are the classes with those features which have the widest regional and social spread. By contrast, for the members of classes B and D a spreading into the standard is much less likely. Regardless of how widespread across non-standard varieties, frequent and entrenched in spontaneous spoken English they may be, many of these phenomena are simply highly stigmatized.

Although they are "familiar to native speakers of English as are the features that are normally considered to be typical of standard English," as Cheshire, Edwards, and Whittle (1993: 83) state for the set of thirteen currently most widespread grammatical features in British urban dialects (1993: 63–4), the majority of these will probably not make it beyond what the authors call a "'standardizing' non-standard variety of English" (1993: 82).

Independent of which of the above features will ultimately make it into the (spoken, perhaps even written) standard in the course of the next decades and centuries, an interesting question will be to what extent class A and C members will also find their way into International English, whose standard will increasingly be determined by non-native (second or foreign language) speakers of English.

7.2 *Regularity, consistency, analyticity*

When leaving aside idiosyncratic features restricted to individual varieties, and looking rather at widely documented syntactic (and morphological) properties, it turns out that there are quite a number of domains of grammar which justify saying that non-standard varieties of English exhibit a higher degree of regularity and consistency (e.g. in terms of a higher degree of analyticity) than Standard English does.

Regularization

Of the features mentioned in sections 2–6, the following exhibit a higher degree of regularization in morphology (typically resulting in a higher degree of simplification):

(VP1) irregular verbs (e.g. normally fewer and/or levelled irregular verb forms compared with Standard English); (A2) inflectional paradigms in the Present Tense: e.g. *have*: in many dialects either in all persons (singular and plural) *-s* (e.g. *I has, you has*) or no *-s* (e.g. *he have*); (P3) formation patterns of reflexives: most English vernaculars consistently use possessive pronoun + *self/selves* (e.g. *hisself, theirself/-ves*), and not the mixed system of Standard English using partly possessive pronouns (*myself, yourself*) and partly the object forms of personal pronouns (*himself, themselves*); negation strategies and negative markers (invariant *ain't* (N2), *don't* (N3)).

Consistency

A more consistent use of analytic constructions can be observed, for example, in those varieties that mark possession with the help of analytic (instead of case-marked) forms (e.g. in relative clauses *what his/what's* or *that his/that's* instead of *whose* (R4)), and in all those (admittedly much rarer) varieties making use of *do*-periphrasis in affirmative statements (recall T5 in section 3). In the relevant varieties (e.g. those in Southwest England), the unemphatic *do* is on its way towards an analytic alternative for coding events in the (inflectionally marked) Present and Past Tense.

But in another respect, too, *do*-periphrasis in these non-standard varieties of English is an instance of a higher degree of consistency: in addition to the Standard English use of *do* as an analytic tense marker in questions, negative statements/questions/imperatives, and emphatic statements, *do* here is also used in unstressed affirmatives, i.e. an important syntactic constraint on *do*-insertion in Standard English has gone. Further examples of a higher degree of consistency in non-standard varieties include the following: (R5) gapping (or: zero-relativization) in object and (!) subject position; (C1) subject-verb inversion in normal and (!) embedded interrogatives; (A6) *was-* or *were-* generalization (in some varieties involving the remorphologization of this distinction described in N6); (A8) loss of subject-verb agreement in negative sentences: the result is a grammar that is more consistent in the sense that in non-standard varieties no negative auxiliary shows agreement, whereas Standard English has some auxiliaries with agreement (*have, be, do*) and some without (i.e. the modals; cf. Hudson 2000: 211). In general, together with the pronounced tendency to make greater use of analytic constructions, the loss of subject-verb-agreement definitely is the most far-reaching property of dialects in terms of consistency. Just recall the bundle of features discussed in section 5, all of which have in common that they either abolish or at least considerably weaken subject-verb agreement.

7.3   Syntactic variation in English from a typological point of view

From a typological perspective, three points are worth noting when looking at variation in the syntax of non-standard varieties of English. First of all, several of the grammatical features mentioned in the previous sections are typologically very rare, or have at least only very rarely, if at all, been described in the typological literature. This applies, in particular, to the Northern Subject Rule (A7) with its type-of-subject and position-of-subject constraints on subject-verb agreement, to the grammaticalization of *do* as a tense and aspect marker (T5 and T6), and to a phenomenon variously known as *gendered pronouns*, *gender animation* or *gender diffusion* (cf. Wagner 2004; Pawley 2004; Siemund to appear). The latter relates to a semantic gender system which is sensitive to the mass-count distinction such that *it* is used only for mass nouns (e.g. in *Pass the bread – it's over there*) and count nouns take *he* (e.g. in *Pass the loaf – he's over there*; *My car, he's broken*) unless they refer to female humans, in which case *she* is used. This assignment of animate gender to inanimate nouns is largely restricted to Germanic dialects. Among varieties of English, gender systems of this kind have only been observed in the English Southwest, Newfoundland, and Tasmania.

Secondly, in quite a number of cases, the grammars of non-standard varieties are typologically "more well-behaved" than Standard English, in that they follow a majority pattern in the world's languages or conform to cross-linguistic tendencies where Standard English does not. Relevant examples include the following: in the domain of tense and aspect, the increasing loss of the (typologically rare) sharp division between the Present Perfect and Simple Past (T3) as well as the development of the progressive into an imperfective (T1). In the domain of negation, non-standard varieties of English follow a frequent pattern in the European and the world's languages in permitting multiple negation (N1). In Europe, for example, only the standard varieties of the Germanic languages do not allow sentence negation to cooccur with negative quantifiers. Another pervasive feature of non-standard varieties, namely the use of invariant negative markers such as *ain't* (N2) and *don't* (N3), appears in a different light, too, when looked at from a cross-linguistic point of view. To start with, obligatory auxiliaries like *don't/doesn't/didn't* in Standard English are an absolute exception in Europe. Apart from English, only Finnic languages exhibit a similar feature, namely inflected negative verbs or auxiliaries literally meaning 'to not.' In these exceptional languages however (for example, in Estonian), these verbs or negative auxiliaries tend to develop into invariable NEG markers. This is exactly the development that led to the spreading use of *don't* as the invariable negated auxiliary for all persons in the present tense (including *he/she/it don't*) and of *ain't*, which does service for *haven't*, *hasn't*, *(amn't,) aren't*, *isn't* (cf. Anderwald 2002: 169–70). Furthermore, the invariant negation markers *ain't* and *don't* are in full accordance with the powerful typological concept of markedness: as was found for many languages, morphological distinctions tend to be reduced under negation. The gapping (or zero) strategy in relative clauses may serve as a last example where Standard English is the odd one out in light of typological principles, whereas the non-standard varieties are in full accordance with them. As was pointed out in section 6.1, Standard English allows gapping only in object position (*The man ___ I saw*), whereas it is a pervasive feature of non-standard varieties to allow gapping also in subject position (*It ain't the best ones ___ finish first*). In doing so, they conform to one of the central constraints on one of the most famous hierarchies in functional typology, namely the Noun Phrase Accessibility Hierarchy formulated for relative clauses: subject > direct object > indirect object > oblique > genitive > object of comparison. According to this hierarchy, if a language can relativize any NP position further down on the hierarchy, it must also be able to relativize all positions higher up, i.e. to the left of it. This constraint is supposed to apply to whatever relativization strategy a language employs. For the gapping strategy, Standard English evidently fails to conform to this constraint, whereas the non-standard varieties do.

When contrasting the syntax of Standard English with that of non-standard differences, a third relevant issue from a typological viewpoint is that, in individual domains of grammar, English would qualify as a different language type if the majority pattern found in the non-standard varieties was taken to represent "the" English language. Two examples may suffice. As pointed out in section 6, the dominant relativization strategy in non-standard varieties is the use of relative particles (e.g. *that, what*), i.e. uninflected relativizers; in typological accounts, however, English is classified as a language using predominantly relative pronouns (i.e. case-marked relativizers like *who* and *whom*). Another striking example is the pervasive loss of subject-verb agreement in non-standard varieties documented in section 5. Indeed, they seem to be on their way towards a system as known from the continental Scandinavian languages. And yet, in a recent typological survey of the European languages, English is classified as a language with strict subject-verb agreement, in contrast to Norwegian and Swedish (cf. map 107.11 in Haspelmath 2001: 1500).

What has been said above about syntactic variation in non-standard varieties of English (and could be said for non-standard varieties in many other languages, too) raises important methodological issues in language typology. In what way, for example, may, or even should, our knowledge of widespread properties of and pervasive tendencies in syntactic variation in non-standard and spontaneous spoken varieties of English influence the views of English as a language type commonly entertained in language typology? This question is relevant for judgments in typological research concerning individual subsystems of English grammar when compared with a large number of languages across the world, such as the language type English represents with regard to relativization or complementation strategies, or ways of marking agreement, negation, tense and aspect. In many of these domains of grammar, the vast range of spontaneous spoken and non-standard varieties differ quite markedly from written Standard American or, especially, British English. And yet these standard varieties are taken to represent English in cross-linguistic comparison, just as, where relevant structural descriptions are available, it is generally the case that the standard (written) varieties are taken to represent "the" languages in typological research. In other words, this is a methodological issue of fundamental importance, all the more so since for many less well described languages, especially those lacking a literary tradition, it is the spoken varieties that serve as the basis of typological observations, generalizations, and explanations (cf. Kortmann 2004c). The study of syntactic variation may thus serve as a corrective in language typology (cf. also Chambers' call (2004) for a new research programme which he labels *variationist typology*).

7.4   *Syntactic variation and linguistic theorizing*

One of the major reasons why at the turn of the twenty-first century the study of syntactic variation has turned into a budding field is a broadening of the perspective taken in recent generative syntactic theory and, still much less pronounced, in functional approaches to syntax, especially functional typology (see for example Black and Motapanyane 1996; Barbiers et al. 2002; Hudson 1999; 2000; Kortmann 2004c). No longer is it cross-linguistic variation only that matters. Variation within individual languages, too, is increasingly attributed important theoretical significance. As a consequence, a strong need was and still is felt to improve the empirical basis for reliable descriptive generalizations and for drawing conclusions for linguistic theory.

In generative linguistics, variation seriously started to matter with the advent of the Principles and Parameters approach in the 1980s, i.e. the idea that Universal Grammar (UG) is an invariant system of highly abstract principles some of which, within a given language, permit at most a specified degree of variation. The (core) grammar of any particular language is considered to consist of these universal principles and the language-specific settings for a small number of parameters. The concept of parametric variation thus accounts for variation observable across languages. In the late 1980s, a crucial step was taken in generative studies from the study of parametric (more exactly, macroparametric) variation to the study of microparametric, i.e. language-internal, variation. Research on microparametric syntax is strongest in Italian and Dutch linguistics, but as yet much less established in English linguistics (cf. Henry 1995 and 2002 for one of the rare exceptions). With regard to the further development of generative theory, the study of microparametric syntax is expected to yield more insights into the form and range of syntactic parameters, as well as into the effects which variation along a single parameter may have. Moreover, it needs to be taken into consideration in "studies of language acquisition based on that theoretical model" (Henry 2002: 280), just as so-called *vernacular universals* may help illuminate the innate set of rules and representations hypothesized to constitute the human language faculty (cf. Chambers 2004: 129).

It can safely be predicted that the study of both macro- and microparametric (i.e. cross- and intralinguistic) variation in syntax will continue to matter also in one of the latest developments of generative linguistics, namely Optimality Theory. This theory may, for example, offer a solution for the following problem. Dialects and non-standard varieties in general, it appears, may let universal principles and language-particular rules compete, allowing also for rivalling outputs. This is a problem of fundamental importance for which generative theory has not yet found a solution. Surely, the basic assumption of a division of tasks between UG principles and language-particular rules should apply to the grammars of all varieties of a language, not just to the grammar of the standard variety.

8   Conclusion

In his book *The dialects of England* (1999a), Peter Trudgill, one of the pioneers of sociolinguistics and modern dialectology, closes his survey chapter on the grammar of English dialects as follows:

> Variation among the Modern Dialects at the grammatical level is certainly still rich and considerable, and happily this diversity seems likely to remain with us as a source of interest, color and enjoyment for the foreseeable future, in spite of the efforts of those in the media and the educational system who would like to see an increase in conformity and uniformity.   (Trudgill 1999a: 108)

The present chapter, in addition, aimed to show what makes the study of syntactic variation, especially from a global perspective, a budding field in linguistics and what a huge potential it holds for a wide range of issues in linguistics and linguistic theory. See also chapter 14, this volume, by Mair and Leech and chapter 28, this volume, by Miller.

NOTE

I would like to thank all of the following for their extremely helpful comments on an earlier version: Bas Aarts, Lieselotte Anderwald, Christian Mair, Peter Trudgill, Susanne Wagner, and an anonymous referee.

FURTHER READING

Butters, R. R. (2001) Grammatical structure. In J. Algeo (ed.), *The Cambridge history of the English language*, vol. 6: *English in North America*. Cambridge: Cambridge University Press, 325–39.

Hickey, R. (ed.) (2004) *Legacies of colonial English: studies in transported dialects.* Cambridge: Cambridge University Press.

Kortmann, B. (2001) In the year 2525 . . . reflections on the future shape of English. *Anglistik* 12, 97–114.

Rohdenburg, G. and Mondorf, B. (eds.) (2003) *Determinants of grammatical variation in English.* Berlin, New York: Mouton de Gruyter.

Tagliamonte, S. (1999) Was/were variation across the generations: view from the city of York. *Language Variation and Change* 10, 153–91.

REFERENCES

Anderwald, L. (2002) *Negation in non-standard British English: gaps, regularizations and asymmetries.* London, New York: Routledge.

Barbiers, S., Cornips, L., and van der Kleij, S. (eds.) (2002) *Syntactic microvariation.* Amsterdam: SAND (www.meertens.nl/books/synmic).

Biber, D., Johansson, S., Leech, G., Conrad, S., and Finegan, E. (1999) *The Longman grammar of spoken and written English.* London: Longman.

Black, J. R. and Motapanyane, V. (eds.) (1996) *Microparametric syntax and dialect variation.* Amsterdam, Philadelphia: Benjamins.

Chambers, J. K., Trudgill, P., and Schilling-Estes, N. (2002) *The handbook of language variation and change.* Malden, MA.: Blackwell Publishers.

Chambers, J. K. (2004) Dynamic typology and vernacular universals. In B. Kortmann (ed.), *Dialectology meets typology: dialect grammar from a cross-linguistic perspective.* Berlin, New York: Mouton de Gruyter, 127–46.

Cheshire, J. (1999) Spoken standard English. In T. Bex and R. J. Watts (eds.), *Standard English: the widening debate.* London, New York: Routledge, 129–48.

Cheshire, J., Edwards, V., and Whittle, P. (1993) Non-standard English and dialect levelling. In J. Milroy and L. Milroy (eds.), *Real English: the grammar of English dialects in the British Isles.* London, New York: Longman, 53–96.

Edwards, V., Trudgill, P., and Weltens, B. (1984) *The grammar of English dialect: a survey of research: a report to the ESRC Education and Human Development Committee.* London: Economic and Social Research Council.

Gachelin, J.-M. (1997) The progressive and habitual aspects in non-standard Englishes. In E. Schneider (ed.), *Englishes around the world.* Amsterdam: John Benjamins, 33–46.

Häcker, M. (1999) *Adverbial clauses in Scots: a semantic-syntactic study.* Berlin, New York: Mouton de Gruyter.

Haspelmath, M. (2001) The European linguistic area: Standard Average European. In M. Haspelmath, E. König, W. Oesterreicher, and W. Raible (eds.), *Language typology and language universals: an international handbook,* vol. 2. Berlin, New York: de Gruyter, 1492–1510.

Henry, A. (1995) *Belfast English and standard English: dialect variation and parameter setting.* New York, Oxford: Oxford University Press.

Henry, A. (2002) Variation and syntactic theory. In J. K. Chambers, P. Trudgill, and N. Schilling-Estes (eds.), *The handbook of language variation and change.* Malden, MA; Oxford: Blackwell Publishers, 267–82.

Herrmann, T. (2004) Relative clauses in English dialects. In B. Kortmann, T. Herrmann, L. Pietsch, and S. Wagner (eds.), *A comparative grammar of English dialects: agreement, gender, relative clauses*. Berlin, New York: Mouton de Gruyter, 21–123.

Hudson, R. (1999) Subject-verb agreement in English. *English Language and Linguistics* 3, 173–207.

Hudson, R. (2000) **I amn't*. *Language* 76, 297–323.

Klemola, J. (2002) Continuity and change in dialect morphosyntax. In D. Kastovsky, G. Kaltenböck, and S. Reichl (eds.), *Anglistentag 2001 Vienna: Proceedings*. Trier: Wissenschaftlicher Verlag, 47–56.

Kortmann, B. (2002) New prospects for the study of English dialect syntax: Impetus from syntactic theory and language typology. In S. Barbiers, L. Cornips, and S. van der Kleij (eds.), *Syntactic microvariation*. Amsterdam: SAND, 185–213.

Kortmann, B. (2004a) *Do* as a tense and aspect marker in varieties of English. In B. Kortmann (ed.), *Dialectology meets typology: dialect grammar from a cross-linguistic perspective*. Berlin, New York: Mouton de Gruyter, 245–75.

Kortmann, B. (ed.) (2004b) *Dialectology meets typology: dialect grammar from a cross-linguistic perspective*. Berlin, New York: Mouton de Gruyter.

Kortmann, B. and Szmrecsanyi, B. (2004) Global synopsis: morphological and syntactic variation in English. In B. Kortmann, K. Burridge, R. Mesthrie, E. Schneider, and C. Upton (eds.), *A handbook of varieties of English*, vol. 2: *Morphology and syntax*. Berlin and New York: Mouton de Gruyter, 1142–1202.

Kortmann, B., Burridge, K., Mesthrie, R., and Schneider, E. (eds.) (2004) *A handbook of varieties of English*, vol. 2: *Morphology and syntax*. Berlin, New York: Mouton de Gruyter.

Kortmann, B., Herrmann, T., Pietsch, L., and Wagner, S. (2004) *A comparative grammar of English dialects: agreement, gender, relative clauses*. Berlin, New York: Mouton de Gruyter.

Miller, J. and Weinert, R. (1998) *Spontaneous spoken language: syntax and discourse*. Oxford: Clarendon Press.

Miller, J. (2004) Problems for typology: Perfects and resultatives in spoken and non-standard English and Russian. In B. Kortmann (ed.), *Dialectology meets typology: dialect grammar from a cross-linguistic perspective*. Berlin, New York: Mouton de Gruyter, 305–34.

Milroy, J. and Milroy, L. (eds.) (1993) *Real English: the grammar of English dialects in the British Isles*. London, New York: Longman.

Murray, T. E. and Simon, B. L. (2004) Colloquial American English. In B. Kortmann, K. Burridge, R. Mesthrie, and E. Schneider (eds.), *A handbook of varieties of English*, vol. 2: *Morphology and syntax*. Berlin, New York: Mouton de Gruyter, 221–44.

Nagle, S. J. (2003) Double modals in the southern United States: Syntactic structure or syntactic structures? In R. Facchinetti, M. Krug, and F. Palmer (eds.), *Modality in contemporary English*. Berlin, New York: Mouton de Gruyter, 349–71.

Pawley, A. (2004) Australian Vernacular English: some grammatical characteristics. In B. Kortmann, K. Burridge, R. Mesthrie, E. Schneider, and C. Upton (eds.), *A handbook of varieties of English*, vol. 2: *Morphology and syntax*. Berlin, New York: Mouton de Gruyter, 611–42.

Pietsch, L. (2005) "Some do and some doesn't": verbal concord variation in the north of the British Isles. In B. Kortmann, T. Hermann, L. Pietsch, and S. Wagner (eds.), *A comparative grammar of British English dialects: agreement, gender, relative clauses*. Berlin, New York: Mouton de Gruyter.

Schneider, E. (2000) Feature diffusion vs. contact effects in the evolution of New Englishes: a typological case study of negation patterns. *English World-Wide*, 21, 201–30.

Siemund, P. (to appear) *Pronominal gender in English: a study of English varieties from a cross-linguistic perspective*. London, New York: Routledge.

Trudgill, P. and Chambers, J. K. (eds.) (1991) *Dialects of English: studies in grammatical variation*. London, New York: Longman.

Trudgill, P. (1999a) *The dialects of England*, 2nd edn. Oxford: Blackwell.

Trudgill, P. (1999b) Standard English: what it isn't. In T. Bex and R. J. Watts (eds.), *Standard English: the widening debate*. London, New York: Routledge, 117–28.

Wagner, S. (2005) Gender in English pronouns: southwest England. In B. Kortmann, T. Hermann, L. Pietsch and S. Wagner (eds.), *A comparative grammar of British English dialects: agreement, gender, relative clauses*. Berlin, New York: Mouton de Gruyter, 211–367.

Wolfram, W. and Schilling-Estes, N. (1996) Dialect change and maintenance in a post-insular island community. In E. Schneider (ed.), *Focus on the USA*. Amsterdam, Philadelphia: John Benjamins, 103–48.

27 Phonological Variation: A Global Perspective

PAUL FOULKES

1 Introduction

Interest in linguistic variation is probably as old as interest in language itself. Comments on variation trace back as far as the Sanskrit grammarian Panini (ca. 600 BC) (Chambers 2002: 6). One of the earliest pronouncements on phonological variation in English comes from John of Trevisa (ca. 1385), who describes an antipathy to northern British accents which is nobly preserved in some quarters even today:

> All the language of the Northumbrians, and especially at York, is so sharp, piercing and grinding, and unformed, that we Southern men can that language hardly understand.   (Freeborn, French, and Langford 1993: 23)

My aim in this chapter is to outline the various causes and effects of phonological variability. In doing this I draw on the methods and findings of phonetics, phonology, dialectology, sociolinguistics, psycholinguistics, pragmatics, language acquisition, and a range of applied disciplines. The integration of work from a variety of academic traditions is intended to highlight some of the areas of overlap and tension between disciplines, as well as to identify areas in which our understanding of variation is limited.

A few caveats are in order before we begin. First, while my focus is on variation in English, the discussion is presented in a more general framework. English examples are used to illustrate general principles and problems in the study of phonological variation. Modern linguistics is so dominated by work on English that much of what we know about variation per se is derived from analysis of English data, and especially data from North American and British varieties. A great deal remains to be learned about varieties of English elsewhere, and about variation in other languages. Second, it will become apparent that we know rather more about how variation is manifested in speech production than about how variation impacts on speech perception. Moreover, within the study of speech production more is known about segmental features than suprasegmental ones. Therefore my review of research is inevitably biased towards work on segmental production. Third, I have interpreted *phonological* in the broad sense of 'pertaining to speech sounds,' so as to include work that deals both with the physical medium of speech and also the cognitive representation of speech 'sounds.' The issue of whether particular variable features are the result of physical (phonetic) or cognitive (phonological) factors is one of the most interesting and important questions to emerge from the study of variation. Fourth, I only discuss language using the vocal medium, although systematic variation is also found in the phonological elements of sign languages (Sutton-Spence, Woll, and Allsop 1990; Bayley, Lucas, and Rose 2002). Finally, given the range of different approaches to variation, the discussion is structured around sources of variation rather than academic tradition. Five broad categories are covered: physical and biological factors, contextual factors, grammatical factors, geographical and social factors, and individual factors. It will, however, become apparent that the factors interact with each other, and that phonological variability must be understood with reference to them all simultaneously.

The sources of variation are discussed in sections 2 to 6. Section 7 then outlines the general contributions made by work on phonological variation to current theoretical debate in linguistics. Section 8 similarly summarizes the relevance of phonological variation for applied fields beyond mainstream linguistics. The final section offers concluding comments and a speculative outlook for future work on phonological variation.

2   Physical and Biological Constraints on Phonological Variation

The first set of factors to consider in understanding phonological variation are not particular to any one language. Rather, they are the direct consequence of differences in the structures of the vocal tract and auditory system. The phonetic form of any utterance is governed to a large extent by the biological and physical components of the *speech chain* (Denes and Pinson 1993). The speech chain encapsulates the discrete stages in production and perception of speech. Any spoken event begins with cognitive processes: the speaker intends to convey a message, and plans the utterance in terms of the linguistic units and structures of the relevant language(s). This plan is then translated into neural motor commands which in turn drive muscular action. The vocal organs are moved into positions to generate the appropriate sounds by channeling airflow through the vocal tract. The acoustic signal thereby created travels to the listener's auditory system, from where it is transmitted by neural response to the cognitive perceptual system. The perceptual system then converts the neural information into linguistic terms to complete the transmission of the message.

This model is clearly universal, applying to all utterances in all languages. Moreover, the model largely defines the study of phonetics, which has developed through investigation of the various 'links' in the chain. Theoretical models have been developed to account for events that occur at particular stages, or in the transition from one stage to the next. Hayward (2000) provides a general introduction to phonetic theory, while thorough reviews of particular links are provided by Kent, Adams and Turner (1996) for speech production, Shadle (1997) for aerodynamics, Fujimura and Erickson (1997) for acoustics, and Moore (1997) for auditory processing. Thorough surveys of the speech perception literature are given by Goldinger, Pisoni, and Luce (1996), Kreiman (1997), and Jusczyk and Luce (2002).

As far as speech production is concerned, there has been abundant work on the effects of context (section 3). Generally speaking, however, the study of variation has played a relatively peripheral role in phonetic theory. In fact, variation has usually been treated by phoneticians as an unwelcome obstacle. Research on speech perception and production has been plagued by the 'lack of invariance problem,' and much effort has been directed at constructing theoretical models to explain it. The 'problem' is the fact that all acts of speaking, and thus all acoustic signals, are unique; yet listeners can understand the same linguistic message even when it is represented in varying acoustic forms. Theoretical models have therefore sought to explain the mapping between production strategies and acoustic forms that are variable, and linguistic units that are assumed to be invariant. No universally accepted solution has been reached, but influential models include the *motor theory* of speech perception (Liberman and Mattingly 1985) and the *direct realism* model (Fowler 1986). For a brief introduction see Goldinger, Pisoni and Luce (1996) and Hayward (2000), and for critical discussion of the models see Mattingly and Studdert-Kennedy (1991) and volume 14 (1) of the *Journal of Phonetics* (1986) respectively. More recent perceptual models, however, have approached the issue of variation from a fresh perspective, taking account of the structured variability in the acoustic signal which results from phonotactic and sociolinguistic factors (see further section 7 below).

In spite of the obvious variation to be found across the speech patterns of individuals, rather little phonetic research has been devoted to understanding the variation inherent to speech production (Mackenzie Beck 1997). The speech chain model does, however, predict variability and provides a partial explanation for why no two utterances are identical. Speech is largely dependent on the physical properties of the vocal-auditory channel, and, of course, no two human beings share exactly the same physical characteristics. Differences in spoken forms may therefore emanate from physical differences in each link in the chain. Furthermore, these physical differences are not only to be found across speakers: individuals are also subject to long- or short-term physical changes in the vocal tract and auditory system, which in turn may yield long- or short-term effects on their speech or hearing.

Mackenzie Beck (1997) surveys the available research on variation in anatomy and physiology of the vocal tract. She notes that differences between individuals may be relatively minor, for example slight variation in dentition which may lead to subtle effects on the acoustic properties of fricatives such as [s]. There may also be much greater physical (and thus phonetic) differences, for example caused by disease or malformation. A detailed consideration of the phonetic effects of speech and language pathologies is beyond the scope of this chapter, but see Weismer (1997) and Howard and Heselwood (forthcoming). The vocal tract of an individual also undergoes substantial physical changes during the life course, with marked developments occurring through childhood and adolescence into adulthood, and further changes emerging as a result of old age. For example, fundamental frequency (F0, which is perceived as the pitch of the voice) lowers from childhood to adulthood, and may undergo particularly dramatic short-term change in the case of adolescent males (the 'breaking' of the voice). In old age the atrophy of muscles and calcification of bones and cartilages may introduce marked phonetic changes (Mackenzie Beck 1997: 258ff), including whispery phonation and further changes in average F0. Smoking may also affect parameters such as F0, and in turn may affect listeners' ability to estimate a speaker's age (e.g. Braun 1996).

All human beings are affected by short-term physical changes, occurring, for example, as a result of the common cold, mouth ulcers or tooth loss. The phonetic effects of such physical changes range from the subtle to the obvious, but all remain under-researched. Mackenzie Beck (1997: 278) points out that this is in part because of methodological difficulties: it is hard to distinguish the effects of physical variability from those which stem from social and cultural influences such as regional accent (see further section 5 below). It is also often impractical to track individuals longitudinally.

Although the study of variation has been peripheral to phonetic theory, models of production, acoustics and perception do enable us to understand the parameters of variability in speech. For example, it has been shown that (all things being equal) vowels differ in intrinsic F0, with close vowels having higher F0 than open vowels. Lehiste and Peterson (1961) demonstrate this in a study of one American informant, while cross-linguistic evidence confirms the effect is genuinely universal (Whalen and Levitt 1995). One suggestion to explain the finding is based on the muscular linkage between the tongue and larynx: close vowels require the tongue to be raised, and the action of doing this may produce a side effect of increasing vertical tension in the larynx. In turn this tension in the vocal folds yields a higher F0 (Ohala 1978). Similarly, voice onset time (VOT) in stop consonants varies in relation to several factors including the place of articulation of the consonant. This has been explained with reference to the variable aerodynamic demands of different vocal tract configurations (Westbury 1983).

The *quantal theory* (Stevens 1998) explains the complex relationship between articulatory configuration and acoustic output. The theory predicts that articulatory variability is constrained by the potentially abrupt (quantal) effects on the acoustic signal. In some cases large articulatory variation results in only small degrees of variation in the acoustic domain. In other cases, however, small articulatory differences can result in quantal changes in acoustic quality. Perkell and Cohen (1989), for instance, studied the production of [i ɑ u] by one American speaker using X-ray imaging. They found that variability in articulation was greatest in the plane parallel to the midline of the vocal tract. Variability in the open back [ɑ] was greater in the vertical dimension, while that for the close vowels [i] and [u] was greater horizontally. Perkell and Cohen suggest that this variability is tolerated because the acoustic effects of variation in constriction *location* are much smaller than those which would result in variation in constriction *degree*. Vertical variation for /i/, for example, would potentially produce formant values similar to lower vowels in the American vowel system such as /ɪ/ or /e/. This would present a potentially confusing acoustic signal to the listener. Variability in articulatory configuration can therefore be said to be constrained by acoustic consequences.

3 Contextual Constraints on Phonological Variation

In addition to the gross effects of the physical vocal system, phonological variation also results from the linguistic context in which a sound appears. Contextual constraints include the effect of sequential articulations upon one another, and also the effect of position within words or syllables.

3.1 Coarticulation

The effect of one sound on another is termed *coarticulation* (for detailed discussion see Farnetani 1997; Hardcastle and Hewlett 1999). Well-known examples in English are the addition of lip-rounding to consonants in anticipation of a following rounded vowel (thus the second /s/ of *see-saw* is likely to be rounded), and the abrupt consonantal changes that may occur across word-boundaries (e.g. assimilation in *dress shop* [dɹɛʃ ʃɒp]). A subtler effect is described by Moreton (2004), who demonstrates that vowel formants vary in relation to whether a following consonant is voiced or voiceless. Cruttenden (2001b: 278ff) discusses many more types of variation caused by syntagmatic context. Anticipatory effects are stronger than perseverative effects, thus sounds are more likely to be influenced by their following neighbours than their preceding ones (Gay 1978).

The variation in the acoustic signal which results from articulatory movement between neighbours is important for speech perception. In consonant+vowel sequences, the formants of the vowel take systematically different routes towards the final target position, depending on the place of articulation of the consonant as well as the quality of the vowel itself (see e.g. Ladefoged 2001:

180). These formant transitions are an important cue to the identity of the consonant (Harris 1958; Mann and Repp 1980), and may help to identify the vowel: Verbrugge and Rakerd (1986) found listeners could easily identify vowels in /bVb/ sequences even when the middle 60 percent of the vowel was replaced by a period of silence. Most perceptual work, however, has concentrated on syntagmatic variation between sounds in stressed syllables, while relatively little work has been devoted to perception of unstressed syllables or domains longer than individual segments (but see e.g. Fowler 1981).

How far assimilatory effects can stretch has been tested in perceptual experiments by West (1999). She found that listeners could distinguish minimal pairs containing /l/ and /r/ (e.g. *mirror/miller*) when the target sound was replaced by noise, presumably by responding to the different coarticulatory effects of /l/ and /r/ on other sounds. The listeners were able to distinguish pairs even when several syllables preceding the target sound were replaced by noise, showing that coarticulation may stretch much further than immediately adjacent sounds. Other studies have also shown non-adjacent effects. Fowler (1981), for instance, showed that unstressed English vowels may take on articulatory and acoustic properties of neighbouring vowels despite the presence of intervening consonants. Fitzgerald (2002) similarly finds evidence for vowel harmony in Buchan Scots.

Assimilatory effects have often been described as resulting from economy of articulatory effort (e.g. Abercrombie 1967: 87). In the course of fluent speech speakers may take 'short cuts' as they move from the production of one sound to another. Support for this explanation comes from studies which have examined the effect on articulation of speaking rate (e.g. Gay 1968; Crystal and House 1988a, 1988b; Perkell, Zandipour, Matthies, and Lane 2002; but see Harris 1978 for contrary evidence). In general, faster speaking rate is characterized by articulations of shorter duration, increased overlap, and greater articulatory undershoot (that is, the articulators do not fully reach their targets). Not all sounds are equally affected by changes in speaking rate, because the various articulators differ in degrees of inertia, and in the basic speed with which they can be moved (Ohala 1983: 207).

However, economy of effort does not tell the full story behind coarticulation. Ohala (1983) argues that some examples are better explained by aerodynamic principles. For example, stops develop into affricates most commonly in the context of close vowels or /j/ (for instance the pronunciation of *tune* as [tʃun] in some varieties of British English). The generation of fricative energy results not from articulatory change, but via the aerodynamic consequences of the vocal tract configuration. In [ti] or [tj] a narrow constriction is created behind the alveolar closure for [t], which in turn causes high velocity airflow to last longer when the stop is released. The long period of high velocity airflow may be perceptible as a fricative (Ohala 1983: 204).

Moreover, it is clear that some coarticulatory effects are not universal. They differ across languages, dialects and individuals (Lindblom 1963; Byrd 1994; Laver 1994). By way of illustration, Received Pronunciation (RP) is said not to show anticipatory voicing assimilation, unlike some Scottish accents where the medial consonant cluster in *birthday* may be [-ðd-] (Laver 1994: 384). Similarly, a contextually-determined difference in vowel duration is reported by Peterson and Lehiste (1960). Vowels before voiceless consonants are on average one third shorter than the same vowel before voiced consonants. Thus *brute* has a shorter vowel than *brood* and *bruise*. However, the effect of the following consonant is not universal (Laver 1994: 446). In Scottish English, for example, some vowels display a pattern known as the Scottish Vowel Length Rule (SVLR; see e.g. Scobbie, Hewlett, and Turk 1999). (SVLR is not in fact restricted to Scotland, being also found in some north-eastern accents in England; Milroy 1995.) In SVLR accents vowels preceding voiced stops are short, and thus pattern with vowels preceding voiceless consonants. Thus, *brood* and *brute* are short, while *bruise* is long. Further contextual differences across English dialects are discussed by Fourakis and Port (1986) and Kerswill (1987), while Nolan and Kerswill (1990) demonstrate similar differences across socioeconomic groups.

These differences across dialects and individuals show that coarticulation is not simply the automatic consequence of 'mechanical necessity' (Laver 1994: 379), but is to some extent planned by speakers. Knowledge of coarticulation can therefore be argued to form part of phonological competence (Whalen 1990; Kingston and Diehl 1994).

3.2 *Prosody*

The examples discussed in section 3.1 concern the simple sequential effects of sounds upon each other. Sounds also vary in response to their prosodic context, that is, their context with respect to higher level units of linguistic organization such as sentences, intonational phrases, words or syllables. Generally speaking, articulations are longer and 'stronger' in initial contexts, and when in stressed rather than unstressed positions. Final contexts and unstressed positions present greater freedom for sounds to reduce or lenite (e.g. Harris 1978; Bauer 1988), although it is also common to find increased duration of segments before major prosodic boundaries (e.g. Wightman, Shattuck-Hufnagel, Ostendorf, and Price 1992).

Evidence for these points is abundant in experimental phonetics (see the review by Shattuck-Hufnagel and Turk 1996). Lavoie (2001), for instance, analyzed acoustic and electropalatographic (EPG) data from American English. She found consonantal features such as VOT to be longer when preceding stressed vowels and when syllable-initial. Similar findings are reported by Pierrehumbert and Talkin (1992) for /h/ and /ʔ/, and by Redi and Shattuck-Hufnagel (2001) for glottalization. Byrd (1996) used EPG to show that there is less overlap between articulatory gestures in syllable onsets than codas, and that onsets are in general less variable than codas. Coda /l/ also has been shown to contain a 'weaker' consonantal gesture than onset /l/ (Sproat and Fujimura 1993). A contrasting example is provided by Vaissière (1988), who showed that the extent of velum lowering in the production of nasal consonants is systematically greater in coda positions than initial positions.

Not all sounds are affected equally by prosodic context, however. In Byrd's (1996) analysis of articulatory timing in consonants, she found that in coda positions plosives reduced in duration more than fricatives, and coronals were overlapped more by following velar gestures than vice versa. Pierrehumbert (1995) discusses variable effects of context on syllable-final glottalization of /t/. She hypothesizes that glottalization is less likely in the context of a following voiceless fricative (e.g. *hat shop*) than other following sounds. This is because the aerodynamic consequences of glottalization are in conflict with the aerodynamic needs of fricatives. Glottalization involves a constriction or closure of the glottis, which therefore restricts airflow passing into the oral tract. Fricatives, however, demand high airflow in order to create turbulence. The data shown in Figure 1 lend support to Pierrehumbert's hypothesis. This figure displays glottalization patterns produced by 32 speakers from Newcastle, England (the speakers are the same group reported in Docherty and Foulkes 1999 and Watt and Milroy 1999). The y axis shows the proportion of glottalized tokens produced for word-final /t/ in pre-consonantal contexts. The data combine glottal stop realizations with those displaying laryngealization (see Docherty and Foulkes 1999, 2005). Data from older (45–67) and younger (15–27) speakers are shown separately. The x axis refers to the consonantal context. We can see that glottalization is lowest in the voiceless fricative contexts, particularly /f, s, ʃ, h/. Stops trigger higher rates of glottalization, but substantially less than approximants and nasals. This pattern is also predicted by Pierrehumbert: stops require sufficient airflow to create plosion, while approximants and nasals can be produced with relatively low airflow rates. Note, however, that figure 27.1 also reveals other factors to be at work in accounting for the variation in the data. In the case of /h, θ, ð, l, r, j/ the younger speakers have significantly higher glottalization rates than the older generation, suggesting that the accent is undergoing change. Indeed, that is precisely what has been found with glottalization in other contexts (Docherty, Foulkes, Milroy, Milroy, and Walshaw 1997).

As with coarticulation, there is some debate on the extent to which prosodic effects are universal. While many effects seem to be found to similar degrees across languages, there are also clear differences between dialects in contextual realization of sounds; hence these differences must form part of speakers' phonological knowledge. For example, in American English it has been suggested that nasal consonants in coda positions are in fact typically realized via nasality on the preceding vowel. This is especially true where the nasal occurs in a cluster with a final voiceless obstruent. As a result, the duration of a nasal consonant in a word such as *tent* may be shorter than that in *ten* or *tend* (Fujimura and Erickson 1997: 105).

The significant age effects in glottalization shown in figure 27.1 also testify that universal explanations for variable patterns (in this case based on aero-dynamic principles) cannot be wholly satisfactory. Instead, aspects of

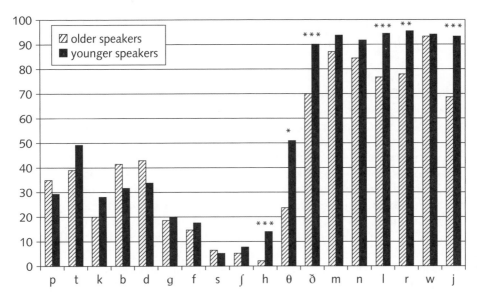

Figure 27.1 Percentage glottalization for pre-consonantal /t/ in Newcastle English
* Indicates $p < .05$, ** $p < .01$, *** $p < .001$; N tokens = 4,883; data for /v, ʧ, ʤ/ are not shown due to small number of tokens.

prosodically conditioned variability may differ across individuals or may correlate with social factors. Further evidence is provided by Docherty and Foulkes (1999, 2004). In an acoustic study of Newcastle English, systematic variation was found in the realization of pre-pausal /t/. In addition to the expected voiceless oral stop variants, we also found variants which contained a continuation of voicing from the previous vowel and pre-aspirated variants which contained a period of high frequency fricative energy before the stop closure. The voiced variants were significantly more common in the speech of older males than any other group, while the pre-aspirated type was strongly associated with young women.

4 Grammatical Constraints on Phonological Variation

It was noted in section 3 that aspects of contextual variation vary across languages and dialects, and are thus arguably represented cognitively in the phonological component of the grammatical system. This section addresses further sources of variation which are unequivocally the result of grammatical factors. Some of these involve the interaction of the phonology with other levels of the grammar (4.1), while others occur as a result of speakers having access to grammars of more than one language or dialect (4.2).

4.1 Interactions between phonology and other levels of the grammar

Several phonetic and phonological studies have discussed the deletion of /t/ and /d/ in English coda consonant clusters. For example, in the phrase *perfect memory* it is common for the /t/ of *perfect* to be deleted, particularly in casual speech (e.g. Cruttenden 2001b: 287; see also Browman and Goldstein 1990, who show via X-ray evidence that the apparent deletion may be a perceptual effect, with the alveolar closing gesture for the /t/ still present but masked by labial closure for the /m/). The deletion of final /t/ and /d/ has also been a common topic in sociolinguistic work (e.g. Guy 1980; Guy and Boyd 1990). It has been shown that the rate of deletion is influenced by several contextual factors, including the phonetic quality of adjacent sounds. However it has also been shown that deletion rate is affected by the morphological status of the target word. Deletion is most likely in monomorphemes (*mist*) than in irregular past tense forms (*kept*), and less likely still in regular past tense forms (*missed*). This pattern is largely consistent across dialects, although differences have been found in a study in York (Tagliamonte and Temple 2005). Similarly, Labov (1989) shows that the use of alveolar [n] for /ŋ/ (e.g. in *jumping*) is influenced by grammatical category. It is least frequent for nouns, but increasingly more frequent for gerunds, adjectives and progressives/participles. Labov claims there is a historical explanation for the patterning, as the modern *-ing* forms derive from two different historical roots, *-inge* and *-inde*.

The differential rate of cluster reduction in pairs like *mist* and *missed* shows that morphological structure may make itself apparent in phonetic form even where the phonological structure of words appears to be identical. Hawkins and Smith (2001) and Hawkins (2003) cite examples where similar differences are found even in canonical speech and without the influence of connected speech processes. In some dialects the pair *mistake* and *mistime* share a similar phonological structure, with a syllable break after /mɪs/. However, for some speakers syllabification of the /t/ differs: it is affiliated with the second syllable in *mistime* but ambisyllabic in *mistake*. As a result of the different syllabic structure the relative durations of acoustic segments may differ. *Mistime* has a more aspirated /t/, for example, because it is in syllable-initial position. The explanation for the difference is that *mistime* contains a morpheme boundary wheras *mistake* does not. Similar differences are found in SVLR accents (see section 3.1): while *brood* has a short vowel in these accents, *brewed* has a long vowel because of its morphological complexity. Hawkins and Smith (2001) predict that listeners should be able to perceive such subtle distinctions and exploit them in speech perception tasks to facilitate lexical access (cf. findings on coarticulatory variation referred to in section 3.2).

A word's grammatical category can also constrain the degree of variability that speakers exercise in producing it. Function words and auxiliaries undergo quite different reduction processes from content words (Ogden 1999; Turk and

Shattuck-Hufnagel 2000; Bell, Jurafsky, Fosler-Lussier, Girand, and Gregory 2003). Usually this means a greater range of reduced forms are found for function words. In English, for example, forms of the auxiliary *have* include [hav, həv, əv, v], but a similar range of reductions is not possible for minimally-different phonological forms such as *ham, heave, Gav.* Ogden (1999) cites this kind of evidence in support of a polysystemic approach to phonological structure (see further section 7 below).

4.2   Interactions between grammatical systems

The anglocentric world of linguistics has tended to treat monolingualism as the norm. It is often neglected that the majority of the world's population is bilingual or multilingual. Research on the phonology of bilinguals, however, shows that the grammatical systems of languages may interact and influence a person's speech production and perception (see e.g. Flege 1995; Flege, Schirru, and MacKay 2003).

In the case of adult learners of a new language, it is of course usual for the new language to conform largely to the phonological patterns of the base language. This is why we tend to display a non-native accent when speaking a language learned in adulthood. Where a large population learns the same language, as is often the case with English around the world, there may be a long-term effect which comes to define the regional accent. For instance, features of South African English such as unaspirated stops and tapped /r/ have been attributed to the interference of Afrikaans phonology (Melchers and Shaw 2003: 117). Jibril (1986) notes regional differences within Nigerian English which appear to be the result of the differing influences of Hausa and Yoruba. Several varieties of North American English are characterized by influence from other languages, including Cajun (French, see e.g. Dubois and Horvath 1998) and Chicano (Spanish, e.g. Fought 2003).

Phonological studies of bilingual children – i.e. who are learning two languages simultaneously – also show that interference may take place between phonological systems (e.g. Leopold 1947). However, Khattab (2002a) shows that such interference may take place only in particular communicative settings (see section 5.6). She also argues that some differences between bilinguals and monolinguals are not the result of interference between the two grammatical systems, even if that may seem to be the case at first glance. In her study of Arabic-English bilinguals, the children did not show much success in producing Arabic pre-voiced stops /b, d, g/. Instead they produced short lag VOT, as is appropriate for /b, d, g/ in English. However, statistical analysis revealed that the children still made significant differences in VOT duration for the two languages, and were therefore not simply transposing the English pattern onto their Arabic productions (Khattab 2002b).

Interaction between two languages has also been shown in perceptual experiments. Elman, Diehl, and Buchwald (1977) found that bilinguals categorized synthetic stimuli differently depending on which of their languages they believed they were listening to. Niedzielski (1999) showed similar effects at a cross-dialect level in experiments with listeners from Detroit. Some subjects were played voice samples and told that they were hearing Michigan English, while others were told they were hearing a Canadian variety. The subjects were then asked to listen to a set of synthesized vowels, and from them choose the best match to the vowels they had heard in the original samples. Listeners made different choices depending on which variety they believed they had heard. Niedzielski's study therefore suggests that knowledge of dialect-specific variation is drawn upon in perceptual tasks.

5   Geographical and Social Constraints on Phonological Variation

One of the most obvious sources of phonological variability is the geographical and social background of the speaker. Speakers learn the dialect of the community in which they are raised. In the case of a global language like English this may result in phonological differences between speakers that are so large as to make communication difficult or even impossible. Furthermore, work carried out in the Labovian sociolinguistic paradigm since the 1960s has revealed differences between speakers of any given dialect as a function of social factors such as gender, social class, ethnicity, age and speaking style (see Chambers 2003 for a review).

The following sections (5.1 to 5.6) outline geographical and social factors in turn, explaining the influence of each factor on phonological variation with reference to key findings from dialectological, sociolinguistic and phonetic research. However, many published sources contribute to our understanding of several of these factors simultaneously. Sociolinguistic studies, for example, usually investigate the effects of various social factors within a geographical location. In addition to the works referred to in the specific sections below, other sources which provide valuable information about geographical and/or social differences across varieties include:

General overviews of regional varieties
Bailey and Görlach (1982), Wells (1982), Cheshire (1991), Burchfield (1994), MacMahon (1998), Melchers and Shaw (2003), Kortmann and Schneider (2004). See also studies reported in the journals *American Speech, English World-Wide, Journal of English Linguistics, Language Variation and Change, World Englishes.*

British Isles
Trudgill (1974, 1988), Macaulay (1977), Bauer (1985), Petyt (1985), Milroy (1987b), Ramisch (1988), Deterding (1997), Pandeli, Eska, Ball and Rahilly (1997), Kerswill and Williams (2000), McClure (2002), Marshall (2003, 2004), Corbett, McClure and Stuart-Smith (2003). Several other studies are collected in Trudgill (1978) and Foulkes and Docherty (1999). Foulkes and Docherty (in press) summarize recent work on phonological variation in England.

United States

Fischer (1958), Labov, Yaeger and Steiner (1972), Pederson (1977), Feagin (1979), di Paolo and Faber (1990), Schneider (1996), Fridland (1999), Thomas (2001), Clopper and Pisoni (2004). A survey of work is provided by Wolfram and Schilling-Estes (1998).

Canada

Chambers (1991), Clarke (1991, 1993), Esling (1991), Woods (1991).

Australia

Mitchell and Delbridge (1965), Horvath (1985), Collins and Blair (1989), Burridge and Mulder (1998), Blair and Collins (2001).

New Zealand

Bauer (1986), Holmes (1997), Burridge and Mulder (1998), Bell and Kuiper (2000), Trudgill, Gordon, Lewis and Maclagan (2000), Watson, Maclagan and Harrington (2000).

Elsewhere

Holm (1983, Central American creoles), Bansal (1990, India), Khan (1991, India), Patrick (1996, Jamaican Creole), Tent (2001, Fiji), Sudbury (2001, Falkland Islands), Aceto and Williams (2003, Caribbean), Simo Bobda (2003, African varieties).

Information on the pronunciation of consonants and vowels is considerably richer than that on suprasegmental features, particularly in sociolinguistic studies. However, works referring to intonational patterns in specific dialects include Bilton (1982), Guy, Horvath, Vonwiller, Disley and Rogers (1986), Britain (1992), Douglas-Cowie, Cowie and Rahilly (1995), Rahilly (1997), Warren and Britain (2000), Daly and Warren (2001), Cruttenden (2001a), Fletcher, Stirling, Mushin and Wales (2002), Sutcliffe (2003) and Walters (2003). Grabe (2002) and Fletcher, Grabe and Warren (2004) compare patterns across dialects, while Cruttenden (1997: 128ff) summarizes dialect-specific intonation work.

Esling (1978, 1991), Henton and Bladon (1988) and Stuart-Smith (1999) show that social factors correlate with variation in *vocal setting*. Vocal setting is defined by Laver (1994: 396) as the 'tendency underlying the production of the chain of segments in speech towards maintaining a particular configuration or state of the vocal apparatus.' Examples of vocal settings include the use of breathy or creaky voice quality. Further comments on regional or social variation in vocal setting and voice quality can be found in Honikman (1964), Trudgill (1974), Catford (1977: 103), Knowles (1978) and Laver (1980: 4). Other suprasegmental aspects to have been analyzed across dialects include pitch accent realization (Grabe, Post, Nolan and Farrar 2000) and rhythm (Low, Grabe and Nolan 2000; Deterding 2001). The works cited on rhythm, for example, show Singapore English to be more syllable-timed than British English.

5.1   *Geographical variation*

There is a long tradition of interest in geographical differences across English dialects, with systematic studies of regional varieties beginning at least as early as the eighteenth century. For example, Pegge's survey of the dialect of Whittington, Derbyshire, began in 1751 (published posthumously as Pegge 1896). Specific phonological interest is exemplified by Ellis (1889) and the editorial additions made by Hallam to Pegge (1896).

The study of geographical variation was formalized in national dialect surveys in the mid-twentieth century (Chambers and Trudgill 1998). Major national projects include surveys of the USA and Canada (Kurath and McDavid 1961; Kretzschmar, McDavid, Lerud and Johnson 1994), England (Orton et al. 1963–70), Scotland (McIntosh 1952), and Ireland (Barry 1981). These surveys yielded detailed descriptive data in the form of local lexical items and pronunciations, often presented as linguistic atlases (e.g. for the USA, Kurath, Hanley, Bloch, and Lowman 1939–43, Allen 1973–6, Pederson, McDaniel et al. 1986–92; for Scotland, Mather and Speitel 1975; for England, Orton, Sanderson and Widdowson 1978, Upton and Widdowson 1996). Such surveys have been criticized for the lack of representativeness in their fieldwork, with the focus usually on accessing the speech of NORMs (non-mobile older rural males). The data thus tell us relatively little about language in urban centers, or variation within communities or within the repertoire of individuals (see e.g. Pickford 1956; Milroy and Gordon 2003: 11ff). Nonetheless, the wealth of descriptive data produced during national surveys remains an extremely valuable resource for research in historical phonology (e.g. Jones 2002).

Logistical and financial constraints, however, mean that national surveys are rare. One of the few ongoing projects is Telsur, which focuses on vowel pronunciations in the USA and Canada, and the results of which are being used to produce an Atlas of North American English (www.ling.upenn.edu/phono_atlas/home.html). Telsur has collected data from a socially heterogeneous sample of over 700 informants, with recordings made via telephone (although telephone speech may itself be problematic – see section 5.6).

The effects of geographical space on linguistic variation are deconstructed by Britain (2002). Britain argues that sociolinguists have overemphasized the effects of *Euclidean* (physical) space, while neglecting *social* and *perceived* space. Maintenance and change in linguistic forms may be constrained not only by physical distance but by the social distance between speakers, viewed in socio-economic or political terms. The political division between England and Scotland, for example, explains why the Scottish–English border remains an abrupt division between dialects (Watt and Ingham 2000). Variation may also be linked to speakers' attitudes, and their perceptions of geographical or social distances (e.g. Britain 2002; Dyer 2002). Britain (2002) shows, for example, that the English city of Peterborough is much more influenced by London speech patterns than the adjacent rural areas of the Fens. The geographical distance from London is similar, but the social link is much closer with Peterborough than the Fens thanks to good road and rail links. Attitudinal factors further enhance the distance between Peterborough and the Fens, with urban dwellers often holding negative perceptions of their rural neighbors, and vice versa. This in turn means there is relatively little interaction between the urban and rural communities, thus further distancing the Fenlanders from London influences.

A number of perceptual studies have tested listeners' abilities to recognize and categorize regional dialects, including Wolfram, Hazen, and Schilling-Estes (1999) (see further Thomas 2002a: 117–20). Clopper and Pisoni (2004) investigate which acoustic cues were utilized by listeners in detecting American regional dialects.

5.2 Social class and social network

Socio-economic status, often abbreviated as 'class,' is usually found to have a very strong influence on linguistic behavior. Typically the class continuum correlates with a linguistic continuum from standard to vernacular, with vernacular forms most prevalent for members of lower social classes. Although many sociolinguistic studies investigate class differences, class itself is a difficult concept to quantify and interpret, particularly where female and child subjects are concerned (Rickford 1986; Ash 2002; Milroy and Gordon 2003). Recent studies tend to avoid the complex measuring systems for class that were used in early work such as Trudgill (1974). Instead, 'class' is often no more than a general label for the type of neighbourhood being investigated.

Our understanding of within-community differences has been enhanced by *sociometrics* and *social network* analysis (e.g. Eckert 2000; Milroy 2002). This is especially true where social class is relatively homogeneous, as in Belfast, for example (Milroy 1987b). Networks describe the type of regular contact a person has with other individuals. A *dense* network is a tight-knit one in which individuals all know each other. The ties between network members are *strong* if the individuals have regular contact with each other. The polar opposite is a *loose* network with *weak* ties between members. Network studies show that dense networks are often characteristic of broadly working-class communities, and that these networks exert strong influences on group members to adhere to the norms of group behavior. One result of this influence is the maintenance of local linguistic patterns. By contrast, looser networks are found in situations where group members are more physically and socially mobile, as is typical of communities higher up the social hierarchy. Such networks exert less influence on group members to conform to in-group norms, in turn rendering group members more susceptible to influence from outside the group. Britain (1997) elaborates on the role of network types and their effect on language use with reference to the effect of *routines*. Routine activities (e.g. regular patterns of work and leisure) promote the maintenance of patterns of behavior. Typical 'middle class' communities are characterized by weaker cycles of routine, since they tend to enjoy greater mobility, which in turn disrupts routine activities.

Milroy and Milroy (1985) argue that loose networks and weak ties act as a conduit for linguistic change, since they increase the chances of exposure to external linguistic patterns (see also Watt and Milroy 1999; and, for critique of the network model, Marshall 2004). The degree to which an individual is central to a group is also influential on the individual's linguistic choices, as Labov, Cohen, Robins and Lewis (1968) showed in their analysis of AAVE speakers belonging to New York gangs. Gang members who were peripheral to the group produced fewer non-standard forms than those who were central.

5.3   Sex and gender

Sex-based phonetic differences between adult speakers are very striking, and result to an extent from marked differences in vocal tract anatomy and physiology (section 2). The larger size of the average male vocal folds explains why male voices typically have lower F0 than women, for example. However, biology is not the only source of variation between males and females. Children are not differentiated by the obvious variation in anatomy and physiology that adults are, and yet it seems that gender-correlated patterns of phonological variation are learned relatively early in childhood. Perceptual studies show that listeners can distinguish boys and girls in speech samples taken from children as young as three years old (Lee, Hewlett, and Nairn 1995). Production studies confirm that children start to manifest the same gender-differentiated phonological patterns as the adults of their community at around three years (Roberts and Labov 1995; Roberts 1997a, 1997b; Docherty, Foulkes, Tillotson, and Watt in press).

Although speaker sex is relatively rarely the focus of attention in laboratory phonetics or phonology (Byrd 1994), sex-correlated differences emerge in almost all sociolinguistic studies. Generally, women are found to adhere more closely than men to norms associated with standard language varieties (see the review by Cheshire 2002). There are, however, exceptions (e.g. Milroy 1987b), and the general correlation between sex and standardness has been shown to be an oversimplification. Milroy and Milroy (1985) redefine the effect of sex in terms of orientation to *non-local* versus *local* forms rather than a standard/non-standard continuum. Their conclusion is based on observations that women and men typically operate in different social network structures: men's networks are usually denser than women's, which explains why men orient more to vernacular norms (see 5.2 above). The local/non-local dimension is better able to capture observed patterns where standard forms appear to play little role. One such finding is described by Watt and Milroy (1999), in their study of vowels in Tyneside English. Their results show that women prefer variants which have a relatively wide currency over northern England, while men show a much higher use of more localized pronunciations.

The distinction between speakers' socially defined gender and the binary distinction of biological sex is often merely an issue of terminology (Cheshire 2002: 423): results tend to be presented and interpreted in binary terms in any case. Eckert (1989, 2000), however, shows that analysis of informants' gender identity offers a much more refined understanding of their linguistic differences (see also Cameron this volume). Eckert's study of vowel variables used by Detroit teenagers revealed that many of the largest differences emerged not between male and female groups but between different groups of girls. She explains this finding in the following terms:

> the primary importance of gender lies not in differences between male and female across the board, but in differences within gender groups . . . a general constraint against competition across gender lines leads people to compete, hence evaluate themselves, within their gender group.   (Eckert 2000: 122–3)

In the perceptual domain rather little attention has been paid to gender-based differences, although a series of experiments have shown that perceptual boundaries between sounds may be adjusted in line with the assumed gender of the talker. Strand (1999) presented listeners with a continuum of synthetic stimuli ranging from a clear [s] at one pole to a clear [ʃ] at the other, with intermediate stimuli gradually decreasing in the low frequency boundary of fricative energy. The listeners' task was to label the stimuli as either /s/ or /ʃ/. While hearing the stimuli, some listeners were presented with a female face but others saw a male face. The category boundary differed for the two listener groups, in line with typical differences in speech production. Those who saw a female face placed the boundary at a higher frequency, since female voices produce fricatives with higher frequencies than male voices. A similar pattern was found in vowel categorization by Johnson, Strand and D'Imperio (1999). These experiments demonstrate that sociolinguistic knowledge may influence basic speech perception tasks (cf. also Niedzielski 1999 on regional dialect differences; section 4.2).

5.4   Race and ethnicity

The relationship between linguistic variation and ethnicity has been a prominent focus for North American sociolinguistics since the 1960s. Labov's early works included investigations of the phonological patterns of the Portuguese and Wampanoag Native American minorities in Martha's Vineyard (Labov 1963), and Puerto Ricans and African Americans in New York City (Labov, Cohen, Robins, and Lewis 1968). Since then a wealth of work has been produced on African American Vernacular English (AAVE) in particular, both describing features of contemporary AAVE and also tracing its development from the early settlement of Africans in North America (see e.g. Wolfram 1969; Mufwene, Rickford, Bailey, and Baugh 1998; Thomas and Bailey 1998; Wolfram, Thomas, and Green 2000; Green 2002; Wolfram and Thomas 2002). Phonological features, however, have been less studied than other aspects of the grammar, and suprasegmentals fare worse still (but see Tarone 1973, Hudson and Holbrook 1982; and brief reviews of work by Green 2002, Wolfram and

Thomas 2002). Furthermore, most work has concentrated on differences between AAVE and other varieties, with relatively little attention being paid to variation within AAVE itself (Wolfram and Schilling-Estes 1998: 174). Overall, however, it appears that AAVE varies relatively little geographically, and AAVE speakers collectively resist participation in major sound changes such as the Northern Cities shift (e.g. Wolfram and Schilling-Estes 1998; Milroy and Gordon 2003).

Other ethnic communities to have been studied in North America include Franco-Americans in New Hampshire (Ryback-Soucy and Nagy 2000), Lumbee Native Americans (Schilling-Estes 2000), Cherokees (Anderson 1999), Irish, Italian and Jewish groups in Boston (Lafarriere 1979), Pennsylvania Germans (Huffines 1984), Orthodox Jews (Benor 2001), and several rural enclaves in Canada (see Chambers 1991). Chicano speakers are perhaps the most extensively studied (Peñalosa 1980; Penfield and Ornstein-Galicia 1985; Fought 1999, 2003; Thomas 2000).

Ethnic differences in phonology have not been so extensively studied elsewhere in the English-speaking world, although there is a growing body of work on differences between Maori and Pakeha (European) English in New Zealand (e.g. Britain 1992; Holmes 1997). In Australia there has been little work on the phonological properties of Aboriginal English, although other ethnic groups have been studied (see Clyne, Eisikovits, and Tollfree 2001 for a review). These include Torres Strait English (Shnukal 2001) and several communities of German and Greek origin (Clyne, Eisikovits, and Tollfree 2001).

In the UK there have been few systematic phonological studies of ethnic varieties. Work in Northern Ireland has investigated differences drawn along religious divisions (Milroy 1987b; McCafferty 1999, 2001). The dearth of work, however, is regrettable in view of the rapidly changing ethnic composition of the UK. There has been a huge rise in immigration since the mid-twentieth century, resulting in very large ethnic minority populations in cities such as Bradford and Leicester. Notable exceptions are Wells (1973), who presents a detailed study of London Jamaican English, and Khan (in progress), who compares phonological patterns across three ethnic groups in Birmingham. Brief information on aspects of Caribbean English in the UK is provided by Sutcliffe (1982), Local, Wells, and Sebba (1985), and Hewitt (1986). Hewitt suggests that features of Caribbean Englishes are filtering into the speech of white adolescents in the south of England, a claim supported in recent work by Hirson, Holmes, and Coulthrust (2003).

Heselwood and McChrystal (2000) present a preliminary study of the accent features of Panjabi-English bilinguals in Bradford. Intriguingly, their results suggest that differentiation from local Yorkshire patterns is much more marked in the speech of young males than females. For example, the males used more noticeable retroflexion in /t/ and /d/ articulations, a feature characteristic of Panjabi itself. It seems that the males may be adapting phonological features of one language for use as markers of ethnicity in the other. This 'recycling' of sociolinguistic features is also reported by Dyer (2002) in her study of the

English steel town, Corby. The town saw a large influx of Scottish steel work-
ers in the 1960s. Subsequent generations have abandoned many of the Scottish
phonological features which characterized the immigrant community. However, certain features are being maintained with redefined social-indexical
values. The use of monophthongs in words such as *boat*, *know*, for example, is
emblematic of Scottish ethnicity for older speakers, but is now being used by
younger speakers as a marker of local Corby identity. In this way young
Corby speakers differentiate themselves from inhabitants of neighboring areas.

Perceptual studies relating to ethnicity are almost all concerned with whether
listeners can identify the ethnic origins of a speaker. Several studies (reviewed
by Thomas 2002a; Thomas and Reaser 2004) show that listeners can indeed
distinguish African Americans from Anglo Americans, although few of these
studies identify which particular phonological features enable listeners to perform the task. An exception is Walton and Orlikoff (1994) who describe ethnic
differences in voice quality, albeit from analysis of very short samples.

5.5　Age

The effect of age on phonological differences is very obvious when comparing
the speech of adults with that of children. Of course, differences in anatomy
and physiology are largely responsible, as we saw in section 2. However,
socially oriented variation also occurs across the course of life. In discussing
such variation, Eckert (1997) shows that culturally-determined life stages are
of greater relevance than biological age. She identifies three key *life stages* –
childhood, adolescence and adulthood. Each of these stages exert quite different influences on linguistic patterns.

Childhood is obviously characterized by relatively immature speech patterns due to incomplete language learning and the ongoing development of
the child's anatomy and motor control. Relatively little work has been carried
out on the acquisition of socially structured variation by children, despite the
obvious variation which is a hallmark of child speech. This lack of study
results in large measure from the dominance in child language work of structuralist and generative frameworks, and the emphasis on searching for the
acquisition of language-specific contrasts (Ferguson 1986: 44). It is clear, though,
that local forms of pronunciation, including quite complex patterns of allophonic
distribution, emerge from the very start of the acquisition process (Roberts
and Labov 1995; Roberts 1997a, 1997b, 2002; Foulkes, Docherty, and Watt
2001; Docherty, Foulkes, Tillotson, and Watt in press). Typically, patterns
characteristic of adult women's speech have the greatest chance of being
acquired by children, as in most societies children will gain the majority of
their linguistic input from female caregivers (Labov 1990).

In adolescence, the role of the peer group becomes very important, and may
overtake the influence of the home. Conformity to peer group norms becomes
increasingly important, and one reflex of this may be the rapid increase in
usage of vernacular features in speech. Individuals may therefore undergo

marked changes in phonological patterns as the influence of the home model wanes. A very clear example is provided in the context of the English new town, Milton Keynes (Kerswill 1996; Williams and Kerswill 1999; Kerswill and Williams 2000). Being a new town, Milton Keynes is characterized by a large number of in-migrants from various quarters of the British Isles and beyond. Children growing up in Milton Keynes are therefore exposed to an unusually wide array of dialects as their initial linguistic input. The variety of input dialects is clearly apparent in the speech of four year olds, who constitute as heterogeneous a linguistic group as their parents. However, by age 12 the pressure to conform to peer norms is such that most of the initial differences have been eradicated, and a strikingly homogeneous local accent has emerged. Eckert (2000) also reveals the important linguistic influence of the peer group on adolescents.

Adulthood, by contrast, is often assumed to be a stable period, with the phonological structure of the language having become fixed. Some studies reveal evidence for ongoing change in adulthood, however, depending on the personal circumstances of the speaker. Obvious situations which induce ongoing change include the learning of a new dialect or language after geographical relocation (e.g. Chambers 1992). Coupland (1980) and Mees and Collins (1999) also show that individual deployment of sociolinguistic variants may change markedly during adulthood, depending on factors such as the social ambition of the speaker. Mees and Collins, for instance, analyze the use of glottal variants of /t/ in a real-time study of four Cardiff women. Glottal variants are not characteristic of Cardiff English, and are thus indexical of supra-local rather than local varieties. Individuals who are content to stay in Cardiff show relatively low use of glottal variants, whereas those speakers who signal an intent to leave the area show an increase in their use of glottals over the period studied. An even more striking example illustrating ongoing change is reported by Harrington, Palethorpe, and Watson (2000), who identify various changes in Queen Elizabeth II's vowel production over several decades. Her pronunciation has gradually shifted from a stereotyped upper-class RP towards a more mainstream RP variety.

5.6   *Communicative context*

Variation in speech may result from many different types of influence emanating from the specific context in which communication takes place. Phonetic forms may be controlled in line with the style or register of speech; they may be tailored according to the relationship between the speaker and listener; they may be designed to provide coherence to a discourse; they may be linked to changes in the ambient physical conditions of the context; and they may be affected by temporary external influences such as alcohol or consciously adopted disguise.

Speaking style has been a long-standing focus in sociolinguistics (see Schilling-Estes 2002 for a review). Many studies have shown that speakers (particularly women) move closer to the standard in more formal styles of speech. Examples include the increased production in formal styles of post-vocalic [ɹ] in New York (Labov 1966), and [h] in British English (Trudgill 1974). Phonological variation may even be linked to quite particular registers, such as pop songs (where features of American accents are often adopted, Trudgill 1983) and horse racing commentary, which is notable for its particular rhythm, rate and intonational features (Horvath 1997).

In early sociolinguistic work speaking style was conceived as a linear continuum from vernacular to standard, with speakers shifting towards the standard pole of the continuum as a reflex of increasing self-consciousness (e.g. Labov 1972: 208). Subsequent work has refined this view somewhat, with researchers recognizing that phonological choices are also affected by the interlocutor, communicative task, and discourse function.

Bell (1984) notes that interlocutors often accommodate to each others' linguistic patterns as a means of establishing solidarity. Trudgill (1986: 8), for instance, found that in the sociolinguistic interviews he carried out in Norwich his own use of glottal forms of (t) correlated with that of the interviewees. Alternatively, linguistic differences may be enhanced to create distance between speakers. In both cases phonological variation results not simply from the speaker's self-consciousness but from the relationship between the interlocutors in the communicative context. As such, speech is therefore subject to what Bell terms *audience design*. A similar conclusion is reached in phonetic work by Lindblom (1990), who claims that the structure of spoken discourse varies along a continuum from *hyper-speech* to *hypo-speech*. The former is characterized by relatively canonical pronunciation, and is generated when the listener's needs in the communicative setting demand clear speech from the speaker (for example when conditions are noisy, or detailed new information is being given). Hypo-speech is characterized by increased rapidity and greater degrees of underarticulation. It is produced when the communicative context permits the speaker to be more egocentric, such as in narratives. Variation according to addressee was demonstrated very clearly in a study of the speech of one individual, Carol Meyers, in a range of situations (Labov 2001: 438ff). Meyers' vowels differed quite radically depending on whether she was in a work or social context. Differences in phonological variant patterns have also been found in studies comparing speech between adults to that between adults and children (see Foulkes, Docherty, and Watt 2005). Degrees of hyper- and hypo-articulation have furthermore been shown to depend on a word's relative frequency, and on the number of close phonological neighbours it has (Luce and Pisoni 1998; Wright 2003).

Research with bilinguals supports the view that situational context is an important influence on phonological choice, in that patterns of interference between languages depend upon the type of *language mode* being used (Grosjean 1998). In some circumstances a bilingual is likely to use just one language, such as speaking to a monolingual. In a monolingual mode, any interference between the speaker's two languages is minimal. However, in interaction with other bilinguals code-switching often emerges. That is, speakers engage in a bilingual mode where both languages are used and structures from one language may well be transposed onto the other. Khattab (2002a, 2002b) provides evidence for mode-related phonological differences in Arabic–English bilingual children.

In addition to variation according to addressee, speakers exploit phonological choices for pragmatic and conversational purposes. For example, in Tyneside English fully-released non-glottalized voiceless stops seem to play a role in signaling transitions in speaking turns (Local, Kelly, and Wells 1986; Docherty, Foulkes, Milroy, Milroy, and Walshaw 1997). Turn transitions may also be controlled by intonational patterns that vary markedly across dialects. Local, Wells, and Sebba (1985) describe patterns of pitch movement as a cue to turn-endings in London Jamaican English, while the use of high rising tone has been identified as a turn-holding mechanism in Australia (Guy, Horvath, Vonwiller, Disley, and Rogers 1986) and New Zealand (Britain 1992; Warren and Britain 2000). Other studies reveal very fine control of phonetic parameters to give coherence to discourse, including timing, overlap between interlocutors, speech rate and F0 level (e.g. Couper-Kuhlen and Selting 1996; Curl 2003; Local 2003; Walker 2003).

Given communicative contexts may generate short-term effects on phonological patterns. Some of these result from the speaker's attitude to the addressee, topic of discourse or situation. Speakers usually indicate paralinguistic intent via suprasegmental features such as voice quality or intonation (reviewed by Ní Chasaide and Gobl 1997). Boredom, for instance, is typically conveyed by a narrow intonational range and low overall F0. Some such features are clearly voluntary, although the phonetic effect of others such as anger and fear appear to be largely beyond the speaker's control. Individuals nevertheless vary in the effects they manifest. Perceptual experiments show that listeners can detect attitudinal factors, and also that variation in paralinguistic voice qualities may affect speech perception and voice recognition (Mullennix, Bihon, Bricklemyer, Gaston, and Keener 2002).

Other short-term effects may result from temporary changes in ambient conditions, or through the presence of external influences such as intoxicating substances. Chin and Pisoni (1997) review work on the variable phonetic consequences of alcohol intake. Speech in noisy conditions, meanwhile, is often modified to counteract the effects of background noise. The *Lombard reflex* typically leads to louder speech, which results in various side-effects including higher F0 and complex modifications to vowel formants (Lane and Tranel 1971; French 1998). A similar response also typifies speech via telephones where the limitations of the transmission medium lead speakers to increase loudness (as anyone who has witnessed people using mobile phones will recognize) (Künzel 2001).

Variation resulting from factors such as telephone speech, alcohol, and emotional states is a particular problem in forensic phonetics (Nolan 1997; Rose 2002). A frequent task in the application of forensic phonetics is to compare a speech sample with criminal content (e.g. a threatening message) with a sample from a known suspect, to assess the likelihood that the two samples were produced by the same person. However, the majority of criminal samples in real cases involve telephone calls, often made in emotional circumstances, and not infrequently by people who have had a few drinks. The phonological effects of these factors must all be catered for in the comparison with the suspect's sample, which is likely to have been recorded in quite different conditions (usually an interview in police custody). Active attempts to disguise a voice may further exacerbate analytic problems (Hollien, Majewski, and Doherty 1982).

Perceptual effects of situational influences on speech have also been found, and again have particular relevance for the practices of forensic phonetics. It has been shown, for example, that identifying a known individual's voice is more difficult when the speech is heard through a telephone (Rathborn, Bull, and Clifford 1981). Foulkes and Barron (2000) found in an experiment with phone samples that individuals who know each other well may fail to recognize each others' voices, and even their own voices.

What is perhaps most striking about the effect of communicative context is the sheer range of different influences on speech that can be found. In view of that, our understanding of how such factors are handled in phonological knowledge remains relatively poor. Work in experimental phonetics and theoretical phonology has largely ignored the sorts of factors outlined in this section, focusing instead on canonical materials collected in laboratory settings or 'neutral' interactional styles.

6 Individual Constraints on Phonological Variation

Phonological differences between individuals have been alluded to throughout the previous sections. We have seen, for example, that differences may result from idiosyncracies in vocal tract anatomy, or, in the case of Carol Meyers and others, the effects of personal interactions.

It is probably true, in fact, that individual differences are demonstrated in every empirical study of speech production or perception, even if these differences are rarely the subject of much discussion. An obvious counter-example is the field of forensic phonetics, where there is a prime concern in identifying features particular to an individual (Nolan 1997). By contrast, the number of laboratory phonetic or phonological studies which draw attention to inter-speaker differences is very small (but see e.g. Abbs 1986; Vaissière 1988; Johnson, Ladefoged, and Lindau 1993; and Allen, Miller, and DeSteno 2003). Socio-linguistic studies likewise tend to focus on group patterns in favor of descriptions of general or average patterns within the group under investigation (but see e.g. Mees and Collins 1999; Llamas 2000).

While the lack of explicit interest in individual patterns is understandable, it does mean that we have only limited understanding of the parameters of variation across individuals. Johnstone and Bean (1997: 236) acknowledge that factors such as region, class and gender all have an important influence on speech, but point out that such factors 'do not *determine* how people sound.' Instead, the array of structured variation available to an individual, coupled with other factors such as ideology, can be seen as a rich resource from which the individual can choose elements in order to project their own identity. Johnstone and Bean's study of two Texan women discusses their self-expression with reference to lexical, syntactic and discourse structures. Studies of the role of phonological variables in the contruction of identity include Bucholtz (1998, focusing on [t] production by female nerds), Benor (2001, [t] production by Orthodox Jews) and Podesva, Roberts, and Campbell-Kibler (2002, phonetic patterns in camp gay male speech).

Llamas (2000) takes a similar approach with reference to phonological variation in the speech of 32 inhabitants of Middlesbrough, England. Changes in English local government divisions have seen the official political identity of Middlesbrough change four times since 1968. At one time it was part of Yorkshire, but after two other reorganizations it is now an independent city borough. Llamas's analysis shows that speakers' use of phonological variants is intertwined with their differing perceptions of the regional identity of the city. These largely correlate in a predictable way with age, for instance with older speakers showing greater use of variants characteristic of Yorkshire. However, there are also individual differences in variant use, which Llamas argues are linked to the speakers' own degree of affiliation to the city, and their experience of other dialects. The work of Llamas takes a significant step towards explaining how phonological variability is exploited by people in the construction of their identity, and is singular in its attempt to do so with a relatively large sample of speakers. It is to be hoped that further work in this direction is undertaken, not only for sociolinguistic purposes but because understanding the scope and nature of individual variability may have wide-ranging implications for issues at the core of phonology and phonetics such as phonological representation and speech perception. Support seems very likely to come for the position adopted by Mufwene (1994: 208), who argues that there is 'no compelling justification for assuming that [individuals] develop identical speech strategies or that their competences do not vary from one speaker to another' (see also Hawkins 2003).

7   Theoretical Implications of Phonological Variation

As we have seen in the preceding sections, different traditions in linguistic research have focused on different aspects of variability, while in some traditions variability has generally been factored out of research designs or marginalized in interpreting results.

This section aims to summarize the contribution of phonological variation to aspects of linguistic theory. It also highlights areas in which an understanding of variation may prove more profitable than it has hitherto been.

The role of variation in shaping theory is most evident in sociolinguistics. The recognition that much variability is structured rather than random has enabled great strides to be made in understanding how linguistic change originates, and how it spreads through communities and grammars (e.g. Milroy 1992; Trudgill, Gordon, Lewis, and Maclagan 2000; Kerswill and Williams 2000; Chambers 2003). Labov's work has been particularly influential in this sphere (see e.g. Labov 1994, 2001; and for critiques Gordon 2001; Thomas 2002b). Experimental phonetic work has further contributed to explaining the origins of regular sound changes (Ohala 1983). Dialect geography, too, although sometimes uncharitably depicted as a theory-free zone, has often had an eye on understanding change. The Survey of English Dialects, for instance, was largely geared to tracing the development of the Middle English vowel system (Orton, Sanderson, and Widdowson 1978).

Sociolinguistic studies have, however, made only limited impact on grammatical theory. This is unsurprising in view of the general aims of twentieth-century linguistic theory to describe synchronic grammars of particular languages, and the universal parameters of possible grammars. Few phonologists have therefore accorded a central place to issues of variation in the development of theory, although Lexical Phonology (e.g. Carr 1991; McMahon 1991) and Government Phonology (Harris 1994) are exceptions, and Articulatory Phonology is well equipped to deal with many of the types of variability discussed in section 3 (Browman and Goldstein 1989, 1990). Various phonological models have been applied to variationist data at some time or other, though, including the currently dominant model of Optimality Theory (OT) (e.g. Anttila 1997; Nagy and Reynolds 1997). Such applications, however, serve just as often to reveal the deficiencies of the models. OT analyses of variable data, for example, seem to be characterized by the discovery of a wide range of new constraints needed to account for the data, which sits rather uncomfortably with the tenet that all OT constraints are universal and innate (see McMahon 2000 for a thorough critique of OT and its devices for dealing with variation). That said, it is equally true that sociolinguistics has been slow to profit from advances within theoretical phonology (cf. Honeybone 2002: 414). Much sociolinguistic work refers to organization at the level of the phoneme, an approach which has been superseded by many alternatives in phonological theory, some of which have radically different conceptions of what the basic phonological units are and how they are organized into lexical representations.

Like phonology, phonetic theory has also advanced with relatively little interest in variation beyond the contextual types discussed in section 3. Exceptions are the contribution of cross-dialect research to intonational phonology (Grabe 2002), and Shockey's (2002) detailed analysis of English in casual speech.

Generally phonetic research is dominated by analysis of carefully controlled materials, usually canonical forms in standard dialects of American or British English, and gathered from few speakers under laboratory conditions. There are some departures from this norm, as exemplified by Byrd (1994), who analyzes the effects of dialect and sex on reduction processes using the 630-speaker TIMIT database. The general concentration on small speaker samples is largely due to practical constraints: commonly used methodological techniques are often expensive and/or invasive (such as electropalatography, fibroscopy, or electromyography), and results may be difficult to quantify in such a way as to permit cross-speaker comparisons. Researchers are therefore often forced to investigate their own speech, or that of a small number of subjects. Obvious disadvantages, however, are that findings may potentially be unrepresentative of the speech community at large, and the methods do not permit investigation of how phonological variation is handled by the cognitive system.

Recent trends, though, have started to show that speech production, and particularly speech perception, are affected by detailed knowledge of structured variability. New theories are therefore emerging, along with new methods designed to test those theories. *Exemplar*, *episodic* or *multiple trace* models of lexical representation have been proposed as a radical alternative to traditional models (Pisoni 1997; Goldinger 1997; Lachs, McMichael, and Pisoni 2002). The perceptual work of Strand (1999) and Niedzielski (1999) and others, referred to earlier, have contributed to the development of these models. So too have psycholinguistic experiments which show that detailed features of speakers' voices are stored in long-term memory. For example, Nygaard, Sommers, and Pisoni (1994) tested word recognition using stimuli drawn from a set of talkers. Listeners who had been trained to recognize the individual voices performed better than a control group who were encountering the voices for the first time in the test. Previous exposure to the voices thus aided subsequent perceptual processing of new words from those talkers, which suggests that highly specific information about the voices is accessed in the process of speech perception. Lexical representations are therefore argued to contain speaker-specific details, rather than being stored solely in abstract, invariant, symbolic forms. More specifically, exemplar models propose that the cognitive representation of a word is richly detailed, and in fact consists of a potentially vast store of detailed individual traces. These traces reflect the detailed acoustic properties of tokens that a speaker has heard, and by extension articulatory properties of tokens the speaker has uttered. Exemplar models thus echo the view of sound structure espoused by the neogrammarians in the nineteenth century (e.g. Paul 1880/1978). Here the cognitive representation of a sound is seen as a set of 'memory pictures,' based on articulatory and acoustic sensations and clustered around an average or prototype value.

Support for exemplar models comes from several quite disparate sources. Studies of second language learners support the view that experience of multiple talkers improves lexical recognition (Lively, Logan, and Pisoni 1993).

Studies of child language have also stated support for exemplar models, both via perception experiments (Nathan, Wells and Donlan 1998) and production analyses (Docherty, Foulkes, Tillotson, and Watt in press). In speech production studies with adults, Pierrehumbert (2002) finds effects on phonetic form linked to the frequency of occurrence of words. Common words are typically produced faster and less clearly than rare ones. The implication of this finding is that the on-line planning of speech is tailored differently according to the specific word involved, implying in turn that speakers have knowledge of frequency distributions for words and their phonological elements. Such a conclusion is compatible with the view that speakers have access to a store of individual exemplars of words – large sets for common words and smaller sets for rare ones (see further Coleman 2002 and Bod, Hay, and Jannedy 2003). Further evidence is supplied by studies which show that phonetic realization of words varies according to grammatical category (e.g. Ogden 1999; see section 4.1). While not explicitly supportive of exemplar models, Ogden adopts Firthian prosodic analysis, one tenet of which is that grammars are polysystemic. That is, rather than being seen as a single monolithic system, a language is held to be the product of numerous interwoven systems in which contrasts and the phonetic instantiations of those contrasts may vary from system to system. The perceptual model proposed by Hawkins and Smith (2001) and Hawkins (2003) combines exemplar representations with the polysystemic approach.

Exemplar models entail several important implications, many of which are themselves compatible with the various strands of work dealing with phonological variation that have been outlined throughout this chapter. Exemplar models may therefore potentially be the best candidates for a unitary account of the disparate sources of variation we have discussed. If so, one implication is that individuals possess their own unique lexical store (cf. Mufwene 1994; Hawkins 2003). Another is that lexical representations need not be stored in canonical form, as is usually assumed in phonological models. Furthermore, lexical and indexical information may not be stored as two separate knowledge bases, but as a single composite store of knowledge about sound in general (Pisoni 1997; see also Docherty, Foulkes, Tillotson, and Watt in press). Thus phonological knowledge is not only a source of information about lexical contrast, it also contains information about specific voices, encompassing details of age, gender, dialect, contextual allophony and so on. Note that the 'lack of invariance problem' (section 2) is largely solved, since there is no cognitive stage at which invariant and abstract symbolic representations need to be mapped onto variable and continuous speech signals (Docherty and Foulkes 2000).

Modern exemplar models are, however, still in relative infancy, and while they appear advantageous in some respects they are problematic in others. The bulk of evidence in support of the models comes from speech perception: it is less clear how a vast store of exemplars is manipulated in the course of speech production. Pierrehumbert (2002) suggests that production goals are driven by exemplars that are most heavily weighted in perception, although no formal model of how weighting takes place has yet been proposed beyond simple statistical observations. Presumably there must also be weighting in respect of factors such as sociolinguistic preferences, stylistic choices, attitude and attention (Pierrehumbert 2002: 135). It is not clear either to what extent the store of traces is subject to abstraction, what form that abstraction takes, or what role (if any) the abstract representation plays in speech production or perception. What is clear, though, is that exemplar models reignite the cognitive storage/computation debate of the 1970s (see e.g. Ladefoged 1972; Linell 1979). In generative models and their derivatives one aspect of the evaluation metric for grammars is that simpler and better grammars minimize storage at the expense of complex processes of derivation or manipulation. OT provides a clear illustration of this assumption, with invariant input forms (cf. generative underlying forms) filtered through a dense network of constraints en route to physical output. Exemplar models are diametrically opposed, with major demands on cognitive storage but little on-line computation. Much work therefore remains to be done to test and refine exemplar models, but they are at least to be welcomed for their fresh perspective on established issues.

8   Wider Significance of Phonological Variation

Understanding phonological variation is not only important for linguistic theory but for a range of interests beyond mainstream linguistic theory. Speech technology, for example, must cater for social, regional and contextual variability to generate natural-sounding synthesized speech and to ensure speech recognition systems can tolerate natural variability (Hoequist and Nolan 1991; Laver 1995). Speech therapists benefit from informed views of language variation, enabling them to distinguish genuine pathology from natural non-standard variability (Milroy 1987a: 208ff; Ball 2005).

Information on variability is critical for practical casework in forensic phonetics. Comparison of criminal recordings with a suspect's speech involves making allowances for the effects of factors such as accent, style shifts, disguise, stress, emotion, and telephone speech. In other cases, for example the receipt of a call or tape from a kidnapper, there may only be a criminal recording. The analyst's task is therefore to create a *speaker profile* to help narrow the field of suspects (see e.g. Ellis 1994). The strength of conclusions that can be reached is largely dependent on the state of descriptive reference material, including the likely geographical origins of particular features and the frequency of speech disorders and other idiosyncrasies throughout the population. A similar technique is currently being applied to assess the claims of asylum seekers, by analysing their speech to verify their country or region of origin (Simo Bobda, Wolf, and Peter 1999). Worryingly, this is often done by government agencies or private companies rather than professional linguists.

Pedagogical issues are clearly informed by debate on phonological variation, most (in)famously perhaps in the case of the Ebonics debate in the USA (see Wolfram and Schilling-Estes 1998: 169ff; and volume 26 (2) of the *Journal of English Linguistics*, 1998). On a wider platform, models of English for teaching as a foreign language are constantly being revised in line with changes in British and American standard varieties, as well as in respect of the development of influential new standards such as Australian in east Asia (Melchers and Shaw 2003: 101).

More widely still, it has been shown that people often develop strong attitudes, negative and positive, to features of linguistic variation (see Honey 1989 and Milroy and Milroy 1998 for a stimulating debate). These attitudes may affect communication between groups of people (Lambert, Hodgson, Gardner, and Fillenbaum 1960; Gumperz 1982), job prospects (Lippi-Green 1997), and may be consciously tapped into for purposes of advertising and marketing (Bell 1991: 135ff). Lippi-Green (1997) also highlights the subliminal effects of linguistic stereotyping with reference to the use of accents for characterization in films. She shows, for example, that in Disney films 'good' characters usually have standard accents, with AAVE and foreign accents largely reserved for negatively-portrayed characters. Similar examples of language stereotyping abound in film and television, as witnessed, for instance, by the Cockney-sounding Orcs in the film versions of *The Lord of the Rings*.

9   Conclusion and Outlook

We have seen that phonological variation results from many sources. The physical form of any utterance is governed simultaneously by the speaker's anatomy and physiology, the nature of airflow through the vocal tract, linguistic context, the social and regional background of the speaker, communicative context, and a range of psychological factors. We have seen also that the full range of effects are rarely countenanced together within academic pursuits. Phonetics, phonology and sociolinguistics have tended to focus on particular aspects of variability to the exclusion of others, or in some cases to peripheralize the study of variability.

Developments in recent years have started to recognize the importance of variability for our understanding of the structure and functioning of linguistic systems as well as for issues outside linguistic theory. There is a growing awareness that systematically controlled variation is something that must be learned in the course of language acquisition, and thus that it represents an aspect of knowledge about sounds and sound structure. Phonological models of varied hues are making progress in addressing issues in social and geographical variability, while new models are emerging which place some types of variability in center stage. Sociolinguistic data are being more widely exploited as a testing ground for theoretical claims. The expanding field of 'sociophonetics,' while somewhat ill defined and encompassing an eclectic range of approaches, nevertheless testifies to the growing interest in the inter-relationship between linguistic theory and variable data. This field is likely to continue to grow, thanks to a large extent to rapid changes in technology. Acoustic analysis of large data samples is now cheap and speedy, while newer articulatory techniques such as ultrasound (Gick 2002) and will provide new perspectives on variability in speech.

The most intriguing challenge remains how to weave together the various strands of knowledge about lexical forms and variability of all kinds into a unified theoretical framework. But the best chance of achieving this is by viewing variability not as a nuisance but as a universal and functional design feature of language.

NOTE

My thanks to Gerry Docherty, Ghada Khattab, Helen Lawrence, April McMahon, Rachel Smith, Ros Temple, Erik Thomas, Dominic Watt, and an anonymous reviewer for their comments on draft versions of this chapter.

FURTHER READING

General introductions to phonetic theory and methods: Denes and Pinson (1993), Hayward (2000), Ladefoged (2001). On physical and biological constraints: Mackenzie Beck (1997). On contextual constraints: Hardcastle and Hewlett (1999), Shattuck-Hufnagel and Turk (1996).

General introductions to sociolinguistic theory and methods: Chambers (2003), Milroy and Gordon (2003). Sources on geographical variation are listed by region at the start of section 5.

BIBLIOGRAPHY

Abbs, J. H. (1986) Invariance and variability in speech production: a distinction between linguistic intent and its neuromotor implementation. In J. S. Perkell and D. H. Klatt (eds.), *Invariance and variability in speech pocesses*. Hillsdale, NJ: Lawrence Erlbaum Associates, 202–19.

Abercrombie, D. (1967) *Elements of general ponetics*. Edinburgh: Edinburgh University Press.

Aceto, M. and Williams, J. P. (eds.) (2003) *Contact Englishes of the eastern Caribbean*. Amsterdam: John Benjamins.

Allen, H. B. (1973–6) *Linguistic atlas of the upper midwest* (3 vols.).

Minneapolis: University of Minnesota Press.

Allen, J. S., Miller, J. L., and DeSteno, D. (2003) Individual talker differences in voice-onset-time. *Journal of the Acoustical Society of America* 113, 544–52.

Anderson, B. L. (1999) Source-language transfer and vowel accommodation in the patterning of Cherokee English /ai/ and /oi/. *American Speech* 74, 339–68.

Anttila, A. (1997) Deriving variation from grammar. In F. Hinskens, R. van Hout, and W. L. Wetzels (eds.), *Variation, change and phonological theory*. Amsterdam: John Benjamins, 35–68.

Ash, S. (2002) Social class. In J. Chambers, P. Trudgill, and N. Schilling-Estes (eds.), *The handbook of language variation and change*. Oxford: Blackwell, 402–22.

Bailey, R. W. and Görlach, M. (eds.) (1982) *English as a world language*. Ann Arbor: University of Michigan Press.

Ball, M. J. (ed.) (2005) *Clinical sociolinguistics*. Oxford: Blackwell.

Bansal, R. K. (1990) The pronunciation of English in India. In S. Ramsaran (ed.), *Studies in the pronunciation of English: a commemorative volume in honour of A.C. Gimson*. London: Routledge, 219–30.

Barry, M. V. (ed.) (1981) *Aspects of English dialects in Ireland*. Belfast: Institute of Irish Studies, Queen's University Belfast.

Bauer, L. (1985) Tracing phonetic change in the received pronunciation of British English. *Journal of Phonetics* 13, 61–81.

Bauer, L. (1986) Notes on New Zealand English phonetics and phonology. *English World-Wide* 7, 225–58.

Bauer, L. (1988) What is lenition? *Journal of Linguistics* 24, 381–92.

Bayley, R., Lucas, C., and Rose, M. (2002) Phonological variation in American Sign Language: the case of 1

handshape. *Language Variation and Change* 14, 19–53.

Bell, A. (1984) Language style as audience design. *Language in Society* 13, 145–204.

Bell, A. (1991) *The language of news media*. Oxford: Blackwell.

Bell, A., Jurafsky, D., Fosler-Lussier, E., Girand, C., and Gregory, M. (2003) Effects of disfluencies, predictability, and utterance position on word form variation in English conversation. *Journal of the Acoustical Society of America* 113, 1001–24.

Bell, A. and Kuiper, K. (eds.) (2000) *New Zealand English*. Amsterdam: John Benjamins.

Benor, S. B. (2001) The learnèd /t/: phonological variation in Orthodox Jewish English. *University of Pennsylvania Working Papers in Linguistics* 7, 3, 1–16.

Bilton, L. (1982) A note on Hull intonation. *Journal of the International Phonetic Association* 12, 30–5.

Blair, D. and Collins, P. (eds.) (2001) *English in Australia*. Amsterdam: John Benjamins.

Bod, R., Hay, J., and Jannedy, S. (eds.) (2003) *Probabilistic linguistics*. Cambridge, MA: MIT Press.

Braun, A. (1996) Age estimation by different listener groups. [*Forensic Linguistics:*] *The International Journal of Speech, Language and the Law* 3, 65–73.

Britain, D. (1992) Linguistic change in intonation: the use of high rising terminals in New Zealand English. *Language Variation and Change* 4, 77–103.

Britain, D. (1997) Dialect contact and phonological reallocation: 'Canadian Raising' in the English Fens. *Language in Society* 26, 15–46.

Britain, D. (2002) Space and spatial diffusion. In J. Chambers, P. Trudgill, and N. Schilling-Estes (eds.), *The handbook of language variation and change*. Oxford: Blackwell, 603–37.

Browman, C. P. and Goldstein, L. (1989) Articulatory gestures as phonological units. *Phonology* 6, 201–51.

Browman, C. P. and Goldstein, L. (1990) Tiers in articulatory phonology, with some implications for casual speech. In J. Kingston and M. E. Beckman (eds.), *Papers in laboratory phonology I: Between the grammar and physics of speech.* Cambridge: Cambridge University Press, 341–76.

Bucholtz, M. (1998) Geek the girl: language, femininity, and female nerds. In N. Warner, J. Ahlers, L. Bilmes, M. Oliver, S. Wertheim, and M. Chen (eds.) *Gender and belief systems: Proceedings of the fourth Berkeley women and language conference.* Berkeley: Berkeley Women and Language Group, 119–31.

Burchfield, R. (ed.) (1994) *The Cambridge history of the English language, volume V: English in Britain and overseas: origins and development.* Cambridge: Cambridge University Press.

Burridge, K. and Mulder, J. (1998) *English in Australia and New Zealand.* Melbourne: Oxford University Press.

Byrd, D. (1994) Relations of sex and dialect to reduction. *Speech Communication* 15, 39–54.

Byrd, D. (1996) Influences on articulatory timing in consonant sequences. *Journal of Phonetics* 24, 209–44.

Cameron, D. (this volume) Language and gender. In B. Aarts and A. M. S. McMahon (eds.), *The handbook of English linguistics.* Oxford: Blackwell.

Carr, P. (1991) Lexical properties of postlexical rules: postlexical derived environment and the Elsewhere Condition. *Lingua* 85, 41–54.

Catford, J. C. (1977) *Fundamental problems in phonetics.* Edinburgh: Edinburgh University Press.

Chambers, J. K. (1991) Canada. In J. Cheshire (ed.), *English around the world.* Cambridge: Cambridge University Press, 89–107.

Chambers, J. K. (1992) Dialect acquisition. *Language* 68, 673–705.

Chambers, J. K. (2002) Studying language variation: an informal epistemology. In J. Chambers, P. Trudgill, and N. Schilling-Estes (eds.) *The handbook of language variation and change.* Oxford: Blackwell, 3–14.

Chambers, J. K. (2003) *Sociolinguistic theory,* 2nd edn. Oxford: Blackwell.

Chambers, J. K. and Trudgill, P. (1998) *Dialectology,* 2nd edn. Cambridge: Cambridge University Press.

Cheshire, J. (ed.) (1991) *English around the world: sociolinguistic perspectives.* Cambridge: Cambridge University Press.

Cheshire, J. (2002) Sex and gender in variationist research. In J. Chambers, P. Trudgill, and N. Schilling-Estes (eds.), *The handbook of language variation and change.* Oxford: Blackwell, 423–43.

Chin, S. B. and Pisoni, D. B. (1997) *Alcohol and speech.* San Diego: Academic Press.

Clarke, S. (1991) Phonological variation and recent change in St John's English. In J. Cheshire (ed.) *English around the world.* Cambridge: Cambridge University Press, 108–22.

Clarke, S. (ed.) (1993) *Focus on Canada.* Amsterdam: John Benjamins.

Clopper, C. G. and Pisoni, D. B. (2004) Some acoustic cues for the perceptual categorization of American English regional dialects. *Journal of Phonetics* 32, 111–40.

Clyne, M. Eisikovits, E., and Tollfree, L. F. (2001) Ethnic varieties of Australian English. In D. Blair and P. Collins (eds.), *English in Australia.* Amsterdam: John Benjamins, 223–38.

Coleman, J. (2002) Phonetic representations in the mental lexicon. In J. Durand and B. Laks (eds.), *Phonetics, phonology, and cognition.* Oxford: Oxford University Press, 96–130.

Collins, P. and Blair, D. (eds.) (1989) *Australian English: the language of a new society*. St. Lucia: University of Queensland Press.

Corbett, J., McClure, J. D., and Stuart-Smith, J. (eds.) (2003) *The Edinburgh companion to Scots*. Edinburgh: Edinburgh University Press.

Couper-Kuhlen, E. and Selting, M. (eds.) (1996) *Prosody in conversation: interactional studies*. Cambridge: Cambridge University Press.

Coupland, N. (1980) Style-shifting in a Cardiff work-setting. *Language in Society* 9, 1–12.

Cruttenden, A. (1997) *Intonation*, 2nd edn. Cambridge: Cambridge University Press.

Cruttenden, A. (2001a) Mancunian intonation and intonational representation. *Phonetica* 58, 53–80.

Cruttenden, A. (2001b) *Gimson's pronunciation of English*, 6th edn. London: Arnold.

Crystal, T. H. and House, A. S. (1988a) The duration of American-English vowels: an overview. *Journal of Phonetics* 16, 263–84.

Crystal, T. H. and House, A. S. (1988b) The duration of American-English stop consonants: an overview. *Journal of Phonetics* 16, 285–94.

Curl, T. S. (2003) The phonetics of repetition in other-initiated repair sequences. In M. J. Solé, D. Recasens, and J. Romero (eds.), *Proceedings of the 15th international congress of phonetic sciences*. Barcelona: Universitat Autònoma de Barcelona/Causal Productions, 1843–6.

Daly, N. and Warren, P. (2001) Pitching it differently in New Zealand English: speaker sex and intonation patterns. *Journal of Sociolinguistics* 5, 85–96.

Denes, P. B. and Pinson, E. N. (1993) *The speech chain: the physics and biology of spoken language*. New York: W. H. Freeman.

Deterding, D. (1997) The formants of monophthong vowels in Standard Southern British English pronunciation. *Journal of the International Phonetic Association* 27, 47–55.

Deterding, D. (2001) The measurement of rhythm: a comparison of Singapore and British English. *Journal of Phonetics* 29, 317–30.

di Paolo, M. and Faber, A. (1990) Phonation differences and the phonetic content of the tense-lax contrast in Utah English. *Language Variation and Change* 2, 155–204.

Docherty, G. J. and Foulkes, P. (1999) Newcastle upon Tyne and Derby: instrumental phonetics and variationist studies. In P. Foulkes and G. J. Docherty (eds.), *Urban voices: accent studies in the British Isles*. London: Arnold, 47–71.

Docherty, G. J. and Foulkes, P. (2000) Speaker, speech, and knowledge of sounds. In N. Burton-Roberts, P. Carr, and G. J. Docherty (eds.) *Phonological knowledge: conceptual and empirical issues*. Oxford: Oxford University Press, 105–29.

Docherty, G. J. and Foulkes, P. (2005) Glottal variants of (t) in the Tyneside variety of English: an acoustic profiling study. In W. Hardcastle and J. Mackenzie Beck (eds.), *A figure of speech: a festschrift for John Laver*. London: Lawrence Erlbaum, 173–99.

Docherty, G. J., Foulkes, P., Milroy J., Milroy L., and Walshaw, D. (1997) Descriptive adequacy in phonology: a variationist perspective. *Journal of Linguistics* 33, 275–310.

Docherty, G. J., Foulkes, P., Tillotson, J., and Watt, D. J. L. (in press) On the scope of phonological learning: issues arising from socially structured variation. To appear in L. Goldstein, D. H. Whalen, and C. T. Best (eds.), *Laboratory Pphonology 8*. Berlin: Mouton de Gruyter.

Docherty, G. J. and Watt, D. J. L. (2001) Chain shifts. In R. Mesthrie (ed.), *The concise encyclopedia of sociolinguistics.* Amsterdam: Pergamon, 303–7.

Douglas-Cowie, E., Cowie, R., and Rahilly, J. (1995) The social distribution of intonation patterns in Belfast. In J. Windsor Lewis (ed.), *Studies in general and English phonetics: essays in honour of Professor J. D. O'Connor.* London: Routledge, 180–6.

Dubois, S. and Horvath, B. M. (1998) Let's tink about dat: interdental fricatives in Cajun English. *Language Variation and Change* 10, 245–61.

Dyer, J. M. (2002) 'We all speak the same round here': dialect levelling in a Scottish-English community. *Journal of Sociolinguistics* 6, 99–116.

Eckert, P. (1989) The whole woman: sex and gender differences in variation. *Language Variation and Change* 1, 245–67.

Eckert, P. (1997) Age as a sociolinguistic variable. In F. Coulmas (ed.), *Handbook of sociolinguistics.* Oxford: Blackwell, 151–67.

Eckert, P. (2000) *Linguistic variation as social practice.* Oxford: Blackwell.

Ellis, A. J. (1889) *On early English pronunciation, part V: the existing phonology of English dialects.* Oxford: Oxford University Press.

Ellis, S. (1994) The Yorkshire Ripper enquiry: part 1. [*Forensic Linguistics:*] *The International Journal of Speech, Language and the Law* 1, 197–206.

Elman, J. L., Diehl, R. L., and Buchwald, S. E. (1977) Perceptual switching in bilinguals. *Journal of the Acoustical Society of America* 62, 971–4.

Esling, J. H. (1978) The identification of features of voice quality in social groups. *Journal of the International Phonetic Association* 7, 18–23.

Esling, J. H. (1991) Sociophonetic variation in Vancouver. In J. Cheshire (ed.), *English around the world.*

Cambridge: Cambridge University Press, 123–33.

Farnetani, E. (1997) Coarticulation and connected speech processes. In W. J. Hardcastle and J. Laver (eds.), *The handbook of phonetic sciences.* Oxford: Blackwell, 371–404.

Feagin, C. (1979) *Variation and change in Alabama English: a sociolinguistic study of the white community.* Washington, DC: Georgetown University Press.

Ferguson, C. A. (1986) Discovering sound units and constructing sound systems: it's child's play. In J. S. Perkell and D. H. Klatt (eds.), *Invariance and variability in speech processes.* Hillsdale, NJ: Lawrence Erlbaum Associates, 36–51.

Fischer, J. N. L. (1958) Social influences on the choice of a linguistic variant. *Word* 14, 47–56.

Fitzgerald, C. M. (2002) Vowel harmony in Buchan Scots English. *English Language and Linguistics* 6, 61–79.

Flege, J. E. (1995) Second-language speech learning: theory, findings and problems. In W. Strange (ed.), *Speech perception and linguistic experience: theoretical and methodological issues in cross-language speech research.* Timonium, MD: York Press Inc., 233–72.

Flege, J. E., Schirru, C., and MacKay, I. R. A. (2003) Interaction between the native and second language phonetic subsystems. *Speech Communication* 40, 467–91.

Fletcher, J., Grabe, E., and Warren, P. (2004) Intonational variation in four dialects of English: the high rising tune. In S.-A. Jun (ed.), *Prosodic typology: the phonology of intonation and phrasing.* Oxford: Oxford University Press, 390–409.

Fletcher, J., Stirling, L., Mushin, I., and Wales, R. (2002) Intonational rises and dialog acts in the Australian English Map Task. *Language and Speech* 45, 229–53.

Fought, C. (1999) A majority sound change in a minority community: /u/-fronting in Chicano English. *Journal of Sociolinguistics* 3, 5–23.

Fought, C. (2003) *Chicano English in context*. Basingstoke: Palgrave.

Foulkes, P. and Barron, A. (2000) Telephone speaker recognition amongst members of close social network. [*Forensic Linguistics:*] *The International Journal of Speech, Language and the Law* 7, 180–98.

Foulkes, P. and Docherty, G. J. (eds.) (1999) *Urban voices: accent studies in the British Isles*. London: Arnold.

Foulkes, P. and Docherty, G. J. (in press) Phonological and prosodic variation in the English of England. To appear in D. Britain (ed.), *Language in the British Isles*, 2nd edn. Cambridge: Cambridge University Press.

Foulkes, P., Docherty, G. J., and Watt, D. J. L. (2001) The emergence of structured variation. *University of Pennsylvania Working Papers in Linguistics* 7, 3, 67–84.

Foulkes, P., Docherty, G. J., and Watt, D. J. L. (2005) Phonological variation in child directed speech. *Language* 81, 177–206.

Fourakis, M. and Port, R. (1986) Stop epenthesis in English. *Journal of Phonetics* 14, 197–221.

Fowler, C. A. (1981) Production and perception of coarticulation among stressed and unstressed vowels. *Journal of Speech and Hearing Research* 46, 127–39.

Fowler, C. A. (1986) An event approach to the study of speech perception from a direct-realist perspective. *Journal of Phonetics* 14, 3–28.

Freeborn, D., French, J. P., and Langford, D. (1993) *Varieties of English*, 2nd edn. Basingstoke: Macmillan.

French, J. P. (1998) Mr Akbar's nearest ear versus the Lombard reflex: a case study for forensic phonetics. [*Forensic Linguistics:*] *The International Journal of Speech, Language and the Law* 5, 58–68.

Fridland, V. (1999) The southern shift in Memphis, Tennessee. *Language Variation and Change* 11, 267–85.

Fujimura, O. and Erickson, D. (1997) Acoustic phonetics. In W. J. Hardcastle and J. Laver (eds.), *The handbook of phonetic sciences*. Oxford: Blackwell, 65–115.

Gay, T. (1968) Effect of speaking rate on diphthong formant movements. *Journal of the Acoustical Society of America* 44, 1570–5.

Gay, T. (1978) Articulatory units: segments or syllables? In A. Bell and J. B. Hopper (eds.) *Syllables and segments*. Amsterdam: North-Holland, 121–31.

Gick, B. (2002) The use of ultrasound for linguistic phonetic fieldwork. *Journal of the International Phonetic Association* 32, 113–21.

Goldinger, S. D. (1997) Words and voices: perception and production in an episodic lexicon. In K. Johnson and J. W. Mullennix (eds.), *Talker variability in speech processing*. San Diego: Academic Press, 33–66.

Goldinger, S. D., Pisoni, D. B., and Luce, P. A. (1996) Speech perception and spoken word recognition: research and theory. In N. J. Lass (ed.), *Principles of experimental phonetics*. St. Louis: Mosby, 277–327.

Gordon, M. J. (2001) Investigating mergers and chain shifts. In J. Chambers, P. Trudgill, and N. Schilling-Estes (eds.), *The handbook of language variation and change*. Oxford: Blackwell, 244–66.

Grabe, E. (2002) Variation adds to prosodic typology. In B. Bel and I. Marlin (eds.), *Proceedings of the speech prosody 2002 conference*. Aix-en-Provence: Laboratoire Parole et Langage, 127–32.

Grabe, E., Post, B., Nolan, F. J., and Farrar, K. (2000) Pitch accent realization in four varieties of British English. *Journal of Phonetics* 28, 161–85.

Green, L. J. (2002) *African American English: a linguistic introduction.* Cambridge: Cambridge University Press.

Grosjean, F. (1998) Studying bilinguals: methodological and conceptual issues. *Bilingualism: Language and Cognition* 1, 2, 131–49.

Gumperz, J. (1982) *Discourse strategies.* Cambridge: Cambridge University Press.

Guy, G. (1980) Variation in the group and individual: the case of final stop deletion. In W. Labov (ed.), *Locating language in time and space.* New York: Academic Press, 1–36.

Guy, G. and Boyd, S. (1990) The development of a morphological class. *Language Variation and Change* 2, 1–18.

Guy, G., Horvath, B., Vonwiller, J., Disley, E., and Rogers, I. (1986) An intonational change in progress in Australian English. *Language in Society* 7, 23–51.

Hardcastle, W. J. and Hewlett, N. (eds.) (1999) *Coarticulation: theory, data and techniques.* Cambridge: Cambridge University Press.

Harrington, J., Palethorpe, S., and Watson, C. I. (2000) Does the Queen speak the Queen's English? *Nature* 408, 927–8.

Harris, J. (1994) *English sound structure.* Oxford: Blackwell.

Harris, K. S. (1958) Cues for the discrimination of American English fricatives in spoken syllables. *Language and Speech* 1, 1–7.

Harris, K. S. (1978) Vowel duration change and its underlying physiological mechanisms. *Language and Speech* 21, 354–61.

Hawkins, S. (2003) Roles and representations of systematic fine phonetic detail in speech understanding. *Journal of Phonetics* 31, 373–405.

Hawkins, S., and Smith, R. (2001) Polysp: a polysystemic, phonetically-rich approach to speech understanding. *Rivista di Linguistica* 13, 99–188.

Hayward, K. (2000) *Experimental phonetics.* London: Longman.

Henton, C. and Bladon, A. (1988) Creak as a sociophonetic marker. In L. Hyman and C. N. Li (eds.), *Language, speech and mind: studies in honor of Victoria A. Fromkin.* London: Routledge, 3–29.

Heselwood, B. and McChrystal, L. (2000) Gender, accent features and voicing in Panjabi-English bilingual children. *Leeds Working Papers in Linguistics and Phonetics* 8, 45–70 (www.leeds.ac.uk/linguistics).

Hewitt, R. (1986) *White talk, black talk: inter-racial friendship and communication amongst adolescents.* Cambridge: Cambridge University Press.

Hirson, A., Holmes, F., and Coulthrust, B. (2003) Street talk, England 2003. Paper presented at the Annual Conference of the International Association for Forensic Phonetics, Vienna.

Hoequist, C. and Nolan, F. J. (1991) On an application of phonological knowledge in automatic speech recognition. *Computer Speech and Language* 5, 133–53.

Hollien, H., Majewski, W., and Doherty, E. T. (1982) Perceptual identification of voices under normal, stress and disguise speaking conditions. *Journal of Phonetics* 10, 139–48.

Holm, J. (ed.) (1983) *Central American English.* Heidelberg: Julius Groos Verlag.

Holmes, J. (1997) Maori and Pakeha English: some New Zealand social dialect data. *Language in Society* 26, 65–101.

Honey, J. (1989) *Does accent matter?* London: Faber and Faber.

Honeybone, P. (2002) Review of *Urban voices,* ed. P. Foulkes and G. J.

Docherty (London: Arnold, 1999). *English Language and Linguistics* 6, 408–16.

Honikman, B. (1964) Articulatory settings. In D. Abercrombie, D. B. Fry, P. A. D. MacCarthy, N. Scott, and J. L. M. Trim (eds.), *In honour of Daniel Jones*. London: Longman, 73–84.

Horvath, B. (1985) *Variation in Australian English*. Cambridge: Cambridge University Press.

Horvath, B. (1997) An empirical study of textual structure: horse race calls. In G. R. Guy, C. Feagin, D. Schiffrin, and J. Baugh (eds.), *Towards a social science of language. Papers in honor of William Labov. volume 2: social interaction and discourse structures*. Amsterdam: John Benjamins, 103–20.

Howard, S. and Heselwood, B. C. (forthcoming) *Analysing disordered speech*. San Diego: Academic Press.

Hudson, A. I. and Holbrook, A. (1982) Fundamental frequency characteristics of young black adults: spontaneous speaking and oral reading. *Journal of Speech and Hearing Research* 25, 25–8.

Huffines, M. L. (1984) The English of Pennsylvania Germans. *German Quarterly* 57, 173–82.

Jibril, M. (1986) Sociolinguistic variation in Nigerian English. *English World-Wide* 7, 47–74.

Johnson, K., Ladefoged, P., and Lindau, M. (1993) Individual differences in vowel production. *Journal of the Acoustical Society of America* 94, 701–14.

Johnson, K., Strand, E., and D'Imperio, M. (1999) Auditory-visual integration of talker gender in vowel perception. *Journal of Phonetics* 27, 359–84.

Johnstone, B. and Bean, J. M. (1997) Self-expression and linguistic variation. *Language in Society* 26, 221–46.

Jones, M. J. (2002) The origin of definite article reduction in Northern English dialects: evidence from dialect allomorphy. *English Language and Linguistics* 6, 325–46.

Jusczyk, P. W. and Luce, P. A. (2002) Speech perception and spoken word recognition: past and present. *Ear and Hearing*, 23, 2–40.

Kent, R. D., Adams, S. G., and Turner, G. S. (1996) Models of speech production. In N. J. Lass (ed.), *Principles of experimental phonetics*. St. Louis: Mosby, 3–45.

Kerswill, P. E. (1987). Levels of linguistic variation in Durham. *Journal of Linguistics* 23, 25–49.

Kerswill, P. E. (1996) Children, adolescents and language change. *Language Variation and Change* 8, 177–202.

Kerswill, P. E. and Williams, A. (2000) Creating a new town koine: children and language change in Milton Keynes. *Language in Society* 29, 65–115.

Khan, A. (in progress) Dialect levelling and innovation in the English of adolescents of Asian, black and white ethnicities in Birmingham. Ph.D. dissertation, University of Reading.

Khan, F. (1991) Final cluster simplification in a variety of Indian English. In J. Cheshire (ed.), *English around the world*. Cambridge: Cambridge University Press, 288–98.

Khattab, G. (2002a) /l/ production in English-Arabic bilingual speakers. *International Journal of Bilingualism* 6, 335–53.

Khattab, G. (2002b) VOT production in English and Arabic bilingual and monolingual children. In D. B. Parkinson and E. Benmamoun (eds.), *Perspectives on Arabic linguistics XIII–XIV*. Amsterdam: John Benjamins, 1–37.

Kingston, J., and Diehl, R. L. (1994) Phonetic knowledge. *Language* 70, 419–54.

Knowles, G. O. (1978) The nature of phonological variables in Scouse. In P. Trudgill (ed.), *Sociolinguistic patterns in British English*. London: Arnold, 80–90.

Kortmann, B. and Schneider, E. W. (eds.) (2004) *A handbook of varieties of English* (2 vols.). Berlin: Walter de Gruyter.

Kreiman, J. (1997) Listening to voices: theory and practice in voice perception research. In K. Johnson and J. W. Mullennix (eds.), *Talker variability in speech processing*. San Diego: Academic Press, 85–108.

Kretzschmar, W. A. Jr., McDavid, V. G., Lerud, T. K., and Johnson, E. (eds.) (1994) *Handbook of the linguistic atlas of the middle and south Atlantic states*. Chicago: University of Chicago Press.

Künzel, H. J. (2001) Beware of the 'telephone effect': the influence of telephone transmission on the measurement of formant frequencies. [*Forensic Linguistics:*] *The International Journal of Speech, Language and the Law* 8, 80–99.

Kurath, H., Hanley, M., Bloch, B., and Lowman, G. S. Jr. (1939–43) *Linguistic atlas of New England* (3 vols.). Providence, RI: Brown University Press.

Kurath, H. and McDavid, R. I. (1961) *The pronunciation of English in the Atlantic states*. Ann Arbor: University of Michigan Press.

Labov, W. (1963) The social motivation of a sound change. *Word* 19, 273–309.

Labov, W. (1966) *The social stratification of English in New York City*. Washington, DC: Center for Applied Linguistics.

Labov, W. (1972) *Sociolinguistic patterns*. Oxford: Blackwell.

Labov, W. (1989) The child as linguistic historian. *Language Variation and Change* 1, 85–94.

Labov, W. (1990) The intersection of sex and social class in the course of linguistic change. *Language Variation and Change* 2, 205–54.

Labov, W. (1994) *Principles of linguistic change. Vol. 1: Internal factors*. Oxford: Blackwell.

Labov, W. (2001) *Principles of linguistic change. Vol. 2: Social factors*. Oxford: Blackwell.

Labov, W., Cohen, P., Robins, C., and Lewis, J. (1968) *A study of the non-standard English of Negro and Puerto Rican speakers in New York City*. New York: Columbia University Press.

Labov, W., Yaeger, M., and Steiner, R. (1972) *A quantitative study of sound change in progress: report on national science foundation project no. GS-3287* (2 vols.). Philadelphia: US Regional Survey.

Lachs, L., McMichael, K., and Pisoni, D. (2002) Speech perception and implicit memory: evidence for detailed episodic encoding. In J. S. Bowers and C. J. Marsolek (eds.), *Rethinking implicit memory*. Oxford: Oxford University Press, 215–35.

Ladefoged, P. (1972) Phonetic prerequisites for a distinctive feature theory. In A. Valdmann (ed.), *Papers in linguistics and phonetics to the memory of Pierre Delattre*. The Hague: Mouton, 273–85.

Ladefoged, P. (2001) *A course in phonetics*, 4th edn. Fort Worth: Harcourt.

Lafarriere, M. (1979) Ethnicity in phonological variation and change. *Language* 55, 603–17.

Lambert, W. C., Hodgson, R. C., Gardner, R. C., and Fillenbaum, S. (1960) Evaluational reactions to spoken language. *Journal of Abnormal and Social Psychology* 60, 44–51.

Lane, H. and Tranel, B. (1971) The Lombard sign and the role of hearing in speech. *Journal of Speech and Hearing Research* 14, 677–709.

Laver, J. (1980) *The phonetic description of voice quality*. Cambridge: Cambridge University Press.

Laver, J. (1994) *Principles of phonetics*. Cambridge: Cambridge University Press.

Laver, J. (1995) Voice types in automated telecommunications applications. In

J. Windsor Lewis (ed.), *Studies in general and English phonetics: essays in honour of Professor J. D. O'Connor*. London: Routledge, 85–95.

Lavoie, L. (2001) *Consonant strength: phonological patterns and phonetic manifestations*. New York: Garland.

Lee, A., Hewlett, N., and Nairn, M. (1995) Voice and gender in children. In S. Mills (ed.), *Language and gender: interdisciplinary prespectives*. Harlow: Longman, 194–204.

Lehiste, I. and Peterson, G. E. (1961) Some basic considerations in the analysis of intonation. *Journal of the Acoustical Society of America* 33, 419–25.

Leopold, W. F. (1947) *Speech development of a bilingual child*. New York: AMS Press.

Liberman, A. M. and Mattingly, I. G. (1985) The motor theory of speech perception revised. *Cognition* 21, 1–36.

Lindblom, B. (1963) Spectrographic study of vowel reduction. *Journal of the Acoustical Society of America* 35, 1173–81.

Lindblom, B. (1990) Explaining phonetic variation: a sketch of the H&H theory. In W. J. Hardcastle and A. Marchal (eds.), *Speech production and speech modelling*. Amsterdam: Kluwer, 403–39.

Linell, P. (1979) *Psychological reality in phonology*. Cambridge: Cambridge University Press.

Lippi-Green, R. (1997) *English with an accent*. London: Routledge.

Lively, S. E., Logan, J. S., and Pisoni, D. B. (1993) Training Japanese listeners to identify English /r/ and /l/: the role of phonetic environment and talker variability in learning new perceptual categories. *Journal of the Acoustical Society of America* 94, 1242–55.

Llamas, C. (2000) Middlesbrough English: convergent and divergent trends in a 'part of Britain with no identity.' *Leeds Working Papers in Linguistics and Phonetics* 8, 123–48 (www.leeds.ac.uk/linguistics).

Local, J. (2003) Variable domains and variable relevance: interpreting phonetic exponents. *Journal of Phonetics* 31, 321–39.

Local, J., Kelly, J., and Wells, W. H. G. (1986) Towards a phonology of conversation: turntaking in Tyneside. *Journal of Linguistics* 22, 411–37.

Local, J., Wells, W. H. G., and Sebba, M. (1985) Phonology for conversation: phonetic aspects of turn delimitation in London Jamaican. *Journal of Pragmatics* 9, 309–30.

Low, E. L., Grabe, E., and Nolan, F. J. (2000) Quantitative characterizations of speech rhythm: syllable-timing in Singapore English. *Language and Speech* 43, 377–402.

Luce, P. A. and Pisoni, D. B. (1998) Recognizing spoken words: the neighbourhood activation model. *Ear and Hearing* 19, 1–36.

Macaulay, R. K. S. (1977) *Language, social class, and education: a Glasgow study*. Edinburgh: Edinburgh University Press.

Mackenzie Beck, J. (1997) Organic variation of the vocal apparatus. In W. J. Hardcastle and J. Laver (eds.), *The handbook of phonetic sciences*. Oxford: Blackwell, 256–97.

MacMahon, M. K. C. (1998) Phonology. In S. Romaine (ed.), *The Cambridge history of the English language, volume IV. 1776–1997*. Cambridge: Cambridge University Press, 373–535.

Mann, V. A. and Repp, B. H. (1980) Influence of vocalic context on perception of the [ʃ] – [s] distinction. *Perception and Psychophysics* 28, 213–28.

Marshall, J. (2003) The changing sociolinguistic status of the glottal stop in northeast Scottish English. *English World-Wide* 24, 89–108.

Marshall, J. (2004) *Language change and sociolinguistics*. Basingstoke: Palgrave.

Mather, J. Y. and Speitel, H. H. (1975) *The linguistic atlas of Scotland*. London: Croom Helm.

Mattingly, I. G. and Studdert-Kennedy, M. (eds.) (1991) *Modularity and the motor theory of speech perception*. Hillsdale: Lawrence Erlbaum.

McCafferty, K. (1999) (London)Derry: between Ulster and local speech – class, ethnicity and language change. In P. Foulkes and G. J. Docherty (eds.), *Urban voices: accent studies in the British Isles*. London: Arnold, 246–64.

McCafferty, K. (2001) *Ethnicity and language change*. Amsterdam: John Benjamins.

McClure, J. D. (2002) *Doric: the dialect of north-east Scotland*. Amsterdam: John Benjamins.

McIntosh, A. (1952) *An introduction to a survey of Scottish dialect*. London: Nelson.

McMahon, A. M. S. (1991) Lexical phonology and sound change: the case of the Scottish Vowel Length Rule. *Journal of Linguistics* 27, 29–53.

McMahon, A. M. S. (2000) *Change, chance and optimality*. Oxford: Oxford University Press.

Mees, I. M. and Collins, B. (1999) Cardiff: a real-time study of glottalisation. In P. Foulkes and G. J. Docherty (eds.), *Urban voices: accent studies in the British Isles*. London: Arnold, 185–202.

Melchers, G. and Shaw, P. (2003) *World Englishes*. London: Arnold.

Milroy, J. (1992) *Linguistic variation and change*. Oxford: Blackwell.

Milroy, J. (1995). Investigating the Scottish Vowel Length Rule in a Northumbrian dialect. *Newcastle and Durham Working Papers in Linguistics* 3, 187–96.

Milroy, J. and Milroy, L. (1985) Linguistic change, social network and speaker innovation. *Journal of Linguistics* 21, 339–84.

Milroy, J. and Milroy, L. (1998) *Authority in language*, 3rd edn. London: Routledge.

Milroy, L. (1987a) *Observing and analysing natural language*. Oxford: Blackwell.

Milroy, L. (1987b) *Language and social networks*, 2nd edn. Oxford: Blackwell.

Milroy, L. (2002) Social networks. In J. Chambers, P. Trudgill, and N. Schilling-Estes (eds.), *The handbook of language variation and change*. Oxford: Blackwell, 549–72.

Milroy, L. and Gordon, M. (2003) *Sociolinguistics: method and interpretation*. Oxford: Blackwell.

Mitchell, A. G. and Delbridge, A. (1965) *The speech of Australian adolescents*. Sydney: Angus and Robertson.

Moore, B. C. J. (1997) Aspects of auditory processing related to speech perception. In W. J. Hardcastle and J. Laver (eds.), *The handbook of phonetic sciences*. Oxford: Blackwell, 539–65.

Moreton, E. (2004) Realization of the English postvocalic [voice] contrast in F1 and F2. *Journal of Phonetics* 32, 1–33.

Mufwene, S. S. (1994) Theoretical linguistics and variation analysis: strange bedfellows? In K. Beals, J. Denton, R. Knippen, L. Melnar, H. Suzuki, and E. Zeinfeld (eds.), *Papers from the parasession on variation in linguistic theory*. Chicago: Chicago Linguistic Society, 202–17.

Mufwene, S. S., Rickford, J. R., Bailey, G., and Baugh, J. (eds.) (1998) *African-American English: structure, history and use*. London: Routledge.

Mullennix, J. W., Bihon, T., Bricklemyer, J., Gaston, J., and Keener, J. M. (2002) Effects of variation in emotional tone of voice in speech perception. *Language and Speech* 45, 255–83.

Nagy, N. and Reynolds, B. (1997) Optimality theory and variable word-final deletion in Faetar. *Language Variation and Change* 9, 37–55.

Nathan, E., Wells, W. H. G., and Donlan, C. (1998) Children's comprehension of unfamilar regional accents: a preliminary investigation. *Journal of Child Language* 25, 343–65.

Ní Chasaide, A. and Gobl, C. (1997) Voice source variation. In W. J. Hardcastle and J. Laver (eds.), *The handbook of phonetic sciences*. Oxford: Blackwell, 427–61.

Niedzielski, N. (1999) The effect of social information on the perception of sociolinguistic variables. *Journal of Language and Social Psychology* 18, 62–85.

Nolan, F. J. (1997) Speaker recognition and forensic phonetics. In W. J. Hardcastle and J. Laver (eds.), *The handbook of phonetic sciences*. Oxford: Blackwell, 744–67.

Nolan, F. J. and Kerswill, P. E. (1990) The description of connected speech processes. In S. Ramsaran (ed.), *Studies in the pronunciation of English: a commemorative volume in honour of A.C. Gimson*. London: Routledge, 295–316.

Nygaard, L. C., Sommers, M. S., and Pisoni, D. B. (1994) Speech perception as a talker-contingent process. *Psychological Science* 5, 42–6.

Ogden, R. A. (1999) A declarative account of strong and weak auxiliaries in English. *Phonology* 16, 55–92.

Ohala, J. J. (1978) The production of tone. In V. A. Fromkin (ed.), *Tone: a linguistic survey*. New York: Academic Press, 5–39.

Ohala, J. J. (1983) The origin of sound patterns in vocal tract constraints. In P. F. MacNeilage (ed.), *The production of speech*. New York: Springer-Verlag, 189–216.

Orton, H. and Barry, M. V. (1969) *Survey of English dialects, vol. 2: the west Midland counties*. Leeds: Arnold.

Orton, H., and Halliday, W. J. (1963) *The survey of English dialects, vol. 1: the six northern counties and the Isle of Man*. Leeds: Arnold.

Orton, H., Sanderson, S., and Widdowson, J. (eds.) (1978) *The linguistic atlas of England*. London: Croom Helm.

Orton, H., and Tilling, P. M. (1970) *The survey of English dialects, vol. 3: the east midland counties and east Anglia*. Leeds: Arnold.

Orton, H., and Wakelin, M. F. (1967) *The survey of English dialects, vol. 4: the southern counties*. Leeds: Arnold.

Pandeli, H., Eska, J. F., Ball, M. J., and Rahilly, J. (1997) Problems of phonetic transcription: the case of Hiberno-English slit-t. *Journal of the International Phonetic Association* 27, 65–75.

Patrick, P. (1996) The urbanization of creole phonology: variation and change in Jamaican (KYA). In G. R. Guy, C. Feagin, D. Schiffrin, and J. Baugh (eds.), *Towards a social science of language: Papers in honor of William Labov. Volume 1: variation and change in language and society*. Amsterdam: John Benjamins, 329–55.

Paul, H. [1880] (1978) On sound change. Translated and reprinted in P. Baldi and R. N. Werth (eds.), *Readings in historical phonology: chapters in the theory of sound change*. University Park: Pennsylvania State University Press, 3–22.

Pederson, L. (1977) Studies of American pronunciation since 1945. *American Speech* 52, 262–327.

Pederson, L., McDaniel, S. L., et al. (eds.) (1986–92) *Linguistic atlas of the Gulf states* (7 vols.). Athens, GA: University of Georgia Press.

Pegge, S. (1896) *Two collections of Derbicisms*. London: English Dialect Society.

Peñalosa, F. (1980) *Chicano sociolinguistics: a brief introduction*. Rowley, MA: Newbury House.

Penfield, J. and Ornstein-Galicia, J. L. (1985) *Chicano English: an ethnic contact dialect*. Amsterdam: John Benjamins.

Perkell, J. S. and Cohen, M. H. (1989) An indirect test of the quantal nature of speech in the production of the vowels /i/, /a/ and /u/. *Journal of Phonetics* 17, 123–33.

Perkell, J. S., Zandipour, M., Matthies, M. L., and Lane, H. (2002) Economy of effort in different speaking conditions. I: a preliminary study of intersubject differences and modeling issues. *Journal of the Acoustical Society of America* 112, 1627–41.

Peterson, G. and Lehiste, I. (1960) Duration of syllabic nuclei in English. *Journal of the Acoustical Society of America* 32, 693–705.

Petyt, K. M. (1985) *Dialect and accent in industrial west Yorkshire*. Amsterdam: John Benjamins.

Pickford, G. R. (1956) American linguistic geography: a sociological appraisal. *Word* 12, 211–33.

Pierrehumbert, J. B. (1995) Prosodic effects on glottal allophones. In O. Fujimura and M. Hirano (eds.), *Vocal fold physiology*. San Diego: Singular Publishing Group, 39–60.

Pierrehumbert, J. B. (2002) Word-specific phonetics. In C. Gussenhoven and N. Warner (eds.), *Laboratory Phonology 7*. Berlin: Mouton de Gruyter, 101–39.

Pierrehumbert, J. B. and Talkin, D. (1992). Lenition of /h/ and glottal stop. In G. J. Docherty and D. R. Ladd (eds.), *Papers in laboratory phonology II: gesture, segment, prosody*. Cambridge: Cambridge University Press, 90–119.

Pisoni, D. B. (1997) Some thoughts on 'normalization' in speech perception. In K. Johnson and J. W. Mullennix (eds.), *Talker variability in speech processing*. San Diego: Academic Press, 9–32.

Podesva, R. J., Roberts, S. J., and Campbell-Kibler, K. (2002) Sharing resources and indexing meanings in the production of gay styles. In K. Campbell-Kibler, R. J. Podesva, S. J. Roberts, and A. Wong (eds.), *Language and sexuality: contesting meaning in theory and practice*. Stanford: CSLI Publications, 175–89.

Rahilly, J. (1997) Aspects of prosody in Hiberno-English: the case of Belfast. In J. L. Kallen (ed.), *Focus on Ireland*. Amsterdam: John Benjamins, 109–32.

Ramisch, H. (1988) *The variation of English in Guernsey/Channel Islands*. Frankfurt-am-Main: Peter Lang.

Rathborn, H., Bull, R., and Clifford, B. R. (1981) Voice recognition over the telephone. *Journal of Police Science and Administration* 9, 280–4.

Redi, L. and Shattuck-Hufnagel, S. (2001) Variation in the realization of glottalization in normal speakers. *Journal of Phonetics* 29, 407–29.

Rickford, J. (1986) The need for new approaches to social class analysis in sociolinguistics. *Language and Communication* 6, 215–21.

Roberts, J. (1997a) Acquisition of variable rules: a study of (-t,d) deletion in preschool children. *Journal of Child Language* 24, 351–72.

Roberts, J. (1997b) Hitting a moving target: acquisition of sound change in progess by Philadelphia children. *Language Variation and Change* 9, 249–66.

Roberts, J. (2002) Child language variation. In J. Chambers, P. Trudgill, and N. Schilling-Estes (eds.), *The handbook of language variation and change*. Oxford: Blackwell, 333–48.

Roberts, J. and Labov, W. (1995) Learning to talk Philadelphian. *Language Variation and Change* 7, 101–12.

Rose, P. (2002) *Forensic speaker identification*. London: Taylor & Francis.

Ryback-Soucy, W. and Nagy, N. (2000) Exploring the dialect of Franco-Americans of Manchester, New Hampshire. *Journal of English Linguistics* 28, 249–64.

Schilling-Estes, N. (2000) Investigating intra-ethnic differentiation: /ay/ in Lumbee Native American English. *Language Variation and Change* 12, 141–74.

Schilling-Estes, N. (2002) Investigating stylistic variation. In J. Chambers, P. Trudgill, and N. Schilling-Estes (eds.), *The handbook of language variation and change*. Oxford: Blackwell, 375–401.

Schneider, E. W. (ed.) (1996) *Focus on the USA*. Amsterdam: John Benjamins.

Scobbie, J. M., Hewlett. N., and Turk, A. E. (1999) Standard English in Edinburgh and Glasgow: the Scottish Vowel Length Rule revealed. In P. Foulkes and G. J. Docherty (eds.), *Urban voices: accent studies in the British Isles*. London: Arnold, 230–45.

Shadle, C. H. (1997) The aerodynamics of speech. In W. J. Hardcastle and J. Laver (eds.), *The handbook of phonetic sciences*. Oxford: Blackwell, 33–64.

Shattuck-Hufnagel, S. and Turk, A. (1996) A prosody tutorial for investigators of auditory sentence processing. *Journal of Psycholinguistic Research* 25, 193–247.

Shnukal, A. (2001) Torres Strait English. In D. Blair and P. Collins (eds.), *English in Australia*. Amsterdam: John Benjamins, 181–200.

Shockey, L. (2002) *Sound patterns of spoken English*. Oxford: Blackwell.

Simo Bobda, A. (2003) The formation of regional and national features in African English pronunciation: an exploration of some non-interference factors. *English World-Wide* 24, 17–42.

Simo Bobda, A., Wolf, H. G., and Peter, L. (1999) Identifying regional and national origin of English-speaking Africans seeking asylum in Germany. [Forensic Linguistics:] *The International Journal of Speech, Language and the Law* 6, 300–19.

Sproat, R. W. and Fujimura, O. (1993) Allophonic variation in English /l/ and its implications for phonetic implementation. *Journal of Phonetics* 21, 291–311.

Stevens, K. N. (1998) *Acoustic phonetics*. Cambridge, MA: MIT Press.

Strand, E. (1999) Uncovering the role of gender stereotypes in speech perception. *Journal of Language and Social Psychology* 18, 86–99.

Stuart-Smith, J. (1999) Glasgow: accent and voice quality. In P. Foulkes and G. J. Docherty (eds.), *Urban voices: accent studies in the British Isles*. London: Arnold, 203–22.

Sudbury, A. (2001) Falkland Islands English. *English World-Wide* 22, 55–80.

Sutcliffe, D. (1982) *British black English*. Oxford: Blackwell.

Sutcliffe, D. (2003) Eastern Caribbean suprasegmental systems. In M. Aceto and J. P. Williams (eds.), *Contact Englishes of the eastern Caribbean*. Amsterdam: John Benjamins, 265–96.

Sutton-Spence, R., Woll, B., and Allsop, L. (1990) Variation and recent change in fingerspelling in British Sign Language. *Language Variation and Change* 2, 313–30.

Tagliamonte, S. A. and Temple, R. A. M. (2005) New perspectives on an ol' variable: (t,d) in British English. *Language Variation and Change* 17, 281–302.

Tarone, E. E. (1973) Aspects of intonation in Black English. *American Speech* 48, 29–36.

Tent, J. (2001) Yod deletion in Fiji English: phonological shibboleth or L2 English? *Language Variation and Change* 13, 161–91.

Thomas, E. R. (2000) Spectral differences in /ai/ offsets conditioned by voicing of the following consonant. *Journal of Phonetics* 28, 1–26.

Thomas, E. R. (2001) *An acoustic analysis of vowel variation in new world English*. Durham, NC: Duke University Press.

Thomas, E. R. (2002a) Sociophonetic approaches of speech perception

experiments. *American Speech 77,*
115–47.

Thomas, E. R. (2002b) Instrumental
phonetics. In J. Chambers, P. Trudgill,
and N. Schilling-Estes (eds.), *The
handbook of language variation and
change.* Oxford: Blackwell, 168–200.

Thomas, E. R. and Bailey, G. (1998)
Parallels between vowel subsystems of
African American Vernacular English
and Caribbean anglophone creoles.
Journal of Pidgin and Creole Languages
13, 267–96.

Thomas, E. R. and Reaser, J. (2004)
Delimiting pereceptual cues for the
ethnic labelling of African American
and European American voices. *Journal
of Sociolinguistics* 8, 54–87.

Trudgill, P. (1974) *The sociolinguistic
differentiation of English in Norwich.*
Cambridge: Cambridge University
Press.

Trudgill, P. (ed.) (1978) *Sociolinguistic
patterns in British English.* London:
Arnold.

Trudgill, P. (1983) *On dialect: social and
geographical perspectives.* Oxford:
Blackwell.

Trudgill, P. (1986). *Dialects in contact.*
Oxford: Blackwell.

Trudgill, P. (1988) Norwich revisited:
recent linguistic changes in an English
urban dialect. *English World Wide* 9,
33–49.

Trudgill, P., Gordon, E., Lewis, G., and
Maclagan, M. (2000) Determinism in
new-dialect formation and the genesis
of New Zealand English. *Journal of
Linguistics* 36, 299–318.

Turk, A. E. and Shattuck-Hufnagel, S.
(2000) Word-boundary-related
duration patterns in English. *Journal
of Phonetics* 28, 397–440.

Upton, C. and Widdowson, J. D. A.
(1996) *An atlas of English dialects.*
Oxford: Oxford University Press.

Vaissière, J. (1988) Prediction of velum
movement from phonological
specifications. *Phonetica* 45, 122–39.

Verbrugge, R. R. and Rakerd, B. (1986)
Evidence of talker-independent
information for vowels. *Language
and Speech* 29, 39–57.

Walker, G. (2003) 'Doing a rushthrough':
a phonetic resource for holding the
turn in everyday conversation. In
M. J. Solé, D. Recasens, and J. Romero
(eds.), *Proceedings of the 15th
international congress of phonetic sciences.*
Barcelona: Universitat Autònoma de
Barcelona/Causal Productions,
1847–50.

Walters, J. P. (2003) 'Celtic English':
influences on a South Wales valleys
accent. *English World-Wide* 24, 63–87.

Walton, J. H. and Orlikoff, R. F. (1994)
Speaker race identification from
acoustic cues in the vocal signal.
Journal of Speech and Hearing Research
37, 738–45.

Warren, P. and Britain, D. (2000)
Intonation and prosody in New
Zealand English. In A. Bell and
K. Kuiper (eds.), *New Zealand
English.* Amsterdam: John Benjamins,
146–72.

Watson, C. I., Maclagan, M., and
Harrington, J. (2000) Acoustic evidence
for vowel change in New Zealand
English. *Language Variation and Change*
12, 51–68.

Watt, D. J. L. and Ingham, C. (2000)
Durational evidence of the Scottish
Vowel Length Rule in Berwick
English. *Leeds Working Papers in
Linguistics and Phonetics* 8, 205–28
(www.leeds.ac.uk/linguistics).

Watt, D. J. L. and Milroy, L. (1999)
Patterns of variation and change in
three Tyneside vowels: is this dialect
levelling? In P. Foulkes and G. J.
Docherty (eds.), *Urban voices: accent
studies in the British Isles.* London:
Arnold, 25–46.

Weismer, G. (1997) Motor speech
disorders. In W. J. Hardcastle and
J. Laver (eds.), *The handbook of phonetic
sciences.* Oxford: Blackwell, 191–219.

Wells, J. C. (1973) *Jamaican pronunciation in London*. Oxford: Blackwell.

Wells, J. C. (1982) *Accents of English* (3 vols.). Cambridge: Cambridge University Press.

West, P. (1999) Perception of distributed coarticulatory properties of English /l/ and /ɹ/. *Journal of Phonetics* 27, 405–26.

Westbury, J. R. (1983) Enlargement of the supraglottal cavity and its relation to stop consonant voicing. *Journal of the Acoustical Society of America* 73, 1322–36.

Whalen, D. H. (1990) Coarticulation is largely planned. *Journal of Phonetics* 18, 3–35.

Whalen, D. H. and Levitt, A. G. (1995) The universality of intrinsic F0 of vowels. *Journal of Phonetics* 23, 349–66.

Wightman, C. W., Shattuck-Hufnagel, S., Ostendorf, M., and Price, P. J. (1992) Segmental durations in the vicinity of prosodic phrase boundaries. *Journal of the Acoustical Society of America* 92, 1707–17.

Wolfram, W. (1969) *A linguistic description of Detroit Negro speech*. Washington, DC: Center for Applied Linguistics.

Wolfram, W., Hazen, K., and Schilling-Estes, N. (1999) *Dialect change and maintenance on the outer banks*. Tuscaloosa: University of Alabama Press.

Wolfram, W. and Schilling-Estes, N. (1998) *American English*. Oxford: Blackwell.

Wolfram, W. and Thomas, E. R. (2002) *The development of African American English: evidence from an isolated community*. Oxford: Blackwell.

Wolfram, W., Thomas, E. R., and Green, E. W. (2000) The regional context of earlier African American speech: evidence for reconstructing the development of AAVE. *Language in Society* 29, 315–56.

Woods, H. B. (1991) Social differentiation in Ottawa English. In J. Cheshire (ed.), *English around the world*. Cambridge: Cambridge University Press, 134–49.

Wright, R. (2003) Factors of lexical competition in vowel articulation. In J. K. Local, R. A. Ogden, and R. A. M. Temple (eds.), *Phonetic interpretation: papers in laboratory phonology 6*. Cambridge: Cambridge University Press, 75–87.

28 Spoken and Written English

JIM MILLER

0 Introduction

The study of spoken English is exciting, challenging, and controversial: exciting, because new and unexpected constructions keep turning up; challenging, because some syntactic constructions of spoken language resist analysis; controversial, because not all researchers recognize the study of spoken language as legitimate, far less its results. The very title of this chapter is controversial, since spoken language *tout court* does not differ from written language and analysts recognize genres or dimensions applying to both speech and writing (see section 4). Nonetheless, spontaneous spoken language (Miller and Weinert 1998) or conversation (Greenbaum and Nelson 1995a) is very different from other genres and that is the focus of this chapter.

The contrast between spoken and written language has long interested linguists, particularly linguists of the Prague School, who from the 1930s on have investigated the characteristics and functions of speech and writing. Teachers of English as a second language have always been aware that learners do not learn to *speak* like natives by reading books. Scholars pondering the relationship between language and society (including literacy) have to deal with spoken and written language. In societies with a standard and non-standard language, typically only the standard has an elaborated written variety; a central issue is the effect of written language on the spontaneous speech of individuals with long exposure to formal education.

Despite the interest, it is only in the past thirty years that the detailed and accurate study of spoken language has become possible through new technology: genuinely portable cassette recorders, small but high-fidelity microphones, foot controls enabling the analyst to listen many times to particular portions of a recording. Thanks to computers and concordance programs analysts can quickly and accurately retrieve data from digitized transcriptions. Interestingly, much of the detailed work on spoken language has been done by investigators of non-standard varieties; little micro-analysis has been carried out on spoken standard English in the UK, and what counts as spoken standard English is not clear (see section 7).

Spoken language is more fundamental than written language; it appeared before written language in the general evolution of human beings, children acquire it before they learn to read and write and all the societies with a known history had spoken language before they had writing. What is coming out of the research with modern technology is that spontaneous spoken language is far more different from (formal) written language than had been suspected and every area of language is affected – morphology, phrase and clause syntax and the organization of discourse.

1   Content of the Chapter

Since most published work on English deals with the written language, this chapter takes the structures and functions of written English merely as a point of orientation and focuses on spontaneous or unplanned spoken English. Section 2 outlines the dimensions established by Biber which demonstrate that there is no boundary dividing all spoken language from all written language. It points out that, Biber notwithstanding, unplanned speech is a distinctive genre. Section 3 demonstrates the different typical constructions of spoken and written English, drawing on the quantitative analyses in Biber et al. (1999), Miller and Weinert (1998), Greenbaum and Nelson (1995), Macaulay (1991), and Thompson (1988). Section 4 deals with objections to any analysis of unplanned speech. Sections 5.1 and 5.2 cover two general properties of unplanned speech, the irrelevance of the sentence and unintegrated syntax, while section 5.3 sketches the salient features of discourse organization in unplanned speech. Section 6 briefly discusses major problems emerging from recent work on unplanned speech: what constructions are non-standard and the fact that some constructions require different analyses in unplanned speech and planned writing. The conclusion in section 7 lists areas of research for which the study of unplanned speech has important implications.

2   Genres and Dimensions

It is essential to begin by making clear what data is under analysis. The central fact is that there is no single boundary dividing all spoken texts from all written texts. Different genres must be recognized, such as conversation, news broadcasts, conversation, and academic texts as used by Biber et al. (1999). There is space here to discuss only one recent and important development in the study of genres. Abandoning the usual genres, Biber (1988) established six dimensions cutting across speech and writing, six sets of properties correlating positively or negatively with certain major properties of texts and their producers. For example, Dimension 1 has to do with involved versus informational production, i.e. whether the text-producer is participating in face-to-face conversation with instant on-line production or writing carefully edited texts conveying carefully organized information; Dimension 3 has to do with explicit versus situation-dependent reference, i.e. with whether the text-producer is setting out all the information in detail or leaving the listener/reader to fill in details from context.

Grammatical properties that correlate positively with Dimension 1 are, in descending order of weighting, adverbial clauses of reason and cause, propositional relative clauses (*Julia has resigned, which I think is unwarranted*), adverbial clauses of condition and WH complements (*I believed what she told me*). Grammatical properties that correlate negatively, i.e. which are not found in unplanned speech, are prepositional phrases, attributive adjectives, past participial phrases and present participial phrases. The positive correlations match the number and type of adverbial clauses found by Miller and Weinert and the occurrence of complement clauses; the negative correlations match the types of noun phrases listed in table 28.1. Biber (1988: 104–8) interprets the properties as reflecting the strategies adopted by speakers conveying a lot of information in unplanned speech: speakers avoid compressed, highly integrated structures such as participial phrases which are cognitively expensive.

Grammatical properties correlating positively with Dimension 3 are WH relative clauses in object positions (*the house which we have bought*), relative clauses introduced by Preposition + WH (*the house in which we are going to live*), WH relative clauses in subject position (*the people who sold us the house removed all the light fittings*), phrasal coordination (*Sue and Sheena*, as opposed to *Sue bought a car and Sheena sold her motorbike*, which is an example of clause coordination), and nominalizations, i.e. words ending in *-ity*, *-ment*, *-ness*, and *-tion*. Biber interprets these properties as reflecting referential explicitness, which is typically connected with precise writing but also with prepared spoken texts such as lectures and speeches.

In spite of the complexities outlined above, researchers continue to find spontaneous or unplanned speech very different from other types of text. Picking up the key points made above, however, we recognize that the key distinction is not speech versus writing but planned versus unplanned production of speech and writing. Planned production includes speech based on writing, such as lecturing, giving a sermon and delivering a prepared speech. Unplanned production includes conversation, extempore narration, and impromptu discussion, but also writing activities such as composing personal e-mails or personal letters. Some speech production is semi-planned; for example, speakers narrating events which they have described previously and for which they have in memory ready-made phrases and clauses.

Unplanned spoken language has essential properties which determine certain characteristics of spoken texts. Spontaneous speech

i   is produced in real time with little or no planning and editing (many
      written texts are planned and edited);

ii   is subject to the limitations of short-term memory;
iii is typically produced by people talking face to face;
iv   involves the use of pitch, amplitude, rhythm and voice-quality;
v   is accompanied by gestures, eye-gaze, facial expressions and body postures, all of which signal information.

The above properties engender certain linguistic properties:

a   A small quantity of information is assigned to each phrase and clause.
b   Speakers do embed clauses inside other clauses, but a typical pattern is one in which clauses are merely adjacent.
c   The syntax is less integrated than the syntax of planned writing.
d   Phrases contain fewer words and clauses contain fewer phrases.
e   The range of vocabulary, particularly Greco-Latinate, is less than in planned writing.

In addition:

f   Constructions occur in unplanned speech which are not used in writing, and vice-versa.
g   The organization of discourse involves a number of devices that are absent or infrequent in writing.

3   Differences between Spontaneous Speech and Writing

This section discusses the general grammatical properties that distinguish unplanned speech from other types of text. The following sections look at particular properties, the abandonment of sentences and the unintegrated syntax of unplanned speeech.

3.1   *Settings, topics, and informants*

Consider (1) and (2).

(1)   New York's **an incredible place** we went through the Bowery . . . and we had to keep the windows locked through there but it's **an incredible city** it's **mind-boggling** and the negroes are **fantastic** the clothes they wear they are **so magnificently turned out** flamboyancy that they just seem to carry off I was very impressed with the way that they dressed . . . it's **a marvelous city**

(2)   However defective our knowledge may be, we have ample evidence to show that great empires rose and fell in India, and that, as in religion, art, literature and social life, so in political organization, India produced her own system, distinctive in its strength and weakness.

(1) and (2) illustrate some of the differences between unplanned speech and planned writing. (1) is a narrative from spontaneous conversation and (2) is from Basham's *The Wonder That Was India*. (1) consists of a series of short main clauses. There is one subordinate clause, a contact relative clause, in the noun phrase *the way that they dressed*. Its structure is simple, a pronoun subject and an intransitive verb. The noun phrases are simple too; mostly pronouns or article + noun, and two with an adjective, *incredible*. There is a complex noun phrase, *flamboyancy that they just seem to carry off*, but it stands on its own and is not part of a clause.

(2) is typical of planned writing. It has three subordinate clauses – *however . . . may be, that great . . . India, that . . . weakness* – and a main clause, *we have . . . weakness*. In the first subordinate clause the complement of *be, however defective*, is untypical of speech, where we would expect *no matter how defective*. The third subordinate clause contains a complex correlative construction, *as . . . life, so . . . organization*, quite untypical of planned speech, never mind unplanned. The passage contains a very complex noun phrase – *her own system, distinctive . . . weakness*, a type unknown in unplanned speech.

Are the differences between these texts typical of the differences between unplanned speech and writing? Early investigations produced different answers. Some analysts reported that spoken discourse had significantly more subordination, elaboration of syntax and adverbs. Others reported that written narratives contained more subordinate constructions than spoken narratives but fewer coordinate constructions. Halliday (1989: 76–91) proposed that written language has compact but simple syntax loaded with lexical items, whereas spoken language has intricate syntactic structure with many subordinate clauses but a small number of lexical items per clause.

Beaman (1984: 76–91) resolved the contradictions by suggesting that the different results reflected differences in formality (setting, topic and participants). These indeed seem to be part of the answer. One study concluding that spoken language has complex syntax was based on interviews with university students about school and university and essays about the students' life-plans. In the the interviews, figures of authority, academics, inquisited people of junior status, students, in an institutional setting. They focused on one topic and invited narrative monologues from the students. These are ideal conditions for complex syntax because narrators have the floor in a formal setting and can concentrate on the narrative without interruptions.

Another factor is amount of exposure to formal written texts. The people with most exposure to writing experiences are typically (but not necessarily) those with the longest exposure to formal education; significantly, the above-mentioned study analyzed the language of speakers who had successfully undergone a long process of formal education to reach university. Halliday's (1989) examples of speech have complex syntax and vocabulary and sound very typical of speakers in command of written English (see Miller and Weinert 1989: 18–20.) Unfortunately, samples of speakers have usually been organized with respect to gender, age and social class, but not length and type of formal education or reading habits.

A third factor is experience of unplanned speaking in formal situations. Consider the use of propositional relative clauses such as *The noise went on all night, which we thought outrageous*. Millard (2003), analyzing transcripts of radio discussions and phone-in programmes, found that presenters and regular members of discussion panels produced ten such relative clauses but that non-regular members produced none. Miller and Weinert found none, nor did they find non-restrictive relative clauses such as *the girl, who acted very courageously, was praised by the police*. In Millard's data non-restrictive relative clauses were produced by regular speakers and presenters. Finegan and Biber (1994: 337–8) sum up the view adopted here: speakers who engage in literate activities more often tend to use complex 'literate' syntax and vocabulary more often in unplanned speech, and vice-versa for speakers who do not engage often in literate activities.

3.2   *Morphology*

Derivational morphology is of direct relevance to the issue of planned and unplanned speech. English has a very large stock of lexical items built from Greco-Latinate roots which occur more frequently in planned texts, especially formal written texts but also in speeches, news broadcasts and academic discourse. They are much less frequent in unplanned speech. Even Biber, working on conversations involving middle-class, middle-aged, university-educated males (1986: 389 n. 4), found that abstract nouns ending in *tion, -ity* were relatively infrequent. Similarly, in a different corpus of speech from a wider sample of speakers Biber et al. (1999) found that in conversation *-tion* occurred around five hundred times per million words; the others occurred less frequently. *-tion* was three times as frequent in fiction, nine times as frequent in news broadcasts and eighteen times as frequent in academic texts. *-ity* was twice as frequent in fiction, six times as frequent in news broadcasts and ten times as frequent in academic prose. A similar pattern held for compound nouns.

3.3   *Syntax*

Many syntactic constructions are used both in speech and writing but there are significant differences. There are constructions typical of speech but not writing and excluded from copy-edited written text. The constructions that occur in both speech and writing often differ in complexity, frequency of occurrence, function and position. The most controversial question is whether spontaneous speech can be analyzed as having sentences. This is discussed in section 4.

3.3.1   *Noun phrases*

Judgments of complexity are based on two properties: the number of words in a phrase and phrases in a clause, and the depth of embedding. Noun phrases provide good illustrations. Miller and Weinert (1998: 146) found that in a

Table 28.1   Noun phrases in different types of text

	Adjective+ noun	Noun + prepositional phrase	Noun + relative clause	Complex noun phrase
	% of Noun Phrases belonging to each type			
Conversation (Miller and Weinert)	5.6 *a big adventure*	6.6 *the book on the table*	3.2 *the book that I liked*	0 *a new proposal from the agency which is likely to be rejected*
Letters to newspaper	19.7	18.8	3	3 *a rigorous and valid examination on applied economics that consists of three papers*

sample of monologue 50 percent of the noun phrases consisted of a pronoun and another 7 percent consisted of a single non-pronominal word. When NPs consisting only of a numeral (*give me two please*) or a quantifier (*I'd like more*) were counted, the percentage of one-word NPs rose to 64. Few NPs contained other constituents, as shown in table 28.1. Note the different percentages found in letters to a quality newspaper (Miller and Weinert 1998: 154).

Counting types of NPs is not sufficient; where they occur in clauses is also important. The main tendency is clear: in subject position speakers use simple NPs. In Thompson's (1988) data the subject NPs of transitive clauses did not have adjectives, although some subject NPs of intransitive clauses did. Likewise in the monologue analyzed by Miller and Weinert no adjectives occurred in subject NPs. This pattern accords with the findings of Crystal (1979: 164) working on conversations in the Survey of English Usage (later the London-Lund Corpus). He found that 77 percent of the clauses had as subject a pronoun or an empty word such as *it* and *there*. The pattern is confirmed in Biber et al. (1999: 235–7).

3.3.2   Clause constructions

Certain clause constructions are quite untypical of spontaneous speech and do not occur in Miller and Weinert's data. Examples are shown in table 28.2.

Gerunds and infinitives occurred but only very simple ones: *I like skiing* and *I love to go skiing*. Biber et al. (1999: 754) found that infinitives and gerunds are relatively rare in conversation and most common in fiction, followed by news broadcasts and academic prose.

Table 28.2 Constructions typical of writing and not attested in Miller and Weinert's spontaneous spoken data

Type of construction	
Gapping	Jim washed, and Margaret dried, the dishes
Accusative and infinitive	We consider her to be the best candidate
Possessive gerund	His having resigned before he even took up the post astonished everyone
Free participle	Browsing in the bookshop, I came across a book on Peter the Great
Participial phrase	the book rejected by the publisher the plane sitting on the runway at Heathrow
Infinitive as clause subject	To see Naples and die would be pretty stupid
Gerund as clause subject	Skiing in summer is difficult

Other constructions, such as relative clauses, occur in speech and writing but with different frequencies and in partly different forms, as shown in table 28.3.

Macaulay (1991: 64) comments that in his middle-class interviews 20 percent of the relative clauses are non-restrictive but only 5 percent in the working class interviews. (Non-restrictive relative clauses are typical of planned writing and there is some connection between social class and length of formal education.) Biber et al. (1999: 610) found that contact relative clauses were proportionately most common in conversation. Biber et al. found a miniscule number of relative clauses with *whom* and even fewer with *whose*. Other differences concern the use of shadow or resumptive pronouns and the occurrence of subject gaps. These are discussed in section 5 below.

Miller and Weinert (1998: 93) found more complement clauses than relative clauses in their conversational data. Sixty-six percent of the former were contact complement clauses. Biber et al. (1999) do not provide directly comparable figures but they do comment that post-predicate *that* clauses are particularly common in conversation (*It is essential that this is done immediately* as opposed to *That this be done immediately is essential*). Examples such as the latter are also absent from Miller and Weinert's conversational data. The ratios of finite subordinate clauses to the total number of finite clauses in samples of speech and writing show interesting patterns. See table 28.4.

Table 28.3   Types of relative clause in a sample of Miller and Weinert's spontaneous spoken data

Type of relative clause	Number	Example
WH	0	the book which we gave her the girl who phoned
TH	35	the house that they bought the student that complained
Contact	37	the house they bought the town they live in
Non-restrictive	0	We met her brother, who plays golf. [She has only one brother. Incidentally, he plays golf.] (Compare the restrictive relative clause We met her brother who plays golf. [She has several brothers; we met the golf-playing one.])
Whom, whose	0	the lawyer whom we know the friend whose car we bought

Table 28.4   % of finite subordinate clauses in different text-types

Conversation	Fiction	Quality newspaper	Semi-academic journal
25	26	41	45

Source: from Miller and Weinert 1998

Finite adverbial clauses present a complex pattern. Thompson (1984) carried out a study of finite and non-finite adverbial clauses and non-restrictive relative clauses in databases of informal speech, informal writing and formal writing. (Both types of clause are peripheral, i.e. not embedded in other constituents but are loosely attached to their host clause.) Thompson found that informal speech had the highest proportion of finite adverbial clauses. Greenbaum and Nelson (1995: 186) found a lower percentage of finite adverbial clauses in spoken English, a higher percentage in informal written texts and the highest in formal written texts, but whereas they analyzed monologues, broadcast discussions and conversation, Thompson confined herself to monologues. Biber et al. (1999: 826) also found that finite adverbial clauses were (marginally) more frequent in conversation. See table 28.5.

Table 28.5 Number of finite adverbial clauses per million words

Conversation	Fiction	News	Academic prose
11,000	10,500	7,500	6,300

Source: Biber et al. 1999

Looking at different types of adverbial clause, they found that in conversation the most frequent types of finite adverbial clause were condition, reason/ cause and time in decreasing order of frequency; Miller and Weinert (1998: 93) found the same types but in reverse order of frequency. Clauses of concession, result, purpose and manner are much less frequent in Biber et al.'s data and Miller and Weinert found no adverbial clauses of concession at all.

4   Can Unplanned Speech be Analyzed?

In spite of the word, phrase and clause constructions described above, the study of unplanned speech is not uncontroversial. The very possibility of studying spoken language has been called into question. Huddleston and Pullum (2002: 11–12) – henceforth H&P – invoke the many disfluencies in conversation. In contrast, Labov (1972: 203) described as myth the ungrammaticality of everyday speech. He had to edit only 10 percent of the utterances produced by his sample of non-academic speakers discussing familiar subjects, which matches Miller and Weinert's (1998: 383) experience with their conversation data. Academics discussing complex topics in complex language produce far more disfluent utterances.

H&P worry that word sequences resulting from slips might be wrongly taken to represent grammatical facts and that actual utterances reflect only imperfectly 'the system that defines the spoken version of the language.' This worry is met by the rules of fieldwork. Single examples are treated with caution until the analyst collects more examples and checks the data against the findings of other analysts. (See the salutary lesson of *sat* and *stood* below.) A final check is whether a construction occurs in writing that is unplanned because it is produced within strict time limits or is very informal, e.g. personal letters, e-mails, and even newspaper reports and articles, which are produced to deadlines and without the rigorous sub-editing of pre-computer days. Many constructions begin life confined to spoken language but make their way into writing, particularly texts that are not subject to the scrutiny of teachers and publishers' editors. For instance, H&P (2002: 1069) say that the example *It is unreasonable what she suggests* is incorrect, but the author has noted the same construction, as in *It's unfair what they're doing to the union*, in conversation, radio discussions and examination scripts. Copy-editors would exclude it, but in speech it is very common.

Halliday (1989) observes that the production of written language also presents disfluencies – restarts, repetitions and anacolutha. Editorial tidying-up removes them, but they can be seen in, e.g., handwritten personal letters and examination scripts. Analysts of written language also have to deal with unique examples, particularly of lexical items; they ensure the item is clearly labeled with its technical term, *hapax legomenon*. One-off syntactic structures are relegated to footnotes in reference grammars or annotated editions of literary texts.

5   General Syntactic and Discourse Properties of Unplanned Speech

5.1   *Sentences and clauses*

Sentences are the traditional basic unit of syntax. Many analysts propose to keep sentences for the analysis of written language but to analyze spoken language as consisting of clauses and combinations of clauses, or 'clause clusters,' to use the term introduced by Halliday (1989).

There are three major reasons why sentences are not suited to the analysis of spoken language. One is that speakers do not share intuitions about what counts as sentences in spoken language. Wackernagel-Jolles (1971) found that senior undergraduate students listening to a recording and provided with an unpunctuated transcript of the words did not agree on sentence boundaries; for one narrative they agreed that twenty-nine sentences were possible but agreed on final boundaries for only six.

Another is that there are no reliable criteria for recognizing sentences. Speakers do not always pause between one putative sentence and the next, and intonation contours may include more than one main clause. Finally, speakers typically produce loosely connected phrases and clauses unlike the neat hierarchical structures associated with formal written language and courses in syntax. Indeed, utterances may consist of fragments of clauses but be perfectly interpretable; they belong to a particular text and context which support the interpretation.

Miller and Weinert (1998: ch. 2) observe that what counts as a text sentence varies from one language culture to another and has varied from one century to another in English. They point out that text sentences do not correspond neatly to the system sentences of linguists, system sentences being units within which analysts can handle constituent structure and dependency relations. In any case, the traditional tests for constituent structure apply inside single clauses and while a few dependency relations cross clause boundaries, the densest networks of dependency relations occur within single clauses. The abandonment of the sentence for the analysis of spontaneous speech seems only sensible.

Nonetheless, some analysts remain neutral or change their mind. Crystal (1979: 159) concluded strongly in favor of the clause and against the sentence for spoken language but later (Crystal 1995: 214–15) he asserted that we do speak in sentences but that speech and writing differ in sentence organization. McCarthy (1998: 79–82) points to various problems: utterances interpretable as the realization of sentences but produced by two or more speakers; clauses introduced by *cos* or *if* which do not modify a main clause and function like main clauses; the general absence of well-formed sentences from spoken discourse. He does not explicitly abandon the sentence but does declare that grammar becomes discourse when sentence-based units of description fail to account for the facts, and he does focus on discourse.

Chafe (1994: 139–45) regards sentences as viable for spoken language but redefines them as corresponding more to short paragraphs. Central to this view are prototypical intonation units consisting of a single coherent intonation contour, possibly followed by a pause and stretching over a maximum of six words. These contours and sequences of words may correspond to clauses, phrases or simply fragments of syntax. Each intonation contour encompasses one piece of information. However, speakers regularly deal with conglomerates of information, which Chafe calls 'centers of interest'; they use one intonation pattern to signal that a given conglomerate has not been completed and another pattern to signal that it has. Chafe identifies the latter pattern with sentence-final intonation.

Greenbaum and Nelson (1995: 5) reject Chafe's analysis because the recognition of centers of interest is subjective and unreliable Presumably Chafe would counter that what is crucial is the pattern of intonation signalling completion of a given chunk of utterance, but his sentences nonetheless correspond to paragraphs. The proponents of clauses claim that clauses can be recognized by picking out verbs (finite or non-finite) and their modifiers. The debate over sentences and spoken language will continue.

5.2   *Integrated and unintegrated syntax*

The syntax of formal written language is said to be integrated while that of spontaneous spoken language is unintegrated. Consider the following examples.

(3)   If you've got some eggs about whose age you are not sure here's a useful test

(4)   if you've got some eggs you're not sure about their age here's a useful test   (cookery programme on New Zealand television)

In (3) the noun *eggs* is modified by the relative clause *about whose age you are not sure*. *About whose age* is the complement of *sure* but is at the front of the clause. The relative pronoun *whose* connects the relative clause to *eggs*. Crucially, the relative clause immediately follows the head noun *eggs* and is held to be embedded; that is, in process terms, the basic noun phrase is *some eggs*, the direct object of *'ve got*. Into that noun phrase is inserted the relative clause.

In (4) the relative clause is replaced by *you're not sure about their age*. This looks like a main clause; there is no relative pronoun and the clause is linked to *eggs* by the personal possessive pronoun *their*. *About their age* is the complement of *sure*, which it follows, as is normal for adjective complements in main clauses. All the evidence indicates that *you're not sure about their age* is a main clause which is adjacent to *some eggs* but not embedded in it. The differences are summed up by saying that the second clause is integrated into the noun phrase in (3) but not in (4).

(5) is an example of a relative clause embedded in a noun phrase but with no overt pronoun linking it to the head noun.

(5) I only wear shoes that I'm not thrown forward on my toes   (BBC radio
     discussion)

The relative clause is *that I'm not thrown forward on my toes*. It modifies the head noun *shoes* and is linked to it by the complementizer *that*. But inside the relative clause there is no WH pronoun or even an ordinary pronoun linking with *shoes*. A formal written English equivalent is *shoes by which I am not thrown forward on my toes* and a possible spoken version is *shoes that I'm not thrown forward on my toes by them*. In the former *which* provides the link, in the latter *them*.

Another type of integrated construction is in (6).

(6) Only Nato forces stand between what that man is doing and a huge
     tragedy

The integrated syntax lies in the complement of *between*. The noun phrase [*what* [*that man is doing Ø*]] is coordinated with the noun phrase *a huge tragedy*. The actual spoken version of (6), from a BBC radio discussion, is in (7).

(7) Only Nato forces stand between that man what he's doing and a huge
     tragedy

In (7) the basic complement of *between* is *that man and a huge tragedy*. Interpolated between the two noun phrases is the free relative clause *what he's doing*. The free relative is not embedded in another constituent; it is simply adjacent to *that man*. Its subject, *he*, is co-referential with *that man*. (7) puts the human protagonist at the center of the event, *that man* being the 'direct object' of *between*; he is mentioned first and then the relevant characteristic is mentioned, what he is doing.

Other examples are . . . *Everybody knows Helen Liddell how hard she works* [radio discussion] and *I've been meaning to phone and ask about the new baby and Alan how they're getting on*. The construction is far from new; (8) is from the Authorized Version of the New Testament and is a straight calque of the New Testament Greek. (See Miller and Weinert 1998: 362.)

(8)   Consider the lilies of the field how they grow

The New Testament is a written text but it is a written record of what was spoken. Later groups of translators seem to have considered the unintegrated syntax of (8) unsuitable for writing. The Good News Bible has *Look at how the wild flowers grow* and the Revised English Bible has *Consider how the lilies of the field grow.*

The classic WH cleft construction offers a good example of integrated syntax, as in (9).

(9)   What they will do is use this command to save the data

Is links the clauses *what they will do* and *use this command to save the data.* The second clause can be thought of as integrated into the overall structure by losing its subject and its tense. The typical WH construction in spontaneous speech is exemplified in (10). No integration has taken place; the clause following *is* has a subject and its own tense.

(10)   right, well, what you're doing is you're drawing a line

As a final example of unintegrated syntax consider the examples in (11).

(11)   a.   It's unfair what they're doing to the union   (radio discussion)
       b.   it has been well documented the effect "phONEday" had on both
            business and domestic users   (article in *The Independent*)

It is the subject of *is unfair* in (11a) and *has been well documented* in (11b). What is unfair or well documented is conveyed by the free relative clause *what they're doing to the union* and the noun phrase *the effect* . . . In formal writing, and this is why (11b) is surprising, we would expect the free relative clause and the long noun phrase to be the subjects: *what they're doing to the union is unfair* and *the effect "phONEday" had* . . . *has been well documented.*

(12) shows another construction typical of spontaneous speech but not of (planned and edited) writing.

(12)   this older woman in the class she likes to kid us all on

(12) begins with the noun phrase *this older woman in the class* and continues with the complete clause *she likes to kid us all on.* The subject of the clause, *she,* is co-referential with the initial noun phrase. The explanation of the noun phrase–clause structure as a way of dealing with complex subject phrases looks plausible for examples such as (13) but not at all plausible for (14), with a very short Noun Phrase.

(13)   the people who are listening to this many of them will not understand
       the complexities   (radio discussion)

(14)   the driver you get a good laugh with him   (conversation)

Occasionally the construction is used to contrast two referents, as in (15), from a road report on Classic FM.

(15)   there's been an accident in Kent on the M26 but the earlier accident on the A28 that's now been cleared

Speakers could use the construction to escape from a syntactic mix-up but most examples do not display any signs of syntactic breakdown such as hesitations and repetitions. The primary function of the structure is to establish referents and make them salient; its secondary function is to enable speakers and listeners to handle complex referring expressions. (13) enables listeners to establish the referent of *the people who are listening to this* and then to decode the clause *many of them will not understand the complexities*. *Them* provides the link to *the people who are listening to this*.

Classic indirect question clauses are integrated with the main clause.

(16)   I asked where the new form came from

The WH complement of *asked* conveys a question. It begins with the interrogative *where* but the rest of the clause has declarative constituent order. Compare (17a,b), in which the WH complements have the word order and structure of a WH interrogative clause with subject-auxiliary inversion. (17a) is from conversation and (17b) is from a university final examination script. (This type of indirect question is generally ignored in discussions of English syntax, but note (18) from an article in the newspaper *Scotland on Sunday*.)

(17)   a.   I can't remember now what was the reason for it
       b.   The question centers on where did this new form come from

(18)   No one is sure how long are the passages leading off from this center.

This section concludes with examples of a further three spoken constructions: relative clauses with shadow pronouns in (19), clauses with preposed prepositional phrases and shadow pronouns in (20), and clauses in which what looks like a complementizer is separated from the rest of the clause by a pause, as in (21).

(19)   I'm one of these people that I don't like to be surprised

(20)   out of the twenty four traditional medicine shops they visited rhino horn was for sale in nineteen of them [radio report]

(21)   a.   Plus, the lack of ordered rules means that OT analyses are not burdened with various intermediate levels of representation
       b.   Although, English has been the most successful language in becoming a lingua franca

5.3 The organization of spoken discourse

Speakers and writers combine clauses into larger chunks of text. Whatever the type of a written text (see section 2) its writer(s) and reader(s) are not face to face and writers typically have more time than speakers to edit their text. Some types of spoken text are also edited, and may be partly or wholly scripted. Examples are talks on radio or television, lectures, and sermons. Other types of spoken text are produced face-to-face and in real time with no scripting; examples are informal conversation, interviews and impromptu narratives.

The differences are reflected in the use of different syntactic devices for various discourse functions in unplanned and unscripted texts. (The functions of intonation and amplitude are ignored here.) Speakers use syntax (as descibed above) that can be produced online but listeners need texts that they can interpret online. Information is carefully staged with a small quantity of information assigned to small syntactic units and highlighted to make sure the listener's attention is engaged. For example, new entities may be introduced in written discourse by means of indefinite direct objects – *In this section I discuss a difficult construction*. New entities in unplanned (and even planned) speech are introduced, and thereby highlighted, by means of special structures – *there's a difficult construction I want to discuss*. Speakers use a range of highlighting devices for introducing new entities or reintroducing entities (which can be individuals or entire events). Examples are *I've got a friend who . . .* – or (reintroduction) *(you) see the bridge over the river you have to cross it very slowly* or *you know the bridge over the river you have to cross it very slowly . . .* where *the bridge* is highlighted by being the direct object of *see* and *know*. Entire clauses can be highlighted: *you know when we get home can we watch tv?*

Given entities (e.g., people and things in the immediate context or previously mentioned) are regularly introduced into a conversation by means of the NP-Clause construction exemplified in (12), repeated here as (22).

(22)   this older woman in the class she likes to kid us all on

The construction helps to ensure that discourse referents are clearly established. The NP fixes the referent and the clause conveys the relevant information about the referent. Not so frequent, but playing a similar discourse role, is the Clause-NP structure as in *it's not very good the wine*; the final NP both clarifies and firmly establishes the referent of *it*. In Macaulay's (1991: 81) Scots data the clause subject and the final NP can be pronouns, as in *He was some man him*. Macaulay analyzes *him* as reinforcing the referent of *he*. Neither construction is used in writing (except in written dialogue). Carter and McCarthy refer to heads – *this older woman . . .* , and tails – *. . . the wine*, and Biber et al. (1999), use 'preface' (but not 'epilogue'). The construction which H&P find incorrect, *It's unfair what they're doing to the union*, achieves the same effect, establishing the important property and then clarifying and reinforcing the referent of *it*. (See too the discussion of (7) in section 5.2.)

In unplanned speech speakers introduce topics, move from one part of a conversation to another, correct what they have just said (mistakes or misleading accounts are not infrequent in unplanned speech) and draw a line under sections of conversation. Consider the excerpt from conversation in (23).

(23)   A   what is it you're after anyway
       B   we're after everything I mean not not not the phonetics because that's fairly well known anyway em it's the syntax we're after.

Speaker A introduces a new sub-topic with a WH question, simultaneously signalling with *anyway* that he is lacking a crucial piece of information in spite of B's previous account. In his reply speaker B uses a typical phrase, *I mean*, to revise the information he has just given. He uses the spoken negative construction *not* plus NP to cancel one piece of information and an IT cleft to highlight the important information – *it's the syntax we're after*.

Speaker A could have introduced a new topic with a WH cleft, integrated or unintegrated; the first utterance in a politician's speech was *what I thought I'd do Chairman: the most important issue is the poll-tax.* (Example from Regina Weinert.) Reverse TH clefts are used to finish off a stretch of speech, say a chunk of narrative: *and this was him landed with a broken leg* – Macaulay 1991: 78).

Example (1) in section 3.1 is a good example of information being staged. A possible written version is *New York is an incredible, mind-boggling city where the black people are magnificently and flamboyantly turned out.* This is an economical version but it lacks the effect of the spontaneous spoken version in which the adjectives are piled on one by one and even repeated and in which the opening clause *New York's an incredible place* is echoed in the clause that completes the description *It's a marvelous city.*

Finally we note that speakers have to keep signaling their attitude towards the propositions they are conveying or receiving. They achieve this by means of a large number of particles such as *actually, well, anyway, in fact, really* and so on. (See Schiffrin 1987 and the text commentaries in Carter and McCarthy 1997.)

6   Questions Arising from the Study of Unplanned Speech

6.1   *The boundaries of standard English*

Better knowledge of the constructions of unplanned speech has alerted analysts to the fact that constructions previously considered non-standard are in fact used in spontaneous speech by speakers of standard and non-standard English alike. It can be difficult to say what constructions count as standard English. Unquestionably standard are *the young women whom I met* and *the young women who walk the dogs*, but *the young women what I met* is definitely non-standard.

Many linguists admit *the young women who I met* as standard or *the young women that walk the dogs*, which would be rejected by many ordinary educated users. Controversy keeps breaking out over *the data are* vs *the data is, I never got the essay started till nine o'clock* [preferred: *I did not get . . .*] and *Even if they had arrived on time, they may have missed the accident* [preferred: *. . . they might have . . .*]

Comrie (1999: 88) does not himself use *Remember the man that's house got burnt down* but considers it acceptable colloquial standard speech. Some of his colleagues disagreed and many people simply reject spoken data. A referee reviewing a paper for the *Journal of Pragmatics* declared the WH cleft *what you're going to do – you're going to go up past the allotments* a performance error. The construction is so frequent in spoken texts (planned and unplanned) that it clearly belongs to the system of spoken English.

The construction does not always receive adequate analysis. One dialogue in Carter and McCarthy (1997) contains *I'd 've thought the first thing you do when it gets as dark and as wet and as miserable as this. You turn your lights on. . . .* Why is the utterance is represented as two sentences, one of which is incomplete? The authors describe the comments ('clauses') as chained together by association and state that written English requires more complex linking, i.e. integration as discussed in section 5.2: *. . . the first thing you do is to turn your lights on* (Carter and McCarthy 1997: 113).

This section concludes with a caveat: it is dangerous to rely on one's own intuition when labeling structures as non-standard or as incorrect. With respect to *the pilot was sat in one of the seats*, Carter and McCarthy (1997: 34) comment that the speaker spoke Yorkshire dialect and that standard English requires *was sitting*. Cheshire, Edwards and Whittle (1993: 70–1) observe that BE *sat/stood* had been reported as used in certain specific areas of England. Their research showed that the structure was widespread and characteristic of 'a general non-standard or semi-standard variety of English,' although Burchfield (1981), writing for the BBC, declared *was sat/stood there* unacceptable in any circumstances. Twenty years on the structure is widely used by, e.g., reporters on the BBC *News at Ten* (though not by the presenter) and seems to be characteristic of unplanned speech. Many structures considered 'non-standard' may be misclassified.

6.2   Problems of analysis

A given construction may require different analyses in spoken and written language.

Consider (24).

(24)   It's the wine that I was complaining about (not the food)

That I was complaining about looks like a relative clause – compare *It's wine which I was complaining about* and even *It's the wine about which I was complaining*. Consider now (25)–(27).

(25)   It was because he was ill (that) we decided to return

(26)   It was in September (that) I first noticed it

(27)   It was in the restaurant that he proposed to her

That cannot be replaced by *which* – **It was because he was ill which we decided to return*, etc. – and the *that* clauses modify an adverbial clause of reason *because he was ill* and the prepositional phrases *in September* and *in the restaurant*. Quirk et al. (1985: 1387) propose that the *that* clause in IT clefts is not a relative clause (relative clauses modify nouns) but an annex clause.

Q&G discuss another major property that (allegedly) distinguishes relative clauses from annex clauses. In (28) *that* is omitted.

(28)   It was the President himself (that) spoke to me

Since *the President* is the understood subject of the relative clause, say Q&G, the complementizer cannot be omitted, as shown by (29a)

(29)   a.   *I'll lend you the book kept me awake
       b.   I'll lend you the book that kept me awake

In the presentative-existential construction in (30) *that* is absent, although *something* is the understood subject of the final clause Ø *keeps upsetting him*.

(30)   There's something (that) keeps upsetting him

Q&G are consistent; since *that* in (30) is omissible, Ø *keeps upsetting him* is an annex clause. They contrast (30) with (31), which they do analyze as having a relative clause.

(31)   *I know a man lives in China

In fact (31) is acceptable and normal in spontaneous spoken English and has a presentative-existential function. The complementizer can be omitted in other presentative-existential structures such as (32), uttered by a theatre manager, and (33), uttered by a teacher. (NB *had* in the context was not causative.)

(32)   I had a witch disappeared down a trap (= trapdoor in the stage)

(33)   we've got plenty of kids know very little about English

To sum up, Q&G's concept of annex clauses applies to formal written English but not to spontaneous spoken English. (Note the non-standard *He's a man likes his beer* where *man* is the understood subject of Ø *likes his beer*.)

(26) and (27) are also untypical of spoken English, which has the construction in (34) and (35), not mentioned in Q&G (1985), H&P (2002) or Biber et al. (1999).

(34)   It was in September when I first noticed it

(35)   It was in Edinburgh where we found the picture

Note the free relative clauses *when I first noticed it* and *where we found the picture*. *It was in September* establishes a temporal referent. *When I first noticed it* picks up the referent, adds information to it and can be glossed as 'at which time I first noticed it' or even 'that's when I first noticed it.' This structure simply bypasses Q&G's difficulties.

7   Conclusion

The syntax and discourse-organization of spontaneous speech are important for descriptions of English and for teaching non-native learners to 'speak like a native.' They are important for other reasons. Children acquire spoken language but learn written language and any adequate theories of first language acquisition must take into account the data presented above. Questions arise, legitimate but not easily answered, about how useful theories are which are based on sentences, given the difficulties in recognizing sentences in spontaneous speech.

The differences between the syntactic structures of speech and writing are relevant to typology; for instance, spontaneous spoken English and written English occupy different locations in a typology of relative clauses. The differences are also relevant to accounts of historical change, since many syntactic changes begin in spoken language and spread into writing. Last, but for many scholars first, theories of the evolution of language must take account of the central fact that spoken language evolved first, not written language.

FURTHER READING AND REFERENCES

Beaman, K. (1984) Coordination and subordination revisited: syntactic complexity in spoken and written narrative discourse. In D. Tannen (ed.), *Coherence in spoken and written discourse*. Norwood, NJ: Ablex, 45–80.

Biber, D. (1986) Spoken and written textual dimensions in English: resolving the contradictory findings. *Language* 62, 384–414.

Biber, D. (1988) *Variation across speech and writing*. Cambridge: Cambridge University Press.

Biber, D., Johansson, S., Leech, G., Conrad, S., and Finegan, E. (1999) *Longman grammar of spoken and written English*. London: Longman.

Burchfield, R. W. (1981) *The spoken word: a BBC guide*. London: BBC.

Carter, R. and McCarthy, M. (1997) *Exploring spoken English*. Cambridge: Cambridge University Press.

Chafe, W. (1994) *Discourse, consciousness and time*. Chicago: University of Chicago Press.

Cheshire, J., Edwards, V., and Whittle, P. (1993) Non-standard English and dialect levelling. In J. Milroy and L. Milroy (eds.), *Real English*. London: Longman, 53–96.

Comrie, B. (1999) Relative clauses: structure and typology on the periphery of standard English. In P. Collins and D. Lee (eds.), *The clause in English*.

Crystal, D. (1979) Neglected grammatical factors in conversational English. In S. Greenbaum, G. Leech, and J. Svartvik (eds.), *Studies in English linguistics*. London: Longman, 153–66.

Crystal, D. (1987) *The Cambridge encyclopaedia of language*. Cambridge: Cambridge University Press.

Crystal, D. (1995) *The Cambridge encyclopaedia of the English language*. Cambridge: Cambridge University Press.

Finegan, E. and Biber, D. (1994) Register and social dialect variation: an integrated approach. In E. Finegan and D. Biber (eds.), *Sociolinguistic perspectives on register*. New York: Oxford University Press, 315–47.

Greenbaum, S. and Nelson, G. (1995a) Clause relationships in spoken and written English. *Functions of Language* 2, 1–21.

Greenbaum, S. and Nelson, G. (1995b) Nuclear and peripheral clauses in speech and writing. In G. Melchers and B. Warren (eds.), *Studies in Anglistics*. Stockholm: Almqvist and Wiksell, 181–90.

Halliday, M. A. K. (1989) *Spoken and written language*. Oxford: Oxford University Press.

Huddleston, C. D., Pullum, G., et al. (2002) *The Cambridge grammar of the English language*. Cambridge: Cambridge University Press.

Labov, W. (1972) The logic of nonstandard English. In P. Giglioli (ed.), *Language and social context*. Harmondsworth: Penguin, 179–215.

McCarthy, M. (1998) *Spoken language & applied linguistics*. Cambridge: Cambridge University Press.

Macaulay, R. K. S. (1991) *Locating dialect in discourse: the language of honest men and bonny lasses in Ayr*. Oxford: Oxford University Press.

Millard, S. (2003) Relative clauses in spoken English. MA Honours dissertation, University of Edinburgh.

Miller, J. and Weinert, W. (1995) The function of LIKE in spoken language. *Journal of Pragmatics* 23, 365–93.

Miller, J. and Weinert, W. (1998) *Spontaneous spoken anguage: syntax and discourse*. Oxford: Clarendon Press.

Milroy, J. and Milroy, L. (1993) *Real English*. London: Longman.

Nattinger, J. and DeCarrico, J. (1992) *Lexical phrases and language teaching*. Oxford: Oxford University Press.

Pawley, A. and Syder, F. (1983) Two puzzles for linguistic theory: Nativelike selection and nativelike fluency. In J. C. Richards and R. W. Schmidt (eds.), *Language and communication*. London: Longman, 191–226.

Quirk, R., Greenbaum, G., Leech, G., and Svartvik, J. (1985) *A comprehensive grammar of the English language*. London: Longman.

Schiffrin, D. (1987) *Discourse markers*. Cambridge; Cambridge University Press.

Thompson, S. A. (1988) A discourse approach to the cross-linguistic category "adjective." In J. A. Hawkins (ed.), *Explaining linguistic universals*. Oxford: Basil Blackwell, 167–85.

Wackernagel-Jolles, B. (1971) *Untersuchungen zur gesprochenen Sprache: Beobachtungen zur Verknüpfung spontanen Sprechens*. Göppingen: Alfred Kümmerle.

Weinert, R. (1995) The role of formulaic language in second language acquisition: a review. *Applied Linguistics* 16 (2), 180–205.

Wray, A. (2002) *Formulaic language and the lexicon*. Cambridge: Cambridge University Press.

29 The Grammar of Conversation

PAULO QUAGLIO AND DOUGLAS BIBER

1 Introduction

Conversation has long been recognized as the most basic form of human communication, and as a result it has received a great deal of attention from scholars in linguistics, sociology, anthropology, and philosophy. These scholars have developed several different approaches to the study of conversation. Perhaps the best known of these has come to be known as Conversation Analysis. This approach, with its focus on 'talk-in-interaction,' has made important contributions to our understanding of how speakers interact by examining conversational constructs such as turn-taking (e.g., Ford, Fox, and Thompson 2002; Sacks, Schegloff, and Jefferson 1974; Schegloff 2000a, 2001), repair (e.g., Schegloff 1997a, 1997b, 2000b; Wong 2000a), and adjacency pairs (e.g., Schegloff and Sacks 1973).

Pragmatics, through its 'meaning-in-interaction' perspective, is another subfield which has contributed much to our understanding of conversation. Among other topics, this approach has focused on speech acts (e.g., Austin 1962; Sbisa 2002; Searle 1969), implicature (e.g., Grice 1975, 1989; Horn 1984), conversational relevance (e.g., Sperber and Wilson 1986a; Wilson and Sperber 2002), politeness (e.g., Bargiela-Chiappini 2003; Brown and Levinson 1987; Kasper, 1990), and cross-cultural pragmatics (e.g., Blum-Kulka, House-Edmondson, and Kasper 1989; Boxer 2002; Spencer-Oatey and Jiang 2003). Descriptive studies in pragmatics range from a focus on the meanings of individual expressions to the overall organization of conversations. For example, some studies have focused on the pragmatic functions of discourse markers (e.g., Condon 2001 on *OK*; Erman 1986 on *you know, you see,* and *I mean*; Schiffrin 1987 on a range of discourse markers; Schourup 2001 on *well*), formulaic expressions (e.g., Ward and Birner 1993 on *and everything*), and conversational routines and phraseology (e.g., Aijmer 1996; Altenberg 1998; Coulmas 1981). At the other extreme, some studies of conversation have focused on information flow (e.g., Chafe 1987; Fox 1987; Fox and Thompson 1990; Prince 1981), and topic and cohesion (e.g., Hardy 1996; Tannen 1984, 1989).

Surprisingly, it has been less common to investigate the grammatical characteristics of conversation as a variety or 'register.' However, a comparison of conversation to other registers shows that it is as distinctive in its characteristic grammatical features as it is in its exchange structure and interactive pragmatics. In the present chapter, we survey these distinctive grammatical characteristics of conversation.[1]

2 Characteristic Grammatical Features of Conversation

In the present section, we survey the typical grammatical characteristics of conversation. Although these features could occur in any register, in actual use they are especially common in conversation. For example, the three basic clause types – declarative, interrogative, imperative – are equally grammatical in any register. In actual use, however, we find that two of the clause types are strongly associated with conversation: interrogative and imperative clauses are relatively common in conversation but rare in most other registers.[2]

Several studies have undertaken detailed investigations of specific grammatical features in conversation. Table 29.1 surveys some of the most important of these studies.

A comprehensive survey of the typical grammatical features of conversation is given in the *Longman grammar of spoken and written English* (Biber, Johansson, Leech, Conrad, and Finegan 1999). The LGSWE describes the range of grammatical features in English and compares the use of these features in four major registers: conversation, fiction, newspapers, and academic prose. The register comparisons are based on analysis of a representative corpus of texts (the LSWE Corpus) containing approximately 5 million words from each register (1999: 24–35). This approach enables empirical investigations of the extent to which grammatical features are characteristic of a given register. For example, returning to the use of interrogative and imperative clauses in conversation, corpus analysis in the LGSWE shows that there are over 20,000 questions per million words in conversation, compared to only around 500 per million words in newspapers or academic prose (1999: 211). Similarly, there are about 10,000 imperatives per million words in conversation versus only 1,000 per million words in newspapers or academic prose (1999: 221). Thus, these grammatical features can be considered characteristic of conversation by virtue of their distribution: although they can be used in all registers, they turn out to be much more common in conversation.

A survey of the findings reported in LGSWE shows that conversational features come from most structural categories. Table 29.2 lists several of the major grammatical features that are especially common in conversation. Three word classes are especially prevalent in conversation: verbs, adverbs, and pronouns. For verbs, there are several specific features that are characteristic of conversation. For example, mental verbs (e.g., *know, think, see, want, mean*), phrasal verbs, modal and semi-modal verbs, present tense, and progressive

Table 29.1 Selected studies that describe typical grammatical characteristics of conversation

Author/study	Type of study	Selected findings
Aarts, F. (1993). Who, whom, that and ø in two corpora of spoken English.	Empirical Corpora: SEU and LLC	• In subject position, *who* is far more frequent than *that* in both corpora. • In direct object position, *that* or ø (54 instances) are more frequent than *who* or *whom* (13 cases).
Aarts, F. (1994). Imperative sentences in a corpus of English conversation.	Empirical Corpus: LLC	• 87% of imperative sentences are (– LET type).
Altenberg, B. (1991). Amplifier collocations in spoken English.	Empirical Corpus: LLC	• Of the 21 maximizers analyzed, only 9 occur in recurrent combinations. Five (*quite, absolutely, perfectly, entirely, completely*) account for 95% of the examples. • Most frequent maximizers: *quite* (230 tokens, 45 combination types), *absolutely* (70 tokens, 24 combination types), *perfectly* (39 tokens, 10 combination types). • Of the 15 boosters analyzed, 7 (*very, so, very much, terribly, jolly, extremely, awfully*) account for 98% of the examples. • Most frequent boosters: *very* (1669 tokens, 204 combination types), *so* (372 tokens, 66 combination types), *very much* (134 tokens, 6 combination types), *terribly* (39 tokens, 14 combination types).
Altenberg, B. (1993). On the functions of *such* in spoken and written English.	Empirical Corpora: LLC and LOB	• Relative frequencies of intensifiers *such* in LLC: 75.9 per 500,000 words. • Relative frequencies of intensifiers *such* in LOB: 10.0 per 500,000 words.
Bäcklund, I. (1986). Beat until stiff: conjunction-headed abbreviated clauses in spoken and written English.	Empirical Corpora: LLC and LOB	• Clauses introduced by conditional *if* are considerably more frequent in speech (semantic category). • Verbless clause is the most frequent type in speech (usually formulaic: e.g., *if necessary; as soon as possible; if so*) (structural type).

Table 29.1 (*continued*)

Author/study	Type of study	Selected findings
Biber, D. and Conrad, S. (1999). Lexical bundles in conversation and academic prose.	Empirical Corpus: LSWEC	• Conversation: (a) 90% of lexical bundles are declarative or interrogative clause segments; (b) 50% of these begin with a personal pronoun; (c) most frequent 4-word lexical bundles: *I don't know what, I don't want to, I was going to.* • Academic prose: (a) 60% of lexical bundles are parts of noun phrases or prepositional phrases (e.g., *as a result of*); (b) most frequent 4-word bundles: *in the case of, on the other hand, one of the most, the nature of the,* etc.
Biber, D. (2004). Conversational text types: a multi-dimensional analysis.	Empirical Corpus: LSWEC	Three major 'dimensions' of variation distinguish among conversational text types: 'Informational versus involved discourse,' 'stance-focused versus context-focused discourse,' and 'narrative-focused discourse.'
Carter, R. and McCarthy, M. (1999). The English get-passive in spoken discourse: description and implications for an interpersonal grammar.	Empirical Corpus: CANCODE	• BE passive seems to be the unmarked form. • GET passive highlights stance and occurs mostly in negative circumstances, as judged by the speaker.
Greenbaum, S. and Nelson, G. (1995). Clause relationships in spoken and written English.	Empirical Corpora: subsets of spoken and written texts from the British component of ICE	• 50.4% of clauses in conversation: *paratactic clauses* (tag questions or parenthetics), *fragments* (NPs or Prep phrases that serve as responses to a previous clause), *non-clauses* (hesitations, interjections, etc), and *incomplete clauses.* • Major differences are found in text categories within each mode (written and spoken): conversation: 63.2% of clauses are simple (as opposed to 44.7% in the written mode). conversation: 60.9% of clauses are clusters without subordination (as opposed to only 31% in the written mode).

Table 29.1 (*continued*)

Author/study	Type of study	Selected findings
		• Factors other than the speech/ writing differences affect the use of coordination and subordination in discourse. These might include the degree of planning and formality.
Meyer, C. (1995). Coordination ellipsis in spoken and written American English.	Empirical Corpora: Brown and ICE	• Overwhelming preference in speech for full unellipted forms: 60% of the total of 63 (full ellipsis + partial ellipsis + full forms). • High frequency of full forms makes repetition much more important in speech. • When ellipsis occurred, all were in the beginning of the second conjunct (e.g., *He stopped doing that and* [ ] *spoke strange words . . .*).
Stenström, A-B (1999). He was really gormless – She's bloody crap: girls, boys and intensifiers.	Empirical Corpus: COLT	• Most frequent adjective premodifiers: *really* (659), *bloody* (70), *fucking* (40). • Items occur predominantly with adjectives in predicative position. • Regarding semantic prosody: all premodifiers (including *completely* and *absolutely*; excluding *really*) predominated in negative context. • Intensifiers were more frequent in the girls' conversations (in a subcorpus of 21,000 words).
Taguchi, N. (2002). A Comparative analysis of discourse markers in English conversational registers.	Empirical Corpora: LSWEC and T2K-SWAL	• Discourse markers *you know* and *I mean* were more prominent in family and professor-student conversations compared with service encounter dialogues, reflecting the length of discourse and high personal involvement. • *OK* was much more common in service encounter dialogues, marking transitions in service exchanges. • *Oh* appeared most frequently in family/friends conversations because the conversations often involved multiple topics, providing more occasions for signaling topic shifts.

Table 29.1 (*continued*)

Author/study	Type of study	Selected findings
Tao, H. and McCarthy, M. (2001). Understanding non-restrictive *which*-clauses in spoken English, which is not an easy thing.	Empirical Corpora: CANCODE and CSAE	• Preferred syntactic configuration of NRRCs: *which* + modal expressions (including discourse markers) + *is* with the discourse function of *evaluation*. • Functional types: 62% of NRRCs are evaluative; 31% expansion. • 96% produced by the same speaker.
Tottie, G. (1986). The importance of being adverbial: adverbials of focusing and contingency in spoken and written English.	Empirical Corpora: subset of LLC and subset of LOB	• Inverse relationship between focusing and contingency adverbials: Spoken (117 focusing vs. 245 contingency adverbials); written (146 focusing vs. 208 contingency adverbials). • *Just* was the most frequent exclusive adverbial in conversation: 67% (61/91). • Most common meanings of *just*: simply, merely, only. • Much more common in conversation: condition and reason/cause; reason/cause: finite clauses (*because*); adverbials of condition: finite *if* clauses.
Tottie, G. (1991). Conversational style in British and American English: the case of backchannels.	Empirical Corpora: CSAE and LLC	• Most frequent (American): *yeah* (40%), *mhm* (34%), *hm* (11%), *right/unhhunh/uhuh* (4%). • Most frequent (British): *yes* (44%), *m* (36%), *yeah* (4%). • Backchannels are more common in American conversation (16 per minute vs. 5 per minute in the British data).
Viitanen, O. (1986). On the position of *only* in English conversation.	Empirical Corpus: LLC	• 83% of adjunct *only* were in pre-verbal position. • Most frequent focusing adjuncts: *only* (90% of total of 211), *merely*, *alone*, *solely*.

CANCODE: Cambridge and Nottingham Corpus of Discourse in English
COLT: The Bergen Corpus of London Teenage Language
CSAE: Corpus of Spoken American English
ICE: International Corpus of English
LLC: London-Lund Corpus (spoken)
LOB: Lancaster-Oslo/Bergen Corpus (written)
LSWEC: Longman Grammar of Spoken and Written English Corpus
SEU: The Survey of English Usage Corpus
T2K-SWAL: TOEFL 2000 Spoken and Written Academic Language Corpus

aspect verb phrases are more common in conversation than other registers. Adverbs and pronouns show similar patterns of use. For example, simple adverbs are more common in conversation than in most other registers, especially when they express stance meanings. Pronouns are also prevalent in conversation, especially first and second person pronouns. Sometimes these patterns of use can be very specific. For example, the demonstrative pronoun *that* is very common in conversation but rare in most other general registers; in contrast, the demonstrative pronoun *this* is common in the written registers. Thus compare:

Conversation

(1)   I don't want to think about <u>that</u>.

(2)   I don't know if we can change <u>that</u> or not.

Academic writing

(3)   <u>This</u> can be seen in the spectrum of benzyl acetate . . .

Many of the grammatical features typical of conversation reflect the dense use of short, simple clauses (e.g., verbs, adverbs, and pronouns instead of complex noun phrases). However, it is more surprising that several dependent clause features are also much more common in conversation than other registers. These are mostly complement clauses controlled by verbs, especially *that*-clauses and *WH*-clauses. These features are often used to express 'stance' in conversation: the controlling verb expresses the stance, while the complement clause contains the new information. For example,

(4)   I <u>think</u> [that the kids will learn to like that].

(5)   I <u>hope</u> [that uh Kathleen faxed that order].

(6)   I <u>know</u> [what you're talking about].

Certain kinds of adverbial clauses are also typical of conversation, especially conditional clauses and reason/cause clauses. In contrast, postnominal clauses and noun complement clauses are relatively rare in conversation.

3   Functional Correlates of Conversational Features

The characteristic grammatical features of conversation listed in tables 29.1 and 29.2 are not arbitrary; rather, these features are functional, associated with

Table 29.2 Grammatical features that are especially common in conversation

Feature	Pattern of use
Verbs and verb phrases	
Lexical verbs: overall pp. 65, 359	Almost 1/3 of all content words in conversation are lexical verbs. Verbs are much more common in conversation than in informational written registers
Lexical verbs: specific verbs pp. 374–8	The verbs *get, go, know, think* are extremely common in conversation
Mental verbs pp. 366, 368	Mental verbs (e.g., *know, think, see, want, mean*) are more common in conversation
Copular verb *get* pp. 438, 444	Common only in conversation; e.g., *get ready, get worse.*
Main verb *do* pp. 432	Common only in conversation; e.g., *you do it*
Phrasal verbs pp. 409, 424	Common in conversation and fiction
Present tense pp. 456ff	c. 70% of all verb phrases in conversation are present tense
Progressive aspect pp. 462ff	Common in conversation and fiction
Modal verbs pp. 486ff	Much more common in conversation than in the written registers; especially *can, will, would*
Semi-modal verbs pp. 486ff	Common only in conversation; especially *have to, (had) better, (have) got to, used to*
Adverbs	
Simple adverbs pp. 540–2	Most common in conversation
Adjectival forms used as adverbs pp. 542–3	Common only in conversation; e.g., *It's running real good*
Amplifiers pp. 564–6	Most common in conversation, especially *very, so, really/real, too*

Table 29.2 *(continued)*

Feature	Pattern of use
Adverbs for place deixis pp. 796, 799	Most common in conversation, especially *there, here*
Restrictive adverb *just* pp. 796, 798–9	Common only in conversation
Stance adverbs pp. 859, 867–71	Most common in conversation, especially *really, actually, like, maybe*
Simple adverbs as linking adverbials pp. 880, 884–9	Most common in conversation, especially *so, then, though, anyway*
Pronouns	
Personal pronouns pp. 92, 235, 237, 333, 334	Most common in conversation, especially *I, you, it*
Demonstrative pronoun *that* pp. 349–50	Extremely common only in conversation
Pronoun *one* with specific reference pp. 353–4	Most common in conversation, e.g., *that one, the other one*
Simple clause features	
Questions pp. 211ff	Common only in conversation
Imperatives pp. 221–2	Common only in conversation
Stranded prepositions in WH-questions pp. 106–7	Most common in conversation
Coordination tags pp. 116–17	Common only in conversation, e.g., *or something* (But note the use of *etc.* in writing)
NOT negation pp. 159ff	Most common in conversation
AND as clausal (vs. phrasal) Coordinator p. 81	The preferred use in conversation (80% of all occurrences of *and* connect clauses)

Table 29.2 *(continued)*

Feature	Pattern of use
Dependent clause features	
Verb + *that* complement clause pp. 668–70, 674–5	Most common in conversation, especially *think, know, guess* + *that*-clause
Complementizer *that* omission (vs. retention) pp. 680–3	The preferred use in conversation (over 80% of all *that*-clauses omit the complementizer)
Verb + WH complement clauses pp. 688–9	Most common in conversation, especially *know* + WH-clause
want + *to*-clause pp. 710–13	Extremely common in conversation; rare in expository writing
try and + VERB (vs. *try to* VERB) pp. 738–9	Common only in conversation
keep/start + *-ing* complement clause pp. 746–7	Most common in conversation
Conditional adverbial clauses pp. 821ff	Most common in conversation
Reason/cause adverbial clauses pp. 821ff	Most common in conversation
Other features	
Lexical bundles pp. 993–4, 996–7	Most common in conversation, especially bundles with a verb
VERB *and* VERB binomial phrases pp. 1031–2	Most common in conversation
Contractions pp. 1128–32	Common only in conversation
'Special' features of conversation Chapter 14	Found only in conversation (and fictional dialogue); e.g., pauses, repeats, repairs, blends, tags, inserts (e.g., greetings, attention signals, response forms, expletives), vocatives

Source: Based on a survey of the *Longman Grammar of Spoken and Written English*

the distinctive discourse circumstances of conversation. As McCarthy and Carter (1995: 211) put it, "speakers regularly make [grammatical] choices which reflect the interactive and interpersonal nature of the communication." For example, because conversation is inherently interactive, it is one of the few registers to make extensive use of questions (a grammatical feature that normally requires a specific addressee). Because it is produced in real time, conversation is characterized by many different grammatical reductions and omissions (e.g., contractions, ellipsis).

Chapter 14 in the LGSWE describes the situational characteristics of conversation and provides a detailed survey of distinctive grammatical features associated with those characteristics. Four of the most important situational characteristics are:

- conversation takes place in real time;
- conversation takes place in a shared context and therefore avoids elaboration or specification of meaning;
- conversation is interactive;
- conversational participants talk about their own feelings and attitudes; they express stance and employ a vernacular range of expressions.

In the present section, we identify grammatical features that are especially prevalent in conversation because they have a functional relationship to one or more of these situational characteristics. Several of these features can be associated with more than one situational characteristic; we point out examples of this type in the following sections. The examples here are taken from the American English conversation subcorpus of the LSWE Corpus.

3.1   *Conversation takes place in real time*

Perhaps the most obvious situational characteristic of conversation is the pressure resulting from the quick production of language. Speakers simply do not have time to plan or edit their utterances. As a result, speakers rely on a wide range of reduced structures and features that have vague reference. It is easier and quicker to produce a reduced form (such as a contraction) than a fuller grammatical form. Similarly, it is easier to choose a vague reference (e.g., *that kind of thing*) than to be explicit about the specific reference. Given the pressures of real-time production, speakers tend to opt for these easier and more efficient forms. Further, the need for precision in conversation is much less important than in written registers.

In addition to contractions, conversation relies heavily on other reduced forms, including complementizer *that* omission, ellipsis, and non-clausal utterances. Conversation also makes extensive use of devices with vague reference, including pronouns, vague nouns (e.g., *stuff, thing*), hedges (e.g., *sort of, kind of, like*), and coordination tags (e.g., *and stuff like that*).

The shared context of conversation allows speakers to use these reduced/ vague forms and still be understood. Out of context, many of these devices would not be meaningful, but listeners usually have no difficulty understanding the intended meaning in context. We thus return to a discussion of several of these features in 3.2 below.

The real-time pressure of conversation is also reflected in special grammatical features that are unique to spoken language (and some written representations of speech). These are referred to as 'performance phenomena' in Biber et al. (1999: ch. 14). These features include: dysfluencies, the add-on strategy, and non-clausal units.

Dysfluencies

(7) A: I haven't done the any of *the the* {repeat} follow thank you stuff to Janet <name> *um* {hesitator} and that was *I I* {repeat} just had that on my list to do because *um* . . . {pause}want to finalize the date for that other stuff, but that needs to be copied to whole slew of people <unclear>

　　B: Speaking of Janet <name> you know something, I still don't have <unclear> videos for front of <unclear>. I mean if she {incomplete sentence}

　　A: Did he give it to you?

(8) A: This is really neat. This is um . . . {false start} can I get this?

　　B: Probably.

Examples (7) and (8) show instances of dysfluencies, which include pauses, hesitators, repeats, incomplete sentences, and false starts (labeled in {}). Pauses, hesitators, and repeats give the speaker more time to think about what he/she wants to say, reflecting the pressures of real-time production; these features can also reflect underlying attitudes, such as insecurity. Incomplete sentences often occur in the end of a turn as a result of an interruption by the interlocutor, as in (7). False starts are essentially incomplete sentences that become reformulated as a more meaningful utterance, expressing a change in the discourse path of the speaker, as in (8).

The add-on strategy

Another performance phenomenon is the *add-on strategy*, where speakers produce long utterances that consist of a sequence of finite clause-like units; for example:

(9) I think probably of the reason why Gloria and I are still so close is because . . . when I ca = when I divorced my husband and moved out here from New Jersey she was just divorcing her husband and I moved into one half of the duplex and she moved into the other half and for five years we were neighbors and raised our kids together.

Speakers produce utterances like (9) with little difficulty, and listeners also have no problem understanding these structures. One possible explanation is that these utterances should be understood as sequences of clause-like chunks, rather than a single structure with multiple levels of embedding (Biber et al. 1999: 1068; see also Chafe 1994).

Because conversation takes place in real time, speakers also often use 'utterance launchers' as attention getters, providing a frame for the listener to interpret the following information; for example:

(10) A: Yeah I know. It takes up this much room and they're big.
      B: *I tell you what*, those things are really thick.

Non-clausal units

Non-clausal units include inserts (e.g., discourse markers, polite formulas), minimal responses, ellipses, non-clausal questions, and vocatives. These forms reflect the real-time production pressures of conversation, but they also serve important discourse organizing functions. For example:

(11) A: *Well* let's see, tonight should be much more active I think.
      B: *Well* let me be off on my little rounds.
      A: *Okay.*
      B: *Good luck* with the survey.
      A: *Thanks.*

(12) A: It's eighty there tomorrow.
      B: *Wow.*
      A: And rain.

Example (11) illustrates how these features are frequently used together in conversation: *well* and *okay* are discourse markers; *good luck* is an example of ellipsis; and *thanks* is a polite formula. Example (12) shows a simple response form that expresses speaker stance.

Condensed directives and statements can also be considered non-clausal units that reflect the pressures of real-time production:

Condensed directive

(13) ... There you go. Throw it. *Careful of Mia's head.*

Condensed statement

(14) A: I would like a, an egg and a whole wheat English muffin.
      B: You keep doing this to me. *No more cooking eggs in my kitchen.* It grosses me out.

Such non-clausal units reflect other functional considerations besides real-time production: shared context, avoidance of syntactic elaboration, 'interactiveness,' and expression of stance. In addition, non-minimal responses (e.g., *right* or *good*) are used to indicate good listenership (McCarthy 2002).

Lexical bundles

Conversation relies heavily on prefabricated sequences of words that are used as extended lexical building blocks; one type of prefabricated expression is referred to as 'lexical bundles' in LGSWE (ch. 13). For example:

(15) A: There's his birthday cake, *I don't know why*, *I don't know what* got in these pictures, that's his fifth birthday.
      B: Oh, you made this?
      A: Mhm.

Lexical bundles facilitate real-time production, but they also serve important discourse functions (relating to stance, discourse organization, and referential functions; see Biber, Conrad, and Cortes 2004).

Finally, repetitions can also be regarded as a reflection of real-time production. However, repetitions can also serve interactive purposes, reflecting speaker involvement, and conveying participatory or ratifying listenership (Tannen 1989; see also Johnstone 1994). For example:

(16) A: Or do you want to take this and roll for a full house? Or there's two pairs isn't there?
      ?: <unclear>
      B: *There's no two pair.*
      A: *There's no two pair.*

3.2 *Conversation takes place in a shared context and therefore avoids elaboration of meaning*

Shared context is a major factor associated with the use of conversational features. Speakers in conversation share the same physical location and the same time; as a result, they can make direct reference to that shared place and time. Speakers also usually share some background knowledge about one another: past histories, likes and dislikes, etc. This personal shared knowledge is also part of the larger context of conversation.

This shared knowledge is often reflected linguistically in the simplification of grammatical structures. In addition to the high frequency of pronoun reference (especially *I* and *you*), conversation is characterized by a high frequency of ellipses, substitute pro-forms (e.g., *one/ones*, *do it/that*), deictic expressions (e.g., *this, that, there*), hedges, and vague language (e.g., vague coordination tags, nouns of vague reference).

Examples (17), (18), and (19) illustrate three types of ellipsis: situational, across turns, and in sequences of questions and answers.

Ellipsis/deictic expressions

(17)   A: ↔ think you could fall asleep there?
       B: Yeah ↔.

(18)   A: What ↔ you gonna order, Bry?
       B: ↔ a cheeseburger.

(19)   A: You ↔ better go check it Wayne.
       B: Oh, I can't ↔ because I don't have enough gas to go out there.

Situational ellipsis is characterized by the omission of content words and auxiliary verbs in unstressed positions, which are usually easily retrievable from the context. The first turn in example (17) shows the omission of the auxiliary *do* and the pronoun *you*; the auxiliary *are* is omitted in the first turn of example (18); and the first turn in example (19) omits the unstressed contraction *'d*.

In (18), speaker B responds only with the new information (*a cheeseburger*), rather than repeating the full clause (*I'm going to order . . .*), illustrating an instance of ellipsis in a question and answer sequence. In (19), speaker B similarly does not feel the need to repeat the full verb phrase (*go check it*) from the preceding turn. This type of ellipsis does not occur in the first turn of an adjacency pair; rather, it is as a reaction or response to a previous utterance. In this case, the first turn in the adjacency pair establishes the context and the basis for comprehension, allowing ellipsis in the second turn (Eggins and Slade 1997).

Ellipses are highly characteristic of spontaneous speech. They contribute functionally to speeding up the communicative process as they allow the speaker to reduce the length of the turn and avoid unnecessary repetitions. As a consequence, elliptic utterances have the effect of 'keeping the conversation alive' as interlocutors implicitly (perhaps unconsciously) reveal their interest in one another's participation in the communicative event.

Examples (17) and (19) also contain instances of deictic expressions (*there* and *out there*, respectively), which are also very common in conversation. Deictics require a specific context for the speaker to identify the intended reference. The shared context of conversation provides that information. These deictic elements are often accompanied by paralinguistic information, such as gestures, identifying the specific aspects of the context that should be considered.

Substitute pro-forms
Substitute pro-forms are also often deictic and recoverable only from the context; for example:

(20)   A: *It* looks the best on you Kate with your long hair.
        B: I like it better when it's standing up straight. Could you do *that* one
             more time?

In (20), Speaker A is pointing at some object, referred to as 'it.' (The specific reference of 'it' was not identified in the preceding discourse.) Kate then performs some action, and Speaker B asks her to do 'that' again. Here again, the action is never identified in language, but the participants understand the reference of 'that' from the context.

Conversational hedges

Because conversational participants rely heavily on shared context, they also tend to avoid elaboration or precise specification of meaning. Elaboration of meaning can, in fact, be perceived as a hindrance to the communicative process because it requires longer turns and reduces the need for clarification, which, ultimately, reduces the interactiveness of the communicative event. This lack of precision is reflected in the high frequency of hedges, which create a sense of vagueness.

(21)   It's *sort of* a an honor system we're doing here.

(22)   I think he's *kind of* getting burned out on everything. I can't say for certain but that's just a feeling I get.

(23)   I'd hate to *like* get in a problem while she's gone.

Although *sort of* and *kind of* express vagueness, they can at the same time "make it easier for the listener to pick out the specific referent the speaker has in mind if the linguistic expression is not exact" (Aijmer 1984: 122). For example, in (21), *honor system* might not have been perceived by the speaker as the most adequate term for the situation. By using *sort of* the speaker acknowledges the inadequacy of the expression and counts on the interlocutor to interpret the term based on the context shared by them.

As pointed out earlier, grammatical devices can be related to more than one of the discourse circumstances of conversation. Hedges, for example, are also used to "achieve intimacy with the listener and to maintain the informal tone of the conversation" (Aijmer 1987: 5). Such informality, together with the explicit marking of vagueness, can lead interlocutors to engage more actively in the conversation (e.g., by asking for clarification), thus making the communicative process more interactive.

Hedges also have the effect of mitigating some potential threats to face resulting from overly direct statements (McCarthy and Carter 1997). Interestingly, the speaker in (22) adds an 'explanation' to the hedged statement, in an apparent attempt to further reduce the potential threat to face (*I can't say for certain but that's just a feeling I get*). In (23), the use of *like* has the effect of minimizing the impact that *get in a problem* could create. However, in many instances, it is not clear if *that* is used as a hedge, a filler (allowing for processing time), or as a marker of focus (see Dailey-O'Cain 2000 and Underhill 1988).

Quantifying hedges

Quantifying hedges are often expressed with *like* and the suffix *-ish* added to quantities (especially time expressions):

(24)   There were *like* four girls behind the counter and there were only two clients . . .

(25)   A: Okay so what time will you be back on Sunday?
        B: We're going to try to get out of there about six so probably figure about *oneish*, *twoish* and if you got something going on then I'll just you know.

In (24), *like* has the sense of *about* as *four girls* contrasts with *only two clients*. Example (25) illustrates a form of hedge that is becoming more and more common in American English. Instead of using *about* or *around* a particular time, the speaker adds *ish* to the numeral (one*ish*). Interestingly, in this example, the speaker uses two hedges, adding to the inaccuracy of the utterance (*about oneish, twoish*). These hedges create a sense of vagueness that can only be interpreted on the basis of shared context: the interlocutor has to interpret the 'time span' that the suffix *ish* represents by relying on the broader context and the personal relationship he/she has with the speaker.

Vague coordination tags

Vague coordination tags are also frequent in conversation; for example:

(26)   So like I'm getting really good at at Excel. [laugh] I'm making charts and *stuff like that* you know.

(27)   There are some things that are <unclear> watching sports and watching news and *things like that*.

(28)   And they must have done all kinds of tests *and stuff*.

(29)   We could all go to the gym *or something* I suppose.

Coordination tags can take many forms, including *stuff like that* (26), *things like that* (27), *and stuff* (28), and *or something* (29). These forms not only suggest vagueness, but are also a form of reduction as the speaker refrains from itemizing other examples of the same thing he/she is talking about. *Or something* in (29) also suggests flexibility in the interpersonal relationship as the speaker privileges the interlocutor's preferences. This simplification addresses the requirements of face-to-face conversation as it speeds up the communicative process by reducing the potential length of the turn. It is up to the interlocutor(s) to 'fill in the gaps' created by these expressions and interpret them according to what the context suggests.

Nouns of vague reference

Elaboration of meaning is also avoided through the use of nouns of vague reference:

(30)   Then we have *stuff* for stir fry

(31)   Diane, did you want this *thing* kept?

(32)   My mother was very, is very superstitious. We walk down the street, she won't step on cracks, she won't split, <laugh> and I thought that *stuff* used to drive me crazy.

Thing(s) and *stuff* are extremely common in conversation. In addition to creating a sense of vagueness, the lack of specification saves processing time; the shared context usually allows the interlocutor to understand what the speaker means by these nouns. However, in (32) the use of *stuff* also suggests that there were other things that his/her mother used to do, perhaps piquing the interlocutor's curiosity to ask for more detailed information.

3.3   Conversation is interactive

Conversation is interactive: it is co-constructed by all participants, who take turns building the discourse. It also makes direct reference to those participants. Thus, we find frequent first and second person pronouns (referring to the two immediate participants), and frequent questions and imperatives (clause types that make direct reference to the addressee). Biber et al. (1999, ch. 14) also point out that this interactiveness is reflected in the high frequency of features such as negatives, sequences of question-answer, attention signals, backchannels, vocatives, and non-clausal fragmented questions.

Non-clausal questions

(33)   A: Back the van into the door.
      B: *What for?*
      A: So I can load up some glass <unclear>

(34)   A: Cokes and *what else?*
      B: Orange juice.

(35)   A: . . . Are they hiring?
       B: Yeah. <unclear>
       A: *Really?*
       B: So is the Red Bull.

The non-clausal questions in (33), (34), and (35) are related to the need to speed up the communicative process. *"Really?"* (35) also adds stance to the utterance as it suggests not only interest in what the interlocutor is saying, but also surprise (see Stenstrom, 1986 for a comparison of *really* in speech and writing).

Vocatives

(36)   Hey *guys* keep uh, this, this Saturday at nine open.

(37)   Hey, *dude*, we getting tickets today, huh?

The vocatives in (36) and (37) have an attitudinal function implying familiarity and adding to the informality of the discourse as they "establish or maintain a social relationship between the speaker and the addressee(s)" (Leech 1999: 108).

Discourse markers

(38)   A: Did he shake you?
       B: *Well I mean* he was like pushing on the bed *you know*, so I must have been.

(39)   A: *Yeah.* And I talk to Carol a little bit more often, *you know.*
       B: *Yeah.*

Another important group of features associated with the interactive nature of conversation is discourse markers, such as *well*, *you know*, and *I mean. Well* usually occurs in initial position, as in (38), providing a discourse frame for the interpretation of the following utterance (see Schiffrin 1985). *I mean* and *you know* (39) can have a 'softening effect' (Altenberg 1984) and usually occur in the middle of an utterance (see Erman 1986 for a discussion of *you know*, *I mean*, and *I see*). Discourse markers "are typically used to signal the pragmatic or discoursal role of the speaker's utterance, dynamically shaping it to the ongoing exchange" (Biber et al. 1999: 1046).

Utterance final so . . .

(40)   A: Do you know what they are?
       B: Started the time I came back to Santa Fe and they have the smog
            so . . .
       A: I know . . .

(41)   A: irreplaceable. I mean, they can't bring any of those back and there
            were no copies, *so* . . .
       B: They're somewhere, you know. [unclear]

The use of *so* as a discourse marker at the end of an uninterrupted turn is a
common conversational feature in American English. In (40) and (41), the
speakers reach the end of their utterances as if they were going to conclude
with an explanation. Instead, they give the interlocutor the task of understanding what they mean from the context. In addition, this use of *so* marks the
end of an utterance, an indication that the floor is being transferred to the
interlocutor. This is an interesting form of reduction at the discourse level
and a clear indication of how speakers perceive the communicative process as
interactive and co-constructed, as potential silence gaps are avoided and the
conversation is thus 'kept alive.'

3.4   Conversational participants talk about their own feelings and attitudes; they express stance and employ a vernacular range of expressions

In conversation, speakers often express their feelings, attitudes, concerns, and
evaluations. Biber et al. (1999: ch. 12) describe how a range of grammatical
constructions are utilized to convey such assessments of stance. Several of
these devices are especially common in conversation (see 1999: 978–86),
including modals/semi-modals, stance adverbials (e.g., *really*, *actually*), and
certain kinds of complement clause (especially *that*-clauses controlled by
mental verbs such as *think*, *know*, and *guess*).

In addition, several common speech acts in conversation reflect stance, such
as requests, greetings, offers, and apologies. These are often associated with
formulaic openings (e.g., *would you* . . . , *could you* . . .) and inserts marking
politeness (e.g., *thanks*, *please*, *sorry*). Stance can also be expressed through the
use of interjections and exclamations, which "express a mental reaction to a
stimulus" (Aijmer 1987: 61) and often co-occur with evaluative adjectives:

(42)   *Oh*, what a *beautiful* house.

Stance adverbs

(43)   That feels good *actually*.

(44)   I think. I don't *really* know enough about it. It's *probably* too subtle for
       me . . .

Actually (43), *really*, and *probably* (44) are some of the most frequent stance
adverbs in conversation. *Probably* expresses doubt, and *really* and *actually* can
have different pragmatic functions depending on factors such as intonation

and position in the utterance (see Aijmer 1986 for a description of *actually*). Conrad and Biber (2000) note that the high frequency of these adverbials is "consistent with several contextual characteristics of conversation, particularly the focus on interpersonal interactions, the conveying of personal assessments and opinions, and the lack of time for planning or revision which makes precise word choice difficult" (2000: 65).

Expletives

Like interjections, expletives are often utilized by speakers to show stance:

(45)   Huh, *damn* garden. I don't think I'm gonna grow a garden this year.

(46)   A: He's gonna create it too and we'll all finally be fabulously wealthy.
       B: *Fuck you.* [laugh]
       A: [laugh]

These forms are instrumental not only in the production of insults, but also in the establishment of an informal, friendly atmosphere between interlocutors. In (45) the speaker expresses his personal (negative) feelings toward the garden. In (46) the expletive, reinforced by the presence of laughs, is not intended as an insult, but rather as an expression of informality signaling closeness of relationship between the interlocutors. (See Stenstrom 1991 and Wachal 2002 for a fuller discussion of taboo expressions/expletives.)

New uses of ALL and SO

New forms are constantly being introduced in conversation, often for stance functions. The words *all* and *so* have recently taken on new grammatical functions that correspond to new stance-related functions:

(47)   So, that was nice 'cause she was *all* impressed with everything I did.

(48)   He's *all* making it sound innocent . . .

(49)   There are days where I'm just like *so wanting* to capture everything I think and just feel god, it's amazing.

(50)   A: Oh, look at that.
       B: This is *so* the symbol of <unclear>, this here.

(51)   A: How long does it take?
       B: A very short time.
       A: *So not* long.

One of the new uses of *all* in American English functions as "a marker of the speaker's upcoming unique characterization of some entity in the discourse"

(Waksler 2001: 128). This marker functions as an intensifier, denoting attitudinal stance. In (47) and (48) the speakers prepare the 'attitudinal setting' with *all* to make sure that their interlocutors understand the emphasis they wish to add to the statement. Having a similar effect in the discourse are the new grammatical functions of the adverbial intensifier *so* modifying a verb (49), a noun (50), and an adjective split by the negator *not* (51). The marked position of *so* enhances the emphatic content of the statement.

Vernacular expressions

In addition to stance expressions, speakers in conversation tend to employ 'vernacular' expressions. The definition of 'vernacular' is problematic; vernacular is opposed to 'standard,' but "in practice, there is a continuous range of acceptability [of these expressions]. At one extreme we find widely used and widely accepted colloquialisms . . . ; at the opposite extremes there are stigmatized forms" (Biber et al. 1999: 1121). We provide several examples below, mostly of morphosyntactic variants, since "morphosyntax is the area where most differences occur between standard and vernacular grammar" (1999: 1125).

Stigmatized variants

The variants *ain't*, *Me and* . . . (in subject position), and double negatives are examples of stigmatized forms:

(52)   A: I'm unavailable
       B: For what reason
       A: <laugh> *it ain't* my fault

(53)   . . . I was hoping that maybe *me and Greg* could like travel once a year . . .

(54)   A: I *don't* have *no* money.
       B: You're too old to whine . . .

Ain't is often used to convey humor, and can also be used to express the speaker's awareness of inadequacy (52). *Me and* . . . (53) is stigmatized for two reasons: the accusative personal pronoun (*me*) is used in subject position, and it is fronted. The use of double negatives, as in (54), is also considered non-standard. These stigmatized forms are completely absent in formal writing and also restricted in speech to particular social or regional dialects.

There's + plural notional subject

(55)   There's a lot of hospitals in Santa Barbara.

Example (55) illustrates the lack of verb agreement commonly found with existential *there* followed by a plural notional subject. Interestingly, this lack of concord occurs much more often with contracted *there's* than with non-contracted *there is*. In addition to the obvious phonological simplification (typical of online production), this seems to indicate that *there's* could be in the process of becoming grammaticalized in conversation as a general expression of existence, irrespective of number (singular or plural) of the logical subject (see Crawford, 2005).

Regional dialects

Regional dialect forms can also provide examples of non-standard grammar:

(56)   A: Is it working?
      B: Now *y'all* know I didn't break it.
      A: Alright, don't be scared of me.

(57)   A: Like what? I *done called* everybody.
      B: Who did you call? Who did you call?

Both the second person pronoun *y'all* in (56) and the use of the auxiliary verb *done* in (57) have been identified as features of the southern regional dialects of American English (see Feagin, 1991). These non-standard grammatical constructions also have a strong social function, as they are sociolinguistic markers of group membership and solidarity among speakers.

3.5   *The relationship between structural and functional correlates of conversational features*

In the sections above, we have isolated specific situational characteristics of conversation, describing how particular linguistic features are associated with each characteristic. However, conversations obviously are constructed from the interaction of all these situational characteristics, and as a result, we usually find many characteristic linguistic features co-occurring in a given conversation, as in the short extract of conversation below. The labels in curly brackets identify several of these features.

(1)   A: Where'd {contraction} you {2nd person pronoun} put everything? {question}

(2)   B: In the closet, in there. {ellipsis + deictic item}

(3)   A: That's good. {deictic item/demonstrative pronoun + contraction + evaluative adjective}

(4)   B: I don't wanna {medial ellipsis; want + *to*-clause; mental verb; present tense; lexical bundle} put the computer you know {discourse marker + incomplete sentence} I've wan = well {discourse marker} when we put the, {false start} what I did was folded up that {deictic item} metal de = uh {hesitator} table and {clausal coordinator} we'll

{contraction + modal} just {restrictive adverb} put the desk out on the porch. It's {contraction + pronoun *it*} a little high, but it's {contraction + pronoun *it* (vague referent)} better than putting it downstairs.

(5) A: Oh {discourse marker} I {1st person pronoun} agree {present tense} with that {demonstrative pronoun} Okay. {non-clausal unit, discourse marker}

(6) B: And uh . . . {hesitator + pause} let me scoot this {deictic item} out.

(7) A: You {2nd person pronoun} did all that {deictic item/demonstrative pronoun} while I was on the phone? {question}

(8) B: What? {non-clausal question}

(9) A: You {2nd personal pronoun} did all that {deictic item/demonstrative pronoun} while I was on the phone? {repetition}

(10) B: Yeah. {non-clausal response}

Lines (1), (7), (8), and (9) are examples of interrogatives. Sequences of questions and answers reflect the interactive nature of conversation as interlocutors show their interest in each other's contributions to the communicate event. The non-clausal question (8) helps to speed up the communicative process as it avoids unnecessary elaboration. The combination of deictic items (2, 4, 6, 7, 9) and ellipsis (2, 4) reflects the shared context in which conversation takes place. Line (4) has one of the most frequent mental verbs (*want*) followed by a *to*-complement clause within a frequent lexical bundle (*I don't want to*). The controlling verb (*want*) expresses stance which is emphasized later in the utterance by the presence of a modal (*will*) and a restrictive adverb (*just*). The false starts, incomplete sentences, and hesitator in (4) along with the pause in (6) and contractions in (1, 3, 4) are a result of the pressures of online production. The discourse markers in (4, 5) also reflect interactiveness and allow for additional processing time. These features (plus others) illustrate the complex interactions among situational functions and their associated linguistic characteristics in conversation.

4   Television and Dialogue

Scripted dialogue has also been studied as a representation of face-to-face conversation, especially in historical research. Rey (2001), for example, used the American television show *Star Trek* for a diachronic study of language and gender. Rey (2001: 138) claims that popular media is an appropriate source for the study of sociolinguistic differences, noting that "while the language used in television is obviously not the same as unscripted language, it does

represent the language scriptwriters imagine that real women and men produce." In a similar vein, Biber and Burges (2001: 158) describe the artificial
dialogue of fiction and drama as "useful representations of historical spoken
language." Tannen and Lakoff (1994: 139) believe that "artificial language may
represent an internalized model or schema for the production of conversation."

There is no doubt that the best way to study and describe the features of
conversation is through the analysis of naturally-occurring spoken data. However, because there are few publicly-available corpora of naturally-occurring
conversation, some scholars (e.g., Washburn, 2001) have suggested the use of
television language (especially situation comedies) for the purposes of English
as a second language (ESL) language teaching and learning.

Initially motivated by ESL purposes, Quaglio (2002, 2004) describes the
language of the American television situation comedy *Friends* (based on
analysis of a corpus comprising nine seasons of the show). The analysis
shows that *Friends* shares many of the typical linguistic features of face-to-face
conversation. For example:

(1)   Woman: **I'll** {contraction} see you tomorrow.
(2)   Ross: **Okay!** {non-clausal unit} **Hey!** {insert used as greeting}
(3)   Chandler and Joey: **Hey!** {insert used as greeting}
(4)   Ross: I just asked **that** {deictic item} girl out.
(5)   Chandler: **Nice!** {non-clausal unit + evaluative adjective}
(6)   Joey: **Nice!** {non-clausal unit + evaluative adjective} **Yeah!** {discourse
      marker used as an interjection} Is that part of your resolution, {ellipsis}
      your new thing {noun of vague reference} for today?
(7)   Ross: Yes, it is. **See?** {ellipsis}
(8)   Chandler: Elizabeth Hornswoggle?
(9)   Ross: That**'s** {contraction} right, **uh**, {hesitator} Elizabeth Hornswoggle.
(10) Chandler: Horn-swoggle.
(11) Joey: {ellipsis} You Okay **Chandler** {vocative}? {ellipsis} something funny
      about **that** {deictic item} name?
(12) Chandler: **No. No**, {repeat} I just think that **maybe** {hedge} **I-I'd** {repeat
      + contraction} heard it somewhere before.
(13) Joey: **Oh really?** {interjection + non-clausal question} **Where?** {non-clausal
      question} **Somewhere funny** {non-clausal unit} **I'd** {contraction} bet!
(14) Ross: **Hi**, {greeting} **Phoebs!** {vocative}
(15) Phoebe: **Hey!** {insert used as greeting}
(16) Ross: **Oh-oh** {insert + repeat}, **guess what?** {preface} **I-I** {repeat} have a
      date with Elizabeth Hornswoggle.
(17) Phoebe: Hornswoggle? Ooh, **this** {deictic item} must be killing
      you.   (Excerpt from NBC's *Friends*, episode 518, season 5)

At the same time, there are distinctive characteristics of television dialogue
imposed by the televized medium. For example, *Friends* has almost no overlaps, to avoid the possibility of misunderstandings by the audience. At the

discourse level, there are far fewer repetitions and interruptions than in natural conversation. As Cameron (2001: 26) suggests, television may be a convenient source for spoken data, but "broadcast talk has special characteristics which arise from the nature of the medium and the relationship it produces between speakers and addressees."

Despite these differences, the general similarities between television dialogue and face-to-face conversation suggest that television has the potential to provide researchers and teachers with a convenient source of spoken language data (see Quaglio 2004). Further, a corpus of television dialogue can be sampled in a continuous manner over a period of years, providing detailed data for investigations of language change in progress (such as the new uses of *so* as an adverbial intensifier; see section 3.4).

5 Conclusion

Conversational analysis studies usually focus on exchange structure and the overall organization of conversation. We have instead focused here on the typical grammatical characteristics of conversation. We first identified a set of features that can be considered 'conversational' because they occur more commonly in conversation than in other registers. A few of these features are essentially restricted to conversation (e.g., dysfluencies, false starts, hesitations) due to the characteristics of the spoken medium. We then shifted our attention to situational/functional characteristics of conversation, showing how these same linguistic features have strong functional associations with the typical situations and communicative purposes of conversation. Finally, we suggested that television dialogue provides interesting data for linguistic analysis, as a surrogate for natural conversation, and as an object of study in itself.

Most conversational features can also be found in some written registers, like e-mails or letters. We would argue that there are few, if any, absolute linguistic differences between conversation and other registers. Rather there is a cline of use which reflects the communicative needs of speakers and the characteristics of the spoken medium. It turns out that there are many grammatical features that occur much more commonly in conversation than in other registers, because of the distinctive situational characteristics of this register.

NOTES

1 There is of course also linguistic variation within conversation, associated with differences in communicative task or purpose (see Biber 2004; Carter and McCarthy 1997; McCarthy 1998; Quaglio 2004). However, these differences are small when compared to the full range of

spoken and written registers. In the present survey, we focus on the grammatical characteristics that are generally shared among conversational texts, rather than internal patterns of variation within conversation.

2   There are, of course, other specialized registers that use imperative and/or interrogative clauses frequently to serve specific communicative purposes. For example, instruction brochures often use many imperative clauses. The main point here, though, is that conversation uses these features much more frequently than other general registers (such as newspapers or academic prose).

FURTHER READING

1   Biber, D., Johansson, S., Leech, G., Conrad, S., and Finegan, E. (1999). *Longman grammar of spoken and written English*. London: Longman.

The authors take a corpus-based approach to describe English grammar from both structural and use perspectives. The patterns of use across four registers are compared (i.e., conversation, fiction, news, and academic prose) and natural corpus examples are presented to illustrate the grammatical features discussed throughout the book. A separate chapter is dedicated exclusively to spoken English (ch. 14, *The grammar of conversation*).

2   Aijmer, K. (1996). *Conversational routines in English: convention and creativity*. New York: Longman.

This is a comprehensive, corpus-based study of some of the most frequent conversational routines (e.g., apologies, requests, offers) in English. Examples from face-to-face conversations, radio discussions, and telephone conversations illustrate these expressions from a grammatical and pragmatic perspective.

3   Eggins, S., and Slade, D. (1997). *Analysing casual conversation*. New York: Continuum.

An interdisciplinary (sociology, linguistics, semiotics) approach is taken by the authors to analyze the grammatical and discourse features of casual conversation, including conversational genres such as storytelling and gossip.

4   Carter, R., and McCarthy, M. (1995). Grammar and the spoken language. *Applied Linguistics* 16 (2), 141–158.

In this article, Carter and McCarthy emphasize the importance of describing spoken grammar and bringing authentic spoken data to the ESL/EFL classroom. The analysis of selected grammatical features shows that there is a discrepancy between real conversation and how it is depicted in pedagogical grammars.

5   Leech, G. (2000). Grammars of spoken English: new outcomes of corpus-oriented research. *Language Learning*, 50 (4), 675–724.

Leech surveys current corpus-based research on spoken English grammar commenting on the strengths and limitations of the corpus-based approach. Comparing the grammar of spoken and written English, the author discusses the existence of one or two different systems. Pedagogical implications are drawn.

REFERENCES

Aarts, F. (1993) *Who, whom, that* and Ø in two corpora of spoken English. *English Today* 9, 19–21.

Aarts, F. (1994) Imperative sentences in a corpus of English conversation. *Leuvense Bijdragen* 83, 145–55.

Aijmer, K. (1984) *Sort of* and *kind of* in English conversation. *Studia Linguistica* 38, 118–28.

Aijmer, K. (1986) Why is *actually* so popular in spoken English? In G. Tottie and I. Backlund (eds.), *English in speech and writing: a symposium*. Studia Anglistica Upsaliensia 60, Stockholm: Almqvist and Wiksell, 119–29.

Aijmer, K. (1987) Discourse variation and hedging. *Costerus* 57, 1–18.

Aijmer, K. (1996) *Conversational routines in English: convention and creativity*. New York: Longman.

Altenberg, B. (1984) Lexical and sex-related differences in spoken and written English: some results of undergraduate research at Lund University. In H. Ringbom and M. Rissanen (eds.), *Proceedings from the Nordic conference for English studies*. Lund: Lund University Press.

Altenberg, B. (1991) Amplifier collocations in spoken English. In S. Johansson and A.-B. Stenstrom (eds.), *English computer corpora: selected papers and research guide*. Berlin: Mouton de Gruyter, 127–47.

Altenberg, B. (1993) On the functions of *such* in spoken and written English. In N. Oostdijk and P. de Haan (eds.), *Corpus-based research into language: in honour of Jan Aarts*. Amsterdam: Rodopi, 223–40.

Altenberg, B. (1998) On the phraseology of spoken English: the evidence of recurrent word-combinations. In A. P. Cowie (ed.), *Phraseology: theory,* *analysis, and applications*. Oxford: Clarendon Press, 101–22.

Austin, J. L. (1962) *How to do things with words*. New York: Oxford University Press.

Bäcklund, I. (1986) Beat until stiff: conjunction-headed abbreviated clauses in spoken and written English. In G. Tottie and I. Bäcklund (eds.), *English in speech and writing: a symposium*. Uppsala: Almqvist and Wiksell, 41–55.

Bargiela-Chiappini, F. (2003) Face and politeness: new (insights) for old (concepts). *Journal of Pragmatics* 35, 1453–69.

Biber, D. (1988) *Variation across speech and writing*. Cambridge: Cambridge University Press.

Biber, D. (2004) Conversational text types: a multidimensional analysis. In C. Fairon, L. Lebart, and A. Salem (eds.), *Proceedings of the 7th International Conference on the Statistical Analysis of Textual Data*.

Biber, D. and Conrad, S. (1999) Lexical bundles in conversation and academic prose. In H. Hasselgard and S. Oksefjell (eds.), *Out of corpora: studies in honour of Stig Johansson*. Amsterdam: Rodopi, 189–90.

Biber, D. and Burges, J. (2001) Historical shifts in the language of women and men: gender differences in dramatic dialogue. In S. Conrad and D. Biber (eds.), *Variation in English: multi-dimensional studies*. London: Longman, 157–70.

Biber, D., Conrad, S., and Reppen R. (1998) *Corpus linguistics: investigating language structure and use*. New York: Cambridge University Press.

Biber, D., Conrad, S., and Cortes, V. (2004) *If you look at . . .* : Lexical bundles in university teaching and textbooks. *Applied Linguistics* 25, 371–405.

Biber, D., Johansson, S., Leech, G., Conrad, S., and Finegan, E. (1999) *Longman grammar of spoken and written English*. London: Longman.

Blum-Kulka, S., House-Edmondson, J., and Kasper, G. (1989) *Cross-cultural pragmatics: requests and apologies*. Norwood, NJ: Ablex.

Boxer, D. (2002) Discourse issues in cross-cultural pragmatics. *Annual Review of Applied Linguistics* 22, 150–67.

Bright, K. S., Kauffman, M., and Crane, D. (executive producers) (1994) *Friends* [Television series]. New York: National Broadcasting Company.

Brown, P. and Levinson, S. C. (1987) *Politeness: some universals on language usage*. Cambridge: Cambridge University Press.

Cameron, D. (2001) *Working with spoken discourse*. London: Sage.

Carter, R. and McCarthy, M. (1997) *Exploring spoken English*. Cambridge: Cambridge University Press.

Carter, R. and McCarthy, M. (1999) The English get-passive in spoken discourse: description and implications for an interpersonal grammar. *English Language and Linguistics* 3 (1), 41–58.

Chafe, W. (1987) Cognitive constraints on information flow. In R. S. Tomlin (ed.), *Coherence and grounding in discourse*. Philadelphia: John Benjamins, 21–51.

Chafe, W. (1994) *Discourse, consciousness, and time: the flow and displacement of conscious experience in speaking and writing*. Chicago: University of Chicago Press.

Condon, S. L. (2001) Discourse ok revisited: default organization in verbal interaction. *Journal of Pragmatics* 33, 491–513.

Conrad, S. and Biber, D. (2000) Adverbial marking of stance in speech and writing. In S. Hunston and G. Thompson (eds.), *Evaluation in text:*

authorial stance and the construction of discourse. Oxford: Oxford University Press, 56–73.

Coulmas, F. (ed.) (1981) *Conversational routine: explorations in standardized communication situations and prepatterned speech*. The Hague: Mouton.

Crawford, W. (2005) Verb agreement and disagreement: a corpus investigation of concord variation in existential *there+be* constructions. *Journal of English Linguistics* 33, 1–27.

Dailey-O'Cain, J. (2000) The sociolinguistic distribution of and attitudes toward focuser *like* and quotative *like*. *Journal of Sociolinguistics* 4, 60–79.

Deirdre, W. and Sperber, D. (2002) Truthfulness and relevance. *Mind* 111 (443), 583–632.

Eggins, S., and Slade, D. (1997) *Analysing casual conversation*. New York: Continuum.

Erman, B. (1986) Some pragmatic expressions in English conversation. In G. Tottie and I. Backlund (eds.), *English in speech and writing: a symposium*. Studia Anglistica Upsaliensia 60, Stockholm: Almqvist and Wiksell, 131–47.

Feagin, C. (1991) Preverbal *done* in southern states English. In P. Trudgill and J. K. Chambers (eds.), *Dialects of English: studies in grammatical variation*. New York: Longman, 161–90.

Ford, C. E., Fox, B. A., and Thompson, S. A. (2002) *The language of turn and sequence*. New York: Oxford University Press.

Fox, B. A. (1987) *Discourse structure and anaphora: written and conversational English*. Cambridge Studies in Linguistics, Cambridge University Press.

Fox, B. A. and Thompson, S. A. (1990) A discourse explanation of the grammar of relative clauses in English conversation. *Language* 66, 297–316.

Greenbaum, S. and Nelson, G. (1995) Clause relationships in spoken and written English. *Functions of Language* 2 (1), 1–21.

Grice, H. P. (1975) Logic and conversation. In P. Cole and J. Morgan (eds.), *Speech act: vol. 3 of syntax and semantics*. New York: Academic Press, 41–58.

Grice, H. P. (1989) *Studies in the way of words*. Cambridge: MA: Harvard University Press.

Hardy, D. E. (1996) Topic versus cohesion in the prediction of causal ordering in English conversation. *Discourse Processes* 21, 237–54.

Horn, L. (1984) Toward a new taxonomy for pragmatic inference: Q-based and R-based implicature. In D. Schiffrin (ed.), *Meaning, form and use in context: linguistic applications*. Georgetown: Georgetown University Press.

Johnstone, B. (1994) *Repetition in discourse: Interdisciplinary perspectives*, vols.1 and 2. Norwood, NJ: Ablex.

Kasper, G. (1990) Linguistic politeness: Current research issues. *Journal of Pragmatics* 14, 193–218.

Leech, G. (1999) The distribution and function of vocatives in American and British English conversation. In H. Hasselgard and S. Oksefjell (eds.), *Out of corpora: studies in honour of Stig Johansson*. Amsterdam: Rodopi, 107–18.

Martinez Insua, A. E. and Palacios Martinez, I. M. (2003) A corpus-based approach to non-concord in present day English existential *there*-constructions. *English Studies* 3, 262–83.

McCarthy, M. (1998) *Spoken language and applied linguistics*. Cambridge: Cambridge University Press.

McCarthy, M. (2002) Good listenership made plain: British and American non-minimal response tokens in everyday conversation. In R. Reppen, S. Fitzmaurice, and D. Biber (eds.), *Using corpora to explore linguistic variation*. Amsterdam: John Benjamins, 49–71.

McCarthy, M. and Carter, R. (1995) Spoken grammar: what is it and how can we teach it? *ELT Journal* 49 (3), 207–18.

McCarthy, M. and Carter, R. (1997) Written and spoken vocabulary. In N. Schmitt and M. McCarthy (eds.), *Vocabulary: description, acquisition and pedagogy*. Cambridge: Cambridge University Press, 20–39.

Meyer, C. (1995) Coordination ellipsis in spoken and written American English. *Language Sciences* 17, 241–69.

Prince, E. F. (1981) Toward a taxonomy of given-new information. In P. Cole (ed.), *Radical pragmatics*. London: Academic Press, 223–5.

Quaglio, P. (2002) The language of NBC's *Friends*: implications for ESL/EFL teaching and materials development. Paper presented at the Fourth North American Symposium on Corpus Linguistics, Indianapolis, IN.

Quaglio, P. (2004) The language of NBC's *Friends*: a comparison with face-to-face conversation. Unpublished Ph.D. dissertation, Northern Arizona University.

Rey, J. M. (2001) Changing gender roles in popular culture: dialogue in *Star Trek* episodes from 1966 to 1993. In S. Conrad and D. Biber (eds.), *Variation in English: multi-dimensional studies*. London: Longman, 138–55.

Sacks, H., Schegloff, E. A., and Jefferson, G. (1974) A simplest systematics for the organization of turn-taking for conversation. *Language* 50, 696–735.

Sbisa, M. (2002) Speech acts in context. *Language & Communication* 22, 421–36.

Schegloff, E. A. (1997a) Practices and actions: boundary cases of other-initiated repair. *Discourse Processes* 23, 499–545.

Schegloff, E. A. (1997b) Third turn repair. In G. Guy, C. Feagin, D. Schiffrin, and J. Baugh (eds.), *Towards a social science of language. Papers in honor of William Labov*, vol. 2. Philadelphia: John Benjamins, 31–40.

Schegloff, E. A. (2000a) Overlapping talk and the organization of turn-taking for conversation. *Language in Society* 29 (1), 1–63.

Schegloff, E. A. (2000b) When 'others' initiate repair. *Applied Linguistics* 21 (2), 205–43.

Schegloff, E. A. (2001) Accounts of conduct in interaction: interruption, overlap and turn-taking. In J. H. Turner (ed.), *Handbook of sociological theory*. New York: Plenum, 287–321.

Schegloff, E. and Sacks, H. (1973) Opening up closings. *Semiotica* 8, 289–327.

Schiffrin, D. (1985) Conversational coherence: the role of *Well*. *Language* 61, 640–67.

Schiffrin, D. (1987) *Discourse markers*. Cambridge: Cambridge University Press.

Schourup, L. (2001) Rethinking *well*. *Journal of Pragmatics* 33, 1025–60.

Searle, J. R. (1969) *Speech acts*. Cambridge: Cambridge University Press.

Spencer-Oatey, H. and Jiang, W. (2003) Explaining cross-cultural pragmatic findings: moving from politeness maxims to sociopragmatic interactional principles (SIPs). *Journal of Pragmatics* 35, 1633–50.

Sperber, D. and Wilson, D. (1986a) *Relevance: communication and cognition*. Oxford: Blackwell.

Stenström, A-B. (1986) What does *really* really do? Strategies in speech and writing. In G. Tottie and I. Backlund (eds.), *English in speech and writing: a symposium*. Studia Anglistica Upsaliensia 60, Stockholm: Almqvist and Wiksell, 149–63.

Stenström, A-B. (1991) Expletives in the London-Lund corpus. In K. Aijmer and B. Altenberg (eds.), *English corpus linguistics: studies in honour of Jan Svartvik*. London: Longman, 239–53.

Stenström, A-B. (1999) He was really gormless – she's bloody crap: girls, boys and intensifiers. In H. Hasselgard and S. Oksefjell (eds.), *Out of corpora: studies in honour of Stig Johansson*. Amsterdam: Rodopi, 69–78.

Taguchi, N. (2002) A comparative analysis of discourse markers in English conversational registers. *Issues in Applied Linguistics* 13 (1), 41–68.

Tannen, D. (1984) *Coherence in spoken and written discourse: advances in discourse processes*. Norwood, NJ: Ablex.

Tannen, D. (1989) *Talking voices: repetition, dialogue, and imagery in conversational discourse*. Cambridge: Cambridge University Press.

Tannen, D. and Lakoff, R. (1994) Conversational strategy and metastrategy in Bergman. In D. Tannen (ed.), *Gender and discourse*. New York: Oxford University Press, 137–73.

Tao, H. and McCarthy, M. (2001) Understanding non-restrictive *which*-clauses in spoken English, which is not an easy thing. *Language Sciences* 23, 651–77.

Tottie, G. (1986) The importance of being adverbial: adverbials of focusing and contingency in spoken and written English. In G. Tottie and I. Backlund (eds.), *English in speech and writing: a symposium*. Studia Anglistica Upsaliensia 60, Stockholm: Almqvist and Wiksell, 93–118.

Tottie, G. (1991) Conversational style in British and American English: the case of backchannels. In K. Aijmer and B. Altenberg (eds.), *English corpus linguistics*. London: Longman, 254–71.

Underhill, R. (1988) *Like* is, like, focus. *American Speech* 63, 234–46.

Viitanen, O. (1986) On the position of *only* in English conversation. In G. Tottie and I. Backlund (eds.), *English in speech and writing: a symposium*. Studia Anglistica

Upsaliensia 60, Stockholm: Almqvist and Wiksell, 165–75.

Wachal, R. S. (2002) Taboo or not taboo: that is the question. *American Speech* 77, 195–206.

Waksler, R. (2001) A new *all* in conversation. *American Speech* 76, 128–38.

Ward, G. and Birner, B. J. (1993) The semantics and pragmatics of *and everything*. *Journal of Pragmatics* 19, 205–14.

Washburn, G. (2001) Using situation comedies for pragmatic language teaching and learning. *TESOL Journal* 10, 21–6.

Wilson, D. and Sperber, D. (2002) Truthfulness and relevance. *Mind* 111 (443), 583–632.

Wong, J. (2000a) Delayed next turn repair initiation in native-nonnative speaker English conversation. *Applied Linguistics* 21 (2), 244–67.

30 Gender and the English Language

DEBORAH CAMERON

1 Gender and Its Relationship to Language

The term *gender* is used in this chapter primarily to refer to the social condition of being a man or a woman. For linguists, of course, the same word also denotes a grammatical category: in many languages nouns are divided into gender classes and the classification determines their agreement with other words such as adjectives and pronouns. How this works in English is a relevant question and will be discussed later on, but it is not the main subject of the chapter. Rather I will consider a number of ways in which the English language is affected by gender in the 'men and women' sense.

In modern feminist theory it has been traditional to distinguish *gender* from *sex*. *Sex* is used in connection with the biological characteristics that mark humans and other animals as either male or female, whereas *gender* refers to the cultural traits and behaviors deemed appropriate for men or women by a particular society. The sex/gender distinction is important for feminists because it challenges the belief that everything about women, men, and the relationship between them is a matter of biology. Being cultural, gender can take varying forms in different societies and historical periods: what is considered 'masculine' in one time or place may be understood as 'feminine' in another, and have no special gendered significance in a third.

Recently, some feminist postmodernists, notably the philosopher Judith Butler (1990), have argued that the sex/gender distinction itself concedes too much to biology, and that sex, like gender, is a socially constructed category. Her point depends on the idea that all human knowledge is profoundly shaped by the sociocultural beliefs and practices of the knowers: what are presented as the scientific 'facts' about biological sex must inevitably have been filtered through the scientists' experiences of gender as a social phenomenon. This theoretical argument has influenced some recent discussions in linguistics (see e.g. Bergvall and Bing 1997). But while there are areas of linguistic inquiry where biological sex differences might be considered relevant (e.g.

neurolinguistics), the research tradition I review in this chapter is located in fields which focus specifically on the sociocultural dimension of language, such as sociolinguistics and linguistic anthropology. Whatever stance is taken on the distinction between sex and gender, this tradition is clearly concerned with men and women as social beings – in other words, it deals with gender.

What are the issues that need to be addressed in a chapter about gender and English? For some readers, perhaps many, it will seem obvious that the key question must be, 'do men and women use English differently?' or even 'what is it that differentiates the English used by men from that used by women?' Such questions reflect a set of preconceptions about what gender is, how it works and what is interesting about it, which it is necessary to examine critically before we proceed.

Gender is often seen as a particularly fundamental attribute of human individuals (when a baby is born, its status as a boy or a girl is often the first piece of information to be announced). Gender also differs from many of the other attributes which are culturally (and linguistically) salient in being, or appearing to be, a binary opposition. We do not think of it as a continuum, like age, or as a multivalued variable like geographical origin or ethnicity, but as a system in which there are only two possibilities: a person must be either a woman or a man, not both and not neither. This encourages the perception that studying gender means studying the *differences* between men and women – differences which we imagine to be clear-cut and consistent. Our cultural preoccupation with gender differences is as strong in the sphere of language as elsewhere. Consider the current popularity of books like *Men are from Mars, Women are from Venus* (Gray 1992), which purport to describe the different languages of men and women; or the interest generated by a recently developed text-analysis tool called the 'Gender Genie,' whose designers claim to be able to tell from a 500-word sample of English text whether the author is a man or a woman. The popularity of this website points not only to a widespread fascination with gender differences in language, but also to the strength of the belief that a person's gender influences their language-use in such clear and predictable ways, it will be readily identifiable from any small random sample of their output.

But many contemporary language and gender scholars have questioned the assumption that gender manifests itself linguistically through clear-cut binary differences – 'men do this, women do that' (see, e.g., Benor, Rose, Sharma, Sweetland, and Zhang 2002; Bergvall, Bing, and Freed 1997; Eckert and McConnell-Ginet 2003; Hall and Bucholtz 1995). They have argued that where researchers focus exclusively on differences between men and women, they are distorting the picture in two ways: by downplaying the extent of similarity and overlap between the two groups, and by disregarding the variation that exists *within* each gender group. People are never *just* men or women, they are men and women of particular ages, classes, ethnic and geographical origins, occupational categories, social roles and statuses, religious and political beliefs. The form gendered behavior takes is affected significantly by these other dimensions of identity and experience. Older and younger women, or working-class and middle-class women, may be as different from one another as from their male peers; each of these groups may be defining its femininity more by contrast with the femininity of some other group of women (for instance, their mothers) than in opposition to masculinity. This is still a question of gender, but it is not simply about differences between men and women.

A lot of the research I discuss in this chapter is informed by the binary difference approach, since it dominated the field until quite recently. However, my presentation will acknowledge that it is now debated among language and gender scholars. To avoid foreclosing the debate, I have refrained from organizing this chapter around a question which inherently presupposes the binary model, such as 'what differentiates men's use of English from women's?' Instead I address a more open-ended question: how does the social phenomenon of gender in English-speaking societies impact on the use and structure of the English language? I have also preferred the term 'gender-linked variation' over 'gender difference,' since the former term can more easily accommodate the view, held nowadays by an increasing number of researchers, that gender is not a *single* 'difference.'

This chapter is specifically about gender-linked variation in *English*, but in many cases the patterns found in English are known or believed to exist in other languages too. Though a detailed examination of the cross-linguistic evidence is beyond the scope of this chapter, some researchers would argue that certain patterns identified in English are expressions of gender-linked tendencies that are far more general, or even universal (see e.g. Holmes 1993).

2   Gender as a User Variable in English

In this section I consider how English is affected by the fact that its *users* are socially differentiated by gender. There is a longstanding belief that this differentiation is consequential for the development and use of languages. Eighteenth-century commentators on English often alluded to the differing roles played by men and women in advancing the cultivation of the language or conversely hastening its degeneration. The Danish linguist Otto Jespersen (1922) argued that women and men's differing speech-habits push linguistic development in different directions: men innovate where women conserve, and women avoid 'indelicate' language where men embrace the 'vigor' of vernacular speech. Jespersen thought the proper development of a language depended on maintaining a balance between these opposing tendencies. While contemporary linguists eschew such judgments, many would agree that men and women tend to make different choices from the available linguistic repertoire and exert different kinds of influence on the process of change. Below I discuss the evidence for that belief in two areas of English-language linguistics: variationist sociolinguistics, which specializes in the quantitative analysis of (mainly phonological) variation and change; and the study of what I will term 'discourse style,' where researchers seek to identify clusters of features which give a particular group of language-users – in this case men or women – their allegedly distinctive style of speaking or writing.

2.1   *Variation and change in English*

In modern sociolinguistics it is axiomatic that variability is an inherent characteristic of languages, that the variation found in linguistic behavior is highly structured, and that this structured variation provides the seedbed for language change. What we call a linguistic change is not the result of everyone suddenly substituting a different consonant, say, for the one they used before, but of a shift over time in the balance between two existing variants. Change, then, is a subtype of variation rather than a different phenomenon entirely.

Gender has consistently been found to be an important influence on variation: statistical analysis reveals gender-linked patterns for sociolinguistic variables in many or most speech communities. This arguably tells us something of general interest about the purposes variation serves. As William Labov has commented (2001: 262), the pervasiveness of gender-linked variation challenges what might seem to be a logical assumption, that the linguistic differences between groups will be greatest where the contact between them is least. Men and women in the same community interact with one another regularly and in some contexts intimately, but their linguistic behavior remains distinct in measurable ways. This reflects the fundamental significance we accord to gender as an element of identity, and the use we make of linguistic variation as a resource for constructing identity and difference.

How are gendered identities marked in English? Probably the most familiar of all variationist claims on this subject is that women are 'more standard' speakers than men. The meaning of this claim, however, is frequently misunderstood. It does not mean that women in general, or greater numbers of women, are monodialectal speakers of standard English. It means that when there are two ways to pronounce a certain sound (for instance, sounding or not sounding the /r/ in 'farm'; pronouncing the /t/ in 'bottle' as a [t] or as a glottal stop), one of them closer to the prestige or standard pronunciation and the other further away, there will be a statistical tendency for women as a group to show higher frequencies of the prestige variant than the men with whom they are compared.

In fact, the claim that women use higher frequencies of standard English variants has recently been modified. After reviewing the evidence from studies conducted in a range of speech communities (many but not all of them English-speaking), Labov (1990; 2001) formulated some general principles relating to gender, variation and change:

(1)   Where sociolinguistic variables are stable (not involved in change), men use higher frequencies of nonstandard variants than women.

(1)   a.   Where there is change from above (i.e. people are aware of the existence of the competing variants and of the prestige of one relative to the
other) women lead in the adoption of the incoming prestige variant.

(2)   Where there is change from below (i.e. one variant is gaining ground
from another without speakers being aware of it), women are further
advanced than men in their use of the innovative variant.

These principles suggest that the 'women are more standard' claim only holds
in certain circumstances: where a variable is not involved in any change and
where there is change in the direction of the standard. Some of the most far-
reaching changes, however, exemplify a third possibility – change from below,
which is not conscious and does not involve a move towards more standard
pronunciation. In these cases women typically lead in adopting the new, shifted
variants. Consequently we cannot maintain that overall men are innovative
and women conservative, or that overall, women favor prestige and men vernacular pronunciations. Rather there seems to be what Labov calls a 'gender
paradox': women 'conform more closely than men to sociolinguistic norms
that are overtly prescribed, but conform less than men when they are not'
(Labov 2001: 293).

Both these tendencies, and therefore women as a group, play an important
role in variation and change in English – though there are some changes
which do not bear out the predictions made by the principles (one example of
a change from below led by men rather than women is reported by Dubois
and Horvath 2000). Where the generalizations set out in Labov's principles do
hold, though, what is it that causes them to hold? Various explanations have
been proposed (see Labov 2001 for a discussion), but one answer that has the
merit of being able to account for both conservative and innovative behavior
among women is suggested by Penelope Eckert (2000; see also Eckert and
McConnell-Ginet 1999, 2003; Nichols 1997).

Eckert conducted research in a high school near Detroit, one of a number of
major cities in the northern USA (others include Chicago, Cleveland, Buffalo
and Rochester) where the vowel system is undergoing the 'Northern Cities
Shift.' The effect is to change the phonetic realization of a number of vowel
phonemes, as shown by the examples in table 30.1.

These however are not separate and discrete sound changes, but part of a
single 'chain shift': the initial movement of one sound into the phonetic space
of another causes the sound whose position is encroached on to shift in order
to maintain its distinctiveness, and this displaces yet another sound, and so
on. The trajectory of the Northern Cities Shift is shown in figure 30.1, where
the arrows indicate the direction in which the vowels are moving and the
numbers indicate the temporal sequence of their movements.

The social life of the high school students Eckert studied is organized around
a contrast between two subcultural groups, 'jocks' and 'burnouts.' Jocks embrace the official culture and values of the school: studying and getting good
grades, taking part in sports and other extra-curricular activities, going on to

Table 30.1 The effect of the Northern Cities Shift in four English vowels

Word	Vowel in unshifted dialects	Vowel of Northern Cities Shift
<u>st*u*ck</u>	[ʌ]	[ɔ]
<u>st*a*lk</u>	[ɔ]	[ɑ]
<u>st*o*ck</u>	[ɑ]	[a]
<u>st*a*ck</u>	[æ]	[eæ]

Source: From the Language Samples Project 2001: www.ic.arizona.edu/~lsp/LSProject.

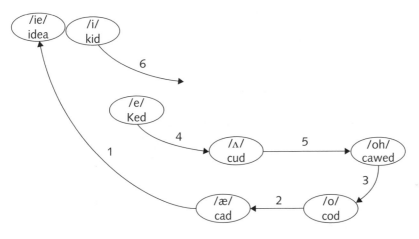

Figure 30.1 The Northern Cities Shift
Source: Labov 1996

college and to a successful professional career. Burnouts reject these goals and aspirations. This difference is also expressed in all kinds of symbolic ways, from the style of a student's jeans to the statistical patterning of her or his vowels.

Eckert found that vowel variables involved in the Northern Cities Shift were used differently by jocks and by burnouts. But she also found that in each group, it was the girls who were the most 'extreme' users of whatever variants marked their subcultural identity – linguistically, girls were the 'jockiest jocks' and the most 'burned-out burnouts.' Eckert relates this finding to the way gender affects an individual's status within their peer-group. Boys can demonstrate their jock or burnout credentials through what they do, e.g. excelling in athletics or being successful fighters. For girls, however, peer-group status depends more on factors like attractiveness and popularity – what a girl 'is like' rather than what she does. Eckert argues that for that reason, girls make more use than boys of *symbolic* resources, like clothing and language, for presenting themselves as 'good jocks/burnouts.' Their symbolic self-presentation needs to be more 'extreme' because they cannot earn their peer-group credentials in other ways. Eckert also suggests that this symbolic imperative is not confined to adolescent subcultures, but affects women in many other social groups and settings. Perhaps, then, women's tendency to be more 'extreme' than men in both conservative and innovative linguistic behavior has to do with the greater importance of symbolic resources in the construction of socially approved feminine identities.

Some linguists believe that the tendencies identified in variationist sociolinguistics are linked to biological sex differences. Chambers (1992) has suggested that they may reflect women's greater 'stylistic flexibility,' which he argues is an expression of the innately superior verbal ability of females. The postulate of female verbal superiority is an old one, recently re-emphasized by evolutionary psychologists in connection with their argument that natural selection has produced 'hard-wired' differences in the minds as well as the bodies of men and women (e.g. Baron-Cohen 2003; Dunbar 1996). However, a meta-analysis of the relevant research literature (Hyde and Linn 1988) found the evidence for women's superior verbal ability to be weak and inconclusive. Similarly inconclusive, not to say highly speculative, is the suggestion made by Gordon and Heath (1998) that males and females are likely to be instrumental in different kinds of sound changes, because of a biologically based tendency for females to gravitate toward a phonological system with maximum dispersion of sounds in phonetic space, while males do the opposite.

2.2   *Gender and discourse style*

It is not generally supposed by variationists that the pronunciations favored by men or women express particular masculine or feminine qualities: since individual phones have no inherent semantic value, these variants are meaningful in gender terms only insofar as they become markers of membership in a gender category. In the case of what I am calling 'discourse style,' by contrast, the assumption has often been that the linguistic markers of 'men's style' and 'women's style' are not arbitrary, but functionally linked to the personality traits and preoccupations which are supposedly typical of men and women.

One of the best-known attempts to delineate a gendered discourse style in English (though on the basis of the analyst's own intuitions rather than empirical investigation) was made by Robin Lakoff (1975). Lakoff proposed the existence of a style which she labeled 'women's language' (WL), whose characteristic linguistic features included the following:

1   A preference for milder over more strongly tabooed expressions (e.g. 'fudge' rather than 'fuck').

2   An elaborate color vocabulary (e.g. 'mauve' and 'lilac' rather than just 'purple').
3   Use of 'empty' adjectives ('lovely,' 'divine') and intensifiers ('so nice,' 'such a good time').
4   Hedging to reduce the force of an utterance and/or the speaker's degree of commitment to it ('I've got a bit of a headache,' 'It was sort of the wrong color').
5   Phrasing statements as questions, using rising intonation and/or end-of-sentence question tags ('that's a nice one, isn't it?' 'dinner's at six, OK?').
6   'Superpoliteness' (e.g. 'excuse me, I was just wondering if you could possibly . . .').

This formally rather ill-assorted cluster of features becomes more coherent if one considers the functions they fulfill. Many of them, Lakoff argued, communicate insecurity: a lack of confidence in one's own opinion, a desire to avoid giving offence, and a need to seek approval from other people (e.g. 1, 4, 5, 6); others (e.g. 2) signal a preoccupation with trivia. Lakoff saw insecurity and triviality as traits women were socialized to develop in order to conform to mainstream notions of femininity. As a feminist, she linked these notions of femininity to women's subordinate status: WL, from her perspective, was essentially a display of women's culturally imposed powerlessness in a male-dominated and sexist society.

Later researchers have followed Lakoff in looking for clusters of linguistic features linked functionally to the differing roles, traits and preoccupations of men and women, but in other ways their approach is different. Lakoff distinguished 'women's language' not from 'men's language' but from 'neutral language': in language as in society more generally she understood femininity to be the 'marked' gender position, not just different but unequal. Her successors by contrast have more often taken the view that linguistically, men and women are simply different: their characteristic discourse styles reflect a fundamental difference in their orientations to the world, with women oriented mainly to people and relationships while men are more oriented to objects and information. Deborah Tannen (1990) has popularized this view in her distinction between men's 'report talk' and women's 'rapport talk.' Janet Holmes (1993; 1995) has suggested that women focus more on the 'affective' as opposed to the 'referential' dimension of verbal communication and use more linguistic devices whose function is to maintain harmonious relations in talk (e.g. politeness phenomena, including hedges, apologies and compliments). Jennifer Coates (1996; 2003), working with data from all-male and all-female friends' talk in British English, concludes that women talking to women engage in more personal self-disclosure than men talking to men. Coates's British work also echoes the earlier research of Barbara Johnstone (1993) on US midwesterners' conversational narratives, which found that male narratives tended to feature male protagonists and to be organized around themes of contest, whereas women's stories featured both men and women and foregrounded themes of community.

Another approach to the identification of gendered discourse styles is associated with corpus linguistics. Though this has theoretical similarities with the approaches just discussed, it is radically different methodologically. Whereas the researchers cited above specialize in the qualitative microanalysis of spoken interactive discourse, corpus linguists typically carry out statistical analyses of very large data samples, which in many cases consist of written text. This is the approach that has produced the Gender Genie, the interactive tool for identifying authorial gender which I mentioned above; to illustrate it I will refer to the work of the scholars whose research the Genie is based on (Argamon, Koppel, Fine, and Shimoni 2003).

Argamon et al. worked with a large (604 document, 25 million word) subset of the British National Corpus (BNC), a collection of English-language texts which is subdivided into genres and in which every word has been 'tagged' using a 76-category grammatical classification. The researchers were interested in formal written genres, on which it had been suggested that gender would exert little or no influence. Their dataset contained both fiction and nonfiction texts, with equal numbers of male and female-authored texts in each category. Initially, statistical analyses were made of around 1,000 lexical and grammatical features to identify those that were most reliable in discriminating between the male and female-authored texts in the sample. Around 50 such features were found, of which a small number stood out as particularly significant. Male-authored texts were discriminable by high frequencies of determiners (e.g. *a, the, that, these*), and quantifiers (e.g. *one, two, more, some*), while high frequencies of personal pronouns, particularly *I, you, she,* and their variants, were strong indicators of female authorship. The researchers found that quantifying these variables enabled them correctly to attribute authorial gender for 80 percent of unseen texts. (The Gender Genie, using what is described on its site as a simplified version of Argamon et al.'s algorithm, has significantly lower accuracy rates.)

Argamon et al. identified their markers using purely statistical methods, without regard to their meaning or function, but they argue that what they found supports the distinction others have made between 'affective' women and 'referential' men, or men's 'report talk' and women's 'rapport talk.' They suggest that women's use of first and second person pronouns is a corollary of their concern with persons and relationships – especially, in this case, the relationship between writer and reader – while men's use of determiners and quantifiers is a corollary of their concern with specifying the properties of objects. The features identified here as gender markers are also markers of the 'involved–informational' contrast that has emerged in other research as an important dimension of register variation in written English (Biber 1995). Argamon et al. found higher frequencies of other 'involved' features, such as verb contractions and present-tense verbs, in women's texts; conversely, they found higher frequencies in men's texts of 'informational' features such as prepositional phrases with *of* post-modifying nouns (e.g. 'shelf of books').

These claims about gendered discourse styles in written English are not unproblematic. One question they raise is whether the markers are really stable gendered characteristics of writers, or whether they are primarily associated with clusters of textual characteristics (genre, subject-matter, formality, interactivity, etc.), which are linked to gender in a more indirect way. Such a link might arise because of a cultural tendency for men and women to specialize in particular kinds of writing rather than because of context-independent differences in the way men and women write. Though Argamon et al. attempted to control for genre or topic effects by selecting a sample in which men and women each contributed 50 percent of the texts in each genre and subject category, arguably the BNC classifications of genre and topic are not delicate enough to ensure that this strategy produces a consistent comparison of like with like. Many subject classifications are very general (e.g. 'world affairs,' 'leisure') and encompass a considerable range of both genres and subject-matter. 'World affairs' for instance includes celebrity biographies alongside political treatises, and several different subgenres of history (popular, scholarly, local, etc.). So the possibility cannot be discounted that the BNC sample reflects the tendency for women and men to dominate subtly different areas of textual production, and that consequently Argamon et al. have not sufficiently discriminated 'user' variables from 'use' ones.

The question I have just raised in relation to Argamon et al.'s work – whether they have assumed a direct link between language and gender when in fact the link is indirect, mediated by another variable or variables – is in the spirit of an influential essay by the anthropologist Elinor Ochs (1992). Ochs argues that there are very few instances in which the link between language and gender is direct and unequivocal. In most cases, speakers 'index' ('point to') gender by using features whose primary association is with a certain role (e.g. caring for infants) or trait (e.g. modesty, deference), but which become gendered by association, because the role or trait in question is culturally understood as gender specific and/or is typically played by members of a particular gender group. If the issue of gendered discourse styles is approached in this way, it might imply that the various gender-markers proposed by researchers are better conceived as primarily markers of affective/involved or referential/ informational orientation, which may index gender indirectly but whose relationship to gender is not exclusive or invariant. This reformulation allows us both to acknowledge the gender-linked patterning revealed by research on English, and to deal in a more principled way with cases which do not exhibit the expected pattern.

Some language and gender researchers take a more sceptical view of the quest to identify gendered discourse styles, and have made various criticisms of the approaches discussed above. I have argued, for instance (Cameron 1997a, 1997b), that these approaches, based as they are on the assumption that what genders language is the producer's (speaker's or writer's) selection of stylistic features that carry gendered meanings, overlook the pragmatic role of the interpreter (hearer or reader). Since gender is a highly salient social division, language-users are likely to bring gendered 'scripts' – pre-existing assumptions about masculinity and femininity – to bear on the interpretation of utterances by men and women. That is why, for instance, we may be reluctant to hear of a group of men as 'gossiping' even though they are talking in a manner we would call gossip if the speakers were women (see Cameron 1997a), and why a woman who objectively swears as much as a man may be judged subjectively to swear far more: we read these behaviors through cultural preconceptions about gender and gender difference. Discourse may thus be gendered as much through the interpretive frame its recipients use to make sense of it as by the stylistic choices its producers make.

Other scholars, most notably Penelope Eckert and Sally McConnell-Ginet (1992, 1999), are critical of the discourse styles approach because its perspective on gender is 'global' rather than 'local.' They argue that ways of using language (be they what I am calling 'discourse styles' or styles in the variationist sense) are not just reflexes of large-scale sociological abstractions like gender and social class, but emerge out of people's participation in particular local 'communities of practice' (CoPs). CoPs are groups constituted by engagement in some joint endeavor, like religious worship, political campaigning, playing a sport, learning a language, working in an office, etc. For Eckert and McConnell-Ginet, it is the habitual doing of certain things with certain groups of people that most directly influences our linguistic behavior. The CoP, as the locus for this doing, is thus a key analytic concept.

Where is gender in this approach? As Eckert and McConnell-Ginet point out, being a man or a woman tends to affect both the range and type of CoPs someone belongs to and the terms on which they participate. Eckert's work with adolescent peer groups, discussed above, illustrates the point: though girls and boys are both engaged in the local practices of the jock or burnout CoPs, they are not engaged in exactly the same ways, nor do they participate on equally favorable terms. Consequently there are differences as well as similarities in the speech of girls and boys within each group. Crucially, however, these are *local* differences: the fact that gender works like this in one community does not entail that it must work the same way in all others. That makes the CoP approach very different from the quest for gendered discourse styles, which precisely looks for features differentiating men-in-general from women-in-general. Gender is conceived as a 'global' identity, given in advance of and transcending any particular local setting. By contrast, the CoP approach says that femininities and masculinities, and the ways of speaking associated with them, are local phenomena, as diverse as the local practices through which they are constituted.

3   The Representation of Gender in English

Language-users construct gender identities through their ways of using and interpreting language, as discussed in the previous section; but they also construct gender as a salient category of reality through their verbal representations of the world beyond the self. This section considers the resources English provides for representing gender, the uses made of those resources in English-speaking communities, and the influence of changing attitudes to gender on the recent history of English.

The question of how gender is represented in language is not just about gender as a grammatical category. Grammatical gender is only one of the linguistic resources that may be used to mark social gender. Languages in which gender is not a grammatical category, such as Finnish, are not by that token lacking any means to represent the distinction between men and women. Even in languages where gender is a pervasive grammatical category – all nouns are assigned to gender classes and there is extensive agreement marking on, for instance, adjectives and articles – it may not be used consistently or exclusively to mark social gender, either because the noun classification is based on another semantic distinction (e.g. animate/inanimate, as in Algonquian languages) or because it is based on formal rather than semantic criteria (leading to 'anomalies' like the German *Mädchen*, 'girl,' which is neuter rather than feminine, as are all nouns ending in *-chen*). In modern English gender is a grammatical category, based largely on the semantic features of animacy and sex/gender reference, but it is not particularly pervasive: agreement (the defining feature of a grammatical gender system) is limited to third person singular pronouns. These pronouns are significant for the representation of gender in English, but they are not the whole story.

Many of the resources used by English-speakers to differentiate men and women are lexical rather than grammatical. Since gender is an attribute of persons, terms that name, address and categorize persons are often gender-differentiated. An obvious example is kinship terminology: in English we have *(grand)mothers* and *(grand)fathers*, *sisters* and *brothers*, *aunts* and *uncles*, *daughters* and *sons*, *nieces* and *nephews* (though *cousin* is undifferentiated). Gender is also commonly marked in the selection of personal names, titles and other address terms. Take my own personal name, *Deborah*. Like most names chosen by English-speaking parents, it indicates my gender clearly. People who know me usually call me *Debbie*, a type of diminutive nickname that is very common for women (cf. *Katie, Cathy, Becky, Jenny, Christie*) but less so for adult men, who are more given to the monosyllabic diminutive: *Bob, Jim, Mike, Pete, Tom*. (Add a *-y* and the effect is not so much to feminize as to infantilize. That is also what *-y* diminutives do to women, but we do not perceive the same incongruity between femininity and childishness). People who don't know me and need to address or refer to me more formally use a gender-marked title such as *Miss/Mrs/Ms*, or *Madam/Ma'am*. People who know me intimately – or who don't but who choose to address me in familiar terms – select endearments that are gendered or have overtones of gender: *cupcake, honey, sweetie, doll*. And people who want to insult me often do it using clearly gendered words: *bitch, cow, dyke*.

This is not to say there are no ungendered English address terms: one interesting case is the now widespread, at least in American English, use of *guys* to address or refer to a group of either gender or both, as in 'hey, you guys.' This usage exemplifies another common pattern in the representation of gender: a term like *guy*, originally referring to men only, can become generalized to encompass women, but the opposite pattern of generalization is rarely observed, because applying female-referring terms to men implies a downgrading of status which is resisted. Thus when a masculine personal name is widely adopted to name girls, it will generally lose its currency as a name for boys (cf. *Beverley*, *Evelyn*, and increasingly, *Robin*). This kind of pattern suggests that the linguistic marking of gender is not just a matter of distinguishing men and women, but may also be about marking their relative *status*. Indeed, it has been argued that the cultural perception of gender as a hierarchical relationship exerts a systematic influence on the process of semantic change in English. Muriel Schulz (1975) drew attention to the existence of pairs such as *governor/governess* and *lord/lady*, in which feminine terms that were originally equivalent in meaning to their masculine counterparts had undergone downgrading, so that the equivalence had been lost. *Lady* no longer refers only to aristocratic women; *governess* would no longer be a suitable term for the woman in charge of a US state or the Bank of England. Schulz also noted the tendency for feminine terms to acquire specifically sexual meanings. *Mistress*, for example, remains parallel to *master* in some contexts but is strongly sexualized in others.

It is this issue of status, rather than simply gender differentiation, that has prompted recent feminist concerns about the workings of grammatical gender in English. As noted above, obligatory grammatical gender-marking in English is limited, applying only to the third person singular personal pronouns *he, she, it*. In the case of specific referents, the gender of a third person singular pronoun must match that of the antecedent NP ('my father . . . he,' 'my mother . . . she,' 'my car . . . it'). Limited though this is by comparison with the requirements imposed by many other languages, it does mean that English speakers have to work quite hard to talk about a person without specifying their gender, and there has been a long history of (failed) proposals for a common gender alternative such as *per* or *tey* to obviate this necessity (see Baron 1980 for a list and discussion).

But the kind of pronominal gender marking that has caused most controversy in English relates not to specific but to indefinite or generic reference, where the pronoun's antecedent is formally third person singular but indeterminate as to gender, as in the following examples:

(1)   has *everybody* done ____ homework?

(2)   *the average citizen* seems to think ___ will be wasting ___ time by voting in local elections.

Prescriptive English grammarians since the early modern period have held that the 'correct' pronoun to put in the empty slots in these examples is the relevant form of the masculine pronoun (*he, him, his, himself*). In recent times this has tended to be explained by stating that the masculine is formally the 'unmarked' gender in English. Among feminist critics, however, it is seen as another instantiation of the general principle that masculine terms have higher status than feminine ones. Ann Bodine (1975) points out that in the early grammars where the rule was first codified, prescribers made no secret of the ideological basis for their ruling. Rather than appealing to arguments about markedness, they argued that the order of precedence in grammar should be the same as in society generally, i.e. men before women. The more specifically linguistic argument advanced by early prescribers concerned not gender but number agreement, for the variant that competed with *he* in indefinite/generic contexts was not *she*, but the third person plural *they*. *They* was (and in spoken English still is) especially common with antecedents like *everybody*, which though formally singular has a strong semantic plurality (hence the dubious acceptability of 'everybody came and I was very glad to see him'). Bodine sought to demonstrate using historical evidence that the 'unmarked' status of *he* was not an integral part of English grammar, but merely an artefact of earlier prescriptive interference.

The generic masculine pronoun is not the only instance where English linguistic convention has historically treated men as prototypical of the human species. The same principle is operative in relation to a subset of English nouns which denote people by office or occupation. One significant group of these terms uses the suffix -*man*, which in Old English had the meaning 'person' but in present-day English is clearly masculine. Examples include *fireman, salesman, alderman, chairman*. Some of these terms have variants in -*woman* (e.g. *alderwoman*); others do not, because traditionally the positions they denote were not occupied by women. Another group of terms do not contain the morpheme -*man* but are gender-differentiated morphologically, yielding pairs like *actor/actress, waiter/waitress, usher/usherette*, where the feminine term is marked with respect to the masculine, both formally (i.e. something is added to the masculine form to make the feminine) and in the sense that only the masculine form can be used generically. A mixed-gender group of people who belong to the acting profession are 'actors,' not 'actresses.'

It is of course true that in many of the cases I have just cited there are also gender-neutral terms in existence, some of which are now as familiar as the older gender-marked terms. For instance, it is now standard practice to talk about *firefighters* rather than *firemen*. *Chairperson* and *chair* are familiar alternatives to *chairman/woman* (though the latter terms, especially *chairman*, remain in widespread use), and in some communities it is possible to encounter *waitperson* or *waitron* as substitutes for *waiter/waitress*. The existence of these terms, and of alternatives to generic *he*, illustrates the influence on English of the recent social trend towards gender egalitarianism. This influence is felt particularly in the area of occupational terms, because in English-speaking countries such as the US, UK, Canada, and Australia, one key expression of gender-egalitarian principles has been legislation outlawing gender discrimination in employment. In this context it is problematic that unmarked or generic occupational terms are also often masculine: an advertisement for a 'fireman' or a 'salesman' leaves room for doubt about whether the job is open to women. Consequently, advertisers have been required to describe occupations in terms that unambiguously apply to either sex. This has created a need for new terminology, and a pressure for new terms to be adopted as standard in at least some domains.

However, you do not necessarily solve the 'male as norm' problem just by getting rid of the morphological vehicles through which it has traditionally been manifested. Language-users may simply reimpose the old structure on new content. One study (Dubois and Crouch 1987) found that this had apparently happened with *-person*. In a sample of job-change announcements from the US *Chronicle of Higher Education* the researchers observed that men who held a certain position in academic departments were generally described as 'chairmen' whereas women who held the same position were generally described as 'chairpersons.' Instead of replacing generic *-man* and/or the marked/ unmarked pairing *-woman/-man*, *-person* in this dataset appeared selectively to have replaced *-woman*, while *-man* remained untouched. Another case where something similar has happened is that of the title *Ms*. This title was not intended to be gender-neutral, but it was meant to be neutral regarding a woman's marital status, and as such to provide a direct parallel with the male title *Mr*. It seems though that not all English speakers have found this aim consonant with their own ways of making sense of social reality. Some speakers have restructured their system of titles in the way feminists hoped, by using *Ms* instead of *Miss* and *Mrs*. Others seem to have restructured along different lines, by constructing a three-term system: *Miss* for young unmarried women, *Mrs* for married women and *Ms* for 'anomalous' women – older but still unmarried, divorced, militantly feminist or lesbian (Schwarz 2003).

These examples illustrate the difficulties that can arise with attempts to change a language from the top down: as Anne Pauwels (1998) reminds us, the shift towards greater gender-egalitarianism in English usage has been less a matter of 'natural' evolution than a case of language planning. Pauwels also makes the point that feminist language planners' goals and strategies were in some respects quite limited. Generally they shared the folk-view of languages as collections of words, and their reforming efforts focused on vocabulary, with some attention (inevitably) to morphology. Their main strategy was, and remains, what Pauwels terms 'form replacement,' the replacement of one word or morpheme by another (e.g. substituting *they* for *he*, or *-person* for *-man*). This strategy has no purchase on gender-linked patterns at the level of syntax or discourse, and in these areas there has been little institutional pressure for change. Guides to non-sexist language rarely discuss, for instance, the recurrent pattern (ideologically analogous to the precedence of *he* over *she*) whereby men tend to appear before women in conjoined phrases (*John and Sue*, *Mr and Mrs Gupta*, *men and women*, *husbands and wives*, etc.). And the guides say nothing about the kinds of lexicogrammatical patterns uncovered by recent corpus studies, for instance Elizabeth Manning's (1998) finding that verbs denoting sexual acts, such as *fuck* and *shag*, show a tendency to have male subjects and female objects, though no grammatical rule prevents the opposite ordering, and reciprocal constructions (*they fucked*; *we shagged each other*) are also possible.

There is no doubt that since the 1970s, gender-egalitarianism and feminism have had an impact on the way gender is represented in English, but it would be misleading to suggest that this has produced a wholesale change in the language. Innovations do not magically cause older usages to be abandoned: eventually that may happen, but meanwhile new forms coexist with older ones, obliging speakers to make choices in contexts where once there was no choice. The outcome is new patterns of socially meaningful variation. Just like the phonological and stylistic variation discussed earlier in this chapter, variation in the use of pronouns, titles, occupational terms, and so forth points to the continuing salience for users of English of gender as a sociocultural phenomenon. It also underlines, however, that gender is not a monolithic construct understood and expressed or represented in exactly the same way by every member of the speech community. Consequently, the influence of gender on the English language is a more complicated issue than its popular representation, in 'Mars and Venus' literature or on the Gender Genie website, might suggest.

FURTHER READING

Cameron, D. (ed.) (1998) *The feminist critique of language: a reader*. London: Routledge.

Coates, J. (ed.) (2000) *Language and gender: a reader*. Oxford: Blackwell.

Holmes, J. and Meyerhoff, M. (eds.) (2003) *The handbook of language and gender*. Malden, MA: Blackwell.

REFERENCES

Argamon, S., Koppel, M., Fine, J., and Shimoni, A. R. (2003) Gender, genre and writing style in formal written texts. *Text* 24, 321–46.

Baron, D. (1980) *Grammar and gender*. New Haven: Yale University Press.

Baron-Cohen, S. (2003) *The essential difference: men, women and the extreme male brain*. London: Allen Lane.

Benor, S., Rose, M., Sharma, D., Sweetland, J., and Zhang, Q.

(eds.) (2002) *Gendered practices in language*. Stanford, CA: CSLI Publications.

Bergvall, V., Bing, J., and Freed, A. (eds.) (1997) *Rethinking language and gender research: theory and practice*. London: Longman.

Biber, D. (1995) *Dimensions of register variation: a cross-linguistic comparison*. Cambridge: Cambridge University Press.

Bodine, A. (1975) Androcentrism in prescriptive grammar: singular *they*, sex-indefinite *he*, and *he or she*. *Language in Society* 4, 129–46.

Cameron, D. (1997a) Performing gender: young men's talk and the construction of heterosexual masculinity. In S. Johnson and U. Meinhof (eds.), *Language and masculinity*. Oxford: Blackwell.

Cameron, D. (1997b) Is there any ketchup, Vera? Gender, power and pragmatics. *Discourse & Society* 9 (4), 437–55.

Chambers, J. (1992) Linguistic correlates of gender and sex. *English World-Wide* 13 (2), 173–218.

Coates, J. (1996) *Women talk: conversation between women friends*. Oxford: Blackwell.

Coates, J. (2003) *Men talk: stories in the making of masculinities*. Oxford: Blackwell.

Dubois, B. L. and Crouch, I. (1987) Linguistic disruption: *He/she, S/he, He or She, He-She*. In J. Penfield (ed.), *Women and language in transition*. Albany, NY: SUNY Press, 28–36.

Dubois, S. and Horvath, B. (2000) When the music changes, you change too: gender and language change in Cajun English. *Language Variation and Change* 11, 287–313.

Dunbar, R. (1996) *Grooming, gossip and the evolution of Language*. London: Faber.

Eckert, P. (2000) Gender and sociolinguistic variation. In J. Coates (ed.), *Language and gender*. Oxford: Blackwell, 64–75.

Eckert, P. and McConnell-Ginet, S. (1992) Think practically and look locally: language and gender as community-based practice. *Annual Review of Anthropology* 12: 461–90.

Eckert, P. and McConnell-Ginet, S. (1999) New generalizations and explanations in language and gender research. *Language in Society* 28, 185–201.

Eckert, P. and McConnell-Ginet, S. (2003) *Language and gender*. Cambridge: Cambridge University Press.

Gordon, M. and Heath, J. (1998) Sex, sound symbolism and sociolinguistics. *Current Anthropology* 39, 421–49.

Gray, J. (1992) *Men are from Mars, women are from Venus*. New York: HarperCollins.

Hall, K. and Bucholtz, M. (eds.) (1995) *Gender articulated: language and the socially constructed self*. London: Routledge.

Holmes, J. (1993) Women's talk: the question of sociolinguistic universals. *Australian Journal of Communication* 20 (3), 125–48.

Holmes, J. (1995) *Women, men and politeness*. London: Longman.

Hyde, J. and Linn, M. (1988) Gender differences in verbal ability: a meta-analysis. *Psychological Bulletin* 104, 53–69.

Jespersen, O. (1922) The woman. In D. Cameron (ed.) (1998), *The feminist critique of language*. London: Routledge, 225–41.

Johnstone, B. (1993) Community and contest: midwestern men and women constructing their worlds in conversational storytelling. In D. Tannen (ed.), *Gender and conversational interaction*. New York: Oxford University Press, 62–80.

Labov, W. (1990) The intersection of sex and social class in the course of linguistic change. *Language Variation and Change* 2, 205–54.

Labov, W. (1996) The organization of dialect diversity. Paper delivered to the International Conference on Spoken Language Processing, Philadelphia; available on the website of the Phonological Atlas of North America.

Labov, W. (2001) *Principles of linguistic change, vol. II: Social factors*. Oxford: Blackwell.

Lakoff, R. (1975) *Language and woman's place*. New York: Harper & Row.

Manning, E. (1998) Kissing and cuddling: the reciprocity of romantic and sexual activity. In K. Harvey and C. Shalom (eds.), *Language and desire*. London: Routledge, 43–59.

Nichols, P. (1997) Black women in the rural South: Conservative and innovative. In J. Coates (ed.), *Language and gender: a reader*. Oxford: Blackwell, 55–63.

Ochs, E. (1992) Indexing gender. In A. Duranti and C. Goodwin (eds.), *Rethinking context: language as an interactive phenomenon*. Cambridge: Cambridge University Press, 335–58.

Pauwels, A. (1998) *Women changing language*. London: Longman.

Schulz, M. (1975) The semantic derogation of woman. In B. Thorne and N. Henley (eds.), *Language and sex: difference and dominance*. Rowley, MA: Newbury House, 64–75.

Schwarz, J. (2003) Quantifying nonsexist language: the case of Ms. In S. Sarangi and T. van Leeuwen (eds.), *Applied linguistics and communities of practice*. London: Continuum, 169–83.

Tannen, D. (1990) *You just don't understand: Men and women in conversation*. New York: Morrow.

31 Language and Literature: Stylistics

PETER STOCKWELL

1 Introduction

It might seem obvious to the non-specialist that literature, the most culturally valued and aesthetically prestigious form of language practice, is best studied using the resources developed in the field of linguistics. However, this truism has not always been obvious to a wide range of disciplines, all of which claim a different stake in the study of the literary. Much of this contentiousness has arisen out of the historical baggage accumulated by institutionalized disciplines, out of territorial self-interest, and (it must be said) out of intellectual laziness, as well as the legitimate arguments around the validity and scope of linguistics. Stylistics is the discipline that has bridged these areas, and stylisticians have found themselves engaged in arguments not only with literary critics, cultural theorists, philosophers, poets, novelists and dramatists, but also with practitioners of linguistics. On the one hand it is argued that the artistic endeavor of literature cannot be amenable to the sort of rigorous analytical procedures offered by linguistic analysis; on the other hand it is argued that descriptive linguistics cannot be applied to artificial texts and readerly interpretations. For one group, stylistics simply and reductively dissects its object; for the other, the object simply cannot be described in a scientifically replicable and transparent manner.

The multivalent position of stylistics has its roots in the histories of language study and literary criticism, and the institutional make-up of modern universities and department divisions which fossilize particular disciplinary boundaries and configurations. Stylistics has therefore come to be regarded as an essentially interdisciplinary field, drawing on the different sub-disciplines within linguistics to varying degrees, as well as on fields recognizable to literary critics, such as philosophy, cultural theory, sociology, history, and psychology. However, by the end of this article, I would like to argue that stylistics is in fact a single coherent discipline: in fact, is naturally the central discipline of literary study, against which all other current approaches are partial or interdisciplinary. In order to arrive at that position, we must consider the history of stylistics, the status of stylistic analysis, some examples of stylistic practice, and a review of the latest paradigms and principles in stylistics research.

2   A Brief History of Stylistics

Broadly viewed as the analysis of linguistic form and its social effects, stylistics can be seen as a direct descendant of rhetoric, which constituted a major part of the training of educated men for most of the past two and a half millennia. Specifically, stylistics overlaps considerably with 'elocutio,' the selection of style for an appropriate effect. (The other four divisions of rhetorical skill were: invention, the organization of ideas, memory, and delivery). It is important to note the dual aspect in the discipline: rhetoric was concerned not only with linguistic form but also inextricably with the notion of the appropriacy of the form in context. The context was typically and primarily for spoken discourse, though rhetorical discussion was also applied to written texts. In the course of the twentieth century, stylistics developed with an almost exclusive focus on written literature, while at the same time the link between formalism and readerly effects became weakened.

According to Fowler (1981), there were three direct influences which produced stylistics: Anglo-American literary criticism; the emerging field of linguistics; and European, especially French, structuralism. Early twentieth-century literary criticism tended either to be historical and based in author-intention, or more focused on the texture of the language of literary works. The latter, though also encompassing textual editing and manuscript scholarship, mainly focused on the 'practical criticism' of short poems or extracts from longer prose texts. Such 'close reading' was largely informed by a few descriptive terms from the traditional school-taught grammar of parts of speech. This British practical criticism developed in the US into the 'New Criticism.' Where the former placed readerly interpretation first with the close reading to support it, the New Critics focused on 'the words themselves.' Famous essays by Wimsatt and Beardsley (1954a, 1954b) and others argued for the exclusion of any considerations of authorial intention or the historical conditions of contemporary production of literary works, and also against any psychologizing of the literary reading experience.

Despite the rather uncompromising stance taken by New Criticism, the belief that a literary work was sufficient unto itself did not amount to a purely descriptive account of literary texts. Interpretative decisions and resolutions simply remained implicit in terms of the social conditions and ideologies that informed them, while being dressed up in an apparent descriptive objectivity. A more rigorous descriptive account was being developed in the field of linguistics. As Fowler (1981) points out, Bloomfieldian structural linguistics evolving between the 1920s and 1950s offered a precise terminology and framework for detailed analyses of metrical structure in poetry. Chomskyan transformational-generative grammar from 1957 onwards provided a means of exploring poetic syntactic structure with far more sensitivity to detail than had ever been possible in literary criticism. And Hallidayan functionalism added a socio-cultural dimension that began to explain stylistic choices in literary texts.

The third area which influenced stylistics was European structuralism, arising out of Saussurean semiology and Russian Formalism through the work of Jakobson, Barthes, Todorov, Levi-Strauss, and Culler, among others. Branded 'formalists' by their detractors, many of the main concerns of modern poetics were in fact developed by the Moscow Linguistic Circle, the St Petersburg group *Opayaz*, and later the Prague School linguists. These concerns included studies of metaphor, the foregrounding and dominance of theme, trope and other linguistic variables, narrative morphology, the effects of literary defamiliarization, and the use of theme and rheme to delineate perspective in sentences. The Formalists called themselves 'literary linguists,' in recognition of their belief that linguistics was the necessary ground for literary study.

Stylistics began as a distinct approach to literary texts in the hands of Spitzer (1948), Wellek and Warren (1949), and Ullmann (1964), for example, but it really emerged from the 1960s onwards as the different influences mentioned above came to be integrated into a set of conventions for analysis. From Formalism and practical criticism came the focus of interest on literature and the literary, and from linguistics came the rigor of descriptive analysis and the scientific concern for transparency in that description. Though stylistic analysis could be practiced on any sort of text, much discussion involved the specification of 'literariness' and the search to define a 'literary language' – this preoccupation dominated to such an extent that stylistics has come to be identified very strongly with the discussion of literature, with non-literary investigations delineating themselves separately as 'critical linguistics' or 'critical discourse analysis' or 'text linguistics,' and so on. Of course, the notion of literariness makes no sense within a formalist or structuralist paradigm, since a large part of what is literary depends on the social and ideological conditions of production and interpretation. Nevertheless, stylistic analyses flourished in the 1970s, especially explorations of the metrics and grammar of poetry, and explanations of deviant or striking forms of expression in prose.

Concerns with literariness, the investigation of artificial rather than natural language, and the spectre of capricious interpretation all served to make theoretical and applied linguists in other areas of linguistic study rather suspicious of stylistics. At a time when the other branches of linguistics were claiming prestige and institutional funding as social sciences, those who were interested in literary analysis tended to be regarded as operating at the 'soft' end of the discipline. Equally and contrarily, literary critics and philosophers tended to regard the practices of stylisticians as being mechanistic and reductive. Since stylisticians often worked in literature departments, the most heated debates occurred with literary critics: traditional liberal humanist critics attacked a perceived irreverence for literary genius and its ineffable product; critics excited by the rise of literary theory as a discipline attacked stylistics for claiming to be merely a method without an ideological or theoretical under-pinning. Notorious examples of the antagonism include the debate between the stylistician Roger Fowler and the literary critic F. W. Bateson (see Fowler, 1971 for an account), centering on the question of rigorous descriptiveness against literary sensibility; or the attack by Stanley Fish and defence by Michael Toolan (see Fish 1980; Toolan 1990), circling around the status of interpretation in literary reading.

Although vigorous defences of stylistics continued to be raised in the 1970s, the field largely sidestepped the theoretical quagmire by taking an explicitly practical approach in the form of 'pedagogical stylistics.' This was a natural consequence of teaching (English) language using literary texts: foreign language learners took most readily to a linguistic approach to literature without importing any undue concern for theoretical niceties nor any misplaced reverence for the literary artefact. Teaching language through literature mirrored stylistics very clearly: texts tended to be those of contemporary literature; stylistically deviant texts were popular because they were fun and made it easy for the teacher to illustrate a specific point of usage; grammar and lexical choice were discussed as a motivating means of accessing the literature, rather than studied rather dryly for their own sake. Stylistics thus took itself out of literature departments and found adherents in education and modern language study around the world, enthusiastically supported by the international cultural promotion agency of the UK government, the British Council. (See Widdowson 1975, 1992; Brumfit 1983; and McCarthy and Carter 1994.)

At the same time, advances in pragmatics, sociolinguistics and discourse analysis in the 1970s allowed stylistics to move beyond the analysis of short texts and sentence-level phenomena. Studies involving speech act theory, norms of spoken interaction, politeness, appropriacy of register choice, dialectal variation, cohesion and coherence, deictic projection, turn-taking and floor-holding all allowed stylistics the opportunity of exploring text-level features and the interpersonal dimension of literature, especially in prose fiction and dramatic texts. New labels for a host of sub-disciplines of stylistics blossomed: 'literary pragmatics,' 'discourse stylistics,' 'literary semantics,' 'stylometrics,' 'critical linguistics,' 'schema poetics,' and so on. Stylistics came to identify itself as virtuously interdisciplinary, though it should perhaps properly be seen in this period as 'inter-sub-disciplinary.'

By the early 1980s, stylistics had established itself as a coherent set of practices largely based in Europe, mainly in Britain and Ireland, with strong centers in the Germanic and Scandinavian countries, representation in Spain as a major EFL destination for British teachers, with a separate tradition of *stylistique* operating in France, Italy, Greece and Turkey. Stylistics also developed where teaching links to Britain were strongest: in Australasia, India, Japan, and parts of Africa in the Commonwealth. The term 'stylistics' was nowhere near as widely used in North America, where generative grammar maintained its paradigmatic hold on linguistics, and post-structuralist theory enthralled those literature departments that aspired to more than character-study and a simple historicism.

3   The Status of Stylistic Analysis

One reason for the historical debates around stylistics has been the difficulty of defining 'style.' Even in its most simple sense of variation in language use, many questions instantly arise: variation from what? varied by whom? for what purpose? in what context of use? The different sub-disciplines that have been drawn on in stylistics have also brought along different senses of the term. Variationist sociolinguists treat style as a social variable correlated with gender, or class, for example, and have developed a cline of formality on this dimension. Anthropologists and ethnomethodologists have identified style with the contextual 'domain' in which the language variety is used, so that style has developed a wider sense close to that of 'register.' Style as an interpersonal feature involves psychological and socially motivated choices, so style can be seen as the characteristic pattern of choices associated with a writer's or projected character's 'mind-style,' or the pattern associated with particular periods, genres or literary movements. Most broadly, since every dimension of linguistic expression represents a choice – whether idiosyncratic or socially determined – the limits of 'style' can be seen to be the limits of language itself, which is not very helpful.

One central tenet in modern stylistics has been to reject the artificial analytical distinction between form and content. Contrary to the practice of traditional rhetoric, style cannot be merely an ornamentation of the sense of an utterance, when it is motivated by personal and socio-cultural factors at every level and is correspondingly evaluated along these ideological dimensions by readers and audiences. Style is not merely free variation. Even utterances which are produced randomly (as can be seen in surrealist and nonsense works) are treated conventionally against the language system in operation. Moreover, there can be no synonymy in utterances, since the connotations even of close variations are always potentially significant. Taking this argument to its logical end, even the same sentence uttered twice is 'stylistically' non-synonymous since the context of the second occasion of utterance is different from that of the first.

Clearly, the sense of 'stylistic' being used here has moved on a great deal from the earlier formalist sense of 'the words themselves.' The sorts of things stylisticians have been doing over the last twenty to thirty years have added more and more dimensions to the strictly 'linguistic' level, encompassing more of what language is while not losing sight of the necessity to ground descriptions in tangible evidence. Socio-cultural and psychological factors have become part of stylistic considerations.

Since the early 1980s, stylistics has continued in an expansive phase. Criticized for constantly focusing on deviant or odd texts, stylisticians shifted to the analysis of less stylistically striking writing, and presented variation in terms of norms and patterns that were internally marked in the literary work. The search for a linguistic definition of literariness was largely abandoned, with the literary being located in contexts of production and interpretation. The emphasis turned to examining the continuities between literary creativity and everyday creativity, and to how literary reading is continuous with the reception of language in general. Sociolinguistic findings informed literary analysis. Cognitive psychological aspects fed into stylistic exploration. Developments in pragmatics and discourse analysis continued to offer new tools and areas of investigation for stylistics. Insights into language use provided by corpus linguistics were drawn on, and computational techniques applied to literary works. Through the 1990s, stylistics in its most broad sense became one of the most dynamic and interdisciplinary fields within applied linguistics.

In response to its invigorated position within literary studies, stylistic practice has recently attracted a new series of methodological attacks, as well as debates between stylisticians themselves around theoretical issues and ideologies. However, the key arguments and issues being discussed can still be seen as rehearsals of concerns that have been of interest throughout the history of poetics. For example, there have been several variations on the theme of the position of stylistics as a science or as part of a more artistic endeavor. Most stylistics adheres to the scientific practices of presenting rigorous and systematic method and being explicit about its assumptions. Studies mainly conform to a Popperian approach to scientific method: they are transparent, explicit in their hypotheses and expectations, and are therefore falsifiable in the sense that other readers can compare their own readings and see how they differ from the stylistician. Only the principle of the replicability of the study is problematic in stylistics, since the reading experience is unrepeatable. For integrationalists (such as Harris 1980, 1981, 2000; and Toolan 1996), this is a serious problem: in rejecting the Jakobsonian 'code' model of language as involving what they scornfully term 'telementation,' in effect they remove any possibility of stable or comparable analyses. Mere formalism is not an analysis of language as communication, they argue, but then the move of stylistics towards encompassing more context ultimately renders the products of analysis merely as idiosyncratic readings, little different from the intuitive expressions of traditional literary criticism.

The key issue here is the question of interpretation, and the importance of noticing a difference between the textual object, reading, and interpretation. As I have argued elsewhere in response to the integrationalist critique (see Stockwell 2002b), stylistics can be regarded theoretically as a form of hermeneutics. Texts exist as autonomous objects, but the 'literary work' is an actualization of that object produced only by an observing consciousness (in the terms used by Ingarden 1973a, 1973b). The object of stylistic analysis (the literary work as opposed to the material literary text) comes into existence only when read. Since readers come with existing memories, beliefs, and both personal and social objectives, the context of the literary work is already conditioned by interpretation, even before reading begins (see Gadamer 1989). This means that reading is the process of becoming consciously aware of the effects of the text in the process of actualization: reading is inherently an analytical process, in this sense. Stylistics is simply the formal and systematic means of recording the same process and making it available for comparison.

As Toolan (1990: 42–6) points out, stylistics can be used for a variety of purposes, including the teaching of language and of literature. It can also be used as a means of demystifying literary responses, understanding how varied readings are produced from the same text; and it can be used to assist in seeing features that might not otherwise have been noticed. It can shed light on the crafted texture of the literary text, as well as offering a productive form of assistance in completing interpretations, making them more complex and richer. Stylistics can thus be used both as a descriptive tool and as a catalyst for interpretation.

These two possible functions of stylistics have been debated as if they were mutually exclusive: is stylistics a type of descriptive linguistics or is it a type of critical theory? The sense of exclusivity arises only if it is assumed that description is non-ideological. There are some stylisticians who argue that stylistics is simply a tool which can then be used in the service of a range of critical and interpretative positions. For example, it is an objective fact that a certain poem has a certain set of noun phrases from a particular semantic domain. Or it is a fact that the viewpoint in a certain novel is consistently a first person focalization. However, I would argue against this position, firstly on the theoretical dimension set out above that interpretation at least partly precedes analysis, and secondly on the practical dimension: since stylistics as a tool can only be manifest by being used, the fact that it is a descriptive tool in an ideal state is true but irrelevant in practice. As soon as stylistic analysis is undertaken, it partakes of ideological motivations, from the nature of the reading to the selection of the particular work and particular linguistic model for analysis. Examining noun phrases in the poem, rather than verb phrases, or describing them as a semantic domain, or choosing to explore focalization are all matters of ideological selection. So we might as well admit the fact and accept the ideological foundations on which we are operating.

Such debates within stylistics indicate that the field is far from settled at the theoretical level. It is a strange fact that the emphasis on practical application has meant that stylistics has a generally accepted method and approach while theoretical disagreements about the status of the discipline have continued around a relatively consistent analytical practice. Any differences in stylistic approach tend to arrange themselves along a cline from 'linguistic stylistics' to 'literary stylistics' (see Carter 1997), reflecting the motivations of the researcher rather than any programmatic political attachment. Linguistic stylisticians tend to be interested in exploring language using literature; literary stylisticians tend to be interested in exploring literature through analysis of its language. The former are more likely to be language teachers and the literary text is the equivalent of the data in applied linguistics. The latter are more likely to be cognizant of critical theoretical issues. However, the best stylisticians, in my view, are those who perceive an animating value in both positions.

4 Some Examples of Stylistic Practice

A consequence of the expansion of stylistics into matters of socio-cultural and readerly context is that stylistics has also come to be interlinked with related fields such as narratology, social semiotics, critical discourse analysis, cognitive poetics, and other approaches concerned with literary and culturally important texts. To attempt to represent this diversity, even for illustrative purposes only, in a short article such as this would be impossible. In this section, then, I will simply indicate the sort of practical work that has been undertaken under the umbrella of stylistics. For convenience here, examples will be arranged roughly along the linguistic rank scale, and according to the areas of linguistics set out in this *Handbook*, though it is important to remember that few modern stylistic studies are so exclusively focused. Work in, for example, the point of view of fictional characters might involve an analysis of how lexical choices, modal expressions, the directionality of verbs and other deictic features combine to produce the overall effect and characterization.

Early stylistic studies (as mentioned above) were often in the area of poetic metrics, and there has been a recent resurgence of interest in matters of prosody and phonology in poetry. Traditional descriptions of 'feet' and metre were enriched by 'generative metrics,' which sought to establish the transformational rules by which well-formed stress patterns in poetry were related to an abstract metrical pattern (see Chomsky and Halle 1968; Chatman 1964; and more recently Attridge 1982, 1995; and Fabb 1997). Stylistics shifted attention from metrics as a descriptive labelling to a consideration of the foregrounding patterns in verse: this involved an explanation of how certain features were made more salient than the background pattern, often through repetition, parallelism, positioning or co-occurrence with thematically significant syllables, words or phrases. This allowed phono-aesthetic effects to be explored, without resorting to simplistic equations of sound and sense. The point here was to demonstrate the poet's craft in organizing the texture as a literary feature in support of the developing meaning of the work.

To illustrate with a very simple example, here is the first part of Thomas Hardy's 'The Darkling Thrush':

> I leant upon a coppice gate
>   When Frost was spectre-gray,
> And Winter's dregs made desolate
>   The weakening eye of day.
> The tangled bine-stems scored the sky
>   Like strings of broken lyres,
> And all mankind that haunted nigh
>   Had sought their household fires.

Written on New Year's Eve, 1900, the poem continues to describe the apparent death and starkness of the landscape, explicitly symbolic of the old century's end. A stylistic analysis would note the uniformly regular rhythm in the prosody here, supported by the repetitions of /p/ in the first line, /s/ in the second, /d/ in the third, and so on. These produce an unremittingly strong emphasis throughout, with heavy pauses at the end of each line in spite of the syntax which runs across the line-endings. In particular there are repetitive consonant clusters /sk/, /st/, /zd/ which often coincide with stressed syllables. Almost every word is mono- or disyllabic, leaving the heaviest emphasis to fall on key content words: 'Frost,' 'spectre,' 'Winter,' 'dregs,' 'tangled,' 'scored,' 'haunted,' and so on. The two exceptions are 'weakening,' which is itself prosodically weakened in context towards a disyllabic pronunciation as 'weak'ning,' and the only other key polysyllabic word which is thus prominent in this stanza: 'desolate.' In everyday speech, this word would take heavy stress on the first syllable, and contrastive lighter stress on the second and third syllables. The metre and end-line rhyme position in the poem forces attention on the word, making it difficult to read – especially for inexperienced readers – without a temptation to emphasize the final syllable as 'late.'

After a second stanza which largely hammers home the same effect as the first, the third stanza begins:

> At once a voice arose among
>   The bleak twigs overhead
> In a full-hearted evensong
>   Of joy illimited;
> An aged thrush, frail, gaunt, and small,
>   In blast-beruffled plume,
> Had chosen thus to fling his soul
>   Upon the growing gloom.

The contrast here is striking, and a stylistic analysis would again draw attention to the differences apparent here against the phonological norms set up by the poem so far, such as the obvious multiple repetition of the vowel in the first line. Notice, too, how lexis is being selected to maintain the patterns already established: 'illimited,' not 'unlimited'; 'plume,' not 'plumage.' Where the repetitions of consonants and consonant clusters in the first stanza were largely embedded within word boundaries, here they are more properly alliterative as word-initial elements ('blast-beruffled,' 'growing gloom'). The third line of this stanza breaks the monotonous rhythm at the same time as the lexical choices begin to shift from the semantic field of superstition ('spectre,' 'haunted') to that of religion ('evensong,' 'soul,' and in the next stanza, 'carollings' and 'blessed Hope'). Again, a stylistic discussion would notice the correspondences between metrics and thematics here, in order to support a particular interpretative line and demonstrate the reading.

Though such phonological exploration of poetry most typically remains focused at the micro-level, stylistics has also investigated suprasegmental and sociolinguistic aspects of the phonological dimension in, for example, the representation of accents in prose fiction. Given that novelists tend not to write in phonetic notation, the graphological creativity involved in representing Scots (Hugh MacDiarmid, Irvine Welsh, James Kelman), a Dorset accent (Thomas Hardy), Mississippi (Mark Twain) or West African (Ken Saro-Wiwa) forms of pronunciation are all of interest to stylisticians. Again, such studies would not treat the literary representation as dialectological data but as a symbolic representation in which language establishes identity, develops characterization, conveys realist texture, and asserts a political ideology.

Notice, of course, how even my simple illustrations here inescapably spill out of the purely phonological level, drawing in semantics, graphology, and syntax however briefly. In a similar way, stylistic analyses which focus on lexical choices are also likely in reality to draw in aspects of syntax and grammar. My own studies of science fictional neologisms, for example, necessarily paid attention to the syntactic positioning, the word-class and the derivations and inflections in context that increase the sense of plausibility and verisimilitude in those science fictional worlds (see Stockwell 2000). Often, the interaction between different linguistic levels serves to signal some literary complexity. For example, surrealist poetry might have a highly normative syntactic form but a highly unusual set of lexical collocations: Philip O'Connor's 'Blue bugs in liquid silk/talk with correlation particularly like/two women in white bandages' is syntactically well-formed and is even suggestive of an explanatory register, except that the semantic sequence is extremely odd. Several W. H. Auden poems set up a serious topic (cancer, death, state repression) in lexical choices from coherent and consistent semantic fields, only to undermine them by setting the poem to a nursery-rhyme style of prosody, in order to signal irony, satire or bathos. These few examples illustrate that both deviant texts and relatively normative texts are amenable to stylistic study, even narrowly at the level of lexis.

The lexical choices made in a poem or ascribed to a character in fiction serve as clear markers of the imagined speaker's perspective, opinions, and identity. Naming and pronominal choices, expressions of modality, the selection from among synonyms, and idiomatic forms are often deployed to be consistent with lexical collocates, and with grammatical organization. Stylistic analysis can reveal very subtle differences between characters' styles of speaking and thinking; when those styles are highly deviant from typical everyday discourse, a stylistic analysis can illuminate the micro-craft of the literary work, suggesting connections between parts of the text that might otherwise have been only subconsciously realized. For example, Steve Aylett's (1999) novel, *The inflatable volunteer*, presents a first person narrative that is either set in a rich fantasy world or represents the hallucinatory imagination of the focalizer, Eddie. Eddie's narrative style generates a sense of discomfort and unease in most readers of the novel; my students describe it impressionistically as very weird, but not weird enough to be completely mad:

Bone midnight Eddie – the little red lizard curled up in a rose. Yeah there's nightmares and nightmares – you know what I'm saying. I've taken part in some where the curtains have caught fire off the devil's roll-up and the clueless bastard ghosts have barged in late and we were all of us shuffling apologies to the poor sod on whom we were meant to be slamming the frighteners. Torment's not what it was. Subjective bargaining and the bellyflop of the old smarts flung a spanner in the works an age ago Eddie. That and lack of imagination. Nothing like a spider in the mouth to get you thinking.   (Aylett 1999: 5)

Here Eddie is talking to himself, and his lexical choices include phrases which are genuine casual idiomatic expressions ('you know what I'm saying,' 'spanner in the works'). However, these are also mixed up throughout the novel with lexical clusters that sound almost idiomatic ('slamming the frighteners' = 'putting the frighteners on'?), as well as a great number of phrases that have the flavor of idioms but seem to be newly invented ('the devil's roll-up,' 'Nothing like a spider in the mouth'). The effect of the entire novel is a disconcerting defamiliarization of the world, accompanied by the disorientating effect of the prose style. These effects can be locally identified and explained at the lexical level, where the style of the novel plays a major part in its success.

Again, though an analysis focusing on the lexical and phrasal levels would be the most interesting here, a stylistic account of representative passages from the novel would also need to explore the more global features of narratological style and the various shifts in point of view. Even a micro-analysis of selected passages would probably draw in matters of lexico-grammar more broadly, including the syntactic organization and matters of transitivity, for example. Indeed, Hallidayan functional grammar has been a very productive approach in the field of stylistics over the past thirty years. One of the earliest and still most famous such studies was that presented by Halliday (1971), in which he investigated the unusual patterning of transitivity in William Golding's 1955 novel, *The inheritors*. Large parts of the novel are written from the point of view of Lok, a neanderthal man living in a community which encounters a more technologically advanced group he calls 'the new people.' Halliday shows firstly how Lok's limited world view is represented by his inability to name new technology: bows and arrows, for him, are unlexicalized, and he has to explain the effect of a stick becoming shorter and longer and a tree next to him acquiring, with a click, a new branch. Halliday develops these observations at the lexical level into an analysis of the transitivity relations in the clauses used by Lok. His focalization is dominated by material action processes and intransitives, in order to represent a simple world view with a limited sense of abstraction, generalization, and cause and effect. As Halliday (1971: 360) points out, 'In *The inheritors*, the syntax is part of the story.'

Clearly, in setting out to explore the texture of novels, any stylistic analysis of readable length cannot possibly be exhaustive, and I have mentioned that a process of selection and excerpting of key passages is necessary. This unavoidable selection is part of what makes stylistics an interpretative enterprise rather than a mechanistic or purely descriptive approach. Scenes or passages that appear intuitively to be key parts of the text, or which create oddities in readerly sensation, are often good places to begin a more systematic stylistic analysis. It could even be said that the mark of a good stylistician is someone who selects a particular analytical tool best suited to the passage in hand. Sometimes this selection is very obvious: it makes sense to investigate the murder scenes in crime novels in order to discern elements of blame, justification, motive, disguise of the identity of the murderer, and other narratological factors crucial to the novel's suspense or psychological tension. Carter (1997) for example, explores the transitivity relations in the murder scene of Joseph Conrad's 1907 novel *The secret agent*, showing how the agency is deflected from the victim's murderer and it is inanimate objects and disembodied limbs which appear to act. The murder is thus depersonalized and blame is shifted away from the murderer.

For illustration, here is another murder scene:

Just after 8.15 p.m. that same evening a man was taking the lid off the highly-polished bronze coal-scuttle when he heard the knock, and he got slowly to his feet and opened the door.

'Well, well! Come on in. I shan't be a minute. Take a seat.' He knelt down again by the fire and extracted a lump of shiny black coal with the tongs.

In his own head it sounded as if he had taken an enormous bite from a large, crisp apple. His jaws seemed to clamp together, and for a weird and terrifying second he sought frantically to rediscover some remembrance of himself along the empty, echoing corridors of his brain. His right hand still held the tongs, and his whole body willed itself to pull the coal towards the bright fire. For some inexplicable reason he found himself thinking of the lava from Mount Vesuvius pouring in an all-engulfing flood towards the streets of old Pompeii; and even as his left hand began slowly and instinctively to raise itself towards the shattered skull, he knew that life was ended. The light snapped suddenly out, as if someone had switched on the darkness. He was dead.   (Dexter 1991: 517)

The reader of this terrifying passage in the crime novel, *The silent world of Nicolas Quinn*, knows the identities neither of the victim nor his murderer. However, there are several clues in the style of the passage that might pass into the reader's awareness and can be illuminated through a stylistic analysis.

For example, the identity of the victim is kept secret by the careful selection of referential style in the cohesive chain of noun phrases. He is first unspecified as 'a man,' then co-referred to simply using the pronouns 'he' and 'his,' suggesting this is the reader's first encounter with him (in fact, this is a red herring, since we later find out the victim is Mr Ogleby, a character we have met previously). However, certain definite noun phrases then signal a point of view shift into the man's head: the proximal deictics of 'that same evening,' 'the lid,' 'the . . . scuttle,' 'the knock,' 'the door' and 'the tongs' all suggest his familiarity with the contents of the room. In particular, 'the knock' (rather than 'a knock' here) suggests that the visitor (and his/her knock at the door) was expected and also known to the victim.

The reader might even begin to gain a sense of characterization in the style of the passage. Someone who, rather redundantly, specifies 'Just after 8.15 p.m. that same evening' appears to be someone who likes precision and is rather fastidious – note also how his coal-scuttle is highly-polished. As the psychological viewpoint in the narrative, he also likes the specification offered by multiple adjectival modifiers: 'highly-polished bronze,' 'lump of shiny black,' 'enormous,' 'large, crisp,' 'weird and terrifying,' 'empty, echoing,' and so on. These aspects of his life contrast sharply with the stark unmodified statement, 'He was dead.' The phatic greeting ('Well, well!') suggests not only familiarity with the visitor, and a certain warmth ('Come on in' rather than, say, 'Come in,' or 'Do come in'), but also offers inferences to be made about the speaker's age and social class: 'shan't' also supports my sense of an upper middle-class middle-aged educated and rather pedantic man. This sense of his level of education is also perhaps confirmed by the erudite reference to the ancient destruction of Pompeii. In fact, as we later discover, the victim, Mr Ogleby, is an Oxford academic responsible for the examinations system. We discover his murder at the same time as the detective, Inspector Morse, and so even though we have been given access to this striking passage, we share some of Morse's shock at the news. The subtlety of stylistic clues in the passage also reflects, of course, the piecing together of clues by the detective in the crime novel.

In the long third paragraph, noun phrases denoting the parts of his body are used metonymically to stand for him: he is already being stylistically dis-embodied at the moment of his murder. Furthermore, a quick analysis of the predicate processes in this paragraph reveals that the disembodied limbs are the active participants in material processes ('right hand held,' 'left hand began to raise'). Mostly, though 'he' is distanced from the action by being placed as a participant in relational and mental processes: 'seemed,' 'sought,' 'willed,' 'knew.' The main actions take place in conditional or subordinate level clauses, relativized by 'as if.' The outcome of all of this textual organization is that the victim's conscious mind is immobilized in his dying body, and his desires for action are rendered unproductive. The first five sentences of the paragraph are extremely hypotactically complex; the final sentence consists of a single clause expressing, ironically, an existential process: 'He was dead.' The choice of past tense for the verb here generates particular horror: the sentence plays out for the reader the realization in the mind of Ogleby that in fact he has been dead for the duration of the paragraph.

This brief illustrative stylistic analysis, focusing on lexico-grammar, connects the selected passage with matters of characterization, suspense and point of view. In the process, I have drawn briefly on pragmatics, discourse analysis, sociolinguistics, narratology and the cognitive effects of cohesion. At these macro-linguistic levels, it is easy to see the possible linkages to be made with more purely literary concerns such as characterization, narrative structure, tone and atmosphere, genre, texture, realism and viewpoint, for example. From the standpoint of more well-established branches of linguistics, this practice might look hopelessly eclectic. However, for stylistics to account fully for the organizational patterns and readerly effects of literary works, such a wide-ranging approach is essential, since the object of study itself is various, protean and complex. As a result of its interdisciplinary contact with critical and cultural theory, modern stylistics is currently addressing itself to providing a principled account of the textural complexity of literature.

5   Emerging Work in Stylistics

There is a growing body of work in stylistics which marries up detailed analysis at the micro-linguistic level with a broader view of the communicative context. Indeed it is this integrative direction that seems to me to characterize the various emerging concerns of the discipline. Of the numerous different developments that I outline below, all have in common the basic stylistic tenets of being rigorous, systematic, transparent and open to falsifiability. All set out to draw the principled connections between textual organization and interpretative effects. In short, they present themselves as aspects of a social science of literature, rather than a merely poetic encounter with the literary. Modern stylistics continues the century-old tradition of denying any separation of interpreted content from textual form, and it is interesting to note books and courses appearing which exchange the term 'stylistics' for the term 'literary linguistics,' reappropriating the Russian Formalists' term for themselves.

In this respect, stylistics *necessarily* involves the simultaneous practice of linguistic analysis and awareness of the interpretative and social dimension. The act of application is what makes stylistics a fundamentally singular discipline of applied linguistics, arguing that formal description without ideological understanding is partial or pointless. If there is a paradigm in stylistics, it is this, and it seems to me to make stylistics a unified discipline at heart, with spin-offs into history, social study, philosophy, and literary archaeology, as practiced in literature departments around the world.

The discipline of stylistics is currently drawing much of this work to itself. For example, studies of the sociolinguistics of writing have led to a renewed emphasis on the various literatures of the world in different international Englishes. The ways that writers use different vernaculars to represent a greater richness of cultural voices are being explored stylistically. These studies include explorations of particular authors and communities around the world, as well as more theoretical work on how 'voice' is represented in literature. The holistic sense of 'voice' involves many of the historical concerns of stylistics: mind-style, character viewpoint, deixis, modality, and so on. In some respects, the current interest in voice represents a re-evaluation of these textual patterns renewed through the readerly construction of the psychology of the speaker.

Also along the readerly dimension, a major evolution in stylistics has been the development of 'cognitive poetics' (also called 'cognitive stylistics'). Applying the growing field of cognitive science to the experience of literary reading has been generating many interesting new insights into literature. These range from the almost purely psychological to the almost purely textual, but the vast majority of cognitive poetic studies combines our understanding of readerly cognitive processes with textual reality in the stylistic tradition (see Stockwell 2002a; Gavins and Steen 2003; and Semino and Culpeper 2002).

Cognitive poetics adds new facilities to stylistics, enabling the field to address key current issues such as a principled account of 'texture,' an understanding of how the thematics of reading a literary text works, or how a piece of literature can generate and sustain emotion. These developments simply extrapolate the continuing evolution of stylistics towards encompassing matters that were traditionally the ground of literary critics alone.

Underlying much of this principled interest in social and psychological context is a renewed sense of *ethics* in stylistic research. Non-literary stylistic analysis has developed through critical linguistics and critical discourse analysis alongside stylistics: the interaction between the two fields has been constant and close and consequently very productive (see Fairclough 1995; and Mills 1995, for example). Along with the ethical awareness that the literatures of the world ought to be studied sociolinguistically, fields such as feminist linguistics have worked to remind stylisticians (and all applied linguists) of our ethical responsibilities and the impossibility of an ideologically neutral linguistic theory.

Stylistics has also continued to draw on methodological innovations in linguistics. In particular, corpus linguistics and the use of computerized concordances and other empirical analytical tools have revolutionized the systematic study of literary texts. (See Thomas and Short 1996.) The continuities between literary creativity and the creativity apparent in everyday discourse have been revealed in all their complexity largely out of the fruitful interaction of stylistics and corpus linguistics. New methods such as these can be used to explore levels of language from lexical collocations right up to narrative organization. At the same time, the pedagogical element in stylistics has also developed strongly. Stylistic methods are now the paradigmatic approach in the foreign language classroom, and the applied study of creativity is becoming standard in native-speaker language teaching too.

Stylistics, as a discipline, is therefore very much in its heyday. It is a progressive approach in the sense that stylisticians strive constantly to improve their knowledge of how language works, while at the same time being aware of the useful insights of its own tradition. Its challenges arise from an apparently boundless appetite for drawing in the different disciplines and levels of language study, and the desire of its practitioners to be at once rigorously disciplined and also engaged and passionate about verbal art.

FURTHER READING

Bex, T., Burke, M., and Stockwell, P. (eds.) (2000) *Contextualised stylistics*. Amsterdam: Rodopi.

Carter, R. (ed.) (1982) *Language and literature: an introductory reader in stylistics*. London: Allen & Unwin.

Carter, R. and Simpson, P. (eds.) (1989) *Language, discourse and literature: an introductory reader in discourse stylistics*. London: Unwin Hyman.

Culpeper, J., Short, M., and Verdonk, P. (eds.) (1998) *Exploring the language of drama: from text to context*. London: Routledge.

Fowler, R. (1996) *Linguistic criticism*, 2nd edn. Oxford: Oxford University Press.

Pope, R. (1995) *Textual intervention: critical and creative strategies for literary studies*. London: Routledge.

Short, M. (1996) *Exploring the language of poems, plays and prose*. Harlow: Longman.

Simpson, P. (2004) *Stylistics: a resource book for students*. London: Routledge.

Verdonk, P. (ed.) (1993) *Twentieth century poetry: from text to context*. London: Routledge.

Verdonk, P. and Weber, J.-J. (eds.) (1995) *Twentieth century fiction: from text to context*. London: Routledge.

Wales, K. (ed.) (2001) *A dictionary of stylistics*, 2nd edn. Harlow: Longman.

Weber, J.-J. (ed.) (1996) *The stylistics reader*. London: Arnold.

Journals

Genre
Journal of Literary Semantics
Language and Literature
Language and Style
Poetics
Poetics Today
Social Semiotics
Style

REFERENCES

Attridge, D. (1982) *The rhythms of English poetry*. Harlow: Longman.

Attridge, D. (1995) *Poetic rhythm: an introduction*. Cambridge: Cambridge University Press.

Aylett, S. (1999) *The inflatable volunteer*. London: Phoenix House.

Brumfit, C. J. (ed.) (1983) *Teaching literature overseas: language-based approaches*. Oxford: Pergamon.

Carter, R. (1997) *Investigating English discourse*. London: Routledge.

Chatman, S. (1964) *A theory of metre*. The Hague: Mouton.

Chomsky, N. and Halle, M. (1968) *The sound pattern of English*. New York: Harper & Row.

Dexter, C. (1991) *The silent world of Nicolas Quinn*. London: Macmillan.

Fabb, N. (1997) *Linguistics and literature*. Oxford: Blackwell.

Fairclough, N. (1995) *Critical discourse analysis*. Harlow: Longman.

Fish, S. (1980) What is stylistics and why are they saying such terrible things about it? In S. Fish (ed.), *Is there a text in this class? The authority of interpretative communities* (pp. 68–96). Cambridge, MA: Harvard University Press.

Fowler, R. (1971) *The languages of literature*. London: Routledge & Kegan Paul.

Fowler, R. (1981) *Literature as social discourse*. London: Batsford.

Gadamer, H. G. (1989) [1965] *Truth and method*. Trans. J. Weinsheimer and D. G. Marshall. New York: Crossroad Press.

Gavins, J. and Steen, G. (2003) *Cognitive poetics in practice*. London: Routledge.

Halliday, M. A. K. (1971) Linguistic function and literary style: an inquiry into the language of William Golding's *The inheritors*. In S. Chatman (ed.), *Literary style: a symposium*. London: Oxford University Press, 330–65.

Harris, R. (1980) *The language myth*. London: Duckworth.

Harris, R. (1981) *The foundations of linguistic theory*. London: Routledge.

Harris, R. (2000) When will stylistics ever grow up? Paper presented at the 20th PALA conference, Goldsmith's College, London, July 2000.

Ingarden, R. (1973a) [1931] *The literary work of art: an investigation on the borderlines of ontology, logic, and theory of literature*. Trans. G. Grabowicz. Evanston, IL: Northwestern University Press.

Ingarden, R. (1973b) [1937] *The cognition of the literary work of art*. Trans. R. A. Crowley and K. Olson. Evanston, IL: Northwestern University Press.

McCarthy, M. and Carter, R. (1994) *Language as discourse: perspectives for language teaching*. Harlow: Longman.

Mills, S. (1995) *Feminist stylistics*. London: Routledge.

Semino, E. and Culpeper, J. (2002) *Cognitive stylistics*. Amsterdam: Benjamins.

Spitzer, L. (1948) *Linguistics and literary history: essays in stylistics*. Princeton, NJ: Princeton University Press.

Stockwell, P. (2000) *The poetics of science fiction*. Harlow: Longman.

Stockwell, P. (2002a) *Cognitive poetics: an introduction*. London: Routledge.

Stockwell, P. (2002b) A stylistics manifesto. In S. Csábi and J. Zerkowitz (eds.), *Textual secrets: the message of the medium*. Budapest: Eötvös Loránd University, 65–75.

Thomas, J. and Short, M. (eds.) (1996) *Using corpora for language research*. Harlow: Longman.

Toolan, M. (1990) *The stylistics of fiction: a literary linguistic approach*. London: Routledge.

Toolan, M. (1996) *Total speech: an integrational linguistic approach to language*. Durham, NC: Duke University Press.

Ullmann, S. (1964) *Language and style*. Oxford: Basil Blackwell.

Wellek, R. and Warren, A. (1949) *Theory of literature*. Harmondsworth: Penguin.

Widdowson, H. (1975) *Stylistics and the teaching of literature*. Harlow: Longman.

Widdowson, H. (1992) *Practical stylistics*. London: Oxford University Press.

Wimsatt, W. K. and Beardsley, M. C. (1954a) The affective fallacy. In W. K. Wimsatt (ed.), *The verbal icon*. Lexington, KY: University of Kentucky Press, 21–39.

Wimsatt, W. K. and Beardsley, M. C. (1954b) The intentional fallacy. In W. K. Wimsatt (ed.), *The verbal icon*. Lexington, KY: University of Kentucky Press, 3–18.

32 English Usage: Prescription and Description

PAM PETERS

1 Introduction

1.1 *Definitions of* usage

The French loanword *usage* has always been polysemous in English, referring to the customary way of doing something, as well as accepted practice or a body of rules associated with a group or an occupation. The earliest application of *usage* to "the established or customary use of language" was, according to the *Oxford English dictionary* (1884–1928), by Defoe. Yet the citation from Defoe's essay on *Essential projects* (1697) is caught up in an argument for establishing an English academy like the Academie Française, and the hope that "the voice of this society [i.e. the English academy] should be sufficient authority for the usage of words." Defoe's authoritarian approach to language *usage* contrasts with the OED's citation from Paley (1785) that "all senses of words are founded upon usage." Eighteenth-century commentators often echoed Horace's dictum that common usage is the ultimate arbiter of language: "usus quem penes arbitrium est et jus et norma loquendi" (*Ars Poetica* ll. 71–2), literally ". . . usage, in which lies the arbiter, law and rule of speech." Yet few recognized its full implications (Leonard 1962: 139–65), and the century goes down in English language history as "the age of correctness," not achieving the scientific advances of other contemporary disciplines such as botany or mathematics.

Though the *Oxford dictionary* project provided an enormous stimulus to empirical approaches to usage in the nineteenth century, the tug-of-war between descriptive and prescriptive approaches to English usage only intensified during the twentieth century. Prescriptive appraisals of usage resurfaced with Henry Fowler's *Dictionary of modern English usage* (1926), whose strong discriminations between usage he found acceptable or abhorrent made it and him a household word. The judgmental stance on *usage* is spelled out in Eric

Partridge's title *Usage and abusage* (1942), and others like the *Concise dictionary of correct usage* (Phythian 1979). While the second edition of the *Oxford English dictionary* (1989) maintains the original definition of *usage* ("established or customary use of language"), it adds that the word is often used attributively in *usage guide* etc., where its application is usually prescriptive: very few usage guides published in the second half of the twentieth century take a descriptive stance (see below, section 2.2).

Descriptive and prescriptive senses are visibly merged in the *New Oxford dictionary*'s (1998) definition of *usage*, formulated as "the way in which a word or phrase is normally and correctly used," and foregrounding the attributive use where the distinction between "normal" and "correct" usage is neutralized. Compare the definition given by a similar-sized American dictionary such as *Merriam-Webster collegiate* (2000): "the way in which words and phrases are actually used . . . in a language community," where only the descriptive sense is noted. Reflections of this British–American divergence will emerge in the discussion below. Meanwhile, let us note the comprehensiveness of the *Canadian Oxford dictionary*'s (1998) definition of *usage* as: "established or customary use of words, expressions, constructions etc . . . , as opposed to what is prescribed," where the difference between descriptive and prescriptive approaches to language usage is clearly on the table.

1.2   *The scope of* English usage

The two different understandings of *usage* just discussed make for enormous differences in scoping the subject. By the descriptive, neutral approach, the subject of *usage* research is the English language at large – a vast, multilayered system. By the prescriptive approach only selected elements of the language are considered, those on which judgments may be brought to bear.

From Fowler's *Modern English usage* (1926) on, the subject typically entails a miscellany of linguistic cruces including spelling, pronunciation, lexical semantics, collocation, and grammar, which are mostly treated in isolation, without systematic appraisal of their place in the language. Fowler's alphabetical list of topics is varied by later commentators on usage, especially those who wrote in different parts of the English-speaking world. But the "old chestnuts" are usually there, as if no usage guide could do without them, even though the tide of usage (in the other sense of the word) may have passed them by. English usage commentary has thus something in common with the medieval complaint tradition, as noted by Milroy and Milroy (1999). Burchfield in his *New Fowler's Modern English usage* (1996) maintains critiques of words such as *aggravate*, *alright*, *enormity*, *hopefully*, *unique*, though it must be said that he added substantially to Fowler's inventory (Delbridge 1997). Yet whatever the selection, the alphabetical format of usage books seems to reduce the subject to a limited set of items on which pronouncements can be made. They are of course the tips of icebergs, crystallized out of the larger dynamics of the English language.

Apart from limiting the scope of the subject and atomizing it, prescriptive approaches to *usage* imbue the subject with polarized values of right and wrong. Fowler was "an instinctive grammatical moralizer" (Jespersen, quoted in Gowers 1965: viii), a consequence of his years in the classroom. But it tends to preempt interest in natural linguistic variation, and reinforces the ideology of standardization (Milroy and Milroy 1999). More crucially, it disregards or ignores lexical and grammatical research which illuminates the very issues that usage commentators like to address. The lack of lateral referencing in many usage books (Peters and Young 1997: 317–19) suggests their remoteness from linguistic research, and a reluctance to refer even to the work of other usage commentators. The right to make one's own judgments is assumed.

All this explains why the prescriptive commentator on English usage and the descriptive linguist have been poles apart for most of the twentieth century. They have scoped the subject quite differently, worked in and published for different communities of practice. The large research endeavors of descriptive linguists rest on methodologies unknown or unavailable to prescriptive commentators. Their different products will be reviewed below in sections 2 and 3. Section 4 then brings linguistic-descriptive methods to bear on usage prescription, to discuss the impact of usage commentary on the actual usage of particular constructions. Section 5 considers the diversification of usage throughout the English-speaking world, and implications for the lexicography of usage.

2   Research on Usage Writing in Britain and North America

2.1   *Usage writers from the eighteenth to twentieth century: the quest for authority*

The first prescriptive accounts of English usage were a byproduct of eighteenth-century efforts to codify the grammar of the language. Earlier comments on points of interest in the emerging English vernacular can be found in the sixteenth century (Tucker 1961), and the earliest attempt to schematize such things as the English future tense is in Wallis's *Grammatica Linguae Anglicanae* (1653). But the eighteenth century saw an explosion of writing on English grammar, idiom, and points of usage which challenged those attempting to bring order to the vernacular chaos. The most comprehensive review of these endeavors, found in Sterling Leonard's *The Doctrine of Correctness 1700–1800* (1929/1962) contextualized them in terms of the philosophical and cultural movements of their time. Most pertinent in relation to usage discriminations was the quest for authority, sought initially from Latin and Greek grammar, which sanctioned basics such as the eight "parts of speech" into which English words have traditionally been classified, as well as nineteenth-century extrapolations such as proscription of the "split infinitive" and the "preposition" at the end of a sentence/clause. The applications of the classical models to English idiom were, however, limited, and the grammarians also turned to "universal grammar" or mathematical logic to rationalize their judgments, e.g. the disallowance of negative concord on grounds that two negatives make a positive, beginning with Lowth (*A short guide to English grammar*, 1762). But external reference points were few, and many points of usage were evaluated ad hoc with *ipse dixit* judgments, as grammarians affirmed their own individual authority. Usage judgments were then often contradictory, as Leonard (1962: 251–307) shows in a remarkable table which lines up authors who approved and those who disapproved of particular elements of grammar.

The contradictoriness of usage judgments, and the quest for authority, are recurrent aspects of usage writing in the nineteenth century, both in England and America. Baron (1982) charts them under the heading of "schoolmastering the language," and the demands of applying the diverse prescriptions of eighteenth-century grammarians to the needs of teaching English in the classroom. Amid rising interest in "scientific lexicography" in Victorian England (Willinsky 1994: 14ff), *ipse dixit* judgments were more readily challenged, as in the very public controversy over the attempt by Henry Alford, Dean of Canterbury to claim the royal imprimatur for his usage selections, which he published as "the Queen's English" (1863). His appeal to royal authority was pilloried in a volume titled *The Dean's English* (1864) by George Washington Moon, a Fellow of the Royal Society of Literature, and the London-born son of American parents. Against Alford's often usage-based preferences, Moon published his own set of rule-governed prescriptions, and was able to point out anomalies in Alford's position. He reacted also to anti-American aspects of Alford's preferences (Baron 1982: 190–7). The controversy was followed with interest on both sides of the Atlantic, but it added little fresh substance to the canon of English usage.

More lasting success in claiming royal authority went with the Fowler brothers (Henry and his older brother George), and their much larger reference on grammar and usage, titled *The King's English* (1906). From correspondence with the publisher we learn that this title was not the one originally proposed: it was the less arresting formula *The new solecist: for sixth form boys and journalists*, which would have tied the book too closely to the classroom and the newspaper office. The royal title addresses a more universal readership, and served also to divert attention from the scholarly limitations of the book, about which the authors were unapologetic in a letter (July 10, 1905) to the publisher.

> As to the expert, we have done our best to keep out of his danger; that is, we have practically based no arguments on historical grounds, have made no pretensions whatever to technical knowledge, and have occasionally implied that our authority is only that of a hour's start.   (quoted in Burchfield 1979: 9)

This extraordinary affirmation of the *ipse dixit* principle was no impediment to the success of *The King's English*, pace the title. It ran to second and third editions (1907, 1931), suggesting that it satisfied the pedagogical market, where its use no doubt lent educational authority to the usage tradition. In Britain as in the US, usage issues were most keenly examined in the classroom.

The King's English anticipates Henry Fowler's *Dictionary of modern English usage* (1926) in various ways, in its didactic and sometimes hectoring stance, and in exhibiting examples of bad writing, especially from the daily press, to make a point. But the alphabetically organized *Dictionary* provided easier access to the widened range of lexical and syntactic raw material, and additional topics such as affixes, spelling, and selected pronunciations. The miscellany of items, the alphabetic format, and the didactic stance of Fowler's *Dictionary of modern English usage* became the generic model for prescriptive usage books by others as the century progressed. Yet there have been few critical appraisals of Fowler's work. Monographs by Burchfield (1979) and McMorris (2001) have been largely biographical, not to say hagiographical. Quirk ventured a few iconoclastic remarks in an article "The toils of Fowler and moral Gowers" (1972), but otherwise the critique of Fowler's prescriptions has been left to descriptive language analysts (see below, sections 3 and 4).

Fowler's undeniable legacy can be seen in the sequence of usage guides published after him (Peters and Delbridge 1997). His very title is emulated in several others: *Dictionary of modern American usage* (Horwill 1935); *Dictionary of American English usage* (Nicholson 1957); *Dictionary of modern American usage* (Garner 1998), as well as *Dictionary of modern Australian usage* (Hudson 1993), and Burchfield's *New Fowler's modern English usage* (1996), all published by Oxford University Press. The Oxford imprint no doubt helped/helps to associate these books with the *Oxford English dictionary* and its monumental scholarship, and to lend its genuine authority to them. However their actual connections with the *Dictionary* are tenuous, except in Burchfield's case.

2.2 The lexicography of usage after Fowler: new sources of authority

Critical research on usage guides of the twentieth century takes off in the 1970s with Roy Copperud's *American usage: the consensus* (1970). There Copperud sought to synthesize the divergent opinions of contemporary American usage writers and dictionaries. His conclusions were subverted by the subjectivities of the raw material, yet his was a first attempt to compare the spectrum of prescriptive opinion.

A much more rigorous analysis by Thomas Cresswell (*Usage in dictionaries and dictionaries of usage*, 1975) compared usage material from 10 dictionaries and 10 usage books to see how far they coincided with each other and especially with the usage notes of the *American heritage dictionary* (1969/71) (= *AHD*). Cresswell was able to show that the "consensus" of these works was very limited, both in the range of items that they covered and their judgments about them. Of the 318 items compared, only 5 (= 2 percent) were treated in all 20 works (1975: 123), and opinions diverged on their acceptability. Their acceptance by members of the *AHD* usage panel ranged from 16 percent to 70 percent. The *AHD* usage panel had been specially created by the American Heritage Publishing Company to lend authority to the *Dictionary's* stance on usage, so as to set itself apart from *Webster's third new international dictionary (WIII)*, (1961). In its constitution the *AHD* panel was more like an Academie Française than a body of consulting experts, with high profile authors and social commentators such as Isaac Asimov, Jacques Barzun, Alistair Cook, Walter Lippmann among the original membership of 165. They seemed to constitute a kind of "cultured elite" (Landau 1979: 4) whose usage might provide a model for the upwardly mobile. Few were linguistic specialists or language historians. Rather there was a bias toward writers, editors and columnists who had been outspoken in their criticisms of *WIII*, as had the *AHD* editor himself, William Morris (Morton 1994: 228–30). The panelists' votes were quite erratic, but skewed toward the negative on most items of grammar and idiom (Cresswell 1975: 40–4). The fact that they were asked to provide opinions on each particular usage, rather than assess its general currency, would no doubt have fostered this response (cf. Marckwardt and Walcott 1938: 59). The usage panel's ratings (with some reconstitution of its membership) have remained a feature of subsequent editions of *AHD*. With the panel members' average age estimated at 61+ (Nunberg 1990: 481), a prevailing conservatism was assured, although changes in the panel's approval ratings are sometimes commented on in *AHD* notes. See for example the usage note in *AHD* 4 (2000) on the verb *premiere*, showing the decline in its disapproval rating: now 49 percent where it was 84 percent in *AHD 1* (1969/71). The publishers presumably see it as vindicating the panel's sensitivity to usage, rather than belatedly acknowledging its trends, and prefer to retain the panel as an "authority" which they alone can invoke.

A usage panel of 136 persons was also retained for the *Harper dictionary of English usage*, edited by William Morris and Mary Morris (1975). There were some overlaps in membership with the original *AHD* panel, but it consisted more of media "personalities" (Landau 1979: 4). Their outspoken comments are attached to more than 100 entries in the book, lending it the tone of "a very average talkshow" according to the American Library Association's *Booklist* review (1976). But they allude interestingly to other local language "authorities" in the US, such as Harvard University, and the *New York Times* (see *finalize*).

The American usage panel can nevertheless be seen as a methodological innovation of the twentieth-century usage book industry – remarkable as a collective means of supporting conservative positions on usage. No other usage guide among the 40 surveyed by Peters and Young (1997), published in the US, UK, or Australia between 1950 and 1995, had such resources. Those surveyed were typically written by one or two authors, and took for granted the *ipse dixit* right to pass their own judgments on usage. This went hand in hand with the lack of lateral referencing already noted (only 20 percent of those surveyed contained a bibliography). The data provided for discussion was quite often used for negative exemplificatiaon (found in 40 percent of publications surveyed), whether the examples were concocted, or derived from published texts. *The right word at the right time* (1985) highlighted its judgments of right/wrong/questionable usage with red ticks, crosses and question marks on the quotations of published authors – who might be surprised at their treatment there. No one would welcome being cited in Hudson's *Dictionary of diseased English* (1977), or the subsequent *Dictionary of even more diseased English* (1983).

The usage guides surveyed by Peters and Young (1997) were also examined on their judgments on 11 points of usage, in terms of whether they found them "unacceptable," usable under "restricted" circumstances, or quite "acceptable" (extending Cresswell's (1975) dichotomy of "restricted"/"acceptable"). As a set, the 20 British books surveyed were more consistently conservative than the (16) American or the (6) Australian, which both presented a wider range of positions and one or two descriptively oriented examples, discussed below (next paragraph). But profound conservatism could also be found among the American examples, most notably *The careful writer*, by Theodore Bernstein (consulting editor to the *New York Times*), who espoused British rather than contemporary American usage on questions such as use of the subjunctive; and Wilson Follett, who dubbed "promiscuous" the acceptance of usage alternatives by descriptive linguists (1974: *Introduction*). Both were among the most conservative of the usage authors analyzed by Thomas Cresswell (1975), returning a negative on more than 80 percent of the usage items they discussed.

Apart from the American usage panel, the only methodological innovation among the usage guides surveyed by Peters and Young (1997) was the use of corpus data, found in two (three) isolated cases. One of these was the *Dictionary of contemporary American usage* (1957), by Bergen and Cornelia Evans, who used a purpose-built corpus of journalistic texts and undergraduate writing to support their description of American usage. The other corpus-based publication was Peters's *Cambridge Australian English style guide* (1995), which made use of the Australian Corpus of English (ACE). The *Webster's dictionary of English usage* (1989) refers very occasionally to data from the American Brown corpus, but otherwise uses its large collection of citations held in the *Webster's dictionary* files, to describe usage trends. It is worth noting that these, and other corpus-based usage guides published since 1995, such as the *Guide to Canadian English* (Fee and McAlpine 1997), and the *Cambridge guide to English usage* (Peters, 2004) have all have been written outside Britain.

Few of the usage books published in the second half of the twentieth century are empirically oriented towards language data. On Algeo's (1991: 6–13) scale of usage books, most site themselves towards the "subjective, moralizing" end, rather than the other where "objectivity and reportage" of usage are the author's goals. Algeo makes Fowler (1926) the exemplar of the first, and *Webster's dictionary of English usage* (1989) exemplar of the second. More recent publications such as Burchfield (1996) and Garner (1998), still seem to sit more towards the subjective end of the scale, despite the large volumes of citational data presented. What is telling is the authors' tendency to use their data only in support of a priori judgments about correct use – or to identify negative examples (see for example Burchfield's treatment of *alright*). They show only occasional, grudging acceptance of usage trends, and otherwise affirm the prescriptive approach. Like their predecessors, they provide no access to the findings of contemporary linguistic research into regional, social, generic variation in usage.

3   Descriptive Approaches to English Usage in the Twentieth Century

3.1   *Lexical and grammatical description*

Descriptive and empirical appraisals of English usage can be found throughout the twentieth century, amid research into every level of the language. They shed light from time to time on points of usage discussed by prescriptivists, without it being their prime concern. Major projects on the English lexicon and English grammar have been supported by large British or American publishing houses, notably Oxford, Merriam-Webster, and Longman. But seminal work on English grammar has also been carried out by individual researchers, as discussed below. All have contributed important data to the analysis of usage.

Empirical work on the history of the English lexicon reached a climax in the 1930s with the publication of the final volumes of the *Oxford English dictionary* (1884–1928) and the 1933 *Supplement*. The *Dictionary*'s entries on words such as *disinterested/less/none/than* are illuminated by a wealth of historical citations, providing long, dispassionate records of their semantics and collocational properties, and incidentally showing how narrow and arbitrary the comments of prescriptivists have been. The recency of usage prescriptions comes to light by comparison with the *Dictionary*'s much longer perspective. For example: its original note on *like* (from the first edition): "Now generally condemned as vulgar or slovenly, though examples may be found in many writers of standing" still stands as a benchmark for the descriptive approach, which is generally maintained in the second edition. See for example the uses of *comprise* added to the 1972 supplement, but treated as "disputed or erroneous" by Burchfield (1996). Perceived weaknesses in the range of sources in the first edition were addressed in work toward the second (Willinsky 1994: 162–89), with citational material taken increasingly from texts published outside Britain and North America.

Webster's third new international dictionary (1961) edited by Philip Gove, also embraces a wealth of citational evidence, using it to drive definitions, and to register a full range of alternative forms, such as the alternative past tenses for *sink, spring* etc. It provides occasional notes to contextualize variants, as in the case of *ain't*, which became highly contentious in the furore over *WIII's* documentation of marginal and nonstandard usages (Morton 1994: 158–63). Though a natural consequence of its descriptive stance, it was represented as "permissiveness" by the media (Morton 1994: 172–3); and the backlash was successfully exploited by the *American heritage dictionary* (1969, 1971) with its usage panel. Fortunately, the accumulated data of *WIII* could be accessed and effectively used by Gilman et al. in the writing of the *Webster's dictionary of English usage* (1989).

Controversial elements of English usage were treated by Danish philologist Jespersen, in his large descriptive grammar of English (1909–49, 7 vols.). Like the OED, its makes extensive use of historical citations, to show the evolution of English grammatical practices, and bring to light the more idiomatic aspects of grammar, which were made controversial by prescriptivists. Jespersen was able to demonstrate the long history of such things as hypercorrect *whom* in parenthetic clauses (vol. iii: 198); of relative *whose* applied to nonhuman antecedents (vol. iii: 129); and of variations to formal patterns of concord (vol. ii: 66, 152, 181–2). His source material justifying *alright* and the use of the accusative with the gerund-participle proved powerful in much publicized controversies with Fowler through the Society for Pure English (tracts no. 18, 1924, and no. 25, 1926). Jespersen's historical data was used by Marckwardt and Walcott (1938) along with other authorities to recalibrate the usage findings of Leonard's 1928 elicitation experiments.

Useful data on usage issues also comes from Charles Fries's very original, descriptive *American English grammar* (1940). This was a radical departure from traditional grammars, using the inductive methodology of field linguistics to develop grammatical categories for the English language, rather than simply applying those handed down from the Greeks. The *Grammar* was totally based on data from a large corpus of bureaucratic correspondence to the US Veterans Department during World War I. The corpus contained more than 3,000 letters by more and less educated correspondents, divided into three categories which he labeled Standard, Colloquial, Vulgar, based on the education and occupations of the writers (Fries 1940: 26–33). Despite obvious limitations of the corpus, the *Grammar* is an object lesson in how it could be used to drive grammatical description, to profile grammatical variation, and to address usage controversies such as those discussed below (section 4.1.1 and 4.1.4). His interest in sociolinguistic divergence – when the dominant paradigm still foregrounded regional divergence – anticipates research on sociolects of speech by several decades. He provides the first breakdown of more and less "standard" usage in English grammar.

In descriptive grammars of the later twentieth century, data from more heterogeneous corpora than Fries's play an increasingly central role. The *Comprehensive grammar of the English language* (1985) by Quirk, Greenbaum, Leech and Svartvik makes occasional reference to University College London's Survey of English Usage, along with occasional references to regional and stylistic differences in usage. Some sections are also supported by elicitation studies (see below). All are reminders of variation within English usage, and serve to explain some of the variants. Corpus data is very systematically used in the later *Longman grammar of spoken and written English* (1999), by Biber, Johansson, Leech, Conrad, and Finegan. With the large Longman corpora, they are able to profile variation across written and spoken usage, and to systematically contrast British and American differences in conversational style. Longman data will also be introduced in the discussion of usage (sections 4.1.1 and 4.1.4 below).

These major ventures in describing the English lexicon and grammar were all founded on large volumes of data, from citational archives or from databases of texts (i.e. corpora) – both lending the authority of actual usage to the description of the language. The computerized corpus is perhaps the single most important development for the description of English usage. See also McEnery and Gabrielatos (this volume).

3.2   New methods for gathering linguistic data on usage

The earliest computer corpora (compiled with printed material from 1961) were designed to profile generic rather than social or intra-regional differences. Hence the different text types of the Brown and Lancaster-Oslo-Bergen corpora and their analogues, with 500 samples taken from the daily press, magazines, government and academic publications, and a 3:1 ratio of non-fiction to fiction. The generic range of these "sample" corpora has supported numerous contrastive studies of usage, and sheds light on the elements of style used in different contexts of writing. Because of their parallel structure, the Brown corpus and its regional analogues also support studies of regional difference in English usage; and short-term intra-regional developments in American and British usage can now be profiled with the help of the matching Frown and FLOB corpora, compiled at Freiburg University in Germany with data from the 1990s. The lack of spoken material in these corpora has been addressed in the expanding set of ICE corpora (International Corpus of English), but intercomparisons with data from the American ICE corpus are not yet possible, hence the continuing value of the earlier set of corpora. Larger corpora, such as the Longman corpus (used by Biber et al. 1999) and the British National Corpus now provide volumes of transcribed speech, to facilitate contrastive studies of spoken and written usage. A diachronic corpus of spoken present-day English (DCSPE) constructed at University College London allows searches of grammatical patterns over several decades.

Corpus resources allow us to map the variable landscape of English usage, with data of known provenance. This remains their great value, despite the very large volumes of data that usage researchers may garner from the internet. Through corpus data we gain a synoptic view of trends in usage in different communicative contexts, and across a range of styles. The adoption of colloquial elements of usage in what are regarded as more "serious" types of writing offers the chance to see larger trends such as the widespread conversationalization of usage (see Mair and Leech, this volume), with impacts on grammar as well as lexical choices.

Despite their advantages, corpus data from written sources tends to foreground the usage of those with access to publishing, thus typically that of the older generation (Peters 1998: 101; Minugh 2002: 72) Sociolinguistic variation in usage has been illuminated by other research methods developed during the twentieth century, most notably elicitation tests conducted among known groups of language users. This experimental technique was used for example by Greenbaum (1977) to investigate certain grammatical variables among American and British university students, they being provided with example sentences, and asked to insert their preferred form. The questionnaires returned allow the researcher to quantify results in terms of the user's age, education etc., which are not necessarily available with corpus material, and are especially useful for researching rarer morphological variants, such as the attachment of foreign plurals to English words (this was the focus of one of the six Langscape surveys, run by Peters (1998–2000) through the journal *English Today*). Elicitation provides a controlled context for researching spoken usages, which are otherwise subject to unpredictable pragmatic variables.

The same technique has been used to elicit acceptability judgments on disputed usages, by researchers such as Leonard (1932; Marckwardt and Walcott 1938), who asked his 229 judges (including linguists, teachers, authors, editors, businessmen) to rate 230 items on a scale from "literary" to "standard, cultivated, colloquial" to "vulgar." The judges' decisions converged on 173 of the items, but on the remainder, the judgments of professional linguists tended to be more favorable than those of others. Mittins et al. (1970: 18) noted a similar tendency among the English teachers and lecturers included in his 450 judges. They were asked to assess the acceptability of a set of 50 usage items in terms of spoken and written English, with formal/informal subcategories within each. Elicitation tests provide alternative lights on the status of usage variants, targeting community language attitudes and values which constitute the climate of usage practice. In combination with corpus data, elicitation techniques give us triangulation on the state of usage, and a means of assessing stylistic trends, in the shorter and longer term. For a case study, see below 4.1.4.

4 The Impact of Prescriptive Writing on English Usage

4.1 Case studies of the relationship between prescription and common usage

Despite the occasional findings of descriptive researchers discussed in section 3.1 above, there has been little research focusing on the interplay between prescriptive and descriptive approaches to language usage – on (1) how far the prescriptive guides reflect common usage in the judgments they make;

and (2) how far common usage seems to respond to their prescriptions. Tottie (1997) addresses the second question, though not the first, in her study of British/American divergence over the use of *that/which* in restrictive relative clauses. On countless points of usage, research is needed to examine both questions, to see whether prescriptive publications are in tune with the language practices of their time; and whether or not common usage subsequently falls into line. Let us now examine four grammatical issues, where empirical data can be brought to bear on usage practices contemporary with the prescription, and afterwards, providing some measure of its longer term influence on the English language.

4.1.1   *Future* shall *and* will

C. C. Fries's (1925) research on *shall* and *will* made use of dramatic texts over three centuries (from 1560 to 1920), to chart their interrelationship in expressing the English future tense, which puzzled generations of grammarians. The earliest formulation, that of Wallis (1653), was to prescribe *shall* as the future auxiliary for the first person, and *will* for the second and third persons. His "rules" were confined to declarative statements in main clauses, and extended idiosyncratically by others to cover subordinate clauses and questions. Fowler (1926) elaborates them further. Yet Fries's data enabled him to show that the "rules" assigning *shall* and *will* to different persons for the future were never really in touch with the interactive spoken discourse of contemporary drama. Instead, *will* is always the dominant usage for the 1st person, and the major variant for the third. *Shall* was the major variant for the second person only up to the later eighteenth century. Recent research by Biber et al. (1999), based on the Longman corpus of British and American English, shows *will* always in the ascendant in declarative syntax, with *shall* in the majority only for first person polite questions/suggestions. This limited application is the only outcome of centuries of prescription, in situations where there is considerable sociological pressure on the forms of communication. But otherwise our primary questions on the relationship between the rules for *shall* and *will* and actual usage yield only negative answers. The prescriptive rules did not reflect common usage of their time, nor have they had any durable effect on common usage of the two modals. Any conformity to the prescriptive rules seems to be highly context-dependent.

4.2.1   *The English subjunctive*

The decline of the subjunctive was a commonplace of usage commentary from the eighteenth century on, though the fate of the past subjunctive (*were*) is not always distinguished from that of its various present forms, as in the mandative construction "asked that they *be* informed." Fowler (1926) provided a pot pourri of comments on several forms (identified as "alives," "revivals," "survivals" and "arrivals"), but his judgment was that the system had broken down, and his advice – the course of least resistance – to avoid using it at all. Low levels of use of the present subjunctive in Britain after world war II are documented in corpus-based research by Johansson and Norheim (1988), which might indeed seem to reflect Fowler's influence on this aspect of English usage. However, their data from the LOB and Brown corpora also showed that American use of the present/mandative subjunctive was much higher; and subsequent studies (Peters 1998; Hundt 1998a) have confirmed this result with comparative data from elsewhere (the US, as well as Australia and New Zealand). Thus in "settler" Englishes outside Britain, use of the mandative has held steady in standard usage, whereas it had become confined to the formal fringe, according to British grammarians (see Quirk, Greenbaum et al. (1985)). With fresh evidence from a longitudinal corpus of literary texts from 1900 to 1990, Gerd Overgaard (1995) was able to show that use of the mandative subjunctive was low, but relatively stable in Britain up to the end of world war II. Nothing in her findings suggested the impact of Fowler's advice – only that British use of the construction was substantially lower than American use during the first half of the century. The transatlantic difference had in fact been noted by Gowers (1973 [1954/62]), who foreshadowed its possible impact on British usage. This is shown very graphically in Overgaard's data for the second half of the twentieth century (1995: 39), with a sharp rise in British use from 1960 to 1990. The increase was confirmed by Hundt (1998b), using comparative data from the Freiburg updates of LOB (FLOB) and Brown (Frown). British use of the mandative subjunctive begins to revive in tandem with lexical influences from the US, noted by Strang (1970: 37). So this post-world war II stimulus to British use of the mandative subjunctive seems to have far outweighed Fowler's advice to avoid it. In this remarkable case of major dialects in contact, we may also find the effects of koineization (Trudgill 1986). Where regional and international usage diverge, we might expect the latter to exercise more influence than local, prescriptive advice in the longer run.

4.1.3   *Conjunctive* like

Regional divergences contribute to the still unsettled status of *like* as a conjunction. Though rooted in the history of English, its use seems to have increased substantially during the nineteenth century, and to have been anathema to some, as the OED comments (see above, section 3.1). Fowler (1926) was relatively detached about it, allowing readers to decide for themselves which way to go; as was the American usage commentator Perrin (1942), commenting that despite the efforts of editors and publishers, it "increasingly appears in print." But Strunk and White (1959, 1972) made no bones about conjunctive *like* being the style of the "illiterate," and Bernstein (1958, 1965) likens it to wearing shorts to dinner at a restaurant. Follett (1966) and Morris and Morris (1975) also find it unacceptable. The prescriptive position on *like* thus seems to have been hardening in the US, thrown into the public arena through the controversy over the grammar of a cigarette advertisement: *Winston tastes good, like a cigarette should.* Corpus data from the 1960s (from Brown and LOB) provides an interesting foil to the furore – showing that American writers were then rather more tolerant of this use of *like* than their British counterparts (Peters 1993). Thirty

Table 32.1   Relative frequency of conjunctive *like* in two pairs of matching corpora of American and British English

	Brown *(data from 1961)*	*LOB* *(1961)*	*Frown* *(1991)*	*FLOB* *(1991)*
Nonfiction	9 (0.024)	0	10 (0.026)	4 (0.011)
Fiction	42 (0.336)	13 (0.104)	49 (0.392)	14 (0.112)
Totals	51	13	59	18

The figures in brackets normalize the raw numbers relative to the number of samples in nonfiction (375) and fiction (125) sections of the corpora. (Calculations based on the respective totals of words: 750,000 and 250,000 words, produce minuscule values.)

years on, with comparative data from matching British and American corpora, the overall picture for the use of conjunctive *like* with personal pronoun subjects is much the same: see the totals in table 32.1.

Though American writers are clearly more comfortable than the British with conjunctive *like*, the normalized figures show that both use it much more freely in fiction. Its use is thus stylistically stratified on both sides of the Atlantic, but the effect is much more marked in British English, where it hardly appears in nonfiction. This is somewhat paradoxical, inasmuch as the position taken by American usage commentators was quite uncompromising by comparison with that of Fowler (reproduced without change in the Gowers edition (1965)). Yet the corpus data show that the distribution of conjunctive *like* correlates with stylistic practice on both sides, that while American and British writers (and editors) allow it to render relaxed, speech-like discourse, they avoid it in more formal, serious writing. It shows also how the advice of prescriptive commentators tends to privilege the high style (which eschews conjunctive *like*), and endorses its practices as if they were "common usage." Alternative and colloquial constructions are relegated to the opposite end of the stylistic scale, in that unhappy dichotomy between written and spoken usage which underlies much of the ideology of "standard" English (Milroy and Milroy 1999). Yet corpus data show that conjunctive *like* is an element of common usage in the US, produced especially in clausal structures following the verbs *seems/sounds/ looks*, etc. (Peters 2004), which have their place in nonfiction as well as fiction. Perhaps they will serve as idiomatic "leaders" of the construction, to strengthen the conjunctive role of *like* across the stylistic board in the US, and establish it in more serious styles in the UK during the twenty-first century.

4.1.4   *Pronoun selections with the gerund-participle*

Stylistic and sociolinguistic stratification seem now to be key factors in the question of whether the genitive or accusative personal pronoun should be used to precede a gerund-participle. Some eighteenth century grammarians

Table 32.2 Frequencies (raw scores) of pronouns accompanying gerund-participle constructions in five matching corpora representing American, British and Australian English, all consisting of 1m words

	Brown (1961)		LOB (1961)		ACE (1986)		Frown (1991)		FLOB (1991)	
	gen.	acc.	gen.	acc.	gen.	acc.	gen.	acc.	gen.	acc.
Nonfiction	21	0	27	6	11	9	17	4	21	8
Fiction	19	6	14	10	4	11	6	5	10	7
Totals	40	6	41	16	15	20	23	9	31	15

The data are confined to instances where the gerund-participle follows a preposition, so as to avoid constructions which are predisposed to the accusative, e.g. verbs of perception (Biber et al. 1999: 750).

e.g. Lowth (1762) accommodated its "amphibious" behavior, but others such as Webster (1789) insisted on the genitive as the "genuine English idiom." Fowler (1926) agreed that it should be "they spoke of my being there," and disparaged the accusative construction "they spoke of me being there" as the "fused participle." He did however allow that the genitive was less satisfactory with nouns and indefinite pronouns, as in "they spoke of the secretary's/ everyone's being there." Jespersen (1909–49, vol. 5: 133–40) provides ample examples of the use of the accusative pronoun by well known writers from the nineteenth and early twentieth century – enough to show its currency, at least in speech-like discourse. In American data from the earlier twentieth century, discussed by Fries (1940), the two structures are almost equally represented in the "Standard" samples of correspondence (just 52 percent of examples had the genitive pronoun), whereas the accusative prevailed by 66 percent in data from the "Vulgar" samples. These modest statistics suggest that the accusative construction was ordinary American usage in the first half of the twentieth century, whereas the genitive construction prescribed by Strunk and White (1959/1972) was the style of the "educated" American. Corpus data in table 32.2 confirm that although use of the genitive pronoun was strongly preferred by American writers of the 1960s, the gap has narrowed in the ensuing thirty years, and the superiority of the genitive construction was never so keenly felt among British writers. If there was any immediate impact from the prescriptions of Fowler and Strunk and White, the effect is fading.

The totals from Brown, LOB, Frown and FLOB show that the genitive is definitely preferred in both northern hemisphere varieties of English, whereas the data from ACE show an overall preference for the accusative in the southern hemisphere. Accusative constructions are evidently acceptable in Australian nonfiction, and much preferred by fiction writers (The extent of the difference is clear when we normalize the raw scores for fiction, multiplying by 3 to bring them up to parity with the figure for nonfiction, because of the unequal amounts of data on which the fiction and nonfiction figures are based. See note under table 32.1 above). There is thus a stylistic dimension to the Australian preference for the accusative construction – as well as a sociolinguistic dimension, articulated by the pioneer usage writer Stephen Murray-Smith (1987: 89): "people of a literary bent may feel uneasy if the possessive [genitive] is not used [. . . , yet] others may regard it as an unnecessary affectation." So in Australia, use of the genitive construction is calibrated on the high side of common usage, while the accusative has at least as much claim to be "common usage." Popular preference for the accusative has been confirmed by an *Australian style* survey (2003: 10–11), where it was endorsed by a large majority across the age spectrum, but especially by the under 45s. This broad use of the accusative with gerund-participles is an element of the general trend towards colloquialization in Australian usage, and the ready accommodation of informal idiom in writing (Delbridge 2001: 313–14). At any rate, there is less stylistic pressure to use the genitive with the gerund-participle than in northern hemisphere. Even there, the data from Frown and FLOB suggest that the gap is narrowing, and Biber et al. (1999) present the choice between accusative and genitive as equal options. There is no suggestion that the genitive construction is superior, as it was according to Fowler and Strunk and White.

The four cases discussed show the great value of primary language data from synchronic and diachronic corpora in analyzing the extent to which prescriptivists mirror the language of their times, and the relative influence and/or durability of their prescriptions. Their effects, if any, seem to coincide with stylistic discriminations which are fluid and local, and can therefore be destabilized by alternative usage from elsewhere, or neutralized by sociolinguistic changes within the language. But without corpus data and other empirical evidence, there is no way to calibrate the accuracy or artificiality of the prescription in relation to common usage.

4.2   *Pervasive power of prescriptivism*

Whatever the connections between particular language prescriptions and common usage, the signs are that prescriptivists, language *shamans* (Bolinger, 1980), "usageasters" (Algeo 1991), and "language mavens" (Pinker 1994) do have a pervasive influence on popular attitudes to usage and style. They predispose the community to accept that there may be good/bad usage wherever there are variants to consider. In public discussions of usage as on talkback radio, the alternatives are rarely seen as neutral. The expectation is that only one of them is "correct," only one can be good for you (Peters 2000: 99–100). It feeds insecurities (Baron 1982), and can create a kind of "moral panic" (Cameron 1995).

This more general impact of the prescriptive tradition shows up in the expanding range of usage cruces from the nineteenth to the twentieth century – despite, or perhaps because of, broader access to the multiplicities of usage through communication technologies. The hardening of attitudes to some particular issues, and the expansion of their frontiers, is another symptom of the prescriptive culture. A noteworthy example is the *split infinitive*, which was tolerated by Fowler (1926) and Gowers (1965) with the advice to "use it if you have to . . ." But Fraser in his 1973 revision of Gowers *Complete Plain Words* takes a harder line, as did Bernstein (1965) in the US, and both speak of it as "taboo." Both writers note the further anxiety about putting an adverb between an auxiliary and the lexical verb (Bernstein 1965: 427; Gowers and Fraser 1973: 219) – further extended to the avoidance of using an adverb between *to* and a gerund (Nunberg 1990: 473). Fowler's modulated advice was thus hardened up by later exponents of the tradition, and overgeneralized into additional constraints. Fowler's model for the use of *that/which* is another example (using *that* for restrictive relative clauses and *which* for nonrestrictive ones). He himself presented it as an ideal: "it would be idle to pretend that it is observed . . . ," but it has become a rule in the hands of some publishers' editors, especially in the US (Tottie 1997; 2002: 166). The details of Fowler's actual position have been neglected, turned into proscription or black-and-white prescription in these two cases.

Attempts by linguists to alleviate popular anxieties about correct usage have not necessarily been well received. Robert Hall Jr.'s *Leave your language alone* (1950) was ridiculed, though its title may have done some misservice to his purpose. The negative public reaction was exploited by Bernstein in a string of cautionary titles (*Watch your language* (1958), *More language that needs watching* (1962) and *The careful writer* (1965)), all encouraging the public to mistrust their intuitions about usage. In the UK, the first of Jean Aitchison's 1996 Reith lectures on "The Language Web" drew some bizarre negative reactions – presumably because her liberating line on the oppressive role of usage prescription ("the web of deceit") challenged entrenched language values in some listeners.

By contrast, the voices of non-linguistically trained prescriptivists seem to gain remarkable prominence and public endorsement. The voices of the shamans who write regular newspaper columns on usage "problems" chime with those who publish whole monographs on "paradigms lost" (John Simon 1980) and "the language trap" i.e. liberal approaches to language (John Honey 1983). Honey's combative approach to "standard English and its enemies" (1997) is a rallying cry like that of Lynne Truss (2003) drumming up support for all-out "war" on bad punctuation. The publication of such books bespeaks a reading public ready to enlist on usage concerns.

The publishing industry itself, and the editorial profession, are not neutral parties in maintaining public awareness of usage sanctions, as Cameron (1995) points out. They have a gatekeeper role in enforcing selected usage practices, and exercise constraints on their authors through a "house style," sometimes justified as a kind of corporate identity. Style and usage in government documents are similarly constrained, at least in US and Australia, by government style guides. Electronic style checkers are a further device for holding the line on points of usage, especially spellings and grammatical issues on the surface of language, such as split infinitives.

Educational institutions are still expected to be mediators of standard English and bastions of "correct" usage, and taken to task when any liberalization of the English language curriculum is mooted. Strong criticism of the Kingman report (1988) and the Cox report (1989) on the UK English language curriculum showed the gulf between expert linguistic opinion and conservative educational politics (Cameron 1995: 87–93). Educators themselves in some cases (e.g. Honey) insisted on the need to focus purely on standard English in ELT, denying any value in trying to embrace the lectal variation of students in the classroom. This British reaction makes an interesting parallel to the "Ebonics" controversy in California in 1996, which had been intended to enhance federal support for African-American English-speaking students in the classroom (McArthur 1998). A strong emphasis on standard English only is also typical of ESL teaching by British and American educational institutions. Pennycook (1994) puts the spotlight on the role of the British Council in this regard; but American publishers and educational institutions are engaged in similar activities in non-Commonwealth countries such as Japan and China. As "dominant" nations in Clyne's (1993: 4–5) taxonomy, they naturally focus on their own standard forms, maintaining the two codes in their respective spheres of influence.

All these centripetal, normative forces exercise considerable restraints on the forms of English used in particular regions and institutions. They provide structural support for prescriptive positions on usage, though they are not necessarily concerned with its particularities. The pervasive conservatism generated by prescriptive attitudes to usage is still a force to reckon with, for those who engage with the dynamism of common usage.

5   Diversification of English Usage, New Descriptive Challenges

The description of English usage in the twenty-first century presents larger challenges than ever because of centrifugal forces in the language itself. L1 users of the language are accessing it from ever further afield, and more freely. What was previously mediated is now continuously available through the internet. L2 users can construct their own amalgam out of the Englishes with which they come into contact. Thus the *China Daily* newspaper and other Chinese English language publications blend elements of British and American usage as part of their written code (Peters 2003: 36–7). This is part of the evolutionary process for new Englishes (Schneider 2003), adding to the family of "English languages" (McArthur 1998).

On the opposite side of the coin, language descriptivists are empowered with the array of methodologies developed in twentieth-century linguistics, and quantities of data that lend the strength of common usage to their work. Computerized data is more voluminous, but computer tools to deal with it more sophisticated. We are better placed now than ever before to provide accurate accounts of regional, social and generic variation. Usage dictionaries mounted on the web will be able to sustain links from individual entries to clustered treatments of topics, and thus escape the tyranny of the alphabet. The limitations of the prescriptive usage book will thus have been transcended within less than a century of Fowler's *Modern English usage.*

FURTHER READING

Aitchison, J. (1996) *The language web: 1996 Reith lectures.* Cambridge: Cambridge University Press.

Baron, D. (1982) *Grammar and good taste: reforming the American language.* New Haven and London: Yale University Press.

Cameron, D. (1995) *Verbal hygiene.* London and New York: Routledge.

Honey, J. (1997) *Language is power: the story of standard English and its enemies.* London, Faber.

McArthur, T. (1997) *The English languages.* Cambridge: Cambridge University Press.

Morton, H. C. (1994) *The story of Webster's Third: Philip Gove's controversial dictionary and its critics.* Cambridge: Cambridge University Press.

Pennycook, A. (1994) *Cultural politics of English as an international language.* Harlow: Longman.

Pinker, S. (1994) *The language instinct.* London: Penguin/Allen Lane.

REFERENCES

Algeo, J. (1991) Sweet are the uses of diversity. *Word* 42, 1–17.

American heritage dictionary (2000) Boston: American Heritage Publishing Company/Houghton Mifflin, 4th edn. (1969, 1971, 1st edn.).

Australian style (2003) Feedback report 11 (2), 10–11.

Bernstein, T. (1958) *Watch your language.* Great Neck, NY: Channel.

Bernstein, T. (1962) *More language that needs watching.* Great Neck, NY: Channel.

Bernstein, T. (1965) *The careful writer.* New York: Atheneum.

Biber, D., Johansson, S., Leech, G., Conrad, S., and Finegan, E. (1999) *Longman grammar of spoken and written English.* Harlow: Longman.

Bolinger, D. (1980) *Language: the loaded weapon.* London and New York: Longman.

Burchfield, R. (1979) *The Fowlers: their achievements in lexicography and grammar.* London: The English Association.

Burchfield, R. (1996) *New Fowler's modern English usage.* Oxford: Clarendon Press.

Canadian Oxford dictionary (1998) Toronto: Oxford University Press.

Clyne, M. (1993) Australian English as an example of a world phenomenon: pluricentric languages. In P. H. Peters (ed.), *Style on the move.* Sydney: Dictionary Research Center, Macquarie University.

Cresswell, T. J. (1975) *Usage in dictionaries and dictionaries of usage.* Publication of

the American Dialect Society.
University of Alabama, 63–4.

Delbridge, A. (1997) Review of
Burchfield's *New Fowler's modern
English usage, Australian Style* 5, 2, 10.

Delbridge, A. (2001) Lexicography and
national identity. In D. Blair and
P. Collins (eds.), *English in Australia.*
Amsterdam: John Benjamins.

Evans, B. and Evans, C. (1957) *A
dictionary of contemporary American
usage.* New York: Random House.

Fee, M. and McAlpine, J. (1997) *Oxford
guide to Canadian English usage.*
Toronto: Oxford University Press.

Follett, W. (1966; 1974) *Modern American
usage: a guide.* New York: Hill and
Wang.

Fowler, H. W. (1926) *A dictionary
of modern English usage.* Oxford:
Clarendon Press.

Fowler, H. W. and Fowler, F. G. (1906)
The king's English. Oxford: Clarendon
Press.

Fraser, E. (1962), see Gowers (1973).

Fries, C. C. (1925) The periphrastic
future with "shall" and "will" in
modern English *Publications of the
Modern Language Association* 40,
963–1024.

Fries, C. C. (1940) *American English
grammar.* New York: Appleton,
Century, Crofts.

Garner, B. A. (1998) *A dictionary of
modern American usage.* New York:
Oxford University Press.

Gowers, E. (1973) *The complete plain
words,* 2nd edn. B. Fraser (ed.).
Aylesbury: Pelican (1954, repr.
1962).

Gowers, E. (ed.) (1965) *Fowler's modern
English usage.* Oxford: Clarendon Press.

Greenbaum, S. (1977) *Acceptability in
language.* The Hague: Mouton.

Honey, J. (1983) *The language trap: race,
class and the standard English issue in
British schools.* Middlesex: National
Council for Educational Standards.

Hundt, M. (1998a) *New Zealand English
grammar: fact or fiction.* Amsterdam:
John Benjamins.

Hundt, M. (1998b) It is important that
this study (should) be based on the
analysis of parallel corpora. In H.
Lindquist et al. (eds.), *The major
varieties of English: papers from MAVEN
97.* Växjö: Växjö University.

Jespersen, O. (1909–49) *A modern
grammar on historical principles.* 7 vols.
Heidelburg: Carl Winter.

Johansson, S. and Norheim, E. H. (1988)
The subjunctive in British and
American English. *ICAME Journal* 12,
27–36.

Landau, S. (1979) The egalitarian spirit
and attitudes towards usage. *American
Speech* 54, 3–11.

Leonard, S. A. (1929; 1962) *The doctrine
of correctness in English usage 1700–
1800.* New York: Russell and Russell.

Leonard, S. A. (1938) *Current English
usage.* Published in Marckwardt and
Walcott.

Lowth, R. (1762) *A short introduction to
English grammar.* London.

Marckwardt, A. and Walcott F. (1938)
Facts about current English usage.
New York: Appleton, Century, Crofts.

McMorris, J. (2001) *The warden of English:
the life of HW Fowler.* Oxford: Oxford
University Press.

Merriam-Webster's collegiate dictionary
(2000) Merriam-Webster, 10th edn.

Milroy, J. and Milroy, L. (1985; 1999)
Authority in language, 3rd edn. London:
Routledge and Kegan Paul.

Minugh, D. (2002) The Coll corpus:
towards a corpus of web-based college
student newspapers. In P. Peters,
P. Collins, and A. Smith (eds.), *New
frontiers of corpus linguistics.*
Amsterdam: Rodopi.

Mittins, W. H., Salu, M., Edminson, M.,
and Coyne, S. (1970) *Attitudes to
English usage.* London: Oxford
University Press.

Moon, G. (1864) *The dean's English: a criticism on the Dean of Canterbury's essays*. London: Hatchard.

Morris W. and Morris M. (1975) *The Harper dictionary of contemporary usage*. New York: Harper and Row.

Murray-Smith, S. (1987; 1989) *Right words*. Ringwood, Victoria: Viking.

New Oxford dictionary of English (1998) Oxford, Clarendon Press.

Nunberg, G. (1990) What the usage panel thinks. In C. Ricks and L. Michaels (eds.), *The state of the language*. London: Faber & Faber.

Overgaard, G. (1995) *The mandative subjunctive in American and British English in the 20th century*. Uppsala: Uppsala University Press.

Oxford English dictionary (1884–1928; 1989) 2nd edn. Oxford: Clarendon Press.

Perrin, G. (1942) *Writers' guide and index to English*. New York: Scott.

Peters, P. (1993) Corpus evidence on some points of usage. In J. Aarts, P. de Haan, and N. Oostdijk (eds.), *English language corpora: design, anlysis and exploitation*. Amsterdam: Rodopi.

Peters, P. (1995) *Cambridge Australian English style guide*. Melbourne: Cambridge University Press.

Peters, P. (1998) The survival of the subjunctive: evidence of its use in Australia and elsewhere. *English World-Wide* 19 (1), 87–103.

Peters, P. (2000) Compelling judgements: the language of prescriptive usage commentators. In P. H. Peters (ed.), *Style in context: language at large*. Sydney: Dictionary Research Center, Macquarie University.

Peters, P. (2003) What is international English? In P. H. Peters (ed.), *From local to global English*. Sydney: Dictionary Research Center, Macquarie University.

Peters, P. (2004) *Cambridge guide to English usage*. Cambridge: Cambridge University Press.

Peters, P. and Delbridge, A. (1997) Fowler's legacy. In E. W. Schneider (ed.), *Englishes around the world 2: Studies in honour of Manfred Goerlach*. Amsterdam: John Benjamins.

Peters, P. and Young, W. (1997) English grammar and the lexicography of usage. *Journal of English Linguistics* 25 (4), 315–31.

Quirk, R. (1972) The toils of Fowler and moral Gowers. In *The English language and images of matter*. London: Oxford University Press.

Quirk, R., Greenbaum, S., Leech, G., and Svartvik, J. (1985) *A comprehensive grammar of the English language*. Harlow: Longman.

Right word at the right time, The (1985) London, Reader's Digest.

Schneider, E. W. (2003) The dynamics of new Englishes: from identity construction to dialect birth. *Language* 79 (2).

Simon, J. (1980) *Paradigms lost: reflections on literacy and its decline*. New York: Clarkson N. Potter.

Strang, Barbara. (1970) *A history of English*. London: Methuen.

Strunk, W. and White, E. B. (1959; 1972) *The elements of style*, 2nd edn. New York: Macmillan.

Tottie, G. (1997) Literacy and prescriptivism as determinants of linguistic change: a case study based on relativization strategies. In U. Boker and H. Sauer (eds.), *Proceedings/Anglistentag: 1996 Dresden*. Trier: Wissenschaftlicher Verlag.

Tottie, G. (2002) *An introduction to American English*. New York: Blackwells.

Trudgill, P. (1986) *Dialects in contact*. New York: Blackwells.

Truss, L. (2003) *Eats, shoots and leaves*. London: Profile Books.

Tucker, S. (1961) *English examined: two centuries of comment on the mother*

tongue. Cambridge UK: Cambridge
   University Press.
Webster's dictionary of English usage
   (1989) Springfield, MA: Merriam-
   Webster.

Webster's third new international dictionary
   (1961) Springfield, MA: Merriam-
   Webster.
Willinsky, J. (1994) *Empire of words:
   the reign of the OED*. Princeton, NJ:
   Princeton University Press.

Subject and Key Names Index